Organic Mental Disorder NOS

Sedative, Hypnotic, or Anxiolytic
- Intoxication
- Uncomplicated Sedative, Hypnotic, or Anxiolytic Withdrawal
- Withdrawal Delirium
- Amnestic Disorder

Other or Unspecified Psychoactive Substance
- Intoxication
- Withdrawal
- Delirium
- Dementia
- Amnestic Disorder
- Delusional Disorder
- Hallucinosis
- Mood Disorder
- Anxiety Disorder
- Personality Disorder
- Organic Mental Disorder NOS

Organic Mental Disorders Associated with Axis III Physical Disorders or Conditions, or Whose Etiology is Unknown

Delirium
Dementia
Amnestic Disorder
Organic Delusional Disorder
Organic Hallucinosis
Organic Mood Disorder
Organic Anxiety Disorder
Organic Personality Disorder
Organic Mental Disorder

PSYCHOACTIVE SUBSTANCE USE DISORDERS

Alcohol
- Dependence
- Abuse

Amphetamine or Similarly Acting Sympathomimetic
- Dependence
- Abuse

Cannabis
- Dependence
- Abuse

Cocaine
- Dependence
- Abuse

Hallucinogen
- Dependence
- Abuse

Inhalant
- Dependence
- Abuse

Nicotine
- Dependence

Opioid
- Dependence
- Abuse

Phencyclidine (PCP) or Similarly Acting Arylcyclohexylamine
- Dependence
- Abuse

Sedative, Hypnotic, or Anxiolytic
- Dependence
- Abuse

Polysubstance Dependence
Psychoactive Substance Dependence NOS
Psychoactive Substance Abuse NOS

SCHIZOPHRENIA

Types: Catatonic
Disorganized
Paranoid
Undifferentiated
Residual

DELUSIONAL (PARANOID) DISORDER

Delusional (Paranoid) Disorder
Types: Erotomanic
Grandiose
Jealous
Persecutory
Somatic
Unspecified

PSYCHOTIC DISORDERS NOT ELSEWHERE CLASSIFIED

Brief Reactive Psychosis
Schizophreniform Disorder
Schizoaffective Disorder
Induced Psychotic Disorder
Psychotic Disorder NOS (Atypical Psychosis)

MOOD DISORDERS

Bipolar Disorders

Bipolar Disorder
Cyclothymia
Bipolar Disorder NOS

Depressive Disorders

Major Depression
Dysthymia (or Depressive Neurosis)
Depressive Disorder NOS

Abnormal Psychology

G. Terence Wilson
Rutgers University

K. Daniel O'Leary
State University of New York at Stony Brook

Peter E. Nathan
University of Iowa

PRENTICE HALL, Englewood Cliffs, New Jersey 07632

Library of Congress Cataloging-in-Publication Data

Wilson, G. Terence, ( )
Abnormal psychology / G. Terence Wilson, K. Daniel O'Leary, Peter Nathan.
p. cm.
Includes bibliographical references and index.
ISBN 0-13-005802-5
1. Psychology, Pathological. I. O'Leary, K. Daniel, ( ).
II. Nathan, Peter E. III. Title.
[DNLM: 1. Mental Disorders. WM 100 W748a]
RC454.W543 1991
616.89—dc20
DNLM/DLC
for Library of Congress 91-28842
CIP

Production Editor: Shelly Kupperman
Acquisitions Editor: Susan Finnemore Brennan
Editor-in-Chief: Charlyce Jones Owen
Development Editor: Marilyn Miller
Senior Development Editor: Leslie Carr
Marketing Manager: Tracey McPeake
Copy Editor: Nancy Savio-Marcello
Design Director: Florence Dara Silverman
Cover and Interior Design: Howard Petlack/A Good Thing Inc.
Photo Editor: Lorinda Morris-Nantz
Photo Researcher: Ilene Cherna
Prepress Buyers: Debra Kesar and Kelly Behr
Manufacturing Buyer: Mary Ann Gloriande
Supplements Editor: Sharon Chambliss
Editorial Assistant: Jennie Katsaros
Cover photo: *Seated Woman* by Diana Ong, 1940. Photo from *Super Stock.*

Printed in the United States of America
10 9 8 7 6 5 4 3 2 1

ISBN 0-13-005802-5

Prentice-Hall International (UK) Limited, *London*
Prentice-Hall of Australia Pty. Limited, *Sydney*
Prentice-Hall Canada Inc., *Toronto*
Prentice-Hall Hispanoamericana, S.A., *Mexico*
Prentice-Hall of India Private Limited, *New Delhi*
Prentice-Hall of Japan, Inc., *Tokyo*
Simon & Schuster Asia Pte. Ltd., *Singapore*
Editora Prentice-Hall do Brasil, Ltda., *Rio de Janeiro*

Overview

Contents

Jan Sawka, *A Yellow Letter* (1984–85). Acrylic (mixed on masonite). Courtesy of the artist.

Chapter 3: Diagnosis and Clinical Assessment 55

Chapter 4: Research Methods in the Study of Abnormal Behavior 77

Diego Rivera, *Young Man with a Stylograph, Portrait of Best Mangard* (1914). Oil on canvas, 31¾ × 25⅝ inches. Courtesy of Private Collection, Mexico.

Jay Burch, *Untitled Still Life Study* (1989). Pastel on paper. Courtesy of Govinda Gallery, Washington, D.C.

Pablo Picasso, *Seated Woman (after Cranach)* (1958). Color linoleum cut, block: 25 11/16 × 21 5/16 inches. Collection, The Museum of Modern Art, New York. Gift of Mr. and Mrs. Daniel Saidenberg.

Jan Sawka, *The Negotiations* (1984). Acrylic on masonite, 75 × 48 inches. Courtesy of artist.

Preface

Abnormal thoughts and behavior are some of the most unusual and interesting phenomena we encounter in life. These thoughts and behaviors, which cause considerable trauma and grief, are intrinsically interesting; both professionals and amateurs have been fascinated by the field of abnormal psychology for years. Abnormal behavior also poses a tremendous challenge to those who have searched for a way to help. Our own intense involvement with the etiology and treatment of abnormal behavior has allowed us to remain on the cutting edge in the field. Whatever your own reason is for inquiry into this exciting subject, we will lead you through the central themes of abnormal psychology.

In 1975, two of us (O'Leary and Wilson) published our first book with Prentice Hall entitled *Behavior Therapy: Application and Outcome.* The second edition of the behavior therapy book appeared in 1987. Our next book, *Principles of Behavior Therapy* (Wilson and O'Leary) was published in 1980. At the urging of our editors, we then decided to broaden our sights and write an abnormal psychology book. Our interests and expertise complement each other well. Terry Wilson participates in clinical and research activity on alcohol abuse, eating disorders, anxiety disorders, sexual disorders, behavioral medicine, and individual therapy. Dan O'Leary is active in clinical research on child assessment and treatment, marital and family therapy, and the etiology and treatment of depression and wife abuse. Nevertheless, keenly aware of the formidable task we were undertaking, we sought the help of Peter Nathan, a colleague and friend for many years. Peter Nathan is well-known for his numerous research contributions to substance abuse diagnosis, prevention, and treatment, as well as to diagnostic assessment more broadly and to the training and regulation of mental health professionals. We are now a trio, and we hope that the diversity of our experience is reflected in this text.

Each of us has been involved in clinical practice, teaching, and research in this field for over twenty years. The integration of research and scientific findings into our clinical practices has led us to classify ourselves as scientist-practitioners. This classification helps us to combine the latest research findings with clinical case material in our text, bringing our subject matter to life and allowing students to put themselves in the mind of a practitioner. Our case studies are diverse and fascinating; they include Anne M., a young, depressed college student whose story illustrates the DSM diagnostic process, brief case histories of victims of Alzheimer's Disease and Korsakoff's Disorder, cases of such diverse subjects as the "Hillside Strangler," and Ryan White as well as:

- Abraham Lincoln, who had such severe bouts of depression he was unable to appear at his own wedding
- Anna O., or Bertha Pappenheim, a woman often associated with dependent, hysterical females, but who in fact was an early feminist who stated that if there were any justice in the world, men would raise the children and women would make the laws
- Janet Whitehall, a physician who recently described how frightening it can be to live with a husband who psychologically and physically abuses her. Her story demonstrates that physical abuse affects women in all social classes
- Stuart Sutherland, a distinguished psychology professor who coped with extreme obsessional thoughts and the problem of "going crazy"

Our own clinical work with individuals, couples, and families gives us an extensive body of knowledge about the possibilities and limitations of therapy. We, therefore, carefully integrate methods of treatment with the discussion of each disorder, so that the disorder and treatment work in tandem to enhance understanding. Treatment is not relegated to one chapter early or late in the text; rather, it is integrated throughout. The text describes the clinical disorders, discusses treatment methods, and analyzes the results of treatment all within the same chapter. In addition, we have provided integrative chapters on biological, psychological, and social treatments at the end of the text.

The therapeutic process requires practitioners to be alert to the biological, psychological, and social factors that may have interacted to produce an abnormal behavior. Indeed, few psychologists or psychiatrists today focus on biological, environmental, or social factors alone when they set out to understand and treat a psychological disorder. In our text, we provide the student with an approach to abnormal behavior, the biopsychosocial approach, which integrates these influences and helps the student to better understand disorders and their treatments.

Our text gives convincing evidence that biological predispositions interact with psychological and sociological factors in almost all major disorders we discuss. This biopsychosocial perspective allows us to shed light on recent exciting advances in each of the three areas. Examples of recent research areas which illustrate the biopsychosocial perspective are:

- Affective and anxiety disorders (biological factors), poor self-esteem and lack of social skills (psychological factors), and sexual and physical abuse (social factors) place an individual at risk for developing borderline personality disorders.
- Genetic predispositions as reflected in parental histories of excessive drinking and antisocial behavior (biological factors), rewards for being aggressive, strong punishment, models of aggressive behavior, lax and inconsistent discipline, and marital discord (psychological factors), and large family size, overcrowding, and inability to obtain child care (social factors) place an individual at risk for developing oppositional defiant and conduct disorders.
- Higher concordance rates for the disorder (biological factors), family disturbances, restrained eating, and negative emotional states (psychological factors) and cultural emphasis on being thin (social factors) place an individual at risk for developing anorexia nervosa and/or bulimia nervosa.

We believe that the field of abnormal psychology has been plagued for too long with one-sided advocacy for one perspective or another. It is often difficult to take a broader perspective than one's own training and expertise permit; however, there is general agreement that any comprehensive analysis of abnormal behavior done today requires a biopsychosocial perspective.

Finally, we wanted to present an empirically-based account of abnormal behavior in a "reader friendly" way. Developments in biology, psychology, and social fields are occurring at an extremely rapid pace, and, although a voluminous amount of research and clinical literature could be included in an abnormal psychology text, we resisted the pressure to cover too much. We feel the students will benefit from our coverage of major clinical disorders and such fascinating questions as:

1. Can the immune system be influenced by psychological factors? If so, can it be influenced enough to prevent or treat diseases such as cancer and AIDS?
2. Are women overdiagnosed for psychological disorders?
3. Are some psychotherapies better than others? Can some psychotherapies actually harm rather than help?
4. Is electroconvulsive therapy a treatment of choice for certain types of depression?
5. Is medication the most effective treatment for children with attention deficit hyperactivity disorder?
6. When, if ever, can an alcoholic consider "controlled drinking" as a safe alternative to abstinence from alcohol?
7. Is suicidal behavior modeled by adolescents? If a relative or popular figure commits suicide, does the risk for suicide increase?
8. Is marriage a mental health risk for women?

Answers to the above questions may vary depending upon the investigator and his or her theoretical biases. In fact, many, if not most, issues are controversial because there is no simple answer. These very issues make abnormal psychology challenging and intriguing. While reading this book, we hope you share our own excitement about this complex and exciting field.

SUPPLEMENTS

We believe the quality and expertise that went into *Abnormal Psychology* by Wilson, O'Leary, and Nathan is matched in the superb supplemental package which accompanies the text. The following materials are available to enhance the teaching and learning experience:

Instructor's Resource and Testing Manual—This manual includes the following information for each chapter of the text: abstracts of recent research articles, activities, and discussion topics, suggested further readings, chapter summary, key terms, film and video descriptions, and a list of film and video distributors. The test item file, also in the manual, contains over 1600 questions, both conceptual and applied, with page references to the text. The types of questions are multiple choice, true/false, and essay and they range in level of difficulty.

Video Cases in Abnormal Psychology—Patients as Educators—our videocases program features 10 interviews of patients with such disorders as schizophrenia, obsessive-compulsive disorder, depression, and more. Each interview is preceded by a brief history of the patient and a synopsis of some major symptoms of the disorder. Each interview ends with a summary of the interview and a brief analysis. This exciting teaching and learning tool was developed by James H. Scully, Jr., M.D., Chief Resident of Psychiatry at the University of Colorado's Medical Center as well as Denver Veteran's Hospital, and Alan M. Dahms, licensed Clinical Psychologist and Professor of Psychology at Metropolitan State College in Denver. This video program is free to adopters of our text.

Prentice Hall DataManager—Unmatched by any other computerized testing software, Prentice Hall DataManager is a state-of-the-art classroom management system. The program contains three key components that will help you efficiently organize vital information: Test Manager, Grade Manager, and Study Manager. All components are easy to learn and use.

MAC Test Manager—This program streamlines the test design process and offers greater flexibility in actual test generation. Incorporating questions taken directly from the test item file or from your own files, MAC Test Manager enables the instructor to create, refine, update, store, and print a variety of tests.

Telephone Test Preparation Service—Select up to 200 questions from the Test Item File and call us toll-free at (800) 842-2958. Prentice Hall prepares the test, and an alternate version if requested, on bond paper or ditto master within 48 hours of your call. We mail the test with a separate answer key directly to the professor.

Prentice Hall Transparencies for Abnormal Psychology, Series I—Our transparency set consists of 30 full-color transparencies exploring various key topics found in the text, such as "Symptoms of Depression," "Reaction to Stress," "Sex Differences in Personality Disorders," "Varying Degrees of Paranoid Thinking," and many more.

Handout and Transparency Masters—These versatile questionnaires and activities can be handed out in class or made into overhead transparencies to involve and stimulate your classroom discussion.

A Contemporary View—Abnormal Psychology-Prentice Hall and The New York Times have joined forces to bring your students the perfect complement to *Abnormal Psychology*. Each student will receive a free student newspaper supplement which contains recent articles pertinent to the study of abnormal psychology. These articles, taken from *The New York Times* and printed in newspaper format demonstrate the applied nature of this fascinating field.

Study Guide and Workbook—Each chapter of this student aid includes a chapter review, learning objectives, key concepts/terms with definitions, self-tests including multiple-choice and true/false questions, and activities to enhance the topics presented in the text.

THE NEW YORK TIMES and PRENTICE HALL are sponsoring A CONTEMPORARY VIEW: ABNORMAL PSYCHOLOGY, a program designed to enhance student access to current information of relevance in the classroom.

Through this program, the core subject matter provided in the text is supplemented by a collection of time-sensitive articles from one of the world's most distinguished newspapers, THE NEW YORK TIMES. These articles are gathered into a special, complimentary student supplement to demonstrate the vital, ongoing connection between what is learned in the classroom and what is happening in the world around us. Also, to enjoy the wealth of information in THE NEW YORK TIMES daily, a reduced subscription rate is available. For information, call toll-free: 1-800-631-1222.

PRENTICE HALL and THE NEW YORK TIMES are proud to co-sponsor A CONTEMPORARY VIEW. We hope it will make the reading of both textbooks and newspapers a more dynamic, involving process.

ACKNOWLEDGMENTS

We wish to thank a number of people for their contributions to the preparation and production of this book. The following colleagues and students read different drafts of the text and provided valuable input about style and content:

Maureen Acker, State University of New York-Stony Brook
James Alexander, University of Utah
Ileana Arias, University of Georgia
Johnston Beach, U.S. Military Academy
Nelson Butters, University of California-San Diego
Edward Craighead, Duke University
Anthony Davids, Brown University
Nancy Fagley, Rutgers University
Donald Fowles, University of Iowa
Catherine Green, University of Miami
Steen Halling, Seattle University
Rolf Jacob, University of Pittsburgh
Daniel Klein, State University of New York-Stony Brook
Robert Lavallee, St Michael's College
Roger C. Loeb, University of Michigan-Dearborn
Chris Lonigan, Vanderbilt University
John McCauley, College of Du Page
Shannon Lee Meyer, State University of New York-Stony Brook
Kathleen Much, Center for Advanced Study in the Behavioral Sciences-Stanford, California
Chris Murphy, University of Maryland-Baltimore County

Michael W. O'Hara, University of Iowa
Anne O'Leary, Rutgers University
Michael O'Leary, Duke University
Susan O'Leary, State University of New York-Stony Brook
Peggy Pittas, Lynchburg College
Ronald Prinz, University of South Carolina
Michael L. Raulin, State University of New York-Buffalo
Lyn Rehm, University of Houston
Kathryn K. Rileigh, Pembroke State University
Cline J. Robbins, Duke University Medical Center
Raymond C. Rosen, Robert Wood Johnson School of Medicine-Piscataway, New Jersey
April Sato, University of Houston
Michael Saxe, University of Iowa
Michael Sayette, University of Pittsburgh
Forrest Scogin, University of Alabama
Janet Simons, Central Iowa Psychological Services
Patricia B. Sutker, VA Medical Center-New Orleans
Robert Woolfolk, Rutgers University
Robert D. Zettle, Wichita State University

We also express our appreciation to the many anonymous reviewers who caught many of our mistakes and offered useful and constructive criticism of our coverage.

Other individuals were invaluable in helping us with such time-consuming but important tasks as gathering information, checking references, and securing permission from other authors and publishers for reprinting figures and text. In particular we are grateful to the following:

Margaret Amara, librarian at the Center for Advanced Study in the Behavioral Sciences, Stanford, California
Mary Samios, State University of New York-Stony Brook
Karin Schlee, State University of New York-Stony Brook
Elaine Wilson, Princeton, New Jersey

In addition, Karin Schlee and Mary Samios provided valuable editorial feedback on many chapters and facilitated their progression through the various stages of the editorial process. We thank our editors at Prentice Hall for their support and professional expertise:

Susan Finnemore Brennan, Senior Acquisitions Editor
Shelly Kupperman, Production Editor
Leslie Carr, Senior Development Editor
Marilyn Miller, Development Editor

G. Terence Wilson
K. Daniel O'Leary
Peter E. Nathan

About the Authors

G. Terence Wilson

After receiving his Ph.D at the State University of New York at Stony Brook in 1971, Terry Wilson moved to Rutgers University in New Jersey where, in 1985, he was appointed Oscar K. Buros Professor of Psychology. In addition to teaching undergraduate and graduate students, he is a practicing clinical psychologist. Terry Wilson has co-authored or co-edited a number of books, including *Behavior Therapy: Application and Outcome* (with K.D. O'Leary), *The Effects of Psychological Therapy* (with S. Rachman), *Annual Review of Behavior Therapy: Theory and Practice* (with C.M. Franks), and *Evaluation of Behavior Therapy: Issues, Evidence, and Research Strategies* (with A.E. Kazdin). A past-President of the Association for Advancement of Behavior Therapy, his academic honors include the Distinguished Scientist Award from Section III of the Division of Clinical Psychology of the American Psychological Association, and Fellowships at the Center for Advanced Study in the Behavioral Sciences at Stanford in 1976-77 and 1990-91. His current research interests focus on alcohol use and abuse and eating disorders.

K. Daniel O'Leary

Dr. O'Leary is a Distinguished Professor of Psychology at the State University of New York at Stony Brook. In 1989 and 1990, the graduating senior psychology majors at Stony Brook elected him "Teacher of the Year." Dr. O'Leary received his Ph.D. at the University of Illinois in Urbana in 1967, and afterwards he went directly to Stony Brook where he was chair of the department from 1978 to 1981. He is also a practicing clinical psychologist.

Dr. O'Leary is an Associate Editor of the *Journal of Abnormal Child Psychology* and he serves on a number of editorial boards including the *Journal of Family Violence, The Journal of Interpersonal Violence,* and the *Journal of Family Psychology.* He has written a number of books including, *Depression in Marriage* (with S. Beach and E. Sandeen, 1990), *Assessment of Marital Discord* (1987), *Behavior Therapy: Application and Outcome* with G.T. Wilson [1975; 1987], and *Mommy I Can't Sit Still: Coping with the Aggressive and Hyperactive Child* (1984). His major research interests include spouse abuse and the interaction of marital discord and depression. He has long been involved in treatment research for problems of both children and adults surrounding issues of depression and aggression.

Peter E. Nathan

After receiving an A.B. in Social Relations with Honors from Harvard College and a Ph.D. in Clinical Psychology from Washington University, Peter E. Nathan spent seven years on the faculty of Harvard Medical School. During this time he began his studies of the causes of alcoholism that continue to this time. He moved to Rutgers University in 1969 to become Professor and Director of Clinical Psychology Training and was named Henry and Anna Starr Professor of Psychology and Director of Rutgers' Center of Alcohol Studies in 1983. Dr. Nathan left Rutgers in 1987 to become Senior Health Program Officer for the MacArthur Foundation. Two years later, he assumed his present position, Vice President for Academic Affairs, Dean of the Faculties, and Distinguished Professor of Psychology at The University of Iowa.

A member of the *DSM-IV* Work Group considering new diagnostic criteria for the substance use disorders, Dr. Nathan also served eight years as Associate Editor of *American Psychologist* and seven years as Executive Editor of *Journal of Studies on Alcohol.* He is a past-President of the Division of Clinical Psychology of the American Psychological Association.

Josef Levi, *Still Life with Titian & Jawlensky* (1987). Acrylic & graphite/canvas, 37.5 × 54 inches. Courtesy of OK Harris, New York.

1

ABNORMAL BEHAVIOR: CONCEPTUAL AND HISTORICAL PERSPECTIVES

Abnormal behavior has fascinated human beings for centuries. In the seventeenth century, Shakespeare wrote plays in which characters exhibit mental disorders recognizable to us today. In the nineteenth century, composers of operas wrote "mad scenes" for their heroines to show off their voices. And in our own century, television programs regularly portray such disorders as multiple personality, paranoia, and depression. Abnormal behavior is so commonly discussed nowadays that the technical language of psychology has become pervasive. "He's a sadist," we may say, or "She's neurotic." "He's narcissistic"—or paranoid or compulsive or phobic. Obviously, we think that we can recognize abnormal behavior when we see it.

But can we? As this chapter suggests, it is not so easy. In the following pages, we consider what abnormality is and how we define it. We also take note of its relative commonness in the modern world.

The chapter also reviews the education, training, and responsibilities of members of the four core mental health professions—clinical psychology, psychiatry, psychiatric social work, and psychiatric nursing. This information will be especially valuable to those of you who may consider entering one of these professions.

To enable you to put this material—as well as the information contained in subsequent chapters—in historical perspective, a brief history of our efforts to understand, diagnose, and treat psychopathology, from ancient times to our own, concludes the chapter.

WHAT IS ABNORMAL BEHAVIOR?

How do we decide whether our own behavior—or that of others—is normal or abnormal? In some cases, symptoms are so dramatic or unusual as to leave little doubt that a person is no longer behaving normally. A man who believes that his thoughts are being broadcast by the local talk radio program or that the League of Women Voters is trying to wire his car with explosives, is clearly not thinking normally. Similarly, a woman who regularly converses aloud with deceased members of her family as she walks down the street has, to some degree, lost touch with reality. But other cases are more subtle. What about a woman who becomes so upset over a supervisor's criticism that she quits her job, causing herself great financial hardship? Or a man who occasionally enjoys dressing up in women's clothing, although he is happily married and seems in other respects an average, well-adjusted person? As these examples suggest, it is not always easy to decide when behavior is abnormal. The following two cases illustrate the range of behavior that clinicians are called on to evaluate.

Clifford Beers was thirty years old when he wrote *A Mind That Found Itself* (1905). The following ex-

Clifford Beers was the author of A Mind That Found Itself, *which graphically described his serious mental disorder.*

cerpts describe with great clarity the author's serious mental disorder, which would be diagnosed today as bipolar affective disorder.

Although Beers had experienced striking alterations of mood in childhood, his first severe depression began shortly after graduating from Yale College.

> *What I had long expected I now became convinced had at last occurred. I believed myself to be a confirmed epileptic. . . . From that time my one thought was to hasten the end, for I felt that I should lose the chance to die should relatives find me in a seizure of the supposed malady. . . . Soon my disordered brain was busy with schemes for death. I distinctly remember one which included a row on Lake Whitney, near New Haven . . . I then thought of severing my jugular vein . . . During these three or four days I slept scarcely at all . . . By a process of elimination, all suicidal methods but one had at last been put aside. On that one my mind now centered. . . . The sills of my windows were a little more than thirty feet above the ground. . . . It required no great amount of calculation to determine how slight the chance of surviving a fall from either of these windows. . . . It was now or never for liberation. . . . With my fingers I clung for a moment to the sill. Then I let go.* (pp. 15–19)

Beers's depression and attempted suicide were followed first by a period of hospitalization, then a time of relative normality at home, and then a period of mania, for which he was again hospitalized.

> *My large and varied assortment of delusions of grandeur made everything seem possible. There were few problems I hesitated to attack . . . Many times a day I would instruct the attendants what to do and what not to do, and tell them what I should do if my requests, suggestions, or orders were not immediately complied with. . . . During the latter part of that first week I wrote many letters, so many, indeed, that I soon exhausted a liberal supply of stationery . . . It was now at my own suggestion that the superintendent gave me large sheets of manila wrapping paper. These I proceeded to cut into strips a foot wide. . . . More than once letters twenty or thirty feet long were written; and on one occasion the accumulation of two or three days of excessive productivity, when spread upon the floor, reached from one end of the corridor to the other—a distance of about one hundred feet.* (pp. 85, 89, 102)

After his mania subsided, Beers was redischarged from the hospital. Although he continued to experience periods of depression and mania throughout his life, he was also able to devote a substantial portion of his energies and intelligence to mental hospital reform.

The following contemporary case illustrates a problem less bizarre than Clifford Beers's.

> *Billy Ainsworth was a 21-year-old senior in a southwestern university. He requested treatment at the university counseling center because of difficulties that he had been having since his girl friend, Jill, broke up with him three months previously. The relationship with Jill had been "a real love relationship." Nonetheless, they decided to date other people, and eventually she came to prefer another man.*
>
> *Since the breakup Billy had lost interest in his schoolwork, was not able to concentrate on his studies, and as a result had accumulated several "incompletes." He also had trouble sleeping and was preoccupied with thoughts about Jill, for whom he still cared. When thinking about her he felt sad, but at other times he was able to enjoy himself with friends and to pursue his interests in sports and politics.*
>
> *In addition, he complained of difficulties in making a career choice. It was the fall of his senior year, and he had not yet decided whether he would go to graduate school, and if so, whether it would be law school or business school.* (Spitzer et al., 1983, p. 195)

Was Clifford Beers' behavior abnormal? Was Billy Ainsworth's? You probably would agree that Clifford Beers's behavior was abnormal, even without knowing which diagnostic label to attach to it or why he acted this way. Someone who experiences such extreme swings in moods, you would say, is behaving abnormally. Additionally, you also would probably agree that such a person ought to consult a psychiatrist or a psychologist, so that his or her disorder can be diagnosed and treated.

But what about Billy Ainsworth's behavior? Was his brief, disruptive period of depression over the loss of a significant relationship abnormal? Should he have been labeled clinically depressed and referred to a mental health professional for evaluation? These questions are harder to answer, partly because the feelings and behaviors that bothered Billy—sadness, indecisiveness, trouble sleeping—are more familiar to us, and, therefore, more difficult to label as abnormal.

Moreover, in contrast to Clifford Beers's dramatic excesses of mood, thought, and behavior—which led him to be admitted repeatedly to a hospital—Billy Ainsworth's turmoil was mainly private: The changes in his sleep patterns, his feelings about the future, and his inability to concentrate did not really affect anyone else. Most significantly, nothing inside Billy forced him to act on his distress, as Beers ultimately did—for example, Billy neither dropped out of college nor attempted suicide. Moreover, unlike Beers's mood swings, Billy's depression, although personally painful, did not cause catastrophic changes in his plans or prospects.

We use a variety of standards to judge whether behavior—our own and that of others—is normal or abnormal, healthy or pathological. [That judgment about behavior is important for several reasons.] For example, during times of stress, grief, or illness, we may worry that our behavior has become so unusual or abnormal that it requires not simple attention from ourselves or time or solace from friends but professional consultation. Or we may observe troubling changes in the behavior of a friend or a family member. We wonder whether we should speak up and urge that person to obtain help for suicidal feelings, excessive drinking, or some other problem.

Such judgments are often complicated because the standards people use to judge the adequacy or appropriateness of behavior vary a great deal from subgroup to subgroup within our complex society. Such standards vary even more widely between societies separated by time, climate, or continents. For example, today we would consider the harsh physical punishments once routinely imposed on children to be child abuse. Similarly, only a few generations ago, divorced people were considered shockingly deviant. No wonder we find labeling someone's actions abnormal so difficult.

Are there hard-and-fast rules for deciding a behavior is abnormal? For example, should we rely on *statistics* and consider a behavior to be abnormal only if it is infrequent or unusual? This approach to defining abnormality is appealing since it employs numbers and relies on research findings. It is *objective*, less subject to our own biases. But behaviors are not easily reduced to numbers—and certain abnormal behaviors (including some revealed by the epidemiological surveys reviewed later) are both common *and* abnormal—for example, depression and anxiety.

Or should we define abnormality *contextually*? That is, should we first understand the environmental and social context of the behavior before deciding if it is normal or abnormal? This position has some merit. Behaviors considered perfectly normal in some societies are clearly abnormal in others. For example, in our culture the drive to succeed is considered not only normal but an asset. Yet in some non-Western societies, it is viewed as both a sign of exceedingly bad taste and of emotional disorder. But some other behaviors, including Clifford Beers's mania and depression, are recognized as abnormal regardless of when and where they occur.

Because of the complexity of the task, most modern societies depend on mental health professionals to differentiate the abnormal, or **psychopathological**, from mere eccentricity, cultural deviance, or variations in lifestyle. On their clinical judgments rest such vital decisions as whether someone ought to receive psychological or psychiatric treatment, where it should occur, and what it should consist of. Later in this chapter, we discuss who these professionals are, how they are trained, and what each mental health profession contributes to the understanding and treatment of the emotionally disturbed.

WHY STUDY ABNORMAL BEHAVIOR?

Psychopathology has affected human life for at least as long as human history has been recorded—and probably longer. The study of psychopathology, therefore, provides historical and contemporary perspectives on an element of the human experience as central today as it was when Julius Caesar's epilepsy influenced his conduct of the Roman wars of conquest (by clouding his perception of the likelihood that his army would emerge victorious), when King George III's preoccupation with the symptoms of his tertiary neurosyphilis (a viral infection of the brain) led him to ignore the troublesome American colonies in the early 1770s, and when Abraham Lincoln's recurrent bouts of depression affected his military leadership of the North during the American Civil War. (In the midst of these severe depressions, he was unable to make tactical decisions.) To the extent that psychiatric disorder has afflicted the great and the ordinary, its study yields insights into history and humanity available from few other sources.

Another reason to study abnormal behavior is more personal. As noted earlier, all of us have occasionally asked ourselves, especially during periods of stress, whether we are going to "lose it" or "go off the deep end." The normal strains of life inevitably create situations that cause us pain and concern. Despite the turmoil we may be in, our depression, anxiety, and fears usually live out their brief lives and then

Julius Caesar, Abraham Lincoln, and George III suffered from mental disorders serious enough to have affected the course of history.

disappear, without leaving significant traces or meriting formal diagnosis. Although we may decide to seek help during particularly troublesome periods—such as on experiencing the loss of a key relationship, experiencing difficulties with parents or friends, or making a tough vocational choice—we may realize later that living through our distress was a necessary step toward greater self-understanding and maturity.

Many of you have probably also witnessed the impact of mental disorder on a close friend or relative. Alcoholism and drug abuse, depression and anxiety, even the serious forms of mental disorder we call the **psychoses** (conditions involving an actual break with reality, like that experienced by Clifford Beers), are sufficiently common for every American to know someone who suffers from one or another of them. Learning about these conditions in this text will give you some understanding of how they originate, are diagnosed, and can be treated. You will also learn if the social circumstances of your life, as well as your family's history of medical or psychiatric disorder, increase or decrease your chances of developing a mental disorder.

Finally, the authors of this text hope that the study of psychopathology will enable you to appreciate—perhaps for the first time—the vital interplay of biology, psychology, and the environment in the determination of behavior. We stress throughout this volume that all behavior—normal and abnormal—is the consequence of a wide range of influences, some internal, others external. We want to share with you this **biopsychosocial perspective**. We employ this term throughout the text to highlight the simultaneous impact on behavior of *biological* factors—including normal biology and disease processes as well as genetic influences—*psychological* factors—our thoughts, feelings, and perceptions—and *social* and *environmental* factors—the characteristics of the social setting we live in. To understand psychopathology, we believe you must understand the biopsychosocial perspective.

THE INCIDENCE AND PREVALENCE OF PSYCHOPATHOLOGY

How many Americans suffer from a psychiatric disorder? What are the most common forms of mental illness? Is emotional disorder increasing or decreasing in our society today? Do such factors as age, sex, race, and socioeconomic status influence incidence and prevalence?

Most of you probably assume that mental health professionals have clear-cut answers to these questions. The training of clinical psychologists, psychiatrists, psychiatric social workers, and psychiatric nurses is lengthy, as indicated by our overview of their professional education later in this chapter. Therefore, we might reasonably assume that they devote much of that time to learning the bases for diagnostic agreement. Yet, as discussed in Chapter 3, only in the last two decades have we begun to develop methods enabling clinicians to agree on a patient's diagnosis.

Because of the problems in achieving diagnostic agreement, consensus on the incidence and prevalence of psychopathology in this country has been difficult to reach. (The **prevalence** of a disorder is the total number of people within a given population who suffer from it; the **incidence** refers to the number of people within a given population who have acquired the disorder within a specific time period, usually a year.)

Our failure to agree on the extent of psychopathology in the American population is also surprising in view of the five landmark **epidemiological surveys** of psychiatric disorder conducted since World War II. Epidemiological surveys are focused studies of large groups of people designed to answer questions relating to incidence and prevalence of illness (in this context, psychopathology) in particular populations.

The landmark surveys of psychiatric epidemiology include the Stirling County Study (Hughes et al., 1960), the Baltimore Morbidity Survey (Pasamanick et al., 1962), the New Haven Study (Weissman & Myers, 1978), the Midtown Manhattan Study and the NIMH Epidemiologic Catchment Area (ECA) Program. Each of them was considered a landmark because its researchers drew on the best survey methodology of their day to design a study yielding data that could be generalized widely across the United States. Most of these surveys, especially the most recent, have yielded unexpectedly high prevalence figures.

A comparison of the data from the two most recent and comprehensive epidemiologic surveys of mental health and mental disorder in this country (the Midtown and the ECA surveys) reveals the scope of the problem of abnormality in America.

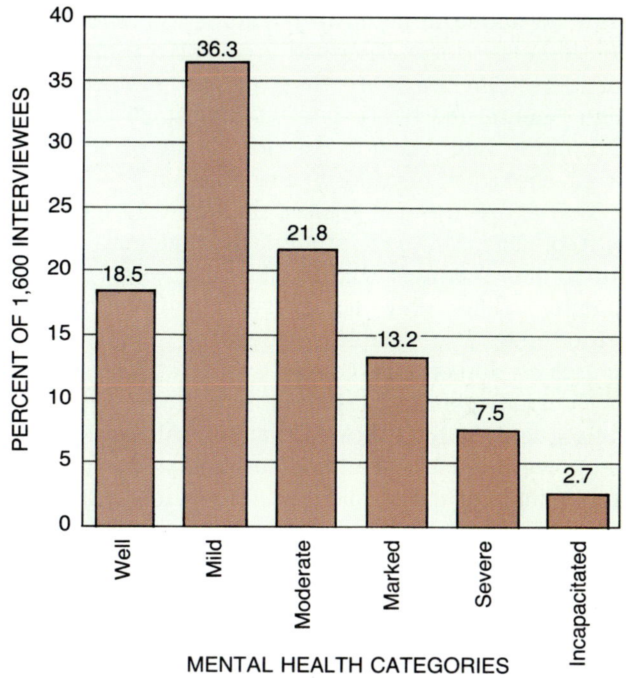

Figure 1.1 Prevalence of psychopathology in the Midtown Manhattan Study.

Source: From Srole, L. et al. (1962). *Mental health in the metropolis: The Midtown Manhattan Study.* New York: McGraw-Hill. By permission of the author.

The Midtown Manhattan Study

The **Midtown Manhattan Study** was an eight-year (1952 to 1960) investigation of mental health problems and resources among the residents of this area of New York City (Srole et al., 1962). It was, for its time, an extremely ambitious epidemiologic survey of mental health and mental illness.

TABLE 1.1 Diagnostic Categories in the Midtown Manhattan Study

Diagnostic Category	Definition
Well	No significant symptom formation
Mild	Mild symptom formation but adequate functioning
Moderate	Moderate symptom formation with no apparent interference in life adjustment
Marked*	Moderate symptom formation with some interference in life adjustment
Severe*	Serious symptom formation, and functioning with great difficulty
Incapacitated*	Serious symptom formation; functioning with great difficulty or inability to function

* Interviewees in these categories are considered impaired.

Source: From Srole, L. et al., (1962) *Mental health in the metropolis: The Midtown Manhattan study.* New York: McGraw-Hill. By permission of the author.

The study employed interviews based on a 200-item questionnaire given to 1,660 residents of Mid-Manhattan. Subjects were selected to represent the 750,000 residents of Midtown as closely as possible in age, sex, and ethnic, racial, and socioeconomic status. By this selection process, the researchers hoped to maximize the likelihood that data from the survey would be valid for all the residents of this part of New York City.

The mental health of Midtown residents was categorized by a six-point scale (Table 1.1). Figure 1.1 shows the percentages of Midtown residents who fell into each of these six categories. These judgments were made by two psychiatrists after reading the completed interviews.

The final three ratings in Table 1.1 ("Marked," "Severe," and "Incapacitated") were combined to form a single category that the Midtown investigators called "Impaired." Persons in one of these ratings were assumed to have experienced, at least to some degree, difficulties working, going to school, meeting ordinary family obligations, and the like. More than 23 percent of the persons interviewed at home fell into this category. Because the researchers considered interviewees as representative of the entire Midtown population, and the Midtown area as representative of the entire New York metropolitan area, they concluded that more than 23 percent of the several million people living and working in the New York metropolitan area were emotionally impaired. When the researchers than added in Midtown residents who had been continuously hospitalized for a psychiatric disorder for more than five years, they reported a startlingly high "mental morbidity rate" of almost 26 percent. (Morbidity rate refers to the prevalence of physical or psychological disorder in a population.)

This figure was far greater than anyone had expected. The Midtown study's methodology, measures, data analyses, and implications were, consequently, thoroughly scrutinized, and ultimately criticized by those unable to accept the validity of the figures on impairment.

The study generated even more controversy when subsequent analysis showed that poor Midtown residents were much more likely to be judged impaired than middle or upper-middle class residents. Since a principal aim of the study had been to examine the effects of urban stress on psychopathology, the obvious conclusion from these findings was that such stress most burdens the poor. Charges ranging from racism on the part of the interviewers—the poor were disproportionately black and Hispanic in Midtown—to insensitivity on the part of politicians who systematically ignored the plight of the poor were byproducts of these findings. A more positive consequence of the study was the impetus it gave to the development of federal programs during the presidency of Lyndon Johnson (1963–1969) to address the problems facing the urban poor that led to their extremely high rates of mental disorder.

The NIMH Epidemiologic Catchment Area (ECA) Study

The NIMH **Epidemiologic Catchment Area (ECA) Study** surveyed the psychiatric status of more than 20,000 persons residing in five U.S. cities and towns in the early 1980s (Eaton et al., 1984; Regier et al., 1984).

This study was designed to obtain rates of specific mental disorders rather than rates of impairment, as in the Midtown and other earlier epidemiologic studies (Regier & Burke, 1987). This goal became possible following the development of a standardized interview schedule, the *Diagnostic Interview Schedule (DIS)* (Robins et al., 1981). Not only did the DIS provide reliable diagnostic information on the most common psychiatric disorders, it could be administered by trained nonprofessionals.

Another valuable feature of the ECA study was the size, diversity, and representativeness of its sample population. Drawn from five sites (Baltimore, Maryland; Durham, North Carolina; Los Angeles, California; New Haven, Connecticut; and Saint Louis, Missouri), survey subjects came close to being as diverse geographically, economically, socioculturally, and ethnically as the country as a whole. The study's findings, consequently, can be considered representative of the entire country.

Initial reports from the ECA survey contrasting prevalence rates for urban versus rural interviewees

An urban homeless person may be the victim of alcohol or drug abuse or of a serious mental disorder.

and Mexican American versus non-Hispanic white interviewees justify the researchers' careful selection of survey sites. Data from the Durham site (Blazer et al., 1985), which includes surrounding rural areas as well as the city of Durham, reveal significantly more major depressive episodes and drug abuse/dependence among Durham residents than among those in the rural areas outside it. By contrast, alcohol abuse/dependence was a greater problem for inhabitants of the rural areas outside Durham. These findings confirm the widely held view, supported by data from the Midtown survey, that where people live affects whether they are likely to suffer from psychopathology and, if they do, what form it takes.

Data from the Los Angeles survey site (Burnam, et al., 1987), where significant numbers of Mexican Americans live, indicate that this ethnic group displayed higher rates of severe cognitive impairment (generally, impairment in intellectual capacity) than non-Hispanic whites. The ECA researchers suggest that this finding might reflect American society's ethnic and educational bias in defining adequate cognitive functioning largely in terms of scores by middle-class whites on IQ tests. (This matter is considered in detail in Chapter 3.) By contrast, non-Hispanic whites had higher rates of drug abuse/dependence than Mexican Americans or interviewees at other ECA sites. The ECA investigators concluded that ethnicity may be a factor in the distribution of psychopathology, a finding the Midtown survey also had highlighted.

TABLE 1.2 Six-Month Prevalence of Psychiatric Disorders in Three Communities (in Percentages)*

	New Haven	Baltimore	Saint Louis
Men			
18–24 years	23.8	25.1	18.9
25–44	18.9	23.5	19.8
45–64	11.9	18.7	9.4
65+	12.3	15.3	8.8
Total Men	16.7	21.1	15.4
Women			
18–24 years	24.6	26.6	17.8
25–44	21.2	27.1	17.2
45–64	10.3	21.5	10.9
65+	13.2	17.8	8.8
Total Women	17.1	23.6	14.3
Men and Women	16.9	22.5	14.8

* The psychiatric disorders included in this table include the affective disorders, panic disorder, obsessive-compulsive disorder, substance abuse/dependence, somatization disorder, antisocial personality disorder, schizophrenia, schizophreniform disorder, and cognitive impairment. All produce significant impairment in functioning.

Source: From Myers, J. K. et al., (1984), Six Month Prevalence of Psychiatric Disorders in Three Communities. *Archives of General Psychiatry,* 41, p. 959. Copyright 1984, American Medical Association.

Tables 1.2 and 1.3 show, respectively, six-month and lifetime prevalence rates at three survey sites for the mental disorders the ECA research team thought were most likely to impair functioning significantly. We will study each of these disorders in later chapters of this book. The six-month prevalence rates (Table 1.2) show the percentage of persons in each of the three cities diagnosed as having one of the listed disorders at any time during the six-month study period. The lifetime prevalence rates (Table 1.3) indicate the percentage of persons in the same cities diagnosed as suffering from the disorders at any time in their lives.

Table 1.2 shows percentages of impairment for survey subjects by age and sex. Impairment rates—ranging from a low of 14.3 for women in Saint Louis to a high of 23.6 for women in Baltimore—are similar

TABLE 1.3 Lifetime Prevalence Rates of DIS/DSM-III Disorders (in Percentages)

Disorders	New Haven	Baltimore	Saint Louis
Any disorder	28.8	38.0	31.0
• Substance use disorders	15.0	17.0	18.1
• Schizophrenic/schizophreniform	2.0	1.9	1.1
• Affective disorders	9.5	6.1	8.0
• Anxiety/somatoform disorder	10.4	25.1	11.1
• Eating disorder	0.0	0.1	0.1
• Antisocial personality	2.1	2.6	3.3
• Cognitive impairment—severe	1.3	1.3	1.0

Source: From Robins et al., (1984). Lifetime Prevalence Rates of DIS/DSM-III Disorders. *Archives of General Psychiatry,* 41, p. 952. Copyright 1984, American Medical Association.

Interviews were major sources of data in both the Midtown Manhattan and ECA studies.

to those in the Midtown Manhattan Study. This suggests comparability across both time and geography for the two surveys. Table 1.3 indicates that, during their lifetimes, about one third of the persons studied in the same three communities met interview criteria for one or more of the formal psychiatric diagnoses investigated in this epidemiologic study—from a low of 28.8 percent in New Haven to a high of 38.0 percent in Baltimore. Because none of the earlier epidemiologic surveys studied lifetime prevalence rates, this figure cannot be compared to earlier figures. It is nonetheless extremely substantial.

Much of the data from the ECA study confirm the Midtown Manhattan findings. This result is surprising, given the differences in the two studies' sampling procedures, data collection methods (the *Diagnostic Interview Schedule* led to far greater diagnostic agreement among interviewers), and methods of data analysis. Nonetheless, separated by time, geography, and level of methodologic sophistication, the two surveys agree that large numbers of Americans suffer significant impairment from stress, distress, and emotionally related problems. Moreover, men and women demonstrate comparable prevalence rates which vary with age, socioeconomic status, and race and ethnicity.

Additionally, the Midtown and ECA surveys confirm that the material covered in this textbook is relevant to you, the reader. What is described here has been or will be a part of your life or the lives of your family and friends.

THE MENTAL HEALTH PROFESSIONS

Several distinct professions have arisen to diagnose and treat the various mental disorders. Clinical psychologists, psychiatrists, psychiatric social workers, and psychiatric nurses are all members of the **core mental health disciplines**, the mental health team. Differences in education, training, and experience guarantee that each of the four professions makes unique contributions to the understanding and care of the mentally disordered.

Clinical Psychology

Clinical psychologists undergo a lengthy period of training and education. On graduating from a four-year college, usually with a major in psychology or another social or natural science, clinical psychologists-to-be apply for admission to a graduate program in clinical psychology.

Graduate study in clinical psychology leads to either a Ph.D. or a Psy.D. Most doctoral programs in clinical psychology require four or five years of academic work plus a minimum of a year in a clinical internship. Such programs typically require coursework in basic areas of psychological theory and research, along with courses in clinical assessment, diagnosis, and treatment. Extensive practicum experiences, in which students work beside experienced clinical psychologists in hospitals, outpatient clinics, and other institutions, are a regular and essential part of the training of clinical psychologists.

Most Ph.D. programs in clinical psychology provide training in both research and clinical practice. Dr. Betsy Oldmeyer, the young clinical psychologist whose typical workday is described in Box 1.1, graduated from a Ph.D. program in clinical psychology. Graduates of such programs generally complete several pieces of research during their four or five years in graduate school. Their culminating project, the dissertation, an extensive research project, is accomplished under the supervision of a senior faculty member. Ph.D. students also take a variety of clinical

BOX 1.1 A Day in the Professional Life of a Young Clinical Psychologist

A long and difficult day stretched ahead of Dr. Betsy Oldmeyer. A new Ph.D. in clinical psychology from a large midwestern university, Dr. Oldmeyer had just become an assistant professor of psychology in the Department of Psychiatry at the medical school where she had interned two years before.

Dr. Oldmeyer's day began with a two-hour diagnostic conference, at which the staff on the inpatient psychiatric unit reviewed its new admissions, made tentative diagnostic decisions, and preliminarily planned treatment. Her special role included sharing with other staff members results from the psychological tests she had given to several new admissions. In some instances these indicated the extent and nature of the deterioration in thinking patients had suffered because of their disorder. In others, the findings helped the therapists to identify issues they might want to ask their patients to begin to deal with.

After the conference—and before a "brown bag" lunch with colleagues at a departmental research seminar—Dr. Oldmeyer saw two behavior therapy patients, both of them admitted to her unit about two weeks ago. The first was a moderately depressed young man, the second, a young woman with a severe eating disorder. Both had begun to respond to the behavioral treatment methods that Dr. Oldmeyer knew from the literature had been quite effective with other patients with similar disorders. While she anticipated them, because the concrete diminishment in her patients' distress was gratifying, she also knew the two therapy sessions would demand a great deal from her.

Dr. Oldmeyer devoted the afternoon to her research. Assisted by a graduate student, she was engaged in a treatment outcome study. Patients admitted to the unit with diagnoses of mild to moderate depression had been assigned randomly to one of two treatments, either antidepressants alone or with a modification of the "standard" behavioral treatment for depression. Dr. Oldmeyer and her younger colleague wanted to know if adding the behavioral treatment to the medication regimen hastened the disappearance of depressive behaviors and the return of normal functioning.

One of the best things about her job, Dr. Oldmeyer reminded herself, was the challenge of doing excellent clinical work and excellent research. On graduation she had been offered jobs that involved only the one or the other. But both prospects seemed equally tempting. Therefore, she had willingly decided to spend part of each day wrestling with the complex questions posed by clinical assessment and treatment and the rest of it attempting to clarify such issues through clinical research.

courses and invest in extensive practicum training.

Psy.D. programs in clinical psychology are a relatively new development; the first graduated less than twenty years ago. Emphasizing clinical training, they aim to produce competent clinical professionals rather than psychologists who combine expertise in clinical research and clinical practice.

On completing their four or five years at the university, clinical psychology students spend at least another year in a full-time internship. In this capacity they function as junior staff persons under supervision, working with patients and polishing their clinical skills. After this training period, the Ph.D. or Psy.D. is awarded and the graduate can begin working as a clinical psychologist. If the new clinical psychologist desires to establish a private practice, he or she must also meet state requirements for a license as a psychologist. In most states these requirements include a Ph.D. or Psy.D. from an accredited training program, an internship, and satisfactory performance on a written and an oral examination.

Clinical psychology is a new profession. Although psychologists worked in clinical settings as experts on the assessment of intelligence and personality during the early decades of this century (Chapter 3 reviews this history), it was not until the psychiatric casualties of World War II overwhelmed existing mental health resources that clinical psychology was born. The numbers of clinical psychologists have grown subsequently from a handful in 1945 to more than 50,000 in 1989. All fifty states now have licensing laws governing the practice of clinical psychology.

Clinical psychologists are proud of their extensive training in assessment, both of cognitive (intellectual) functioning and of personality. Many value equally the extensive training in research they received in graduate school. Historically, assessment

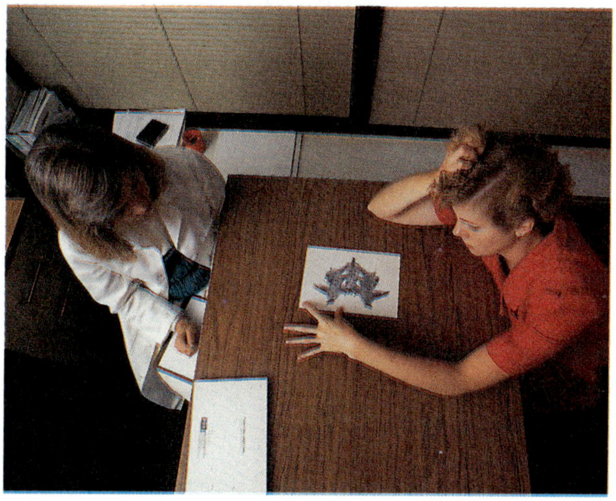

A young psychologist administering a personality assessment measure.

and research are the two unique contributions of clinical psychologists to the mental health team. Clinical psychologists have recently also been trained more extensively than other mental health professionals in psychotherapy and behavior therapy. Therefore, in many clinical settings clinical psychologists are authorities on the "talking therapies."

Psychiatry

Psychiatry is a branch of medicine. Persons intent on becoming **psychiatrists**, medical doctors who specialize in the diagnosis and treatment of mental problems, must first complete four years of college. During this time they take the usual premedical curriculum, including courses in biology, physics, and chemistry, as well as liberal arts courses. They must then be admitted to—and complete—four rigorous years of medical school. There they generally receive a basic medical science education during the first two years, followed by two years of clinical training designed to integrate the first two years of academic work with "hands-on" practical clinical work with patients.

On graduation from medical school, psychiatrists-to-be generally spend a year in an internship in a medical setting, then three or more years in a psychiatric residency. During it they assume increasing responsibility for the care of inpatients—most of them seriously disturbed—and outpatients. They learn how to diagnose psychiatric disorders, differentiate them from physical disorders with which they may share symptoms, and treat both psychotherapeutically and somatically (by physical means, including drugs). Intensive supervision of their clinical work by senior psychiatrists forms a key part of the training of psychiatric residents.

The unique contributions of psychiatrists to clinical work with mentally disordered patients stem from their education and training as physicians, which gives them a special appreciation for the impact of physical health and disease on behavior and psychopathology. Since some physical disorders masquerade as behavioral or psychiatric disorders and certain behavioral or psychiatric disorders resemble physical disorders (Chapter 8 considers some of these conditions in detail), such contributions can be tremendously useful.

Moreover as part of their training as physicians, but particularly during their psychiatric residency, psychiatrists study **psychopharmacology**, the use of drugs to treat mental disorder. During the past thirty years, drug therapy has been increasingly employed in treating the more serious psychiatric disorders. The ability to prescribe the right drug for a condition responsive to it—and to know when a drug is not the treatment of choice—is a valuable part of the psychiatrist's role.

Psychiatric Social Work

Psychiatric social workers generally complete four years of college and then two additional years at a university-based school of social work, from which they receive the Master of Social Work (M.S.W.) degree. During the two years of graduate training, social work students learn about group and social processes and development, public policy and social organization, research methods involved in the study of social organizations, and the various enabling pro-

Family therapy brings together a skilled therapist and two or more family members to focus on the issues disrupting family functioning.

BOX 1.2 A City Hospital Psychiatric Social Worker

Tony Veterno has served for more than a decade as the chief of social work in the Psychiatry Service of the City Hospital in the large northeastern city he lives in. Despite the grinding poverty that surrounds the hospital, the devastating effects of alcohol and drug abuse on many of his patients, the modest paycheck he receives every two weeks, and the hospital's bureaucracy, he would not trade his job for any other. He works hard, finds his patients endlessly fascinating, and believes he really helps them.

Tony Veterno's responsibilities include attempting to make contact with the family or friends of every new patient admitted to the Psychiatry Service inpatient unit. His purpose is to gather as much additional information about the patient as possible and to induce those involved to visit. This part of his job is often difficult. Many of the hospital's patients are either homeless or estranged from their families and friends. But it is necessary, for the information he gathers about patients' previous psychiatric and medical hospitalizations, drug and alcohol use, and job and family history is frequently tremendously helpful in planning treatment.

Tony Veterno is the Psychiatry Service's best-trained, most experienced family therapist. Besides carrying a number of families himself in therapy, he conducts a family therapy training program for psychiatry residents, psychology interns, and social work students. The program's weekly three-hour time block is typically divided into two parts. In the first hour trainees watch him conduct therapy behind a one-way mirror. In the next two hours, he joins them to analyze the session they have witnessed.

The most important of his activities, Tony Veterno believes, is his input at the weekly diagnostic conference. Every Friday morning, a senior clinician interviews newly admitted patients in a conference attended by the entire Psychiatry Service staff. A thorough discussion of the patient's history, diagnosis, and treatment always follows the interview. Tony Veterno then usually presents additional social information about the patient, with a commentary on its significance. Since most of the hospital's patients are poor and many are members of minority groups, he feels the need to emphasize to his colleagues—especially, residents, interns, and students—how the stresses of poverty, racial and ethnic bias, and other social factors affect the development of their patients' disorders. Since most of the professional staff are white and middle class, he believes that it is essential to ask them to consider the social issues they may otherwise ignore.

grams federal, state, and local governments develop to help persons who cannot help themselves. They also study psychology, sociology, and other social science disciplines. Additionally, social work students with particular interests in working in psychiatric settings learn psychopathology, assessment, and treatment. They also devote substantial numbers of hours to practicum training in hospitals and clinics, where they work with individuals and families under the supervision of psychiatric social workers.

Psychiatric social workers bring unique skills in *group work*, or the assessment of and intervention in problems affecting groups of people—families, marital couples, and organizations, for example—to the clinical setting. They also contribute their detailed knowledge of the community and its support structures to others in the mental health team. This knowledge enables psychiatric social workers to help patients receive financial and social support from their communities. Psychiatric social workers are also frequently experts on the environmental factors that may facilitate or interfere with patients' ability to live independently.

Many psychiatric social workers receive extensive training in individual and group psychotherapy and devote a substantial portion of their career to providing psychotherapeutic services (Box 1.2).

Psychiatric Nursing

Psychiatric nurses generally receive a B.S. degree and a diploma in nursing upon graduation from the four-year curriculum in nursing offered at many American universities. Graduates of this kind of program are then licensed as registered nurses.

Psychiatric nursing students return to the university to spend an additional two years pursuing a Masters degree in Psychiatric Nursing, during which they learn psychopathology, diagnosis, and treatment. Special emphasis is given to psychopharmacology, for nurses often are the ones responsible for dispensing medications to psychiatric patients.

Extensive practicum training during the Masters program ensures that the nursing student acquires therapeutic skills, frequently with patients in inpatient settings, where most psychiatric nurses work. Family therapy is one of the therapeutic approaches to which psychiatric nurses have significantly contributed. Another contribution of theirs has been to the "therapeutic milieu," also termed the "therapeutic community." Helped and supported by the nursing staff, psychiatric patients in a therapeutic community establish and enforce the rules governing their unit and regulating their interactions with each other. In this way, many professionals believe, even seriously disturbed patients can start reassuming responsibility for their own behavior and reestablishing social relations with others.

ABNORMAL BEHAVIOR THROUGHOUT HISTORY

Humanity's earliest ideas about abnormal behavior are lost in prehistory. We have no certain way of knowing whether strange behavior was attributed to natural causes, such as sickness or a blow to the head, or to supernatural causes, such as demonic possession or punishment by the gods. Possibly, the two kinds of explanations coexisted, as they do today. Throughout recorded history the natural and the supernatural have struggled for ascendency as explanations for abnormal behavior. Only during the last century have most people come to believe that mental disorders are caused by natural forces—genetic influences, disease processes, and environmental and psychological factors—rather than supernatural ones. Previously, people tended to believe that the gods, especially demons, caused every event beyond human understanding or control—earthquakes, avalanches, hurricanes, pestilence, famine, eclipses, and the seasons of the year, as well as psychosis, mental retardation, and epilepsy.

Many disorders that ancient and medieval peoples attributed to supernatural forces were **psychotic disorders**. The psychoses (Chapters 7 and 14) involve behavior that deviates dramatically from normality. These conditions are signalled by delusions and hallucinations (which Clifford Beers suffered from), bizarre behavior, and unusual or incomprehensible speech and thought. Psychosis and insanity are equivalent terms, although the first is a clinical term and the second is a legal one. We can easily understand why ancient peoples were frightened by behavior they could not comprehend and why, lacking the discoveries of modern science, they created mythic explanations to account for it and often employed harsh measures to "treat" or eliminate it. Mental retardation and epilepsy (Chapter 15) also induced behavioral abnormalities that isolated their victims from others and led to their persecution.

The Ancient World

A few societies before our own challenged the prevailing acceptance of supernatural explanations for the psychiatric and behavioral disorders. For example, almost three milennia ago—during the seventh century B.C.—Chinese physicians concluded that an imbalance in the essential natural forces they called *yin* and *yang* shared responsibility for physical and mental illness. (When yin and yang were in balance, physical and mental health resulted.)

The ancient Greeks held a similarly naturalistic view of the causes of disease. Hippocrates (c. 460–377 B.C.), the "father of medicine," believed that disease—mainly brain disease—was responsible for mental disorders. He prescribed natural treatments for these conditions, including rest, abstinence from sexual activity, solitude, and good food and drink.

Most common mental disorders, Hippocrates believed, derived from an imbalance in the four essential fluids, or *humors,* circulating through the body. When one of the four—blood, phlegm, yellow or black bile—predominated, mental symptoms developed. Too much black bile caused depression. An overabundance of yellow bile produced anxiety and irritability. An excess of phlegm resulted in lassitude and fatigue. Too much blood was associated with great changeability in mood.

Besides developing this theory of imbalance in the body's chemistry—echoed in modern discoveries of the biological components of mental disorder—Hippocrates recognized other natural causes for abnormality. Among them were stress, diet, heredity, a blow to the head—and even family problems.

Hippocrates also contributed to the diagnosis of medical and psychiatric disorders. Although the most

Hippocrates (c. 460–377 B.C.) believed that natural forces—an imbalance in the four humors—caused mental disorder.

rudimentary diagnostic instruments, including the stethoscope and the thermometer, had not yet been invented, and knowledge of human anatomy was extremely primitive (dissection of the body was not practiced), Hippocrates described some disorders familiar to us today, such as mania, melancholia (depression), and paranoia. His careful observation of his patients—in itself an innovation—permitted the description of these conditions.

Other Greek thinkers also emphasized compassionate treatment of disturbed persons. Although Plato (429–347 B.C.) and Aristotle (384–322 B.C.) were philosophers, not physicians, they were influential in promoting a naturalistic approach to mental disorders. They also believed that disturbed people, being ill, should be treated humanely and not held accountable for their actions.

The ancient Greeks recognized the behavioral effects of pathological aging, describing the symptoms of what we now call Alzheimer's disease (see Chapter 15) as well as the psychological and behavioral effects of alcohol abuse (Chapter 11). Two of the behavioral problems that most concern us were apparently as troublesome 3,000 years ago. Yet the behavioral effects of pathological aging were seen much earlier among the ancient Greeks, whose life expectancy was less than thirty years.

Nevertheless, most ancient societies—including Babylonia, China, and Egypt, as well as other centers of civilization—basically accepted the view that supernatural, not natural forces, caused abnormal behavior, disease, bad fortune, and natural catastrophies.

A witch being burnt at the stake.

The Middle Ages

The influence of Greek views of mental disorder persisted into Roman times, but after the fall of the Roman empire in the fifth century, efforts such as Hippocrates's and Galen's (c. 130–200 A.D.) to discover natural causes for abnormal behavior virtually ceased. During the Middle Ages, religion dominated all aspects of European life. Thus, people often explained episodes of mental disorder in supernatural terms. Troubled persons were seen as being punished for sin or perhaps possessed by demons. Although it was still occasionally recognized that a troubled person might best be considered sick, and humanely cared for at home, gruesome persecutions also occurred. Exorcisms were frequently performed—attempts to drive out the "devils" possessing the person. The ill person might be shouted at, deprived of food, flogged, or tortured in some other manner.

In the later Middle Ages, the fairly stable medieval world began to change. Wars, peasant revolts, and, finally, the Black Death (the plague epidemic that eventually killed half the population of Europe) encouraged the idea that powerful evil forces existed. One result was the phenomenon known as the witch craze. By 1484 Pope Innocent VIII issued a papal bull encouraging the persecution of witches. In 1487 two Dominican monks, Johann Sprenger and Heinrich Kraemer, published a treatise designed to establish the relationship between sin—a life devoted to sexual and criminal excess—and mental disorder.

The Witches' Hammer (Malleus Malleficarum) proved enormously influential. It precipitated the torture and death, usually by the most painful means, of thousands of people, some of them psychotics, epileptics, and mental retardates. Believing that persons suffering from mental disorder had sinned, and hence "deserved" their affliction and its consequences, justified widespread efforts by religious and civil authorities in the Middle Ages to destroy the evil spirits that had taken over the souls of the insane. Historians now believe that witch hunting was not simply a movement to persecute the insane. Instead, many of the accused were simply poor or disreputable or disliked by their neighbors. But probably many "witches" were also insane, epileptic, or mentally retarded, and were tortured or killed because their afflictions were attributed to the devil.

Even when insane persons escaped persecution and accusations of witchcraft, their lives often proved extremely difficult. The most fortunate were cared for by their families or took refuge in monasteries. Otherwise, local authorities tended to treat the insane as criminals, imprisoning them in degrading and inhumane conditions.

The Renaissance

The period known as the Renaissance, stretching from the fifteenth to the seventeenth centuries, saw the climax of the witch craze. It also marked the beginning of the reaction against such persecutions, and the movement toward more humane treatment of disturbed persons. The Swiss physician and philosopher Paracelsus (1493–1541) criticized the notion that demons could possess people. Instead, he believed that the stars and planets affected the actions of the brain—specifically that the phases of the moon were related to abnormal behavior. (This notion is preserved today in the word *lunacy, luna* being the Latin word for moon.) As Paracelsus's ideas suggest, Renaissance science remained comparatively ignorant of the workings of the human body. But at least people considered to be under the influence of the moon seemed unlikely candidates for burning at the stake.

Another critic of witch hunting was the German physician Johann Weyer (1515–1588). Having personally witnessed the torture and death of "witches," he wrote a treatise (published in 1563) in which he argued that many of those put to death were mentally unbalanced persons who could not be held responsible for their actions. Although the church banned his work and it received widespread condemnation, a few academics and intellectuals shared Weyer's skepticism. In 1584 the Englishman Reginald Scot (1538–1559) published a book called *Discovery of Witchcraft.* It argued that demons and evils did not cause mental disorders; instead, abnormal behavior was the result of illness.

This contemporary engraving of London's Bethlehem Hospital portrays 17th-century society's view of the chaos and confusion of the "madhouse".

Asylums and Reforms

The earliest institutional care for the mentally disturbed was provided by religious orders, which would sometimes shelter them inside monasteries. Early hospitals, too, occasionally accepted mental patients. By the mid-sixteenth century institutions known as **asylums**, or "madhouses," were established specifically to house the mentally ill. Perhaps the best known was London's Bethlehem Hospital, whose name was commonly contracted to "Bedlam," a term meaning chaos and confusion. Residents were chained to walls and otherwise mistreated; the public purchased tickets to see them, as if they were animals in a zoo. Bedlam and other contemporary asylums seemed more like prisons than like hospitals. The first asylums established in the United States opened in the late 1700s. Conditions in these institutions were not much better than those in the madhouses of Europe.

Reforms in the care of mental patients followed the American and French revolutions, each of which spread ideas about individual rights and human dignity. Humanitarian ideas characterized this age, and a few reformers became aware of the subjection and mistreatment of asylum residents.

The first notable reform occurred at La Bicêtre, a large asylum in Paris. Through the efforts of Philippe

Pinel (1745–1826), physician-in-chief at La Bicêtre, and his staff, patients found themselves in improved conditions. Pinel unchained patients, allowed them outdoor exercise, ordered their cells cleaned, and prohibited attendants from beating them. Under this regimen many patients improved—even seemingly hopeless cases.

Pinel continued to expand his reform efforts, first, at La Bicêtre and, later, at another large mental hospital in Paris, La Salpêtrière. He trained hospital attendants to treat their charges humanely, contrary to their previous harshness, and organized a rigorous and authoritarian routine for residents that he believed would be therapeutic. Pinel's reforms gradually spread through Europe and America.

While Pinel was reforming La Bicêtre, an Englishman, William Tuke, (1732–1822) set up York Retreat, an asylum in a country house in the north of England. A Quaker, Tuke believed that a haven of rural quiet and considerate treatment would benefit mental patients. At York Retreat, patients prayed and worked together, took walks, and rested. Many apparently recovered and went home.

In America, the most prominent mental health reformer was Benjamin Rush (1745–1813), known as "the father of American psychiatry." While associated with the Pennsylvania Hospital in Philadelphia, Rush, a famous doctor, wrote the first treatise on psychiatry to be published in America and established the first medical course in psychiatry. His medical theories were primitive. For example, he believed that astronomy influenced the brain, and regularly employed bloodletting, on the theory that too much blood in the brain caused disturbed behavior. Yet Rush's interest in the scientific study of his patients and his insistence on humane treatment remained positive influences.

Benjamin Rush (1745–1813), "the father of American psychiatry."

Dorothea Dix (1802–1887) played a central role in the reform of mental hospitals in 19th-century America.

Another effective American reformer, Dorothea Dix (1802–1887), was a Massachusetts schoolteacher. Dix became aware of the conditions in the asylums of her day after she taught women inmates in a prison. She traveled around her state, and then across the country, attempting to improve conditions inside mental institutions and to raise money to build new ones. Through her efforts more than thirty mental hospitals were built.

The Rise of the Scientific Model of Mental Disorder

The founding of asylums for the insane toward the end of the eighteenth century brought together, for the first time, sizable groups of mental patients under a single roof. Not only did asylums provide more humane conditions, they gave physicians their first opportunity to observe and contrast the behavior of large groups of seriously disordered patients. Philippe Pinel was one of the first to take advantage of this new opportunity.

Pinel's Classification System. Pinel's detailed observations of his patients led him to divide their disorders into *melancholia* (severe depression), *mania* (marked agitation, grandiose thinking, and elation) *without delirium* (delirium involves a loss of awareness of the environment, time, and the self), *mania with delirium, dementia* (a chronic disabling disorder marked by memory loss, personality change, and deterioration in judgment and personal habits), and *idiotism* (mental retardation). This classification system, based on Pinel's careful clinical observation of his patients' behavior and complaints, was one of the first modern psychiatric nomenclatures.

Kraepelin and the German Classifiers. German physicians working in the latter half of the nineteenth century, about sixty years after Pinel's reforms, led a growing effort to develop more systematic methods for classifying and categorizing mental disorder. The most influential of these workers was Emil Kraepelin (1856–1926). He combined previously distinct diagnostic observations of psychotic conditions into a single diagnostic category, which he called **dementia praecox** (literally, "premature dementia," meaning deterioration of the personality unconnected with advanced age). Kraepelin further characterized this disorder—the Swiss psychiatrist Eugen Bleuler (1857–1930) subsequently renamed it schizophrenia—by carefully detailing several of its subtypes. (They are described in Chapter 14.)

The emergence of schizophrenia as a recognized disorder with several identifiable subtypes constituted a great advance. It marked the first time a clinician willing to adopt a scientific approach to the process had subjected a common and serious psychiatric disorder to detailed investigation.

In his *Textbook of Psychiatry* (1883), Kraepelin argued persuasively that many of the most common mental disorders are disorders of the brain. He included dementia praecox; manic-depressive psychosis, now called *bipolar affective disorder*, (Chapter 7), and the *organic brain disorders* (Chapter 15). Considering the centuries of belief in nonscientific causal factors in mental disorder that preceded Kraepelin, his views on etiology were revolutionary.

Kraepelin's careful and extensive medical and psychiatric histories of patients, his development of the mental status examination (to assess the patient's mental state), and his emphasis on thorough behavioral observation of patients' symptoms in order to enable their diagnosis have influenced generations of mental health professionals.

During the same decades of the nineteenth century, Louis Pasteur postulated the *germ theory* of disease. Tiny organisms and viruses infected the body, producing external symptoms. The germ theory ultimately guided medical scientists in their search for the causes of many of the infectious diseases which had devastated humankind. Soon bacterial diseases with behavioral consequences—syphilis was among the first to be studied—began to receive scientific attention. Their causal agents were identified and, ultimately, effective antibacterial treatments were discovered for some of them. The acceptance of the idea that bodily diseases had identifiable biological causes strengthened the notion that mental problems, too, might eventually prove to be disease states.

The Psychoanalytic Revolution

The end of the nineteenth century witnessed the rise of another view—one that is still with us today. Known as psychoanalytic theory, it was developed by the Viennese physician Sigmund Freud (1856–1939). As a young man, Freud studied in Paris under the famous neurologist, Jean-Martin Charcot, who had investigated the possible role of emotional factors in producing neurological disorders. Among Charcot's experimental techniques was hypnosis. He and his associates found that patients apparently lost their neurological symptoms while hypnotized. Though Charcot believed that both hysteria and susceptibility to hypnosis were the result of nervous system degeneration, his student, Freud, diverged from his mentor when he concluded that patients lost their symptoms during hypnosis because psychological factors, not bodily disease, caused their mental problems. In the language of the day, patients with neurological disorders suffered from "hysteria."

Returning to Vienna after his studies with Charcot, Freud worked with another physician, Josef Breuer (1842–1925), who was treating patients with hypnosis. Breuer had discovered that disturbed patients frequently recovered after talking about their problems under hypnosis. He called this method the "cathartic" method, or "talking cure," since "hysterical" patients seemed to undergo an emotional catharsis, or cleansing, during discussion of their problems under hypnosis (Jones, 1953). Freud later abandoned hypnosis, simply encouraging the patient to talk freely in his presence. The emotional conflicts at the root of the patient's problems would, he believed, eventually reveal themselves in free association, in which patients simply talked of whatever came to their minds.

Studies in Hysteria (1895), written by Freud and Breuer, initiated the psychoanalytic revolution. The book developed several revolutionary ideas:

1. Psychological factors affect behavior in very powerful ways.
2. A "talking" treatment could be more effective for

disordered behavior than the harsh physical and moral treatments then in use.

3. Behavior is influenced by thought patterns, impulses, and wishes the individual is largely unaware of.
4. Nonpsychotic behavioral disorders like anxiety and phobic behavior are worthy of attention and treatment by psychiatrists.

These tenets of psychoanalytic theory (Chapter 2) continue to influence the thinking of mental health professionals.

Adolf Meyer's Psychobiology

During the initial decades of this century, clinicians impressed by the horrors of World War I and its psychiatric casualties played a significant role in the development of psychiatry. Adolf Meyer (1866–1950), a German psychiatrist who emigrated to America, was a notable figure. His view—that organic, psychological, and environmental factors contributed to psychopathology (1906)—greatly influenced the clinical methods and procedures of his era. Meyer's **psychobiology** continues to exert an influence, notably in clinicians' universal practice of taking a detailed personal, social, psychiatric, and family history of every patient, in *DSM-III-R*'s *multiaxial* approach to diagnosis (Chapter 3), and in the increasingly influential idea that unidimensional perspectives on etiology (entirely biological or entirely psychological) are less productive than biopsychosocial views.

Adolf Meyer (1866–1950) emphasized psychobiology—the role of biological, psychological, and environmental factors in mental illness and influenced a generation of mental health workers.

Research on Etiology

Kraepelin, Freud, and Meyer proposed theories on the **etiology**—explanations of the causes—of the psychiatric disorders that still influence many mental health workers. Both the biological position on etiology articulated by Kraepelin and the psychodynamic position espoused by Freud are discussed in detail in Chapter 2, along with the biopsychosocial position Meyer advocated.

As Chapter 2 and other chapters throughout the book suggest, recent decades have witnessed striking advances in the understanding of etiology. These advances required the development of new investigative techniques and procedures, including imaging, genetics, and longitudinal research strategies. The etiologies of such common and disabling disorders as schizophrenia, bipolar affective disorder, alcoholism, and some of the organic brain disorders, consequently, are better understood. Etiologic understanding, in turn, is likely to lead to more effective prevention and treatment.

Advances in Treatment

Only in the last two centuries, following Pinel's reforms of psychiatric institutions, have psychiatric patients received treatment. Before Freud it consisted mainly of ineffective physical measures, such as special diets, baths, and bloodletting. After Freud, psychological treatments—the "talking therapies"—became far more widely used.

Following Freud, a continuing stream of psychoanalytic theorists and clinicians modified psychoanalytic theory and technique. These developments are summarized in Chapter 2, which also describes the development of other psychological theories of abnormal behavior, including the behavioral and humanistic models. Both influenced the development of psychological treatment methods still in use.

A variety of physical treatments for the psychiatric and behavioral disorders have also been developed, particularly in recent decades. Many early physical methods, including insulin coma therapy, fever therapy, psychosurgery, and hot and cold packs (immersion in cold or warm water for long periods), ultimately proved ineffective. Recent advances in pharmacotherapy, however, have begun to restore many seriously disturbed persons to independent living. Drug treatments for schizophrenia and bipolar affective disorder, for example, represent modern miracles. Continuing research on medication to treat other conditions, including nonpsychotic but troubling conditions like attention deficit and anxiety disorders, as well as mild and moderate depressive disorders, also offer promise. These contemporary approaches to the physical treatment of the psychi-

Wartime psychiatric casualties such as these "shell-shocked" soldiers of World War I forced a radical rethinking of prevailing diagnostic conceptions during World War II.

atric and behavioral disorders, mostly developed during the past three decades, are detailed in Chapter 17.

Diagnosis and Classification

As indicated, one of the first advances in treating mentally disordered persons was the recognition that some patients behaved differently from others but in predictable ways. Patients were not simply more or less "crazy," they had specific symptoms, and these could be identified by careful observation. With the notion that distinctive psychological disorders existed came that of diagnosis—determining the particular problem the patient possessed. Accurate diagnosis is crucial, since, as with physical disease, proper treatment depends on correct identification of the problem.

The First American Diagnostic Nomenclature. A psychiatric classification system designed specifically for use in the United States was first developed in the mid-1930s by an association of state hospital superintendents. Previously, almost every hospital caring for psychiatric patients had its own, individual diagnostic system. The lack of a standard system created enormous difficulties in communication among professionals working in different hospitals.

The new system strongly (and predictably) reflected the most pressing needs of the large state psychiatric hospitals where most of the country's mental patients were hospitalized. Clinicians in those facilities needed to make diagnostic sense of the bewildering array of psychoses demonstrated by their patients.

Diagnosing Wartime Psychiatric Casualties. A diagnostic system designed for severely disordered state hospital patients was, however, of little use when, a decade later, America entered World War II. In 1941 a new classification system had to be developed for the many American soldiers who had developed behavioral symptoms under the profound stress of combat. Their symptoms differed greatly from the psychotic behaviors exhibited by the patients for whom the diagnostic system had originally been constructed. A system to categorize the psychiatric casualties of war, one that emphasized disorders reactive to the stress of combat rather than chronic psychosis, needed to be developed. The U.S. War Department undertook this task.

The Diagnostic and Statistical Manuals. In 1946 representatives of the state hospitals, the War Department, and the Veterans Administration met to discuss the creation of a contemporary diagnostic system. Their goal was a system that would be useful with long-term psychotic patients and those whose disorders seemed to be reactions to the stresses of modern life. The result, in 1952, was the first edition of the *Diagnostic and Statistical Manual of Mental Disorders (DSM-I). DSM-I* has since been followed by *DSM-II* (1968), *DSM-III* (1980), and *DSM-III-R* (1987).

As the previous discussion suggests, *DSM-I* was the product of more than a century of debate and discussion beginning with Pinel and Kraepelin. Clinicians had taken that long to appreciate the need for a consistent classification system for all psychiatric and behavioral disorders. Its creation also required the shock of recognition that occurred when the existing diagnostic system failed to classify 90 percent of the psychiatric casualties of World War II.

All four editions of the *DSM* show Kraepelin's influence. Thus, each calls for the careful observation of signs and symptoms of psychiatric disorder, assumes that many of these disorders derive from central nervous system damage, and separates the major psychotic disorders into subtypes based on the same signs and symptoms he identified. Adolf Meyer's psychobiology also has influenced the *DSM.* (As this book proceeds, you will probably be impressed by how thoroughly Meyer's emphasis on the interactive roles of biology, psychological states, and the environment guides the thinking of many contemporary researchers and clinicians.)

By introducing a diagnostic system that enabled all mental health professionals in this country to employ a common language, the first two editions of the *Diagnostic and Statistical Manual of Mental Disorders* represented a great step forward. But once in use, serious deficiencies became visible. These slim volumes (each about 125 pages) provided only brief descriptions of each disorder, together with one or two short paragraphs listing distinguishing signs and symptoms. This information was insufficiently detailed for clinicians to make reliable diagnoses. A reliable diagnosis is one that different clinicians assessing the same patient will agree on. *DSM-I* and *DSM-II* diagnoses, therefore, were highly unreliable (Beck, et al., 1962; Gauron & Dickinson, 1966). The reliability of a diagnosis directly affects its usefulness. Thus, the failure of clinicians to agree on *DSM-I* or *DSM-II* diagnoses made these diagnoses impossible to use to plan treatment, predict outcome, or investigate etiology (causation), three of the key functions of diagnosis (Foulds, 1955; Pinsker, 1967). Chapter 3 discusses why *DSM-III-R,* the latest successor to *DSM-I* and *DSM-II,* is a far more reliable diagnostic system than its predecessors.

SUMMARY

1. The chapter begins with a discussion of how mental health professionals decide whether a person's behavior is normal or abnormal. Among the criteria for this determination are the unusualness of the behavior, whether it is public or private, the social and environmental circumstances in which it occurs, and the behavioral standards of the community where the person lives.
2. Among the reasons for studying abnormal behavior are its influential role in human history, the likelihood that most readers have friends or relatives who have experienced mental turmoil, and the fact that the study of psychopathology illumines the interplay of biology, psychology, and the environment in the determination of behavior.
3. The prevalence of a disorder refers to the total number of persons within a given population who suffer from the disorder. A disorder's incidence relates to the number of people in a population sample who have acquired the disorder within a specific period of time.
4. The Midtown Manhattan Study and the Epidemiologic Catchment Area Study were influential epidemiological surveys designed to assess the incidence and prevalence of psychiatric disorder in selected areas of the United States. Both revealed unexpectedly high rates of mental disorder in their sample populations. The two surveys also found that rates of mental disorder are highest among minority groups and the poor. Reliable age- and gender-based differences in incidence and prevalence of psychopathology were also found in these surveys.
5. The core mental health professions include clinical psychology, psychiatry, social work, and psychiatric nursing. The training, professional emphases, and career patterns of the four professions differ widely, even though each primarily serves psychiatric patients and their families.
6. Many ancient and medieval societies concluded that mental disorder was a product of supernatural influences. A notable exception were the ancient Greeks. Hippocrates, the "father of medicine," stressed the role of brain disease and an imbalance in the body's four essential fluids (humors) in the etiology of these disorders. During the Middle Ages, psychotics and other persons who behaved oddly were often persecuted; some were put to death in the belief that this was the only way the evil spirits responsible for their behavior could be exorcised. The Renaissance saw the criticism of persecution and the recognition that some mentally disturbed persons were ill.
7. Philippe Pinel, a French physician influenced by the new sense of human dignity sweeping his country during the late eighteenth century, freed the mental patients in his charge from physical restraints and horrific conditions. He also developed and implemented a plan to reform and humanize the care of institutionalized psychiatric patients which gradually spread to other European countries and America.
8. Emil Kraepelin was the most influential of the German diagnosticians who worked during the second half of the nineteenth century. A strong advocate of the view that brain disease causes psychiatric disorder, he was also the first to study what are now called schizophrenia and bipolar affective disorder with careful and thorough observational methods that diagnosticians today continue to employ.
9. Sigmund Freud's development of psychoanalysis represented a strong counterforce to Kraepelin's emphasis on brain disease as the cause of psychiatric disorder. Adolph Meyer, who followed Freud, emphasized the value of the biopsychological approach to both research and treatment, an approach the authors of this text endorse.
10. The first American diagnostic system was developed in the 1930s by state hospital clinicians who focused on psychotic disorders they saw in their own hospitals. During World War II, an expanded diagnostic system was developed to include the disorders seen in military personnel. Thus, the first *Diagnostic and Statistical Manual of Mental Disorders* was published in 1952, followed by revised versions in 1968, 1980, and 1987.

Jan Sawka, *A Yellow Letter* (1984–85). Acrylic (mixed on masonite). Courtesy of the artist.

2 MODELS OF ABNORMAL BEHAVIOR

The study of abnormal behavior illuminates a broad sweep of human experience. Its domain includes behavior that deviates imperceptibly from the normal and behavior that is grossly abnormal; it also encompasses the causes, treatments, and prevention of mental disorder. One way humans have attempted to make sense of the puzzle of psychopathology has been to create **models** to help them understand how abnormal behavior originates and how to treat and prevent it. Models generalize our observations from the specific instance to the general instance. The earliest models of mental disorder stressed the role of supernatural influences in its development. Later models assessed the impact of natural causes—including disease—social causes—including criminality, poverty, and immorality—and psychological causes—primarily emotional turmoil.

The models of abnormal behavior proposed through the centuries have changed greatly, with the increasing accumulation of real knowledge. Yet models continue to be proposed because they are still useful. This chapter considers in detail several contemporary approaches to the understanding of psychopathology. Despite our relative sophistication and vastly increased knowledge, these six models focus on the same broad factors—biological, social, and psychological—familiar to the scientists and physicians who proposed their own models centuries ago.

Models are representations or approximations of the real world designed to help clarify and explain it for us. Thus, model trains and model airplanes are miniatures of the real thing; some are built to be extremely detailed and accurate approximations of an actual railroad train or airship. Architects' models are small-scale representations of buildings; they allow architects to test out arrangements of space and building materials before translating their designs into bricks and mortar. Chemists and physicists construct models of natural phenomena permitting them to explore the complex interaction of atoms and molecules more easily than in the laboratory or the real world.

Models help us clarify and organize complicated phenomena. They are especially useful when gaps exist in our understanding of those phenomena. For example, some biologists have proposed that the human circulatory system can be modeled after the network of local, state, and interstate roadways. In this model of the cardiovascular system, major veins and arteries are compared to the interstate highways and transcontinental toll roads, while smaller blood vessels are seen as state and local roads connecting regional cities and towns. Comparing the movement of cars and trucks within the United States to the circulation of blood in our bodies in this way helps clarify the structure and function of the parts of the circulatory system. While no one takes literally this comparison of blood vessels to the concrete and asphalt of streets and roads, the roadway model nonetheless helps us understand the cardiovascular system better.

Each of the six contrasting approaches to understanding abnormal behavior has supporters among today's scientists and clinicians and has contributed to our current understanding of psychopathology. The **biological model** emphasizes the role of physiological and neurochemical processes in understanding the causes and treatments for psychopathology, while the **psychodynamic model** and the **humanistic model** stress the importance of internal psychological processes. The **social-consequence model** and the **behavioral model** focus on the interaction of social and psychological factors to explain psychopathology. Finally, the **biopsychosocial model**, the explanatory model the authors of this text find especially helpful, emphasizes the interaction of all three sets of factors—the social, the psychological, and the biological—in explaining abnormal behavior.

THE BIOLOGICAL MODEL

The biological model of mental disorder assumes that the causes and the most effective treatments for abnormal behavior are biological and somatic. Because this model likens abnormal behavior to a disease, it has also been termed the *disease model.* We prefer the term biological model, though, because the analogy to disease states, as noted throughout the text, is only apt for certain mental disorders.

The history of the biological model of abnormal behavior is venerable. For virtually as long as humans have recognized and written about the existence of abnormality, they have believed that an important cause of psychopathology is something gone wrong with the body. The historical overview in Chapter 1 shows that the biological model of mental disorder has been influential through history. The biological model was developed by the ancient Romans and Greeks, whose understanding of the biological mechanisms responsible for psychopathology has been proven, understandably enough, largely incorrect. This model was kept alive by Chinese and Arab physicians during the Middle Ages, despite the cruel logic of an alternative model, which assumed that demons and other supernatural beings rather than biological factors caused mental disorder.

The biological model of mental disorder began to regain influence in the seventeenth and eighteenth centuries, coincident with the beginnings of modern science. It was especially strongly emphasized by Emil Kraepelin (1856–1926) and the other German diagnosticians in the latter part of the nineteenth century. Their focus on the role of brain disorder in emotional abnormality coincided with critical discoveries in bacteriology and infectious diseases. In our own times, as discussed in several chapters, an explosive advance in understandings of brain mechanisms responsible for several mental disorders has occurred.

Basic Assumptions of the Biological Model

Biomedical scientists today understand many forms of psychopathology to involve excesses or deficits in biochemical substances in the brain called **neurotransmitters**. Scientists increasingly believe that many of these excesses or deficits are transmitted genetically from parent to child. Surprisingly, the underlying assumptions of the biological models of the ancient Greeks and those of modern neurobiologists share striking parallels. They include the following: (1) Impairment or dysfunction of the brain is mainly responsible for mental disorder; (2) Accurate diagnosis consists of identification of the genetic/biochemical/metabolic cause(s) of the impairment in brain function; and (3) Proper treatment requires the attempt, with drugs or other somatic treatments, to lessen or eliminate the brain dysfunction.

Current Data on Disorders of the Brain

The organic mental disorders, first described by Hippocrates, involve disturbances in the functioning of the brain. These serious disorders (caused by the aging process, the abuse of drugs and alcohol, and injury, infection, and other diseases of the brain) exert pronounced effects on behavior. The evidence that these disorders stem directly from either short- or long-term changes in brain function is overwhelming. Few scientists today question the validity of considering these conditions products of brain disease (Chapter 15).

More recently, the role of biological disturbances in the brains of persons with serious psychiatric disorders previously thought to be of psychological or environmental origin has also been investigated. Advances in investigative techniques, including molecular genetics (Coryell & Zimmerman, 1988; Merikangas, 1987; Potter, Rudorfer, & Goodwin, 1987) and noninvasive imaging (Weinberger & Kleinman, 1986), have set the stage for these productive explorations.

The results of these studies have been revolutionary. Such major disorders as schizophrenia (Woods, Kinney, & Yurgelum-Todd, 1986), the affective disorders, including both manic-depressive psychosis and major depressive disorder (Blehar et al., 1988), and alcohol and drug abuse (Cadoret et al., 1985) now seem likely to derive, at least partially, from genetically transmitted disturbances in brain function. Research suggests that even some of the less serious mental disorders, including those primarily characterized by fearfulness and anxiety, long considered products of environmental and psychological factors, may stem partially from genetic alterations in brain functioning (Kaye et al., 1984; Pauls et al., 1986; Rosenbaum et al., 1988).

Biological Bases of Normal and Abnormal Behavior

To appreciate the recent advances in biological research on psychopathology reviewed through the text, you need to know something about the structure and function of the central nervous system. That information is summarized here.

The Brain and Nervous System. Our nervous system controls our every move and thought. A properly functioning nervous system permits us to perceive the environment, integrate our perceptions with memories of prior experiences, and then make appropriate and effective responses to what we have seen and heard.

Neurons and Neurotransmitters. Our nervous system contains many billions of nerve cells or *neurons.* These specialized cells serve two crucial functions:

1. *They receive information* (via systematic changes in the composition of cell chemicals) from *sensory receptors*—which include the eyes, ears, and skin—as well as specialized receptors that obtain information on the state of internal bodily organs.
2. *They transmit messages* to other neurons or to *effectors,* which include the muscles and glands.

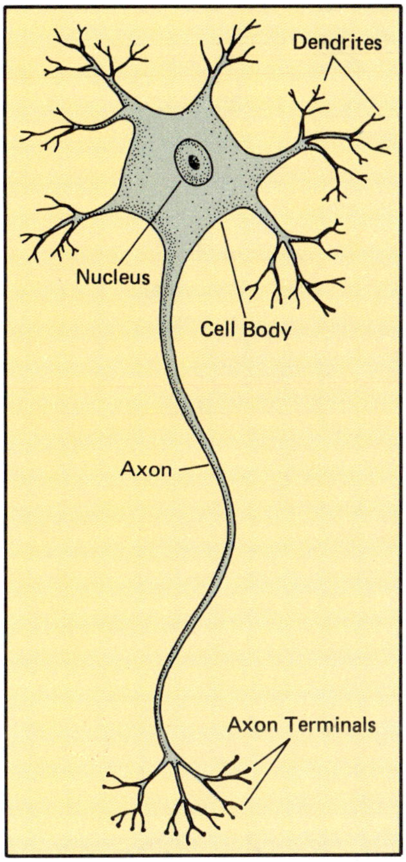

Figure 2.1 Drawing of a nerve cell or neuron. *Neuronal messages are transmitted from the axon terminal of one neuron to the tip of the dendrite of another across the synapse. The bulb of the axon terminal releases a chemical substance, the neurotransmitter, into the synapse to convey the neuronal information across the synaptic gap.*

Figure 2.1 shows a typical neuron. As the figure indicates, it consists of a cell body, branched extensions called *dendrites,* which receive nerve impulses from other neurons, and other extensions, called *axons,* which transmit nerve impulses to other neurons. The extraordinarily minute space between the axon of one neuron and the dendrite of another is called the *synapse.* Nerve impulses are conveyed across the synapse when infinitesimal amounts of neurotransmitters are released from the axon tip and travel across the synapse to the dendrite tip. On making contact with its tip, these substances excite the dendrite and *propagate* the nerve impulse along the new neuron.

Neuroscientists now employ in their research measuring instruments whose sensitivity exceeds that of any known as recently as a decade ago. This research has confirmed the central significance of neurotransmitters to the coordinated functioning of the nervous system. Different brain regions that control different bodily functions, it seems clear, function by means of concentrations of different neurotransmitters.

For example, it is now reasonably well established that regions of the brain regulating the autonomic nervous system (which is responsible for the expression of emotion) are high in concentrations of at least two neurotransmitters, acetylcholine and norepinephrine. Of specific relevance to psychopathology, neuroscientists have also concluded that excesses or deficits in the neurotransmitters norepinephrine, serotonin, and dopamine, which impair transmission across synapses in certain regions of the brain, apparently influence the symptomatology of schizophrenia and depression (Chapters 7 and 14).

The Central and Peripheral Nervous Systems. As Figure 2.2 indicates, the nervous system is divided into the **central nervous system** and the **peripheral nervous system**. The brain and the spinal cord constitute the central nervous system. The two process information on our internal and external environments received from the sensory receptors and, if necessary, transmit instructions for action.

The peripheral nervous system is also divided into two parts. The **somatic nervous system** controls

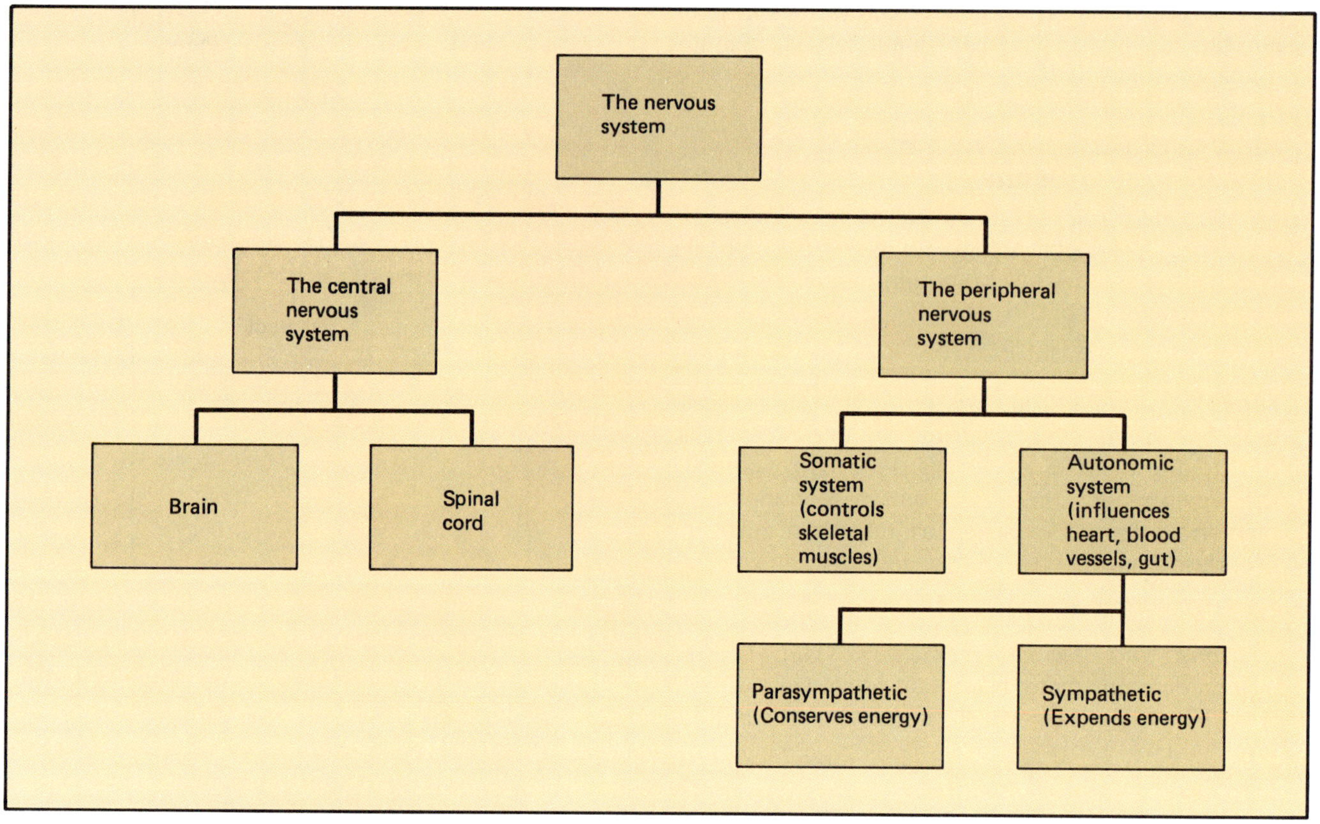

Figure 2.2 Components of the nervous system. *The central nervous system encompasses the brain, spinal column, and peripheral nervous system. The peripheral nervous system includes the somatic nervous system, which serves the skeletal muscles, and the autonomic nervous system. The autonomic nervous system is composed of sympathetic and parasympathetic divisions; both serve the heart, viscera, and other internal organs.*

the skeletal muscles, which permit voluntary behavior like walking and talking. The **autonomic nervous system** regulates the glands, heart muscle, blood vessels, and viscera.

The autonomic nervous system (ANS) is divided into the *sympathetic* and *parasympathetic* divisions. Though they link the brain and spinal column to many of the same organs of the body, the two divisions sometimes act in opposition to each other, by means of different nerve pathways (Figure 2.3), especially during times of stress. During such times, the sympathetic nervous system energizes or activates organs to enable the body to respond to emergency situations. For example, your body's emotional reaction to a "near-miss" auto accident represents a sympathetic division response to a potential threat. Your heart beats faster, you breathe more quickly, you begin to perspire, and you feel "shaky" and lightheaded. All are sympathetic arousal responses to a threatening situation.

By contrast, the parasympathetic division regulates normal bodily functions—"housekeeping" functions—like digestion. Mobilization of the sympathetic division of the autonomic nervous system during emergencies is associated with a reciprocal decrease in the level of activity of the parasympathetic division. When, consequently, we experience emergency situations requiring sympathetic division activation, such parasympathetic activities as digestion diminish. This is why we get "knots" in our stomach during times of emotional stress.

The Brain. Composed of billions and billions of densely packed neurons, the brain is the most complex organ in the nervous system. It is divided into three parts that differ in both function and structure. The three include the *hindbrain*, the *midbrain*, and the *forebrain*.

The hindbrain controls autonomic nervous system functions like the actions of the heart and digestive tract. The midbrain contains the *reticular activating system* (RAS), which also extends down into the hindbrain. The RAS, the brain's "sleep-wake" center, also mediates attentional processes and may play a role in such devastating psychiatric disorders as childhood autism (Chapter 12).

The forebrain controls our capacities to speak, think, plan, and remember. Virtually all psychiatric

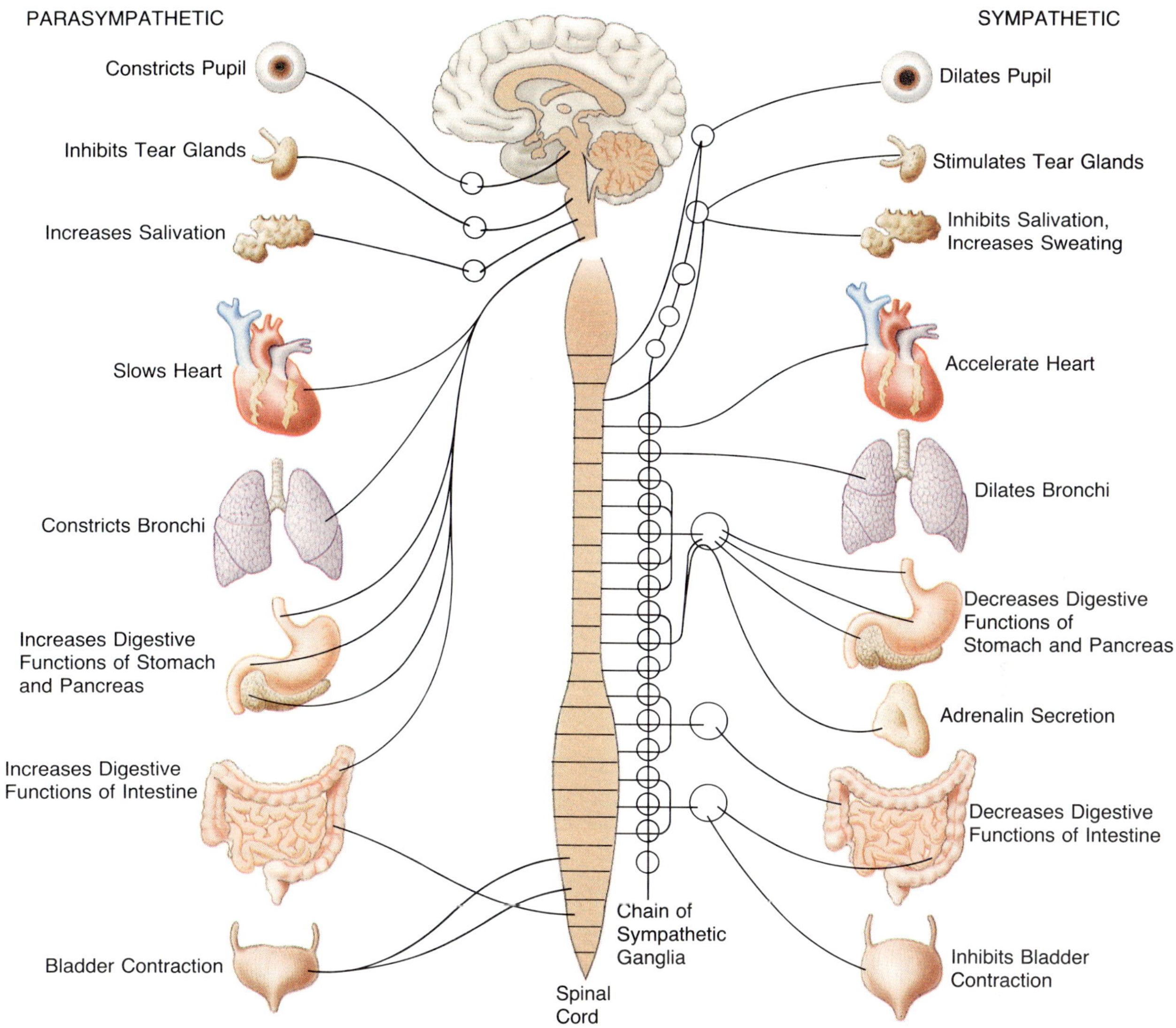

Figure 2.3 The two divisions of the autonomic nervous system. *The sympathetic division activates internal organs in response to stress. After the stress has ended, the parasympathetic division controls the normal functioning of the organs.*

disorders of known biological etiology involve some kind of forebrain dysfunction. Infants born without a forebrain, a rare condition of newborns called *anencephaly*—"brainlessness"—

> often can maintain vegetative and other basic functions. Indeed, these infants can even learn primitive conditioned responses. One anencephalic boy was able to regulate his body temperature and maintain respiration, and displayed near-normal fear and startle responses. (Willerman & Cohen, 1990, p. 201)

Because they do not possess a forebrain, however, these infants could never think, speak, or display any other distinctively human behaviors (although, almost always, they die before such behaviors could develop).

The forebrain consists of the *thalamus* and *hypothalamus,* together commonly termed the *diencephalon,* and the *cerebrum,* called the *telencephalon.* The thalamus and hypothalamus, along with parts of the cortex, mediate the experience of emotion, pain and pleasure, and aggression. These structures compose the *limbic system.* This system is markedly affected by many varieties of psychopathology, because it controls the physical expression of emotion—the changes our body undergoes in the face of emotional extremes—as well as the expression of such basic drives as hunger, thirst, sex, and aggression.

The cerebrum is the largest part of the human brain. Its outer layer, the **cerebral cortex**, the locus of our ability to think, feel, perceive, and reflect, chiefly mediates our most human intellectual capabilities.

The Cerebral Cortex. The human cerebral cortex performs sensory, motor, and associational functions. In its sensory function, it receives information from the sense organs and processes them for storage or action. In its motor function, it controls the movements of our muscles.

The most complex—and uniquely human—function of the cerebral cortex, though, is that of *association,* the linking together of all parts of the cerebral cortex in a myriad of interconnections that far surpasses, for example, any metropolitan telephone system. These interconnections of associational neurons permit uniquely human reasoning, planning, memory, creativity, and problem solving.

The cerebral cortex is divided into symmetrical halves called *hemispheres* (Figure 2.4). Each hemisphere contains four lobes, the **temporal**, **parietal**, **occipital**, and **frontal**. Recent advances in *imaging technology* permit more accurate representation of the structure and the functions of the lobes of the cerebral cortex (Chapter 3).

The temporal lobes control visual information pro cessing, long-term memory, the experience of emotion, and the recognition of sounds. The parietal lobes mediate touch recognition. A portion of the left parietal lobe is also involved in speech. The occipital lobes are primarily concerned with visual perception. The frontal lobes are the seat of the capacity to solve problems flexibly, a capability which calls upon high-level reasoning and remembering. They are also involved in "social cognition," or knowledge of the rules governing social conduct. As this text proceeds, you will understand that the abnormal behavior of the victims of many mental disorders is mediated largely by neurotransmitter dysfunctions centered in the frontal lobes.

Recent research has suggested that, though the two hemispheres appear identical, they mediate different cognitive functions and have different roles in psychopathology. Both hemispheres apparently carry out independent learning, memory, and perceptual functions. But the left hemisphere, dominant in most right-handed persons, is responsible for the analytic, cognitive, and language-based processes that are most essential to our functioning as intelligent be-

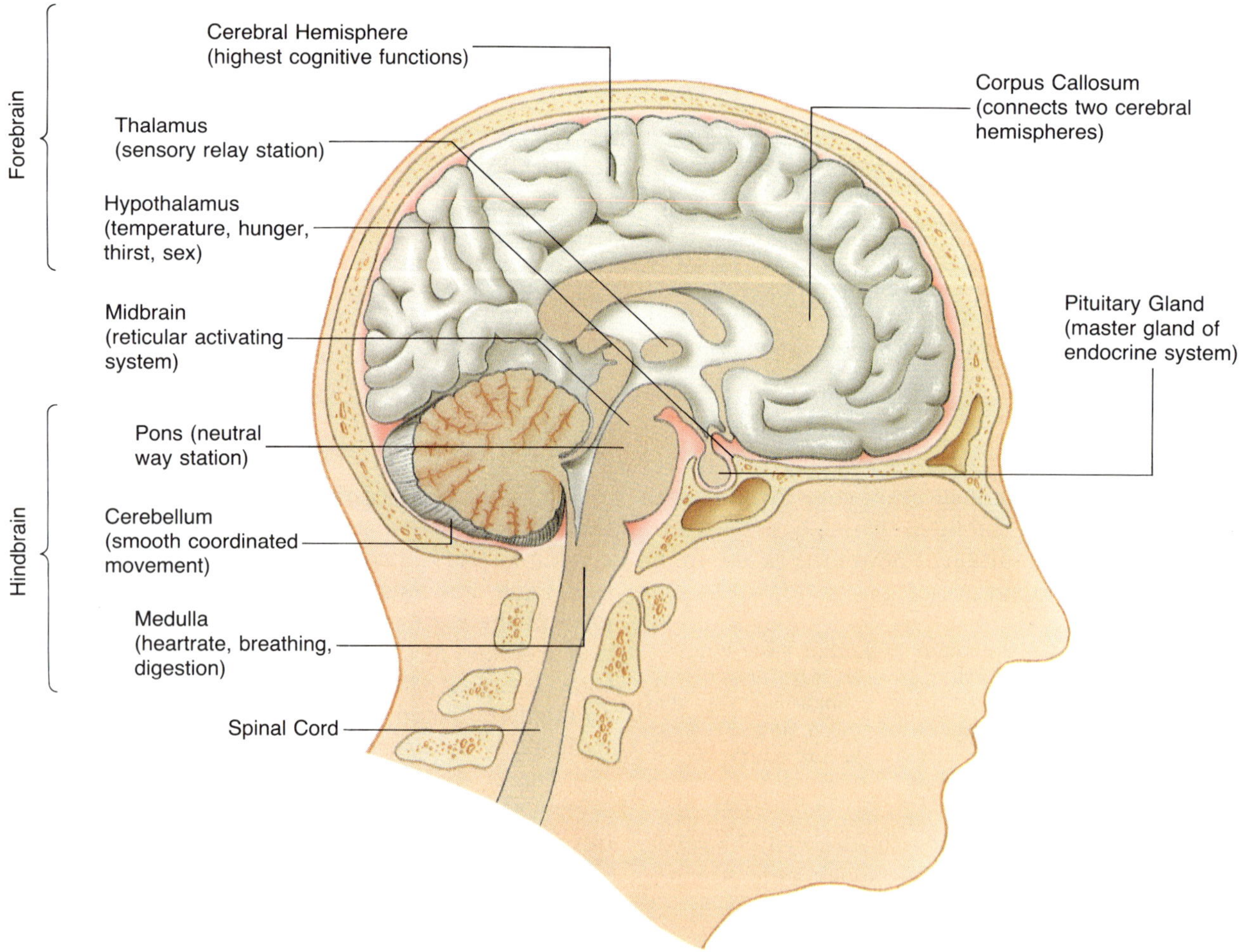

Figure 2.4 Side view of the human brain, showing the cerebral cortex.

ings. By contrast, the right hemisphere is more involved in global perceptions and in comprehending language (rather than in expressing it). The language functions of most people reside in the left hemisphere. Imagery and spatial relations are more often located in the right hemisphere.

The relevance of hemispheric differences in function to psychopathology remains uncertain. Yet recent research suggests that autistic children may suffer from a severe left hemisphere dysfunction, since so many of their significant behavioral deficits are mediated by that hemisphere. Schizophrenic patients too show behavioral deficits and excesses indicative of left hemisphere damage and demonstrate more left than right hemisphere activation (Gur, 1978).

The Endocrine System. The *pituitary, thyroid, adrenal,* and *gonadal* glands are *endocrine organs.* Each produces substances called **hormones**, chemical messengers secreted by the glands directly into the bloodstream and designed to act on other organs in the body. The hormones help regulate the body's physiological processes and coordinate internal bodily processes with external events. They function very much like neurons, except that their route of message transmission is the bloodstream rather than the axons and dendrites.

Prolonged stress, including that associated with significant psychopathology, can cause temporary or permanent dysfunction in the endocrine system, thereby increasing the stress-induced physical and emotional distress experienced by psychiatric patients. Stress can also impair immune system function, making the individual more susceptible to disease. The complex relationships linking stress and other environmental and psychological factors, on the one hand, and autonomic nervous system activity, including endocrine and immune system functioning, on the other hand, is discussed in Chapter 8.

Genetic Factors in Normal and Abnormal Behavior

Every human being began when a sperm and an ovum united to create a single viable cell. Your entire biological inheritance was determined the moment your mother's ovum encountered one of the many millions of your father's sperm to initiate the process of human development. Your development from that single fertilized cell to the young adult reading these words was an enormously complex process that fortunately functions normally in most instances—but is capable of going seriously wrong.

The role of genetic dysfunction in such major disorders as schizophrenia, the bipolar affective disorders, and alcohol abuse and dependence has been studied intensively in recent years by means of increasingly sophisticated molecular genetics techniques. The influence of genetics on psychopathology is a recurrent theme in this text. To make these discussions more understandable, this section of this chapter reviews the mechanisms of heredity and outlines recent advances in investigative techniques used in genetics research.

Genes and Chromosomes. Everything we inherit from our parents and their parents is transmitted by many millions of genes, the chemical units of heredity. Genes are arrayed in a specific order, almost like numbered beads on a string, along chromosomes. Most human beings possess forty-six chromosomes, identical sets of which are located in all cells in the body except the sperm and ova. Every cell's chromosomes are grouped into twenty-three pairs, one member of each having been contributed by each parent.

When humans reach adolescence, his testes and her ovaries produce a *gamete* (a sperm cell or an ovum). Each of these reproductive cells receives only one member of each pair of chromosomes. The union between egg and sperm during reproduction thus restores the full human set of forty-six chromosomes.

The only time two people inherit precisely the same genetic material is when identical twins are created. Otherwise, the millions of genes arranged along our chromosomes guarantee each person's genetic uniqueness. Identical twins develop from the same fertilized ovum or *zygote*; as a result, **identical twins** are also termed **monozygotic twins**. They differ genetically from **fraternal (dizygotic) twins**, who are conceived simultaneously but grow from separate fertilized ova. One percent of all children born are twins; one twin set in three are identical twins. As indicated later, the identical genetic composition of identical twins makes them useful to scientists investigating the effects of heredity and environment on development and psychopathology.

Phenotype and Genotype. If a person inherits the genes for brown hair from one parent and the genes for blond hair from the other parent, he or she will have brown hair. This happens because the genes for brown hair are **dominant** over the genes for blond hair, which are **recessive**. When someone inherits a dominant gene and a recessive gene, he or she will demonstrate the feature or characteristic conveyed by the dominant gene, though the person's cells will also contain the recessive gene. That explains why brown-haired persons can have blond-haired children (if his or her mate also contributes the gene for blond hair, so the child inherits two recessive genes for blond hair).

To express the difference between actual physical appearance and heredity, we refer to **phenotypes** and **genotypes**. The term *phenotype* refers to someone's observable characteristics, like hair, eyes, skin color, height, and weight—and temperament and personality. Genotype refers to the array of genes a person possesses. While the transmission of a recessive characteristic like blond hair is unimportant to the mental health professional, a number of significant mental disorders, including some psychoses and certain forms of mental retardation, are transmitted recessively (Chapters 7, 14, and 15).

Nonhereditary factors can also influence phenotype. Take weight, for example. Though we inherit the predisposition to be lean or rotund, our diet, family-eating pattern, and socioeconomic status powerfully affect the expression of the phenotype. A similar relationship between phenotype and genotype almost certainly affects the expression of certain forms of psychopathology. That is, some persons are born with or later develop a predisposition to develop a particular kind of psychopathology. Whether they actually develop it, though, may depend on their environment and life experiences.

This theory, the *stress-diathesis theory* (Meehl, 1962), assumes that some people inherit or develop a *predisposition* (diathesis) to disorders like schizophrenia and the substance use disorders. The disorder itself, however, will not be expressed unless environmental stress—death, divorce, serious interpersonal or vocational problems, and the like—or biological stress (like disease or injury) is sufficiently intense to interact with the predisposition to produce the disorder.

Gene-Environment Interactions

Extraordinary advances in investigative methods for studying gene-environment interactions have occurred during the past decade. For example, major strides have been made in methods for studying genetic influences on normal behavior and psychopathology. These studies now call on one of four principal investigative techniques, the *family method*, the *pedigree method*, the *twin method*, and *adoption studies*.

The family method represents an early epidemiologic approach to the study of genetic factors in mental disorders. This method assumes that even if a mental disorder does not obey the established laws of inheritance, it is hereditary if it occurs more often in the families of **index cases** or **probands**. (Index cases represent patients who suffer from the disorder.) While still useful—it informs scientists about which disorders run in families—the family method is inadequate as a means of separating the respective influences of heredity and environment. That is because emotional disorders can run in families for either hereditary or environmental reasons.

The pedigree method involves the tracing of the distribution of a disorder among nuclear (close) and collateral (distant) relatives of an index case. This technique shows whether the disorder is distributed in accordance with the Mendelian laws of inheritance (that is, in accordance with the influence of dominant and recessive genes) and whether the responsible gene or genes are dominant, recessive, or sex-linked.

The pedigree method is employed most frequently in conjunction with molecular genetic studies of the genes responsible for specific disorders: When large pedigrees of families in which such disorders as depression, schizophrenia, or alcohol dependence have been identified, genetic "markers" that help researchers localize the genes possibly responsible for the disorders can sometimes be discerned in the genetic material of affected individuals (Figure 2.5).

The twin method controls for environmental factors that neither pedigree nor family methods can. The method's effectiveness depends on the fact that monozygotic twins share all genetic material (because they developed from a single fertilized ovum) while dizygotic twins (who developed from separately fertilized ova) share only some genetic material. Identical twins, therefore, will be significantly more *concordant* for genetically transmitted disorders—that is, more likely to share the disorder—than will fraternal twins. Because identical and fraternal twins reared apart vary systematically—both genetically and environmentally—they are a particularly interesting subset of experimental subjects for genetics research.

Adoption studies represent the most recent method for epidemiologic research on genetic factors in mental disorders. They have been especially instructive in the study of genetic factors in alcoholism (Chapter 11). These studies involved the comparative diagnostic study of adults with and without a family history of alcoholism who, as children, were adopted out of their nuclear families. Study subjects with an alcoholic biological parent were significantly more likely than subjects without an alcoholic biological parent to develop an alcoholism problem as adults. These findings strongly support a role for genetic transmission in the development of alcoholism in some persons.

Recent research by Plomin (1986, 1989) demonstrates the contributions of genetic factors to individual differences in behavioral development. Paradoxically, this research also emphasizes the impact of environmental factors on development. Reviewing this research, Plomin (1989) concludes that intellectual factors (e.g., IQ, academic achievement, and mental retardation), personality factors (e.g., emotionality, activity level, and sociability), and psychopathology (e.g., schizophrenia, the affective disorders, delinquency, and alcoholism) are all influenced

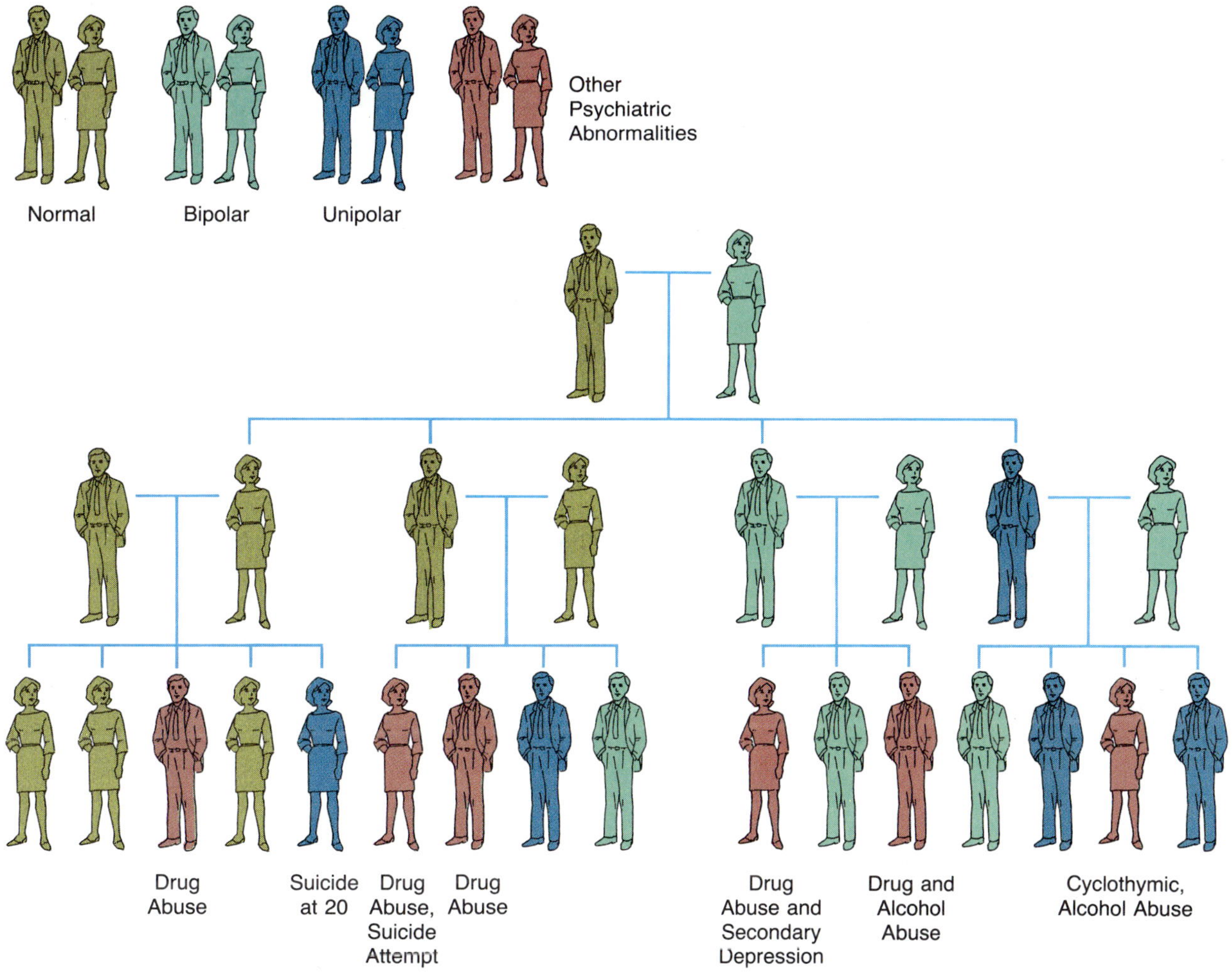

Figure 2.5 Pedigree chart. *A grandmother who suffered from unipolar depression had a son who developed bipolar affective disorder and nine grandchildren who experienced bipolar affective disorder, unipolar depression, and alcohol and drug abuse. This family's pedigree has enabled researchers to explore genetic factors in mental illness.*
Source: Courtesy of E. S. Gershon, Clinical Neurogenetics Branch, National Institute of Mental Health.

significantly by genetic factors. But Plomin also observes that in every instance genetic factors alone are insufficient to explain the development of such behaviors. Nongenetic factors, primarily environmental, are also responsible for these and other complex behaviors, like psychopathological behavior.

In pursuing an answer to this paradox, Plomin asks why children in the same family differ so greatly from one another, since they share so much genetic material. His answer stresses the impact of their *nonshared environments*, those experiences they do not share with their brothers and sisters. Nonshared environments include differences in how parents treat each child in a family, in the friends each child has, and in the number of accidents and illnesses each child experiences. All these make children in the same family different, often unpredictably, despite their shared environments and genetics.

Advances in Molecular Genetics

Advances in molecular genetics investigative procedures now permit genetics researchers to localize the gene or genes responsible for certain mental disorders. Though the process is long and labor-intensive, much progress has been made in identifying, for example, the chromosome and, more recently, the gene location of Huntington's Chorea, a devastating organic brain disorder (Chapter 15). There have also been advances in localizing the gene or genes for Alzheimer's Disease (Chapter 15), manic-depressive illness (Chapter 7), and schizophrenia (Chapter 14), though completing these localization efforts will probably take years.

Once the gene or genes responsible for a disorder have been localized, their biochemical composition can then be studied to yield clues to the nature of the metabolic dysfunction they cause. That is, molecular genetics research to localize genes mediating psychiatric disorders promises to aid in the discovery of their causes and in effective prevention and treatment.

Contributions and Shortcomings of the Biological Model

The biological model of mental disorder represented a distinct step forward when Kraepelin reintroduced it a little over one hundred years ago. Viewing mental patients as sick, not immoral, eased the moral stigma that was attached to mental disorder through the ages. The biological model represented a humane advance.

The biological model's ties to medicine, moreover, encouraged empirical inquiry, careful observation of abnormal behavior, and respect for reliable diagnosis. Scientific research began, consequently, to be directed to uncovering the causes of disorders and to finding treatments for them.

The biological model also raised the standing of the mental health professions, especially psychiatry. Bright young people became more interested in choosing psychiatry or the other mental health professions rather than, as before, leaving the job of working with psychiatric patients to people who could find no other employment.

Recent advances in our understanding of the role disturbances in brain functioning play in some psychiatric disorders have led to marked improvements in diagnosis and treatment. An example is research on the molecular genetics of neurotransmission in the brain. Insights gained this way into the causes of disorders have improved treatment. Another example is psychopharmacological research, which has produced drugs to modify brain dysfunction that are more effective in treating the severe psychiatric disorders than other methods.

But these advances also could constitute a potential problem. For example, they might conceivably lead us to view *all* behavioral and psychiatric disorders through the lens of the disease model. Preferable, in our view, is the biopsychosocial perspective on mental disorder, which permits a fuller appreciation of the diverse factors contributing to the causes and treatments for these conditions.

For example, rigid allegiance to the biological model obscures the clear impact of social variables—for example, racial, ethnic, and sociocultural factors—on the lives of many persons in our society. Simply by considering such common consequences of poverty and discrimination as drug and alcohol dependence, antisocial personality disorder, and the conduct and learning problems of ghetto children as diseases, it is possible to conclude that societal problems have not influenced the development of these disorders. Many believe, to the contrary, that they have.

THE PSYCHODYNAMIC MODEL

Basic Assumptions of the Psychodynamic Model

All psychodynamic approaches to the understanding of human behavior share the fundamental belief that it is strongly influenced by unconscious factors—internal, irrational conflicts, impulses, and motives of which the individual is unaware. The psychodynamic model also assumes that all behavior, both normal and abnormal, results from the interaction of inherited and environmental factors. Psychodynamic theorists stress the crucial impact of the child's earliest years, believing that events occurring then exert lifelong effects.

Because the **psychoanalytic theory** of Sigmund Freud continues to influence subsequent psychodynamic theories strongly, we highlight it here, though our review of the psychodynamic model also touches on some of the more influential of its later variants.

Freud's Psychoanalytic Theory

The Structure of Personality. Freud's *structural theory of personality* (1917, 1923) divides what he called the *psychic apparatus*—the mind or psyche—into three parts, the familiar **id**, **ego**, and **superego**. Each is responsible for a distinct set of psychological functions.

Dominant during the earliest months of life, the id, a reservoir of primitive drives and desires untouched and unaffected by the real world and its "civilizing" influence, is the first of the elements of personality to make itself felt. Energizing the id are two basic drives. The first is the **life instinct**, or **libido**, composed of sexual impulses and drives. The second is the *death instinct,* or *thanatos,* the id's aggressive and destructive drives that lead to eventual death. In the id—as in human behavior—generative life instincts oppose regressive death instincts.

Unsocialized, primitive, and selfish, the id is preoccupied with the gratification of the sexual and aggressive instincts energizing it. The **pleasure principle**, whose only aim is to maximize pleasure and reduce tension without concerning itself with morality or reality, guides the operations of the id. Therefore, id impulses sometimes conflict jarringly with society's rules and expectations. They do so, partly because they are guided by **primary process** thinking, irrational and illogical thinking characterized by sexual preoccupations and fantasies, anger, jealousy, selfishness and envy.

Sigmund Freud (1856–1939), the founder of psychoanalysis.

The basic elements of id are present in every infant. This belief—that infants and children possess strong sexual and aggressive feelings—embroiled Freud in a great deal of controversy when he first proposed his theory. Written during a time when even adult sexual impulses were largely denied or ignored (the prim and proper Victorian era), Freud's conviction that two- and three-year-old children experienced sexual feelings outraged many contemporaries.

The ego, which modifies the id's primitive drives and impulses so they conform more closely to reality, emerges from the id after a few months of life. It emerges when the infant must begin to respond and adapt to the realities of its external environment. This is the time when the infant begins to notice that all of its needs for food, comfort, and warmth are not gratified immediately—although the infant's unsocialized id demands immediate gratification.

The ego subsequently assumes the additional responsibility of bringing the id's primitive impulses into greater conformity with society's moral and ethical standards. The ego is the principal means by which human beings meet these societal standards, by struggling to adapt the contents of the id to and compromise them with the demands of reality.

In contrast to the id—and the pleasure principle it operates by—the ego is guided by the **reality principle**. The reality principle recognizes society's realistic demands, which the ego undertakes to meet "by the rules." In doing so, the ego employs **secondary process** thinking, reason and logic. Anything that impairs the reality principle on which the ego depends, by interfering with its accurate assessment of the real world—like drugs or serious emotional disturbances—weakens the ego and strengthens the id.

Because it manages the functioning of the person just as a chief executive officer manages the functioning of a corporation, the ego has been called the executive of the personality. This metaphor is especially apt: The ego must balance the demands of the real world with the energies of the insistent id, just as the chief executive officer must coordinate and channel the energies and talents of the company's employees to enable it to compete successfully.

Psychoanalysts believe that successful resolution of the conflicting demands made on the ego permit us to engage in such high-level intellectual pursuits as learning to write, compose music, or create art; sensing, perceiving, then reflecting on our sensations and perceptions; remembering, comparing, and thinking; and comparing reality to our expectations of it.

As the child grows, the ego assumes an additional role, that of dealing with the superego, what we call conscience, or our ability to distinguish right from wrong. The superego emerges gradually, as the child begins to learn the rules his or her parents use to interpret society's expectations by learning the consequences of failure to follow those rules. Parents serve this essential function until the child evolves his or her own internal set of standards.

The superego also makes demands, which the ego must manage. These demands can be excessive in a child raised by extremely critical, punitive, and judgmental parents. In such cases, the superego may become so restrictive that it prevents the child from enjoying the normal, innocent pleasures of life. When children with punitive superegos grow to adolescence and experience puberty's marked increase in sexual feelings and desires, they may experience even more difficulty handling the demands of the superego. Anxiety and depression are common consequences of excessively strong superego demands.

The dynamic interplay of id, ego, and superego form the basis for the **psychodynamic model**. The model reflects Freud's belief that every healthy human being is capable of three distinct kinds of behavior. They comprise (1) irrational, primitive sexual and aggressive drives and wishes; (2) a set of internalized standards that enable the person to live according to society's rules; and (3) an "executive" that mediates, monitors, and continuously adjusts the balance between the outside and inside worlds. Like

Sigmund Freud as a young man, shown with his mother, Amalie. Some biographers have speculated that Freud's close relationship with his mother influenced his formulation of certain aspects of psychoanalytic theory.

these three behaviors, the ego, id, and superego are inherently in conflict because of their differing goals and methods. If the id or superego becomes so strong that it overwhelms the ego, the result will be **intrapsychic conflict**. If this conflict between the ego, id, and superego remains unresolved, it can lead to mental disorder.

Freud's early clinical work was with patients who suffered from puzzling physical and psychological symptoms. His patients' inability to explain their symptoms led him to conclude that much of our behavior is controlled by mental processes we are unaware of. He ultimately concluded that the contents of the id and superego remain largely **unconscious**, or out of awareness throughout our lives (Freud, 1895, 1940). By contrast, Freud believed, the ego operates primarily at the conscious level, in its role as executive of the personality and principal thinker and planner.

Unconscious materials include impulses and desires beyond our awareness. Though material from the unconscious enters awareness and becomes conscious only rarely and under special circumstances—in dreams and fantasies, during psychoanalysis, in jokes, or through slips of the tongue—it is a powerful determinant of behavior. If the sexual and aggressive impulses of the id and the punitive and judgmental products of the superego are neither modified and brought to conscious awareness (as occurs in psychoanalysis) nor controlled by the ego's defenses, they can precipitate irresponsible, irrational, and maladaptive behavior. The ego's **defense mechanisms**, which are designed to defend the ego against attack by the id or the superego, are detailed later in this section.

Within immediate, conscious awareness are thoughts about current experiences. The memories, feelings, and fantasies which can be brought to consciousness by shifting attention or changing environment, which might include information on how you spent last weekend or what you've planned to do the coming summer, is stored in the *preconscious*. You can bring it to conscious experience simply by shifting your attention to it.

The Stages of Psychosexual Development. Freud's theory of psychosexual development (1905, 1920) portrays the development of the personality as proceeding in distinct and successive stages, each distinguished by a different means of gratifying libidinal (sexual) needs.

The first, or **oral stage**, extends from birth to the age of eighteen months. The infant's predominant physical need during this period is for the food necessary to sustain rapid growth. The infant's mouth, lips, and tongue are, consequently, invested with libido, so that during eating they become **erogenous** parts of the body that give pleasure. This arrangement, Freud believed, ensures that the infant will want to eat and thus be nourished.

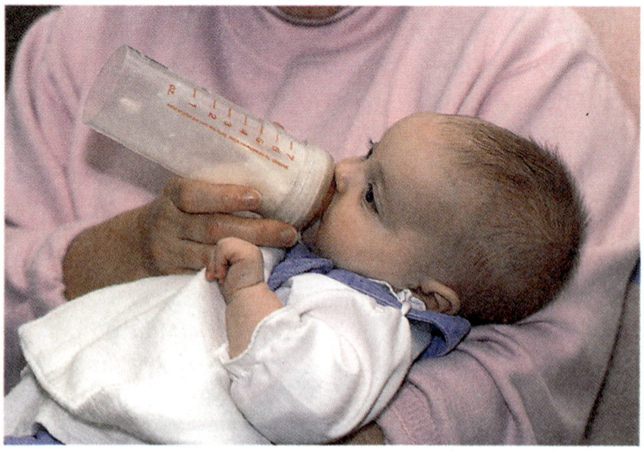

During the oral stage of psychosexual development, the infant's mouth, lips, and tongue become erogenous zones capable of giving pleasure, thereby ensuring adequate nourishment.

Freud also recognized that psychological and cognitive growth characterizes each of the psychosexual stages. In the oral stage of development, for example, infants must learn that they are not the center of the universe—that they cannot be fed, held, or comforted whenever they wish. They must also learn that their impact on the world around them—including on their parents—has clear limits.

The second, or **anal stage**, lasts from about eighteen months to the third year. The bodily—and libidinal—focus is now on the anal and urinary sphincters, which control the elimination of waste products and become erogenous zones. During this psychosexual stage, the child learns that it is pleasureable physically to withhold and expel feces. This pleasure is nature's way of focusing the child's attention on the need to learn these basic bodily skills. In the process, the child acquires new ways to control parents' behavior, by learning (and then demonstrating) that there are parts of his or her body (the bladder and the bowels) and behavior (urination and defecation) they cannot expect to control.

In one of his most controversial statements, Freud wrote that from about the third to the sixth year, the child's principal source of libidinal pleasure derives from manipulating his or her genitals. He believed that, during this period—the third, or **phallic stage**—boys confront the dilemma of the well-known **Oedipus complex**. Impressed by how many of his patients recalled childhood fantasies of incest with the opposite-sex parent, accompanied by jealous, sometimes murderous, rage at the same-sex parent, Freud named this scenario for the mythical Greek King Oedipus. As a youth, Oedipus learns that he is doomed to play out a great tragedy, by killing his father and marrying his mother. Despite his best efforts, the tragic forecasts come true.

During these early years, Freud observed, a boy becomes preoccupied with power and strength—and the size and function of his penis. He wants to become stronger, bigger, and more powerful—and, symbolically, to take the father's place in the mother's bed. Loving the father, yet fearing his wrath, the boy must repress his longings for his mother. The crucial lesson of the phallic stage of development is learned when the child resolves his conflicting feelings of love for and anger at his father, along with his feelings of dependence on and lust for his mother.

Freud also speculated on the existence of a counterpart in girls of this age. He called it the **Electra complex**, after another famous Greek tragedy. Recognizing that they do not possess penises like their brothers and fathers, girls of this age wish symbolically to possess their fathers—and thereby gain a penis. Girls resolve this conflict when they realize they will ultimately have a man—a mate—and then a baby that will substitute for a penis. (Freud's statement of the Electra complex has been strongly criticized in recent years by many women, who feel both that it is sexually demeaning as well as an inaccurate description of the feelings of women and girls in our time.)

The Oedipal complex represents the central challenge of the phallic stage. It forces boys to confront—and resolve—the profound and conflicting feelings they have toward both parents.

Between the ages of six and twelve, the child enters the fourth, or **latency stage**, an extended period of psychosexual quiescence. The child now devotes him or herself to consolidation of the psychological and interpersonal lessons learned and behaviors acquired during the oral, anal, and phallic stages.

The onset of puberty marks the beginning of the fifth, or **genital stage**. Adolescents now learn the pleasures—and perils—of adult sexuality. How much pleasure and how much peril the adolescent experiences depends on how well he or she has progressed through the earlier developmental periods. Central to psychoanalytic theory is the belief that the events of the oral, anal, and phallic stages largely determine both the personality and the emotional status of the adult.

The Ego's Mechanisms of Defense. The ego initiates defensive maneuvers when confronted by anxiety generated by threats from the id or superego. **Neurotic anxiety** arises when id impulses threaten to overwhelm the ego. Even when repressed, they are still capable of causing emotional distress. Anxiety generated by guilt and shame, products of a harsh and punitive superego, is termed **moral anxiety**. **Objective anxiety** refers to the realistic apprehension we experience when confronted by real danger.

Freud postulated the existence and traced out some of the specifics of the devices the ego employs to defend itself against attacks by the id or superego.

Anna Freud (1895–1982), Sigmund Freud's daughter, as a young woman. Anna Freud's writings on the role of the ego in determining mental health and illness, especially The Ego and the Mechanisms of Defense *(1936), strongly influenced the development of ego psychology.*

Freud's daughter, Anna, subsequently developed these ideas fully in *The Ego and the Mechanisms of Defense* (1936). The volume stressed the importance of the ego to our psychological lives—and the consequent necessity of protecting and nurturing it. It also detailed the elaborate series of defense mechanisms the ego employs to ensure its central role in the psychic apparatus.

The ego's protective tactics are unconscious. They operate beyond our control or awareness. When, however, we deny that a recent argument has upset us, or that we have displaced anger from one person onto another, or that we cannot remember a painful incident, we may become aware of our use of these devices. Are any of the defenses described in Table 2.1 familiar to you?

A useful means to adjust to the inevitable stresses of our lives, the defense mechanisms have a downside as well. Excessive reliance on them, especially on such maladaptive defenses as fixation and regression, can become self-perpetuating, rendering us incapable of dealing directly and effectively with even minor problems in the environment. Many of the signs and symptoms of emotional disorder, including anxiety and depression as well as the signs and symptoms of psychosis, stem, Anna Freud believed, from inappropriate reliance on these defensive maneuvers.

Other Contributors to Psychodynamic Theory

Freud's was the most influential psychodynamic theory of personality. It has not been the only such theory proposed, however. Several of Freud's contemporaries, a few of his students, and a number of later clinicians and theorists have proposed their own dynamic theories. Some of the theories remained close to Freud's thinking, others deviated markedly from it. But despite their differences, each of these psychodynamic theories emphasize the dynamic interplay between conscious and unconscious experience in behavior and psychopathology.

Defectors from Freud's "Inner Circle." Carl Gustav Jung (1875–1961), Alfred Adler (1870–1937), and Otto Rank (1885–1939) were young psychiatrists Freud worked closely with during the first two decades of the twentieth century, the years in which he was developing psychoanalytic theory. All three ultimately were unable to accept Freud's conviction that infants and young children possess unconscious sexual feelings for their parents that, unresolved, may cause mental disorder.

Each of the three, therefore, developed substitute theories to explain the development of psychopathology. Jung believed its development should be traced

TABLE 2.1 Some of the Ego's Mechanisms of Defense

Regression
Avoids the experience of painful thoughts and feelings from the past by returning psychologically to an earlier, less stressful period. (Common and harmless regressions include crying and childlike expressions of anger and resentment when frustrated; more problematic regressions are psychotic hallucinations and delusions in response to insoluble life problems.)

Fixation
Keeps potentially threatening thoughts and feelings aroused by environmental or psychological stressors from consciousness by remaining psychologically at an earlier, less painful stage. (The young man "who has never grown up" and continues to evade adult responsibility, like Peter Pan, has fixated at an earlier, less stressful level of development.)

Repression
Prevents painful, potentially disruptive thoughts, feelings, memories, and impulses from reaching consciousness, although they may reach consciousness in dreams, or slips of the tongue, or during psychoanalysis. (The young woman in psychoanalysis who suddenly recalls the guilt she felt at her sexual feelings for her father during her childhood is forced to deal with a repressed emotion.)

Identification
Defends against threatening feelings aroused by the behavior of another person by experiencing a strong sense of psychological linkage between that person and oneself. (Willy Loman, the salesman in Miller's tragic play *Death of a Salesman,* identifies with the ambitious, magnetic, and successful peers he has never been able to emulate.)

Projection
Involves attributing an emotion or feeling that one fears or finds threatening in oneself to another person, thus denying its existence. (The college student who believes that every other student is working at maximum intensity in order to best him academically thereby attributes motives to them he finds difficult to admit to in himself.)

Reaction Formation
Avoids the turmoil aroused by conflicting feelings about someone by excluding these negative feelings from consciousness and focusing on positive ones. (The young man who emphasizes his love for and pride in his father's achievements thereby defends himself against unconscious feelings of competition and rivalry.)

Sublimation
Transforms the psychological energy associated with threatening sexual or aggressive feelings and impulses into socially acceptable pursuits, like art, music, politics, or intellectual activities. (The local politician who devotes himself to the welfare of his constituents may be defending himself against anxiety from unconscious sexual or aggressive conflicts.)

Rationalization
Involves an "after the fact" set of rational and logical reasons for a behavior whose causes were actually irrational and unconscious. (Rationalization is a favorite defense of college students and their professors; it sometimes produces heated arguments which, because they focus on the intellectual and the scholarly, protect participants from anxiety-arousing competitive emotions.)

to problems the patient's parents had when the patient was a child. Adler chose to emphasize the negative consequences of feelings of inferiority every child experiences in relation to bigger, wiser, more powerful adults. Rank conjectured that the emotional consequences of the trauma of birth—the infant's shock at having to forsake the security and warmth of the womb for the confusion and uncertainty of the external world—were responsible for psychopathology.

The Impact of Culture and Society on Personality. In the early 1930s, while economic depression gripped most of the world, Europeans began to experience the results of Adolf Hitler's fascism and his government's denial of rights to many Germans. In response, a group of European personality theorists modified psychoanalytic theory to emphasize the impact of culture and society on the development of personality and psychopathology. These theorists included Karen Horney (1885–1952), Erich Fromm (1900–1980), and Erik Erikson (1902–1988).

Horney based her theory on the belief that anxiety and depression, common signs of psychopathology, develop following one of three basic interpersonal conflicts: "moving toward people," "moving against people," and "moving away from people."

Fromm's most famous book, *Escape From Freedom,* was published in 1941, at the height of the Nazi threat to the world. Puzzled by the appeal of fascism to many Central Europeans, Fromm concluded that the boundless opportunities for choice in life-style and individual freedom available in modern societies was the problem. So great, he felt, was the discomfort many citizens of free countries had felt at their unlimited freedoms that they had chosen to "escape from freedom" (the title of Fromm's book) by embracing Hitler's totalitarian regime.

Erikson—with Freud the most influential psychodynamic theorist—has also emphasized the role of

Carl G. Jung (1875–1961), Alfred Adler (1870–1937), and Otto Rank (1885–1939) were the earliest defectors from Freud's "inner circle."

social and cultural factors in influencing personality and behavior. His belief that personality continues to grow and develop through a series of eight developmental stages extending from the beginning to the end of life has struck an especially responsive chord in recent decades. Humans face social and psychological conflicts, Erikson suggested, at every stage of their lives. At each, the individual must resolve a specific conflict. His or her success in doing so significantly impacts on personality development and psychopathology.

Of Erikson's eight stages of development, *intimacy vs. isolation* is the psychosocial challenge young adults—most college students are young adults—must resolve (Figure 2.6). The young adult is challenged to deal satisfactorily with his or her need for sexual and emotional intimacy with another or, failing to resolve the dilemmas that result from trying, to settle for a lifelong pattern of sexual and emotional isolation.

In Escape From Freedom, *Erich Fromm (1900–1980) speculated on why fascism appealed to so many Central Europeans during the 1920s and 1930s.*

The Ego Psychologists. A third group of neo-Freudian theorists, Heinz Hartmann (1894–1970), René Spits (1887–1974), and Margaret Mahler (1897–1985), are called ego psychologists because their theories stress the importance to personality development and psychology of the ego and its defenses. The ego psychologists were strongly influenced by Anna Freud's *The Ego and the Mechanisms of Defense,* one of the first and still most influential statements of the basic beliefs of ego psychology. These theorists emphasize the role of the strong, mature ego in enabling adults to adapt effectively to changing external environments as well as internal challenges from the id and super-ego.

Margaret Mahler emphasized the importance for normal development of the child's ego's separation from the mother's during early childhood, partly by using the mother's example to make sense of the world. Mahler's theory has influenced subsequent views of normal as well as pathological child development. For example, her concept of *psychological birth,* which occurs later than physical birth, corresponds to the emergence of the child's individuality, and is facilitated by maternal encouragement, has been especially influential. Mahler's belief in the importance for the child's ego development of the early relationship with the mother, well before the Oedipal period, stands in sharp contrast to Freud's conviction that the child's separation from parents comes several years later.

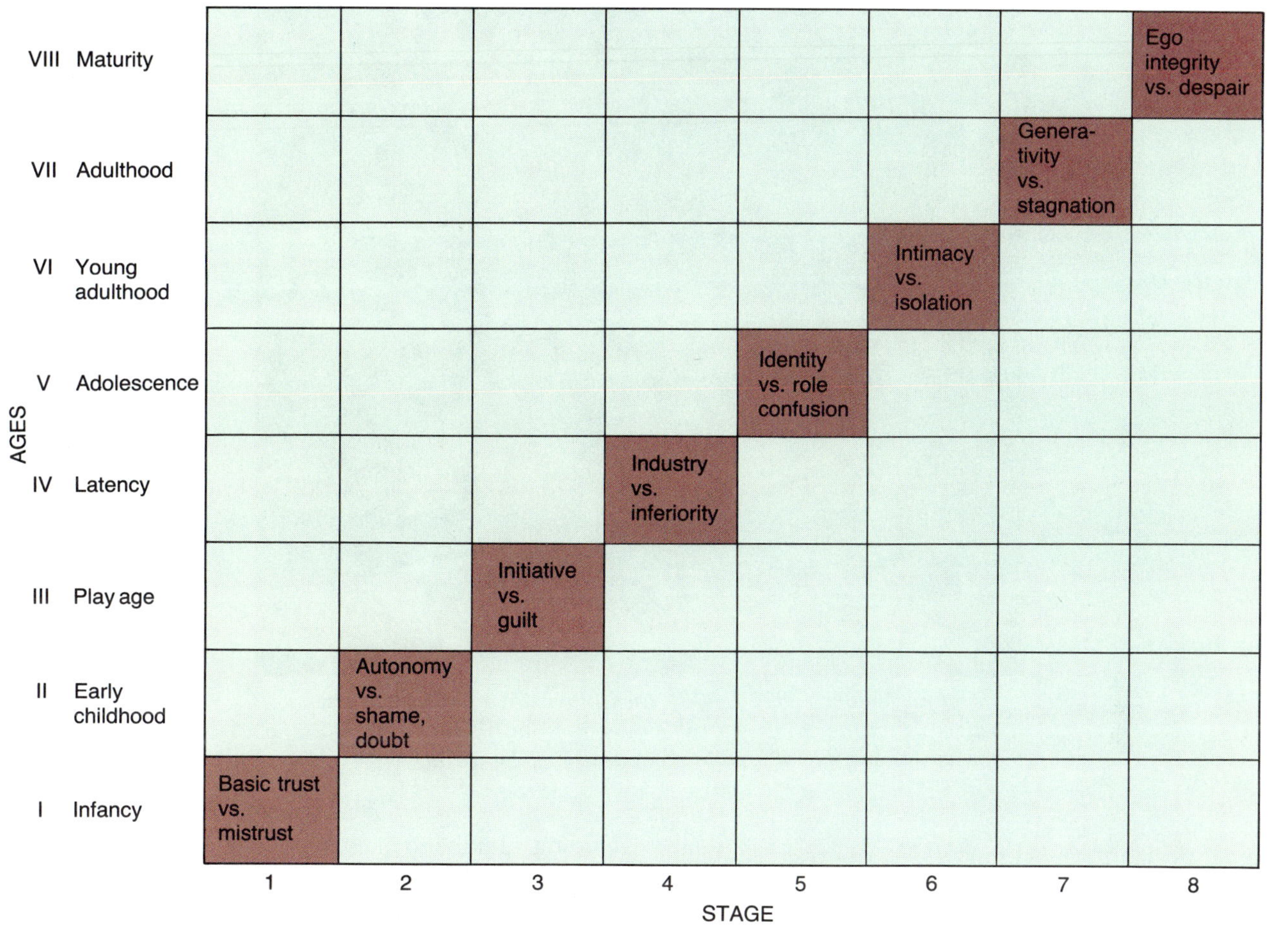

Figure 2.6 Erikson's eight stages of personality development. *The first five stages correspond to Freud's five stages of psychosexual development. According to Erikson, successful resolution of the developmental tasks facing the child during this period, roughly the first eighteen years of life, enables the adult to deal effectively with the three remaining developmental tasks of adulthood.*

Source: From Erikson, E (1950). *Childhood and society.* New York: W. W. Norton & Co., Inc. Reprinted with permission.

Heinz Kohut (1913–1981) extended psychoanalytic theory beyond the ego psychologists' emphasis on the developmental centrality of the ego to develop *self-theory,* one of the most actively-developing current psychoanalytic views of human nature. To Kohut, both normal and abnormal development depend on how we assess our successes and failures in confronting life's inevitable ups and downs. Kohut has been especially concerned with the "narcissistically disturbed," including persons given the diagnosis of Narcissistic Personality Disorder (see Chapter 10). These individuals, Kohut believes, are fixed at such an early developmental stage that fear of the loss of the love object (a parent, for example) predominates. For such individuals the psychoanalytic transference relationship is central to therapeutic growth. The relationship with the therapist can be the most important way these persons can learn to separate their senses of self from those of other important historical figures in their life, most importantly, their parents.

Contemporary Research on Psychodynamic Theory. Like many psychoanalytic concepts, the ego's defensive maneuvers have defied empirical study through the years. Recently, however, two groups of psychoanalytic researchers have reported promising results from efforts to investigate this central feature of psychodynamic theory.

Vaillant (1977) and Vaillant, Bond, and Vaillant (1986) have developed a nine-point scale designed to assess the maturity—essentially, the defensive effectiveness—of the most common ego defenses. Carefully selected clinical descriptions of adaptive human behavior in times of crisis were converted into realistic scenarios, each illustrating one of fifteen different defenses. Each defense was then categorized by a panel of experienced psychoanalysts as immature, intermediate, or mature.

Validity studies of the questionnaire revealed that the maturity of these defenses in 307 middle-aged men (Vaillant, Bond, & Vaillant, 1986) and 188 older

Margaret Mahler (1897–1985), an influential ego psychologist, believed that the child separates his ego from his mother's by using her as an example of how to make sense of the world.

men (Vaillant & Schnurr, 1988) correlated highly with independently assessed measures of maturity. In other words, Vaillant and his colleagues seem to have been able to "operationalize" a key psychodynamic concept to make it amenable to study. Their effort represents a first step for psychoanalytic researchers.

Approaching the same task from a different perspective, Horowitz and his colleagues (1988a, 1988b) have developed a computer system permitting the simultaneous display and analysis of patient's and therapist's verbal, psychomotor, and physiologic behaviors throughout each therapy session, as well as ratings and evaluations of the significance of those behaviors by independent rater-clinicians. The ultimate goal of this research is to be able to test empirically some of psychoanalysis's most firmly held convictions about the impact of unconscious phenomena on the progress of psychotherapy.

Contributions and Shortcomings of Psychoanalytic Theory

Freud's psychoanalytic theory represents a lasting contribution to the understanding of human behavior. His theory of psychosexual development ingeniously tied the physical and emotional tasks of childhood to the organs of the body by which they must be effected. In the process, the theory alerted clinicians to the crucial impact of childhood experiences, including childhood sexuality, on later development and psychopathology.

Freud's structural theory of personality brilliantly complemented his developmental theory by portraying the dynamic interaction among the facets of personality represented by the metaphorical id, superego, and ego. Moreover, Freud's readiness to acknowledge the impact of the unconscious on human behavior was courageous and his discoveries penetrating. By explaining both normal and abnormal behavior as the result of unconscious interaction among the ego, id, and superego, he stressed the continuity of normality and abnormality. In doing so, Freud demystified mental illness in a time when the causes of emotional disorder were virtually unknown. But his emphasis on the role of unconscious processes in behavior and his rejection of biological factors in psychopathology has been criticized.

A keen observer of clinical phenomena, Freud's insights into the interpersonal phenomena that characterize psychotherapy relationships—the thoughts and feelings patient and therapist develop for each other, respectively termed **transference** and **countertransference**—have influenced generations of psychotherapists. His detailed clinical narratives added markedly to the existing store of chronicles of psychotherapeutic studies when they were published. A number of the psychoanalytic techniques Freud developed, quickly incorporated into the existing clinical armamentarium, also continue to be employed.

Freud developed psychoanalytic theory from his observations of his own patients. Yet these very origins have made psychoanalytic theory resistant to empirical investigation. Because Freud thought clinically rather than empirically, it has proven extraordinarily difficult to translate key elements of psychodynamic theory into operational terms and researchable topics. Researchers have been unable to agree on how to operationalize psychoanalytic concepts—to redefine and reconstruct them so that they can be subjected to empirical examination. Though such efforts were initiated shortly after Freud began to develop his theory, the results have been disappointing. This explains why the promising findings of Vaillant and Horowitz have attracted such interest. (Freud himself thought that it was neither possible nor necessary to validate his theory since he believed that his observations and insights were self-evident.)

Perhaps because Freud developed his theory in the consulting room rather than the laboratory, it emphasizes abnormality rather than psychological health. Clear in its vision of how psychopathology develops, the theory is less certain about what early events and child-rearing practices yield psychological health. Psychodynamic theory, therefore, has contributed little to efforts to develop prevention or early intervention methods. Psychodynamicists have also been faulted for their pessimism about human nature, as well as for not acknowledging that human beings can change and grow emotionally on their own.

Freud's conviction that the interpersonal phenomena he observed were universal through time and place has been similarly questioned. Are the stages of psychosexual development and the Oedipus complex invariable accompaniments of the lives of children everywhere, as Freud believed? Or were they mainly products of the time and place in which he lived? Are Freud's century-old observations of the psychological lives of children and their parents as valid in the 1990s as they were in the 1890s? Are they as descriptive of modern urban children, their working mothers, and the single-parent families in which so many live as they were of middle-class Viennese children of 100 years ago, whose fathers always worked and whose mothers almost always stayed home? Many observers have concluded that Freud's insights were more valid in his time than they are in ours.

THE HUMANISTIC MODEL

Basic Assumptions of the Humanistic Model

The humanistic model of behavior, first developed after World War II, underscores the significance and worth of every individual. It highlights the uniqueness and value of each person—the special qualities each of us possesses, regardless of our status, position, power, or influence. The belief that most human beings can expect to grow emotionally and intellectually and realize their full potential is another major element of the humanistic tradition.

In contrast to the psychodynamic tradition, which it reacted against and differs sharply from, the humanistic model is optimistic and future oriented. It stresses the capacity of humans to look after their own welfare and act in their own best interests.

Rogers's Person-Centered Theory of Personality

The **Person-Centered Theory of Personality** of Carl Rogers (1902–1987) assumes that personality and behavior develop from the person's perceptions and interpretations of the world as well as from biological or innate factors and from learning. Rogers's humanistic theory emphasizes the potential of all of us to improve ourselves and our personal environment (Rogers, 1942, 1961). Even the name Rogers chose for his theory reflects this conviction: It emphasizes the central importance of the person—his or her value, worth, and individuality—in understanding his or her behavior.

Throughout his theory are signs of the great respect Rogers holds for the worth, dignity, and power of the individual. In his writings, he focuses on a few such key beliefs: Acting genuinely and openly in relationships facilitates them, as does being open to understanding and accepting others; trusting one's experiences and ability to evaluate them works out

Carl Rogers (1902–1987), founder of the person-centered theory of personality, conducting a group therapy session during his later years.

well; emphasizing one's uniqueness and worth is especially valuable. The discussion of Rogers's person-centered therapy in Chapter 16 shows clearly how heavily it draws on these aspects of theory.

Maslow's Theory of Self-Actualization

Abraham Maslow (1908–1970), like Carl Rogers, was a psychologist, humanist, and optimist who believed that people are basically good. He prescribed the means by which men and women can achieve their unrealized potential—he called it **self-actualization**—despite the frustrations and anxieties of modern life.

Maslow's major theoretical contribution was his description of the **hierarchy of needs**. At the base of the hierarchy are physiological needs—for food, water, sex, and shelter. These needs must be met first to ensure survival of the self and the species. Further up the hierarchy are basic social needs like those for friendship and affiliation. At the top of the hierarchy are the most complex, difficult, and "human" of needs—for love, self-esteem, and self-actualization.

Contributions and Shortcomings of the Humanistic Model

The optimism of Rogers's and Maslow's theories contrasts sharply with the pessimism of the biological and psychodynamic models. These models attribute more of the responsibility for our lives' success or failure to factors beyond us. As a theory of personality and a basis for psychotherapy, the humanistic model encourages individuals to take advantage of every human potentiality, in the quest for full realization of their own potential.

Abraham Maslow (1908–1970). Maslow was a humanistic psychologist like Carl Rogers, who believed that every person has the capacity to achieve self-actualization despite life's inevitable trials and tribulations.

The humanistic model is not based on elaborate and comprehensive theories of personality. Therefore it must be seen differently from the other models in this chapter. We should probably view the humanistic model as a set of uniquely personal theories of living created by humane persons whose optimism about the potential of human beings to realize their full value in life is designed to encourage and reassure, rather than as scientifically defensible models of behavior, to which facts can be added as they are discovered.

THE BEHAVIORAL MODEL

Basic Assumptions of the Behavioral Model

John B. Watson (1878–1958), the founder of the behavioral movement in psychology, defined it clearly in 1913.

> Psychology as the behaviorist views it is a purely objective experimental branch of natural science. Its theoretical goal is the prediction and control of behavior. . . . It needs introspection as little as do the sciences of chemistry and physics. (Watson, p. 158)

In this revolutionary behavioral manifesto, Watson rejects *introspectionism,* or the subjective analysis of one's own consciousness, introduced by Wilhelm Wundt (1832–1920), founder of the first experimental psychology laboratory in 1879 in Leipzig. In taking such a strong stand against the most influential psychological method of the time, Watson wanted to redirect his infant science away from thoughts and feelings, the objects of introspection. Thoughts and feelings, he felt, were impossible to measure with precision. Instead, Watson wanted psychologists to focus on *behavior* which, like chemical and physical phenomena, was observable, quantifiable, and objectifiable.

The behavioral model of personality and psychopathology contrasts sharply with biological and psychodynamic models. The models differ most on the sources of behavior. The biological model emphasizes genetic factors, brain injury, and disease in explaining psychopathology. The roles of learning, the environment, and psychological processes are minimized. In contrast, the psychodynamic model hypothesizes a continuing dynamic interchange among conscious and unconscious psychological processes, the environment, and constitutional factors to explain normal

John B. Watson (1878–1958). Founder of the behavioral movement in psychology, Watson implored psychologists to focus on observable behavior rather than thoughts and feelings.

and abnormal behavior. Moreover, the psychodynamic model emphasizes the crucial role of early experience in determining behavior and minimizes the impact of later learning.

In contrast, the behavioral model accords learning the key role in the development of behavior. Three principal modes of learning, **classical (respondent) conditioning**, **operant (instrumental) conditioning**, and **observational learning** are crucial to acquisition of new behavior and modification of existing behavior. Because these three modes of learning were identified mainly in psychological laboratories, the behavioral model relies most heavily on directly observable behavior, obtained in the study of the stimuli, reinforcing conditions, and responses constituting the learning sequence.

This emphasis on observable data is very different than the psychodynamic model's reliance on hypothetical constructs in personality. While the current biological model, like the behavioral model, is built on data, in the not-too-distant past, philosophers and physicians had to assume the existence of biological factors that could not be confirmed with the technology then available.

Another legacy of the laboratory origins of the behavioral model is its orientation to normal processes of learning and behavior. Thus, the learning-based origins of psychopathology have only recently begun to be studied.

Classical Conditioning

Historical Background. Ivan Pavlov (1849–1936) was professor of physiology at the Military Medical Academy of St. Petersburg between 1895 and 1924. During the first years of this period, he completed the research on digestive secretions and emotion which won him, in 1904, one of the first Nobel prizes in medicine and physiology.

Afterward, as a virtual by-product of his Nobel prize–winning research, Pavlov reflected on the robust influence environmental events appeared to have on gastric and salivary secretions in dogs. He undertook a series of experiments that ultimately succeeded in establishing the principles of what is now called classical conditioning. It is one of the three principal ways humans and other animals learn.

Pavlov's discovery of the principles of classical conditioning followed an unexpected observation: His dogs, who were given meat powder in his studies of digestion, actually started salivating—anticipating the powder—when they first heard the footsteps of and then saw the laboratory assistants who brought the powder, before they could see or smell it. Intrigued, Pavlov set out to study these unexpected observations systematically (1904).

The Classical Conditioning Process. The classical conditioning process (Figure 2.7) starts with an **unconditioned stimulus** (UCS) that elicits an innate, unlearned behavior called the **unconditioned response** (UCR). In Pavlov's original experiment, the UCS was meat powder and the UCR was salivation. When a **conditioned stimulus** (CS) that bears a significant relationship to the unconditioned stimulus is then introduced (in Pavlov's experiment, it was the

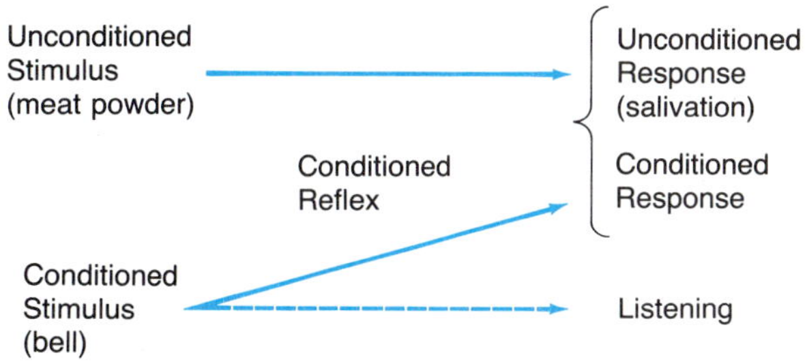

Figure 2.7 *Pavlov's historic demonstration of classical conditioning repeatedly paired a bell (the conditioned stimulus) with meat powder (the unconditioned stimulus) to elicit salivation (initially an unconditioned response; later, a conditioned response) in dogs hearing the sound of the bell alone.*

Source: From Nathan, P. E. & Harris, S. L. (1980). *Psychopathology and society,* 2nd Edition. New York: McGraw-Hill. Reprinted with permission.

Ivan Pavlov (1849–1936), who established the principles of classical conditioning, in his laboratory at the Military Medical Academy of St. Petersburg.

sound of a metronome that preceded the appearance of the meat powder), the UCR may ultimately be elicited and become a **conditioned response** (CR). The repeated pairing of metronome and meat powder ultimately led Pavlov's dogs to salivate at the sound of the metronome alone.

Generations of learning researchers have believed that *contiguity*—a close temporal or spatial relationship between conditioned and unconditioned stimuli—was crucial to the classical conditioning process. Yet a recent article (1988) by Rescorla, a leading learning researcher, reviews convincing evidence that these and other long-held beliefs about how and why classical conditioning occurs are probably wrong. For example, Rescorla concludes that the simple temporal pairing of two events—for example, the sound of a metronome and the sight of meat powder in Pavlov's experiment—is not fundamental to classical conditioning. Instead, classical conditioning involves the learning of *relations* and *contingencies* among events. Pavlov's dogs presumably learned *the complete sequence of events* that ultimately led them to see and smell their food, rather than simply the sequence bell—laboratory assistant—meat powder. They also learned that the sound of a step or of a bell as well as their experience of hunger bore certain contingent relations to the appearance of meat powder, since all three of the former reliably predicted the latter.

Classical conditioning, Rescorla also observes, does not simply teach an association between a single stimulus and a single response. Instead, "a broad range of associations among a wide variety of stimuli" are formed. Thus, we may assume that Pavlov's dogs learned to associate the bell with the room in which the meat powder was given, the persons who provided it, the time of day it was offered, and so on. We may also assume that each of these stimuli ultimately came to have differing capacities to elicit the conditioned response.

Rescorla and others are now convinced that classical conditioning is far more complex than previously believed. It is not invariably automatic and beyond awareness. Instead, it may involve a range of processes that previously were thought to be bypassed by this mode of learning. In humans, cognitive processes are sometimes involved (Baker, Sherman, & Morse, 1987). Baker and his colleagues distinguish between "automatic" conditioning (they think fear conditioning in humans may be of this kind) and "controlled" conditioning, the more complex kind which may involve awareness and other cognitive processes.

Pavlov did not confine his research on classical conditioning to associations between bell, meat powder, and salivation. His interests were wide, centering eventually on the exploration of brain mechanisms responsible for conditioning. Although he was not a clinician, toward the end of his career, Pavlov even attempted to explain human psychosis by means of conditioning theory and brain dysfunction (Pavlov, 1957).

Several generations of learning psychologists have subsequently employed a wide variety of animal species and a broad array of conditioned and unconditioned stimuli to study the effect of respondent conditioning or human behavior (Kimble, 1985; Rescorla, 1988). This research has yielded valuable data on the rules that govern the acquisition and extinction of conditioned responses, and these rules are relevant to an understanding of normal and abnormal human behavior.

Conditioned responses are acquired gradually. The rapidity with which a response is acquired and the strength of the conditioning depend on (1) whether the conditioning trials are *massed* (presented one right after another) or *spaced*; (2) the *value* of the unconditioned stimulus to the organism (food, water, and sex are among the most effective unconditioned stimuli); and (3) whether the CS is *relevant* to the UCS. (Generally, the more relevant the CS is for the UCS, the more predictable the conditioning; for example, a parent's voice is a relevant signal for dinnertime, especially if the parent is the cook, while it is likely to be irrelevant for basketball practice.)

Though many real-life illustrations of the impact of relevance on conditioning exist, a single example must suffice here. Cancer patients suffering from one of the common side effects of radiation therapy, nausea and vomiting, typically reexperience those feelings on viewing the hospital where they receive their radiation treatment. Even other hospitals sometimes bring on those feelings. The relevance of the side effects of radiation treatment to cancer patients—they tend to preoccupy patients' lives during treatment—clearly affects significantly the development of the conditioned relationship between the sight of the hospital and the development of nausea. So does a self-arousal process (Bandura, 1977), in which the patient probably consciously generates anticipatory feelings of anxiety in response to the prior experience with the radiation side effects.

Anxiety and fear, many behavioral clinicians believe, are also acquired by classical conditioning (Lang, 1985). The thoughts, feelings, and bodily responses of fear and the appearance of a stimulus relevant to the fear-inducing stimulus (a person, an animal, or a situation) can produce the sensation of fear even when the originally frightening person or animal is neither seen nor heard.

The process by which classically conditioned behaviors are lost is called **extinction**. Pavlov's dogs' salivation to the sound of a bell gradually extinguished when it was rung repeatedly without being accompanied by meat powder. Stated technically: Conditioned responses extinguish when CS and UCS are no longer paired or when the relevance of the CS to the UCS is lost. A number of the behavioral treatment methods employed to treat anxious and phobic behavior (Chapter 5) are supposed to work by extinguishing the association between the experience of fear and the objects in the environment responsible for it.

By means of *stimulus generalization,* some conditioned responses are linked *both* to the conditioned stimuli with which they were associated *and* to similar stimuli not originally a part of the conditioning. Stimulus generalization probably significantly affects the development of phobic and anxious behavior (Foa, Steketee, & Young, 1984; McNally, 1987). Once the cognitive, subjective, and physiological sensations of fear and anxiety become related to one or more CS (including a punitive father or a critical mother), it can generalize to all males, all females, or all people, thereby producing a generalized phobia that seriously interferes with normal functioning.

Higher-order conditioning is a respondent conditioning phenomenon of special relevance to human behavior and psychopathology. Through it, a CS effectively becomes a UCS—because a "second-order" conditioned association is formed. Higher-order conditioning is said to occur when the impact of the UCS generalizes from the stimulus object itself (such as a punitive father or a critical mother) to thoughts or memories of the object.

For example, assume that a woman has acquired an association between the experience of fear and anxiety and the sight of her abusive ex-husband. That association eventually may generalize to all men who remind her of him. Through higher-order conditioning, even her ex-husband's first name or words like "husband" or "man" elicit the fear and anxiety previously associated only with his physical presence.

Operant Conditioning

Historical Background. Around the time Ivan Pavlov began to explore the conditioned reflex and John B. Watson described psychology as the science of behavior, Edward L. Thorndike (1874–1949) demonstrated the **law of effect** (1911). It states that behaviors associated with satisfying consequences are strengthened by those consequences and, hence, more likely to be repeated, while those linked to unsatisfying consequences are weakened and, therefore, less likely to be repeated. For example, the child who is praised by her teacher for verbal activity is more likely to ask questions the next time, while the child whose questions are ignored is less likely to ask them again.

Watson and Thorndike strongly influenced Burrhus F. Skinner (1904–1990), who, beginning in the early 1930s, established the principles of operant conditioning (so named because this behavior "operates on" the environment). Skinner probably did more than any other psychologist to promote the "behavioral revolution" that characterized psychol-

Burrhus F. Skinner (1904–1990) established the principles of operant conditioning in The Behavior of Organisms, *published in 1938.*

ogy during the decades of the fifties, sixties, and seventies.

Skinner set down the basic principles of operant or instrumental conditioning in his classic research monograph, *The Behavior of Organisms* (1938). Early in the monograph, he responded to Pavlov's oft-stated conviction, shared by other psychologists of his time, that animals and humans learn only by classical conditioning. "There is a large body of behavior," Skinner observed, "that does not seem to be elicited, in the sense in which a cinder in the eye elicits closure of the lid" (p. 19). This "large body of behavior" differs, because they are emitted, from those behaviors acquired by classical conditioning, which are elicited.

In the more than fifty years since Skinner published *The Behavior of Organisms,* the impact of operant conditioning on experimental and clinical psychology, psychiatry, education, social and community planning, and corrections (some of it discussed later on in this volume) has been enormous. Though his ultimate aspirations for operant conditioning—the prediction and control of behavior for a better world—have not been realized, Skinner became one of American psychology's most revered figures before his death.

Another lasting legacy of Skinner's work, the *single-case design,* arose from his research strategy of studying single animals intensively under a variety of environmental conditions. By doing so, Skinner explored systematically many of the environmental factors influencing the animal's operant behavior. Behavioral researchers studying human psychopathology via single-case designs do essentially the same thing. By first modifying one and then another part of a disturbed child's environment and then studying the consequences on the child's behavior, they can learn what controls the behavior and what might be done to modify it for the better.

The Operant-Conditioning Process. In the operant-conditioning paradigm (Figure 2.8), reinforced behaviors are likely to increase in frequency, while punished or ignored behaviors are likely to decrease in frequency. The initial term in Figure 2.6, **discriminative stimulus** (S^D), refers to the information our environment provides us about the likelihood that our responses will be rewarded, ignored, or punished. The second term, **operant response** (R), relates to the behavior we emit and to the **schedules of reinforcement** which link the behavior and its consequences. The third term, **reinforcing stimulus** (S^R), describes those consequences—the reinforcing or punishing outcomes our behavior earns us.

The Discriminative Stimulus. The discriminative stimuli which affected the behavior of Skinner's pigeons (e.g., Ferster & Skinner, 1957; Skinner, 1938, 1969)—colored lights illuminating transparent plastic disks—informed the pigeons whether a series of pecks on the disk would yield food reinforcement and what sequence of pecks was required for the reinforcement.

Most of the discriminative stimuli humans depend on, though, are more subtle and complex. A smile, a frown, a nod of the head, each lets us know whether our behavior is likely to yield a payoff from the person who provides the *social cue* (another phrase for SD). Though our environments have their formal equivalents for the pigeons' colored disks (e.g., stop-

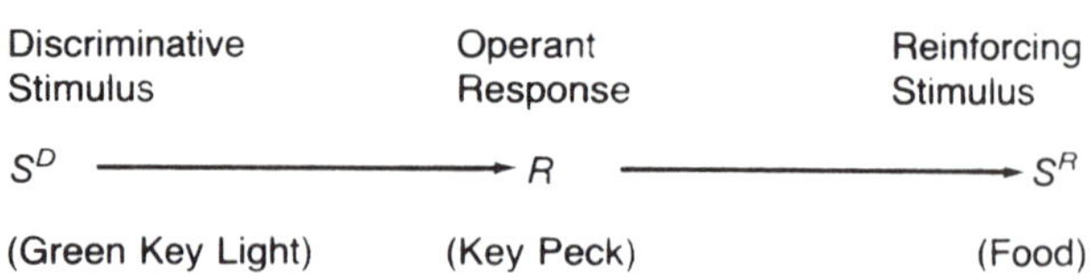

Figure 2.8 *By Skinner's operant conditioning, a pigeon learned to peck repeatedly at a key (a disk lit by a green light) to obtain grain. In the example shown, the green disk served as a discriminative stimulus, the key pecks were operant responses, and the grain was the reinforcing stimulus.*

Source: From Nathan, P. E. & Harris, S. L. (1980). *Psychopathology and society,* 2nd Edition. New York: McGraw-Hill. Reprinted with permission.

lights and stop signs, warning labels on cigarette packages, and grades) most of the information we receive from our environment consists of social cues. One of the key tasks of childhood is learning to read and understand these cues—and accurate perception of them is one of the earliest human capacities to break down in the face of serious mental disorder.

Schedules of Reinforcement. The relationship between operant responses (Rs) and their reinforcing or punishing consequences (S^Rs) is complex. Yet by the time we have become adults, we take for granted the diversity of these schedules of reinforcement.

The Reinforcing Stimulus. Operant behavior yields one of two consequences or S^Rs:

Reinforcement

- A pattern of responses followed by satisfying consequences tends to increase the likelihood the pattern will be repeated. When an instructor praises a piece of written work, the student will likely produce more writing of the same kind. When a child is rewarded for good behavior, he or she will probably repeat that behavior.

Punishment

- A response followed by an aversive or unwelcome behavioral consequence tends to decrease the likelihood of a similar pattern of responses in the future. It generally takes only a single "no" from a person we want to date to convince us that we ought to focus our attentions elsewhere. A poor grade on a midterm exam can radically decrease partying behavior if we want to do better on the final.

Psychopathology and Operant Conditioning. Operant mechanisms appear to affect the development of many of the disorders discussed in this book, as several of the following chapters suggest. There is also good evidence that operant principles are involved in the maintenance and modification of several forms of abnormal behavior. Therefore, operant conditioning has significantly impacted on treatment, specifically, on the design of therapeutic programs. Programs to train parents and teachers to modify the behavior of aggressive, mentally retarded, or psychotic children, for example, extensively use operant principles (Kazdin, 1989; Park & Gaylord-Ross, 1989; Patterson, 1982). By teaching parents and teachers when and how to reward such children for appropriate behavior (it initially occurs very infrequently), behavioral clinicians have helped countless parents and teachers who would otherwise despair of ever bringing their children's behavior under suitable control.

Contributions and Shortcomings of the Behavioral Model

The emphasis by supporters of the behavioral model on research and data has been an impetus to mental health professionals to move in the same direction. Even those with a primary allegiance to other models of psychopathology have accepted the usefulness of this view. Similarly, the value behavioral clinicians and researchers attach to observable behavior rather than to theory or conjecture has influenced others to examine the bases for their own clinical and experimental judgments.

The behavioral model emphasizes environmental and learning variables in explaining behavior, though it does not ignore biological and individual factors. This model has therefore served as a counterweight to the biological model's strong emphasis on biological mechanisms and the psychodynamic model's on intrapsychic ones.

Critics of the behavioral model fault its emphasis on learning and environmental determinants of behavior, especially in view of current findings pointing to the role of genetics in disorders once thought to be learned. Others criticize behavioral researchers and clinicians for deemphasizing cognitive factors and self-control in their efforts to demonstrate the power of the environment to affect behavior. (Cognition refers to the uniquely human mental processes of thinking and reasoning, perceiving and recognizing, judging and conceiving.)

Because of these concerns, cognitive concepts and strategies were energetically incorporated into the framework of what is now termed social-learning theory, primarily during the 1970s and 1980s.

Social-Learning Theory

Observational Learning. Until the early 1960s, most learning theorists believed that classical and operant conditioning were responsible for essentially all human and animal learning. But then Albert Bandura and his colleagues at Stanford University began to study what they came to call modeling, or observational learning. Observational learning is now recognized as a basic mode of learning, distinct from either classical or operant conditioning. Bandura's early research on observational learning demonstrated that, simply by watching others engaging in various kinds of behavior, without engaging in those behaviors themselves, children acquired entirely new response patterns (Bandura, 1973, 1977; Bandura, Ross, & Ross, 1961, 1963).

Behavioral researchers have continued to explore the limits of observational learning. Their efforts have convinced behavioral scientists that modeling is a variety of cognitive learning that strongly influences

Albert Bandura (1925–). Bandura's early research on observational learning and modeling led to the development of social-learning theory and its emphasis on the role of cognitions in learning and behavior.

the development of normal and abnormal behavior. Even in the absence of overt reinforcement, complex behaviors and cognitions are acquired by observing others. Bandura (1986) has detailed the mechanisms by which these processes influence behavior.

Recent studies by Mineka and her colleagues (1984) and Cook and his coworkers (1985) suggest that observational learning influences the acquisition of emotional behavior in animals. Rhesus monkeys raised in laboratories generally do not demonstrate fear of snakes. But, after watching monkeys who were born in the wild show strong innate fear reactions to the snakes, they also become similarly fearful. The fear the animals raised in laboratories acquire, simply by watching the fearful behavior of others, persists. Its intensity depends very much on the intensity of the fear they witness.

The impact of modeling on the acquisition of behavior of relevance to psychopathology in humans has focused on alcohol consumption. This research indicates that the intensity of alcohol consumption by a drinking companion strongly influences the intensity of one's own drinking, although neither person is apparently aware of this influence (Caudill & Lipscomb, 1980; Rosenbluth, Nathan, & Lawson, 1978).

Therapeutic applications of the research findings on modeling initially focused on its use to modify or eliminate the fearful behavior of phobic children and adults. More recently, its use has expanded to a variety of situations where the unwanted behavior of primates (Mineka & Cook, 1986) and children (Thase & Moss, 1976) is modified on exposing them to models demonstrating more appropriate and adaptive behavior.

Self-Control. The concept of *self-control,* or *self-regulation,* derives from a three-stage model of self-observation that developed out of Bandura's empirical and conceptual work (Bandura, 1977). Kanfer (1977) also made key contributions to self-control theory. This concept set the stage for a number of subsequent developments in theory and therapy.

The self-control concept developed in recognition that behavior is not simply a function of external rewards and punishments, whether experienced directly or by watching others. A central feature of the cognitive-behavioral approach to treatment, described later, is that people can learn to regulate their own behavior. They can make active choices among behavioral alternatives by choosing to pursue one and ignore others. We self-regulate when we establish self-rewards and self-punishments that depend on our ability to meet our own performance standards.

The self-control concept encompasses a sequential model that includes, first, *self-observation*—the capacity to view one's own behavior as it occurs. Next is *self-evaluation.* This involves setting standards for evaluating the adequacy of one's behavior, as well as the continuous conscious monitoring of it, according to those standards, in order to evaluate the degree to which one does or does not meet them. *Self-reinforcement,* which follows, depends on both preceding self-control strategies; it permits the person to reward (or punish) him- or herself as a function of the judged adequacy of performance. The self-control model has generated much clinical research that has furthered the development of cognitive-behavioral approaches to treatment.

Reciprocal Determinism. *Reciprocal determinism* describes Bandura's belief in the reciprocal interaction of behavior, cognitive factors, and environmental influences (1977, 1989). The concept highlights his notion that people affect and are affected by their environment. Behavior, then, is the result of factors that both influence and are influenced by each other.

Bandura's concept of **self-efficacy** (1977, 1989), detailed below, is derived from his views on reciprocal determinism.

Self-Efficacy. Bandura defines self-efficacy as "people's beliefs about their capabilities to exercise control over events that affect their lives" (1989, p. 1175). Those beliefs influence *motivation*—for example, the motivation to undertake a difficult or novel task, the *feelings* associated with the task (the attitudes and expectations the person has about it), and the *behaviors* (the actions) necessary to complete the task.

Bandura also reminds us that reciprocal determinism ensures that the outcome of the effort to complete a task—the relative success or failure of the effort—influences our continuing reassessment of self-efficacy. In other words, self-efficacy affects behavior and is affected by it.

Contributions and Shortcomings of Social-Learning Theory. Social-learning theory emphasizes the mediating role in our behavior of the thoughts and feelings we have about ourselves. Psychiatric patients, for example, have attitudes and expectations about how their disorders developed and the prospects for their effective treatment. To fail to explore these beliefs—and, if necessary, dispute them—is to ignore a significant factor in patients' continuing turmoil. When the insights of social-learning theory are added to the behavioral model's emphasis on environmental and learning factors, an impressively comprehensive view of normal and abnormal behavior results.

Some behavioral critics of social-learning theory, however, are concerned by its willingness to recognize the significance of cognitive factors, which are not observable and are difficult to measure. They see this as an unfortunate return to the psychodynamic model's emphasis on theoretical constructs of personality and its rejection of the value of empirical enquiry. Biologically oriented critics maintain, moreover, that the theory fails to provide insight into the origins of faulty thinking and neglects the role of genetics and biological factors in psychopathology.

The Cognitive-Behavioral Approach

Basic Assumptions. The cognitive-behavioral approach to treatment draws on insights and data from behavioral and social-learning theory. It emphasizes precise definition and, when possible, operationalization of concepts. It also stresses subjecting treatment methods to empirical study—and retaining only those which can be experimentally supported.

The cognitive-behavioral approach to treatment depends on two uniquely human capacities. The first is the ability to *self-regulate,* or to exert self-control over one's own behavior. This attribute was detailed in our discussion of social-learning theory. It is central to the cognitive-behavioral approach because, while all of us can self-regulate some behaviors, most of us must learn to self-control other behaviors. Some cognitive-behavioral treatments teach self-control strategies.

The second element of the cognitive-behavioral approach relates to humans' manipulation of *symbolic events,* the thoughts and feelings we attach to past, present, and future experiences. Our cognitive capabilities affect classical and operant-conditioning processes and the choices we make among potential behaviors (Bandura, 1986).

Attributional processes are significant symbolic events. They are the explanations we offer ourselves of past successes and failures. Attributing a failure to events beyond our control is clearly more constructive personally than blaming it on our own incompetence. Attributing a success to our own actions, similarly, is more positive than attributing it to a circumstance over which we had no control. Attributional processes appear to influence depression (Chapter 7) and our response to stressful situations (Chapter 8).

Cognitive-Behavioral Treatment. Cognitive-behavioral treatment focuses on current problems. Its main goal is to help patients make the changes they desire in their behavior and lives by enabling them to learn more adaptive ways to relate to their social environments. Learning more effective problem-solving techniques is an especially important part of cognitive-behavioral treatment.

Cognitive-behavioral treatment is time limited and its goals are mutually agreed on. Unlike other therapies, patient and therapist work collaboratively to identify problems, plan treatment strategies, and evaluate outcomes.

Numerous examples of cognitive-behavioral treatment are offered throughout this text. It is a treatment of choice for some of the anxiety disorders (Chapter 5), some forms of depression (Chapter 7), some of the psychological factors affecting medical disorders (Chapter 8), and some of the sexual disorders (Chapter 9).

THE SOCIAL-CONSEQUENCE MODEL

Basic Assumptions of the Social-Consequence Model

The social-consequence model emphasizes the impact of belonging to certain groups in our society on the behavior and psychopathology of group members. Proponents of the model believe that society's attitudes and behavior toward certain persons because of their gender, ethnicity, race, and socioeconomic status affect their behavior and psychopathology.

Gender, ethnicity, and race, of course, also define biological, behavioral, and psychological differences between groups. These factors, therefore, also interest the proponents of other models of psychopathology. In contrast to those models, the social-consequence model focuses on the impact of *society's attitudes and reactions* to gender, ethnicity, race, and other social factors on psychopathology.

Data from Epidemiologic Research

Selected results from the two epidemiological surveys reviewed in detail in Chapter 1 support the social-consequence model.

The support given the model by the Midtown Study (Srole et al., 1962) stems from its finding that interviewers were more likely to consider poor residents of Midtown Manhattan impaired psychiatrically than middle or upper-middle class residents. One interpretation of this finding is that the stresses of poverty heighten the risk of psychopathology. Another is that Midtown interviewers were more inclined to view as abnormal the behavior of the poor than that of the middle class. Both explanations suggest how social factors help define or determine psychopathology.

By design, data from the Epidemiologic Catchment Area (ECA) Study (Eaton et al., 1984; Regier et al., 1984) offer even stronger support for the social-consequence model. As indicated, systematic differences in disorder prevalence rates for urban and rural, Mexican American and non-Hispanic subjects were found. Major depression and drug abuse/dependence appeared most frequently among urban residents, while alcoholism abuse/dependence flourished in the countryside; Mexican Americans had especially high rates of severe cognitive impairment, while the comparison group had higher rates of drug abuse/dependence.

Gender and Psychopathology

The ECA study also revealed systematic differences between men and women in rates of depression, alcohol and drug abuse/dependence, and antisocial behavior. Throughout this text, detailed consideration is given to these and other gender-linked differences in rates of psychopathology. While it weighs the impact of gender on biological and psychological differences affecting behavior and psychopathology, the text also considers the effects of society's differing attitudes toward and treatment and expectations of men and women on their behavior. These societal attitudes and reactions, for example, may influence the differential rates of depression, alcohol and drug abuse/dependence, and antisocial behavior among men and women revealed by the ECA Study.

Race and Psychopathology

How can race affect psychiatric status? Black leader Malcolm X offered the following personal view of a possible mechanism linking the two in his *Memoirs* (1966):

> I truly believe that if ever a state social agency destroyed a family, it destroyed ours. We wanted and tried to stay together. Our home didn't have to be destroyed. But the Welfare, the courts, and their doctor, gave us the one-two punch. . . . (Little, 1966, p. 22)

Throughout his life Malcolm X remained convinced that the employees of a state social service agency, believing the worst about his mother's ability to care for her children, too readily placed her children in foster care and thereby destroyed the family. The price Malcolm X paid for his chaotic childhood, he felt, was drug dependence and depression.

Chapter 8 considers a number of the conflicting hypotheses that attempt to explain racial differences in rates of psychosomatic disorder. Differences in ab-

Black power advocate Malcolm X (1925–1965) was convinced that the oppression of blacks in America has exerted a profound negative impact on their social, economic, and psychological welfare.

solute levels of stress, in the ability to cope, and in social support could conceivably all contribute to the greater incidence of autonomic nervous system dysfunction, including high blood pressure, in black males.

Additionally, Lex (1985) and others have asked if elevated rates of drug abuse/dependence and antisocial behavior among minority groups in the United States are one of the ways in which these groups have chosen to deal with the discouraging social and psychological conditions many of them live in.

Poverty and Psychopathology

Another element of the social-consequence model inquires into the effects of poverty on psychopathology. Anthropologist Oscar Lewis (1961, 1969), closely identified with this question, initiated the idea that a "culture of poverty" has arisen among the poor in our society that helps explain their stigmatization and self-blaming. Lewis linked the traits of the culture of poverty, a few briefly noted here, to psychopathology as well as other social ills.

Economic traits of poverty include underemployment, child labor, no savings, and a constant struggle for survival. Social and psychological traits consist of crowded quarters, violence, little sense of history, and strong feelings of marginality, helplessness, and dependency. Other traits include resignation and fatalism, relatively high death rates, and high-tolerance for psychological pathology. All these constitute the array of factors that Lewis, with many others, thought were poverty-linked precursors to abnormal behavior.

In considering the traits of the culture of poverty, however, two complementary questions arise. On the one hand, do these traits of poverty, as Lewis believed, induce psychopathology? On the other hand, do psychopathology and its effects make it impossible for individuals to survive economically in our society? Chapter 14 discusses this question in relation to the chronic mentally ill homeless, many of whom are schizophrenic.

Contributions and Shortcomings of the Social-Consequence Model

The social-consequence model forces us to consider the impact of our society's treatment of and attitudes toward certain groups—the poor, racial and ethnic minorities, and women, for example—on behavior and psychopathology. Thus, the social-consequence model counterbalances an exclusive biological or psychodynamic understanding of the development of

A strong relationship between poverty and the incidence and prevalence of psychopathology has been demonstrated repeatedly in epidemiologic surveys of mental health and illness in the United States.

psychopathology. Instead of relying solely on biological factors like neurotransmitter dysfunction or only on psychodynamic factors like inadequate ego defenses, the model asks society to accept some of the responsibility for psychopathology.

Despite the appeal of its logic, the social-consequence model has proven extremely difficult to confirm. Though relationships between poverty, for example, and heightened risk of psychopathology of certain kinds have been demonstrated in several epidemiological studies, they do not prove that poverty causes psychopathology. As noted, perhaps it is the other way around. Perhaps people afflicted with certain forms of psychopathology are less able to earn a living than those who are not. Or, also as noted above, perhaps middle-class interviewers are simply more apt to judge the behavior of the poor as abnormal because it is different from behavior more familiar to them.

Systematic and controlled research necessary to enable a definite answer to this question—that of the antecedents and consequences of selected social factors on the incidence and prevalence of psychopathology—has not yet been undertaken. The validity of the social-consequence model is uncertain, though its emphasis on society's contribution to psychopathology is welcome.

THE BIOPSYCHOSOCIAL MODEL

Evidence presented in this chapter in support of the role of biological factors in the etiology of some of the most serious and disabling of the mental disorders is formidable. Convincing data indicate the role of biological and genetic factors in such disorders as schizophrenia, serious affective disorder, and the substance use disorders.

The significance of learning in the development of behavior and psychopathology is also strongly supported by data reviewed in this chapter. The behavioral and social-learning models of psychopathology, consequently, muster convincing empirical support for the notion that learning factors influence the development of some depressive disorders, the anxiety disorders, the stress disorders, and the substance use disorders.

As indicated, the epidemiologic evidence presented in Chapter 1 attests to the impact of social factors on the incidence and prevalence of psychopathology. Society's attitudes toward race, gender, age, and sociocultural and socioeconomic status all seem to influence the chances of becoming mentally ill. By helping determine who we work and live with, how we treat each other, and the satisfaction with which we view ourselves, these consequences of social group membership powerfully affect our behavior.

The psychodynamic and humanistic models of abnormality are not as well supported by empirical data as are the behavioral, social-consequence, and, especially, the biological models. Nonetheless, several generations of clinicians have concluded that psychological processes have the power to create as well as to remediate disordered behavior.

Despite the compelling individual logic of each of these models, none seems by itself sufficient to explain the development of any psychopathologic condition. Consider the following two patients.

The first is the victim of a serious automobile accident and has suffered brain damage, memory loss, and behavior change. Although the brain disorder this young woman has experienced is severe, she continues to be responsive to the world around her. She is still capable of caring for family and friends, behaving appropriately in social situations, and feeling emotions like happiness and sadness. Additionally, she benefits emotionally from her supportive, understanding family. Their continued involvement in her life helps her remain productive, maintain an optimistic attitude, and work hard at rehabilitation.

Now consider the middle-aged Vietnam veteran who suffers from **posttraumatic stress disorder** (PTSD). This disabling condition (see Chapter 5), characterized by severe anxiety and depression, was caused by the profound environmental stresses during this man's period of combat in Vietnam twenty years ago. Complicating his condition—which was caused by environmental and psychological factors alone and involved no known central nervous system damage or disease—are a variety of physical symptoms. They include a continuously aroused autonomic nervous system that makes him feel, he says, like "it's Vietnam all over again inside."

The point of our contrast between the young accident victim and the Vietnam veteran is that the behavior of neither can be understood fully without an appreciation for the interaction among the social, psychological, and biological systems that influence all of our behavior. A single model of behavior and psychopathology is insufficient to permit full understanding of any mental disorder, unless the model accords weight to all three systems.

Although clinical scientists have generally acknowledged the interactive role of psychological, environmental, and biological factors in understanding and treating psychopathology, their evidence for this interaction has come mainly from the kind of clinical anecdotes we have just shared. But a prominent researcher has provided a theoretical rationale—and some suggestive data to support it—for the interaction of these elements in alcoholism.

Psychiatrist Robert Cloninger, who recently proposed an innovative, empirically-derived biopsychosocial theory of alcoholism.

Robert Cloninger, whose work has led most scientists to agree that there is a genetic component to alcoholism, recently published an article which brought together diverse streams of data to propose a biopsychosocial theory of alcoholism also of relevance to other disorders (1987). Impressed by data, some of it his own, separating alcoholics into two groups based on family history of alcoholism and signs and symptoms of the disorder, Cloninger concludes that the two groups may also differ systematically along biological, psychological, and social dimensions.

Table 2.2, from Cloninger's 1987 article, illustrates his conviction that three of the brain's principal neurotransmitters—dopamine, serotonin, and norepinephrine—modulate three categories of brain-behavior relationships: behavioral activation, inhibition, and maintenance. These three brain systems, in turn, respond with heightened sensitivity to different social stimuli—stimuli which encourage or support novelty seeking, harm avoidance, and reward dependence—to yield different social and behavioral consequences. Genetic factors, Cloninger believes, determine which neurotransmitter (and brain region, since each of the three neurotransmitters is concentrated in a different region) is most influential in a particular person's life. A similar interactive system, he suggests, may help explain other serious mental disorders.

As noted, Cloninger has distinguished two types of alcoholics. They differ in pattern of inheritance of the disorder, with Type 2 alcoholics (Table 2.3) significantly more likely than Type 1 alcoholics to have had a family history of alcoholism.

Table 2.3 lists five of the alcohol-related problems and the three personality traits which differentiate the two types of alcoholics. By implication, the principal monoamine neuromodulators mediating the personality traits of Type 1 alcoholics are serotonin and norepinephrine (because they are high in the traits modulated by these neurotransmitters), while Type 2 alcoholics depend more on dopamine.

Cloninger's biopsychosocial theory proposes that the alcohol-related problems differentiating these two kinds of alcoholics result from differing patterns of interaction among the biological, psychological, and social factors that distinguish them. While biolog-

TABLE 2.2 Three Major Brain-Systems Influencing Stimulus-Response Characteristics

Brain System (Related Personality Dimension)	Principal Monoamine Neuromodulator	Relevant Stimuli	Behavioral Response
Behavioral activation (novelty seeking)	Dopamine	Novelty; Potential rewards or their conditioned signals; Potential relief of: Punishment or monotony or their conditioned signal.	Exploratory pursuit Appetitive growth
Behavioral inhibition (harm avoidance)	Serotonin	Conditioned signals for: Punishment, novelty, or frustrative nonreward.	Escape Active avoidance
Behavioral maintenance (reward dependence)	Norepinephrine	Conditioned signals for reward or relief of punishment.	Passive avoidance Extinction Resistance to extinction

Source: From Cloninger, C. R., (1987), Neurogenetic Adaptive Mechanisms in Alcoholism, *Science 236,* p. 413. Copyright 1987 by the AAAS.

TABLE 2.3 Distinguishing Characteristics of Two Types of Alcoholism

Characteristic Features	Type of Alcoholism Type 1	Type 2
Alcohol-related problems		
Usual age of onset (years)	After 25	Before 25
Spontaneous alcohol seeking (inability to abstain)	Infrequent	Frequent
Fighting and arrests when drinking	Infrequent	Frequent
Psychological dependence (loss of control)	Frequent	Infrequent
Guilt and fear about alcohol dependence	Frequent	Infrequent
Personality traits		
Novelty seeking	Low	High
Harm avoidance	High	Low
Reward dependence	High	Low

Source: From Cloninger, C. R., (1987), Neurogenetic Adaptive Mechanisms in Alcoholism, *Science 236,* p. 411. By permission of the publisher.

ical factors—a predominance of one neurotransmitter system over another—are extremely important, they are insufficient in themselves to produce different alcohol-related problems. Required, additionally, are the distinct social and psychological consequences of the behaviors produced by these differences in predominant neurotransmission. Fights and arrests during periods of intoxication, loss of control, and guilt and fear about alcohol dependence are clearly all distinct behaviors whose presence or absence affects others' reactions to alcoholics as well as their view of themselves.

Cloninger has imaginatively incorporated a biopsychosocial model into a comprehensive, though still untested, theory of alcohol abuse. At present both the biopsychosocial model and Cloninger's theory of "neurogenetic adaptive mechanisms" are hypothetical; they need to be confirmed more fully by extensive additional research. But in theory and, increasingly, in fact, the biopsychosocial model of behavior seems to have a present and a future deserving of attention and support.

SUMMARY

1. Models help clarify complicated relationships and interactions. They are especially useful when significant gaps exist in understanding. Because the mechanisms by which both normal and abnormal behavior develop have not been determined, despite a lengthy history of efforts, a variety of models providing theoretical explanations of these phenomena have been proposed.
2. The biological model of mental disorder has a long history that has culminated, in recent decades, in extraordinary advances in molecular genetics and neurobiology. Those discoveries have strongly implicated biological disorder as the cause of many serious mental disorders. Specifically, an increasing number of psychopathologic conditions are now thought to be caused by the genetic transmission of neurotransmitter dysfunction.
3. The psychodynamic model assumes that human behavior is strongly influenced by unconscious factors. At the heart of Freud's psychoanalytic theory—a psychodynamic theory—is the structural theory of personality. That theory divides the psyche into three parts. The first part to appear, the id, is a reservoir of primitive drives, including the libido, unmodified by civilization and guided by the pleasure principle. The ego, which arises out of the id, is guided by the reality principle and strives to channel id impulses into actions that are more attuned to reality's demands. The superego, which incorporates society's rules and expectations, serves as the seat of the conscience. If ego, superego, and id become imbalanced, they precipitate unconscious intrapsychic conflict. This conflict may require the mobilization of ego defenses, to protect the ego against being overwhelmed by excessively strong id or superego demands.
4. Freud's theory of psychosexual development envisioned a series of successive developmental periods—the oral, anal, phallic, latency, and genital stages. Each of the first three involves a different means of gratifying libidinal needs. The theory links the resolution of discrete physiological tasks (eating, eliminating wastes, handling sexual feelings) with the tasks of learning related interpersonal lessons (learning one is not the center of the universe, how to control others' behavior, how to resolve conflicting emotional feelings for parents.) Freud believed that events occurring during the oral, anal, and phallic stages largely determined the emotional status of the subsequent adult.
5. The humanistic model is an optimistic theory that emphasizes the significance and uniqueness of every human being. Carl Rogers's client-centered theory—a humanistic theory—stresses every person's potential to change for the better. Abraham Maslow believed that people can attain their unrealized goals by working through a hierarchy of needs to realize the most human and most valuable needs—those for love, self-esteem, and self-actualization.
6. The behavioral model accords learning a key role in the development of behavior. The model encompasses three principle learning modes, classical or respondent conditioning, operant or instrumental conditioning, and observational learning or modeling. The behavioral model relies most heavily on directly observable behavior obtained in the study of the environmental stimuli, reinforcing conditions, and responses that constitute the learning sequence.
7. Classical conditioning, first investigated by Pavlov, involves the learning of relations and contingencies

among events. This principle mode of learning forms a broad range of associations among a wide variety of stimuli, so that each, ultimately, becomes capable of eliciting the conditioned response. Classical conditioning is more complex than was previously believed; it is not invariably automatic and beyond awareness. Instead, in humans, cognitive processes are probably involved. Operant conditioning, the principle mode of learning studied most intensively by Skinner, depends on the fact that behaviors which are reinforced are likely to increase in frequency, while those which are punished or ignored are likely to decrease in frequency.

8. Social-learning theory developed from the behavioral model when the crucial role of cognitions in learning was recognized. Elements of social-learning theory include observational learning or modeling, by which behavior is acquired in the absence of explicit reinforcement, simply by watching another person; self-control, by which persons can ultimately learn to self-reward or self-punish themselves as a function of the adequacy of their behavior; and reciprocal determinism, which describes the reciprocal interaction of behavior, cognitive factors, and environmental influences. The cognitive-behavioral approach, which developed from social-learning theory, emphasizes symbolic events and self-regulation and has led to the development of methods to treat a range of serious psychopathological conditions.
9. The social-consequence model of psychopathology points to differences in the incidence and prevalence of certain mental disorders to justify the view that society's attitudes toward certain groups influence psychopathology. Gender, race, age, and sociocultural and socioeconomic status seem to influence the chances of becoming mentally ill.
10. The biopsychosocial model illuminates the crucial interaction of social/environmental, psychological, and biological factors in the development of normal and abnormal behavior. It may yield a more accurate picture of behavioral development and represent a more adequate model for conceptualizing treatment than any of the more restrictive models discussed in the chapter.

David Hockney, *Gary and Doug* (1982). Courtesy of Art Resource.

3 DIAGNOSIS AND CLINICAL ASSESSMENT

Thirty-two staff and trainee psychologists, psychiatrists, social workers, and psychiatric nurses attended a regularly scheduled clinical conference sponsored by the Psychiatry Service of Boston City Hospital a few years ago. The conference that day centered on a recently admitted thirty-six-year-old married white male. A heavy drinker for more than twenty years, he had been a patient there once before, about a year earlier, after a prolonged drinking bout. He had been seriously depressed and suicidal.

The patient detailed a number of serious concerns and problems during the interview conducted as part of the clinical conference. He shared the conviction that there were people living in his home he could not identify. As a result, he had called the police several times, but they had been unresponsive to his concerns. The patient also admitted to recent intense feelings of unfamiliarity with his surroundings at home.

While watching television a few months earlier, the patient reported, he had become confused, lost consciousness, and experienced a convulsive seizure. He had also become convinced in recent months that he was a serial murderer though, when pressed, he was unable to explain why he believed this. Alone in his bedroom at times during the past year, the patient had begun hearing indistinct voices and seeing animals, including a white horse surrounded by a red glow.

Responding to a pain in his chest, the patient had begun collecting the knives and razor blades he would need to operate on himself if doctors refused to take his complaints of pain seriously.

Following the interview, the patient's psychologist, psychiatrist, and social worker in turn reported on the results of their assessment efforts, designed to make sense of this puzzling array of symptoms. Reports were given on psychological testing, including intelligence and personality assessments; on the

results of a detailed series of laboratory tests of bodily functioning, including the central nervous system; on the patient's mental status; and on his personal, family, social, medical, and psychiatric history.

The intelligence test results indicated that the patient was of average intelligence and that his chronic alcohol abuse had probably reduced his ability to perform certain high-level cognitive tasks like problem solving. Results of personality assessment testing indicated the patient was suffering from a severe personality disorder that also affected his behavior. The mental status examination revealed moderate to severe psychopathology.

Laboratory tests were negative, with the exception of abnormal liver function tests, reflecting the long-term consequences of the patient's abusive drinking. An electroencephalogram (EEG) revealed an abnormal pattern of electrical activity in the brain, suggesting the possibility of brain damage induced by chronic alcohol abuse.

The likeliest diagnostic possibilities given the symptoms and test results included organic brain disorder, alcohol dependence, and depressive disorder. (Adapted from Nathan et al., 1969)

Mental health professionals *diagnose* and *assess* mental disorders in a variety of ways. These two clinical procedures provide the information mental health professionals need to plan for their patients. Their usefulness—in understanding etiology, planning treatment, and predicting disease course—has increased markedly since the clinical conference cited above.

Diagnosis is the act of identifying and naming a state or condition according to an agreed-on system of categorization. Although we also use the word for other purposes (an auto mechanic "diagnoses" the reason your car doesn't start), here we refer specifically to the process mental health professionals use to determine if a patient has a behavioral or psychiatric disorder and, if so, what it is.

Clinical assessment is the process clinicians use in gathering information in order to diagnose, plan treatment, and predict the future course of a behavioral or psychiatric disorder. In the assessment process, clinicians evaluate personality, intelligence, vocational, and academic skills by amassing detailed information on the patient's personal, medical, psychiatric, and family history. This generally includes a thorough physical examination, perhaps even studies of brain structure and function, to determine if physical disease or dysfunction is partly responsible for the patient's condition.

DIAGNOSIS

The best-known classification systems were developed centuries ago to categorize animals, plants, elements, and other natural phenomena. **Nosologies** enable scientists to communicate their observations without having to describe every distinguishing characteristic of each plant, animal, or element. Exact systems for categorizing physical illnesses and, later, behavioral and psychiatric ones produced similar results. They became shorthand communication methods permitting clinicians to share knowledge about the causes, treatments, and differentiating signs and symptoms of a vast number of disorders. Without these systems, every disorder and case would be unique, without precedent.

In diagnosing a physical disease, physicians most often rely on past and present **signs** and **symptoms**. A disease sign is a characteristic feature a patient may be unaware of that is noted by the clinician, such as an elevated temperature, an increased white blood cell count, or swollen glands. A disease symptom is something a patient recognizes and may complain about, like a sore throat, a headache, or blurred vision.

Mental health clinicians look for behavioral and psychological as well as physical signs and symptoms in order to make a diagnosis. Certain kinds of psychopathology, such as the organic brain disorders, are signaled by characteristic changes in blood chemistry or electroencephalographic ("brain wave") patterns. However, diagnosis of these and other behavioral disorders is more often made from past and present observed behavior, which might be examined during a clinician's interview of the patient. Also a medical or psychosocial history (the latter traces the person's friendship and relationship patterns) or a family member or friend might provide the necessary detailed information about a behavior. The biopsychosocial model of psychopathology (Chapter 2) purports that important diagnostic and treatment information can be uncovered by a thorough examination of the psychological, social, and biological factors that may be present in any disorder.

We may think of diagnosis as a two-part process. In addition to collecting the physical and behavioral data on signs and symptoms described above, the clinician must also find some way to interpret that information. Just as physicians have developed a set of disease labels they apply to particular sets of physical signs and symptoms, so too have clinical psychologists and psychiatrists developed a system for classifying behavioral disturbances. First developed in 1952, that system is incorporated in the *Diagnostic and Statistical Manual of Mental Disorders.*

The Diagnostic and Statistical Manual of Mental Disorders

DSM-III-R (1987), a revision of the 1980 edition of the *Diagnostic and Statistical Manual of Mental Disorders,* features three notable innovations—operational criteria introduced first in the 1980 *Man-*

ual, multiaxial diagnosis, and increased scope and detail. Each was incorporated to make the 1980 and 1987 *DSMs* more useful as diagnostic instruments than their predecessors, which only briefly described each disorder.

Operational Criteria. The **operational criteria** in *DSM-III-R* outline and briefly describe the behaviors associated with the diagnosis of each disorder. The information was largely derived empirically from extensive studies of patients. These studies were designed to pinpoint ways signs and symptoms of psychopathology cluster together in psychiatric patients with the same diagnosis.

Box 3.1 shows the *DSM-III-R* operational criteria for **dysthymia**, a common depressive mood disorder sometimes afflicting college students. To illustrate how diagnosticians employ the operational criteria, an excerpt follows from the case of Anne M, a twenty-year-old college student when she was diagnosed.

Dysthymia is a common depressive mood disorder that afflicts college students and interferes with the ability to work, study, and enjoy life.

Multiaxial Diagnosis—The Five Axes of DSM-III. To improve the usefulness of diagnosis, the drafters

BOX 3.1 DSM-III-R Operational Criteria for Anne M's Dysthymia

A. Depressed mood for most of the day, more days than not, as indicated either by subjective account or observation by others.

- Anne admitted to feeling sad most of the time she had been in college, and for several years before that. On comparing her prevailing moods to those of her friends, Anne almost always concluded that they were happier much more often than she.

B. Presence, while depressed, of at least two of the following:

(1) poor appetite or overeating
(2) insomnia or hypersomnia (abnormally long sleeping)
(3) low energy or fatigue
(4) low self-esteem
(5) poor concentration or difficulty making decisions
(6) feelings of hopelessness

- Anne frequently complained of "having no pep," especially when she got up in the morning. Moreover, she clearly suffered from low esteem: She thought poorly of herself, her ability to do her schoolwork, to make and keep friends, and to be the kind of daughter her parents expected her to be. And she often became exasperated when, on sitting down to do homework, she couldn't concentrate long enough to read and understand her assignment.

C. During a two-year period of the disturbance, never without the symptoms in A for more than two months at a time.

- Though Anne hadn't kept careful track, she could not recall more than a day or two at a time during the past several years when she hadn't felt sad and pessimistic. Her therapist agreed that, during the eighteen months he had known her, she had been moderately depressed the entire time.

D. No evidence of an unequivocal major depressive episode during the first two years.

- Anne had not shown the serious symptoms of this disorder (see Chapter 7) at any time.

E. Has never had a manic episode or an unequivocal hypomanic episode.

- Anne had never shown any symptoms of mania or hypomania, which include increased activity levels, euphoria, and grandiosity. (These behaviors are discussed in detail in Chapter 7.)

F. Not superimposed on a chronic psychotic disorder, such as schizophrenia or delusional disorder.

- Anne had never shown symptoms of psychosis, such as hallucinations, delusions (false beliefs), or disordered thinking (see Chapter 14).

G. It cannot be established that an organic factor initiated and maintained the disturbance.

- No organic factor affecting brain function responsible for Anne's condition has been identified (Chapter 15).

of *DSM-III* developed a **multiaxial diagnostic system**. It rates each patient on five distinct behavioral dimensions, or **axes**, rather than—as in earlier editions of *DSM*—only one, abnormal behavior. Consequently, the clinician has much more information available about each patient, much of it useful for planning treatment.

The multiaxial system is controversial in that it divides abnormal behavior into two separate axes. Axis I codes all common mental disorders except the personality and developmental disorders. These long-term disorders may persist for a lifetime and are included in Axis II. Distinguishing them from Axis I disorders, which generally last for shorter periods of time, highlights the impact of long-term psychological conditions on shorter-term ones. (The distinction is similar to "chronic" versus "acute" physical conditions.) For example, the *conduct disorder* of a ten-year-old boy—he has great difficulty getting along with other children and often disobeys his parents—is diagnosed on Axis I, while his *moderate mental retardation* is diagnosed on Axis II.

Axis III codes the physical diseases or conditions relevant to understanding or treating the patient. Box 3.2, which lists and details Anne M's complete *DSM-III-R* multiaxial diagnosis, illustrates such a relationship—between an Axis I diagnosis, *dysthymia*, and an earlier physical disorder, *a series of viral infections*, which interfered with Anne's transition to a new school during ninth grade. Axis IV rates the severity of stressors in the patient's environment; it helps clinicians decide whether early treatment of an Axis I condition should focus on removal or on alleviation of environmental stress. Finally, Axis V asks diagnosticians to assess patients' current level of functioning; this axis represents a point for comparison—a *baseline*—by which to compare treatment-induced behavioral changes.

The multiaxial material in Box 3.2 provides a more complete picture of Anne M and her disorder than the diagnosis of dysthymia alone (Box 3.1) did. This fuller view not only gave her therapist some initial ideas on where to focus treatment but also provided a "benchmark"—a comparison point—to compare Anne's progress against as therapy continued.

Increased Scope and Detail. To enhance the usefulness of the manual, the drafters of *DSM-III-R* markedly increased the number of diagnostic categories available to diagnosticians, continuing the trend of each previous revision of *DSM*. Table 3.1 lists the

BOX 3.2 DSM-III-R Multiaxial Diagnosis of Anne M

Axis I (Most psychopathological disorders): Dysthymia, primary type, early onset, moderate.

- Anne met all the operational criteria for *Dysthymia* listed in Box 3.1. Her condition is of the *primary type*, meaning it isn't related to any other condition which might cause depression (e.g., substance abuse or anxiety disorder). Early onset means that it began before Anne was twenty-one. Moderate means the depressive symptoms interfere with schoolwork and social life to a moderate degree.

Axis II (Personality disorders and developmental disorders of childhood): No diagnosis.

Axis III (Physical diseases or conditions which might be relevant to understanding or managing the patient): Recurrent viral infections during ninth grade.

- These recurrent viral infections caused Anne to miss almost half of that school year. Hence, she found it difficult to keep up with her schoolwork and to develop new social relationships during that crucial year of entering high school. Significantly, she dates the onset of her depressed mood to this period. It is also possible that these infections affected central nervous system functioning enough to interfere with Anne's ability to do her schoolwork and to participate fully in extracurricular activities at school for a few months.

Axis IV (This axis asks the clinician to describe and rate the severity of stressors in the patient's environment during the past year): Moderate.

- During the past year Anne had been subjected to the normal stresses of college life and the knowledge that her parents might decide to divorce, after a lengthy period of marital discord. While these stresses did not cause Anne's depression, which probably began during the first year of high school, they may have contributed to its persistence and intensity.

Axis V (This axis asks the clinician to judge how well the patient is functioning psychologically, socially, and occupationally on a scale which assesses mental health and illness): Patient generally functioning pretty well.

- Although depressed, Anne does better than average work at school, has a few good friends, provides support to her parents and siblings during a difficult time for them, and manages the everyday details of her life reasonably well. However, both she and her therapist believe that Anne would be able to function at a superior level were she not depressed.

TABLE 3.1 Major Diagnostic Categories and Subcategories in DSM-III-R

Disorders Usually First Evident in Infancy, Childhood, or Adolescence
- Developmental disorders (including mental retardation, autism—a childhood psychosis, and reading, writing, and language disorders)
- Disruptive behavior disorders (disorders affecting attention and conduct)
- Anxiety disorders of childhood and adolescence
- Eating disorders (unreasonable fear of becoming fat leading to marked weight loss, binging, and self-induced vomiting)
- Gender identity disorders (conditions that involve uncertainty about sexual identity)
- Tic disorders
- Elimination disorders (including bedwetting)
- Speech disorders not elsewhere classified
- Other disorders of infancy, childhood, or adolescence

Organic Mental Disorders
- Dementias arising in the senium and presenium (the severe, irreversible behavioral and cognitive disorders that affect some older persons)
- Psychoactive substance–induced organic mental disorders (including the irreversible behavioral and cognitive disorders caused by chronic alcohol and drug abuse)
- Organic mental disorders associated with Axis III physical disorders or conditions, or whose etiology is unknown (including the severe behavioral and cognitive disorders caused by brain injury and disease)

Psychoactive Substance Use Disorders (alcohol and drug abuse and dependence)

Schizophrenia

Delusional (Paranoid) Disorders

Psychotic Disorders Not Elsewhere Classified

Mood Disorders
- Bipolar disorders (the manic-depressive disorders)
- Depressive disorders

Anxiety Disorders (the panic, phobic, obsessive-compulsive, and stress disorders)

Somatoform Disorders (physical symptoms that are caused by psychological factors)

Dissociative Disorders (alteration in identity, memory, or consciousness caused by psychological factors)

Sexual Disorders
- Paraphilias (sexual arousal by nonhuman objects, suffering or humiliation, or children or other nonconsenting persons)
- Sexual dysfunctions (disruption of one or more parts of the complete sexual response cycle)
- Other sexual disorders

Sleep Disorders
- Dyssomnias (disturbance in the amount, quality, or timing of sleep)
- Parasomnias (an abnormal event during sleep or at the threshold between wakefulness and sleep)

Factitious Disorders (intentionally produced physical or psychological symptoms)

Impulse Control Disorders Not Elsewhere Classified (including intermittent explosive disorder, the inability to resist stealing, pathological gambling, and fire-setting)

Adjustment Disorder (inability to adjust to a known psychosocial stressor)

Psychological Factors Affecting Physical Condition (the psychosomatic disorders)

Personality Disorders (a maladaptive, enduring pattern of perceiving, relating to, and thinking about the environment and oneself)
- Paranoid, schizoid and schizotypal disorders
- Antisocial, borderline, histrionic, and narcissistic disorders
- Avoidant, dependent, obsessive-compulsive, and passive-aggressive disorders

seventeen major diagnostic groupings and twenty-two subgroupings in Axes I and II of *DSM-III-R.*

The drafters of the newer diagnostic manuals also tripled the length and greatly enhanced the detail of the accompanying text. In fact, *DSM-III-R:*

1. Provides much more descriptive detail on the signs and symptoms of abnormality.
2. Offers additional information about each disorder's frequency in the population.
3. Explains how to distinguish it from similar disorders.
4. Shows how the disorder changes over time.
5. Discusses treatment options.

Providing clinicians a wider range of diagnostic possibilities ideally enables them to be more precise in diagnostic labeling, thereby increasing diagnostic reliability and usefulness. Nonetheless, some respected observers have complained that the drafters of *DSM-III* may have gone too far. Psychologist Norman Garmezy (1978) criticized the vastly expanded section of a draft of *DSM-III* dealing with disorders of childhood and adolescence, for example. He was fearful that the addition of so many new diagnostic labels would tempt clinicians to attach ones to unusual but normal behaviors of childhood. This would inappropriately stigmatize disturbed children simply acting like children.

Issues in Diagnosis and Classification

Diagnostic reliability, diagnostic validity, and diagnostic bias are the most important issues a diagnostic system must confront and resolve.

Diagnostic Reliability. A **reliable diagnostic system** leads to diagnoses clinicians can agree on whereas an unreliable classification yields diagnoses clinicians disagree about. If clinicians cannot agree on precisely how to diagnose a disorder, their views on who suffers from that condition will be different. Therefore, they would probably be unable to examine its causes, develop appropriate treatments for it, or predict its outcome. However, if all clinicians base their diagnoses on the same sets of operational criteria, those diagnoses will be more likely to agree.

In an early study that reported higher diagnostic reliability for a draft of *DSM-III,* Robert Spitzer, chair of the task force responsible for developing *DSM-III,* and two colleagues conducted field trials in which 274 mental health clinicians evaluated 281 adult patients (Spitzer, Forman, & Nee, 1979). Patients in in- and out-patient settings at a range of institutions, including hospitals, mental hospitals, and outpatient mental health centers, were diagnosed. Most clinicians evaluated two patients each and every patient was seen by at least two clinicians. Clinicians reached significantly higher levels of diagnostic agreement than those in reliability studies of *DSM-I* and *DSM-II*.

Diagnostic Validity. Progress has accelerated toward the goal of a common clinical language because of the improved diagnostic reliability of *DSM-III-R*. Reliability and validity of diagnosis are specifically related: The more reliable a diagnostic system is, the more likely it will lead to valid diagnostic distinctions.

The **diagnostic validity** of *DSM-III-R*—its capacity to identify and predict behavioral and psychiatric disorders accurately—has only recently begun to be investigated. Research has already confirmed the capacity of *DSM-III* to distinguish depressed from nondepressed persons (Fabrega, Mezzich, Mezzich, & Coffman, 1986), hypochondriacal from nonhypochondriacal medical outpatients (Barsky, Wyshak, & Klerman, 1986), and persons dependent on alcohol or drugs from those who are not (Rounsaville et al., 1987).

Diagnostic Bias. *DSM-III* and *DSM-III-R* have also been examined for hidden biases which might affect their usefulness. In an attempt to tie psychiatry more closely to medicine, *DSM-III* may have overemphasized an organic view of causes and a medical orientation to treatment (Schacht & Nathan, 1977) when the available data did not support such a position (Schacht, 1985).

Another potential source of bias concerns how diagnosticians use the *Diagnostic and Statistical Manual.* Studies have shown that clinicians are more likely to make certain diagnoses of patients whose sex, race, and socioeconomic status conform to their expectations about the kinds of people who experience such disorders. For example, Warner (1978) asked 175 mental health professionals of both sexes to diagnose a patient from a summarized case history. Some subjects were told the patient was male, others that she was female. Gender of the patient turned out to make a substantial difference in the diagnosis given (though gender of clinician did not): When subjects thought the patient was female, they were more likely to diagnose hysterical personality; when they believed the patient to be male, the more likely diagnosis was antisocial personality.

Concerns regarding sex bias within the *DSM* have recently been raised with the inclusion of a provisional diagnosis, *late luteal phase dysphoric disorder,* in *DSM-III-R.* The usefulness of this provisional diagnosis will determine whether the diagnosis is retained as an accepted diagnosis in *DSM-IV.* The condition, more familiarly known as *premenstrual syndrome,* is characterized by depression, irritability, and other symptoms of increased stress typically occurring just prior to menstruation and lasting a day or two. The controversy is over the legitimacy of attaching a label indicating dysfunction and disorder to symptoms some women experience only once or twice a month—and the possible use of the diagnostic label to justify systematic exclusion of women with the condition from certain desirable jobs (Gallant & Hamilton, 1988).

Clinicians are not immune to bias regarding race and socioeconomic status (Abramowitz & Dokecki, 1977; Pavkov, Lewis, & Lyons, 1989). Investigating this issue, Morey and Ochoa (1989) asked 291 mental health professionals to diagnose and describe a composite patient with symptoms of borderline personality disorder (so-named because its symptoms place it on the borders of several serious psychiatric disorders). This disorder is one of the most commonly misdiagnosed—and most controversial—of all the personality disorders. Symptoms include a pattern of unstable and intense interpersonal relationships, impulsiveness, rapid shifts in mood, inability to control anger, chronic feelings of emptiness and boredom, and recurrent suicidal threats, gestures, or behavior.

Table 3.2 shows that inexperienced clinicians, female clinicians, and psychodynamically oriented clinicians in general were likely to diagnose a patient as borderline more often than the symptoms justified. This misdiagnosis was particularly possible if the patient was poor, white, or female. Male clinicians were less likely to diagnose a patient as borderline, particularly if the patient was wealthy.

TABLE 3.2 Factors Leading to the Misdiagnosis of Borderline Personality Disorder

Factor	Direction
Overdiagnosis	
Clinician experience[1]	Less experienced overdiagnose
Clinician sex	Females overdiagnose
Clinician orientation	Psychodynamic overdiagnose
Patient income	Poorer overdiagnosed
Patient race	Whites overdiagnosed
Patient sex	Females overdiagnosed
Underdiagnosis	
Clinician experience	More experienced underdiagnose
Clinician profession	Psychologists underdiagnose
Clinician sex	Males underdiagnose
Patient income[2]	Wealthier underdiagnosed

[1] *Explanatory Note:* Less experienced clinicians significantly more often diagnosed ("Over-diagnosed") borderline personality disorder than more experienced clinicians.

[2] *Explanatory Note:* Wealthier patients were significantly less often diagnosed ("Under-diagnosed") borderline personality disorder than less wealthy patients.

Source: From Morey, L. C. & Ochoa, E. S. (1989), An Investigation of adherence to diagnostic criteria: Clinical diagnosis of the *DSM III* personality disorders. *Journal of Personality Disorders 3*, 180–192. By permission of The Guilford Press, New York.

Diagnosis to Plan Treatment

Physicians diagnose illnesses and the right diagnosis often leads to the most effective treatment. Diagnosing certain physical disorders reliably (for example, many fractures and infections) is easier than behavioral or psychiatric disorders (Skodol & Spitzer, 1987). To diagnose the latter disorders, clinicians must often use only behavioral signs and symptoms, difficult to pin down and subject to errors of observation, interpretation, and bias. For example, the restrained, withdrawn, and self-effacing behavior of a normal person with a generally pessimistic approach to the world would probably be considered evidence of depression in someone who is usually outgoing and optimistic. Nonetheless, valid and reliable *DSM* diagnoses can help mental health professionals plan treatment by enabling them to choose the treatment that has achieved the best results with patients given one of those diagnoses.

Diagnosis to Conduct Research

Accurate diagnosis is also very important to research. Mental health professionals frequently assess the effectiveness of their treatments. To do so they must feel confident upon examining the success or failure of a given treatment that all patients given the treatment had the same disorder.

Diagnosis is also crucial in the study of etiology, the search for the causes of a disorder. For example, in order to test the theory that the inability to learn to read at a normal pace plays a central role in causing childhood depression, a clinician would select a group of patients who have been diagnosed as suffering from childhood depression. For comparison purposes, additional groups comparable to the patient group along every other characteristic except the diagnosis would also be identified and studied. That way, if the findings indicated that only the children with childhood depression, not the children with phobias or anxiety, had troubles learning to read, the clinician would be on firmer ground in concluding that reading difficulties may play a causal role in depression in young children.

Research on the prevention of physical or psychiatric disorders also requires an accurate diagnostic system. The confirmed diagnosis of a disease in a large number of individuals of a particular sex, age, life-style or behavioral pattern helps public health workers focus their prevention efforts on the population at heightened risk. A recent example is research leading to the identification of life-style patterns associated with increased risk of contracting the AIDS virus.

PSYCHOLOGICAL ASSESSMENT

The psychological assessment methods described here include interview methods, personality measures, and techniques for assessing intelligence. Data gathered from psychological assessment, especially assessment of personality, are valuable to clinicians for diagnostic purposes and in planning treatment for their patients (Matarazzo, 1990).

Interview Methods

Interviews are a precious tool of the mental health professional. **Diagnostic interviews** produce information on the patient's past and present behavior—normal and abnormal—that may be available from no other source. **Assessment interviews** take a variety of forms, including those to assess personality, interpersonal behavior, or the functioning of a family unit.

Individual therapy interviews bring patient and therapist together in an extended relationship based on the patient's willingness to recount and reevaluate past and present behavior, feelings, and attitudes. Therapy interviews represent a continuing series of assessment interviews, as more and more data on the patient's thoughts, beliefs, and behavior are continuously gathered and updated.

Some interviews are **highly structured** by a detailed set of questions prepared and tested before the interview and always asked in a predetermined order. One such interview, the Diagnostic Interview Schedule, or DIS (Robins et al., 1981), poses questions about symptoms of panic and anxiety. For example, "Have you ever had a spell or attack when all of a sudden you felt frightened, anxious, or very uneasy in situations when most people would not be afraid?" Interviewees who answer this question in the affirmative are then asked, "During this spell: Did your heart pound? Did you have tightness or pain in your chest? Did you sweat? Did you tremble or shake?" Because the diagnostic information is always gathered in precisely the same way, structured diagnostic interviews like the DIS yield very reliable *DSM-III* diagnoses (Antoni et al., 1987; Carr, Sweet, & Rossini, 1986). **Research interviews**, among the most focused of interviews, typically center on a specific research question (e.g., the subject's attitude toward the issue being studied or the frequency with which the subject behaves in a particular way).

Other interviews are **semistructured**: They follow an outline but do not prescribe specific questions or require a particular ordering of questions. Table 3.3 outlines a typical **mental status examination**, a semistructured interview to establish the current status of a patient's thinking, feeling, sensing, and perceiving. The results of such examinations are used to diagnose (mental status is an important diagnostic criterion for such conditions as schizophrenia and mood and anxiety disorders) and to plan treatment.

Therapy interviews are **unstructured**. Regardless of a therapist's theoretical orientation, a treatment session generally involves a continuing assessment of the patient's current concerns and preoccupations. Although therapists respond to each patient in a manner consistent with their theoretical orientation (for example, psychoanalysts are almost always less active in therapy than behavior therapists), they rarely know what issues a patient will want to discuss in advance of a particular session.

TABLE 3.3 Outline for a Mental Status Examination

General Appearance and Manner Is the patient clean and neat? Does he or she show peculiarities of posture (the way the patient stands) or movement? How easily and appropriately does the patient interact with the interviewer?
Speech Characteristics Does the patient show abnormalities of speech, like making up words or repeating the same word or phrase over and over?
Mood Is the patient's mood excessively happy, sad, or somewhere in between? Is it appropriate to what is being discussed?
Content of Thought Does the patient dwell on a particular topic or topics, excluding others? Is the patient delusional (having false beliefs), or does he or she show paranoid thinking (believing someone or something wishes one harm)?
Orientation, Memory and Learning, Attention and Concentration, and Information Does the patient know who and where he or she is, and what time and date it is? Does the patient pay attention to the interview? Does he or she have an adequate store of information on current and past events? Is the patient's memory intact?
Insight and Judgment Does the patient have insight into his or her behavior? Do his or her decisions reflect sound judgment?

Personality Measures

What traits of character, personal attributes, skills, abilities, and competencies make one person different from another? Better or worse at adjusting to adversity? More or less successful in a particular environment? Prone or invulnerable to mental disorder?

There have been varied answers to these questions through the years. This reflects the diversity in views on what constitutes **personality**, the concept psychologists use to explain the fact that past and present behavior often predicts future behavior (Buss & Finn, 1987; Digman & Inouye, 1986).

The Projective Tests. One way of assessing personality is to present individuals with standard ambiguous stimuli (Lerner, 1984). The Rorschach Inkblot Test is probably the most familiar of these *projective tests,* which share one common feature: unstructured, ambiguous test stimuli that respondents impose their own structure and meaning on.

Whereas clinicians have studied and used the **Rorschach Inkblot Test** and the **Thematic Apperception Test** (TAT) (discussed below) most extensively, they have also employed many others. For example, a variety of **sentence completion measures** are commonly used (e.g., Lanyon & Lanyon, 1980; Rotter & Rafferty, 1950). Developers of these tests assume that, by asking people to complete an open-ended sentence beginning "My mother was . . ." or "The happiest time was . . .", respondents will shape their responses less than when an interviewer asks them more structured questions on the same topic. Some clinicians also ask people to draw familiar objects or people (Gynther & Gynther, 1983; Sutker & Allain, 1988). The assumption behind these **projective drawings** is that the content or the form of pictures made without explicit instruction will provide uncensored information about personality traits (Stricker & Healey, 1990).

Hermann Rorschach, a Swiss psychiatrist, was influenced by psychoanalytic pioneer C.G. Jung's description of personality types, especially **introverted** and **extraverted** (Jung, 1923). (According to Jung, introverted people tend to be quiet, shy, and uncomfortable in social settings whereas extraverted persons, more receptive to influence from the environment, are gregarious, social, and open.)

In 1921, to separate his patients according to these two Jungian personality types, Rorschach developed the Rorschach Test. It was made of inkblots, some black and white, some in color, all sufficiently ambiguous that no viewer sees precisely the same things. Rorschach's aim was to study people's *projections*—the meanings they put—onto the ambiguous inkblots to gain insight into the unconscious determinants of their behavior. The absence of obvious "right" or "wrong" answers, Rorschach hoped, would lead people to respond from the depths of their personalities, as in psychoanalysis, to reveal how their behavior is driven by introversive or extroversive personality factors.

The Rorschach technique consists of ten cards, each with one inkblot design. Shown one card, or blot, at a time, the respondent tells everything he or she sees. The examiner notices which parts of the inkblot the person describes, any reference to colored objects or objects that have some texture or are unusual, the shape of what is seen, and what the shape is "doing."

What you see in this inkblot and how you see it gives psychologists experienced in projective testing information on personality and psychopathology.

Shortly after they began using the Rorschach technique, clinicians considered particular responses to be signs of specific mental disorders. Respondents who saw people in the inkblots who possessed both male and female characteristics, for example, were assumed to have homosexual tendencies, while those who preferred the black-and-white cards to the colored ones were considered depressed. Ultimately, the test was considered a diagnostic instrument, although Rorschach himself had rejected its use for that purpose. He was convinced that it was more sensitive to unconscious influences on behavior than to overt behavior, including psychopathology.

Despite Rorschach's opposition to the diagnostic use of the technique, diagnostic signs for organic brain damage (Piotrowski, 1937), neurosis (Harrower-Erikson & Steiner, 1945), and schizophrenia (Beck, 1938) on the Rorschach were reported many years ago. Even today, despite considerable evidence supporting Rorschach's initial position, clinicians continue to find clusters of Rorschach signs they believe are associated with the *DSM* diagnoses (e.g., Blatt, 1986; Piotrowski, Sherry, & Keller, 1985).

A new system for interpreting and scoring Rorschach responses (Exner, 1986) has revitalized respect for empirical findings among clinicians using the Rorschach. Exner's scoring system produces greater reliability (agreement among scorers) than other Rorschach scoring systems. And because his system is based on large **standardization samples** of respondents grouped by age, gender, diagnostic category, and personality structure, the validity (accuracy) of clinical judgments and personality assessments made from Rorschach responses scored by it may also turn out to be superior.

The Thematic Apperception Test (TAT) was created by personality researcher Henry Murray in 1938, seventeen years after Rorschach developed his test. The TAT is still one of the most widely used projective tests worldwide (Piotrowski & Keller, 1989; Sweeney, Clarkin, & Fitzgibbon, 1987). Like the Rorschach, it was designed to uncover respondents' unconscious mental processes.

The TAT consists of thirty-one stimulus cards. Thirty are drawings of ambiguous scenes that largely involve people; the remaining card is blank. Usually, twenty cards chosen with the respondent's age and sex in mind are shown, one at a time. The respondent is to "tell as dramatic a story as possible" about each card, including what led up to the event in the picture, what is happening now, what the people in the story are thinking and feeling, and what will happen next.

Murray (1938) made two important assumptions about TAT responses.

1. The behavior and feelings respondents attribute to the main character in a TAT story represent their own tendencies toward such behavior and feelings.
2. Respondents react to the aspects of the pictures that are most similar to important aspects of their own environment.

Murray proposed a scoring system to evaluate every TAT story along two dimensions—the respondent's **needs** (for food, affection, dominance, sex, and the like) and **presses** (e.g., poverty, emotional impoverishment, discrimination because of race or gender, and so forth). He maintained that presses prevent people from meeting their needs. Despite extensive research on the TAT as a diagnostic instrument (Weiner, 1983; Western, Lohr, Silk, Gold, & Kerber, 1990) and as a measure of personality (Atkinson, 1983; McClelland, 1980), its usefulness for both has been questioned (Lanyon, 1984). One reason is the difficulty psychologists have had developing a reliable system for categorizing and scoring TAT responses (Entwisle, 1972; Lundy, 1985). Murray's system proved complicated and cumbersome to use. Subsequent systems developed by others have also failed to be reliable. Clinicians, therefore, interpret their patients' TAT productions according to their own unique systems, making generalization of findings extremely difficult. Still, some clinicians continue to believe that TAT responses provide valuable information about their patients, especially about the unconscious roots of their behavior.

The Personality Inventories. Personality inventories pose questions about respondents' behavior, attitudes, experiences, and beliefs. Most of them have been **standardized**: Before publication, they were administered to large groups of subjects whose responses were analyzed according to age, gender, socioeconomic status, diagnostic category, and the like. Standardization of these instruments means two things. First, the questions are written simply and clearly, increasing the likelihood that respondents will answer them accurately, as intent will be understood. Second, respondents' responses are more likely to be **valid**, because they can be compared to

A psychologist administering the Thematic Apperception Test.

similar responses by similar individuals in the standardization sample.

The most widely used objective measure of personality and behavior is the **Minnesota Multiphasic Personality Inventory (MMPI)**. Other well-known personality measures include the California Psychological Inventory (Gough, 1969), the Sixteen Personality Factor Questionnaire (Cattell & Stice, 1957), the Eysenck Personality Inventory (Eysenck & Eysenck, 1969), the Edwards Personality Inventory (Edwards, 1967), and the Millon Clinical Multiaxial Inventory (Millon, 1986). All of them share a set of features and assumptions about how to measure personality functioning. Above all, respondents to each supply direct and objective reports—of memories, attitudes, beliefs, and feelings about past, present, or future behavior—enabling clinicians to assess personality and predict behavior. As indicated, a person's responses to all these instruments can be compared to previously gathered norms—collections of responses to the same instrument given by persons similar in age, gender, socioeconomic status, and, in some instances, diagnosis.

The reliability and the validity of direct measures of behavior such as personality inventories are superior to those of indirect measures of behavior like the projective techniques (Costa et al., 1986; Finn, 1986; Hogan, DeSoto, & Solano, 1977). These findings suggest that objective tests are apt to be more helpful than projective tests for diagnostic and predictive purposes (e.g., Lanyon & Goodstein, 1982; Preng & Clopton, 1986).

A true-false self-report questionnaire, the MMPI asks subjects to mark a lengthy series of statements "true" or "false" as each applies to them. The 566 items in the first version (Hathaway & McKinley, 1943) were selected from an original pool of 1,000 items. These items were chosen during its standardization because groupings of them (the clinical scales, illustrated in Table 3.4) differentiated among eight different diagnostic groups as well as a control group of nonpatients.

TABLE 3.4 The Clinical Scales of the MMPI

The MMPI's eight clinical scales and sample items from them are shown below. A plus sign after an item means that persons in the 1943 standardization sample diagnosed with the disorder associated with the clinical scale were likely to endorse the item; a minus sign means that they were unlikely to do so.

Hypochondriasis

This condition is characterized by excessive concern with bodily functions and imagined illness.

- I do not tire quickly. (−)
- The top of my head sometimes feels tender. (+)

Depression

The term *depression* is used in the conventional sense to imply strong feelings of "blueness," despondency, and worthlessness.

- I am easily awakened by noise. (+)
- Everything is turning out just as the prophets of the Bible said it would. (+)

Hysteria

The development of physical disorders such as blindness, paralysis, and vomiting as an escape from emotional problems is termed *hysteria*.

- I am not likely to speak to people until they speak to me. (+)
- I get mad easily and then get over it soon. (+)

Psychopathic Deviance

An individual who lacks "conscience," who has little regard for the feelings of others, and who gets into trouble frequently is called a psychopathic deviate.

- My family does not like the work I have chosen. (+)
- What others think of me does not bother me. (+)

Paranoia

Extreme suspiciousness to the point of imagining elaborate plots is paranoia.

- I am sure I am being talked about. (+)
- Someone has control over my mind. (+)

Psychasthenia

The term *psychasthenia* indicates strong fears and compulsions.

- I become impatient with people easily. (+)
- I wish I could be as happy as others seem to be. (+)

Schizophrenia

Bizarre thoughts and actions, out of communication with the world, characterize schizophrenia.

- I have never been in love with anyone. (+)
- I loved my mother. (−)

Hypomania

Overactivity and inability to concentrate on one thing for more than a moment are typical of hypomania.

- I don't blame people for trying to grab everything they can get in this world. (+)
- When I get bored, I like to stir up some excitement. (+)

Source: From Nunnally, J. C. (1984). Self-report measures of personality traits. In N. S. Endler & J. M. Hunts (Eds.), *Personality and the Behavior Disorders*, pp. 221–260. New York: John Wiley & Sons. By permission of the publisher.

A 1989 revision of the MMPI has added new items to and removed some old items from the original 550, to create a test of 567 items, increased the reliability of the original clinical scales of the MMPI, created new scales, and extended the range of disorders covered (Butcher et al., 1989; Butcher & Hostetler, 1990).

The MMPI also contains three "validity" scales. They reveal the respondent's attitude toward test taking, specifically whether he or she read the questions carefully and answered them truthfully. These scales help examiners decide if their conclusions are likely to be valid.

Not long after it was introduced, the MMPI's suitability for diagnostic purposes began to be questioned (Dahlstrom, Welsh, & Dahlstrom, 1972, 1975). High scorers on the clinical scales of the 1943 version of the MMPI—most of which correspond roughly to diagnostic categories in *DSM-I* and *DSM-II*—seldom met the diagnostic criteria for those categories. Psychologists, however, discovered that upon analyzing relationships among scores on the eight clinical scales, the MMPI did yield useful clinical discriminations and personality formulations for individuals and groups (Lanyon & Goodstein, 1982; Webb & McNamara, 1978). For example, a person who scores highest on the Depression scale, next highest on the Hypochondriasis and Hysteria scales, is likely to be much less troubled than someone who also scores highest on the Depression scale but next highest on the Schizophrenia and Psychasthenia scales.

The MMPI is more reliable than the projective measures of personality because it asks direct, understandable questions demanding equally direct answers (Burisch, 1984; Werner & Pervin, 1986). But the MMPI's validity and usefulness is less certain. It appears to distinguish between broad diagnostic groups. For example, it correctly labels persons as either psychotic or not psychotic about 75 percent of the time (Skinner & Jackson, 1978). The MMPI also distinguishes persons suffering from serious medical problems from those with psychiatric ones (Davis et al., 1980); patients with symptoms of posttraumatic stress disorder (an anxiety disorder experienced by people, particularly soldiers, who have experienced prolonged and/or highly traumatic stressful events) from those with other emotional disturbances (Penk et al., 1989); individuals with a personality disorder diagnosis from those with a medical disorder or another psychiatric disorder (Dubro & Wetzler, 1989); and suicidal persons who eventually kill themselves from those who do not (Leonard, 1977). Yet the instrument has been unable to differentiate sex offenders from other violent and nonviolent criminals (Levin & Stava, 1987), alcoholics from nonalcoholics (Nathan, 1988; Preng & Clopton, 1986), or among patients with different schizophrenia diagnoses (Young, 1972).

Assessment of Intelligence

Intelligence plays a crucial role in our success relating to our environment. The effect of intelligence on our ability to adapt well to the complexity of modern life is a key theme in the recently developed theories of intelligence we review in this section.

Although intellectual performance is sometimes impaired by psychopathology, high intelligence does not appear to predispose us to or protect us directly from mental illness (Cronbach, 1984; Sternberg & Berg, 1986). Nevertheless, the success of our adaptation to our environment plays a role in many behavioral disorders, from alcoholism and drug dependence to the anxiety and depressive disorders.

Historical Perspective. Pursuing an abiding interest in human heredity, English biologist Sir Francis Galton undertook one of the first scientific studies of intellectual ability in 1883. He attempted to compare and contrast aspects of intelligence in biologically related and unrelated persons. Galton ultimately concluded, as most of us do today, that intelligence runs in families. He also decided that sensory discrimination—the ability to respond quickly to environmental stimuli—is the most valid measure of intelligence. Galton studied simple reaction time, the speed with which subjects responded to a tone or a flash of light. He also measured intelligence by asking subjects to discriminate between tones, weights, and painful stimuli of different intensities.

At the beginning of the twentieth century, French psychologist Alfred Binet developed a series of tests of intelligence which continue to influence our thinking about the nature and measurement of intelligence. The tests were to determine which Parisian schoolchildren would benefit from a public school education and who required special schooling. Binet believed that children's intelligence grows and develops as they do. The older they are, the better their ability to reason and understand, make judgments, and come to rational decisions.

Binet evaluated specific children's intelligence by comparing their performance on tests of their judgment, comprehension, and reasoning to norms from a large standardization sample of children. The *Binet Scale* yielded an estimate of intelligence called the **intelligence quotient**, or **IQ**. By dividing the child's **mental age** (which corresponded to the number of age-grouped tests and problems the child passed) by his or her **chronological age**, the IQ is determined. Extensively revised through the years (Terman & Merrill, 1960, 1973), the *Stanford-Binet Scales*, the legacy of Alfred Binet, are still used to test children's intelligence.

The Wechsler Intelligence Tests. Psychologist David Wechsler (1939, 1955, 1958) devised a series of tests to replace the Binet tests for two reasons. First, the Binet Scales were originally developed to test the intelligence of children. They provide an estimate of intelligence based on age-grouped tests, of doubtful value in assessing adult intelligence. Second, the single score that the tests yield—the intelligence quotient—does not highlight an individual's intellectual strengths and weaknesses.

In 1939 Wechsler developed the *Wechsler Adult Intelligence Scale*, or *WAIS*, permitting the separate examination of diverse intellectual abilities, in adults, which most experts believe constitute intelligence.

The latest of his tests is the *Wechsler Adult Intelligence Scale—Revised (WAIS-R)*, published in 1981, designed for adolescents and adults. It tests eleven separate abilities, six of them verbal, five of them performance. The six verbal measures assess general information, the ability to think abstractly, short-term memory, arithmetic ability, the capacity to act on well-learned societal rules and expectations, and vocabulary. The five performance measures test the capacity to solve puzzles, reproduce designs, and manipulate objects, symbols, and numbers (Kramer, 1990; Waller & Waldman, 1990).

Other Wechsler measures of intelligence include the *Wechsler Intelligence Scale for Children—Revised (WISC-R)*, published in 1974 and designed for children between five and sixteen, and the *Wechsler Preschool and Primary Scale of Intelligence (WPPSI)*, published in 1967 and intended for preschool children. All three measures conceive of intelligence as the sum of several separate abilities, some verbal, others performance.

Two New Concepts of Intelligence. During the past century, controversies have raged over intelligence: how to define and measure it, if it is largely acquired or inherited, and the role it plays in success or failure and behavioral health or disorder. Recently, experts have questioned the prevailing conceptions of intelligence, including those underlying Binet's and Wechsler's intelligence tests. Instead of accepting the familiar answer to the question "What is intelligence?"—as simply "what intelligence tests measure," psychologists have begun to propose alternatives. These new theories return to some of the thinking in the late 1800s that led Galton to consider sensory responses crucial to intelligence. Today, psychologists Howard Gardner and Robert Sternberg have proposed theories of intelligence that owe more to Galton than to Binet and Wechsler.

Gardner (1983, 1986) asserts that the best way to understand and assess intelligence is to study the spontaneous processes of thought accompanying our efforts to adapt to our everyday environment. He conceives of multiple, independent intelligences rather than a single intelligence. People differ greatly

A young boy puzzling over the solution to the block design subtest of the revised Wechsler Intelligence Scale for Children.

in their pattern of strengths and weaknesses across the seven intelligences Gardner has identified: linguistic, logical-mathematical, musical, spatial, bodily kinesthetic, interpersonal, and intrapersonal. Gardner believes these seven intelligences, separately and together, determine the success of our interaction with our environment so that assessment of intelligence is best achieved in real-world interactions between the individual and the environment. Above all, Gardner emphasizes the successes diverse individuals can achieve, both within and between cultures, as a function of intelligence (Gardner, 1983).

Robert Sternberg is convinced that intelligence determines (1) where and how we choose to live, (2) how we adapt our lives to those choices, and (3) how we shape our choices to suit the way we want to live our lives (Sternberg, 1984a). Sternberg's *triarchic theory of human intelligence* (Sternberg, 1984b, 1985) emphasizes, even more than Gardner, the central role of intelligence in helping us adapt to the world.

The first of the three aspects of Sternberg's triarchic theory are the *componential* aspects of intelligence. Comprising the mental processes or skills most theories of intelligence emphasize, they determine how well we learn to do things and acquire new knowledge. The second, *experiential* aspects of intelligence, help us adjust to new intellectual demands, to explore and use new concepts, and to adjust quickly to new situations and challenges. The third, *contextual* aspects of intelligence, enable us to choose environments in which we can succeed, to adapt to them if necessary, and to structure them to our own needs.

While Sternberg's theory has attracted widespread attention, it has not yet been confirmed empirically.

ASSESSMENT OF BRAIN DISORDER

Virtually every disorder of the brain affects behavior. Minor disturbances in brain function, like those caused by two or three alcoholic drinks, yield barely perceptible, short-lived changes in a person's thinking and behavior, whereas major changes in the brain produce profound and permanent behavioral changes. Clinicians working with the brain damaged need a reliable assessment of these changes in the way the brain works to confront the changes in behavior that have already taken place and to prevent further deterioration.

Most brain disorders cannot be diagnosed simply from mental status examination and diagnostic interview, as most behavioral disorders are diagnosed, because of the overlap in signs and symptoms between the brain and behavioral disorders. Instead, diagnostic information from multiple assessment sources—diagnostic and specialized interviews, neuropsychological tests, the electroencephalograph (EEG), and the brain imaging techniques—is required if brain disorder is suspected.

Neuropsychological Test Batteries

The use of neuropsychological test batteries in diagnosing organic brain disorders is detailed in Chapter 15. These psychological instruments require persons suspected of brain damage to perform memory, problem-solving and psychomotor tasks which reveal subtle brain damage before it begins to affect behavior.

Several subtests of the *WAIS* and *WAIS-R* are sensitive to presence or absence of brain damage (Whipple, Parker, & Noble, 1988; Zarantonello, 1988). Because of this sensitivity and because clinical psychologists who want to administer and interpret the more specialized neuropsychological measures of brain damage must receive prior specialized training, the Wechsler tests—which every clinical psychologist studies in graduate school—are commonly used for this purpose. When confirmation or greater specification of the dimensions of a deficit in memory, reasoning, or problem-solving is required, the specialized batteries are often used.

The two neuropsychological test batteries in widespread use in America today are the *Halstead-Reitan Neuropsychological Battery* (Halstead, 1947; Reitan, 1959; Reitan & Davison, 1974) and the *Luria-Nebraska Neuropsychological Battery* (Golden, Hammeke, & Purisch, 1980).

The Halstead-Reitan Battery was initially developed more than forty years ago. Despite the development of newer test batteries in recent decades, it remains the most widely used measure of the cognitive and behavioral consequences of brain damage. The instrument assesses the full range of cognitive functions affected by brain damage with ten subtests to evaluate the status of those cognitive and behavioral functions—verbal and psychomotor—most affected by central nervous system injury or disease.

The newer Luria-Nebraska Battery is based on concepts and techniques developed by Aleksander Luria (1902–1977), the famous Soviet neuropsychologist. It profiles cognitive functioning in fourteen areas, including some—like memory and problem solving—tapped by the Halstead-Reitan Battery and others—like writing—unique to the Luria-Nebraska Battery. Design of the instrument was guided by Luria's conviction that while local areas of the cortex control specific skills, even the simplest human behavior calls on a variety of such skills and must, accordingly, be connected to several cortical centers. Hence, the neuropsychologist must look across brain areas and specific skills to achieve the most accurate picture of the disturbances in brain structure and function, which this neuropsychological test battery is especially well suited for.

Diagnostic distinction between chronic brain damage and chronic psychosis are very important. The signs and symptoms of each greatly overlap, yet their causes and, often, their treatment differ.

A report on the Luria-Nebraska Neuropsychological Battery revealed it as sensitive to some of the cognitive differences between brain-damaged patients and patients suffering from chronic psychosis (Moses, Cardellino, & Thompson, 1983). All but 19 percent of the sample (about twenty patients) were correctly identified as brain damaged or chronically psychotic on the basis of their Luria-Nebraska Neuropsychological Battery scores.

Electroencephalography (EEG)

Electroencephalography (EEG) detects abnormalities in the electrical activity of the brain. The electroencephalogram is recorded by placing pairs of electrodes in several locations on the patient's scalp. These electrodes send a signal corresponding to the difference in the voltage from the brain between the pair to one of several EEG recording channels.

The EEG of a normal, conscious but relaxed adult shows regular, oscillating waves (moving up and down) called **alpha waves** (see Figure 3.1). Other patterns of electrical activity replace them when the person becomes excited, is asleep, or falls into a deep coma. Abnormal conditions of the brain are frequently (but not always) associated with particular EEG patterns. For example, irregular, slow waves, known as **delta waves**, are typically recorded from damaged localized areas of the brain. However, an epileptic seizure (Chapter 15) may be signaled by extremely rapid, irregular "spikes," dramatic manifestations of the disorganized activity of the brain during the seizure.

The value of EEG studies of psychopathology is limited because most forms of psychopathology, including those without evident brain pathology, are not associated with specific EEG patterns. Even the organic brain disorders do not produce consistent EEG findings unless they are caused by or associated with localized brain damage or specific kinds of epilepsy, which do yield positive findings under certain circumstances. The EEG remains very useful for other purposes, though, including the investigation of sleep patterns.

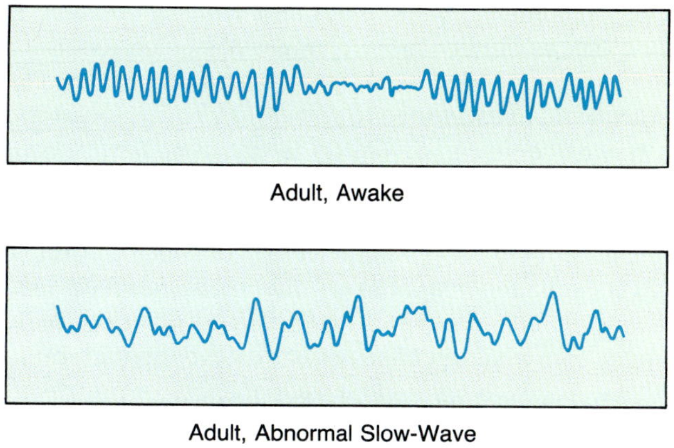

Figure 3.1 *Alpha waves are regular and oscillating; they represent EEG patterns shown by normal, conscious, relaxed adults. By contrast, delta waves are irregular and slow; they may signal localized brain damage.*

Imaging Techniques

Advances have been made over the past decade in the development of both invasive and non-invasive procedures for studying the anatomy and physiology—the structure and function—of the brain. (Invasive techniques require physical entry into the body while non-invasive procedures do not.) When brain damage is suspected, clinical assessment now generally involves one or more of the following procedures.

Computerized Axial Tomography (CAT). A big advance in brain imaging technology moved clinical radiology ahead in the early 1970s. To that time, X rays of the brain, using a contrasting substance that outlined blood vessels *(angiography),* were helpful in diagnosing circulatory diseases. They were not helpful, however, in localizing brain lesions because no contrast substance was able to capture differing brain tissue densities. Beginning in the early 1970s, however, sophisticated, high-speed computers capable of solving many equations simultaneously allowed information from multiple X-ray exposures of the brain from different angles, after a radioactive substance had been injected into the bloodstream, to be displayed in a single reconstructed image reflecting a cross-section or "slice" of that brain. The development of this technology, called *computerized axial tomography* (CAT), revolutionized the clinical investigation of many brain diseases. It permits detailed, undistorted images of the gross anatomy of the living brain by means of a non-invasive, painless, and quick procedure (Jaskiw, Andreasen, & Weinberger, 1987).

One of the first achievements of CAT technology confirmed a long-held suspicion that certain groups of schizophrenic patients show enlarged lateral and third ventricle spaces of the brain and of some cortical surface markings. The net result of these enlargements is a reduction in the mass of brain tissue. Aged persons, especially victims of Alzheimer's disease, show the same kinds of changes to a lesser extent. This reduction in brain volume, called *cortical atrophy,* is presumably associated with a shrinkage in the volume of brain neurons. Precisely what mechanisms are responsible for this decrease in the size of neurons in some schizophrenics and some of the aged is unclear, as is how these changes affect behavior.

Magnetic Resonance Imaging (MRI). *Magnetic resonance imaging* (MRI) is an even newer noninvasive technology, available only since the early 1980s. MRI might ultimately displace CAT as the imaging technology of choice for the localization of structural abnormalities of the brain (Jaskiw, Andreasen, & Weinberger, 1987). MRI provides a finely detailed visual reconstruction of the human brain that resembles three-dimensional slices of preserved brain. Unlike X ray and CAT, MRI does not involve radiation (instead, it measures nuclear magnetic movements of ordinary hydrogen nuclei in the body's water and fat), so repeated scans can be made without worrying about overexposure to radiation.

MRI studies at the University of Iowa provide precise data on brain disorder's role in schizophrenia (Andreasen, et al., 1985). Setting out to compare the brains of thirty-eight patients suffering from schizophrenia with those of forty-nine normal control subjects, these investigators ultimately focused their MRI investigations on the frontal lobe. (Many of the behaviors of schizophrenic patients resemble those of patients with known frontal lobe damage, e.g., decreased spontaneity and fluency of speech, reduced voluntary motor behavior, and difficulties with mood and emotions, including apathy, indifference, and shallowness.) Comparing the sizes of the frontal lobes of members of the two groups (requiring precision only achievable with MRI), the Iowa researchers found that schizophrenics had significantly smaller frontal lobes than did the controls (Andreasen et al., 1985).

Positron Emission Tomography (PET). While X rays, CAT, and MRI allow successively more precise representations of brain *structure,* one of the newest imaging technologies, *positron emission tomography* (PET), permits direct imaging access to information on brain *function* for the first time (Morihisa, 1987). When used in conjunction with CAT or MRI, PET helps clinicians localize a structural abnormality in a specific region of the brain and then test for possible causes of that abnormality, such as reduced blood flow or oxygen utilization.

The subject of a PET study is injected with a chemical substance carrying radioactive isotopes that interact with electrons in the brain to generate

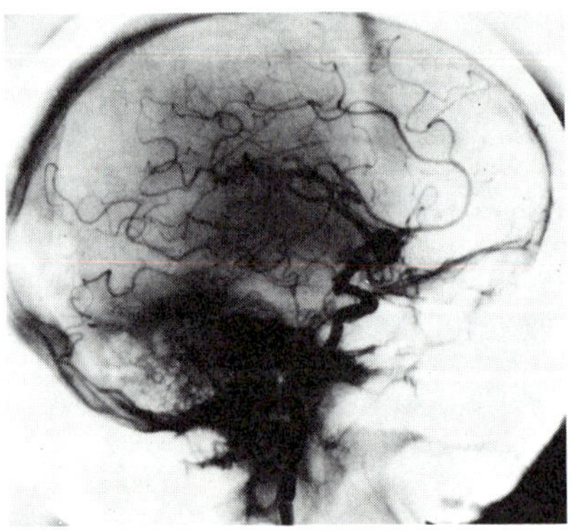

A. *Angiogram*

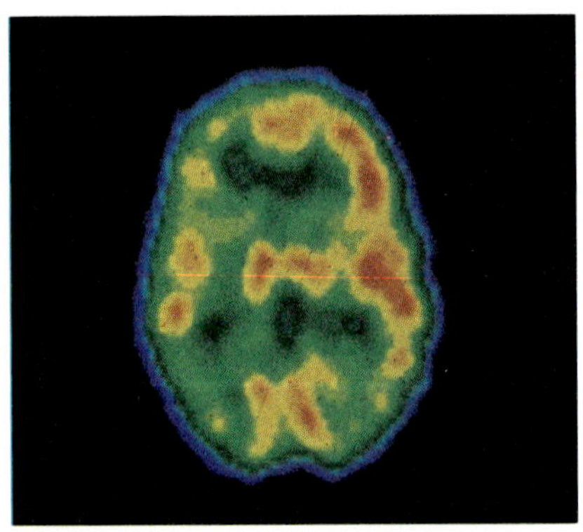

B. *CAT Scan*

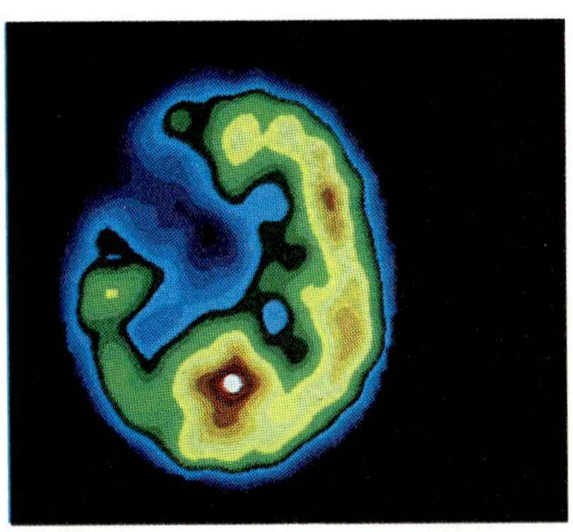

C. *PET Scan*

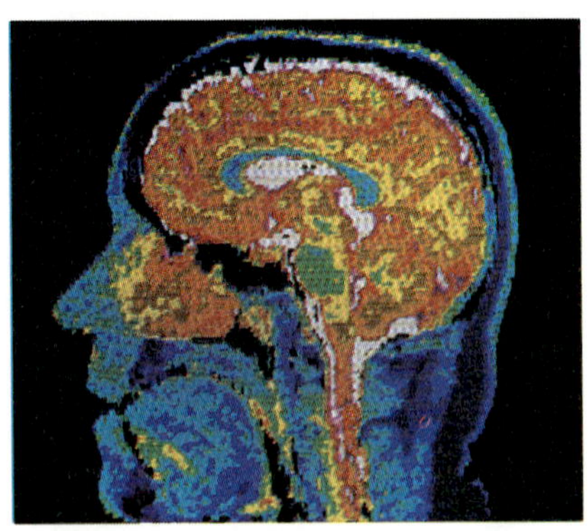

D. *MRI*

Angiography, computerized axial tomography (CAT), magnetic resonance imaging (MRI), and positron emission tomography (PET) provide invaluable information on the living brain's structure and function.

gamma rays. These rays reflect actual brain function in the living human being. This new technology makes possible blood flow studies, studies of oxygen utilization, and research on other processes necessary to the functioning of brain cells.

BEHAVIORAL ASSESSMENT

Behavioral assessment, a new approach to assessment, stems from behavior therapy and focuses on the current environment and the patient's current behavior, thoughts, feelings, and attitudes. Behavioral clinicians need to determine when and how often a disturbed or disturbing behavior occurs and the conditions which precede and follow it in order to try to modify those conditions or the person's attitude toward them to change the behavior.

Behavioral assessment developed for two primary reasons. First, many clinicians (not simply behavior therapists) had become impatient with the unreliability and uncertain validity of the traditional personality measures. They wanted more reliable and potentially useful ways to assess personality and behavior (Goldfried & Kent, 1972; McFall, 1986; Nelson, 1983). Second, many clinicians needed assessment procedures which provide information pertinent to behavioral treatment techniques in much the same way projective test results lend themselves to planning for psychodynamic treatment.

Antecedents, Target Behaviors, and Consequences

Behavioral assessment focuses on specific, troubled aspects of a person's behavior, such as fearful behavior, maladaptive interpersonal interactions, inadequate social skills, or unassertiveness. Few contemporary behavioral assessment approaches survey the entire person as that would not be specific enough to help behavior therapists plan treatment.

Behavioral clinicians typically emphasize the following three sets of data in their assessments:

- A detailed description of the disturbed behaviors themselves, as well as the thoughts and feelings that accompany them—*the target behaviors*.
- The events and circumstances typically preceding the target behaviors—*their antecedents*.
- The events and circumstances typically following the target behaviors—*their consequences*.

The detailed behavioral description of Anne M's behavior in Box 3.3 is a useful supplement to her *DSM-III-R* multiaxial diagnosis of dysthymia in Box 3.2 on page 58.

Behavioral Interviews and Direct Observation Methods

Behavioral clinicians most often develop specific assessment instruments for certain conditions and disorders, rather than assuming that a single battery of tests (such as the WAIS, MMPI, Rorschach, and TAT, which are often given together as part of a standard assessment procedure) is suitable for every condition (Gottman, 1985; Moskowitz, 1986).

This difference mirrors the varying assumptions dynamic and behavioral clinicians make about intervention. Dynamic clinicians stress how consistently traumatic events during the patient's early years result in later emotional disorder; behavioral clinicians see the patient's specific form of psychopathology as the consequence of the unique interplay of immediate environmental stressors, his or her particular learning history, and associated constitutional factors (such as energy level, intelligence, and physical prowess). As a result, whatever behavioral assessment reveals is very often the basis of treatment.

A behavioral interview is usually a first step in behavioral assessment. The interview gathers information on the sequence of events preceding and following development of the client's problems, as well as on the target behavior itself. Anne M's therapist (Box 3.3) chose to organize her behavioral assessment interview around the three elements of behavioral analysis (Antecedents, Target Behaviors, and Consequences) that many clinicians have found useful. She could also have tailored an interview to what she knew of Anne's situation.

Behavioral clinicians also try, whenever possible, to observe their patients' troubled behaviors personally. Witnessing these behaviors and, if possible, the events which precede and follow them, can be extraordinarily revealing, even more than descriptions of episodes by the patient.

Comprehensive plans for observing the behavior of several specific clinical populations have been developed. For example, guides for the systematic observation of troubled children—including the autistic or hyperactive—are used regularly to identify environmental variables, such as the behavior of parents, siblings, and friends, that may elicit the desired or undesired behavior of these children (Mash, 1987; Petit et al., 1987). Valid observational systems have also been developed to identify the behavior of partners in troubled marriages, members of disturbed families, and adults suffering from various kinds of disorders (Kolotkin et al., 1983; Margolin, 1983; Weiss & Tolman, 1990). Often these focus on observable behaviors such as angry, aggressive, or critical statements by marital partners or members of disturbed families to spouses, parents, children, or other family

BOX 3.3 A Behavioral Assessment of Anne M's Behavior

Antecedents

Anne M possesses a full and adequate "behavioral repertoire." That is, she is interpersonally skilled, sensitive to others' feelings, appropriately assertive, conscientious, hard working, bright, and energetic. But in certain circumstances, she visibly recedes into the background and ceases being the competent, intelligent, and effective person she is at other times. When this occurs (as it does once or twice a week), she withdraws from friends and family and her withdrawal is typically accompanied by self-critical thoughts and feelings of depression and worthlessness.

Meeting someone new, especially a peer, often precipitates social withdrawal and self-deprecatory feelings in Anne. These feelings, according to Anne, depend on who this person is, how the person behaves, and who else Anne is with. Thus, Anne says she might conclude that the new person is brighter, more skilled interpersonally, attractive, or interesting than she is. While, objectively, this is rarely the case, Anne quite often believes this.

Anne's interactions with her parents precipitate similar behavior and accompanying feelings even more predictably. When she is with them for any period of time, she reexperiences feelings of incompetence she felt as a child. Anne says her parents tend to treat her like the sick child she was in ninth grade, rather than the competent, independent adult she has become.

Anne's episodes of social withdrawal and self-critical cognitions began in her first year of high school when she lost a good deal of time from school because of recurrent viral infections. She says a doctor told her parents at the time that she may also have suffered temporary brain damage because of these infections. This, she feels, may have been the cause of her frequent inability to concentrate and thereby complete her schoolwork. Ever since, especially in academic settings and with peers, Anne has told herself that she doesn't measure up intellectually or socially.

Target Behaviors

When she is with friends or her parents and has begun to feel troubled, Anne withdraws markedly. She speaks much less than usual even though, when she speaks, others listen. She laughs or jokes rarely at those times even though, when she is not upset, she tells jokes well and says she likes to laugh. Following a disturbing social encounter, Anne avoids her friends for a day or more. With her parents, Anne, at times like this, becomes visibly more childlike, permitting her mother to do things for her she has long since done for herself.

During Anne's self-critical periods, she berates herself for her (imagined) social incompetence, unattractiveness, inability to do her schoolwork (during these times, even though Anne continues to study, she complains she cannot concentrate), and failures as a friend and a daughter.

Consequences

By withdrawing from others, Anne is never in a position to learn how inaccurately she assesses her intellect, social skills, and maturity. That is, Anne's friends generally respect her wish to be alone during these times, although they do persist in asking if they could help. Anne rarely shares her negative feelings about herself with friends. When she does, they are clearly unwilling to support her view of herself as incompetent or unworthy.

At home, Anne's parents strongly reinforce her view of herself as delicate, sickly, socially inept, and intellectually weak.

Treatment Plan

Behavioral treatment should focus on **cognitive restructuring**—direct feedback to Anne on her very positive impact on others, their clear desire to spend time with her, and the strength of her academic transcript. Consistent repetitions of these facts will make it more difficult for her to persist in denying them. Her therapist, then, should help Anne change her negative self-perceptions, to bring them into better alignment with others' very positive assessment of her and her strong academic achievements. Behavioral family therapy sessions designed to align her parents' perceptions of Anne with her current skills and achievements (rather than those of the fourteen-year-old Anne) also seem necessary.

members, or the fearful, depressed, or bizarre behavior of disordered adults.

Self-Monitoring and Self-Report Measures

The best way to gather information about people usually is to ask them. As noted, interviews are one way clinicians gather information about patients. Self-report measures are another. For example, behavior therapists treating substance abusers ask them to make detailed records of cigarettes smoked, drinks consumed, or drug "hits" made: when, where, and with whom, along with the feelings and thoughts that accompany use (Foy, Cline & Laasi, 1987; Wurtele & Martin, 1987). Behavioral clinicians treating persons with eating disorders ask them to keep similar track of their eating circumstances (Dubbert & Brubaker, 1987) and clinicians treating marital couples ask them to report conflictual situations (O'Leary, et al., 1989). And behavior therapists treating depressed persons ask their clients to **self-monitor** thoughts, feelings, and other cognitions by means of **self-report measures** (Jacobson, 1985; Lehrer & Woolfolk, 1982), to become aware of the sequence of events leading to self-defeating or self-damaging cognitions (Finney, 1985; Last & Blanchard, 1982; Wincze, 1982).

Behavioral clinicians also track therapeutic progress through self-report measures. For example, decreases in the frequency of negative self-statements and increases in positive self-statements (such as a person who says to him- or herself less often, "I could never do that" and more often thinks, "Maybe I should at least give it a try") can signal therapeutic success or failure (Lewinsohn & Lee, 1981). Self-reports can also reveal changes in the intensity of phobic, obsessive, or anxious thoughts during and after treatment.

In recent years, procedures have been extensively developed to chronicle patients' cognitions during and after therapy to track treatment success. This emphasis reflects the view of cognitive-behavior therapists and theorists (discussed in detail in Chapter 2) that the thoughts and feelings accompanying troubled behavior are most influential in maintaining it. Accordingly, behavior therapists need to know and understand what patients are thinking about their behavior and their chances of benefitting from treatment.

The validity of self-reports may be questionable at times. For example, psychologist Linda Sobell and her colleagues have carefully examined the reliability of self-reports of drinking by alcoholics and problem drinkers (Maisto, Sobell, & Sobell, 1982; Sobell & Sobell, 1990). They conclude that if there are no adverse consequences for accurate reporting, alcoholics will provide it. But if the consequence of an accurate self-report is perceived as negative, like a coerced return to treatment or an institution, the self-report is likely to be untrue, thus invalid. This raises the question whether persons in treatment for any of a number of disorders, particularly substance abuse, give their therapists accurate self-monitoring information, when they believe doing so will disappoint or anger the therapist (Babor, Brown, & Del Boca, 1990).

Assessment of Physiological Functioning

Behavioral clinicians rely on measures of bodily functioning—primarily autonomic nervous system activity and muscle tension—to track treatment response, plan interventions, and sometimes actually intervene. Behavior can be expressed—and should be measured—in three ways (Lang, 1971):

1. The overt behavior itself (our words and deeds).
2. Subjective feelings and attitudes about it (how we interpret the behavior to ourselves).
3. Our body's accompanying physiological responses (how the autonomic nervous system and other bodily systems reflect the behavior).

Sometimes the three kinds of responses are in synchrony (agreement), sometimes not. Nevertheless, measurement of all three response systems is worth doing if possible.

As we will discuss in detail in Chapters 5 and 8, measures of autonomic nervous system activation reflect a person's stress level. Heart and respiration (breathing) rate, galvanic skin response (measuring perspiration) and blood pressure are used for this purpose. In one common measurement situation, a patient listens to a description (and may see a still or moving picture) of objects or situations the therapist believes are particularly stressful for the patient, and the therapist takes several measures of autonomic nervous system level. For example, when confronted with fear-inducing stimuli, phobic patients may show dramatic increases in level of autonomic activity (Hayes, Nelson, & Willis, 1982; Last & Blanchard, 1982). This increase can help the clinician identify phobia-inducing stimuli to focus on in treatment. *Ambulatory monitoring of psychophysiological indicators of stress*—measurements that permit patients to go about their everyday lives while they are taken—is a recent development which promises greater correspondence between stress and stressors.

Electromyographic assessment—measurement of the level of activation of muscle groups—is also valuable in certain situations. Patients suffering from chronic pain, for example, may react to the description of a particular situation by tensing muscle groups that exacerbate their pain. Such behavior indicates that those situations help maintain the chronic pain and, thus, enables the clinician to focus the therapy more effectively (Blanchard, 1981).

To chart patients' progress, behavior therapists measure autonomic activation, muscle group activation, and the activity of the endocrine system (which also reflects stress level) before, during, and after treatment. For example, comparing heart rates generated by frightening stimuli before, during, and after behavioral treatment of a phobic patient supplies concrete evidence on the effectiveness of therapy in reducing or eliminating the problem (Sturgis, 1984; Taylor & Agras, 1981).

Chapter 8 details how **biofeedback techniques** employ physiological monitoring methods to reduce chronic pain and modify the intensity of stress-related physical conditions.

Reliability and Utility of Behavioral Assessment

Reflecting their belief that direct observation methods and behavior therapy go hand-in-hand, behavioral clinicians developed the methods for each simultaneously. From the start, behavioral assessment methods were designed for planning and evaluating a treatment's success or failure.

A reliable method of behavioral observation enables clinicians to observe the behavior of a group of disturbed children and agree on the nature of their observations. A reliable self-report of smoking behavior accurately reflects the number of cigarettes smoked. An assessment's **usefulness** is gauged from the assistance clinicians get from it in planning or evaluating treatment. A physiological measure of stress is useful, for example, if it informs the clinician that a patient is no longer severely stressed in a previously stressful social situation.

So that assessment techniques would not suffer from the low reliability of the projective techniques and some of the objective tests, behavior therapists developed measures that focused very closely on the target behavior (Patterson & Bank, 1986). For example, these measures did not require patients to interpret their own behavior, respond to ambiguous test stimuli, or give responses to open-ended questions, like sentence completion measures. Consequently—and predictably—those being assessed usually give the same answer to a behavioral assessment instrument despite the passage of time. Exceptions occur if they are asked questions about the behaviors targeted for therapeutic change (e.g., drug addicts don't always give accurate self-reports on drug use); when what is assessed occurs across too vast a timespan (e.g., asking a depressed person about his or her mood six months earlier); or if the behavior is too complex to capture in words (e.g., expecting a person to describe complex details of a brief interaction with another person).

Another problem that confronts behavioral assessment as well as personality assessment relates to the measurement process itself. The direct observation of a patient's problematic behavior is clearly costly and often impractical. Clinicians, therefore, have to undertake assessments in situations comparable to the patient's actual environment. But the assessment situation and the real-life situation may be different enough—despite their similarities—that the resulting assessment is not **ecologically valid**. Though a person may appear to be appropriately assertive on a paper-and-pencil test of assertiveness (where the patient is to indicate how he or she would respond to a series of situations that demand assertiveness), the situations included in the measure may have little to do with those in which the patient lacks assertiveness.

The usefulness of behavioral assessment also depends on whether the clinician shows **observational bias**. Without knowing or recognizing it, all of us introduce our own biases into what we hear and see even though, as clinicians, we try not to. Clinicians are only human and assess what they hear and see from their own perspective, which includes their own learning history, experiences, attitudes, and, sometimes, racial and ethnic stereotypes. That assessment, filtered through the clinician's perspective, may not be completely valid.

SUMMARY

1. Clinical assessment is the process clinicians use in gathering information to diagnose, plan treatment, and predict the future course of a disorder. Diagnosis is the act of identifying and naming a disorder according to an agreed-upon system of categorization.
2. *DSM-III-R* (1987) is the United States's accepted diagnostic system for mental disorders. It features three innovations first introduced in 1980: operational criteria, a multiaxial diagnostic system, and enhanced scope and detail. All three confront the low reliability and limited validity of earlier *DSM* editions.
3. A reliable diagnostic system leads to diagnoses clinicians agree on. A valid diagnostic system permits the accurate identification and prediction of behavioral disorder. Without diagnostic agreement, a diagnosis is neither useful nor valid.
4. Interviews are an important source of clinical assessment data. Some interviews are highly structured, like the recently developed *Diagnostic Interview Schedule*. Others, including the mental status examination, are semistructured. Still others, like most individual therapy interviews, are unstructured.
5. Projective tests are designed to provide clinicians access to determinants of behavior, including traits of personality, of which we may be unaware. They present respondents with unstructured, ambiguous test stimuli on which they impose their own structure. The projective tests include the Rorschach Inkblot Test, the Thematic Apperception Test, projective drawings, and a variety of sentence completion measures.
6. Personality inventories are standardized, paper-and-pencil measures which ask about respondents' behavior, attitudes, experiences, and beliefs. The most widely used personality inventory is the Minnesota Multiphasic Personality Inventory, newly revised in 1989.
7. Efforts to measure intelligence trace a substantial history. English biologist Galton undertook an early study of intellectual ability in 1883, concluding that intelligence runs in families. French psychologist Binet developed a series of tests of children's intelligence at the turn of the century, introducing the term *intelligence quotient* (IQ) based on mental age. In the late 1930s, psychologist David Wechsler devised a series of tests to replace the Binet tests, permitting the separate examination of the diverse intellectual abilities which constitute intelligence.

8. Information from multiple assessment sources—diagnostic and specialized interviews, neuropsychological tests (including the Halstead-Reitan and Luria-Nebraska batteries), the electroencephalograph (EEG), and the brain imaging techniques (computerized axial tomography, magnetic resonance imaging, and positron emission tomography)—is required if brain disorder is thought to be responsible for disordered behavior.

9. Behavioral assessment techniques focus on the current environment as well as the patient's present behavior, thoughts, feelings, and attitudes. Behavioral clinicians typically assess the target behaviors themselves, their antecedents, and their consequences. Behavioral clinicians also rely frequently on measures of bodily functioning—primarily, autonomic nervous system activity and muscle tension—to track treatment response and plan interventions.

Frank Kupka, *Architecture philosophique* (1913). H/T 143 cm c 112 cm. Courtesy of Galerie Louis Carre & Cie, Paris.

4 RESEARCH METHODS IN THE STUDY OF ABNORMAL BEHAVIOR

There is something of the psychologist in all people as we observe what others do and often try to understand their actions. We also try to predict and even change others' behavior, or even our own. This is especially likely to be true when we experience abnormal behavior in other people or ourselves. What sets apart the amateur psychologist or layperson from the professional psychologist is the latter's training in the scientific method for studying behavior and human experience.

Although it is not the only approach, as noted in Chapters 1 and 2, the scientific method is the dominant means of studying abnormal behavior today. Inspired by scientific advances in medicine and other fields of human inquiry, psychologists have adapted a variety of scientific research methods to the study of abnormal behavior. The main features of these research methods that define the scientific study of abnormal behavior are examined in this chapter. And in succeeding chapters, how the use of these research methods has produced notable progress in the understanding, prevention, and modification of different forms of abnormal behavior will be shown.

THE SCIENTIFIC STUDY OF ABNORMAL BEHAVIOR

The scientific approach is a method for systematically studying normal and abnormal behavior. It is designed to identify general laws about behavior. Simply gathering many facts about different forms of behavior is insufficient: The scientific approach attempts to discover the laws that explain these apparently diverse bits of behavior. For example, writers over the centuries have observed the widely varying effects on different people of alcohol consumption. If we assume that the many different behaviors following alcohol consumption were previously held in check (inhibited) by a common brain mechanism, and that alcohol functions to release these behaviors from inhibitory control, then all these apparently unrelated effects are explainable by a single mechanism of action (Gray, 1985).

Researchers using the scientific approach must describe and define the phenomena they study in precise terms which other investigators can clearly understand. For example, *anxiety* is possibly the most widely used concept in abnormal psychology. It can have several different meanings, ranging from arousal of the autonomic nervous system (e.g., increased heart rate and blood pressure) to subjective self-report of fear (i.e., "I feel uptight"). These different **operational definitions** suggest ways of measuring a phenomenon reliably and usefully but do not always refer to the same thing. Thus two researchers may both use the term *anxiety* but be talking about partially different phenomena if one is measuring heart rate and the other self-report of fear (Lang, 1969).

A **scientific theory** is an explicit and formal state-

Psychological testing frequently involves completing questionnaires.

ment of a set of propositions designed to explain a particular phenomenon. A theory must meet explicit criteria.

1. A theory must be stated clearly to be tested. The value of any theory, no matter how convincing it seems, ultimately depends on the findings of rigorous experimental tests.
2. A theory should explain and integrate the information currently known about the phenomenon in question.
3. A theory should stimulate research leading to new findings.

Theory plays an important role in scientific method as it guides research and helps determine what will be discovered. As social psychologist Kurt Lewin (1935) once said, there is nothing as practical as a good theory. Theories can also play an important role in guiding therapists in clinical practice as they seek to understand their patients' problems and devise useful assessment and treatment strategies.

Scientific findings must be reliable or replicable. Before they can be accepted, research results must be repeated under carefully specified conditions, ideally by different investigators in different research centers. Science depends on publicly observed evidence.

Scientists are commonly divided into two camps of scientific method. The first approach is the **hypothetico-deductive method**. These scientists are more theoretical or speculative and use imagination and intuition to arrive at a theory and then test their hypothesis by experiment or observation. For example, eating disorders occur predominantly in female adolescents and young adults. Such disorders also appear to have greatly increased in prevalence during the 1980s. Behavioral and social scientists have asked why these particular disorders mainly afflict young women, and why at an accelerated rate during this particular decade (Striegel-Moore, Silverstein, & Rodin, 1986).

To explain these related phenomena, Striegel-Moore and her colleagues proposed several hypotheses, one of which was that cultural norms during the 1980s pressured women, far more than men, to be thin and physically attractive. Women, because of their social role, are susceptible to this cultural pressure, and therefore engage in unhealthy diets which place them at risk for eating disorders. The researchers then deduced specific experiments to test their hypothesis. For instance, those women who are most subject to sociocultural pressure for thinness (e.g., fashion models) should have especially high rates of eating disorders (see Chapter 13).

The second method is the **inductive approach.** Many scientists accumulate data first to develop a theory explaining a phenomenon. The logic behind the inductive approach is spelled out by that legendary master of analytical reasoning and detection, Sherlock Holmes: "It is a capital mistake to theorize before one has data. Insensibly one begins to twist facts to suit theories, instead of theories to suit facts." Most researchers, in reality, combine elements of both the hypothetico-deductive and inductive approaches as the scientific approach to abnormal behavior offers a variety of different, flexible strategies for studying specific phenomena.

Why Adopt a Scientific Approach?

Scientific research has advanced our understanding of some of the most puzzling phenomena in the field of abnormal behavior. Additionally, it has forced researchers to revise strongly held theories about a number of clinical disorders—theories which seemed believable but had no empirical support. For example, as discussed in Chapter 14, it was once popular to view schizophrenia simply as a different or unconventional way of coping with stress, not as a major mental disorder (Szasz, 1960; Ullmann & Krasner, 1969). The view was that the actions of schizophrenics made sense if the social context in which they lived were taken into account (Laing & Esterson, 1969). It was not that schizophrenics were disturbed but rather that their behavior was disturbing to a society that then sought to control them through drugs and by other means (Ullmann & Krasner, 1969). Laing, a British psychiatrist with a large popular following in the United States in the late 1960s, even argued that schizophrenics had superior mental capacity to "normals." Subsequently scientific research established that schizophrenia is a mental disorder, which is determined in large part by genetic influences, and has identifiable brain abnormalities.

The scientific approach is not strictly objective. There is creativity and guesswork in generating testable hypotheses, excitement and personal satisfaction in discovering new knowledge, and intrigue and detective-like know-how in tracking down an elusive mechanism causing abnormal behavior or accounting for a treatment's success. And there is frustration in failed experiments and in encountering dead ends.

THE CASE STUDY

The case study is perhaps the method used the longest to study abnormal behavior. The clinician observes and records the individual's current behavior and gathers information about his or her past, including family history, education, employment, crucial social relationships, and general level of psychological adjustment. This information is typically based on an interview with the person, possibly supplemented by psychological tests and material obtained from family members. The goal of the case study is to describe the patient's problem, relate it to his or her present and past functioning, and provide a hypothesis about its causes.

The case study has been one of the most influential research methods in the study of abnormal behavior. For example, the Freudian or psychodynamic model once dominated our understanding and treatment of abnormal behavior and still remains one of the most influential approaches. And it was a small number of enormously influential case studies that transmitted Freud's impact (described in Chapters 5 and 6). All models of abnormal behavior—even the behavioral model—have relied upon the case study. For example, it was Masters and Johnson's (1970) report of a series of case studies on the nature and treatment of sexual dysfunction that ushered in the era of sex therapy in the 1970s (see Chapter 9).

Advantages

Case studies make important contributions to the study of abnormal behavior. Their scientific function provides a useful source of hypotheses which can be tested employing more powerful experimental research methods. For example, psychologists used to view obsessive-compulsive disorder as a function of unresolved psychological conflicts experienced in early childhood. Then a handful of clinical case studies reported the sudden onset of the disorder following head injuries (McKeon et al., 1984). In a particularly unusual case, a man with obsessive-compulsive disorder shot himself in the head in a suicide attempt. He survived, and his obsessive-compulsive problems promptly disappeared, leading researchers to speculate that those areas of the brain which had been damaged may have been responsible for the disorder. These case studies helped focus researchers on brain neurochemistry rather than childhood conflicts as a possible cause of obsessive-compulsive disorder (see Chapter 5). A clinical function of case studies allows the report of therapeutic innovations and the description of clinical methods and strategies applied to particular clients. Consider, for example, the following case report:

> *A forty-two-year-old housewife erroneously believed she was suffering from cardiac disease. Negative medical tests and reassurance from her physician failed to modify this belief. When asked what evidence she had for the idea that she had cardiac disease, she said that she noticed her heart more frequently than did her husband or colleagues at work and she thought this must indicate that there was something seriously wrong with it. The therapist suggested an alternative interpretation that the problem was her belief that there was something wrong with her heart. This belief then led her to selectively attend to her body, which in turn increased her awareness of her heart. When asked what she thought of this alternative, she said, "You psychologists are very good at thinking of clever explanations, and this would, no doubt, apply to some people, but I don't think that the effects of attention could be strong enough to account for my sensations." Rather than argue with this assertion, the therapist said, "You may be right. But perhaps to get more information it would be good if we did an experiment to see how strong the effects of attention are for you." In this experiment the patient was asked to close her eyes and concentrate on her heart for five minutes. To her great surprise, she found that simply attending to her heart enabled her to detect the pulse in her forehead, neck, arms, chest, and legs without touching these parts of the body. Furthermore, when she was subsequently asked to describe out loud the contents of the room for five minutes, she ceased to be aware of her heart. This demonstration reduced her belief that she had cardiac disease, increased her belief in the alternative explanation, and encouraged her to use distraction as a coping technique when she subsequently felt panicky.* (Clark, 1989, p. 85)

This case report not only helps explain the nature of the woman's abnormal fear of heart disease but also provides details of how to treat such a fear. The clinical detail and practical focus of a good case study make it especially appealing to practitioners. To serve this clinical function case studies must meet some basic criteria:

1. Treatment methods must be described with sufficient detail and precision to allow replication by other therapists.
2. The methods must be applied to specific problems.
3. Any relevant personal characteristics of the patient(s) must be reported.

Disadvantages

Case studies cannot show that one event causes another nor prove theories about the etiology of a clinical disorder nor establish that treatment cures a disorder. The problem is that alternative explanations of the results cannot be ruled out; A case study may be described as *uncontrolled.* The findings may be limited to the particular patient in question, or they may be due to the specific interaction between a particular clinician and patient. Because of these limitations, there is no certainty that the findings can generalize to other patients with apparently similar problems.[1]

The danger of depending on uncontrolled clinical reports instead of well-controlled research studies has been repeatedly demonstrated in the history of abnormal psychology. For example, Breuer's treatment of his patient Anna O was a key element in the development of psychoanalysis. Yet not only was his diagnosis incorrect, but Freud erroneously reported that Breuer's treatment methods had cured Anna O (see Chapter 6). The danger of relying too heavily on uncontrolled case studies has not been confined to psychoanalysis as examples exist in all therapeutic systems. In 1967, Richard Stuart published an account of the behavioral treatment of eight obese patients. The results were the best ever reported in the treatment of obesity—all eight continued to lose twenty pounds or more during the year following therapy. Subsequent research has shown that behavioral treatment of obesity is only modestly effective; it does not have the dramatic and uniform outcome effects suggested by Stuart's eight cases (Wadden et al., 1988). Reliance on case studies alone, then, would falsely inflate the effects of behavioral treatment of obesity, misleading patients about what to expect. For ethical and clinical reasons (Chapter 8), obese patients must be alerted to the limited effectiveness of obesity treatment.

[1] Freud was perhaps the most brilliant and influential exponent of the clinical case study in abnormal psychology. His use of the case study illustrates its advantages and disadvantages. On the positive side, the theory and practice of psychotherapy was influenced by the clinical insights and therapeutic strategies of his case studies. On the negative side, Freud generalized too much from a single case. Ernest Jones, Freud's loyal biographer, commented on the positive and negative aspects of Freud's use of case studies as follows: "His great strength, though sometimes also his weakness, was the quite extraordinary respect he had for a singular fact. . . . That is the way Freud's mind worked. When he got hold of a simple but significant fact he would feel, and know, that it was an example of something general, and the idea of collecting statistics on the matter was quite alien to him" (cited in Sulloway, 1979, p. 84).

Why have case studies been so influential despite their many limitations? Richard Nisbett and Lee Ross (1980) studied why researchers, including social scientists, assign importance to different data or sources of information. People believe information presented dramatically or vividly is more important, they conclude. Researchers will thus ignore or pay too little attention to valid information presented as a summary of well-controlled studies, whereas they will base their judgments on less valid information which is more vivid, such as a fascinating case history with personal details.

CORRELATIONAL METHODS

Correlational methods assess the extent to which two or more events are related. A **correlation coefficient** is the mathematical expression of the degree of relationship between two variables, or two sets of data, and ranges from -1 to 1. A correlation of 0 means no association between two variables; the relationship is totally random. The closer to 1, the stronger the *positive correlation,* indicating the degree to which subjects have the same relative standing in the distributions of the two variables. The closer the coefficient is to -1, the stronger the *negative,* or *inverse, correlation.* For example, there is a strong, inverse correlation between obesity and social class[2] (Goldblatt, Moore, & Stunkard, 1965). As shown in Figure 4.1, the lower the social class, the greater the incidence of obesity. This conclusion has been replicated in more than thirty subsequent studies and stands as one of the most secure findings in the field of obesity (Stunkard, 1989). For reasons discussed below, however, this does not mean that a person's social class in some way causes or prevents obesity.

Researchers extensively employ correlational methods in the study of abnormal behavior, particularly those in the field of clinical psychology (Cronbach, 1957). Even the case study is a crude type of correlational method. For example, the clinical case studies cited earlier described how a man's obsessive-compulsive disorder disappeared following a self-inflicted (gunshot) brain injury. The disappearance of the clinical symptoms covaried with the head injury. This covariation led to the hypothesis that physical brain abnormalities may cause obsessions and compulsions.

Most case studies are limited to a single patient, whereas correlational research methods typically in-

[2] More generally, mental health is inversely correlated with social class—the lower the social class, the greater the degree of mental illness (Srole et al., 1962).

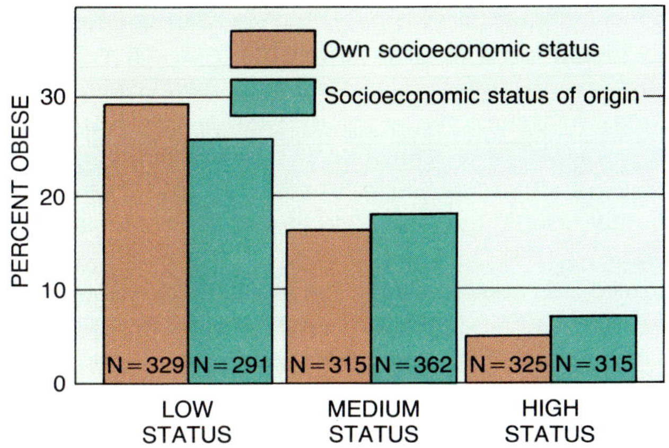

Figure 4.1 *Decreasing prevalence of obesity with increase in own socioeconomic status (SES) and SES of origin.*

Source: From "Social factors in obesity" by P.B. Goldblatt, M.E. Moore, & A.J. Stunkard, 1965, *Journal of the American Medical Association*, 192, p. 1034. Copyright 1965, American Medical Association. Reprinted with permission.

volve more systematic analyses of the characteristics or performance of entire groups of subjects. Research on personality theory illustrates the systematic nature of the correlational method. For example, an individual scores highly on a questionnaire measure of extraversion. According to the trait theory of personality, how this extraverted person will behave in different situations should be predictable. To test the accuracy of these predictions, the personality researcher measures the individual's behavior in different situations and determines if these measures are significantly correlated with his or her score on the questionnaire measure of extraversion. The higher the correlation, the more confidence we can have that the questionnaire is measuring the trait of extraversion.

Correlation and Causality

Correlational methods are limited to showing that two or more events are associated with each other. Like case studies, they cannot indicate anything about causality—whether one event causes the other. For example, patients with eating disorders show high levels of depression whereas normal dieters do not (Levy et al., 1989). In other words, eating disorders are correlated with depression. This correlation can reflect different relationships between the two clinical disorders. There are three possible relationships.

The first possibility is that depression causes the eating disorder. This formulation is one of the most influential theories of the nature of bulimia nervosa (Pope & Hudson, 1988). The second possibility is that depression is the consequence of the eating disorder. The third possible interpretation is that neither depression nor the eating disorder causes the other—both are the product of some third variable or disorder. For example, some individuals may have a genetic predisposition to react to stressful life experiences with both depression and an eating disorder, perhaps because of abnormal biochemical functioning. According to this interaction these two disorders are correlated coeffects of the third variable. The three *C*'s help interpret a correlation: One of the two variables in a correlation might be the *cause*, the *consequence*, or the *correlate* of the other variable.

Sophisticated and powerful research tools are needed to sort out which of the three interpretations is correct and to identify the cause of eating disorders. Through experimental methods the depression could be treated and the eating disorder monitored for change. If the disorder changed, the view that depression caused the eating disorder would be favored. Or the eating disorder could be treated directly and the depression observed. If the depression were altered, depression as the consequence of the eating disorder would be likely. This kind of research showing that depression is typically the consequence, not the cause, of eating disorders is discussed in Chapter 13 (Laessle et al., 1988).

Epidemiological Research. **Epidemiology** is a correlational method that studies the prevalence, etiology, and consequences of physical disease and mental disorders in a population. Epidemiological methods have been used most widely in research on how psychological or behavioral factors (e.g., hostility, cigarette smoking) can influence physical disease (e.g., heart disease) (see Chapter 8). Epidemiological research studies the social conditions correlated with the prevalence of specific physical and mental disorders and identifies individuals and groups at high risk for developing these disorders.

The now-famous Framingham Heart Study is an illustration of epidemiological research. Framingham is a town in Massachusetts where, for the last thirty-five years, a substantial percentage of the adult men and women have been regularly tested for the development of heart disease. Nearly all of these people were healthy when the study began. By continuing to assess their health-related behavior and its association with heart disease over the years, researchers have revealed the role of high blood cholesterol, high blood pressure, cigarette smoking, obesity, and other **risk factors** in the development of heart disease.

Epidemiological research is also crucial in the study of mental health. The results of epidemiological research showing the prevalence of different forms of abnormal behavior in the United States were summarized in Chapter 1. Epidemiological family studies have examined the interaction between genetic and environmental factors in the development of abnormal behavior (Weissman et al., 1986). Studies of high-

The research team from the famous Framingham study.

risk subjects focus on the children of a parent with a clinical disorder. The adult (parent) with the disorder is called the **proband**. The children of probands are at higher risk for developing the disorder than comparable children of parents without the disorder. For example, this is true of children of a depressed or alcoholic parent (see Chapters 11 and 13). The children are studied *longitudinally*—that is, information is repeatedly collected on them over a period of years. By studying changes in these children over time, risk factors that precede the development of a problem may be identified. Once this is done, researchers try to devise ways to help the children cope with their situation, thereby preventing the development of abnormal behavior. Epidemiological studies can thus form the basis of prevention and treatment programs. Researchers may also use epidemiological studies to investigate the role of factors that protect the children at risk from developing the disorder.

In **case-control studies**, the person with the clinical disorder is matched with a control, namely someone without the disorder but similar in respects such as age, race, sex, and socioeconomic status. The prevalence of the disorder among the family members of the proband is then compared to that among the relatives of the control. A case-control study may show a higher prevalence of the disorder among family members of those with a disorder, in other words, that the disorder runs in the family. This evidence of family aggregation does not prove that the disorder is transmitted genetically because family members also share a common environment. Yet evidence from family epidemiological studies improves our understanding about how disorders are transmitted. If a disorder is transmitted within a family, more powerful experimental designs for separating genetic and environmental determinants of behavior can be used (e.g., twin or adoption studies, Chapter 2).

Epidemiological studies can never prove particular risk factors cause a disease; they can show only varying degrees of association or correlation and suggest which risk factors researchers should analyze experimentally (see Box 4.1).

EXPERIMENTAL METHODS

Since causation cannot be inferred from correlation, experimental methods are needed to establish that one event causes another. In an "experimental" study a variable (the **independent variable**) is manipulated, or controlled, by the researcher in order to measure the effects on other variables (the **dependent variables**). An experimental effect is demonstrated when the manipulation of the independent variable produces reliable effects on the dependent variable.

Consider the following example. Based on uncontrolled case studies, clinicians have long hypothesized that anxiety interferes with or decreases sexual arousal (Masters & Johnson, 1970). David Barlow and his colleagues set out to test this hypothesis with a laboratory experiment (Barlow et al., 1983). The subjects were three groups of normal, male college students who watched an erotic film. Group 1 were told that if they did not become sexually aroused, they stood a 60 percent chance of receiving a harmless but painful electric shock to the hand. Group 2 were told that they might be shocked, regardless of whether they became sexually aroused. Group 3 were not exposed to the threat of shock. Sexual arousal was assessed by measuring penile erection. See Figure 4.2 on page 84. Contrary to the researchers' hypothesis, anxiety did not decrease sexual arousal—rather, it increased arousal.

In this experiment anxiety was the independent variable. To manipulate it in the laboratory, the experimenters defined anxiety in terms of the threat of an electric shock. This is an example of an operational definition. (No subject was ever actually shocked—it was the threat of receiving a shock that was manipulated.) Sexual arousal was the dependent variable. The experimenters defined sexual arousal as changes in penile tumescence (see Chapter 9).

BOX 4.1 From Correlation to Cause

Epidemiological studies link specific behaviors to disease. For example, numerous studies have demonstrated that cigarette smokers have a much greater chance of dying from cancer and other diseases than nonsmokers. One of these other diseases is ischemic or coronary heart disease. (*Ischemia* is an inadequate blood flow to a part of the heart. If this inadequate flow is prolonged, a heart attack or myocardial infarction may result.) Health professionals have concluded that cigarette smoking is harmful to the heart, but tobacco companies have denied their findings. They have claimed that these studies show only a correlation and that no direct evidence proves that smoking damages the heart.

Direct evidence of this kind has now been reported (Barry et al., 1989). These researchers had patients with heart disease wear a Holter monitor, a small recording device which assesses the frequency and duration of episodes of myocardial ischemia. Patients wear this device twenty-four hours a day to obtain a complete and continuous record of heart activity. (The same type of sophisticated electronic monitoring of physiological functioning has been used to study other types of abnormal behavior, such as panic attacks.)

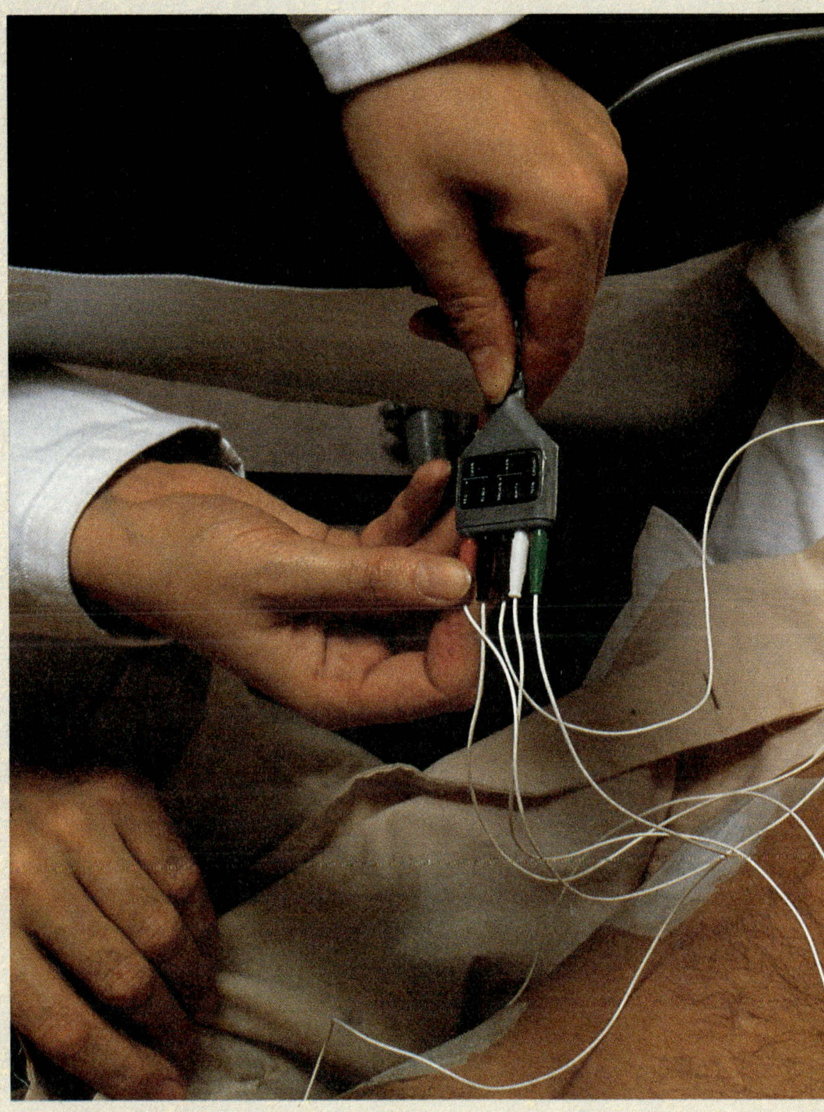

A halter for 24-hour monitoring of heart rate.

The results in the study by Barry and colleagues were dramatic: a twelve-fold increase in the duration of ischemic episodes. Most of these episodes were "silent," i.e., the patient experienced no pain. This evidence clearly shows that cigarette smoking harms the heart. Tobacco companies might still argue that it is only in certain types of people that smoking increases ischemia. The final study that would reject this argument—and establish that smoking *causes* heart disease—would be when patients who quit smoking show a significant decline in ischemia (Cohn, 1989).

Elements of Experimental Design

Hypotheses. The **hypothesis** is what the experiment is designed to test. Because it leads to new experiments and observations, the hypothesis is the main intellectual instrument in research. Hypotheses must be testable in order to specify conditions under which they can be proved wrong, that is, disconfirmed. We test hypotheses by specifying an independent variable to manipulate in the experiment. In the Barlow et al. (1983) experiment cited above, anxiety was operationally defined as the threat of an electric shock. An hypothesis cannot be so vague that investigators are able to explain away findings inconsistent with their theory.

Researchers generate hypotheses in different ways. Systematic observation of behavior by clinical

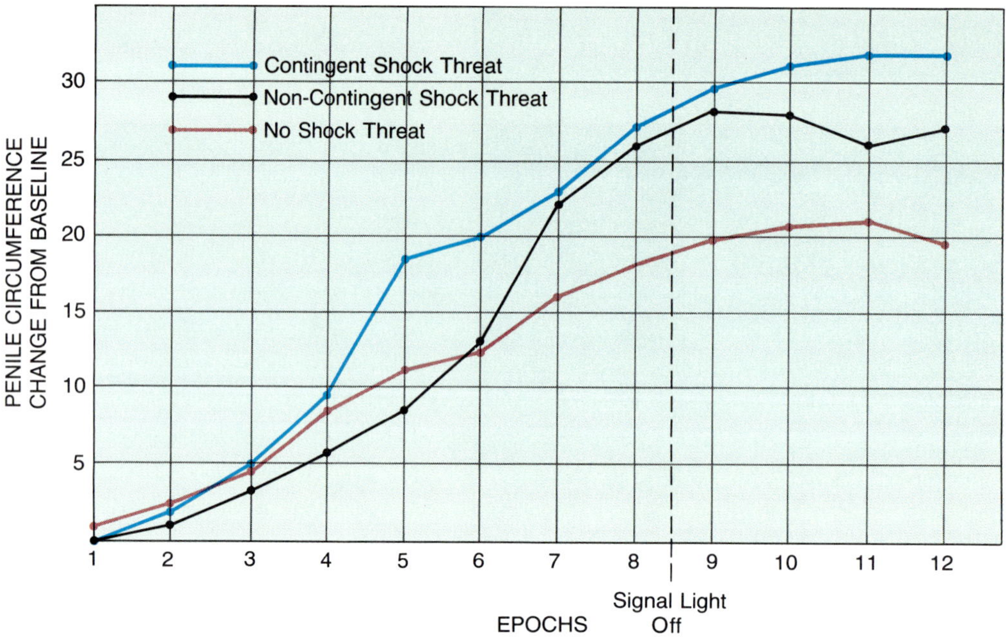

Figure 4.2 *Average penile circumference change in millimeters for each 15-s epoch during each of three conditions: no shock threat, noncontingent shock threat, and contingent shock threat.*

Source: From "Anxiety Increases Sexual Arousal" by D.H. Barlow, D.K. Sakheim, and J.G. Beck, 1983, *Journal of Abnormal Psychology, 92,* p. 52. Copyright 1983 by the American Psychological Association. Reprinted by permission.

researchers and practitioners has been a principal source of hypotheses in the study of abnormal behavior. For example, psychodynamically oriented investigators have derived a wealth of hypotheses from clinical observation of individual patients. Other researchers derive hypotheses from reading the published literature.

Hypotheses are most useful when they lead to experimental research. As a result, even wrong ones can generate experimental findings that advance our knowledge of the problem under investigation. For example, psychologists now believe that Type A behavior pattern itself may not cause heart disease. Instead, hostility, usually associated with Type A behavior pattern, may be one of several causes. And it was the research triggered by the original Type A behavior pattern hypothesis that led to this discovery. Hypotheses, then, are useful even if later discarded or revised when contradictory evidence appears.

Internal Validity. The *internal validity* of a study is the degree to which change in the dependent variable is due to the manipulation of the independent variable. The researcher seeks to exclude all alternative explanations of the effects on the dependent variable in order to conclude that the independent variable caused the change in the dependent variable. Ruling out alternative explanations of the results increases the internal validity of the experiment.

Suppose a hypothesis that a particular psychological therapy cures depression needs to be tested. A sample of depressed subjects is selected and assessed as to the extent of their depression on various measures. This is known as the **pretreatment assessment**. The particular therapy is applied to the subjects for the next four months, then they are reassessed on the same measures as before—the **posttreatment assessment**. The subjects are significantly less depressed at posttreatment than they were at pretreatment. Did the therapy cause the improvement?

The results are consistent with the hypothesis that the therapy is effective in curing depression. Success could, however, also be attributed to other factors. For example, over the four-month period the subjects may have improved by themselves in the absence of any therapy. There is good evidence that this happens—it is called **spontaneous remission** (Rachman & Wilson, 1980). The possibility of it in the hypothetical experiment is quite good. Depression is often a cyclic disorder—it frequently comes and goes. Perhaps at the posttreatment assessment patients were at the point in their cycle when depression had dropped spontaneously.

There are other possible explanations of the results of the hypothetical experiment. For example, repeated testing of the subjects may have had some unintended therapeutic effect. Perhaps repeated testing prompted the patients to reflect on their problems and become more aware of thoughts and activities that were making them depressed. This in-

BOX 4.2 The Birth of an Experimental Hypothesis

In the early 1950s two cardiologists in San Francisco, Meyer Friedman and Ray Rosenman, proposed that a particular form of behavior can cause heart disease. This was the well-known Type A behavior pattern hypothesis, which succeeded in generating numerous experimental studies and significantly changing our views of preventing and treating heart disease (Chapter 8).

How did two cardiologists arrive at a psychological hypothesis for explaining a physical disease? In their book, Friedman and Rosenman (1974) explained that they first searched the medical literature vainly for an explanation of heart disease. Problems such as high blood pressure and cholesterol levels, they knew, could cause heart disease. But these and other medical causes did not, by themselves, appear to explain the prevalence and pattern of heart disease. The cardiologists began to examine the personalities of their patients to determine anything that might be related to heart problems. An interview with one of the women with whom they discussed the problem was the final link:

> "I told you right from the first," she said, "that you would find that we are eating exactly as our husbands do. If you really want to know what is giving our husbands heart attacks, I'll tell you."
>
> "And what is that?" we asked, possibly a bit patronizingly (as doctors can't help behaving at times when confronted with laymen who are certain that they know the immediate answers to age-old medical puzzles).
>
> "It's stress, the stress they receive in their work, that's what's doing it," she quickly responded.
>
> And that's when our concept of Type A Behavior Pattern and its probable relationship to coronary heart disease was born (pp. 72–73).

sight might have enabled them to make some changes that decreased their depression. The point is that these alternative causal explanations of the results cannot be eliminated. The results could be due to variables other than the independent variable. These alternative explanatory variables are *confounds*, and they undermine the internal validity of the experiment.

Use of a control group rules out confounds and alternative causal explanations to the hypothesis that the therapy caused the reduction in depression. A **control group** is functionally the same as the experimental (treatment) group on all relevant dimensions except the one being manipulated. In the Barlow et al. (1983) experiment, the control group consisted of subjects of the same age, sex, and college status as their peers in the two experimental groups. The only difference between the control and experimental groups was that the latter were exposed to the threat of an electric shock.

To improve upon the hypothetical study of the treatment of depression just described, depressed patients would be assigned to either an experimental or a control group, ideally on a random basis. *Random assignment* means that each subject has an equal chance of being in either the experimental or control group. It is frequently used to ensure no differences between subjects in the experimental and control groups prior to the experimental treatment or manipulation when the number of subjects is sufficiently large. The control group would be tested at the same time as the experimental group but not receive the psychological therapy. At posttreatment assessment the experimental (treatment) group would be evaluated as significantly more or less depressed than the control group.

If the experimental group were significantly less depressed than the control group, a strong conclusion would be that therapy caused the improvement. The possible confounding role of spontaneous recovery or the effects of repeated testing could be eliminated. Also, the random assignment to groups would rule out explanation in terms of different subject characteristics prior to treatment.

Control Groups. Researchers employ different types of control conditions depending on the independent variable being manipulated. The study of the effects of drugs on behavior illustrates several of the issues investigators must consider in choosing appropriate control groups.

Studies of alcohol—and all other drugs—have traditionally compared it with a chemically inert substance known as a *placebo* for an experimental analysis of alcohol's effects on behavior. Figure 4.3 shows this comparison as Group I versus Group II, where the experimenter's goal is to hold everything constant except the active chemical agent—the alcohol. Subjects in Group II are led to believe they are consuming the "real thing" to control for their expectations and beliefs—the subject's cognitive set—about drug effects. If the results of the experiment show that Group I differs from Group II, this difference can be attributed to the effects of alcohol.

But what if the researcher believes that variables such as expectations about the drug affect behavior independently or interact with the drug? To answer this question it is necessary to manipulate expecta-

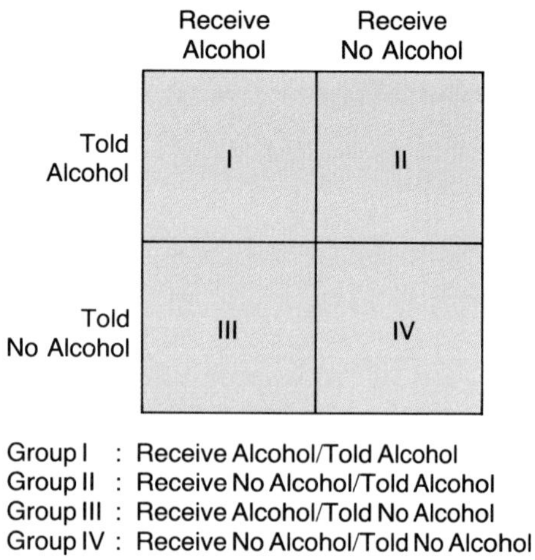

tions experimentally, and Figure 4.3 describes such a design. Known as the ***The Balanced Placebo*** , it is constructed to evaluate the separate and interactive effects of alcohol and the subject's cognitive set (Marlatt & Rohsenow, 1980). As Figure 4.3 shows, this requires the addition of Groups III and IV to the traditional comparison between alcohol and a placebo drink. These two groups are led to believe they have consumed a nonalcoholic beverage, whereas Groups I and II believe they have consumed alcohol. In this design, both the actual consumption of alcohol and beliefs about its effects are experimentally manipulated. In all alcohol and drug administration studies it is essential that the researchers who give the drink (or drug) to the subject do not themselves know whether the drink contains the real thing or simply a placebo control. This *double-blind* control prevents the researcher from inadvertently giving the subject clues about the nature of the drink (or drug).

Use of the balanced placebo design has produced some surprising and important findings (see Chapter 11). For example, investigators have used this design to study the effects of alcohol on sexual arousal. Clinical and survey findings show that acts of sexual aggression are often correlated with intoxication (Wilson, 1981). To better understand this, Briddell and his colleagues (1978) conducted an experiment randomly assigning male college students to the four groups of the balanced placebo design. All subjects listened to one audiotape describing mutually enjoyable heterosexual intercourse and another depicting forcible rape. Sexual arousal was measured by degree of penile erection while subjects listened to the tapes. The results showed that the belief that they had been drinking, but not actual alcohol consumption, produced changes in subjects' sexual arousal. As might be expected, subjects who believed that they were sober showed substantial arousal to the audiotape describing mutually consenting heterosexual intercourse and little arousal to the forcible rape tape. In contrast, subjects who believed they had been drinking showed almost the same level of sexual arousal to both the mutually consenting and the forcible rape tapes (Figure 4.4). These disturbing findings led the researchers to conclude that "normal heterosexual males who believe that they have been drinking may exhibit sexual arousal patterns indistinguishable from identified rapists" (Briddell et al., 1978, p. 427).

External Validity. The *external validity* of a study is the degree to which the findings are generalizable to other individuals in different settings. For example, it is unclear whether the findings from the Briddell et al. (1978) study described above, and other similar laboratory experiments, generalize to behavior in the real world. Sexual arousal in the laboratory—an artificial setting—might not adequately reflect a person's typical response in more natural settings.

Conducting experimental research in real-life settings—sometimes referred to as **field research**—is exceedingly more complex and costly than doing it in the laboratory. External validity is vital for research on the effects of treatment of abnormal behavior. The most direct way to study the effects of treatment would be to design an experiment in which experienced therapists treated actual patients under clinical conditions. This is difficult to do for several reasons. From a methodological point of view, experimenters find it hard to conduct highly controlled research in such service–delivery settings. From a practical point of view, recruiting experienced therapists with the time or desire to participate in such research is difficult. Finding sufficiently large numbers of similar clients with common problems is a formidable task. Finally, from an ethical point of view, it is difficult to assign clients to control groups not receiving the most effective form of treatment particularly if the disorder is a serious, even life-threatening one, as in suicidal depression, anorexia nervosa, or AIDS (O'Leary & Borkovec, 1978).

An alternative research strategy to studying the clinical situation directly is to evaluate specific treatment methods applied to well-defined, circumscribed problems under controlled laboratory conditions, commonly called analogue research. For example, subjects with intense anxiety (phobias) about small animals are used to study the nature of anxiety and its treatment (Chapter 5). This approach has several advantages: (1) The treatment method can be standardized and a wide range of subjective and objective measures of behavior change obtained. (2) The se-

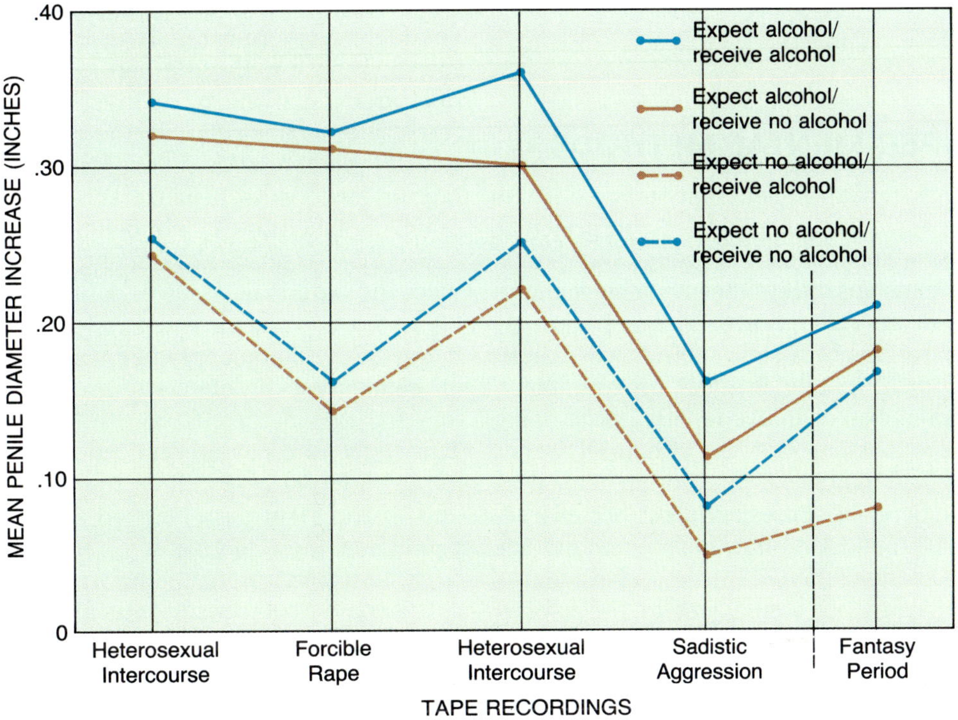

Figure 4.4 *Mean penile diameter of each experimental group for the erotic stimulus conditions and fantasy period.*

Source: From "The effects of alcohol and expectancy set on male sexual arousal" by D. Briddell, D. Rimm, G. Caddy, G. Krawitz, D. Sholis, & R. Wunderlin, 1978, *Journal of Abnormal Psychology*, 87, p. 424. Copyright 1978, American Psychological Association. Reprinted with permission.

lection of a homogeneous subject population with the same problem behavior permits evaluation of the particular problem for which the specific treatment is best suited.

Analogue research is an ideal way to develop and test theories about the mechanisms whereby treatment changes behavior. For example, the concept of self-efficacy, described in several chapters of this book, originated in research on snake phobic subjects in a laboratory setting (Bandura, 1986). Subjects can also be randomly assigned to different treatment and control conditions. Unlike the actual clinical situation in which the therapist is ethically and professionally obliged to offer the client the most effective treatment in the most efficient manner possible, specific elements of therapy or even therapy itself can be selectively withheld in the laboratory setting. Once a treatment method is effective in analogue research, it must then be tested under more typical conditions of clinical practice with real patients.

Recruiting subjects by advertising the program and contacting physicians and other appropriate treatment facilities has been a common tactic in research on treatment effectiveness. Critics have charged that subjects recruited this way are intrinsically different from individuals seeking therapy on their own (Gurman, Knudson, & Kniskern, 1978; Marks, 1978). However, if care is taken to demonstrate that subjects recruited for clinical research are as severely distressed and motivated to change as their counterparts in the natural clinical setting are, this objection should be less of a problem. Studies with phobics, depressed patients, and obese individuals have in fact failed to show differences in treatment effects between individuals recruited for clinical research and those who initiated treatment without such prompts (Foreyt, Goodrick, & Gotto, 1981; Grey, Sartory, & Rachman, 1979).

Whether the findings of a research study are generalizable to therapeutic situations applies to all clinical research, including studies conducted with patients in actual therapeutic settings. In evaluating therapy outcome research, the critical question is to what degree do the conditions of the study approximate the clinical situation? The generalizability of a study needs evaluation along several different dimensions, including the kind of problem being studied or treated, the type of subject, subjects' motivation for treatment, therapist characteristics and training, nature of the treatment method and how it might vary from the way it is usually administered in clinical practice, assessment of treatment effects, and so on (Kazdin & Wilson, 1978). Researchers generally assume that the more similar the study to the clinical situation, the greater the generalizability of the results.

QUASI-EXPERIMENTAL METHODS

By randomly assigning sufficient numbers of subjects to different groups, we ensure, at least in principle, that the experimental and control groups are alike on all relevant dimensions except the one being manipulated, or tested. In reality, however, it is frequently impossible to randomly assign subjects to experimental and control groups. Imagine, for example, a study of the effects on cognitive functioning of being a child of an alcoholic parent (COA). Children cannot randomly be made the biological offspring of an alcoholic or a nonalcoholic. Preexisting subject characteristics (i.e., being a COA) inevitably confound the experimental manipulation. A true experiment—which demands random assignment to the experimental variable—cannot, therefore, be conducted.

Then quasi-experimental methods are used to study preexisting individual differences. In a **quasi-experiment** membership in a class or category defines the experimental group. Typical groups in research on abnormal psychology would be subjects who are COAs, subjects who share common psychopathology (e.g., schizophrenics), or subjects who have experienced a common life event (e.g., divorce or bereavement).

The control group is selected to match the experimental group on known personal characteristics that might confound interpretation of results except the independent variable. In studying the effects of being a COA on cognitive functioning, then, a control group of non-COAs would match the experimental COA group in terms of age, gender, socioeconomic status, current drinking status, and degree of psychopathology, among other factors.

Even with a carefully chosen control group, there is no guarantee that the two groups are identical except with respect to the independent variable. Thus, even if COAs (the independent variable) score more poorly on a test of cognitive functioning (the dependent variable), being a COA cannot be inferred as the cause. The experimental and control groups may have differed in terms of another, unknown confounding variable. A good example of a quasi-experimental study is the Stanford Three Community study (Chapter 16). It was designed to reduce risk factors for heart disease (e.g., stopping cigarette smoking, reducing blood pressure, and decreasing dietary fat) in an entire community. The psychosocial intervention program (the independent variable) aimed at changing these health-related behaviors was implemented in two rural communities, with a third serving as the no-intervention control group. The three communities were carefully matched on relevant dimensions prior to the intervention, such as frequency of cigarette smoking, blood pressure, and dietary patterns. We cannot rule out the possibility, however, that the communities differed among each other in one or more ways because subjects were not randomly assigned to the independent variable.

Because a quasi-experimental design does not meet the criteria of a true experiment, it is not possible to draw strong inferences about causation. Confidence in the finding obtained will ultimately depend on eliminating the effects of group differences that may have been correlated with the observed result. This requires repeated replication of the basic finding by different research groups with different samples. If the result is replicated under these varying conditions, there is greater confidence that it is not confounded with some unknown, correlated variable.

Criteria for subject selection are essential in interpreting the results of any study. As discussed, if the experimental and control groups differ in any way other than the experimental manipulation there is a confound across the two groups. But depending on the subject-selection criteria, a confound may also exist within the experimental group. For example, researchers comparing COAs with non-COAs try to select only those subjects showing no drinking problem. The presence of any problem drinking would make attributing any difference observed between COAs and non-COAs to the presence of an alcoholic parent impossible. Yet Sher (1985) has shown that by excluding COAs who are problem drinkers, researchers diminish their chances of demonstrating real differences between COAs and non-COAs. By eliminating individuals showing drinking problems as young adults, those particular high-risk subjects who were the initial focus of experimental interest may be lost.

Despite their inherent limitation, quasi-experimental designs are vital to the study of abnormal behavior. Kenny (1975) has neatly summarized their value and constructive use by informed researchers.

> We would all prefer to have the testimony about an event from a sighted man over a blind man. But when we have only the blind man, we would not dismiss his testimony, especially if we were aware of his biases and he had developed faculties of touch and hearing that the sighted man could have developed but has neglected. The difference between the true experiment and the quasi-experiment is of the magnitude of the difference between sight and blindness. We must often grope in the darkness with quasi-experimental designs, but this blindness both forces us to compensate for biases and helps us develop a new found sensitivity to the structure of data. Finally, it makes us appreciate the clarity of true experimental inference (p. 360).

ANIMAL MODELS

An *animal model* of abnormal behavior is an experimental attempt to reproduce some of the basic characteristics of a human disorder in nonhuman subjects (Suomi, 1982). At best an animal model is only a simplified approximation of a clinical disorder, useful to the extent that the findings generalize from the animal laboratory to the human disorder.

Researchers use animal models for several reasons. First, they can conduct experiments on animals that they cannot do with human subjects for both practical and ethical reasons. The development of new medical or surgical procedures and drugs always begins with animal research. Similarly, studies of biological bases of abnormal behavior requiring experimental surgery, direct analysis of brain mechanisms, or experimental drug administration necessarily rely on animal subjects. For example, animals have been made dependent on heroin or cocaine so that researchers may study experimentally the process and treatment of drug dependence.

A second reason is that researchers can conduct *prospective studies* by inducing clinical disorders in animal subjects. For example, certain strains of mice can be made diabetic, enabling researchers to analyze this widespread disorder and test different forms of treatment (see Chapter 8). Such practices would be ethically impossible in human subjects. Researchers would have to resort to quasi-experimental designs in which they would compare subjects who were already diabetic with some nondiabetic control group.

A monkey clinging to a surrogate "mother" in Harlow's primate laboratory at the University of Wisconsin.

Animal rights groups have vigorously opposed the use of animals in experimental research, objecting to the suffering animal subjects sometimes experience. A minority of animal rights activists totally oppose the use of animal subjects, and some have even resorted to violence to show their opposition. The more moderate majority, however, have campaigned successfully to reduce the number of animal subjects and ensure their humane treatment. Many in the biomedical and behavioral research community share these objectives. Using animals as research subjects raises complex moral and ethical questions: Should a chimpanzee—or even a rat—be sacrificed in order to understand and treat physical and mental disorders in people? (See Chapter 18.)

Learned Helplessness

The development of the concept of **learned helplessness** provides a revealing illustration of the contributions of animal models to the study of abnormal behavior. In the 1960s Martin Seligman and his colleagues were conducting laboratory research aimed at understanding avoidance learning in dogs. They observed that dogs who experienced unavoidable shocks during their experiments subsequently showed serious psychological deficits in learning tasks where incorrect responses were associated with shock. Those dogs subject to unavoidable—and hence uncontrollable—shock developed motivational, cognitive, and emotional difficulties; they became passive, failed to learn simple tasks, and showed symptoms of marked emotional distress. Seligman (1975) labeled this pattern of responses *learned helplessness*. With keen insight, he recognized that the deficits these dogs displayed resembled the symptoms of depressed patients, and he proposed that the learned helplessness concept might provide a model of human depression (see Chapter 8). Seligman's observations are a good example of the role in science of making an unexpected finding in the course of working on something else.

Seligman and his students next showed that their animal findings generalized to laboratory studies with humans. College students who experienced events beyond their control showed motivational, cognitive, and emotional effects similar to those of the dogs. Generalizing from the animal model to clinical de-

Martin Seligman, Ph.D. Well-known experimental/clinical psychologist noted for his research on learned helplessness.

pression in people revealed critical limitations in learned helplessness theory. In a major reformulation, Abramson, Seligman, and Teasdale (1978) modified the theory to include causal attributions: The effect of uncontrollable events on people depends on how they explain those events. Drawing on attribution theory, the researchers hypothesized three critical dimensions people use to explain events: internal–external ("Is it me or the situation?"); stable–unstable ("Is this permanent or a passing event?"), and global–specific ("Is it my whole life or only this one situation?") (Abramson et al., 1978). This reformulated theory may help explain illness and disease in healthy individuals (Chapter 8). Specifically, people with a negative explanatory style—those who attribute negative events to internal, stable, and global factors—develop significantly more illnesses than their peers with a more optimistic explanatory style (Peterson et al., 1988). Individuals with a pessimistic explanatory style also show poorer functioning of their immune system—the body's defense against infectious disease (Rodin, 1988).

SINGLE-CASE EXPERIMENTAL DESIGNS

The major limitation of the clinical case study, as discussed, is that it is uncontrolled. A significant contribution of the operant-conditioning approach has been the development of a single-case experimental methodology to conduct controlled research and treatment. The clinical adaptation of these designs shows that behavior change in an individual patient is the result of specific treatment interventions, not simply the passage of time, placebo reaction, or some other uncontrolled event.

There are many variations of single-case experimental designs. The basic principles can be illustrated by the two most commonly used designs—the reversal and the multiple baseline designs.

The Reversal Design

In the **reversal design,** following a period of baseline observation (A) during which no treatment of any kind is attempted, a treatment phase (B) is introduced while the behavior in question is continuously observed. The behavior usually will show change in the desired direction, after which the treatment is discontinued in a return to the baseline procedure (A). If the treatment per se was responsible for the observed change, then the behavior should generally return to almost its former level during the original (A) period.

A pioneering study by Ayllon and Azrin (1965) provides a variation of the reversal design. These investigators first increased the level of participation in rehabilitation activities of a group of hospitalized schizophrenics by making positive reinforcement contingent on participation in phase A of the study. Then, as Figure 4.5 shows, in phase B, reinforcement was administered on a noncontingent basis. In this procedure patients received tokens at the beginning of each day regardless of their performance. This broke the relationship, or contingency, between the reinforcer (token) and the response (participation) without eliminating the reinforcer completely. This had the benefit of ensuring that the amount of social interaction between the attendants and ward staff, who administered the tokens and the patients, remained unchanged. If any deterioration in sociability was found, then it would be directly attributable to only one thing: the relationship between behavior and reinforcement. During phase C the researchers returned to contingent reinforcement, as in phase A. It was clear that the treatment made a difference. The results showed that the specific reinforcing contingency, the tokens for group participation, maintained these schizophrenics' behavior.

The study illustrated in Figure 4.5 demonstrates another characteristic of single-case experimental designs: They typically focus on the behavior of the individual patient. The type of experimental arrangement rather than the number of subjects studied, nevertheless, defines this methodology. The number of subjects may vary widely; there were forty-four in

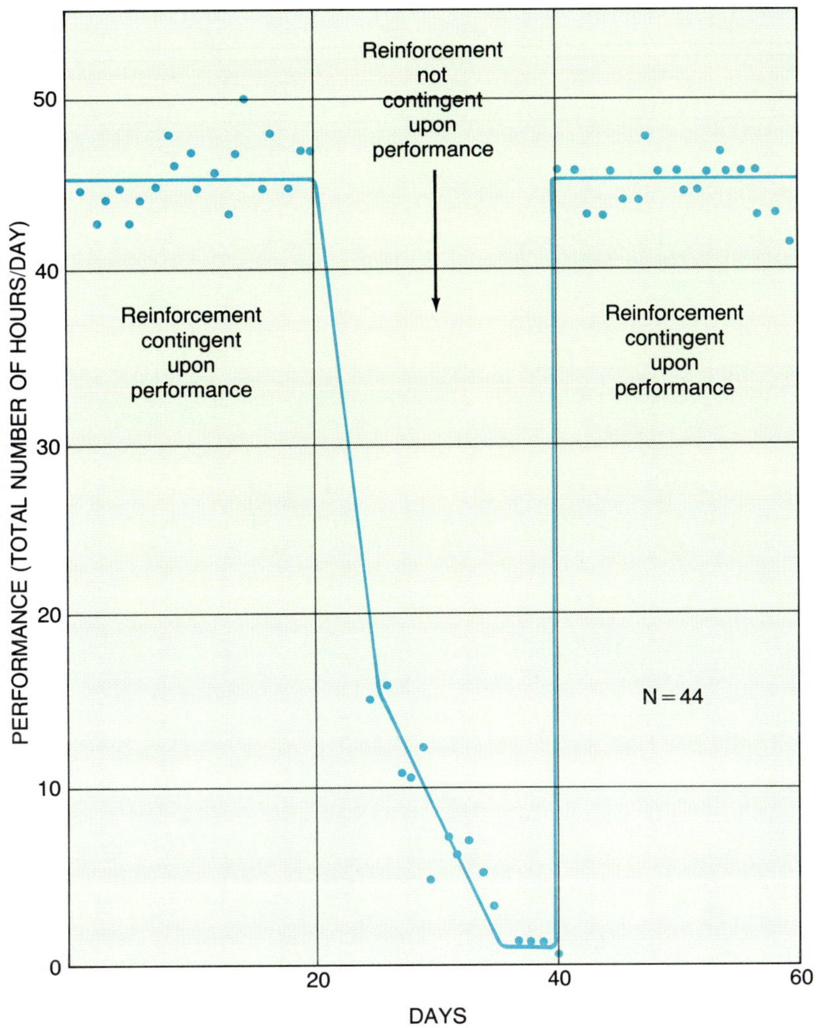

Figure 4.5 *Total number of hours the group of 44 schizophrenics participated in rehabilitative activities on the ward under conditions of both contingent and noncontingent positive reinforcement.*

Source: From Ayllon and Azrin (1965). The measurement and reinforcement of behavior of psychotics. *Journal of the Experimental Analysis of Behavior, 8,* 373. Copyright 1965 by the Society for the Experimental Analysis of Behavior. Reprinted by permission.

the Ayllon and Azrin study. The key point is that this group was treated as a single case.

One limitation of reversal design is its requirement that the treatment effect is reversible and that the target behavior returns to baseline level once treatment is withdrawn. But it is often ill-advised or unethical to return to a baseline condition after an effective treatment. For example, when a self-destructive child has responded to a particular intervention, such as praise from attendants for positive interactions with other children on the ward, it may be very detrimental to the child's physical and mental health to ask attendants to withdraw their praise. A second problem is the reversal design's limitation to readily reversible treatment conditions. There are certain treatments that lead to relatively permanent changes in behavior. For example, if enuretic children (bedwetters) are given certain toilet training, their bladder size increases. They no longer wet the bed, and the withdrawal of the treatment does not lead to a return to a baseline condition. This limitation applies especially to the learning of new skills. After a child has learned to read, removal of external incentives to read will not make the child illiterate. In cases like this, investigators can never reinstate the original baseline. If the behavior of interest shows no reversal, little of significance can be concluded.

The Multiple Baseline Design

In the **multiple baseline across behaviors design**, several responses are identified and measured over time to provide a baseline to evaluate changes

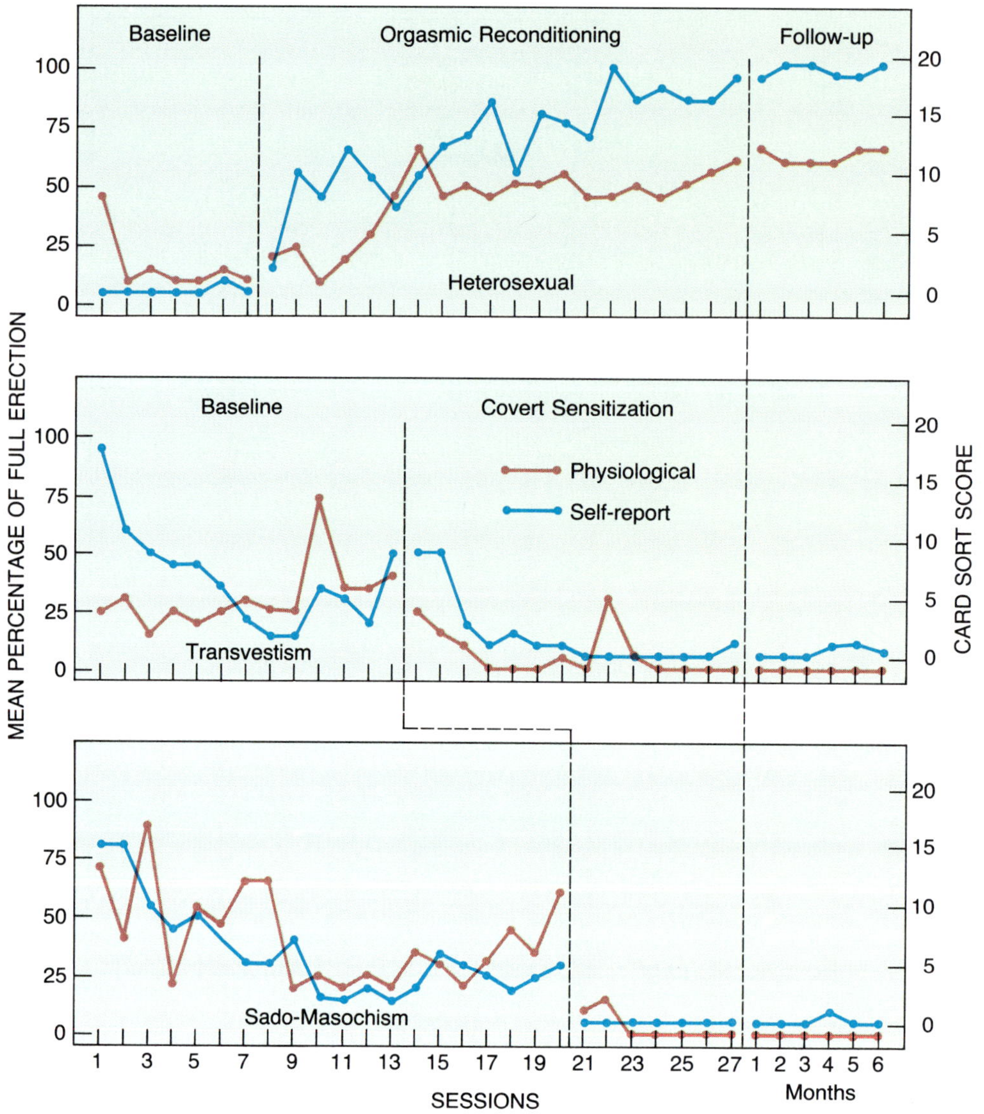

Figure 4.6 *Mean penile circumference changes and card sort ratings of sexual arousal in response to deviant and heterosexual stimuli for Subject 5.*

Source: Brownell, K.D., Hayes, S.C., and Barlow, D.H. [1977]. Patterns of appropriate and deviant sexual arousal: The behavioral treatment of multiple sexual deviations. Reprinted with permission from *Journal of Consulting and Clinical Psychology, 45,* 1144–1155. Copyright 1977 by the American Psychological Association.

against. Each response is then successively modified in turn; if each behavior changes maximally only when specifically treated, then a cause–effect relationship can be reliably inferred. Figure 4.6 illustrates the procedure in the treatment of a patient with the sexual disorder transvestism with sadomasochism (Brownell, Hayes, & Barlow, 1977). The specific treatment of **orgasmic reconditioning** was first used to increase the patient's heterosexual responsiveness. Such reconditioning left his transvestism and sadomasochism unaffected. A second treatment technique, known as **covert sensitization**, was then used to decrease transvestism, while baseline measures of sadomasochism showed no effect (see Chapter 9). Finally, sadomasochism was treated and successfully reduced. The different dimensions of this man's sexual disorder changed only when directly treated.

The multiple baseline design is useful if highly specific treatment effects occur, as in Figure 4.6. But what if more than one baseline (i.e., more than one type of sexual response) had simultaneously changed? These changes could indicate generalized effects of the specific treatment or nonspecific effects of variables other than the treatment itself (e.g., placebo effects).

Advantages and Disadvantages

Like any type of experimental design, single-case experimental designs have advantages and disadvantages (Kazdin, 1981). One advantage is continual assessment of behavior over time. The target behavior is assessed regularly before, during, and after treatment intervention, often daily. This provides immediate information on treatment progress and makes possible data-based decisions about whether to continue or modify treatment. A second advantage is that intervention effects are replicated within the same subject over time. Subjects act as their own controls, and comparisons of their performance are made as different interventions are made. Hence, the treatment of individual patients can be evaluated objectively. The personal quality of the clinical case study is largely preserved without sacrificing experimental rigor. Investigators can therefore study clinical problems that would be otherwise rejected as unsuitable for group methodology.

Another limitation of single-case experimental designs is the difficulty of studying the possible interaction of subject variables with the specific treatment technique. Since only a single subject is investigated, the effect of different subject characteristics on the treatment procedure cannot be directly assessed. For example, the treatment might be effective only for a certain type of patient, and not for others. To assess these different patient characteristics requires a group design. Another disadvantage is that it is hard to generalize findings. Perhaps a particular patient responds well to a certain treatment; others may not. One answer to this problem is for the same therapist to apply the same technique under the same conditions, to more than one patient. If this technique is consistently successful and the results can be replicated in all cases, then interpretation of the results is clear-cut. If the results are mixed or inconsistent, as frequently occurs in clinical research, problems in interpretation arise. Interpretation of these designs depends on visual inspection of graphs, such as those shown in Figures 4.5 and 4.6. The idea is that reliable effects should be seen directly without resorting to statistical analysis. However, the problem is there is an absence of rules about what constitutes a true or reliable experimental effect. Visual inspection of graphs without statistical analysis invites subjectivity and inconsistency in interpreting data (Kazdin, 1981).

EVALUATING TREATMENT OUTCOME

Evaluating the effects of psychological and drug treatments on abnormal behavior is a complex task with specific methodological challenges. For example, what type of control group would a treatment, as the experimental condition, be compared to? An obvious possibility would be a group of patients who received no treatment, yet it is unethical to withhold therapy from patients in need of treatment.

Another possibility is to use what is called a **waiting-list control group**. Patients in this group are promised treatment at the end of a certain waiting period, corresponding to the time taken to administer therapy to the treatment group in the study. A limitation of the waiting-list control group is that treatment can be compared to no treatment only during the period in which treatment is administered. Any follow-up comparison between the treatment and no-treatment groups is impossible because the latter eventually receives treatment. The different implications that no-treatment and waiting-list control groups may have for the evaluation of treatment outcome is illustrated in a study by Kent and O'Leary (1976); a behavioral program for children with conduct disorder greatly improved behavior both in the home and at school relative to a no-treatment control group. The effects of treatment were, however, no longer significant on a number of dependent variables at a nine-month follow-up. The no-treatment group improved over the follow-up interval across diverse measures, with some exceptions. In this study, the conclusions would have differed had researchers used a waiting-list rather than a no-treatment control group.

The most powerful experimental designs for evaluating treatment outcome are comparative experiments. A **comparative treatment study** compares two or more treatments with neither treatment condition being viewed as a formal control group. For example, in a landmark study, Paul and Lentz (1977) compared three programs in the treatment of chronic schizophrenic patients in a mental hospital:

1. Cognitive-behavioral therapy, using learning principles to modify patients' behavior.
2. Milieu therapy, or creating a therapeutic community in the institution. The focus was on the communication of positive expectations and group cohesiveness and group pressure directed toward normal functioning.
3. Routine hospital therapy, emphasizing chemotherapy combined with custodial care and little psychological treatment.

Both cognitive-behavioral therapy and milieu therapy produced greater improvement than routine hospital therapy on a number of different measures of patient functioning.

Comparative outcome studies require clearly defined alternative treatments because procedural differences between contrasting techniques make interpreting results difficult. A well-designed study should include independent measures of whether alternative treatments were distinct from one another and of **treatment integrity,** that is, the degree to which treatment was implemented as planned (Kazdin & Wilson, 1978). In the Paul and Lentz study, for example, continuous assessment of the behavior of the staff of the treatment programs indicated that the social-learning therapy and milieu therapy approaches were being faithfully implemented, consistent with their original guidelines. The clear procedural differences between these two programs made it possible to attribute the superior outcome of the subjects in the social-learning program to the specific treatment. In other studies treatment sessions have been audiotaped and later analyzed to ensure that the alternative treatments were correctly administered. The ultimate goal of comparative treatment studies is to determine which method appears most effective with particular clinical disorders.

Evaluation of treatment success must address short-term and long-term effects. Two treatments may produce equal improvement immediately following the end of therapy. One, however, may be associated with rapid relapse shortly after posttreatment, whereas the other has lasting benefits. In such circumstances, the treatment of choice is clearly the one producing durable or long-term improvement. For example, drug therapy is effective in the treatment of bulimia nervosa yet once the drug is discontinued, patients rapidly relapse and return to binge-eating and purging. In contrast, psychological treatment produces comparable short-term effects which are maintained over time (Fairburn, 1988). Given this pattern of effects, psychological treatment would seem the therapy of choice.

Carefully planned treatment outcome studies can have both theoretical and practical value. They not only establish which form of therapy is most effective for a particular clinical disorder but also shed light on the nature of the disorder in question. Consider, for example, panic disorder. The biological model states that panic disorder is caused by a neurochemical abnormality successfully treated only with medication; psychological treatments, because they do not directly address this hypothesized neurochemical abnormality, are said to be incapable of reducing panic (Klein et al., 1987). Yet recent treatment studies have convincingly shown that psychological treatment does consistently reduce if not eliminate panic attacks (Barlow, 1988). Accordingly, a better model of panic disorder now necessarily includes a psychological component—an emphasis on the importance of the patient's cognitive appraisal of bodily sensations (see Chapter 5).

SUMMARY

1. Investigators use a variety of methods to study abnormal behavior, ranging from speculative theorizing to scientific experimentation. The scientific approach identifies general laws about behavior. It requires researchers to define the phenomena they study in precise, operational terms so that other investigators can repeat their experiments. A scientific theory is a formal statement of propositions designed to explain a phenomenon. To be useful, a theory should be testable, integrate known information, and stimulate new research. Scientific research has produced several breakthroughs in our understanding of abnormal behavior.
2. There are several different methods for studying abnormal behavior. In the case study the clinician gathers information about the individual's past and present functioning using an interview and possibly psychological tests. The case study provides detailed description of clinical methods and generates hypotheses that can be tested by other methods. However, it cannot establish that one event caused another and the findings cannot be generalized to other individuals with the same problem.
3. Correlational methods assess the degree of relationship between two or more events. The correlation coefficient is a mathematical expression of the extent to which two variables are associated. Correlation does not imply causation. Epidemiological research is a type of correlational method defined as the study of the prevalence, etiology, and consequences of physical disease and mental disorders in the population. Epidemiological research identifies risk factors which precede the development of a disease or disorder.
4. Experimental methods are needed to show that one event causes another. In an experimental study the independent variable is manipulated or controlled by the researcher to measure its effect on the dependent variable. Hypotheses are ideas that the experiment is designed to test. An experiment is internally valid if it allows the researcher to rule out explanations of the observed effects other than the manipulation of the independent variable. To eliminate other explanations requires the use of control groups.
5. A control group is functionally the same as the experimental group on all relevant dimensions except the one being manipulated. Subjects are randomly assigned to experimental and control groups, meaning each subject has an equal chance of being assigned to either group. In a quasi-experimental design, the nature of the independent variable makes it impossible to randomly assign subjects to the experimental variable. Therefore, a control group is selected by matching the experimental subjects with controls with similar personal characteristics. The external validity of a study is the degree to which its findings are generalizable to other subjects in other settings.
6. Animal models have been useful in generating

hypotheses about abnormal behavior in people. Single-case experimental designs allow experimental manipulation of the independent variable in an individual patient. Evaluation of treatment effects pose particular methodological challenges. The treatment under evaluation can be compared against no treatment, a waiting-list control which receives the treatment after a set period of time, or alternative treatments. Treatment outcome research not only establishes which methods are most effective with which clinical disorder but also may illuminate the nature of the disorder in question.

Edvard Munch, *Red Virginia Creeper,* Norwegian (1863–1944). Photograph by Superstock.

5 ANXIETY DISORDERS

Everyone experiences anxiety from time to time, but for many, anxiety is so severe that it is a clinical disorder. Recent findings show anxiety disorders as the most common mental health problem in the United States (Barlow, 1988). Anxiety is also a key symptom in or a contributory cause of some other clinical syndromes, such as alcoholism and sexual disorders. Optimistically, exciting new developments in the study and treatment of the anxiety disorders have been made. These significant advances in research on their psychology and biology have provided knowledge about their nature and, most importantly, promising new methods to treat them with.

THE CONCEPT OF ANXIETY

There is no more basic concept in the study of abnormal behavior than anxiety. As Freud himself observed, ". . . the problem of anxiety is a nodal point, linking up all kinds of the most important questions; a riddle, of which the solution must cast a flood of light on our whole mental life" (1917, p. 401). All major theories of human behavior converge on anxiety, for its explanation is fundamental to psychodynamic, behavioral, and humanistic theories of abnormal behavior.

The Biological Perspective

Imagine this scenario: A car is racing toward you. Your breathing quickens and becomes shallow. Your heart pounds, you feel "butterflies" in your stomach. Your palms become sweaty, your knees are weak and wobbly. These bodily symptoms indicate you are experiencing fear or anxiety.[1] Their presence is often also a criterion for diagnosing an anxiety disorder; then they are triggered not by real dangers such as a runaway car but by seemingly innocuous objects or situations. Such symptoms underscore the significance of biology in understanding and possibly treating anxiety disorders.

We have two nervous systems. The skeletal nervous system consists of the muscles attached to our skeleton and is under voluntary control. The autonomic nervous system activates organs such as the heart, the stomach, and the adrenal glands. These glands release adrenalin (epinephrine), a hormone that produces the physiological reactions noted previously. Directly or indirectly reducing autonomic arousal is a common target of therapy.

Anxiety originates in the brain. Sophisticated measures of brain function such as the PET scan allow researchers to identify the neuroanatomical correlates of anxiety in the brain. For example, PET scans

[1] Some writers distinguish between fear and anxiety. They use *fear* to describe normal or reality anxiety, and reserve the term *anxiety* for what Freud and May called neurotic anxiety. There is no consistent usage in the literature, and in this book we refer to fear and anxiety interchangeably, indicating when the emotion is unrealistic and excessive (i.e., neurotic) or when it is not.

are recorded before and during the experimental induction of anxiety. Researchers can then see which specific areas of the brain become active in response to the anticipation or actual experience of anxiety, and determine if there is any brain function abnormality (Reiman et al., 1989). Other neurochemical research has identified specific brain cells that seem closely linked to anxiety. They are in a portion of the brain stem known as the *locus ceruleus.* Electrical stimulation of these cells triggers fear whereas their destruction inhibits it. These cells have specific receptors for such anxiety-reducing drugs as Librium and Valium. The receptors are like locks and the drugs like keys that fit only these locks because they have the right molecular structure. These research breakthroughs have raised some provocative questions: What is the natural function of these brain cell receptors? Does the brain make its own Librium-like substances? If so, does a deficiency in this neurochemistry result in some people developing anxiety disorders? And can we synthesize drugs that unlock these brain receptors and thereby selectively reduce or prevent anxiety? (Goodwin, 1986)[2] Finally, there is persuasive evidence indicating a genetic or biological predisposition for developing anxiety disorders (Barlow, 1988).

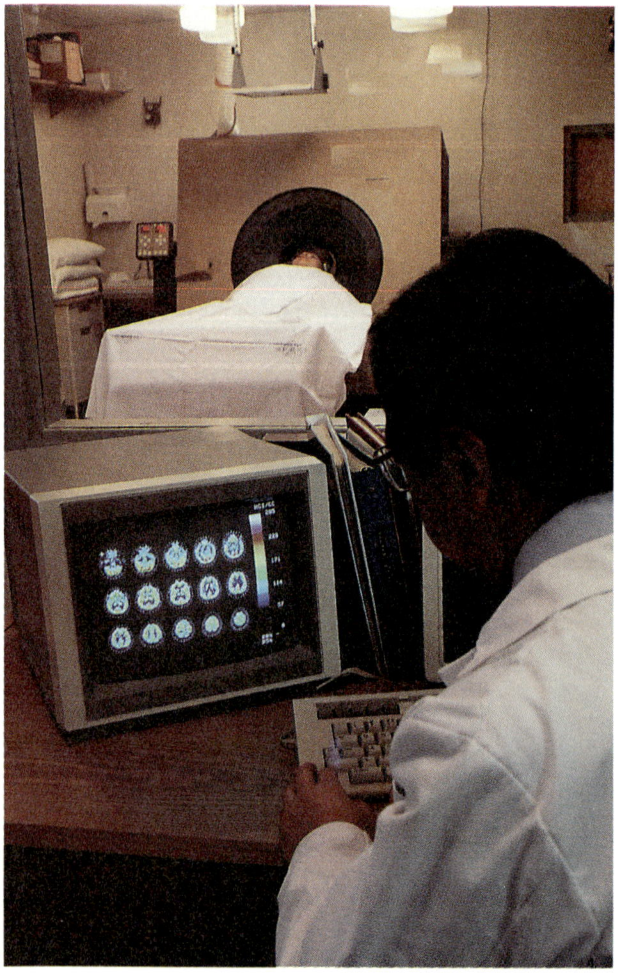

The PET scan provides measures (computer generated pictures) of neural activity in specific regions of the brain when the person is asked to engage in some mental process.

The Psychodynamic Perspective

Freud distinguished between reality and neurotic anxiety. In the former, the person perceives danger in the external world and experiences anxiety, a state of painful tension which he or she seeks to reduce. In the latter, anxiety is traced to early childhood conflicts. The child has aggressive and sexual impulses that cannot be directly expressed because they will be met by the parents with punishment or the withdrawal of love. Hence, the child learns to fear these impulses and develops ways to defend against them. **Repression** is the most fundamental defense mechanism by allowing the ego to exclude threatening impulses from conscious awareness.

However, a weak ego and only partly successful repression cause neurotic anxiety, signaling that the threatening impulses are starting to break through the defenses. The impulses are then expressed indirectly or symbolically in ways disguised from the person and others. These defenses may be healthy (e.g., sublimation, in which the anxiety leads to good works) or unhealthy. The different neurotic disorders are all self-defeating ways of coping with anxiety. For example, phobias are anxiety displaced onto some external, neutral object. Anxiety that cannot be expressed in terms of specific symptoms such as phobia or obsessions, is experienced as "free-floating."

Freud saw sexual and aggressive impulses as the basis of neurotic anxiety. Later psychoanalysts expanded this view to include other sources. Alfred Adler emphasized *power,* Karen Horney *dependency,* and Harry Stack Sullivan *security* needs as the unconscious core of neurotic conflict or what we call anxiety disorders today.

According to the psychodynamic model, we must delve into an individual's early childhood conflicts to understand anxiety and the disorders it causes. The overt symptoms through which neurotic anxiety is expressed provide only clues about the real underlying disorder. The therapist acts as a psychic detective, exploring and tracking down these different clues.

[2] Goodwin (1986) draws our attention to Aldous Huxley's well-known book, *Brave New World.* In that far-reaching, futurist fiction, Huxley, "with amazing prescience, fantasized a drug called soma which tranquilized and did nothing else: exactly what pharmaceutical companies around the world are searching for—and will almost certainly find" (p. 78).

The Cognitive-Behavioral Perspective

This approach's key assumption is that anxiety is a product of classical conditioning and other forms of cognitive learning, such as modeling (Bandura, 1986). Anxiety—considered a set of loosely coupled response systems—can be directly measured (Lang, 1985). These response systems are the verbal report of feelings of distress and apprehension, the presence of physiological arousal predominantly involving the autonomic nervous system, and overt escape and avoidance behaviors. But because anxiety is not a single phenomenon, these systems often fail to correlate with each other, which is known as *desynchrony.* For example, following treatment, a phobic may freely approach situations she had previously avoided but still show high levels of physiological arousal.

Bandura (1986) has provided a detailed account of how the three systems of thought, emotion, and behavior interact with and influence each other. Thought creates physiological and emotional arousal and provides cognitive labels for it. Arousal can, in turn, influence thought. The relative influence of these three sets of interlocking factors varies in different individuals depending on the circumstances. Self-efficacy determines the reciprocal interaction among action, affect, and thought. Self-efficacy is the person's perceived ability to cope with a threatening situation. According to Bandura (1986), the stronger an individual's sense of self-efficacy, the less his or her avoidance, autonomic arousal, and subjective anxiety will be. It postulates the conditions under which both synchrony (high strength of self-efficacy) and desynchrony (low strength of self-efficacy) among different measures of anxiety will occur.

In this model, understanding and altering anxiety require us to identify the external (environmental) and internal (cognitive) factors currently maintaining the anxiety. In contrast to the psychodynamic model, the focus is on the here and now.

The Humanistic Perspective

We live in a time that has been called the "age of anxiety," the title of a famous poem by W.H. Auden in 1950. Auden, like many intellectuals of that time, was influenced by existentialism. In fact, Rollo May, a prominent existentialist, published the book *The Meaning of Anxiety* the same year Auden published his poem. May distinguished between "normal" and "neurotic" anxiety in the same way Freud differentiated between reality and neurotic anxiety. Existentialists argue that life reduces to one choice after another—between good and evil. This burden of continual choice causes inescapable anxiety, part of the human condition.

Why did existentialism and the age of anxiety come to the fore after World War II? Some argue that our modern, postwar society lost faith in religion and reason. Without the basic reliance on these to guide existence, there was nothing fundamental to believe in. Consequently, people became alienated and confused about values and acceptable standards of conduct. Yet as a society we were healthier and more prosperous than ever before. Freed from the concern of day-to-day survival we had the "luxury" of worrying about anticipated events and being anxious. Nevertheless, over the centuries anxiety has been recorded as a human emotion and different anxiety disorders have been documented.

THE ANXIETY DISORDERS

Before the introduction of *DSM-III* in 1980, anxiety disorders were known as neurotic disorders. Each of the neuroses was seen as a different, symptomatic expression of underlying neurotic anxiety. *DSM-III* changed this view by simply describing the problems without making judgments about their etiology and nature. As part of this attempt to be more descriptive, *DSM-III* preferred the term *anxiety disorders* to that of *neurotic disorders.*

Simple Phobia

Characteristics. The *DSM-III-R* criteria for simple phobia include the following:

1. Persistent, excessive, and unreasonable fear of a specific object or situation.
2. Avoidance or endurance with intense anxiety of the object or situation.
3. Recognition that the fear is unreasonable.

Animal phobias are the most common. Other prominent examples include fear of closed spaces (claustrophobia), heights (acrophobia), illness, flying in planes, vomiting, injections, and the sight of blood. Phobias are often highly specific. For example, fear of heights is really the fear of falling or loss of support. Pilots may have this fear but be perfectly comfortable in the cockpit of their plane at 30,000 feet because the closed-in space provides a sense of security. Simple phobias may begin at any age. Animal phobias, however, typically start in childhood, blood-injury phobias in adolescence or early adulthood, and illness phobias later in life. Phobias are common in the general population: It is estimated that 7 out of every 100 Americans have phobias (U.S. Department of Health and Human Services, 1986). Since phobic objects or situations can usually be avoided, many phobics never seek treatment. Also, a large number of phobias appear to disappear naturally; about half of early onset phobias vanish within five years. More

BOX 5.1 Fear of Flying: The Case of John Madden

John Madden, the well-respected former head coach of the Oakland Raiders football team, has become a national figure as a football analyst on CBS and an easily recognized participant in the Miller Light beer commercials. John Madden is also a claustrophobic. The following is his description of phobic anxiety:

> I settled into my first-class seat . . . across from the big door that was swung back while the passengers got on. But as soon as the flight attendant slammed that door shut, I got woozy again. Worse than ever. That cold sweat and that weakness in my legs. I thought, jump up and open that door and get the hell off this plane. And then I thought, No, don't make an ass of yourself. I was arguing with myself now—get off, stay on . . . get off, stay on. I stayed on. That two-hour flight to Houston was the most miserable experience of my life. As soon as we took off, I felt more woozy than usual. I broke into a cold sweat. My legs were weak. I glanced at the seat-belt sign, thinking maybe there was some turbulence I hadn't noticed. But the sign wasn't lit. The takeoff had been smooth. . . . I bolted out of my aisle seat and hurried to the rest room. Not to throw up. Just to be on my feet. I must have stayed in there half an hour, staring into the mirror at the cold sweat glistening on my forehead. After a while, I felt a little better. But as soon as I returned to my seat, the same wooziness came over me and the same cold sweat broke out. I got up and walked back and forth in the middle of the first-class cabin. But when some of the other passengers began to glance up at me, I disappeared into the rest room for the rest of the flight.

John Madden no longer travels by plane. At one time, he thought of resigning from his lucrative television job for CBS because he has to travel around the United States. Instead of resigning, he decided to take the train wherever he went—even from California to New York—no matter how long it took. He now travels in a specially outfitted bus, the Madden-mobile. Madden recalls having claustrophobic tendencies as a child: "At dinner, I had to sit at one end of the table or the other, not in the middle. At a movie, I always sat on the aisle" (p. 43). When he was coach of the Raiders he had to travel by air, as there was no alternative, and managed to endure the anxiety. When he retired from coaching, he began to avoid flying. His phobia immediately worsened to the point where he abandoned air travel completely. His story illustrates a common clinical phenomenon—avoidance feeds on itself and leads only to more avoidance.

Source: Reprinted with permission from *Hey Wait a Minute, I Wrote a Book* by John Madden. New York: Villard Books, 1984, pp. 34–35.

women than men are generally diagnosed as having simple phobias.

Causes

The Biological Model. Normal fear is partly under genetic control. Identical twins, compared to fraternal twins, are more similar as infants in their fear of strangers, and as children and adults on measures of emotionality, shyness, and fears, and on physiological measures such as blood pressure (Marks, 1987). Accordingly, it would not be surprising to discover genetic influences on the development of simple phobia. Some researchers have hypothesized that humans as a species are biologically "prepared" to develop fears or phobias to selected classes of stimuli (Seligman, 1971). People commonly have phobias about heights, flying, blood, small animals, and so on, but not about inanimate objects such as hammers, electric sockets, or typewriters. To account for this nonrandom distribution of phobias, the preparedness hypothesis states that our evolutionary past has prepared us to acquire fears about objects or situations at one time associated with danger to the species.

The preparedness hypothesis predicts that when specific "prepared" stimuli are associated with an aversive event, more rapid and stronger learning will result than with "unprepared" stimuli. The following example illustrates the typical laboratory study used to test this prediction. Based on classical conditioning procedures, Hugdahl (1978) paired pictures of either snakes and spiders (a biologically prepared stimulus) or circles and triangles (an unprepared stimulus) with either electric shock or threat of electric shock as the UCS. The dependent measure, or CR, was a change in skin conductance, which marks arousal of the autonomic nervous system and hence is widely used as a measure of fear. All four subject groups showed equal speed and strength conditioning. During extinction, when subjects were informed that no further shock would be given, the two groups conditioned to the unprepared CS showed an immediate reduction in fear response. In contrast, the two groups who had experienced the prepared CS indicated resistance to extinction. This resistance is consistent with the preparedness hypothesis. Similar results were obtained using social stimuli. The prepared stimuli were pictures of angry faces, the unprepared stimuli pictures of neutral or happy faces (Ohman, 1986). It is argued that these data fit an evolutionary explanation because to survive we need to learn which individuals are potentially dangerous to us.

We can reasonably conclude that certain stimuli

produce stronger learning of fear reactions than others. The preparedness or evolutionary hypothesis is, nevertheless, only one possible explanation of these findings. An alternative view, emphasizing differential social-learning experiences, is discussed below.

The Psychodynamic Model. A phobia is simply one way in which intrapsychic, neurotic anxiety is unconsciously transformed into an external fear of a specific object or situation. The model can be illustrated with reference to one of Freud's classic case studies, that of Little Hans,[3] who developed a phobia about horses when he was five years old. He also reported the following dream: "There was a big giraffe in the room and a crumpled one; and the big one called out because I took the crumpled one away from it. Then it stopped calling out; and then I sat down on the top of the crumpled one." The boy was interviewed once by Freud, who then talked to his father, a physician and an admirer of Freud's views. The father asked Hans questions and made notes, which he sent to Freud. Goodwin (1986) neatly summarized the way Freud explained the boy's phobia as follows:

> 1. *Hans lusted for his mother.*
> 2. *He was jealous of his father, a rival with a larger penis.*
> 3. *He could not express his jealousy because of fear, specifically fear that he would be punished by the father for lusting for the mother. The punishment would take the form of castration (a punishment he assumed was common, based on his observation that little girls lacked penises, presumably because they, too, had lusted for a parent).*
> 4. *The fear was so great that he actively "forgot" (repressed) the whole business. For further protection, his unconscious mind performed the following maneuvers:*
> 5. *He projected his hostility onto the father: The father became the aggressor. Then he displaced his aggressive feelings from the father to something safer, more neutral: horses. Horses became the objects to be feared and avoided. Horses were a symbol for the father, but Hans did not know this. He certainly did not connect his fear of horses with incestuous sex (p. 43).*

In the boy's fantasy the big giraffe was his father and the crumpled one his mother. In the dream or fantasy Hans took his mother away from his father and the father unsuccessfully objects. A phobia about snakes is seen as castration anxiety in males and as penis envy (the female counterpart of castration anxiety) in women. A phobia about crowds or open spaces may conceal an unconscious desire to exhibit oneself.

The problems with this model illustrate the general criticisms of the psychodynamic approach. First, the evidence is restricted to clinical case studies. Other interpretations—both psychodynamic (e.g., Brown, 1965) and nonpsychodynamic (e.g., Wolpe & Rachman, 1960)—of these cases are equally plausible. Second, the model predicts that treatment failing to unravel the early childhood conflicts that cause the disorder will be ineffective or incomplete. Although its overt expression will be eliminated, other symptoms (i.e., ego defenses) will take their place. Research has shown that this does not occur (O'Leary & Wilson, 1987) as phobias can be effectively treated without understanding their origins.

The Cognitive-Behavioral Model. According to this model, the phobic object or situation has been associated with some threatening event by the person. One way this is learned is through classical or Pavlovian conditioning in which an object or situation is paired with a traumatic event. Such experiences create learned expectations in the person about what cues predict what events.

Observing some other person behaving fearfully or being harmed is another way to acquire phobic anxiety. This cognitive process of **modeling** helps explain how people can develop phobias although they have never had direct contact with the feared situation or object. Strong evidence of the role of modeling comes from a study of primates (Mineka, Davidson, Cook, & Keir, 1984). Young monkeys acquired severe and lasting fear of snakes after observing their wild-reared parents behave fearfully in the presence of one. The degree of behavioral disturbance (fear) shown by the parental models was more significant than their behavioral avoidance in determining an observer monkey's fear.

The cognitive-behavioral model can be illustrated by showing how it would explain the case of Little Hans. The boy had been exposed to several aversive experiences with horses. To quote Bandura (1986, p. 203),

> *He had been frightened at seeing horses being beaten at a merry-go-round; he was warned to avoid horses, for they might injure him; he was frightened when a friend was hurt while playing horses; and in the episode that immediately preceded the onset of the phobic behavior, Hans was terrified at witnessing a bus accident in which he believed a large bus-horse[4] was killed. . . . There were three important elements in the final, traumatic incident—large horse,*

[3] For years there was speculation about the identity of "Little Hans." Recent research reveals that he was Herbert Graf, the son of a Viennese musicologist (*The New York Times,* March 6, 1990, page C1).

[4] The setting was 1908 in Austria. The language describes a horse-drawn carriage.

heavily loaded transport vehicle, and horse and vehicle traveling at high speed. The occurrence and intensity of Hans's phobic reactions varied as a function of the specific patterning of these three predictive cues. He was more frightened of large dray horses than of small horses, more frightened of heavily loaded vehicles than of empty ones, and more frightened when a horse-drawn cart made a turn which increased the risk of turning over. Indeed, transport vehicles were as much, or more of, a factor in Hans's fear than were horses per se. As he described, "I'm afraid of buses and luggage-carts, but only when they're loaded up, not when they're empty. When there's one horse and the cart's loaded full up, then I'm afraid; but when there are two horses and it's loaded full up, then I'm not afraid."

The psychoanalytic interpretation fails to explain the discriminative patterning of the boy's phobic behavior. For example, Bandura (1986) asks "How can a horse phobia be attributed to an underlying Oedipus complex and projected castration fears if a person responds phobically to one horse pulling a heavy loaded vehicle, but is relatively unafraid of two horses drawing a loaded vehicle?" (p. 13) Nor does it explain why Hans also feared heavily loaded vehicles and locomotives, phobias which reflect generalization from the transport-vehicle incident. These phenomena fit well with the learning or behavioral model. Psychoanalysts, however, would contend that the model does not explain the boy's dream and its connection with the phobia.

We need to go beyond classical conditioning and modeling to understand the nature of phobias, however. Many people who are exposed to intense fear-provoking conditions do not develop phobias (e.g., not all people involved in car or plane crashes become fearful of cars or planes). Some people are apparently predisposed to acquiring phobic reactions. Both genetic and early learning experiences probably contribute to this predisposition. As we have indicated, normal fear and at least some phobias have a genetic component. J.B. Watson himself, the extreme behaviorist, hypothesized that "constitutional inferiority" (i.e., genetic background) might help explain the maintenance of phobic reactions (Eysenck, 1982).

Two central concepts in explaining phobic and other anxiety reactions to specific events are predictability and controllability. The more people feel capable of predicting and potentially controlling aversive events, the less anxious they become (Bandura, 1986). It follows that the greater a person's self-efficacy, the less vulnerable he or she is to developing a phobic reaction in response to a traumatic experience. Self-efficacy is a product of the individual's specific social-learning history.

Support for the significance of self-efficacy in the development of phobic reactions comes from an experiment with primates showing that a history of personal control or mastery over one's environment critically influences the development of fear (Mineka, Gunnar, & Champoux, 1986). One group of infant monkeys, the "Masters," were reared in an environment where they controlled when they received their food, water, and special treats. A second group, the "Controls," living in an identical environment, obtained the same rewards. The only difference between the groups was that the Controls received their food, water, and treats automatically whenever the Masters chose theirs. Between ages seven and nine months, both groups were subjected to fear tests with a fear-provoking mechanical toy monster, as well as playroom tests in a novel situation to assess fear and exploratory tendencies. The Masters were significantly more willing to approach the toy monster and less fearful in the novel situation. The authors of this study raise the interesting possibility that the higher prevalence of phobias in women than in men may partly be due to differences in gaining a sense of control over the environment in the course of development.

A major criticism of a learning analysis of phobia is that classically conditioned fear reactions typically extinguish quickly if the conditioned stimulus (CS) is repeatedly presented without the unconditioned stimulus (UCS). Yet people with phobias frequently come into contact with situations or objects they fear (the CS) without any adverse effects (the absence of an UCS), and their phobias remain intact. For example, John Madden, as Box 5.1 describes, traveled in airplanes for several years with little reduction in his fear of flying. Self-efficacy theory helps explain both the persistence and modification of phobic reactions. Whether phobic behavior is eliminated by exposure to feared situations will depend on the nature of the information the person derives from exposure to them. If individuals conclude they can cope effectively, and thereby their learned expectations of aversive outcomes are disconfirmed, they will stop their avoidance behavior and overcome their fear. But no change will occur if individuals cannot cope and instead experience unnerving anxiety. By strengthening phobics' expectations that they are unable to cope, exposure might even enhance phobic sensitivity.

Another criticism of the learning model is that it does not explain the nonrandom distribution of phobias—why phobics fear only some stimuli but not others. In contrast to the view that people are biologically prepared to acquire certain fears, social-learning theory states that in our culture we learn to react differently to salient, fear-relevant stimuli like snakes or angry faces than to stimuli like circles and triangles (Bandura, 1986).

Laboratory studies have been made of the merits of these competing explanations. Pictures of spiders were compared to pictures of a handgun pointed at the subject as conditioned stimuli (Hugdahl & Johnsen, 1989). The assumption here was that guns are not evolutionary but culturally fear-relevant stimuli—we learn to fear guns. Subjects rated the two sets of stimuli as equally fearful, contrary to the explanation based on our evolutionary heritage. Apparently, people are differentially susceptible to developing fear reactions to certain stimuli. Social-learning experiences rather than innate biological "wiring" determine this susceptibility.

The preparedness hypothesis also predicts that prepared fears (i.e., phobias) should be unusually resistant to extinction. Yet research summarized in this chapter shows that phobias are rapidly eliminated when the appropriate learning conditions are arranged. In a clinical test of the preparedness hypothesis, de Silva, Rachman, and Seligman (1977) rated sixty-nine phobic and eighty-two obsessional patients for the preparedness, or evolutionary significance of their fears, and related these measures to therapeutic outcome. The results showed that the preparedness ratings failed to predict treatment outcome, stimulus generalization, severity of the problem, suddenness of the onset of fear, or age of onset. This finding shows that even a phobia influenced by genetic factors is not necessarily resistent to behavioral modification.

Treatment. Clinical research has consistently shown behavior therapy efficient and effective in treating simple phobias (O'Leary & Wilson, 1987). Joseph Wolpe's technique of **systematic desensitization** illustrates this general approach. Phobic patients are first trained in progressive relaxation—taught to concentrate on systematically relaxing different muscle groups—resulting in lowered physiological arousal and a comfortable subjective feeling of calmness. Next, a hierarchy of the phobic object or situation is constructed, ranging from mildly stressful to highly threatening items. Finally, the patient is asked to use visual imagery to picture these items while relaxed. This is repeated systematically until the patient can visualize the scenes without undue anxiety. In a more effective variation of systematic desensitization, called **exposure treatment,** patients are asked to confront their phobic situations in real life rather than in imagination (Barlow, 1988).

Exposure methods are the most effective for treating phobic disorders, though the theoretical mechanisms responsible for this success are still debated. Contrary to the predictions of classical conditioning, amount of exposure is a poor predictor of outcome. Neither self-report of anticipated anxiety nor physiological arousal predict outcome well. Instead, evidence suggests that exposure treatments are effective because they increase patients' perceived self-efficacy—their expectations and belief that they can cope successfully with the phobic object or situation (Bandura, 1986). The relative merits of the conditioning and self-efficacy theories of why exposure treatment works have been tested in a series of studies by Bandura and his colleagues (1977) at Stanford University. In a typical experiment, subjects phobic about harmless snakes received either one of two exposure treatments or no treatment at all. In the more powerful of the two exposure treatments (guided exposure), subjects learned how to cope with their fear while systematically being exposed to the snake. In the less powerful treatment, subjects rehearsed coping responses in imagery for approaching the snake (imaginal exposure). As predicted, guided exposure produced stronger efficacy expectations and the greater change in phobic behavior as compared with imaginal exposure. The latter, in turn, produced greater self-efficacy and behavior change than the no treatment control condition. As shown in Figure 5.1, increased self-efficacy was closely linked to reductions in phobic behavior. The greater the increase in self-efficacy, the greater the change in behavior regardless of whether the treatment involved a behavioral (guided exposure) or imaginal (imaginal exposure) procedure. In other studies, (Bandura, 1986) showed that if different subjects achieved the same degree of change in phobic behavior at the end of treatment, but reported different levels of self-efficacy, the expectations and not the behavior predicted subsequent behavioral perfor-

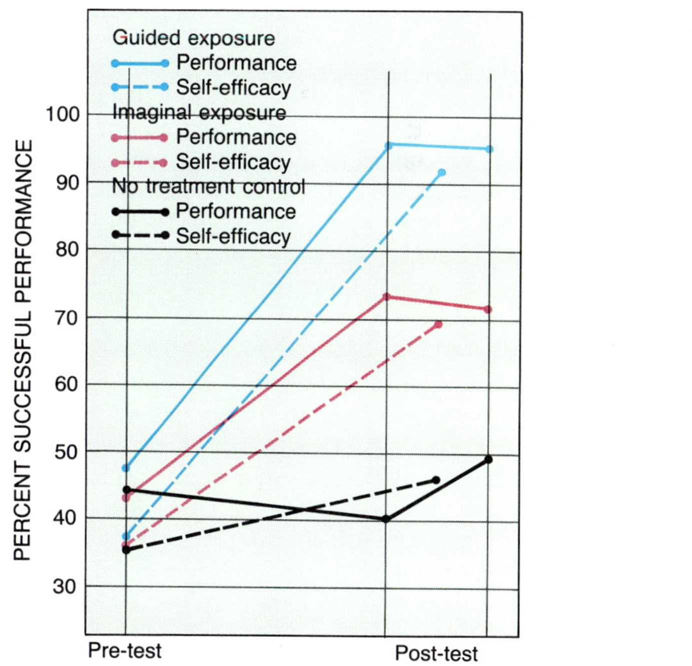

Figure 5.1 *Level of efficacy expectations and approach behavior displayed by subjects toward threats after receiving exposure treatment or no treatment.*
Source: From A. Bandura, N. Adams, & J. Beyer (1977). "Cognitive increases mediating behavioral change," *Journal of Personality and Social Psychology,* 35, 126–139. Copyright © 1977 by the American Psychological Association. Reprinted with permission.

mance. These results support the theory that treatment changes phobic behavior by increasing efficacy expectations, rather than by extinguishing a conditioned anxiety response. Comparable results have been obtained with other phobic disorders (Williams, 1987). Some critics have argued that self-efficacy is only correlated with treatment-induced changes in phobic behavior, and does not cause the behavior change (Borkovec, 1978; Marks, 1987). In answer to this criticism, Bandura et al. (1982) treated snake phobic subjects until they reached predetermined levels of low, moderate, or high self-efficacy. This was done by assessing subjects' efficacy levels after they completed each step of the behavioral avoidance test used to measure phobic behavior. In a separate study, low, moderate, or high levels of self-efficacy were successively induced within the same subjects. Both the between-group and within-group experimental designs showed that phobic behavior varied according to the level of subjects' self-efficacy. Bandura (1986) interprets this systematic covariation between efficacy expectations and phobic behavior as evidence of the causal nature of self-efficacy.

Self-efficacy is related to measures of fear arousal other than self-report and behavioral performance. Phobics with little self-efficacy who engage in feared activities show increases in blood pressure and heart rate. In contrast, phobics with high levels of self-efficacy who engage in the activities show no increase in blood pressure and heart rate. Self-efficacy is also related to neuro-endocrine processes underlying stress reactions (Bandura, Taylor, Williams, Mefford, & Barchas, 1985). Phobics reporting only moderate levels of self-efficacy about specific tasks showed significant increases in plasma epinephrine and norepinephrine. After they increased their self-efficacy through behavioral treatment, they completed the previously feared tasks with little increase in endocrine activity.

One advantage of this theory is that it explains the success of behavior therapy techniques and also of effective non-behavioral treatments (Klein, Zitrin, Woerner, & Ross, 1983). Self-efficacy can be increased not only through behavioral performance but also via vicarious experience, physiological arousal, and verbal persuasion. In this theory, exposure is not a necessary condition for anxiety reduction. Behavioral performance is, however, the most effective means of increasing self-efficacy and thus overcoming phobic disorders (Bandura, 1986).

Freud originally advocated a similar sort of treatment. He stated that "One can hardly ever master a phobia if one waits till the patient lets the analysis influence him to give it up." Freud recommended that the therapist modify the usual psychoanalytic method and actively encourage the patients to expose themselves to their phobic situations. It seems, however, that Freud did not always take his own advice. He was fearful about trains and avoided them (Goodwin, 1986).

Social Phobia

Characteristics. *DSM-III-R* defines *social phobia* as a "persistent fear of one or more situations in which the person is exposed to possible scrutiny by others and fears that he or she may do something that will be humiliating or embarrassing" (p. 241). Social phobics fear being looked at. The woman who is unable to sign a check at the bank teller's window if people are around is a social phobic. Typical symptoms of social phobics who are exposed to feared social situations include tachycardia (elevated heart rate), trembling, blushing, sweating, and shortness of breath, all indicating heightened autonomic arousal. The phobia may be specific (e.g., fear of speaking in public) or general (e.g., fear of virtually all social situations). The fear and avoidance interfere with the person's job or usual social relationships. Social phobia occurs in approximately 1.2 percent to 2.2 percent of the population (Myers et al., 1984).

The disorder is illustrated in the following case example:

> *The patient, Mary M., a 29-year-old female, married with a three-year-old child, referred herself for treatment of "social anxiety," consisting of avoidance of all social situations involving "one-on-one" contact with another person other than her husband or daughter. She reported being socially isolated with no friendships. She occasionally interacted with a group of other mothers in her daughter's nursery school but was only able to do so if it was a group situation. She avoided one-to-one contact fearing that she would inevitably disappoint the other person, leading to embarrassment, rejection, and humiliation. She reported that when she was in a social situation, she was obsessively preoccupied with the perceived negative evaluations of those she was with. For example, when she took her daughter to the pediatrician, she became upset wondering whether the physician thought she was an "uptight, insecure, and incompetent mother." She wondered further whether the pediatrician would side with her "if anyone thought I was an unfit mother and tried to take my daughter away." She reported that when in such situations, she would become very conscious of tension in her facial muscles and would then look for signs in the other person's face that they noticed her anxiety, and became uncomfortable. She and her husband did not socialize with other couples, largely due to her anxiety about such encounters. She reported a fervent desire to have friends, and frequent depression and crying spells over the difficulties she was having"* (Taylor & Arnow, 1988, p. 231).

Simple phobics typically cope by avoiding their feared situations. Social phobics have more difficulty doing this, because complete avoidance of social interaction is often impossible. Thus, they do not completely avoid their feared situation but engage instead in social interactions they find distressing and painful (Lang, Levin, Miller, & Kozak, 1983). Social phobics show other psychiatric symptoms, most notably more general anxiety and depression, than do simple phobics, with alcohol abuse often a problem. This phobia typically begins in late childhood or early adolescence and follows a chronic course unless treated. It is more common in males than females.

Most people experience some anxiety if they have to give a speech in public. And many men feel uneasy if they have to urinate in a public restroom with a long line forming behind them. Are these and other normal reactions totally different from a social phobic's concerns? Some investigators suggest that social phobic is simply at the extreme end of a continuum of shyness or social performance anxiety (Barlow, 1988). Others reject the idea of a continuum and argue that there is a qualitative difference between social phobia and "normal" shyness or performance anxiety. Recent research on temperament in children is relevant to this debate. About 15 percent of two-year-olds are consistently shy and emotionally inhibited in unfamiliar situations, whereas another 15 percent are sociable and uninhibited (Kagan, 1989). These children remain this way at eight years of age. There is no continuum between these two extremes—they appear to be separate categories.

Causes. Studies of families of social phobics indicate a genetic predisposition for developing the disorder. Torgersen (1983) found monozygotic twins significantly more alike, or concordant, for such social phobic features as discomfort when eating with strangers or when being watched working, writing, or trembling, suggesting a genetic contribution to social anxiety. Kagan's (1989) landmark research on temperamental differences in young children shows that extreme shyness is inherited rather than created by early experience. The parents of social phobics are much more socially fearful and worried about the opinions of people than those of other phobics (Barlow, 1988), although this is consistent with either a genetic or a social-learning interpretation.

The psychodynamic view is the same as that for simple phobia, namely, a transformation of intrapsychic anxiety into external anxiety via the defense mechanism of displacement, although no empirical evidence is available to test the theory. The behavioral account emphasizes learning processes in the development of social phobia, as in the case of simple phobia.

Treatment. Cognitive-behavioral therapy has successfully treated social phobics. The key components of this treatment are

1. Cognitive restructuring, in which patients are helped to identify anxiety-eliciting thoughts, to challenge them, and to rehearse more constructive alternatives.
2. Relaxation training.
3. Guided exposure, in which patients are helped to participate actively in situations they have been avoiding.

In an illustrative study, Butler and her colleagues (1984) compared two forms of treatment to a waiting-list control group. One method was exposure, in which patients were encouraged to systematically confront situations they had been avoiding. The other method was exposure plus anxiety management training, combining relaxation training with cognitive restructuring. Both treatment groups improved significantly more than the waiting-list control group, which showed no improvement on most measures. Treatment effects were maintained or increased at a six-month follow-up.

Drugs are commonly used to treat social phobia. Benzodiazepines—minor tranquilizers such as Librium or Valium (see Chapter 17)—provide short-term relief, but may be abused by patients. Another type of anti-anxiety drug, phenelzine, which is an MAO-inhibitor, is also effective (Levin et al., 1989). A combination of drug and psychological therapy is recommended in treating social phobia.

Panic Disorder

Characteristics. *DSM-III-R* distinguishes between **panic disorder** with and without agoraphobia. (Agoraphobia is discussed later in this chapter.) Panic disorder without agoraphobia is a chronic condition characterized by unexpected recurrent attacks of intense anxiety, occurring in apparent absence of identifiable anxiety-eliciting situations. A patient described the experience of what it is like to have a panic attack in the following words:

> Imagine that you are walking a tightrope between two skyscrapers like the World Trade Center. You are halfway across when a gusty wind starts to blow. You feel your footing go. You look down. It's a long, long drop to the street below. Try to capture the feelings in your body and mind in that situation. The spontaneous panic attack is even worse, and here's why. On the tightrope you know why you're anxious: you can identify things that need to be done to cope. The danger is clear. You are also expecting to feel fear and anxiety. There are no big surprises. On the other hand, with the spontaneous panic attack, it can strike unexpectedly at any time. And worse, you can't identify any good reason for it. You can't pin it on anything. It's a nameless terror. It comes from nowhere and you don't know when it will stop, if ever. Since it can strike any time, anywhere, you are never really safe anywhere. If you invented Hell, you'd have to include this part of the package (Sheehan, 1983, p. 42).

Panic is a terrifying emotional experience that can cause people to think that they are about to die.

To be diagnosed as panic, at least four of the following symptoms must have occurred during an attack: shortness of breath, dizziness, heart palpitations, trembling or shaking, sweating, choking, nausea, depersonalization, numbness or tingling sensations, flushes, chest pain, fear of going crazy.

Heart and respiratory symptoms are typical complaints of patients with panic. Thus they frequently consult physicians or go to hospital emergency rooms because they believe they are having a heart attack, as illustrated in the following example:

> *A fifty-one-year-old electrical engineer was brought to an emergency room by ambulance complaining of severe left frontal chest pain. His breathing was labored and he complained of numbness and tingling in his lips and fingers. His pulse was 110. He was perspiring heavily and obviously frightened. The electrocardiogram was normal. His blood chemistry was normal. Nevertheless, the patient was admitted to the intensive care unit. He was observed for twenty-four hours and then discharged free of symptoms.*
>
> *The patient had first experienced severe chest pain at the age of twenty-one while watching a movie. He had many subsequent episodes of chest pain accompanied by dyspnea (difficulty breathing) and anxiety and had been taken to an emergency room on at least ten previous occasions. Although the examinations were always normal, he had undergone a variety of cardiovascular procedures, including cardiac catheterization* (Goodwin, 1986, p. 115).

Freud described panic at the turn of the century. He referred to what we now know as panic as an "anxiety state," which he differentiated from free-floating (generalized) anxiety and phobic anxiety.

Until recently, our understanding of panic disorder was limited to patients' retrospective accounts of panic attacks. Then Barr Taylor and his colleagues at Stanford Medical School developed a convenient means of electronically recording patients' heart rate on a twenty-four-hour basis. They were able to distinguish between changes in it caused by physical activity and those associated with a panic attack (Taylor et al., 1986). Panic attacks resulted in an average increase in heart rate of almost forty beats per minute. Panic, as measured by heart rate increase, lasted an average of twenty minutes and occurred most frequently between the hours of 1:30 A.M. and 3:30 A.M.—when patients were in bed asleep.

The lifetime prevalence of strictly defined panic disorder is roughly 1.5 percent of the population (Karno et al., 1987), although specific panic attacks are much more common. They occur relatively frequently in the general population, in other anxiety disorders, and even in affective disorders (Barlow, 1988). Adolescents experience panic attacks as well as adults. A major study of 2,375 college students found that 2.36 percent met *DSM-III-R* criteria for panic disorder and approximately 12 percent reported having experienced at least one unexpected panic attack. It is equally common in men and women (Telch et al., 1989).

Panic disorder with agoraphobia is diagnosed if, in addition to the criteria for panic disorder, the patient also meets the criteria for agoraphobia. The prevalence of panic disorder with agoraphobia is as high as 5 percent of the population and far more common among women than men.

Recent research has revealed a serious complication of panic disorder. People with panic disorder are almost three times as likely to attempt suicide as those with other psychological disorders, including major depression (Weissman et al., 1989). Moreover, people who experience panic attacks, even though they do not meet the criteria for the diagnosis of panic disorder, are nearly twice as likely to try suicide as those with any other psychological disorder.

Causes. Currently, the two most promising and influential theories of panic disorder are the biological model and the cognitive-behavioral model.

The Biological Model. According to this model, panic is qualitatively different from the anxiety that defines phobia and other anxiety disorders (Klein, 1981). Panic is an unlearned alarm reaction activated by a biochemical dysfunction. Other forms of anxiety are said to be learned. Psychological stress, which might be associated with the onset of panic, is viewed as only a nonspecific influence that might worsen but never cause the problem.

Panic differs from anticipatory and generalized anxiety both in the specific thoughts associated with the anxiety and in physiological responsiveness. Patients suffering from panic report more thoughts about illness, dying, or collapsing than patients with other anxiety disorders (Holt & Andrews, 1989). Panic patients also show greater physiological arousal than other anxiety disorder patients (Barlow, 1988). For example, when they monitored patients' heart rates around the clock, Taylor et al. (1986) found that panic was associated with a big increase in heart rate yet intense anticipatory anxiety was not.

Panic disorder patients have been found to differ physiologically from normal people. A number of pharmacological and physiological reactions (e.g., hyperventilation and inhalation of carbon dioxide) trigger panic in panic patients but not in other people. For example, lactic acid in the blood of panic patients rises to higher levels after exercise than in normals. Lactic acid injected directly into the bloodstream of panic patients typically makes them panic whereas normal controls do not. Research using PET scans of the brain has shown differences between patients who panic following lactate infusion and those who do not (Reiman et al., 1989). In the nonpanic state before lactate infusion, patients who subsequently experienced panic attacks showed an abnormal metabolic rate for oxygen in a particular region of the brain called the parahippocampal gyrus. During panic, however, they showed the same increase in neural activity in the temporal poles of the brain as normal volunteers anticipating an electric shock.

Some proponents of a biological model assume that panic is qualitatively different from other anxiety disorders, and hence should respond selectively to a particular class of drugs (tricyclic antidepressants and MAO inhibitors), but not to the benzodiazepines. The latter are supposed to be effective with anticipatory and generalized anxiety but not with panic. The evidence is mixed on the specificity of drug treatments, however, as antidepressants tend to have broad effects on different forms of anxiety and dysphoric feelings and on panic (Margraf, Ehlers, & Roth, 1986). Moreover, benzodiazepines can reduce not only anxiety but also panic (Noyes et al., 1984).

Anxiety disorders run in families; they occur significantly more frequently in the relatives of patients with anxiety disorders than among controls. The biological model assumes (1) that a genetic basis exists for panic disorder and (2) that it is independent of other anxiety disorders. The evidence is generally consistent with these assumptions. About 50 percent of people with panic disorder have relatives with the same disorder, higher than the rate in the general population. Noyes et al. (1987) found that the high frequency of panic disorder among the relatives of panic disorder patients was not seen in the families of people with other anxiety disorders, such as generalized anxiety disorder (GAD). These and other findings indicate that familial risks for panic and GAD are independent. Moreover, familial transmission of panic disorder appears to be genetically influenced. Monozygotic (MZ) twins are more likely to be concordant than dizygotic (DZ) twins, although the absolute rate of concordance was low, indicating environmental factors are also influential (Torgersen, 1983). The major weakness of the biological model is its prediction that panic disorder is treatable only by specific drugs that alter underlying biochemical dysfunction so that psychological methods are assumed incapable of reducing panic (Klein et al., 1987).

The Cognitive-Behavioral Model. This model postulates that panic attacks result from the individual's catastrophic misinterpretation of certain bodily sensations. The misinterpreted sensations are mainly those involved in normal anxiety responses (e.g., palpitations or breathlessness) but also include some others (e.g., bodily changes in response to excitement or anger). These sensations are perceived as much more dangerous than they really are and sometimes as indicative of immediate impending disaster (Clark, 1988). For example, a healthy person might interpret palpitations as evidence of an impending heart attack. Figure 5.2 illustrates this model. Stimuli that are interpreted as a threat cause anxiety, which involves different physical sensations. These sensa-

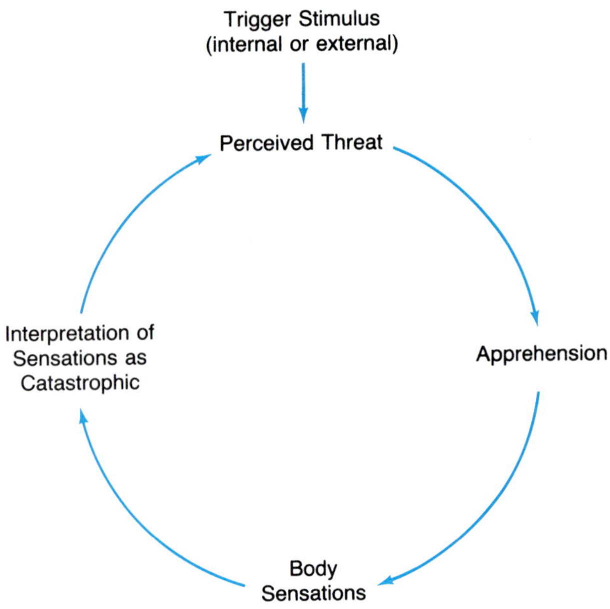

Figure 5.2 A cognitive model of the sequence of events in a panic attack.

Source: From D.M. Clark (1986). A cognitive approach to panic. *Behaviour Research and Therapy, 24,* p. 463. Oxford: Pergamon Press. Reprinted with permission.

tions are then interpreted by the person in a catastrophic way that further increases anxiety. This response in turn causes a further increase in negative physical sensations in what becomes a vicious circle. Panics are viewed as unexpected, or coming "out of the blue," because the triggering sensation, such as emotional excitement or that brought on by drinking coffee, may be unrelated to anxiety. Also, the person fails to distinguish between the physical sensation that initially triggers the reaction and the attack itself. For example, if a man believes something is wrong with his heart, he will interpret the palpitations that trigger his panic and the panic itself as aspects of the same thing—a heart attack or a close call.

The cognitive-behavioral model is consistent with the view that biological abnormalities predispose individuals to panic but differs in postulating that these abnormalities do not directly cause panic. They have to be misinterpreted in a catastrophic fashion. This cognitive reaction is seen as a necessary condition for panic. The cognitive model also differs from a related psychological explanation of panic, namely the **fear of fear** hypothesis. According to this hypothesis, panic patients will panic when they become anxious, yet this does not always happen. The cognitive model explains how a panic patient can become anxious and not panic. If the patient attributes anxiety to an understandable cause (e.g., a job interview), he or she does not become panicked. Panic follows only when the patient attributes anxiety to physical sensations he or she interprets as signaling impending disaster, though panics are not always triggered by anxiety.

Several lines of evidence support the cognitive-behavioral model. First, the model predicts that panic patients should be significantly more likely to misinterpret bodily sensations catastrophically than other individuals. Studies comparing panic patients to other anxious patients and normal controls have supported this prediction (Rachman & Maser, 1988). Second, studies have also supported that eliciting catastrophic cognitions in panic patients should lead to panic. Clark (1988) had panic patients read aloud a series of word pairs consisting of a bodily sensation and a catastrophic interpretation (e.g., palpitations–dying, breathlessness–suffocation, and so on). Compared to former panic patients who had been successfully treated and normal controls, only the panic patients experienced panic symptoms after reading the word pairs. Other indirect support for this model comes from a study in which panic patients and normal controls were given false feedback indicating a sudden rise in heart rate. Only the panic patients showed a real increase in heart rate and anxiety in response (Margraf et al., 1986).

Third, treatment that corrects or changes patients' catastrophic misinterpretation of bodily sensations should reduce panic attacks. As noted later, initial evidence indicates that this does occur. The following experiment by Rapee, Mattick, and Murell (1986) shows the importance of altering a patient's cognitions. Panic patients were asked to inhale a mixture of carbon dioxide and oxygen that typically produces a panic reaction. One half were given a minimal explanation about the procedure, whereas the other half received a detailed explanation of all possible sensations attributed to effects of the gas. This explanation was intended to block patients' naturally occurring tendency to catastrophically interpret the sensations produced by the gas. Consistent with the cognitive model, subjects given no explanation experienced significantly more panic than those whose cognitions had been altered by the detailed explanation.

To summarize, several important findings are consistent with the cognitive-behavioral model. This model takes the well-documented role of biological factors into account but assigns them an indirect rather than a direct function.

Treatment. Anti-anxiety drugs are the most widely used treatment for panic disorder. The drugs are believed to directly remedy the biochemical abnormality causing panic attacks through pharmacological action (Levin, Schneier, & Liebowitz, 1989). Although several studies have shown that these drugs reduce panic attacks (Zitrin et al., 1983), negative findings have also been reported (Marks et al., 1983).

Psychological treatments can reduce panic attacks. Exposure treatment reliably reduces panic attacks, although we do not know the mechanisms through which it achieves its therapeutic effects (Barlow, 1988). Cognitive-behavioral therapy is also promising. It was first developed for patients with panic associated with hyperventilation (Clark, Salkovskis, & Chalkley, 1985). Treatment consists of

1. Brief, voluntary hyperventilation intended to induce a mild panic attack.
2. Explanation of the effects of overbreathing and reattributing a patient's attacks to hyperventilation.
3. Training in slow breathing incompatible with hyperventilation.

Clark et al. (1985) obtained substantial reductions in frequency of panic attacks within two weeks, despite the documented absence of subjects' exposure to feared situations might have confounded the treatment. Therapeutic improvement was maintained at a two-year follow-up. Other studies have similarly shown that cognitive-behavioral treatment combining exposure to feared physical sensations, cognitive restructuring, and relaxation training produces dramatic reductions in frequency of panic attacks compared to untreated control patients (Barlow, 1988).

Cognitive-behavioral treatment involves more than the patients' mere exposure to internal anxiety-eliciting stimuli. In the Rapee et al. (1986) study both groups received equal exposure to anxiety-eliciting sensations but only the group provided with a noncatastrophic interpretation of these symptoms responded without panic. This finding underscores the value of the cognitive component of treatment.

Agoraphobia

Characteristics. *DSM-III-R* defines **agoraphobia** as the "fear of being in places or situations from which escape might be difficult (or embarrassing) or in which help might not be available in the event of suddenly developing a symptom(s) that could be incapacitating or extremely embarrassing" (p. 241). Agoraphobics are anxious about losing control, going insane, fainting, or having a heart attack. This anxiety is often referred to as **anticipatory anxiety.** Although groundless, it results in agoraphobics avoiding public transportation; confined places, including tunnels, bridges, restaurants, and movie theaters; and being away from home or in places where help is not readily available. Some agoraphobics become housebound. They tend to dread crowded shopping centers and supermarkets especially. To combat this, agoraphobics usually require someone—spouse, family member, or trusted companion—to accompany them when they go places.

Agoraphobics are often depressed but this is secondary to the agoraphobia. Successful treatment of agoraphobia usually leads to the lifting of depressive symptoms. A sizable minority of agoraphobics abuse alcohol, although it is not always clear whether their agoraphobia preceded their alcoholism (Bibb & Chambless, 1986). Age of onset is typically in the twenties or thirties, and without treatment the disorder persists for years. Between 2.7 percent and 5.8 percent of the adult population in the United States suffers from agoraphobia, with far more women than men affected.

Causes. Modern clinical thinking views agoraphobia as a secondary consequence of panic disorder. The avoidance behavior of agoraphobia is seen as simply a culturally determined effort to cope with anxiety about the occurrence of a panic attack (Barlow, 1988). There is good evidence to support this recent reformulation of agoraphobia. Patients with panic disorder alone or panic disorder with agoraphobia appear identical in terms of descriptive characteristics, such as age of onset and panic frequency (Telch et al., 1989). Virtually all who seek clinical treatment for agoraphobia report developing avoidance behavior after an initial panic attack (Thyer, Himle, et al., 1985). Yet this clinical evidence conflicts with epidemiological findings from the general population showing that 25 percent to 50 percent of agoraphobics do not report panic attacks (Weissman et al., 1986). These epidemiological data are the reason *DSM-III-R* (1987) included agoraphobia as a separate category. The reason for the discrepancy between the clinical and epidemiological evidence is unknown.

The onset of agoraphobia may be gradual or sudden. Evidence consistently shows agoraphobia developing against a background of stress. Whatever the cause of the initial experience of acute anxiety (or panic attack in agoraphobics with panic), the agoraphobic subsequently increasingly avoids the original and related situations. The more the person avoids them, the more difficult it is to break out of this self-defeating pattern. Also family members and friends may inadvertently help maintain this pattern of avoidance behavior by taking over the agoraphobics' responsibilities.

The Biological Model. Where panic is present, the phobic anxiety and avoidance that defines agoraphobia is seen as a secondary consequence of panic disorder, which, as we have seen, is hypothesized to be the result of some biochemical abnormality. The biological view of agoraphobia without panic attacks is less well developed. Biologically oriented theorists point, however, to evidence indicating agoraphobics have unusually high levels of autonomic nervous system arousal and are more sensitive to stressful stimuli; hence, they respond more readily to stressful events than the average person. We do not know whether this physiological arousal is a cause or an effect of the disorder.

Agoraphobia runs in families, particularly among the female relatives of agoraphobics. Harris, Noyes, Crowe, and Chaundry (1983) found the risk for all anxiety disorders to be 32 percent among first-degree relatives of agoraphobics, compared to 15 percent among nonanxious controls. Risk of anxiety disorder was increased by more than twice among female relatives of agoraphobic probands, whereas male relatives were also at higher risk for alcoholism. Whether this familial transmission is the product of genetic or environmental influences remains unknown.

The Psychodynamic Model. Current psychodynamic theory postulates that individuals who became extremely anxious whenever separated from their parents, as children, seem likely to develop agoraphobia later in life. This early childhood anxiety, real or feared, is known as **separation anxiety.** Gittelman-Klein and Klein (1984) have reported that 42 percent of agoraphobic patients had a history of separation anxiety. The theory explains why agoraphobics avoid situations that threaten separation from a loved one and why they can often function well if accompanied by a spouse or family member.

This theory has not gone unchallenged. Contrary to Gittelman-Klein and Klein's (1984) results, other better-controlled studies have found no differences in reported incidence of separation anxiety between agoraphobic patients, other anxiety patients (e.g., simple phobics), and normal controls (Buglass et al., 1977; Thyer, Nesse, Cameron, & Curtis, 1985).

The Family Systems Model. According to this theory, agoraphobia is a product of a pathological marriage or family system. For example, a wife might develop the disorder as a subtle way of controlling her husband. He would then have to spend considerable time with her and take over some of her activities; he could not become angry at her without appearing uncaring because of her "sickness." Alternatively, the husband might unconsciously encourage in his wife the dependency and limited social functioning that is part of agoraphobia as a way of controlling her. Or by focusing on her problems he might be shifting attention away from his.

Although this systems approach is popular among many clinicians, research evidence is lacking. In a major study, Buglass et al. (1977) compared thirty married agoraphobic women and normal controls matched for age, sex, social class, and marital status and found no significant differences between them across a wide range of measures, including decision making, domestic organization, social relationships, and problems in their children. Both husbands and wives of each group described their marriages in similar terms before the onset of agoraphobia or during the comparable period among the control group. Nor could Buglass and colleagues unearth evidence indicating that spouses were reinforcing dependency in the agoraphobic partners. Arrindell and Emmelkamp (1986) compared female agoraphobics and their husbands with three comparison groups: nonphobic female psychiatric patients and their husbands, maritally distressed couples, and happily married couples. In terms of marital adjustment, agoraphobics and their spouses were most similar to the happily married couples. By comparison, the nonphobic psychiatric controls reported significantly more marital distress and resembled the maritally distressed couples. These results indicate that agoraphobia is a problem emerging independently from the interpersonal, or marital, context. Marital factors can, however, influence treatment and the maintenance of treatment effects, as discussed later.

The Cognitive-Behavioral Model. The cognitive-behavioral model of panic attacks is described in the section on panic disorder. Once the initial panic or anxiety attack has occurred, the person increasingly avoids the original and related situations. A learning history of dependence as opposed to self-reliance then predisposes the person to continue avoiding rather than confronting his or her fears attributed to various external circumstances. The agoraphobic pattern is maintained by the **negative reinforcement** of avoiding anxiety-provoking situations and possibly by positive reinforcement of such behavior by significant others in his or her environment.

Sex Role and Agoraphobic Avoidance. Perhaps the most striking feature of agoraphobia is that studies from different parts of the world consistently show 75 percent or more of agoraphobics are women. Remember that panic disorder without agoraphobia is equally common in men and women. The greater the degree of avoidance behavior among panic disorder patients, the greater the proportion of women among these patients (Reich et al., 1987).

There is no evidence to suggest that biological differences—such as hormonal fluctuations at stressful periods—predispose women to agoraphobia. The more common explanation of this sex ratio difference is that women are more easily able to cope with anxiety or panic by avoiding fear situations and staying home. Men may experience the same anxiety or panic, but because of societal expectations they cannot avoid feared situations as easily, resorting instead to alcohol as a means of "self-medicating" their anxiety (Barlow, 1988). Consistent with this view is that the less "masculine" either male or female agoraphobics scored on a measure of sex role, the more avoidance behavior they showed (Chambless & Mason, 1986).

Agoraphobics are more dependent and less assertive than nonagoraphobic controls. Women, generally, are more likely to be dependent than men, and the passive avoidance behavior shown by female agoraphobics may be an exaggeration of their stereotypical role (Fodor, 1974). For example, if a young woman feels trapped in her marriage, has no emotional outlet, and cannot be assertive for fear of losing her husband, she may become fearful and avoidant in an effort to cope. Under the stress of the marital relationship, some married women who appear to have accepted the dependent wife role develop agoraphobia.

This theory leaves several questions unanswered. Why do some otherwise independent and assertive women develop the disorder, and many dependent and passive women do not? Moreover, the existence of an "agoraphobic personality" has yet to be demonstrated. Agoraphobics are less assertive and report feeling more powerless and helpless when compared to normal controls (Fisher & Wilson, 1985). But differences of this kind between patients with the disorder and normal controls are difficult to interpret. The lack of assertiveness may be the cause or the consequence of the disorder or may simply be correlated with it. Buglass et al. (1977) found no differences in dependency between agoraphobics and matched nonagoraphobic controls prior to the onset of the disorder. The only definitive way to disentangle cause from consequence is to carry out prospective studies of people before they develop the disorder (see Chapter 4).

Treatment. Although a wide range of individual, group, and family therapies are used with agoraphobics, the two treatments producing the best outcomes are pharmacotherapy and behavioral exposure therapy. Medication, specifically tricyclics or MAO inhibitors, are typically recommended in cases of agoraphobia with panic attacks because proponents of this approach believe panic is the underlying biological cause of the disorder, as discussed previously.

The most effective psychological treatment is *in vivo* exposure. Patients are encouraged to systematically and gradually confront the situations they fear and avoid (see Box 5.2). Exposure treatment reliably reduces phobic anxiety and avoidance behavior, as well as panic attacks. The benefits of this treatment usually extend to other aspects of the patient's life.

BOX 5.2 An Example of Exposure Treatment

Exposure treatment is more effective when patients are provided with a written manual detailing homework assignments between therapy sessions. These homework sessions are carried out under the therapist's direction. The following is an example of the contents of such a manual:

Summary of Treatment Plan

1. Practice facing the feared situations every day.
2. Plan progress from easier to difficult situations.
3. Expect to experience some fear when practicing; the point of the exercise is to cope with the feelings instead of overreacting to them.
4. Avoid relying on others or dwelling on your own problems and symptoms. Concentrate on help that leads to doing things for yourself.

Which would be the *wrong* thing to recommend for someone with agoraphobia?

a. Doing things one step at a time.
b. Practicing going out every day.
c. Having help from others with things like shopping.

---

a. Doing things one step at a time.

This is a good thing to recommend for someone with agoraphobia, as it builds up confidence for more difficult items. The question asked which was the wrong thing.

b. Practicing going out every day.

It is only by practice in facing the feared situations that the fear will be overcome, and it is important to get into the habit of doing this daily, so this cannot be wrong.

c. Having help from others with things like shopping.

Correct. It is not helpful in the long run to get someone else to do the shopping. It simply makes it easy for you to stay at home and makes the habit of avoidance stronger.

To help patients follow through with homework assignments, it is useful for a spouse or a former agoraphobic to accompany them to treatment and to assist in it, after having received training. Such individuals are provided with their own manual.

Source: From Mathews A.M., M.G. Gelder, & D.W. Johnston (1981). *Agoraphobia: Nature and treatment.* New York: Guilford Press. Reprinted with permission.

One group of prominent clinical researchers summarized these effects as follows: "We found a significant improvement in the quality of their lives; better functioning at home and at work, increased social life, expanded interests and activities, and improved interpersonal relationships. In general, there was a greater richness in the fabric of their lives" (Klein et al., 1983, p. 169).

Marital factors influence the maintenance of treatment effects. A caring spouse may provide emotional support that helps the agoraphobic persist in confronting rather than avoiding treatment situations (Arnow, Taylor, Agras, & Telch, 1985). Agoraphobics with good marriages at the onset of exposure treatment maintain the reductions they make on phobic anxiety and avoidance better than their counterparts with poor marriages (Bland & Hallam, 1981). Including husbands in their agoraphobic wives' exposure treatment program (couples training) produced superior results to treating wives alone (Barlow et al., 1983).

Just as a complete understanding of panic disorder and agoraphobia requires a biopsychosocial perspective, so too might the most effective treatment involve a combination of drugs and behavior therapy. For example, Telch et al. (1985) found that the combination of exposure treatment and medication (imipramine) produced better results than either the drug alone or exposure plus a drug placebo.

Generalized Anxiety Disorder

Characteristics. *DSM-III-R* defines **generalized anxiety disorder** (GAD) as unrealistic and excessive anxiety about two or more life situations (e.g., family, finances or job) for a period of six months or longer. Symptoms include motor tension (e.g., feeling shaky), autonomic hyperactivity (e.g., shortness of breath or dizziness), and extreme vigilance (e.g., difficulty concentrating). GAD involves what has been called **free-floating anxiety,** or anxiety that is not attached to any specific stimulus or situation. Age of onset is variable, although usually in late adolescence or early adulthood. This disorder is illustrated in the following clinical case study:

> *Ray is a thirty-two-year-old rock musician. About five years before his evaluation at the clinic, he had begun to feel very anxious and nervous and found it difficult to sit still. He also found himself worrying constantly about his career, although he had more bookings than ever and had achieved financial independence. Although he had previously been a heavy cocaine user, he found that cocaine caused him to be intolerably nervous. Also, he found that marijuana and alcohol which used to calm him down no longer did so. He reported most* DSM-III-R *symptoms of motor tension, including trembling, twitching or feeling shaky, muscle tension and restlessness, and autonomic hyperactivity; he exhibited extreme vigilance and scanning during the interview. He was able, however, to sit in the chair for the entire interview. He often felt irritable and had more trouble dealing with frustration than before this episode began* (Taylor & Arnow, 1988, p. 104).

The population prevalence of GAD is about 4 percent, with men and women equally affected. The incidence of GAD is roughly four times that of panic disorder yet analyses of patients treated in anxiety clinics indicate that panic disorder is seen far more frequently (Barlow, 1988). It appears that GAD patients only seek specialized psychological or psychiatric care when their physical symptoms become too severe. Otherwise, they are likely to put up with their "worrying" or see a general medical practitioner.

Causes. As with other anxiety disorders, GAD runs in families. Relatives of people with GAD show a higher frequency of it than relatives of control, panic disorder, and agoraphobic patients (Noyes et al., 1987). Unlike panic disorder, however, there is no difference in the frequency of anxiety disorders among MZ and DZ twins of people with GAD (Torgersen, 1983). Compared to panic disorder, GAD is associated with fewer physical symptoms and has an earlier and more gradual onset. Also, GAD patients experience more secondary depression than patients with panic (Noyes et al., 1987).

GAD is characterized by excessive worry. The cognitive dimension of anxiety seems especially prominent in this disorder so psychologists have studied the way people with GAD cognitively process information related to perceived threat or danger. Research has shown that such individuals react more sensitively to threat cues than do normal controls. In a study by Mathews and MacLeod (1986) two groups of subjects, one of patients with GAD and the other normal controls, participated in a test of divided attention, called a dichotic listening task. Subjects attended to a list of words presented in one ear (the attended channel) and were asked to repeat them aloud as they heard them (known as shadowing). Subjects also had to complete a reaction time task as they listened to the words. Both neutral and threat words were presented in the other ear (the unattended channel). Examples of the threat words were *emergency, desperate,* and *terrified.* Results showed that the threat words, not the neutral words, interfered with GAD patients' shadowing and slowed their responses on the reaction time test. They were attending selectively to the threat cues, resulting in impaired performance on the attended channel. In contrast, normal control subjects were unaffected by the threat words. That subjects did not recognize the words in the unattended channel is of particular significance. Their attentional bias in cognitive processing occurred before the words entered their awareness. But people with GAD are unaware of selectively attending to threat cues in their environment. This attentional vigilance for perceived threat, nevertheless, elicits the anxiety they experience.

A subsequent study has shown that although GAD patients selectively attend to threat cues, once perceived they then inhibit or cognitively avoid them (Mogg, Mathews, & Weinman, 1987). This secondary avoidance prevents patients from accurately evaluating threat cues and learning they have no reason to worry. Thus the vigilance–avoidance pattern of cognitive processing helps maintain generalized anxiety.

Treatment. The most frequent treatment for GAD has been the use of drugs, specifically benzodiazepines, though they have short-lived effectiveness (Salzman, 1989). Cognitive-behavioral treatment of GAD is similar to that of social phobia, combining relaxation training, cognitive restructuring to help patients identify and alter specific anxiety-provoking thoughts, and guided exposure for overcoming avoidance behavior. Fully two thirds of GAD patients report avoidance behavior which is more diffuse than in simple phobia (Butler et al., 1987). Cognitive-behavioral treatment of this sort is significantly more effective than no treatment (Borkovec et al., 1987) but may not be more effective than other forms of psychological treatment (Borkovec & Mathews, 1988).

A classic study by Sloane et al. (1975) comparing psychoanalytic psychotherapy with behavior therapy and a waiting-list control group, contained a number of patients who would have been diagnosed as suffering from GAD. Overall, psychotherapy and behavior therapy produced equal success rates of roughly 80 percent, and both were superior to the control group with a 48 percent success rate. These findings suggest that different forms of psychotherapy may be effective in treating GAD.

Posttraumatic Stress Disorder

Characteristics. *DSM-III-R* diagnostic criteria for **posttraumatic stress disorder** (PTSD) are

1. The occurrence of a recognizable stressor or trauma (e.g., military combat).
2. The reexperiencing of the stressor (e.g., recurrent nightmares).
3. Persistent avoidance of stimuli associated with the stressor (e.g., attempts to block out thoughts or feelings about the trauma).

PTSD is caused by a range of life-threatening or personally devastating experiences, including experiences associated with war (combat, bombing, or torture); natural disasters such as floods or earthquakes; and airplane crashes, fires, and criminal assaults. Davidson and Baum (1986) assessed the impact of the nuclear accident at Three Mile Island in Pennsylvania on individuals living near the plant. They compared people living close to (within 5 miles) or far from (greater than 80 miles) the plant and found that those living close to it experienced significantly more symptoms of chronic stress and PTSD. Additionally, a link appeared between exposure to the stressor and the development of PTSD such that people who had experienced greater levels of stress subsequently showed higher levels of PTSD symptoms.

Symptoms may occur immediately after the traumatic event or emerge months, even years later. PTSD may produce mild to total impairment in functioning and involves biological as well as psychological and behavioral disturbance. Suicide and suicide attempts are not infrequent. A study of U.S. Army combat veterans of Vietnam found that within five years after returning to civilian life, they had an overall death rate 45 percent higher than veterans who had served elsewhere (Korea, West Germany, or the United States) during the same period. The suicide rate for the Vietnam combat veterans in the first five years after their separation from the military was 72 percent higher than that of other veterans of the Vietnam era who did not serve there (The Centers for Disease Control Vietnam Experience Study, 1987).

PTSD is illustrated in the following clinical case history:

Mr. K, a 43-year-old Vietnam combat veteran, was the second-oldest child from a working-class family dominated by a harsh father. His mother died of cancer when he was 13 and his father remarried a year later. Although Mr. K did well in school, he dropped out of school at age 17 to join the Navy for 4 years. During his Navy tour he married the first woman he had ever dated. They produced two children. Following discharge from the Navy he had difficulty finding satisfactory civilian employment and decided to join the Army.

After 6 years in the Army, he was sent to Vietnam as a staff sergeant in charge of a vehicle maintenance team. This tour of duty was punctuated with frequent traumatic combat experiences, including the death of a close friend, his shooting a Vietcong soldier at close range, seeing the death of a truck mate during a convoy attack, finding a burned crew inside a disabled tank, finding the remains of a driver inside a disabled personnel carrier, and witnessing the demolition of a village. The death of his close friend by sniper fire in a "safe" area was particularly traumatic; Mr. K felt personally responsible for their having been in an avoidable dangerous situation.

When he returned from Vietnam his marriage ended in divorce and he began drinking heavily. He received several Army disciplinary actions, usually for going absent without leave. After 3 years, Mr. K volun-

The Vietnam War Memorial in Washington, D.C. In addition to the thousands who lost their lives in this tragic war, it has been estimated that 0.5 to 1.2 million of the 2.8 million men and women who served in Vietnam may have suffered from posttraumatic stress disorder (PTSD).

> *teered for a second tour in Vietnam, which, in contrast to the first tour, was relatively uneventful.*
>
> *Following his second Vietnam tour he took a discharge from the Army. During the next 15 years, his life seriously deteriorated. He had two short marriages, lived in five different states, and had a long series of various jobs. He began having Vietnam-related nightmares and flashbacks. His abusive drinking became chronic, resulting in several stints on skid row. In addition to numerous alcohol treatments, there were several psychiatric hospitalizations for depression, anxiety, paranoia, and suicide attempts* (Foy et al., 1987, pp. 369–370).

A widely recognized group of people with PTSD are combat veterans from the Vietnam War. Of the 2.8 million Vietnam era veterans who served, 0.5 million to 1.2 million may have suffered from PTSD (Wolfe, Keane, Lyons, & Gerardi, 1987). Diagnosis of PTSD in patients seeking treatment is as high as 70 percent for veterans who participated in combat and were wounded, but much lower (25 percent) for those with little combat exposure (Foy et al., 1987).

The prevalence of PTSD in the general population was assessed in an epidemiological study by Helzer, Robins, and McEvoy (1987), with interviews of more than 2,493 household residents in the St. Louis area, selected as a representative sample of the U.S. population. This study's strength was its sampling of not only a group known to be at special risk for PTSD (e.g., Vietnam veterans) but also the general population. Among the population as a whole only 5 men and 13 women per 1,000 had met the criteria for PTSD at some point in their lives. Considerably more people had experienced some criteria without meeting the full diagnostic criteria. For men the main causes were combat in Vietnam; for women it was threat (e.g., physical attack such as rape) or seeing someone hurt or die. The most common symptoms were nightmares, a feeling of jumpiness, and trouble sleeping. Two symptoms, included because they were thought to characterize the Vietnam syndrome—emotional numbing and guilt at having survived or having done the acts necessary to survive—were rare, even among combat veterans. Men or women with PTSD were twice as likely to have some other disorder as were persons without it. The most commonly associated disorders were obsessive-compulsive disorder, chronic depression, and manic-depressive disorder.

Causes. Classical conditioning helps to explain the development of PTSD as stimuli associated with a severe trauma (the unconditioned stimulus) elicit stress responses that were part of the original trauma. The more severe the trauma, the greater the likelihood of PTSD (Foy et al., 1987). Moreover, repeated exposure to stimuli associated with the trauma in the ensuing months reduces distress, just as we would expect from the extinction of a conditioned response (Wirtz & Harrell, 1987). Exposure to a traumatic event, nevertheless, is a necessary but insufficient condition for the development of PTSD. As with phobias, not everyone who experiences a traumatic event shows symptoms of the disorder. For example, the majority of Vietnam combat veterans did not develop PTSD, and many actually felt that their experience strengthened them emotionally.

A variety of physical, psychological, and social factors help determine the onset of the disorder. For example, preexisting clinical problems facilitate its development. In their comprehensive study, Helzer et al. (1987) found that individuals with behavioral problems before age fifteen (e.g., stealing, lying, truancy, fighting, and substance abuse) were significantly more likely to develop PTSD or some of its symptoms than those without these childhood problems. Similarly, individuals with a family history of psychiatric problems are much more likely to develop PTSD if exposed to military combat than those with no such background (Foy et al., 1987). On the positive side, social support protects against PTSD. The stronger their social network of family or friends, the less chance of developing the disorder (Barlow, 1988).

A Historical Note. PTSD was first studied in nineteenth-century England following a series of railway accidents (Goodwin, 1986). In World War I it was known as *shell shock,* and in World War II and the Korean War as *combat exhaustion* or *combat fatigue.* The diagnosis and the disorder have always been controversial. In World War I, the response to it was both disciplinary and medical. The German Army outlawed shell shock and declared that victims would be shot. The result was that no cases were reported! (Goodwin, 1986) Other punitive measures were taken by French and British authorities against soldiers who succumbed to shell shock without being exposed to bursting artillery shells. During this period, however, Freud advanced the concept of **repetition compulsion** to explain many of the features of PTSD. According to Freud, recurrent, intrusive dreams were an attempt to overcome psychological fixation on the traumatic event. Perhaps partly because of these ideas, PTSD was treated more humanely in World War II, Korea, and Vietnam. Mental health experts learned that immediate counseling was the most effective way to help soldiers suffering from it. This would be as close to the battle scene as possible, with the expectation to return to duty quickly.

In 1980, after considerable debate, the American Psychiatric Association included the diagnosis of PTSD in *DSM-III.* The Veterans Administration agreed that veterans with PTSD could be financially compensated since their problems were now regarded as service-related, even if they appeared long after discharge from the military. Some critics were skeptical, using the term *compensation neurosis* to describe the delayed onset of stress symptoms. But PTSD had been reported well before it became compensatable; Freud had even described the delay between the trauma and the appearance of symptoms.

The unusual nature of the war probably contributed to the delayed onset of PTSD in Vietnam veterans. Because of the war's unpopularity in the United States, veterans were ignored rather than welcomed as heroes on their return. Only late in the 1980s did the country and its government formally recognize the sacrifices of those who had served in Vietnam. Apparently, it is important for society to provide returning soldiers with some sort of ritual welcome and acceptance (e.g., a ticker-tape parade or triumphal march, a national monument, and so on). Even primitive cultures had their rituals for returning warriors. These rituals help to alleviate the guilt of soldiers who have killed in battle and symbolize their reintegration and acceptance into society.

Treatment. PTSD has responded to a variety of treatments. "Rap" groups, a form of self-help group therapy, have been widely adopted to treat Vietnam veterans with PTSD. Because all members have shared the same kind of experiences, they are also able to share feelings and to develop a unique sense of understanding and trust. For the average case of PTSD, brief psychological treatment, possibly combined with an anti-anxiety drug to reduce the arousal and hyperalertness, is often sufficient.

Based on extensive clinical experience, Horowitz (1989) has developed a brief, twelve-session psychodynamic treatment for PTSD. The therapist first works to establish a trusting relationship with the patient. Within this "safe" therapeutic relationship, the patient is encouraged to explore self-identity and achieve increasing levels of self-awareness. The goal is for the patient to recognize and accept thoughts about the traumatic event that he or she had warded off. The therapy is illustrated in the following case of a twenty-five-year-old lifeguard at a neighborhood pool:

> *A small boy was drowned one hectic summer day before he realized anyone was in trouble. Subsequently, the lifeguard experienced guilt, anxiety, and a fear of dying himself. He had difficulty concentrating, and avoided pools and children. He developed recurrent nightmares about the event, and began to have difficulty relating to his friends.*
>
> *The beginning phase of psychotherapy was marked by his apathetic and distant response to the psychotherapist. This was ameliorated as the psychotherapist indicated an empathic recognition of the various experiences that the young man reported. The therapist's ability to link his experiences to responses of other persons who had traumatic events also seemed to encourage an increase in cooperation.*
>
> *In the middle phase of therapy an important and repetitive activity was to attempt to disentangle the realistic aspects of his responsibility as a lifeguard*

for the safety of everyone in the pool, and his fantasy elaborations of reasons why he was terribly guilty. In order to do this it was necessary to get beyond his surface statements that he had already worked through this issue, that it was the fault of others that there were too many people at the pool, and that he had acted in the best possible way under the circumstances and now was no longer remorseful. Part of this activity, after patiently going over all the events and associations, was to ask how much remorse he had to have, and to separate the issue of making up to others in whatever way he could for what had happened, from the need to be self-punitive, as in seeking to fail in his current career efforts.

This working through process led to turbulent feelings in which there was rage at the pool managers for putting him in an overly demanding situation, as well as rage at himself for not having acted sooner. During the same period of therapy the patient was encouraged to confront the neighborhood, the pool, and even the gravesite in a gradual manner, taking on whatever task he felt he could, and going there with companions. This led to some reaction towards the therapist, including rage that the therapist was expecting too much of him, and a warded off but gradually emergent feeling that "recovery was too good for him." It was also important to work through memories of how he had piled toys onto his unwanted younger brother in an effort to get rid of him when the patient was only four years old himself.

As termination approached he became very frightened that his improvement would prove to be dependent on being with the therapist, and that he would quickly relapse after the treatment ended. Nonetheless by the next to last session he himself felt that he could stop at the appointed time, provided he could return for follow up visits if needed (Horowitz, 1989, pp. 2078–2080).

Behavioral methods, particularly imaginal exposure and densensitization, have also proved useful in treating PTSD (Keane & Kaloupek, 1982). The patient is asked repeatedly to conjure up detailed imagery of the events associated with the traumatic experience and to focus on it until the initial anxiety decreases. Repeated exposure of this kind under a therapist's guidance results in clinically significant reductions in the patient's subjective and physiological arousal in response to the imagery prior to therapy. Disappearance of the intrusive thoughts and sleep disturbance typically follows.

Chronic PTSD, especially with marked depressive symptoms, has also been treated with antidepressants. Both tricyclics and MAO inhibitors have been associated with a decrease in intensity and frequency of prolonged nightmares, flashbacks, panic attacks and episodes of anxiety as well as an improvement in mood and the ability to modulate anger.

Obsessive-Compulsive Disorder

Characteristics. **Obsessions** are unwanted intrusive and repetitive thoughts, images, or impulses. For example, a highly religious person might be plagued with blasphemous thoughts; a gentle, nonviolent individual might have repeated images of mutilated corpses; or a concerned parent might experience reoccurring impulses to injure a loved child. Obsessional impulses are often associated with the fear of losing control. They are almost never acted upon, and the person typically tries to suppress or neutralize them with some other thought or action. Unwanted, unacceptable thoughts are called *ego-dystonic*. The person realizes the obsession is a product of his or her own mind. This quality, and that the individual actively resists thinking obsessively, distinguishes an obsession from a psychotic delusion.

The most common obsessions involve themes of aggression, dirt and contamination, sex, religion, and doubt. The following case is an example of obsessive doubt. Ted was a college sophomore who became unable to drive a car:

Despite being a careful driver with no history of any accident, he obsessed about having hit something or someone. Often he would pull over to the side of the road to check his car. Also, after he arrived home he would check the car for any marks. This would be followed by phone calls to the local newspaper, police station, and hospital to see if any hit-and-run accident had been reported. In addition, he would continually ask his mother if she thought he had hit someone. [Demands for repeated reassurance are common among obsessive-compulsive individuals.] All these attempts to neutralize his thoughts of having hit someone had, however, only transitory effects. He continued to be worried about driving. His anxiety became so intense that he began to avoid it entirely (Authors' Files).

Roughly half of the patients with this disorder have more than one obsession. For example, Ted would also obsessively worry about whether he had turned off all the electrical appliances whenever he left his house. And he would spend hours worrying about having said something rude or offensive which would make someone angry with him, even though he was a very polite, gentle person.

Compulsions are repetitive, stereotyped, and intentional acts. The two main types of compulsive acts, or rituals, are cleaning and checking. The classic example of the first type is the compulsive hand washer; a common example of the second is the person who compulsively checks the security of appliances and of entrances to his or her home. Compulsive acts are to neutralize or prevent either discomfort or some feared event. Patients realize their behavior is unreasonable or excessive though, when pressed, some will insist that the obsession or compulsion has a rational basis. For example, a compulsive hand washer might argue that without this activity he could contract an illness ("It's better to be safe than sorry"). This is known as an **overvalued idea.** Yet, even here the person will admit the behavior is excessive.

Compulsive rituals may be covert as well as overt. Patients use mental strategies like thinking a "good thought" or conjuring up a particular image to neutralize distressing obsessional thoughts or images.

Obsessive-compulsive disorder not only causes severe personal distress but also impairs social, occupational, and sexual functioning. The following case illustrates the devastating effects of the disorder:

> *The patient was obsessed with the fear of contamination by germs. As a result she engaged in prolonged and intensive washing and cleaning rituals. Her young child was restrained in one room of the four-bedroom house, as it was the only one that she could keep satisfactorily free from germs. Three of the rooms were kept permanently locked because she was incapable of ensuring that they were sufficiently sterile. She used an extraordinarily large amount of disinfectants to clean her house and to wash herself and her child. As is common with many of these patients, she was particularly agitated by contact with doors and doorknobs, and therefore learned how to open a door with her feet in order to avoid contaminating her hands. The large and complicated series of rituals that had to be carried out in preparing food meant that the family was kept on a restricted diet. Meals were seldom complete and rarely ready on time. The patient's fear of contamination made her virtually housebound, and her child was not permitted to leave the house except on a very few essential occasions. On returning from work each day, her husband was obliged to go through a series of decontaminating-cleaning rituals. Their sexual relationship, never satisfactory, had been abandoned because of her fears of contamination. Their social life was damaged beyond repair, and they had lost all but one of their friends; even the members of their families could neither visit them nor be visited by them. Although the patient had been a competent, trained secretary, returning to work was out of the question* (Rachman & Hodgson, 1980).

On average, obsessive-compulsive patients have superior intelligence (Rachman & Hodgson, 1980). Among those who have suffered from this disorder were such noted figures as the seventeenth-century English writer John Bunyan (author of *A Pilgrim's Progress*) and Howard Hughes, the American billionaire. Bunyan, who became deeply religious following a morally lax early life, coined the term *pollution of the mind* to describe the unacceptable and blasphemous thoughts that tormented him. In his final years, Hughes constructed a sterile, isolated environment to keep his contact with potentially contaminating

Howard Hughes was one of America's most colorful and successful billionaires. An airline pioneer and tycoon, he developed a severe obsessive-compulsive disorder later in his life and secluded himself in a sterile, isolated environment to avoid direct contact with people or certain objects.

people to a minimum, avoided touching any person or object directly, and covered himself with paper tissues and other protective materials.

The typical age of onset of this disorder is late adolescence or early adulthood. The epidemiologic catchment area study of five U.S. communities shows prevalence of obsessive-compulsive disorder ranging from 1.9 percent to 3.3 percent of the general population (Karno et al., 1988). Equal numbers of men and women develop the disorder, and it is less common among African-Americans. The impact on the family can be devastating as family members find it difficult if not impossible to avoid being drawn into the patient's obsessive-compulsive rituals, as the case of the woman with the germ obsession shows. Many obsessives do not marry, and those who do have a greater than average incidence of marital and sexual problems.

Obsessions and compulsions are on a continuum from those that are clearly abnormal to those that are normal. Not only patients with obsessive-compulsive disorder but also a majority of people experience obsessions and compulsions. Normal obsessions generally reported by nonclinical individuals resemble abnormal obsessions in patients in form and content. But abnormal obsessions are more frequent, are more intense, cause more personal distress, and cannot be controlled. A large study of college students, for example, showed that 10 percent to 15 percent reported rates of compulsive checking that were within the clinical range. Another 40 percent reported more limited compulsions (Frost, Sher, & Geen, 1986). Significantly, nonclinical checkers were more depressed and anxious than noncheckers. These results support the view that obsessions and compulsions are a response to psychological stress and represent attempts to establish some form of personal control.

Obsessive-compulsive disorder must be distinguished from **compulsive personality.** A study of ninety-six patients with obsessive-compulsive disorder showed that only six patients met the diagnostic criteria for compulsive personality disorder (Baer et al., 1990). Compulsive personalities are unusually tidy, orderly, and even rigid in their daily routines. Yet, they do not regard their behavior as unwanted, unacceptable, or distressing. Nor are patients with an obsessive-compulsive disorder necessarily compulsive in all aspects of their functioning. Rachman and Hodgson (1980) note this inconsistency in their description of the homes of these patients:

> We learned to expect that the homes of compulsive cleaners would contain a bizarre mixture of excessively clean areas and indescribably dirty parts as well. In the same home, the lavatory might be brightly clean and strongly disinfected while parts of the kitchen were caked with month-old food remains. (Incidentally, this peculiar contrast is often encountered in the patients themselves—a compulsive cleaner who washes her hands 200 times per day may leave her legs and feet unwashed for months and wear the same dirty underwear for weeks on end.) In some cases the accumulation of debris and dirt was directly attributable to the patient's inability to come into contact with dirty or contaminated objects. In other cases the dirt and disarray reflected the patient's inability to cope with the daily requirements of living (Rachman & Hodgson, 1980, p. 65).

The Biological Model. A high proportion of the families of individuals with obsessive-compulsive disorder have reported psychological disorders. For example, McKeon and Murray (1987) studied relatives of fifty obsessive-compulsive patients and those of carefully matched control subjects who had no psychiatric disorder. The first-degree relatives of the obsessive-compulsive patients had a significantly higher rate of lifetime psychiatric disorders than the relatives of the nonpsychiatric control patients. For example, the former showed markedly greater rates of depression and generalized anxiety disorder than the latter. The two groups of relatives did not, however, differ in prevalence, which was very rare, of obsessive-compulsive disorder. Among the 149 relatives of the obsessive-compulsive patients and the 151 relatives of the controls, only one case of it in each group was diagnosed. McKeon and Murray concluded that a "neurotic tendency," not obsessive-compulsive disorder, is transmitted from first-degree relatives to patients. Evidence of a genetic rather than a socially learned origin of this transmission comes from twin studies showing that the concordance rate for anxiety disorders between MZ twins is higher than that for DZ pairs. There is little evidence that this higher concordance applies to obsessive-compulsive disorder. McKeon and Murray speculate that the inherited neurotic tendency appears in a subclinical form in the preexisting (i.e., premorbid) personality difficulties of obsessive-compulsive patients, with the final expression of the disorder determined by stressful life events.

Recent research using PET scans has revealed that specific parts of the brain of patients with obsessive-compulsive disorder metabolize glucose (i.e., burn energy) more rapidly than the same brain areas in patients with other mental disorders (Baxter et al., 1987). The brain areas are the basal ganglia, particularly the **caudate nucleus** (see Figure 5.3). Identifying brain mechanisms involved in obsessive-compulsive disorder does not address the causes of the problem. But the research has shown that brain chemistry abnormalities seem to play a role, and it provides scientists a powerful tool for further study of causes and treatment.

The neurotransmitter **serotonin** is involved in the pathophysiology of obsessive-compulsive disorder.

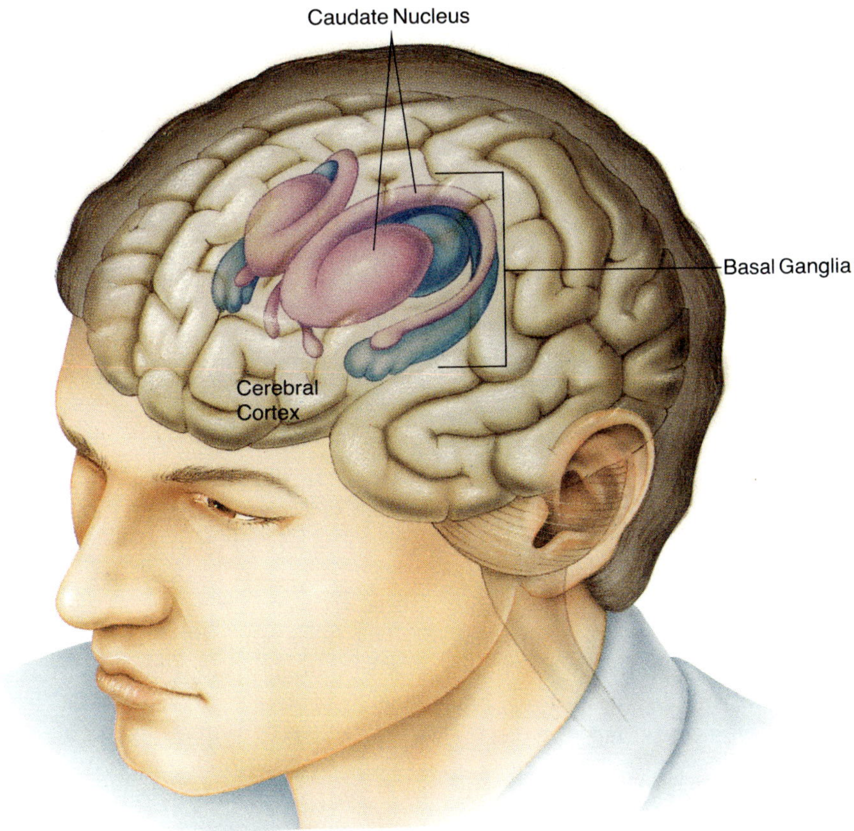

Figure 5.3 Specific brain areas involved in obsessive-compulsive disorder.

Source: From *The New York Times* (1988), Vol. 137, March 8, page C1. Copyright © 1988 by *The New York Times Company.* Reprinted with permission.

The brain areas that show abnormal activity in obsessive-compulsives depend greatly on serotonin. Drugs that have shown the best results in treating obsessive-compulsive disorder increase the amount of serotonin in the brain (Zohar & Insel, 1987). To test this serotonin hypothesis, Zohar et al. (1987) administered either a serotonin **agonist** or a placebo to groups of obsessive-compulsive patients and matched healthy patients. An agonist is a drug or chemical that stimulates activity in particular nerve cells—just as a key might open a lock. Subjects who received it increased their production of serotonin. The serotonin agonist, not the placebo, produced a significant increase in patients' obsessive-compulsive symptoms, self-rated anxiety, depression, dysphoria, and self-reality (i.e., feeling out of touch with reality and having unusual thoughts). In contrast, the agonist had no effect on the healthy controls.

If directly increasing serotonin causes obsessive-compulsive disorder to worsen, why does indirectly increasing it by administering clomipramine result in the patient's improvement? Zohar et al. (1987) point to animal studies showing that long-term treatment with the drug helps shut down post-synaptic serotonin receptors. So even if more serotonin is available for neural transmission, its effects are decreased.

Obsessive-compulsive symptoms frequently occur among patients with **Gilles de la Tourette's syndrome** (TS), characterized by intermittent tics (i.e., sudden jerks of the head and other body parts), sounds (e.g., barks or yelps), and words (e.g., obscenities). The rate of obsessive-compulsive disorder among the first-degree relatives of patients with TS is significantly higher than estimates from the general population and a control sample of adoptive relatives (Pauls et al., 1986). This suggests some common causal genetic relationship between the two disorders.

The Psychodynamic Model. The psychodynamic view is that obsessive-compulsive disorder occurs in people with a particular type of personality—what Freud called an **"anal-erotic" personality.** A triad of traits—*orderliness, stinginess,* and *obstinacy*—characterize such people. These character traits result from fixation of psychosexual development at the anal stage of personality growth. Toilet training occurs during the anal stage, providing the child's first experience of externally imposed control over an instinctual impulse, that is, defecation. Severe toilet training is said to lead to a child's pleasure in retaining feces, expressed symbolically later in life in the traits of orderliness, obstinacy, and stinginess.

The evidence indicates that the three traits identified by Freud do cluster together, and there is a loose relationship between the occurrence of the disorder and obsessional traits that existed prior to it as predicted by psychodynamic theory (Fisher & Greenberg, 1977). Yet many people become obsessive-compulsive without ever having displayed premorbid obsessional traits. A concern with orderliness does not discriminate obsessive-compulsive patients from other nonobsessive anxiety disorder patients (Rachman & Hodgson, 1980). Orderliness does not appear to be a specific precursor of obsessive-compulsive disorder. Perhaps most critically, the psychodynamic formation has failed to produce an effective treatment for obsessive-compulsive disorders.

The Cognitive-Behavioral Model. This model begins by assuming a nonspecific genetic predisposition to experience anxiety. It further hypothesizes that the individual grows up in an overcontrolling home environment, leading to rigid standards of personal conduct and vulnerability to self-criticism. These early learning experiences result in a low threshold for regarding certain thoughts and images as unacceptable, whereas the same thoughts would be acceptable to nonobsessive people (Rachman & Hodgson, 1980). Consider, for example, sexual thoughts or images. They often form the content of clinical obsessions because patients find them unacceptable. Yet, virtually all college students view them as acceptable. Over 75 percent of the college student population report thinking about sex every day (Eysenck, 1976).

Stressful events and depressive mood precipitate obsessions. Depressed mood is commonly associated with the onset of obsessions. Although depression is not a necessary factor, it may be a sufficient condition for causing obsessions. Also, obsessions can lead to depression (Weiner et al., 1976) as illustrated in the following case:

Stuart Sutherland is an experimental psychologist at the University of Sussex, England, with an international reputation in his field. In the early 1970s he suffered a severe mental breakdown. When he recovered, he wrote a revealing book, Breakdown *(1976), describing his disorder and the treatment he received.*

His breakdown began when his wife disclosed to him that she had been having an affair with a close colleague and friend of his. At first, he experienced intense anxiety and obsessive jealousy. He described his obsession as follows: "It was as though only a single track in my brain was operating—whatever I tried to do led back to the same agonizing groove of jealousy. I was obsessed with visions of Josie's affair, and for hours on end my mind would be crowded with a succession of hideously detailed visual images of the sexual activities that she had (engaged in). . . . At times I did fight to regain some measure of control. I would drag myself into my office for two or three hours at a time thinking I was being very courageous. When I went to work, I could do none.

In response to his anxiety and obsessive jealousy, Sutherland "was seized by a compulsion to tell my wife not merely of every disloyal act that I had ever committed but of every disreputable thought that had ever crossed my mind. I knew I should not do this, but unprompted, some incident would come to mind and I would shake with anxiety as I struggled not to reveal it" (Sutherland, 1976, p. 6).

Sutherland finally became seriously depressed and was hospitalized.

As a result of their genetic heritage and personality, obsessives seem more vulnerable to these stressors. They are less able to resist the obsessions and are more distressed by and have greater difficulty dismissing them.

The behavioral model of the etiology of compulsions is similar. Additional assumptions are that compulsive cleaners come from an overcontrolling and protective environment (which fosters a fearful, noncoping disposition) and that checkers came from overcontrolling and overcritical families (an environment which fosters obsessional doubt and the need to check "to make sure"). This account of etiology remains speculative. Empirical support is lacking, particularly with regard to hypothesized familial influences.

The behavioral model has been more helpful in understanding the maintenance of compulsive behavior. It assumes that compulsions constitute a form of escape or avoidance behavior, as they reduce anxiety, reinforcing the compulsion (Walton & Mather, 1963). Preventing obsessives from engaging in or completing a compulsive ritual will increase their anxiety. (Under the influence of psychodynamic theorizing, it is widely believed that interrupting compulsive rituals will have harmful consequences for the person). This prediction follows from the assumption that compulsions are a form of psychic defense, which if removed, would lead to emotional turmoil in the individual.

Rachman and his colleagues at the Institute of Psychiatry in London carried out a series of studies to test the anxiety-reduction theory. In the basic experiment, obsessive-compulsive patients agreed to touch an object considered "contaminated." They were allowed to wash their hands either immediately or after periods of thirty and sixty minutes. Their self-reported anxiety and heart rate were measured before they touched the object, during the time they were waiting to wash their hands, and after washing. Figure 5.4 summarizes the results. As predicted, touching the contaminated object increases anxiety

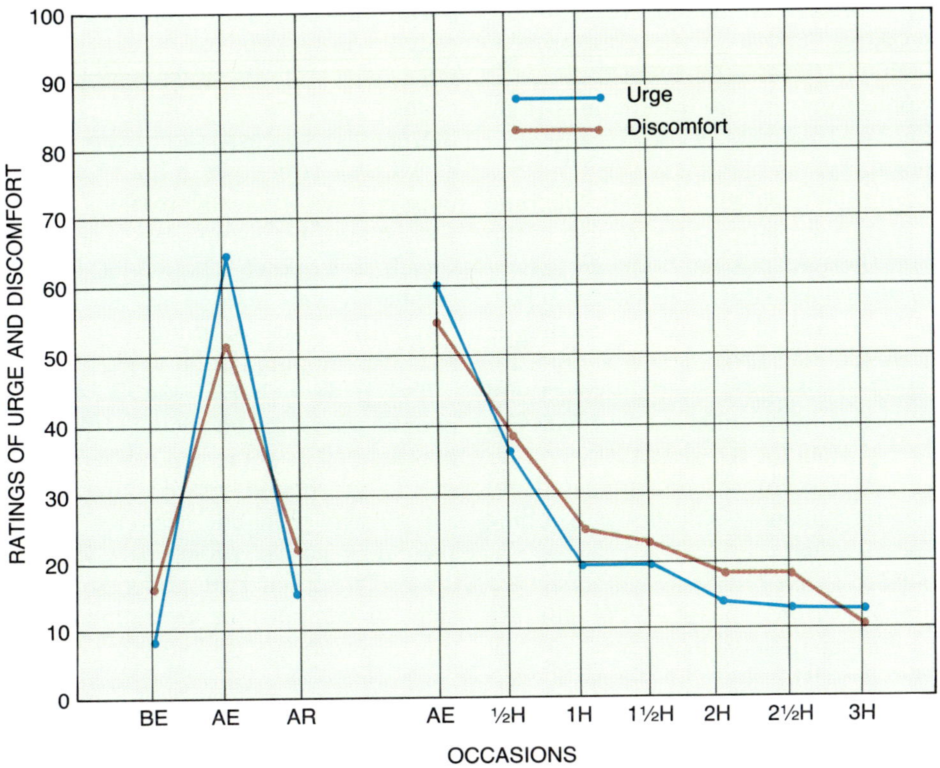

Figure 5.4 Mean ratings of urge and discomfort before and after exposure to a provoking stimulus. *(BE = before exposure; AE = after exposure; AR = after ritual).*
Source: From Stanley J. Rachman & Ray J. Hodgson, (1980), *Obsessions and Compulsions.* Englewood Cliffs, NJ: Prentice-Hall. Reprinted with permission.

or discomfort,[5] and completion of the compulsive activity reduces anxiety/discomfort. But interrupting the compulsive washing did not increase anxiety/discomfort, contrary to the behavioral and psychodynamic models' predictions.

Compulsions usually reduce anxiety or discomfort, but compulsive rituals persist in some individuals even though they fail to reduce anxiety and may even increase it. These data are difficult to reconcile with the anxiety-reduction theory. One possibility is that although some compulsions produce short-term anxiety, they prevent even greater long-term anxiety. For example, a checker may be willing to tolerate the discomfort and effort of compulsively checking whether electrical alliances are turned off to forestall the threat of a disaster like fire at some time in the future. The cognitive-behavioral perspective emphasizes that our behavior is influenced more by anticipated consequences than by immediate consequences (Bandura, 1986).

Obsessions, like phobic stimuli, elicit anxiety and discomfort. Why then do obsessions persist? They do not extinguish over time as the learning-based behavioral model predicts. While nonobsessional people can control and dismiss their normal obsessions, obsessive-compulsive patients cannot control theirs. Acquiring such control requires more systematic and prolonged exposure to them than is the case in the naturally occurring disorder.

Treatment. Obsessive-compulsive disorders have been difficult to treat and success rates were very poor until recently. Virtually all forms of physical and psychological therapy have been attempted. Traditional psychotherapy has proved ineffective and is not recommended (Goodwin, 1986; Rachman & Wilson, 1980).

A significant advance was made in the 1970s with the development of specific behavioral methods for treating cleaning and checking compulsions. The most effective treatment is exposure and **response prevention,** which can be illustrated with compulsive hand washers. The different objects or activities leading the patient to wash his or her hands are first identified through behavioral assessment. Then, following a thorough explanation of the technique and its rationale, and with the patient's fully informed consent, touching objects that trigger hand washing is systematically encouraged. This is the exposure part of treatment. Once the patient has touched what

[5] Rachman and Hodgson (1980) refer to anxiety or discomfort because some of their parents reported a negative feeling that was not accurately described as anxiety. The broader term *anxiety/discomfort* takes this into account.

is unrealistically viewed as contaminated, he or she refrains from washing. This is the response prevention part of treatment. In some inpatient treatments using strict response prevention, the therapist may ask the patient before treatment begins to consent to having no opportunity for hand washing. The patient's anxiety typically rises after initially touching the object and then decreases over the course of the session. Focusing the patient's attention on fear of contamination assists the treatment (Steketee & Foa, 1985). Note that the result of reduction in anxiety is contrary to those theories predicting a serious increase in emotional turmoil if the compulsive activity is prevented. The goal of treatment is to break the negative reinforcing value of the compulsion, extinguish the anxiety elicited by the contaminated object, and enhance the patient's self-efficacy in coping with this kind of situation.

Imaginal exposure is used in cases when *in vivo* exposure is impractical or impossible. Patients are instructed to conjure up detailed imagery of compulsive activities and stay with these images until their anxiety decreases. Box 5.3 shows how this is used in treating an obsessive-compulsive hand washer.

A combination of *in vivo* and imaginal exposure seems to provide optimal results. Foa et al. (1980) tested the effects of combined *in vivo* and imaginal exposure versus *in vivo* exposure only. Although at the end of treatment no differences between groups were observed, the combined techniques were superior in maintaining improvement.

Controlled research and uncontrolled clinical reports from different countries consistently show roughly 65 percent to 75 percent of obsessive-compulsives are cured or markedly improved following cognitive-behavioral treatment (Barlow, 1988). This therapeutic success is maintained during follow-ups as long as two years after treatment. Therapeutic improvement typically extends beyond the obsessive-compulsive symptoms to include occupational, social, and sexual functioning. Exposure treatment commonly eliminates or reduces the frequency of the compulsive rituals and improves marital or interpersonal functioning (Cobb et al., 1980).

Two patient characteristics have been linked to a poor outcome in behavioral treatment. The first is depression. In depressed patients, their depression should be reduced before addressing their obsessive-compulsive problem (Steketee & Foa, 1985). The second negative prognostic factor is overvalued ideas: The more that patients believe their obsessions or compulsions are rational, the more difficult they are to treat (Steketee & Foa, 1985).

Although *in vivo* exposure and response prevention seem essential in eliminating compulsive rituals, effective treatment must frequently include supplementary behavioral strategies. The clinician usually needs to involve family members in the treatment process, especially if they are to help the patient with exposure and response prevention. We have already emphasized the inevitable impact of obsessive-compulsive disorder on the individual's family. Spouses or family members are not always easily co-opted into the treatment program, and marital or family therapy

BOX 5.3 Imaginal Exposure in the Treatment of an Obsessive-Compulsive Hand Washer

The patient, Steve, felt contaminated by feces, urine, sweat, and contact with others. He feared contracting a debilitating disease. Each treatment session included exposure in imagery to contaminants and disastrous consequences.

Scene 1

Steve was asked to imagine touching newspapers, doorknobs, and other objects, all of which elicited moderate to severe anxiety. He was also asked to imagine that after touching these objects, he contracted hepatitis and became seriously ill.

Scene 2

Steve was asked to imagine touching newspapers and doorknobs with the addition of sweat. Fears of disease and debilitation are incorporated as above.

Scene 3

The patient was requested to imagine contact with newspapers, doorknobs, sweat, and toilet seats from public bathrooms along with feared disastrous consequences.

Scene 4

Steve imagined contact with newspapers, doorknobs, sweat, toilet seats, and urine. Feared consequences were incorporated into the scene.

Scene 5

Steve imagined contact with items from session 4 with the addition of feces from a soiled piece of toilet paper. Feared diseases and their effects were focused upon in detail.

Additional scenes were constructed as needed to include fears described by Steve. Imagined contact with the three most disturbing contaminants under various circumstances was continued during each treatment session and lesser contaminants were included periodically until they no longer evoked discomfort. Each session was taped on a cassette, recorded, and given to the patient to be played again at home that day (p. 135).

Source: From Steketee, G., and Foa, E. 1985. Obsessive-compulsive disorder. In D. H. Barlow (Ed.) Clinical handbook of psychological disorders: a step-by-step treatment manual. New York: Guilford Press, pp. 69–146. Reprinted with permission.

may be necessary to produce treatment effects and to help maintain therapeutic improvement.

A wide range of different drugs has been used to treat obsessive-compulsives with limited success. The most effective is clomipramine, a tricyclic antidepressant (see Chapter 17). Clomipramine is superior to other tricyclic drugs (Leonard et al., 1989) and has specific antiobsessive and anticompulsive effects. Yet only two thirds of the patients treated with clomipramine respond, and even they are not free from obsessions and compulsions (Zohar et al., 1989).

Aside from its limited effects, clomipramine has negative physical side effects, such as the loss of sexual function in most male and female patients. Relapse typically occurs upon withdrawal of the drug. For these reasons, it is recommended to combine drug therapy with exposure and response prevention.

The newest drugs used to treat obsessive-compulsive disorder are fluoxetine and fluvoxamine. Initial studies indicate that both are more effective than placebo treatment and also superior to another antidepressant drug (desipramine) that does not increase serotonin in the brain as strongly and directly (Goodman et al., 1990).

The intractable nature of some obsessive-compulsive disorders has resulted in radical treatments, even **psychosurgery,** involving surgical destruction of certain neural pathways in the brain. In leucotomy, the most commonly used surgery, the nerve pathways between the frontal cortex and the hypothalamus are severed. The justification for this treatment is that it often succeeds where other methods have failed (Tippin & Henn, 1982). No one has explained why psychosurgery has specific therapeutic effects on obsessions or compulsions.

SUMMARY

1. Anxiety is a central concept in the study of abnormal behavior. The biological perspective emphasizes that anxiety originates in the brain, where specific brain cells are activated or inhibited by specific chemical substances. Messages from the brain arouse the autonomic nervous system which is responsible for many of the signs of anxiety, such as increased heart rate and blood pressure.
2. The psychodynamic perspective traces anxiety to unconscious impulses stemming from early childhood conflict. These impulses threaten the ego and are repressed. Anxiety occurs when the impulses break through the defense of repression.
3. According to the cognitive-behavioral perspective, anxiety is a learned response based on aversive or stressful circumstances. Anxiety includes the different response systems of avoidance behavior, physiological arousal, and subjective self-report.
4. Anxiety disorders are the most common mental health problem in the United States. Simple phobia is the excessive fear and avoidance of specific situations or objects. Vulnerability to becoming phobic seems to be associated with a social-learning history of unpredictable events over which the individual feels little control, or self-efficacy. Phobias can be rapidly and effectively treated using exposure therapy in which phobics learn to confront and cope with feared situations or objects.
5. Social phobia is a persistent fear of doing something embarrassing when observed by other people. There exists a genetic predisposition for developing the disorder. Social phobics have more associated clinical disorders than simple phobics. Treatment involves both anti-anxiety drugs and psychological methods.
6. Panic disorder, which may be diagnosed with or without agoraphobia, is defined by repeated attacks of intense anxiety which typically involve symptoms of heart palpitations, shortness of breath, or dizziness. The biological view hypothesizes that panic is a product of biochemical abnormality. Evidence indicates that panic occurs only when patients misinterpret benign physical sensations as a sign of some catastrophe. Panic disorder offers a good example of the need for a combined biopsychological model of abnormal behavior. Treatment involves anti-anxiety drugs and cognitive-behavioral treatment.
7. Agoraphobia is the avoidance of situations in which the individual fears some incapacitating event, such as a panic attack. Clinicians believe that agoraphobia develops in response to an initial panic attack, although epidemiological studies suggest that the disorder may occur even in the absence of panic attacks. Agoraphobia occurs predominantly in women. Cognitive-behavioral methods has proved most effective in treating this disorder.
8. Generalized anxiety disorder is excessive and unrealistic anxiety about two or more life situations lasting six months or longer. Treatment typically consists of tranquilizing drugs, or different psychological methods which appear equally effective.
9. Posttraumatic stress disorder (PTSD) is the fear and avoidance of specific stimuli associated with exposure to a traumatic event, such as military combat in Vietnam. PTSD is associated with other clinical disorders including depression and suicide. Preexisting psychological problems in childhood and adolescence predispose individuals to develop PTSD when confronted with a traumatic experience. A wide range of psychological treatments are used to treat PTSD.
10. Obsessions are repetitive thoughts or images which the person cannot dismiss. The most common obsessions involve themes of aggressions, doubt, sex, and contamination. Depression is often associated with obsessions. Compulsions are repeated and stereotyped rituals, such as hand washing, which temporarily reduce anxiety. Obsessions and compulsions typically occur together. Patients realize their behavior is irrational but are unable to stop it. Obsessive-compulsive disorder has devastating effects on the patient's personal and social functioning. It is one of the most difficult clinical disorders to treat. Compulsions are treated successfully with cognitive-behavioral methods, and new anti-anxiety drugs show some promise of therapeutic effects.

Diego Rivera, *Young Man with Stylograph, Portrait of Best Maugard* (1914). Oil on canvas, 31 3/4 × 25 5/8 inches. Courtesy of Private Collection, Mexico.

6 SOMATOFORM AND DISSOCIATIVE DISORDERS

Everyone has experienced the occasional ache, pain, or other unpleasant bodily sensation. For the most part, these real or perceived bodily sensations come and go with no ill effect. On occasion, however, they might be more serious and provide a bodily signal about illness or disease that requires medical treatment. Most of us can make this distinction fairly easily. Yet others seem more sensitive to real or perceived bodily sensations, interpret them as symptoms of undetected physical illness or disease, and continually seek medical treatment.

The clinical disorders explored in this chapter contributed to abnormal psychology's development at the turn of the century. Analysis and treatment of the somatoform and dissociative disorders were critically important in the emergence of psychoanalytic theory and therapy and helped shape the growth of the field of abnormal psychology. And these disorders remain some of the most intriguing but least understood clinical disorders.

SOMATOFORM DISORDERS

Soma means body, and **somatoform disorders** are the presence of symptoms typically associated with physical diseases, but no known organic basis or physiological mechanisms for them can be demonstrated. By exclusion then, the symptoms are linked to inferred psychological processes. Individuals with these disorders believe their symptoms are serious despite the absence of any physical disease. These patients may be distinguished by their scores on Cloninger's (1986) personality dimensions (see Chapter 2). Unlike patients with anxiety disorders, those with somatoform disorders are very high on novelty seeking. This means, for example, that they tend to be impulsive and vulnerable to pain, behavioral tendencies linked to a low neurobiological level of dopaminergic activity. An estimated 30 percent to 80 percent of patients who visit primary-care physicians complain of symptoms not fully explained by any physical problem (Barsky & Klerman, 1983). Patients with somatoform disorders do not initially seek psychological treatment, and only a small fraction come to the attention of a clinical psychologist or psychiatrist. They are referred for psychological help only after physical causes have been excluded.

DSM-III-R lists five somatoform disorders: body dysmorphic disorder, somatoform pain disorder, somatization disorder, hypochondriasis, and conversion disorder. **Body dysmorphic disorder** is characterized by a preoccupation with an imaginary defect in physical appearance. Common complaints concern excessive facial hair or the shape of the nose, mouth, or jaw. In some cases, an individual's concern is greatly exaggerated about a slight physical anomaly. People with this disorder repeatedly consult physicians (e.g., plastic surgeons or dermatologists) to correct the imaginary problem. The age of onset is in adolescence and early childhood. A person with **somatoform pain disorder** is preoccupied with pain that cannot be accounted for by any known pathophysiology. Impairment may be extreme and the patient may adopt the role of an invalid. The disorder occurs almost twice as frequently in women as in men.

Somatization Disorder

Somatization disorder is also known as *Briquet's syndrome*, after the French physician who first described it in 1859. Its defining feature is the pattern of recurrent, long-standing somatic symptoms causing patients to consult one doctor after another without finding any pathophysiological basis. Common symptoms include gastrointestinal problems (e.g., vomiting, stomach pain, nausea); pain (e.g., in the extremities or back); or cardiopulmonary difficulties (e.g., shortness of breath, dizziness, chest pain other than during a panic attack). Anxiety and depression are commonly associated with somatization disorder, and patients often threaten or attempt suicide. Antisocial behavior and marital and interpersonal difficulties are frequently present. Abuse of different medications also typically occurs. These patients are frequently hospitalized and often undergo unnecessary surgery. The onset of the disorder occurs before age thirty, usually during adolescence. More women than men suffer from this disorder. DSM-III-R requires thirteen unexplained somatic symptoms for the diagnosis of somatization disorder. But somatization can be viewed as a continuum of disturbance as well as a discrete disorder as in DSM-III-R. A study of psychologically distressed, high utilizers of medical services found that patients with nine to twelve symptoms were almost as disturbed as those with thirteen or more (Katon, et al., 1991). Anxiety and major depressive disorders were comparable in these two groups, and far more common in these groups than in patients with fewer than six unexplained somatic symptoms.

Both genetic and early environmental influences predispose to somatization disorder. Women with this disorder are more likely to have first-degree female relatives with the same disorder than women in the population at large (American Psychiatric Association, 1987). Somatization disorder is also more common in women whose biological parents had antisocial or substance abuse disorders (Sigvardsson et al., 1984). This familial association between somatization disorder and antisocial personality disorder may be important because the two disorders seem completely separate entities (Guze, Cloninger, Martin, & Clayton, 1986). Guze et al. (1986) have speculated that the two disorders are linked etiologically, with somatization disorder occurring mainly in women, and antisocial personality disorder primarily in men.

On the environmental side, childhood experience with pain or serious illness in a family member increases the risk of developing somatization disorder

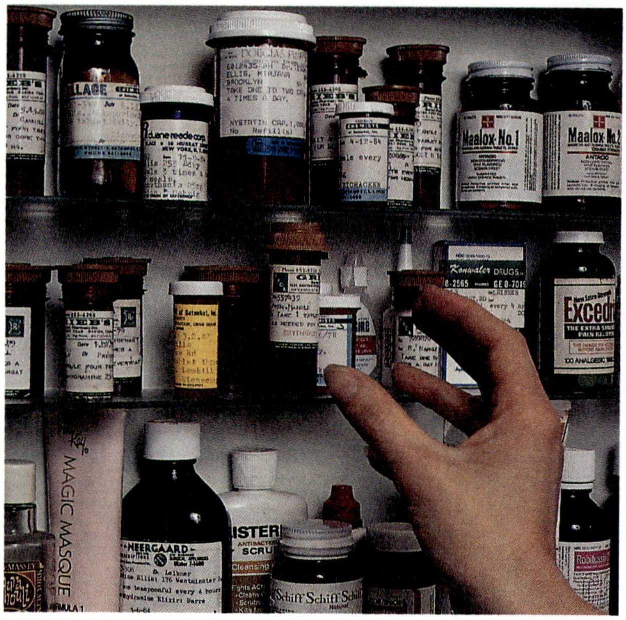

People with somatization disorder often abuse medication.

in adulthood (Hartvig & Sterner, 1985). We can interpret the association between anxiety and depressive disorders on the one hand, and somatization on the other, in at least three ways as Katon et al. (1991) point out. As in other cases of a correlation between two disorders that we note in this book, both the anxiety/depressive disorders and the somatization might be a product of some third, underlying physiological abnormality. Alternatively, either anxiety or depression might lower the patient's threshold for being disturbed by perceived physical complaints. Finally, chronic physical symptoms, such as pain, might cause anxiety or depression.

The per capita cost of health care for patients with somatization disorder is up to nine times the average in this country. Excessive and inappropriate hospitalizations contribute heavily to this increase in healthcare cost. Smith et al. (1986) conducted a controlled study showing that psychiatric consultation with these patients can reduce soaring health costs without affecting the quality of care.

Patients with somatization disorder were randomly assigned to either a treatment or a control group and studied for eighteen months. The treatment group's physicians had detailed information available about the nature of somatization disorder and were instructed to change their typical management of these patients. For example, they regularly scheduled appointments every four to six weeks to avert patients' developing new symptoms as a means of getting appointments. Researchers explained that patients were not consciously making up their symptoms and urged physicians not to tell patients "It's all in your head." The physicians were also encouraged to avoid hospitalization, expensive laboratory tests, and surgery unless clearly indicated. The control group received routine medical care.

Smith et al. (1986) found no evidence that the psychiatric consultation improved patients' mental or physical health. They found that the treatment significantly reduced health-care costs without affecting patients' self-rated health status or their satisfaction with care. The findings demonstrate psychiatric consultation's value in reducing medical-care costs.

Hypochondriasis

The core feature of **hypochondriasis** is the anxiety of having, or the belief that one has, a serious physical illness, despite contrary medical evaluations. The following transcript of a psychologist interviewing a patient with hypochondriasis illustrates the problem:

Therapist: So you believe that you have a serious physical problem that the doctors haven't picked up. Is that right?

Patient: Yes that's right.

Therapist: So that thought is very upsetting, and makes you unhappy in a variety of ways. The main ways it affects what you do is it interferes with you being on your own, and it stops you doing things you enjoy, such as tennis. It also has stopped you from eating very much, which might be making eating still more difficult. Is that right?

Patient: Yes. Sometimes I will be on my own, but I won't if I can help it.

Therapist: Right. In general, when people have fears, they usually have reasons for those fears. In your instance, the reasons for your fear about your health are the pains you get, your loss of weight, difficulty eating and swallowing, and bowel problems. These all suggest to you that you are ill, especially as they come every day. Is there any other evidence that makes you think you are ill?

Patient: Yes, it's not a lump, it's a horrible feeling in the throat, tight, when it gets to here it's sore. My doctor checked me, but this has only got worse since I had the X-rays, not before; then it didn't stop me from eating. My waterworks are a problem too. It's very frightening, I can't deal with it. Those are the main things, they make me think I have the same as my mother.

Therapist: Right; so these all make you think the worst; you think you have cancer, like your mother.

Patient: Yes. (Salkovskis, 1989, p. 254).

Hypochondriacs perceive symptoms where there is no physical basis or they react excessively to normal bodily sensations (see Figure 6.1). The hypo-

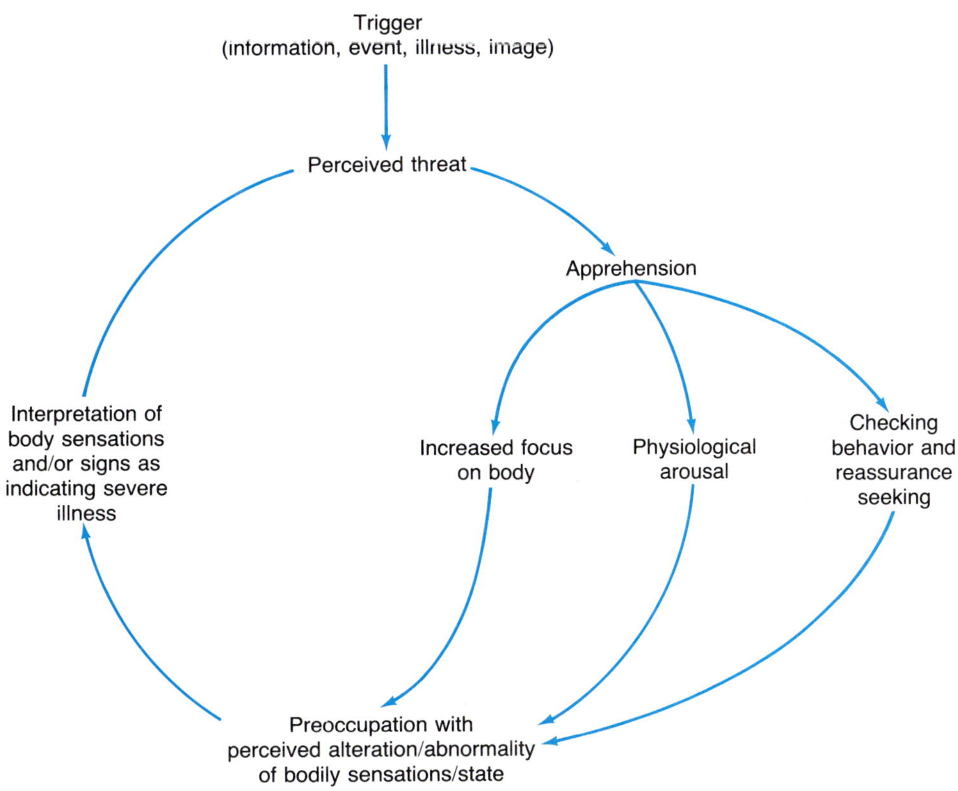

Figure 6.1 A Model of the Psychological Mechanisms in Hypochondriasis.
Source: From P.M. Salkovskis (1989). Somatic problems. In K. Hawton, P.M. Salkovskis, J. Kirk, & D.M. Clark (Eds.), *Cognitive behaviour therapy for psychiatric problems.* New York: Oxford University Press. Copyright © Oxford University Press, 1989. Reprinted with permission.

chondriac views a physical sensation as a threat to health and responds with increased physiological arousal. By focusing attention on the sensation the person may produce further physiological change. For example, the patient described in the excerpt worried he had cancer of the throat. His repeated swallowing to prove that he was all right only made swallowing more difficult. The patient became preoccupied with other bodily sensations misinterpreted as some undiagnosed physical illness. He then stopped engaging in several activities, such as tennis, and cut back on eating.

Hypochondriasis is highly correlated with what Barsky et al. (1990) call *somatosensory amplification,* namely, the tendency to experience bodily sensations as unusually intense, aversive, and distressing.

Hypochondriacal patients have a marked fear of aging and dying and are particularly concerned about their physical appearance (Barsky & Wyshak, 1989). We do not know whether hypochondriacs have increased rates of medical illness or psychological disorders in their families. Evidence of physical illness in childhood, however, suggests that hypochondriacs may be reinforced for adopting a "sick role" (Barsky, Wyshak, & Klerman, 1986).

Conversion Disorder

Characteristics. The best known and most studied of the somatoform disorders, **conversion disorder**, involves the loss or alteration of physical functioning that suggests physical disease, but no underlying pathophysiology can be found. Classic cases show symptoms linked to neurological disease (e.g., paralysis of some body part), anesthesia (loss of physical sensations), or parathesia (sensations of tingling or creeping on the skin). Partial or complete blindness, or loss of voice (aphonia) are other typical problems of patients. Conversion disorder used to be known as hysterical neurosis.

The term *hysteria* comes from the Greek word meaning uterus. This reflects the early belief that the uterus of a woman who had no sexual relations or was childless could dry out and "wander" through the body, symbolizing the desire for procreation. Where the uterus settled would determine the specific symptom. For example, if the uterus lodged in the throat, the person would feel like choking. This indicates that hysteria, including conversion disorder, was believed to be a disorder of women. Yet evidence suggests between 20 percent and 40 percent of conversion disorder cases occur in men (Chodoff, 1974). Age of onset is usually in adolescence or early adulthood but can also occur much later in life.

Freud coined the term *conversion* when he assumed that anxiety was transformed (converted) into a somatic symptom to prevent it from breaking into the conscious part of the mind. Converting the underlying anxiety into a physical symptom allows the anxiety's release without its being consciously experienced. It works the same way as other means of symbolically coping with anxiety, such as the displacement of anxiety onto an external object in the form of a phobia (see Chapter 5). Both mechanisms defend the self against unacceptable anxiety.

Conversion disorder develops suddenly, usually under severe psychological stress. Often a prior history of some physical problem provides a model or prototype for the symptom. An hysterical or dependent personality disorder may increase and also predispose the person for developing conversion disorder (see Chapter 10). Patients with conversion disorder are significantly more likely to show an hysterical personality style[1] (Wilson-Barnett & Trimble, 1985). No clear link has, however, been shown between hysterical personality and conversion or dissociative disorders. Conversion symptoms occur in patients with all kinds of different personalities (Wilson-Barnett & Trimble, 1985).

Conversion disorder has apparently declined in prevalence. During the late nineteenth century, Charcot in France and Freud in Austria treated a large number of hysterical patients with conversion symptoms. Today such symptomatology is rarely seen. Smith-Rosenberg (1972) has proposed the following theory for the disappearance of the disorder: In the nineteenth century, hysteria was confined primarily to women facing oppressive and rigidly sexist social customs. In contrast, society today offers women more freedom and opportunity to control their lives. It is argued that women no longer need these symptoms to escape oppressive life circumstances.

DSM-III-R distinguishes between conversion disorder and **malingering** (faking). The malingerer shows the same pattern of behavior to consciously and intentionally obtain some reward or avoid some unpleasant situation. In contrast, motivation of the patient with conversion symptoms is unconscious. This distinction is often difficult to make. Common clinical guidelines are based on malingerers voluntarily controlling their symptoms; they can switch back and forth between normal and abnormal behavior more easily and quickly than patients with conversion disorder.

Conversion disorder must also be distinguished from *factitious disorder with physical symptoms,* where the person intentionally produces symptoms with an actual physiological basis, for example, ac-

[1] The hysterical personality, diagnosed most frequently in women, is characterized by overly dramatic, superficial, manipulative, and attention-seeking behavior.

cepting a penicillin injection while aware that it will cause a toxic reaction. A specific form of this disorder is *Munchausen syndrome,* where the patient devotes his or her life to getting admitted to hospitals. These attempts to be hospitalized may even cause such an individual to journey to numerous cities and states.

The concepts of conversion disorder and hysterical neuroses have always been controversial. Some critics have charged that they do not exist (Slater, 1965). According to this skeptical view, the term *conversion reaction* or *hysterical neurosis* is merely a label for symptoms without a satisfactory physical explanation, which the clinician could detect with more advanced knowledge.

Some support for this radical view comes from a study of eighty-five patients with the diagnosis of conversion disorder (Slater & Glithero, 1965). A follow-up study revealed that actual illnesses became evident in all but twenty-one of the patients. In many subjects the physical illness they had developed had symptoms similar to those originally diagnosed as hysterical. This suggests that conversion disorder diagnosis was mistakenly applied to patients with physical diseases. In a subsequent study by Watson and Buranen (1979), forty patients with conversion symptoms were followed up over a ten-year period. Their medical records were compared to those of a control group of patients with different, nonhysterical anxiety disorders. Significantly more of the patients with the conversion disorder diagnosis developed physical illnesses. The authors concluded that physical disease was misdiagnosed in 25 percent of cases. This figure is much lower than in the Slater and Glithero study yet still represents a substantial minority of patients.

Some physical illnesses may be misdiagnosed as conversion disorder. The behavior labeled conversion disorder cannot, nevertheless, be adequately explained by reducing it to an underlying physical illness.

The following case study illustrates many of the characteristics of conversion disorder.

A forty-year-old veteran from rural Indiana suddenly became blind in both eyes three days before Christmas (Brady & Lind, 1961). Repeated medical evaluation showed no physical basis for his blindness. He was able to get around without difficulty, indicating that he must have had sight, and showed neither anxiety nor alarm about his blindness. The veteran was hospitalized and diagnosed as suffering from conversion disorder.

He was working nights and weekends under the direction of his wife and mother-in-law when the blindness occurred. His personal history revealed a pattern of constant harassment by his family; he was a dependent personality unable to assert himself in dealing with his wife and mother-in-law. Nonetheless, he spoke of his wife in "endearing terms." Brady and Lind inferred that the patient converted his unconscious anger toward his controlling family into the conversion symptom of blindness. Additionally, his blindness allowed him the secondary gain of not having to work under their supervision. The patient's background revealed a medical history of damage to his right eye, resulting in reduced vision in that eye and a medical discharge from the military with a small pension. In the twelve years following discharge and the onset of his total blindness, he had received treatment for a recurring eye infection three times. As a child he had two aunts who were blind. Brady and Lind suggested that this history explained why he had developed blindness as a symptom.

The researchers used operant-conditioning procedures to analyze the patient's disorder. To earn rewards (special privileges in the hospital), he was given the following experimental task. He was asked to press a button at eighteen- to twenty-one-second intervals. A response during these intervals earned a reward. An error started another time interval and thus delayed reward. After a practice period, a light signaling the correct response was introduced into the experimental situation. Brady and Lind reasoned that if the patient used the visual cue to regulate his responses and thereby earn rewards, it would prove he was able to see, and this is exactly what happened. The patient increasingly employed the visual cue to make correct responses until he finally reported he could see again. The introduction of the visual stimulus also provoked strong anxiety in him for the first time. Brady and Lind suggested that this was consistent with psychodynamic theory. According to this view, the ingenious situation Brady and Lind had devised "exposed" the patient's use of blindness as a symptom. The removal of the symptom, which defended against the underlying anxiety, brought the anxiety to the surface. Brady and Lind reported that the patient could see well at the end of this experimental analysis. He was discharged from the hospital, seemed to be coping better with his family responsibilities, and had found a job.

In 1965, Grosz and Zimmerman published a follow-up and further study of this patient. He had relapsed shortly after Brady and Lind reported on his status. Three years later the patient was hospitalized again, claiming to be totally blind. Grosz and Zimmerman questioned whether he had a conversion disorder or was malingering. The latter possibility was suggested by his excessive manipulative behavior before, during, and after Brady and Lind's experimental analysis. To test this possibility, Grosz and Zimmerman had the patient indicate which of three visual stimuli was the odd one. The performance of a genuinely blind person would be at a chance level. The patient, however, scored at a level significantly below chance, suggesting that he did see and was deliberately making errors.

To test this hypothesis, the investigators did the following: The research assistant, who had been detached, now began talking to the patient and expressed sympathy for his condition. The assistant "confided" that the doctors did not believe the patient was blind due to his scoring at below chance levels. The assistant informed the patient what number of correct responses would be expected by chance in someone who was blind. The purpose of this intervention was to see if the patient would then alter his behavior to fit what he now believed to be the social role of a blind person. This is precisely what happened.

Does this clever experiment by Grosz and Zimmerman prove that the man was really a malingerer? Although the results are suggestive, they concluded that it is probably impossible to differentiate reliably between conversion disorder and faking: "What makes the differential diagnosis even more difficult to resolve is the generally recognized possibility that hysteria and malingering may gradually and imperceptibly supersede one another, or, for that matter, coexist in the same patient at the same time." (Grosz & Zimmerman, 1965, p. 258)

Causes

The Psychodynamic Model. Conversion disorder (and the dissociative disorders) seem to fit the psychodynamic model. It is the only existing well-developed psychological theory of these puzzling disorders. Its key assumption is that individuals derive *primary gain* from the symptom because it keeps intrapsychic anxiety or conflict out of their awareness. Additionally, the *secondary gain* from the symptom allows them to avoid unwanted activities and receive support from others that might otherwise be unavailable.

This psychodynamic model results from Freud's early work with Joseph Breuer, an Austrian physician, described in their classic book, *Studies in Hysteria* (1895). Breuer and Freud told of the treatment of Anna O, who had been Breuer's patient. This single case study not only contributed greatly to the psychodynamic theory of hysterical disorders but also critically influenced the clinical development of psychoanalysis.

Anna O, whose real name was Bertha Pappenheim, began to show severe psychological disturbance when she was twenty-one years old. In nursing her dying father, she experienced great stress. Her conversion symptoms included rigid paralysis and loss of sensation in the right side of her body; occasional paralysis in parts of her body on the right side; sporadic deafness; and loss of her ability to speak German, although she retained perfect command of English. In addition to her conversion symptoms, Anna O also suffered from personality alterations. She could switch abruptly from her normal personality to what she called her "bad self." Today, she would be diagnosed as a multiple personality.

Breuer treated Anna O for eighteen months. During his therapy he hypnotized her and discovered that the symptoms would disappear if he allowed his patient to give a detailed account of her symptoms and the events surrounding their onset. Anna O called this her "talking cure," and, jokingly, "chimney sweeping." Breuer called it "catharsis." For example, the last of her symptoms, paralysis of the right arm, was eliminated only after she recalled and reported the details of this hallucination: Sitting at her father's bedside, she saw a large black snake. She tried to ward it off with her right arm but was unable to move. She was capable only of reciting an English-language prayer. With this final verbal report, her paralysis disappeared and her ability to speak German suddenly returned. Breuer reported his patient cured and able to resume a normal life.

Impressed by this success, Freud adapted Breuer's approach with his own patients. After confirming the effectiveness of the method, Freud soon discarded hypnosis completely and simply asked patients to detail verbally their early experience. The talking cure became known as **free association,** a fundamental element of contemporary psychoanalytic therapy.

Most previous accounts of the famous case of Anna O have ended on this inspiring note yet these are badly incomplete. In fact, Anna O was not "cured." She suffered many relapses and was institutionalized (Ellenberger, 1972). A year after he discontinued his treatment of the case, Breuer even expressed the hope that his former patient might die and so be released from her suffering. Five years after Breuer's contact with her had ceased, she still had occasional hallucinations when evening approached (Sulloway, 1979).

Bertha Pappenheim did eventually recover. More than ten years after her therapy with Breuer had ended, she founded a League of Jewish Women in 1904 and a home for unwed mothers in 1907. Committed to the causes of women and children, she can be considered an early feminist. She wrote that "If there is any justice in the next life, women will make the laws and men will bear the children!" (cited in Sulloway, 1979). In 1954 the West German government issued a commemorative postage stamp in her honor. The woman indelibly associated with a disorder once widely regarded as the exclusive domain of dependent females ironically proved to be an independent person.

What did Bertha Pappenheim think about her therapy, which would later be routinely cited in textbooks as one of the great breakthroughs in psychiatry? Sulloway (1979) reports that she remained "cool, she never spoke to anyone of her experience with Breuer, and she later refused to allow the girls under her care to be psychoanalyzed" (p. 57).

Strongly influenced by Breuer's description of the case of Anna O, Freud began to believe that all conversion disorders (indeed, virtually all neuroses) were the product of early, unresolved sexual conflicts. Breuer agreed that sexual conflicts were an important cause of hysterical symptoms but rejected Freud's insistence that they were at the root of every

The famous "Anna O" whose treatment led Freud to develop the technique of free association. Her real name was Bertha Pappenheim.

case. This disagreement was a major cause of the personal and scientific rift between these two pioneers in abnormal behavior (Sulloway, 1979). Modern psychodynamic theory is more in accord with Breuer's original position. Any anxiety or conflict, sexual or otherwise, can be repressed and subsequently find overt expression in the form of symptoms such as conversion disorder.

Consider a major prediction of the model—that patients with conversion symptoms should show no anxiety. This absence of anxiety or distress has historically been referred to as *la belle indifference. DSM-III-R* has modified this extreme position by noting that not all patients show an absence of anxiety. Nonetheless, the relationship between the conversion symptoms and anxiety remains a key feature of the psychodynamic model.

To test this assumption, Lader and Sartorius (1968) compared patients with conversion disorder with two control groups: a matched group of patients with nonhysterical anxiety disorders and nonanxious, normal subjects. The patients with conversion symptoms showed significantly more physiological arousal and subjective anxiety than the nonhysterical anxiety disorder patients, who, in turn, exhibited greater anxiety than the normal controls. Contrary to the notion of la belle indifference, the patients with conversion symptoms reported great concern about their problems. These findings have been replicated (Rice & Greenfield, 1969; Wilson-Barnett & Trimble, 1985).

Such research challenges a key prediction of the psychodynamic model. One way to reconcile the apparent discrepancy is to argue that patients with conversion symptoms might be even more anxious without them. This is plausible, but if taken too far the theory becomes difficult if not impossible to refute. These experimental findings must also be balanced by clinical observations to the contrary. For example, the patient described in the Brady and Lind (1961) case study, who at first was unconcerned about his blindness but then became very anxious as therapy began to restore his vision, fits the Freudian model.

The psychodynamic approach to conversion disorders and other somatoform disorders is to look for unconscious conflicts that may cause physical symptoms. Unless the patient is assumed to be malingering, we cannot make sense of phenomena such as conversion symptoms without inferring the existence of unconscious processes significantly influencing behavior. Not only Freudian theory but also modern cognitive psychology has clearly shown that our behavior is influenced by unconscious processes, as Box 6.1 discusses.

The psychodynamic model postulates that some mental anxiety or conflict is transformed into a physical symptom. What is the mechanism by which this conversion takes place? The theory has been criticized as having no acceptable biological basis (Chodoff & Lyons, 1958). Psychodynamic treatment follows the classic approach to all anxiety disorders. Exploring and uncovering childhood trauma or conflict underlying the hysterical symptoms helps the patient gain insight into these underlying unconscious processes. It is assumed that working through them will eliminate the disorder.

The Behavioral Model. The behavioral approach suggests that people with conversion disorders are adopting a social role whereby their behavior matches those whose symptoms are caused by physical disease (Ullmann & Krasner, 1969). Two key questions about conversion disorders have guided behavioral research: First, are people capable of

BOX 6.1 Unconscious Processes and Behavior

Modern cognitive psychology has confirmed long-standing clinical observations that behavior is influenced by factors we are unaware of. Current experimental research on priming further illustrates the effect of unconscious processes on behavior.

Priming refers to the speeding up of response to a stimulus by the earlier presentation of that same stimulus or an associated one. Bower (1986) notes that "Priming reflects a kind of memory, since it depends on recent experience with a familiar stimulus. However, it is a most curious kind of memory since people can show priming due to prior experience, but yet they may have no conscious recollection of the experience that primed their perceptual performance. That is, they may show memory according to one index, and forgetting according to another . . . priming may be more sensitive than is conscious recollection in revealing an effect due to weak or subliminal stimulation" (p. 27). Eich (1984) demonstrated this effect in the following experiment: College students rapidly repeated word for word, a prose passage they heard over the right ear of a headphone—a difficult task, requiring intense concentration. While repeating words heard in the right earphone, subjects were told to ignore word-pairs presented in the left earphone. The relevant pairs were composed of a homophone and a modifier that biased one of its spellings, such as rabbit HARE and deep SEA. Bower points out that the word-pairs from the left earphone

> enter sensory memory and contact their word units for a fraction of a second, but then disappear from consciousness as the person continues shadowing. At the end of the session, Eich's subjects had no recollection of the unattended words. However, when given a spelling test, they tended to spell the homophones in the manner biased by the context words presented on the unattended ear. Thus the RABBIT context caused them to spell the sound hare as HARE, and so on. This illustrates remembering without awareness: material that's only briefly perceived, that causes no conscious recollection later, nonetheless causes a later unconscious bias in the meaning assigned to an ambiguous sound.
>
> (Bower, p. 27)

This experiment shows a dissociation between conscious and unconscious memory. Srull and Wyer (1979) showed a similar dissociation in social perception when they first primed college student subjects by having them complete either a hostile or nonhostile verbal task. Next, in what subjects were led to believe was a separate study, they were to form an impression of a man, Donald, after reading about his behavior in different situations. The behavior was designed to be ambiguous so that it could be viewed as either hostile or assertive. Subjects who had received the hostility priming saw Donald's behavior as hostile. The more hostile priming they had had, the more hostile they rated him. Perhaps most importantly, subjects were unaware of the influence of the priming on their social judgments. They did not connect the two experiments. When asked why they rated Donald as hostile, subjects answered that it was obvious to see.

In addition to their research on priming, Nisbett and Ross (1980) summarize numerous studies from social-cognitive psychology showing that we are often unaware of the causes of our actions, even though we think we know them. Research of this nature shows that unconscious processes can influence behavior.

According to psychoanalysis, unconscious material is purposely repressed because it is threatening to the conscious portion of the personality. Psychoanalysis then is a motivational theory of the unconscious—the mind wants to keep material out of awareness. Nisbett and Ross (1980) have proposed an alternative, nonmotivational theory of unconscious processes, arguing that some cognitive processes are inaccessible to conscious introspection. It is not that the material is repressed, but simply that we do not have the cognitive machinery to uncover the causes of some of our behavior. When asked to explain our actions, we give reasons that really reflect shared social explanations of why someone would engage in them. People deny a psychological fact about themselves because it is inconsistent with their learned social explanations, not because it is repressed. These two theories of unconscious processes have different implications for psychotherapy.

In the Freudian view of the unconscious, therapy's goal is to make conscious what is unconscious—to help patients achieve insight into the hidden causes of their actions. In contrast, the goal of a cognitive-behavioral approach to treatment is to involve patients in a collaborative process where they test their assumptions or theories about their behavior and its causes. The aim is to help patients develop a more adaptive understanding of themselves and their world than their previous dysfunctional pattern of thought and behavior.

---

adopting such a social role? Second, under what conditions will people act this way?

In answer to the first question, behaviorists have claimed that individuals can mimic hysterical symptoms without being either unconsciously motivated or consciously malingering. To support this assumption they point to studies showing that people are responsive to **demand characteristics** in social situations (Orne, 1962). In other words, people are suggestible and will respond in ways assumed appropriate to specific situations. In answer to the second question, behaviorists suggest that a person must have had experience with the symptom, and also be reinforced for such behavior. For example, the patient from the Brady and Lind (1961) case study described earlier, had a history of real eye damage and, as a result of developing hysterical blindness, avoided work and harassment by his family.

According to the behavioral model, conversion symptoms are not unconsciously motivated, although they are functionally the same as malingering. How then can the two be distinguished from each other? Behaviorists argue that this is a nonissue. They do not differentiate between conscious and unconscious processes and suggest the absence of any real dichotomy between conversion disorder and malingering. They focus only on observable behavior and its environmental antecedents and consequences. Although some investigators would agree that it is unproductive to try to distinguish between the "real disorder" and malingering (Grosz & Zimmerman, 1965; Miller, 1987), others adhere to the view that important differences exist between the two (APA, 1987).

Focusing only on overt behavior fails to address the cognitive processes involved in somatoform disorders. The riddle of hysterical blindness is patients behaving in a way that proves they are using visual cues, yet insisting they cannot see. The same pattern is shown in hypnotically induced blindness—the phenomena of hypnosis and hysteria have been closely linked since the time of Charcot (see Box 6.2). Bryant and McConkey (1989) used hypnotically induced blindness, therefore, as a model of hysterical blindness in the following experiment.

One group of subjects was hypnotized and told they were blind, whereas a second group were simply instructed to simulate hypnotically induced blindness. Adopting the same procedure Grosz and Zimmerman (1965) had employed to study hysterical blindness, Bryant and McConkey found no difference in the behavior of the hypnotized and the simulating groups. Their actions proved they were using visual cues, though the two groups differed in their cognitive styles. The hypnotized subjects reported a constructive cognitive strategy illustrated in this response: "It's hard knowing that something's there and yet you're not allowed to see it. I concentrated on not letting myself see it by looking at the black screen instead of the lights on the screen. If you look at the detail of the lights you know it's there, so I just looked beyond the lights" (p. 75). Simulating subjects were more passive and less genuine—they simply reported an inability to focus on the visual cues. This difference shows that the behavior of the hypnotized subjects cannot be attributed to the demand characteristics of the situation as the behavioral model predicts.

The main shortcoming of the behavioral model is that it is more a description than an explanation of the disorder (Miller, 1987). Among the questions the model leaves unanswered are how and why do only some people adopt this social role in the face of stressful situations? The behavioral model rejects any mention of conscious and unconscious processes, partly as a reaction against what was seen as speculative and untestable Freudian notions about the unconscious. But recent cognitive research has demonstrated that unconscious processes can be studied scientifically (see Box 6.1).

Treatment. Because of the relative rarity of conversion disorder and other somatoform disorders, there are no controlled studies of treatment and thus we do not know how effective therapy is.

Behavioral treatment includes a range of different strategies. The particular methods the clinician uses depends on a detailed assessment of the individual case. The goals of therapy usually are (1) to help the patient cope more constructively with the stressful circumstances typically preceding the appearance of the disorder; and (2) to alter the patient's reinforcement contingencies so that the maladaptive, hysterical behavior is no longer reinforced. This multifaceted treatment approach is illustrated in a case described by Meichenbaum (1966).

> *The patient, Mr. S, was a forty-three-year-old veteran who had reported headaches and blurred vision for the previous two years. His most recent symptom, an inability to keep his eyes open, caused him to lose his job. Neither opticians nor a physician could find any physical basis for his complaint. Careful assessment suggested that interpersonal stress was, however, an important antecedent. Mr. S's major situational stress was the conflict between his mother and wife over their different religious beliefs. His mother insisted his son be raised a strict Catholic; his wife, who was not a Catholic, refused. Mr. S responded to this interpersonal conflict with denial and withdrawal. The first stage of therapy concentrated on reducing Mr. S's immediate stress. He was taught progressive relaxation to relieve physical tension and promote mental calmness (see Chapter 16). Mr. S improved to keeping his eyes open 75 percent of the time, permitting his discharge from the hospital. The second stage of therapy involved systematic desensitization, where he imagined stressful situations while remaining relaxed. Following this second stage, Mr. S further improved and was able to return to work.*
>
> *Mr. S reported the recurrence of his problem whenever confronted with an important decision or domination by his wife or mother. Mr. S was obviously too submissive or unassertive in interacting with key figures in his life. Thus in the third stage of treatment, the therapist introduced assertion training to make Mr. S less dependent and more self-confident in coping with interpersonal situations (see Chapter 16). The therapist role-played specific situations with Mr. S; they rehearsed how he might respond more assertively to his wife, mother, and employer. The results were dramatic: Mr. S obtained a better job, reached a compromise solution with his wife about the religious upbringing of their son, and coped more confidently with his family. The conversion symptom of closing his eyes under stress disappeared.*

BOX 6.2 Hypnosis and Abnormal Behavior

The history of hypnosis is intertwined with the study of abnormal behavior. The development of hypnosis from Mesmer's claims about animal magnetism to its use by Charcot, Janet, and Breuer in treating patients with hysterical problems toward the end of the last century was described in Chapter 1. Two historically evident features of hypnosis are still prominent today. The first is that hypnotism undoubtedly helped many patients with hysterical disorders. Physicians also employed it to block patients' pain during surgery. Hypnosis continues to be useful in the diagnosis and treatment of somatoform and dissociative disorders. It is also still used as an effective analgesic in surgery and dentistry (Turk, Meichenbaum, & Genest, 1983). The second feature is the controversy surrounding explanations of hypnosis. Mesmer's notion of animal magnetism was rejected by his fellow professionals. He was dismissed as a charlatan and lost his right to practice medicine. Roughly a century later the nature of hypnosis is still debated.

There are currently two contrasting views of hypnosis. The dissociation view considers hypnosis as an altered state of consciousness. Hypnotic induction procedures create a dissociated state or trance during which people will perceive, feel, and act in ways different from their normal behavior when not hypnotized (Hilgard, 1986). The opposing social psychological view rejects the concept of an altered state of consciousness. Hypnotized people adopt a social role where they react to cues in ways no different from their normal behavior (Barber, 1969), responding to what Orne (1962) has called the demand characteristics of the situation. This viewpoint's critical prediction is that any behavior seen in hypnotized subjects (during the so-called trance state) can also be seen in subjects simulating the role of a hypnotized person.

The controversy has fueled a large number of studies. Yet even these well-designed and sophisticated experiments have failed to produce a consensus about the mechanisms responsible for hypnotic phenomena. Among these phenomena are the following: heightened suggestibility; enhanced imagery and imagination, including the ability to recall vivid images from the past; increased tolerance for pain; and the willingness to accept various perceptual distortions that would be rejected as illogical in the nonhypnotized state. Moreover, naive subjects can simulate deep hypnosis so convincingly that it may be impossible to tell that they are not really hypnotized. For example, Dr. Milton H. Erickson, a famous psychotherapist known for his mastery of hypnosis and experience in hypnotizing many thousands of subjects, was unable to discriminate between deeply hypnotized subjects and simulators (Orne, Dinges, & Orne, 1984).

What are popularly believed to be unique characteristics of hypnosis are often myths. For example, it is widely believed that hypnosis can be a sort of "lie detector" the hypnotist can use to bypass the subject's defenses and get to "the truth." But subjects can lie when under hypnosis as well as when they are simulating. Confessions obtained during hypnosis cannot be used in the United States. Courts in several states do not allow a witness to testify about memories elicited during hypnosis (Coons, 1988).

Despite the marked degree of overlap between hypnotized subjects and simulators, Orne and his coworkers (1984) claim that it is possible to differentiate between the two groups in the laboratory. One means of telling the difference is through using trance logic. In the double hallucination test, subjects are asked to hallucinate a person and talk to him or her. When asked where the person is, subjects point to the hallucination in front of them. When asked to turn toward the real person who had previously been outside of their field of vision and to name him or her, simulators typically respond that they do not know the person or that no one is there. When no longer in the simulating role, these subjects explain that in order to preserve this role as hypnotized and hallucinating someone in front of them, they could not admit to seeing the same person in another place at the same time. Deeply hypnotized subjects are not bothered by a logical impossibility and correctly report seeing the same person twice.

Not everyone accepts Orne and his coworkers' (1984) conclusion that simulators can be distinguished from deeply hypnotized subjects. The controversy, which is over 100 years old, continues.

A patient being hypnotized.

The case of Mr. S resembles the patient from the Brady and Lind (1961) case study. If that patient had been treated with behavior therapy, the therapist probably would have focused on his lack of assertiveness in dealing with his wife and mother-in-law. Increased independence would presumably have reduced his stress and made it unnecessary for him to resort to hysterical blindness to cope with social pressure.

Note the similarities between his behavioral approach and psychodynamic treatment. Both try to reduce stressful events believed to precipitate the hysterical symptom. The differences are in how the stress is viewed and what methods are used to treat it. The psychodynamic therapist sees childhood conflicts as the cause of the problem. The behavior therapist focuses on current stressful events in the patient's life. Although the patient's current dependency and lack of assertiveness are probably influenced by early learning experiences, the behavior therapist believes that the most fruitful treatment strategy is to concentrate on feelings and behavior in the here and now. The two approaches differ most in how the stress is treated. Psychodynamic therapists rely on nondirective, verbal psychotherapy to achieve insight into the origin of the problem. Behavior therapists take a directive approach in using specific techniques, such as progressive relaxation and assertion training.

DISSOCIATIVE DISORDERS

The common theme among these disorders is an alteration in the normal, integrated functions of a person's identity, memory, or consciousness. *DSM-III-R* lists four dissociative disorders: psychogenic amnesia, psychogenic fugue, depersonalization disorder, and multiple personality disorder.

Psychogenic Amnesia

Psychogenic amnesia is a sudden loss of memory for important personal information not caused by organic deficits. The two most common forms of the disorder are (1) *localized amnesia*, memory loss of all events in a specific period of time; and (2) *selective amnesia*, failure to remember some but not all events during a period of time. Far less common are *generalized amnesia*, where memory loss extends to the person's entire life, and *continuous amnesia*, where the individual experiences total memory loss following a specific point in time. The state of amnesia is characterized by disorientation and confusion lasting several hours or even years. When the amnesia is about past events, people are usually aware of their lack of recall.

The disorder occurs most frequently in female adolescents and young adults. It has also been reported in young men during war as it is usually preceded by severe stress. The disorder disappears as suddenly as it appears, with complete recovery and rare instances of recurrence.

The following case report by Kaszniak et al. (1988) illustrates the nature of generalized amnesia.

> *Mr. M, a twenty-seven-year-old white male, was found lying in a busy road stating he wanted to die. He was admitted to the emergency room of a hospital, not knowing his name or anything else about his past. Neurological and other medical tests revealed no physical abnormality. Mr. M was distressed by his amnesia, alternating between hostility and withdrawal. During psychological testing, he was shown a picture from a projective test (the Thematic Apperception Test) depicting one person apparently attacking another from behind. He became so agitated that testing was stopped, and shortly afterward he tried to hang himself in his room. Hypnosis was then used to probe into Mr. M's identity.*
>
> *In the first three hypnosis sessions, the patient was gradually able to remember his first name and some details about his childhood and recent past. Not until the fourth session did he recall what had happened immediately prior to his admittance to the hospital. He had been lured to an isolated place by two men promising him a job and then raped. During this session, he remembered being overcome with shame and guilt immediately after the attack. When no longer hypnotized he still remembered the rape but refused to discuss it. During a fifth and final session of hypnosis, he recalled his last name and other autobiographical details. When told his name after coming out of his trance, Mr. M reported a sudden "flooding" of memories about his past.*[2] *For the next ten days his depression increased, and he repeatedly threatened to "kill all faggots." Subsequently, his distress began to subside. Follow-ups at three months and fifteen months after discharge from the hospital showed that he was no longer obsessed with the rape, did not express hostility toward homosexuals, and was successfully employed. But he reported mild depression and increased alcohol consumption.*

In cases of generalized amnesia (and all dissociative disorders), the question of whether the patient is faking must be considered. A sizable number of amnesia cases turn out to be simulated. Schacter et al. (1982) suggest the following guidelines for making this diagnostic distinction: (1) faked cases last longer (e.g., weeks or months) than genuine cases typically limited to a week or less; (2) in faked cases the

[2] A well-known case of amnesia in which hypnosis apparently did not produce recall of the precipitating event is that of Sirhan Sirhan, the man who assassinated Bobby Kennedy in 1968. Under hypnosis Sirhan could recall the details of shooting Kennedy. This material apparently was unavailable to Sirhan when not hypnotized, and initially he denied committing the murder. He eventually agreed that the evidence showed that he did it, but still reported no recall of the event (Bower, 1981).

patient is trying to escape from some financial difficulties or criminal prosecution; and (3) in genuine cases a traumatic event that presumably precipitated the amnesia can be identified. By these criteria Mr. M was clearly a genuine amnesic.

Psychogenic Fugue

The diagnostic criteria for **psychogenic fugue** are suddenly and unexpectedly traveling away from home, taking on a new identity, and failing to recall these actions after recovery. Fugues may be as brief as a few hours or days or may last months. During a fugue a person may travel extensively and participate in complex social activities without any sign of psychological disturbance. The new identity the person assumes may be partial or complete. The alteration in identity usually involves an inhibited person becoming more social and uninhibited, with rare episodes of violent behavior.

The disorder is rare, and the age of onset is variable. Major psychosocial stressors such as military combat, natural disasters, marital conflict, and personal crises typically precede a fugue. The effect on the individual depends on the length of the fugue and the acts committed during it. Relatively brief fugues have only minimal impact on the person.

Depersonalization Disorder

People suffering from **depersonalization** have the sense of being an outside observer of their own thoughts and feelings. In this dream-like state, sense of detachment from their body is accompanied by a feeling of not being in full control of their actions, although reality-testing remains intact. This altered sense of self causes personal distress and is chronic or recurrent. Depersonalization disorder is not diagnosed if the depersonalization is a symptom of panic disorder or agoraphobia (see Chapter 4).

The onset of depersonalization disorder is sudden and usually confined to adolescence or early adulthood. As many as 70 percent of young adults may experience brief spells of depersonalization, but the prevalence of clinically diagnosable cases is unknown (APA, 1987).

Multiple Personality Disorder

Characteristics. People with **multiple personality** show evidence of possessing two or more distinct personalities or personality states. *DSM-III-R* defines *personality* as "a relatively enduring pattern of perceiving, relating to, and thinking about the environment and one's self that is exhibited in a wide range of important social and personal contexts. Personality states differ only in that the pattern is not exhibited in as wide a range of contexts" (1987, p. 269). The alternative personalities are usually fully integrated with distinctive patterns of behavior, attitudes, responses to psychological tests, and even physiological reactivity.[3] They are usually virtual opposites in their behavior and emotional makeup. This sharp contrast among personalities is illustrated by the famous case of Chris Costner Sizemore, described in Thigpen and Cleckley's (1954) classic book, *The Three Faces of Eve.*[4]

One personality was named Eve White. She sought therapy, complaining of severe headaches often followed by "blackouts." Eve was a sweet, conservatively dressed, and inhibited person who was a conscientious worker and a devoted mother to her four-year-old daughter. Eve Black, who first appeared during a therapy session, was the opposite. She was coarse, seductive, impulsive, and searching for adventure. Eve White had an allergy to nylon, reacting with a skin rash; Eve Black had no allergy. After about eight months of treatment a third personality, Jane, emerged. Jane presented a more self-confident, capable, and spontaneous person than Eve White.

The number of different personalities may vary greatly. According to *DSM-III-R*, roughly half of recently described cases have ten or more personalities. The number is not necessarily fixed and may be difficult to determine precisely as new personalities often emerge over time and during treatment. In subsequent autobiographical accounts, Chris Costner Sizemore reported that over twenty new personalities emerged and then disappeared after she had initially been considered cured by Thigpen and Cleckley (Sizemore, 1986; Sizemore & Pittillo, 1977). She describes her last three personalities as the "Purple Lady," the "Strawberry Girl," and the "Retrace Lady." The Purple Lady thought she was fifty-eight years old, needed eyeglasses to read, and wore purple clothes. The Strawberry Girl thought she was twenty-one, read without glasses, wore red, and ate only strawberries. The Retrace Lady was forty-six years

[3] For example, the different personalities of an individual with this disorder have been shown to have distinctive and stable electroencephalograph (EEG) patterns (Putnam, 1984). Normal control subjects instructed to fake multiple personalities did not show the same EEG patterns. These findings may reflect neurophysiological differences in perception between different personalities. However, there are other possible explanations. For example, the findings may simply reflect the different emotional states that characterize the separate personalities.

[4] Chris Costner Sizemore is the real name of the patient given the alias of Eve White and Eve Black by Thigpen and Cleckley (1954). The book, *The Three Faces of Eve,* was later made into a movie of the same name with Joanne Woodward in the Oscar-winning role. Chris Sizemore (1989) has written another book, *A Mind of My Own,* describing her life since her final integration, which she allegedly wanted to make into a movie starring Sissy Spacek (*The New York Times,* February 7, 1989).

Chris Costner Sizemore, the woman behind the "Three Faces of Eve."

old (Chris Sizemore's actual age) and would never repeat anything she did—as though trying to avoid previous mistakes. Sizemore reports having had three personalities at any one time and they followed a definite pattern. Her personalities finally integrated in 1975 at the age of forty-six (Sizemore, 1986). The continuing changes this woman experienced underscores the complex and changing nature of multiple personality disorder.

To be diagnosed as having this disorder at least two of the personalities must repeatedly take full control of the person's behavior. Different personalities can, however, influence behavior even when they are not dominant and in executive control of the individual. The personality present for treatment usually has no awareness of the other personalities. Yet the patient does have an awareness of gaps in time during which period another personality is dominant. The separate personalities may be aware of each other and even interact. For example, Eve Black teased Eve White, and when she finally emerged as the dominant personality, Evelyn White mourned the loss of the two Eves as though they were two sisters.

Transitions from one personality to another are sudden, precipitated by stress or some identifiable pattern of social or environmental cues. When she first consulted Thigpen and Cleckley, Eve White was under considerable pressure, one source of which was serious marital conflict with a husband from whom she had separated and subsequently divorced. A dramatic instance of a specific set of cues eliciting a transition from one personality to another is seen in the case of Sally Beauchamp, the first multiple personality reported in the United States by Morton Prince in 1906. Her three major dissociations appeared after a personal crisis involving a death of someone for whom she felt some responsibility, when the weather was gloomy and rainy, and on a particular day—June 7 (Rosenzweig, 1988).

Age of onset for multiple personality disorder is almost always during childhood, although it usually does not come to professionals' attention until the patient's adolescence or adulthood. Looking back on her life, Chris Costner Sizemore (1986) reports she knew she was different from other people as a small child. She experienced frequent headaches, feelings of weakness, and periods of amnesia—symptoms associated with dissociation. Her case was originally misdiagnosed as amnesia. Usually chronic multiple personality disorder also has varying effects on the individual's functioning, depending on the relationships among the different personalities and their associated psychopathology. One or more of the different personalities may show symptoms indicating a mood, anxiety, or personality disorder. It is frequently unclear whether these symptoms are associated features of multiple personality disorder or separate, coexisting disorders. The extent of this associated psychopathology is shown in a study by Coons and Milstein (1986). They compared twenty patients with multiple personality disorder with twenty, nonschizophrenic control patients hospitalized for mood and personality disorders. Table 6.1 summarizes the findings. The results reveal a consis-

TABLE 6.1 History and Presenting Symptoms in Multiple Personality Disorder (in Percents)

History and Presenting Symptoms	Multiple Personality (N = 20)	Controls (N = 20)
Amnesia	100	0
Depression	75	70
History of childhood sexual abuse	75	5
Fugue	60	0
Suicide attempts	60	80
Auditory hallucinations	60	0
History of drug abuse	55	40
History of childhood physical abuse	55	5
Sexual dysfunction	55	25
Headaches	55	10
Child personalities	45	0
History of alcohol abuse	45	50
History of conversion disorder (any type)	40	0
History of rape	30	0
Opposite sex alternatives	25	0
Visual hallucinations	20	0
Organic seizures	10	5
Conversion paralysis	5	0
Conversion anesthesia	5	0

Source: Adapted from Coons, P.M., & Milstein V. (1986). Psychosexual disturbances in multiple personality: Characteristics, etiology, and treatment. *The Journal of Clinical Psychiatry, 47*, 107. Copyright Physicians' Postgraduate Press, Inc. Reprinted with permission.

tently high degree of psychopathology in these patients. Moreover, they had a significantly greater level of symptoms than psychiatric controls.

Diagnosis. Until recently, multiple personality disorder was thought to be a rare problem, ignored in the scientific literature. But the number of reported cases has increased dramatically since the early 1970s. This puzzling disorder has once again caught the attention of clinical investigators and continues to cause controversy.

Critics dispute the alleged increase in prevalence. Thigpen and Cleckley (1984), Eve White's therapists, report having been referred hundreds of patients diagnosed as multiple personalities but who, in their opinion, were not. They contend that what is diagnosed as multiple personality disorder is usually one of the following:

1. Some form of secondary gain an individual consciously adopts to avoid responsibility.
2. A genuine schizophrenic reaction.
3. Partial dissociations or shifts in emotions and behavior that occur in several different disorders but do not merit the diagnosis of multiple personality disorder.

Some therapists see far more cases of multiple personality disorder than others. Other investigators maintain that the prevalence is much higher than critics allow.

One argument is that multiple personality disorder has been misdiagnosed in the past, primarily as schizophrenia (Kluft, 1987a). In a study of 100 cases of multiple personality disorder, Putnam et al. (1986) reported the average patient had been inaccurately diagnosed more than three times before being properly diagnosed. Some symptoms do overlap, and Kluft (1987b) describes several instances of this. For example, one of schizophrenia's common symptoms is the feeling that some external force is withdrawing one's thoughts. Patients with multiple personality disorder often report their minds going blank and explain this as other personalities blocking their access to the material being discussed. Kluft cites the example of one patient, who, when asked about her dead mother, answered: "'She was a good woman. . . . Doctor, I'm sorry it's like something just took the thoughts out of my mind. What were we talking about?' Her mother, in fact, had abused her severely and described these activities in her diary, which was discovered later" (p. 259).

Other patients might be misdiagnosed because they are functioning reasonably well, as the following case study illustrates:

A 30-year-old female physician applied to a psychoanalytic clinic. Two periods of less intensive psychiatric treatment had failed to change masochistic tendencies in her relationships with men. Her evaluation included interviews with a senior candidate and two graduate analysts and discussion of their findings by an analyzability committee of approximately six other graduates and candidates. No treating psychiatrist, evaluator, or committee member raised consideration of a dissociative disorder.

Once analysis began, she was very resistant. Latenesses were frequent. She claimed she lost track of time and suddenly realized she was already late for her session. As the transference intensified, she became quite uncomfortable. The latenesses increased in frequency and duration. Long silences became commonplace. Midway through her fourth year of analysis, during a session she abruptly got up from the couch, turned to the analyst, and said, "You can analyze HER, but I'm leaving!" The patient spoke in a markedly different voice that was familiar to the analyst, but which he, until that moment, had attributed to transient regression. The analyst regained his composure and responded, "You are in analysis too. Please return to the couch and let us continue." After several minutes of indecision, the patient did go back to the couch.

The personality the analyst recognized as his patient returned a few minutes later, complaining of a headache and vaguely aware that "something upsetting" had occurred. A few weeks later, she showed the analyst diaries in handwriting she did not recognize as her own. She talked about several occasions on which the analyst had commented on her out-of-character clothing and told him that on those days she did not recall dressing. There were garments in her possession that she could not remember buying. She feared she might have multiple personalities. Within weeks, four additional personalities entered the analysis. One readily admitted she opposed the analysis and had acted obstructively in the hope that the analyst would give up on the patient. Once she became cooperative, the lateness and silences ceased.

The painfully good and constricted woman had one personality that led a separate life with drastically different friends, clothes, and habits. A third occasionally took over. When out, she functioned within the patient's usual personal and professional relationships, but was far less inhibited. Both were quite distinct. The other two included a punitive alternate ego who frequently inconvenienced the patient, but never interacted openly with other individuals, and a child personality that rarely emerged. The patient had been aware of many evidences that suggested she had MPD (multiple personality disorder) but had withheld them. For example, she offered extensive rationalizations for her amnesias or behaved so as to appear contrary rather than amnestic. She integrated gradually, and showed no signs of MPD during the last 2 years of a 7.5-year classical psychoanalysis. (Kluft, 1986, p. 723)

The difficulty of accurately diagnosing multiple personality disorder is compounded because most individuals with the disorder try to hide it. Moreover, as the case of the female physician described above shows, the different personalities may often be in relative harmony. Only under specific stressful conditions will they conflict with one another and present the classic signs permitting diagnosis (Kluft, 1987a).

Multiple personality disorder must also be differentiated from malingering although such a discrimination is often difficult and controversial. Box 6.3 critically analyzes this issue in the case of the notorious "Hillside Strangler."

To summarize, multiple personality disorder's prevalence is not known. It is unclear whether the number of cases has increased, whether diagnostic criteria have changed, or whether clinicians are simply more sensitive to the disorder. One reliable finding is that multiple personalities are diagnosed significantly more often in women than in men.

Causes

The Psychodynamic Model. Pierre Janet, a French pioneer of hypnosis, hysteria, and multiple personality in the early 1900s, first developed the theory of dissociation as a means of keeping painful events out of consciousness. Viewing dissociation as a defense against such experiences is the key element of psychodynamic explanations of all dissociative disorders. In multiple personality disorder the dissociated feelings of pain become entrenched as separate selves or personalities. Spiegel (1986) describes a patient's report of the first time a second personality emerged when her father took off his necktie, tied her to the bed, and raped her. "'Come be with me,' this dissociated person said, 'You don't want to be with him, that no good bum!' In this way, she dissociated the pain and fear that she experienced at the time" (p. 125).

Consistent with this model, a strikingly high percentage of multiple personality disorder patients have experienced serious childhood abuse. Putnam et al. (1986) found that 83 percent of the 100 patients they studied reported sexual abuse in childhood; 63 percent had been the victims of incest; 75 percent had been physically abused; and 45 percent had witnessed a violent death, often of a parent or sibling. These findings must be viewed cautiously because the study had several shortcomings including the lack of a control group. Yet a study by Coons and Milstein (1986) revealed similar results (see Table 6.1).

Although most patients with multiple personality disorder have been abused as children, not all victims of child abuse develop multiple personalities. Victims of child abuse are at risk for developing a wide range of mental health problems, including depression, substance abuse, and sexual dysfunction. Patients who develop multiple personality disorder must have the capacity to dissociate. They have been shown to be highly hypnotizable (Spiegel, 1986). This capacity presumably helps them separate themselves from early traumatic experiences. Individuals who lack this capacity, and, therefore, cannot dissociate easily, may resort to denial or repression as defenses against intolerably painful experiences.

The dissociated separate identity or personality is a dynamic rather than a passive force. In Spiegel's patient who was raped by her father, for example, the alternative personality acquired many of the characteristics of her sadistic father, planning the patient's suicide and suggesting various types of self-injurious behavior over the years. A similar formulation was advanced in studies of the multiple personality disorder of the Hillside Strangler, Kenneth Bianchi (Orne et al., 1984; Watkins, 1984). According to this view, Ken was an abused child, who created an imaginary playmate as a defense. The playmate became the repository of all of his anger while he, Ken, remained a controlled and conforming boy. As a result of this unexpressed anger, Ken developed different psychosomatic symptoms. In early adulthood the suppressed personality of Steve, full of anger, became

BOX 6.3 The Los Angeles "Hillside Strangler": Multiple Personality Disorder or Malingering?

During a four-month period in 1977 to 1978, ten young women were brutally raped and murdered (strangled) in the Los Angeles area. Their naked bodies were conspicuously left on hillsides, so that the killer was dubbed the "Hillside Strangler." Almost a year later, two women were murdered in a similar fashion in the state of Washington. Twenty-seven-year-old Kenneth Bianchi was quickly arrested for these two murders. Fingerprinting then linked him to the Los Angeles murders. Despite strong evidence of his guilt, Bianchi continued to claim his innocence. This prompted his lawyer to bring in a psychiatrist and a clinical psychologist to evaluate whether he should plead not guilty by insanity. The clinical psychologist, Dr. Watkins, hypnotized Bianchi. During the hypnosis, Watkins asked to speak to another "part" of Ken. In response, a personality calling himself "Steve" emerged. Steve acknowledged killing the women and described details of the murders that only the killer could have known. He claimed to hate his mother, stating that murdering women was an appropriate act. He denied that Ken, whom he also hated because he was so nice, knew about the murders. After hypnosis Ken denied knowledge of Steve and continued to maintain his innocence. Dr. Watkins and three other psychiatrists diagnosed Bianchi as suffering from multiple personality disorder, and the defense entered a plea of not guilty by reason of insanity.

Was Bianchi faking a disorder to avoid a possible death penalty or a lengthy prison term? Several pieces of information raised this possibility. Bianchi had a history of lying and using false names and identities. His activities included stealing, pimping for prostitutes, and misrepresenting himself as a movie agent and as a psychologist. He had forged documents to obtain a license to practice psychology and was familiar with hypnosis and previous multiple personality cases. The court asked Martin Orne, a distinguished authority on hypnosis and dissociative disorder, and five other clinical experts to evaluate the possibility that Bianchi was malingering. Orne (Orne et al., 1984) set forth the following criteria for discriminating multiple personality disorder from malingering:

1. Was Bianchi really hypnotized or was he simulating? Orne concluded that when under hypnosis, Bianchi gave responses typical of a simulator, not a deeply hypnotized person. For example, the suspect responded to the double hallucination test in a way uncharacteristic of a hypnotized person (see Box 6.2). His simulating hypnosis encouraged the view that he might also be faking multiple personality disorder symptoms.
2. Could Bianchi's personalities be modified by a casual comment designed to unobtrusively alter the demand characteristics of the situation? Until Orne hypnotized him, Bianchi had always reported only two personalities—Ken and Steve. Orne then indicated that the "real" disorder typically involved at least three personalities. Shortly thereafter a new personality, called Billy, emerged. Orne concluded that Bianchi had "far greater control over the management of his ego boundaries than he admitted to, or than would be expected in a patient with multiple personality disorder" (p. 144).
3. Did any independent corroboration of the existence of the different personalities occur before Bianchi's arrest? Extensive interviews with Bianchi's mother, wife, and former coworkers failed to uncover any evidence of preexisting personalities. Nor could his lawyer, social worker, priest, or prison authorities report ever observing the behavior characteristic of either Steve or Billy.
4. Did psychological tests show differences among the personalities? Experts who evaluated tests such as the Rorschach agreed that evidence did not support a multiple personality disorder diagnosis.

Based on the foregoing, Orne and his colleagues concluded that Bianchi was not a multiple personality. Their diagnosis was antisocial personality disorder (see Chapter 10). Of the six court-mandated consultants, four diagnosed Bianchi as having multiple personality disorder. (Watkins [1984] summarizes the view that Bianchi was a genuine case of multiple personality disorder). Orne and one other expert argued that he was malingering. The court agreed with Orne's reasoning, and Bianchi was found guilty and sentenced to life imprisonment.

Kenneth Bianchi, the infamous "Hillside Strangler."

dominant and raped and killed women who symbolized the mother who had abused Ken. Steve obtained sexual gratification from killing women. The Hillside murders began during his wife's pregnancy and ended with the birth of his son. His loss of sexual interest in his pregnant wife, together with his ambivalence about her becoming a mother (which perhaps stirred up his hostility toward his mother) apparently led directly to the murder spree.

The psychodynamic model dominates clinical thinking and practice in these disorders. It is supported by a wealth of clinical experience, but direct empirical confirmation of its theoretical assumptions is still lacking.

The Behavioral Model. Behaviorally oriented investigators have largely neglected dissociative disorders. The only model is the same as that for somatoform disorders. It suggests that individuals with multiple personality, or any other type of dissociative disorder, are playing a social role (Ullmann & Krasner, 1969). The patient has learned the particular role through prior modeling or exposure to information about the disorder, and maintains it by reinforcement of that behavior. The role involves selective attention to certain stimuli and inattention to others. Each personality is defined by the specific behavior in response to a set of restricted situational cues. Behaviorists reject the special states of consciousness and malingering and focus only on observable behavior and its consequences.

To test this model, Kohlenberg (1973) conducted the following study. First, he assessed the baseline rates of occurrence of the behaviors of the three personalities of a hospitalized patient. Then he selectively reinforced the behaviors of one personality. Predictably, these behaviors increased in frequency and then decreased when reinforcement was withdrawn—an example of an ABA single-case experimental design (see Chapter 4). This case study shows that reinforcement contingencies can influence the behavior of a multiple personality, but nothing about etiology can be inferred.

Spanos, Weekes, and Bertrand (1985) have described a social psychological model of multiple personality that is fundamentally the same as the behavioral formulation. To demonstrate that normal subjects can adopt the social role of a person with a multiple personality under the appropriate circumstances, they conducted a laboratory experiment modeled on the Los Angeles Hillside Strangler case (see Box 6.3). They found that if they knew enough, normal college students could take on the role of a separate personality to cope with a personally threatening situation.

In this study, three groups of normal college students were instructed to play the role of an accused murderer claiming his innocence. They would also participate in a psychiatric interview which might involve hypnosis. Following this standard description of the experiment, each group was issued different instructions. A brief hypnotic induction and an interview taken virtually word-for-word from Dr. Watkins's with Kenneth Bianchi was given to Group A. As in that interview, subjects were asked, "Pat, are you the same thing as Harry or are you different in any way. . . ?" Hypnosis was explained to Group B as a means of uncovering thoughts and feelings "walled off" in a different part of them but the direct question asked of Group A was left out. Group C were not hypnotized but told that personality often involved walled-off feelings.

The results showed that more than 80 percent of the subjects in the so-called Bianchi condition (Group A) adopted an alternative personality, a significantly greater number than either Group B or C. Group A subjects showed many of the classic symptoms of multiple personality disorder. They displayed posthypnotic amnesia, that is, after the interview they denied awareness of the other personality. The different personalities were opposite in tastes, emotionality, and behavior; they even performed differently on psychological tests. Spanos and his colleagues concluded that subjects knowledgeable about the multiple personality role can use it to achieve their own ends.

The behavioral model fails to provide an adequate account of multiple personality disorder or the other dissociative disorders as it describes rather than explains the disorders. It cannot predict who will adopt such a strange "social role" as a multiple personality nor why they would do so. The model neither accounts for nor explains the remarkably high incidence of childhood trauma in patients with multiple personality disorder. Nor does it explain the different forms of psychopathology associated with the disorder. By rejecting any dichotomy between multiple personality disorder and malingering, the model fails to address the important diagnostic and legal issues discussed in Box 6.3. The laboratory experiment by Spanos et al. (1985) cleverly demonstrated that normal subjects could adopt the role of a person with multiple personality disorder. This is what Orne and his colleagues (1984) claimed Kenneth Bianchi was doing—faking it. They then spelled out ways in which the "real disorder" might be differentiated from role playing or faking. It would be interesting to apply these criteria to the normal students in the study by Spanos and his coworkers. Presumably, it would reveal that they were merely role playing.

The model predicts that therapists who use hypnosis to diagnose multiple personality may unwittingly encourage patients to show the disorder. Hypnosis may elicit fragments of different personalities, but there is no evidence that hypnosis can create the full clinical disorder (Coons, 1988; Kluft, 1987a). Because of these shortcomings, the behavioral model has had little impact on either research or therapy in this area.

The Cognitive Model. Research findings in cognitive psychology point toward an understanding of dissociative disorders (Bower, 1981). The first finding is that of mood, or *state-dependent memory.* People remember an event best if at the time of recall they can return to the same emotional state they learned it in. For example, in the basic experiment, college students are hypnotized to feel happy or sad. During their happy mood they recall happy personal events during the preceding few weeks; conversely, during their sad mood they recall events that made them sad. The second finding of mood congruity effect means that people learn selectively about material that agrees with their current mood. For example, students are hypnotized to feel happy or sad just before imagining themselves in a number of briefly described situations. Some of these situations are designed to elicit happiness, others sadness. Students are then returned to a neutral mood and asked to recall the situations. Subjects who had been happy during the task learned more about the happy situations, those who had been sad, more about the sad situations. These results show that selective learning has occurred.

Bower has proposed an associative network theory to explain such results. An emotion as a unit in the memory system becomes associated with events the individual perceives as causing that emotion to be aroused. When the emotion is rearoused later, even if by another means, it activates its associated memories. Bower (1981, 1986) has speculated that multiple personalities "may be particularly compelling role enactments that have become suffused with distinctly different moods, with the role's behavior perpetuating its mood . . . a distinctive mood, emotional tone, or set of emotional conflicts associated with a role could easily cause events occurring during enactment of that role to be partially dissociated from, and inaccessible to other states of the person" (pp. 146–147). Consistent with this view is the finding that the multiple personalities typically are characterized by intense and markedly different emotions.

The speculative nature of this approach to multiple personality disorder must be emphasized. Moreover, Bower (1987) has reported some failures to replicate some of the basic findings on mood and memory. At best, this is an incomplete account of multiple personality disorder. Although these findings do suggest how dissociated memories and feeling states might form and be cognitively organized, they do not address why people would dissociate. The apparent motivational or defensive function nature of dissociation is ignored. This explanation, of course, is the unique contribution of the psychodynamic model.

Treatment. A range of different therapies have been used to treat multiple personality disorder, including antidepressant and antianxiety drugs. The two most common treatment methods, however, are hypnosis and psychodynamic psychotherapy (Coons, 1986).

Hypnosis is employed to make the primary personality aware of the other personalities. Posthypnotic suggestions encourage the patient's separate personalities to share memories and feelings to eventually fuse them into an integrated whole.[5]

Psychodynamic therapy focuses on producing insight into the underlying childhood trauma that caused the dissociation. Making the patient aware of these painful experiences should eliminate the need for a dissociated self and help in personality integration. A classic illustration of this is the treatment of Chris Costner Sizemore. In one pivotal therapy session, "Jane who had never had a childhood, who had no knowledge of personal happenings during growing-up years, told [Dr. Thigpen] of the frightening experience of being forced to kiss her dear grandmother good-bye; and she told it in a five-year-old voice. The thin, piping voice, laced with gulping sobs, related the moment of hysterical horror" (Sizemore & Pittillo, 1977, p. 307).

When the therapist later tried to contact either Eve White or Eve Black, Jane reported that they were no longer there. They were gone and she was now alone. It appeared as though getting in touch with this terrifying childhood memory forged an integrated personality. Yet such integration did not occur as separate personalities of Chris Sizemore continued to emerge for several years following this insight.

The goals of treatment for all dissociative disorders consist of developing coping strategies so that patients no longer need to rely on dissociation, and to assist them in integrating their personality. Spiegel (1986) has identified the following strategies for achieving these therapeutic goals:

1. *Confront the trauma.* To have patients alleviate self-blame, identify the trauma that led to the dissociation. In treating a rape victim, for example, "a therapist who chooses to focus on oedipal conflicts instead of effects of the rape, reinforces the patient's fantasy that she was somehow responsible for the rape instead of a victim of it,

[5] Proponents of the behavioral or social psychological model reject hypnosis as able to break down the barriers of dissociated states. They interpret the therapeutic use of hypnosis as providing a legitimate context to display different personalities (Spanos et al., 1985, p. 374).

thereby enhancing the need to dissociate the experience of the rape from her view of herself" (p. 128).

2. *Condense the traumatic experience.* Have patients focus on a specific image that reflects the traumatic experience. Hypnosis is especially valuable here. "For example, a combat veteran who suffered a two-day fugue episode in Vietnam after discovering the body of a boy he had adopted, learned to picture an image of the boy's grave next to that of a party he had given him. These two images helped him grieve over the loss by interweaving it with moments of shared pleasure" (p. 128).
3. *Confession.* Help patients disclose their feelings about the traumatic experience.
4. *Make conscious the dissociated material.* Both hypnosis and psychodynamic therapy share this goal.
5. *Therapist support.* The therapist must develop a supportive relationship with patients.
6. *Control.* Patients should feel a sense of control in accessing previously repressed memories.

Controlled evaluations of treatment outcome are lacking. Current evidence comes from uncontrolled clinical observations. Coons (1986) followed up twenty patients with multiple personality disorder for a mean of 39 months (range = 3 to 129 months). Only five (25 percent) had achieved full personality integration, while another two were partially integrated. Patients who failed to improve had experienced significantly more emotional trauma during treatment than those who achieved integration. Roughly two thirds of both the patients and their therapists thought that the patients had shown moderate to marked improvement. Antipsychotic medication had either no effect or made patients worse. Antidepressant drugs were rated as more useful. These modestly successful reports indicate the difficulty of treating this complex disorder.

SUMMARY

1. Somatoform disorders involve the presence of physical symptoms with no identifiable physiological basis. Patients with these disorders repeatedly seek medical treatment. In conversion disorder (once known as hysterical neurosis) patients develop symptoms linked to neurological disease or lose their sight or voice. Although some physical illnesses may be misdiagnosed as conversion disorder, the problem seems to demand a psychological explanation.
2. The psychodynamic model assumes that intolerable anxiety is unconsciously transformed into physical symptoms to prevent it from breaking into consciousness. The model derives from Freud's pioneering work with Breuer, largely based on the famous but questionable case study of Anna O. Freud's formulation of this disorder was one of the cornerstones of psychoanalysis. He proposed that virtually all anxiety (neurotic) disorders were the product of unresolved childhood sexual conflicts. Psychodynamic treatment is aimed at identifying and resolving the underlying psychological conflict responsible for the physical symptoms.
3. The behavioral model speculates that patients learn to adopt the symptoms as a way of coping with life's stresses. It fails to explain why only a small number of people adopt such a "sick role." Treatment is designed to develop more constructive coping skills and reinforce more adaptive behavior.
4. Dissociative disorders involve serious disruption in the person's identity, memory, or consciousness. Multiple personality is the best known of these disorders. Individuals with this disorder have two or more distinctive and integrated personalities, each with its own pattern of cognitive, emotional, and behavioral responses. The personalities are typically opposite in nature and unaware of each other.
5. Once considered rare, the number of reported cases of multiple personality disorder has increased dramatically. Critics allege that this increase is spurious and due to misdiagnosis. Proponents of the greater prevalence of the disorder argue that it is real and due to improved diagnoses. The psychodynamic model explains this and all other dissociative disorders as a defense against overwhelmingly painful early experience. Dissociative reactions develop if the patient has the capacity to split off thoughts and feelings from awareness. If not, the conflict is repressed in some other form. Consistent with this view, the vast majority of multiple personality patients have been seriously abused as children.
6. The behavioral model of multiple personality disorder is similar to that for somatoform disorders and shares the same limitations. It does not explain why particular individuals would adopt such a "sick role." Psychiatric diagnosis distinguishes between conversion and dissociative disorders and malingering, namely, the conscious adoption of a role to satisfy some personal need. The behavioral model focuses only on overt behavior and draws no distinction between the real disorder and malingering. Nor does it distinguish between hypnotically induced behavior and the clinical disorder. Psychodynamic and cognitive approaches do differentiate between conversion and dissociative disorders on the one hand, and malingering or hypnotically induced behavior on the other.
7. The customary treatment for multiple personalities is hypnotherapy or psychodynamic therapy, with the goal of identifying and resolving the trauma which triggered the original dissociative reaction.

Pablo Picasso, *Brooding Women* (1904). Watercolor on paper, 10⅝ × 14¼ inches. Collection, The Museum of Modern Art, New York. Gift of Mr. and Mrs. Werner E. Josten.

7 MOOD DISORDERS

Feeling gloomy, despondent, broken-hearted, dejected, and sad are depressive emotional states. "I've got the blues" is a common expression of depression, and the "blues" is a type of folk music characterized by minor harmony and a slow jazz rhythm. The titles of songs such as "Against All Odds" by Phil Collins and "I'm Down" by John Lennon also reflect coping with emptiness and depressive mood states.

William Styron, Pulitzer prize winning author of *Sophie's Choice* and *The Confessions of Nat Turner*, recently completed *Darkness Visible: A Memoir of Madness* (1990) chronicling his struggle with depression.

> The pain of severe depression is quite unimaginable to those who have not suffered it, and it kills in many instances because its anguish can no longer be borne. The prevention of many suicides will continue to be hindered until there is general awareness of this pain. Through the healing process of time—and through medical intervention or hospitalization in some cases—most people survive depression, which may be its only blessing; but to the tragic legion who are compelled to destroy themselves there should be no more reproof attached than to the victim of terminal cancer (p. 33).

These examples of depression from ordinary speech, popular music, and literature only begin to suggest the problem's prominence and related affective states in our lives. People of all races and socioeconomic levels suffer from depression. Many noted politicians such as Abraham Lincoln, Theodore Roosevelt, and Winston Churchill had depressive episodes. Creative artists such as the painter, Vincent Van Gogh, and the writer, Ernest Hemingway, had severe bouts with depression. In fact, musicians, artists, and writers are much more likely to have depressive disorders than the average person (Goodwin & Jamison, 1990). On the other hand, it should be emphasized that many creative writers and artists have no significant psychopathology.

Our popular press has called depression "the common cold of mental illness" (Gelman, 1987). Indeed, community survey data indicate that only the various anxiety disorders are more common than depression (Myers et al., 1984). Its frequent occurrence should not lead us to minimize depression's serious consequences. In fact, 60 percent of suicides are committed by depressed individuals (see Figure 7.1).

Each of us may show symptoms of depression at times: An elderly man may be depressed following the death of his spouse. A woman may cry frequently, lack motivation, and fight with her husband as she struggles with a drinking problem. A college student may become despondent about failure to refrain from bingeing and purging food. Although each shows symptoms of depression, it is secondary to another problem: The elderly man is suffering from bereavement, the woman from alcoholism, and the student

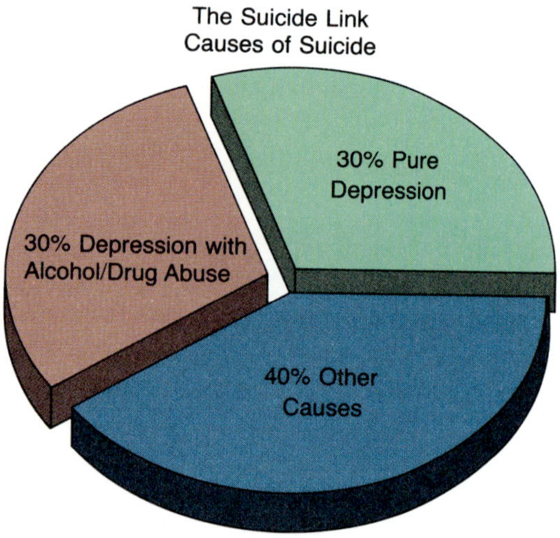

Figure 7.1 *This figure shows that 60 percent of suicides are related to depression.*
Source: Klerman, G., *Newsweek*, May 4, 1987, Artist: C. Blumrich.

from an eating disorder. The focus of this chapter, however, is depression as the primary problem.

Unipolar depression (depression alone) and bipolar disorder (depression and mania) are the main types of mood disorders seen in mental health clinics and psychiatric hospitals. They are officially called (1) major depressive disorder, or unipolar disorder and (2) bipolar disorder. Unipolar disorder is more common, occurring almost fifteen times as frequently.

People with unipolar disorder are overwhelmed by depressive feelings extending into many parts of their lives. They show decreased interest in everyday activities, lack motivation to accomplish all but the most minor tasks, feel worthless, and occasionally have suicidal thoughts. Exhibition of these symptoms with sufficient severity for extended periods is diagnosed as **depressive disorder,** or unipolar disorder.

Bipolar disorder (often called manic-depressive disorder), the second major type of mood disorder, is characterized by mood shifts between extreme highs (mania) and lows (depression). People with bipolar disorder swing from periods of very high energy to periods of severe despondency and little energy. During their high times they may be amusing and entertaining, however, they often are very irritating and get into other people's business. Constantly in motion, they talk loudly and incessantly. During their low or depressed phases, almost all aspects of their thought and behavior (speech, sexual activity, and motor behavior) slow down. Further, they often seriously contemplate and, indeed, plan and attempt suicide (Winokur, 1981).

Ernest Hemingway suffered from bipolar disorder and his biographer, Carlos Baker (1969), described Hemingway's mood swings in the following way:

> [He] is the temperamental manic-depressive . . . who spoke seriously of suicide at intervals throughout his life, yet possessed enormous powers of resilience and recuperation that could bring him back from the brink to the peak within days and sometimes within hours.
>
> He could be lifted from the depths by early morning, the time of the sunset, breezy sunlight, crisp cold hills, and mountains, and the sea (p. viii).

This chapter will define depression and then discuss its prevalence, causes, and treatment. The symptoms associated with unipolar and bipolar disorders will be explored, as will the following topics:

1. The reasons for the disproportionately high rate of major depressive disorder among women.
2. The distinction between mood disorders and other disorders such as anxiety.
3. Genetic theories based both on twin and family studies.
4. Psychological theories of depression focusing on cognitive and marital/interpersonal difficulties.
5. The biological and psychological treatment of depression as well as suicide.

DEFINITIONS

Unipolar Depression

According to *DSM-III-R*, when individuals experience either a depressed mood or a loss of interest in all activities for at least two weeks, they are exhibiting some of the symptoms of the unipolar depression

More women than men become depressed and relationship problems are often precipitants of depression. Lethargy, feeling blue, and loss of interest in daily activities are among the common symptoms of depression.

diagnosis. Besides these two primary symptoms, people with major depression must display a number of the following associated symptoms: appetite disturbance, change in weight, sleep disturbance, psychomotor agitation or retardation, decreased energy, feelings of worthlessness or excessive inappropriate guilt, difficulty thinking or concentrating, and recurrent thoughts of death or suicide; they may also attempt suicide.

The most common symptoms, depressed mood and loss of interest, are apparent in depressed people's daily activities. They may stop their hobbies and have little interest in work. If depressed individuals do go to work, they may have difficulty making decisions, interacting with others, and completing tasks. They may avoid the real work of the day by filing papers, cleaning equipment, and talking about inconsequential matters. Depressed people often find it hard to concentrate on any reading material. Thus, depression impairs performance in college students and others who need to concentrate for long periods on written documents. Even activities that normally would be of special value to them, such as showing affection, having intercourse, and watching movies, become uninteresting.

Although some people sleep more when depressed, more people report trouble falling asleep because they worry about the past day's events. More severely depressed people, once they finally manage to fall asleep, often awaken two to three hours before usual. Lack of deep sleep—as reflected in brain wave patterns—and more awake time during the night often characterizes depressed people. Most depressed individuals, if they have dreams, report them to be sad and unpleasant. For these reasons, it is not surprising that depressed people frequently wake not feeling refreshed.

Suicidal thoughts are also common in depressed people. The suicide rates of depressed teen-agers are particularly disturbing due to marked increases recently (see Chapter 13). Suicide rose significantly in the 1980s to become the third most common cause of teenage death, with only automobile accidents and homicide as more frequent (Berman & Jobes, 1990).

Depressed individuals are very self-critical. They dwell on past failures, attribute their problems to their lack of skill, and focus on negative events that occur to them and to others.

Fortunately, many people with serious depression do recover and return to normal functioning within a year, even if untreated. A majority of depressed people, however, have to cope with bouts of depression throughout their lives (Frank et al., 1990). The extreme anguish and suicidal risk of the seriously depressed person is illustrated by Abraham Lincoln's wish to die if he did not recover from his bout of depression (see Box 7.1).

Bipolar Depression

As noted earlier, a critical sign of bipolar disorder is if the individual undergoes one or more manic episodes, that is, periods characterized by either an elevated expansive mood or irritable mood. Most bipolar disorder patients also have major depressive episodes. The name *bipolar* implies the two poles, or opposites, of manic and depressive episodes. Those in a manic state are hyperactive, exhibit boundless energy, feel "high," often have grandiose ideas, and may even feel all-powerful. They may also see themselves as extremely sexually attractive and engage in a spree of sexual activity. Similarly, during a manic episode, they may write what they believe to be the beginning of a perfect essay or novel or spend money recklessly (see Box 7.2). In brief, the judgment of someone undergoing a manic episode is impaired. Reflecting this deficit in judgment, manic episodes often interfere markedly with an individual's family and occupational functioning, often to the point of requiring hospitalization. Manic episodes are, however, usually much briefer than episodes of unipolar depression. A manic episode generally lasts from only a few days to a few months, whereas unipolar depression may last from many months to several years.

Clinicians and researchers have viewed bipolar, or manic-depressive, disorder, as mainly a biochemical problem. Convincing evidence suggests that genetic factors are critical in the etiology of bipolar disorders (Baldessarini & Cole, 1988) and medications are effective in their treatment. This biological perspective, coupled with the relative infrequency of the disorder, has resulted in much less psychological research on bipolar disorders than on unipolar disorders.

The association of unipolar and bipolar depression is frequently debated. Some experts see the two disorders as very distinct entities. Others see them as lying on a continuum called the depressive spectrum—with bipolar depression being simply a more severe form of depression. Recent researchers believe the distinctiveness of the two disorders has been overdramatized because of such data as that indicating relatives of bipolar depressives are more likely to suffer from unipolar depression than bipolar depression (Goodwin & Jamison, 1990).

PREVALENCE

Prevalence rates indicate the percentage of a population suffering from a specific disorder. Point prevalence is the percentage of individuals with the disorder at the particular point in time the population was sampled. The measurement of lifetime prevalence is the percentage of individuals who have ever had the disorder at any time in their lives. As you might ex-

BOX 7.1 Abraham Lincoln: The Fatal First of January 1841

Abraham Lincoln was to be married on January 1, 1841, but never showed up for the wedding. His fiance, Mary Todd, and the wedding party anxiously waited for him. But, because Lincoln did not arrive at all, the wedding banquet was left untouched, and Mary Todd cried herself to sleep that fateful first of January.

Lincoln's biographer, L. Pierce Clark, described his mood that January of 1841:

> Where can Abraham Lincoln be? Has he not looked forward to this, his wedding day? No; to Lincoln it is almost his death day. By daybreak [of January 2], after persistent search Lincoln's friends find him. The mental strain he has manifested all through the engagement now drives him with restless agitation into a state bordering on melancholia . . . (p. 55).
>
> After a few days, during which he scarcely eats or sleeps, Lincoln appears less agitated, but his thinking is labored and his actions are similarly slow. Periods of silence are broken by lamentations and listlessness. He is indifferent to his surroundings, interrupted by short-lived periods of a pressure of activity as though he were laboring under an intense inner conflict. His thoughts are filled with gloomy forebodings. On the days when he is less perturbed he is able to attend the sessions of the legislature, yet he is clothed in a constant mood of apathy and gloom. His friends encourage him to attend these sessions, as this activity may take his mind from his recent misfortune [his depression and wedding cancellation].
>
> A few weeks later, he writes Stuart in Washington, "I have within the last few days, been making a most discreditable exhibition of myself in the way of hypochondriasm." And a few days later, in answer to a letter from his partner, he states, "From the deplorable state of my mind at this time, I fear I shall give you but little satisfaction," but he is able to give his partner briefly the political news. Yet even this little attention to the issues at hand fatigues Lincoln, and he ends, "I am now the most miserable man living. If what I feel were equally distributed to the whole human family, there would be not one cheerful face on the earth. Whether I shall ever be better, I cannot tell; I awfully forebode I shall not. To remain as I am is impossible; I must die or be better. . . ."

Source: From Clark, L.P. (1933). *Lincoln—A Psycho-Biography*. Charles Scribner's Sons: New York, 57. Reprinted with permission.

Lincoln's depression was so pronounced that he did not show up for his wedding to Mary Todd. Later in her life, Mary Todd Lincoln was declared insane by a jury and she then attempted suicide.

pect, the lifetime prevalence rate is higher than the point prevalence rate.

The lifetime prevalence rate of unipolar depression is 15 percent to 20 percent for women and 8 percent to 10 percent for men. The point prevalence rate is approximately 7 percent to 8 percent for women and 3 percent for men (American Psychiatric Association, 1987). As might be expected, women are hospitalized more frequently than men. The rates of depression for male and female college students are about equal, with about 10 percent of students exhibiting moderate depression while 5 percent are severely depressed (Craighead, 1984). Contrary to popular belief, depression is not most frequently found among the elderly; rather, it is most common among the eighteen- to forty-four-year-old groups (Myers et al., 1984).

People who were adolescents and young adults from 1960 to 1975 were especially affected by depression (Weissman & Klerman, 1977). The social upheaval of the 1960s and 1970s, the Vietnam War (1964–1975), the return of thousands of alienated veterans, the rapid rise in divorce, and the continued loosening of family ties in the past few decades all may have contributed to increasing rates of depression among adolescents and young adults.

Approximately fifteen percent of college students report moderate or severe depression. Academic and relationship pressures are among the most common stressors that lead college students to question their worth and in turn feel depressed.

HOW TO DISTINGUISH DEPRESSION FROM OTHER DISORDERS

In differential diagnosis, the clinician discriminates or differentiates one disorder from another in a patient. A patient often has symptoms of two or more disorders. For example, in outpatient mental health clinics, anxiety and depression are two of the most common problems occurring together which can be differentiated.

The correlation between anxiety and depression is usually quite high. For example, in one study this correlation was .60 (Beck et al., 1987). The strength of this association has led to a debate about whether anxiety and depression are separate disorders or actually part of the same disorder. However, despite the relatively high correlation between anxiety and depression, major depressive disorders and generalized anxiety disorders can be reliably differentiated using structured clinical interviews. Additionally, Beck (1976) argues that specific types of cognitions distinguish depressed people from anxious people. He and his colleagues found that self-criticism and negative attitudes about the past and the future characterize the thoughts of depressed individuals. In contrast, the thoughts of anxious people center around possible imminent harm and danger, often overestimating the intensity and probability of the possible harm surrounding an event.

The clinician must take a careful developmental history of the patient's problems to differentiate between unipolar and bipolar disorders. Since the presence of a manic phase, either concurrently or in the past, is central to the diagnosis of bipolar disorder, the clinician must probe for a history of manic episodes.

Dysthymia is a chronic depressed mood disturbance differing in severity and duration from major depression. Symptoms such as loss of interest and hopelessness characterize dysthymia—just as they do major depressive disorder—but dysthymia's symptoms are less intense and last longer. They usually last two years or more and are evident during the majority of the days during this period. The dysthymic individual in the depressed phase shows some or all of the following symptoms: poor appetite or overeating, insomnia or hypersomnia, fatigue, low self-esteem, poor concentration, and feelings of hopelessness. Dysthymia is often diagnosed as secondary to other problems such as anorexia nervosa, anxiety disorders, and substance abuse.

A disorder clinicians must distinguish from bipolar disorders is **cyclothymia.** Cyclothymia refers to a chronic mood disturbance that has lasted at least two years. It is characterized by loss of interest in activities but to a lesser extent than major depressive disorders. Like the mania of a bipolar disorder, the cyclothymic exhibits expansiveness, irritability, and/or elevation. However, the manic-like episode (often called **hypomania**) is more mild than mania, and such an episode is not severe enough to markedly impair a person's social or occupational functioning or to require hospitalization. Thus, clinical judgment is required to distinguish between cyclothymia and bipolar disorder, with the diagnosis hinging in part on the severity of impairment.

DIFFERENCES IN RATES OF UNIPOLAR DEPRESSION IN MEN AND WOMEN

Women display much higher rates of depression than men across a variety of different studies and across many diverse cultures. The reasons for these sex-differences in rates of depression are not clearly understood and have intrigued researchers for decades. Biological, psychological, and social factors have been offered in debates among biologists, psychologists, and sociologists. These debates usually center around the difference in rates in men and women

BOX 7.2 Coping with Mania

This patient—a poet who has published in nationally recognized sources—provides commentary about her experience with mania. She describes her mania's influence on her creativity and her ability to write but also her terror of losing control. Finally, she shows how the slide down into depression following the manic period is associated with total exhaustion and an inability to work.

> I must be manic to work effectively. For me to write prose, I must empathize with my characters. I must become them. I can excuse these manic episodes in a controlled way. I lock myself in my room and I allow myself to get smarter and smarter. (I have always perceived my depression as a form of stupidity, and my highs as a form of intelligence—a blinding intelligence.) What is difficult for me to do if I am to succeed as a novelist is not to go so high that my powers of organization leave me. To quote my therapist, "The idea is not to create tossed salad."
>
> As a poet I have depended upon my mania to keep me functioning at a level high enough to capture not just ideas alone, but the emotions that color and heighten one's sense of reality. The need is to make the mania last: To keep the sense of super-competence from shifting downward into anxiety and aggression, to at all costs remain productive; though in truth I have no idea of how long my productivity will actually last.
>
> Eventually the slippery highs produce a frustrated sense of not being able to be in control. And from there a sense of anxiety quickly develops followed by an even stronger feeling of terror. One becomes too alive, feels wired all the time and desperately wants all the dizzying terror to stop. And finally (though only after one has slid far enough down), it does. One becomes exhausted, too stupid, too depressed to move, the very thought of any creative kind of work seeming both threatening and absurd.

Source: From the files of Dr. Susan O'Leary.

with unipolar depression since no substantial sex differences exist in the rates of bipolar disorders.

Women outnumber men in rates of unipolar depression in most Western and industrialized countries. More specifically, women are approximately twice as likely to be depressed as men in industrialized countries (McGrath, et al., 1990). On the other hand, women do not differ from men in rates of being treated for depression in countries such as India, Iraq, New Guinea, and Zimbabwe (Weissman & Klerman, 1977), but they do differ in rates of depression reported in clinical surveys. The fact that women have higher rates of depression in developing countries but receive treatment only as often as men, may simply reflect the ability of men to get professional help more readily than women (Kleinman, 1988; Levenson, 1988).

EXPLANATIONS FOR THE DISPROPORTIONATE SEX RATIO

Biological

Two general biological hypotheses have been advanced to account for the sex differences in depression. The first, the hormonal hypothesis, is partly derived from the observation that women are at the greatest risk for depression when their estrogen or progesterone levels change significantly. The premenstrual period, the postpartum period following the birth of a child, and the menopausal period are the most noteworthy examples of great hormonal change. Although the hormonal hypothesis has received considerable attention, the evidence is either inconsistent or counter to it (Janowsky & Rausch, 1985). For example, when women were asked to use a daily mood checklist, there was no association between mood ratings and the menstrual cycle (Abplanap, Haskett, & Rose, 1979; Persky, O'Brien, & Kahn, 1976). While it is too early to totally discount a hormonal explanation for sex differences in depression, current evidence does not support this hypothesis.

The second biological hypothesis, the genetic hypothesis, is based on two facts: (1) unipolar depression runs in families, and (2) the concordance rate for depression in monozygotic twins (same egg) is greater than the rate for dizygotic twins (separate egg) (Allen, 1976). Females have two XX chromosomes, and some mutation in the X chromosome accounts for the observed sex differences. Some supporters of the sex-linked genetic theory argue that females should be at higher risk for depression because they have two X chromosomes. The sex-linked chromosome hypothesis is based on complex blood group typing and the specific location of certain gene abnormalities. Evidence, nonetheless, does not support this biological hypothesis in women with unipolar depression (Gershon & Bunney, 1976).

Psychological

Stress has also been hypothesized to account for sex differences in depression, partly because many clinicians have noted that stressful events often occur before the onset of depression. Although there is an association between stress and severity of psychiatric symptoms, women do not report a greater occurrence of more stressful events than men (Unlenhuth,

Lipman, Balter, & Stern, 1974). In addition, when evaluating specific stressors, women do not perceive these events as more stressful than men.

Learned helplessness, or perceived lack of control over events in one's life, has also been posited to explain sex differences in depression. This hypothesis is based on the assumption that women, as compared to men, believe their behavior is less effective in making good things happen. Women, in fact, are more likely to attribute success on academic tasks to luck or the favor of others (Dweck, 1975) and to attribute failures to lack of ability. Although these findings might lead us to expect women to have more depression than men, they have involved populations where sex differences in depression have not been typically found (e.g., children and university students). Thus, there has been no direct test of the learned helplessness model as a cause of sex differences in depression.

Another possibility for the observed sex differences in depression is women's different coping strategies, characteristic ways of responding to certain events or stimuli. A number of researchers have found that women respond differently than men to feelings of depression (Nolen-Hoeksema, 1987). Presented with a "list of things people do when depressed," college students were asked to indicate how likely they were to engage in them. Men scored higher on items such as the following: "I avoid thinking of reasons why I am depressed," "I do something physical," "I play a sport," and "I take drugs." In contrast, women scored higher on items such as: "I try to determine why I am depressed," "I talk to other people about my feelings," and "I cry to relieve the tension." In other words, men tend to distract themselves from the depressed mood whereas women tend to focus and maintain attention on it. If focusing on depressed feelings intensifies them, then this response style may make women more likely than men to become clinically depressed. This hypothesis has not been tested directly but supportive evidence suggests its validity. For example, men who use coping strategies more common in women—focusing on their negative feelings—are more likely to become clinically depressed at a later date than men who employ distraction coping strategies (Wood et al., 1989).

CAUSES

Biological models of depression predominated during the 1950s and 1960s and continue to influence the field. Nevertheless, individual psychological models of depression became accepted in the 1970s and 1980s. In the 1980s, interpersonal or marital and family models of depression began to receive significant attention.

Biological Theories of Depression

The argument for depression's genetic transmission was introduced by the English author, Robert Burton, in 1621 in his book, *The Anatomy of Melancholy.* He asserted that the "inbred cause of melancholia is our temperature, in whole or part, which we receive from our parents" and "such as the temperature of the father is, such as his son's, and look what disease the father had when he begot him, his son will have after him" (p. 184). For Burton centuries ago, temperature meant bodily temperature which he thought caused mood changes. More important, his observation that diseases are passed from one generation to the next continues to be advanced. Over time, the particular form of this argument and the technology used in making it have grown increasingly sophisticated. Family studies and twin studies have been used to investigate the role of genetic variables in the etiology of depression.

Family Studies. Studies of family inheritance patterns provide useful leads in genetic and biochemical research. The poet, Lord Byron, and the composer, Robert Schumann, were both afflicted with bipolar depression, and biographical accounts of their families indicate that many of their relatives were similarly affected (Goodwin & Jamison, 1990).

In the late 1970s, the National Institute of Mental Health launched a large study of the psychobiology of different types of depression (Andreasen, Rice et al., 1987). Approximately 600 depressed subjects and 3,000 of their first-degree relatives (children, brothers, sisters, and parents) were observed across five cities: Boston, Chicago, Iowa City, New York, and St. Louis. The researchers divided their depressed subjects, the vast majority of whom were hospitalized, into various groups.

As expected, relatives of bipolar subjects had a higher lifetime prevalence rate of bipolar disorder than relatives of unipolar patients. Relatives of bipolar depressives, however, also displayed higher rates of unipolar depression than did the relatives of unipolar probands. Thus, from this study and related evidence (Gershon, 1990), we can conclude relatives of hospitalized bipolar depressives are at significant risk for developing either bipolar or unipolar depression. Indeed, Gershon (1990) stated "The most frequent affective disorder in relatives of bipolar patients is not bipolar illness but unipolar illness" (p. 379).

Family studies also indicate that relatives of hospitalized unipolar depressives have a much higher rate of depression than we would generally expect in the population. The likelihood of bipolar disorders in relatives of patients with unipolar disorders is very low (Andreasen & Block, 1991; Gershon, 1990).

In summary, family studies suggest that unipolar depression "breeds true." That is, relatives of unipolar depressives have a very significant risk of developing unipolar depression but they have very little risk of developing bipolar depression. In contrast, the picture is not as clear-cut with bipolar disorders, since relatives of bipolar disorders have a greater likelihood of developing unipolar depression than for developing bipolar depression.

We want to address the risk of developing depression if you have a relative with symptoms of depression who was not hospitalized for it. If the relative is your parent, brother or sister (not a twin), the likelihood that you will have depressive symptoms is roughly the same as or only slightly higher than someone with no depressed relatives (Kendler et al., 1987). This information helps extend the notion of the depression spectrum with mild to moderate unipolar depression being on one end of the continuum, severe unipolar depression for which people are hospitalized being in the middle, and bipolar depression at the severe end of the continuum. As one moves from one end to the other, the likelihood of a relative developing depression increases.

It is difficult to separate hereditary factors from environmental factors in biographical accounts and family inheritance studies. If a daughter, mother, and grandmother were all depressed, an observer might conclude that depression in this family is "in the genes." But, alternatively, these women may have lived in depressing environments. Further, they may have married depressed men, leading them to feel depressed. In fact, we know that depressed persons are more likely than the average person to marry other depressed individuals (Merikangas, 1982). In any particular case of depression, it is impossible to know whether hereditary or environmental factors were more important in determining the depression.

Twin Studies. Twin studies of mood disorders show a clear-cut relationship between unipolar depression and genetic variables. Research with unipolar depressives yields monozygotic twin concordance rates of about 40 percent and dizygotic concordance rates of approximately 10 percent (Allen, 1976). In other words, with one monozygotic twin diagnosed as a unipolar depressive, there is a 40 percent chance that the other twin will also be depressed. In contrast, there is only a 10 percent chance that a dizygotic twin would be depressed if the other twin were diagnosed as depressed. Recall that the likelihood of an individual in the general population having unipolar depression is 7 percent to 8 percent for women and 3 percent for men, yielding an overall prevalence rate of approximately 5 percent. Therefore, with one twin in dizygotic pairs depressed, the other twin is roughly twice as likely to be depressed as the average person, and in monozygotic pairs the other twin is roughly eight times more likely to be depressed than the average person. Genetic factors clearly play a significant role in depression.

Heredity's role is even more apparent in the twin studies of bipolar depressives. With bipolar disorders, the monozygotic concordance rates are about 70 percent, whereas the dizygotic concordance rates are only 10 percent to 20 percent (Nurnberger & Gershon, 1982). While some researchers initially believed bipolar disorders were caused by a dominant gene on the X chromosome, much evidence suggests these disorders probably obey a more complex inheritance pattern (Farone, Kremen, & Tsuang, 1990).

Research on genetic factors in depression has derived almost solely from studies with hospitalized depressed patients. Studies of nonhospitalized twins with unipolar depression generally have not supported genetic theories (Torgersen, 1986; Kendler et al., 1987). That is, monozygotic and dizygotic concordance rates of clinical depression did not differ. Genetic factors, however, determine whether individuals may develop psychological symptoms of depression and anxiety. Development of depression or anxiety symptoms will also be determined by environmental factors (Torgersen, 1986; Kendler et al., 1987).

Adoption Studies. Twin studies strongly suggest a predisposition for inheriting depression, but twins may possibly create similar environments for themselves. Twins reared in the same family look similar, often develop their own special means of communicating, and spend a great deal of time with one another as children. Thus, similarities in their personalities could be due in part to these environmental factors. Adoption studies assess genetic influences and avoid the similarity of environments of the twin studies. Adoption studies compare those people who were adopted out of their biological families to both their biological relatives and their adoptive family members. Such research is often conducted in Western European countries with socialized medicine because detailed medical records beginning at birth are kept on all citizens. Thus, with special approval from the government, a researcher may be able to obtain hospital and mental health clinic records of both biological and nonbiological family members of the adopted person.

Adoption research further supports the view that genetic factors play an important role in the etiology of depression. Mendelewicz and Rainer (1977) assessed Belgian bipolar patients who had been adopted and ones who had not been adopted. They then determined whether the biological and nonbiological (adoptive) relatives of the depressed patients had ever been depressed. As expected, they found that more biological relatives of the patients were depressed than nonbiological relatives. Wender et al. (1986) assessed relatives of depressed patients and of nondepressed people in Denmark. They found depression more frequent among biological relatives of depressed subjects as compared to control cases. In brief, adoption research provides more support for the importance of genetic factors in the development of both unipolar and bipolar depression.

Inheritance of Bipolar Depression: Is It a Single Dominant Gene? An isolated religious community of Old Order Amish lives near Lancaster, Pennsylvania, consisting of approximately 12,500 people who live on farms and shun modern technology. They do not use motor-driven machinery, electric lights, nor telephones. They use horse-driven implements and dress in black or dark blue. Most Lancaster County Amish are descended from fifty couples who arrived in Pennsylvania in the mid-1700s from Germany. Alcoholism, drug use, and homicide are very uncommon among the Amish. They generally avoid social contact with the rest of the world and have values clearly different from those of general society. In addition, the Amish marry almost exclusively among themselves and keep careful family history records. This unique situation allows researchers to accurately study inheritance patterns of depression in the Amish.

Using very specific criteria to diagnose bipolar depression, Jean Endicott and her research team interviewed the Amish bipolar depressives and their relatives, studying family histories and their lines of descent (Hofstetter, Egeland, & Endicott, 1983). Like manics in other cultures, the Amish bipolar depressives overdo things. For example, when an Amish man was manic, his friends said he spoke so fast that nobody could understand him, he drove his horse and buggy at breakneck speed, and he was loud and boastful. The researchers' diagnostic and DNA marking techniques suggested that people inherited bipolar disorders through a single dominant gene, but not every individual with that one dominant gene developed the disorder. This situation is called **incomplete penetrance.** The term *penetrance* refers to the likelihood of having the disease if you have the dominant gene.

In addressing the issue of risk for developing bipolar depression in first-degree relatives, Endicott and her research team (Kolata, 1987) found that if an Amish individual had bipolar disorder, the likelihood of a relative being similarly diagnosed was 35 percent to 55 percent. These percentage rates are much higher than those in family studies of bipolar depression, namely 6 percent. Therefore, genetic determinants for bipolar depression were much stronger in these Amish families than in the general population.

Given the apparently strong genetic influence on bipolar depression in this community, a research team searched for a specific genetic marker for bipolar disorder among the Amish. A genetic marker is a particular site on a chromosome governing the presence or absence of a physical or behavioral characteristic. In the Amish with bipolar disorder, a portion of chromosome 11 was believed to be the genetic marker for depression (Egeland et al., 1987; Kolata, 1987). With additional analyses, however, this specific marker has proven questionable; a recent review of this research indicates that while there is some support for a single genetic marker, the results are not always consistent (Farone, Kremen, & Tsuang, 1990; Kelso et al., 1989; Merikangas et al., 1989).

Even if a genetic marker for depression exists in the Amish population, we should not conclude that the same marker would have equal penetrance in other populations with greater mating diversity. The Amish marry almost solely within their own community, and genetic factors in highly inbred communities can have greater influences than in other communities. There have not been attempts to replicate the research with the Lancaster County Amish in other Amish communities. Nonetheless, the results of this Amish community study (Hofstetter, Egeland, & Endicott, 1983) received considerable attention in the scientific and popular press, and the search for specific genetic markers of bipolar disorders as well as other psychiatric disorders was given increased impetus.

Biochemistry and Neurobiology of Depression

As early as the second century, depression was thought to be caused by a biochemical excess, black bile. It was not until the introduction of antidepressant drugs approximately thirty years ago, however, that much research on the biochemistry of depression occurred. In the 1960s, studies suggested that these antidepressant medications worked at least partly through effects on catecholamines, a class of chemicals that help transmit messages in the central nervous system. Following the research on transmission of messages came the study of the reception of messages in the central nervous system. Finally, in the 1980s, research developed on neuroendocrine abnormalities and sleep disorders in depression.

Neurotransmission. In the 1960s researchers intensely studied the transmission of electrical impulses in the brain, hoping to discover a biochemical explanation for depression. Electrical impulses are transmitted from one nerve cell, or neuron, to another. For transmission to occur across the tentacle-like nerve cells, chemicals called neurotransmitters are produced to carry the impulse, or message. Early investigators felt that one class of neurotransmitters, the catecholamines, held the key to depression. Too much catecholamine, especially norepinephrine, was thought to cause mania and too little to cause depression. Researchers quickly found, however, that a number of other neurotransmitters, such as dopamine and serotonin, are involved in depression, too.

Following these studies, depression research focused on the reception of messages in the transmission process. Almost immediately after a patient takes antidepressant medication, certain neural transmissions are increased. Despite this immediate action at the transmission site evidenced by biochemical activity, the psychological effects of the medication are not seen until two to three weeks afterward. This lag led many to believe that the receptor neurons are at "fault" in the production of depression. That is, though the messages may be sent properly, a problem may exist in how receptor neurons act on them.

Most researchers have not directly measured neurotransmitters in the brain. Instead, they measured by-products, or metabolites, of neurotransmitters in the cerebrospinal fluid and urine. Such research indicates that a metabolite of serotonin (5-hydroxyindolactic acid [5-HIAA]) is present in low amounts in the cerebrospinal fluid of depressed individuals. Longitudinal studies of bipolar patients have also shown that a metabolite in the urine [MHPG] appears in higher levels during bipolar patients' manic states as compared to their depressed states (Goodwin & Jamison, 1990). Attempts to demonstrate abnormalities in norepinephrine and serotonin activity in depressed persons have recently produced conflicting data. When the combined action of neurotransmitters such as norepinephrine, serotonin, and dopamine are considered together, however, prediction of response to antidepressant medication was enhanced. A strong association existed between the various neurotransmitters (norepinephrine, serotonin, and dopamine) in responders to antidepressant medication. In contrast, there was a lack of correlation between the various neurotransmitters in patients who did not respond to antidepressant medication. Thus, it appears that depression in many individuals is not simply a function of a single neurotransmitter deficiency but is caused by an abnormality in the interaction of various neurotransmitters (Hsiao et al., 1987).

Neuroendocrine Abnormalities. Current thought regarding the biochemistry of depression is that answers to the etiology of depression must be sought not only in the brain and in neurotransmitters but also in neurochemical processes involving endocrine glands. Work in this area was prompted by the observation that patients with endocrine diseases such as hypothyroidism often have symptoms of depression. In addition, development of biochemical tests allowing detection of very small amounts of hormones helped the field rapidly expand.

Initial research in this area indicated that over half of hospitalized depressed patients have an excess of the hormone cortisol in their blood and urine. As important, severely depressed patients often had relatively high levels of cortisol in their blood throughout the day whereas normals or nondepressed people have high levels of blood cortisol in the morning and lower levels the remainder of the day (Carroll et al., 1981). Of special interest to clinicians, moreover, was that patients recovering from depression have cortisol levels similar to those of nondepressed people.

The test for cortisol secretion, Dexamethasone Suppression Test (DST), was even used to predict response to treatment. There is some evidence, though not consistent, that patients with a cortisol abnormality respond best to antidepressant medication (Schildkraut, Green, & Mooney, 1985). It has become evident that patient groups such as schizophrenics and anorexics have abnormal DSTs, and the DST is no longer used as a general diagnostic test. Research on varied endocrine functions was stimulated by work on DST, and growth hormones and prolactin have recently received special attention (Goodwin & Jamison, 1990).

As they progressed in analyzing hormones' role in the development of depression, researchers sought to determine the specific place of the hormone disturbances; they wanted to find out where endocrine problems developed in a long complex chain called the HPA (hypothalmic-adrenal-pituitary) axis. It is hoped that study of this chain will help solve some of depression's mysteries appearing to result from the activation and inhibition of various brain areas as they activate and are activated by various hormones.

Research in depression's biochemistry proceeds at a very rapid pace, and there will likely be classifications of depressive disorders based on biochemistry. At present there is no biochemical test to guide a psychiatrist selecting a clinically effective medication certain to work on the first trial. However, recent research strides indicate such a test may be developed within the next decade.

Sleep Disorders. Depressed patients usually have sleep abnormalities reflected on EEG. They have less deep sleep (slow wave sleep) and longer periods of sleep time where dreams and nightmares occur (REM sleep). These abnormalities reflect many of the sleep problems mentioned by depressed people discussed earlier (Andreasen & Block, 1991). Depressed

BOX 7.3 Seasonal Affective Disorder (SAD)

Herbert Kern, a research scientist suffering from depression, recorded the timing of his moods and noted his mood changes seemed to be related to seasonal changes and/or length of daylight. In 1972, he joined the American Society of Photobiology in search of information regarding light's effect on the brain. In 1978, he unsuccessfully attempted to treat himself with brief exposures of ultraviolet light. Because of an interest in biochemical markers relating to mood swings, he contacted Dr. Alfred Lewy at the National Institute of Mental Health, who had reported a method of assessing melatonin, a chemical possibly regulating biological rhythms.

In the winter of 1980, Kern was successfully treated for his depression with full spectrum light simulating the sun's natural spectral qualities. This account of seeking a remedy to one's own problems documents the first successful treatment with bright artificial light (Kern & Lewy, 1990).

People with a subtype of major depressive disorder, called winter depression or **seasonal affective disorder (SAD),** display classic symptoms of depression in the winter and then often recover in the spring, even without specific treatment. The most common features of SAD are weight gain, low energy, and hypersomnia. In 1984, bright light therapy in the morning and evening for several weeks was found to be effective in reducing the winter depression of one patient. Since that time many people with winter depression have similarly been treated successfully in various centers across the country (Sack et al., 1990).

The effectiveness of light treatment in various settings, raises the question of why it works. Bright light in the morning, but not in the evening, reduces depressive symptoms. The exact reasons for this effectiveness of light treatment are not clear, but chemical analyses reveal that melatonin production is prompted by the morning light (Wehr & Rosenthal, 1989). In turn, melatonin production affects the body's circadian rhythms governing the awakening cycle. Presumably, depression is more likely to occur if circadian rhythms are delayed. Thus, the exposure to simulated sunlight seems to help people with winter depression by stimulating delayed circadian rhythms.

In the light therapy studies just discussed, people with SAD were moderately depressed as judged by their self-reports of depression, and they had few other symptoms. Further, they were not depressed at a follow-up in the summer. Thus these results suggest that people with winter depression can be successfully treated solely with full spectrum light.

people have EEG sleep abnormalities that can be distinguished from people with insomnia, anxiety disorder, and panic disorder. You may recall that serotonin and norepinephrine abnormalities have been found in many depressed patients, and these neurotransmitters are involved in the induction and maintenance of non-REM sleep. Thus excesses of these neurotransmitters may underlie the sleep problems of depressed people (Thase, Frank, & Kupfer, 1985).

Psychological Theories of Depression

As noted earlier, experts believe bipolar depression has a genetic/biochemical basis. Thus, psychological accounts of bipolar depression will be presented briefly later in this chapter. A discussion of the major psychological explanations of unipolar depression shows each account emphasizing individual variables.

Cognitive Theories

Cognitive Distortion and Negative Self-Schemata. According to Beck (1967; 1976), cognitions of depressed individuals reflect varying levels of cognitive distortions, which cause many if not most of a person's depressed states. Several of the most important follow:

Arbitrary inference is an individual's process of drawing a conclusion from a situation, an event, or an experience when no evidence supports the conclusion or when it is contrary to the evidence. For example, a woman concludes her boss hates her because he seldom makes positive remarks about her.

Overgeneralization refers to an individual's pattern of drawing conclusions about his or her ability, performance, or self-worth based on a single incident. An example is when a man concludes he is worthless because he is unable to find his way to a particular address, even though he has numerous other skills.

Magnification and **minimization** are an individual's gross errors in evaluation. Magnification refers to exaggeration of negative events and minimization to devaluation of positive events. For example, if a woman has a minor car accident, erroneously concludes her car is a wreck, and she must purchase a new one, she is guilty of magnification. Conversely, if a college student receives an A on an exam, and he says the test was easy and he was lucky, he is guilty of minimization.

According to Beck, these distortions or depressive cognitions are automatic, occurring without reflection or forethought. Many patients emphasize that they have these depressive thoughts even though they have resolved not to. The depressed person accepts these distorted thoughts as accurate and realistic although others would clearly not view them as such.

A number of different studies have confirmed the premise that depressed people operate with a negative cognitive bias (Hollon & Kendall, 1980). However, the specific cognitive distortions described by Beck (1967) are often difficult to distinguish reliably. Thus for research purposes, these categories had to be grouped into one overall negative cognitive category (Cook & Peterson, 1986). Investigators found that depressed persons make more self-critical or self-deprecating statements than nondepressed individuals. They also observed that depressed persons use more illogical justifications for their beliefs about causes of things than nondepressives. For example, a coed may argue that she had a horrible time on a date at a fraternity party because "the last time I had a date at that fraternity house they played loud heavy metal music."

Beck's theory does more than just list and categorize negative cognitions. He also describes how negative beliefs and knowledge about oneself are organized. Called **self-schemata,** these belief systems are hypothesized to operate like memory banks serving to process and organize information. Kovacs and Beck (1978) believe depressed persons have negative self-schemata which they use to organize information about themselves. In turn, they argued that depression occurs as a result of the original activation of these depressive schemata in childhood.

A person's early experiences, such as deprivation or the loss of a close relative in childhood, can result in depressive schemata. Later, the individual is vulnerable to depression in response to specific stresses resembling these earlier experiences. According to Beck (1967), stress activates depressive schemata and fosters negative beliefs about the self, the world, and the future. These beliefs, the **negative cognitive triad,** are maintained by cognitive distortions.

Research suggests that cognitive distortions, irrational beliefs, and negative statements about oneself are often related to depression. In comparison to the nondepressed, depressed persons evaluate their behavior more negatively and remember more negative events. We may, however, question whether cognitions measured by scales that assess depressive attitudes are really specific to depression and not to other disorders such as anxiety. Further, it is unclear if negative cognitions actually cause depression or are simply associated with it. Reviewing the evidence of the predictive role of negative cognitions, Hammen (1985) concluded that "in terms of longitudinal studies of depressive cognitions, there appears to be no evidence of depressive cognitions apart from a depressed state" (p. 35). For example, when depressives were assessed at admission to a hospital and at discharge with tests measuring stable negative cognitive biases, their scores at discharge resembled those of nondepressed comparison people. That is, depressed individuals no longer showed evidence of stable negative beliefs. Nevertheless, Hammen suggests that depressogenic cognitions could influence or cause depression, but evidence from longitudinal studies does not support such a position at present.

Negative Attributions. Learned helplessness originally referred to a condition in animals resulting from repeated exposure to unavoidable shocks. After a period of inescapable shocks, experimenters allowed the animals an avenue of escape yet the latter acted helplessly, failing to respond in avoidance of electrical shocks and their discomfort. The animals looked visibly upset and depressed (Seligman, 1975). In extending the learned helplessness model to human research, Seligman argued that individuals exposed to uncontrollable situations are likely to develop beliefs that outcomes have nothing to do with their behavior. They then generalize these beliefs to situations that are controllable. Attributions about behavior and events and one's control over them thus become central etiological factors in the development of depression. The attributional reformulation of learned helplessness (Abramson, Seligman, & Teasdale, 1978), along with formulations by Weiner and Litman-Adizes (1980), states that an individual's feelings of helplessness and perceived lack of control predict his or her lack of self-esteem and severity of depressive reactions. According to the learned helplessness model, depressed people have an internal, stable, and global attributional style (Seligman et al., 1979):

1. **Internal attribution.** They attribute the causes of negative events to their own internal failings or incompetency.
2. **Stable attribution.** They believe the causes of negative events remain consistent across time (i.e., whatever causes negative events won't go away).
3. **Global attribution.** They see the causes of negative events having a broad effect in many areas of their lives.

Attribution researchers study the reasons or causes individuals offer for certain events and behavior. Depressed people attribute experiences of failure to internal characteristics such as incompetence (DeMonbreum & Craighead, 1977; Kuiper, 1978). While attributional theorists hypothesized that depressed subjects would perceive less control over events than nondepressed subjects, there is conflicting evidence about this assumption (Huesmann & Morikawa, 1985). Actually, attributions of depressed

BOX 7.4 Are Depressives "Sadder but Wiser?"

Some studies have shown that depressed persons have relatively realistic attitudes and nondepressed persons have positive biases (Alloy & Abramson, 1979; Lewinsohn et al., 1980). Depressed college students estimate the negative feedback they receive reasonably accurately, whereas nondepressed students actually underestimate or distort the negative feedback they receive. In short, the depressed students may be more accurate and in turn sadder.

Researchers assessed judgments about the social competence of clinically depressed and nondepressed individuals (Lewinsohn et al., 1980). The depressed population was a group of moderately to severely disturbed unipolar depressives. Subjects in the control group did not have depression scores in the clinical range on a standardized personality test, the MMPI, and did not appear depressed based on the semistructured clinical interview.

Both depressed and nondepressed subjects were assigned to small groups of five: a depressed person, a nondepressed person, and three research assistants. With the group seated in a circle, each member introduced himself or herself in a three-minute monologue. Then the group continued conversing for twenty minutes. All participants were told of the researchers' interest in finding out how strangers relate to one another.

Following the group sessions, both the depressed and nondepressed subjects rated themselves on different social competence dimensions. These self-ratings were then compared to ratings made by specially trained coders after observing videotapes of the group's interactions. Of special interest was that depressed subjects' ratings of their own social competence were more similar to those of the trained coders than were the ratings of nondepressed subjects. In other words, depressed subjects were more accurate in their self-perceptions than nondepressed subjects. The nondepressed subjects were less accurate because they rated themselves more positively than the coders did. The researchers pointed out that the results—documenting a "warm illusory glow" of nondepressed subjects—confirmed a consistent theme of depressed people appearing "sadder but wiser" in their self-judgments than nondepressed people (Alloy & Abramson, 1979). "In sum," the authors noted, "to have good feelings about ourselves we may have to judge ourselves more kindly than we are judged."

Source: Lewinsohn et al., 1980, p. 212.

individuals about themselves and their behavior seem more important than perception of control of others or external events.

The role of attributions in the *etiology* of depression is less clear. Before fully embracing an attributional model of depression, a number of critical questions are now being addressed: First, do individuals typically make causal attributions for most or all of their behavior? If they do not frequently make causal statements to themselves about their behavior, attributions may have little to do with becoming depressed. Second, are these attributions consistent across time? Basic research is necessary about the moment-to-moment thought processes in daily living before drawing conclusions about any causal role of attributions and depression. Contrary to the attribution model, attribution styles are not very consistent across time and do not typically generalize across situations (Hammen, 1985). Third, do attributions cause depression, result from depression, or interact in a more complex way than is currently understood? There is no consistent evidence that attributions about negative events predict depression. A number of studies have failed to prove that negative attributions predict depression when initial levels of depression are controlled statistically. Yet, college students with negative attributions are more likely to become depressed than college students without such attributions, especially when combined with specific measures of stress (Alloy, Clements, & Kolden, 1985).

According to attributional theorists, depressive attributional styles are influential across time and situations, similar to personality traits. However, research on depression has not generally supported this view. One problem with such generalizations is that most early research demonstrating consistent attributional styles occurred within achievement contexts predicting academic failure. That is, most of the subjects were college students asked about their ability to succeed in academic tasks to determine their attributional style. As Hammen (1985) has argued, however, there may be issues such as interpersonal relationships that are more important to some people than achievement. Barthe and Hammen (1981) found that depressed persons experiencing difficult romantic relationships did not have stable and internal negative attributions. For example, some individuals may become seriously depressed when they lose a lover even if they do not generally see themselves negatively. The attributional model, therefore, may have to be reformulated with greater emphasis on relationship issues.

Recent research has clearly documented different vulnerability to depression depending on whether individuals viewed interpersonal relationships or achievement issues as more critical to their self-esteem (Hammen et al., 1989). People who considered interpersonal relationships most important did not become depressed when they encountered academic failure. On the other hand, these same individuals were likely to become depressed if they encountered social failure. Conversely, individuals who find academic achievement critical to their self-esteem become depressed as a result of academic problems, but not social relationship problems. In sum, in predicting depression, it is a matter of matching particular problems in life with specific views of oneself.

Attributional theories have been extremely influential in promoting research on the cognitive factors in depression. The reformulation of the learned helplessness model into the attributional model served researchers well for over a decade. It prompted many studies documenting the different cognitives styles of depressed and nondepressed people, and it continues to spur revisions of the theory based on subtypes of depression. Reflecting these reformulations, hopelessness is now seen by some as a critical cause of—as well as a symptom of—certain depression (Abramson, Metalsky, & Alloy, 1989).

Researchers now question whether negative attributions are stable, and evidence for the critical etiological role of attributions in depression is mixed. Research on mood and cognition has led to cognitive-mood models which are bidirectional: In some instances, the way we think may cause us to feel depressed, but in other instances the way we feel can cause us to have depressive thoughts. It is becoming increasingly apparent that no single factor—cognitive or otherwise—is likely to explain all depression.

Script Disruption and Self-Criticism. Early behavioral models of depression focused primarily on elevated rates of negative events and scarcity of reinforcement in the depressed individual's life (Lewinsohn et al., 1982). This model had three main hypotheses about the causes of depression:

1. *Availability* of few positive reinforcers and a surplus of punishers in the person's environment.
2. *Skill deficiencies* that make it difficult for a person to obtain positive reinforcers or to cope with negative events.
3. *Susceptibility* by the person to negative events and the reduced impact of positive events.

Lewinsohn provided reasonable support for the notion that depressives experience more aversive events and less reinforcement than nondepressives. This model, often referred to as a **reinforcement model of depression,** led to successful group treatments for depression (Brown & Lewinsohn, 1984; Lewinsohn & Arconad, 1981; Hoberman, Lewinsohn, & Tilson, 1988). Extensive clinical experience, however, suggested that depressed individuals' attention is very self-focused and negative. A new model of depression incorporates both positive and negative external events and takes into account internal events such as attention directed toward oneself. This model assumes a central role for disruption of scripted or automatic behavior patterns and for a critical self-focus (Lewinsohn et al., 1985). Figure 7.2 shows this model of depression.

Sociologists and psychologists have discussed **scripted behavior** for many years as patterns of behavior following social expectations in a predictable fashion, like a movie or theater script. Scripted behavior often becomes well developed and automatic. For example, in a grocery checkout line, everyone knows his or her role, and what happens in it is quite predictable. Work routines, family interactions, and leisure activities also often follow an orderly predictable script. Lewinsohn et al. (1985) argue that depression-evoking events occurring in a person's life disrupt expected, automatic patterns of behavior and are likely to elicit a depressed mood. This in turn leads to a reduced rate of positive reinforcement and/or an elevated rate of aversive experience. If this script disruption continues, a heightened state of self-awareness leads to self-criticism and withdrawal, with a major depression developing.

Self-criticism and self-focus have become important subjects in depression research and theory. Duval and Wickland (1972) postulated that focusing attention on the self initiates a self-evaluative process. When we focus on ourselves, we compare how well we do in a certain area with how well we wanted to do. When we focus attention on ourselves and have not met our goals, the self-focus can produce negative emotion. Reviewing the self-focus literature, Pyszczynski and Greenberg (1987) presented both correlational and experimental evidence in support of this idea. Self-focusing style appears to be a key factor in the maintenance or etiology of depression. As discussed, elevated self-focusing in females was one possible explanation for the 2 : 1 ratio of depression for females and males (Nolen-Hoeksema, 1987).

Elevated levels of self-focus characterize mild depression in both college samples and clinically depressed persons (Ingram et al., 1987). Persistence in self-focusing occurs when the individual experiences a loss in the personal, social, or work sphere (Pyszczynski & Greenberg, 1987). Actually, sometimes there may be no objective loss but the depressed person feels that there is (e.g., my boyfriend doesn't love me anymore; my boss doesn't talk to me like he did last year). Pyszczynski & Greenberg (1987) propose that "depression occurs to the extent that the individual who experiences a loss fails to disengage

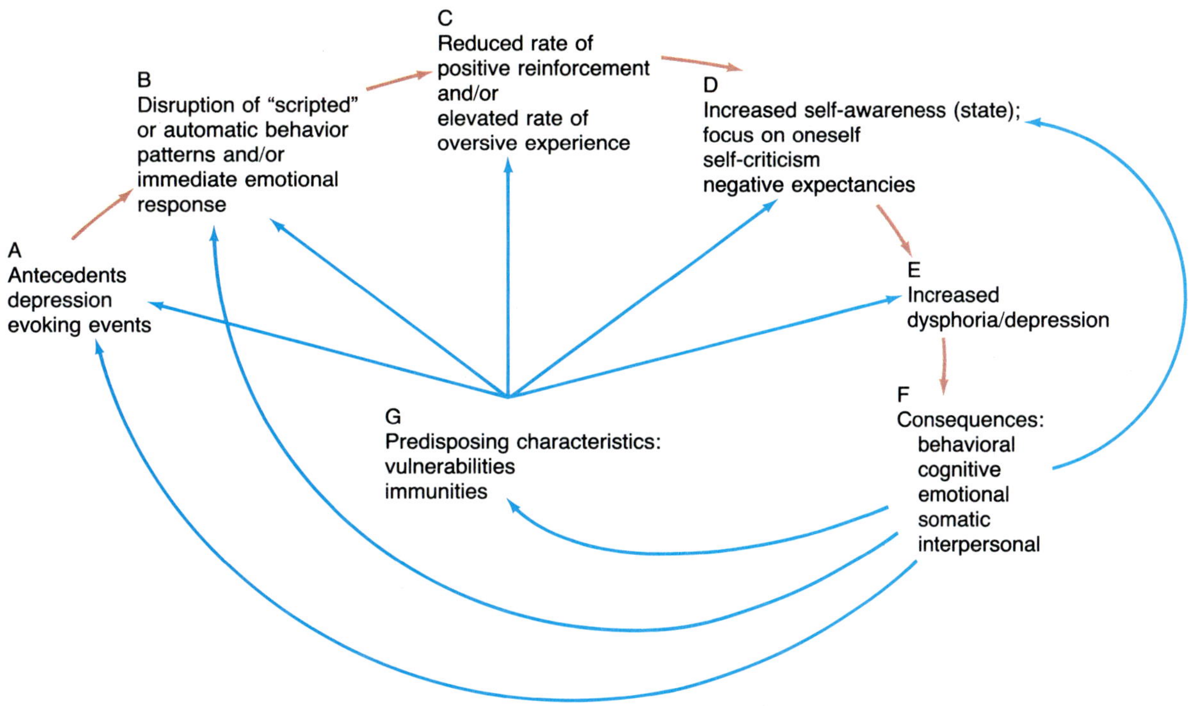

Figure 7.2 *Lewinsohn's schematic representation of the variables involved in the occurrence of unipolar depression. The causes of depression include genetic predisposition (predisposing characteristics), stressful events, disruption of normal behaviors, fewer reinforcers, and increased self-focusing.*

Source: Lewinsohn, P.M., Hoberman, H.M., Teri, L., and Hautzinger, M. (1985). An integrative theory of depression. In S.R. Reiss, and R. Bootzin (Eds.), *Theoretical issues in behavior therapy,* 343. New York: Academic Press.

the cycle and continues to self-focus" (1987, p. 127). Self-focus over the loss persists long after it would have been adaptive for the individual to direct his or her attention elsewhere.

Self-control. Of the many views on self-control, the one discussed next is that presented by Kanfer (1970), then extended by Rehm (1977).

When individuals perceive that some form of behavior is not functioning or will not be able to function to achieve desired outcomes, a feedback sequence of self-monitoring, self-evaluation, and self-reinforcement is engaged. Self-monitoring involves observation of one's own performance including its antecedents, consequences, and concomitants (Rehm, 1987, p. 81). Self-monitoring refers simply to self-observation. Self-evaluation is the comparison of one's performance to an external standard. Based on this self-evaluation, a person will decide whether his or her behavior should be reinforced (self-reinforcement). Rehm proposed that the development of depression centers on deficits in the individual's self-monitoring, self-evaluation, and self-reinforcement abilities.

According to Rehm (1977), depressed individuals selectively attend to negative outcomes and to immediate rather than delayed outcomes. These researchers believed that depressed individuals focus more on negative events than positive events. However, on the basis of a series of studies about memory for positive and negative events, DeMonbreum and Craighead (1977) concluded that depressed people consistently underestimate positive feedback, especially when given at high rates. Lack of attention to positive events, not a focus on negative events, most clearly appears to distinguish depressed from nondepressed people.

Contrary to Rehm's original hypothesis, depressed people do not attend to immediate outcomes more than nondepressed people (Rehm & Plakosh, 1975). Further attention to positive or negative events has little effect on the mood of normal subjects. O'Hara and Rehm (1979) asked subjects to attend selectively to positive or negative events. During a four-week period, some subjects were requested to record positive events while others were asked to record negative events. To the investigators' surprise, there was no change in the subjects' moods whether they recorded positive or negative events. However, *clinically depressed* people do record more negative events and fewer positive events in their daily experiences. Clinically depressed individuals often do have more negative events in their lives. Rehm (1988) summarized a decade of research by indicating that depressed people may not have a consistent distorted perception of life events, but they may spend different amounts of time attending to negative and positive events than nondepressed people do.

According to Rehm (1977), depressed individuals set excessively stringent standards for themselves—too high in an absolute sense or too high relative to their skills and abilities. In an early study in this area, depressed individuals rated their performances as poor even though they were identical to that of nondepressed individuals (Loeb et al., 1967). A related study established an association between high standard-setting and low self-esteem in males (Warren, 1976). Thus, research provides indirect support for the causative role of excessively high standards in the etiology of depression (Rehm, 1988). On the other hand, high standard-setting is not a consistent enough factor to argue self-evaluation is critical in the depression's development. This research's impact on standard-setting and self-evaluation will likely be seen in an integration with basic research on memory process and how depressed individuals may be able to gain access to and keep positive thoughts in their mind (Teasdale, 1983).

Self-reinforcement and self-punishment appear to distinguish depressed people from nondepressed individuals. Depressed college students indulged in self-reinforcement or self-reward less frequently than nondepressed students in learning tasks where they could take a reward of money for a correct answer (Nelson & Craighead, 1977). Depressed psychiatric patients reinforce themselves less often on memory tasks and punish themselves more than nondepressed subjects. There is not enough evidence yet to determine whether self-reinforcement problems cause depression or are simply correlated with it.

The self-control model of depression is similar to cognitive models emphasizing (1) negative schemata and cognitive distortions, (2) negative attributions, and (3) disruption of scripted behavior and negative self-focus. Rehm's focus on selective attention to negative events, common to the other three cognitive models, most closely resembles the self-control model. This obvious overlap generates debate about the self-control model's distinct usefulness. Critics like Hollon and Beck (1979) argue that the self-control model "adds little to existing cognitive models and consists, at best, of a semantic rewording of cognitive theory into behavioral terminology." Moreover, Hollon and Beck believe the self-control model underestimates the role of individual differences in information processing. An alternative view is that there are various ways to successfully understand and treat depression. Rehm's emphasis on overt behavioral factors coupled with his successful treatments (O'Leary & Wilson, 1987) challenge those who argue for one specific set of cognitive factors in depression.

Interpersonal Factors in Depression

Several trends in recent decades have led to an increased focus on interpersonal factors in depression. Many influential neo-Freudian therapists such as Harry Stack Sullivan and Erik Erickson shifted their emphasis away from deep unconscious processes and childhood toward current interpersonal relationships. The ascendance of marital, family systems, and social therapies in the 1960s and 1970s highlighted the importance of interpersonal relationships in a variety of psychological disorders (Chapter 16). This was followed up by critical attention from researchers in the 1980s. Three aspects have gained special notice as having important etiological and treatment significance.

1. Loss or disturbance in close relationships
2. Social support
3. Marital discord

Loss or Disturbance in Close Relationships. Psychoanalytic views of depression have typically emphasized loss of love and emotional security as key variables in depression. This was first postulated in Freud's (1917) classic paper, "Mourning and Melancholia." In it, he suggested that melancholia, like mourning, occurs after the loss of a loved object either in actuality by death, or emotionally by rejection. Freud hypothesized that the individual who lost someone became angry at that person—for example, boyfriend or girlfriend, husband or wife. Because this anger at a loved one causes dangerous or threatening feelings, it is redirected toward the self, experienced first as self-hate and ultimately as depression. Since Freud's original paper, many revisions of his position have been made, including some of his own where he later stressed the severity of the superego in the development of depression (Bemporad, 1985). Nonetheless, psychodynamic therapists often link depression and anger in one form or another (Mendelson, 1982; Rosenberg, 1985).

As psychodynamic theory has changed, so have conceptualizations of depression, with an increasing emphasis on loss of self-esteem rather than loss of a loved object or person. To learn about the etiology of depression, researchers have examined factors leading to a loss of self-esteem, for example, poor body image or lack of skill in various areas (Jacobson, 1971). According to psychodynamic theory, the first root of poor self-esteem is a *pathological* self-concept. For example, a woman may see herself as being very overweight even though she is, objectively, within normal weight limits. Second, a **primitive superego,** which has not modified internalized parental expectations from childhood, makes the individual vulnerable to depression in adulthood when she or he fails to live up to the internalized parent's standards. Third, an unrealistic **ego-ideal** (ideal image of oneself) may lead to unhappiness with oneself, thus increasing vulnerability to depression. In addition to these three main causes of poor self-esteem, other problems could occur, according to Jacobson, because of failure, poor health, loss of affection, or neglect during the earliest periods of a person's life.

Klein (1940) suggested a predisposition to depression stemming from poor mother-infant relationships. Klein held that until infants can become secure in their mother's love, they interpret every removal from the breast and every frustration as a loss of a "good object." Klein felt that all infants experience a depression in which they fear sorrow and loss of loved objects, and children who never feel sufficient love are later predisposed to depression.

As there are numerous versions of psychodynamic theory, no one empirical test of psychodynamic theory is possible. Moreover, Freud's original conceptualization of depression as anger turned inward has not received much support from research. For example, dream analyses show incompetence and failure as the most common themes in dreams of depressed individuals, not internalized anger (Beck, 1963). Observations of interactions with strangers or marital partners have indicated that depressed individuals are openly negative and hostile with others; they do not simply internalize their negative feelings. On the other hand, psychodynamic conceptualizations of depression focusing on self-esteem and unrealistic ego-ideals (high standard-setting) have, as already indicated, received some support. The importance of developing a close mother-infant attachment has proven useful in the construction of a successful treatment of depression—interpersonal therapy—that focuses interpersonal loss and familial factors (Klerman et al., 1984).

Social Support. Social support refers to a social network's ability to satisfy an individual's interpersonal needs and to provide support during stressful times. Social support problems can arise if the individual has too few contacts, is not close enough to confide in other people, or perceives that others don't care. In a large epidemiological study in Britain, Brown and Harris (1978) found that individuals experiencing a large number of stressful life events were less likely to become depressed if they had close and confiding relationships. A related Australian study by Henderson, Byrne, and Duncan-Jones (1981) noted that depressed individuals had fewer close friends and contacts outside the household and a higher proportion of negative interactions with support group members. Beach, Arias, and O'Leary (1986) observed risk for depression as thirteen times greater in socially isolated community members (in the bottom 20 percent of the sample) than in those not socially isolated.

The association between depression and lack of social support has been replicated in at least a half dozen studies (Brown & Harris, 1986). This research on depression risk has been integrated into a broader theoretical framework including cognitive factors, specific stressors, and the particular type of depressive symptoms observed. Other research has also analyzed specific types of interactions characterizing depressed people and their social networks.

Depressed individuals maintain less eye contact, are less verbal, speak more softly and monotonously, make more negative statements about things, and take longer to respond to others' verbalizations than do nondepressed people (Gotlib & Robinson, 1982). In response, nondepressed persons are less likely to be positive when speaking to depressed individuals than they are to others; they smile less, talk less, and make fewer supportive comments. Depressed people seem to enter a vicious cycle in which their own negativity and distance results in less positive attention from others. In turn, this may make them more unhappy. Coyne's (1976) theorizing has been an impetus for others to investigate the role of friends and family in maintaining depressive symptoms.

Marital Discord. Considerable documentation exists for an association between marital discord and depressive symptomatology (Beach, Arias, & O'Leary, 1986; Colman & Miller, 1975; Weiss & Aved, 1978). This is significant for men and women, with a moderate correlation between marital discord and depression in samples from the general population (ranges from .30 to .50). Research has also assessed the relationship between these two variables in clinic samples showing a 50 percent overlap between depression and marital discord. That is, in a maritally unhappy clinic sample, about half the couples will include one clinically depressed member. In a depressed sample, about half of the subjects will meet the criterion for serious marital discord (Beach, Jouriles, & O'Leary, 1985).

At times marital discord can lead to depression, but there are also times when depression can lead to marital discord. Based on clinical risk, general marital discord appears more likely to lead to depression than vice versa (O'Leary & Christian, 1990). However, if depression is low-level and long-standing (dysthymia), the risk of marital discord may increase (Beach, Arias, & O'Leary, 1990).

Is Marriage a Mental Health Risk for Women?

The role of marriage in mental illness is hotly debated. Sociologists such as Bernard (1972) concluded that men like to be married because it is good for them; marriage provides care for their children, household maintenance, and often cooked meals. Consequently, Bernard argued that marriage should be particularly good for men. On the other hand, she felt marriage would often mentally harm women because of their service to their husbands and lack of emotional and financial support from employment. In his book, *Marriage and Mental Illness: A Sex Role Perspective* (1986), Julian Hafner provided some support for Bernard's view in concluding that the *combination* of marriage and lack of employment outside the home is a critical ingredient in causing depression in young wives. Bernard and Hafner reached their conclusions based on lower rates of mental illness and depression in single, divorced, and widowed women than in *men* in these same categories (Weissman & Klerman, 1977). Married women employed full-time outside the home, however, report levels of depression similar to married men. We should not, however, jump to the conclusion that marriage and not working outside the home are unequivocally bad for all women (i.e., a very high risk for depression in women). Most critical is if the marriage is close and confiding and if a wife feels she must work or feels supported in that role by her husband (Barling, 1990).

Many findings support the link between marital discord and depression. Among women entering treatment, one of the most common elements in their lives during the previous six months is marital discord. Acutely depressed women report considerably more problems in marital intimacy than matched controls. If depression subsides following treatment with medication, marital problems often remain. Female depressed patients indicate that they feel the greatest impairment in their roles as wives and mothers (Weissman & Klerman, 1977). The interactions of a depressed person with a spouse reveal a pattern of hostile and negative interactions, similar to a depressive's interactions with nonfamily members, discussed earlier. Husbands of depressed women report feeling detached and hostile toward their partners following discussions with them (Arkowitz, Holliday, & Hutter, 1982; Gotlib & Colby, 1987; Beach, Sandeen, & O'Leary, 1990).

Coyne's (1976) family systems model suggests that depressive symptoms represent a cry for reassurance and support. When a person initially makes such a plea, it is granted. Yet repeated pleas made by the depressed person are perceived as demands and become aversive to family members. After feeling obliged to provide support for weeks or months, the family member may become angry and hostile. Utterance-by-utterance analyses of interactions of depressed wives and their husbands reveal that depressive talk by the wives may "turn off" criticism and negative feedback from the husbands (Biglan et al., 1985). In short, in some instances the depressive behavior of wives reduces the aversive behavior of their husbands and may maintain depressive symptoms. In turn, their husbands feel resentment and anger toward their wives. Depressed women may be unaware of their behavior's impact on their husbands, and the women's actions may be partly a function of an unsupportive husband.

Stress

Even if someone has a family or genetic background making depression more likely, some environmental event or stressor must prompt it. This interaction of biological and social events is the **diathesis-stress model.** The diathesis is the biological or psychological predisposition and the stress is the particular problem the individual encounters. For example, someone with a family history of depression (the diathesis) later laid off from a job (the stress) is more likely to become depressed than someone without the interaction of these two factors. To evaluate the role of stressors in the development of depression, Paykel et al., (1969) compared the histories of 185 depressed patients with 185 control subjects from the community (matched with the patients for age, sex, and education). The depressed individuals reported having almost three times as many undesirable life events as community control subjects, although the groups did not differ on desirable life events such as promotion, engagement, or marriage.

Interpersonal problems or loss are common critical events preceding depression such as problems in relationships or death of a family member. However, individuals who become depressed generally experience a variety of stressors prior to their depressive episode. Other stressors commonly found prior to depression are changes in work conditions and serious personal illness (Lloyd, 1980; Paykel, 1982). Finally, sometimes having a newborn child or the departure of a son or daughter for college precipitates depression.

Some differences between depressed and nondepressed individuals found in research on stressful life events could be due to memory distortion. Depressed people may simply remember more negative things. In addressing this issue, Paykel et al. (1969) noted, however, that depressed patients were not interviewed until after their depression had lessened. More importantly, the researchers recorded stressful *events*—for example, separation and divorce—not the perception of these events.

The stress of coping with a newborn child along with the absence of contact with co-workers during maternity leave often leads to depression in young women.

Social stressors may cause changes in brain functioning, which in turn seem to produce depression. As Siegel (1986) writes: "The common denominator in all depression is a lack of love or a loss of meaning in life, at least as perceived from the depressed person's point of view. Illness then often functions as an escape from the routine that has become meaningless" (p. 76). Recent research confirms that both depressed patients and people undergoing severe life stressors show reductions in some of their natural immune function of about 50 percent (Irwin et al., 1990). The particular immune functions associated with depression vary somewhat from study to study, and depression does not effect immune functions consistently. However, when it has an affect, it lowers immune functions (Schleifer & Keller, 1989; O'Leary, 1990; Stein, Miller & Trestman, 1991).

From a social stress perspective, individuals from lower social classes and minority groups might be expected to be more stressed and, consequently, have more depression. Actually, depression is not dependent upon race, social class, or educational group. Epidemiological studies of prevalence rates of psychiatric disorders have been conducted in Mexican-American populations in Los Angeles (Karno et al., 1987) and in Hispanic populations in Puerto Rico (Canino et al., 1987). They indicated that rates of major depressive disorder were not higher for these populations than for non-Hispanic whites in Los Angeles or Puerto Rico. To the surprise of researchers, in Los Angeles, non-Hispanic whites had higher rates of major depressive disorder than Mexican-Americans. Moreover, in Puerto Rico, where education and poor living conditions were assessed, these variables were not associated with depression.

Is There a Psychology of Manic-Depression?

Manic phases of a patient with manic-depressive disorder are so unusual and powerful that for many years researchers have sought their origins almost exclusively in biochemistry and genetics. The appearance of mania is sudden, and the patients' energy and racing thoughts seem endlessly driven. Sleep appears totally unnecessary. Since a manic episode can develop within an hour and often without an apparent precipitating event, searches for biochemical causes seem reasonable. Indeed, as seen earlier, genetic models of manic depression have definite support. Further, there is consistent evidence of increased secretion in manic patients of aldosterone, a hormone produced by the adrenal glands, yet its specific role in producing mania is unclear (Carroll, 1979).

Psychological factors may also be important, though they have been much less studied. Research is not clear whether specific precipitating events are critical in the development of mania. In some studies specific stressors did not predict mania or depressive episodes in bipolar individuals (Lloyd, 1980; Hammen et al., 1989) whereas in other studies they did (Ambelas, 1979; Kennedy et al., 1983). One major problem with studies of precipitating events of manic episodes is the retrospective reports of events, which the manic patient may slant. Yet based on a review of fourteen studies, Goodwin and Jamison (1990) provided considerable support for the importance of stressful events in the initial onset of episodes in bipolar patients. However, they also noted that as manic episodes reoccur, they appear less and less influenced by environmental events.

Clinicians nevertheless generally believe that social support and understanding during a manic episode is crucial. More manic depressive patients get divorced than unipolar depressives, but this may be a result not a cause of the mania (Krauthammer & Klerman, 1979). Whether or not a manic depressive patient gets divorced may not even be the most crucial issue. Because they often spend large sums of money, act promiscuously, and indulge in other impetuous behavior during the manic phases, they certainly often have very unsatisfactory marriages.

While no specific psychotherapy has proven effective with manic patients, many experts argue that psychotherapy and family therapy are necessary adjuncts to pharmacotherapy (Andreasen & Block, 1991; Goodwin & Jamison, 1990). The clinical impression is that spouses with a clear understanding of the manic-depressive illness are better able to support the patient. Indeed, bipolars with families displaying low levels of expressed negative emotion are less likely to relapse following discharge from the hospital than bipolars with negative family atmospheres (Miklowitz et al., 1988). While systematic research on the psychological aspects of families of bipolars has only begun, this research's similarity to the work on schizophrenia relapse and family environment (Chapter 14) underscores the role of psychological variables even in situations where a disorder has a clear genetic component.

Psychodynamic theorists see the onset of mania as a defense against severe depression. If this is the case, a manic patient may feel and *report* reasonably strong feelings of self-esteem, yet have poor self-esteem when judged independently. Winters and Neale (1986) found just these results. Manic-depressives reported higher self-esteem than unipolar depressives. Yet when their self-esteem was measured in a task the manic-depressive and unipolar-depressive subjects thought to be about memory, the manic depressives had lower self-esteem scores. The researchers concluded that the manic-depressive subjects try to defend against an underlying low level of self-esteem.

TREATMENT

Unipolar Depression

A number of treatments for unipolar depression have been developed including anti-depressant medication, electroconvulsive-shock, psychotherapy, and marital therapy. The most common treatments are anti-depressant medications and psychotherapy.

Medications

Antidepressants. Tricyclic antidepressant medication—with a chemical structure containing three rings—has been used successfully for more than two decades to reduce or alleviate depressive symptoms of many patients. Antidepressant medications have been compared with placebos (nonpsychoactive pills for the condition being treated, such as sugar pills) because some patients may improve based on the therapeutic setting of a physician's office and/or the simple belief that the pill can help them. In general, antidepressant medication, such as imipramine (Tofranil), one of the most commonly prescribed treatments, is successful with about 65 percent of patients with unipolar depression, whereas only 30 percent of patients respond to placebos (Davis, 1985). Patients may experience some undesirable side effects such as dryness of the mouth, constipation, blurred vision, and difficulty urinating. When such side effects occur, the physician may alter the dosage or consider another type of medication.

A second antidepressant medication frequently used is amitriptyline (Elavil). Several studies have shown that imipramine and amitriptyline are approximately equally effective, and both can be taken for several years without problems. Although the body rapidly absorbs antidepressants, often they take several weeks to decrease depression.

Prozac is now the most frequently prescribed medication for the treatment of depression by psychiatrists. Developed for use in the late 1980s, many mental health professionals view it as the wonder drug of the 1990s (*Newsweek,* July 27, 1990) because it has few negative side effects. It is a potent and selective serotonin uptake inhibitor; that is, it keeps serotonin in circulation by blocking its reabsorption (Hudson & Pope, 1990). It clearly decreases depression. Because 13 percent of patients also lose six to eight pounds, it is now being evaluated in clinical research trials as a weight reduction treatment. Despite the belief by some that Prozac will be the new wonder drug of the mental health field, Prozac is not without critics. Some professionals believe its use makes suicide more likely in a small number of patients. Yet even some critics such as Jerrold Rosenbaum of Harvard University, who conducted research on Prozac and believes that suicide was a side effect in 4 percent of individuals taking Prozac, admitted that "for many depressed people it is the best thing they ever had" (*Nightline,* ABC TV, July 27, 1990). Nonetheless, in a few cases, depressed patients become violent after taking Prozac, and we do not know if there are long-

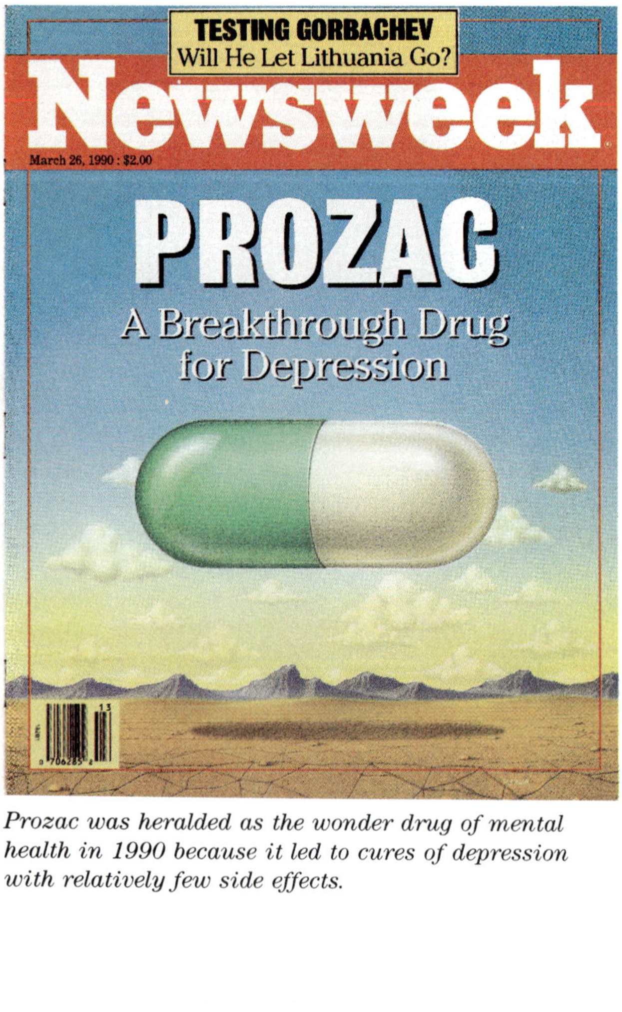

Prozac was heralded as the wonder drug of mental health in 1990 because it led to cures of depression with relatively few side effects.

term side effects of this medication. These effects, if they exist, will become known only after controlled clinical experimentation with thousands of patients.

MAO Inhibitors. When depressed patients do not respond to tricyclic antidepressants, monoamine oxidase inhibitors (MAO inhibitors) are another option (e.g., Nardil, Parnate). They appear to work best for patients with a combination of anxiety and depression. The MAO inhibitors are equal to or somewhat less effective than the tricyclic medications (Davis, 1985) and must be used with great caution. Taken with some foods or drinks, such as cheese and alcohol, they actually can lead to severe hypertension and occasional deaths. Therefore, patients taking MAO inhibitors must adhere to special dietary restrictions. Whereas MAO inhibitors are superior to placebos in alleviating depression, they are obviously not the medication of first choice for most depressed patients (Klerman, 1982).

Regardless of the effectiveness of medications for depression, one should not assume depression will not reoccur after the patient has stopped taking the medication. Once a person has a depression, he or she is at significant risk of becoming depressed again, approximately 20 percent become chronically depressed (Andreasen & Block, 1991). We need, therefore, to know how to minimize the occurrence and/or reoccurrence of depression through treatment, education, and early intervention.

Electroconvulsive Therapy. Electroconvulsive therapy (ECT) is sending electrical charges through a person's body to alleviate a particular emotional disorder. In the 1920s, clinicians believed that the electrical discharges emitted in the brains of epileptics prevented them from becoming schizophrenic. This led clinicians to introduce electrical charges into the bodies as a treatment for schizophrenia. Epileptic-like seizures were induced by injections of a chemical, camphor, and later by direct electrical current.

Currently, ECT is provided by a medical team that monitors the induction of electrical current and the patient's brain functioning. Electrodes are placed on the patient's head and a short-acting barbiturate puts him or her to sleep. In addition, a powerful muscle relaxant prevents possible bone breakage from convulsions. The electric shock is administered for .1 to .5 seconds. One minute after receiving the shock, patients have convulsions. As the anesthetic wears off, they are able to reason and converse. ECT usually takes between four to twelve sessions to complete. Although the induction of seizures seems barbaric to many, some highly suicidal patients may be excellent candidates for it. In such cases, a physician may not want to wait the three weeks for antidepressant medication to take effect. While we do not know why ECT reduces the depression symptoms, approximately 80 percent of depressed patients show significant improvement after ECT treatment. Although patients undergoing the early ECT treatment experienced severe memory loss, the current practice of placing the electrodes on the nondominant side of the brain usually causes only minor and transient memory loss (Fink, 1979).

The controversy over ECT has been intense. Many experts, nonetheless, feel that "ECT is probably the safest and most effective treatment available for depressive illness" (Andreasen, 1985, p. 208). Although used primarily with severely depressed hospitalized patients, ECT may also be effective in treating patients with a history of heart problems, as tricyclics are ill-advised in such cases. ECT will undoubtedly continue to have its supporters and detractors (Andreasen, 1985). Any patient considering it should be informed of its positive and negative effects (Chapter 16) and the existing alternatives. While 87 percent of depressed patients in well-monitored ECT treatment believed it was very helpful in reducing or alleviating their depression, only 26 percent would be very willing to have ECT again (Maletzky, 1981).

The decreases in depression following ECT are as great or even greater than any other treatment for depression. Dramatic refinements have been recently recommended by the American Psychiatric Association (1990) in their guide, *The Practice of Electroconvulsive Therapy.* The length and intensity of the electrical charge has been reduced—ten or fewer treatments are typically recommended—and gender

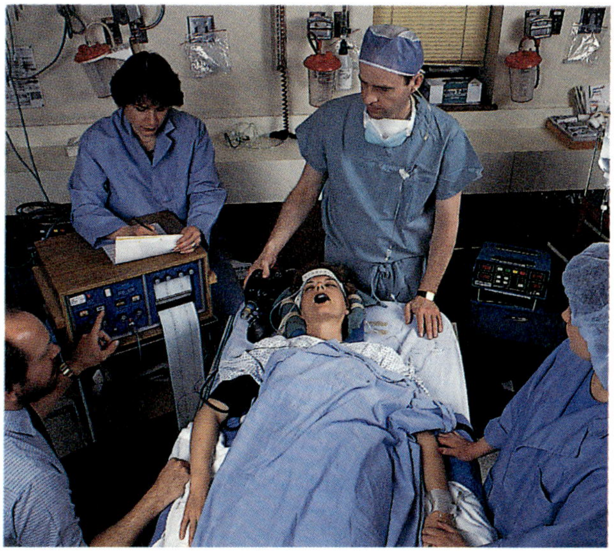

Electroconvulsive therapy is one of the most effective treatments for depression, and in the late 1980s it became more commonly accepted as it was demonstrated that it can have few side effects if administered properly.

and size differences are considered in selecting the appropriate level of electroshock.

Psychotherapy. Psychotherapy is now clearly established as an effective treatment for unipolar depression. It can be used as either an alternative or an adjunct to medication because many individuals who positively respond to medication often refuse to continue its use because of adverse side effects. In studies of antidepressant medication, for example, dropout rates in the medication groups are sometimes as high as 35 to 40 percent. Secondly, many mental health professionals and consumers of mental health services recognize that medication does not address life stress or the problems leading to depression. Many individuals desire a nonmedicinal way of coping with depression.

A number of studies in different clinics show two major types of effective psychological therapies in treating depression. The most well-investigated is individual cognitive or cognitive-behavioral psychotherapy (Neitzel et al., 1987). This type of therapy changes cognitive distortions, negative self-schema, negative attributions, script disruption, self-criticism, and self-control. The second treatment, interpersonal therapy, has also received large-scale evaluation as an individual therapy emphasizing coping with important past and present relationships (Elkin et al., 1989). A third treatment, conjoint marital therapy, is effective with unipolar depressives who are also maritally discordant (O'Leary & Beach, 1990; Whisman et al., 1988). This type of therapy enhances communication, reduces negative interchanges between partners, and increases the likelihood of the depressed person feeling loved by his or her partner.

Cognitive Therapy. Cognitive therapy for depression has been identified with its originator, Aaron Beck, because he presented a treatment rationale and format in his book, *Depression: Causes and Treatment* (1967). According to Beck, the therapist teaches the cognitive model of depression to patients in a straightforward didactic manner. Patients learn to analyze the associations between their thoughts, affect, and behavior, and to view their depression as the product of dysfunctional thoughts. The therapist and patient jointly explore the connection between various dysfunctional beliefs and depressed feelings. Beck called the relationship between the patient and the therapist a **collaborative set.** By the end of treatment, the patient learns specific techniques to change faulty beliefs and thought processes.

The identification of dysfunctional thoughts per se aids patients. They begin to gain some "distance" from these thoughts and can then evaluate their reality, checking them against real life data. However, more than simple identification of dysfunctional thoughts is necessary for successful treatment. Therapists must carefully and specifically question patients to help them uncover maladaptive thoughts and beliefs. For example, a therapist may ask questions to help patients discover the maladaptive consequences of assuming that a person should *always* work up to his or her potential.

Patient: I guess I believe I should always work up to my potential.

Therapist: Why is that?

Patient: Otherwise, I'd be wasting time.

Therapist: But what is the *long-range* goal in working up to your potential?

Patient: (Long-Pause) I've never really thought about that. I've just assumed that I should.

Therapist: Are there any positive things you give up by always having to work up to your potential?

Patient: I suppose it makes it hard to relax or take a vacation.

Therapist: What about "living up to your potential" to enjoy yourself and relax? Is that important at all?

Patient: I've never really thought of it that way.

Therapist: Maybe we can work on giving yourself permission *not* to work up to your potential at all times. (Young & Beck, 1982)

A second strategy for changing dysfunctional thoughts is to list the advantages and disadvantages of altering an assumption. After making the list, the

Dr. Aaron Beck developed cognitive therapy for depression and in 1972 wrote the famous book, Depression: Causes and Treatment, *which served as a clinical guide for clinicians throughout the world.*

therapist and patient collaboratively evaluate it. Additionally, the patient may simply weigh the long-term effects of holding onto the assumption.

As a third strategy, the therapist may help the patient overcome a number of "shoulds" that restrict activities. For example, a patient may feel she "should" not take time for herself to read or jog because she has so many chores that "have" to be completed. To aid her in overcoming "shoulds," the therapist helps her devise experiments to suggest what will happen if she spends time reading or jogging.

In addition to the cognitive strategies used to change dysfunctional thoughts, the therapist employs behavioral techniques, such as scheduling activities and giving concrete assignments. Activity scheduling is the simple and straightforward daily and hourly planning of endeavors. It is particularly helpful because the depressed person and his or her family often believe the depressed person can do very little. Realizing that daily accomplishments are possible encourages depressed people to believe they can actually do important, though small, things. Recording each activity is part of the therapeutic intervention. To avoid having depressed patients feel that they have not met goals, the therapist encourages them to be flexible in following their activity plans.

Cognitive therapy was originally evaluated by Rush et al. (1977) on primarily college-educated individuals in their mid-thirties. They found it superior to the antidepressant medication, imipramine, on both self-ratings and clinicians' ratings of depression. The dropout rate for the cognitive therapy group was much lower than for the medication group. This study stimulated a great deal of cognitive therapy research for depression and served as the springboard for a large government study comparing various therapies.

Another well-researched cognitive treatment for depression was originally designed by Lewinsohn and colleagues (Lewinsohn, Sullivan, & Grosscup, 1982). Lewinsohn initially emphasized low rates of reinforcement and high rates of punishment in a behavioral theory of depression. His later expanded model included cognitive or cognitive-behavioral factors in the etiology of depression.

This treatment has a well-proven record of success (Lewinsohn, Sullivan, & Grosscup, 1982). The five-step treatment plan consists of the following.

1. Daily Monitoring

Patients learn to graph and interpret their daily monitoring of events and moods. Apparently, patients often readily see the relationship between negative events and an unpleasant mood but seldom see the clear relationship between pleasant events and an elevated mood. For example, a woman may go to the beach, feel relaxed and pleasant, yet fail to see that being at the beach may have led to her feeling good. However, seeing depression clearly related to many observable events in life often helps clients understand their depression and comforts them. As Lewinsohn et al. (1982) noted, "Patients, in a very real sense, learn to diagnose their own depression."

2. Relaxation Training

Patients are taught that tension can maximize the impact of negative situations and interfere with pleasant situations. They are reminded that people under high stress often see things negatively and are prone to be critical. These findings on stress, anger, and misperception are then discussed as they apply to the depressed individuals in the group. They are assigned a book on learning how to relax (e.g., Benson, 1975), instructed how to tense and relax major muscle groups, and asked to practice relaxation twice per day and keep a record of their relaxation. Finally, they are aided in ascertaining which situations make them feel most tense.

3. Managing Aversive Events

Cognitive strategies for decreasing unpleasant events are also part of the Lewinsohn et al. (1982) treatment. Patients are taught to think positively and constructively after events that might prompt feelings of depression. They are taught not to take things personally and how to deal with aversive encounters. They learn how to use self-instruction by talking to themselves in a way that enhances their coping efforts and reduces the impact of failure experiences. Basically, patients are taught to think and talk to themselves in constructive and positive ways, rather than destructive and negative ways.

4. Time Management

Depressed persons often have difficulty managing their time. They do not adequately prepare for daily events and need guidance in how to plan their days so the therapy helps them do this.

5. Increasing Pleasant Activities

Patients are helped to increase pleasant activities. They set concrete goals and develop specific plans for what they expect to do. Patients first develop lists of pleasant activities such as watching TV, cooking a special meal, or calling a friend. Next, they develop specific plans of when they expect to engage in the pleasant activities and whether any preparation is necessary—such as buying the food to cook the special meal.

This behavioral treatment is essentially educational intervention. The therapist teaches the patient techniques to trace the specific causes of depressed feelings and ways to ameliorate them and establishes and discusses specific goals and graduated steps to realize them throughout the treatment.

Because of its proven success, Lewinsohn's therapy has been expanded to a course format composed of lectures, class activities, homework assignments, and a textbook, *Control Your Depression* (Lewinsohn, 1987). Research suggests that the course works as well as individual therapy to alleviate depression. This treatment program has aided hundreds of individuals, with the majority showing significant clinical improvement. Approximately 20 percent have, however, remained depressed. Those who remained depressed had suicidal ideation and very high levels of depression before treatment. Even with this proviso, the course offers a low, cost-effective method of dealing with depression.

There are similarities in Beck's and Lewinsohn's psychotherapies to treat depression. Both teach patients how to interpret their affect and behavior and the factors that influence both. Both involve changing cognitions and activities that may cause depression. Finally, both enable clients to develop a sense of mastery over some aspects of their behavior and affective state. Lewinsohn's psychotherapy differs from Beck's treatment in that

1. It has more emphasis on increasing reinforcement through pleasant activities.
2. It includes relaxation training.

Dr. Peter Lewinsohn developed a very successful group treatment now outlined in a textbook, Control Your Depression *(1987). The treatment is essentially a low cost educational intervention that helps people to understand the specific causes of their depressed feelings and to learn ways of coping with these feelings.*

Interpersonal Therapy. This successful treatment approach emphasizes coping with grief, interpersonal disputes, interpersonal deficits, and changes in roles such as entering a full-time job outside the home after fulfilling the job of a mother. It also places importance on family background issues as they relate to current functioning (Weissman et al., 1974). This individual psychotherapy approach was influenced by psychodynamic theorists such as Harry Stack Sullivan and Adolf Meyer, who emphasized the interpersonal environment in the etiology of disorders. Interpersonal therapy also was influenced by John Bowlby's studies of attachment, and it stresses the importance of how the disruption of attachment bonds can initiate depression.

In contrast to classic psychodynamic therapy, interpersonal therapy is directive and time limited, lasting from twelve to sixteen weeks. In this model, depression and interpersonal problems interact. Depression predisposes people to interpersonal problems, and in turn, interpersonal problems such as aggression or alcohol abuse predispose people to depression. The overall therapeutic emphasis is on helping the patient cope more effectively with interpersonal issues with the goal of reducing depressive symptoms and improving self-esteem.

Interpersonal therapy has been evaluated in several independent studies (Weissman et al., 1974) and in one large collaborative study on the treatment of depression (Elkin et al., 1989). In both studies, interpersonal psychotherapy was associated with decreases in depression.

Marital Therapy. Approximately 50 percent of depressed women have serious marital problems. Whether depression causes these problems in most cases is unclear. Marital difficulties are, however, the most frequently associated problem of women seeking treatment for depression. Poor marriages are also predictive of depression. Marital problems are likely to minimize the therapeutic value of antidepressant medication (Coyne, 1986).

Beach and O'Leary (1986) developed a marital therapy program more effective than individual cognitive therapy for women maritally distressed and depressed. Other studies have replicated these results (O'Leary & Beach, 1990; Whisman et al., 1988). Marital therapy's effectiveness highlights the social or interpersonal context of depression. Behavioral marital therapy emphasizes increased feelings

Dr. Myrna Weissman was one of the first researchers to show how marital problems placed women at very significant risk for depression. With Dr. Gerald Klerman she also developed Interpersonal Psychotherapy, a very effective individual treatment for depression.

of closeness, open sharing of thoughts and feelings, positive interchanges, and effective problem solving for marital disputes. Because it has become so apparent that marital problems cause or exacerbate depression for many women, marital therapy should be seriously considered for depressed women who want to remain in their troubled marriages.

Comparative Outcome Research. Prompted by promising leads in the treatment of depression with psychological and pharmacological means, the National Institute of Mental Health implemented an unprecedented large therapy outcome study (Elkin et al., 1985; Elkin et al., 1989). The study compared cognitive therapy, antidepressant medication, a psychodynamically based interpersonal therapy, and placebos. The therapies were conducted at three different universities with 240 depressed persons treated by 28 therapists. After four months of treatment, antidepressant medication proved more successful than a condition called *placebo-clinical management.* This no-treatment control condition involved twenty minutes of consultation per week with a psychiatrist. However, the placebo-clinical management condition and the two psychotherapies were not significantly different. This large-scale study has prompted many responses from professionals in the journal the original report was published in (*Archives of General Psychiatry*), and professionals interpret this study's results differently. However, severely depressed patients responded better to imipramine (70 percent recovery rate), moderately well to the two psychotherapies (40 percent to 50 percent recovery rate), and poorly to the placebo-clinical management (10 percent to 20 percent recovery rate). On the other hand, the mild to moderately depressed patients responded equally well to all interventions—implying that support and guidance alone may be sufficient for these patients (Hirschfeld, 1990; Klerman, 1990).

Bipolar Depression

Lithium. Lithium carbonate effectively alleviates manic symptoms (Klerman, 1988). Because it is a simple inorganic salt, lithium is an inexpensive medication. Approximately 50 percent to 80 percent of manic-depressives report full or partial alleviation of depressive symptoms, such as radical mood shifts (Depuc, 1979). However, follow-up evaluations of manic patients approximately two years after their hospitalization indicate that those taking lithium had no better outcome than those not taking lithium (Harrow et al., 1990). A frequent side effect of lithium is significant weight gain, and many depressives undergo serious stress in trying to balance its advantages in relieving their depression with this disadvantage. The difference between effective and toxic doses is, moreover, very small; at toxic levels, lithium may impair kidney and thyroid functioning so patients treated with it must be very carefully monitored. When lithium is unsuccessful or inappropriate for a patient with bipolar depression, several other medications such as Tegretol and Clonopin, two antiseizure medications, are used. Some experts believe anticonvulsants are especially effective for bipolar patients with unusually rapid mood swings.

SUICIDE

Suicide is an extremely relevant subject in a chapter on depression because, as noted earlier, 60 percent of people attempting suicide are depressed. Many suicides involve multiple disorders such as alcoholism and depression or sexual disorders and depression. Suicides also sometimes result from other disorders such as anorexia or substance abuse. But depression is by far the most common precipitant of suicide. Thus it is the most lethal mental disorder.

Some people view suicide as a totally rational act when a person is extremely ill or despondent, but it is generally condemned by church and state. In some states in the United States, suicide is unlawful and many religions view it as a sin. If a death is declared a suicide, insurance policies are voided. Even disregarding the attitudes of church, state, and society, suicide has enormous adverse effects on family left behind who feel overwhelming guilt and shame.

The actual number of people who commit suicide each year is hard to estimate. One-car "accidents," shooting "accidents," and even lethal doses of alcohol are sometimes listed as accidental deaths when they may have been suicides. A general estimate is that 30,000 individuals commit suicide each year in the United States, and approximately ten times as many people attempt it (Andreasen & Block, 1991). Women make twice as many suicide attempts as men, but men succeed three times more often in killing themselves. Alternatively stated, even though women make more suicide attempts, more men die from suicide. The higher rate of suicide attempts in women is probably due to their greater depression rate, and the higher death rate in suicidal men is due to their use of more violent methods.

Why Do People Commit Suicide?

Suicides of noted personalities, often people with wealth and physical well-being, lead us to wonder why anyone would take his or her life. The suicides of actress Marilyn Monroe and author Ernest Hemingway draw attention to this question because both were attractive, wealthy, and famous.

The two most common reasons people commit suicide in the United States are **surcease** and *manipulation.* Surcease is the desire to simply give up because living seems no longer tolerable. Approximately 56 percent of individuals commit suicide for this reason. Another 13 percent commit suicide to manipulate others; for example, a woman trying to prevent a lover from leaving her, or a teen-ager attempting to get his parents to give their car to him. In such cases, the individual may be ambivalent about wanting to die and in fact may not choose to complete the act. In the process of trying to manipulate events, however, he or she may die because, for example, it took too long to call an emergency number. The remaining 31 percent of suicides involve some combination of surcease and manipulation (Kovacs, Beck, & Weissman, 1975). A classic account of the reasons for suicide by the sociologist Emile Durkheim, who wrote in the late 1800s, included altruistic suicide such as hari-kari. Although some individuals have committed suicide for altruistic reasons, especially in wartime, empirical studies have not found it to be a frequent cause.

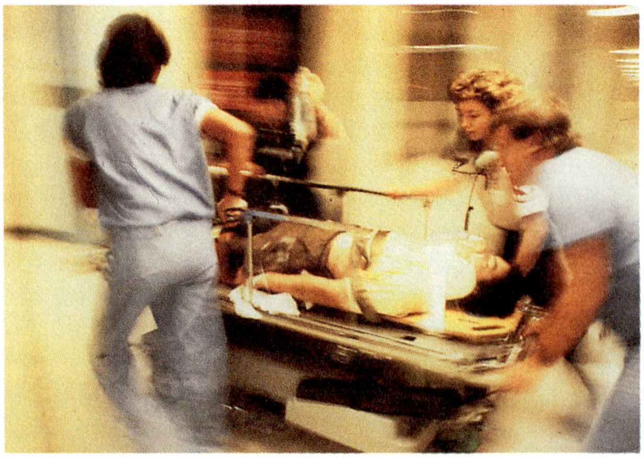

Patients commonly have to be committed to psychiatric hospitals after suicide attempts. Oxygen is often given en route to hospital emergency rooms after such attempts.

Can Suicide Be Prevented?

Suicide can be prevented. Many mental health workers believe they have helped prevent a death when they have taken a call in the early hours of the morning or raced to the emergency room with a client. Do we have solid empirical data to support our belief that suicide is preventable? Such data is difficult to obtain, and the effectiveness of suicide prevention centers and hotline services has not been proven (Dew et al., 1987). Yet if individuals who attempt suicide are referred afterward for psychological or pharmacological treatment, evidence suggests that their suicidal ideation and suicide attempts decrease. Professionals, citizens, and most importantly family members and close friends, however, should be informed about the factors associated with suicide. Many individuals who commit suicide never seek professional help beforehand. In fact, the primary suicide preventors are probably not professionals but family members and close friends able to respond to the need for love and the lack of hope in the person contemplating such an act. The following risk factors are significantly associated with suicide, and if present, should cause you to act (Schneidman, 1985):

1. Unendurable psychological pain.
2. Frustrated psychological needs.
3. Hopelessness.

Any suicidal talk by a friend or relative should be taken seriously! Eighty percent of people who have killed themselves gave specific prior warnings of their intentions. The following suicide note illustrates the psychological pain and frustrated needs of a father whose wish to die and end his pain contrasts markedly with his sincere concern for his family. Despite his worry that his suicide would stigmatize his wife and children, his hopelessness was so great that he could no longer endure life.

> To Tom, Betty, John—The stigma I bring upon you cannot be much more than has already been done. Be good to your mother and do all you can to help as she is a wonderful person. Tom—a rather gruesome thought—Remember when we worked in the yard and

you asked to see a cadaver at the College? Little did we know that I would be the first deceased for you to encounter. I love you and know you will make a wonderful man. Betty—We have been very close to each other. Please don't think too harshly of my actions. Stabilization takes place in time, and I know you will grow up to be one of the best women in the world. My love, dear. Johnny—You came last in our offspring so couldn't know me as well as your brother and sister. Just follow your brother's example, love your sister and help Mother. Remember, I love you, Johnny. Mary—There is no more or less to say than I have already told you—Truth will triumph eventually (pp. 206–207).

Bill

Source: Schneidman, E.S., & Farberow, N.L. (1957). *Clues to Suicide.* New York: McGraw Hill. Used by permission.

TABLE 7.1 Reasons for Committing Suicide

Problems	Females (N = 91)	Males (N = 39)
Marital	68%	83%
Boyfriend/girlfriend	71%	77%
Sexual	14%	15%
Children	25%	17%
Financial	16%	26%
Work	16%	54%
Accident/operation	19%	3%
Alcohol	9%	9%

Source: Bancroft, J., Skrimshire, A., Casson, J., Harvard-Watts, O., & Reynolds, F. (1977). People who deliberately poison or injure themselves: Their problems and contacts with helping agencies. *Psychological Medicine, 7,* 289–303. Reprinted by permission of Cambridge University Press.

Specific Types of Psychological Problems Associated with Suicide

The types of problems, as Table 7.1 shows, were given as reasons for the suicide attempts of 130 individuals in Oxford, England (Bancroft et al., 1977).

Table 7.1 shows that relationship issues are the most common reasons for suicide attempts. Problems in marriage or with a boyfriend or girlfriend clearly top the list of reasons associated with suicide. This information strongly buttresses some of the etiological explanations regarding marital and interpersonal factors in depression.

SUMMARY

1. Depression is one of the most prevalent psychological problems. Approximately 8 to 10 percent of men and 15 to 20 percent of women will face a serious clinical depression at some point in their lives.
2. Depression affects all socioeconomic classes and races about equally.
3. Contrary to popular belief, depression affects young adults more frequently than older persons. Depression among adolescents and young adults has been increasing significantly.
4. The two major types of mood disorder are unipolar depression and bipolar depression. Symptoms of depressive episodes, found in both disorders, include depressed mood, loss of interest in activities, and sleeping or eating problems. In addition, bipolar disorders involve a manic phase characterized by agitation, tremendous energy bursts, and irrationality.
5. Suicidal potential is evident in both unipolar and bipolar depression, with about 60 percent of suicide attempts made by depressed persons.
6. Genetic components of bipolar depression are clearly evident in family and twin studies of depression. Although unipolar depression's genetic components are not as strong as bipolar depression's, biochemical deficits such as norepinephrine and serotonin deficiencies are evident.
7. Cognitive factors are certainly correlates of unipolar depression, but it is unclear whether they cause depression. Cognitive distortion and negative self-schemata, negative attributions, script disruption, self-criticism, and problems in self-control such as critical self-evaluation are characteristics of depressed individuals but their causal role in depression is only beginning to be uncovered.
8. Interpersonal problems such as lack of social support and marital difficulties can cause depression.
9. Many pharmacological treatments of unipolar depression have proven successful, and pharmacological treatment of bipolar depression is effective with the vast majority of patients.
10. Cognitive treatment of unipolar depression has been used successfully for more than a decade; interpersonal treatments are also effective, and marital therapy has proven a successful treatment for maritally discordant depressives.
11. Suicide is a significant risk in every depressed patient, particularly when people experience unendurable psychological pain, when their psychological needs are frustrated, and when they feel hopeless.
12. Data on suicide prevention is difficult to obtain, but family members and friends can help prevent suicide by being aware that most people contemplating suicide give hints of their intentions.

Edvard Munch, *The Voice*. Courtesy of Scala, Art Resource.

8 PSYCHOLOGICAL FACTORS AFFECTING MEDICAL CONDITION

You have only to look at popular magazines and recent best-sellers to discover that people see a link between psychological factors, such as an individual's personality or level of life stress, and the development of different physical diseases (e.g., Siegel, 1986). Scientific surveys also show that people do see life stress causing physical disease (Leventhal, Meyer, & Nerenz, 1980). This belief goes back to ancient times, but is it only folklore, as a few critics have claimed (Angell, 1985), or is there solid scientific evidence connecting stress and illness?

The physical disorders discussed in this chapter are either caused by or significantly influenced by psychological factors. Prior to the *DSM-III-R*'s publication, they were known as psychosomatic, or psychophysiological, disorders. Some common examples are heart disease, hypertension, headaches, arthritis, ulcers, diabetes, and obesity. *DSM-III-R* uses the term *psychological factors affecting physical condition* to describe problems of this sort. But researchers now believe all medical disorders may be significantly influenced by psychological factors (Rodin & Salovey, 1989). Each disorder exhibits clearly evident organic pathology or a known pathophysiological process. In contrast, somatoform disorders have no known pathophysiological basis (see Chapter 6).

DSM-III-R defines *psychological factors* as meaningful environmental stimuli or events, such as interpersonal conflict or the death of a spouse or loved one. A clinician judges that psychological factors can affect a patient's physical condition if they are closely and repeatedly related to it over time. Patients may or may not be aware of the influence of these psychological factors on their condition.

We first trace the historical development of our current understanding of the effects of psychological factors on biological processes and illness. Psychological factors such as stress can influence health and illness either directly by affecting relevant biological processes or indirectly by influencing health-damaging behavior (e.g., cigarette smoking or diet). Finally discussed is the impact of psychological factors on common medical conditions like cancer, heart disease, hypertension, diabetes, and obesity.

HISTORY AND CURRENT STATUS

Psychosomatic Medicine

Origins of the systematic investigation of the links between psychological factors and physical illness can be traced to the development of psychoanalysis. In his pioneering book *Psychosomatic Medicine* (1950), Franz Alexander argued that specific unconscious emotional conflicts cause certain diseases. In gastrointestinal disorders (such as peptic ulcer, diarrhea, and colitis), he suggested an emotional conflict between an unconscious wish to remain passive and dependent—loved and cared for in an infantile sense—on the one hand, and the adult need to be independent and achieving on the other. Ulcer patients overcompensate for their unconscious dependency needs by aggressive and independent real-life behavior, which causes or contributes to an ulcer's development. By contrast, diarrhea and colitis patients compensate for their dependency needs through the unconscious symbolism of excrement. Defecation, viewed by psychoanalytic theory as an infantile form of gift giving or meeting obligations, is an emotional substitute for performance and accomplishment.

Psychosomatic medicine attributed specific emotional conflict in the cardiovascular disorders, such as hypertension and migraine headache, to repressed hostility. Alexander (1950) also linked coronary artery disease to excessive responsibility and mental stress. This clinical observation anticipated the subsequent development of the theory of a Type A behavior pattern, discussed later.

Few studies have evaluated this approach's merit to psychosomatic medicine. In a review of relevant literature, Friedman and Booth-Kewley (1987) examined the association of the five classic psychosomatic diseases of ulcers, headaches, arthritis, asthma, and coronary heart disease with psychological states or personality traits such as depression, anxiety, and anger/hostility. Contrary to psychosomatic medicine's predictions, these different diseases were not linked to specific personality traits or emotional states. Friedman and Booth-Kewley (1987), nevertheless, found the possibility of a general "disease-prone personality" predisposing an individual to any one of a number of different physical disorders.

Consistent with the general psychodynamic view of abnormal behavior, psychosomatic medicine's early approach resulted from clinical observations, not empirical investigation. It explained why different people with various personalities and emotional conflicts developed particular physical disorders. Partially because of the lack of evidence linking specific diseases to particular personalities, and the failure to develop effective methods for changing behavior related to medical problems, this approach to psychosomatic medicine had relatively little influence on either general medicine or the behavioral sciences (Agras, 1982). The emergence of behavioral medicine and health psychology in the 1970s changed this, however, and dramatically altered the study and treatment of health and disease.

Behavioral Medicine and Health Psychology

Behavioral medicine is defined as "the interdisciplinary field concerned with the development and integration of behavioral and biomedical science, knowledge and techniques relevant to health and illness, and the application of this knowledge and these techniques to prevention, diagnosis, treatment and rehabilitation" (Schwartz & Weiss, 1978, p. 250). Behavioral medicine emerged as a field of study in the 1970s, strongly due to behavior therapy's impact. Having demonstrated the effectiveness of behavioral principles and procedures in modifying many traditional psychiatric disorders (e.g., phobias), investigators turned to problems associated with illness and disease (Blanchard, 1982). Biofeedback, the direct modification of physiological responses such as blood pressure, lent itself to the assessment and treatment of different physical problems. Similarly, self-control strategies could be directly applied to preventing and coping with chronic diseases (e.g., coronary heart disease). The medical community quickly accepted the availability of effective methods for changing a wide range of behaviors related to physical conditions, together with strategies for evaluating the resulting effects. Perhaps health-care specialists were receptive because they were often confronted with diverse specific behavioral problems that went well beyond the classic diseases which were the primary concern of the psychosomatic medicine of the times.

Although behavior therapy has always had a seminal influence on behavioral medicine, the field extends beyond the application of behavioral principles and procedures. It encompasses a much broader range of biobehavioral science research from a number of basic and applied disciplines, such as social and physiological psychology, and epidemiology.

Health psychology is the "aggregate of the educational, scientific, and professional contributions of psychology as a discipline to the promotion and maintenance of health, prevention and treatment of illness, and identification of etiologic and diagnostic correlates of health, illness, and related dysfunction" (Pomerleau & Rodin, 1986, p. 485). Health psychology largely overlaps with behavioral medicine since both focus on the influence of psychological factors in health and illness. Yet there are differences. First, behavioral medicine is more closely identified with the modification of specific diseases. In contrast, health psychology is concerned with not only specific interventions but also socioenvironmental factors and individual differences affecting health and illness, and the analysis of health policy and the health-care system. Second, behavioral medicine tends to be more interdisciplinary—medical specialists working with behavioral scientists. In contrast, health psychology is based solely on the discipline of psychology, representing the activities of both basic and applied psychologists.

The development of behavioral medicine and health psychology reflect a significant change in our health and illness models. A biopsychosocial perspec-

Judith Rodin, Ph.D., one of the leading figures in health psychology and behavioral medicine.

tive (Engel, 1977), emphasizing the interactive influences of psychosocial and biological factors, is replacing the traditional biomedical model with its more limited emphasis on biology and disease. With the exception of AIDS, which demands a biopsychosocial approach, infectious diseases have been largely controlled. Current health concerns focus on chronic diseases, such as cardiovascular problems, with behavior and life-style—stress, diet, substance abuse, and physical inactivity—as the main risk factors. Their prevention and treatment necessarily involve psychological factors. People today live longer, and to maximize health as we get older, we must avoid health-damaging behavior and adopt appropriate health habits.

THE RELATIONSHIP BETWEEN MENTAL HEALTH AND PHYSICAL HEALTH

Severe emotional problems such as chronic anxiety or depression, increase the risk of contracting disease and are related to mortality. To show mental health's direct influence on physical health, we need longitudinal data to determine if emotional problems preceded the development of physical illness. If this is a pattern, we can infer a causal relationship. A landmark longitudinal study by Vaillant (1979) showed the relation of mental health to physical illness. The subjects were 204 male Harvard University sophomores first assessed between 1942 and 1944. All were physically healthy and free from any emotional problems. The men were then followed each year or every two years when they would either complete questionnaires or interviews. Based on these measures, the men's mental health status at the 1967 assessment was compared to their physical health at the 1975 examination. The relationship was highly significant. For example, from age twenty-one to forty-six years, only two of fifty-nine men rated with the best mental health became chronically ill or died. Yet eighteen of the forty-eight men with the worst mental health became chronically ill or died.

Table 8.1 lists the factors that defined poor mental health in the men in the 1967 assessment and shows that they occurred significantly more often in the men who later became ill or died. Mental health's effect on subsequent physical health held even when statistical analyses controlled for the possibly confounding influence of alcohol, cigarette smoking, obe-

TABLE 8.1 Association of Psychologic Predictors with Poor Health in Men 53 ± 1 Years Old

Predictor Variables Assessed, 1940–1967	HEALTH 1975	
	Excellent Health (100 Men) (percent)	Ill, Disabled, or Dead (34 Men) (percent)
>10 psychiatric visits	12	56
Heavy use of mood-altering drugs	10	44
Little occupational progress	15	44
Job dissatisfaction	21	44
Little recreation with others	39	76
Marriage unhappy or terminated	31	50
Little vacation	26	50
College psychologic soundness rated poor ("C")	11	29
>5 days sick leave/yr.	14	32
Low income (<$20,000/yr.)	14	26
Total adult adjustment score		
Best scores (10–12)	43	6
Worst scores (16–23)	14	59

Source: From Vaillant, G.E. (1979). Natural history of male psychological health. *New England Journal of Medicine,* 301, 1249–1254. Reprinted with permission.

sity, and parents' longevity. This finding is significant because many studies linking psychological stress with disease have not taken these factors into account. The subjects in Vaillant's study were a homogeneous sample of white, economically advantaged men; we cannot say whether these results generalize to women or other socioeconomic groups. The data, nevertheless, strongly suggest that poor mental health predicts premature aging and deterioration of health. Another way of stating this is that good mental health protects against inevitable decline in physical health of aging. Vaillant concluded that stress in itself does not impair health, but that good mental health improves our health and longevity by allowing us to cope more effectively with that stress.

Stress and Illness

The link between stress and disease is a critical example of psychological factors' impact on physical conditions. Individuals exposed to severe psychological stress are, on average, less healthy and develop more physical illnesses than their peers (Elliot & Eisdorfer, 1982). Evidence from several different sources, such as prospective, epidemiological research studies, demonstrates stress as a **risk factor** for disease (see Chapter 4). A risk factor predicts illness even though the reason for the increased risk is unclear. Once identified, it suggests the type of studies needed to uncover the underlying causes of the disease. Identification also encourages interventions to modify the risk factor and thus reduce the occurrence of the disease.

To analyze psychological stress as a risk factor for illness and disease, we must first understand the concept of stress and its measurement. Stress has been conceptualized in three basic ways.

1. Stress: A Response Model. Stress has been defined in terms of a complex physiological response by Selye (1956), who completed pioneering biological research on it. He conceptualized stress as a provoked, nonspecific body response following predictable stages. The first is an "alarm and mobilization reaction." The second is a state of "resistance" when the body tries to defend against the physiological demands placed on it. The third and final stage, following prolonged exposure to the harmful stimulation, is one of "exhaustion." Subsequent research demonstrated that Selye's complex series of physiological responses occur in response to psychological states as well as to physical stimulation (Weiner, 1977). Box 8.1 summarizes the neurophysiological and hormonal processes involved in stress responses.

2. Stress: A Stimulus Model. Stress has also been defined in terms of stimuli, events, or environmental conditions assumed to influence all or most people similarly. Cohen et al. (1982) have classified these stimuli, or *stressors,* into four broad categories: (a) acute stressors (e.g., awaiting surgery); (b) a stressor sequence triggered by a particular event (e.g., divorce or death of a spouse); (c) chronic stressors (e.g., unemployment); and (d) chronic but intermittent stressors (e.g., weekly contact with family members which reliably produces conflict).

Researchers have tried to measure stress by identifying stressful life events (Holmes & Rahe, 1967). People are asked to recall major life changes that have occurred within a specified period of time, typically one year. Each life event is given a weight—that is, a decision is made about how stressful it was—and the sum of the weighted scores is taken as the degree of stress to which the person was exposed (see Table 8.2). Positive life events, such as marriage, as well as negative events have been assumed to cause stress, because a change from one's normal routine was considered stressful.

Measuring major life events in this manner has increased our knowledge of the association between stress and disease but has been criticized conceptually and methodologically (Dohrenwend & Dohrenwend, 1974; Rabkin & Struening, 1976). One problem is that not all possible stressors are included in the different life event scales; for example, chronic conditions such as sex role conflict, not assessed in the life event approach, are related to health. Additionally, many minor everyday stressors ("hassles") have been linked to health outcomes (Kanner, Coyne, Schaefer, & Lazarus, 1981). A second problem is that it is difficult to know if the occurrence of common stressors (e.g., divorce) preceded illness or was a result of the disease process before the disease was diagnosed. A third problem is that not everyone responds to the same stressful event similarly. Many people feel differently about divorce; for some it may be more traumatic than for others. Finally, many people experience negative life events without becoming ill, a finding that requires a different approach to the assessment of stress.

3. Stress: A Transactional Model. Selye's (1956) view of stress as a unitary response to varied stimuli is no longer tenable. For example, negative life events may have different psychological and physiological consequences from positive events. Negative life events also appear to be better predictors of illness than positive events (Cohen et al., 1982). The evidence clearly shows that different people respond differently to the same noxious stimulus or stressful life event. It is now well established that a number of different biological and psychosocial processes and conditions determine or influence the response of a particular person to a stressor.

TABLE 8.2 The Holmes and Rahe Life Events Stress Scale

Rank	Life Event	Mean Value
1	Death of spouse	100
2	Divorce	73
3	Marital separation	65
4	Jail term	63
5	Death of close family member	63
6	Personal injury or illness	53
7	Marriage	50
8	Fired at work	47
9	Marital reconciliation	45
10	Retirement	45
11	Change in health of family member	44
12	Pregnancy	40
13	Sex difficulties	39
14	Gain of new family member	39
15	Business readjustment	39
16	Change in financial state	38
17	Death of close friend	37
18	Change to different line of work	36
19	Change in number of arguments with spouse	35
20	Mortgage over $10,000	31
21	Foreclosure of mortgage or loan	30
22	Change in responsibilities at work	29
23	Son or daughter leaving home	29
24	Trouble with in-laws	29
25	Outstanding personal achievement	28
26	Wife begin or stop work	26
27	Begin or end school	26
28	Change in living conditions	25
29	Revision of personal habits	24
30	Trouble with boss	23
31	Change in work hours or conditions	20
32	Change in residence	20
33	Change in schools	20
34	Change in recreation	19
35	Change in church activities	19
36	Change in social activities	18
37	Mortgage or loan less than $10,000	17
38	Change in sleeping habits	16
39	Change in number of family get-togethers	15
40	Change in eating habits	15
41	Vacation	13
42	Christmas	12
43	Minor violations of the law	11

Source: From Holmes, T.H., & Rahe, R.H. (1967). The social readjustment rating scale. *Journal of Psychosomatic Research*, 11, 213–218. Copyright 1967, Pergamon Press. Reprinted with permission.

Cognitive Appraisal. Cognitive appraisal of a potentially stressful event helps determine that event's emotional and physiological impact (Lazarus & Folkman, 1984). A stressful event can be appraised three ways. The first is an appraisal of harm—of damage already done. A second appraisal is of threat—of future or anticipated consequences. The third appraisal is of challenge—of future events that might involve personal gain. The student threatened by a pending exam worries about failure. In contrast, the student challenged by the same exam anticipates the opportunity to perform well. Cognitive appraisals are not necessarily rational or conscious; instead they are often automatic, unconscious, and irrational. An example of cognitive appraisal already discussed is Bandura's (1986) self-efficacy theory (see Chapter 5). It is not so much actual exposure to stressful (phobic) stimuli that evokes psychological distress and biological measures of stress, but individuals' perceived confidence about coping with the stimuli.

Another cognitive variable that seems linked to physical illness is pessimistic *explanatory style* or the habitual manner people use to explain their negative life events (Peterson, 1988). These explanations are coded as causes which are stable versus unstable, global versus specific, and internal (due to the self) versus external (due to the environment). Explanatory style is assessed, using either a questionnaire or an analysis of an individual's written or spoken material. Pessimistic explanatory style reflects the belief that bad events are caused by stable, global, and internal factors. In an illustrative study, Peterson, Seligman, and Vaillant (1988) analyzed the explanatory styles of 99 randomly chosen men from Vaillant's (1979) sample of Harvard University graduates described earlier. Pessimistic explanatory style predicted poor health in these Harvard men from ages forty-five through sixty, even when physical and mental health at age twenty-five were controlled. Table 8.3 shows some examples of explanations associated with different health outcomes.

We do not know the mechanisms that link pessimistic explanatory style to poor health, though both direct and indirect influences have been suggested. In the former, people explaining bad events in terms of stable, global, and internal attributions reportedly showed suppression of the immune system later. People with this explanatory style might neglect health care because they have negative, passive views. For example, pessimistic college students who contract colds or influenza may be less likely than their optimistic peers to take steps to ease their recovery, such as sleeping more and drinking more liquids.

Coping. Understanding the nature and effects of stress is linked to the concept of coping. The avail-

TABLE 8.3 Examples of Explanations of Men Who Were Least and Most Healthy at Age 55

Subject	Health (age 55)	Representative Explanation (age 25)
314	Deceased (=5)	"I cannot seem to decide firmly on a career . . . this may be an unwillingness to face reality." (rating = 5.75)
316	Deceased (=5)	"What I feel is characterized more by confusion than by sense." (rating = 5.67)
327	Deceased (=5)	"[I dislike work because I have] . . . fear of getting in a rut, doing the same thing day after day, year after year." (rating = 5.42)
347	Deceased (=5)	"I have symptoms of fear and nervousness . . . similar to those my mother has had. She is still very nervous." (rating=4.67)
301	Healthy (=1)	"My career in the Army has been checkered, but on the whole characteristic of the Army." (rating = 3.92)
315	Healthy (=1)	"I occasionally feel lazy . . . [due to] . . . lack of physical exercise." (rating = 3.75)
301	Healthy (=1)	"I tried to bluff my way through a situation. . . . I didn't know the facts, a situation common to all green junior officers when they are first put in charge of men." (rating = 2.75)
320	Healthy (=1)	"Accused of violating a confidence . . . because the officer had not bothered to get all the facts." (rating = 1.83)

Note: Explanation ratings range from *optimistic* (1) to *pessimistic* (7).

Source: From Peterson, C., Seligman, M.E.P., & Vaillant, G.E. (1988). Pessimistic explanatory style is a risk factor for physical illness: A thirty-five-year longitudinal study. *Journal of Personality and Social Psychology,* 55, 23–27.

ability and use of specific coping mechanisms strongly influences our psychological and physiological responses to stressors. Coping can be how we think about events or how we behave in response to stressors. Both cognitive and behavioral coping strategies can be effective in modifying the effects of life stressors.

Lazarus and Folkman (1984) distinguish between two major forms of coping. In active or *problem-focused coping,* people work to change the situation directly. For example, a college student upset by her roommate's inconsiderate behavior might speak to the roommate, explaining how this behavior is causing difficulty, and suggest alternative arrangements to suit both students. In passive or *emotion-focused coping,* people try to accept and manage their feelings. This form of coping is helpful in situations beyond an individual's control that cannot be changed by appropriate problem solving. For example, coping with terminal illness might be emotion-focused, such as accepting death.

The success of coping ultimately depends on the strategy used, by whom, in what situation, and at which point in the response to a stressor. Active rather than passive coping has often been shown superior in reducing perceived and actual physiological components of stress. Different stressors and problems, nevertheless, require different types of coping.

Personal coping resources significantly affect people's responses to stress. And the effects of different coping styles partly depend on variables such as the specific social and cultural context. Active coping or personal control may occasionally have negative rather than positive effects on health (Folkman, 1984). For example, Dressler (1985) studied the relationships among coping styles, chronic economic stress, and psychosomatic distress symptoms in a rural, southern black community. An active coping style reduced stress's effects on the women but increased its effects on the men. According to Dressler, the social norms within the conservative community where the study was conducted explain this gender-linked difference. Thus in this community, active coping by black men was more likely to conflict with institutionalized racism's barriers. The more they tried to change their economic conditions, the more frustration and failure they met with. They learned to suppress their resentment but only at the cost of increased psychosomatic distress. In contrast, the women's attempts at active coping were confined mainly to improving conditions for the children, efforts which, Dressler observed, were more acceptable within the community and which the women felt more personal control over than men did about their behavior.

Social Support. The environmental factor of **social support** mediates the relationship between stress and illness (Cohen & Syme, 1985). Social support includes showing concern and caring for the individual; communicating acceptance and group inclusion to the person; giving tangible help when needed; and offering advice about coping with problems. Epidemiological research has consistently linked social rela-

BOX 8.1 The Biological Basis of Stress

The human nervous system is organized as a hierarchy of different components. The brain is at the head of this hierarchy. Two parts of the brain exert primary control of emotion and motivation—the *hypothalamus* and the *limbic system*. The hypothalamus is critical to the stress response because it influences the autonomic nervous system and the endocrine system. The sympathetic division of the autonomic nervous system activates key organs such as the heart, blood vessels, stomach, and various glands (e.g., the adrenal glands) (see Chapter 2). In response to emotion or stress it mobilizes the body's resources for emergencies (e.g., by increasing heart rate).

The endocrine system consists of glands secreting hormones into the bloodstream. These hormones allow the brain to send chemical messages to different parts of the body in addition to direct neural transmission. The hypothalamus is itself a gland as well as a center of nerve cells. The chain of influence on the endocrine system initiated by the hypothalamus is shown in Figure 8.1. Its secretion of corticotropin releasing factor (CRF) stimulates the pituitary gland. Together, the hypothalamus and the pituitary control emotional responses, hunger and thirst, digestion, and sexual behavior. The pituitary gland in turn activates the adrenal gland by releasing adrenocorticotrophic hormone (ACTH).

The adrenal gland, which is also stimulated by the autonomic nervous system, consists of two pairs—the inner portion (the adrenal medulla) and the outer portion (the adrenal cortex). In response to stress, the adrenal cortex secretes corticosteroids, whereas the adrenal medulla secretes catecholamines (epinephrine and norepinephrine), the effects of which are summarized in Figure 8.1. These hormones also influence the brain in a complex feedback loop.

The second part of the brain critically involved in regulating emotion is the limbic system. More advanced than the hypothalamus on the evolutionary scale of brain development, the limbic system regulates emotional expression with greater flexibility. The hippocampus of the limbic system plays a major role in memory. The hippocampus seems particularly responsive to corticosteroids released by the adrenal cortex. This feedback action of corticosteroids on the hippocampus helps turn off the stress response.

The close proximity of the major centers of emotion and memory in the brain should be noted. In earlier chapters reciprocal interaction between mood and memory have been described, especially in depression (see Chapter 7). We selectively recall events associated with strong emotion or stress (as in PTSD, for example), and these memories, sometimes traumatic, are often the focus of therapies trying to undo their maladaptive effects on later behavior.

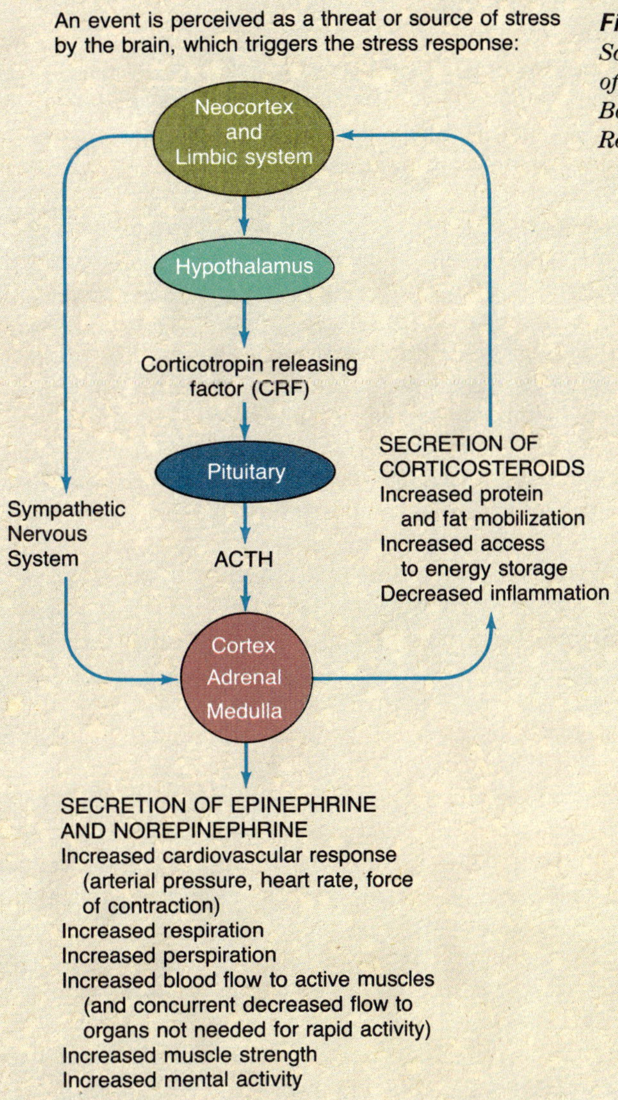

Figure 8.1
Schematic Diagram of the Biological Basis of the Stress Response

tionships with mortality rates. For example, there are higher death rates, from all causes, among unmarried than married individuals. Measures of social relationships—for example, marriage, contacts with extended family and friends, church membership, and other formal and informal social connections—predict subsequent death rates. Thus, in Tecumseh, Michigan, House, Robbins, and Metzner (1982) found measures of social relationships and activities strongly related to death rates during the following ten to twelve years. The relative risk for men was 3.0, for women 1.5. A relative risk for death of 3.0 means that someone who scores low on the measure of interest—in this case the extent of social relationships and activities—is three times as likely to die as individuals high on the measure. These results were obtained even though investigators controlled for the effects of known risk factors such as blood pressure and blood cholesterol, and other biomedical measures such as electrocardiograms. Prospective studies overall have shown the apparent protective effect of social relationships holding for men and women across different populations. But data suggest the effect is greater for men than for women, and possibly for whites more than for blacks (House et al., 1988).

The link between social support and health is established, but the mechanisms explaining it remain to be identified. One view is that social support (e.g., emotional support or practical assistance with challenging tasks) buffers individuals against stress's effects. Bovard (1985) proposed a psychophysiological basis for this effect. In this model, the influence of social relationships in the brain is mediated through the amygdala, leading to the activation of the anterior hypothalamus and the inhibition of the posterior hypothalamic zone. The former effect stimulates release of human growth hormone, whereas the latter inhibits the release of adrenocorticotropic hormone, cortisol, catecholamines, and autonomic reactivity (see Box 8.1).

Another view is that social support enhances health directly in ways unrelated to any buffering effect against stress. Among the hypotheses about social support is that it fosters a sense of meaning or coherence enhancing health, or that it encourages health-promoting behaviors such as sufficient sleep, adequate diet, physical activity, good medical care, and avoidance of alcohol and other substance abuse (Umberson, 1987). Social support might directly enhance immune function and so protect an individual against infection and disease. Among college students experiencing the stress of final exams, those with more adequate social support had superior immune function (Jemmott & Magliore, 1988). The *quantity of social support* a person enjoys is a function of experience. However, how a person perceives the *quality of that social support* is strongly influenced by genetic factors (Bergeman et al., 1990). This intriguing finding suggests that the positive effect of social support on health is a product not only of environmental events, but also of genetic variables which we do not yet understand.

The evidence reviewed should give us pause for thought. It is probably no coincidence that disadvantaged groups such as the elderly, the poor, and the black population in this country are typically the least socially integrated elements of our society and also the least healthy (Williams, 1990). Moreover, as House et al. (1988) point out, changes in marital and child-bearing patterns are progressively leading to an older population and an increase in people living alone—people without a spouse or children whom the elderly have traditionally relied on for support.

PSYCHOLOGICAL EFFECTS ON BIOLOGICAL MECHANISMS

Available evidence consistently shows that factors such as mental health and psychological stress significantly affect physical health. A key question then becomes how these influences are related to the development of illness and disease. How do psychological factors cause the physiological changes that define physical illness and disease? Psychological factors influence health in two major ways. The first is their effects on the basic biological mechanisms and functions that mediate illness and disease. The second is their role in determining specific health-promoting and health-damaging behavior, such as coping better with stress, quitting cigarette smoking, following a healthy diet, or adopting safer sex practices to prevent the spread of AIDS. Stress affects some diseases both directly and indirectly.

With regard to biological functioning, stress may affect any system in the body, including the brain. For example, the glucocorticoids released from the adrenal gland can seriously damage neurons in the hippocampus, a part of the brain critically involved in memory and regulation of the stress response (Uno et al., 1989). The glucocorticoids bind to specific receptors in the hippocampus, which is highly sensitive to their effect, and can combine with other damaging neurological events to kill hippocampus neurons.

To illustrate the direct influence of psychological factors on medical conditions, we will focus on diseases related to the immune system (e.g., cancer), cardiovascular disorders (e.g., heart disease), and metabolic disease (e.g., diabetes). These medical conditions not only afflict large numbers of people but also provide excellent examples of current research in the complex interactions between psychological processes and biological functioning.

Psychological Factors in Immune Function

The **immune system** protects the body against disease. Although immunological functioning is highly complex and not yet fully understood, we should be aware of some of its basic workings. Immune function is measured by drawing blood and analyzing the number and specialized functions of various subgroups of white blood cells, or leukocytes, and their biochemical mediators. The immune system has two main components—the humoral and the cellular—each with different functions. Humoral immunity involves the release into the blood and other body fluids of immunoglobulin, antibodies that defend against bacteria and viruses. They achieve this by combining with and then neutralizing the bacteria or virus. B-cells and their immediate derivatives, plasma cells, are primarily involved in humoral immunity.

Cellular immunity does not involve the release of antibodies and occurs more slowly than humoral immunity. It protects against intracellular viruses, cancer cells, and transplanted tissue—as in heart transplants. T-cells, or lymphocytes, from the thymus gland are primarily responsible for cellular immunity. T-cells eliminate antigens either directly or indirectly by releasing substances in their presence called *lymphokines*. Different T-cell subpopulations have specialized functions: Some destroy tumor cells; others fight infection; still others orchestrate immune responsiveness. For example, helper (T4) T-cells enhance immune responses whereas suppressor (T8) T-cells inhibit them. A common measure of immune functioning is the T4/T8 cell ratio. We normally have twice as many helper as suppressor T-cells. In many immune-related diseases this ratio is changed or even reversed (Borysenko, 1987). Some immune responses depend on complementary actions of T- and B-cells.

Besides T- and B-cells, several other cell types and plasma components are involved in immunological processes. Natural killer (NK) cells, for example, derived from bone marrow and related to T-cells, destroy virus and some tumor cells. In a well-functioning immune system these complex, interdependent components precisely balance each other. When their delicate balance is disrupted, disease may result. Autoimmune disease occurs when the immune cells mistakenly attack the body's normal tissue as if it were foreign matter.

Animal Studies. These studies have generally shown that stress reduces resistance to infection, and enhances the incidence and development of tumors (Shavit & Martin, 1987). Stress's disease-inducing effects appear mediated by immune function. Stress reduces both humoral and cellular immune responses. The relative *controllability* of the stressor seems especially likely to make a difference. Inescapable tail shock suppresses natural killer cell activity and enhances tumor growth in rats, while escapable shock does not (Laudenslager et al., 1979). In other words, the same amount of shock has very different outcomes, depending on the degree of control available to the rat. Helplessness apparently affects the suppression of immune function. The researchers' finding is particularly important given the role of controllability of stressors in the human studies reviewed later. This result, among others, also establishes that stress is not a unitary phenomenon as Selye (1956) had assumed (Shavit & Martin, 1987).

Ader's (1981) pioneering studies of the classical conditioning of immune responses demonstrate the direct control of immune function by psychological factors. In this research environmental stimuli—the conditioned stimuli (CS)—were selectively associated with the administration of a drug causing activation of immune responses—the unconditioned stimulus (UCS). Mere presentation of the environmental stimuli subsequently produced a similar, conditioned, response. Although the clinical significance of this classical conditioning of immune responses has yet to be shown (Ader & Cohen, 1985), its implications are considerable. Research on the interactions between psychological processes and immunology has led to the highly specialized field of **psychoimmunology.**

Human Studies. A variety of stressful events can influence immune function. In one series of studies, Kiecolt-Glaser and Glaser (1987) assessed immune function in medical students one month before and then during final exams. They found significant reductions in a number of immune functions as a result of the stress of examinations, including decreased helper T-cell and NK cell activity. Students taking exams, of course, typically change their behavior in several ways as they sleep fewer hours and eat less well. Either sleep loss or inadequate nutrition rather than stress then may influence immune function itself. Kiecolt-Glaser and Glaser (1987), however, controlled for these potentially confounding factors and concluded that the observed immunological changes directly resulted from examination stress. Although students everywhere might disagree, these investigators argue that examinations are "commonplace" stressors comparable to numerous other common life events. If the researchers are correct, many other instances exist in which we are vulnerable to stress-induced changes in immune function.

Severe and prolonged stressors reliably affect immune function. Bereavement (e.g., the death of a spouse or immediate family member) is usually considered the most powerful of all stressful events and it affects immune function. For example, husbands of women with advanced breast cancer showed significant immunosuppression in the months following their wives' death compared to the months prior to bereavement (Stein, Keller, & Schleifer, 1985). Marital separation and divorce are reliably associated with increased illness and mortality rates. Compared to married controls, separated or divorced women show poorer immune function. Moreover, among separated or divorced women, the greater the attachment to the former spouse, the greater the effect on immune function (Kiecolt-Glaser & Glaser, 1987).

Pessimistic explanatory style affects immune function through illness. As part of a large-scale research program on perceived control's effects on the aging process, Rodin (1988) found that individuals who attributed bad events to global, stable, and internal causes (pessimists) had a significantly lower T4/T8 ratio and responded less well to an immunologic challenge than those with the opposite explanatory style (optimists). These results, showing poorer immune function among pessimistic elderly individuals persisted even when Rodin controlled for potentially confounding factors like current health and depression. This suggests that the well-documented effects of explanatory style on health may be partly mediated by altering immune function.

Perceived self-efficacy directly affects responses of the autonomic nervous system and the immune system. To demonstrate this, Wiedenfeld and her colleagues (1989) used an experimental methodology previously described in phobic disorder treatment (see Chapter 5). Using modeling and guided exposure treatments, researchers systematically increased self-efficacy in snake phobic subjects. They measured immunological responses to the phobic stressor (i.e., the snake) before, during, and after subjects acquired self-efficacy about coping with the snake. The development of self-efficacy enhanced subjects' immunological responses to the stressor.

A study of rheumatoid arthritis also suggests self-efficacy's link to immune function (O'Leary, Shoor, Lorig, & Holman, 1988). Rheumatoid arthritis is a painful and disabling autoimmune disease afflicting 1 percent to 4 percent of the population. Its etiology is unclear, but the pain associated with this disease can be successfully treated with cognitive-behavioral methods. O'Leary and her colleagues (1988) showed that a cognitive-behavioral treatment of relaxation training and self-control strategies produced much greater reductions in pain, inflammation in joints, and stress than a control procedure using an arthritis self-help book about how to cope with the disease. Measures of patients' self-efficacy in coping with pain and physical functioning were correlated with treatment effects, consistent with the view that changes in self-efficacy can influence the effects of cognitive-behavioral treatment (Bandura, 1986). Perceived self-efficacy was also positively correlated with immune function measures directly related to the disease following treatment, although treatment did not alter immune function.

The stress-related personality variable of inhibited power motivation is characterized by a greater need for power than for affiliation, and a high level of self-restraint. As proposed by McClelland (1989), increased stress and disease result when this power need is blocked. Several studies indicate this is associated with both frequency of illness and immune function (Jemmott, 1987). For example, college students high on inhibited power motivation and who experienced power-related life stresses developed more upper respiratory illnesses than other students.

A coping style of passivity, coupled with ready acceptance of the disease, has been specifically linked to risk for and recovery from skin, breast, and cervical cancer. Temoshok et al. (1985) explored the association of emotional expression with malignant melanoma (skin cancer). Researchers found that the less emotionally expressive patients were when interviewed about their feelings, the poorer their immunological response at the site of the cancer. Levy et al. (1985) related coping style both to breast cancer and NK cell activity, an important defense against cancer. Patients less distressed and more accepting of their disease showed decreased NK activity, which in turn was correlated with the spread of cancer nodes at diagnosis.

The strongest evidence to date of psychological factors' influence on breast cancer comes from Spiegel, Bloom, Kraemer, and Gottheil's (1989) study. Researchers found that women who participated in a psychotherapy group and used self-hypnosis to control pain, lived almost twice as long as those in a control group. Both groups received normal medical treatment. Psychotherapy's achievement of this effect remains to be explained, although women in the therapy group reported less anxiety, depression, and pain than the controls. In contrast, a prospective study by Cassileth et al. (1985) found no relationship between psychosocial factors and the course of cancer. The evidence that psychosocial factors can influence cancer outcome is suggestive but not definitive.

The person variables described here differ from each other in several key respects yet they can be seen as related constructs. It is useful to think of them as reflecting different forms of perceived control and active coping in response to stressful conditions—critical to optimal mental and physical health.

Psychosocial Modification of Immune Function. One exciting prospect in the study of psychoimmunology is the potential of developing psychosocial methods for improving immune function. Preliminary results suggest that this is feasible. In geriatric patients, for example, relaxation training significantly decreased stress-related symptoms and enhanced immune function compared to control conditions (Kiecolt-Glaser & Glaser, 1987).

Environmental factors can also modify immune function. Infant monkeys separated from their mothers show marked emotional reactions (separation anxiety). Compared to monkeys allowed to remain with their mothers, separated monkeys, when injected with a virus, exhibited significantly poorer immune function (Coe, 1988). This immunosuppression was eliminated, however, if the separated infant monkey were allowed to remain in its home cage or were housed next to a familiar companion. Both a familiar environment and social companionship helped reverse the bad health effects of a virus.

Psychosocial Factors and Disease

The previous section shows that psychological stress definitely alters immune function. But are these immunologically mediated stress effects clinically significant? Do they lead to or delay recovery from infectious diseases? Increasing evidence suggests that for some diseases the answer to both questions is "yes."

Having shown that examination stress suppresses immune function, Glaser et al. (1987) assessed students' health at three separate exam times during the course of a year. They found a significant increase in self-reported illness—mainly upper respiratory tract infections—at exam time. Glaser et al. (1987) did not report specific correlations between the infections and immune function. Such a correlation would be necessary to prove that stress influences illness directly via its action on the immune system.

Infectious mononucleosis (IM) occurs primarily in young adults and is caused by the Epstein-Barr virus (EBV), a member of the herpes virus group. The virus is usually transmitted through contact with infected saliva by kissing. A prospective study by Kasl, Evans, and Niederman (1979) showed psychosocial factors predicting the onset of and length of hospitalization for IM. They studied an entire class of cadets during their four years at West Point Military Academy. Of the cadets who entered the Academy, 432, or one third, lacked the EBV antibody—that is, they had not been infected with the EBV virus. Twenty percent of these cadets became infected (seroconverted) during the next four years and one quarter of those seroconverters developed the full clinical symptoms of IM. The psychosocial factors predicting IM were (a) a father with "overachieving" values; (b) high motivation for a military career; and (c) poor academic performance. Together, these factors presumably produced increased psychological stress. These psychological factors were even associated with the severity of infection in cadets who seroconverted—that is, contracted the virus—but did not develop clinical IM.

Acquired Immune Deficiency Syndrome (AIDS). AIDS is a particularly deadly disease in which cells of the immune system itself are attacked. The cause is infection with the Human Immunodeficiency Virus (HIV). Although HIV infection is believed to inevitably lead to the full clinical disease of AIDS, a small but possibly growing number of diseased people live five or more years after diagnosis, compared to its average life expectancy ranging from two to eighteen months. Some investigators speculate that psychosocial factors may influence the onset and the course of the disease through their effects on the immune system (Bandura, 1990).

Psychosocial factors might influence the course of AIDS, such as the reduction in number and functioning of lymphocytes due to the effects of stress hormones, by several pathophysiological pathways (Solomon, 1989). One way to test this is to compare patients who had died rapidly following disease onset with those who had survived for two years or longer. A preliminary study indicates that patients who lived longer had higher scores on Kobasa's Hardiness Scale and reached out to obtain more help in solving problems than those who died soon after diagnosis (Solomon, Temoshok, O'Leary, & Zich, 1987). Autonomic arousal was also correlated with greater NK cell activity. Moreover, autonomic arousal measures predicted patients' survival at a three-year follow-up (O'Leary, Temoshok, Jenkins, & Sweet, 1989). These researchers hypothesize that increased autonomic arousal is associated with the release of catecholamines, enhancing NK activity. This is consistent with other research correlating minimal emotional expression with bad outcomes in cancer patients.

Severe stress is commonly believed to speed the deadly progression of AIDS. Yet gay men suffering bereavement over lovers and friends who are AIDS victims do not show different immunological responses to nonbereaved gay men (Kemeny, Cohen, Zegans, & Conant, 1989). And efforts to improve immune function in gay men using relaxation and other stress management strategies have proved unsuccessful (Coates, McKusick, Kuno, & Stites, 1989).

At present there is some evidence that psychosocial factors can influence immune function in AIDS. But the findings are inconsistent and unreliable.

Psychological Factors in Cardiovascular Disease

The cardiovascular system consists of the heart and blood vessels. To illustrate the role of psychological factors in cardiovascular disease,[1] we will focus on the problems of hypertension and coronary heart disease.

Hypertension. Hypertension is chronic, abnormally high blood pressure. A blood pressure measure of 140/90 is defined as borderline hypertension; a measure of 160/95 is definite hypertension.[2] Sometimes hypertension is called the "silent killer" because it is asymptomatic, meaning that you are unaware of it unless you have your blood pressure checked. Affecting roughly 30 million people in the United States, hypertension can cause stroke, heart disease, and kidney damage. Some groups are more at risk for hypertension than others. It is more prevalent in men than women, and twice as common among blacks than whites (Anderson et al., 1989). Risk increases with age, although a large number of adolescents and young adults suffer from hypertension.

Roughly 90 percent of hypertension cases have unspecified causes and are described as essential hypertension. There are probably multiple causes of hypertension, including genetic, dietary, sociocultural, and personality factors. As a result, understanding and treating hypertension requires a biopsychosocial perspective taking into account the separate and interactive effects of different risk factors.

Genetic factors predispose some people to develop the problem with hypertension running in families. Children with at least one parent with hypertension, even if they themselves have normal blood pressure, respond to stress with greater blood pressure increases than those without such a family history. Diet affects blood pressure, and reducing sodium intake is a major intervention for preventing and treating hypertension. Similarly, excessive alcohol consumption is positively correlated with increased blood pressure (Altura, 1986).

Sociocultural factors play a role in hypertension. Cross-cultural research has shown hypertension's strong association with industrialization. It remains uncertain if this is due to increased stress in modern, industrialized societies, or is a function of other variables such as changed dietary practices. Increased blood pressure in response to an acute stressor is a normal biological response of the autonomic nervous system. The higher blood pressure readies the individual to cope with an emergency situation. But constant exposure to stressful conditions, especially in genetically susceptible individuals, might lead to chronically high blood pressure. A highly stressful work environment, for example, might influence hypertension's development.

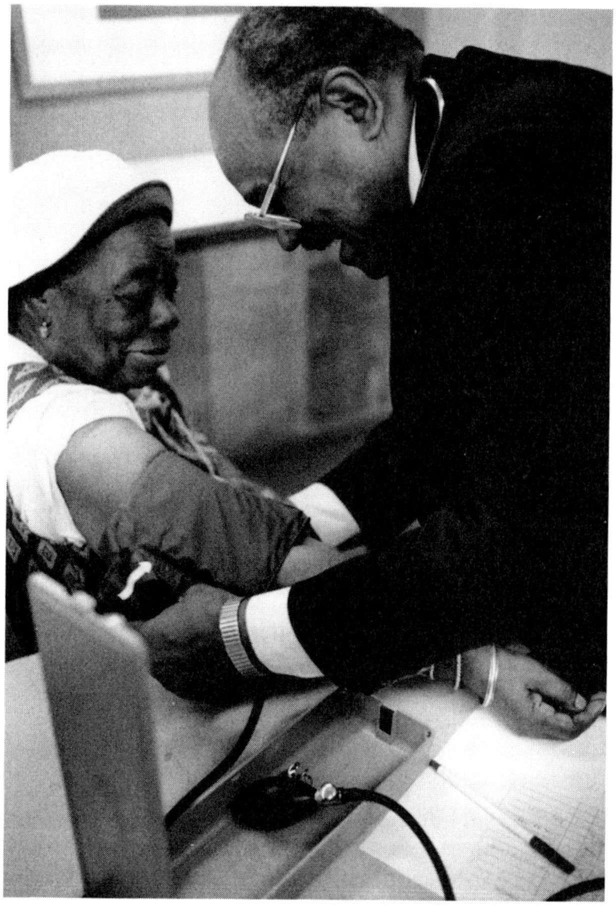

People are unaware of their blood pressure unless it is measured directly.

The view of hypertension as a function of particular personality variables goes back to the emergence of psychosomatic medicine, as discussed earlier. The classic interpretation was that hypertensive individuals have strong hostile and aggressive feelings. Instead of expressing these feelings openly, hypertensives unconsciously suppress them. The strain of suppressing or inhibiting these underlying hostile feelings supposedly transformed into high blood pressure (Alexander, 1950).

The psychosomatic hypothesis was criticized as too speculative and for failing to indicate suppressed feelings' role in altering physiological functioning. Subsequent research has indicated a connection between hostility and aggression and high blood pressure. For example, a personality measure of Harvard students in the early 1950s predicted these men's blood pressure twenty years later (McClelland, 1989). The personality measure was inhibition of the need for power, referred to earlier regarding psychological factors' influence on immune function. A significantly greater percentage of men who scored high on "inhibition of need for power" had developed hy-

[1] Other types of cardiovascular disease include stroke and peripheral vascular disease, such as Raynaud's Syndrome, characterized by vasospasms and coldness in fingers and toes.

[2] The first number refers to systolic blood pressure (i.e., when the heart is actively pumping blood); the second number describes diastolic blood pressure (i.e., when the heart is at rest).

pertension by the 1970s, when the men were in their fifties, than their peers not rated high on this personality variable. Personality's effect was significant irrespective of the men's blood pressure when they were students at Harvard.

The hypothesized association between hostility and cardiovascular functioning receives further support from research on Type A behavior pattern.

Coronary Heart Disease. The suspected link between psychological factors and physical disease is at the heart of the continuing controversy about possible behavioral determinants of heart disease. In the United States and other Western societies, *coronary heart disease (CHD)* is the greatest cause of death, despite a steady decline in CHD mortality over the last twenty years (Levy & Kannel, 1988). This decline is due to improvements in early detection of heart problems and to the identification and modification of biological and psychological risk factors. People have made beneficial changes in their life-styles.

The etiology of CHD[3] is complex. Like hypertension, heart disease runs in the family. Vulnerable individuals inherit a biological tendency for it, which may then interact with different physiological, nutritional, and environmental factors to produce heart disease. Based on epidemiological research in several countries, we have long known that high blood pressure and cigarette smoking are risk factors for coronary artery disease. More recently, serum cholesterol and obesity have also been established as independent risk factors. Despite our knowledge of heart disease's causes, much about its origins is still unknown. Part of the search for additional etiological mechanisms has focused on psychological factors' possible influence.

A classic example of psychological factors potentially influencing heart disease is the now widely known **Type A behavior pattern.** This concept's brief but turbulent history paints a fascinating picture of research's pitfalls, problems, and potential in the link between behavior and heart disease.

Beginning in the 1950s, San Francisco cardiologists Meyer Friedman and Ray Rosenman suggested that people with a particular behavior pattern are at greater risk for coronary artery disease than people without such a behavioral style. They called it Type A behavior pattern. The Type A person responds to stress with hostility or aggression, feels a sense of time pressure (i.e., always has deadlines to meet), and shows competitiveness and ambition. By contrast, the Type B person is less aggressive, more relaxed, and sets fewer deadlines (Friedman & Rosenman, 1974). The two cardiologists also carefully described a structured clinical interview to assess Type A behavior pattern.

Friedman and Rosenman derived their hypothesis from the following observations. First, they argued that biomedical risk factors, such as high blood pressure and cholesterol, by themselves could not explain the heart disease's increasing rate in industrialized societies in the first half of the twentieth century. Second, clinical observations of their patients' hard-driving, competitive behavior patterns led them to suspect psychological stress as a risk factor. One of their early studies (Friedman & Rosenman, 1974) showed stress directly affecting cholesterol level in the blood (serum cholesterol), an established risk factor for heart disease. Friedman and Rosenman measured the serum cholesterol from January to June of one year in a sample of accountants. Cholesterol rose sharply as April 15 approached—the date on which Americans all have to pay taxes! Accountants are under intense pressure to complete tax returns by this stress-inducing deadline. Cholesterol then declined significantly during May and June, when the stress had subsided. Results could not be attributed to changes in the accountants' diet, ciga-

The hard-driven, stressed executive is often thought to show the Type A behavior pattern.

[3] Some definitions will help the reader understand basic heart disease concepts. *Coronary artery disease (CAD)* is the partial or total obstruction of one or more of the coronary arteries with atherosclerosis. *Atherosclerosis* is a plaque of cholesterol, fat, and calcium, which forms in a lesion in the walls of the coronary arteries. Atherosclerotic obstruction can lead to chest pain *(angina)* or heart attack (also known as a *myocardial infarction*). *Myocardial ischemia* is the narrowing of the coronary arteries, producing abnormal function or even a heart attack.

rette smoking, or exercise habits, which remained stable during this period. The impact of psychological stress on serum cholesterol has been replicated (Dimsdale & Herd, 1982).

Evidence for the Type A behavior pattern hypothesis comes from several sources, one being prospective epidemiological studies. Strong support came from the early Western Collaborative Group Study (WCGS) following 3,154 healthy men, aged thirty-nine to fifty-nine, for eight-and-a-half years. As determined by the structured interview, individuals with Type A behavior pattern were twice as likely to develop coronary heart disease than their Type B counterparts (Rosenman et al., 1975). Moreover, the influence of Type A behavior pattern was independent of other known risk factors (Brand, 1978).

A second source of evidence comes from studies of patients undergoing a medical procedure known as **coronary angiography.** This procedure involves inserting a catheter, or fine needle, to inject a special dye into the coronary arteries to examine them under X-ray for the extent of plaque buildup, or atherosclerosis. Initial studies found patients with Type A behavior pattern having more extensive coronary artery disease at the time of catheterization, even with other risk factors held constant (Blumenthal et al., 1978) than patients without this pattern. So convincing did the evidence appear that in 1978 a panel of distinguished medical scientists convened by the National Heart, Lung, and Blood Institute concluded that Type A behavior pattern was an independent risk factor for coronary heart disease.

At this point contradictory findings began to appear (Matthews & Haynes, 1986). For example, a twenty-five-year follow-up of the original WCGS data set subjects showed patients with Type A behavior pattern who had recovered from a heart attack were significantly *less* likely to die of subsequent coronary heart disease than Type B's (Ragland & Brand, 1988). In other words, in subjects who survived a first heart attack, Type A behavior pattern appeared to be a protective factor, not a risk factor.

Studies using angiography have been even more damaging to the Type A behavior pattern hypothesis. After the three initial supportive studies, subsequent investigations failed to show a significant association between Type A behavior pattern and degree of coronary heart disease at the time of catheterization (Dembroski & Costa, 1988).

The epidemiological studies described above tested whether Type A behavior pattern predicted death due to heart disease as a whole. A more recent study showed the importance of specifying the type of cardiac death—Type A behavior pattern predicted sudden but not nonsudden death (Brackett & Powell, 1988). Sudden cardiac death, defined as death within one hour after the onset of cardiac symptoms, causes most deaths in people who have survived an initial heart attack, and is the result of ventricular fibrillation.[4]

Evidence that some element of Type A behavior pattern is related to health comes from a study designed to alter Type A behavior and evaluate its impact on coronary heart disease (Friedman et al., 1984). Patients who had experienced a myocardial infarction were randomly assigned either to a control condition—consisting of standard group cardiologic counseling—or to an experimental condition—consisting of the same counseling plus cognitive-behavioral treatment to reduce Type A behavior. Decreased Type A behavior at the end of three years was observed in 43.8 percent of the 592 patients who received this intervention, a figure higher than for cardiologic counseling alone. That less than half the sample showed reductions suggests this behavior pattern's resistance to modification. The greater reduction of Type A behavior in the experimental group resulted, nevertheless, in a three-year cumulative rate of recurrent cardiac problems (7 percent) that was significantly lower than the 13 percent in the control condition.

In the face of such conflicting results Dimsdale (1988) has arrived at what may be the most balanced conclusion, namely, that "something is going on in terms of the relation between personality and heart disease. The nature of that influence is, however, far more complex than that conveyed by the simple assertion that Type A behavior is a risk factor for coronary heart disease" (p. 112). The current consensus is that not all components of the complex set of reactions labeled Type A behavior pattern are related to coronary heart disease. Only some components may be harmful or "toxic"; others may be neutral or even protective. We should distinguish between the Type A behavior pattern construct and the concept of coronary-prone behavior (Dembroski & Costa, 1988). The latter encourages the identification of more specific—possibly new—behaviors linked to coronary heart disease. To this end, the search to uncover coronary-prone behavior has increasingly centered on the hostility component of the Type A behavior pattern.

Hostility and Heart Disease. In the WCGS data, the hostility component of Type A behavior pattern was the strongest predictor of heart disease (Matthews, Glass, Rosenman, & Bortner, 1977). Other studies have linked a questionnaire measure of hostility to subsequent heart disease and death. For example, 255 physicians who had completed the MMPI in medical school, were assessed twenty-five years

[4] An arrhythmia, or abnormal heart beat rhythm, can lead to death within minutes if not corrected. The ventricles quiver but do not contract, with the result that blood is no longer pumped from the heart.

later (Barefoot, Dahlstrom, & Williams, 1983). Those with high hostility scores on MMPI's Ho scale had a cumulative heart disease rate four or five times higher than those with low scores.

The biological mechanisms linking Type A behavior pattern or some of its components to heart disease are still poorly understood. The leading hypothesis is that individuals with Type A behavior pattern are characterized by excessive cardiovascular and neuroendocrine responsiveness to stressful situations (Contrada & Krantz, 1988).

Psychological Factors in Diabetes. Diabetes is a disorder of carbohydrate metabolism in which individuals have trouble regulating their blood sugar levels. It afflicts roughly 11 million Americans. Uncontrolled diabetes can have a number of serious effects on health. They include a significantly increased risk of heart disease and stroke; blindness (the second leading cause of blindness in the United States); susceptibility to infection, increasing the risk of gangrene, thus resulting in an amputation rate twenty times greater than in nondiabetics; and loss of sexual function in both men and women. Untreated diabetes may lead to a potentially life-threatening condition.

The diabetic's body loses its capacity to produce or use the hormone insulin. In the absence of insulin the body cannot convert sugar, or glucose, into energy to store in cells. High glucose levels collect instead in the bloodstream as an ineffective energy source. In *Type I diabetes*—also known as insulin-dependent or juvenile onset diabetes—the body lacks sufficient insulin because insulin-producing cells in the pancreas degenerate. Thus, the Type I diabetic person depends on daily injections of the hormone. Despite the term *juvenile onset,* adults may also develop it. Onset is related to some form of infection, and Type I diabetes is currently viewed as a form of autoimmune disease.

Type II diabetes is characterized by a sufficient level of insulin which is, however, metabolically ineffective. Roughly 80 percent of all diabetics have the Type II form. It typically occurs among adults and is closely associated with obesity. Figure 8.2 shows the correlation between diabetes and obesity. Researchers speculate that the fat cells of obese people undermine the ability of insulin to regulate blood glucose. Obesity is most likely to lead to Type II diabetes in people with a family history of disease. Weight reduction is an effective way of preventing the expression of diabetes in people who are genetically at risk for the disease. Black Americans, particularly black women, have a significantly higher rate of Type II diabetes than whites (see Figure 8.2). More blacks than whites die from diabetes (Berg, 1991).

Though we have no cure for diabetes, especially the Type II kind can be managed effectively through careful diet, physical exercise, oral (hypoglycemic) medication, and insulin injections. In addition, recent evidence has highlighted the role of psychological stress in exacerbating blood sugar regulation in diabetics.

Physical activity is associated with several health benefits, including lowered blood pressure and cholesterol levels.

Diabetes and Stress. Stress affects diabetes in two ways. An indirect influence impairs adherence to a behavioral treatment program (Fisher, Delamater, Bertelson, & Kirkley, 1982). For example, stress may cause diabetics to eat too much or to eat the wrong foods. This stress-induced failure to adhere to behavioral self-regulation is similar to stress's role in triggering relapse episodes in abstinent patients treated for alcoholism or other forms of substance abuse (Marlatt & Gordon, 1985). The other influence of stress on blood glucose is direct and mediated by the autonomic nervous system.

In response to perceived stress, hormones such as cortisol and the catecholamines are released into the bloodstream to prepare the body for the "flight or fight" response. These "stress hormones" prompt the pancreas to release glycogen, then converted into glucose by the liver; they also block insulin's release from the pancreas, increasing levels of circulating glucose still more.

Studies where stress hormones are directly put into diabetics' blood demonstrate that stress increases blood glucose (Shamoon, Hendler, & Sherwin, 1980). Laboratory studies of stress induction confirm these results. Type II diabetics show increased blood glucose in response to stressful imagery and the threat of electric shock (Goetsch, 1989). Increased blood glucose has also been found

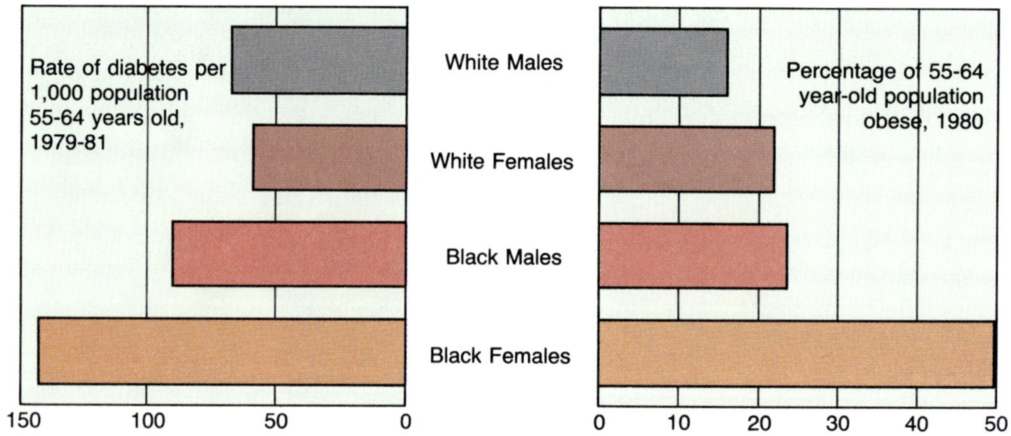

Figure 8.2 *Diabetes is closely correlated with obesity. (Note the high rate among blacks).*

Source: From Closing the Gap, 1990. Office of Minority Health, USDHHS. Reprinted with permission.

in Type I diabetics during stressful video games (Cox, Goner-Frederick, Clarke, & Carter, 1988).

Clinical treatment studies provide additional evidence of a causal stress–blood glucose link. Type II diabetics treated with progressive relaxation, an effective stress-reducing method, show reductions in blood glucose, probably as a function of lowered cortisol levels (Goetsch, 1989). Type I diabetics are less likely to positively respond to relaxation treatment.

Family therapy research has revealed family conflict's influence on diabetes. Minuchin, Rosmon, and Baker (1978) have described repeated hospitalizations of children suffering from diabetic acidosis, a life-threatening condition involving a rise in free-fatty acids (FFA) in the blood. No organic basis for these reoccurrences of acidosis were found. In the hospital the children were easy to care for and showed good control of their diabetes. The problem seemed to be when they returned home, and psychiatric evaluations indicated the children were coping with stress and failed to express their anger. FFA levels were assessed during stressful and nonstressful interviews. The children showed a dramatic rise in FFA level during the stressful interview which, if continued, would have led to diabetic acidosis. In a subsequent study, using a diagnostic interview designed specifically to explore family conflict, Minuchin et al. (1978) showed that these children experienced significantly greater levels of FFA than did those the researchers referred to as "normal" diabetic children. Family therapy aimed at helping the family cope more openly and constructively with conflict initially resulted in even more frequent hospitalizations for diabetic acidosis. After several months of therapy, however, these occurrences disappeared, and the children developed good control of their diabetes.

PSYCHOLOGICAL DETERMINANTS OF HEALTH-PROMOTING AND HEALTH-DAMAGING BEHAVIOR

Psychological factors significantly determine a wide range of behaviors indirectly promoting or damaging health. Substance abuse—alcohol, nicotine, cocaine, or other drugs—has profound damaging effects on health. (The complex biological, psychological, and social factors responsible for substance abuse are described in Chapter 11.) Remember that psychological stress reliably increases cigarette smoking and may also trigger alcohol and other drug abuse (Marlatt & Gordon, 1985). In this way substance abuse can be one of the indirect negative effects of psychological stress on health. Psychological stress not only increases abuse of psychoactive drugs but also affects the elderly's misuse of prescription and over-the-counter medications (Folkman et al., 1987). Misuse of medication—for example, taking the wrong dose or combining drugs which interact negatively with one another—is associated with increased psychological and physical symptoms.

Diet is strongly associated with health. Dietary change is often the first step in the treatment of a range of diseases. Reduced sugar consumption in diabetes and salt intake in hypertension are treatment goals already noted. Serum cholesterol is directly related to heart disease (Lipid Research Clinics Program, 1984) and can be effectively lowered by avoiding food high in cholesterol and saturated fats, also linked to breast cancer (Cooper, 1989).

Physical activity or exercise has been associated with a variety of health-related outcomes (Phelps, 1987). Well-documented benefits of greater physical activity include increased self-esteem and decreased depression; reduced blood pressure and risk of hypertension; reduced cardiovascular risk independent of other factors; maintenance of weight loss in obese patients; and reduced risk of postmenopausal osteoporosis (i.e., brittle bones susceptible to fractures). As with dietary change, however, becoming more physically active and sustaining it can be difficult. In many instances, those who most need to increase their physical activity, such as obese patients, are the least successful in their efforts (Martin et al., 1984). Behavioral scientists have, consequently, increasingly focused attention on how to help people adhere to health-promoting behavior including dietary change and increased physical activity.

Adherence

Adherence, or **compliance** as it is often called, is defined as "the extent to which a person's behavior—in relation to taking medications, following diets, or executing lifestyle changes—coincides with medical or health advice" (Haynes, 1979, pp. 2–3). Some examples illustrate the critical significance of adherence in health care. Ley (1977) found that only about half of all medical patients follow their doctors' advice, even when that advice has major health consequences. Hypertension can be controlled by the appropriate use of medication. Yet 50 percent of patients fail to follow referral advice, over 50 percent drop out of care within one year, and only two thirds of those remaining under it use enough medication to control blood pressure adequately (Vetter et al., 1985). One third of detected cases fail to seek treatment, one third drop out, and one third are uncontrolled. Thus 70 percent of those at risk are uncontrolled (Leventhal, Zimmerman, & Gutmann, 1984). Among other instances of nonadherence, diabetics frequently do not take their insulin as prescribed; roughly half of patients who survive a heart attack drop out of rehabilitative exercise programs within the following year; and only 30 percent to 40 percent of epilepsy patients adhere to their medication schedule (Meichenbaum & Turk, 1988).

Adherence to medical interventions may affect health in still another way. Simply taking medication faithfully, whether or not it is a placebo, seems to improve health. In one study, for example, patients surviving a heart attack were given either medication (propranolol) to prevent another attack or a placebo. As we might expect, patients who adhered to the medication were more likely to be alive at one-year follow-up than poor adherers. What is of particular interest here, however, is that the same pattern was found among patients receiving the placebo. Poor adherers, irrespective of whether they received the active medication or placebo, had an increased risk of death (Horwitz et al., 1990). Moreover, this increased risk of death for poor adherers could not be explained by differences in related health behaviors such as cigarette smoking. The results suggest that adherence can enhance health beyond its function of ensuring that individuals take their medication.

Table 8.4 summarizes the psychosocial factors contributing to nonadherence to doctors' advice and recommendations for life-style changes. Perceived control or self-efficacy affects adherence to health-

BOX 8.2 Sex Differences in Health and Mortality

Health surveys in the United States and Europe reveal that women have higher rates of visits to physicians, disability days, and use of prescription and nonprescription medication than men. Verbrugge (1989) has shown that this is because women suffer from transient, nonfatal illnesses (e.g., arthritis, digestive conditions, and migraine) to a much greater extent than men. Whereas women are more frequently sick (i.e., they have greater morbidity), men are more likely to die from their illnesses. In contrast to women, men have higher rates of fatal medical conditions, such as heart disease. As a result, men have a higher mortality rate.

Based on statistical analyses of health data, Verbrugge concludes that women's higher rate of sickness is due primarily to their social role and attitudes toward health. The psychosocial risk factors predicting greater morbidity in women are their lower level of paid employment, higher levels of emotional stress, feeling of greater vulnerability to illness, and less strenuous physical activity. When these risk factors are statistically controlled, the difference in morbidity between men and women disappears. If anything, men are more likely to get sick and seek medical care. A crucial implication of these findings is that women's health can be significantly improved by psychosocial interventions such as better employment opportunities, reducing stress, and encouraging aerobic activity.

The mortality data tells a different story. Psychosocial risk factors for men include heavier cigarette smoking, alcohol consumption, and greater job hazards. Even when these psychosocial factors are controlled, men still have a higher mortality rate. Why then are men more likely to die? Verbrugge suggests that "we are left with an old but powerful hypothesis—that biological factors are at work in men's poorer long-term health and higher mortality". (p. 295)

TABLE 8.4 Psychosocial Factors Influencing Adherence

1. The patient does not know what to do.
2. The patient does not have the skills or resources to carry out the treatment regimen.
3. The patient does not believe or feel that he or she has the ability to carry out the treatment regimen.
4. The patient does not believe or feel that carrying out the treatment regimen will make a difference (questions the utility).
5. The treatment regimen is too demanding and the patient does not believe that the potential benefits of adhering will outweigh the costs.
6. Adherence is associated with aversive or nonreinforcing events or sensations.
7. The quality of the relationship between the patient and the health care professional is poor.
8. There is no continuity of care.

Source: From D. Meichenbaum & D. Turk (1988). *Facilitating treatment adherence.* New York: Plenum. Reprinted with permission.

promoting behaviors, including cessation of substance abuse, increased physical activity, dietary change, compliance with prescription medication, and dental care (Bandura, 1986; Rodin, 1988). Psychological stress undermines, while social support improves, adherence to health-promoting behavior (Janis, 1983). Knowledge of these psychosocial factors has led to the development of psychological strategies for improving adherence to health-promoting behavior. The clinician or health-care provider usually must show understanding, communicate clearly, and maintain patient motivation to maximize adherence.

Obesity

The importance of adherence to a prudent diet and physical exercise is highlighted in obesity management. Obesity's prevalence in the United States is high—roughly 35 percent of the population. States with the highest prevalence of obesity are Wisconsin, Indiana, West Virginia, and Ohio; those with the lowest are New Mexico, Hawaii, Utah, and Montana (Centers for Disease Control, 1989). Table 8.5 classifies obesity according to its severity.

Evidence suggests that obesity's prevalence in the United States is increasing. Population-based surveys of the Minneapolis–St. Paul metropolitan area in 1980–1981 showed the prevalence as greater than in 1973–1977 (Jeffery et al., 1984). Obesity is increasing faster in black Americans than white Americans. For example, Gortmaker, Dietz, Sobol, and Wehler (1987) reported an increase in obesity of 53 percent in black teenagers over the past 15 to 20 years, compared with a 35 percent increase in white teenagers. Overall, obesity is far more common among blacks than whites (Figure 8.2). The increase in obesity is disturbing because it entails serious medical consequences. Studies have clearly shown relationships between obesity and hypertension, diabetes, pulmonary and kidney problems, osteoarthritis, and complications in recovery from surgery (Van Itallie, 1979). Thus weight reduction is a powerful means of treating hypertension because it reliably reduces blood pressure, controls diabetes, and decreases cholesterol. In addition, obesity has been shown as an independent risk factor for cardiovascular disease in men and women. A prospective study of 115,886 U.S. women between ages thirty and fifty-five showed that even being mildly to moderately overweight increased their risk of heart disease (Manson et al., 1990). Obesity is a serious disease, with health hazards becoming significant at 20 percent or more above desirable weight (National Institutes of Health, 1985). However, it makes a difference where fat is distributed in the body. Irrespective of overall obesity, people whose fat is mainly above the waist are at a significantly higher risk for disease and death than those whose fat is deposited predominantly below the waist (Greenwood, 1989). The pattern where fat is greater above than below the waist is called **abdominal** or **android obesity.** Obese men typically

TABLE 8.5 A Classification of Obesity: Prevalence, Pathology, and Treatment

	Classification of Obesity		
Type	Mild	Moderate	Severe
Percentage overweight	20–40%	41–100%	>100%
Prevalence (among obese women)	90.5%	9.0%	
Treatment	Behavior therapy	Diet and behavior therapy (medical)	Surgical

Source: From A.J. Stunkard & E. Stellar (Eds.), 1984. *Eating and its disorders.* New York: Raven Press. Reprinted with permission.

show this pattern. The pattern where fat is greater below than above the waist is known as **femoral** or **gynoid obesity.** Women show this pattern. People with the abdominal pattern are sometimes called "apples," and those with the femoral pattern "pears"!

Obesity's psychological and social consequences may be as significant as its physical hazards. Society seems biased against overweight people, and obese children, adolescents, and adults often suffer the secondary social effects of rejection, isolation, and job discrimination. Obese people not only are stigmatized by society but also are blamed for their physical condition, commonly viewed as lazy, lacking will power, and gluttonous (Wooley, Wooley & Dyrenforth, 1979). Obese individuals experience depression, loss of self-esteem, and a preoccupation with weight damaging their emotional well-being.

Causes. Obesity runs in families. Both twin and adoption studies have indicated obesity's strong genetic determination. Thus monozygotic twins show significantly greater concordance for overweight than dizygotic twins (Stunkard, Foch, & Hrubec, 1986). Additionally, adopted children are much more likely to weigh the same as their biological than their adoptive parents (Stunkard et al., 1986). Genetic influences on weight seem especially strong between mothers and daughters (Stunkard, 1989).

Weight is under powerful biological control. Studies have shown that most normal-weight individuals are resistant to significant weight loss or gain over the long-term (Keys et al., 1950; Sims et al., 1968). And as discussed later, substantial, lasting weight reduction in obese clients has proved extremely difficult. Our bodies defend a particular weight range. Both obese animals and humans usually do not appear to consume more calories than their leaner counterparts (Bennett & Gurin, 1982).

All individuals have a biologically programmed weight range. Whereas some individuals are naturally lean, others are naturally fat because of the biological setting in their bodies. The mechanism responsible for this biological regulation of weight is still unknown. Clearly, however, genetically determined metabolic rate is a determinant of body weight. A low metabolic rate places one at risk for obesity (Ravussin et al., 1988). Obesity is not simply a learned habit of overeating; it is best regarded as a chronic disease that, like diabetes, has to be continuously managed.

Psychosocial Regulation and Treatment. Evidence of genetic and biological control of obesity does not necessarily indicate that it is unaffected by psychological factors or that obese individuals cannot be helped to lose weight. For example, an inverse correlation exists between obesity and social class. Obesity is six times more common among women of

Obesity runs in families. Obese parents tend to have obese children.

low socioeconomic status than those of high socioeconomic status (Goldblatt et al., 1965). As pointed out in Chapter 4, this correlation does not allow us to infer a causal relationship between obesity and social class. But Figure 4.1 on page 81 gives a clue about what might be happening. Notice that the socioeconomic status into which a woman was born is almost as strong a correlate of obesity as her own status. This suggests that the influence of socioeconomic status on obesity is stronger than the effect of obesity on socioeconomic status (Stunkard, 1989). Since blacks have a lower socioeconomic status than whites, this finding might help explain the greater rate of obesity among blacks. Blacks are also more tolerant of obesity, and do not diet to the same extent as whites. Nevertheless, both genetic and environmental influences probably explain the greater role of obesity among blacks. There are data suggesting that blacks might be more efficient in storing fat and expending energy (Kumanyika, 1987).

Like the diseases discussed in this chapter, obesity is influenced by stress. Stress generally triggers eating in obese subjects, particularly if they have been dieting (Spitzer & Rodin, 1986). As Table 8.6 on page 197 indicates, cognitive-behavioral procedures can effectively treat mild and moderate forms of obesity. The most effective therapies consist of multiple components: behavior modification; nutritional counseling; physical exercise; and self-control strategies designed to achieve life-style change (Brownell &

Foreyt, 1986). In treating the moderately obese, cognitive-behavioral programs are combined with a very-low-calorie diet, thereby producing more rapid and greater weight loss. The most effective treatments to date achieve an average weight loss of thirty pounds to forty pounds over a six-month period (Stunkard, 1989). Although they might have only modest effects on weight loss, behavioral treatments for obesity do have health-promoting effects: reliably reducing depression, enhancing self-esteem, lowering blood pressure, and decreasing cholesterol (Brownell & Foreyt, 1986).

Psychosocial factors, including personality variables, do not predict the outcome of obesity treatments. Biological variables, such as initial percent of body fat or fat cell distribution, are better predictors of outcome. A major limitation of obesity treatment programs is their success in producing long-term weight loss. Roughly one third of patients who have lost weight during treatment have regained it at a one-year follow-up. Evidence of successful maintenance of weight loss after five years is still worse (Wadden, Stunkard, & Liebschutz, 1988). People who rely only on diets to lose weight without making accompanying life-style changes typically regain all of their lost weight. This is known as "yo-yo dieting" or what has also been called the "rhythm method of girth control," and its cyclical pattern of weight loss and gain is in itself a major health risk. Animal studies have shown that weight cycling alters body composition; rats become fatter as a result of this experience. Epidemiological research indicates that weight cycling, independent of obesity, increases the relative risk of disease and death (Brownell, 1988). In pregnant women, a history of weight cycling is strongly correlated with the development of diabetes and hypertension (Rodin, 1989).

Acquired Immune Deficiency Syndrome (AIDS)

As noted earlier, AIDS is a fatal, infectious disease for which there is no cure. AIDS is transmitted only through sexual intercourse with an infected partner, use of contaminated needles in drug infusion, exposure to infected blood, or from infected mother to infant. As many as 20 percent to 50 percent of gay men in cities such as San Francisco and New York are estimated to have the HIV infection. The prevalence of HIV infection among drug abusers in New York City is 50 percent to 60 percent. Although initially concentrated in big cities, the disease is now spreading throughout the United States (Institute of Medicine/National Academy of Sciences, 1988). AIDS has presented society with an unprecedented and deadly threat to public health. We had become accustomed to eliminating infectious disease with vaccines and drugs. With HIV infection there is no "magic bullet"—

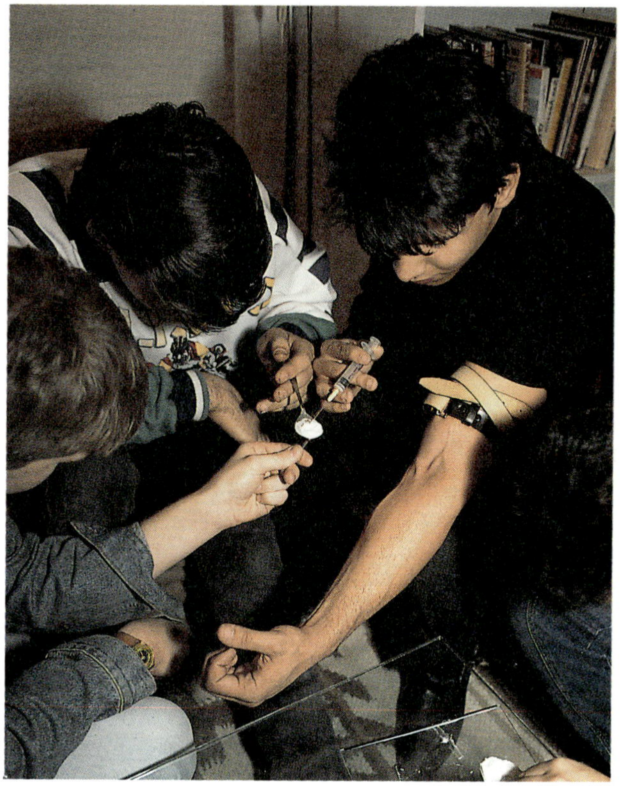

Drug abusers are at risk for contracting AIDS by sharing contaminated needles.

and the prospects of developing one soon are not encouraging. But good news is that the disease is preventable through behavior change.

The AIDS epidemic has produced in the gay male population what a recent report terms "probably the most rapid and extensive change in human behavior in response to a health threat ever observed" (NIMH, 1988, p. 1). In New York City, for example, Martin (1987) interviewed a sample of 745 gay men, ages twenty to sixty-five, to assess the impact of AIDS on their sexual behavior. Sexual activity with different partners had declined by 78 percent; the frequency of sexual contacts involving the exchange of bodily fluids (blood and semen) had decreased an average of 70 percent; and condom use during anal intercourse had increased from 1.5 percent to 20 percent. Comparable changes in sexual behavior have been reported in the San Francisco gay community (McKusick, Horstman, & Coates, 1986).

The success of behavior change efforts among homosexual men is generally attributed to the following psychosocial factors: The gay communities in big cities such as New York City and San Francisco are stable and cohesive. Members educated themselves about the spread of AIDS, devised instructional programs, and were able to disseminate this knowledge throughout the community. Social norms and support were enlisted to cope with despair, encourage safer sex, and reward individuals for making prudent life-style changes. The social-learning principles of modeling and social reinforcement of behavior change are clearly illustrated in these programs. Education alone does not change behavior. The limitations of simply providing information about the disease are illustrated by a study at Stanford University, where an intensive instructional program was conducted, including public lectures, panel discussions, presentations in residence halls, and distribution of condoms. An assessment of the students' beliefs and sexual activities a few weeks later revealed that more than 25 percent did not know what constituted "safer sex," and some had misconceptions that would have exposed them to high-risk sexual activity (Bandura, 1990). Knowledge about AIDS, self-efficacy, and social skill in negotiating safer sex are also linked to low-risk sexual behavior (Emmons et al., 1986; McKusick et al., 1986). Drug and alcohol use have been associated with high-risk sexual activity and noncompliance with safer sex methods (Stall et al., 1986).

Gay men have changed their risky sexual behavior, but it is unclear how well those changes will be maintained over time. Initial research has shown that gay men who return to unsafe sexual practices are very likely to have had frequent sexual interactions with numerous partners, obtained gratification from engaging in high risk sexual behavior, had sex while intoxicated, and were younger than men who continued to follow safe sex methods (Kelly, St. Lawrence, & Brasfield, 1991).

IV drug users are at risk mainly because they share contaminated needles. Efforts to change the behavior of this high-risk group have been less successful (Des Jarlais, 1988). Most IV drug users know about AIDS and how it is transmitted. But they need the means for behavior change, including more effective treatment designed to stop drug use or the availability of sterile needles for "safer injection." The psychosocial

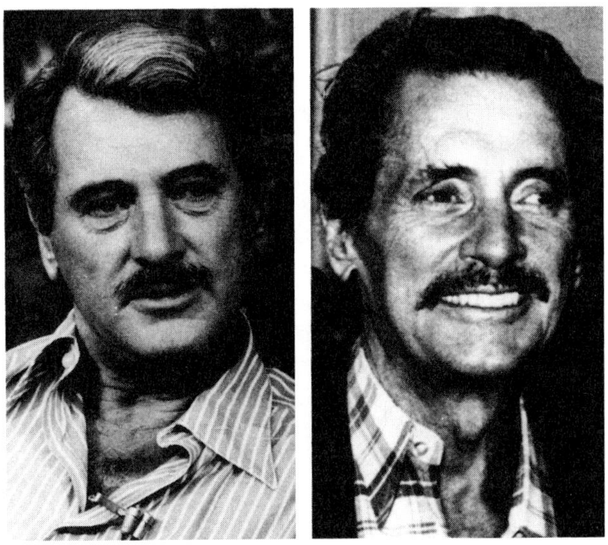

Former film star Rock Hudson before and after he developed AIDS.

factors that facilitated behavior change by gay men are typically absent among IV drug users: They lack educational and financial resources, are caught up in illegal activities, and have little social support.

Even when IV drug users have increased the use of "safer" injections—(e.g., sterilizing needles with bleach)—they have not made commensurate changes in their sexual behavior. This lack of change puts their sexual partners at risk. Studies have found the introduction of condoms as an obstacle to behavior change because it is often associated with the break up of heterosexual relationships. Condoms not only signal that one partner has the HIV infection but also raise concerns about sexual infidelity. The majority of IV drug users are heterosexual males, who may infect female partners, who in turn during pregnancy may transmit the infection to their infants. Minority groups in poor communities with widespread drug use are at particularly high risk for AIDS. At the close of 1987, 38 percent of people with AIDS were black or Hispanic (Freudenberg, 1988).

The AIDS epidemic has highlighted several problems in our social and health-care system. Randy Shilts, in his provocative book *And the Band Played On: Politics, People, and the AIDS Epidemic* (1988), analyzes the first five years of the epidemic (1980–1985). He argues that the United States missed an opportunity to halt the epidemic and blames the Reagan administration, the scientific establishment, gay community leaders, local politicians, and the media for not taking the necessary steps.

But what should our public institutions and leaders have done? A major complication in controlling AIDS was its occurrence in stigmatized groups—gay men, IV drug users, and minority groups. These groups distrust government intervention and were at least initially unreceptive to public campaigns aimed at changing high-risk sexual and drug-taking behavior. Shilts faults the chief medical officer in San Francisco, Mervyn Silverman, for not closing the gay bathhouses—havens for promiscuous, high-risk sexual activities. Yet Silverman delayed taking this action because he felt he had to develop community approval and backing first—without which government action might well have been perceived as further discrimination against gays.

Our societal response to AIDS has been complicated by moralistic assignments of blame because the disease has primarily affected gays and IV drug users. Attempts to impose mandatory screening and other forms of discriminatory social measures have led to a climate of fear and suspicion hindering effective public health actions. Opposition to homosexuality and public discussions of sex have hindered progress. For example, the U.S. Congress cut off funds for educational programs whose candid approach to discussing AIDS was thought to possibly encourage

Programs to prevent the spread of AIDS focus on the use of condoms as part of safer sexual practices.

homosexual activities (IOM/NAS, 1988). And the media have refused to accept commercial advertising for condoms for fear of offending viewing audiences.

PREVENTION AND TREATMENT OF STRESS-RELATED MEDICAL CONDITIONS

Clinicians have used a broad range of psychological approaches to prevent and treat stress-related medical conditions. Psychosomatic medicine in the 1940s and 1950s was a direct application of the psychodynamic model to medical conditions. It followed that some form of psychodynamic therapy was the treatment of choice. Despite the decline of the early psychosomatic medicine approach, psychodynamic therapies continue to be widely used. The basic assumption is that helping patients resolve unconscious psychological conflicts produces improvement in what are presumed to be associated conditions such as diabetes, obesity, and so forth.

Pennebaker, Kiecolt-Glaser, and Glaser (1988) provide an intriguing example of how this psychotherapeutic approach might enhance health. College students were asked to write about the most traumatic experiences in their life for four consecutive days. Consistent with the psychodynamic model, this expression of subjects' feelings was designed to have a cathartic effect of relieving emotional conflict and the psychological cost of inhibiting behavior. Pennebaker and his colleagues found that the subjects showed enhanced immune function and subsequently made fewer visits to the health center than control group subjects.

Cognitive-behavioral methods are frequently used to prevent and treat a variety of medical conditions. Among the most commonly employed, are biofeedback and relaxation techniques.

Biofeedback

Until the late 1960s, it was believed that physiological functions regulated by the autonomic nervous system—for example, heart rate or blood pressure—could be classically conditioned but not brought under direct instrumental or operant control. Then, in a series of dramatic studies, Miller (1969) reported operant conditioning's direct modification of autonomic nervous system responses. The typical experiment to show this in rats involves spontaneous fluctuations in an autonomic response, such as heart rate, that can be shaped or followed by reinforcing consequences. Under these conditions the rat can learn to increase or decrease heart rate—a physiological function previously considered "involuntary." In these experiments, the rat is curarized (paralyzing the skeletal muscles) and maintained on artificial respiration to exclude alternative explanations of the observed changes in heart rate by the indirect effects of skeletal activity or altered respiratory patterns. The rats are rewarded by direct electrical stimulation of rewarding areas in the brain.

Subsequent studies failed to replicate these animal findings and raised questions about the reality of direct operant control of autonomic responses. Miller's ground-breaking research, nevertheless, led to operant-conditioning methods to modify a wide range of human physiological responses including skin temperature; heart rate speeding, slowing, and stabilizing; electrodermal activity; systolic and diastolic blood pressure; skin temperature; peripheral vasomotor responses; EEG rhythms; and penile tumescence (Schwartz & Beatty, 1977). These methods became known as **biofeedback.** Biofeedback equipment continuously monitors physiological responses and converts them into signals such as lights or sounds that the patient can easily perceive. Because we have more difficulty ruling out explanations of results, such as changes in heart rate, in terms of indirect mediating influences like breathing and other skeletal responses, it is unclear if autonomic responses in humans are modified directly. From a practical viewpoint, however, the specific mechanism of change is less important than the fact that different autonomic responses involved in medical disorders are capable of being altered.

The therapeutic use of biofeedback can be illustrated in two of its most common and successful applications—tension headache and hypertension.

Tension Headache. Among the general population, 31 percent of males and 44 percent of females report severe headaches. A study of college students revealed that over 50 percent suffered from headaches at least once or twice a week (Andrasik, Holroyd, & Abell, 1979). The etiology of tension headaches is unclear, but they may result from sustained contraction of skeletal muscles of the face, scalp, neck, and shoulders in response to psychological stress. Biofeedback treatment involves auditory or visual feedback regarding muscle tension, called electromyographic (EMG) feedback. The typical procedure is to attach an electrode to the forehead and provide patients with continuous visual or auditory information signaling reduction in muscle tension. This electronic feedback is then phased out as progress is made. Experimental studies have shown EMG feedback's effectiveness as no greater than that of alternative psychological treatments such as progressive relaxation training or cognitive coping strategies (O'Leary & Wilson, 1987).

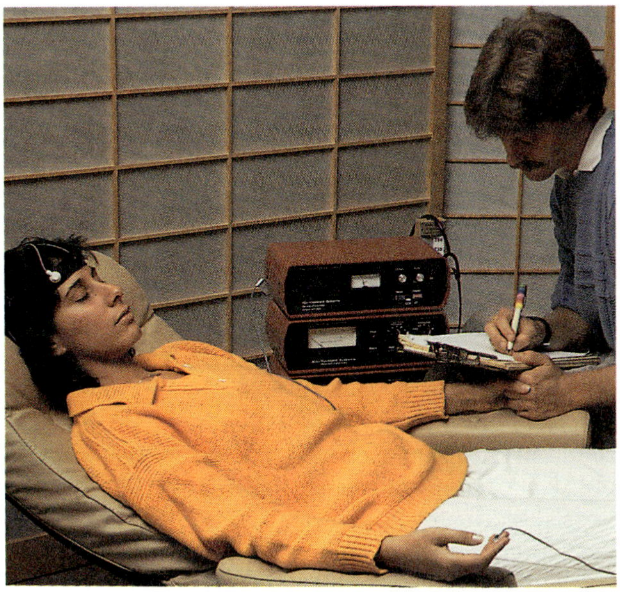

A patient receiving biofeedback treatment.

EMG biofeedback effectively reduces tension headaches, but its mechanism of action is still debated. The original explanation was that this feedback reduced the muscle tension that mediated the headache. Yet tension headaches' successful treatment is often unrelated to changes in forehead muscle tension (Philips & Hunter, 1981). Biofeedback may work, not because it directly changes physiological responsiveness (the original rationale of biofeedback treatment), but because it causes changes in cognitive mechanisms, such as self-efficacy for coping with stress, which then reduce headaches (Holroyd et al., 1984).

Hypertension. High blood pressure is controlled through different pharmacological and nonpharmacological treatments. Standard hypertension treatment relies on different effective drugs that may produce unpleasant side effects. Weight loss, dietary changes (i.e., reduced salt intake), and physical exercise also reduce high blood pressure. Biofeedback aimed at direct control of high blood pressure involves providing patients with information regarding blood pressure on each heart beat. Biofeedback has been shown effective, but little evidence exists of long-term maintenance once treatment is discontinued. Goldstein, Shapiro, Thananopavarn, and Sambhi (1982) compared biofeedback, relaxation training, standard drug treatment, and a control method of blood pressure self-monitoring, in treatment of patients with mild hypertension. The drug treatment produced significantly greater reductions in blood pressure measured in patients' homes than the other methods did. Laboratory measures of blood pressure indicated that biofeedback was as effective as drug treatment. This finding underscores a significant point about the treatment of hypertension: When and in what situation should blood pressure be assessed? Recent research has shown that blood pressure assessment at home or at work is the most sensitive in predicting health problems (Shapiro & Goldstein, 1982).

Relaxation Methods. **Progressive relaxation** is the most widely used relaxation method in treating stress-related disorders. Adapted from a technique originally described by Jacobson (1938), it consists of teaching an individual to systematically tense and relax different muscle groups of the body. These tensing-relaxing procedures help the person learn to become especially attentive to tension feelings and to substitute feelings of relaxation for tension. The typical brief method—taught in four to ten sessions—emphasizes suggestion of relaxation. (It has, therefore, a cognitive thrust.) In contrast, Jacobson's

BOX 8.3 Psychology and Health: A Cautionary Note

The extent to which psychological factors influence physical illness is controversial. At one extreme, some medical scientists remain skeptical; they reject any clinically significant relationship (Angell, 1985). At the other extreme, some health-care professionals go beyond available data in emphasizing the critical role of psychological factors in health and illness. For example, in his best-selling book, *Love, Medicine, and Miracles* (1986), Bernie Siegel, a surgeon at Yale Medical School, argues that self-love is as important as accurate medical diagnosis and treatment in surviving cancer. Siegel believes that cancer is despair experienced at the cellular level. "If we ignore our despair," he writes, "the body receives a die message. If we deal with our pain and seek help, then the message is 'Living is difficult but desirable' and the immune system works to keep us alive" (p. 29). (An early version of this notion was proposed by Wilhelm Reich who attributed Freud's dying of cancer to his sexually unfulfilling and unhappy marriage [Sontag, 1977]). Moreover, Siegel contends that our failure to face psychic conflict results in cancer in the organs where those conflicts are "somatized" or focused. Thus, he writes, "women who have unhappy love relationships are especially vulnerable to breast or cervical diseases." (p. 29)

We believe that assertions of this kind cannot currently be supported by behavioral medicine research. As described in this chapter, some physical states are significantly influenced by psychological factors and may even be altered using psychological treatments. But statements that love can cure cancer only invite skeptical reactions and premature rejection of the possible influence of psychological factors on cancer and other diseases. Perhaps more important is the unintended impact of these much-publicized pronouncements on those unfortunate individuals who are afflicted with disease. Susan Sontag, in her book *Illness as Metaphor*, argues that simplistic psychological theories of this sort place the blame on the patient for the disease. Siegel and others deny that they are blaming the patient. But as Ignatieff (1988) observes, Siegel writes that

> a patient's guilt about his own illness is "not entirely destructive for it often leads to a more realistic sense of participation in the onset of disease." The upbeat message of Siegel's book is Promethean: you can cure yourself. The downbeat message is punitively Puritan: if treatment fails, you have nobody to blame but yourself. (p. 29)

Models of Disease and Attributions of Responsibility

Different models of disease and its treatment assign varying degrees of responsibility to the patient. Brickman et al. (1982) identify four different models of attributions of responsibility for problems and their treatment as summarized in Table 8.6. According to this view, the traditional medical model assigns little or no attribution of responsibility to the patient for developing or treating the problem. Behavioral medicine, as we have described it, is closer to the "compensatory model." Patients are not blamed for their problems. They are viewed as responsible for adopting realistic health-promoting actions under their voluntary control, such as quitting cigarette smoking, taking antihypertensive medication, using safer sex practices, and the like. Although patients are encouraged to exercise personal responsibility for what they can realistically change in their behavior, they are also helped to accept what they cannot change. At present, many of the dread diseases afflicting people fall into this latter category.

---

technique takes months, even years, to master and is exclusively somatic, based on acquiring the skill of muscle relaxation. Progressive relaxation is used as an active coping skill, in which patients are taught to identify early warning signs of stress and to respond with their relaxation skills.

Transcendental Meditation (TM) is another form of relaxation training. Benson (1975) developed a simplified form of TM in which the person becomes comfortable in a quiet environment, assumes a passive attitude, and repeats a word or mantra with each exhalation. He called this simple method the "relaxation response," and it has typically been used in behavioral medicine.

Progressive relaxation training has been employed successfully with a remarkable range of different disorders, such as some of the anxiety disorders in Chapter 5. Other applications include asthma, tension headache, migraine, hypertension, Type A behavior pattern, chronic pain, and insomnia (Lehrer & Woolfolk, 1984; O'Leary & Wilson, 1987). As many as 25 percent of cancer patients treated with chemotherapy acquire conditioned aversive (nausea) reactions to this treatment. They experience profound nausea and vomiting before drug administration, often in response to approaching the hospital, seeing the nurse who gives the injection, or even talking about their chemotherapy. Antiemetic drugs used to control this anticipatory or conditioned nausea are often ineffective. Psychological procedures, including hypnosis and variations of relaxation training and guided imagery, have, consequently, been used to counteract this nausea. Relaxation, as the primary component of these procedures, reliably reduces distress (Redd & Andrykowski, 1982). The effects of relaxation treatment, moreover, appear superior to nonspecific factors, such as expectations of help and the nurse–patient relationship (Lyles, Burish, Kro-

TABLE 8.6 Consequences of Attribution of Responsibility in Four Models of Helping and Coping

Attribution to Self of Responsibility for Problem	Attribution to Self of Responsibility for Solution: High	Attribution to Self of Responsibility for Solution: Low
High	**Moral Model**	**Enlightenment Model**
Perception of self	Lazy	Guilty
Actions expected of self	Striving	Submission
Others besides self who must act	Peers	Authorities
Actions expected of others	Exhortation	Discipline
Implicit view of human nature	Strong	Bad
Potential pathology	Loneliness	Fanaticism
Low	**Compensatory Model**	**Medical Model**
Perception of self	Deprived	Ill
Actions expected of self	Assertion	Acceptance
Others besides self who must act	Subordinates	Experts
Actions expected of others	Mobilization	Treatment
Implicit view of human nature	Good	Weak
Potential pathology	Alienation	Dependency

Source: From Brickman, P., Rabinowitz, V.C., Karuza, J., Coates, D., & Kidder, L. (1982). Models of helping and coping. *American Psychologist*, 37, 368–384. Copyright 1982 by the American Psychological Association. Reprinted by permission.

zely, & Oldham, 1982). Progressive relaxation and transcendental meditation generally seem to be equally effective.

Multiple Risk Factor Interventions

Thus far we have described treatments of individual risk factors for ill health and disease. But optimally effective interventions for reducing coronary heart disease's occurrence would require programs that simultaneously target multiple-risk factors for modification.

The MRFIT Study. A broad-scale heart disease prevention program is the Multiple Risk Factor Intervention Trial (MRFIT) (Multiple Risk Factor Intervention Trial, 1982). This study included 12,866 healthy men between ages thirty-five and fifty-seven assessed at high CHD risk because of their blood pressure, smoking habits, and elevated cholesterol. Their levels of these three risk factors placed them in the top 10 percent of risk scores for developing heart disease. The men were randomly assigned either to a special intervention (SI) program or to a control group (UC) comprising their usual health-care sources in the community. The SI program consisted of formal attempts to lower high blood pressure through the use of antihypertensive medication, to reduce cigarette smoking through behavior modification, and to lower blood cholesterol levels through behavioral and dietary means.

An average seven-year follow-up evaluation showed risk factor levels decreased in both groups though to a greater (although statistically nonsignificant) degree in the SI group. Mortality from CHD was 17.9 deaths per 1,000 in the SI group and 19.3 per 1,000 in the UC group. The multiple risk factor intervention program's failure to produce a statistically significant improvement over usual health care was disappointing. One reason for this lack of difference was the unanticipated change in risk factor levels and lower-than-expected death rate in the UC group. This finding is consistent with other data indicating CHD on the decline in the United States. Although changes in risk factor levels, as a result of public education and awareness, might be responsible for this encouraging trend, the reasons have not been determined.

The Stanford Three-Community Study. In this well-known study, Meyer et al. (1980) sought to evaluate the effects of a social-learning–based intervention program for reducing the risk of CHD in three northern California communities. Using a quasi-experimental design, one community (Gilroy) received a media-based intervention. A second (Watsonville) received the media-based intervention supplemented by an intensive program of face-to-face instruction in behavior change for participants judged at high risk for CHD. The third (Tracy) served as a control community in which no intervention, only survey assessments, were conducted. To evaluate the impact of the interventions, sample surveys gathered baseline and yearly follow-up data from a random sample of adults ages thirty-five to fifty-nine in all three communities. Each survey included a behavioral interview and a medical examination of each subject. The behavioral interview assessed subjects' knowledge and self-reported change in risk factors; the medical examination included measures of plasma cholesterol and triglyceride concentrations, blood pressure, relative weight, and electrocardiograms. Both behavioral and medical data were combined into a single-risk factor estimate based on one developed in the Framingham Heart Study that predicts a person's probability of developing CHD within the next twelve years.

The content of the intervention programs was based on social-cognitive theory and behavioral self-control principles such as self-monitoring modeling, and reinforcement. Media campaigns were presented in both English and Spanish using a variety of media materials. Over two years, about 3 hours of television programs and over 50 television spots were produced, as well as about 100 radio spots, several hours of radio programming, weekly newspaper columns, and newspaper advertisements and stories. Printed materials of many kinds were sent via direct mail to the participants and posters were used in buses, stores, and work sites.

The face-to-face intensive instruction intervention, conducted with 107 high-risk individuals and their spouses in the Watsonville community, consisted of a ten-week program of weekly, then semimonthly, sessions. The therapists carrying out this instruction were mainly college graduates who received four weeks of training in the counseling methods.

Results showed that subjects in both intervention communities significantly gained knowledge about risk factors for CHD. The media campaign also produced changes in self-reported consumption of cholesterol and fats. As shown in Figure 8.3, the intensive instruction plus media program achieved the best results after three years, significantly lowering risk for CHD, predominantly through reduction in number of cigarettes smoked (Meyer et al., 1980). Compared to the control community, the treated communities showed significant reductions in systolic blood pressure and dietary cholesterol. The Watsonville community also had significantly lowered plasma cholesterol.

Several features of this innovative study require emphasis. First, Meyer and his associates (1980) based their intervention on a community rather than individual treatment model. Second, they used the local media to achieve maximal exposure and make the intervention cost-effective. The researchers' success in involving the media and community in an orchestrated program of behavior change contrasts sharply with the problems in treating AIDS. As noted previously, attempts to control AIDS through public health community programs has been complicated by conflicting social attitudes and values about a controversial disease.

Changes in life-style can actually reverse coronary heart disease. Ornish and his colleagues (1990) showed that a combination of a low-fat vegetarian

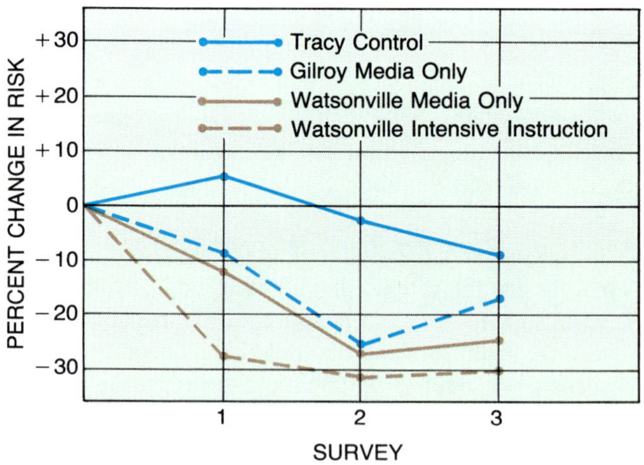

Figure 8.3 *Percentage of change from baseline in risk of cardiovascular disease after the three annual follow-up surveys.*

Source: From Meyer, A.J., Nash, J.D., McAlister, A.L., Maccoby, N., & Farquhar, J.W. (1980). Skills training in a cardiovascular health education campaign. *Journal of Consulting and Clinical Psychology,* 48, 129–142. Copyright 1980 by the American Psychological Association. Reprinted with permission.

diet, stopping smoking, stress management training, and moderate exercise led to reduced atherosclerotic plaque buildup in the coronary arteries of twenty-eight patients after only one year. These dramatic life-style changes may not be applicable to the general population. Nevertheless, the results suggest the possibility of reversing even severe coronary heart disease without the use of cholesterol-lowering drugs, and emphasize still further behavior change's importance in the prevention and treatment of cardiovascular disease.

SUMMARY

1. Psychological factors, defined as meaningful environmental stimuli or life events, can significantly influence medical disorders, including cardiovascular disease and other well-known illnesses. Psychoanalytic clinicians linked psychological factors to physical illness as psychosomatic medicine developed in the 1940s and 1950s. Different medical disorders were seen as expressions of specific personality types.
2. The development of the fields of behavioral medicine and health psychology in the 1970s went beyond the psychoanalytic approach in emphasizing the use of behavioral science's methods for assessing, preventing, and treating medical conditions. These developments reflect an important change in our thinking about health and illness. Instead of the traditional biomedical model with its limited emphasis on biology and disease, we now have a broader biopsychosocial perspective emphasizing the interactive influences of psychological and biological factors in health and illness.
3. Serious emotional problems, such as anxiety or depression, increase the risk of developing disease and are associated with mortality. People exposed to severe stress in their life, on average, are less healthy than those not severely stressed. Psychological stress involves more than mere exposure to stressful life events such as bereavement. It also includes how people cognitively appraise such an event, their coping mechanisms, and their social support. Appraisal, coping, and social support all determine whether a specific life stressor elicits stress. Different people respond very differently to the same life stressors.
4. Psychological factors affect medical disorders in two ways. The first is through their direct effects on biology; the second is through their indirect effect of behavior related to health and illness, such as cigarette smoking.
5. One direct biological effect of psychological factors affecting health and illness is on the immune system protecting the body against infection and disease. Psychoimmunology, the study of this interaction, in animal and human research shows psychological stress impairing immune function and enhancing disease risk. Both environmental factors (e.g., how predictable or controllable a stressor is) and person variables (e.g., self-efficacy and explanatory style) influence stress's effect on immune function. Mononucleosis is an example of this influence.
6. Stress directly affects cardiovascular diseases such as hypertension and coronary heart disease (CAD). Type A behavior pattern—characterized by aggressiveness, time urgency, and the need to control—has been linked to CAD. The evidence on this relationship, however, is inconsistent. Type A behavior pattern may relate only to some types of CAD, namely sudden death from a heart attack. Also, only one component of the Type A pattern, namely hostility, may be related to CAD. Diabetes is another disease directly influenced by stress.
7. Psychological factors significantly determine a wide range of behaviors that indirectly promote or damage health. Substance use and abuse, diet, body weight, and physical exercise all have been shown as risk factors for cardiovascular disease and other problems. Adherence, or the extent to which medical advice is followed (e.g., taking medication to control high blood pressure), affects health.
8. Obesity is a genetically determined, chronic disease linked to numerous medical problems and mortality. Although obesity is refractory to change, obese individuals can reduce weight and manage their condition in ways which either promote or damage health. AIDS is a fatal disease for which there is still no cure. The emphasis must be on prevention, usually meaning behavior and life-style change. Successful changes in patterns of sexual activity in gay communities have significantly reduced the spread of this killer disease.
9. Women have higher rates of illness and consult physicians more than men do. If psychosocial factors such as employment and emotional stress are taken into account, this disadvantage for women disappears. Men, however, have higher mortality rates than women, probably because they are more biologically vulnerable.
10. Different psychological methods are used to prevent and treat medical conditions influenced by psychosocial factors. These interventions range from individual therapy for specific problems (e.g., biofeedback for tension headache) to community-based programs targeted at life-style change (e.g., changes in diet, physical exercise, cigarette smoking, and alcohol use designed to lower the risk of heart disease.

H. Toulouse Lautrec, *"Le Lit" (The Couple).* Courtesy of Giraudon/Art Resource.

9 SEXUAL DISORDERS

Sex is not just another form of human behavior. It has unique personal and social significance. It helps define our personal identity and sense of self and affects some of our closest interpersonal relationships. Not surprisingly, therefore, the consequence of impaired or highly unusual sexual response is often serious emotional distress.[1] *DSM-III-R* divides the different sexual disorders into the following categories: sexual dysfunction, paraphilias, gender identity disorder, and ego-dystonic homosexuality. We begin with the most common sexual disorders, namely, the dysfunctions.

SEXUAL DYSFUNCTION

Changing Concepts of Sexual Dysfunction: From Freud to Modern Sex Therapy

The formal, scientific study of sexual pathology can be traced to late-nineteenth-century Europe. Richard von Kraft-Ebing, professor of psychiatry at the University of Vienna, helped to found the scientific study of sexual disorders as an independent field of inquiry. His great work, *Psychopathia Sexualis* (1886), is generally credited with ushering in the scientific analysis of sexual disorders as an important, yet controversial, branch of medical psychology. It was, however, Kraft-Ebing's colleague in Vienna, Sigmund Freud, whose concepts and pioneering clinical observations dominated the field in the first half of this century.[2] Freud and his followers' continuing emphasis on human sexuality in the study of clinical disorders is a major contribution of psychoanalysis. The following features characterized the Freudian framework.

1. Sexual disorders were viewed as symptoms of an underlying (unconscious) emotional conflict.
2. Treatment was directed at these hypothesized underlying personality conflicts, not at the symptom or sexual problem itself.
3. Consistent with this approach, women with low sexual desire or unable to reach orgasm were

[1] Not all couples with a sexual problem, however, experience emotional conflict. Some report happy relationships despite the sexual problem (Frank, Anderson, & Rubinstein, 1978).

[2] Historical analysis has shown that many discoveries attributed to Freud by his followers had been described or suggested well before he published his own theories. Sulloway (1979) points out how "terms and constructs like libido, component instincts, erotogenic zones, autoerotism, and narcissism—all generally associated in twentieth-century consciousness with Freud's name—were actually brought into scientific circulation between 1880 and 1900 by other contemporary students of sexology" (p. 277). Nor was Freud the first to observe infants' normal experience of sexual sensations (e.g., erections, masturbation) as he himself claimed and is still widely believed. Sulloway shows that other scientists before Freud, in his celebrated *Three Essays on the Theory of Sexuality* (1905), clearly described the evidence of childhood sexuality.

Zoologist and pioneering sex researcher Alfred Kinsey (1894–1956), seated in the middle of the group, with his staff at Indiana University.

labeled frigid; men who failed to get an erection were called impotent. These vague terms tell us more about the presumed character of the individual than his or her actual sexual problem. They had negative implications about the individual's personality, suggesting that such a woman was cold, unresponsive, and even hostile, and such a man weak and helpless—not a "real man." The impact on self-esteem of these negative, global labels was especially damaging, adding to the suffering caused by the sexual inadequacy itself.

4. There was no scientific study of sex and its disorders. Knowledge was based on a mix of clinical inference and prevailing social values.

After Freud the next great name in sex research is Alfred Kinsey, the American biologist. Kinsey's (1948, 1953) famous surveys of American men and women's sexual preferences and practices broke through the social taboos about investigating sexual behavior, produced the first reliable information of the American population's sexual behavior, and paved the way for the objective study of sexual activity. Kinsey's surveys were based on the self-reports of people during interviews. Self-reports, particularly of sensitive and intimate information, are always open to the criticism that they may be biased. Thus subsequent investigators directly observed actual sexual behavior. In 1966, in *Human Sexual Response,* William Masters and Virginia Johnson published the results of their detailed observations and recordings of a variety of explicit sexual acts such as masturbation, intercourse, and oral sex. Their book, and its sequel on therapy, *Human Sexual Inadequacy,* published in 1970,[3] fundamentally changed the field. Masters and Johnson added significantly to our knowledge about sex and its disorders, shattered some of the myths about sexual function, and helped to make the study of sexual behavior a legitimate scientific subject. The following are some of their contributions.

1. They defined the physiological basis of the normal sexual response. This begins with an increase in sexual tension (the excitement phase), builds to a plateau, increases to orgasm if stimulation is strong enough, and ends in the resolution phase (release of tension). Men and women respond similarly.
2. They helped prove that women were no less sexual than men. Women were shown to be at least as sexually responsive as men. For example, they were capable of multiple orgasms in response to

[3] Both of these works headed the list of best-selling books in the United States for several weeks.

William Masters and Virginia Johnson whose laboratory studies of sexual behavior led to the "new sex therapy."

effective sexual stimulation. Society's double standard—denying women their sexual equality—rather than their biology was the limiting factor of their sexual response.

3. They exploded the myth of a difference between **clitoral** and **vaginal orgasms.** Freud (1917/1963) declared that in childhood the clitoris was the focus of the little girl's sexuality and had a "special excitability" which enabled her to gain sexual satisfaction through masturbation (p. 318). For the girl to become a woman and achieve psychosexual maturity the clitoris had to "hand over its sensitivity, and at the same time its importance, to the vagina" (Freud, 1932/1964, p. 118). This, allegedly, would allow the woman to experience mature sexual satisfaction through vaginal intercourse rather than masturbation that was seen as the hallmark of psychosexual immaturity. Sexual dysfunction was predicted if the clitoris retained its sensitivity (Freud, 1917/1963, p. 318). Through their research Masters and Johnson (1966) showed that the physiological basis of *all* orgasms is the stimulation of the clitoris, either directly during masturbation or indirectly during vaginal intercourse. The sensitivity of the clitoris is vital to healthy sexuality. With hindsight, the Freudian view can be seen as sexist, and it is sobering to reflect on the possibly harmful consequences to many women who underwent unnecessary psychotherapy to overcome their alleged "arrested psychosexual development."
4. They clarified other misconceptions. For example, the goal of simultaneous orgasm during sexual intercourse is both unrealistic and unnecessary for mutually satisfying sex. Additionally, penis size is unrelated to the satisfaction both partners derive from intercourse.
5. Finally, as discussed next, Masters and Johnson identified the different forms of sexual dysfunction and developed and evaluated strategies for treating these directly rather than automatically viewing them as symptoms of some other emotional conflict.

The Cultural Context. The dramatic change in how we have viewed sexual dysfunction over this century highlights cultural values' importance in defining and treating sexual disorders. Masters and Johnson's research appeared during the 1960s, a period of intense social unrest and change in the United States—the era of Woodstock, swinging couples, open marriage, the birth of gay activism, and widespread student unrest with traditional societal customs. Talk was of a *sexual revolution* in which sexual attitudes became more liberal. Previously prohibited pursuits such as premarital and extramarital sex became more acceptable to many people. Women, freed from the fear of unwanted pregnancy by the development of the pill and other birth control methods, became increasingly independent in their career choices and social roles and began to demand sexual equality. The accompanying heightened expectations increased pressures for sexual performance, and sexual dysfunction was seen as more serious than ever before.

The Nature and Causes of Sexual Dysfunction

Transitory sexual difficulties are not uncommon for both men and women to experience at some point in life. For example, a survey of 100 well-educated, happily married couples—who had not sought therapy—showed 36 percent of the men reporting difficulties with ejaculating too quickly, and 16 percent reporting problems with obtaining or maintaining erections

(Frank, Anderson, & Rubenstein, 1978). Most men manage to cope with such problems. Yet when these difficulties persist and cause distress, they become clinical dysfunctions requiring treatment. *DSM-III-R* divides sexual dysfunctions into four major categories: (a) desire disorders; (b) arousal disorders; (c) orgasm disorders; and (d) pain disorders. These different categories correspond to the different phases of the sexual response cycle. Desire refers to how often or strongly a person wants sex; arousal to how excited someone becomes once sex is initiated; and orgasm to the male's ability to ejaculate and the female's capacity to reach climax after arousal. For men and women, orgasm is an intensely satisfying physiological reflex releasing sexual tension. Sexual pain refers to any genital discomfort during sexual intercourse.

Sexual dysfunction is diagnosed only if it is not the result of some other disorder, such as major depression. Any sexual dysfunction may be lifelong or acquired following a particular life event; it may be generalized to all sources of sex or specific to a particular person or situation.

Sexual Desire Disorders. Hypoactive or **low sexual desire** is marked by the absence of sexual fantasies and wish for sexual activity. A professional clinician makes the diagnosis, taking into account "factors that affect sexual functioning, such as age, sex, and the context of the person's life" (*DSM-III-R*, p. 165). **Sexual aversion** is the avoidance of all or almost all genital sexual contact with a partner.

Defining low sexual desire is difficult because there are no objective standards of "normal" or "healthy" desire, or whether interest in sex is "too low" or "too high." How much sex is there in stable marriages? One study found that of 100 couples, 8 percent reported intercourse less than once a month, 23 percent two to three times a month, 24 percent once a week, 31 percent two to three times a week, 12 percent four to five times a week, 1 percent daily, and 2 percent never (Frank et al., 1978). Clinical experience indicates that some people with low desire may not view it as a dysfunction—it is their partners' dissatisfaction that leads them to seek help. When a couple complains about low desire the problem may be *desire discrepancy,* in which one partner wants sex more often than the other (Zilbergeld & Ellison, 1980). For example, is a man who engages in sex on average only once or twice a month, but whose wife would like sex almost daily, suffering from a "disorder"? Before the 1960s sexual revolution the answer would have been a clear "no"; since then the answer has become less obvious. Another complication caused by today's society's emphasis on sex—especially by the mass media—is some people questioning if a relative lack of interest in sex could be "abnormal." This question illustrates how definitions of sexual problems are partly rooted in the values of specific individuals and cultures.

Despite problems in defining low sexual desire, some people clearly have pathologically low levels of sexual desire distressing to them and their partners. Therapy is recommended in these cases. In making the diagnoses of hypoactive sexual desire, behavioral and subjective aspects must be taken into account. One definition of low sex desire is when "individual or partner sexual experiences (including oral,[4] manual, or penile or vaginal stimulation) occur every two weeks or less *and* there is evidence of lack of subjective desire for sexual activity (including sex with mate, with other partners, masturbation, sexual dreams), [and] lack of fantasies. . . ." (Friedman & Hogan, 1985, p. 423). More women than men were initially treated for desire disorder, but recent statistics show its prevalence in men in conjunction with other disorders (Leiblum & Rosen, 1988). In a study of 152 couples seeking sex therapy, 38 percent of husbands and 49 percent of wives were diagnosed with desire disorder (Schover & LoPiccolo, 1982). In the women, 18 percent of the cases involved sexual aversion. Desire discrepancy between partners is the most common problem of couples seeking therapy (Kilmann et al., 1986).

Causes of Low Sexual Desire. Sexual function in general, and desire in particular, is a complex product of biological, psychological, and sociocultural influences. A wide range of physical and psychological factors can, therefore, disrupt it. Illness, disease, or surgery all may chronically or temporarily lower sexual desire. For example, adjusting to rehabilitation from a heart attack and coping with cancer can decrease sexual desire. Lowered desire is not only the direct physical response to these circumstances but also the response to the resulting psychological scars (Anderson & Wolf, 1986). Evidence has also linked sexual desire to levels of androgens, especially testosterone, often called the sex hormone; yet administering androgens to healthy individuals does not remedy their sexual desire disorder (Rosen & Leiblum, 1987). Depression and severe stress may also cause low sexual desire. Both involve physiological as well

[4] Clinicians view desire for oral sex and orgasm through oral sex as functional or "normal." Many women who cannot reach orgasm through penile-vaginal intercourse experience orgasm during cunnilingus—oral stimulation of the female genitals (Hite, 1976). Surveys have shown that the majority of men and women in the United States regularly practice and enjoy oral sex (Wolfe, 1981). In one survey women practicing frequent oral sex were more likely to rate their marriages and sex lives as satisfying than those who rejected oral sex (Tavris & Sadd, 1977). Oral sex is, nevertheless, a crime in twenty-five states in the United States. As recently as 1988, a man in Atlanta, Georgia, was sent to prison for two years after admitting to having oral sex with his estranged wife (*The Miami Herald,* August 6, 1989).

as psychological determinants. A person's sexual desire often returns to normal when a depression lifts or stressful life circumstances change, but occasionally negative sexual consequences of these conditions persist.

Psychological causes of lowered desire include negative early learning about sex as sinful or dangerous, traumatic experiences such as childhood sexual abuse, or rape (Becker, Skinner, & Abel, 1983). Men and women's sexual problems are frequently caused by or become enmeshed with anxiety, anger, jealousy, and guilt. Intrapsychic conflicts can trigger what Kaplan (1979) calls the "turn-off" mechanism. Based on her clinical experience, she argues that people may unconsciously and involuntarily suppress sexual desire by focusing selectively on the negative characteristics of their partners or the situation. Motivating this sexual turn-off is an unconscious fear of intimacy; sexual intimacy is too threatening. In psychodynamic terms, the fear originating in unresolved childhood conflicts transfers to the person's sexual partner. For example, a woman may see her husband as the father with whom sex is forbidden. These patients suppress sexual desire because it would not feel psychologically "safe."

Apfelbaum (1988), an ego-analyst, theorizes that many cases of desire disorder represent a fear of not becoming sexually aroused. Given the pressure in today's world to respond positively as a sexual partner, the fear of not getting excited leads to suppression of desire. This is consistent with desire disorders first coming to clinicians' attention in the late 1970s, in the aftermath of the sexual revolution and its demands for more and better sex for both men and women.

Interpersonal problems, particularly underlying hostility and conflict, are a major cause of all sexual disorders. Sex is often used as a weapon in power struggles between partners (e.g., withholding sexual contact). Sexual desire may also wane because of boredom within the relationship. Desire discrepancy is especially likely to cause problems in a troubled relationship. A couple otherwise happy in a good relationship can more easily overcome a problem of sexual desire discrepancy than partners experiencing marital discord.

The following case illustrates how relationship problems may cause sexual desire disorder.

> *Max and Carol, a couple in their mid-twenties, had been living together for three years. Max, a third-year medical student, felt frustrated by Carol's growing lack of interest in sex. Although Carol was able to become aroused and have orgasms, she was seldom in the mood for sex and rarely initiated it. Carol, a laboratory assistant, felt equally frustrated by Max's preoccupation with his medical-school training. His school pressures had become so great that the couple spent little time together. Carol also complained that when they had sex, Max was usually impatient and rushed through foreplay. Max agreed that during the week they saw too little of each other but usually planned to make it up on the weekends. By the time the weekend began, he said, he'd been bottling up his desire all week and generally felt very horny. When Carol showed no interest in his advances, he became angry because of the tension, and the couple often found themselves arguing about something. Max saw Carol's low level of sexual desire as a major problem for them.* (Rosen & Hall, 1984, p. 373)

Sexual Arousal Disorders. **Male erectile disorder** is defined as either (1) persistent or recurrent failure to attain or maintain an erection until completion of sexual activity, or (2) persistent lack of subjective sexual excitement and pleasure during sexual activity. Prior to *DSM-III*'s publication in 1980, men who experienced problems in obtaining or maintaining an erection were called *impotent*. This unfortunate term, as noted previously, had perjorative implications about an individual's personality. Erectile dysfunction's new terminology offers a more precise and objective way of describing these problems, although *impotence* is still used sometimes (Krane, Goldstein, & DeTejada, 1989).

Primary erectile dysfunction means that a man has never been able to achieve a sufficient erection to have either vaginal or rectal intercourse with a partner. Cases of this severity seem relatively rare. In *secondary erectile dysfunction*, the man is currently unable to achieve a sufficient erection to engage in sexual intercourse, either vaginally or rectally, but had been able to do so at least once in the past. Men experience erectile problems in a variety of ways. Kaplan (1974) gives a good synopsis.

> Some men cannot achieve an erection during foreplay. Others attain an erection easily, but lose their erection and become flaccid subsequently at specific points in the sexual response cycle, e.g., at the moment before entry, or upon insertion, or during intercourse. Other men are impotent during intercourse, but can maintain an erection during manual manipulation or oral sex. Some can have an erection while clothed, but become flaccid as soon as their penis is exposed to view. Some men become excited and have erections during foreplay when they know that intercourse is not possible, but lose their potency when they are involved in situations where intercourse is not only feasible but is expected. Some men can become erect only if the woman dominates the sexual situation, while others become impotent if their partner tries to assume control. (p. 256)

Causes. It was previously believed that roughly 90 percent of all erectile failure cases were psychogenic, that is, caused by psychological factors. Yet recent analyses have suggested organic factors cause 30 percent to 50 percent of erectile dysfunction (Van Arsdalen, Malloy, & Wein, 1983). Organic factors can precipitate erectile dysfunction, such as illness (e.g., diabetes), surgery (e.g., prostatectomy), drugs (e.g., antihypertensive or antidepressant medications), and prolonged alcohol abuse. These factors impair the hormones, nerve pathways, or blood supply that form the physiological basis of penile tumescence. Gradual onset despite normal desire is indicative of an organic cause.

Men with erectile problems should consult a urologist, who, through physical examination and laboratory tests, will check their hormone function and other likely organic factors. Where this examination is inconclusive, behavioral scientists have developed a test to determine an organic basis for erectile problems. This test is described in Box 9.1. It is increasingly recognized that some erectile problems may have organic and psychogenic causes.

Erectile disorder's psychological determinants can be divided into historical influences contributing to the person's sexual inadequacy and factors currently maintaining the sexual problem.

Historical Influences. Masters and Johnson (1970) found rigid adherence to religious orthodoxy as the most common factor in the backgrounds of men and women with different forms of sexual dysfunction. Strict religious teaching, regardless of the particular religion, often results in negative attitudes toward sexuality. These dysfunctional individuals had been led to believe that "sex is sin." Deeply religious peo-

BOX 9.1 The Psychophysiological Assessment of Sexual Function

The average healthy adult male during sleep may experience an average of about one erection every ninety minutes. This increase in penile tumescence usually occurs during rapid eye movement (REM) sleep. The term **nocturnal penile tumescence** (NPT) describes these erections. During sleep, this naturally occurring physiological process is unimpaired by the inhibitions, fears, and anxieties affecting erection during the waking state. The absence of NPT usually—but not always—signals an organic cause. As many as 20 percent of patients may be misdiagnosed using NPT (Wasserman, Pollack, Speilman, & Weitzman, 1980). Diagnosis of organic problems can be improved by supplementing NPT with measuring the rigidity of the erection and assessing erectile response to visual erotic stimuli when the man is awake (Kane et al., 1989; Rosen & Beck, 1988).

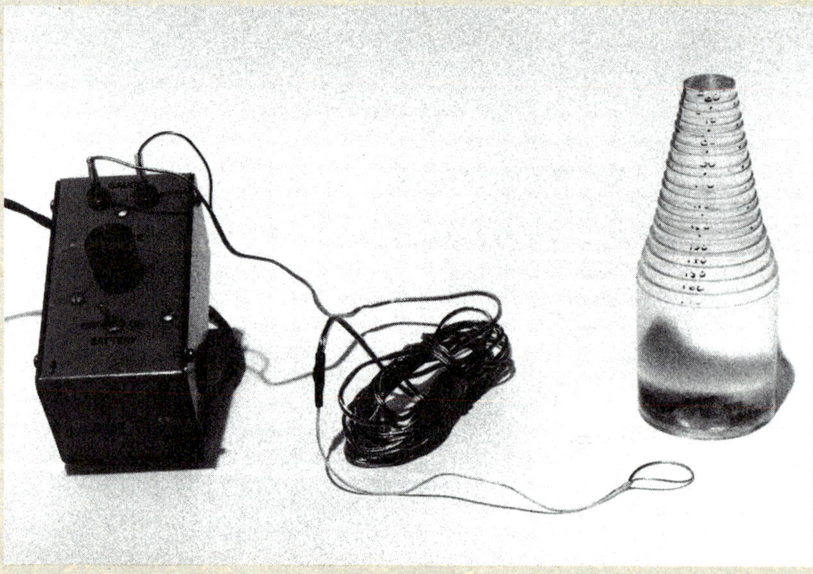

Figure 9.1 *Left: A mercury-in-rubber strain gauge attached to a variable resistance bridge, which is, in turn, connected to a polygraph. Right: A cone device for calibration of the strain gauge over a range of standard circumferences.*

Source: **From Raymond C. Rosen, Ph.D., Robert Wood Johnson Medical School. Reprinted by permission.**

Penile erection, either during the waking or sleeping state, is measured using the penile plethysmograph. As Figure 9.1 shows, this thin rubber gauge is filled with mercury. A very weak electrical current goes from the attached wire and flows through the mercury. The man places the rubber gauge over his flaccid penis, and when the penis becomes erect, the rubber gauge expands, thereby changing the electric current's flow. A polygraph then records these alterations. The penile plethysmograph is safe and relatively simple to use. It is very sensitive—each pulse of blood into the penis can be detected.

In addition to assessing possible organic factors in erectile disorder, the penile plethysmograph has proved useful in the study of men with other types of sexual problems.

The comparable instrument for women is the vaginal photocell plethysmograph (Geer, Morokoff, & Greenwood, 1974). This device looks like a tampon and measures the amount of light reflected from the vaginal walls. The polygraph records the reduction in reflected light from the vaginal blood flow's lubrication. The same physiological process—the pooling of blood in the genital region—is responsible for penile erection and vaginal lubrication. Hence the results from using these two devices are comparable.

ple do not of course necessarily develop sexual dysfunction. Masters and Johnson's findings have been corroborated by other sex therapists indicating that strong religious beliefs and other background factors increase the probability of a person running into sexual difficulties. A dominating, overcontrolling parent who undermines self-esteem; traumatic initial sexual encounters, such as a humiliating failure experience destroying self-confidence and heightening fears of inadequacy; and homosexual leanings that compete with heterosexual arousal are often other underlying causes of primary erectile dysfunction.

Secondary erectile dysfunction's range of causes is broader than that of primary erectile dysfunction. Religious orthodoxy, traumatic sexual experiences, conflicts about sexual identity, and premature ejaculation have been identified as common antecedents of secondary erectile dysfunction. Alcohol abuse impairs the erectile response, and a variety of nonsexual causes, such as inhibited emotional development, can also lead to erectile failure. Sudden onset, typically associated with life stresses, points to psychogenic causes.

Erectile problems may be the cause or the consequence of a desire disorder. Careful diagnosis is required to identify whether they mask such an underlying disorder. Rosen and Leiblum (1987) illustrate this point with the case of Mr. F, a 54-year-old recovered alcoholic, who received a surgical implant (prosthesis) following a diagnosis of organic impotence due to alcoholic neuropathy. Despite the patient's new-found ability to perform intercourse at will, in the two years following surgery he infrequently used the prosthesis. His wife became increasingly distressed by his unwillingness to either initiate sexual contact or respond with any enthusiasm to her overtures. In reviewing the couple's history it became apparent that his loss of sexual desire had preceded the erectile failure and appeared to be the primary problem for treatment. Both the urologist and the patient's wife had incorrectly assumed that once the capacity for intercourse was restored, sexual interest would reemerge unassisted.

Current Causes. Irrespective of the historical causes, which may differ for men and women and from one form of sexual dysfunction to another, the person's current anxiety about sexual performance seems responsible for most forms of sexual dysfunction. According to Masters and Johnson (1970), performance anxiety leads to what they call **spectatoring,** in which the person grows self-conscious and becomes an observer of his or her sexual response as a "third person"—looking for signs of failure. Instead of being open and responsive to the erotic stimulation and enhanced sensory input, he or she is distracted by critical self-evaluation generating anxiety and undermining the body's natural psychophysiological response to erotic cues.

Research by Beck and Barlow (1984) has clarified spectatoring's psychological mechanisms that cause erectile dysfunction. They compared the sexual response of sexually dysfunctional men with that of normally functioning men. In a series of laboratory studies, these two groups viewed erotic movies under various anxiety-eliciting conditions (i.e., threat of an electric shock). Subjects' subjective sexual arousal, erectile responses (measured by the penile plethysmograph), and attentional processes were assessed. The results revealed significant differences between the two groups.

1. The dysfunctional men consistently showed negative emotion in response to the erotic cues, whereas the functionals indicated positive feelings.
2. The dysfunctional men reported less subjective arousal than the functionals even when their erections did not differ.
3. The dysfunctional men were distracted by performance-related sexual stimuli (e.g., instructions to focus on how erect they become), whereas the functional men showed increased arousal to such stimuli.
4. Anxiety inhibited sexual arousal in dysfunctional men but had no effect or even increased arousal in functionals.

Other research is consistent with this general pattern of results. Heiman and Rowland (1983) found that sexually dysfunctional men showed inhibited erections following explicit instructions to try to become aroused but had enhanced erections in response to nondemand instructions. Functionals showed the opposite pattern.

Based on these research findings, Barlow (1986) proposed a psychological model of sexual arousal disorder (see Figure 9.2). The model assumes that any demand for sexual performance elicits anxiety and feelings of inadequacy. Instead of attending to normal erotic cues, the person is distracted and worries about his perceived inability to perform. The resulting cognitive distraction or interference leads to erectile failure. This negative cognitive-affective response to sexual performance is rooted in the historical factors summarized previously as the basis of spectatoring.

Female sexual arousal disorder is defined as either

1. persistent or recurrent failure to be physiologically aroused—that is, to have increased genital blood flow and vaginal lubrication—until completion of sexual activity, or

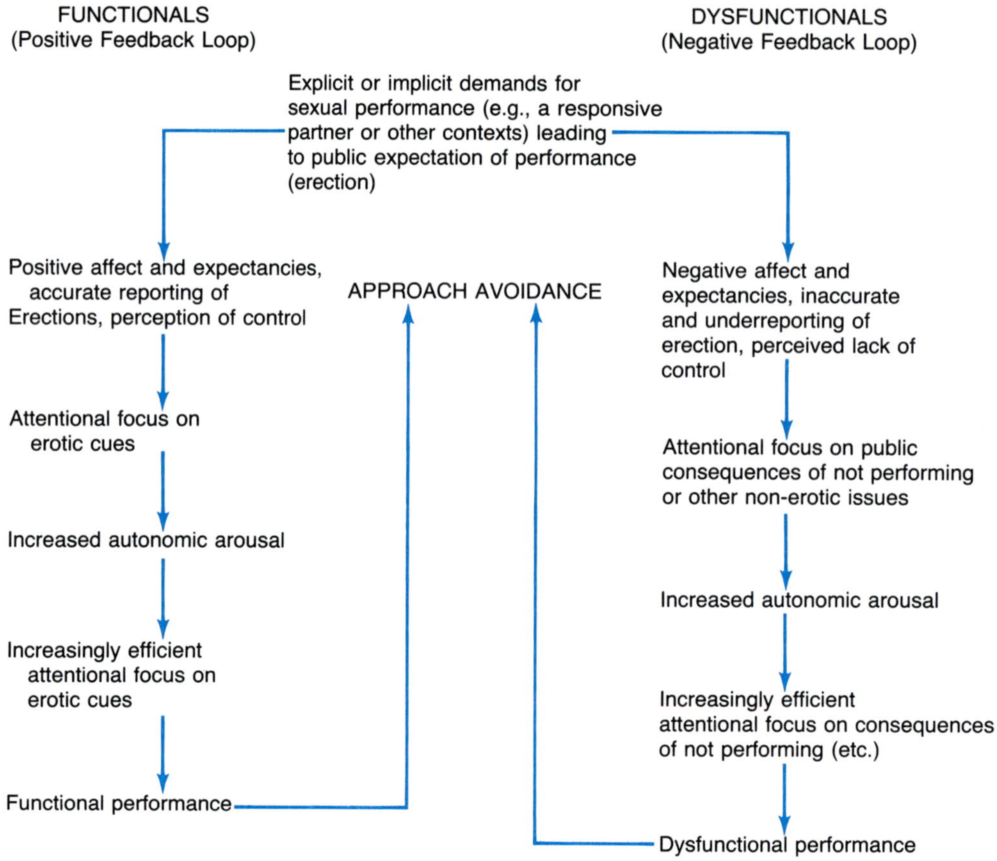

Figure 9.2 Current Causes of Sexual Dysfunction.

Source: From D.H. Barlow, Causes of sexual dysfunction. *Journal of Consulting and Clinical Psychology,* 1986, *54,* 140–148. Copyright © 1986 by the American Psychological Association. Reprinted with permission.

2. persistent lack of subjective sexual excitement and pleasure during sexual activity.

The many factors that can impair sexual arousal in women are discussed in the following section on female orgasmic disorders. Barlow (1986) suggests that the sexual arousal disorder model in Figure 9.2 may also apply to women. Although not directly tested in women with this dysfunction, data from studies comparing functional with sexually dysfunctional women are consistent with the model (Morokoff & Heiman, 1980).

Orgasm Disorders. **Inhibited female orgasm** is the persistent or recurrent delay in or absence of orgasm following sexual arousal judged by the clinician to be adequate in intensity and duration. Many sex therapists, following Masters and Johnson, differentiate between the *primary orgasmic dysfunction* and *situational orgasmic dysfunction.* Primary orgasmic dysfunction is a woman's failure to have ever had orgasm by any means. Situational orgasmic dysfunction occurs when a woman is orgasmic in only very limited circumstances—for example, with masturbation but not during intercourse.[5] Roughly one out of ten women have never had an orgasm (de Bruijn, 1982). Since many of them can learn to achieve it, they have also been called preorgasmic (Barbach, 1975).

Among the most common causes of orgasm disorders identified by Masters and Johnson were the same negative influences responsible for male sexual disorders. Restrictive religious prohibitions, homosexual commitments, and negative family influences leading to what Masters and Johnson termed a "cold, formal, and controlled" childhood all can result in female sexual difficulties. The most frequent source of sexual orgasmic difficulty is the woman's emotional dissatisfaction with her partner. These negative emotional reactions might include shame, re-

[5] *DSM-III-R* notes many women's failure to reach orgasm during intercourse without manual stimulation of the clitoris is "normal variation of the female sexual response." For example, in Hite's (1976) survey of women's sexual behavior, only 30 percent reported achieving orgasm during intercourse without some form of additional clitoral stimulation. Deciding whether this pattern is a normal variation or a clinical disorder requires the clinician to make a difficult and perhaps arbitrary judgment.

sentment, jealousy, boredom, disappointment, even disgust, variously reflecting unhappiness over financial failure, physical appearance, social shortcomings, a lack of affection, and the man's relationships with other women. Sexual problems in women can also result from specific trauma, such as rape or attempted rape, being molested as a child, or severe pain or panic during the first sexual encounter (Crewdson, 1988).

Women are also vulnerable to the negative influences of sexual inadequacy in their partners. Men may not even concern themselves with their partner's sexual satisfaction and are physically able to have orgasm through sexual intercourse regardless of their mate's sexual responsiveness. For a woman to achieve orgasm during sexual intercourse, however, her partner must maintain an erection and control his ejaculation for a sufficient period of time. Even then, a clumsy or insensitive lover may interfere with a woman's orgasmic response, the presence of the necessary sexual mechanics of erection and ejaculatory control notwithstanding. Women also frequently worry about their partner's inability to control ejaculation or maintain an erection, thereby impairing their own sexual response. They might even feel guilty about his erectile failure, doubting their own sexual allure. Of the large number of couples Masters and Johnson (1970) treated in which both partners showed sexual dysfunction, premature ejaculation and orgasmic dysfunction was the most common combination.

Fundamental to most forms of sexual dysfunction in women, according to Masters and Johnson, is society's double standard of sexual values: Male sexuality is culturally sanctioned, if not implicitly encouraged, while a woman's sexual nature (other than to satisfy her husband) has been ignored, even denied. Sexual responsiveness is not simply an innate drive that automatically unfolds as men and women mature physically. The biological potential for sexual responsiveness is elaborated on and probably channeled into different directions depending upon subsequent psychosocial experiences. In short, as Gagnon (1977) has argued, we have to learn to be sexual. If necessary social opportunities for this learning are unavailable, or if the response is systematically punished, a woman will have difficulty in suddenly becoming orgasmic as a result of taking a marriage vow or accepting her first invitation to go to bed with a man.

Related to our society's double standard of sexual mores has been the assumption that the man, as the sexual expert, must take responsibility for initiating and orchestrating sex. A U.S. study of pairs of college students who were seriously dating found that despite the recent easing of the double standard, the male is still expected to make the first move in sexual encounters (Peplau, Rubin, & Hill, 1977). The overwhelming majority of women waited for men to make sexual overtures, although 95 percent of both the men and the women advocated identical moral standards for sex. The reason? The women's fear that they would threaten their partner's ego were they to initiate sex. In their research on customary sexual behavior, Masters and Johnson observed the typical script of the man taking the lead with some form of usually brief, stereotyped foreplay, followed by the ultimate objective of vaginal intercourse. This relatively unvarying pattern among heterosexual couples often places the woman at a sexual disadvantage because the timing may not align with her pattern of sexual responsiveness. This single-minded emphasis on sexual intercourse as the end goal also places unnecessary pressure on the man to perform, which can result in erectile problems.

As with male sexual dysfunction, organic factors can play a role in female orgasmic dysfunction. The biological basis of sexual dysfunction in women has, however, received less direct research attention than disorders in men.

Inhibited male orgasm can take two forms. The first refers to a delay in, or absence of, orgasm following normal arousal during sexual activity judged by the clinician to be adequate in intensity and duration. This problem typically means the inability to ejaculate in the vagina. The second form, **premature ejaculation,** is the more common, and can be difficult to define. Here the male ejaculates "too soon." But what is "too soon"? And according to whom? Any attempt to specify arbitrary time periods seems misguided. Sexually functional women vary greatly in the amount of stimulation required for orgasm; the same woman will vary from time to time depending on a host of changeable physiological and situationally specific psychosocial factors. *DSM-III-R* defines premature ejaculation as ejaculation with minimal stimulation before or shortly after vaginal penetration and before the male wishes it. The clinician takes into account factors affecting duration of the excitement phase, such as age, novelty of the sexual partner, and the frequency of sexual activity.

Many sex therapists emphasize the importance of *both* sexual partners feeling satisfaction with the male's ejaculatory control during intercourse. This development is relatively recent, reflecting the modern trend toward equality between the sexes and the recognition of the sexual needs and wishes of women. Previously, a man with premature ejaculation might not have considered himself to have a problem.

Masters and Johnson's (1970) study of almost 200 premature ejaculators revealed a correlation between a man's educational level and his concern about his wife's sexual satisfaction. The better educated the man, the more likely he was to be troubled by his inability to satisfy his wife sexually. Men who had not completed high school rarely complained about premature ejaculation. It would be unwise to make too much of these preliminary findings, based as they are on a relatively small and nonrandom sample of sexually dysfunctional men. Premature ejaculation seems related to unusually hurried early sexual experiences. The majority of premature ejaculators studied by Masters and Johnson reported early heterosexual encounters where rapid ejaculation was demanded.

The causes of premature ejaculation are poorly understood, although generally assumed to be psychogenic. Ejaculation is controlled by the sympathetic branch of the autonomic nervous system, which is intimately associated with emotion. Performance anxiety, particularly, may lead to this ejaculatory problem.

Sexual Pain Disorders. **Dyspareunia,** or *painful intercourse,* such as aching, burning or itching sensations during intercourse often indicate an absence of adequate vaginal lubrication. (Lubrication is, roughly speaking, the functional equivalent of erection in the male). Lack of lubrication usually means the woman is insufficiently aroused, suggesting some emotional or interpersonal factor is responsible and indicating sex therapy. However, physical factors may be at work. Various types of vaginal infections damage ligaments supporting the uterus (as a result of childbirth or brutal physical assault) and endometriosis (a disease affecting the vaginal lining) are also possible causes of deep pelvic pain during intercourse and require diagnosis by a gynecologist.

Vaginismus refers to the involuntary tightening or spasms in the outer third of the vagina. These spasms can make it difficult if not impossible for the woman to have intercourse. Diagnosis of this disorder is made on the basis of a physical examination in which the presence of the muscle contractions are established by one-finger insertion. Aside from some of the psychosocial causes of sexual dysfunction already discussed, such as punitive religious prohibitions, vaginismus can be the result of rape.

Treatment of Sexual Dysfunction in Heterosexuals

Psychological Methods. The publication of Masters and Johnson's *Human Sexual Inadequacy* in 1970 ushered in the "new sex therapy" and fundamentally changed the treatment of sexual dysfunction.[6] Whereas sexual problems were previously regarded as resistant to treatment, Masters and Johnson showed that most problems could be rapidly eliminated. Current psychological treatment methods are largely derivative of their program. Masters and Johnson view sexual inadequacy as a fear of failure and their program is carefully designed to overcome this fear through a desensitization procedure.

The following key concepts help define the typical sex therapy program.

1. It is recommended that both marital partners participate in the treatment even if only one is clearly dysfunctional. Emphasis on treating the sexually dysfunctional couple reflects the significance attributed to improving effective interpersonal communication. Treating the couple also precludes the possibility of the partner not being seen in therapy engaging in "sexual sabotage," namely, accidentally or purposefully interfering with treatment because of other emotional or interpersonal conflicts.
2. The objective is to reduce the performance anxiety that leads to spectatoring. The first step is to prohibit any sexual activity not specifically sanctioned by the therapists. Thus sexual intercourse is initially forbidden, thereby removing the pressure on the man to perform. Thereafter, the couple is instructed in how to embark upon a carefully graduated program of mutually pleasurable sensual and sexual involvement. As this is conducted at the couple's own pace and involves no explicit goals, performance pressure is effectively undercut.
3. The mutual, non–goal-oriented sensual interactions between partners is known as *sensate focus*—the physical or sensory stimulation of each other's body. The couple are taught to think and feel sensuously by giving and receiving bodily pleasure, first by nongenital contact and then by specific genital stimulation. Although clients develop skills in bodily stimulation, the fundamental goals of sensate focus exercises are to increase the partners' verbal and nonverbal communication and to teach them that sexual gratification does not necessarily depend on intercourse. As sexual arousal spontaneously occurs in these "homework" assignments, the treatment is oriented toward the specific form of sexual dysfunction in question.

Treatment of Male Sexual Dysfunction. The *squeeze technique* is used to treat premature ejaculation. The woman manually stimulates her partner's penis to full erection and then, just prior to ejaculation, using her thumb and first two fingers of the same hand, firmly squeezes the penis for three or four seconds. This pressure eradicates the man's urge to ejaculate, and after about 30 seconds the identical procedure is repeated. The man is then

[6] Masters and Johnson's program included some established behavioral treatment techniques developed previously by Wolpe and Lazarus (1966).

gradually able to maintain increasingly longer erections. The progression next moves from the woman straddling the man and inserting his penis into her vagina while remaining motionless, to slowly building up to vigorous pelvis thrusting. If at any time the man feels that he is going to ejaculate too quickly, the woman, who is in the superior coital position, raises her body, repeats the squeeze technique, and then reinserts the penis. It is vitally important that the man recognize the point at which he is close to ejaculation and communicate this to his partner. By waiting too long he will reach the point of ejaculatory inevitability and will be unable to restrain ejaculation. The man's willingness and ability to make this judgment and communicate it to his partner is critical to the treatment's success.

The treatment of erectile problems is similar to that of ejaculatory disorders. Couples are instructed to continue with sensate focus exercises until erection spontaneously occurs. Thereafter, the wife uses a "teasing technique" in which she manipulates the penis to erection and then relaxes with her partner until the erection disappears. She then repeats the procedure several times, thereby reducing the man's fear of losing an erection and not regaining it during sexual interaction. The therapy continues with the woman making it easy for the man to insert his penis into her vagina without any pressure, followed by progressively more vigorous thrusting until orgasm occurs.

Like any other sexual problem, erectile dysfunction is often embedded in a troubled relationship. Treatment methods, consequently, have to extend beyond specific sexual techniques to address the role of marital difficulties in the maintenance of sexual dysfunction.

Brady (1976) described the case of a twenty-seven-year-old patient treated for secondary erectile dysfunction. Standard sex therapy failed completely. The patient disobeyed the therapist's explicit instructions and drank before a session of sensate focus. (Alcohol consumption can significantly suppress erectile capacity.) His wife also ignored instructions by engaging almost immediately in direct genital stimulation and urging her husband to attempt intercourse. Mutual recriminations inevitably followed these interactions. As soon as this self-defeating pattern of behavior became apparent, the therapist delved more deeply into the nature of the couple's marital relationship. This showed the client plagued by self-doubt and a lack of assertiveness; his wife, while expressing occasional warmth and support, was predominantly critical and aggressive in manner. Therapy was redirected to changing the couple's relationship, and as a result, it improved greatly over the following five months of treatment. The client's erectile problem persisted, however, and he naturally still felt anxiety about his sexual performance. At this stage, the original desensitization program was reintroduced, and the sexual dysfunction eliminated within a few weeks.

This clinical case underscores an important point: Effective treatment of specific sexual disorders will sometimes require therapy for other nonsexual aspects of the couple's functioning, such as competitive tendencies and lack of communication. The temporal relationships between these classes of problems are often impossible to disentangle. Sexual dysfunction flourishes in an unhappy relationship, and problems such as impotence invariably place great strain on any relationship. The pragmatic clinical strategy is to intervene directly in the sexual problem while looking for signs of marital disharmony that may interfere with therapy. As in this case, such a strategy may quickly expose resistances to therapy so that other, related features of the total clinical problem can be identified, assessed, and appropriately treated.

Treatment of Female Sexual Dysfunction. Many of the basic treatment concepts and procedures for dysfunctional men are applicable for dysfunctional women, including reducing performance pressure and developing improved verbal and nonverbal communication. Sensate focus exercises encourage the woman to show her partner what she does and does not find sexually arousing rather than passively allowing him to do what he thinks she wants. The therapist instructs the couple in the details of specific sexual positions for stimulation and intercourse, stressing the importance of timing. For example, Masters and Johnson's observations of heterosexual couples having sex revealed that men typically begin to stimulate their partner's clitoris as soon as sex is initiated. This immediate stimulation may, however, be ineffective if not unpleasant unless the woman is psychologically ready for it.

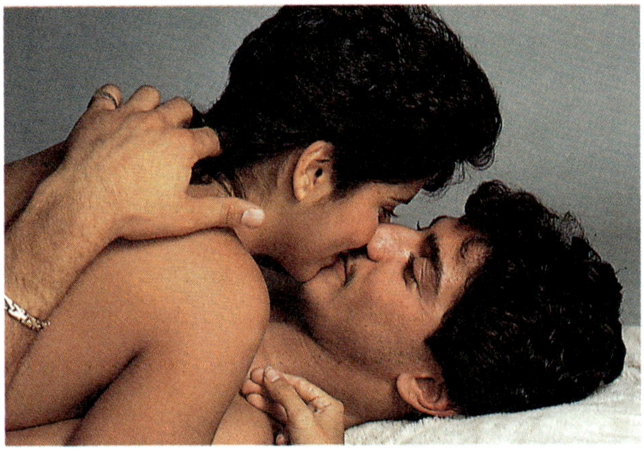

"Sensate focus" involves a couple communicating openly about how to please each other physically.

Instead, the man is taught how to stimulate nongenital areas of his partner's body to build up arousal gradually before moving to more direct genital play. This more varied or imaginative pattern of sexual stimulation, carried out with explicit concern for the woman's sensual and sexual pleasure, markedly contrasts with the more typical sexual script between man and woman. This latter pattern has been characterized as only minimal foreplay followed by a rapid, male-initiated move to have sexual intercourse. Following sensate focus exercises, the couple proceeds gradually to nondemanding penile insertion with the woman in the superior coital position controlling the pace.

As sex therapy has developed, several additional treatment procedures have proved effective in enhancing female sexual responsiveness. A widely used approach with women who have never experienced orgasm is a systematic program of directed masturbation (Heiman, LoPiccolo, & LoPiccolo, 1976). The woman is first taught to familiarize herself with her body, particularly the genital area, and to identify pleasurable sensations. A female therapist then instructs her in the intricacies of masturbation, including the use of electric vibrators. Once the woman reaches orgasm through masturbation, her husband is introduced to the procedure by observing her masturbate. This not only desensitizes the woman to being sexually aroused in his presence but also is a learning experience for him, who, in the next step of the program, masturbates her to orgasm. Although most women become orgasmic in response to direct genital stimulation, far fewer achieve orgasm during intercourse with a partner.

Successful sex therapy for both men and women usefully involves more than using specific methods such as sensate focus, the squeeze technique, or desensitization. Sex may be part of the politics and power arrangements of the marriage. For example, the resolution of a man's erectile failure might drastically alter this balance, thereby threatening an insecure partner for whom the dysfunction served a controlling purpose. Deep-seated hostility or fear can result in resistance. Should a man with erectile dysfunction become functional, his wife is faced with the prospect of greatly increased sexual contact that she may not want or may even fear. Improvement in a wife's orgasmic responsiveness can, conversely, produce erectile problems in a husband, whose own problems were masked by her sexual inhibitions.

Resistance may be motivated by a number of factors, including simple inertia, the belief that treatment will be ineffective, or even what Kaplan (1979) refers to as a "fear of success." In overcoming resistance, the sex therapist(s) have to be especially resourceful. Should continued encouragement and repetition of the treatment instructions to engage in specific homework assignments prove unproductive, the therapist(s) will confront the couple directly. The pattern of failure to follow treatment directives is pointed out, and the issue opened up for mutual questioning and discussion. Providing insight into self-defeating patterns of behavior of which the sexually dysfunctional man or his partner may be unaware usually suffices to overcome resistance. As a result, some sex therapists, such as Kaplan (1974), advocate using the behavioral, Masters-and-Johnson–type techniques previously described, in combination with traditional psychoanalytic psychotherapy. According to this approach, resistance in some cases is a function of intrapsychic unconscious conflicts requiring psychoanalytic interpretive therapy that includes analysis and interpretations linking current behavior to childhood events.

How Well Does Sex Therapy Work? Masters and Johnson (1970) reported originally that of the 790 patients treated, only 19 percent were failures at the end of their two-week therapy program. This outcome assessment has subsequently been criticized as lacking good outcome measures and necessary scientific controls (Zilbergeld & Evans, 1980). Modern sex therapists make more modest claims (LoPiccolo & Stock, 1986). A number of conclusions, some more tentative than others because of a lack of evidence, can be drawn.

1. Behavioral sex therapy has been shown to provide quick and effective treatment for orgasmic difficulties in women, premature ejaculation, and some erectile problems. It reduces sexual anxiety and can increase sexual responsiveness. But data on long-term effectiveness are lacking. The long-term outcome of secondary erectile disorder seems especially unstable. Some degree of relapse frequently occurs (Levine & Agle, 1978).
2. Masters and Johnson's insistence on highly trained two-partner sex therapy teams in all instances is unnecessary. Single therapists appear to achieve comparable success. Nor does the gender of therapist have to match with that of patient, as required by Masters and Johnson (LoPiccolo & Stock, 1986).
3. Following a thorough assessment of each individual patient's (couple's) problems, sex therapy needs to be flexible for best results. Multifaceted treatment programs, including sexual and nonsexual methods, are usually required.
4. Simple sexual problems, uncomplicated by other personal or interpersonal difficulties, are relatively easy to treat, often within a few weeks of therapy. Women can become orgasmic, and males overcome premature ejaculation using

self-help manuals with minimal instruction from a therapist (Morokoff & LoPiccolo, 1986). Clinical experience, nevertheless, shows that relationship problems tend to complicate sex therapy and hinder its success. This is additionally significant if, as sex therapists widely believe, the population seeking sex therapy today is more likely to have fundamental relationship problems than the patients treated in the early 1970s (Friedman & Hogan, 1985). Successful therapy for these more complex cases may take months or even years.

5. Among the contemporary sexual disorders, problems of inhibited desire are particularly challenging. Therapeutic success rates with them are usually said to be much lower than with the other forms of sexual dysfunction discussed previously, although not all therapists agree with this view. For example, both Apfelbaum (1988) and Leiblum and Rosen (1988) claim good results, often better than in treating erectile problems. Kaplan (1979) has argued that whereas short-term behavioral sex therapy is reliably effective for some specific sexual dysfunctions, it is inadequate for sexual problems characterized by greater psychopathology, as in low sexual desire. For the problems of desire, Kaplan advocates a combination of behavioral methods and psychodynamic principles she calls "psychosexual therapy," which, she claims, works where behavior therapy fails. Friedman and Hogan (1985) similarly assert that to treat problems of low desire, therapists must be skilled not only in behavior therapy but also in systems and marital therapy, and able to use techniques from Gestalt and psychodynamic therapies. There are currently too few data to evaluate these claims' validity.

Pharmacological and Physical Methods. Since organic causes of erectile disorders are being increasingly identified, there have been trends toward medical methods of erectile failure treatment. No evidence indicates that medication, such as antidepressant or antianxiety modification drugs, modifies specific forms of sexual dysfunction, although an antidepressant drug, bupropion, produced greater improvement in patients' ratings of sexual desire than a placebo (Crenshaw, Goldberg, & Stern, 1987). Hormone replacement therapy—for example, testosterone—is helpful when the failure is due to a hormonal deficiency, but of little value if the man is within the normal range (Bancroft, 1983). Additionally, penile revascularization is now used to bypass arteries in the penis damaged by atherosclerosis. Surgery is frequently done to implant a *penile prosthesis,* an inflatable or semi-rigid device, in the penis (see Figure 9.3). Prostheses are implanted not only in men whose erectile disorder is organic but also in some men with psychogenic problems judged as poor candidates for sex therapy. Once implanted, the prosthesis produces an erection hard enough for intercourse, and ejaculation is possible. A study of 52 men who received a penile implant showed that the surgery was technically successful and that 90 percent would choose it again if confronted with the same problem

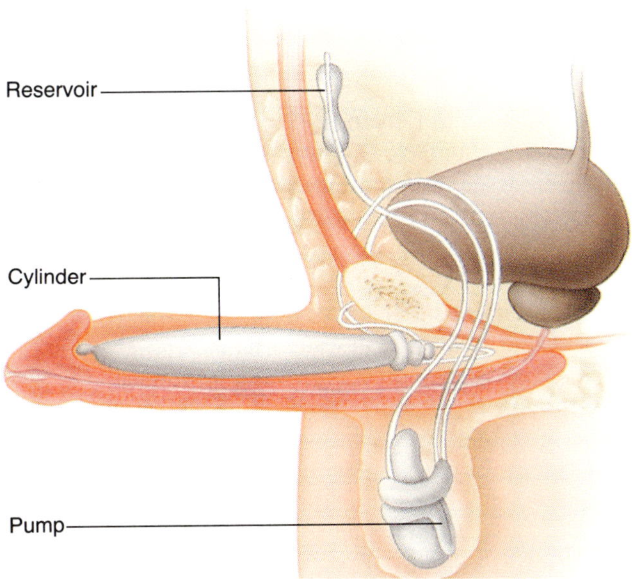

Figure 9.3 Penile Prosthesis with Pump for Inflations *(American Medical Systems, Minneapolis).*

Source: From Rosen, R.C., & Hall, E. *Sexuality,* 1984, p. 366. New York: Random House. Copyright © 1986, Random House. Reprinted by permission.

(Steege, Stout, & Carson, 1986). Yet 25 percent of the men reported significant dissatisfaction with the outcome. They were troubled by the size and stiffness of their erections and decreased sensations during ejaculation.

Another increasingly popular treatment is the injection into the penis of substances such as papaverive hydrochloride and phentolamine. These substances produce partly or totally stiff erections in most cases of either organic or psychogenic erectile dysfunction within fifteen minutes of injection, lasting one to four hours. The physician first determines the correct dose of papaverine/phentolamine through a series of trial injections, then teaches the patient how to inject himself at home. Common physical side effects are bruising and nodules developing on the penis. A minority of men experience priapism, or prolonged erection in the absence of sexual stimulation. Some couples dislike the artificiality of the procedure. Still, a study of these injections' psychological effects showed an increase in quality of erections, frequency of intercourse, and general sexual satisfaction in the men and their partners (Althof et al., 1987).

Treatment of Sexual Dysfunction in Homosexuals

Masters and Johnson's (1979) laboratory studies have shown that despite their differences in sexual orientation, homosexuals exhibit the same physiological pattern of sexual response as heterosexuals. Homosexuals also experience the same sexual dysfunctions as heterosexuals. It follows then that dysfunctional homosexuals may overcome their sexual difficulties by the same methods used to successfully treat heterosexuals. This is precisely what Masters and Johnson and other therapists have shown.

Masters and Johnson treated male and female homosexuals in the same two-week rapid treatment program used to treat heterosexuals. All patients were required to find a same-sex partner willing to participate in the therapy. Masters and Johnson developed definitions of homosexual dysfunctions similar to those of heterosexual dysfunctions. For example, a lesbian with primary orgasmic dysfunction was defined as a person who had never experienced orgasm in response to one of three primary sources of sexual stimulation: masturbation, manual stimulation by partner, or oral sex (cunnilingus). A gay male with primary erectile dysfunction was defined as someone who had never been able to achieve an erection in response to masturbation (either by self or partner) or oral sex (fellatio). The results of Masters and Johnson's treatment of homosexual couples were as good, if not better, than their results with heterosexual couples.

PARAPHILIAS

The study of sex blends modern science with changing moral values and politics. The mix is often the source of controversy. Any analysis of sexual behavior, then, requires us to think seriously about ethics, law, life-styles, different cultural influences, and the psychological and biological bases of behavior.

Most people engage in sexual activities within their particular society's conventions. Some individuals, however, are "turned on" by unconventional acts or odd objects. In street language, this is called "kinky sex." In *DSM-III-R,* these sexual activities are labeled the **paraphilias.** The term comes from the Greek word *para* meaning beyond, or amiss, and *philia,* meaning love. A clinical diagnosis is made only if the person acts on these deviant urges or is distressed by them. Paraphilias had previously been called sexual deviance. The problem with the term *sexual deviance* is the difficulty of defining what is deviant or abnormal. Considerable diversity exists across cultures as to what forms of sexual expression are deviant, and few patterns have been universally disapproved of as abnormal. The term *paraphilia* seems more descriptive and less judgmental. Yet the question of defining what is abnormal remains. Perhaps the most useful approach is to define as abnormal those acts that people feel compelled to engage in, that make them unhappy, or that distress or harm other individuals. This definition acknowledges that something normal in one context may be abnormal in another situation (Rosen & Hall, 1984). The paraphilias described next are all punishable offenses in the United States.

Characteristics of Paraphilias

Obtaining accurate information on paraphilias confronts researchers with unusual difficulties. We must rely on information provided by paraphiliacs themselves. Arrest records are inadequate data sources because most paraphiliacs are not caught and those caught have committed many more offenses than the one for which they were arrested. But because these actions are criminal offenses, paraphiliacs remain understandably reluctant to disclose their behavior. Virtually all available information on paraphilias comes from men imprisoned for their behavior. These incarcerated men risk violence from fellow prisoners if the nature of their crimes becomes known (Abel et al., 1988). Most textbook accounts of the nature of paraphilias, consequently, rely on very limited if not inaccurate information.

Recent research by Abel and his colleagues has overcome the problem of obtaining more accurate information (Abel et al., 1987; Abel et al., 1988). Using a certificate of confidentiality from the federal government, these researchers guaranteed confidentiality to 56 nonincarcerated paraphiliacs seeking voluntary evaluation or treatment at centers in Tennessee and New York City. With this guarantee, these men had little reason to withhold relevant information. The results challenge many long-held assumptions about paraphiliacs, and three findings stand out. First, previous research had suggested the average paraphiliac or sex offender commits fewer than two crimes. Abel et al. (1987) found that the number is much higher. Second, paraphiliacs were thought to engage in only one type of deviant behavior. Abel et al. (1988) found that they participate in as many as ten different forms of paraphilia on the average; in fact, the paraphiliac with a history of only one paraphilia seems rare. Third, paraphiliacs often have normal sexual involvements with adult partners without paraphilic fantasies or activities. Deviant and nondeviant sexual behavior coexist in most paraphiliacs.

Exhibitionism. The exhibitionist, or "flasher," as he is often called, either exposes his genitals to unsuspecting women or has strong and persistent urges and sexually arousing fantasies concerning such exposure. His victims may be adults or children. His average age at conviction is thirty years; approximately one third are married; one third separated, divorced, or widowed; and the remainder have never been married. The exhibitionist acts compulsively in exposing himself and is obsessed with his immediate feelings and intentions. As a result he becomes oblivious to the consequences of his actions and the danger he may be in. Some men masturbate during exposure, but for most paraphilias, the image or memory of the act of exposure typically arouses them when they later masturbate or even have intercourse.

> *Mr. B, a thirty-five-year-old married man, with two sons aged eight and five years, came from a successful, middle-class family. He was also a persistent exhibitionist with a pattern over the past twenty years of exposing his genitals to unsuspecting adult women as often as five or six times a week. Fifteen years of intermittent psychoanalytic treatment, several hospitalizations at psychiatric institutions, and a six-year prison sentence had failed to change his unwanted, but apparently uncontrollable, behavior. At present, he was under grand jury indictment for exposing himself to an adult woman in the presence of young children. He stood to receive a lengthy prison term if a last resort to treatment was unsuccessful in changing his behavior.*
>
> *Analysis of Mr. B's behavior identified several immediate precursors of his exhibitionism. For example, a woman standing alone at a bus stop as he drove past in his car often triggered a pattern of thoughts and images causing him to circle the block and eventually expose himself. Additionally, his anger after a heated argument with his father, which Mr. B could not handle, could elicit the same urge. The more Mr. B thought about exposing himself, the more obsessed he became with a particular woman and her anticipated reactions. As he tuned out everything except his immediate feelings and intentions, he became oblivious to the consequences of his actions. He hoped his victim would express some form of approval, either by smiling or making some sexual comment. Although this did happen periodically, most women ignored him and some called the police.* (Wilson & O'Leary, 1980)

The traditional textbook view is that the majority of exhibitionists tend to be inhibited, conform to society's customs, and show no associated psychopathology. They feel guilty about their problem, are motivated to regain control of their behavior, and respond well to treatment. In contrast to this group of "pure" exhibitionists, a much smaller number have antisocial behavior histories, show personality disturbances, and engage in other illegal activities (Forgac & Michaels, 1982). Yet Abel et al. (1988) found that the exhibitionists in their sample frequently engaged in other paraphilias. For example, as many as 46 percent had molested young girls. Contrary to the traditional view of exhibitionists as harmless nuisances, several of Abel et al.'s (1988) sample reported acts of sexual aggression, and 25 percent said that they had raped someone.

Fetishism. The fetishist is sexually aroused by persistent fantasies about or actual use of nonliving objects by themselves—for example, women's panties. Often the fetishist fondles or smells the object while masturbating. Many men are turned on by a female partner in sexy lingerie—for example, a woman wearing only a garter belt and net stockings is a common pornographic image—but this excitement does not constitute a fetish unless the man cannot function without the object. Fetishists tend to be lonely, withdrawn people lacking appropriate social skills.

Voyeurism. The voyeur, or "peeping Tom" as he is often called, is a male whose preferred or exclusive means of gaining sexual excitement is observing unsuspecting women undressing or engaging in sexual activity. He may masturbate to orgasm either during the voyeuristic activity or afterward in response to his memory of it. The element of risk seems crucial for the voyeur; his victim must be unaware of being observed. The majority of voyeurs tend to be young, single, timid men fearful about direct sexual contact with women. Yet a subcategory among voyeurs who have been arrested are aggressive and may go on to commit sexual assault.

Masochism and Sadism. These two paraphilias are closely related. The masochist is sexually aroused by fantasizing about, or engaging in the act of, being humiliated or beaten. The sadist is aroused by fantasies or actions involving the domination or beating of another person. A sadomasochist is someone who responds to both sources of stimulation.

Sadists and masochists get their stimulation from a range of activities, including whipping, biting, burning, and cutting. These rituals may result in injury and even death. For example, a sadomasochist who administers electric shock to his genitals may inadvertently electrocute himself.

Sadism and masochism occur in heterosexual and homosexuals, and, unlike all other paraphilias, in both men and women. Specialized "S-M" clubs and bars cater to this clientele. Abel et al. (1988) found that 46 percent of the sadists in their sample of nonincarcerated men reported involvement in rape—the highest percentage of rape in any type of paraphilia.

Transvestism. A transvestite is a man who becomes sexually aroused by dressing as a woman. Cross-dressing is usually done in limited circumstances and, for the most part, these men are masculine in appearance and activities. Most are heterosexual and married. The transvestite cross-dresses in secrecy, often with the knowledge of and occasionally the cooperation of his wife.

Brownell, Hayes, and Barlow (1977) describe the case of Jack, a married, thirty-one-year-old police officer, suffering from uncontrollable urges to appear in public dressed as a woman. Besides his transvestism, Jack had a history of sadomasochism. During sexual intercourse with his wife he tied her to the bed, handcuffed her, and had her wear an animal collar and leash. He also tied himself with ropes, chains, handcuffs, and wires while cross-dressed and was concerned that he would injure himself seriously. His wife had threatened divorce as a result of the cross-dressing yet she frequently purchased women's clothing for him and was "compassionate" while he wore it. This collusion by the wife in the patient's deviant sexual behavior is not atypical.

The prevalence of transvestism cannot be gauged with any accuracy. Cross-dressing is most frequently performed in privacy and very few transvestites are ever arrested. Clinical case histories of transvestites usually reveal that during childhood the boy received considerable attention and praise for wearing female clothing.

Child Molesting. Persistent sexual fantasies about sex or actual sexual contact with a prepubescent child (age thirteen or younger) is known as child molesting or pedophilia. The nature of the sexual contact may vary from genital fondling to sexual intercourse with a young girl or homosexual acts with a young boy. Even toddlers may be the target of the pedophile. Russell (1983) interviewed a random sample of women in San Francisco; four in ten reported having been the victim of serious sexual abuse before age eighteen. In July 1985 the *Los Angeles Times* conducted a telephone poll of a random sample of 2,627 men and women from every state in the United States. The results made front page news—27 percent of the women and 16 percent of the men reported having been sexually abused as children (*Los Angeles Times,* August 25 and 26, 1985). Most cases of abuse involved physical contact. Fully one third had never disclosed their history of abuse to anyone; only 3 percent had contacted the police. These numbers indicate how widespread but hidden childhood sexual abuse is. Children may be too frightened to tell their parents. Even if the parents find out, they might be unwilling to inform police for fear of negative publicity and unwanted attention from such a charge. Societal concern is growing that this problem is on the increase with several recent, highly publicized instances of repeated sexual abuse in day-care centers and schools (Crewdson, 1988).

A study of 453 pedophiles by Abel (1989) has cast new light on this disorder's dimensions. Of these men,[7] more had assaulted girls than boys. But those whose victims were boys did so more frequently. Sixty-three percent of all reported victims were males. Many pedophiles abuse boys and girls, and their victims can be within and outside of the family. Like other paraphiliacs, pedophiles may engage in other forms of paraphilia, including rape (Abel et al., 1988). Pedophiles and their victims are drawn from all socioeconomic and educational levels (Abel et al., 1987), with no differences between blacks and whites (Crewdson, 1988). Pedophiles often try to justify their behavior by claiming that a child who does not physically resist really wishes to have sex with them, or that they are performing a service by teaching the child about sex.

Incest. When the pedophile and his victim are related, the offense is incest. Incest occurs at all levels of society, not only in rural areas as once believed. A study of 796 college students in New England revealed that 15 percent of the women and 10 percent of the men recalled some kind of sexual relationship with a sibling. Many of these cases involved a teenager with a younger sibling (Finkelhor, 1979). Father-daughter incest is also more common than once believed. A survey of the general population indicated that roughly one in every one hundred women reported a sexual experience with her father or stepfather (Justice & Justice, 1979).

Public and professional awareness of the alarming incidence of the sexual abuse of children within and outside the family may appear to be a recent phe-

[7] Sex between mother and son is very rare. It is the subject of Louis Malle's well-known film, *Murmur Of The Heart.*

nomenon. But the problem was identified professionally almost 100 years ago—by none other than Freud. Virtually all of his female patients, suffering from what Freud called hysterical illness, reported that they had been sexually abused as children, mainly by their father.[8] Freud hypothesized that childhood sexual abuse was the main cause of adult neurotic behavior. This idea—the *seduction theory* of the neuroses—was widely rejected by Freud's colleagues. Within two years Freud changed his mind by deciding that the incest of his patients had not really occurred—his patients unconsciously wished to have sex with their father (Masson, 1984). The new theory was called the **theory of infantile sexuality** and became a cornerstone of psychoanalysis.

Freud's abandonment of the seduction theory was doubly unfortunate. We now know that Freud was correct the first time—that childhood sexual abuse contributes significantly to later mental disorder (Burnam et al., 1988). We also know that female patients' reports of sexual abuse to their therapists came to be misinterpreted as unconscious fantasies. Consequently, the victims were held responsible for their suffering (Crewdson, 1988).

Textbooks have traditionally differentiated between nonincestuous and incestuous child molesters. The former were said to be attracted to younger victims than the latter. A common stereotype of incest is a man under stress turning to his daughter for the emotional support or sexual expression not available from his wife. But if this were so, why would the man not pursue extramarital affairs with other adult women? Abel et al. (1988) reject this traditional view and conclude that the incestuous pedophile turns to his daughter because he is generally attracted to young girls; or in the case of male incest, because he is generally attracted to young boys. A large proportion of pedophiles who molest their own sons or daughters will molest children from outside the family as well (Abel et al., 1988).

Rape[9]

The Act. A few weeks before Christmas of 1981, the news media in New York City carried the story of the brutal assault by two men on a forty-year-old nun. Not only had she been repeatedly raped and sodomized, but one attacker had cut crosses in her skin in numerous places. The vicious nature of this crime should dispel the myth of rape as a forced sexual encounter that happens to seductive women. Rape victims range from young children to women in their eighties. Whether they resist or not, they are frequently beaten, injured physically, and even killed. Roughly one quarter of reported rapes are committed by more than one man. The woman who lives in an urban, lower socioeconomic environment with a high rate of other crime is the most probable rape victim.

Rape statistics are based on assaults reported to the authorities, which account for only a fraction of the actual incidence. Russell (1983) found that 24 percent of her sample of adult women in San Francisco had been raped, although only 9.5 percent had notified the police about the incident. The alarming scope of rape and related sexual aggression was revealed in a large-scale study of a national sample of 6,159 college students in thirty-two institutions throughout the United States (Koss, Gidycz, & Wisniewski, 1987). The results show how widespread sexual aggression is—a remarkable 27.5 percent of college women reported experiencing rape or attempted rape since age fourteen; 54 percent claimed to have been sexually victimized in some way—for example, kissed or petted against their will. Eight percent of college men reported acts on their part that met legal definitions of rape. Another study found that when college men were asked if they would rape if certain of not being caught, about 20 percent said they would and another 15 percent said they might. These men found tape-recordings of rape incidents highly arousing (Malamuth, 1981).

Most rapists are not strangers, but someone the woman knows (Koss, Dinero, Seibel, & Cox, 1988). For example, **date rape** is a disturbingly common case of sexual coercion and is defined as unwanted sexual intercourse. Men may use physical force or threaten it to subjugate their date, but the most common means of obtaining unwanted sex is by simply ignoring the woman's refusal as illustrated in the following account by a victim of date rape.

> *I was 15. I had heard about rape. I knew I was supposed to be careful and not trust strangers, but nobody told me to be afraid of my date. Tom was a senior on the baseball team and was from a nice, white, middle-class family. I didn't recognize it as rape at the time because he didn't hit me or yell at me; he just ignored me. He had sex with me while I was crying and saying no and asking, "Why are you doing this to me?"* (Muehlenhard, Julsonnet, Carlson, & Flarity-White, 1989, p. 211)

Date rape occurs on all college campuses and is not confined to first dates. Steady dates are even more likely than casual dates to engage in sexual coercion (Muehlenhard et al., 1989). What happened between Cindy and Phil, as described in Box 9.2 on page 219, illustrates some facts about date rape.

Both Cindy and Phil had been drinking. Alcohol

[8] In recent years the possibility that Freud himself was the victim of incest has been debated (Krull, 1986).

[9] Nowhere does *DSM-III-R* list rape as a disorder. Following considerable controversy, it appears to have been omitted so as not to encourage the view that this is a specifically sexual or psychiatric act as opposed to a violent crime.

Women students at Brown University protesting against sexual harassment and rape on campus.

makes men more sexually aggressive. Women who drink are often believed by men to be more sexually available (George et al., 1988). Miscommunication is often an element in date rape. Phil did not see himself as a rapist. He thought Cindy wanted sex. Muehlenhard (1989) points out that we still have a sexual double standard in our society. Males are expected to pursue sex; women, in order not to appear "loose," are expected to offer some resistance. The "scenario where a forceful man continues a sexual advance despite a woman's protests, until she melts in compliance," is a common theme in books and movies. This sexual script, Muehlenhard (1989) contends, may give men the message that although a woman says "no," she really means "yes." Date rape, however, cannot be explained simply as a result of passion, alcohol, or mixed signals. More fundamentally, rape seems related to motives of power and anger and to a lack of respect for women.

Men are also the victims of rape. This behavior occurs most frequently in prisons. Infrequent cases of men being raped by women also have been reported (Sarel & Masters, 1982).

Men Who Rape. There is no "typical rapist" as these men vary in age, intelligence, social and economic background, and marital status. Although rapists have often been drinking, many are sober at the time of the act. The high blood levels of testosterone sometimes found in them probably reflect their tendency toward violence as this hormone's presence in substantial amounts has been linked to violent criminal activities. Men who rape other men in prisons do not see themselves as homosexual, their motivation being to dominate and degrade the usually smaller and less aggressive male.

Why do men rape? No easy answer to this question exists. One traditional view has been that women who are raped really "asked for it" by being seductive or otherwise inviting sexual assault. This unfortunate stereotype has greatly damaged rape victims and is clearly contradicted by the facts. The same theme is a familiar one in novels, pornography, and movies. Many normal women do have sexual fantasies in which rape is often an element. Yet there is no evidence that women have any desire to be raped in real life.

Susan Brownmiller (1975) forcefully presents a different perspective of rape. In her view, men rape as part of their continuing subjugation and intimidation of women. To support her radical position, Brownmiller traces rape's history throughout the centuries. For example, historically the victim was punished as often as her attacker and greater con-

BOX 9.2 Cindy and Phil: The Same Story but from a Male and Female Point of View

Cindy: I'll never forget that night as long as I live. Phil and I had been dating a while and he had always acted like a perfect gentleman—well, we had done our share of kissing but he never gave me any reason not to trust him. The night of the party I wore this gorgeous dress that I borrowed from my roommate. It was little flashier than I normally wear but I thought it was very flattering. At the party I had some beer and it made me really tired so I wanted to lie down. Maybe I shouldn't have suggested we both lie down together but it felt weird to just go upstairs by myself and leave Phil all alone. The next thing I know he was all over me, forcing me to have sex with him. It was horrible. I didn't want to scream and make a fool of myself with all those other people in the next room but I tried to fight him off. I guess I was just too wiped out to be very effective. Needless to say, I never want to see Phil again. He seemed like such a nice guy. What happened?

Phil: I still don't understand what happened. Cindy and I had been dating for about two months and while we had not slept together yet, I had certainly made it clear that I was very attracted to her and eventually expected to have sex with her. We were supposed to go to a party and when she showed up in this sexy low-cut dress I thought maybe this was her way of saying she was ready. At the party we drank some beer, which made her sort of sleepy and sensual. When she said she wanted to go lie down and have me come snuggle with her, what was I supposed to think? Of course I thought she wanted to have sex. Granted, she did grumble a little when I started to undress her but I just figured she wanted to be persuaded. Lots of women feel a little funny about being forward and want men to take responsibility for sex. I don't know. We had sex and it was fine. I took her home from the party and I thought everything was OK. But ever since then she refuses to talk to me or go out with me. I thought she really liked me. What happened?

Source: From J.O. Hughes and B.R. Sandler, "Friends" raping friends. *Project on the Status and Education of Women*, Washington, DC: Association of American Colleges. Copyright 1987 by the Project on the Status and Education of Women, Association of American Colleges. Reprinted with permission.

cern existed for the victims' fathers and husbands than for the victims themselves. Rape viewed as a crime against the woman herself is a fairly new development. Until recently, it was not a crime if a husband raped his wife, as it was assumed she had no right to deny her husband's sexual wishes. The first prosecution of a man for marital rape occurred in Oregon in 1978. He was acquitted (and his wife returned to him), but other men have subsequently been found guilty of this offense.

Experimental research has uncovered three differences between rapists and normal controls

Alcohol consumption is often associated with sexual seduction and coercion.

1. Both rapists and nonrapists become sexually aroused to consensual sexual activity, but only rapists become sexually excited by rape cues (see Box 9.3).
2. Rapists have a callous attitude toward women, with little respect for their rights and feelings. They interpret ambiguous female reactions as come-ons (Lipton, McDonel, & McFall, 1987), and believe that women obtain gratification from sexual assault (Malamuth & Check, 1983).
3. Rapists (and child molesters), compared with normal controls, have difficulty with heterosocial skills such as the ability to express their feelings (Overholser & Beck, 1986).

Adolescents and Sexual Violence. In the spring of 1989 the entire country was shocked by the savage gang rape and near-fatal beating of a young woman jogger in Central Park, New York City, by a group of inner-city youths. Upon arrest, the suspects expressed little remorse and described their behavior as a "wilding." Less than two months later, three eighteen-year-old young men from a wealthy New Jersey suburb, stars of the high school football team, were accused of abusing a seventeen-year-old mentally impaired young woman. The young men allegedly forced her to perform sexual acts and stuck a broomstick into her vagina while eight other youths watched. These disturbing incidents are the tip of the iceberg; widespread sexual violence by teenagers

BOX 9.3 Summary of Experimental Analysis of Rape Cues

The penile plethysmograph has been used to identify specific cues that trigger arousal in rapists. Abel, Barlow, Blanchard, and Guild (1977) asked rapists and nonrapists to listen to two different types of audiotapes. One tape gave a detailed description of mutually enjoyable intercourse with an enthusiastic partner. The other described the forcible rape of the same partner, with the resistant victim expressing physical pain and emotional distress. Both groups showed considerable sexual arousal to the descriptions of mutually consenting, loving sex. Only the rapists, however, showed significant degrees of tumescence in response to the rape cues. Demonstrating the problems in relying only upon sex offenders' verbal reports, the rapists claimed little sexual arousal in response to the description of forcible rape. But their penises gave them away in this instance.

Abel and his colleagues also studied the reactions of rapists to three different audiotapes. The first described a rapist physically abusing a resisting woman but without subsequent sexual intercourse. The second described the rapist engaging in sexual intercourse with the same woman, against her will. The third consisted of a narrative of sexual intercourse with mutual consent. The results showed that the rapists did respond with increases in penile tumescence to the first tape with its emphasis on aggression. But the second and third tapes elicited greater levels of penile tumescence than the first.

The penile plethysmograph may not, however, always yield valid results. Many sex offenders can voluntarily inhibit their erections to pedophilic or rape stimuli. (Hall, 1989).

cuts across racial and socioeconomic lines and seems on the increase.

Crime statistics show that 30 percent of rapes and 50 percent of child molesting are committed by adolescents under age eighteen (Davis & Leitenberg, 1987). The majority of pedophiles report that their sexual attraction to young boys and girls developed before age eighteen (Abel, 1989). Adolescent sex offenders are a heterogeneous group. Some may be "pure" paraphiliacs, whereas others sexually abuse their victims as part of a more general antisocial behavior pattern. A large proportion, particularly rapists, have a high conduct-disorder rate (Becker, 1988).

One of the suspects in the rape and beating of the Central Park jogger.

Why do teenagers commit these crimes? Why does the problem seem to be increasing now? We have no good answers to these questions. Antipornography groups claim one factor is the explicit association between sex and violence in movies, rock videos, and music lyrics. "Slasher" films eroticize the rape, torture, and murder of women. In the song "Predator," Genocide sings of a "heart ripped from the chest decapitated, a meal of vaginas and breasts" (*Time,* June 5, 1989). The cumulative effect of repeated media images may be to blunt teenagers' sensitivity to women and condition sexual arousal to violent activities.

Other Paraphilias. Several other forms of paraphilias have been identified. Among these are *frotteurism* (rubbing against a nonconsenting and unsuspecting person[10]); necrophilia (obsession with corpses); klismaphilia (sexually excited by enemas); coprophilia (sexually excited by feces); and zoophilia (sexually excited by animals).

The Consequences of Sexual Abuse. Sexual abuse victims suffer many negative consequences. A Los Angeles study of a representative sample of 3,132 adults showed sexually abused men and women as two to four times more likely to develop major depression, alcohol or drug dependence, or an anxiety disorder (Burnam et al., 1988). **Sexual abuse,** defined as any forced or pressured sexual contact, had a similar impact on male or female victims. Childhood

[10] Anyone who has spent much time in a crowded, impersonal, and public place—such as the New York City subway—might have witnessed this type of behavior.

One of the youths alleged to have sexually assaulted a mentally handicapped girl in New Jersey.

sexual abuse was a more significant predictor of later mental disorder than abuse as an adult.

Several studies have examined the specific aftermath of rape. Researchers differentiated between the short- and long-term effects. The victim's immediate reaction involves depression, general anxiety, social maladjustment, and frequently sexual dysfunction, as noted earlier. After roughly three months these reactions fade, although sexual dysfunction and rape-specific anxiety remain. The anxiety and sexual dysfunction may continue even after one year, resulting in reduced enjoyment of life (Ellis, 1983; Frank et al., 1988). In a community-based study, Kilpatrick and Calhoun (1988) observed that 57 percent of rape victims developed PTSD (posttraumatic stress disorder) some time after the rape. The traumatic consequences of male rape, including the development of amnesia, are discussed in Chapter 6. Another troubling finding is that sexually abused children are at increased risk for becoming sex abusers themselves (Crewdson, 1988). Even brief psychological treatment can significantly reduce anxiety and enhance self-esteem in rape victims (Resick et al., 1988).

Theories and Causes of Paraphilias

Different theories have been advanced to explain the bizarre phenomena of paraphilias. In the psychodynamic view, all paraphilias are expressions of a common underlying psychopathology, namely, a form of personality disturbance. Thus a pathological sexuality derives from unconscious, intrapsychic conflicts originating in early childhood. For example, the exhibitionist defends himself against underlying castration fears. The observer's reaction to the sight of his genitals supposedly reassures him that he is not castrated. For the transvestite, cross-dressing as a female serves as a symbolical protection against castration. Abel (1989) rejects this theory of specific paraphilias as the product of particular psychological conflicts. He argues instead that evidence shows paraphiliacs suffering from a generalized lack of control over their sexual arousal and behavior.

Robert Stoller, a prominent psychoanalytic authority on sexual disorders, has argued that sexual aggression (e.g., sadomasochism) is simply a more extreme form of the same sexual drive that arouses people engaging in conventional sexual activity. The difference between a love bite and rape is only one of degree. Stoller asserts that "It is hostility—the desire, overt or hidden, to harm another person—that generates sexual excitement" (1979, p. 6). According to this view, sadomasochists and other sexual aggressives act out their unconscious hostility, whereas normals restrict this drive to the fantasy level or subordinate it to positive feelings of affection.

A behavioral or social-learning analysis emphasizes interpersonal and environmental events' importance in the development of paraphilias. Kinsey originally outlined this view.

> Learning and conditioning in connection with human sexual behavior involve the same sorts of processes as learning and conditioning in other types of behavior. . . . From its parents, from other adults, from other children, and from the community at large, the child begins to acquire its attitudes toward such things as nudity, the anatomic differences between males and females and the reproductive functions; and these attitudes may have considerable significance in determining its subsequent acceptance or avoidance of particular types of overt sexual activity. (Kinsey, Pomeroy, Martin, & Gebhard, 1953, pp. 644–45)

Repeated masturbation to deviant fantasies endow these fantasies with exaggerated sexual erotic values which then instigate deviant sexual behavior. Repeatedly pairing sexual arousal with a formerly neutral stimulus can result in the experimental induction of a mild fetish. Rachman and Hodgson (1968) showed that penile erection from pornographic stimuli could be classically conditioned to a previously neutral stimulus, for example, a boot.

Parents may model and maintain deviant sexuality patterns through direct and vicarious reinforcement. Stoller's (1967) study of transvestites, for example, revealed initiation into transvestism by wives and mothers, with strong reinforcement for dressing in feminine clothes.

The following adult transvestite's narrative illustrates social learning's influence on this behavior's development.

> *The highlights of my life as a girl came when I was between the ages of ten and seventeen. I had an aunt who was childless and wanted to take me through the steps from childhood to young womanhood. She knew of my desires to be a girl. I would spend every summer at her ranch. The first thing she would do was to give me a pixie haircut, which always turned out pretty good since I would avoid getting a haircut for two months before I went to her ranch. She then would take me into the bedroom and show me all my pretty new things she had bought me. The next day, dressed as a girl, I would accompany her to town and we would shop for a new dress for me. To everyone she met, she would introduce me as her "niece."*
>
> *This went on every year until I was thirteen years old. Then she decided I should start my womanhood. I will never forget that summer. When I arrived I got the same pixie haircut as usual but when we went into the bedroom there laid out on the bed was a girdle, a garter belt and bra, size 32AA, and my first pair of nylons. She then took me over to the new dressing table she had bought me and slid back the top to reveal my very own makeup kit. I was thrilled to death. She said she wanted her "niece" to start off right and it was time I started to develop a bust.*
>
> *The next morning I was up early to ready myself for the usual shopping trip to town, only this time it was for a pair of high heels and a new dress. I remember I stuffed my bra with cotton, put on my garter belt, and slipped on my nylons with no effort. After all, I became an expert from practice the night before. My aunt applied my lipstick because I was so excited I couldn't get it on straight. Then off to town we went, aunt and "niece." What a wonderful day. I shall never forget it.* (Stoller, 1967, p. 335)

Paraphilias, with the exception of sadomasochism, are confined almost exclusively to men. Instances of these disorders in women are extremely rare, and those women who do commit them have a high rate of mental illness or handicap (O'Connor, 1987). To explain this disparity between men and women, Money and Lamacz (1989) have proposed that in the psychobiology of sexual development, a pattern of brain functioning is established that programs normal erotic imagery and actions. They call this brain program a **"lovemap."** The prenatal, structural differentiation of the male fetus is more complex than that of the female fetus. Sexual development is correspondingly more complex in the male and more subject to errors. These errors involve either the displacement or distortion of elements within the species-specific, or phyletic, sequence of behaviors leading to sexual activity—what Money and Lamacz (1989) call "vandalized lovemaps." For example, fondling a sexual partner is normal but becomes abnormal (a paraphilia) if it is displaced, as when a man becomes aroused by rubbing against an unsuspecting stranger (frotteurism).

The social-learning explanation of the male–female imbalance emphasizes the greater role of visual cues and fantasy in male as opposed to female sexual arousal, as well as men's greater participation in more varied and impersonal sex. Men have more opportunities for learning unusual arousal patterns (Gagnon, 1977). The paraphilias, as Money points out, involve some forbidden image repeatedly enacted in fantasy or in reality.

None of the theories discussed adequately explains the etiology or maintenance of the paraphilias. At present, we have too little scientific evidence to permit anything more than informed speculation.

Treatment

Treatments of paraphilias include psychodynamic, behavioral, family, and drug therapy. Lengthy psychodynamic treatment has not proved effective with these problems, but alternative therapies have been successful.

Behavioral treatments focus on three major areas: the suppression or elimination in the paraphiliac of the unwanted or undesirable sexual arousal; the substitution of a more acceptable source of sexual arousal and behavior; and the development of self-control or coping skills to resist the problem behavior (Abel & Rouleau, 1990).

Aversion therapy suppresses unwanted sexual arousal. Although different methods have been used, the most common employs aversive imagery. In this technique of **covert sensitization,** the patient first imagines engaging in the deviant behavior and then imagines an aversive consequence. For example, an exhibitionist might be instructed to imagine that just as he approaches the woman he plans to expose himself to, a police car with flashing red lights and blaring siren draws up and he is apprehended. One advantage of this technique is its use as a self-control method by the patient any time he senses the urge to expose himself. For the technique to be effective, the patient must repeatedly and actively rehearse this association between his deviant activities and realistic aversive consequences. Maletzky (1980) has reported a success rate of roughly 90 percent in treating exhibitionists with aversive imagery, with follow-up evaluations for up to two-and-a-half years.

Orgasmic reconditioning helps paraphiliacs develop sexual arousal to more conventional heterosexual activities. Consider, for example, the treatment of Jack, the transvestite police officer described earlier. He was instructed to continue to masturbate in his usual fashion to his deviant fantasies of cross-dressing and sadomasochism. Then, just prior to *ejaculatory inevitability*—the point at which the male ejaculates involuntarily—he switched to an erotic fantasy of more conventional heterosexual behavior. To ease this switch to heterosexual arousal, he was given pictures from magazines of nude women. Gradually, Jack made the switch earlier in the sequence until he could initiate masturbation and reach orgasm exclusively using heterosexual fantasies. Prior to treatment he had shown virtually no arousal to conventional heterosexual stimuli. Following approximately twenty sessions with orgasmic reconditioning, he displayed strong erections to it.

Self-control training begins with assessing the thoughts, feelings, and events preceding exposure. The patient is shown how he actively contributes to his problem by focusing on inappropriate thoughts and feelings. He learns to recognize early warning signs of temptation to expose himself and then to institute self-control procedures at that point. If he waits too long and the temptation becomes too strong, his chances of self-control greatly diminish. If tension or anxiety precipitate exposure, the patient is taught relaxation procedures as an alternative to it. Social skills training instructs him how to relate better to adult partners. Finally, treatment emphasizes relapse prevention (Laws, 1989). The risk of relapse following initially successful therapy is high in these disorders, so the therapist coaches the patient to recognize and cope with early warning signs of the return of his deviant behavior. Using this combination of behavior treatment strategies, Abel (1989) reports a 95 percent reduction in child molesting by pedophiles. This impressive success rate does not include pedophiles who dropped out of treatment and might be considered treatment failures. If dropouts are included, the success rate would obviously be lower, and controlled studies are lacking (Rosen & Hall, in press). Some authorities doubt whether pedophiles can ever be cured. No convincing evidence exists of the clinical effectiveness of these methods with rapists.

Family therapy is the most recent treatment approach in this field and is the most widely used method in incest cases (Lanyon, 1986). Interrelationships among family members are assumed responsible for the specific sexual disorder, and that all of them need to be involved in its treatment.

Pharmacotherapy to treat paraphiliacs involves the administration of an antiandrogen drug, Provera. This drug reduces *testosterone* level and may also directly affect brain centers controlling sexual behavior. Because it drastically reduces a person's sexual desire and fantasies, Provera's effects have been called chemical castration. For this reason, its use is controversial. Another major problem is that the unwanted sexual arousal returns once the patient discontinues the drug. The positive effects of Provera, nonetheless, encourage the search for more effective chemical means of controlling behavior often unresponsive to psychological methods.

GENDER IDENTITY DISORDER

Transsexualism

Description. *Transsexuals* believe they are a member of the opposite sex. They identify completely with the opposite sex. This belief—and desire—is summarized in the favorite phrase of the male transsexual: "I'm a woman trapped in a man's body." The ultimate aim of transsexuals is to obtain a "sex change" operation—surgery that will alter their bodies to that of the opposite sex. More men than women initially applied for these operations, but recent reports suggest an equal number of would-be patients are women wishing to become men. Transsexualism is a rare disorder, and its causes are unknown. A rough estimate is that there are 10,000 transsexuals in the United States, with six to eight male transsexuals for each female (Levine & Lothstein, 1981).

Transsexuals should not be confused with transvestites or homosexuals. Transvestites are almost always heterosexuals who achieve specific sexual satisfaction by cross-dressing. They do not make the fundamental and consistent identification with the opposite sex that the transsexual does. Although a transsexual is sexually attracted to other men, the attraction is not homosexual. Instead, the transsexual claims that "she" relates to men as a woman does.

The following excerpt from a clinical interview with Todd, a seventeen-year-old transsexual, illustrates his image of his own body.

Therapist: When you say, "I feel like a woman," do you imagine yourself having a female body?

Todd: Yeah.

Therapist: Do you imagine yourself having a woman's breasts?

Todd: Yeah.

Therapist: Do you imagine yourself having a penis?

Todd: No penis.

Therapist: Do you imagine yourself having a vagina?

Todd: Yeah, I guess.

Therapist: Do you imagine yourself with a vagina, or not?

Todd: Well, I just—yeah, that's—I'm not sure what it is. It's just the sexual part, right?

Therapist: It's the opening and the canal inside.

Todd: Oh, yeah.

Therapist: You imagine that?

Todd: Yes.

Therapist: So when you say you feel like a woman, you imagine yourself with a woman's body?

Todd: Yeah.

Christine Jorgensen, the first person to undergo a sex change operation, in Europe, from male to female. She died in California in 1989.

Another excerpt from the same interview shows that Todd was not homosexual.

Therapist: You don't have to be a woman to have sex with a man.

Todd: Yeah, but it would be kinda gross.

Therapist: Why?

Todd: Because—I don't know—I think that's very gross.

Therapist: But obviously you know there are a substantial number of men who have sex with men without becoming a woman. You know that?

Todd: Yeah.

Therapist: It's not new.

Todd: It doesn't appeal to me too much.

Therapist: So one of the things is that if you were a woman you could have sex with men in a way that you would find more acceptable?

Todd: Yeah.

Therapist: That's one thing.

Todd: That's the basic problem. I want to be a woman before I want to have sexual relations with a man.

Therapist: Do you have strong religious feelings about homosexuality being sinful?

Todd: I don't believe in God.

Therapist: So it's not a religious thing. But there is something else about homosexuality that really disturbs you, as not being right?

Todd: I just—like I said—it's not very important really, sex is just something people do for pleasure. It's not necessary to survive except if you're going to have children, unless you're going to have a baby with them, it's not a big thing.' (Green, 1979, p. 125)

Treatment. In the 1960s, **sex reassignment surgery** became an established form of treatment. In the male-to-female reassignment, the man first takes *estrogens* to develop breasts and other female characteristics. Next, he is castrated and an artificial clitoris and vagina constructed. Women who wish to become men initially take *androgens* to reduce their breasts, develop male characteristics, and stop menstruation. A surgeon then removes the uterus and remaining breast tissue, and constructs a penis, which, however, is unsatisfactory for intercourse and cannot be stimulated to orgasm.

The merits of sex reassignment surgery have been vigorously debated. One influential study found that transsexuals who had undergone surgery were no better adjusted subsequently than those who had not (Meyer & Reter, 1979). This study has been criticized for various methodological inadequacies, including a failure to assess patients' psychological adaptation (Lothstein, 1982). The best estimate is that roughly two thirds of patients show improved adjustment following surgery, with females-to-males faring better (Abramovitz, 1986). The negative outcome rate is significant—about 7 percent request reversal, require psychiatric hospitalization, or commit suicide.

Psychological treatment of transsexuals has been limited primarily to behavioral methods, as illustrated in the following case study by Barlow, Reynolds, and Agras (1973).

> *The patient was a seventeen-year-old male transsexual. Several different measures of his sexual orientation and gender identity were monitored consistently before, during, and after therapy, including attitudinal responses toward transsexualism, such as "I want to have female genitals"; penile circumference changes in response to slides of nude males and females; also a daily record of the number and nature of his sexual fantasies was kept; as well as a detailed behavioral checklist of gender-specific behaviors, like walking and talking.*
>
> *The initial treatment to increase heterosexual arousal by gradually having the client imagine heterosexual*

stimuli while sexually aroused had no effect. Forty-eight daily half-hour sessions of punishment of transsexual fantasies with electric shock also failed to induce any changes. The focus of therapy was then shifted to developing appropriate sex-role behaviors. Modeling, behavior rehearsal, and videotaped feedback were used to modify the most obvious signs of gender identity confusion—the client's excessively effeminate manner of walking, standing, and sitting which elicited social scorn. This gender-role reshaping program was then expanded to incorporate typical masculine interpersonal contacts at high school—for example, discussing football or girlfriends—and finally, to voice retraining. At the end of this three-month phase of therapy, the client liked his newfound masculine manner of acting but still reported feeling socially and sexually like a girl. Moreover, objective measures of his sexual arousal, urges, and fantasies remained at the pretreatment level despite overt behavioral changes.

A direct attempt was accordingly made to develop competing gender-appropriate thoughts and fantasies. A female therapist praised the client for fantasizing sexual involvement with a girl for increasingly longer durations. Transsexual attitudes decreased for the first time, while female fantasies predominated over previous male fantasies. In contrast to these subjective reports of sexual fantasies about females, penile tumescence changes indicated no such arousal. A classical conditioning procedure in which slides of attractive females—as a conditioned stimulus—were paired with attractive male slides—as an unconditioned stimulus—rapidly increased physiological arousal, further enhancing masculine "ways" of sitting, standing, and walking. The client's remaining homosexual arousal was eliminated by aversion therapy, which now proved to be effective.

At a one-year follow-up the client's transsexual attitudes had disappeared, subjective and physiological measures showed sexual arousal to female stimuli, and masculine role behavior remained stable. The client had a steady girlfriend. A follow-up six-and-a-half years after therapy by a psychologist who had not been involved in the original treatment revealed stable progress. (Barlow, Abel, & Blanchard, 1979)

Despite the success in this and a few other cases (Khanna, Desai, & Channabasavana, 1987), very few therapists have adopted it. There is general pessimism about the effects of psychological (including behavioral) treatment with transsexuals, most of whom have severe psychological problems.

Gender Identity Disorder of Childhood

Description. For males, gender identity disorder is marked by a persistent distress at being a boy, coupled with a desire to be a girl. Such a boy finds his genitals disgusting, and his behavior goes well beyond the fairly typical tendency of some young boys, for example, to dress up occasionally in their mother's clothes or assume the role of a girl in play. Here the boy does so persistently, rejecting typical boys' games. Behavior such as cross-dressing is not an isolated act but part of a consistent pattern or syndrome. For girls, gender identity disorder is marked by a comparable unhappiness about their anatomy and the desire to possess a penis and be a boy.

In the following excerpt, a mother describes her eight-year-old son.

Mother: He acts like a sissy. He has expressed the wish to be a girl. He doesn't play with boys. He's afraid of boys, because he's afraid to play boys' games. He used to like to dress in girls' clothing. He would still like to, only we have absolutely put our foot down. And he talks like a girl, sometimes walks like a girl, acts like a girl.

Therapist: How long have you had these concerns?

Mother: For about three years.

Therapist: What was the very earliest thing that you noticed?

Mother: Wanting to put on a blouse of mine, a pink and white blouse which if he'd put it on would fit him like a dress. And he was very excited about the whole thing, and leaped around and danced around the room. I didn't like it and I just told him to take it off and I put it away. He kept asking for it. He wanted to wear that blouse again. And I said, "No, I'm sorry that belongs to me, not to you. You wear your clothes and I wear mine." But he asked many times for it.

Therapist: You mentioned that he's expressed the wish to be a girl.

Mother: I remember distinctly his making this remark. And it's such a dramatic remark that you don't forget it. He'd make it many times.

Therapist: What does he say, exactly?

Mother: "I would like to be a girl. I don't like to be a boy. Boys are too rough. When I play boys' games the ball hurts my legs. I don't want to go to school today because I'll have to play baseball." So he goes and plays gently with the girls.

Therapist: Has he ever said, "I am a girl"?

Mother: Playing in front of the mirror, he'll undress for bed, and he's standing in front of the mirror and he took his penis and he folded it under, and he said, "Look, Mommy, I'm a girl." (Green, 1987, pp. 2–3)

Causes. We do not know what causes gender identity disorder or transsexualism. Among the possible biological influences are the effects of prenatal hormones. Although some findings indicate that young boys whose mothers took female hormones during pregnancy may show fewer "masculine" behaviors (Yalom, Green, & Fisk, 1973), there is no evidence of this resulting in gender identity disorder or adult transsexualism. It is not unusual for young boys to engage in some stereotypically "feminine" activities, and young girls in some "masculine" behavior, without any abnormal gender development.

Both psychodynamic and behavioral theories emphasize the importance of early childhood experiences in psychosexual development. Psychodynamic theorists believe that the child must identify successfully with the parent of the opposite sex. Behavioral theorists focus on parents as role models and sources of social reinforcement (Rosen & Hall, 1984). Yet the family environment seems to have surprisingly little effect on the development of gender disorders. Green (1978) studied sixteen children reared by transsexual parents. Most of the children knew about their parent's sex change, all became heterosexual, and none developed a gender identity problem. We cannot even predict with any certainty that children with such a problem will develop into adult transsexuals. Many become heterosexual (Zucker, Finegan, Deering, & Bradley, 1984), others homosexual or bisexual, as discussed later (Green, 1987).

Treatment. The treatment of gender identity disorder has aroused considerable controversy, as illustrated in the following case study by Rekers and Lovaas (1974).

> *Kraig was a physically normal five-year-old boy referred for treatment by the family physician. He had cross-dressed since the age of two, played with cosmetic items belonging to his mother and grandmother, displayed exaggerated feminine mannerisms, preferred to play with little girls, and emphasized his desire to be a girl. The two therapists, Rekers and Lovaas, helped Kraig's mother alter her behavior to reinforce more masculine activities and decrease gender inappropriate behavior. The result was that Kraig's gender disorder decreased dramatically, and he began to act in a more masculine manner. Using sophisticated methodological control procedures, Rekers and Lovaas were able to show that this behavioral change was due directly to the reinforcement procedures that formed the basis of the treatment program. At a follow-up over two years later, Kraig looked and acted like any other boy his age.*

The therapists justified their treatment program on the following grounds.

1. This sort of exaggerated feminine behavior in boys subjects them to social isolation and ridicule by their peers.
2. Cross-gender preferences predict severe adjustment problems in adulthood. (Most adult transsexuals and transvestites report a history of childhood gender disturbances.)
3. Altering cross-gender preferences is most likely to be successful during early development.
4. The treatment program was consistent with the parents' wishes, the social mores and cultural expectations of the community in which the family lived, the local law, the views of other professionals, with the child himself cooperating throughout the program.

Critics of this sort of program have argued that adult pathology, such as transsexualism, cannot be reliably predicted from highly effeminate behavior in early childhood. Gay activists have gone further condemning Rekers's program as "homosexual genocide." His strongly moralistic descriptions of homosexuality as "an unfortunate perversion" have understandably invited these criticisms. Other objectors have noted the emphasis in these programs on the masculine sex role. As an alternative, they advocate the idea of *androgyny* (Winkler, 1977). Androgyny is neither "masculine" nor "feminine" behavior in the stereotyped sense, but includes supposedly desirable attributes from each—for example, strength and independence from the masculine role, affection and compassion from the feminine role. These critics assert that androgynous behavior is more likely to lead to better adjustment than extreme sex-role typing as masculine or feminine.

Aside from the ethical issues this type of operant-conditioning program has raised, some have also questioned its efficacy. Green (1987) reports far less success in trying to change the sexual identity of these boys. Rekers's approach, he notes, "ignores reasons why they prefer traditionally 'feminine' activities. Why have they chosen to play with dolls and not trucks? Is it only that they have been previously 'conditioned' to make these preferences? Simply conditioning such a boy so that he obtains rewards for alternate behaviors and is punished for earlier preferences may make the child look different. But to what extent is self-concept changed?" (p. 261).

EGO-DYSTONIC HOMOSEXUALITY

The history of homosexuality and its treatment by the medical and psychological professions has been marked by sharp controversy and radically different views. Until the 1970s, the American Psychiatric Association officially listed homosexuality as a major clinical disorder in its *Diagnostic and Statistical Manual of Mental Illnesses (DSM-II)*. In response to pressure from gay activist groups and concerned professionals, a change was made in *DSM-III* in 1980. Homosexuality was no longer inevitably seen as a form of psychopathology. *DSM-III* recognized it as a possible nonpathological, alternative life-style. The category *ego-dystonic homosexuality* was, nevertheless, included as a diagnosis for those homosexuals who, distressed by their sexual orientation, wish to become heterosexuals.

This action by the American Psychiatric Association was a compromise. It reflected the majority view of professionals that homosexuality is a normal variation of sexual life-styles. Research has consistently failed to document the assertion that homosexuals are more disturbed than comparable groups of heterosexuals (Bell & Weinberg, 1978). Moreover, Masters and Johnson (1979) found no physiological differences in sexual arousal and response between heterosexual and homosexual men and women.

The American Psychiatric Association's action did not, however, satisfy lay and professional groups' different objections. For some, it either did not go far enough or went too far. Among professionals, a minority continued to insist that all homosexuality is inherently a form of psychopathology (e.g., Socarides, 1978). Others protested the inclusion of any reference to homosexuality in *DSM-III* and its revision. In concert with gay activist groups, they condemned any approach aimed at altering homosexual preference even if the individual homosexual so desires. As Davison (1976) argued, "the very existence of change-of-orientation programs strengthens societal prejudices against homosexuality and contributes to the self-hate and embarrassment that are determinants of the voluntary desire by some homosexuals to become heterosexual" (p. 157).

Compared to only two decades ago, homosexuals lead more public lives. Gay activist groups and working political alliances increasingly pressure society to change laws and regulations they regard as infringements of their civil rights. Yet, homosexuals remain a minority and often feel the sting of societal discrimination. For example, in an annual national survey of U.S. students entering college in 1986, 52 percent supported laws banning homosexual behavior (*The New York Times,* January 12, 1987). This marked the first time that a majority of students had held such an opinion. Their attitudes were probably influenced by the AIDS crisis, as homosexuals and intravenous drug abusers are the two groups with the highest rates of this disease.

Theories of Homosexuality

Historically, psychodynamic theory has been very influential in shaping clinicians' views. In this view, homosexuality is the product of an overprotective, "close-binding" mother and a distant, ineffectual father. These negative parental influences are said to result in the person getting stuck at an "immature" level of psychosexual development (Bieber et al., 1962). As discussed later, evidence does not support this theory. The behavioral view has emphasized the role of learning principles in the development of homosexuality (Feldman & MacCulloch, 1971). It has been assumed that if heterosexual encounters were aversive, perhaps because of undue anxiety, and early homosexual experiences rewarding, the person would develop a homosexual orientation. This framework seems too general, for it does not specify the critical conditions under which homosexuality would or would not develop.

Gay and lesbian protests have helped to change the way in which homosexuality is perceived by mental health professionals.

Neither the psychodynamic nor the behavioral view denies the contribution of genetic or biological determinants, but they assign little importance to these factors. Recent research findings have, however, pointed to the biological bases of homosexuality. In one study, approximately 1,000 homosexuals and 500 heterosexuals in the San Francisco Bay area were interviewed about their childhood (Bell, Weinberg, & Hammersmith, 1981). There were no differences between homosexuals and heterosexuals in their relationships with their mothers. Homosexual men did not identify more with their mothers than heterosexual men, as predicted by psychodynamic theory. Lesbians identified with their fathers less, not more, than heterosexual women. The only difference between the two groups was that homosexuals recollected more of their early lack of conformity to traditional sex roles. Roughly half of the homosexual men said that they had disliked typical boys' games and liked girls' games. Lesbians had preferred boys' games as little girls. The researchers could find nothing in the family or social backgrounds of these homosexuals explaining this childhood gender nonconformity. They concluded, therefore, that it reflected an innate, biological predisposition.

This study by Bell and his colleagues (1981) must be interpreted cautiously. Their findings rely on childhood memories, which are often biased and influenced by what we presently believe about a subject. Could the participants in this study have reported what they now believed as adults about the origins of their homosexuality, rather than what actually occurred? We cannot know the answer to that question. Furthermore, the researchers arrived at their conclusion about a biological predisposition by a process of elimination. In other words, because they were unable to find any psychosocial explanation, they inferred a biological one. Yet, these results are consistent with other research.

A second study, by Green (1987), followed forty-four extremely feminine boys for fifteen years, from early childhood to adolescence or young adulthood. Three quarters of what Green called these "sissy" boys—boys with what Bell and colleagues termed **childhood gender nonconformity**—later became homosexuals or bisexuals.[11] Only one of a comparison group of typically masculine boys became a homosexual. In cases where parents tried to discourage feminine behavior, their sons' homosexual tendencies were lessened but not reversed. Similarly, treatment by professionals designed to alter this pattern of behavior did not prevent later homosexuality, although the boys did show more typical masculine behavior. No consistent evidence emerged indicating that parents "shaped" their feminine sons. Some, in fact, had other typically masculine sons.

These findings support the view that some children have a biological predisposition to be homosexual. But not all homosexuality can be explained in this way. One quarter of these "sissy boys" became heterosexuals. And many male homosexuals recall typical masculine boyhoods.

Whether this biological predisposition is genetic or the result of prenatal influences appears uncertain, although a higher concordance rate exists for homosexuality between identical twins than between fraternal twins (Cooper, 1978). In a major review of the biology of sexual orientation in animals and human beings, Ellis and Ames (1987) concluded that "complex combinations of genetic, hormonal, neurological, and environmental factors operating prior to birth largely determine what an individual's sexual orientation will be, although the orientation itself awaits the onset of puberty to be activated, and may not entirely stabilize until early adulthood. The involvement of learning, only appears to alter how, when, and where the orientation is expressed" (p. 251).

A critical implication of this biologically based view is that changing an adult's sexual orientation should be difficult if not impossible. It is to this controversial topic that we next turn.

Can Homosexuals Become Heterosexuals? Psychotherapies, including hundreds of hours of intensive psychoanalytic therapy, have proved ineffective (Bancroft, 1974). Behavior therapy has not fared much better, particularly with homosexuals with no history of heterosexual interests (O'Leary & Wilson, 1987). Where behavioral methods have proved effective, the homosexual patients had histories of heterosexual behavior, leading some to suggest that these men were really bisexuals (Ellis & Ames, 1987).

An apparent exception to the ineffectiveness of psychotherapy and behavior therapy is Masters and Johnson's (1979) study. They treated fifty-four men and thirteen women dissatisfied with their homosexuality, using the same intensive two-week treatment program described earlier in this chapter. These patients were accepted for therapy only after careful screening to ensure that they were highly motivated and sincere about changing their sexual preferences. Additionally, all clients had to have an understanding partner of the opposite sex willing to participate in the treatment program. A high percentage were married—61 percent of the men, 54 percent of the women—and all of their spouses participated in the treatment. Masters and Johnson found that two thirds of the sample had become heterosexual following treatment.

The limitations of this study must be stressed in interpreting what appears to be the unusually posi-

[11] Contrary to the researcher's predictions, only one of the feminine boys became an adult transsexual.

tive outcome of Masters and Johnson's treatment. First, their patients were highly motivated, sincere, and fortunate enough to have a willing and able partner of the opposite sex to provide sexual and nonsexual support and guidance critical to making such fundamental behavioral changes. Caution must be exercised in attempting to generalize from these findings to other samples of homosexuals who might seek heterosexual reorientation. Second, Barlow (1980) has pointed out that Masters and Johnson's follow-up data on these dissatisfied homosexuals are not superior to previous reports in the clinical literature. Sixteen of the forty-three men and three of the ten women who had responded to the initial therapy could not be contacted at follow-up. Masters and Johnson did not include their data in the summary statistics, a procedure that probably made the follow-up failure rate of 28 percent appear lower than it actually was. An estimated failure rate of roughly 45 percent is more plausible.

We can conclude that, overall, the psychological therapies appear largely ineffective in helping homosexuals become heterosexuals. This conclusion is consistent with the view that homosexuality is biologically determined. Such a view is contrary to what clinicians have usually believed. It is also inconsistent with what public opinion surveys indicate, namely, that much of the population of the United States believes homosexuality results from various experiences in childhood or adolescence.

SUMMARY

1. Systematic study of sexual disorders can be traced largely to Freud's contributions in the early part of this century. Kinsey's surveys of American men and women's sexual practices were the next advance in our knowledge, but the pioneering research of Masters and Johnson in the 1960s identified the psychobiological bases of the sexual response and its dysfunctions.
2. Sexual dysfunctions are divided into disorders of desire, arousal, orgasm, and pain. Low sexual desire is the absence of sexual fantasies and wish for sexual activity. Male arousal disorders involve impaired erections (a condition also known as *impotence*); female disorders, the absence of vaginal lubrication. Orgasmic disorders refer to a man or woman's inability to reach orgasm following sexual arousal. Painful intercourse, or dyspareunia, and vaginismus are the most common pain disorders. A variety of psychosocial and biological factors can cause the different sexual dysfunctions. A distinction is drawn between historical influences (e.g., a strict religious upbringing that equates sex with sin) and current causes, such as negative self-evaluation and anxiety about sexual performance.
3. Modern sex therapy derives mainly from Masters and Johnson's methods and effectively treats a number of male and female dysfunctions. These psychological methods are also supplemented by medical techniques, particularly in treating difficult erectile problems. Homosexuals experience similar dysfunctions to heterosexual men and women and respond equally well to sex therapy.
4. Paraphilias are deviant sexual activities punishable legally in our society. Until recently, most of our knowledge about paraphilias was obtained from men imprisoned because of their behavior. More recent research, in which paraphiliacs in the community voluntarily seeking treatment were guaranteed confidentiality, shows a broader extent of deviant sexual activities than previously thought. Paraphiliacs often commit numerous offenses, engage in several different kinds of paraphilia, and have normal sexual involvements with adult partners.
5. Sex with someone thirteen years old or younger is known as child molesting or pedophilia. One major study revealed that 27 percent of women and 16 percent of men had been sexually abused as children, and the incidence seems to be increasing. Incest is when the abuse occurs within the same family, typically between siblings or between father and daughter. A large number of pedophiles who molest their own children also abuse children from outside the family. Rape is a violent crime whose victims range from young children to the elderly. The frequency of rape is difficult to estimate because only a fraction of cases are reported to the police. But it occurs often—one study found that 27.5 percent of college women reported rape or attempted rape. Rapists are insensitive to women's feelings and lack social skills compared with normals. Adolescents commit a significant amount of sexual aggression, including rape and child molestation.
6. Men and women who have been sexually assaulted are two to four times more likely to later develop a major mental disorder, especially if the assault occurred during childhood. Victims of rape suffer several negative consequences, including anxiety, depression, social maladjustment, and sexual dysfunction. Psychological treatment can help sexual abuse victims cope successfully with their trauma. Psychological treatment is effective with several paraphilias, such as exhibitionism and pedophilia. Medication, or "chemical castration," has been recommended in especially resistant cases.
7. Transsexualism is a gender identity disorder in which the person believes that he or she is a member of the opposite sex. Sex reassignment surgery is often used to treat these individuals. Gender identity disorder of childhood for boys is the strong desire to be a girl and is marked by cross-dressing and rejection of male anatomy. For girls, it is indicated by comparable unhappiness with their anatomy, and the desire to have a penis and be a boy.
8. Homosexuality in general is no longer generally considered a clinical disorder. Ego-dystonic homosexuality is, nevertheless, still used as a diagnosis for homosexuals who wish to be heterosexuals. Homosexuality seems to be biologically determined, and there is little evidence that even prolonged treatment can alter this sexual orientation.

Patssi Valdez, *The Headache* (1988). Acrylic on canvas, 12 × 19 inches. Courtesy of Daniel Saxon Gallery, Los Angeles.

10 PERSONALITY DISORDERS

All of us have ways of behaving that are hallmarks of our "personality." Most of us have some idiosyncrasies. Our unique styles characterize us to our friends, who describe us to others in terms of these styles. We may be described as shy or extroverted, bold or fearful, conforming or somewhat eccentric. Indeed, social conversations are filled with these general personality descriptions. The abnormalities of personality styles described in this chapter, however, are called personality disorders.

No sharp line divides normal from abnormal or disordered personalities (Millon, 1986). Psychologists study a continuum of personality styles to determine where on this continuum personality disorders begin. **Personality disorders** are maladaptive and inflexible ways of interacting; these rigid personality styles may create serious difficulties for the individual. Research involving structured interviews has estimated approximately 10 percent to 15 percent of the U.S. population may have a personality disorder (Gunderson, 1988; Zimmerman & Coryell, 1989). Believed to begin during childhood, personality disorders become relatively stable in adulthood. These maladaptive interacting styles remain constant in the face of change with age, the particular people a person interacts with, or medication. Although children can be diagnosed as having personality disorders, these diagnoses are typically used with adults. Personality disorders are diverse and range from those with relatively little impact on a person's vocational and professional functioning to those that severely affect every aspect of a person's life. As discussed in greater detail later, personality disorders can be diagnosed along with other clinical syndromes such as alcoholism, depression, and sexual dysfunction. All the personality disorders represent long-established patterns of behavior. In addition, personality disorders have serious implications for interactions with others as they are extremely difficult to change. Finally, they often cause more pain and anguish to others than to the afflicted individual.

Many developmental psychologists hypothesize that early parent–child relationships form the basis for later interpersonal styles and love relationships. Today, these professionals study how children form parental attachments and learn the workings of intimate relationships. This kind of research can be traced to Sigmund Freud's writings on parent–child relationships as models for later relationships. John Bowlby (1973) modified Freud's hypotheses by emphasizing cognitive developmental factors more than the sexual factors central to Freud's views. Current developmental research on attachment focuses on children first forming "working models" of how close relationships should operate and then adopting these models themselves. Indeed, in later relationships, children repeat certain attachment patterns, especially those of being either securely or insecurely attached to their parents (Main & Goldwyn, 1985). Insecurely attached children respond with anxiety to separation, whereas securely attached children handle separation well. Moreover, our relationship patterns with our parents often continue beyond childhood into our intimate adult relationships. Finally, biological and temperament factors are influential in personality development as evidenced by longitudinal studies indicating temperamental factors such as activity/withdrawal as early as age three (Chess & Thomas, 1977).

CLASSIFICATION OF PERSONALITY DISORDERS

The personality disorders are listed as Axis II disorders in the *DSM-III-R* (1987) classification system, whereas the types of disorders discussed so far in other chapters are called clinical syndrome, or Axis I, disorders. Most clinical syndrome disorders, such as major depression and even schizophrenia, have remission periods when symptoms become less intense or even nonexistent. In contrast, the features of personality disorders generally remain extremely stable across time. The differentiation between Axis I (clinical syndrome) and Axis II (personality disorder) is not based on the severity of the patient's symptoms as both types of disorders can seriously affect the afflicted individuals. But personality disorders seem to evolve early in life and are relatively enduring, especially after young adulthood.

The current diagnostic system used by mental health professionals (*DSM-III-R*) mandates that Axis II disorders (personality disorders) be noted in every case. Alternatively stated, every case must be evaluated on both Axis I and Axis II so that the presence or absence of clinical syndromes and personality disorders can be indicated in a diagnosis. Further, when clinicians diagnose, they also note whether the patient is coping with any medical conditions (Axis III) or unusual social stressors (Axis IV) as these conditions may predispose the patient to certain syndromes or disorders. Finally, the clinician provides a global assessment of the client's functioning on Axis V of the multiaxial system.

Considerable controversy has existed within psychology over clinicians' ability to diagnose personality disorders with test and interview information. One main problem for clinicians is that more than half of the individuals with one personality disorder also have at least one other personality disorder. Indeed, the clinicians and researchers who wrote the *DSM-III-R* indicated the absence of distinct boundaries between the various personality disorders. Yet, they believed the categorical system of classifying individuals was most appropriate at present. Here we follow *DSM-III-R*'s guidelines and discuss personality disorders as separate disorders, despite developments in the personality assessment field that may lead to other means of classifying individuals by taking into account the overlap between symptoms in the various personality disorders (Frances & Widiger, 1986; Trull, Widiger, & Guthrie, 1990). We will look into one alternative to the categorical means of assessment at the end of this chapter.

DSM-III-R groups the personality disorders into three main types:

I. Dramatic, emotional, or erratic
II. Anxious or fearful
III. Odd or eccentric

Table 10.1 lists the *DSM-III-R* personality disorders. Until recently, antisocial personality disorder was the only one backed by considerable research, and most abnormal psychology texts only discussed it because severe antisocial behavior causes obvious major problems for family, friends, and society. For example, the police and the judicial system have to deal with assaults and robberies. The legal decisions that must be made about what to do with someone convicted of such behavior, combined with the seriousness of such crimes, has consistently focused psychologists' interest on antisocial behavior's causes.

Despite the relative lack of interest in them until recently, other disorders such as dependent personality disorder and obsessive-compulsive personality disorder can certainly cause tremendous personal turmoil and serious interpersonal difficulty. Additionally, borderline personality disorders may also be ex-

TABLE 10.1 The Classification of Personality Disorders

Dramatic, Emotional, or Erratic Disorders
Narcissistic
Histrionic
Borderline
Antisocial
Anxious or Fearful Disorders
Dependent
Passive Aggressive
Obsessive-Compulsive
Avoidant
Odd or Eccentric Disorders
Paranoid
Schizotypal
Schizoid

Source: American Psychiatric Association: *Diagnostic and Statistical Manual of Mental Disorders, Third Edition, Revised.* Washington, DC, American Psychiatric Association, 1987.

tremely serious. As we shall see, 10 percent of borderline individuals eventually commit suicide. A number of other comparatively neglected personality disorders, detailed herein, are also now receiving considerable attention from researchers. The broad class of odd or eccentric personality disorders (paranoid, schizotypal, and schizoid), however, have not been the focus of much research. *DSM-III-R* states for each of these three disorders that there is "no information" about factors predisposing certain individuals to them. Thus, we shall briefly describe their essential features at the end of this chapter.

DRAMATIC, EMOTIONAL, OR ERRATIC DISORDERS

Narcissistic Personality Disorder

Definition and Symptoms. Do you love yourself? Do you think you are brilliant and attractive? Do you think that you are the kind of person anyone would want for a mate? Do you frequently have fantasies of power and beauty? Do you take advantage of others to achieve your own ends? Do you fish for comments? Do you crave the approval and attention of others? Do you have difficulty taking the perspective of others—to see things through their eyes? An individual with **narcissistic personality** disorder is likely to answer yes to most of these questions.

The word *narcissism* is derived from the Greek myth about Narcissus, a handsome young man told by his mother that he would have a long life if he never looked at his features. Despite her warning, Narcissus gazed into a spring at his reflection and fell in love with his own image. The flower named for him, the narcissus, sprang up where he died vainly trying to see his own image. The myth of Narcissus portrays the Greek view of self-interest as dangerous or even fatal (Bulfinch, 1979). As in the case of the myth, men are more likely to be narcissists than women. Approximately 10 percent of men and 6 percent of women display narcissistic characteristics (Millon, 1987).

Narcissism was described by Freud, yet received little research attention until recently when therapists, especially psychoanalysts, began to recognize common difficulties in their attempts to treat certain kinds of patients. Narcissists, they noted, do not develop close relations with a therapist easily, and they withdraw when the therapist challenges their exaggerated feelings of power, brilliance, and beauty.

Certain narcissistic tendencies may actually serve some people well. For example, to achieve success, actors, rock stars, and athletes may need to feel that others think they are brilliant and attractive. Thus, athletes craving attention and adulation may profit from this style or drive because it spurs them on in athletic play.

Muhammad Ali (previously known as Cassius Clay) was perhaps the best-known athlete in the world in the 1960s and 1970s. He became so famous that *Sports Illustrated* devoted a special cover story on him in 1989 in their Thirty-Fifth Anniversary Issue—the thirty-first time Ali had graced that magazine's cover. Naturally, Ali derived most of his fame from being the world heavyweight boxing champion, but as important, his narcissistic style probably made him even more famous than his sheer athletic prowess. Consider some of his self-descriptive comments:

- "I am *the* greatest!"
- "I am bea-u-ti-ful!"
- "These are my tools," Cassius said, pointing to his legs and his arms. "A good mechanic keeps his tools clean. I keep my teeth clean. I keep my body clean. I keep my hands clean. I keep my tools sharp and clean. . . . I keep every muscle I got sharp. I even do toe exercises. That's why I am so bouncy for my size. My backers own a jewel. I am clean and a sparkling champion." (Olsen, 1967, pp. 245–246)

When reporters in Miami asked Clay why he needed a nine-passenger automobile, he answered, "All big people have chariots. . . . I am the king of the world. I really need ten or fifteen of these things" (Olsen, 1967, p. 22).

After a fight for the championship with Sonny Liston, whom he defeated, Ali regaled news reporters with his poetry:

"Yes, the crowd did not dream when they laid down their money that they would see a total eclipse of Sonny" (Olsen, 1967, p. 20).

Ali's personal physician described him as follows:

> He's a narcissist. He loves himself above all people. You get to such a withdrawn state in narcissism that you begin to love yourself at all times. You'll notice that a narcissistic woman is always touching herself, looking in mirrors, clutching at herself, smoothing at her skirt, and all unconsciously, unaware. Cassius is the same way." (Olsen, 1967, p. 131)

Ali possessed more than a narcissistic style that caused people to either love or hate him. Not only did he have panache, he stood for certain ideas; he danced women off their feet; he recited poetry to the press; he preached; he became a Muslim and visited sick children in hospitals; he informed the U.S. government he was not going to Vietnam. Unfortunately, Ali is now seriously plagued by the brain disorder, Parkinson Syndrome (see Chapter 15). He now has serious memory problems and motor coordination difficulties (*Sports Illustrated,* November 1989).

Muhammad Ali won the world heavyweight boxing championship title. He loved himself, and he continually told the press, "I am the *greatest!"*

While some hated his narcissistic style, the Parkinson Syndrome prevents him from offering the poetry and quips his legion of fans once loved—all part of a personality package that made him "the greatest."

People catapulted into the public eye are probably at risk for developing narcissism—especially when they have certain family backgrounds. In most cases, however, real or imagined success highlights narcissists' basic self-esteem problem, and they become anxious and/or depressed when their sense of self-worth is threatened. Additionally, narcissists frequently become caught in an unending pursuit of adulation. They emphasize exterior trappings of success, such as automobiles, lavish homes, and flashy clothing. In making purchases, their emphasis is on the label or what others will think—not the product's inherent quality. For the same reasons many narcissists pursue money with a vengeance. But narcissism exerts the most obvious toll in intimate relations. When a friend or lover begins to give honest feedback and refuses to feed the narcissist's exaggerated sense of self-importance, the narcissist becomes threatened and withdraws. Table 10.2 shows the difference between a healthy and an unhealthy, or narcissistic, desire for praise and approval.

Narcissists are not simply self-centered. They believe that the world should revolve around them; they exploit others; they expect others to do them special favors without any reciprocity. They do not allow others to get close to them—except superficially. For example, Muhammad Ali, the boxer just discussed, always had an entourage of followers expected to be extremely attentive to him, to applaud his poetry and antics, but he was actually close to only one of these followers, one of his brothers.

The following case describes one narcissist's efforts to impress others and protect his insecure "real self."

> *Mr. X came for treatment because of "marital problems." He considered his wife to be 100 percent wrong. He said, "I feel extremely confident about myself, in charge of myself and the world but over-stimulated." Although he felt good and functioned well in this state, a number of resulting difficulties arose in his career and his relationships. "In order to feel okay, I had to be the best businessman, athlete, lover, etc., best at everything. In sexual relations I was more concerned about how I functioned in the woman's eyes than with my own satisfaction. I had to perform the best there also" (Masterson, 1985, p. 47).*
>
> *"I put on my perfect self in order to manage people. I am interested in impressing them, not relating to them." After he began to see the front he was presenting, he stated to his therapist:*
>
> > *Now that I see that this is a false self, I feel like a hypocrite, I'm a phony. But underneath I feel that the real self is nothing, empty and cannot manage. For example, when I'm in my perfect self, I have no trouble trying to pick up women or seducing them and I feel confident and superior, but when that passes and I'm in my real self, I feel frightened, shy, and self-conscious.*

TABLE 10.2 Approval Seeking

Healthy Style	Unhealthy Style
Appreciates praise, but does not live for it.	Has an insatiable craving for adulation; needs praise to feel momentarily good about self.
May be hurt by criticism, but the feeling passes.	Is enraged or crushed by criticism, and broods for a long period about it.
Feels unhappy but not worthless after a failure.	Failure sets off feelings of shame and worthlessness.
Feels "special" or especially talented to a degree.	Feels far superior to everyone else, and demands recognition for that superiority.
Feels good about himself, even if others criticize.	Requires continual bolstering from others to have a sense of well-being.
Takes life's setbacks in stride, though may be put off balance for a time.	Reacts to the hurts and injuries of life with depression or rage.
Self-esteem is steady in the face of rejection, disapproval or attacks.	Reacts to rejection, disapproval or attacks with sharp rage or deep depression.
Does not feel hurt if no special treatment is given.	Feels entitled to special treatment, that ordinary rules do not apply.
Is sensitive to the feelings of others.	Is exploitative and insensitive to what others need or feel.

Source: *The New York Times* "Narcissism Looming Larger as Root of Personality Woes" (November 1, 1988, pp. C1, 16). Reprinted by permission.

> *I could never assert my real self to approach a woman and I felt that if I did, it wouldn't work. I'm terrified of exposing myself to attack or ridicule. But when I'm in the perfect self, I couldn't care less. I'm not only prepared to be attacked by others, but to attack others if the objective requires it. Although I do enjoy tennis, what I really like or am interested in is the applause of the multitudes, to be the center of an adoring multitude, to dream the impossible dream and to fulfill it."* (Masterson, 1985, p. 47)

In sum, Mr. X's intent was clear. He hid himself from others to protect his poor self-image, fearing he would be discovered as unworthy of approval. He constantly projected an image of superiority to maximize the likelihood of receiving continuous praise.

Etiology of Narcissistic Personality Disorder. In 1914, Sigmund Freud wrote a paper, *On Narcissism: An Introduction*, describing how a child learns to differentiate himself from his mother and enter the world of interpersonal relationships. Most children, according to Freud, go through an initial narcissistic stage in infancy when they are loved for almost everything they do and feel. Therefore, they feel they can do no wrong. Then children progress through the next phase where they learn that love for others is appropriate. If, however, a parent does not love a child reliably, the child may fail to find fulfillment in that stage and thus regress to the earlier narcissistic developmental stage.

About fifty years later, psychoanalyst Heinz Kohut (1971) created a stir in the psychoanalytic community because he differed from Freud by placing less emphasis on an instinctual developmental process. Children, Kohut believed, feel all powerful in early childhood and perceive their parents as all knowing and good. A loving relationship with a mother, beginning as the child becomes attached to her, produces a healthy sense of self. A strong, satisfying attachment gives the child confidence to venture out into

Individuals with narcissistic personality styles try to constantly impress people. They often spend excessive amounts of money on clothing in order to put on their "perfect selves."

the world on his or her own. But if parents do not respond positively to the child, are unaccepting, and do not live up to the child's expectations or fantasies, the child may feel unfulfilled and anxious about facing the world. The child may then venture out on a lifelong search for praise and applause from others as substitutes for the lack of parental adulation. Alternatively stated, in response to the lack of love and the resulting perceived deficiencies, the child develops a "grandiose self," which he or she believes is perfectly lovable.

Another psychoanalyst, Otto Kernberg (1970), also has been influential in the psychodynamic conceptualization of the narcissistic process. Like Freud and Kohut, he believed that cold and rejecting parents influence narcissism's development and that resentful and frustrated parents place their children at special risk for developing narcissistic personality styles.

In contrast to psychoanalytic theorists, theorists with a biopsychosocial orientation believe parents of narcissists are too positive to their children. As Millon (1986) stated, the narcissistic personality "reflects the acquisition of a self-image of superior worth, learned largely in response to the admiring of doting parents" (p. 659). Such parents overrate their offspring and when these children grow up and face the real world, they discover they are not "the greatest" or the "most beautiful." Their images of themselves and how others see them do not match. As Millon (1987) noted, "Early experience has taught them to overvalue their self-worth; this confidence may be based on false premises; that is, it [self-worth] may be unsustainable by real or mature achievements" (p. 28). Another important factor is modeling of a narcissistic style. For example, Mohammed Ali's father was "a quicksilvery little man, the leading player on any stage he visits, a man who does not mind telling you that he is the hippest, the wisest, and the coolest. 'I always wondered where the champion got his quick ad lib,' trainer Angelo Dundee once said, 'and then I ran into his father on the street and then I knew'" (Olsen, 1967, p. 94).

In addition to the early family experiences just discussed, according to social-learning theorists, during certain periods in our culture (such as the 1970s) social philosophers and therapeutic movements urged people to seek immediate gratification and to "look out for number one." Narcissistic styles have thus, at certain times, received such social support. Comparing Americans and Europeans in the book *The Ugly American* (1958), Lederer and Burdick described the greater narcissistic, assertive, and self-indulgent style of Americans. From a social-learning perspective, both parenting and cultural factors influence narcissistic personality's development.

The psychoanalytic and social-learning conceptualizations of narcissism's development clearly differ. Empirical tests have not yet been developed to assess the validity of either theory. Several paths probably lead to narcissism, and, if so, the clinical depictions of the psychoanalysts and social-learning theorists may each be partly true. Thus, psychoanalyst Reuben Fine (1966) incorporates portions of both social-learning and psychodynamic views, arguing for two types of narcissism: healthy narcissism and pathological narcissism. Healthy narcissism, he contends, develops when a child disengages from a loving parental relationship; that is, the parent's love provides the child with the needed confidence to venture out into the world with a positive outlook. In contrast, unhealthy or pathological narcissism derives from disengagement from a hostile unloving mother. Like most psychoanalytic theorists concerned with the development of disorders, Fine (1966) believes pathological narcissism develops as a defensive reaction, that it is a regression to a prior stage of personality development where adulation is more likely.

Treatment of Narcissistic Personality Disorder. Treatment of narcissists appears difficult no matter which conceptualization is used to understand the problem. Narcissists, Freud argued, could not be helped by psychoanalysis because they were not able to form the necessary close relationship with the therapist. In contrast, Kernberg (1974) believed in the use of psychoanalysis to treat narcissism, though, like Freud, he recognized the difficulties of establishing therapeutic relationships with narcissists. Kernberg described narcissists as "lacking in capacity for empathic understanding of others" (1974, p. 215) and "deficient in genuine feelings of sadness and mournful longing; their incapacity for experiencing depressive reactions is a basic feature of their personalities" (1970, p. 53). Therapy for the narcissist is educational and "cures" are not the primary goal of therapy. The therapy is often aimed at providing direct feedback and interpretation about the actions of the narcissist—not at restructuring the way he or she has thought, felt, and acted since childhood. With understanding and improved functioning as the definition of success, an example of successful psychoanalytic treatment, as described by the clinician, follows.

> *Finally the day came when he said, "My real self is beginning to emerge. Although I am not clear who I am, I am no longer a potentate or a star, but there is much more than that, there is something coming out that is authentic and real." He began to experience, as he called it, a profound change in his life style as his real self emerged. He was enjoying his mastery at work, relating more to his colleagues on a real basis and getting good feedback, had more recreational time, had lost his restless, impatient, impulsive actions, was able to view himself and others, particu-*

larly women, more realistically and to experiment with his real self. "I'm trying to contain and think rather than act. I'm less afraid or uncomfortable with myself, more willing to try to understand what others' needs are." (Masterson, 1985, p. 88)

In summary, psychoanalysts aid narcissistic patients in addressing their "real selves." These therapists provide a supportive atmosphere where patients feel comfortable expressing how they perceive themselves and others. Analysts achieve this by helping narcissists discover the negative consequences of their false self-presentation, particularly in intimate relationships. They also place special emphasis on interpretation of the relationship with the therapist (Masterson, 1990). Through this process, narcissistic patients learn to tolerate a certain amount of anxiety and depression and to face themselves for who they are.

Histrionics seek attention in many unusual ways. This man seeks attention through both his tattoos and his hair style.

Histrionic Personality Disorder

Definitions and Symptoms. Individuals with histrionic personalities resemble narcissists in their constant search for the attention of others. Yet unlike narcissists, they are highly emotional and attempt to gain attention in unusual ways; they exaggerate and dramatize, overreact to situations, and often dress in unusual bright-colored garb and have strikingly different hair styles. Also, in contrast to narcissists, who portray themselves as if everything is always all right, histrionics show extreme anger, sadness, and anxiety. Women are much more likely to be diagnosed with **histrionic personality** than men. Approximately 85 percent of individuals with this diagnosis are, in fact, women (Millon, 1986).

Histrionics are impressionable; therefore, they often become enmeshed in fads. They develop convictions based on little real thought or evidence. Histrionics also complain of health problems such as headaches, pains, and feeling weak, and exaggerate their symptoms. When extremely stressed, they may even display psychotic thought, but these symptoms usually last only a few days and generally do not warrant a diagnosis related to the psychotic thoughts.

A number of histrionic symptoms are similar to those characterizing other personality disorders. Like narcissists, histrionics are self-centered and overly concern themselves with physical attractiveness. Like dependent personalities, they rely excessively on the approval and guidance of others. Yet, exaggerated emotionality and dress are key symptoms differentiating the histrionic personality from other personality disorders.

Development of Histrionic Personality Disorder. When children cannot get their parents' attention legitimately, they create scenes to attract attention. They may make unusual demands, spill their juice, or pull pots and pans out of a cupboard during their parent's telephone conversation. If children are often ignored or shunned by parents, they may learn that in order to be seen or heard in most situations, they have to make a scene or exaggerate; a pattern of histrionic behavior may, therefore, begin to emerge. Similarly, adult histrionics often feel successful competition with others on usual grounds is impossible; consequently, they pursue attention in a different or dramatic fashion.

For example, adult histrionics tend to dress seductively and act in sexually promiscuous ways. Because they have not learned to form usual close relationships with significant others, their personal relationships are usually shallow.

From a psychodynamic perspective, the histrionic is preoccupied with being erotically pleasing to others to compensate for feeling unlovable (Gunderson, 1988). Histrionics frequently prompt others to act protectively to them which in turn reinforces their behavior and their insecurities. Extroverted temperaments are known to be partially genetically determined, and such a genetic predisposition influences the likelihood of a person being histrionic if other predisposing factors are also present.

Treatment of Histrionic Personality Disorder. Histrionics reveal their symptomatology in therapy and with people they are in daily contact with. Therapists seeing histrionics have to be careful because of the patients' seductiveness. They are not only physically seductive, but they may also seduce the therapist into spending more than the allotted therapy time and may not want to terminate therapy when they have progressed far enough to do so. Histrionics may even overdramatize the insights they receive from the therapist to defer attention from their real problems. Interpretation and direct feedback to the patient in a supportive environment are necessary, and couples or group therapy is helpful because people other than the therapist can provide this feedback to the patient.

Borderline Personality Disorder

Borderline personalities are characterized by unstable self-image and intense personal relationship problems. Study of this disorder has recently become very popular in clinical and research circles. Although the diagnosis became officially recognized only in 1980, as many as 20 percent of psychiatric patients receive it (Frances & Widiger, 1986). Approximately two thirds of individuals diagnosed with **borderline personality** are women. As we shall see, childhood physical and sexual abuse appear to be critical factors in this disorder's development.

The name *borderline* implies being on the border, or edge, of something; as such, it reflects the instability characteristic of individuals with this personality style. The name itself, however, also reflects some of the controversy surrounding borderline disorders. The term was used originally as a "waste basket" category when a clinician could not make a specific diagnosis. Subsequently, some professionals argued that it appeared to be on the "borderline" of too many other disorders to be seen as a distinct disorder; that is, on the border between schizophrenia and affective disorders. Now, however, most experts view it as a distinct diagnostic category of marginal and unstable individuals (Gunderson, 1984). We will examine this issue in more detail after considering the disorder's primary characteristics.

Defining Characteristics

A key feature of borderline personalities is an identity problem reflected in uncertainty about major issues such as sexual orientation, career choice, friends, or lovers. Lacking a strong sense of identity themselves, women and men with this disorder fear abandonment and often make frenzied efforts to maintain relationships.

Borderline personalities: (*DSM-III-R*, 1987) are characterized by

1. Unstable personal relationships.
2. Impulsiveness.
3. Frequent mood shifts.
4. Inappropriate anger.
5. Recurrent suicidal threats or gestures.
6. Identity disturbance.
7. Chronic feelings of emptiness.
8. Frantic efforts to avoid abandonment.

Clinicians repeatedly observe that some borderline patients appear quite healthy in a clinical interview but score poorly on unstructured tests. As early as 1942, Rorschach, who developed the famous projective inkblot test named for him, reported that certain people score well on structured tests but do poorly on unstructured tests such as the one he developed. He described them as having primitive thinking (i.e., thinking that resembled the thoughts of children). Others noted that when these patients were placed in supportive hospital environments, they often deteriorated and engaged in highly destructive behavior. Psychiatrists reported becoming very angry with or feeling helpless about the borderline patients because of difficulty in pinpointing the exact problem though something about the patients seemed troublesome (Gunderson, 1984).

Two independent lines of investigation in the late 1960s led to a focus on borderline patients. First, Kernberg (1967) was interested in the internal psychological structure, or mental functioning, of these patients. He believed these patients were capable of assessing their impact on others and of behaving within socially acceptable limits (called intact reality testing). On the other hand, these patients had unstable identities and immature or infantile ways of protecting themselves. They could not tolerate anxiety, were often illogical, and showed poor impulse control. Indeed, recent research confirms that borderline patients are not seen as different from patients without borderline disorders by hospital staff observers, but that borderline patients exhibited significantly greater hostility and depression on clinical assessment instruments (Edell, Joy & Yehuda, 1990). Psychoanalytic therapists believe that therapy candidates generally should be capable of good reality testing in both structured (work and school) and unstructured situations (certain psychotherapies). As noted earlier, however, borderlines do not do well in unstructured situations. Disagreeing with the accepted position about the ability to handle unstructured situations well, Kernberg (1967) began to advocate psychodynamic therapy for these patients. Since this theory was the dominant influence in psychiatric hospitals in the 1960s, his description of borderline patients was influential, prompting clinicians to carefully assess and treat them.

A second major impetus for work with borderlines was the systematic collection of data on such patients by Grinker, Werble, and Drye (1968). Through careful clinical description and assessment, they identified four central problems in the "borderline syndrome."

1. Failures in self-identity.
2. Depression stemming from loneliness.
3. Predominance of expressed anger.
4. Severe dependencies.

As you can see, these characteristics are very similar to many of the current diagnostic criteria for borderline personality in *DSM-III-R,* discussed earlier.

Current research on diagnosed borderlines indicates a general agreement across over a half a dozen studies that borderlines have intense unstable interpersonal relationships. Borderlines, according to Gunderson (1984), devalue or discredit certain aspects of relationships, telling themselves other people are not important. They manipulate and yet are also very dependent. These characteristics cause borderlines to establish intense and unstable interpersonal relationships. The centrality of problems in interpersonal relationships is a key factor differentiating this diagnosis from others.

Suicidal gestures, such as wrist slashing or overdosing, are the most common reason for hospitalization of borderlines. Self-destructive behavior distinguishes hospitalized borderlines from other psychiatric inpatients. Table 10.3 shows the variety of self-destructive acts by fifty-seven borderline patients at the McLean Hospital in Belmont, Massachusetts.

Etiology of Borderline Personality Disorder. A disturbed infant–parent relationship is theorized as central in borderline personality's development, which psychodynamic theorists have detailed. Kernberg suggested that some infants became very frustrated in the first year of life. The mother, Mahler (1968) asserted, in fantasy or in reality, does not accept the child, and therefore the child fails to develop an adequate sense of self-esteem. This pathological pattern with the mother beginning in infancy continues into adulthood. This maladaptive relationship is exemplified in the case of Jane, a twenty-two-year-old college student diagnosed as borderline.

Jane complained of several symptoms including depression, anxiety, and feelings that her legs would collapse under her and that she could not swallow. Jane experienced helpless feelings and contacted her mother frequently for reassurance. Her mother idealized the family unit and rewarded Jane for infantile compliant behavior, such as doing chores for her and remaining at home instead of seeking friends. The mother also attacked any display of self-assertiveness by Jane. For example, when she learned that Jane had demonstrated against the war in Vietnam, the mother refused to attend her graduation. The mother also described sexual relations as the "work of the devil." Jane's emotionally distant father functioned largely as a figurehead echoing his wife's opinions.

After Jane began to trust her therapist, she said:

> *I think I'm going to die because I'm growing up. I can envisage no life outside my mother or my family. I'm made up of two parts—one me, one her. The part that she has worked on, taken care of, and given to me. . . . If I move away from her the part that is in me would turn against me. . . . Mother will make it turn against me and will punish me. I don't feel strong enough to battle in spite of myself. Mother insists that I remain helpless and not grow up.*

Later Jane continued:

> *I'm afraid that if I grow up, I'll lose her. I will take away her reason for living. I'll carry out what mother says—I'm an empty shell. Mother puts in values, otherwise I'll be nothing. I'm empty except for her. Mother sees me as a tool for herself. She instructed me in one thing I can't do—grow up and leave her or I'll be punished for it.*
> (Rinsley, 1982, pp. 54–55)

TABLE 10.3 Self-Destructive Acts by Fifty-Seven Hospitalized Patients with Borderline Personality Disorder

Variable	Number of Patients	Noteworthy Patterns
Suicide threats	42	To get attention To cause trouble In rage
Overdose	40	No usual pattern Barbiturates most frequent
Self-mutilation	36	Wrist slashing, body banging, burning, puncturing, hair removal
Drug abuse	38	Polydrug abuse, amphetamines, alcohol binges, marijuana
Promiscuity or alcohol	36	Usually under the influence of drugs
Accidents	14	Reckless driving

Source: Gunderson, J. G. (1984). *Borderline personality disorder.* Washington, DC: American Psychiatric Association, p. 86. Reprinted by permission.

Sexual and physical abuse are also common in the histories of borderline patients. In a recent study, 80 percent of borderlines had been sexually or physically abused or had witnessed serious domestic violence (Herman, Perry, & van der Kolk, 1989). Since girls are at far greater risk for sexual abuse than boys, this finding has tremendous implications for the differential rate of women diagnosed as borderline. (Recall that approximately two thirds of individuals with this diagnosis are females.) Indeed, some professionals believe repeated child sexual abuse may be one of the primary causes of borderline personality disorder (Kroll, 1988). However, physical and emotional abuse of boys—and to a lesser extent sexual abuse—may also be critical in borderline disorders developing in males.

Affective disorders are common in the families of borderlines (Loranger, Oldham, & Tulis, 1982), and assessment of borderlines themselves reveal depressive and anxiety disorders occurring in at least 75 percent of them (Schwartz et al., 1989). Interpersonal relations problems, especially hostility and manipulativeness, are, however, more pronounced in borderlines than depressed individuals, and the disorder generally appears distinct enough to warrant separate diagnosis.

Because borderlines are disproportionately likely to come from families with affective disorders and most borderlines report significant symptoms of depression, the possibility of a genetic link for these disorders arises. Hereditary factors, then, may play some role in the etiology of borderline personality disorder. In summary, borderline disorder's etiology is believed to be rooted in a pathological mother–infant relationship fostering the child's dependency, resulting in a failure to develop an adequate sense of self. Other family stressors such as sexual abuse also appear in the backgrounds of borderlines. Experts from diverse theoretical backgrounds believe that this disorder's development must be viewed from a broad integrative perspective incorporating biological, social, and psychological variables (e.g. Gunderson, 1984; Millon, 1986).

Treatment of Borderline Personality Disorder. Treatment of borderlines is a great challenge for any professional because, as indicated earlier, the borderline vacillates between extreme dependency and great hostility.

The following letter from a patient to her therapist illustrates the pressure the borderline repeatedly places on the therapist. For this reason, therapists treating a borderline patient need considerable supervision and support. A repeated issue for them is how to respond to a patient's frequent suicidal gestures. Consider the case of the suicidal gestures mentioned by the patient to the therapist, Katie.

Dear Katie,

This is to let you know that I'm canceling my appointment this week. And I don't know when I'll be able to make another one. I was originally going to cancel out because we were going out of town. But I'm not going to go. I'll let him and both the kids go.

I don't think you'd like to see me this way. I knew for a long time I was heading for a big downfall. I know you'll be moving soon just like everyone else did and I hate it.

My daughter went to camp for a week, and that's when I realized I was all alone. I was so distraught after dropping her off that I lost control of the car and went off the road. I had to call my girlfriend's boyfriend to come help me.

Lately it's been awful hard to get up in the mornings and go to work or get the kids off to school and daycare. But I haven't missed a day of work because of it. I even received another raise again. So my performance must be good.

We're not getting along too good. He's gone all day working all his side jobs. And he gets upset when I leave when he's home. But I need time away from home and the kids.

I think or should I say I KNOW I want my girlfriend's boyfriend. But I don't know if its worth losing her as a friend. We've been caught in awkward positions by her, but nothing too damaging. And to be honest I haven't slept with him since last year, but would if he wanted to.

I let a lot of myself die. My drawings and sewings have gone downhill. My hands aren't steady enough to do that kind of work any more. Maybe I just don't have the patience any more.

I'm not going to seek help anymore. I'm done with it. I figured I'd get along on my own. I also told my husband I quit seeing you, that I quit the clinic there all together.

Yesterday, I tried to kill myself after an argument again. And today I almost killed myself and one of my kids in a car accident. The worse part is I don't realize I'm doing these things.

Don't worry about me. I'm doing good. You see my girlfriend's boyfriend is taking good care of me. He's trying to get me to stop using drugs. But that's my way of coping and my way of keeping him. (Kroll, 1988, p. 197)

In this case Katie's supervisor encouraged her to write back, telling the patient she enjoyed receiving the letters and suggesting she call to establish another appointment.

Psychodynamic therapists have pioneered in the borderline patient's treatment. They generally employ a combination of support, advice, and cognitive explorations in seeking the causes of their patients' problems. Therapy may occur as often as three times a week and last for as long as four years.

A behavioral treatment for borderlines based on a biopsychosocial approach has been developed by

Marsha Linehan (1987) and described by Linehan and Wagner (1990). This approach addresses three key symptom patterns of the borderline patient: (1) emotional vulnerability, (2) passivity, and (3) unrelenting crises. Linehan assumes a physiological base for the emotional vulnerability due to an inability to regulate emotional responses. To cope with this vulnerability, patients are taught to regulate or control their emotions and/or to tolerate emotional distress until they find a socially appropriate way of dealing with it. To cope with their passivity, patients receive a careful balance of support for their capabilities and confrontation regarding their deficiencies. Alternatively stated, they are taught specific social and behavioral skills to aid them in controlling their emotions and behavior. A basic goal of this treatment, then, is for patients to recognize and address interpersonal problems. This treatment approach has been extremely successful in reducing the intentionally self-injurious behaviors of borderline patients, and few have dropped out of treatment (Linehan, 1987).

The approach described by Linehan and Wagner (1990) is called **dialectical behavioral therapy (DBT)** because of its philosophical underpinnings. This therapy's philosophical framework assumes all things are interconnected and opposing forces operating within us can be brought together to produce therapeutic change. Conflicts are necessary, or at least useful, for change. The dialectic behavior therapy's hierarchy of goals follow: (1) decrease suicidal behavior, (2) decrease avoidant behavior, and (3) teach skill acquisition such as regulating emotional reactions and stress tolerance. Group and individual therapy is conducted, with the group setting used to teach emotional regulation, stress tolerance, and interpersonal skills. The individual therapy teaches the patient how to integrate the skills taught in the groups into the patient's everyday life. Similar to feminist views, this therapeutic approach's premise is that women are often in double-binds, expected to behave and feel in ways that are often actually, or at least seemingly, contradictory. For example, women are expected to be feminine and at the same time to be assertive and independent.

Feminist therapy may have special advantages with borderlines because they often come from families and social environments where they have been socially and emotionally abused—often by men. Feminist therapy focuses on the integration of the subjective and objective life of a woman and of the emotional and rational aspects of life (Mandler, 1977). Central and often unique to feminist therapy is the therapeutic goal of teaching the harmful effects of a sexist society (e.g., job discrimination, academic discrimination in which the skills of women are often unrecognized, and emphasis by men on how a female looks rather than how she thinks). Feminist therapy teaches empowerment by recognition of women's power or potential power. Such therapy focuses primarily on environmental and social origins of behavior, while DBT also focuses on biological determinants of behavior. While there have been no evaluations of feminist therapy with borderline patients, it has certain unique emphases which may prove very useful with these patients (Linehan & Wagner, 1990). Moreover, feminist therapy or its variants are common in treating physically abused women (Adams, 1989). Finally, feminist therapy and cognitive-behavioral therapy procedures can be combined to aid borderlines and other patients suffering from social discrimination. A comparison of feminist therapy and dialectical behavior therapy appears in Table 10.4 below.

TABLE 10.4 Comparison of Feminist and Dialectic Behavior Therapy

Feminist Therapy	Dialectic Behavior Therapy
I. Philosophical Bases	
Integration of subjective and objective Integration of emotional and rational	Emphasis on interconnectness
II. Goals	
Recognize harmful effects of sexist society Teach empowerment Teach social skills	Reduction of suicidal behavior Reduction of avoidant behavior Teach social skills
III. Strategies	
Problem solving Recognize contradictions in society for women Develop relationships with others	Problem solving Recognize power women already have Emphasis on individual therapy relationship and group relationships

Source: Linehan, M. M., & Wagner, A. W. (1990). Dialectic behavior therapy: A feminist-behavioral treatment of borderline personality disorder. *The Behavior Therapist,* January 1990. Copyright by the Association for the Advancement of Behavior Therapy. Reprinted by permission of the publisher and author.

Pharmacotherapy with antidepressant and antipsychotic medications has also proven successful in treating borderline patients (e.g., Turner, 1989). It is, however, controversial because of the risk of intentional drug overdose by self-destructive patients who are not hospitalized. Pharmacotherapy is often employed as an adjunct to psychotherapy in the treatment of borderlines when the clinician believes that either depression or schizophrenic-like behavior needs to be reduced (Kroll, 1988; Cowdry & Gardner, 1989). Even in these situations, however, medication is viewed as adjunctive to psychotherapy, not as a complete treatment in itself. The combination of the antidepressant medication, Prozac, and psychotherapy has been remarkably successful in helping borderlines. Patients treated with this medication "returned to full time work, began to date again, moved out of a parent's home, married, returned to school, quit using drugs and alcohol, and stopped making 'crisis' phone calls to the therapist. Many still need psychotherapy, but they now come an average of once per month instead of once a week, and the therapy is going better" (Norden, 1989). Agitation is Prozac's most serious side effect, but lowering the dosage at any point during treatment usually reduces this.

Current knowledge about the long-term outcome of treatment of borderline patients is limited. The effects of well-developed treatments in varied settings and by a variety of therapists have not yet been studied. What we do know is based on patients who were followed after diverse treatments. The borderline pattern generally appears quite stable across time; poor work performance and unstable relationships are generally the rule—even when the patient has completed treatment. About a third of borderline patients marry, about half of them function well in their jobs and personal life, but as many as 10 percent eventually kill themselves (Gunderson & Sanarini, 1987).

Antisocial Personality Disorder

As noted previously, antisocial behavior has been the subject of more research than any other personality disorder, mainly because of its impact on society. For an **antisocial personality** disorder diagnosis to be made, an individual must display a behavior pattern that violates the rights of others and began before age fifteen. The *DSM-III-R* (1987) criteria are as follows:

1. The person must be at least eighteen years old.
2. By age fifteen, he or she must have had a conduct disorder as reflected in four of the following: truancy; school suspension; stealing; vandalism; initiating fights; repeatedly violating rules at home and at school; an arrest or referral to a juvenile court; running away from home; lying; engaging in sexual intercourse much earlier than his/her peers; and having regularly used alcohol, tobacco, or other drugs.
3. After age fifteen, the antisocial person must exhibit a pattern of irresponsible and antisocial behavior, including several of the following: inability to sustain work, repeated work absenses, harassment, property destruction, physical fighting with people outside the home, spouse or child abuse, financial irresponsibility, lying, lack of remorse, and failure to sustain a monogamous relationship for more than one year.

Like conduct disorders, antisocial personalities are much more common in males than females. Approximately 6 percent of men and 3 percent of women display characteristics of antisocial personality (Millon, 1987).

As you may expect, many incarcerated criminals suffer from antisocial personality disorder. For example, Hare (1983) found that about half of the criminals in two prisons met the criteria for this diagnosis. There are, of course, thousands of people with antisocial personality disorders who have never been arrested nor spent time in jail, and they are unlikely to seek professional help. These people may have conned, duped, swindled, or charmed others into believing they were "the greatest." They are the politicians who proclaim their ethics while being "on the take" from various illegal ventures. They are the physicians who sell unnecessary or even harmful services. They are the television and radio evangelists who amass fortunes for themselves and engage prostitutes while preaching "the good clean life." Most of these antisocial personalities never enter the offices of psychologists or psychiatrists and are never caught for their illegal behavior.

James Bakker was a television preacher who made national headlines in 1989 after the scandal of his $129-million-per-year ministry was revealed. Bakker was accused not only of sexual misconduct with a young woman, but also of having used company funds to purchase mansions, luxury cars, and vacations for himself and selling partnerships in condominiums and lodges when these units actually had already been sold. Prior to his trial, Bakker was committed to a mental hospital after a psychiatrist observed him "lying in the corner of his attorney's office with his head under a couch hiding." Because Bakker was reported to have been hallucinating, the judge suspended his trial awaiting tests of mental competence (*Time,* September 11, 1989). From this brief account, it may seem as if Jim Bakker were an antisocial personality; yet without a developmental history of conduct problems by age fifteen, this diagnosis would be inaccurate. While Jim Bakker displayed some antisocial behavior in adolescence such as spreading gasoline on driveways and setting the gasoline on fire, he did not have a significant history of serious antisocial behavior. In fact, at his trial, psychiatrists did not diagnose him as an antisocial personality. He was a simple criminal with psychopathic features now to be described.

Psychopathy. A subgroup of individuals with antisocial personality disorder are called *psychopaths*. Some professionals do not think this controversial subgroup of psychopaths have a consistent behavior pattern distinguishing them from other antisocial personalities (e.g., Blackburn, 1988). Yet, the term **psychopath** continues to be used in both clinical and research settings, and interest in psychopathy will probably continue as either a subgroup of antisocial personality disorder or as a dimension of the antisocial personality disorder (Quay, 1978). Let us now consider the symptoms or core characteristics of psychopaths.

Psychopaths are thought to behave in ways that reflect a core personality disorder different from what the individuals experienced in their own environments growing up. Although superficially charming, psychopaths coldly engage in antisocial behavior without anxiety, shame, or remorse. Psychopaths do not establish long-lasting relationships with others; they lie and manipulate people. Consider the behavior of Ted Bundy, a slick, good-looking, psychopathic sex offender and murderer (see Box 10.1). Bundy was an example of a particular psychopathic subtype—a hostile psychopath acting senselessly on aggressive and sexual impulses.

Etiology of Antisocial Personality Disorder. As reflected in the diagnostic criteria for antisocial personality disorder, this disorder's causes clearly overlap with those of conduct disorder. Some of the psychological factors associated with conduct disorder's development include modeling of aggressive behavior, strong punishment, rewards for aggressive behavior, and marital discord (see Chapter 12). Additionally, growing evidence suggests an association between abnormalities of the central nervous system and antisocial behavior (Mednick & Moffit, 1987; Wilson & Herrnstein, 1985).

Neuropsychological Factors. Scores of studies indicate that antisocial individuals have impaired ability to concentrate, plan ahead, and inhibit certain behaviors (Wilson & Herrnstein, 1985). Memory impairments have often also been found. Yet, interpretation of these results is problematic, since subjects were generally from highly select groups such as prison inmates or reform school volunteers, hospitalized violent offenders, and offenders referred for psychiatric evaluation. We cannot, therefore, be certain that the same findings would hold for antisocial individuals outside of these groups. However, some findings are now available in research conducted with self-reported delinquent teen-agers as part of a large-scale longitudinal study of health, development, and behavior in Dunedin, New Zealand (Moffit & Silva, 1988). A unique feature of this study is that teenagers were included in the delinquent sample if their parents, a teacher, or a police report corroborated their self-report of antisocial acts. This combined reporting provided some assurance that the adolescents most heavily involved in delinquent activities would be identified. A neuropsychological examination and a test of family adversity (e.g., low parental income, poor maternal health, negative family environment) were administered to 124 delinquents and 726 nondelinquents by psychologists unaware of the delinquent status of some of their subjects. As may be expected, family adversity had the greatest association with delinquency, but neuropsychological variables such as problems in motor and eye-hand coordination also contributed significantly to the correct prediction of delinquency.

Attentional problems, hyperactivity, and conduct disorders have predicted delinquent behavior in studies examining childhood variables associated with later teen-age delinquency status (Cloninger & Gottesman, 1987; Farrington, Loeber, & van Kammen, in press). Additionally, some U.S. longitudinal studies have followed conduct-disordered children and delinquent teen-agers into adulthood. These studies as well as substantial retrospective evidence indicate that factors associated with conduct disorder's development also appear in the development of antisocial personality disorder (Robins, 1966; Kazdin, 1987).

Family Problems. Family background's association with the development of conduct disorders and antisocial personality is now extremely well established. Family factors related to conduct disorders and antisocial personality disorder can be grouped into three general classes: (1) marital discord and divorce, (2) parental rejection and negativity, and (3) modeling of antisocial behavior.

Marital problems and divorce have repeatedly been linked to conduct problems in children, especially boys (Emery, 1982; O'Leary & Emery, 1984). On the other hand, it is important to emphasize that the majority of children of maritally discordant or divorced families do not exhibit clinical levels of behavioral or emotional problems. The presence, nonetheless, of marital discord and divorce do seem critical in the development of conduct disorders, delinquency, and later antisocial personality disor-

BOX 10.1 The Case of Ted Bundy

Ted Bundy was a law school student when he was convicted of killing two Florida State University sorority sisters sleeping in their beds in the Chi Omega sorority house, and a twelve-year-old Lake City, Florida, girl. Bundy also received two additional consecutive sentences of ninety-nine years each for assaulting three other women. Additionally, law enforcement officers linked him to the worst string of sex murders in the 1980s, making him the prime suspect in the murders of over thirty women from coast to coast whose corpses were found in places ranging from beds to hog sheds. Bundy typically stalked coeds at various university campuses in the Northwest, luring them with his good looks and soft-spoken charm; often to gain sympathy, he would bandage his arm.

Just before being electrocuted, Ted Bundy confessed and provided details about sixteen murders. He was on the FBI's "Most Wanted Fugitive" list for being a suspect in thirty-six killings. He said "I am the most cold-blooded son-of-a-bitch that you will ever meet."

Theodore Bundy was born in Philadelphia to Louise Cowell. He was an illegitimate child, and in order to establish a new life, his mother moved to Tacoma, Washington, where she married John Bundy. In first grade, Ted was perceived of as a good student at ease with his classmates. As a child he fantasized about being adopted by Roy Rogers and Dale Evans so that he could have his own pony and be rich enough to have anything he wanted. Some indications of his later psychopathic behavior were present in his boyhood behavior. For example, he roamed his neighborhood searching the trash barrels for pictures of naked women. (While this feature of his sexual behavior fits readily into Bundy's later development, it may not have been central to his psychopathy.) He isolated himself, spending much of his free time in junior high school listening to radio talk shows. In high school, Bundy, a B+ student, was considered amusing, yet he apparently stole ski equipment and devised a scheme to forge ski lift tickets. His fiery temper was evident in adolescence when he shoved a plate in the face of someone who had cut down a small tree. It is chilling to note that Ted Bundy became the assistant director of the Seattle Crime Prevention Advisory Commission and that he wrote a pamphlet on rape prevention the same year he began to commit murder (*The New York Times,* January 25, 1989). In describing himself, Bundy said:

> A lot of my pretensions about being a scholarly type, a person interested in serious studies, was really a defense mechanism. I was accused on a couple occasions of being aloof, arrogant, and snobby. But it was just this defense mechanism to protect my somewhat introverted nature. I used that to compensate for my outright fear of socializing. Maybe, also it was a way to protect myself because I couldn't achieve those kinds of social goals I wanted. (Michaud & Aynesworth, 1989, p. 14)

Contrary to much of Bundy's publicity, he was not a brilliant college student; his grades were fair and he stole repeatedly. A compulsive nail biter and nose picker, he stuttered when nervous and later failed law school. Because of his sense of social inadequacy, he worked hard at maintaining an image of himself as different from others. For example, he thought that he could be unique by mastering an Asian studies curriculum (Michaud & Aynesworth, 1983).

Before trial, Bundy was examined by two psychiatrists; both agreed he had an antisocial personality. He seemed, they noted, thrilled at the opportunity of defying authority. Although they said Bundy displayed poor judgment, they believed him competent to stand trial (Winn & Merrill, 1980).

Throughout his trial and imprisonment, Bundy steadfastly proclaimed his innocence, but just before he died in an electric chair in Florida on January 24, 1989, he supplied police detectives with details about sixteen murders. According to his biography by Stephen Michaud and Hugh Aynesworth, *Conversations with a Killer* (1989), the most apt single-sentence description of Bundy was provided by the man himself: "I'm the most cold-blooded son-of-a-bitch that you will ever meet" (p. 3).

der, since a disproportionate percentage of individuals with these disorders come from discordant or broken homes. Moreover, these effects of discordant and nondiscordant homes exist even after corrections are made for social class.

Investigators have recently noted that parents' antisocial personality disorders may be even more significant in the etiology of children's conduct problems than divorce (Lahey et al., 1988). In a sample of boys referred to a psychological clinic, parental divorce and conduct disorders were not found to be highly related, but parental antisocial personality disorder (especially in fathers) and conduct disorders were. Perhaps, then, the often discussed relationship between divorce and conduct problems and in turn antisocial personality disorders is a misleading one; it may be accounted for by a high divorce rate among adults with antisocial personalities. If so, modeling of antisocial behavior by fathers may contribute significantly to the development of similar behavior patterns in boys.

The family problems noted above must be considered as risk factors for developing antisocial personality disorder. Of course, many individuals do *not* manifest antisocial personality disorder even when exposed to divorce, great family hardship, and parental fighting or violence. Many individuals in such environments rise above those environments—perhaps because they find psychological and social support from friends, teachers, and extended family.

Treatment of Antisocial Personality Disorder. Treatment of individuals with antisocial personality disorders and of psychopaths is extremely difficult. As previously noted, few psychopaths voluntarily seek treatment, and only a small percentage of people with antisocial personality disorders go to psychotherapists. When people with antisocial personalities enter therapy, they often distrust the therapist and/or miss appointments. Unfortunately, most adults with these problems first have significant negative contact with professionals in legal circumstances, probation, reform schools, and prisons.

Even conduct disorders, the precursors to these antisocial personality disorders in adulthood, are very difficult to treat (see Chapter 12). Recent research indicates that the majority of antisocial children treated as inpatients because of highly aggressive and destructive behavior do not fall within the normal range of behavior *after* treatment (Kazdin, Bass, Siegel, & Thomas, 1989). One desirable course of action, consequently, is early preventative efforts consisting of parent training for parents of children displaying significant oppositional and conduct problems, and community action to involve teen-agers in sports and prosocial activities. Other courses of action would be multipronged and also start early in life upon detection of the antisocial behavior; these would include academic remediation and psychological therapy.

Although we do not have promising evidence of the effectiveness of treatment for antisocial personality disorders, we do know that every type of aggressive behavior decreases with age. Families burdened with children afflicted by severe conduct problems or adults with antisocial personality disorder can thus anticipate gradual decrease in the aggressive and unlawful behavior. Yet while waiting for maturation and perhaps some insight into the problems of the person with antisocial personality disorder, families are often split apart by the difficulties such an individual presents: Individuals with antisocial personality disorders ask for loans they never repay. They borrow cars, wreck them (usually while drunk), then cannot afford the repairs. They reluctantly enter therapy, often draining family finances to pay mental health professionals. They break laws and require legal assistance, prey upon parental guilt, and often prompt family members to pay expensive attorneys to help them avoid any real penalty for their misconduct. They thus move the family even further into debt. Because of these stresses, and because the patterns of individuals with this personality disorder gradually improve with time, psychological help for family members may be as beneficial as any aid that can be found for the person with the antisocial personality disorder.

ANXIOUS OR FEARFUL BEHAVIOR DISORDERS

Dependent Personality Disorder

Dr. Rosa L. had been the best student in her medical class at a large northeastern university. She later became a superb resident, who showed great caring for her patients. After her residency, she worked as a practicing physician and an active investigator, presenting research findings at conferences on pediatric medicine. Rosa was pretty, liked by almost everyone, and extremely outgoing.

Rosa's husband, an engineer, left her for another woman shortly after she began her career, at which point she began to call both her male and female friends to talk for hours. Her husband was critical of her as a mother, claiming she overprotected their two young children, and he initiated a legal battle to obtain custody of their children. Rosa then began to question her judgment about child rearing, and tried to persuade her husband to leave his girlfriend and return to her—although she knew that he'd had many extramarital affairs.

In an effort to cope with these pressures, Rosa frequently called her best friend in desperation, terrified that she might lose her children. She also was uncertain about how to handle the many advances she received from men once they knew she was "free." She and her husband contacted a psychologist at the suggestion of a family court judge to provide a report to the court regarding a recommendation for custody and visitation. The psychologist gave Rosa the Millon Personality Test (the Millon Clinical Multiaxial Inventory II), a test frequently used to assess personality style. She had elevated scores on the **dependent personality** scale, indicating she displayed significantly more dependency than most adults. Rosa's high score *along with* the information she provided in the assessment interviews caused the therapist to diagnose her as suffering from a dependent personality disorder.

The key features of dependent personalities are submissive and dependent behaviors generally beginning in adolescence and evident in diverse settings. People diagnosed with this disorder rely on others to make most of their decisions. They lack self-confidence—even when they have social and vocational/professional skills. They ask about how they look with certain hair styles, about what to wear, and for assistance in making decisions on their jobs. They frequently seek the comfort of friends and professionals and do whatever possible to avoid being alone. They will even do other people's "scut" work or mundane jobs as a way of gaining approval. They take criticism poorly—even when it is intended to be constructive.

Clinicians who evaluate people for dependent personality disorders consider the following to be characteristics of this problem (Millon, 1987):

1. Ill-equipped to assume mature roles.
2. Devastated when close relationships end.
3. Fearful of loss or desertion.
4. Highly agitated and anxiously watchful.
5. Tries to keep emotions under tight control.
6. Preoccupied with fears of being alone.
7. Easily persuaded and gullible.
8. Unimaginative and cognitively constricted.
9. Compliant, submissive, and placating.
10. Belittles own aptitudes and competencies.

More women than men are diagnosed as dependent personalities, although perhaps surprisingly, the disorder is not uncommon in men. Using standardized test batteries, about four women for every three men are diagnosed with this problem (Millon, 1987).

Etiology of Dependent Personality Disorder. Dependency seems to be fostered in childhood by extreme overprotectiveness—sometimes by extremely caring parents who want to do everything possible for their children. As children, dependent personalities have what developmental psychologists describe as insecure attachments to their parents (Main, 1989). Insecurely attached children exhibit high levels of anxiety, crying, and fussing when separated from their parents. Fear of venturing out on their own is a common memory of adults with dependent personalities. Dependency may be fostered by parents who model dependent behavior or who actively encourage or reward it. Dependency is also encouraged when parents fail to teach and reward the skills a child needs to feel confident and comfortable in social and vocational settings. The dependent adult, therefore, usually has poor self-esteem and a strong sense of inadequacy. In our culture, dependent behavior is far more likely to be tolerated and encouraged in girls than boys. Though controversial, some also posit that dependent or submissive behavior in females may be genetically caused and has developed because of evolutionary reasons (Gunderson, 1988). These social and biological reasons may explain why women are particularly vulnerable to dependent personality disorder. Because they are most comfortable with people who allow them to behave dependently, young women with this personality style may be prone to select "strong men" as partners. These men may also discourage any attempts by such women to act independently by pursuing a job or additional education. Unfortunately, the relationship's pattern may even evolve into one in which the dependent woman is completely dominated and sometimes abused. In such cases, however, the dependent personality is likely a reaction to the physical and emotional abuse, not necessarily a lifelong personality style or disorder. Thus, some professionals believe that posttraumatic stress disorder more accurately captures the clinical picture the abused women present than the dependent personality diagnosis (Walker, 1989). Answers to this issue await more research on the etiology of spouse abuse.

Treatment of Dependent Personality Disorder. Many psychological treatments exist for people with dependent personalities. Assertiveness training, often in groups, teaches dependent people to feel confident enough to express themselves. Encouragement of assertiveness is the basic component of various self-help groups, such as Divorced and Separated Parents and Women's Health Collectives. These volunteer organizations offer help to women with varied physical and psychological problems and have proven very useful to many. Mental health clinics also conduct assertiveness training workshops for women, and individual therapists often help single clients become more assertive and independent.

Becoming assertive, however, is not the only issue for dependent women. They must also develop enough confidence to seek a new job or learn new

Assertion training involves telling someone what you believe are your legitimate rights. Individuals are taught to voice their opinion, stand up for their rights, and assert themselves with more confidence.

vocational and social skills. Thus, they need to overcome old views of themselves as incompetent and develop in their place self-esteem.

Treatment for women in physically aggressive relationships can take varied forms. Individual or group therapy helps them build self-confidence and learn new skills. In extreme cases, physically battered women receive protection in secret community "shelters." The men in these relationships may receive group therapy in which they are taught to control their anger. Even when abusive males are forced into treatment through court mandates, evidence suggests the effectiveness of such men's groups in reducing anger and physical aggression (Edleson, Miller, Stone, & Chappan, 1985). Couples in physically aggressive, but not life-threatening relationships, may also benefit from marital therapy to help them learn more adaptive styles of communication and to cope more effectively with disagreements. The therapist may sometimes recommend marital therapy in addition to individual treatment for both the husband and the wife (O'Leary & Vivian, in press).

The Battered Wife Syndrome: A Diagnostic Controversy

Women in physically abusive relationships are often described as having dependent personality disorder. Yet another diagnosis, the **"battered wife syndrome"** (Walker, 1989), may be more relevant since many battered women do not have personality disorders. Moreover, even if some do have personality disorders, they may not be dependent personality disorders but other personality problems. Although the battered wife syndrome is not listed as a personality disorder in *DSM-III-R,* it is increasingly being recognized as a unique problem suffered by large numbers of women. Some argue that women beaten by their husbands may also qualify for a provisional *DSM-III-R* diagnostic category, self-defeating personality disorder, in which "the person is drawn to situations or relationships in which he or she will suffer" (p. 430). However, this category does not apply to many abused women for they do not become abused in additional relationships after leaving their abusing partner. Further, empirical evidence for this personality diagnosis was not strong enough to include it as a regular or nonprovisional category in *DSM-III-R* (Walker, 1987; Widiger, 1987). Nonetheless, others argue that the diagnosis may be the most appropriate for abused women. At present, there have been no systematic personality studies of abused women to settle this. Thus there is no definitive answer as to which personality diagnosis, if any, best fits abused women. The commonly observed problems of depression, anxiety, and dependency are often the consequence of abuse and not the cause of a personality disorder. Finally, symptoms of posttraumatic stress disorder, an anxiety disorder diagnosis, such as intense fear, terror, helplessness, and reexperiencing the traumatic event(s) may also apply to some abused women.

Women beaten by their husbands often do not have driver's licenses, their own checkbooks, or jobs outside the home. Observers who know little about the battered wife syndrome are usually puzzled about these women's predicaments, and ask, "Why do they stay with their husbands if they are belittled, sexually abused, and physically abused?" The problems of abused women caught in this dilemma are so severe that the battered wife syndrome is now receiving special attention by mental health professionals and the courts.

In 1984, Susan Baum of Florida, who killed her husband, John, was one of the first women acquitted of murder on the basis of the battered wife syndrome defense. Baum had been repeatedly beaten and threatened by her husband; she testified that her six-month marriage was a horror punctuated by a series of beatings and rapes, including a hospital visit on her wedding night for broken bones. On the last night of their marriage, after she refused to take cocaine with her husband, he demanded, "We'll party or I'll blow your head off." The next morning, Susan Baum dialed the police emergency number, and requested police aid before her husband's return from work, claiming she was afraid he would kill her. John Baum returned home before the police arrived, and finding the door locked by his wife, threatened to kill her. In response, she picked up a .22 caliber revolver and shot him through the door, killing him instantly.

In testimony during her murder trial, Susan Baum said, "In my last call from him, he said that he was going to kill me, that there was no doubt in his mind, that he had a gun, and that he was going to kill me. . . . I was hysterical. I fired about a dozen shots out the window." [*Miami Herald,* Dec. 1, 1984).

Because of her husband's past threats on her life and his efforts to keep her extremely dependent, the defendant was acquitted of murder on the basis of the battered wife syndrome diagnosis (*Fort Lauderdale Sun-Sentinel,* December 5, 1984). Like all battered women, Susan Baum perceived that she had no control over her own safety. And like other victims of repeated past violence, she felt more violence was inevitable.

Besides these two criteria, the battered wife feels depressed, trapped, helpless, as well as angry, and is financially and psychologically dependent (Walker, 1977; 1989). Many battered women meet the criteria for dependent personality disorder. And, as earlier noted, they may also meet the criteria for **posttraumatic stress disorder (PTSD)** (see Chapter 5).

Certainly not all physically abused women are economically or psychologically dependent upon their husbands. However, most abused women lose a great deal of their self esteem, and some fear leaving because of even greater abuse after they leave. The following case presented in Box 10.2 illustrates how women who are abused feel that they are poor wives. It also depicts how spouse abuse can occur to any woman—regardless of her occupational and social status.

Bridgette Showes was one of 111 women who murdered their husbands and was reviewed for clemency by Ohio governor Celeste in 1990. The clemency consideration was based on the "battered wife defense."

BOX 10.2 A Piece of My Mind

I'm awake and in a sweat. I don't need to look at the clock; it's about 5 A.M., and I know I won't sleep anymore. I need all the sleep I can get to be alert for this evening. Yet my body demands I wake up and think. So, like on so many previous mornings, I will lie still here for 2 quiet hours.

What to think about? That's easy. No problem. I am unworthy, a poor excuse for a wife, just an anchor on him. But I will change—be more giving, more caring, more something. Something is wrong, and it's my fault, so I must try harder.

But my mind wanders. Get away! Don't come back! I have thought through elaborate escape plans, but I know that when I really need one I can never get away. . . .

To be on guard for tonight I must get more sleep. Silently I turn over, trying to find a more comfortable position. A bolt of pain shoots from my ear to my eyes. It is strange that even for an instant I could forget my raw left ear: For the last 3 days it had ached to use my stethoscope, but the swelling has lessened now; chewing no longer hurts. I don't dare reposition myself again, or he might wake up.

I always know the day of the last beating. I always hope it was the last. But it never is. Sometimes 2 or 3 days in a row go by. Or 8 or 10 pass, . . . Then, there it is again. Yet all the beatings and bruises fade and blur with time, as do the reasons. The reason for the last one? . . . Perhaps I left a towel hanging crooked . . . or did I forget to turn off a light as I left a room? . . . Maybe I wasn't paying enough attention to him while he was talking to me. . . .

He says I am selfish. . . . I've been called many things . . . but never selfish!

After the bad stuff is over, he tells me I should have known he didn't mean it. . . .

Usually just after the beating is all over, he says such nice things. But first he sort of apologizes, something like, "You weren't listening. I had to slap you out of that foggy state. See how you're paying attention now?" Then he tells me he won't ever do it again—unless I do something mean and selfish. And he'll kiss me and say, "You're the gentlest, sweetest, prettiest woman in the world." . . .

But I never know how long it will last. And why not forever? I know that's what I want. That's what he wants too, but first I must learn to care more, to love more. Yes, what a poor excuse for a wife I am. . . .

Hey, it's working! My ear is just a quiet throb now. . . . Trying not to rustle the blankets, I crawl out of bed . . . gather up my clothes and slip into the bathroom.

I grab my attache case and sneak a peek at him over my shoulder. So calm and peaceful he looks, still asleep. I will make it to work on time today . . . I did OK this morning.

I will call him at lunchtime to see how his morning has gone.

Postscript: Many people know women who live with abuse and ask why: why would a woman stay? I have given you my answer. Fortunately, I had people around me who cared. I was lucky to find a therapist who knew about spouse battering . . . (I later disappeared [from my husband].)

Yes, I know that I am truly lucky to be alive.

Janet A. Whitehall, M.D.*
[A Pseudonym]

Source: Whitehall, J. (1989). A Piece of My Mind: Wife. *Journal of American Medical Association, 261,* Copyright © 1989 by the American Medical Association, p. 3460.

Passive Aggressive Personality Disorder

Jim can really make you mad. You ask him to do something, and you get the impression that he will do it, but he repeatedly thwarts you. He "forgot to do it." He had "other things which came up." You wonder, "How many dumb excuses can he make?" As you interact with Jim more frequently, you suspect he resents being asked to do things in the first place—despite repeated assurances that you can rely on him. He rarely lets you know how he feels directly, engaging instead in passive aggressive acts against you. He covertly shows his anger toward you by letting you down when you need him. In sum, the passive aggressive personality expresses hostility in indirect and nonphysically aggressive ways.

For a diagnosis of **passive aggressive personality** disorder, the individual must behave in at least five of the following ways in a variety of contexts:

1. Procrastinate.
2. Act sulky, irritable, or argumentative.
3. Work slowly when he or she does not want to do something.
4. Protest, without justification, that others make unreasonable demands upon him or her.
5. Avoid obligations by claiming to have forgotten.
6. Believe that he or she is doing a much better job than others think he or she is doing.
7. Resent suggestions from others about how to be productive.
8. Obstruct the work of others by failing to do his or her share.
9. Unreasonably criticize others or scorn people in authority (*DSM-III-R,* 1987).

Passive aggressive personality disorder involves

such a behavior pattern across many situations. For this reason, the passive aggressive actions of politically downtrodden people, such as slowdowns by black workers in South Africa or sit-ins led by Martin Luther King to end racial discrimination in the United States, do not warrant a diagnosis of passive aggressive personality disorder. Persons involved in such protests may behave very differently toward their families, friends, and coworkers.

Passive aggressive behavior can ultimately be self-defeating because it often leads to being fired from jobs, separation from spouses, failure to achieve success, and alienation from friends. A thirty-year follow-up of male college graduates found that passive aggressive personality styles measured during college predicted poor adjustment in middle age (Valliant, 1976).

Passive aggressive personalities frequently experience conflicts between submissiveness and aggressiveness, and thus may behave inconsistently. Millon (1987) describes their conflicts: "These patients get themselves into endless wrangles and disappointments as they vacillate between deference and obedience one time, and defiance and aggressive negativism the next. Their behavior displays an erratic pattern of explosive anger or stubbornness intermingled with periods of guilt and shame" (p. 29). Both men and women are passive aggressive at almost identical rates (Millon, 1987).

Etiology of Passive Aggressive Personality Disorder. Like other personality disorders, the origins of passive aggressive personality patterns can be traced to childhood and adolescence. Psychodynamic theorists generally agree that passive aggressive behavior's core problem is an inability to express anger or hostility more directly. The basic question, however, appears to be "Why is the patient angry?" Usually the anger arises from dependency problems and the parent's failure to gratify these needs, resulting in various psychological consequences. In the extreme, psychotic reactions can occur. In more moderate cases, the frustration can lead to resentful rage expressed in antisocial ways. The child's need is frustrated by the parent in a fashion threatening to the child who cannot express his or her feelings about this treatment directly (Stricker, 1983). A young boy, for example, may be unable to tell his parents to stop acting in restrictive or punitive ways, but he can wet the bed, refuse to eat, or stutter to get back at his parents.

It is not unusual for many children to display passive aggressive behavior toward authority figures. We have all seen children passively resist doing something that they are told to do. They dawdle, walk slowly, and drag themselves toward the task, showing their anger or resentment. For example, a little girl tested her parents almost to the limit by not putting her toys away until they repeatedly threatened to spank her, but then, because of her sensitivity, her parents backed away from the confrontation. A child's dawdling and stalling, if not confronted by parents, can set the stage for a later passive aggressive personality style. This pattern is put in motion by the reinforcement or reward a child receives in getting away with such behavior. As might be expected, seeing parents display passive aggressive behavior also provides models for children to behave similarly. Adults, indeed, often display patterns resembling children's stalling. When Mom and the children are ready to leave on a trip, Dad may find a number of "last-minute" chores that simply *have* to be done.

A key characteristic of passive aggressive personalities is the denial of any hostile intent. According to psychodynamic theorists, the patients are unaware or unconscious of their passive aggressive behavior's underlying meaning. These individuals tend to believe they are unfortunate victims of their circumstances. This view of themselves is called *ego-syntonic,* a view acceptable to the person. In contrast, symptoms of depression, anxiety, or interpersonal problems are a great source of problems to the individual. Thus, they are called *ego-dystonic* and prompt the individual to seek treatment (Stricker, 1983).

Obsessive-Compulsive Personality Disorder

Most of us sometimes check certain things that we do. We return back to the house to see if we turned off the iron. We check our gas gauges and make lists of things to do the next day. Some people check gas gauges frequently or go over completed work several times. Scores reflecting compulsive checking habits similar to the **obsessive-compulsive personality** disorder were found in 10 percent to 15 percent of a college population (Frost, Sher, & Geen, 1986). In a poll of 100 randomly selected physicians, every one of them reported themselves to be "compulsive personalities," and 20 percent actually met criteria for obsessive-compulsive personality disorder (Krakowski, 1982).

What is the difference between normal checking and the checking of the obsessive-compulsives? The latter's checking and perfectionism are pervasive and inflexible. Obsessive-compulsives must try harder and more often, if possible, yet no matter how well they have done, it is not good enough. In their constant striving for perfection, they become preoccupied with trivial matters and procedures. They worry,

Individuals with obsessive-compulsive personality disorders strive for perfection and often spend time on trivial matters such as being extremely neat. This woman even cleans under her rugs.

schedule themselves poorly, and because they spend excessive time on triviality, are often in a frenzy trying to complete tasks.

For example, one graduate student took ten years to finish his doctoral requirements.

> His inability to finish his thesis grew out of his efforts to include everything, so that each new publication, study, or research in his field required him to revise his report. While his friends viewed him as a scholarly man who was intellectually honest and precise, he pursued this endless goal for fear of being rejected because of an inadequate or incomplete thesis. He functioned reasonably well as a parent, but his career was always in jeopardy because of interminable procrastinating, indecisiveness, and perfectionistic drives. **(Adapted from Salzman, 1985, p. 95)**

People described as compulsive are usually neat and punctual; often others perceive them as "uptight" and controlling. Some therapists called them "anal personalities," for according to Freudians, anal characteristics result from conflicts with parents during bowel training in the second to third year of life. When punishment surrounding this toilet training is severe or if the training comes too early, Freudians argue, the groundwork is laid for the obsessive-compulsive personality disorder or the anal retentive character. Like a child who refuses to go to the bathroom because of the erotic control associated with feces retention, anal personalities hold on to things; that is, they are possessive and keep their emotions under tight control. Alternatively, orderliness can also develop during this bowel training period when the child internalizes and accepts the parents' demands for bowel control.

The obsessive-compulsive personality disorder and the obsessive-compulsive anxiety disorder (see Chapter 5) seem similar on the surface. However, the obsessions of the obsessive-compulsive anxiety disorder often are more debilitating than those of the obsessive-compulsive personality disorder. As noted in the beginning of this chapter, anxiety disorders may be very serious yet episodic whereas personality disorders last much longer. Obsessive-compulsives can function socially and vocationally. In contrast, those with obsessive-compulsive anxiety disorder behave maladaptively, often in conflict with social or community standards (Salzman, 1985). Obsessive-compulsives do not feel the immediacy of their compulsion; instead there is little affect associated with it. They also exhibit low levels of general anxiety unlike those with the obsessive-compulsive anxiety disorder (Slade, 1974). Yet obsessive-compulsives may become anxious over circumscribed issues—such as seeing that all the books are not arranged on a shelf properly, or not having a desk arranged with appears in neat piles.

Obsessive-compulsives' fear of making an error and of losing control contributes to problems committing to people or things. This lack of commitment leads them to feel alienated and uninvolved, and they cope with their alienation by displacement—by spending time doing things of minor importance like checking and rechecking lists, travel plans, or the weather.

Their cold, calculating manner and inability to express their thoughts has adverse consequences for obsessive-compulsives in intimate relationships. Sexual difficulties often exist; even when the sex act is adequate, the positive feelings and communication essential to make it truly satisfying for most people are absent. Obsessive-compulsives "often appear to be a competent fornicating machine to their partners, rather than someone engaged in a loving involvement" (Salzman, 1985, p. 22).

Etiology of Obsessive-Compulsive Personality Disorder. Freud's view of obsessive-compulsive personality disorder's origins has had a lasting influence on many professionals. Obsessive-compulsive personality styles, Freud believed, originated in the child's battles with parents over withholding urine and feces. If the parents' toilet training began too young or was too extreme, the child responded with hostile feelings and active rebellion. More recent psychodynamic views recognize the disagreement and the conflicting evidence over bowel training's role in this disorder's etiology. Today, psychodynamic theorists believe the disorder stems from feelings of helplessness and insecurity and the need, therefore, for maintaining order to deal with these insecurities. "The overriding purpose of the behavior is to attempt to achieve some security and certainty for the person who feels threatened and insecure in an uncertain world" (Salzman, 1985, p. 12). Unlike Freud, who argued that obsessive-compulsive behavior represented a way of coping with unacceptable sexual impulses, professionals now believe that obsessive-compulsive behavior aids the individual in controlling any shameful thoughts—whether hostile, sexual, or in some way undesired. Emphasis has shifted, with therapists focusing less on the patient's need for control of explicit sexual thoughts and more on the need for control of any undesired or shameful thoughts.

Some professionals observe that the obsessive-compulsive's controlled, perfectionistic manner results from a conflict between hostility toward others and fear of disapproval. Obsessive-compulsives cope with this ambivalence by attempting to overconform and demanding much of themselves. Such self-restraint helps control their oppositional feelings. "Behind this front of propriety and restraint, however, are intense anger and oppositional feelings that occasionally break through their controls" (Millon, 1985, p. 29). Obsessive-compulsives score high on measures of authoritarian beliefs and holding to conventional attitudes (e.g., strong negative attitude toward communism). They do not respond readily to praise in experimental psychology tasks, and also overestimate time in experiments—presumably because of its special value for them (Pollak, 1979).

Treatment of Obsessive-Compulsive Personality Disorders. Obsessive-compulsives are unlikely to seek any kind of treatment on their own. Some of their compulsiveness, they may even believe, is useful to them: They think they are able to "get more" done. Certain jobs may encourage this type of behavior. For example, we reward proofreaders, accountants, and laboratory technicians for checking and rechecking their efforts. American society also generally rewards perseverance, diligence, and the ability to work hard, characteristics which obsessive-compulsives consider they possess. The serious problems for obsessive-compulsives usually occur in relationships when, for example, the need to check and recheck if all electrical appliances are turned off prevents them and their partner from catching a train. The partner, if sufficiently frustrated, then forces the issue. A "showdown" that leads to therapy—often pushed by the partner—may also occur when the obsessive-compulsive's anger or hostility is provoked in the intimate relationship or on the job.

We have no controlled outcome studies of treatment of the obsessive-compulsive personality disorder, but insight-oriented psychotherapy—either psychodynamic or cognitive behavioral—is probably helpful. Sometimes prompting the obsessive-compulsive through persuasion and encouragement not to engage in the behavior and to evaluate the consequences of *discontinuing* it is necessary. For example, consider the way the compulsiveness of this client, a successful attorney, was changed:

> *The client would get up very early in the morning to review his cases for the day. Several days before a court appearance, he would also review as many questions of the opposing attorney as he could possibly dream up. The client's blackboard would literally be covered with questions that he thought might come up on the trial. If he had a number of cases that might be scheduled for trial within the next week or two, his life became filled with compulsive behavior designed to cover "all his bases" on each case. Finally his wife, furious with coping for years with his checking, asked for a separation. He responded with fears that his life would then be less orderly and that she might leave him for good. Instead of attacking the pathological nature of the compulsiveness, the therapist spent several months providing insight into the useful role the checking had served for the client. Then gradually, the client was asked to systematically stop engaging in certain of his compulsive acts. For example, he was asked not to review cases in his car as he sat waiting for the court house to open; instead he was to get out and chat with other attorneys who were waiting as well. The therapist next*

asked him to skip the Saturday morning work session where he reviewed his cases for a Monday court appearance; instead, he was asked to review them only on his regularly scheduled Sunday review. Later, he was asked to skip the Sunday review as well and to attempt to keep his reviewing hours to 8:30–6:00 P.M., Monday to Friday. This graduated plan of change resulted in very significant reductions in the client's compulsiveness; meanwhile, he was able to see that his law practice had not dwindled. At present, he still obsesses about certain things, has relationship problems to cope with, and is not "cured" of all his problems. His life and work, however, significantly improved. Seeing the changes in him, his wife decided to seek therapy with him to improve the relationship. (K. Daniel O'Leary, 1989)

Avoidant Personality Disorder

As the name implies, avoidant personalities fear and avoid others, especially in situations where they may face failure or rejection. Avoidant personalities are usually shy, fearful, or overly self-critical. Coworkers tend to view them as aloof and distant; such individuals seem overly sensitive to criticism or even the appearance of it.

Avoidant personalities refrain from relationships until they receive clear signs that they will be accepted. In contrast to individuals with the schizoid personality, they desire contact with others. Yet, although they want to be accepted very badly, they avoid the risk of interpersonal relationships. They continually cope with a basic conflict of wanting contact yet running from it. The cycle of the avoidant personality is often vicious: Lacking self-esteem, they avoid others; then, as a result, their self-esteem plummets even further. The following case of a seventeen-year-old high school student illustrates the **avoidant personality** disorder:

The patient reported that her mother frequently criticized her performance of daily household chores irrespective of the quality of her performance. Further, the patient indicated that her older brother often teased her about many things, such as doing poorly on a test at school. Finally, she reported that her father was overprotective and restricted her social life. As a result, the patient reported withdrawing from family interactions and spending an inordinate amount of time in her room.

The patient indicated that her boyfriend broke up with her six months previously. When discussing this, she became tearful and related that she was very upset with his rejection. The patient also indicated that she had a very small network of friends and that approximately one month earlier one of these "turned" on her. She reported feelings of anxiety when she thought or spoke of or actually encountered either of these two individuals. . . .

The patient indicated that she gets extremely nervous when taking examinations at school which interferes with her performance on such tests. . . . The patient reported experiencing daily dull, ache-like pain in the frontal area of her head, which varied in intensity and duration. . . .

The patient reported many feelings of insecurity and viewed herself negatively. (Turkat and Maisto, 1985, p. 514)

Etiology of Avoidant Personality Disorder. We know that predispositions to be fearful and avoidant are inherited and become manifest in childhood and early adolescence. Timid children as young as two years old show heightened autonomic nervous system reactivity after changes in the environment such as when a mother leaves a room or another adult enters it (Alden & Cappe, 1988). Fearful and avoidant behavior in childhood is also influenced by modeling of parents and their direct reinforcement of this behavior (see Chapter 12). Some patients with this disorder also describe emotional and physical abuse in childhood. There is little if any etiological evidence on this specific personality disorder's development; to conceptualize about it, psychologists have relied on general models of the development of anxious and fearful behaviors. Moreover, since clinicians rarely employ it as a primary diagnosis, the disorder's developmental course is unknown. Alternatively stated, we do not yet have enough cases of individuals with avoidant personalities followed over time to assess the disorder's stability (Gunderson, 1988).

Treatment of Avoidant Personality Disorder. A wide variety of psychological treatments can help individuals with avoidant personality disorder. Such therapies' goal is to encourage the patient to confront fearful situations and extinguish the fearful response. Based on research with phobias and generalized anxiety, both short-term psychotherapy and desensitization appear beneficial. Short-term cognitive-behavioral treatment in a group is successful where clients share information and feelings about their problems, establish specific goals between therapy sessions, and attempt to change the focus of their thoughts from fear-related thinking to action. Such treatment results in enhanced self-esteem, less avoidance, and less anxiety. While few individuals report that ten weeks of group therapy completely resolve their problems, the changes noted were clinically meaningful and generalized to their work settings (Alden, 1989).

ODD OR ECCENTRIC PERSONALITY DISORDERS

The very names of the odd and eccentric personality disorders (paranoid, schizotypal, and schizoid) raise questions for many students. Are these disorders mild versions of the similarly named clinical syndrome disorders? For example, are the schizotypal and schizoid personality disorders simply precursors or early phases of the clinical syndrome, schizophrenia? The answer is no. These personality disorders are not emergent or emerging clinical syndromes; they are separate disorders. Like the other personality disorders, the odd and eccentric personality disorders are maladaptive personality styles starting early in childhood and generally remaining stable—at least throughout early adulthood.

Paranoid Personality Disorder

People with **paranoid personality** disorders feel that others are against them. At least by early adulthood, they begin to believe people are somehow exploiting or taking advantage of them. Paranoids feel slighted by little things and are easily hurt by others' small oversights. Often we say that such people make "mountains out of molehills." Paranoids tend to be jealous, secretive, rigid, argumentative, scheming, cold, and frequently sullen; they think they are faultless and attribute their mistakes to others. They even go as far as ascribing sinister motives and behavior to others that caused their mistakes (e.g., my lab partner purposely didn't clean the test tube so that my chem lab experiment would not work). Paranoid personalities are supersensitive to rank, class, and power issues; they envy others who possess things they don't have. All these characteristics originate from a pervasive mistrust and suspicion of others.

According to Gunderson (1988), the paranoid and the schizotypal personality disorders are the most severe of the personality disorders. The paranoid disorder is so-considered because of the resulting problems in relationships with others, especially those in positions of authority. Indeed, the workplace is where the paranoid person typically experiences the most obvious problems. This disorder is very difficult to change.

Etiology of Paranoid Personality Disorder. While its etiology is unknown, Gunderson (1988) believes hostile motives are at the core of the problem and that paranoids project their motives onto others. Other professionals feel that many paranoids have experienced sadistic treatment during infancy and then as children they internalized sadistic tendencies toward themselves and others (Cameron, 1963). Relatively little systematic research exists on the etiology of paranoid personality disorders because research on how to correctly diagnose this disorder is still in its' infancy (Kreiner, Simonsen, & Mogensen, 1990).

Treatment of Paranoid Personality Disorder. Treatment of paranoids usually focuses on trust building rather than direct confrontation. Men are more likely to be paranoid than women yet few men seek therapy for this problem. They do not wish to be in another relationship, like a therapeutic relationship, in which they feel inferior and not in control.

Schizotypal Personality Disorder

Schizotypal personalities are loners who isolate themselves from others. Like the paranoids, they feel suspicious of others, but in contrast they are often odd and eccentric in their dress and appearance. Often, they dress in clothing that is totally out of fashion or in clothing that does not fit with the season (e.g. they may wear layers of clothing on a hot summer day). Schizotypal personalities may also appear unusual to others because of their speech and their perception of the world. For example, they sometimes act as if they were clairvoyant or "others could feel their feelings." They occasionally have illusions such as "I feel that someone else is in the room." But unlike the schizophrenic, their unusual thoughts and speech do not reflect a total loosening of associations so they never lose complete ties with reality.

Schizotypal personalities bear some resemblance to borderlines, and in fact, they were once called *borderline schizophrenics*. Schizotypal personalities, however, do not engage in suicidal behavior as frequently as borderlines, and, as a consequence, they are generally seen in outpatient settings. The schizotypal personality also exhibits more unusual patterns of social behavior such as having unusual dress than the borderline personality.

Etiology of Schizotypal Personality Disorder. Family data reveal an association of **schizotypal personality** with schizophrenia though twin data and adoption studies have not indicated such a relationship (Rutter, 1987). In brief, family data indicate that relatives of schizophrenics appear at risk for a schizotypal personality disorder although family members of people with schizotypal personality disorders are not more likely to be schizophrenic (Gunderson, 1988). No convincing evidence indicates that an individual with schizotypal personality disorder will become schizophrenic, but evidence does suggest that schizotypal personalities will suffer from later social maladjustment.

Treatment of Schizotypal Personality Disorder. Schizotypal personalities (like paranoid personalities) appear to profit best from supportive, nonconfrontational psychotherapy. Intensive psychotherapy directed at exploring the schizotypal individual's central conflicts is often avoided by expert clinicians because of the schizotypal personality's extreme sensitivity (Stone, 1985). Because of their shyness, these patients can profit from group therapy if they do not show severe paranoid tendencies. Those with such tendencies would withdraw from a group. Schizotypal personalities rarely need institutionalization, but specific social skills training is often necessary to enable them to function well in job settings or sheltered workshops. For example, they may need to be taught not to wear certain attire, how to overcome a fear of touching doorknobs, or to avoid spitting in public. The following example illustrates the psychodynamic treatment of a schizotypal patient who showed "slow but steady improvement" over a seventeen-year therapy.

> *I began working with Miss T. when she was 31 years old, and have been seeing her thrice weekly for the succeeding 17 years. She had seen a different therapist for seven years in another city. Briefly married during college, she has remained single since. For a long time, she would seldom see a man beyond the third date, lest she feel constrained to reveal certain things about her past of which she was deeply ashamed. In particular, she felt that no one could accept her, knowing that her chronically schizophrenic mother and her father had died some years ago in a mutual suicide attempt. She assumed others would regard her as somehow to blame—for having "abandoned" them by moving to another city. She supported herself well as a certified public accountant, but led a lonely existence apart from her frequent, though short-lived, relationships. . . . She was markedly eccentric and concretistic in thought and speech, and rather eccentric in dress as well.*
>
> *She was very enamored of psychoanalysis, and peppered her sessions with intellectual interpretations about her various conflicts and peculiarities ("It's because my mother tied me up in the back of the house when her friends came over, isn't it?"). It quickly became apparent the knowledge she had of her dynamics was of little use to her. Despite her protestations . . . I shifted the focus to one of two important areas. She saw me and everyone else as carbon copies of her parents, and needed a great deal of help in recognizing that I (and others) were largely unlike either of them and that she herself was separate and unique (p. 583).*
>
> *Her poor ability either to generalize, or to retain an image of me over any long period of time, contributes to her distress before each interruption in our work. Even after 17 years, separations still lead to intense worries that I will not return, to notions of being "ugly" or "unlikable" (else why would I be "abandoning" her?), and to anger at seeing how little control she has over my comings and goings. . . . Of late, she has been able to sustain romantic relationships for a year or more, though still requiring day-to-day guidance in behavior, lest her eccentricities and irritability alienate those for whom she cares.* (Stone, 1985, pp. 583–584)

Our knowledge of the course of schizotypal personality disorder is based on only two studies. The first is an evaluation of outpatients in a private treatment; they changed very little. The individuals most likely to change were those possessing the capability of expressing warmth and the capacity for empathy. Symptoms of avoidance and suspiciousness showed little change (Stone, 1983).

The second study regarding the treatment of schizotypal personalities was of hospitalized inpatients. Schizotypal personalities do not usually require institutionalization, but this follow-up of hospitalized inpatients involved an analysis of all patients discharged from a famous psychiatric facility, the Chestnut Lodge Hospital in Rockville, Maryland. Most of the discharged patients had been treated for approximately two years at Chestnut Lodge, and they had been released from the hospital an average of fifteen years. The follow-up of hospitalized schizotypal inpatients showed that schizotypal personalities had good intellectual skills, and 50 percent had obtained further education since their hospitalization. On the other hand, they were still withdrawn and reclusive. Half of the patients had been married at some point in their lives (McGlashan, 1986).

Schizoid Personality Disorder

Individuals with schizoid personality disorders are seclusive; they often engage in solitary activities, choosing work with minimal social interactions. They prefer to be alone and avoid expressing their feelings. A shy, introverted temperament may be a predisposing factor to this disorder (Gunderson, 1988). They do not display the same eccentric behaviors as the schizotypal personalities do. They can often form distant but stable relationships at work and play, but they do not form close relationships and seem to have very little desire for sexual experiences. Like the schizotypal personalities, the schizoid personality has little interest in psychotherapy, and, as a consequence, very little is known about treatment of this disorder.

Professionals originally believed that the schizoid personality was a mild form variant of schizophrenia. Yet, a separate diagnostic category was formed for the schizoid personality disorder because psychologists no longer see it as a simple variant of schizophrenia (Gunderson, 1988). The **schizoid personality** disorder is viewed as less severe than the schizotypal personality disorder.

A DIMENSIONAL APPROACH TO ASSESSMENT OF PERSONALITY DISORDERS

Anyone studying the personality disorders may wonder about the overlap among the various personality disorders we have discussed. In one study of this overlap, only 11 percent of inpatients with personality disorders had only one disorder (Widiger et al.

1987). Because of this extremely frequent overlap among the clinical symptom pictures presented by patients, a **dimensional approach** offers an alternative to the categorical system used in the *Diagnostic and Statistical Manual.* The dimensional approach has been used for several decades with children and adults. It involves a statistical analysis of diverse symptoms of all types of patients to understand the basic dimensions or core groups appearing to underlie the diverse symptoms. For example, recall the three general groups of personality disorders in this chapter: (1) dramatic, emotional, or erratic, (2) anxious or fearful, and (3) odd or eccentric. These three are quite similar to the groupings or underlying dimensions or factors found in analyses of ratings of the behavior of outpatients (Kass et al., 1985). Moreover, very similar factors also characterize the ratings of inpatients specifically diagnosed with personality disorders. In brief, similar factors seem to appear in both inpatient and outpatients—confirming a belief that a dimensional approach has special value.

The **categorical approach** of the *DSM-III-R* and the dimensional approach discussed here each have their advantages and disadvantages. The categorical approach's simplicity aids in communication of rich clinical material. It is also consistent with psychiatric and medical formulations of discrete symptoms and disorders. On the other hand, the categorical approach may obscure the actual overlap that exists among symptoms. As just noted, in one study of inpatients, only 11 percent of the population had a single diagnosis. Dimensional approaches to personality have existed for decades and proponents of this system include the famous protégé of Freud, Carl Jung, and others such as Hans Eysenck in England and Raymond Cattell and Theodore Millon of the United States. For the 1990s, the dimensional system appears likely to supplement but not to replace the categorical system utilized in the *DSM-III-R.* Yet, the dimensional approach may have special value in understanding the etiology and relationships among the personality disorders that is not possible with the diagnostic categories. Finally, several new dimensional approaches have been proposed to account for the interaction of personality dimensions, the function of brain systems, and learning phenomena (e.g., Cloninger, 1987). Such dimensional approaches may be in their infancy, but they have advantages of fostering interdisciplinary team research with neuroscientists, psychologists, and psychiatrists.

SUMMARY

1. Personality disorders are stable ways of behaving that generally begin in childhood. They are classified on Axis II of the *DSM-III-R* to distinguish them from the far less stable symptom disorders of Axis I.
2. Individuals with narcissistic personality disorder are characterized by their craving for attention and the feeling that others should cater to them. Narcissists have been of special interest to psychodynamic therapists, who have aided these patients in understanding that they need to confront the etiology of their problems, that is, to understand that their search for attention is maladaptive and that they can accept themselves for who they are.
3. Histrionic personality disorders also seek attention but in unusual ways; they are manipulative and self-centered.
4. Borderline patients are on the border of life in many ways. They are marginal in both personal and vocational adjustment. Their frequent suicidal behavior places them at great personal risk; as many as 10 percent of these patients eventually die from suicide. Both psychodynamic and cognitive-behavioral therapies have been useful with borderline patients, especially in combination with antidepressant medication.
5. Antisocial personalities have very stable personal characteristics. They represent "grown-up" conduct disorders, continuing to display behavior violating the rights of others. They are aggressive and frequently engage in unlawful behavior. Antisocial personalities rarely seek psychological therapy, and the effects are limited even when they do.
6. People with dependent personality disorders are characterized by their submissiveness and persistent need for assurance. Dependent personalities require psychotherapeutic aid to enhance their self-esteem and social skills. Women may receive this diagnosis or a diagnosis of self-defeating personality after being physically beaten by their spouses, but it must be recognized that these personality styles may be a reaction to violence, not necessarily a lifelong personality style or disorder. Consequently, the anxiety disorder, posttraumatic stress disorder, and a new proposed diagnosis, "battered wife syndrome" may be most relevant in these cases.
7. Passive aggressive personalities are distinguished by resisting the requests of others. Instead of overtly telling someone directly that they do not want to do something, they take more time than expected or find excuses for not doing it.
8. Individuals with obsessive-personality disorders preoccupy themselves with attempts to be perfectionistic; they often spend time redoing what they have already completed for fear they have not done it well enough.
9. People with avoidant personality disorders are noted for their fearful avoidance of others. Psychotherapy and cognitive-behavioral therapy can help avoidant personalities by aiding the patients to directly face what they are avoiding.
10. Individuals with paranoid personality disorder believe that others are taking advantage of them. They are often jealous, secretive, scheming, and they distrust almost everyone. The paranoid per-

sonality disorder has severe consequences in the workplace where the mistrust leads to accusations about others' motives. Paranoids are extremely hard to change.

11. Individuals with schizotypal personality disorders are characterized by isolation from others, suspiciousness, and unusual speech and dress. But, unlike the schizophrenic, they never lose complete touch with reality. The schizoid personality, like the schizotypal personality, is characterized by seclusiveness, but schizoid personalities do not display as much eccentric behavior as schizotypal personalities.

12. An alternative diagnostic system to the *DSM-III-R* is the dimensional system accounting for the frequent overlap of diagnoses seen in actual practice. Varied dimensional approaches have existed for decades, and they continue to influence the conceptualization of disorders — especially the basic dimensions or factors that may underlie or cut across them. Although the categorical system, nevertheless, appeals to clinicians because of its descriptive simplicity, the dimensional systems may be used as adjuncts to them.

Raul Guerrero, *"Borracho en el Ancla"* (1989). Oil on linen, 41½ × 49½ inches framed. Courtesy of the Daniel Saxon Gallery, Los Angeles.

11 PSYCHOACTIVE SUBSTANCE USE DISORDERS

Most people in this country drink alcoholic beverages and many use drugs. While most drinking and drug use is legal, some is not. Many people drink and use other drugs without serious consequences, yet some people's abuse of these substances causes themselves and their families enormous problems. For these reasons, psychoactive substance abuse and dependence are among the nation's major public health problems.

Consider the following data on the effects of alcohol and drug abuse in the United States.

- In 1990, alcohol abuse cost almost $137 billion. More than half stemmed from lost employment and reduced productivity, while another quarter paid for health-care costs (National Institute on Alcohol Abuse and Alcoholism (NIAAA), 1990).
- Forty-eight percent of all persons convicted of a crime in 1983 had consumed alcohol before committing the crime (NIAAA, 1987).
- In 1990, alcohol use and abuse was either the main cause or a contributing factor in more than 100,000 deaths (NIAAA, 1990).
- Between 20 percent and 36 percent of suicide victims had a history of alcohol abuse or were drinking shortly before their suicides (Colliver & Malin, 1986).
- Approximately one half of the fatal traffic crashes during 1987—killing 46,386 people—were alcohol-related (National Highway Traffic Safety Administration, 1988).
- The economic cost of drug abuse was at least $60 billion in 1983, including both direct costs (e.g., health-care costs) and indirect costs (e.g., lost productivity) (Siegel, 1988).
- Smoking now claims more than 390,000 lives a year. The average male smoker is twenty-two times more likely to die from lung cancer than a male nonsmoker (National Institute on Drug Abuse (NIDA), 1989).
- Experience with illegal drugs in the early 1960s was restricted to 2 percent or less of the population. By 1982, almost one third of the household population over age twelve had had some experience with them (American Psychiatric Association Committee on Drug Abuse, 1987).
- Ten percent of violent crimes are drug-related. One third of all federal prisoners and over one half of all state prisoners are narcotics addicts (Goldstein, 1985).
- Among eighteen- to thirty-four-year-old women (those in the primary childbearing ages) in 1987, 30 percent used an illicit drug at least once and 18 percent used an illicit drug at least once in the past month (NIDA, 1989).

A BRIEF HISTORICAL PERSPECTIVE

Alcohol and drug abuse have long been part of human history. The Old Testament of the Bible, for example, describes such diagnostic features of alcoholism as physical and psychological dependence, alcohol-induced memory problems, and withdrawal's sometimes-fatal consequences. The authors of the Old Testament severely criticize those lacking the moral strength to resist drink's temptation. In the First Book of Samuel, for example, the High Priest Eli condemns Hannah's weakness when he discovers her, in an apparently intoxicated state, mumbling at the shrine of Shiloh.

Chronic alcohol abusers were stoned to death for their weakness in Old Testament times. During the Middle Ages, along with psychotics, mental retardates, and those believed possessed by demons, alcoholics were tortured and burned at the stake. Those who escaped the stake could be confined indefinitely to prison or the almshouse, in the conviction that people who abused alcohol or displayed psychotic behavior did so from choice—and an impaired moral sense.

Only in the past several decades of the twentieth century has a more enlightened view of alcoholism developed (well after psychiatric patients had begun to be treated with greater humanity). It took the effects of World War II—in which as many soldiers fell victim to substance abuse and psychiatric disorder as to enemy gunfire—to convince Americans that alcoholism was not simply a moral issue.

Alcoholics Anonymous (AA), the newly formed self-help group, also helped change public attitudes toward alcoholism at about the same time. AA's fellowship ultimately convinced many Americans of alcoholism's being more a medical and social problem than a moral one. Continuing advances in scientific understanding of alcoholism's causes have helped make this evident to more people.

Until very recently, alcohol has been the principal drug abused in Western society. Although opium, "the flower of happiness," had been cultivated in the Middle East's Fertile Crescent 2,000 years before the birth of Christ and its use had become well established in India and China by A.D. 800, it was essentially unknown in the Western world before Paracelsus created "laudanum"—tincture of opium—in the fifteenth century. Up to the end of the eighteenth century, most Western opium addicts were either survivors of battlefield trauma or victims of chronic pain; in both instances, they had become dependent on one of the pain-killing drugs in the opium family. Until the Pure Food and Drug Act and the Harrison Narcotic Act were passed in the early twentieth century, opium, morphine, and heroin were widely available without restriction in the United States (Kissin, 1982) because, in the absence of systematic studies of their long-term effects on the body, they were believed no danger to their users.

Drug and alcohol abuse and dependence have long been an important part of human history.

The abuse of drugs of dependence other than alcohol and the opiates in Western countries began to increase sharply in the early nineteenth century when (1) veterans of Napoleon's Egyptian campaign introduced marijuana and hashish into French society on their return, and (2) cocaine, the potent alkaloid of the coca leaf, was isolated and introduced to Europe and later America. Sigmund Freud's favorable review of cocaine's analgesic and sedative properties in the late 1800s and the popular fictional detective Sherlock Holmes's use of cocaine as a mental stimulant contributed to its appeal—and the perception that it, like opium, was not dangerous.

By the end of the nineteenth century, alcohol was not the only drug Europeans and Americans abused. That pattern has escalated during the twentieth century to include the other drugs of abuse considered in this chapter.

DIAGNOSIS OF THE PSYCHOGENIC SUBSTANCE USE DISORDERS

Earlier Diagnostic Conceptions

The symptoms of *alcohol* and *drug addiction* were described in *DSM-I* (1952), the first formal American nomenclature. They were considered varieties of **sociopathic personality disturbance,** a catchall diagnostic category including antisocial behavior and the sexual deviations. *DSM-II* (1968) categorized these four conditions the same way. The implication of the 1952 and 1968 diagnostic manuals was that people exhibiting any of these four behavioral patterns were a threat to society's moral fabric.

DSM-III's developers (1980) moved away from the implicit moral judgment characterizing those portions of *DSM-I* and *DSM-II* devoted to substance abuse, antisocial behavior, and the sexual deviations. *DSM-III* placed the *substance use disorders* in a separate category, avoiding the "guilt of association" of the 1952 and 1968 versions. In addition, *DSM-III* highlighted research findings implicating sociocultural and genetic factors in the etiology of these disorders and emphasized the role scientists and physicians had begun to play in their study and treatment.

The Substance Dependence Syndrome

DSM-III-R (1987) retains many of *DSM-III*'s diagnostic advances while introducing some new diagnostic elements. The most striking change is the decision by *DSM-III-R*'s drafters to base the diagnosis of substance dependence on the empirically derived **substance dependence syndrome,** which includes the following diagnostic criteria.

- The person takes more of the substance over a longer period of time than he or she intends.
- While recognizing that he or she uses the substance to excess, and despite trying to control its consumption, the person cannot do so.
- The person spends much of his or her time obtaining and ingesting the substance and then recovering from its effects.
- The substance's effects, including intoxication and withdrawal, interfere with the person's ability to work, study, and meet family obligations.
- The person puts substance use ahead of important social, job-related, and recreational activities.
- Despite experiencing significant problems from substance use, the person continues to use it.
- Because tolerance to the substance has developed, the person must ingest increasing amounts to achieve the same subjective effect as previously.
- When, after continued use, the person stops ingesting the substance or markedly reduces its level of ingestion, he or she experiences characteristic withdrawal symptoms.
- To avoid the unpleasant experience of withdrawal, the person must continue taking the substance.

Persons who meet three or more of these criteria merit the *DSM-III-R* diagnosis of **psychoactive substance dependence.** Those who fail to meet at least three of these criteria but (1) have used a substance for a month or more even though it caused them significant problems or (2) use substances in physically hazardous circumstances (e.g., while driving a car) meet criteria for **psychoactive substance abuse.**

Tolerance and Withdrawal. Through the years, clinicians have considered tolerance and withdrawal key symptoms for the diagnosis of alcohol or drug dependence. For example, the diagnosis of alcohol or drug dependence required one or both in *DSM-III.* Though the drafters of *DSM-III-R* have diminished the diagnostic importance of these symptoms, in part because of clinicians' problems observing them reliably, the behaviors are still vital to anyone attempting to understand alcohol and drug dependence.

Tolerance refers to a phenomenon probably occurring at the cellular and psychological levels. That is, cells adjust to chronic alcohol or drug challenge by altering certain biochemical processes, even as the thinking human learns to expect certain behavioral and psychological consequences of regular alcohol or drug ingestion (see discussion of learned tolerance later in this chapter). Tolerance forces those using alcohol or a drug for a period of time to increase their dosage to maintain the pleasurable feelings which originally accompanied ingestion. It also produces a gradual reduction in those feelings when the drug's dosage remains constant.

Withdrawal refers to the interrelated physical and psychological consequences accompanying cessation of drug or alcohol intake after a long enough period of heavy enough ingestion to create dependence—and, usually, tolerance. Withdrawal symptoms, like tolerance, are influenced by physical as well as psychological factors.

Strengths of the Current Diagnostic System

One of the most important features of *DSM-III-R* is its reliance on a solid body of empirical research. That research, for example, identified the so-called "alcohol dependence syndrome" in a large number of alcoholic patients (Edwards, Arif, & Hodgson, 1981; Edwards, Gross, Keller, & Moser, 1976). Another positive feature is that *DSM-III-R* does not require clinicians to make a categorical choice between alcohol or drug abuse or dependence, as *DSM-III* and its predecessors required. Instead, by the current system, the clinician places the patient at a point on the *continuum* of dependence, called the substance dependence syndrome. That point can vary from mild (e.g., if the person displays only three diagnostic symptoms) through moderate to severe (e.g., if the person shows multiple symptoms).

The substance dependence syndrome judges all psychoactive substances according to a consistent set of criteria for abuse and dependence. The same diagnostic criteria weigh the long-term behavioral consequences of the abuse of such different drugs as alcohol, cocaine, the opioids, and the hallucinogens. In this way clinicians are now able to judge the severity of simultaneous dependence on several drugs (an increasingly frequent phenomenon).

The Classes of Abused Substances

DSM-III-R lists nine classes of substances that induce both abuse and dependence.

- Alcohol
- The amphetamines and other substances with amphetamine-like effects
- Cannabis and marijuana
- Cocaine and crack
- The hallucinogens
- The inhalants
- The opioids
- Phencyclidine (PCP) and similarly acting drugs
- The sedatives and similarly acting drugs

A tenth drug, nicotine, induces dependence but not abuse.

These ten substance groups can also be classified by predominant effect.

- Substances that decrease central nervous system activity (alcohol, the opioids, and the sedatives).
- Substances that increase central nervous system activity (cocaine and crack, the amphetamines, the inhalants, and nicotine).
- Substances that induce psychotic-like behavior (the hallucinogens and PCP).

Cannabis and marijuana have both sedative and hallucinogenic effects.

ESTIMATING THE NUMBER OF SUBSTANCE ABUSERS

How many Americans suffer from psychoactive substance dependence? Estimates are that somewhere between 6 percent and 8 percent of our population, or between 15 million and 20 million people, have a serious alcohol problem (Helzer, Burnam, & McEvoy, 1990). Louise, whose story is related in Box 11.1, was such a person.

It is less clear how many Americans abuse substances other than alcohol. This lack of clarity derives, at least partially, from the widespread availability of the five classes of drugs abused in this country. They include:

1. Psychoactive drugs for which a physician's prescription is necessary. (About 30 percent of all prescriptions are for drugs that act upon the brain; many of these drugs are abused.)
2. Over-the-counter drugs intended to treat minor illnesses; they do not require a prescription.
3. Caffeine and nicotine; both induce dependence, though many users are unaware of this fact.
4. Compounds sold for nondrug purposes which are nonetheless abused; they include airplane glue, certain herbs, and the seeds of certain plants.

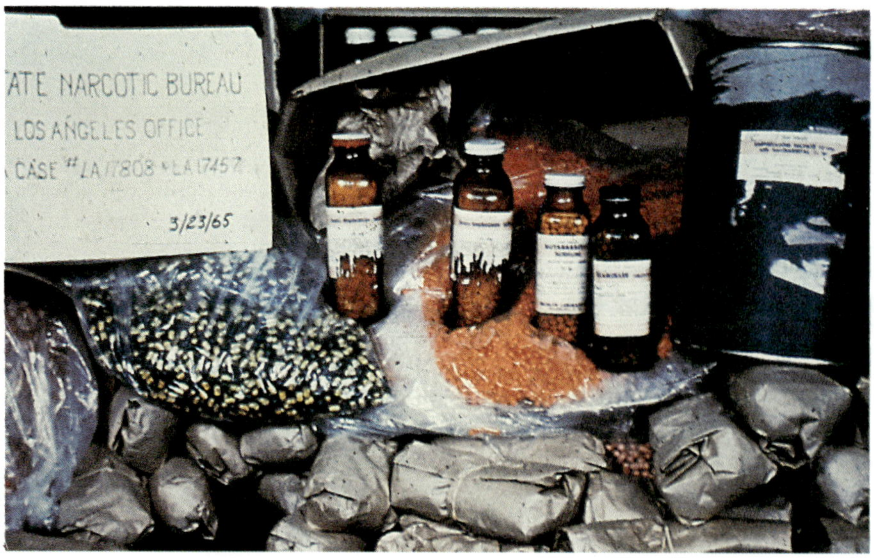

This photograph shows a small sample of the available drugs of abuse.

BOX 11.1 Louise Is an Alcoholic

Louise was forty seven but looked a good deal older when she came to one of the authors of this book for alcoholism treatment. Her decision to seek treatment was motivated by her new husband's ultimatum that either she stop drinking or he would take immediate steps to end their two-year marriage. Because Louise wanted the marriage to continue, she agreed to treatment for her drinking problem.

Louise related a long history of efforts to control her drinking. They began shortly after she took her first drink, when she was a sophomore in a small liberal arts college near her Midwestern hometown. The first night she drank, she drank enough to get drunk—and very sick. Louise's parents were lifelong abstainers, partially because each had an alcoholic parent.

Louise began using alcohol to deal with the stresses of college life. She drank almost every day and got drunk at least a couple of times a week. She became concerned about her drinking a few months after graduation, when she realized that it had begun to affect her position as a newspaper reporter, a job she had always wanted. Working for a small Midwestern paper not far from her hometown, Louise began missing assignments when hangovers made it impossible for her to leave her apartment to cover a story.

Following several unsuccessful efforts to control her drinking, Louise began attending a local Alcoholics Anonymous meeting. Louise ultimately abstained from alcohol for several years but only after several anguished months of inner debate over whether she could actually give up drinking for the rest of her life. The AA philosophy of "one day at a time" made it a good deal easier to stop drinking, because sobriety for a day was much easier for Louise to imagine than abstinence for a lifetime.

After a failed marriage, caused partially by a return to abusive drinking, Louise moved East, where she began working for a weekly newspaper in the New York metropolitan area and tried to stay sober. Shortly after the move, she met Morris, and they subsequently married. Two years afterward, with the marriage in serious trouble because of a return to drinking, Louise sought help again for her drinking.

Louise had no trouble remaining abstinent during the day. Her drinking began at night, usually after eight o'clock, when she started consuming great quantities of vodka and orange juice. A frequent result was marked behavioral change: Louise would chide Morris for real and imagined wrongs, something she did not do when sober. In reaction, Morris retreated from Louise physically and psychologically, causing her to complain, when drunk, of an even greater list of wrongs. And so the vicious cycle had been going when Louise entered treatment.

5. Illegal psychoactive drugs like marijuana, cocaine, crack, heroin, and LSD; these are the drugs of greatest concern to our society.

Polydrug abuse, often involving both alcohol and one or more other drugs, being more the rule than the exception nowadays makes it even more difficult to attain an accurate picture of the numbers of drug abusers.

The 1987 National High School Senior Survey, conducted for the National Institute on Drug Abuse, provides one answer to this question (NIDA, 1987). It reveals that 50 percent of American high school seniors reported ever using marijuana, 19 percent inhalants, 10 percent hallucinogens, 8 percent LSD, 15 percent cocaine, 6 percent crack, 10 percent heroin and other opiates, 21 percent stimulants, 9 percent sedatives, 11 percent tranquilizers, 92 percent alcohol, and 67 percent cigarettes. More significant—because they probably identify heavy users—are figures indicating that 21 percent of these high school seniors had used marijuana during the month preceding the survey, 66 percent had used alcohol, and 29 percent had smoked cigarettes. No other drugs were used by more than 5 percent of the seniors during the same time period.

The story of Derek, detailed in Box 11.2, illustrates one of this country's most troublesome recent substance dependence problems, crack cocaine abuse.

ALCOHOL ABUSE AND DEPENDENCE

Nature of Alcohol Abuse and Dependence

All alcoholic beverages result from fermentation processes. Certain yeasts acting on sugar and water ferment and under certain circumstances produce alcohol. Most fruits (including grapes) contain sugar, so they can be fermented to produce an alcoholic beverage called wine. Cereal grains contain starch rather than sugar so their starch must be converted to sugar before fermentation; this process of malting is an essential part of brewing beer, which is generally made from corn, barley, malt, and hops.

Beer customarily contains from 3 percent to 5 percent alcohol by volume. Most wine contains about 12 percent. Substantially greater concentrations of alcohol are only possible by a process called *distillation:* An alcohol-containing solution is heated (distilled) to vaporize the alcohol, which is then collected in a separate container in concentrated form. Scotch, bour-

BOX 11.2 Derek, Crack, and a Life on the Streets

Derek was eleven years old when he first tried crack. He was an impressionable boy with most of his free time spent in the streets of the urban ghetto where he, his four older siblings, and his mother lived. Most of Derek's older friends regularly used drugs. The man he most admired, Jonathan, had been dealing drugs off and on for as long as Derek could remember. Jonathan wore expensive clothing, he always seemed to have spending money, the girls clearly liked him, he drove an expensive car, and he was always smiling and laughing. Derek thought he wanted to be like Jonathan when he grew up, even though his mother told him that Jonathan was bound to get into serious trouble with the law.

Derek first tried crack a few months after he had had his first drink of alcohol and about the time he first smoked marijuana. An older boy in the neighborhood shared a small bag of the delicate white powder; when he inhaled the crack smoke into his lungs, an intense euphoria, coupled with freedom from the stresses of his life on the streets, overcame him and he knew he had to experience it again.

Crack's powerful effect on Derek ultimately led him to make everything else in his life secondary to the effort to get money to buy it. And when money couldn't be earned, it had to be stolen, from old people on the street, other children in the neighborhood, and, ultimately, the proprietors of the stores Derek and his friends held up at gunpoint. During one of these armed robberies, Derek was caught by a police officer on stakeout. Tried and convicted, Derek is now serving an indeterminate juvenile sentence likely to stretch to his eighteenth birthday. Though he has completed a drug program in the juvenile detention center which he was sent to, he isn't certain he can withstand crack's lure when he returns to the streets, though he would very much like to be able to do so.

bon, vodka, and gin are distilled spirits whose alcohol concentration customarily varies between 40 percent and 50 percent.

Once in the stomach and small intestine, a beverage's alcohol is directly and quickly absorbed into the blood. The blood carries the alcohol to the brain, where alcohol's effects on behavior are mediated.

At moderate doses, alcoholic beverages initially produce a mild sense of stimulation and enhanced well-being, followed by relaxation and calm. At higher doses, alcohol interferes with cognitive functioning, balance and coordination, judgment, memory, and perception. At extremely high doses, alcohol's sedative effects can interfere with respiration and breathing and cause death from respiratory failure.

Table 11.1 summarizes some of alcohol's most common behavioral effects at differing concentrations in the blood. These data help explain why the acute effects of substantial quantities of alcohol not only exert direct toxic effects on the body but also lead to a variety of indirect results. These include automobile accidents, frequently caused by drunken drivers, other alcohol-related accidents and injuries, crimes resulting from the disinhibition intoxication causes, and marital and family discord and abuse.

Even more devastating than the acute effects of high doses of alcohol are its long-term effects. Several of these effects are components of the substance dependence syndrome, upon which *DSM-III-R*'s diagnosis of alcohol and other drug abuse and dependence is based. Chronic alcohol abuse also leads to permanent brain function changes that reflect alcohol's direct toxic effects on the brain (see Chapter 15). Moreover, as briefly noted already, chronic alcohol use is associated with a variety of life-threatening physical disorders, affecting vital organs like the heart, liver, and gastrointestinal tract (Hasen, Grant, Harford, Hilton & Endicott, in press).

Since alcohol is a dangerous drug exacting a terrible price for its abuse, why do human beings so often abuse it? The following discussion of theories about and research on the causes of alcoholism attempts to answer that challenging question.

Causes of Alcohol Abuse and Dependence

Genetic/Biological Factors in Alcoholism. It is well-known that alcoholism and drug abuse run in families. The data supporting the view of a genetic predisposition to the disorder transmitted from alcoholic parent to child are reviewed here.

Concordance Rates in Twins. The study of twins is productive in examining the possible genetic basis for alcoholism. In an early study, Kaij (1960) reported the concordance rate for alcohol abuse among Swedish monozygotic (identical) twins was 54 percent whereas among dizygotic (fraternal) twins it was 28 percent. Partanen, Bruun, and Markkanen (1966) reported Finnish monozygotic twins as more highly concordant for normal drinking patterns than dizygotic twins. In a study of 850 pairs of like-sex twins—American high school juniors at the time—Leohlin (1977) observed identical twins as more often concordant for heavy drinking than fraternal twins.

Though these studies suggest a genetic basis for alcoholism, they can be criticized. While identical and fraternal twins are presumed to share their environ-

TABLE 11.1 Behavioral Effects of Blood Alcohol Levels

Percent Blood Alcohol Level	Behavioral Effects
0.05	Lowered alertness; usually good feeling; release of inhibitions; impaired judgment
0.10	Slowed reaction times; impaired motor function; less caution
0.15	Large, consistent increases in reaction time
0.20	Marked depression in sensory and motor capability; decidedly intoxicated
0.25	Severe motor disturbance; staggering; sensory perceptions greatly impaired; smashed!
0.30	Stuporous but conscious; no comprehension of the world around them
0.35	Surgical anesthesia; minimal level causing death
0.40	About half of those at this level die

Note: A 160-pound man will achieve a blood alcohol level of 0.05 in the course of an hour by consuming about two beers or two 5-ounce glasses of wine or two highballs, each containing an ounce of Scotch, bourbon, vodka, or gin. A blood alcohol level of 0.10 will be achieved by consuming roughly twice that amount of beverage alcohol during an hour, or 25 percent more during two hours (because alcohol metabolizes or disappears from the system at the constant rate of about 0.015/hour).

Source: From Ray, O. & Ksir, C. (1990), Behavioral Effects of Blood Alcohol Levels, *Drugs, Society, and Human Behavior* (5th Ed.). St. Louis: Times Mirror/Mosby College Publishing. Reprinted by permission of the publisher.

ments equally (i.e., presumed to differ only in amount of shared genetic material), identical twins may actually share more features of the environment than fraternal twins because their parents and the world treat them as more alike than fraternal twins. Thus, the environmental side of the environment-heredity equation for identical twins may differ from that for fraternal twins.

Adoption Studies in Children of Alcoholics. Adoption studies hold environmental influences constant (something twin studies may not be able to do) while systematically varying genetic factors. As a consequence, they may provide the best perspective on genetic factors' role in alcoholism.

The most influential of these was a series of Danish studies by Goodwin (1976, 1979, 1985) comparing four groups of young adult children of alcoholics. The first group was sons of alcoholics who had been raised by nonalcoholic foster parents; the second group sons of alcoholics raised by their biological parents; the third and fourth groups daughters of alcoholics raised, respectively, by nonalcoholic foster parents and by their biological parents. Paired with each of these four groups was a control group matched for age and adoption status. All adoptees had been separated from their biological parents during the first few weeks of life and then adopted by nonrelatives.

These extensive studies yielded two principal findings.

1. Sons of alcoholics were about four times more likely than sons of nonalcoholics to become alcoholic adults *regardless of whether they had been raised by their own alcoholic biological parents or by nonalcoholic adoptive parents.*
2. The influence of genetics on the daughters of alcoholics was not nearly as strong as on the sons of alcoholics.

Subsequent Swedish research on adopted children has confirmed Goodwin's initial conclusions on the role of genetic factors in male alcoholism (Bohman, Cloninger, von Knorring, & Sigvardsson, 1984). It has also suggested, more strongly than did Goodwin's data, that genetic factors significantly affect female alcoholism.

The Swedish research also implied the presence of at least two forms of inherited alcoholism. After analyzing data from 2,000 Swedish adoptees, these researchers (Bohman, Sigvardsson, & Cloninger, 1981; Cloninger, Bohman, & Sigvardsson, 1981) identified two groups of alcoholics. Although the more common Type I alcoholics begin drinking in their mid-twenties to thirties, they typically do not develop alcohol problems until middle age, they have a high risk of liver disease, and they show little antisocial behavior and relatively few social and occupational problems. Children of Type I alcoholics are twice as likely to develop alcoholism themselves as children without a family history of alcoholism; sons of Type I alcoholics raised in troubled adoptive homes are at even greater risk to develop alcoholism. In contrast, Type II alcoholics, whose alcoholism begins very early, experience profound social and occupational problems but relatively few medical difficulties. Their adopted sons—but not their adopted daughters—are nine times more likely to become alcoholics, regardless of environmental influences.

Electrophysiological Studies of Children of Alcoholics. Two electroencephalographic (EEG) techniques commonly used to study the brain's electrical activity—the evoked potential (EP) and the event-related potential (ERP)—have been employed to study genetic influences on alcoholism. EP techniques measure the brain's electrical response to external stimuli, like flashes of light or loud sounds. ERP techniques measure electrical events that arise during the brain's processing of information.

Noting substantial evidence that EP waveforms are genetically determined, Begleiter, Porjesz, Bihari, and Kissin (1984) hypothesized that a particular kind of ERP, the P3 wave deficit, may be a genetically determined forerunner of alcoholism rather than its consequence, as had previously been believed. Begleiter and his colleagues (1984) tested this hypothesis by comparing the ERPs of twenty-five 12-year-old boys with alcoholic fathers with those of twenty-five boys with no history of paternal alcoholism. Significant differences in P3 voltage were found between the two groups (see Figure 11.1). Interestingly, the boys with a paternal history of alcoholism showed a pattern of significantly reduced P3 voltage similar to a pattern previously seen in abstinent chronic alcoholics (Porjesz & Begleiter, 1983). This coincidence strengthened the case for this deficit's role in the development of alcoholism.

A Biological/Genetic Basis for Alcoholism? Do these findings prove that the children of alcoholics are doomed to follow in their parents' footsteps? Absolutely not. Most children of alcoholics do not become alcoholics and most alcoholics are not the children of alcoholics. A genetic basis for alcoholism simply implies a heightened predisposition to develop the disorder—an increase in the chances of developing it—if one's father or mother was or is alcoholic (Merikangas, 1990).

Children of Alcoholics. Some authorities believe children of alcoholics bear an additional burden be-

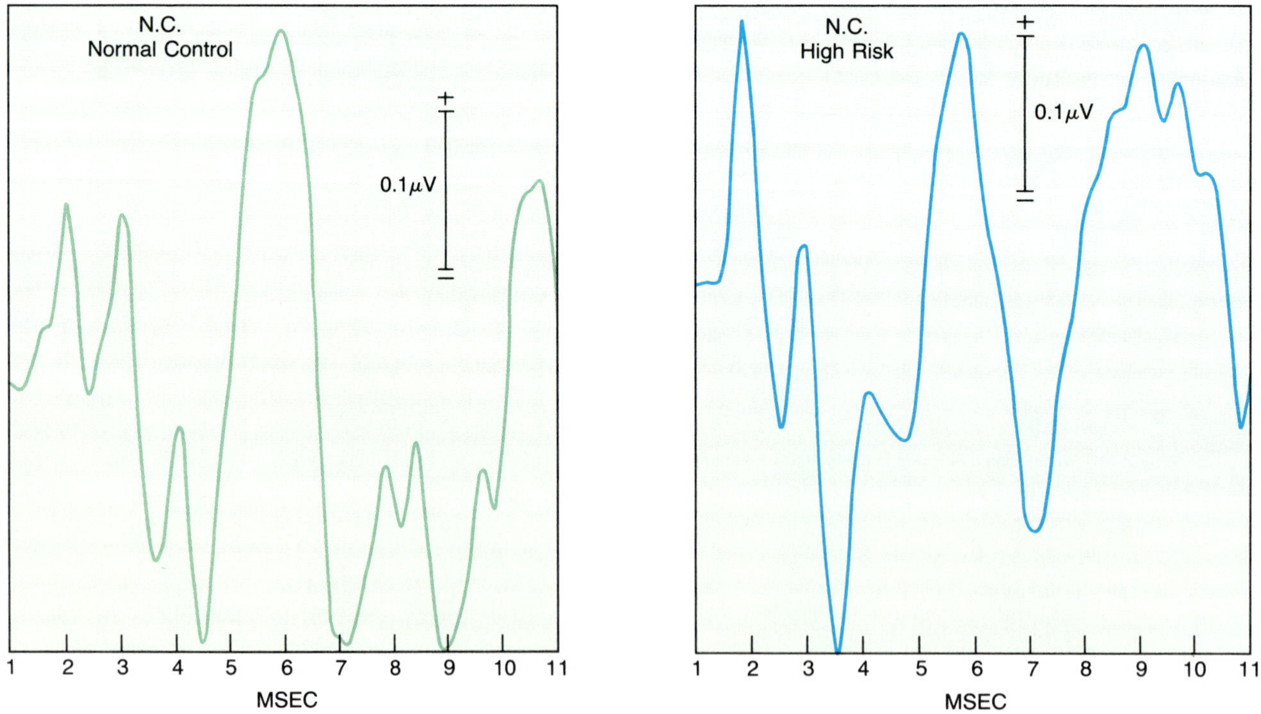

Figure 11.1 *This figure illustrates the marked difference in event-related responses shown by a normal control subject and a high risk subject studied by Begleiter and his colleagues.*

Source: From Begleiter, H., Porjesz, B., & Bihari, B. (1987). Auditory brainstem potentials in sons of alcoholic fathers. *Alcoholism: Clinical and Experimental Research, 11,* p. 478. By permission of the Research Society on Alcoholism.

yond their heightened risk of developing alcoholism. They claim that adult children of alcoholics suffer disastrous behavioral consequences from their parents' alcoholism, even if they do not themselves develop the disorder. Dr. Timmen L. Cermak, himself the adult child of an alcoholic, put together a list of the most common characteristics of adult children of alcoholics (1988). They include the following:

- Hard-driving; workaholic; always preoccupied by projects and things that "have to be done"; rarely satisfied with accomplishments; in denial of feelings, relationships take a back seat.
- Defensive; fearful of closeness to others; play cards close to the vest; unable to deal honestly on an emotional level; longing for relationships; chronic anger.
- Overwhelmed by feelings; buffeted by emotional storms; desperately trying to get other people to behave properly; often unable to work effectively.
- Alcohol and drug addiction.
- Depressed, with a chronic sense of emptiness within; lacking a sense of direction in life; apathy; low self-esteem; may be self-destructive.
- Confused sense of identity; unable to separate from family; always taking on the characteristics of others.
- Victim identity; constant sense of being attacked, misunderstood, ignored, and betrayed—all of which justifies an angry, demanding attitude toward others.
- Martyr identity; long-suffering; unwilling to take care of oneself; constantly excusing the faults of others; willingness to submit oneself to painful situations for others' sake.
- Generous, helpful, and thoughtful—to a fault.
- Constantly searching for answers, rules, and guidelines for finding happiness and social/emotional success.

Even though a great number of people believe parental alcoholism produces these troubling behavioral effects in offspring, empirical research has not validated this view. One reason is that behaviors like some listed above tend to be found in many people, not just children of alcoholics.

Researchers who have studied the problem and surveyed the existing literature question the existence of a discrete set of behavioral consequences of parental alcoholism. The data gathered suggest instead that the majority of adult children of alcoholics resemble most other people and that if there is a lasting effect of parental alcoholism, it is not distinguishable from the effects of living with a parent who suffer from any other chronic, recurrent disorder (Berkowitz & Perkins, 1988; Sher, in press; Werner, 1986).

The Role of Sociocultural Factors in Alcoholism. Your sociocultural group—that is, your racial, religious, national, and/or ethnic group—is important in determining many of your behaviors, including your drinking behavior. This is hardly surprising. Your parents' own membership in these groups influenced their child-rearing patterns in many important ways. Cultural group identification also directly affects your childhood and adult behavior as you emulate your elders and those you admire. Still, it may surprise you to learn that, whereas group membership's influence on many kinds of human behavior is strong, its impact on alcohol and drug use and abuse may be strongest (Bales, 1946; Kandel, 1984; Kandel, Davies, Karns, & Yamaguchi, 1986).

The widely differing rates of alcohol consumption across this country's regions summarized in Table 11.2 effectively illustrates cultural patterns' effects on alcohol consumption. These differences in consumption rates (and, almost certainly, alcoholism rates) reflect regional population differences in the religious, ethnic, and racial makeup of our American

TABLE 11.2 Apparent Alcohol Consumption by Geographic Region for the Total U.S. Population over 21

Geographic Region	Percentage of Adult Population over Age 21 Who Drink	Apparent per Capita Consumption Based on Total Population over Age 21 (gallons)	Adjusted Apparent per Capita Consumption Based on Drinking Population over Age 21 (gallons)
Northeast	78.1	3.22	5.79
Midwest	72.2	3.00	5.86
South	51.6	2.91	8.01
West	66.0	3.42	7.34
U.S. total	67.0	3.14	6.75

Source: (NIAAA, 1987, p. 4)

Alcoholic beverages are consumed in many places, including neighborhood taverns like the one shown in this photograph.

"melting pot." For example, in the Midwest, a region with large numbers of Northern Europeans, groups whose parents and grandparents came from countries with high alcoholism rates, a much higher percentage of adults drink than in the South, a region with a substantial number of Southern Baptists, for whom drinking is proscribed.

How is it that different groups can effect such major influences on alcoholism rates? It is not simply because one group discourages any consumption of alcohol while another especially encourages it. In fact, distinct subcultures in this country with low rates of alcoholism—including Italian-Americans, Jewish-Americans, and Chinese-Americans—generally show low rates of abstinence as well. The opposite is also true: High rates of alcoholism and high rates of abstinence characterize Irish-Americans, black Americans, and Americans from Eastern Europe. At first paradoxical, these findings suggest that cultural patterns stressing moderate use of alcohol, especially in a family or religious context, lead to use by a high percentage of the group's members and low rates of alcoholism. In contrast, cultural groups which focus on both the dangers and the allure of intoxication tend to produce a greater percentage of group members who abstain from alcohol—and a greater number who drink to excess (Lex, 1985; Lowman, Harford, & Kaelber, 1983).

Gender and Alcoholism. A recent population survey of alcohol abuse and addiction in five sites across the globe—in St. Louis, Missouri; Edmonton, Alberta, Canada; Puerto Rico; Seoul, South Korea; and Taipei City, Taiwan—confirms gender as a major risk factor for alcoholism (Helzer et al., 1990), just as it is for such other common disorders as depression (Chapter 7) and antisocial personality disorder (Chapter 10). The marked disparity in lifetime prevalence findings between men and women in all five geographically diverse sites, shown in Figure 11.2, suggests gender as a probable risk factor for alcoholism virtually everywhere. (Lifetime prevalence means, for example, that 29 percent of the men and 4 percent of the women interviewed in St. Louis had been diagnosed alcoholic at some point in their lives.) These data confirm other studies (e.g., Fillmore, 1987; Hammer & Vaglum, 1989) that reported similar differences in alcoholism rates between men and women in the United States.

Scientists have offered a variety of theories to explain these marked differences between men and women in alcohol abuse and dependence, and two explanations have become most widely accepted. First, many observers explain the consistently lower alcoholism rates among women as a result of most societies' lower tolerance for heavy alcohol use by women, probably because of women's traditional child-care role.

Second, recent empirical data on differential rates of metabolism of alcohol by men and women (Frezza, DiPadova, Pozzato, Terpin, Baraona, & Lieber, 1990) suggest that women may possess smaller amounts than men of a crucial enzyme that detoxifies alcohol in the stomach and small intestine. Such a gender-based difference in this enzyme's amounts would explain why alcohol consumed in equivalent doses by men and women has consistently greater behavioral and physiological effects on women (Gallant, 1987; Jacobsen, 1986). Simply put, fewer women than men may drink to excess because alcohol in large quantities produces especially negative behavioral and bodily consequences for women.

Learning-based Causes of Alcoholism

Classical Conditioning. The effort to link learning to substance abuse began more than four decades ago with Conger's pioneering research (1951, 1956). Rats subjected to conflict (they had to risk painful electric shock to gain access to food) drank more of an alcohol-water solution than conflict-free rats. Conger explained this behavior as classically conditioned tension-reduction, suggesting tension-reduction as human beings' primary reason to consume alcohol to excess.

What came to be known as the **tension-reduc-**

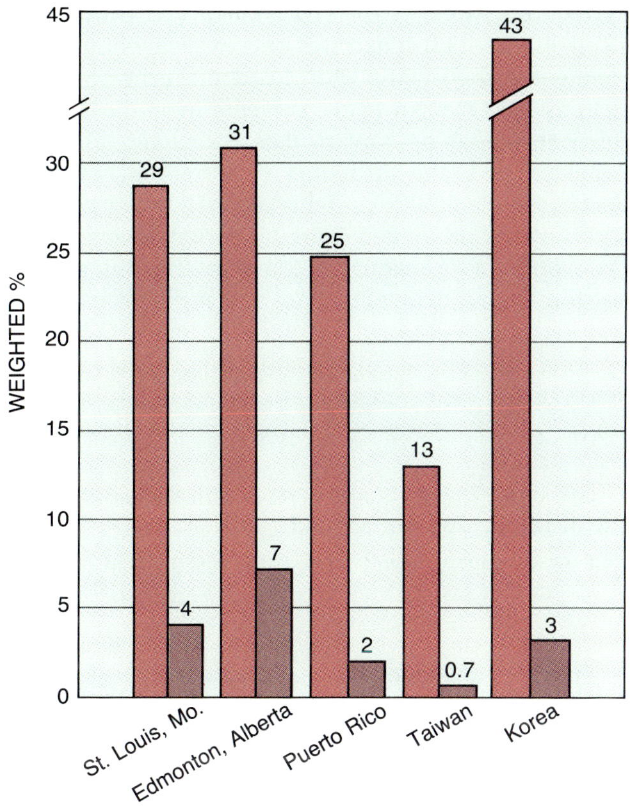

Figure 11.2 *Helzer and his colleagues found striking differences between men and women in lifetime prevalence rates for alcoholism in all five of the sites they studied. Prevalence rates for men and women in Korea were most disparate.*

Source: From Helzer, J.E., Canino, G.J., Yeh, E.-K., Lee, C.K., Hwu, H.-G., & Newman, S. (1990). Alcoholism—North America and Asia. *Archives of General Psychiatry, 47*, p. 315. Copyright 1990, American Medical Association.

tion hypothesis (TRH) was not directly tested in humans until nearly two decades later, when alcoholics in experimental laboratory settings were permitted to drink as much alcohol as they wanted under varying stress levels. These studies (Mendelson & Mello, 1966; Nathan et al., 1970) yielded results directly opposed to those predicted by the TRH: Human alcoholics actually became substantially more anxious, depressed, and angry when they drank in the experimental laboratory settings.

Clearly, learning theorists needed a more complex learning-based model of human alcohol abuse than the tension-reduction hypothesis alone. That model, as the rest of this section indicates, now incorporates operant, modeling, and cognitive social-learning elements to more accurately reflect the complexity of the determinants of human behavior. At the same time, as the learning model has evolved, it has retained a tension-reduction component, because both clinical experience and research suggest that some alcoholic drinking is clearly designed to diminish stress.

Levenson, Oyama, and Meek (1987) studied the "stress-dampening" (tension-reducing) effects of alcohol, finding them more pronounced in young adults with a family history of alcoholism than in those without such a background. This suggests the existence of a mechanism—perhaps learned, perhaps inherited—which mediates individual responses to alcohol's stress-dampening/tension-reducing properties. It helps explain why for some people (perhaps including children of alcoholics), alcohol is a particularly potent stress-dampener while for others it is not.

Another recent test of the TRH systematically manipulated stress in groups of alcoholics drinking in a tavern setting (Langenbucher, Nathan, & Niaura, 1991). The results suggested the need to again revise the hypothesis. Subjects not exposed to intense experimental stress during four-hour drinking sessions held on four successive evenings became progressively more relaxed and happier as drinking progressed; those subjected to a stress-induction procedure, by contrast, became much more anxious, depressed, and angry as drinking proceeded. These findings suggest that the TRH may be valid for persons who are not feeling stressed when they begin to drink.

Classical conditioning mechanisms have also been implicated in the development of alcohol withdrawal symptoms, craving, and behavioral tolerance that accompany dependence on alcohol and other psychoactive substances. The *conditioned withdrawal model* (Wikler, 1965) was an early classical conditioning model of addiction. It emphasized the power of withdrawal's extremely unpleasant environmental or internal cues to increase the addict's motivation to seek the drug to alleviate these withdrawal feelings. Logically extending this theory, Ludwig, Wikler, and Stark (1974) proposed that the physiological and cognitive accompaniments of *craving*—a state often leading recovering alcoholics to return to drinking—represent a form of conditioned withdrawal.

A series of experiments using both alcohol (Crowell, Hinson, & Siegel, 1981) and morphine (Siegel, 1978) demonstrated that rats which had developed tolerance maintained the tolerance only when tested under the same environmental conditions previously associated with drug or alcohol administration. These experiments led Siegel and his colleagues to propose the *conditioned compensatory response model*, another classical conditioning model of addiction. Siegel (1978) argued that environmental stimuli preceding drug intake combined with the drug's effects on the body ultimately elicit a conditioned response opposite to the drug's effect, a compensating response designed to maintain bodily homeostasis (balance). As this conditioned homeostatic response increases in magnitude with continued drug intake, the drug's effect continues to decrease, that is, tolerance develops.

The *conditioned appetitive motivational model* is a more recent classical conditioning model of alcohol and drug addiction (Stewart, deWit, & Eikelboom, 1984). It explains drug-seeking and -ingesting behavior by focusing on conditioned stimuli associated with the positive reinforcing effects of drugs (for example, the smell, sounds, and lighting of a familiar neighborhood tavern) rather than on those associated with withdrawal or tolerance. According to this theory, following conditioning, conditioned stimuli become capable of eliciting a positive motivational state similar to the one elicited by the drug itself. This state, in turn, creates strong urges to seek and use the drug. This theory explains the great difficulty former abusers have maintaining abstinence when they must return to the environments associated with their abuse.

Operant Conditioning. By the late 1960s, the classical conditioning explanation of alcohol's tension-reducing effect was clearly insufficient to explain alcohol abuse and dependency's development and course. As a result, learning researchers began to explore the role of operant or instrumental mechanisms in alcohol abuse. The assumption was that operant mechanisms are involved when alcohol or drug consumption is reinforced by its consequences and drinking or ingestion rate increases as a consequence.

One of the first studies of the operant-conditioning mechanisms involved in alcohol self-administration by humans was reported by Nathan and O'Brien in 1971. Figure 11.3 illustrates the experimental environment in the Boston City Hospital ward where Nathan and O'Brien's (1971) subjects lived during the thirty-three-day operant studies. Social and affective behavior and the drinking patterns of matched groups of alcoholics and nonalcoholics were compared over a prolonged drinking period. Researchers used operant procedures to assess the differential reinforcement value of alcohol and social interaction, two extremely powerful reinforcers. Subjects had to press an operant panel's push-button repeatedly, on a high fixed-ratio schedule, to earn points to "purchase" alcohol, time out of their rooms in a social area, or both.

The following were observed upon comparison of the alcoholic and nonalcoholic groups.

1. Alcoholics worked much longer and harder to earn points to purchase alcohol. As a result, though both alcoholics and nonalcoholics reached the same high blood-alcohol levels early in drinking, the alcoholics remained at these levels longer and returned to them more frequently. They drank almost twice as much as the nonalcoholics.
2. Nonalcoholics worked much longer and harder to earn points to permit them to interact with each other. By contrast, the alcoholics were social isolates before, during, and after drinking.
3. Once drinking began, the alcoholics became significantly more depressed and less active and demonstrated significantly more psychopatho-

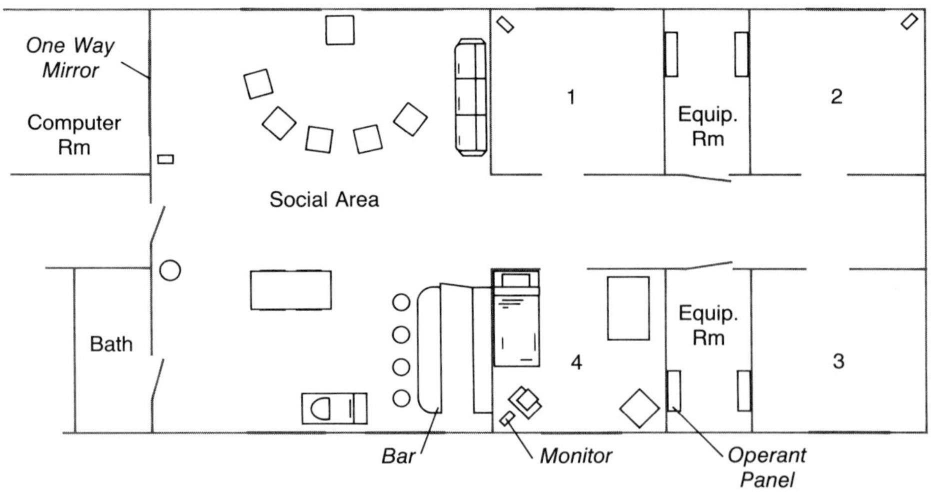

Figure 11.3 The experimental environment in the Boston City Hospital experimental ward. *Each of the four bedrooms was furnished with a bed, chair, table, operant panel, and television monitor. The dayroom contained a dining table, bar, driving machine, and large social area.*

Source: From Nathan, P.E. & O'Brien, J.S. (1971). An experimental analysis of the behavior of alcoholics and nonalcoholics during prolonged experimental drinking. *Behavior Therapy, 2,* p. 459. By permission of the publisher.

logy (including anxiety, manic behavior, depression, paranoia, and phobic and compulsive behavior) than the nonalcoholics.

This research program ultimately led other clinical researchers to test out operant schedules that would reinforce alcoholics for reducing or stopping their drinking. Bigelow and his colleagues (Bigelow, Cohen, Liebson, & Faillace, 1972; Bigelow, Liebson, & Griffiths, 1974), for example, reported marked reduction in alcoholics' drinking in the laboratory by reinforcing subjects with money and other rewards for limited periods of abstinence.

These findings in turn led other behavioral researchers to wonder whether rewarding alcoholics for sobriety and other desirable behaviors in their home environments might be a viable approach to alcoholism treatment. As described more fully below, Hunt, Azrin and their colleagues (1973) did report limited success in such an effort.

Modeling and Vicarious Reinforcement. Many people drink as their parents and others in their environment drink. Our earlier reviews of alcoholism's sociocultural and genetic factors reviewed data that help explain this well-known effect. During the early 1970s, Bandura's research (1969; 1977) established its learning-based mechanism. That research, much of it with children, demonstrated that new behaviors and new knowledge can be acquired and existing knowledge and behavior modified simply by watching other people and events. It isn't necessary to engage in these behaviors oneself and the consequences of these behaviors needn't affect the observer. Learning can occur *vicariously,* by *modeling* the behavior of others.

For theorists interested in alcoholism, vicarious reinforcement and modeling offered learning-based explanations for the finding that some children of alcoholics themselves drink abusively. They also helped explain the impact of social group membership on drinking rates and patterns.

Attitudinal/Expectancy Variables. The past decade has witnessed a marked increase in attention to cognitive factors' role in alcohol and drug use and abuse. Along with similar developments in other areas of psychology—where the so-called "cognitive revolution" has also been strong—these studies suggest a person's expectations about alcohol's effects on sexual, aggressive, and social behavior directly influence those behaviors independent of alcohol's effects (Marlatt & Rohsenow, 1980; Wilson, 1981). It is also clear that expectations about one's ability to benefit from alcoholism treatment can play an important role in determining whether one benefits from the treatment (Marlatt & Gordon, 1985).

One of the most active research programs on young adults' expectancies of alcohol effects has been developed by Goldman and his colleagues. In a 1985 study of adolescent alcohol expectancies, Christiansen, Goldman, and Brown found that, during the crucial years from thirteen to eighteen, adolescents increasingly come to believe that alcohol improves social behavior, increases arousal, and decreases tension. In a related study, the same investigators (Goldman, Brown, & Christiansen, 1987) reported that adolescent alcohol abusers differ from nonabusers in what the two groups expect alcohol to do for them. When 116 adolescents, including both alcohol abusers and nonabusers as well as people with and without a family history of alcoholism, filled out the *Alcohol Expectancy Questionnaire,* striking differences in expectancies distinguished these four groups. The adolescent alcohol abusers anticipated significantly more reinforcement from drinking than their nonabusing peers. Adolescents with an alcohol-abusing parent expected more cognitive and motor enhancement from alcohol than did those without a family history of alcoholism. It is clear that alcohol use pattern and family history affected adolescent attitudes toward drinking.

This finding, which has been replicated (Brown, Creamer, & Stetson, 1987), suggests that a family history of alcoholism and an early pattern of heavy drinking may affect later development of alcoholic drinking by magnifying the stress-relieving effects of alcohol in people for whom those effects thus become increasingly attractive. Table 11.3 lists some of the key items on the Alcohol Expectancy Questionnaire.

Psychiatric and Personality Factors in Alcoholism

Comorbidity. Psychiatric explanations of substance abuse assume that the abuse occurs, at least partially, because of the presence of one or more associated **comorbid** psychiatric disorders. A substantial amount of research suggesting that alcoholics are much more likely than nonalcoholics to suffer from other psychiatric conditions supports this widespread view (Gerstley, Alterman, McLellan, & Woody, 1990; Khantzian & Treece, 1985). Most commonly associated with substance abuse are depression and antisocial personality disorder; others include schizophrenia, anxiety disorders, and sleep disorders (Schuckit, 1989).

To explain the coincidence of substance abuse and other psychiatric disorders, researchers must first resolve the "chicken–egg" problem by determining if the symptoms of the other disorders (1) precede the substance abuse and thereby influence its development, (2) are the consequences of the troubled life of the substance abuser, or (3) both. Empirical data to

TABLE 11.3 Selected Items from the Alcohol Expectancy Questionnaire

Factor I. Alcohol improves cognitive and motor functioning
- Drinking can make me more satisfied with myself.
- Alcohol makes me feel better physically.
- I feel more creative after I've been drinking.

Factor II. Alcohol promotes relaxation
- I am not as tense if I am drinking.
- At times, drinking is like permission to forget problems.
- Alcohol decreases muscular tension.

Factor III. Alcohol enhances sexuality
- After a few drinks, I am more sexually responsive.
- I am a better lover after a few drinks.

Factor IV. Alcohol increases social assertiveness
- When I drink, it is easier to open up and express my feelings.
- A few drinks make me feel less shy.

Factor V. Alcohol improves and elevates mood
- Alcohol makes me feel happy.
- Drinking helps me get out of a depressed mood.

Factor VI. Alcohol increases arousal
- After a few drinks, I feel brave and capable of fighting.
- I drink when I am feeling mad.

Factor VII. Alcohol promotes sleep
- Alcohol helps me sleep better.

Source: From Christiansen, B. A., Goldman, M. S., & Brown, S. A. (1985). The differential development of adolescent alcohol expectancies may predict alcoholism, *Addictive Behaviors, 10,* p. 303. Copyright (1985), Pergamon Press plc.

answer this question have been equivocal. The weight of the evidence seems to suggest, however, that antisocial behavior frequently precedes substance abuse and may help trigger its onset, whereas depression as often follows as precedes substance abuse, leaving its causal role uncertain (Meyer & Hesselbrock, 1984; Schuckit, 1986; Vaillant, 1983).

Personality Factors. The psychodynamic model of alcohol abuse and dependence represented an early effort to portray personality factors' function in the disorder's development. It viewed abuse and dependence as ultimately unsuccessful efforts to satisfy strong dependency needs in adulthood unmet in infancy and early childhood. According to this view, the alcoholic has substituted abusive drinking's oral gratification for the satisfaction of oral dependency needs (Khantzian, 1985). The psychodynamic explanation for substance dependence is less influential than it was several decades ago because it has not been confirmed empirically.

Controversy over personality factors' role in alcoholism continues (e.g., Graham & Strenger, 1988; Nathan, 1988; Sutker & Allain, 1988). Supporters of personality factors' role point to data suggesting that alcoholics share certain behaviors and personality characteristics differentiating them from nonalcoholics (Morey & Skinner, 1986; Sutker & Allain, 1988). Opponents of this view (e.g., Nathan, 1988) claim that the personality factors distinguishing substance abusers from others are actually consequences, not causes, of these disorders so they played no role in their development.

Cloninger's theory of "neurogenetic adaptive mechanisms" (1987) is one of the most interesting developments in this dialogue (see Chapter 2). According to Cloninger, genetic, neurobiological, and personality factors interact to yield persons at substantially higher risk to develop alcohol dependence than persons without these predisposing factors. This biopsychosocial theory appears to constitute stronger support for personality factors' function in the etiology of alcoholism because it ties these factors to measurable variations in associated biological and behavioral variables.

A Biopsychosocial Model of Alcoholism. Alcohol abuse and dependence very comfortably fit a biopsychosocial causal model. The data on the role of genetic factors in alcoholism are strong; they suggest that individuals with a family history of alcoholism are at heightened risk to develop the disorder. But the fact that most individuals with that history do not go on to develop the disorder and that most of those who do develop it do not have the history demands explanation. That explanation comes, partially, from the contemporary cognitive social-learning model, by now impressively buttressed with empirical findings (summarized in NIAAA, 1990). The explanation also comes from the long-accepted findings about sociocultural factors' impact on drinking pattern.

It is clear that neither biological factors alone, nor sociocultural factors alone, nor learning factors alone can explain the onset and course of alcohol abuse and dependence as convincingly as the three together (Cloninger, 1987; Nathan, 1990).

Treatment of Alcohol Abuse and Dependence

Individual Psychotherapy. Traditional one-to-one psychotherapy, psychodynamic in orientation, remains mental health professionals' predominant treatment mode of substance abusers. Most clinicians are trained to offer patients psychodynamic psychotherapy's "talking therapy," hence its popularity. Many clinicians continue to accept psychodynamic formulations of alcohol and drug dependence, despite the absence of empirical support for them.

The psychodynamic psychotherapy treatment

process for substance abusers is similar to that for patients suffering from other disorders. One important difference is the therapist's uncertainty of the patient's abstaining from alcohol or other drugs of abuse, even though he or she may appear drug-free during the therapy session. Hence, trust becomes particularly important in the treatment of the substance abuser. Actually, the issue of trust is two-sided: Since many alcohol and drug abusers have learned that their behavior does not incline friends and relatives to trust them, they cannot in turn trust friends, relatives, or therapists.

Once rapport between patient and therapist has been established, the two begin the arduous process of trying to understand how the patient's presumed early dependency problems contribute to current behavior, including substance abuse. The ultimate aim is enabling the patient to appreciate that his or her self-destructive behavior may be a response to long-ago childhood events with no real relationship to the current life situation.

Group and Family Therapy. During the past two decades, group and especially family therapy have become treatments of choice for many substance abusers. Group therapy first gained popularity because it offered therapists a way to confront their patients' denial of the seriousness of the problem of abuse in a strong, effective, and direct manner uncompromising of the all-important therapeutic relationship. In many instances, substance abusers can confront fellow patients' efforts to deny their abuse problems with greater credibility and impact than a therapist can. The following illustrates just such a confrontation during a group therapy session attended by eight young men, most of them alcohol abusers, convicted of drunk driving.

Roy: You guys have got it all wrong. Sure I drink. In fact, I'd had something to drink the night of the accident. But it was raining and the roads were slick and my old car wasn't too good going around curves in the best road conditions. So for you to say . . .

Thomas: Roy, you're giving us a bunch of bullshit . . .

Roy: . . . that I'm an alcoholic just because I had an accident is ridiculous. I can control my drinking whenever I want. I always drink with friends, never alone, I've never had blackouts . . .

Thomas: . . . because you won't take responsibility for anything, for the accident, for being alcoholic, for beating up on your wife when you're drunk, for anything.

William: Roy, we've been where you are. It took losing my child and wife and the best job I ever had for me to face up to the possibility that maybe something I was doing was responsible for my troubles, that maybe it was my drinking . . .

Roy: Why are you all after me, what'd I do to deserve this? Why don't you pick on somebody else?

Thomas: Because if we don't call you on this, you're going to do it again. And when you do, you might kill somebody in that old car of yours!

Group therapy has become a popular treatment for alcohol abuse and dependence.

During the past decade family therapy has also become an accepted treatment for alcoholism. Despite the relative absence of empirical data supporting its superiority to other treatments, many therapists are convinced of its value. An appealing feature of family therapy is its insight that substance abuse is not the abuser's problem alone. Because it affects every member of the family, all ought to participate in treatment. In some ways, these views parallel those of Alcoholics Anonymous and its related self-help groups for spouses and children, Alanon and Alateen. In other ways, though, family therapy differs markedly from them.

According to its supporters, family therapy powerfully permits family members to share with the substance abuser the effects of his or her behavior on them. The warmly supportive atmosphere of the family therapy session makes it easier for children and spouse to relate the emotional impact of the abuser's behavior on them. This ventilation enables family members to confirm a deeply felt, long-hidden truth. But it may be even more important for abusers since, afterward, it is more difficult for them to deny the impact of their behavior on those they claim to love.

Supporters of family therapy as an effective treatment for substance dependence believe that alcohol and drug abuse is a "family disorder," caused and maintained by disordered family relationships. The wife who drinks to blot out her husband's unfaithfulness, the husband who drinks to forget about his wife's disinterest in sex, or the adolescent who drinks because the family has made him the scapegoat for an older brother's failure to meet parental expectations represent typical family patterns thought to lead to abusive drinking.

What follows is an excerpt from a long and intimate statement written by a recovering female alcoholic who traces her sobriety to understandings she achieved in family therapy.

> *In the four years that I've been sober, one of the changes that has taken place is my attitude toward my childhood and family. I am now 35, and have a brother, 39, and a half sister from my father's second marriage who is 28; we are just getting to know each other. My mother is still living, but my father died about 15 years ago. While I was drinking I laid the blame for my failures squarely at my mother's feet and tried in various ways to scare or coerce her into showing love. It was convenient to use her, my parents' divorce, and my brother's hostility when we were children as an excuse for my insanities. I did not seem capable of seeing my mother as a separate person who also happened to be my mother and who had a life and problems of her own. This attitude of self-pity and blame has changed to a better evaluation of where my own sickness lay; I have been able to extract from the past just where my confusions were and find out how to begin to sort them out. Whatever anger I have is confined to the present; I do not see my family as the villains I once did, nor myself as the victim.* (Kaufmann & Lilly, 1979, p. 245)

Behavior Therapy. In the past two decades, behavioral approaches to the understanding and treatment of alcohol and drug abuse and dependence have become well accepted. They are based on the belief that some of the maladaptive behavior of the substance abuser is learned. Behavior therapists working with substance abusers attempt to help them unlearn inappropriate or maladaptive behavior associated with their abuse and learn more appropriate behaviors unrelated to it.

Aversive Procedures. *Chemical aversion,* based on classical conditioning principles, was the first behavioral treatment for alcoholism. Clinicians began using it in the late 1930s and early 1940s (e.g., Lemere & Voegtlin, 1950; Voegtlin, 1940). Today it is an accepted, though controversial, treatment. Chemical aversion involves repeated pairing of the sight, smell, and taste of the patient's preferred alcoholic beverage with drug-induced nausea and vomiting in order to establish a conditioned aversion to the beverage. This permits the patient to enjoy a "craving-free" interval of two or three months, during which he or she and a therapist can work on a more lasting solution to the substance abuse. The data on outcomes of chemical aversion treatment have consistently been among the most promising of all approaches to the treatment of the substance use disorders (Nathan & Skinstad, 1987; Wiens & Menustik, 1983). However, the great motivation required to participate in a treatment as demanding as chemical aversion may explain, at least in part, its high rates of success (Holden, 1987; Miller, 1985).

Skill Training Methods. Community reinforcement counseling (Azrin, 1976; Hunt & Azrin, 1973) provides chronic male alcoholic inpatients with social skills training to improve long-standing vocational, interpersonal, and family problems preventing them from breaking the cycle of dependency. Detailed, focused training procedures to help these socially isolated men learn to deal more effectively and successfully with family, job, and friends were used. The men were taught the social skills necessary to interact successfully with family and friends. They were also reminded of employers' expectations of punctuality, diligence, reliability, and trustworthiness. Training resulted in behavior changes that led employers, family, and friends to begin to respond to these men with warmth, affection, and concern rather than the previous rejection and disdain. After a time, continued access to family, job, and friends, which had become reinforcers, was made contingent on the maintenance of sobriety. In the two studies published, eight and ten alcoholics in treatment were doing significantly better at six-month follow-up in both drinking and social adjustment than nontreated alcoholics. Unfortunately, the short follow-up interval and lack of independent replication only permit us at present to view these preliminary data as promising.

Oei and Jackson (1980) trained alcoholic subjects in six different social skills. Two groups of eight received this training; two other groups received "traditional supportive treatment" for comparison purposes. Whereas the therapists instructed members of one group of alcoholics in a group setting, they trained the other group's members individually. Training continued for three weeks, with subjects attending 12 two-hour a day sessions. They were trained in

1. Nonverbal expression (e.g., eye contact, smiling, frowning, etc.).
2. Refusing unreasonable requests.
3. Making difficult requests.
4. Expressing and receiving positive feelings.
5. Replying to criticism.
6. Initiating conversations.

The therapists supplemented modeling of these skills by therapist-subject role-playing. Videotapes of the role-plays permitted corrective feedback and behavior modification. Between sessions, subjects completed homework assignments. On measures of social skills, alcohol intake, and assertiveness, the two groups given social skills training improved significantly more than those receiving traditional supportive treatment. Group social-skills subjects performed better than individual social-skills subjects on all measures but alcohol intake.

Broad-Spectrum Behavioral Treatment Procedures and Goals of Treatment. Several broad-spectrum behavioral treatment programs were designed in the 1970s to deal simultaneously with alcoholics' abusive drinking and its associated maladaptive behaviors. The best-known of these programs, *Individualized Behavior Therapy for Alcoholics* (IBTA), was the first broad-spectrum behavioral treatment program designed for inpatient chronic alcoholics. It tested a revolutionary concept: Nonabstinent outcomes for treated alcoholics.

What was new about IBTA was its focus on modifying the environmental factors associated with the alcoholics' abusive drinking. Until the time of the study, alcoholism treatment had tended to emphasize more nonspecific goals, like "personality change." The effort to induce alcoholics to develop and practice alternatives to drinking was especially exciting; this was a critical focus, because most alcoholics' lives center on obtaining and consuming alcohol.

Evaluation of the IBTA study (Sobell & Sobell, 1973; 1976) involved the determination of whether groups of patients treated by IBTA methods performed better at regular follow-up intervals than those treated by standard hospital procedures. Overall, the behavioral treatment package did yield better outcomes over two years than the standard package. In part, this outcome may have reflected the young team of clinicians' enthusiasm and commitment.

Much more controversial were results suggesting that the group of alcoholic patients that had done best had received both the behavioral treatment package and the assigned treatment goal of controlled social drinking, rather than the traditional goal of abstinence. Box 11.3 considers the resultant controversy over controlled drinking treatment goals.

Although controlled drinking goals for chronic alcoholics are rejected by most clinicians nowadays, these goals may make better sense for early-stage problem drinkers. Heavy drinkers who have only begun to experience problems because of their drinking are usually unwilling to stop drinking altogether. Yet, if they can be helped to acknowledge these problems, they might agree to enter a treatment program to help them resume moderate drinking and avoid future drinking-related problems. The few treatment studies of early-stage problem drinkers (e.g., Sanchez-Craig, Annis, Bornet, & MacDonald, 1984; Taylor, Helzer, & Robins, 1986) have established this approach's feasibility for treating these drinkers.

A one-year follow-up in self-reported alcohol consumption by young adults, most of them college students participating in a "cognitive-behavioral alcohol skills training" program is also encouraging (Kivlahan, Marlatt, Fromme, Coppel, & Williams, 1990). Trained to estimate intoxication level during drinking, set limits on drinking before each drinking occasion, and respond effectively to occasional lapses from this plan, the students reported substantial reductions in alcohol consumption a year after treatment ended.

Joint Hospitalization of Alcoholic and Spouse. McCrady and her colleagues (McCrady, Moreau, Paolino, & Longabaugh, 1982; McCrady, Paolino, Longabaugh, & Rossi, 1979) designed an innovative study to evaluate joint hospitalization of couples in which one partner is alcoholic. The treatment program consisted of a wide range of ward therapeutic activities, weekly behavioral couples group therapy, and individual behavioral group therapy during and after the hospital stay. The couples were divided into three groups: Each couple in the first group was hospitalized at the same time for a period of inpatient treatment. Couples in the second group received

BOX 11.3 The Controlled Drinking Controversy

Strong historical, conceptual, and practical reasons justify abstinence as the sole treatment goal for alcoholics. Abstinence is associated with positive outcomes for many alcoholics, it enables the body to recover from the physical ravages of chronic alcohol abuse, and it gives talking therapies a better chance to work (Nathan & McCrady, 1987). While most clinicians and researchers agree on these facts today, there was much less agreement in the early 1970s. That's why the results of the Sobells' IBTA study (1973; 1976) and those from a handful of other studies exploring the same issue, aroused so much interest – and controversy.

Results of the IBTA study encouraged controlled drinking as a possible treatment goal for chronic alcoholics. For this reason, the study was subjected to very close scrutiny. Ultimately, the integrity of the study's authors was also questioned (Pendery, Maltzman, & West, 1982). Several independent groups investigated these charges. All concluded that the research had been conducted as it was described, though they criticized aspects of the study's research design, methodology, and data analysis.

It is ironic that so much furor continues to surround the findings of this study even today (Maltzman, 1989; Sobell & Sobell, 1989). By the beginning of the 1980s, the early promise of controlled drinking as a treatment for chronic alcoholism had been largely discounted, because few treatment studies with nonabstinent goals had actually yielded outcomes superior to those with the goal of abstinence.

Source: Nathan, 1981; Nathan & McCrady, 1987.

couples therapy, though only the alcoholic spouse was hospitalized. In the third group, individual treatment (and inpatient treatment) was given to the alcoholic spouse alone.

At two- and six-month follow-up periods (McCrady, Moreau, Paolino, & Longabaugh, 1982), all three groups had improved on several measures, including the alcoholic spouse's drinking and the couples' satisfaction with their relationship, but only the joint admission and couples therapy groups reported significant decreases in consumption. Four years later, however, no differences among the groups were reported on any measure. These data illustrate a common finding in research on treatment of substance abusers: Initial promise at the six-month or one-year mark often gives way to significantly less promise at later follow-up intervals.

Relapse Prevention. Marlatt and Gordon (1985) argue convincingly that treatment for alcoholism should not end when the newly sober patient has been released from inpatient hospital treatment. At that time, he or she will still have to confront the environmental risks that can induce *relapse,* a return to alcohol abuse. These risks are maximized when the person returns to a previous job and to old friends and family, all of which may have been associated, before treatment, with alcohol abuse.

Marlatt and Gordon's *relapse prevention model* (also considered later regarding treatments for smoking) stresses the importance of identifying the cues in the recovering person's environment associated with relapse (situations which elicit anger, depression, or anxiety typically precede a return to alcohol abuse). The model also focuses on the coping strategies (many of them are cognitive and involve self-statements about the person's capacity to confront risky situations without relapsing) the recovering person uses to deal with these situations. A growing number of clinical researchers (e.g., Annis, 1986; Rankin, 1986) have developed relapse prevention programs to extend active alcoholism treatment into the period following inpatient treatment.

Detoxification. Most clinicians agree that, before treatment for substance abuse of any kind can commence, the patient must be detoxified—withdrawn completely—from alcohol, drugs, or, as is now commonly the case, both. Besides safeguarding the patient's physical health, detoxification increases treatment efficacy. The ability of persons dependent upon a psychoactive substance to cooperate with their treatment is likely to be impaired. In fact, two to three months must pass after dependent abusers have been detoxified before their thinking processes have returned to their predependence state. Some older patients never fully recover their cognitive abilities after a lengthy period of heavy drug or alcohol abuse (see Chapter 15).

An increasingly controversial question is whether it is necessary to follow the three to five days of detoxification from alcohol with a prolonged period of inpatient treatment. Miller and Hester (1986), among others, have pointed to the absence of data supporting the widespread and expensive practice of routinely treating alcoholics in an inpatient setting. Miller and Hester cite data indicating that, overall, alcoholics do as well when detoxification is followed by outpatient treatment. There are certainly some alcoholics—and many drug addicts—whose dependence on and craving for their substance of choice is so intense that they require a period of time away from alcohol- or drug-related stimuli before they return to confront them. But there may well be others for whom this enforced absence from home, family, and work is neither necessary nor helpful.

Antabuse. The drug Antabuse (its chemical name is *disulfiram*) blocks the chemical breakdown of alcohol. Individuals who have ingested Antabuse cannot metabolize alcohol beyond the point at which their bodies have broken it down chemically to a substance called *acetaldehyde,* which is toxic to the body in minute quantities. Even when a small amount of alcohol has been ingested by someone on Antabuse, an acetaldehyde reaction occurs. The alcoholic immediately experiences a set of extremely unpleasant bodily sensations including nausea, vomiting, profuse sweating, and markedly increased respiration and heart rate. Alcoholics who have experienced an Antabuse reaction report it as among the most unpleasant experiences they have ever had.

But it is precisely because of this unpleasant reaction that the drug has been used for several decades as a treatment for alcoholism. Patients who take Antabuse every day cannot consume alcohol without experiencing the Antabuse reaction. In this way, patients are "protected" against the impulse to drink when alcohol-related cues tempt them. Because of the severity of the Antabuse reaction, physicians only prescribe it to patients who are physically fit, want to stop drinking, and fully appreciate the consequences if they drink alcohol while Antabuse is in their systems.

Some experienced clinicians swear by Antabuse; others find it ineffective. The empirical data are equivocal (Kofoed, 1987). In general, clinicians use Antabuse to give the alcoholic a recovery "window" which reduces their risk of succumbing to craving; presumably, this grace period permits further psychological and behavioral gains, so that the Antabuse can later be discontinued safely.

Tranquilizing Drugs. A decade ago, professionals routinely treated many alcoholics and some drug addicts with the minor tranquilizers Librium and Valium. They assumed that these antianxiety agents would either cause patients to stop their drinking or drug use entirely or at least help them lower their consumption level. Instead, many substance abusers added abuse of Librium or Valium to their abuse of alcohol and other drugs. Both Librium and Valium are dependency-inducing; addiction to them complicates withdrawal from the original dependency. As a result, these dependency-inducing drugs are now given far less often to persons already dependent on alcohol or drugs. Yet patients whose severe anxiety interferes with their functioning and causes them to self-medicate with alcohol or sedative drugs may receive anxiolytic drugs, including Librium or Valium, albeit under careful supervision.

Nonetheless, therapists continue to use some drugs in conjunction with the treatment of alcohol and drug abuse. For example, they give tranquilizers to ease withdrawal pains. They may also administer drugs to substance abusers whose abuse may be partially a function of another psychiatric disorder. For example, patients who drink to diminish their schizophrenic hallucinations may receive phenothiazine drugs to achieve the same effect. Similarly, patients who drink or abuse drugs to alleviate recurrent or chronic depression may take antidepressant medication.

Alcoholics Anonymous, Alanon, and Alateen

> *This is not the story of my life. It is the story of how I got drunk, and how I got sober. I have told it before, many times: at A.A. meetings, and to my A.A. sponsor, and to other close A.A. friends gathered in coffee shops—what we in A.A. call "the meeting after the meeting." But I have never before told it in full. By tradition, no speaker leading an A.A. meeting runs over thirty minutes. I will tell it as I would at an A.A. meeting, in the same spirit. My name is Nan, and I am an alcoholic.* (Robertson, 1988, p. 238)

This excerpt is from a compelling first-hand account of the workings of Alcoholics Anonymous written by Nan Robertson, a reporter for *The New York Times.* In her book, published in 1988, the author describes her struggles with alcohol and ultimate recovery by means of the fellowship of Alcoholics Anonymous.

The best-known, biggest, and most influential of the self-help groups is Alcoholics Anonymous (AA). By its own estimate, AA served more than 750,000 alcoholics in this country last year. Worldwide, the figure was more than 1.5 million. The organization has grown dramatically since it was founded in 1935 in Akron, Ohio, by Doctor Bob and Bill W, two alcoholics who came together to share their suffering and find a solution to their misery.

Alcoholics Anonymous seems to work best when people determined to do something about their drinking problem commit as much time as possible to attending meetings. One commonly espoused goal for newly sober recovering alcoholics is "90 meetings in 90 days," reflecting the view that a meeting every night during the crucial initial recovery period may work best. AA serves as a protected, alcohol-free social environment for the alcoholic. Its commitment to nonjudgmentalism is particularly helpful for individuals whose actions have caused family, friends, and themselves to judge their behavior—and themselves—harshly.

A typical AA meeting begins and ends with a period of socialization over coffee. When the meeting begins, members who have remained abstinent for a significant period of time—ranging from ninety days to thirty years or more—will talk about their experiences with alcohol, including family, job, and personal losses as well as new-found gains of sobriety. New members quickly realize they are not alone, that what has happened to them has happened to others (a surprise to many), and that they can look forward to a different kind of life (though AA cautions about the hazards of looking beyond the next twenty-four hours of sobriety, believing that no one is ever cured of alcoholism.)

Meetings of Alanon, an offshoot of AA, provide spouses and partners of alcoholics the welcome reassurance that the responsibility for the alcoholic's condition lies with the alcoholic. This message comforts the spouse who believes, as many do, that it is his or her behavior that maintains the drinking partner's alcoholism. Freeing spouses from the burden of guilt for their partners' alcoholism also helps the alcoholics, by forcing them to take more responsibility for their drinking.

Meetings of Alateen, another affiliate of Alcoholics Anonymous, permit children of alcoholics to share their burden of guilt and anger over parental drinking. In this way the children can be helped to understand that they deserve neither guilt nor blame, that their anger is appropriate, and that the drinking parents must bear the major burden of responsibility for their drinking problem.

Alanon typically brings together many adult children of alcoholics. This photograph shows a therapy session involving adult children of alcoholics.

Although AA is a major factor in alcoholism treatment, its impact has been hard to quantify. This partially reflects the organization's decentralized nature. While broadly conforming to AA traditions, each group is free to develop its own focus, traditions, and helping procedures. Though this philosophy has maintained AA as a vital, continuously renewing organization, it also makes the coordinated study of treatment outcomes across groups extremely difficult.

The modest amount of research on AA's effectiveness suggests an abstinence rate of between 25 percent and 50 percent at one year, within the range of outcomes from other treatments (NIAAA, 1987). A recent membership survey (1989) reports an average sobriety length of fifty months for those attending meetings regularly (an average of four meetings a week by the typical member). The survey also found that about half of those who come to AA do not remain for more than three months.

DRUG ABUSE AND DEPENDENCE

Nature of Drug Abuse and Dependence

The Amphetamines and Other Stimulants. The amphetamines are central nervous system (CNS) stimulants. Methamphetamine hydrochloride—"speed" or "meth"—is the best-known and most commonly used member of this family of drugs. It is also the most potent. These psychoactive drugs increase the brain's level of activity, especially the reticular activating system (RAS). The RAS, located in both the mid- and hindbrain, plays a central role in the sleep-wake cycle.

For many years, the most common use of the amphetamines was to help control appetite; that use is now illegal because the drugs were so often abused by dieters. Another frequent therapeutic application was to reduce fatigue and heighten concentration in military personnel and others unable to sleep regular hours; that use, too, is uncommon nowadays because of the drugs' high abuse potential. The amphetamines are still used, however, to control the agitated behavior of hyperactive children, whom they calm by their *paradoxical action* (i.e., by acting on children in a direction opposite to their effect on adults).

Besides the amphetamines, caffeine—the sympathetic nervous system stimulant that gives coffee its "kick"—is a member of this family of stimulant drugs. Some scientists also consider some antidepressant drugs to be stimulants, since their behavioral actions mimic those of the amphetamines and the other CNS stimulants.

Elevated mood and increased mental alertness typically follow ingestion of low to moderate doses of a stimulant; enhanced feelings of happiness, including euphoria, are also common. At higher doses, and especially with repeated use, stimulant intoxication may involve irritability and motor restlessness, insomnia, disturbed speech, and anxiety.

Withdrawal from a stimulant, especially when a substantial amount has been ingested, typically involves a "crash"—a period of despair and depression. Marked agitation, concentration difficulties, hostility, and paranoid delusions are not uncommon upon repeated use of increasing doses of these drugs for an extended period of time. These behaviors may ultimately develop into a psychoticlike reaction, called *toxic psychosis,* resembling paranoid schizophrenia.

Tolerance develops to the stimulants' euphoriant and energizing properties, resulting in more and more of the drug taken to achieve the same subjective effect. Tolerance explains why high doses of the drug, ones that lead to very serious consequences, are taken. Withdrawal symptoms, including various CNS and gastrointestinal abnormalities, accompany the profound, prolonged depression typical of abrupt cessation of heavy stimulant use.

Cocaine and Crack. Cocaine is a short-acting, powerful stimulant whose effects are very much like the amphetamines, only shorter lived and more intense. A natural substance refined from the coca plant, cocaine has long been used by South American Indians to induce euphoria and counteract fatigue. Coca leaf chewing by Indians in the Andes is still very common. The only therapeutic use of cocaine is as a topical anesthetic for minor operations.

When taken by mouth, cocaine's potency is significantly reduced. As a result, it is generally inhaled ("snorted"), smoked, or injected. When snorted, cocaine's peak effects occur in about twenty minutes; they diminish within an hour or less. An intense though short-lived feeling of well-being, the "rush," makes cocaine ingestion so sought after (Gawin & Ellinwood, 1988).

Crack, the recent source of an epidemic of stimulant use in many U.S. cities, is the dried mixture of cocaine, water, and baking soda that is "free-based"—smoked to yield a very intense twenty- to thirty-minute high. Arnold Washton, a psychologist with long experience treating drug dependencies, considers crack ". . . the most addictive drug known to man right now. It is almost instantaneous addiction. . . . There is no such thing as the 'recreational use' of crack" (Morganthau, 1986, p. E1).

Cocaine and crack induce dependence extraordinarily rapidly. The reason is two-fold:

1. The euphoria they produce is very reinforcing.
2. Because this effect is so short lived and so often followed by depression, the abuser may ingest another dose very rapidly, both to regain the high and postpone the low.

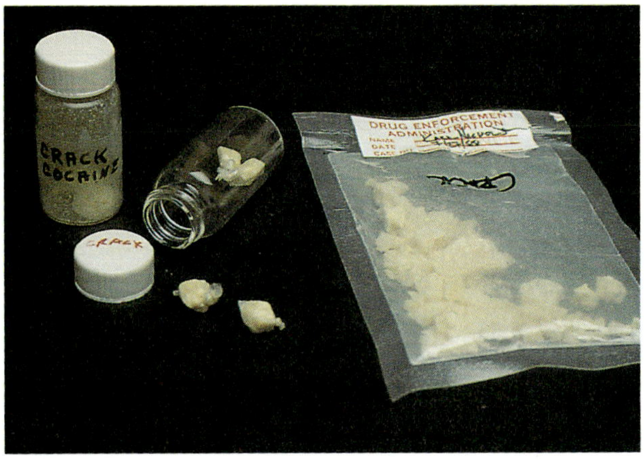

Ice (an extremely fast-acting form of cocaine), crack, and cocaine.

In other words, the vicious cycle so often associated with psychoactive drugs is instituted with unparalleled swiftness when cocaine and crack are involved:

> While alcoholism takes its toll over the course of years, coke, free-basing, and crack are causing people to bottom out within months. "It's very simple," says Paul, a 45-year-old real-estate broker with a large investment firm, who became a born-again Christian when he kicked his coke habit. "There's a line you cross when it becomes impossible. It usually takes twenty years with alcohol, ten to fifteen years with pot, five years with snorting cocaine, six months for shooting it, and a matter of weeks for crack." (*New York Magazine,* February 20, 1989, p. 40)

Besides the catastrophic psychological and psychiatric consequences of cocaine and crack addiction—many shared with the other stimulants—free-basing of cocaine and crack can lead to significant cardiovascular and lung damage. Cocaine has also been implicated in pregnancy complications and with birth defects. As well, financial incentives behind the cocaine/crack epidemic have led to drug wars, numerous murders involving rival drug suppliers, and the virtual siege of drug-infested areas of some large cities. The problem of drug dependence in our cities is no longer primarily a problem of heroin; crack and cocaine are strong contributors.

Wider public recognition of cocaine's harmful effects is reflected in NIDA's 1987 National High School Senior Survey of the perceived harmfulness and current use of cocaine by this national sample of young people. These data, graphed in Figure 11.4, may foreshadow a meaningful reduction in cocaine abuse during the next few years.

Nicotine. The number one public health problem in this country is not cocaine or crack. It is not heroin. It

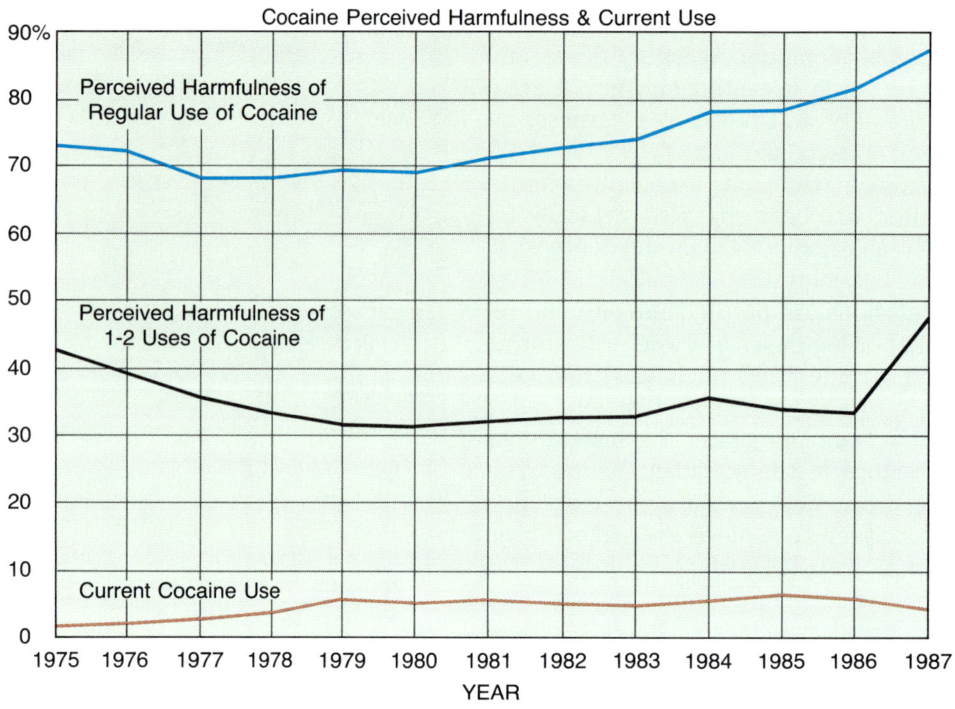

Figure 11.4 *Between 1975 and 1987, perceived harmfulness of both regular and infrequent use of cocaine by high school seniors increased. Although current cocaine use also increased slightly overall, it actually began to decrease the last two years of the period.*

Source: From the 1987 National High School Senior Survey, conducted by the University of Michigan Institute for Social Research, for the National Institute of Drug Abuse.

is not even alcohol, as severely as that drug tests our society. The number one public health problem in the United States is tobacco, a dangerous component of which is nicotine. Costing the country almost 400,000 lives a year, cigarettes also exact very substantial costs for lost productivity when smoking-related illnesses, many life threatening, cause workers to stay home from work or seek hospitalization.

Cigarette smoking has declined in the United States since 1964, when the Surgeon General issued his initial report on smoking's catastrophic health consequences. However, as Figure 11.5 shows, this decrease has been very uneven: Whites, college graduates, and males have substantially decreased their smoking rates while blacks, females, and high school dropouts have shown surprisingly little change.

Nicotine is chemically related to the amphetamines. It causes both withdrawal symptoms and tolerance, so it is dependency-inducing. While the tars and other toxic components of cigarette smoke are fully as dangerous as nicotine, it is the nicotine in cigarettes which ensures that people dependent on it will continue to smoke.

Contrary to belief, nicotine is an extremely potent compound. Fortunately, its potency is diminished somewhat because it is not ingested in purified form. Once inhaled, up to 90 percent of nicotine is absorbed through the lungs. At low doses, nicotine acts as a mild CNS stimulant. At higher doses, it causes agitation, irritability, and a variety of other bodily effects. Chronic nicotine ingestion is associated with serious cardiovascular disease.

The Barbiturates and Other Sedatives. The sedative-hypnotic drugs depress the central nervous system by dampening brain activity, especially the reticular activating system. As a consequence, reduction in the usual level of the brain's chemical-electrical activity results in a comparable reduction in awareness level. These drugs are used therapeutically to sedate and calm (at low doses) and to induce sleep (at higher doses).

Alcohol is a sedative-hypnotic drug, as are the barbiturates and certain nonbarbiturate drugs sold over the counter. Among the sedative-hypnotics requiring a prescription, besides the barbiturates, are such common sleeping medications as Quaalude, Doriden, and Noludar. Like barbiturates, they are most commonly used to sedate or induce sleep. The minor tranquilizers, including Librium and Valium, are also classified as sedative-hypnotics; they are prescribed as muscle relaxants and to induce relaxation.

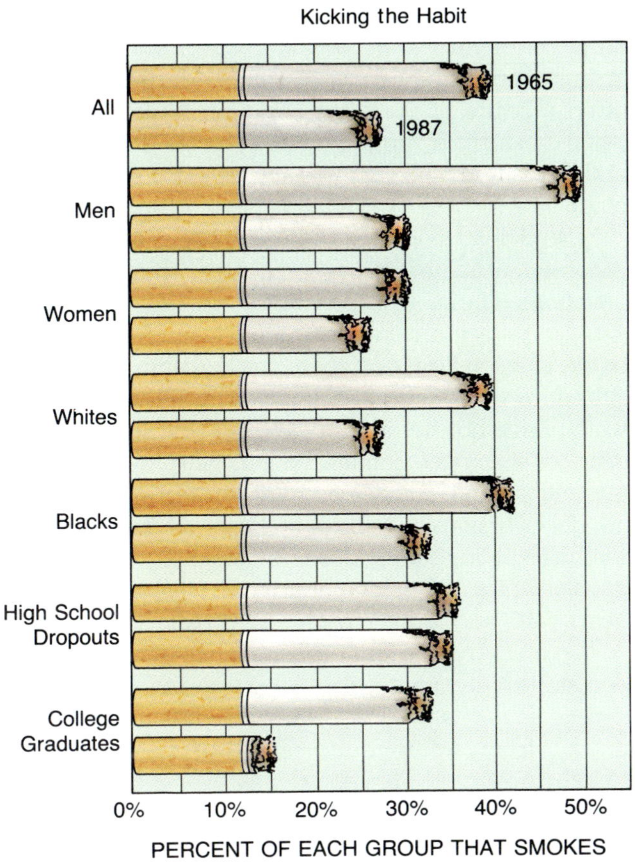

Figure 11.5 *Cigarette smoking by all groups in this figure declined between 1965 and 1987. Sharpest declines were shown by men, whites, and college graduates while women, blacks, and high school dropouts showed smallest declines.*

Source: Adapted from data from the United States Public Health Service.

The abuse potential is quite high for most sedative-hypnotic drugs. At lower doses, they induce mild sedation, relaxation, and a feeling of well-being; they are abused for those effects. However, most of these drugs, including the barbiturates and Librium and Valium, also induce marked physical dependence and tolerance, with the result of ingesting ever-increasing amounts of these drugs to maintain their reinforcing effects. Unfortunately, these higher doses can induce behavioral and CNS depression, respiratory failure, and death. Because these drugs produce marked tolerance, abrupt withdrawal can cause a variety of life-threatening consequences, including convulsions, coma, and death. Because tolerance to these drugs is typically so marked, withdrawal from the minor tranquilizers and, especially, the barbiturates can be extremely dangerous.

The sedative-hypnotic drugs are *additive*, meaning that people who combine them (a common, sometimes lethal, mixture is alcohol and barbiturates) experience greater effects than that of either taken alone. The result has been fatal in many instances when the combinative effects of two sedatives depress respiration and CNS functioning.

The Natural and Synthetic Opioids. Three groups of powerfully addicting drugs are included in this drug class. They are (1) the *natural opiates*, drugs like morphine and codeine, derived directly from the opium poppy; (2) the *semisynthetic opiates*, including heroin, which are chemical derivatives of morphine or codeine; and (3) the *synthetic opiates*, manufactured drugs whose actions are like those of the opiates; these drugs include methadone, Darvon, and Demerol.

The actions of the dried exudate of the opium poppy cut seed pod have been known for virtually as long as humankind has recorded its history. The Sumerians, almost 6,000 years ago, wrote of a "joy plant," which was likely the opium poppy. The opiates' actions include euphoria and a profound sense of well-being, passivity, and warmth, a striking subjective sense of removal from physical reality into a dreamlike state, and very effective dampening of pain. The therapeutic use of these drugs centers on the last effect: Morphine, a premier analgesic for two centuries, continues in use for that purpose today, especially for the severe pain of orthopedic surgery and some forms of cancer.

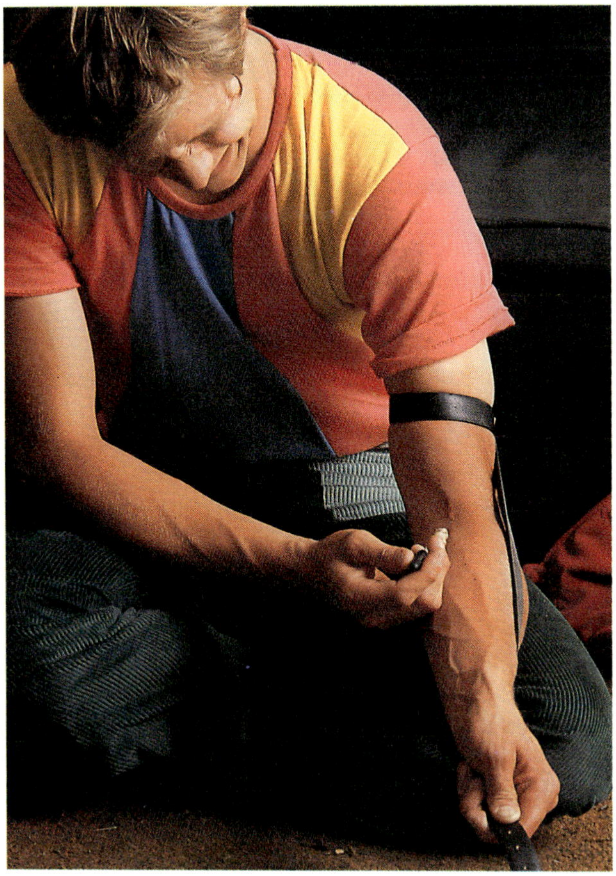

A young heroin addict "shooting up".

Heroin is the most commonly abused opiate, in part because it is several times stronger than morphine. A white, odorless, bitter powder, when injected (the preferred route of action because of its rapid effect) heroin produces a powerful "rush" of relaxation, dreaminess, and well-being. Many users have compared the heroin high to orgasm.

Natural and synthetic opiates are profoundly addicting. They induce tolerance and physical dependence rapidly and typically produce a most unpleasant period of physical withdrawal, characterized by nausea, vomiting, psychomotor irritability, and insomnia. The opiates also cause respiratory depression and sedation; significant numbers of deaths occur every year when stronger than intended heroin doses effectively shut down breathing and cause death by asphyxiation. A variety of untoward consequences also accompany the injection of heroin and its adulterants, often because of dirty or dull needles. Recently, the most profound consequence has become HIV infection: The most rapidly growing group of AIDS victims are intravenous drug abusers, most of them heroin addicts.

The Hallucinogens. The hallucinogens include LSD, psilocybin, morning glory seeds, mescaline, and phencyclidine (PCP). They are ingested to induce hallucinations—visual and auditory distortions of the environment—distancing the user from the environment and, sometimes, forcing a rethinking of his or her relationships. This "altered state of consciousness" is reinforcing to some young people, sufficiently so in certain cases to cause them to focus their lives on the hallucinogens rather than on home, school, family, and friends.

Through history hallucinogens have been used, often by religious leaders, as "mind expanding" agents seeming to bring the user into closer contact with the "cosmic forces" of the universe. Used on a very occasional basis, they are unlikely to cause damage. But when used frequently, they can cut the abuser off from the real world, further alienating a person who may be estranged from society to begin with. These drugs also have the potential to permanently alter the brain and, possibly because of these brain function changes, to cause paranoid and other delusional psychoses that may be prolonged and very difficult to treat.

How is it that the desire to experience hallucinations, which seem to most of us to be totally undesirable, would cause someone to risk the consequences of repeated ingestion of a hallucinogen? The first-person accounts of drug-induced hallucinatory experiences in Box 11.4 on page 284 provide some insight.

Cannabis, Hashish, and Marijuana. Cannabis and marijuana are related, both chemically and by action, to the hallucinogens. The psychoactive ingredient in both, tetrahydrocannabinol (THC), is concentrated in the resin of the *Cannabis* plant. Marijuana is the dried mixture of the leaves and seeds of this plant while hashish, a more potent form of THC, is the highly resinous mixture of the flowering tops of the plant.

In sufficient amounts, both marijuana and hashish can induce hallucinations and, less often, paranoid delusions. The more usual subjective effects of these substances are a clear sense of relaxation and well-being and, on occasion, behavioral disinhibition, resulting in things seeming humorous, silly, or offbeat which have not before appeared in that light. These drug effects may enhance conviviality, one reason marijuana is often ingested in group settings. Moderate doses of marijuana have behavioral effects similar to those of moderate doses of alcohol. Marijuana's physical effects include increased respiration and heart rate, and a dry mouth and throat.

The most troublesome consequence of marijuana's heavy chronic use is called the *amotivational syndrome.* It is characterized by great difficulty rousing oneself from the profound self-absorption to return to reinvolve oneself with friends, work, family, and school. There is considerable scientific dispute over whether long-term marijuana use is associated with other untoward psychological or physical consequences.

Figure 11.6 graphs data from the 1987 National High School Senior Survey of perceived harmfulness and daily use of marijuana. The figure shows that regular use of marijuana has been perceived by a greater number of high school seniors as harmful through the last decade. Through the same period, fewer and fewer seniors have used the drug on a daily basis.

Causes of Drug Abuse and Dependence

The bulk of research on the actions of the psychoactive substances, as well as on the causes and treatments of the associated disorders, has been on alcohol. This reflects that the other psychoactive drugs have not been perceived as major problems for most people in society until relatively recently. As a result, they were not studied extensively. In turn, our discussion of the causes of drug abuse and dependence is less extensive than our discussion of the causes of alcohol abuse and dependence.

Genetic Factors in Drug Abuse and Dependence. In one of the few empirical studies of genetic factors' role in the development of drug abuse, Cadoret, Troughton, O'Gorman, and Heywood (1986) reported significant relationships among parental alcoholism, antisocial behavior, and drug problems developing in

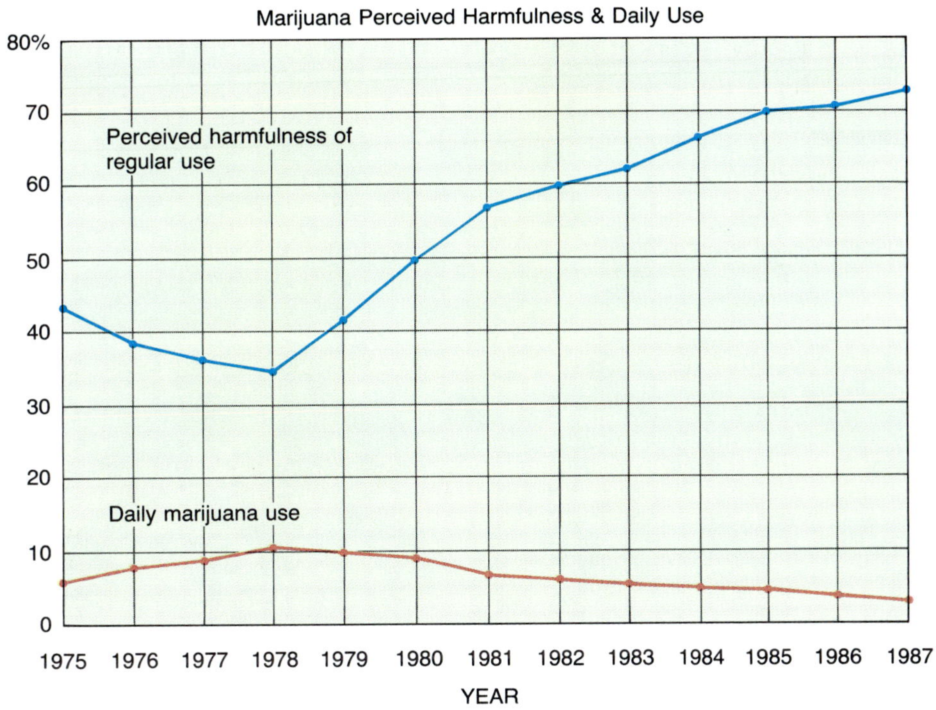

Figure 11.6 *Perceived harmfulness of regular use of marijuana by high school seniors increased sharply between 1975 and 1987. Daily marijuana use decreased slightly during the same period.*

Source: From 1987 National High School Senior Survey, conducted by the University of Michigan Institute for Social Research, for the National Institute of Drug Abuse.

adopted-out children. As both antisocial personality and parental alcoholism have been associated with the development of drug abuse (Helzer et al., 1990), these data suggest an indirect link between parental drug abuse and drug abuse in these children. The paucity of other studies exploring genetic factors' role in drug abuse, however, makes it impossible to draw firm conclusions.

Sociocultural Factors in Drug Abuse and Dependence. Drug use in this country has long been related to ethnic identity. Heroin use is largely, though by no means entirely, confined to poor, largely black and Hispanic, urban ghetto dwellers (NIDA, 1986). By contrast, the abuse of prescription drugs is largely, though not entirely, a phenomenon of middle-class women whose physicians originally prescribed these drugs to alleviate depression, anxiety, and insomnia. In contrast, middle-class whites appear to use cocaine much more often nowadays than do other groups, though crack seems to appeal to abusers across a wide range of socioeconomic categories (Newcomb & Bentle, 1990).

It is tempting to conclude from these data that poor people and minority group members in this country abuse drugs at higher rates than others as an escape, however temporary and dangerous, from the reality of their existence. Many have made that argument. However, in the absence of related empirical data, we can only continue to ponder the question—and hope for empirically based answers as soon as possible.

Psychiatric Disorder and Marijuana. Some researchers have speculated that the heavy use of marijuana causes psychiatric disorders. The evidence for this link, a convincing argument against the heavy use of the drug, is, however, slim. When 100 regular marijuana users were followed for six to seven years, researchers failed to observe a higher incidence of psychopathology in the users than in a comparison group of fifty young men and women who were not marijuana users (Weller & Halikas, 1985).

As noted above, marijuana does cause an amotivational syndrome in some chronic users, interfering significantly with their ability to function. As a result, it might be recognized as a significant psychiatric disorder at some future time.

Cocaine Abuse and CNS Dysfunction. More and more data in recent years support the view that substance use disorders are partly due to central nervous system dysfunction. Figure 11.7 on page 285 illustrates one theory of cocaine addiction. It hypoth-

BOX 11.4 First-Person Accounts of Drug-Induced Hallucinations

The Magic Mushroom

What is happening to you seems freighted with significance, beside which the humdrum events of every day are trivial. All these things you see with an immediacy of vision that leads you to say to yourself, "Now I am seeing for the first time, seeing direct, without the intervention of mortal eyes." On doing so, my spirit seems to soar and leave the hut, and with the speed of thought, to travel where it listeth, in time and space, accompanied by the shaman's singing . . . at last you know what the ineffable is, and what ecstasy means. Ecstasy! (Crahan, 1969, p. 17)

Gage Taylor, *Mescaline Wood* (1969). Oil on canvas.

Peyote

The display which for an enchanted two hours followed was such as I find it hopeless to describe in language which shall convey to others the beauty and splendor of what I saw. Stars, delicate floating films of color, then an abrupt rush of countless points of white light swept across the field of view, as if the unseen millions of the Milky Way were to flow in a sparkling river before my eyes . . . zigzag lines of very bright colors . . . the wonderful loveliness of swelling clouds of more vivid colors gone before I could name them. (De Ropp, 1957, p. 34)

Psilocybin

On the whole, if I had to describe the visions in one word, I should say that they were living arabesques. There was generally a certain incomplete tendency to symmetry, the effect being somewhat as if the underlying mechanism consisted of a large number of polished facets acting as mirrors. It constantly happened that the same image was repeated over a large part of the field, though this holds good mainly of the forms, for in the colors there would still remain all sorts of delicious varieties of experience, which constituted an essential part of these sensory manifestations. . . . It is true that at one stage of mescal intoxication, and more especially in quite healthy persons, there is a feeling of well-being, and even of beatitude, accompanied by an illusory sense of quite unusual intellectual activity; but there is no stage of maudlin emotionality; on the whole there is a condition of fairly unimpaired and alert intellect, untiringly absorbed in the contemplation of the strange world of new sensory phenomena into which the subject has been introduced.

Source: From Ellis, H. (1902). Mescal: A study of a divine plant. *Popular Science Monthly, 61,* 59, 65. Reprinted by permission of the publisher.

esizes that the drug blocks the reabsorption of dopamine, one of the key brain neurotransmitters. In doing so, cocaine simultaneously induces euphoria and lays the groundwork for one of its principal negatives, the "crash" that may lead to profound depression on withdrawal. A key unanswered question is whether some people are more liable than others to the allure of cocaine's euphoria, to the depression accompanying withdrawal, or both. One or both those vulnerabilities, presumably, would reflect some sort of inborn abnormality in neurotransmission metabolism.

Treatment of Drug Abuse and Dependence

Individual, group, and family therapy continue to be popular treatments for drug abusers, as they are for alcoholics. However, as we observed in considering treatments for alcoholism, empirical data attesting to the usefulness of these treatment methods with drug dependent persons are scarce.

Though a wide variety of smoking cessation programs are offered this country's smokers, approximately 95 percent of those who stop smoking do so on their own, without a formal program (Garvey, Heinold, & Rosner, 1989).

The results of formal smoking cessation programs have been disappointing, in that most smokers resume smoking soon after treatment. Women, especially young women, have been resistant in recent years to smoking cessation efforts. A recent survey of strategies employed by men and women in smoking cessation treatment (Blake et al., 1989) revealed women as more tentative and less committed to quitting smoking entirely and less confident of their ability to quit than men.

One reason—of particular interest to young women who are more likely than young men to be concerned about their weight—may be that smoking seems to diminish appetite and inhibit weight gain. As a result, young women who continue to smoke can successfully maintain diets and avoid gaining weight. The rate at which women initiate cigarette smoking nowadays, generally during adolescence, is also higher than the rate for men (Center for Disease Control, 1987).

Behavioral Treatment Methods. *Aversion techniques* were among the first formal treatments for smoking. Such aversive stimuli as painful electric shock, nausea-inducing drugs, and aversive images actually do succeed in inducing smokers to stop smoking when they predictably accompany smoking. But once they no longer do so, smoking tends to return to pretreatment levels quickly.

Cigarette smoke has also been employed therapeu-

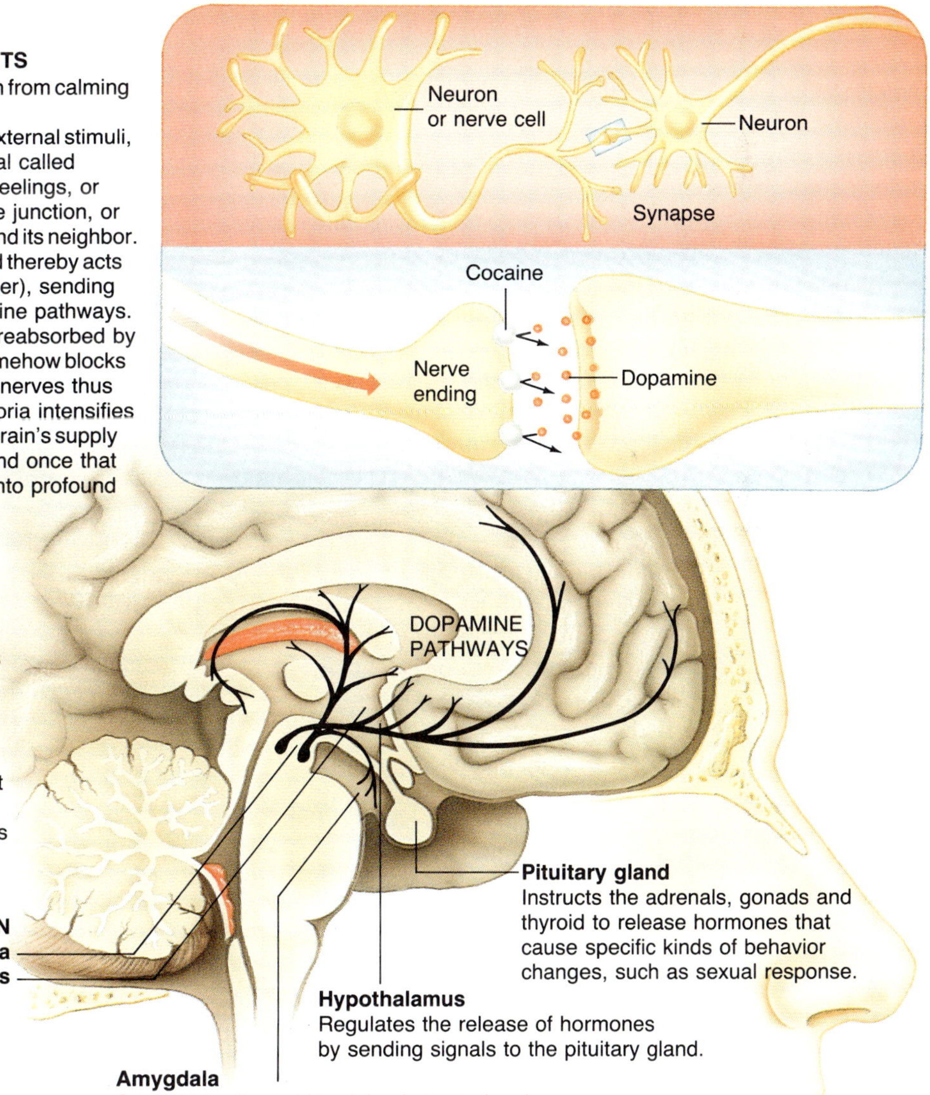

Figure 11.7 *This figure illustrates one theory of cocaine addiction—that cocaine prevents the brain from calming itself down.*
Source: From *The New York Times*, 8/24/89, p. B7. Copyright 1989 by The New York Times Company. Reprinted by permission.)

tically. Smokers are required to smoke several cigarettes in rapid succession, drawing deeply and repeatedly on each, to induce an aversion to the highly concentrated dose of nicotine and tars. While this *rapid smoking* has achieved some success in inducing short-term abstinence, its long-term consequences have been disappointing (Lichtenstein & Mermelstein, 1984).

Various *behavioral self-control strategies* have also been incorporated in smoking cessation programs, largely to modify smokers' cognitions about their ability to cope with urges to smoke. Self-monitoring (keeping a careful record of urges to smoke and cigarettes consumed before, during, and after treatment), contingency contracting (arranging consequences, usually monetary ones, for maintaining abstinence), and self-management training (rearranging the smoker's environment to decrease the likelihood it will encourage a return to smoking) are typical components of self-control strategies for smoking cessation (e.g., Stevens & Hollis, 1989).

Pharmacological methods, including nicotine gum or tablets and lobeline, a drug related to nicotine, diminish nicotine-induced withdrawal symptoms that help prevent a return to smoking by the newly abstinent. These drugs have achieved moderately positive results (e.g., Hjalmarson, 1985) but only with smokers highly motivated to change their behavior (West, Hajek, & Belcher, 1986). *Nicotine fading*—making smokers smoke cigarettes that contain successively lower concentrations of nicotine (and tars)—has also been tried, generally in conjunction with behavioral self-control programs, with mixed results (Burling et al., 1989).

Nicotine gum successfully confronts another common impediment to continued abstention from cigarettes, the weight gain that often follows (Gross, Stitzer, & Maldonado, 1989). Smoking cessation often results in increased food intake (Stamford, Matter, Fell, & Papanek, 1986), it changes food preferences in favor of sweet, high-caloric foods (Grunberg, 1985), and it causes a reduction in energy output (Hofstetter, Schutz, Jequier, & Warren, 1986). As indicated above, the likelihood of weight gain following smoking cessation may be especially influential in convincing young women who are smokers not to attempt to stop smoking (Streater, Sargent, & Ward, 1989) and those who are nonsmokers to begin smoking.

A large-scale smoking relapse prevention trial (Killen, Fortmann, and Newman, 1990) evaluated the usefulness of psychological treatment methods combined with nicotine gum. While 42 percent of the 1,096 study participants maintained their weight during an 8-week treatment program, 43 percent of them gained more than 2.2 pounds (1 kilogram). Those who completely stopped smoking during treatment (only some of the participants did) gained more than four times the weight relapsers gained. Participants who used nicotine gum gained significantly less weight than those who did not.

Efforts to change public attitudes toward smoking have enjoyed marked success during the past twenty-five years, in contrast to the modest results of formal treatment. From the Surgeon General's *Report on Smoking and Health* (1964), a variety of public figures, including a recent Surgeon General, have led an ultimately successful campaign to alter public attitudes toward smoking, especially smoking in public settings. This is evidenced by the involvement of entire communities in community-wide smoking cessation programs (LeFebvre, Cobb, Goreczny, & Carleton, 1990); by increased public concerns about passive smoking's effects (inhaling someone else's cigarette smoke); and by the willingness of society to support the imposition of health warning labels on cigarette packages, restrictions on smoking in public places, including restaurants and airplanes, and prohibitions on advertising of tobacco products. A significant reduction in smoking has resulted in this country: Only 29 percent of adults now smoke, as against 40 percent in 1965. Men have stopped smoking at the highest rates: 50 percent smoked in 1965; fewer than a third do today.

Relapse Prevention. As indicated earlier in the chapter, Marlatt and Gordon (1985) have proposed a cognitive behavioral approach called relapse prevention (RP) to treat alcohol and drug dependence, including cigarette smoking. It focuses on the crucial maintenance period *after* detoxification and intensive treatment, a period often ignored by other clinicians. Its developers describe a flexible and comprehensive program.

> RP procedures can be applied either in the form of a specific maintenance program to prevent relapse or as a more global program of lifestyle change. In the former case, the goals of the program are (1) to anticipate and prevent the occurrence of a relapse after the initiation of a habit change attempt (e.g., to prevent a recent ex-smoker from returning to habitual smoking); and (2) to help the individual recover from a "slip" or lapse before it escalates into a full-blown relapse. Such RP procedures can be used regardless of the theoretical orientation or intervention methods applied during the initial treatment phase. . . . In the second more general application of the RP model, the purpose is to facilitate global changes in personal habits and daily lifestyle so as to reduce the risk of physical disease and/or psychological stress. (Marlatt, 1985, p. 4)

The relapse prevention model (illustrated in Figure 11.8) helps patients dependent on alcohol, cocaine, amphetamines, and nicotine deal with the inevitable challenges of a return to the everyday

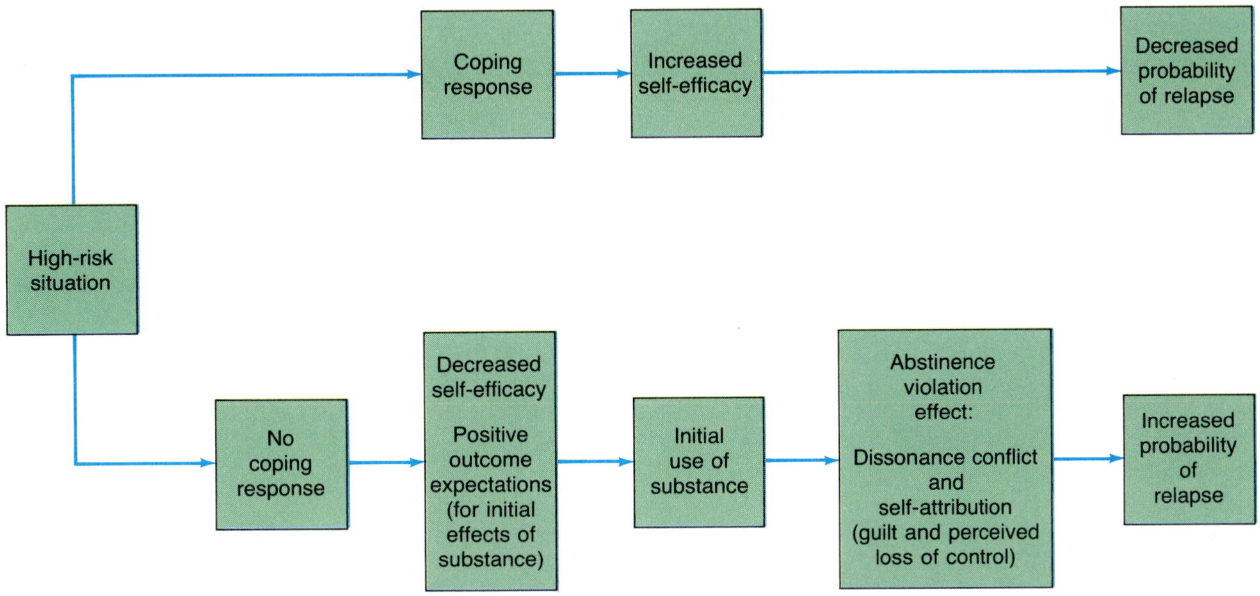

Figure 11.8 Marlatt and Gordon's Relapse Prevention Model.
Source: From Marlatt, G.A. & Gordon, J.R. (1985). *Relapse prevention.* New York: Guilford Press, p. 38. By permission of the publisher.

environment *without* the drug or drugs that were previously an integral part of that environment. Craving, "slips," help or hindrance from friends and family are all dealt with in this model.

RP represents a *cognitive* approach to treatment because it emphasizes the role, in maintaining positive treatment gains, of such cognitions as self-efficacy, outcome expectancies, and attributions. It is *behavioral* because it emphasizes behavioral change in the effort to modify these cognitions and increase the likelihood of maintaining treatment gains. Behavioral change through relaxation training and training in coping and social skills is designed to bring about cognitive change, which in turn will help maintain abstinence from substances. Some of those techniques were employed in the following effort to induce smoking cessation through relapse prevention.

> *Mr. L, who had been ordered by his doctor to stop smoking, was a veteran of several smoking cessation programs. Each time he applied himself vigorously to quitting, but was not able to maintain abstinence for very long. He complained that, after a while, not smoking so interfered with his ability to work that he was "forced" to start smoking again. A discussion of Mr. L's self-monitoring data was a stimulus for a discussion of his lifestyle. Mr. L was a classic "workaholic." He typically worked 12-hour days 6 days a week and found little time for anything else. He reported that he nearly always felt rushed and . . . agreed that his two-pack-a-day habit helped him maintain this lifestyle.*
>
> *A "want-should" analysis of Mr. L's life showed a nearly total absence of wants (i.e., reinforcers). While Mr. L easily identified several behaviors that might become wants for him (gym workouts and tennis were high on the list), he claimed that all were too time consuming given his busy schedule. Mr. L's therapist forcefully pointed out that this issue was critical to Mr. L's success in quitting smoking, and that he had been willing to commit substantial time and energy to this project. Mr. L contracted to work out three times a week on a trial basis. With Mr. L's permission, the therapist contacted Mrs. L and encouraged her to engage Mr. L in positive conversation about his workouts. Mr. L reported a slight decrease in tension on the workout days. When the clinic ended, Mr. L was unwilling to commit firmly to continuing his workouts. However, his wife reported that he seemed to be enjoying them and thought he would continue.* (Shiffman et al., 1985, p. 515)

Detoxification. Detoxification from some drugs can take place safely outside hospitals, whereas withdrawal from others requires resources available only to inpatients. People with a long history of heavy drinking currently consuming substantial daily quantities of alcohol, people dependent on and tolerant to barbiturates, and people with acquired tolerance to the synthetic sedatives, including Valium and Librium, are at particular risk in attempting withdrawal outside a hospital.

Withdrawal in these situations requires a gradual daily-dose reduction over several days or weeks. Otherwise, life-threatening withdrawal symptoms may develop. Abrupt cessation of the barbiturates and the other sedative-hypnotic drugs, for example, may precipitate withdrawal seizures, which can cause brain damage, coma, and death. Although highly unpleasant, withdrawal from the other drugs of abuse is not usually associated with life-threatening withdrawal symptoms. The individual's physician is the best judge of where and how detoxification ought to take place.

Methadone and Naloxone. Methadone, a treatment for heroin addiction, is even more controversial than Antabuse, a treatment for alcoholism. A synthetic opiate, methadone essentially replaces heroin in the addict's central nervous system opiate receptors. Consequently, heroin's reinforcing effects are markedly reduced. For most users, methadone produces a less powerful "high" than heroin; therefore, addicts on methadone maintenance have consented to give up heroin's strongly positive effects for a life free from the necessity to maintain their heroin habit.

Critics of methadone maintenance point out, however, that because it produces a moderate high, it creates an active and illegal market. However, the usual methadone maintenance procedure requires addicts to report to a treatment center for their daily oral dose of the drug to be consumed in the staff's presence. This reduces the possibility of taking the drug from the center and selling it on the street.

Critics also argue that methadone maintenance substitutes one addicting substance for another: Addicts on methadone are no more free from dependency than addicts on heroin. In response, supporters of methadone maintenance point out that one of the major social problems associated with heroin dependence—the necessity for most addicts to commit crimes continuously for money to support their habit—is largely eliminated when it is substituted for heroin.

Another controversial drug treatment for opiate dependence involves narcotic antagonists such as naloxone. Narcotic antagonists precipitate immediate withdrawal from a narcotic drug. When addicts on a maintenance dose of naloxone "slip" and ingest or inject an opiate like heroin, they will not experience its reinforcing effects because the heroin is rapidly dissipated from the body: Narcotic antagonists abolish or greatly diminish all the effects pleasurable to heroin addicts.

Like Antabuse, narcotic antagonists should be given only to patients wishing to break their dependence. Otherwise, they might take substantial amounts of their drug of choice despite being on the narcotic antagonist, with effects that are almost as unpleasant and sometimes as dangerous as the Antabuse reaction.

Like Antabuse, methadone and naloxone have supporters and detractors. Empirical data have not yet answered the all-important question of their therapeutic utility.

Synanon and Narcotics Anonymous. Just about the only similarity between Narcotics Anonymous and Synanon is that both are self-help treatments for drug addiction. Otherwise, the two differ profoundly.

Narcotics Anonymous is modeled after Alcoholics Anonymous. In slightly altered form, it espouses the Twelve Steps of AA as keys to recovery. It seeks to involve heroin abusers in daily meetings, to convince them to put their trust for the purposes of recovery in a "higher being," to shed their overwhelming guilt, and to take responsibility for renewing their lives drug-free. Though data on outcomes of Narcotics Anonymous are difficult to obtain, many believe it is a viable approach to the notoriously difficult task of inducing narcotics and cocaine abusers to give up their drug of abuse.

Synanon offers a very different approach to treatments though its goal—permanent abstinence from drugs—is the same. Treatment requires a lengthy period of residence in a Synanon House, where residents confront each other in the constant effort to

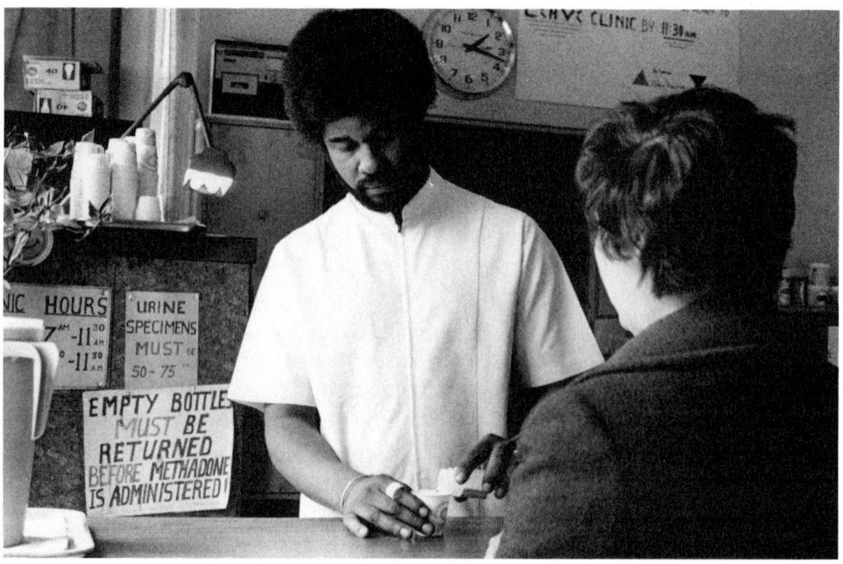

Administration of a heroin addict's daily dose of methadone at an outpatient methadone clinic.

break down defenses and denial. Synanon's basic assumption is that the addict's denial of the consequences of and personal responsibility for use is a key factor in his or her decision to continue drug use. In some ways, alcoholics use the same kind of denial system, though the manner in which Alcoholics Anonymous seeks to break through it is less direct, though no less central to treatment.

Virtually every day of a resident's time at the Synanon House includes a group therapy session attended by all residents. The meeting's focus shifts from person to person, but it always emphasizes the group's need to see the people it focuses on beginning to take more responsibility for their behavior, especially their drug-using behavior, and to confront realistically that behavior's impact on those around them. Implicit in this choice of group confrontation as the touchstone of Synanon treatment is the assumption that abusers will continue their drug abuse until or unless they face up to its consequences for themselves and others.

As with Alcoholics Anonymous, reliable data on outcomes of Synanon treatment are generally unavailable. Hence, we are unable to compare outcomes to other treatment approaches. The movement's dramatic growth in recent years attests to its acceptance by those most concerned, the abusers it seeks to help.

New Treatments for Cocaine and Crack. Cocaine and crack's urban epidemic has led many policymakers and clinicians to rethink existing approaches to and funding for treatment. A recent editorial in a leading newspaper lauding the federal government for finally recognizing the extent of our cities' drug problem also had the following to say about federal treatment efforts:

> As for treatment, Mr. Bennett (federal drug policy director) calls for an expansion of program capacity and contemplates adding a hefty $304 million to the current Federal treatment budget of $621 million. Studies suggest that about half the estimated six million Americans with serious drug problems might benefit from treatment, yet programs now enroll fewer than a million. A variety of approaches are now known to work for some addicts, and there is reason to believe success rates might improve dramatically with more careful matching of addicts to programs. (*The New York Times*, August 4, 1989, p. A26)

Two approaches, one new, the other not so new, have recently been heralded as promising treatments for cocaine and crack addiction. The new approach involves using one of the recently developed antidepressant drugs said to reduce the addict's craving during initial withdrawal, when craving is often so overwhelming addicts feel no choice but to return to the drug.

The other approach to crack and cocaine was announced in a front-page newspaper article under the two-column head, "Experts Finding New Hope on Treating Crack Addicts." The article begins:

> Drug experts now believe that the extreme difficulties they face in treating crack addiction stem far more from the setting and circumstances of the users than the biochemical reaction the drug produces. . . . Researchers are finding that crack addiction, under the right circumstances, can be successfully treated. Some studies suggest that crack is no more intrinsically addictive than other drugs that addicts have been able to quit. (*The New York Times*, August 24, 1989, p. A1)

Illustrating clinicians' new recognition that addicts cannot be returned to the environments which they originally developed their habit in is the compelling story of Derrick J.

> *Derrick J., a 28-year-old crack dealer who was recently released from prison and lives in a badly decayed apartment in West Harlem, is a one-man example of key factors in the saga of quitting or not quitting drugs: being physically removed from the surroundings of drug use; being cut off from the cues that trigger the craving; being returned to an environment without a job or friends who do not use the drug. . . . In an interview, Derrick said that crack was readily available in prison and that he smoked it during the first few months he was there; that he then stopped using it for about a year and had no trouble stopping because it lost its allure; that it was not so enjoyable to him when he was smoking alone in his cell; that when he was released from prison, he took up the habit again, mostly because crack addicts were the only friends he had, and that selling crack was the best way he knew to make money.* (*The New York Times*, August 24, 1989, p. B7)

More and more cities are establishing halfway houses permitting crack addicts to leave their old friends and environments, in which crack and other drug use was "the only show in town." Removal from the environment, establishment of new friendship patterns, and the promise of jobs not involving the sale of drugs are all part of this approach to the crack epidemic in our inner cities.

HOW EFFECTIVE ARE PREVENTION AND TREATMENT FOR SUBSTANCE ABUSE?

Preventing Substance Abuse

Most prevention efforts in this country center on school settings. Age-appropriate programs portraying the metabolism and physiology of alcohol and drugs in the body are typically offered to students, along with information on the range of potentially dangerous effects of abuse. These programs also generally consider the causes of substance abuse, the impact on children of parental alcoholism and drug dependence, and the treatments available for substance abuse. Some combine information on alcohol and drug effects with discussion of ways to say no to peer pressure to join in alcohol and drug use and abuse. These efforts share the goal of inducing children and adolescents to consider more seriously than they might otherwise the negative consequences of the decision to begin drinking or using drugs. In this context, they attempt to change attitudes of youthful users about alcohol and drugs, from symbols of emerging adulthood and sophistication to agents of injury, disease and death.

Most available data on the outcomes of preventive education and attitude change programs in secondary schools and colleges reveal success in increasing information level and changing attitudes on use from positive to less positive but failure in changing consumption levels in youths already using drugs (Nathan, 1983).

A police officer using a portable breath analyzer to test a teenage driver's blood alcohol level.

Preventing the Consequences of Substance Abuse

Strategies for reducing the *consequences* of alcohol use have been distinctly more successful. Efforts to limit alcohol's availability to youthful drivers (e.g., by raising the legal age for purchase of alcoholic beverages to twenty-one, and to increase the enforcement of laws pertaining to alcohol sales to underage individuals have succeeded in substantially reducing the number of fatal accidents involving youthful drinkers (NIAAA, 1990)). Similarly, efforts to educate pregnant women about **fetal alcohol syndrome (FAS)**—a syndrome affecting children of mothers who consume heavy quantities of alcohol during pregnancy that can involve mental retardation and physical and emotional disability—have led to significant reductions in the frequency of FAS (NIAAA, 1987).

Both drunken driving and FAS are major public health problems. Drunken drivers kill and injure thousands of Americans and cause millions of dollars of property damage each year. Similarly, victims of FAS number in the thousands; the loss of their full productivity to the country, by virtue of mental retardation and physical and emotional disabilities, is enormous. Hence, the success of efforts to this time to reduce drunken driving and the incidence of fetal alcohol syndrome represents an important public health advance.

Treating Substance Abuse

Though the effectiveness of substance abuse's treatment remains limited, we may be able to anticipate some improvement in the future. Before detailing reasons for this optimism, though, we should examine some apparently gloomy statistics. Though most of them have to do with alcoholism, the message they convey probably holds for other drugs as well.

First, no more than 10 percent of all alcohol-dependent people seek and find treatment in any given year in the United States (NIAAA, 1987). The comparable figure for drug-dependent individuals is unlikely to be any higher; in fact, it is probably lower, given the illegality of most abused drugs.

Adopting the most widely accepted prevalence estimate, between 6 percent and 8 percent of the U.S. population—around 18 million people—suffers from a significant alcohol problem. Combining these two estimates suggests that fewer than 2 million of them enter treatment during any given year. Since the percentage of people addicted to drugs is probably no lower than that for alcohol, and the number entering treatment is probably much lower, comparable figures for drug abusers in treatment are likely even more dismal.

The most widely accepted consensus on treatment outcomes for alcoholism is that an average 30 percent of those who begin a treatment program remain abstinent a year after its end (Miller & Hester, 1986; Nathan & Skinstad, 1987). One important reason is that over 50 percent of patients entering treatment drop out before its conclusion. Another is simply unresponsiveness to treatment. Because the patients in some programs are better prospects for treatment than the average, those programs do better than 30 percent; conversely, those programs treating more difficult patients do worse than 30 percent. If one multiplies this 30 percent average positive outcome figure by 10 percent—the number of alcoholics treated in a year in this country—the product is 3 percent. In other words, only 3 out of 100 of our nation's alcoholics in a year are helped out of their dependency—and the comparable percentage figure for drug-dependent individuals is almost certainly even lower.

Judged by these figures, we treat alcoholism and drug dependence with very modest effectiveness. However, the situation may not be as bad as it seems. The substantial quantity of research on treatment outcomes for substance abuse in the past two decades has begun to yield important results. Data reported during recent years suggests that patient variables and, perhaps, therapist variables appear to be important predictors of treatment outcome, perhaps more important than treatment variables (Loosen, Dew, & Prange, 1990).

Patient variables affecting treatment include a complex of factors that define the quantity and quality of the patient's personal resources. Such variables as marital status, age, education, and employment status predict outcome. More important is the patient's drinking history. Predictably, patients whose abusive drinking has neither progressed to dependence nor involved developing physical disease, patients who have shown themselves able to abstain from alcohol or control their intake for significant periods in the past, and patients with no or minimal involvement with other drugs are better treatment prospects than patients whose abusive drinking is of long duration and has long been out of control (Holden, 1987).

Patients' motivation to change their abusive drinking pattern may be the most important determinant of treatment success (Miller, 1985). For this reason, clinicians are making specific efforts to heighten patients' treatment motivation and to maximize success by selecting individuals most likely to benefit from rigorous treatments.

Another promising attempt to improve treatment success is to match patients both to treatment and to therapist. This is based on pilot research suggesting that particular patients may be motivated to work hardest in a particular treatment setting with a particular kind of therapist (Miller & Hester, 1986; Moos & Finney, 1983). Two of the nation's leading researchers on matching caution us, however, against believing that significant breakthroughs are imminent (Finney & Moos, 1986). Apparently, the conceptual and methodological problems associated with treatment matching are formidable indeed.

Unfortunately, the data on treatment outcomes for drug abuse, considerably less promising, have not been leavened by research suggesting that the situation might soon improve. At present, we do not know how to select drug abusers for treatment, motivate them to benefit from it, or treat them effectively.

SUMMARY

1. Psychoactive substance abuse and dependence are among the nation's leading public health problems.
2. Diagnosis of alcohol or drug abuse and dependence in *DSM-III-R* depends on recognition of behavioral criteria within the substance dependence syndrome. Three or more merit the diagnosis of psychoactive substance dependence. Fewer than three but significant use for a month or more or use in physically hazardous circumstances meet the standards for psychoactive substance abuse. Tolerance involves a gradual reduction in the subjective effects of a dependency-inducing drug on repeated drug administration, while withdrawal symptoms are physical and psychological consequences of cessation of use. Both tolerance and withdrawal symptoms are important signs of dependence.
3. *DSM-III-R* lists nine classes of substances that induce both abuse and dependence: alcohol; the amphetamines; cannabis and marijuana; cocaine and crack; the halucinogens; the inhalants; the opioids; phencyclidine and similarly acting drugs; and, the sedatives and similarly acting drugs. Nicotine induces dependence but not abuse.
4. Research on the causes of alcohol abuse and dependence suggests that some persons may have a genetically transmitted predisposition to develop alcoholism. Also believed to play roles in the etiology of alcohol abuse and dependence are sociocultural influences; learning variables, including classical conditioning, operant-conditioning, modeling and vicarious reinforcement, and attitudinal/expectancy variables; and psychopathological factors.
5. Treatments for alcohol abuse and dependence include individual psychotherapy, group and family therapy, behavior therapy, detoxification, relapse prevention, Antabuse, tranquilizing drugs, and Alcoholics Anonymous. None of these treatments appears markedly more effective than any of the others. More important than treatment variables in predicting positive treatment outcomes for alcohol abuse and dependence seem to be patient and, perhaps, therapist variables.
6. The causes of drug abuse and dependence likely include genetic and sociocultural factors and psychopathology. Treatments include behavior therapy, detoxification, methadone and Naloxone, and Synanon and Narcotics Anonymous. Treatments for drug abuse and dependence seem to be less effective than those for alcohol abuse and dependence.

Jay Burch, Untitled Still Life Study (1989). Pastel on paper. Courtesy of the Govinda Gallery, Washington, D.C.

12 CHILDHOOD DISORDERS

Did you feel depressed because your parents separated?

Did you get cut from a team during tryouts?

Were you often sent to your room for fighting with your brother or sister?

Were you bullied by kids at the bus stop and afraid to go to school?

Did you ever have to repeat a grade in school?

Did you cry yourself to sleep and not know why?

Not all of these problems are serious ones parents would seek professional help for their children for. Yet a hundred years ago, children never received professional services for any such problems. Their mothers may have given them some special attention but more often they were ignored. Fortunately today, children's psychological problems are now taken seriously and considered more than miniature versions of adult problems. Children's reactions to these problems are dubbed abnormal or not depending upon their age and how intense and how long their reactions are. Children with serious problems are usually referred by parents or teachers for professional assistance.

First we will consider the prevalence of the major childhood disorders and how they differ for boys and girls. We then will discuss the development and treatment of the following childhood disorders:

1. Oppositional and conduct disorders.
2. Attention deficit disorder with hyperactivity.
3. Anxiety disorders (separation anxiety, overanxious disorders, and childhood phobias).
4. Enuresis.
5. Specific developmental disorders.
6. Childhood depression.
7. Childhood suicide.
8. Infantile autism.

Prior to 1900, society viewed children's psychological and physical abnormalities as downward extensions of adult problems. Children with extreme abnormalities, especially physical disfigurements, went untreated, often left to die of neglect. And even though their fate was less horrible, children with less-pronounced abnormalities still were seen as a financial and psychological drain on the family. In society's view, children and adolescents engaging in criminal behavior suffered from moral deficits due to physical causes and were sent to special children's prisons. Also considered a burden were children who could not be gainfully employed and thereby contribute to the family economy. Moreover, adults did not generally enjoy children—normal or abnormal—for their playfulness and merriment; instead, grownups treated them as little adults (Aries, 1962). Even the art of the fourteenth through the eighteenth centu-

Diego Velasquez, *Las Meninas (The Maids of Honor)* (1656). Oil on canvas, 10′5″ × 9′ 3/4″. Courtesy of Prado Museum, Madrid.

As evident in the Velasquez painting, The Maids of Honor, children were portrayed as little adults in the 1600s. Their dress was basically a miniature version of the dress of adults.

ries mirrors this attitude. For example, the children in "The Maids of Honor" by Diego Velazquez (1656) wear miniature versions of adult clothing. This prevailing view consequently prevented conceptualizing children's abnormalities as different from those of adults.

One exception to this view was Charles Darwin's 1887 developmental account of his own son in a scientific publication, *A Biographical Sketch of an Infant.* There were very few clinical accounts of, and not a single research publication devoted to, psychological abnormalities of children. Fortunately, Leightner Witmer—founder of the first American psychological clinic at the University of Pennsylvania in 1898—pioneered in the treatment of children. Witmer believed that the causes of children's problems should be sought in their homes, schools, and communities. Then in 1909, Freud published "Little Hans," the first account of the psychoanalytic treatment of a child. Another major event was the 1909 establishment in Chicago of the Healy School (Juvenile Psychopathic Institute), a clinic school for adolescents guilty of illegal behavior. Healy gained prominence as a champion of the idea that adolescent illegal or delinquent behavior did not have a physical cause. Instead, Healy and his school promoted the notion that children learned such behavior in their subculture.

By the 1920s, treatment programs began for children. State universities established child guidance clinics, and by the 1950s, experts agreed that children's emotional disturbances required consideration separate from that of adult disturbances. During this time, the child psychology field began to be established, and many universities started graduate degree programs in developmental psychology. Yet, the number of mental health professionals specializing in adult disorders far outnumbered child psychologists and psychiatrists. The history of child psychology journals also reflected the secondary significance attached to the subject. Thus, although the first major journal in child psychology, *Child Development,* was established in 1930, the *Journal of Abnormal Child Psychology* (publisher of research on psychological disorders of children) did not emerge until 1973. In contrast, the *Journal of Abnormal Psychology,* focusing primarily on adult disorders, began publication in 1906.

Another consequence of this neglect is that ordinarily only one or two chapters of abnormal psychology texts contain information on childhood disorders although professionals have increasingly recognized their diversity over the past two decades. *DSM-III-R* (1987) lists forty-seven separate childhood diagnoses under five major headings; *DSM-III* (1980) had ten separate diagnoses, *DSM-II* (1968) six. Table 12.1 shows the five general categories of childhood problems in *DSM-III-R* with several examples of each subcategory.

Given the number and variety of childhood diagnoses, why then do most abnormal psychology texts

TABLE 12.1 Disorders of Childhood in DSM-III-R

I. Intellectual
    - Moderate mental retardation
    - Severe mental retardation

II. Behavioral (overt)
    - Attention deficit disorder
    - Conduct disorder

III. Emotional
    - Anxiety disorders of childhood or adolescence
        - Separation anxiety disorder

IV. Physical
    - Eating disorders (anorexia nervosa; bulimia)
    - Stereotypic movement disorders (chronic motor disorder; Tourette's disorder)

V. Developmental
    - Pervasive developmental disorders (infantile autism)
    - Specific developmental disorders
        - Developmental reading disorder
        - Developmental arithmetic disorder

devote only a few chapters to them? One reason is that even today fewer psychologists and psychiatrists specialize in children than in adults. Between 1971 and 1976 only ninety-five psychiatrists specializing in childhood disorders graduated in the United States compared to more than four times that number of psychiatrists treating adults (Pardes, 1979). The situation is similar in clinical child psychology: As recently as 1987, no official clinical child psychology degree programs existed in the United States. Forty-four clinical psychology programs did advertise a child clinical psychology specialty, but 126 accredited clinical programs graduating Ph.D.–level clinical psychologists dealt largely with adult disorders (American Psychological Association, 1986). Nonetheless, the number of clinicians and researchers specializing in childhood disorders is growing quickly. The field's rapid expansion is evidenced by the recent publication of at least five abnormal psychology texts on childhood disorders. Prior to 1974 (Ross, 1974), no major publisher had produced a text on abnormal child psychology.

PREVALENCE OF CHILDHOOD DISORDERS

Using *DSM-III* criteria, researchers assessed a representative sample of approximately 800 New Zealand children to ascertain the prevalence of various problems (Anderson, Williams, McGee, & Silva, 1987). The children assessed—all nonretarded and between the ages of eleven and twelve—were part of an ongoing health and developmental study. Table 12.2 lists the prevalence of various disorders and the ratio of male to female children having them.

About 25 percent of the children studied received some diagnosis, and more than half of those diagnosed had multiple disorders. Similarly, more than 50 percent of the children seen in psychological clinics show more than one specific disorder. The most common overlap found in the New Zealand study was attention deficit problems (now called attention deficit hyperactivity disorder, ADHD) combined with conduct disorder (CD) or oppositional problems. Figure 12.1 shows this overlap, 15 children had ADHD and CD, or oppositional problems; 2 had ADHD, CD problems, and anxious or phobic problems; and 8 had ADHD along with CD/oppositional problems and Anxious/Phobic problems with depression. Altogether, 25 of the 53 children (47 percent) with ADHD also had CD/oppositional problems.

Investigators' assessment of the problems parents took their children to private practitioners or clinics for showed the following most common reasons:

1.	Multiple disorder: Primarily conduct/oppositional and anxious/phobic	57%
2.	Attention deficit/hyperactivity disorder (ADHD)	43
3.	Conduct/oppositional	23
4.	Anxious/phobic	22
5.	ADHD and conduct oppositional	13

As Figure 12.1 shows, the majority of children seen by professionals have multiple problems and parents most frequently seek help for their child's conduct problems and hyperactivity (Cerroto & Tuma, 1977). Of course, they also take their child for help with a severe developmental disability such as autism, yet autism is extremely infrequent, affecting fewer than one in 250 children.

TABLE 12.2 Prevalence of Individual Disorders

Disorder	N	Male/Female Ratio	Prevalence
Attention deficit disorder	53	5.1/1	7%
Oppositional disorder	45	2.2/1	6%
Separation anxiety	28	0.4/1	3%
Conduct disorder/aggressive	27	3.2/1	3%
Overanxious disorder	23	1.7/1	3%
Simple phobia	19	0.6/1	2%
Depressive/dysthymia	17	5.4/1	2%
Social phobia	7	0.2/1	1%
Total	219	1.8/1	

Source: From Anderson, J.C. Williams, S., McGee, R., & Silva, P.A. (1987). Copyright © 1987, American Medical Association. DSM-III disorders in preadolescent children; Prevalence in a large sample from the general population. *Archives of General Psychiatry*, 44, 72. Reprinted by permission.

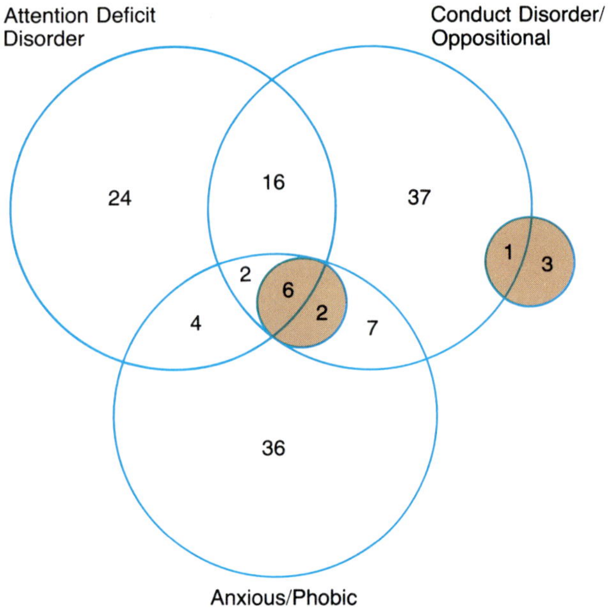

Figure 12.1 Overlap of Childhood Disorders *This figure shows the overlap between four major groups of disorder, showing number of children in each combination of categories: Attention Deficit Disorder, Conduct Disorder, Anxious Phobic Disorder, and Depression and/or Dysthmia (Shaded Circles). As the figure shows, the overlap is greatest for the attention deficit disorder and conduct disorder.*

Source: Anderson, J.C., Williams, S., McGee, R., & Silva, P.A. DSM-III disorders in preadolescent children: Prevalence in a large sample from the general population. *Archives of General Psychiatry, 44,* p. 73, Copyright 1978, American Medical Association.

SEX DIFFERENCES ACROSS DISORDERS

Another fact emerging from the New Zealand data (Anderson et al., 1987) is that in every major category, boys with the problem far outnumbered girls, with the exception of anxieties and phobias. Additionally, for all major disorders, except anxious-phobic problems, parents of boys sought help more frequently than parents of girls. Boys' vulnerability to almost all psychological problems, except depression and anxiety, is apparent across cultures in North America, Western Europe, Australia, and New Zealand. Moreover, their greater vulnerability to physical problems is evident even before birth and during infancy. For every 100 girls conceived, approximately 140 boys are conceived but the ratio of boys' births to that of girls is 106/100 (Klug & Cummings, 1986). Nearly a third of the boys conceived die before birth. More boys than girls also die from birth disorders and diseases in infancy, especially during the first month. By age three, there are fewer males than females because of a greater susceptibility to physical diseases in utero and in infancy, even though boys outnumber girls by 40 percent at conception.

As they mature, boys are also much more likely to be susceptible to family and marital stress. Table 12.3 shows associations between parents' ratings of boys' problems and their own marital discord. There were clear associations between parents' marital troubles and their sons' problems. All types of boys' problems (conduct disorder, personality disorder, inadequate-immaturity, and subcultural deviance) assessed were in fact related to the tensions between parents.

U.S. and British studies have repeatedly demonstrated higher associations between marital problems and problems of boys than of girls, especially conduct problems (O'Leary & Emery, 1983). Although girls are generally more likely to suffer anxiety problems, if their parents are experiencing marital difficulties boys are at greater risk for conduct problems related to anger and aggression than girls, evident from data from psychological and psychiatric clinics. Although it is possible to argue that boys with anger and aggression problems may contribute to their parents' marital problems, complex statistical analyses and longitudinal research suggest the opposite (O'Leary, 1984).

As boys and girls enter late childhood and adolescence, males' far greater vulnerability to psychological problems continues. Learning disabilities of all forms, **stereotypic movement disorders,** alcohol and drug abuse, as well as delinquency are all much more frequent in males than females. More than three times as many adolescent boys as girls kill themselves (see Chapter 13). Moreover, males continue to be more susceptible to physical as well as psychological problems throughout the life span. Between the ages of fifteen and twenty-nine, men die three times as frequently as women (Erhardt & Berlin, 1974), and by age seventy, females outnumber males by almost 35 percent.

TABLE 12.3 Correlations between Parents' Ratings of Boys' Behavioral and Emotional Problems and Their Own Marital Adjustment

Rating of Child's Behavior	Correlations with Parental Marital Adjustment Ratings: Mothers	Fathers
Conduct disorder	−.37	−.40
Personality disorder	−.31	−.24
Inadequacy—immaturity	−.36	−.34
Subcultural deviance	−.33	−.43

Source: From Oltmanns, T.F., Broderick, J.E., & O'Leary, K.D. (1977). Copyright © 1977 by the American Psychological Association. Marital adjustment and the efficacy of behavior therapy with children. *Journal of Consulting and Clinical Psychology, 45(5),* 724–729. Reprinted by permission of the publisher.

OPPOSITIONAL DEFIANT AND CONDUCT DISORDERS

All children sometimes can be defiant and argumentative. However, children diagnosed with **Oppositional Defiant Disorder** behave defiantly and negatively significantly more frequently than their peers (*DSM-III-R,* 1987). Such children often are angry, lose their temper, swear, and defy adult rules. They usually limit their display of defiance to the home and with children they know well. Thus, during an office visit to a pediatrician or psychologist, they may show none of these behaviors. Oppositional defiant disorders typically appear in early to mid-childhood. In serious cases, they may evolve into conduct disorders, usually diagnosed after age twelve.

Children with **conduct disorders** show a "persistent pattern of conduct in which the basic rights of others and major age-appropriate societal norms are violated. The behavior pattern typically is present in the home, at school, with peers, and in the community" (*DSM-III-R,* 1987). Such children usually display their disorder by verbal and physical aggression but may also destroy others' property or treat animals cruelly. As these children become older, their aggression may take the form of mugging and purse snatching, and in the late teens as assault or rape. In contrast to the way children with oppositional defiant disorder behave, children with conduct disorders clearly violate the rights of others. The following reports of parents exemplify the difficulties of children with conduct problems:

> My boy is always fighting with other kids; he is a bully, and he has a chip on his shoulder. He seems to feel my husband and I don't care for him as much as we do for his brothers and sisters.
>
> My ten-year-old boy won't do what I ask him to do unless I threaten him severely; I sometimes wonder whether he has a hearing problem. He refuses to do his homework, yet he is barely passing. I could handle his problems before he went to school, but since first grade he has become unbearable. Now my husband and I argue about how to discipline him, and he is affecting our marriage.
>
> My daughter is 12 years old. She frequently uses foul language at home and she has occasionally gotten in trouble for fighting in the halls at school. She is surly with me but is usually afraid to be disobedient with her dad. She is beginning to drink and smoke with her friends, and she has begun to hide cigarettes in her drawers. She spends more and more time with her friends, and I think she is avoiding me (O'Leary, 1984, pp. 16–17).

A person whose conduct disorder pattern persists beyond age eighteen often indulges in physical fights and reckless behavior, such as driving while intoxicated, speeding or racing cars, promiscuity, and financial irresponsibility. People with conduct disorders lack remorse about their behavior and its adverse effects on others. After age eighteen, such behavior is diagnosed as antisocial personality disor-

Physical fighting is more common among young boys than girls, and the kind of aggressive behavior depicted here is very characteristic of boys with conduct problems.

der. We do not know why, but the most blatent forms of antisocial behavior, such as physical fighting and criminal activity, tend to decrease significantly after age thirty in most individuals.

The Developmental Course of Defiance and Aggression

Table 12.4 shows the common characteristics of defiance and aggression disorders across the age span. For many individuals, a behavior pattern emerges in childhood and unfolds to become much more serious in the teens and during early adulthood. Many children, of course, do not progress from one disorder to another. For example, most juvenile offenders do not move on from minor to more serious crimes. Yet, the roots of antisocial personality disorder for males and females can often be traced to conduct disorders in childhood and are clearly evident by puberty or early teens (see Chapter 10). Also, a disproportionate number of adults diagnosed as drug-dependent had been diagnosed as conduct-disordered in childhood (see Chapter 11). We will discuss later some treatments for the various childhood disorders that decrease the possibility of movement from one disorder to another.

TABLE 12.4 Characteristics of Disorders Associated with Defiance and Aggression

Oppositional Defiant Disorder

(Usually diagnosed between ages eight–sixteen)

- Loses temper/argues
- Refuses requests, such as doing chores
- Angry/resentful
- Deliberately annoys others

Conduct Disorder

(Usually diagnosed after age of twelve)

- Stealing
- Lying
- Runs away from home; school truancy
- Fighting; destruction of others' property; fire-setting
- Cruelty to animals

Antisocial Personality Disorder

(Diagnosed at eighteen years or older)

- Antisocial behavior since fifteen years of age
- Irritable and aggressive
- Poor school/college or work attendance
- Violation of social norms by stealing and harassing others
- Lying and use of aliases

Source: From American Psychiatric Association: Diagnostic and Statistical Manual of Mental Disorders, Third Edition, Revised. Washington D.C., American Psychiatric Association, 1987.

Prevalence of Oppositional Defiant and Conduct Disorders

The exact percentage of boys and girls with oppositional defiant disorders is unclear, but the problem is more common in boys than girls, and the general estimate in the United States is approximately 5 percent of boys and 3 percent of girls (Loney, 1987).

The prevalence of conduct disorders in the United States has been estimated at 7 percent to 9 percent for males and 2 percent for females younger than eighteen years old (*DSM-III-R,* 1987). Although delinquency, or acting unlawfully, is not synonymous with conduct disorders, the two frequently overlap. A delinquent is someone under eighteen who has committed a legal offense, whereas, a young person diagnosed as having a conduct disorder suffers from a psychological/psychiatric disorder. Most habitual youthful offenders do meet diagnostic criteria for conduct disorder. Although youthful offenders are usually males, over the last thirty years the percentage of young females committing crimes has been increasing (Chesney-Lind, 1987). For example, between 1960 and 1975, the percentage of girls arrested for criminal behavior increased over four-fold. Yet as Chesney-Lind (1987) noted, females rarely engage in violent crimes. They were arrested for only 10 percent of violent crimes (murder, forcible rape, robbery, and assault).

In summary, more boys than girls suffer from oppositional defiant and conduct disorders. Although there has been some increase in girls' criminal behavior, boys continue to commit the most serious crimes.

Causes of Oppositional Defiant and Conduct Disorders

Genetic and psychological theories attempt to explain the etiology of oppositional and conduct disorders. Because the common themes in oppositional and conduct problems are anger outbursts, low frustration, and most significantly, aggression, the etiological question is "What causes extreme anger and aggression in children and adolescents?" It is more difficult to answer this because the causes of oppositional defiant disorders and conduct disorders may differ as oppositional disorders are more common than conduct disorders. Moreover, the oppositional defiant disorder diagnostic category did not appear until *DSM-III* in 1980. Much of the available research relating to these two disorders, then, falls under the general heading of conduct disorder.

Genetic Predisposition. A consistent theme of this text is the influence of heredity *and* environment on every human characteristic. We currently do not have any clear evidence of the inheritance of anger outbursts and aggressive behavior. No study of oppositional defiant disorders has specifically addressed the role of genetic and environmental factors. Researchers have, however, found that parents of children diagnosed with conduct disorders frequently displayed an antisocial behavior pattern, such as excessive drinking or criminal activity (Robins, 1966). Additionally, half the adult males diagnosed as suffering from conduct disorders as children met the criteria for what is now termed antisocial personality disorder.

Psychological Determinants

Rewards. It is now very clear that parents and peers often reward aggressive behavior. All children, especially males, are apt to learn of aggression's "payoffs." One study documented rewards for aggressive behavior in nursery school (Patterson, Littman, & Bricker, 1967). Researchers observed thirty-six children over a nine-month period and coded consequences of aggression as positive and negative. Positive consequences included the attacked child's crying, passivity, and/or acting defenselessly. Negative consequences included telling the teacher, retaliating, or asking the teacher to intervene. The results showed the aggressive behaviors of nursery school children were most likely followed by positive consequences. That is, when the child aggressed, the attacked child acted passively, gave in, and/or cried; this rewarded or reinforced the aggressive behavior. In examining children's aggressive behavior patterns in the home, Patterson (1982) distinguished between instrumental aggression and irritable aggression. **Instrumental aggression** is the type just discussed; it is controlled by its positive consequences or rewards. In contrast, irritable aggression is elicited by an aversive event such as someone calling you a name. Irritable aggression is controlled by the stimuli in the environment whereas instrumental aggression is controlled by rewards. Patterson (1982) believes that two thirds of children referred to treatment for conduct problems exhibit instrumental aggression. They thus display coercive behaviors such as whining, yelling, hitting, and noncompliance to obtain a desired response. Positive consequences for these behaviors serve to strengthen and maintain aggressive behavior patterns over time. Although the exact form of aggression may change, aggression is one of the most stable characteristics of human behavior (Olweus, 1978). Intelligence is the only behavioral characteristic known to have greater stability.

Consider the following case illustrating how parents sometimes reward oppositional behavior.

Therapist: *Please describe in detail a recent incident you had with Zack.*

Mrs. D.: *This happened three days ago. We were pretty upset about it and it is really what prompted us to call. Zack has a little battery-operated riding toy. He really loves those kind of toys. My husband had just come home and we were in the backyard. Well, Zack jumped on his car and started riding on the cement patio next to the pool. I asked him to come ride over next to us and he ignored me.*

Therapist: *What did you do then?*

Mr. D.: *I asked him if he had heard what his mother had said. He just looked at me and kept doing what he had been asked not to do.*

Therapist: *What happened next?*

Mrs. D.: *We had been having a pretty good day and I didn't want to spoil it with a fight so I told him he could continue to ride by the pool as long as he kept outside the blue tile line. That seemed to prompt him to ride inside the line.*

Therapist: *Then what did you do?*

Mrs. D.: *I tried to explain to him that I wanted him to ride elsewhere because I was afraid he might fall in the pool. Upon hearing that he turned the car and rode directly into the pool.*

Mr. D.: *After we pulled him out of the pool and saw that he was all right, I really started yelling at him. He really could have been hurt. He just acted like he hadn't done anything wrong.*

Therapist: *Did you punish him?*

Mr. D.: *I told him he could not use any of his riding toys for a week.*

Therapist: *Did you follow through with this plan?*

Mr. D.: *For a day or so.*

An analysis of the data that Mr. and Mrs. D. brought back on their next clinic visit revealed a specific pattern in their interactions with Zack. Zack's noncompliant behavior resulted in a great deal of one-to-one attention [thus rewarding his behavior]. Following an oppositional response, Mr. and Mrs. D. usually explained to Zack the reasons that it was important to follow their instructions. When this failed, they usually threatened him with punishment or tried to persuade him to comply. More important, if their efforts failed to prompt the desired behavior from Zack, they would frequently become frustrated and perform the task themselves [again, rewarding his behavior]. For example, after an argument concerning keeping his toys out of the living room failed to produce the desired effect, Mrs. D. usually put the toys away for him. This sequence of events resulted in his parents' inadvertently reinforcing noncompliant behavior. A similar pattern of experiencing no immediate aversive consequences for inappropriate behavior characterized many of the problem interactions with his teacher (Gross, 1988, p. 182–183).

Modeling. Children learn to do what they observe others do. In a series of studies, Bandura and his colleagues demonstrated that children readily imitate aggressive filmed models (Bandura, 1977). Children who viewed movies depicting children behaving aggressively subsequently displayed more aggressive behavior in their classes than children who had viewed movies without aggressive scenes. Nursery school children learned to display new forms of aggression after simply watching a child model behave aggressively toward a life-sized plastic Bobo doll. The child model sat on the doll, punched it repeatedly, kicked it around the room, and made statements like "Sock him in the nose." Both boys and girls were dramatically influenced by watching aggressive models (Bandura, Ross, & Ross, 1963).

The effects of watching TV aggression and violence on children's behavior have also been observed in the natural environment. In a classic study, Lefkowitz, Eron, Walden, and Heusmann (1977) assessed 400 nine-year-old boys' viewing habits. Ten years later, when they were nineteen years old, those who had watched a high level of TV violence at age nine were more aggressive than those who had not.

Considerable research has been conducted on the effects of observing aggression, and most reviewers of this research conclude that watching aggression by others in real life and in the media leads some people to act aggressively (Heath, Bresolin, & Rinaldi, 1989). In 1982, the National Institute of Mental Health prepared a report for the Surgeon General indicating the pervasive and cumulative effects of watching television. The more aggression children watch, the more likely they are to have a low threshold for it. A predisposition to be aggressive, a violent family environment, and identification with media characters make this modeling effect even more probable. The impact of television aggression is always hotly debated because it suggests the possibility of regulating the television industry. The advent of video cassette recorders and the amount of violent programming available to children alarm some critics even more. First Amendment rights providing freedom of speech have prevented regulation of television programming, but under parental pressure, the TV industry created a "family viewing hour" in which the portrayal of sex and violence was minimal (Prime time: Mon–Sat (8 PM–11 PM) Sun (7–11 PM)). Unfortunately, this family viewing hour was not maintained by the industry, leaving parents themselves to bear the responsibility of monitoring their children's viewing of violent behavior.

Strong Punishment and Inconsistent or Lax Discipline. Parents of children with conduct problems and delinquent behavior tend to resort to strong and frequent punishment (Bandura & Walters, 1963; McCord, McCord, & Howard, 1961; Sears, Maccoby, & Levin, 1957). Childhood aggression is also associated with the frequency of punishment in the home. Matching aggressive and nonaggressive children for age and socioeconomic status, parents of the aggressive children are more punitive, disagree with each other more, and are more cold and rejecting than parents of nonaggressive children (Bandura & Walters, 1959). Children with conduct problems are also more likely to have been physically abused than children referred to clinics who do not have conduct problems (Wolfe, 1987). But if aggressive children are strongly and frequently punished by their parents, why are they then aggressive at school? It seems that even when parents harshly punish aggressive behavior in the home, they often specifically encourage a son's aggression directed at children outside the home (Bandura & Walters, 1959).

Erratic and lax discipline, minimal monitoring or

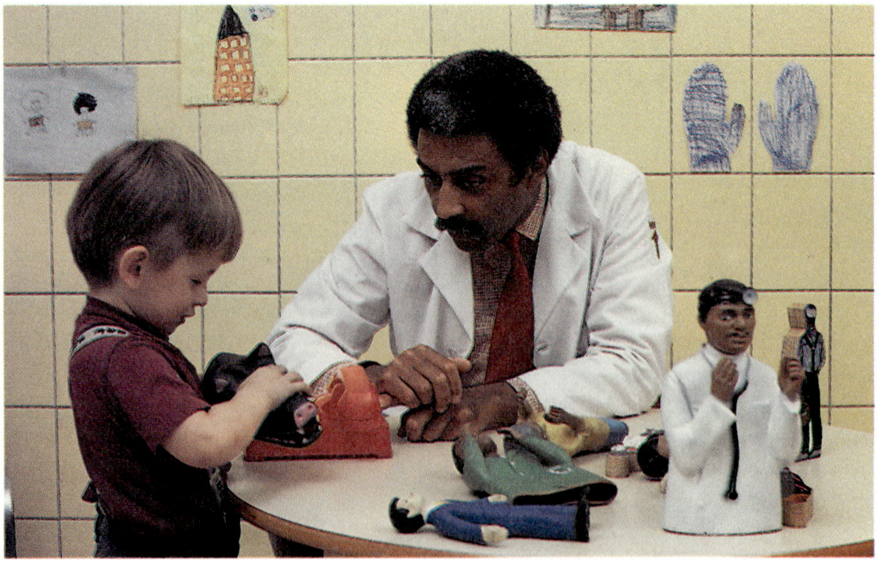

This child psychiatrist is using doll play to assess the child's perceptions of interactions with family members and friends. Doll play sometimes reveals patterns of punishment or discipline that a child will not disclose directly.

supervision of children's activity, are also associated with conduct problems and antisocial behavior. Laxity of discipline and monitoring has been observed in correlational research (Gleuck & Gleuck, 1968; Robins, 1966; Wilson, 1980) and in complex evaluations of a model of antisocial behavior training by Patterson and Bank (1986), as presented in Figure 12.2.

Inept discipline refers to frequent and severe physical punishment such as hitting, grabbing, or beating with an object or a stick as well as scolding and nagging when trivial problems occur. Most importantly, parents who ineptly discipline their children fail to consistently back up their threats. Inept monitoring is a failure to provide supervision and to know what a child is doing at any particular time. It is failing to believe reports by teachers and neighbors of significant misbehavior. It is having an "out of sight, out of mind" attitude.

Coercive children win in negative interactions with others. They persist in tantrums, arguments, and fighting until they get their way. They manipulate their brothers and sisters—as well as their parents. They "teach" others to quit making requests—unless they want trouble. They coerce others to do what they want.

Antisocial behavior, the primary behavior to be predicted (see bottom right of figure), is verbal and physical aggression.

As hypothesized, inept discipline leads to inept monitoring which, in turn, leads to antisocial behavior development in children. Inept discipline and coercive child patterns interact to influence each other. That is, parents who use inept discipline are likely to have children who later become coercive. In addition, coercive children are likely to produce parental reactions such as severe punishment and failure to follow through on threats (inept discipline). In brief, both children and parents cause behaviors in the other.

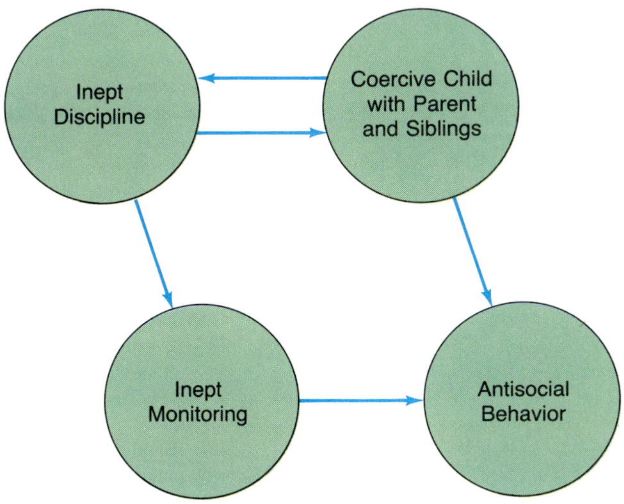

Figure 12.2 Basic Training in the Home for Antisocial Behavior *Patterson and Bank's model illustrates the interaction of a number of variables in the home which lead to the development of antisocial behavior in children. The chain starts with inept discipline leading to inept monitoring, and coercive child interactions. Both the inept discipline and coercive child interactions lead directly to antisocial behavior.*

Source: Patterson, G.R. & Bank, L. (1986). Bootstrapping your way in the nomalogical thicket. *Behavioral Assessment, 8*, p. 56, Pergamon Press. Reprinted with permission.

Marital Discord and Divorce. In the 1950s and 1960s, clinicians and researchers noted that teenagers with divorced parents were more likely to display antisocial behavior and delinquency than teenagers who lived with both their parents. However, subsequent research has shown that teen-agers from divorced homes have a variety of childhood disorders, not simply conduct problems (Rutter, 1970). Further, the studies of the 1950s and 1960s did not examine differences between children whose homes were broken due to death of a parent, institutionalization of a child, or marital problems. As discussed earlier, more recent findings show marital discord associated with conduct problems, especially in boys (O'Leary, 1984). Even so, however, the correlation between marital discord and antisocial behavior in children is not very large. Perhaps separation and divorce will be found as less of an aversive influence on children and adolescents in the 1980s and 1990s than it was in the 1950s and 1960s. Since the divorce rate is much higher now, children of divorced parents may feel less stigmatized. Also because of the high divorce rates, many schools now offer groups for children from broken homes. Finally, whereas marital discord and divorce are common in current American society, many divorced people are able to raise children with little obvious deleterious impact on them. It appears that parental discord, not whether parents are separated, divorced, or living together, is the more significant predictor of childhood problems and antisocial behavior (Emery, 1982; Hetherington, Cox, & Cox, 1982; Rutter, 1970). Indeed, continuation of parental fighting after separation or divorce over custody, visitation, and finances may even be more detrimental for children than the separation or divorce itself. Marital discord is probably a marker or correlate of other problems (e.g., lax discipline, poor supervision, negativity, and scapegoating) that contribute to antisocial behavior. Although divorce may have subtle effects such as late dating and girls' suspiciousness of men (Wallerstein & Kelly, 1980), clearly most children of divorce do not have conduct problems nor become delinquents.

Social Class. Children displaying conduct problems and delinquent behavior come disproportionally from lower socioeconomic levels (West, 1982). But social class, like marital discord, seems to be a marker of other factors relating more directly to conduct problems and antisocial behavior, such as large family size, poor parental discipline, and overcrowding. When these variables are controlled, social class has little or no association with antisocial behavior (Robins, 1978). Yet, we cannot underestimate low socioeconomic levels' impact, since factors such as poor discipline and supervision may be partially caused by the parents' inability to provide or obtain adequate care for their children.

Treatment of Children with Conduct Problems

Patterson and his colleagues at the University of Oregon have repeatedly shown the effectiveness of behavior therapy programs for children with these problems (Patterson, Reid, & Dishion, in press). These treatment programs teach parents to

1. *Reward desirable behavior,* such as sharing and cooperating through praise and other supporting comments.
2. *Ignore certain undesirable behaviors* that annoy them, such as dressing in a way parents consider undesirable.
3. *Punish other undesired behavior,* such as swearing and back-talk, through loss of privileges, or isolation in one's room for a fixed period, or some other negative consequence.

Patterson and Fleishman (1979) reviewed their behavioral treatment programs' effects and found them better than no treatment. Eighty-four percent of the aggressive children functioned in the normal behavior range following treatment. Moreover, after treatment, mothers reduced their amount of punishment and saw their children as more relaxed, less withdrawn, and less aggressive. Factors associated with positive treatment outcomes for aggressive children include the absence of parental psychopathology and severe discord (Strain, Young, & Horowitz, 1981), frequent supportive contacts between mothers and their relatives and friends (Dumas & Wahler, 1985), and parental knowledge and use of social-learning concepts (McMahon, Forehand, & Griest, 1981). Outcome studies of similar behavioral treatments for younger children with oppositional and compliance problems have shown that when parents receive brief training in social-learning or behavioral principles, their children's behavior significantly improves (e.g., Forehand, 1981).

Another approach to treating aggressive behavior problems in children and adolescents focuses on changing the family system. Alexander and Parsons (1973) noted that compared to normal families, deviant families are more silent, share talk-time less equally, make fewer positive interruptions, and are less actively engaged in conversation. The researchers argued, therefore, that a treatment goal should be to increase mutual reinforcement, communication,

BOX 12.1 Parental Alcoholism and Childhood Psychopathology

Parental alcoholism is a risk factor for a host of childhood symptoms and disorders. Children of alcoholic parents are at risk for anxiety, conduct problems, depression, hyperactivity, somatic complaints, and truancy. Most importantly, however, alcoholism of parents, especially of the father, is most closely associated with aggression and hyperactivity problems (West & Prinz, 1987). However, the majority of children of alcoholic parents do not develop specific childhood disorders.

Fortunately, research on the role of parents' alcoholism has gone beyond simple risk analyses regarding whether children of alcoholic parents develop particular disorders. Today, a growing body of research indicates many family interaction patterns are altered in families of alcoholics. There is less cohesion, expressiveness, and husband–wife agreement. Further, the nonalcoholic parent's depression and anxiety are often directly related to this lack of cohesion and expressiveness (Moos & Moos, 1984).

Parental alcoholism's disruptive effect on family life is evident from even casual observation. On the other hand, it is certainly not clear what variables account for the elevated risk for childhood symptoms. Perinatal birth problems associated with maternal alcohol use, marital discord, loss of income associated with job loss, moving, physical abuse, inept discipline, and/or inept monitoring all may be critical factors in producing some childhood problems.

The particular ways in which young children and adult children successfully cope with alcoholic parents is of interest to many as evidenced by the rapid growth of adult group meetings of the national organization, Adult Children of Alcoholics (ACOA). Further, many university campuses have ACOA chapters to provide group support for young adults seeking help in coping with past *or* present problems of alcoholic parents. While no specific psychological profiles for ACOA have been documented, common problems reported by ACOAs include lack of assertion and problems of intimacy–trust (Black, Bucky, & Wilder-Padilla, 1986).

and negotiation. They compared a no treatment control and three treatments:

1. The behavioral family-oriented approach just described.
2. A client-centered treatment where therapists focused discussion on feelings and attitudes within the family.
3. Psychodynamic therapy with insight as the primary goal.

The subjects were thirteen- to sixteen-year-old delinquents who had been arrested or detained for offenses such as running away, truancy, and alcohol or drug possession. After a twelve- to fifteen-week treatment program, the **recidivism** rates were as follows: behavioral family treatment 26 percent; client-centered treatment 47 percent; psychodynamic therapy 73 percent; no treatment control 50 percent. In brief, the behavioral family therapy approach resulted in recidivism rates markedly lower than those of no treatment or alternative treatments. Behavioral family treatment success was associated with more talking, more interruptions (presumably positive) in the family, and more equality of talk-time among members. Additionally, the siblings of adolescents who received the behavioral family treatment had significantly lower referral rates to juvenile courts than siblings of children in the no treatment and alternative treatment groups (Klein, Alexander, & Parsons, 1977).

A third but related approach uses **problem-solving training** to treat aggressive children and adolescents. The therapist focuses on the patient's cognitive processes, such as expectations, self-statements, and problem-solving skills (Spivak & Shure, 1982). Sometimes the therapist works with the adolescent and his or her parents (Foster, Prinz, & O'Leary, 1983; Robin & Foster, 1988). Although the specifics vary, these programs' core is the problem-solving *process* as contrasted with its outcome, or results. That is, the process of arriving at solutions and the emotional reactions of family members become the therapy's focus. Further research is needed to evaluate this approach's effectiveness in reducing severe conduct problems. However, studies employing outcome measures such as court referrals, classroom observations, and teacher ratings have yielded promising results (Kendall & Braswell, 1985; Kazdin, 1987; Robin & Foster, 1988). They indicate that cognitive style, self-reports of behavior at home, and communication have changed as a function of treatment.

In sum, research shows that children with oppositional and conduct problems can be treated successfully when their parents learn to manage them more effectively. Similarly, behavioral family approaches have significantly helped adolescents with aggression and conduct problems. Some evidence suggests that problem-solving approaches may be used successfully with children and adolescents who have conduct problems. It should be noted, however, that the greater the level of aggression and the larger the number of risk factors for severe aggression and delinquency, the dimmer the therapeutic picture. Severe aggression and delinquent behavior thus are difficult to treat no matter the approach (Davidson, Gottschalk, Gensheimer, & Mayer, 1987).

ATTENTION DEFICIT DISORDER WITH HYPERACTIVITY

The following parent report typifies this mother's concern about her hyperactive son, whose problems were evident at one year old:

> *My boy has been a terror since he was able to walk; he was always pulling things from my drawers and cabinets. He never seems able to sit still; he is up and down at the dinner table. He had difficulty learning to print and write, and now he is beginning to fall behind in reading. His teacher feels we should check with a neurologist to see if he has some minor brain damage. What frustrates me is that all his teachers feel he is a bright lad.* (O'Leary, 1984, p. 16)

Doctors Dorothy Ross and Sheila Ross dedicated their scholarly work, *Hyperactivity: Research-Theory-Action* (1976), to "a real stalwart whose warmth, wisdom, and steadfast refusal to accept the school's negative appraisals as final gave a very hyperactive child the support he needed in his troubled years." The stalwart was an English nanny; the hyperactive child was Winston Churchill, later prime minister of England. Early in this century, children were not recognized as hyperactive or as having *attention deficit* problems. Did we create a new group of childhood problems that did not exist previously? The answer is yes. The concept of **hyperactivity** emerged only as formal schooling became required for all children. Children with problems we label today as hyperactive naturally have existed, but the concept of hyperactivity did not become formalized until the 1960s.

Children generally are not diagnosed for hyperactivity until they reach an age when they are expected to sit and attend for a significant period of time. Some mothers describe extremely high levels of activity and restlessness in children as young as two years old, but, hyperactivity usually becomes evident when children have to cope with a structured school environment. In classroom settings, observers of children allowed to complete specific tasks during study times are actually unable to distinguish "hyperactive" from "normal" children (Jacob, O'Leary, & Rosenblad, 1978).

If we created hyperactivity and attention problems by requiring formal structured education, can we eliminate them by allowing children different educational environments or by not requiring them to attend school? Our society is obviously geared toward children attending school. The 1970s, however, witnessed a public educational effort in England and the United States to provide "open" or "informal" schooling in which children could choose to work on whatever subject they wanted at their own pace (Silberman, 1970). Charles Silberman, originator of the "open school" concept, said he rarely saw a "hyperactive child in an informal class." In other words, hyperactive children were not distinguishable from other children in such settings. Despite its claims, informal schooling did not receive strong support in the United States for any extended period because of educators' serious concern that it was excellent for highly self-motivated children but not for those unable to be "self-starters." Further, there was no evidence that open classrooms provided clear academic gains for ADHD children, and there were grave worries that ADHD children would fare academically worse in such classrooms.

In structured classroom settings, ADHD's essential features—inattention, impulsiveness, and hyperactivity—are apparent. Table 12.5 lists items assessed in making a diagnosis of ADHD. At least eight of the fourteen items must have existed for six months to make this diagnosis. The items are placed in order of their usefulness for discriminating children with ADHD from other children.

TABLE 12.5 Characteristics of ADHD Children

1. Fidgets with hands or feet; squirms.
2. Can't remain in seat.
3. Easily distracted.
4. Difficulty awaiting turn in games.
5. Blurts out answers to questions.
6. Difficulty following instructions.
7. Difficulty sustaining attention.
8. Often shifts from one activity to another.
9. Difficulty playing quietly.
10. Talks excessively.
11. Interrupts others; butts into other children's games.
12. Often doesn't listen to what is said to him or her.
13. Often loses pencils or books necessary for school tasks.
14. Often engages in physically dangerous activities without considering negative consequences (e.g., running into street without looking for oncoming cars).

Source: From American Psychiatric Association: *Diagnostic and Statistical Manual of Mental Disorders*. Third Edition, Revised. Washington, D.C., American Psychiatric Association, 1987.

In making a diagnosis of ADHD, the clinician should be aware if the child's problems began before age seven. Taking the child's age into consideration, the clinician must also judge if he or she meets at least eight of the fourteen criteria listed in Table 12.5. Who can make such judgments? Can a pediatrician, a child psychologist, or a child psychiatrist determine this in a brief office visit? There is no single test or observation that an expert can make in a short interview to determine ADHD, except perhaps in extreme cases. Because professionals often continue to make such judgments simply on the basis of a brief office visit, many of these diagnoses are erroneous. As mentioned earlier, children's attention problems and hyperactivity become most pronounced when they enter school and are required to sit still, complete a task without interruption, and listen to a set of teacher's instructions.

For these reasons, teacher input is essential in assessing if a child has ADHD. To assure that the children studied really do have ADHD, researchers often ask teachers to complete a standard rating form describing behaviors characteristic of children with ADHD (Conners, 1969). This rating form has been standardized with thousands of children and has cutoff points indicating whether a child exhibits more of these behaviors than most children. If the resulting score of this rating form filled out by a child's teacher places the child in the upper 5 percent of the population, he or she would be seriously considered for an ADHD diagnosis. Such a diagnosis is actually only possible after considering the child's developmental history for, as noted earlier, such problems should be apparent before age seven. Table 12.6 describes the developmental history of children with ADHD.

The clinician has to differentiate ADHD from conduct disorder, which is not easy to do. As noted earlier, approximately half the children with ADHD also have conduct disorder problems (Anderson et al., 1987). In such cases, the clinician has to decide which is the primary disorder since the particular diagnosis affects the path of treatment.

The developmental characteristics outlined in Table 12.6 represent a composite of characteristics based on many investigators' research (e.g., Weiss & Hechtman, 1986; Weiss et al., 1971; Douglas, 1983.) Any one hyperactive person would rarely show all of these characteristics. Yet these features differentiate hyperactive individuals from nonhyperactive individuals of the same age. As mentioned earlier, many children with high activity levels and inattention are classified as ADHD. Also, some children diagnosed as ADHD are no longer viewed as hyperactive or inattentive when they reach high school. Some professionals take a differing view, though: They see ADHD

TABLE 12.6 Developmental History of Children with ADHD

Infancy
Extremely frequent crying
Sleep difficulties; restless sleep
Overactivity
Difficult to soothe

Preschool
Inattentiveness
Overactivity
Temperamental; emotional
Misconduct/aggression
Rejection by peers

Elementary School
Overactivity
Impulsivity
Inattention
Fidgeting
Poor school achievement
Low self-esteem
Slightly lower IQ than average; variable scores on subtests of IQ tests
Motor clumsiness
Disorganization

High School
Restlessness
Poor grades
Failure to complete high school
Rebelliousness
Difficulty studying
Lying/defiant
Alcohol Use

Post High School
Restlessness, poor concentration; impulsivity
Accidents in automobiles and motorcycles
Alcohol abuse
Antisocial personality problems
Low self-esteem
Emotional/behavioral problems

as a potentially lifelong problem requiring long-term professional attention and medication (e.g., Wender, Reimherr, & Wood, 1980). The long-term outcome for children with ADHD seems to depend partly on evidence of conduct problems and aggression since aggressive behavior may persist into adulthood. In such circumstances, aggression is a better predictor of long-term clinical outcome than are hyperactivity or attention problems (Paternite & Loney, 1980).

In *DSM-I* and *DSM-II*, children with the problems we have discussed were diagnosed as hyperkinetic. The term *hyperkinesis* comes from the Greek words *hyper*, meaning over, and *kinesis*, meaning motion. Thereafter, a change in the official diagnosis occurred because research suggested attentional deficits as these children's primary problem. *DSM-III*, therefore, included two relevant diagnostic categories: ADD with hyperactivity and ADD without hyperactivity. By *DSM-III-R*'s publication in 1987, it became apparent that only one category was needed, since almost all children with attention deficit problems also had overactivity problems. Thus, Attention Deficit Hyperactivity Disorder (ADHD) became the official *DSM-III-R* diagnostic category.

Causes of Attention Deficit Hyperactivity Disorder

Genetic Predisposition. Children of active, impulsive, aggressive parents frequently display the same traits. Such parents actually often report that they feel their children inherited their "bad" characteristics from them. These parental reports led researchers to investigate genetic factors' role in determining activity levels. Studies suggest that the activity levels of monozygotic, or same egg, twins are more similar than those of dizygotic, or different egg, twins. The correlation between activity levels is 0.92 for monozygotic twins and 0.60 for dizygotic twins (Willerman, 1968). Basically, these twin data make clear that genetic factors have a role in activity level.

In another method of studying genetic predisposition, researchers compared self-reports of natural parents of hyperactive children who were adopted with self-reports of the children's foster parents. These self-reports indicated that the hyperactive children's natural parents had higher activity levels as children than the foster parents did (Morrison & Stewart, 1973). Thus, both research avenues strongly suggest genetic factors' role in hyperactivity's development. On the other hand, they do not appear responsible for the hyperactivity and attentional problems of many children. For example, Morrison and Stewart (1971) found that only 20 percent of hyperactive children had a hyperactive parent although even fewer children in a control group (5 percent) did. In brief, genetic factors may play a role in ADHD's etiology, but they account for problems in only a small percentage of children with it.

Dietary Influences. In the last two decades, researchers have become increasingly concerned about the adverse effects of various foods on behavior. One of the first to point to the negative role of dyes and additives in foods, beverages, and medicines was allergist Dr. Benjamin Feingold, whose book, *Why Your Child Is Hyperactive* (1975), reached a wide audience. After seeing a woman who displayed uncontrollable overactive behavior and who took large doses of aspirin, Feingold thought she might be allergic to aspirin and other compounds containing salicylate, a type of salt. He, therefore, put her on a salicylate-free diet resulting in a marked decrease in her frenetic behavior. Feingold then reasoned that many of the children he was treating might be hyperactive because of a similar physiological sensitivity to salicylates, as well as to food additives, like red and yellow dye, and food preservatives. To test his theory, he placed all his hyperactive child patients on diets free of these substances. According to Feingold, 30 percent showed a "dramatically positive response" to the special diets and another 18 percent had a "very favorable response." Subsequent controlled studies comparing the **Feingold diet** to alternative diets, however, showed no clear evidence that it led to any improvement (Conners, 1980). Diet affected hyperactivity only when children consumed extremely large amounts of dye (100 to 150 milligrams) or were selected because of a presumed dye sensitivity (Swanson & Kinsbourne, 1980). According to the U.S. Food and Drug Administration, about 10 percent of children between ages five and twelve consume approximately 150 milligrams of food dye daily. It is entirely possible that some of them might adversely react to dye. Yet, not all children suspected of having food sensitivity react adversely to additives even when they consume as much as *150 milligrams of dye*. No more than 2 percent to 5 percent (Conners, 1980) have such reactions, but, even if a very small number of children are affected, it seems reasonable to ask the food industry to eliminate additives. They have no nutritional value, and, in countries like France and Italy, gourmets do not find their cuisine less aesthetically appealing or palatable without them.

Individual subject designs are especially useful in determining if a particular food or beverage has a negative effect on someone. Children are given challenge diets, or diets containing an ingredient suspected of some adverse effect. They stay on the challenge diets for a specified amount of time or use them on alternating days. Research on diets free of salicylates, food dyes, and preservatives has shown that only a very small number of children have definite adverse reactions to these substances. For most children with the disorder, ADHD does not seem to be a function of food sensitivities. The behavior of certain children is, however, markedly influenced by diet changes. During classroom observations, Rose (1978) measured on-task, aggressive, and out-of-seat behavior in an individual subject design with two eight-year-old girls suspected of physiological sensitivity to salicylates. During a baseline period, the girls were not on a special diet; they ate what they normally ate. They were subsequently placed on diets that contained color additives and then taken off such diets several times. Neither the teachers nor the observers recording the girls' behaviors knew of the days they were on or off the special diet. The results showed that for both girls, a color-free diet resulted in increases in rates of on–task behavior. Figure 12.3 shows one girl's rates of change for on–task behaviors when she was off or on the color-free diet (neutral condition).

In sum, the Feingold diet is not warranted as a general treatment for ADHD children. Nevertheless, comprehensive reviews of the research indicate that we cannot dismiss the possibility of food coloring's adverse effects on individual children (Prinz, 1985).

Lead Poisoning. In old buildings, paint chips containing lead sometimes fall from ceilings and walls. Children who eat these paint chips can suffer lead poisoning, leading to neurological problems and severe hyperactivity. A child may acquire lead poisoning through repeated ingestion of small amounts of lead over several months. Unfortunately this is a common occurrence in large cities in old and poorly maintained housing. Fortunately, lead-based paints are produced much less frequently today, and when paint contains lead, it is noted on the labels. Additionally, with increased awareness of the problems posed by lead-based paints, some U.S. towns now require lead-painted buildings to be stripped and repainted if children live there. Some clinics also offer free diagnostic tests to assess lead amount in children's bloodstream. Children with high lead levels are then treated with a chemical (chelating or iron-binding compound) reducing these levels.

Besides lead in the bloodstream, children carry lead in their teeth. A group of dentists and psychologists (Needleman et al., 1979) working together found lead levels in children's baby teeth were related to their disruptive behavior and their short attention span in school. The lead in these children's systems was the result of inhalation of fumes containing lead. Based on this important research,

> the government closely monitors industrial pollution from lead-processing plants and foundries. Across the country, cities and towns are gradually eliminating lead pipes for domestic water use. Meanwhile, oil producers are also offering lead-free gasolines. These policy changes were clearly warranted for recent evidence indicates that adverse effects of lead poisoning were found in England and the effects of lead poisoning such as behavioral and neurological problems persist even into young adulthood. (Needleman et al., 1990)

Brain Dysfunction. In 1902 when Dr. George Still observed children with meningitis and other physical disorders frequently becoming overactive, he reasoned correctly that brain damage could cause both hyperactivity and attentional problems. Many professionals, agreeing with Dr. Still, subsequently began to

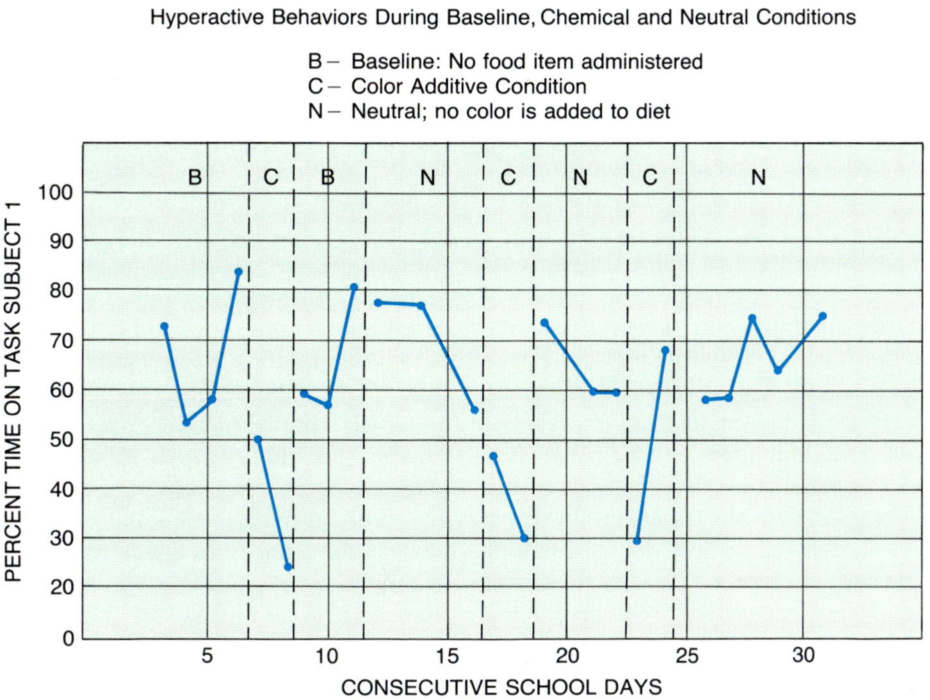

Figure 12.3 Hyperactive Behaviors During Baseline, Chemical and Neutral Conditions *As evident in the figure, color additives (C Condition) are associated with a decrease in attentive or on-task behavior.*

Source: Rose, T.L. (1978). The functional relationship between artificial food colors and hyperactivity. *Journal of Applied Behavior Analysis, 11,* p. 444.

view brain dysfunction as "the" cause of hyperactivity. After Hans Berger's invention of the electroencephalograph in 1929 (Davis, 1975), however, it became apparent that most hyperactive children had no unusual brain wave patterns, although a significant percentage, but not a majority, showed motor coordination problems revealed in writing, maze tracing, and their use of small mechanical objects. The search for causes of hyperactive children's motor coordination problems led medical professionals in the 1960s and 1970s to view hyperactivity as synonymous with **minimal brain dysfunction** (*MBD*). In other words, although neurological exams or EEGs revealed no obvious brain dysfunction in most hyperactive children, researchers hypothesized that some minimal brain dysfunction caused their hyperactivity and motor coordination problems. Today, use of the term *MBD* is waning because little or no evidence exists to support it (O'Leary, 1984). Some respected experts in the hyperactivity field such as Keith Conners (Conners & Wells, 1986), nevertheless, still believe neurological difficulties are at the root of many children's attentional and activity problems. But the failure to find consistent evidence of clear brain dysfunction on EEGs has led to a search for more sophisticated ways of assessing brain dysfunction in hyperactivity. Recent evidence suggests that neurological dysfunction may indeed cause severe problems of inattention and overactivity. For example, Lou, Henriksen, and Bruhn (1984) monitored hyperactive children's brain blood flow and found it is reduced in the frontal lobes. Additionally, medication used to treat attentional problems results in increased blood flow to the central frontal areas of the brain thought to regulate attention and impulse control.

Many clinicians believe children with attentional problems and hyperactivity need medication that stimulates the brain's inhibitory control systems while activating its attentional system. As discussed later, psychostimulant medication appears to stimulate children's attentional processes. But, as seen in a later discussion of treating children with ADHD, the exact process which motor activity is inhibited by is unknown. Whether children with ADHD can be reliably subclassified according to blood flow to specific areas of the brain is also unclear, but evidence suggests that such subtypes could form a basis for research on the etiology and treatment of ADHD (Conners & Wells, 1986).

Psychological Causes of ADHD

Modeling. Yando and Kagan (1968) observed that problem-solving styles modeled by teachers may affect children's extent of displaying an impulsive problem-solving style. The researchers studied normal children in first grade (ages six to seven) exposed to either impulsive or reflective teachers during a school year. By the end of the school year, children exposed to teachers with rapid response styles acquired a pattern of solving problems quickly and impulsively. Conversely, children exposed to teachers with slower problem-solving styles learned to solve problems more slowly and carefully. Although the subjects were not hyperactive, the study demonstrates how children may learn impulsive problem-solving approaches. Experienced, reflective teachers had the greatest impact on their students. Although the evidence is highly suggestive, we cannot conclude that modeling alone caused these students to change their response styles. These teachers may also have encouraged the children in their classes to inhibit and delay their behavior throughout the school year. Whether modeling itself or modeling plus encouragement of reflective problem solving brought about the children's behavior changes, it is nevertheless clear that children's problem-solving styles can be altered (O'Leary, 1984).

Formal versus Informal Classrooms. As previously mentioned, Silberman (1970), the advocate of the "open classroom," or informal school system, observed that he seldom, if ever, saw a hyperactive child in an informal school. In essence, Silberman felt that formal classrooms produced hyperactivity. Some hyperactive children would have presumably attended such informal schools, so that we may in fact partly attribute the absence of hyperactive behavior to the lack of rigid rules. And studies have shown that hyperactive children placed in an informal classroom where they chose the academic tasks they wanted to do, were indistinguishable from nonhyperactive children. In contrast, when hyperactive and nonhyperactive children were required to do tasks such as reading and math at specific times, the behavior of the two groups differed (Jacob, O'Leary, & Rosenblad, 1978; Flynn & Rapoport, 1978). This research suggests that hyperactive children should be placed in regimented learning situations only when necessary. A highly structured learning situation simply makes them stand out or seem different from their classmates. A word of caution here: Informal classrooms were never meant to be totally unstructured. Instead, their proponents felt that the organizational structure would be less apparent and therefore less restrictive to allow children to work at their own pace. Hyperactive children certainly need structure and the teacher's aid in completing tasks. But, if teachers can impose structure less rigidly than they often do today, hyperactive children will be less easily distinguished from their peers.

Positive and Negative Attention. For two decades, educators believed praise and other forms of positive teacher attention such as smiles, winks, hugs, or encouraging words helped children with hyperactivity and aggression problems. Scores of studies found that children with such problems showed increases in attention and problem completion in response to positive feedback (Madsen & Madsen, 1970). Yet recent evidence suggests that at least some negative feedback for inappropriate behavior is critical for maintaining appropriate classroom behavior of hyperactive children. For example, one study showed that when teachers of hyperactive children omitted all types of punishment such as reprimands or loss of recess, the children's level of attending dropped markedly over a five-day period. Yet after the teachers resumed negative feedback for inappropriate behavior, the children's level of attention increased again (Rosen et al., 1984). When teachers of hyperactive children do not use any negative consequences, hyperactive children engage in high rates of antics and fail to complete their classwork. These results suggest that parental and teacher failure to provide negative consequences for hyperactive children's misbehavior contributes to the development or exacerbation of their problems. Of course, providing such consequences is not the sole answer to this complex issue; there are clearly many causes of ADHD.

Family Influences. Some researchers have distinguished primary, or core, symptoms of ADHD, such as hyperactivity and inattention, from secondary symptoms, such as aggression and low self-esteem (Paternite, Loney, & Langhorne, 1976; Paternite & Loney, 1980). In a sample of over 100 children referred to a clinic for hyperkinesis, the core symptoms of inattention and overactivity were not consistently associated with any family and environmental factors. In contrast, researchers found the secondary symptoms of aggression and self-esteem problems were related to five family and environmental factors:

1. Short temper of father.
2. Over-busy parents.
3. Poor parent–child relationship.
4. Urban residence.
5. Low socioeconomic status.

Of related interest is research on children labeled "at risk" for minimal brain dysfunction (MBD) at birth in 1955. These children, so classified because of birth complications such as lack of oxygen and prematurity, were assessed later at age ten (Werner, 1980). At risk children whose families were rated as having high emotional support, structure, and organization displayed the lowest rates of behavior problems at age ten. In contrast, hyperkinetic children whose families were characterized by poor parental mental health, poor mother–child relationships, and punitive child-rearing practices were more likely to be aggressive in young adulthood (Weiss et al., 1971; Hechtman, Weiss, Perlman, & Amsel, 1984).

In sum, a convincing array of research demonstrates that parental factors and low socioeconomic status predict problems of aggression and hyperactivity in children. Investigators are beginning to recognize that hyperactive children significantly affect their parents' behavior. That is, some of the presumed parental factors previously associated with ADHD may really be due to the ADHD children's effects on their parents. For example, mothers of hyperactive children behave in more coercive, controlling, and critical ways when their children are unmedicated than when they are medicated. Thus, as the children respond to medication and are more attentive, the mothers become less coercive and controlling. Yet even when these children become more attentive and compliant, such parents do not increase their rewarding or supportive comments (Barkley & Cunningham, 1979; Mash & Johnston, 1983). Perhaps such children simply elicit fewer positive behaviors from their parents than other children do. One confirmation of this hypothesis is that mothers of children with ADHD are able to respond well to the appropriate behavior of other children in their family. The precise ways in which hyperactive children and their parents influence each other is unclear, but obviously many parents of children with ADHD have to cope with difficult and often incessant behavior.

Pharmacological Treatment of ADHD

The most dramatic treatment for children with inattention and hyperactivity problems is stimulant medication, which generally produces immediate and obvious effects. Such medication appears to increase certain brain functions in a manner that improves attention span and fine motor control (as shown in Figure 12.4). Teachers, classmates, and independent observers can frequently detect these changes within an hour after the children have received one dose of stimulant medication. These effects, observed in many well-controlled studies, have been known since Dr. William Bradley (1937) found that children with severe behavior problems showed a "great increase in interest in school material" after receiving the dose. The children called the medication "arithmetic pills" because they felt they could complete their arithmetic assignments more readily when they were taking them (Bradley, 1937). Approximately forty years later, some children still feel that stimulant medication helps them a great deal. Consider this child's feelings:

SKILLS WITH MEDICATION

These handwriting samples show how medication can help a hyperactive child. The Teacher wrote the top line, the child the middle one before taking medication. After taking medication, the child wrote the bottom line—an obvious improvement.

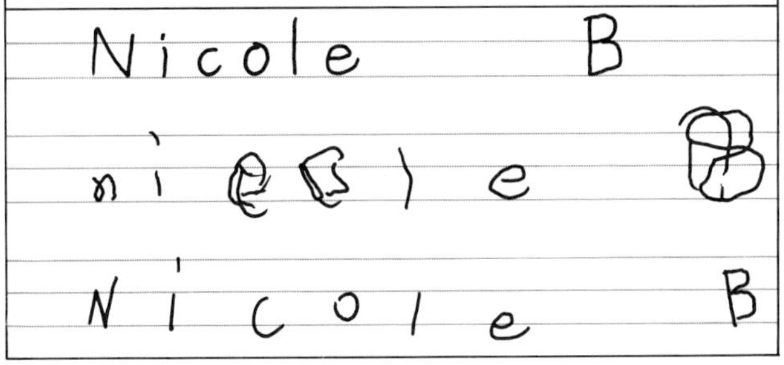

Figure 12.4 Handwriting Skills On and Off Medication *As evidenced in Figure 12.4, some children who are given psychostimulant medication often show dramatic improvement in their motor skills. In this case, handwriting showed great improvement. Reprinted by permission of Medical Economics Publishing.*

Interviewer: How can you tell when you forget to take **Ritalin?**

Child: When I can tell that I'm not concentrating in school. Like she'll [the teacher] give us a half hour to do a math page, like there's about 20 problems, and I'll get about 6 done in 20 minutes, a half hour. But if I take it, I can get them all done in 10 minutes, 20 minutes, and have 10 minutes free.

Interviewer: This is an "imagination" question. Let's say you stopped taking Ritalin altogether.

Child: Oh wow, I'd stay home from school.

Interviewer: How come?

Child: Because I know what would be happening if I didn't. I wouldn't get my work done at all.

Interviewer: How about your friends?

Child: Nobody would like me then, if I didn't take it. They'd think in their minds, "Gosh, she doesn't even want to play. What a baby!"

Interviewer: Pretend that a friend of yours was about to start taking Ritalin and she asked you what you thought. . . .

Child: They'd ask me, like "What does it do?" I'd just tell them, "Well, it helps you concentrate, get more friends, and you want to join in the games more. And you'd be invited more places." (Whalen & Henker, 1980, pp. 27–28)

Despite the dramatic effects observed in children after taking **psychostimulant medication,** many professionals have questioned its use. After Dr. Bradley's initial work, it was hypothesized that children with attentional and hyperactivity problems had deficits, or deviations, in their central nervous system functionings (Clements, 1966; Wender, 1971). Many medical professionals believed that psychostimulant medication's effect was to stimulate the recticular activating system of the brain, a portion of the central nervous system. They called this effect the paradoxical effect of psychostimulant medication, because of the purported stimulation or activation of an inhibitory center of the brain. In 1978 this explanation was challenged when children with average intelligence and no attention or overactivity problems, having been given psychostimulant medication, showed effects similar to those of children with ADHD (Rapoport et al., 1978). Attention and fine motor skills thus improved, even in children who did not display deficits in them before receiving psychostimulant medication. The psychostimulant drug effect then may stimulate the inhibitory center of the brain, but the effect is not specific to children with attention and hyperactivity problems. In brief, psychostimulant medication's use has its intended clinical effect but not because ADHD children have some unique brain dysfunction specifically and uniquely treated by psychostimulants. The precise effects of psychostimulant medications are difficult to determine, since ADHD children's neuropsychological problems may vary widely, and studies typically measure only one or two problems (Conners & Wells, 1987). Children with ADHD may respond to drugs differently according to the nature of their neuropsychological profiles; those with certain profiles may be responsive to drug treatments while others might not. Moreover, the particular symptoms responsive to drugs may be different for children with different profiles.

Behavioral Treatment of ADHD

In classrooms, where ADHD children's difficulties are most apparent, behavior therapy interventions have successfully reduced levels of problem behavior and ratings of hyperactivity (O'Leary, 1984). In these programs teachers generally

1. Praise ADHD children's appropriate behavior (e.g., attending to school work and completing academic problems).
2. Ignore their inappropriate behavior (e.g., calling out answers).
3. Make the classroom rules explicit and review them daily.
4. Give negative feedback privately to these children, so that only they can hear it.
5. Set daily goals with ADHD children each morning.
6. Provide daily feedback to parents on how well their children met the stated goals (daily report system).
7. Request that parents reward their children when they meet daily goals.

The above procedures have been used successfully with ADHD children who were never medicated, as well as medicated children whose parents or pediatricians agreed to withdraw medication at the outset of the behavioral intervention (O'Leary, Pelham, Rosenbaum, & Price, 1976; O'Leary & Pelham, 1978).

Combined Pharmacological and Psychological Treatment of ADHD

In one study examining the effects of psychostimulant medication and behavior therapy on ADHD children, those who received medication only scored better on teacher ratings and independent observations of classroom behavior than children who received behavior therapy only, though both groups showed significant improvements. Moreover, a third group of children, receiving a combination of behavior therapy and medication did better than the group receiving behavior therapy by itself on only one variable, global teacher ratings of classroom behavior (Gittleman-Klein et al., 1976).

There has been one study of a "total push," or multimodality treatment program, that is, a program involving psychostimulant medication and behavior therapy for ADHD children, along with tutoring, family therapy, and individual therapy for their parents (Satterfield, Cantwell, & Satterfield, 1979; Satterfield, Satterfield, & Cantwell, 1980; 1981). Treatment was individualized so that each family had the type(s) of therapy deemed most appropriate for its members. This study showed what can happen in actual clinical practice, since it covered a two-year period and allowed treatments to be tailored to each family's needs. As the authors indicated, there was an "unexpectedly good outcome" as children showed academic gains of approximately 1.6 years in mathematics and reading.

Clinicians and researchers have continually debated about the right treatment for children with ADHD. Some strongly advocate psychostimulant medication, others ardently recommend behavior therapy, and still others suggest a combination of the two. The heterogeneity of symptoms appearing to have both biological and environmental causes, seems to indicate that combinations of behavior therapy and psychostimulant medication are probably most effective when a child has a full complement of ADHD problems including aggression (Conners & Wells, 1986; Pelham & Murphy, 1986). Clinical judgment is necessary, however, to aid parents in deciding whether a particular child's treatment should be behavior therapy, psychostimulant medication, dietary change, tutoring, family therapy, individual therapy for the parents, or some combination thereof. When aggression and conduct problems predominate, clinicians will probably give greatest consideration to behavior therapy. Where attentional problems and overactivity are most obvious, they may suggest psychostimulant medication as the treatment of choice.

SEPARATION ANXIETY, OVERANXIOUS DISORDER, AND CHILDHOOD PHOBIAS

Fears and worries are common among young children. Lapousse and Monk (1959) found that 43 percent of a sample of six- to twelve-year-olds in the United States reported having seven or more fears and worries. More fears and worries were found in girls than boys, black children than white children, and children from lower socioeconomic levels than children from higher socioeconomic levels. The investigators did not find any association between the presence of fears and other forms of pathological behavior or personality disturbance. Similar results have been reported in studies of children in other cultures, such as Japan and Europe (Orvachel & Weissman, 1986). Anxiety and fears severe enough to warrant clinical diagnoses are naturally much less common in children than mild fears and worries. As mentioned earlier, approximately 3.5 percent of children in the United states have *separation anxiety* disorder, 3 percent have **overanxious disorders,** and 1 percent exhibit *social phobias.* Only 1 percent to 4 percent of clinical referrals of children in the United States and England occur in response to a specific fear (Graziano, DiGiovanni, & Garcia, 1979). Yet, children's anxiety problems represent 22 percent of the major problems for which parents seek professional help for their children (Anderson et al., 1987).

During childhood, anxieties and fears change. A classic study by Jersild and Holmes (1935) showed that in the first two years of life, fears of noises, strange persons, and objects predominate, becoming much less frequent by age four. In contrast, fears of imaginary creatures and objects, the dark, robbers, and death are markedly more common between ages four and six.

Some retrospective reports of adults with agoraphobia and panic disorders indicate that 30 percent to 50 percent of them had childhood histories of fearfulness, dependency, separation anxiety, and phobias (Gittleman-Klein & Klein, 1973; Sheehan, Sheehan, & Minichiello, 1981). Other more recent retrospective accounts of childhood experiences of agoraphobics have not indicated higher rates of separation anxiety problems (fear of being away from mother) than normal control subjects (see Chapter 5) (Thyer et al., 1985). Longitudinal studies on the development of anxieties and fears have not yet been conducted, but some retrospective accounts imply that childhood anxieties and fears, especially severe ones, may presage similar adulthood difficulties. Increasing evidence also suggests that children who have difficulty separating from their mothers at twelve months of age are more dependent and less flexible when they become preschoolers and school-age children (Lewis, Feiring, McGuffog, & Jaskir, 1983; Sroufe, 1983).

As indicated earlier, fears and anxieties usually are more common in representative samples of girls than boys in diverse cultures (Gittleman, 1986). One reason why boys usually present less frequently for problems of anxiety than girls may simply be that girls express fears and anxieties more readily than boys. In our culture, this expression is certainly less acceptable for boys than for girls.

Perhaps one reason children with fear and anxiety problems are seen less frequently in clinics than those with conduct problems is that such emotions are more difficult to recognize than the more overt behavior problems of fighting, temper tantrums, and verbal aggression. Many children do not readily express their worries to their parents. In short, the numbers of children brought to mental health clinics because of anxieties and fears is probably not a reliable indication of the percentage of children suffering significant worries and fears in the population as a whole.

Causes of Anxiety, Overanxious Disorders, and Fears

Genetic Predisposition. Family studies indicate that anxiety symptoms appear more commonly among children of anxious parents than among children of depressed parents. Parents with panic disorders are also more likely to have children with anxiety symptoms than parents with generalized anxiety problems (Weissman et al., 1984). Because of such family studies, we cannot argue that genetic factors per se affected anxious behavior's presence in the children studied, because they could have learned such behaviors directly from their parents. However, evidence does in fact indicate that specific fears of children, such as fears of dogs, are often associated with similar parental fears (Bandura & Menlove, 1968). In addition to these data, recent twin studies have provided convincing evidence of genetic factors in the development of fears, anxiety, and shyness in children (Coleman, 1986).

Psychological Determinants

Conditioning and Learning. In 1920, John B. Watson, the famous radical behaviorist, and his graduate student, Rosalie Rayner, published the first conditioning experiment on emotional behavior (see Chapter 5). In the presence of Albert, a healthy nine-month-old infant, Watson and Rayner paired the sound of a large hammer striking a steel bar with the presence of white furry objects. Since young infants generally display fright in response to loud noises, it was predicted that Albert would react fearfully to the noise of the hammer, and further, that pairing of the noise with white furry objects (e.g., pieces of cotton, wool, a white rabbit) which he was unafraid of would lead him to fear them as well. The researchers' hypothesis proved correct: Albert did show changes in breathing, a startle reflex, and a lip tremble when presented with a series of these objects and the sounding of the hammer. One week later after many pairings of the hammer and the white objects, he reacted fearfully to the presence of the white objects alone. A month later, Albert, after again being presented with the white objects, showed fearful, though less extreme, behavior than previously. Thus, Watson and Rayner (1920) believed that fears learned through conditioning could persist and affect an individual's personality throughout life.

Following Watson and Rayner's very influential work, several studies in the 1930s failed to replicate the conditioning findings with infants. Despite this problem, the conditioning model remained a major theoretical view of childhood fear development because this explanation was so well in tune with the general conceptualizations of fear development. In the 1970s, however, the conditioning view was modified to include the notion that humans are biologically prepared to react to certain stimuli such as snakes and spiders but not to others such as geometric shapes or wall sockets (Garcia & Koelling, 1966; Seligman, 1970). As discussed in Chapter 5 (Ohman, 1986), some evidence supports the explanatory values of the preparedness hypotheses, especially based on evidence that humans take longer to extinguish fearful reactions to "prepared" stimuli.

Modeling. Clinicians have long known that many children display similar kinds and numbers of fears as their mothers (Hagman, 1932). Among a sample of dog-phobic children, 35 percent of their parents also had serious phobias and fears (Bandura & Menlove, 1968). In an experimental study, Venn and Short (1973) showed that children exposed to filmed models displaying fears of relatively neutral objects, acquire an avoidance response simply by watching the models. Because of obvious ethical concerns, children cannot be placed in experimental conditions likely to evoke strong fears. Experiments with animals, therefore, have special relevance here. Research with adolescent monkeys shows that they acquire intense and persistent fears of snakes after observing their wild-reared parents interact with a real or model snake for a brief period (Mineka, Davidson, Cook, & Keir, 1984). Ample clinical evidence indicates that children can also acquire the *specific* fears that their parents have by simply observing these fears displayed.

Reinforcement. A child fearful of leaving home and venturing into new situations whose parents say, "Don't worry, you don't have to go out," is then rewarded for avoiding new situations. A child afraid of dogs whose mother praises the child for staying away from them, is rewarded for the fear of dogs. One of the authors saw a boy referred for **school phobia** who was allowed to remain home instead of going to school. The house was very modern with an electric pinball machine with which the boy enjoyed playing. The clinician hypothesized that being allowed to play with toys and the electric pinball machine reinforced the child for staying home. Instead of following the psychologist's advice to put the pinball machine away, the boy's mother said she would not stop her son from playing with it. By her actions then, she clearly rewarded him for avoiding school and he, picking up her cues, refused to attend even after several therapeutic attempts to get him to return. Parents of school-phobic children frequently allow them to remain at home and watch TV or engage in other interesting activities (Johnson & Melamed, 1979). This behavior fits with psychodynamic interpretations of school phobia maintaining that the "phobic" behavior represents a dependency problem reinforced by parental attention.

In sum, constitutional and learning factors seem to influence children's fears. Although research has not established the specific role of genetic or constitutional factors, both twin and family studies of human fears and animal research strongly suggest that genetic factors also significantly affect development of children's anxiety and fear. Learning is also clearly another factor; conditioning, modeling, and reinforcement influence children's acquisition of fears and anxiety.

Treatment of Anxiety, Overanxious Disorders, and Fears

Some childhood fears decrease simply as a function of time and maturation. For example, as noted earlier, fears of noises, strange persons, and objects diminish in most children between ages three and four. As Mary Cover Jones (1924) demonstrated in a classic study, exposing children to particular feared objects in the presence of peers clearly helps them lose

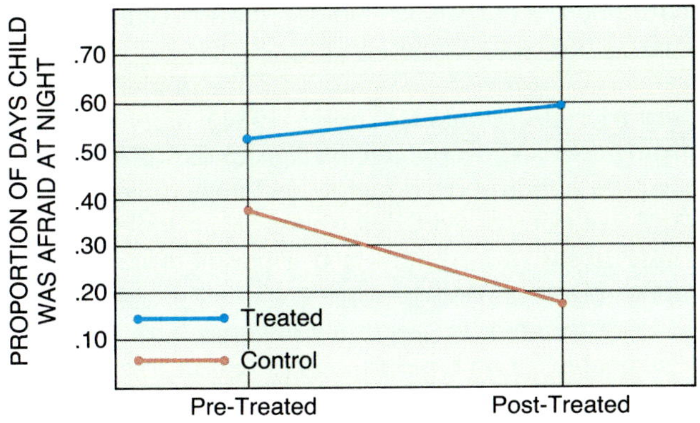

Figure 12.5 Children's Nighttime Fear Reduction *The children treated with a self-statement procedure showed a significant reduction of nights afraid whereas the children who did not receive this intervention (controls) showed a very slight increase in the nights they were afraid.*

Source: Graziano, A.M., & Mooney, K. (1980). Family self-control instruction for children's nighttime fear reduction. *Journal of Consulting and Clinical Psychology, 48,* 206–213.

their fright. Observing filmed models of children gradually approaching feared animals (e.g., dogs), successfully coping with surgery or with receiving an injection is also effective in helping children overcome such fears (Bandura, Grusec, & Menlove, 1967; Melamed & Siegel, 1975; Vernon & Bailey, 1974). Fear of the dark has been successfully treated by having children with this fear recite self-statements such as "I am brave," or "I can take care of myself when alone," and then rewarding them for being brave during the night (Graziano & Mooney, 1980). Figure 12.5 shows this treatment's effects on children's nighttime fears.

Social withdrawal or overanxious disorders are more complex to treat, and the method the clinician chooses will depend upon the problem's severity. One type of treatment effective in increasing the social interactions of withdrawn preschool children involves having other children serve as child "therapists" to interact with the withdrawn child. Furman, Rahe, and Hartup (1979) noted that having withdrawn children play with children twelve to fourteen months younger was more effective in improving their social interactions than was their playing with same-age children or not having any intervention at all. The researchers speculated that the opportunity to initiate and direct social activity in play with younger children was critical to the withdrawn children's improvement. These observations are consistent with the commonly observed phenomenon that shy children on their own often choose to play with younger children. This kind of play provides withdrawn children with occasions to interact without the fear of retaliation they may expect from same-age or older children.

One reason children may be shy or fearful is that they lack skill in perspective taking, that is, the ability to see another point of view (Gottman, Gonso, & Rasmussen, 1975). Socially withdrawn children are also not as likely as average children to respond, especially verbally, to others' initiations (Hops & Greenwood, 1981). Social skills training programs developed for withdrawn children teach them skills such as smiling, greeting, joining, inviting, conversing, and complimenting. To master these skills, the children observe model peers, receive coaching, rehearse the behaviors to be used in critical situations, and discuss how they can employ these skills with their classmates. Children receiving this treatment have been found to initiate more and become less withdrawn compared to children not receiving this treatment (LaGreca & Santogrossi, 1981). The researchers did not, on the other hand, observe any difference in peer ratings of acceptance for likeability as a function of social skills training. From this and related research, it appears that while children's fearful behavior can clearly be changed, children's popularity or peer acceptance is difficult to change.

School phobia has received considerable attention because deleterious social and academic consequences often occur if it is not "nipped in the bud." Young children who refuse to go to school after a

Children with problems of anxiety and children with school phobias are often very dependent upon their mothers. This shy four year old did not want to go to nursery school.

brief illness have been successfully treated with a program developed by Kennedy (1965). This treatment program involves close collaboration between the therapist, parents, and local school personnel. Following a brief period when the child appears to be avoiding school, parents and school personnel exert strong pressure to return the child to school. The program includes pressure to go back to school, a physical exam by a school physician, acceptance and support from teachers. This immediate attention to the problem and pressure to return produce positive results.

In contrast, adolescents who refuse to go to school, claim they are afraid of it, and come from families characterized by marital discord have not been successfully treated with psychological methods. The use of tricyclic medication (antidepressants) seems to be more helpful than placebos in inducing their return to school and in reducing their other physical and psychological symptoms of both anxiety and depression. Antidepressant medication use for anxiety problems is based on the notion that children and adolescents with severe anxiety problems are actually in pain, unhappy, and depressed (Gittelman & Koplewicz, 1986). Although this position is controversial, antidepressant medication has allowed as many as 85 percent of school phobics to return to the classroom (Rabiner & Klein, 1969). At present, nevertheless, there is no unequivocably effective treatment for adolescent school phobics or refusers used by different investigators in different settings. Clinicians must carefully assess for the numerous possible causes of school refusal in adolescents, such as poor academic or social skills, fears of failure or rejection, fear of physical attack, and resistance to leaving home because of concerns about parental fighting or sickness. Because school phobias are complex, they require clinicians' utmost skill in the assessment and treatment phases.

ENURESIS

Enuresis is diagnosed for children between ages five and six when bedwetting or involuntary discharge of urine occurs at least twice per month (*DSM-III-R*, 1987). Older children or adolescents who wet at least once per month may also be said to be enuretic.

In Western countries, approximately 85 percent to 90 percent of children learn to be continent, or stop wetting their beds, by the age of five. By the age of ten, approximately 95 percent are continent, and by adulthood over 98 percent of the population are. Like the majority of childhood psychological disorders, enuresis is much more typical in boys than girls. Twice as many boys wet their beds as girls at age five (7 percent of boys, 3 percent of girls). Moreover, in adulthood, enuresis is almost nonexistent for females, but approximately 1 to 2 percent of males remain enuretic, as estimated from samples of military recruits (Houts & Liebert, 1984). More children from lower socioeconomic backgrounds suffer from it than do children from higher socioeconomic classes. And consistent evidence shows that children are more likely to be enuretic if a parent was also enuretic (Doleys, 1989).

Because enuresis generally declines with age, it is reasonable for an enuretic child's parent to ask "How long will I have to wait until I can quit changing wet sheets?" Approximately 1,200 bedwetters between the ages of five and nineteen were followed over a fifteen-year period to see how long it took them to become dry without medical or psychological treatment (Forsythe & Redmond, 1974). Only 14 percent between the ages of five and nine became dry each year. The percentages were similarly low for older enuretic children and adolescents, with approximately 16 percent of those between the ages of ten and nineteen becoming dry each year. If children are still wetting the bed at five years of age, their likelihood of a spontaneous "cure," or simply "growing out" of the problem is, therefore, only about 15 percent per year. Moreover, on the average, a parent of a five- to six-year-old enuretic may have to wait three to four years for the problem to correct itself without treatment. The likelihood of a spontaneous cure is not any better for older children. For these reasons, parents of most school-age enuretic children are generally advised to seek treatment for this problem.

Enuresis can be troublesome for children who cannot understand why they wet their beds during sleep. Parents who mistakenly believe that the problem is simply one of laziness often exacerbate their children's sense of shame. Soiled sheets anger many parents and embarrass many children. Enuretic children tend to avoid visiting friends overnight, going to camp, or staying with relatives. Those who share a bedroom with siblings are often the subject of relentless teasing. Frustration with this problem is one of the major reasons parents physically abuse their children.

Causes of Enuresis

There are many different causes of enuresis. Parents typically and mistakenly believe bedwetting is caused by emotional problems or by extremely deep sleep preventing the child from detecting bladder pressure (Haque et al., 1981). Diseases and infections also account for only a small percentage of cases with about 10 percent of enuretic children having any bladder disease that causes enuresis. Only 10 percent have a urinary tract infection; yet even when these urinary tract infections are cured, bedwetters usually do not stop wetting their beds (Houts & Liebert, 1984). Evidence indicates that enuretic children's bladders tend to hold less urine than the average child's. This conclusion has been reached in studies where X-ray analyses measured bladder size. Tests measuring the amount of water an enuretic child is able to drink before voiding also confirm this finding.

According to our present knowledge, then, most bedwetters do not have a disease or emotional problems. During sleep or the awaking period, they simply fail to respond to cues from their bladder that it is time to urinate.

Treatment of Enuresis

Several methods have been used to successfully treat enuresis. The common core of the most effective psychological treatments is the bell and pad alarm device awakening a child immediately upon urination. Parents are encouraged to make certain that the child wakes, goes to the bathroom, and voids in the toilet. They then instruct the child to return to his or her bedroom, change the sheets, reset the alarm, and go back to sleep. To monitor the child's progress, the parents keep a daily chart, and for each day he or she is dry, they place a gold star on it. Within three to eight weeks of treatment, the child usually no longer wets the bed. The **bell and pad method** was developed in the 1930s (Mowrer & Mowrer, 1938) and has been widely successful with success rates reported over the past three decades of around 80 percent.

A variation in the bell and pad method involves completing an all-night teaching program of intensive training to become continent during one to two extended overnight sessions with the therapist present. The child drinks large amounts of fluid before going to bed to increase the probability of urinating during the night. Throughout the night, the child then receives practice and positive reinforcement for arising from bed to urinate, positive reinforcement for urinating in the toilet, and punishment for accidents (in the form of reprimands and having to clean and remake the bed). And as in the original bell and pad treatment, a chart marks his or her progress. The all-night training procedure developed by Azrin, Sneed and Foxx (1973; 1974) has been used in several studies with 100 percent success (Bollard & Woodroffe, 1977; Bollard & Nettlebeck, 1981), although in one study only 38 percent of the children were dry at the end of six weeks (Doleys, Ciminero, Tollison, & Wells, 1977). A low-cost, one-hour group treatment program for enuretics and their parents incorporating many of these methods has also proved highly effective, with success in approximately 80 percent of cases (Houts & Liebert, 1984). The beauty of this one-hour program for parents is its cost-effectiveness and efficiency in helping children achieve continence. The relapse rate was only 23 percent, which compares very favorably with other treatment outcomes.

Despite the high success rates usually obtained with enuretics, parents and relatives should know that the 80 percent treatment success rate does not apply to enuretic children attending psychological and psychiatric clinics because of significant behavioral and emotional problems (O'Leary & Wilson, 1987). Some children with multiple problems receiving enuresis treatment display more behavior problems on days after they wet their bed in the night than on days after they are dry (Vivian, Fischel, & Liebert, 1987). Parents and relatives need to be aware that children undergoing enuresis treatment may feel significantly pressured or frustrated when

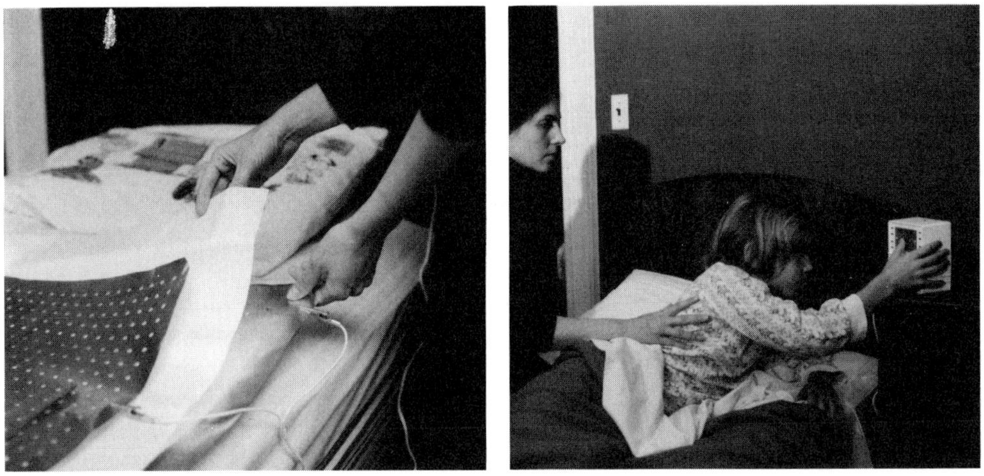

The bell and pad treatment for enuresis involves the use of two metal foil sheets (perforated) connected to the alarm. A cloth pad is inserted between the two metallic sheets, but when the child urinates, a circuit is completed and the alarm rings to awaken the child.

they wet their beds and that successful treatment of those with multiple problems may be a lengthy process.

A final word of caution regarding medication's use as a treatment for enuresis. Following observations that depressed persons treated with imipramine (Tofranil) had trouble urinating, medical professionals began to prescribe imipramine for the treatment of enuresis. Imipramine initially seemed effective in treating enuretic children; they wet their beds less frequently than before receiving the medication. It is now apparent that even though **imipramine** does result in decreased frequency of bedwetting, it does not cure the problem for most enuretic children (Kardish, Hillman, & Werry, 1968). Additionally, children initially treated with this medication are at risk for relapses in other treatment programs; that is, after some period of success, they may begin to wet again (Houts, Peterson, & Liebert, 1984).

SPECIFIC DEVELOPMENTAL DISORDERS

Specific developmental disorders are diagnosed when children evidence inadequate development of certain academic, language, speech, and motor skills. These disorders, commonly referred to as learning disabilities, are not due to low intelligence or inadequate schooling. Instead, for such a diagnosis to be made, a child's skills must be significantly lower than would be expected based on his or her intellectual capacity. Assessment should, therefore, involve administration of a standardized achievement test on the skill area in question along with a standardized intelligence test. Specific developmental disorders tend to occur in conjunction with other clinical disorders. To ensure that they receive adequate attention, they are diagnosed separately on Axis II of *DSM-III-R* (1987).

Four common developmental disorders are

1. *Developmental Reading Disorder.* This disorder is characterized by impaired word recognition skills and reading comprehension. The term **dyslexia,** which means ill (*dys*) words (*lexial*), is often used to describe this disorder. One of the most common problems displayed by dyslexic children is the reversal of letters and words such as using *b* for *d* or seeing the word *saw* as *was*. These reversals occur frequently in normally developing five- to seven-year-olds but are considered as abnormalities when continued beyond the age of seven. During oral reading, dyslexics often omit, add, and distort words. They also tend to read slowly and haltingly.
2. *Developmental Expressive Writing Disorder.* This disorder's essential feature is a marked impairment in the development of expressive writing skills. The diagnosis is made only if the impairment interferes significantly with the child's academic achievement or with his or her daily activities requiring expressive writing skills. When a child with this disorder composes written material, the text is flawed by poor organization and grammatical errors. Although it has received less attention by researchers than dyslexia, this disorder is believed to be as common. The two also frequently occur together.
3. *Developmental Arithmetic Disorder.* Less is known about this disorder than the reading and writing disorders. Perhaps it has received less attention because most individuals who have "difficulties with numbers" can avoid subjects or jobs requiring much arithmetic skill. In contrast, children with reading problems often have difficulty in every academic subject because they all require reading skills. Common characteristics of this disorder include difficulty in understanding mathematical terms and operations and inability to learn concepts such as counting, sequences, and multiplication.
4. *Developmental Articulation Disorder.* This disorder's key feature is a consistent failure to correctly articulate speech sounds. Common misarticulated speech sounds are the ones children acquire last as they learn to speak (e.g., *sh, th, f, z, l,* and *ch*). In severe cases, children also may have difficulty in pronouncing sounds such as *b, m, t, d,* and *n*. Vowel sounds are, however, not problematic to these children. This disorder can often be detected as early as three years of age, but some children's articulation problems do not become obvious until they are six. Boys with articulation disorder outnumber girls by four to one. Children with articulation disorders vary greatly in the extent to which they exhibit other developmental disorders; some children have several other developmental disorders; others have none and may excel both academically and athletically.

Causes of Specific Developmental Disorders

The causes of specific developmental disorders are complex and poorly understood. Although we previously noted they are usually not the result of neurological diseases or disorders, a lack of the precision necessary to detect neurological problems in such children may explain the failure to find any connection. It has been noted that children with ADHD who also have writing and/or coordination disorders im-

BOX 12.2 President Woodrow Wilsons' Disability

President Woodrow Wilson was in school during the Civil War before the diagnosis, developmental dyslexia, was used. However, a neurologist, Dr. Weinstein, (1981) carefully reviewed biographical material, letters, and speeches of Wilson in the book, *Woodrow Wilson: A Medical and Psychological Biography*. Wilson did not learn his letters until he was nine, and he could not read until he was twelve. Wilson was from a learned family, and his father was a Presbyterian minister and a professor. All his family members tried in vain to get him to read. Weinstein concluded that Wilson had developmental dyslexia for several reasons:

President Woodrow Wilson suffered from learning disabilities. He did not learn his letters until he was nine and he did not read until he was twelve. These problems plagued him not only in his own schooling but even when he had to read papers of students when he was a college professor.

1. Wilson was a very slow reader both as a child and as an adult. While in graduate school, he wrote to his fiance that he found steady reading to demand more expenditure of energy than any other sort of work. As a professor at Princeton, he revealed that he found correcting papers an extremely tedious task. Despite years of effort, he could never learn to speak French or German.
2. He was only a fair speller, and he was poor in arithmetic. He hated to add even short columns of numbers and, as an adult, he would ask family members for help with multiplication.
3. When he had a stroke as a middle aged man, his right hand was paralyzed, but within a few days he was able to write very legibly with his left hand. This ability to switch from writing with one hand to the other meant that he had mixed cerebral dominance or a failure to have one side of his brain become dominant. This lack of cerebral dominance is now known to be related to lags in ability to develop verbal and motor skills.

Our former President overcame this disability by having family members read to him very frequently, by his father's focusing on clear thinking, by reviewing speeches of politicians like Daniel Webster, and by sheer determination. Even after dropping out of Davidson College and staying out of school for a year, he entered and later graduated from Princeton.

Source: Weinstein, E.A. (1981). Woodrow Wilson: A Medical and Psychological Biography. Princeton, NJ: Princeton University Press.

prove significantly in these skills when they receive psychostimulant medication, although most of them have not been identified as having neurological problems. As noted in the ADHD section, some experts believe these children do have neuropsychological problems which research will eventually uncover (Conners & Wells, 1987). Others argue that specific disorders simply represent the bottom end of the distribution of abilities. Still others view such problems as the result of developmental delays (Hynd & Cohen, 1983). At present, we can say only that the learning disabled child's brain seems to perceive, process, or remember information in a faulty manner.

Treatment of Specific Developmental Disorders

Treatments for specific developmental disorders vary tremendously and include dietary changes, individual psychotherapy, family therapy, educational tutoring, large-muscle training regimens to aid neurological development, and optometric training. To show improvement, learning disabled children usually receive extensive training in specific skills. A common denominator of treatment for these disabilities is educational intervention. Besides special education services within the public school system, private educational resource centers now exist in many communities to provide tutorial or remedial services for children needing this help. Children with a reading disorder may also benefit from optometric training to aid them in appropriate visual tracking and focusing. Speech therapy may help those with articulation disorder.

CHILDHOOD DEPRESSION

A Controversial Diagnosis

Depression in children has been considered controversial because professionals have disagreed about whether it is a unique phenomenon, distinctly different from depression in adults (Cantwell, 1983). There is no unequivocal evidence to support either position. Whether the symptoms and course of **childhood depression** are similar or quite different from adults, there is increasing recognition that children can be depressed. *DSM-III-R* does not have a separate diagnostic category for childhood depression, but since research on it has increased remarkably over the past decade, we will discuss it separately.

Symptoms of childhood depression include depressed mood, low self-esteem, fatigue, somatic complaints, suicidal thoughts, and a sense of hopelessness (Carlson & Cantwell, 1980). The assessment of children presenting for evaluation in a psychological or psychiatric clinic generally involves a semistructured interview with their parent during which the clinician asks questions about potential symptoms. A semistructured interview for children suspected to be depressed has also been developed and allows the clinician to consider the consistency of parents' and children's reports. Topics covered in these interviews include the child's functioning at school, friends, hobbies, relationships with family members, fears, worries, self-image, mood, somatic concerns, expression of anger, and any unusual thoughts. Besides these interviews, the clinician completes a rating of the child based on observations made during the interview. The child also completes a self-report scale, the Children's Depression Inventory (Kovacs & Beck, 1977), assessing the severity of his or her depression. Laboratory biochemical tests like those administered to depressed adults (see Chapter 7) have not been validated with children and are not routinely employed in the assessment of childhood depression.

Causes of Childhood Depression

Family Factors. Because close relatives of depressed individuals show increased risk of affective disorders or depression (see Chapter 7), investigators have begun to search for family variables associated with childhood depression's onset. Studies examining the relationship between parental depression and that of their children have only recently been conducted. The available evidence suggests that children with depressed parents are more likely to develop problems of depression, substance abuse, poor social functioning, and school problems than children of control subjects (Weissman et al., 1987). Researchers have found a very low frequency of depression in young children of depressed parents (less than one child in one hundred), but have noted a marked increase in the frequency of depression in such children between fifteen and twenty years of age, especially for girls. Yet, even for other children of depressed parents (those between ages fifteen and twenty), the risk for having a major depressive disorder is low in an absolute sense (approximately one in one hundred for boys and four in one hundred for girls). Family studies of childhood depression, then, do not provide conclusive evidence of genetic factors' influence on its development. The increased incidence of depression in adolescent relatives of depressed individuals may, in fact, be a function of high stress levels in families of psychiatric patients. Some support for this position is provided by Weintraub and Neale (1984), who observed an elevated risk for depression for children of depressed patients and children of schizophrenic patients. Comparisons of children of depressed mothers and nondepressed mothers with medical conditions also indicate that the former have more negative thoughts about themselves (Jaenicke et al., 1987). Overall data suggest that psychosocial stressors and genetic predispositions combine to elevate risk for childhood depression.

Psychological Factors. Like depressed adults, depressed children evidence a negative self-concept and low sense of self-worth, which in turn diminishes their belief that they can accomplish certain goals. Depressed children exposed to social stressors seem to personalize them ("I'm always in a bad class"; "I never can do well"), feeling they are unable to cope with such situations successfully. Parental criticism is also highly associated with self-blame and self-critical statements by depressed children (Jaenicke et al., 1987). Moreover, the role of criticism by family members is actually becoming a central focus in much of the research on psychological disorders, since it appears to be associated with a host of etiological factors in child and adult disorders.

Treatment of Childhood Depression

A variety of psychological and pharmacological therapies have been used with depressed children. Common goals of the psychological treatments include changing negative cognitive style, improving self-esteem, and building social skills. Because depressed

BOX 12.3 Childhood Suicide

Children under the age of twelve very rarely commit suicide, but suicidal thoughts occur in about a third of children seen in child psychiatric clinics. Only 5 percent to 8 percent of children seen in psychiatric clinics threaten suicide, and in 1978 only two *childhood suicides* were recorded in the United States (Hawton, 1986).

More boys under twelve years of age actually make suicide attempts than girls. After the age of twelve, suicidal attempts by females are much more common than for males (see Chapter 13).

Separation and divorce are major risk factors for suicide attempts in young children. Adolescent suicide attempters are three times more likely to come from homes with separations and divorces than control subjects. For example, in Australia only 40 percent of parents of child suicide attempters lived together, whereas 82 percent of the parents of the control children lived together (Kosky, 1983). Other important risk factors include psychiatric illnesses of parents, suicidal attempts by relatives, and child abuse.

Treatment of children attempting suicide should generally be implemented with the child and his or her family. Many of these children do not require extensive therapy following an initial assessment. We should not, in other words, automatically assume that every child who makes a suicide attempt should see a therapist regularly. Some children who attempt suicide have problems that are actually not severe. For these children, family support and periodic visits to a therapist often suffice to help them deal effectively with their difficulties. On the other hand, children who are depressed, lonely, and have many conflicts with family members should receive more extensive treatment.

children exhibit such a variety of associated problems (e.g., isolation, anxiety, enuresis), no claims can be made for the superiority of any particular form of psychological therapy.

Rationales for the use of pharmacological treatments for depression in children are largely based on the findings of drug research with depressed adults. Studies of the effects of medication on depressed children have yielded mixed results. Imipramine, an antidepressant used with depressed adults, has shown some promise in treating depressed children, especially those suffering from signs of depression such as weight changes, insomnia, or slowing of thought processes (Petti, 1983). Other research shows, however, little or no beneficial effect of pharmacological interventions. In a review of the literature, Elkins and Rapoport (1983) note that medication may prove less fruitful with depressed children than depressed adults, and that depressed children may more immediately respond to nondrug therapies. At present, we may say that almost all depressed children need psychological help, whereas perhaps only the more severely depressed may need pharmacological treatment as well.

INFANTILE AUTISM

Infantile autism begins before a child is thirty months old, and is one of the most crippling childhood disorders. Along with mental retardation, it is in a subclass of the disorders, severe developmental disabilities (*DSM-III-R*). Autistic children's lack of responsiveness is most troubling to parents. When you try to hug autistic children, they withdraw from you; they squirm away when you try to hold them. They often seem totally uninterested in people. Most autistic children have gross speech deficits. If they speak at all, they parrot others' speech. When you ask, "What's your name?" instead of answering, they parrot back, "What's your name?" The parroting so resembles in tone and pitch what is said to the child that it is termed **echolalia.** Autistics who speak often use pronouns improperly. For example, instead of saying, "I rode in car," the autistic says, "Him rode in car."

Infantile autism is a puzzle to both parents and professionals. Consider the following description of this disorder by a parent:

> *While a father pushes his four-year-old son in cart down the aisle in a supermarket, a heavy, friendly woman stops, bends over toward the son, smiles at him and says, "You're beautiful."*
>
> *"Thank you," says the father.*
>
> *"What's your name?" she asks the boy. He turns his head away making some unintelligible sounds. "What's your name?" she asks again. The boy begins to rock back and forth in the shopping cart. "Don't be shy," the woman continues. "Can't you tell me your name?" "No," says the father, "he can't." The woman looks up with sudden concern. "Doesn't he talk?"*
>
> *"Not any more," says the father.*
>
> *"I'm sorry," says the woman, gently reaching out to pat the boy, who ducks his head away.*
>
> *"What's the matter with him? He's so beautiful."*
>
> *"We don't know," replies the father.*
>
> *As the woman recovers her natural joviality, she*

says, "Don't worry, whatever is bothering him, he'll grow out of it I'm sure."

The father replies, "I wish I could be sure. The boy is my son, Noah."

At the age of four he is neither toilet-trained nor does he feed himself. He seldom speaks expressively, rarely employs his less than dozen word vocabulary. His attention span in a new toy is a matter of split seconds, television engages him for only an odd moment occasionally, he is never interested in other children for very long. His main activities are lint-catching, thread pulling, blanket sucking, spontaneous giggling, inexplicable crying, eye-squinting, wall hugging, circle walking, bed-bouncing, jumping, rocking, door-closing, and incoherent babbling addressed to his finger flexing right hand.

What's the matter with Noah? For the longest time it seemed to depend upon what diagnosis we were willing to shop around for. We'd been told he was mentally retarded, emotionally disturbed, autistic, schizophrenic, possibly brain damaged, or that he was suffering from . . . combinations of these conditions. But we finally discovered that the diagnosis didn't seem to matter. It was all so sadly academic. The medical profession was merely playing . . . games at our expense. For though we live in one of the richest states in the nation, there was no single viable treatment immediately available for Noah, no matter what category he could be assigned to. (Greenfeld, *A Child Called Noah*, 1972, pp. 3–5)

Course of the Disorder (Prognoses)

Leo Kanner, a child psychiatrist at Johns Hopkins University, first described the syndrome of early infantile autism in 1943. The disorder occurs in only 2 to 4 children out of every 10,000. Because of its rarity and relatively recent "discovery," there are no adults older than fifty known with certainty to have had this disorder in infancy. Moreover, most children diagnosed with this disorder in the 1940s to the 1970s did not receive the highly specialized educational and psychological programs currently available for autistics. Our present knowledge about how children diagnosed with early infantile autism fare in adulthood is, therefore, based on their participation in a variety of nonspecialized educational programs. Using this information as background, 42 percent of these children were institutionalized in childhood or adulthood and the majority are educationally impaired. Ten percent to 15 percent were deemed borderline, and 1 percent to 2 percent had recovered enough to be judged normal (DeMyer et al., 1973). Similar follow-up results with autistic children have been obtained in Canada, where about half of the children were eventually placed in institutions and few were able to live independently and hold a job. Most adults diagnosed as autistic during childhood functioned in the mentally retarded range of intelligence (Wolf & Goldberg, 1986). Although general intelligence is one predictor, verbal skill is the best childhood predictor of later functioning for autistic children. Without language skills, many other skills simply cannot be readily acquired. The original cases described by Kanner in 1943 were followed into adulthood by Kanner (1971) himself. Based on these case studies, it seems that autistics who live in environments where their deviance is fairly well tolerated may fare better than others. Donald is one example:

In 1942, his parents placed him on a tenant farm about 10 miles from their home. When I visited there in May 1945, I was amazed at the wisdom of the couple who took care of him. They managed to give him goals for his stereotypes. They made him use his preoccupations with measurements by having him dig a well and report on its depth. When he kept collecting dead birds and bugs, they gave him a spot for a "graveyard" and had him put up markers; on each he wrote a first name, the type of animal as a middle name, and the farmer's last name, e.g.: "John Snail Lewis. Born, date unknown. Died (date on which he found the animal)." When he kept counting rows of corn over and over, they had him count the rows while plowing them. On my visit, he plowed six long rows; it was remarkable how well he handled the horse and plow and turned the horse around. It was obvious that Mr. and Mrs. Lewis were very fond of him and just as obvious that they were gently firm. He attended a country school where his peculiarities were accepted and where he made good scholastic progress.

The rest of the story is contained in a letter from (his) mother, dated April 6, 1970:

"Don is now 36 years old, a bachelor living at home with us. . . . Since receiving his A.B. degree in 1958, he has worked in the local bank as a teller. He is satisfied to remain a teller, having no real desire for promotion. He meets the public there real well. His chief hobby is golf, playing four or five times a week at the local country club. While he is no pro, he has six trophies won in local competition. . . . Other interests are Kiwanis Club (served as president one term), Jaycees, Investment Club, Secretary of Presbyterian Sunday School. He is dependable, accurate, shows originality in editing the Jaycee program information, is even-tempered but has a mind of his own. . . . Don is a fair bridge player but never initiates a game. Lack of initiative seems to be his most serious drawback. He takes very little part in social conversation and shows no interest in the opposite sex. (Kanner, 1971, pp. 121–122)

The few individuals diagnosed with early infantile autism who later assume a relatively normal life offer hope to parents of autistic children everywhere. The retrospective accounts of such individuals provide some insight into their difficulties. One example is Tony, a thirty-six-year-old man who designs livestock facilities for ranches and meat-packing plants. At the time of the following autobiographical account in 1985, he was enrolled in a doctoral program in animal science at the University of Illinois.

At the age of 1-1/2 to 3 I had many of the standard autistic behaviors such as fixation on spinning objects, refusing to be touched or held, preferring to be alone, destructive behavior, temper tantrums, inability to speak, sensitivity to sudden noises, appearance of deafness, and an intense interest in odors. . . .

At the age of 3 to 3-1/2 my behavior greatly improved, but I did not learn to speak until 3-1/2. At the age of 3 to 4 my behavior was more normal until I became tired. When I became tired, bouts of impulsive behavior would return. . . .

In college I was on the Dean's honor list, but getting through the foreign language requirement was difficult. I scraped by with Ds and Cs. Learning sequential things such as math was also very hard. My mind is completely visual and spatial work such as drawing is easy. I taught myself drafting in six months. I have designed big steel and concrete cattle facilities, but remembering a phone number or adding up numbers in my head is still difficult. I have to write them down. Every piece of information I have memorized is visual. If I have to remember an abstract concept I "see" the page of the book or my notes in my mind and "read" information from it. Melodies are the only things I can memorize without a visual image. I remember very little that I hear unless it is emotionally arousing or I can form a visual image. In class I take careful notes, because I would forget the auditory material. When I think about abstract concepts such as human relationships between people, they are like a sliding glass door. The door must be opened gently, if it is kicked it may shatter. If I had to learn a foreign language, I would have to do it by reading, and make it visual. (Grandin, 1987, pp. 144–145)

Causes of Infantile Autism

There is no single known cause of autism. It is a mystery whose answer is being sought in biological, psychological, and social explanations. Because its severe effects occur so early in life, biological explanations seem likely to many. Indeed, twin studies have revealed the concordance rate for monozygotic twins having autism was 32 percent whereas the concordance rate for dizygotic twins was 0 percent. Moreover, when a more liberal category including autism and severe cognitive disorders was used, the concordance rate was 82 percent for monozygotic twins and 10 percent for dizygotic twins (Rutter, 1977). This research strongly indicates that genetics play a key in the development of autism and other severe cognitive disorders. Yet, the siblings of autistic children are usually normal children, and a history of autism is rare in families with an autistic child (Rutter & Garmezy, 1983). Thus autism does not appear to be inherited; instead, there may be genetic predisposition to develop language and cognitive disorders, and autism may be simply one of those disorders.

Numerous biological variables are continuously being studied as possible keys to understanding autism, but no single answer has yet been discovered. One main hypothesis is that some form of brain dysfunction underlies this disorder's problems. Because autistics often do not develop speech or lose what little speech they have acquired, it is believed that the left hemisphere of the brain, housing brain structures important for speech, is somehow involved. Learning to speak is usually so difficult for autistics that sign language is taught to many of them so that they can ask for food, drink, and assistance. The fact that sign language can be learned also implicates the speech area of the brain as a key to this disorder. Endocrine and chromosomal abnormalities have been discovered in some autistic children, but such biological abnormalities are not consistently found. Most professionals believe there are multiple biological causes of autism and that there is no single common pathway by which the disorder develops (Goodman, 1989).

Treatment of Infantile Autism

Educational and psychological interventions are the primary methods of aiding an autistic child. Behavior therapy programs for autistic children have especially proved very valuable in teaching language, social skills, and self-help skills such as dressing and toileting (O'Leary & Wilson, 1987). Teaching simple skills to autistic children can take months and even years. Since they initially do not respond to simple instructions, they have to learn to respond to very simple requests, such as "Come here." To teach such responses, someone has to bring the autistic child to the therapy aid or teacher at the request "Come here." The child is then immediately rewarded with a hug and an edible reward such as a raisin. Hundreds of such trials are repeated until the child comes to the teacher or therapy aid on his or her own. Language instruction for the autistic child typically begins with having the child model simple sounds such as "Ah" or "Mmm." After hours of such teaching, more complex sounds are combined, and finally the child learns the words.

Using a behavior therapy approach, Ivar Lovaas and his colleagues at the University of California at Los Angeles (1987) have been able to teach language and self-help skills to many autistic children. These researchers conducted a large-scale teaching effort where scores of undergraduate teaching aids provided approximately 40 hours per week of teaching per child for two years. The encouraging news from that effort was that the children could in fact learn skills. Unfortunately, the children regressed when they returned to their own homes and no longer received frequent rewards from their teaching aids for appropriate use of language and social skills (Lovaas, 1987). A few of the treated children had to be placed in institutions, having lost almost all of the verbal and social skills they had learned.

Following this effort, Lovaas and colleagues began to implement an early intervention program for autistic children. They hypothesized that if treatment for the disorder was begun by the age of two to three, there would be greater progress and regressions would not be as marked. The intervention involves a forty-hour-per-week training program lasting from two to four years. Selection of the children to be treated considers whether the parents themselves or someone else can provide continuity of the therapeutic program in the home after the formal treatment has been terminated. To date, the program has proved even more successful than anticipated. Roughly half of the children treated have been able to attend regular classes or special education classes in public schools. As Lovaas reported, 47 percent of the children "made substantial recovery with IQ scores within the normal range of functioning and successful first grade performance in public schools" (Lovaas, 1987). Comparisons with a similar group of autistic children treated less intensively (ten hours per week) revealed that only 2 percent of the children had obtained such progress. The message of these treatment efforts seems clear. Intensive teaching of forty hours per week for as much as four years can lead to very substantial progress. While such teaching efforts may seem very costly, consider the fact that an autistic child's long-term institutionalization can cost as much as $2 million. This treatment research of Lovaas and colleagues is controversial. Some professionals feel that the results are spectacular; others question whether the goal of placement in normal classes is appropriate if there are other children in the family and extraordinary resources have to be used to obtain their goal (Goleman, 1987; Schopler, 1987). Whatever the final outcome of the debate over this research, it is a landmark study offering considerable hope to parents of young autistic children.

SUMMARY

1. Psychological disorders of children were not well recognized until the 1950s, and publications such as the *Journal of Abnormal Child Psychology* began only in 1973. The last two decades, however, have witnessed a rapid development of interest in child psychology, and child clinical psychology is now a recognized speciality with over forty graduate programs offering degrees in it.
2. The most prevalent childhood disorders include attention deficit disorder, oppositional defiant disorder, conduct disorder, and anxiety disorders (separation anxiety, overanxious disorder, and phobias). More than half of all children with one disorder also have a second. The greatest overlap in childhood disorders is found with attention deficit disorders and conduct disorders. Attention deficit, oppositional, and conduct disorders are the major types of psychological problems for which parents seek professional help for their children. Boys' problems far outnumber girls' problems in almost every major childhood diagnostic category except for anxiety and phobias. The reasons for boys' greater vulnerability is unclear, but they are more vulnerable than girls to many physical and psychological problems from conception to adulthood.
3. Oppositional defiant disorder and conduct disorder are characterized by persistent conduct violating the rights of others, often in the form of verbal or physical aggression. Oppositional defiant disorder is generally seen in younger children whereas conduct disorder is usually seen in adolescents. There is no clear evidence that aggressive behavior is inherited, but a great deal of data associates psychological and social factors such as rewards, modeling, strong punishment, inconsistent discipline, marital discord, and divorce with aggressive behavior in children. Behavior-management training for parents, behavioral family systems approaches, emphasizing communication and mutual reinforcement, and problem-solving interventions have effectively aided families of children with oppositional defiant and conduct disorders.
4. Attention deficit disorder with hyperactivity (ADHD) is characterized by problems of inattention, distractibility, and overactivity. For most children, problems of extreme overactivity become less problematic as they enter junior and senior high school, but some continue to be restless and have difficulty concentrating even after high school. When aggression and attentional problems coexist, the prognosis is less favorable than if a child has only attentional problems. Both genetic and psychological factors seem significant in the etiology of attentional and aggressive problems, with family and environmental factors most closely associated with the aggressive symptoms associated with ADHD. Neurological problems also appear to play an important role in the development of some children's attentional deficits. Psychological and pharmacological therapies used individually and in combination with one another have been quite successful in aiding children with problems of attention and overactivity.
5. Fears and worries are extremely common in children, but few are referred to clinics for severe specific fears. General problems of anxiety, however, do account for over 20 percent of referrals to professionals, and there is some tendency for girls to present in clinics for these problems more frequently than boys. Although it is unclear whether genetic factors predispose certain children to anxiety problems, these disorders are clearly more common in children whose parent has had similar problems. Conditioning, modeling, reinforcement, and complex cognitive learning also affect the etiology of anxiety. Psychological therapies with anxious children involving training in new cognitive styles and social skills have been effective in reducing anxiety, and both psychological and pharmacological therapies with school phobics have helped children with severe phobias attend school.

6. Enuresis afflicts between 10 percent and 15 percent of children over five years old. Twice as many boys as girls suffer from it. Children are more likely to be enuretic if a parent was also enuretic. Although diverse factors, such as small bladder capacities and emotional problems, have been associated with enuresis, the basic problem is one of failing to respond to cues from the bladder to urinate. Programs involving the use of a bell and pad device to awaken children when they begin to urinate have successfully trained thousands to become continent.
7. Specific developmental disabilities impair the academic and sometimes the social functioning of many children who have at least average intellectual abilities but cannot read, write, or speak without difficulty. The exact causes of the various developmental disabilities are poorly understood, but children with these problems apparently have difficulty processing and/or acting on information efficiently. Treatments for specific developmental disorders include optometric training for visual tracking, neurological programs to develop motor coordination, and psychotherapies. Special training to reduce the specific skill deficits impairing these children's functioning appears essential for promoting improvement.
8. Professional attention has only recently focused on childhood depression, partly because of uncertainty whether it exists as a syndrome significantly different from adult depression. Despite this problem, childhood depression has become a focus of much research in the last decade. Children have a greater likelihood of developing depression if they have a depressed parent. Significant parental strife and criticism also place children at risk for developing depression, with a very few actually attempting suicide. Treatment for childhood depression generally involves psychological therapy directed at changing cognitive styles and social skills. Severely depressed children may also profit from antidepressant medication.
9. Infantile autism is one of the most profound disorders of childhood. Autistic children are often nonverbal and largely asocial. The majority of autistic children followed into adulthood have been retarded and live in institutions or sheltered environments. Yet, recent landmark research with young autistic children suggests that approximately half of them could enter regular schools if they received very intensive treatments.

Joseph Santore, *Anne with Sunflowers* (1989–90). Oil on canvas, 38 × 28 inches. Courtesy of the Edward Thorp Gallery, New York.

13 SPECIAL PROBLEMS IN ADOLESCENTS AND YOUNG ADULTS: DEPRESSION, SUICIDE, EATING DISORDERS, AND DRUG ABUSE

Many adolescents and young adults are depressed: Some commit suicide; others experience intense fears of becoming obese so they starve themselves nearly to death or purge themselves through self-induced vomiting. Large numbers of teens and young adults abuse alcohol and use drugs readily available on the street. Depression, suicide, and drug abuse are not unique to adolescents and young adults, but they appear in very high rates in these populations. Moreover, young people's stresses differ from those at later ages, and the factors causing their problems often differ from the development of similar problems in adulthood.

Eating disorders are almost solely problems of adolescence and young adulthood. Their incidence and that of depression and suicide among young people has risen sharply during the past several decades. Moreover, group suicides among adolescent friends is certainly a problem new to the United States within the last decade. Meanwhile, for other age groups, these problems' prevalence has remained relatively constant. The increases in mental health problems in adolescents and young adults compel us to take a closer look at this group.

THE TRANSITION TO ADULTHOOD

In order to best describe and understand the special problems of young people, we must examine their world. Perhaps you can recall yourself at this period. As an adolescent, you experienced a variety of new stressors (e.g., pressure to have sex for the first time; being left alone for evenings or weekends). You continued to rely heavily on your parents but probably disagreed with at least some of their opinions. You may have felt you had no control over dramatic changes affecting you, such as a divorce or a separation in your family. Your body was changing in ways that may have been difficult to cope with, such as acne, moodiness, and the beginnings of sexual feelings, dreams, and orgasms. You may have worried that your bodily changes were occurring too fast or too slow. Your social skills may have felt woefully inadequate to new demands. You may have felt self-conscious much of the time.

Around the ages of seventeen to twenty-two, when many of you will be reading this material, you may be embarking on another difficult transition: the change from adolescence to adulthood. Now you are half-in and half-out of both worlds. You may feel you want to shed your adolescent self-image and become independent of your parents, yet, you may also wish they would continue some of their financial and psychological support. You may also feel the need to make new friends. During this transitional time, you are trying to establish yourself, to develop your own identity, values, and relationships. Thus, you "try out" the adult world in long-term sexual relationships, jobs, colleges, universities, and in daily living relationships in apartments, dorms, and rooming houses with members of both sexes. You may even have to deal with very difficult issues like pregnancy and whether or not to have an abortion.

For many young people, poised between adolescence and adulthood, these new freedoms and responsibilities can be overwhelming. And sometimes gains do not feel like they offset the losses. During this time, young people often lose the comforts and supports of home and the familiar surroundings of family and friends. They encounter the pressures of school, a job, and maybe even the need to support themselves. Most of their concerns focus on the future and how well prepared they are to meet it.

During the period from about age twenty-two to twenty-eight, young people explore different life options, such as "real world" jobs. They also attempt to create a stable life structure, which may involve searching for a relatively permanent living partner and an occupation. They often get married or, if they haven't already, start some long-term sexual relationship. Frequently, a desire to explore different relationships and different jobs conflicts with pressures from family or a partner to become committed. Many young people also become parents at this time.

Data on depression indicate this period as frequently the most difficult of a person's life. Issues regarding partner selection and career choices become increasingly critical. Additionally, relationship pressures increase intensely during this time: The vast majority of marriages and almost half of all divorces occur in the course of this period of life. Moreover, alcohol and drug abuse patterns may begin or become exacerbated, and criminal behavior, homicide, and nervous breakdowns most commonly occur during this developmental period.

During adolescence many young people experience a variety of new stressors as they are faced with an uncertain future, difficult decisions, and the struggle to establish their identity and independence.

To add to their pressures, young people frequently must cope with their problems without the support or even occasional presence of family members. For many, life is faced *alone* for the first time. Thus, an appreciation of the serious challenges and transitions facing late adolescents and young adults makes it easier to understand their high rates of depression and suicide.

DEPRESSION

Susie was fun-loving and vibrant. The life of the party, she talked frequently and rapidly; talented and successful, she was on the hockey team and the student council. Her friends described her as an "up" person, and guys liked her even though she complained about being slightly overweight. Susie's parents thought she was great, and as a sign of their confidence in her, they gave her full use of the second family car. They were very generous in giving her all the clothes she wanted.

In her junior year of high school, Susie's grades fell sharply, and she began to withdraw from some of her best friends—a frequent early warning sign of depression. Next she started to skip school, and, by midyear, she had failed two subjects and her best grade in the remaining courses was a C. In the third quarter, she dropped one course, believing she could get back on track by lightening her workload. This plan did not work, and her performance continued to decline. Susie became aware that she was depressed but did not know why. Her father responded by becoming angry and accusing her of not working hard enough. Caught between her daughter and her husband, Susie's mother had no idea what to do. The situation deteriorated even further as Susie started to drink beer to put herself to sleep and to dissipate her hopeless feelings. When this did not work, she dreamed of quitting school and going to live with friends. Instead, she entered therapy with one of the authors of this book.

Susie's scenario is hardly unusual. Although childhood depression's existence is debated, adolescent depression has been recognized for centuries. And, in the last two decades, adolescent depression has risen to epidemic proportions in the United States. We will discuss the reasons for this increase later.

Symptoms of Depression in Young People

Dejected mood is depression's prominent feature in young people. Similarly, loss of pleasure from previously pleasurable activities, or **anhedonia,** characterizes at least two thirds of depressed adolescents. Low self-esteem, high self-criticism, and poor body image are also common symptoms. Because of our culture's emphasis on physical attractiveness—especially for young females—feelings about being unattractive can be devastating to many adolescents. Symptoms associated with the loss of motivation are often expressed in behaviors of escape and withdrawal such as drug and alcohol use, and, sometimes in its most extreme forms, in suicidal wishes and attempts. In samples of depressed adolescent inpatients, between 75 percent and 85 percent report thoughts of suicide, and roughly 60 percent have attempted some suicidal act (Albert & Beck, 1975). As we shall see later, however, not all young people who commit suicide are depressed.

Like older depressed persons, adolescents and young adults with depression report loss of appetite, sleep problems, and fatigue. Yet these physical symptoms appear in only half of depressed adolescents. Further, most studies of teen-age depression have used depressed inpatient adolescents as subjects. The symptoms of appetite disturbance, sleep problems, and fatigue may occur less frequently among depressed nonhospitalized adolescents and young adults (Chartier & Ranieri, 1984).

Masked Depression

Some experts (e.g., Glaser, 1981; Lesse, 1981) suggest that teen-age depression may manifest itself very differently from adult depression. They propose that while adults overtly express depression, teenagers may mask or hide theirs through other behavior and symptoms or "depressive equivalents." "Masking" symptoms may include hyperactivity, truancy, sexual promiscuity, drinking, drug abuse, and running away from home.

Researchers have addressed the **masked depression** issue in several ways, sometimes by assessing if behaviors such as aggression and hyperactivity precede depression. If they do precede depression, some support would be provided for the notion of the aggressive and hyperactive behaviors having masked the depression. However, symptoms of masked depression do not regularly precede depression's onset. Instead, aggression and related behaviors may develop simultaneously with or as a secondary reaction to depression (Strober, Green, & Carlson, 1981).

Even if depression's symptoms in adolescence and young adulthood are nearly identical to those of midlife depression, we should not immediately conclude that the *causes* of their depression are the same. Like many other problems discussed in this book, depression is influenced by biological, social, and psychological factors. However, some of the most important factors influencing depression's development in teen-agers and young adults may be quite different than those central to the etiology of depression in adulthood.

Prevalence

The prevalence of depression increases markedly from childhood to young adulthood. Differences in the rates of depression among junior and senior high school students have been studied in England (Graham & Rutter, 1973). At any one time, approximately 11 percent of the ten-year-olds report feeling misery, depression, moodiness, and lack of self-worth. In contrast, almost half of the fourteen-year-olds report such feelings. In the largest U.S. study to date on depression's prevalence during the high school years, 1,700 randomly selected adolescent students in Oregon were carefully assessed with clinical interviews and self-report measures. Results indicated approximately 8 percent of the population was clinically depressed at the time of the assessment. In addition, 20 percent of this population had experienced clinical depression at some earlier point in their lives (Lewinsohn, Hops, Roberts, & Seeley, 1989). Moreover, in this study and in a related epidemiological study of over 5,000 high school students, depression was by far the most common disorder (Whitaker et al., 1990).

Among college students, 7 percent report moderate to severe depression (Bumberry, Oliver, & McClure, 1978). This is similar to the clinical depression just discussed in the studies of high school students since 8 percent of those students reported being depressed at the time of the assessment. In brief, depression is widespread among adolescents and young adults both in the United States and England, and the prevalence rates appear relatively constant after junior high school.

Gender Differences. Females experience depression two to three times more frequently than males (see Chapter 7). Moreover, gender differences in depression's severity seem to emerge by mid-adolescence. Kandel and Davies (1982) administered self-report instruments to over 8,000 adolescents in New York State. They found young women consistently reported higher levels of depressive symptoms (e.g., feeling too tired to do things, feeling hopeless about the future) than young men at each year from thirteen to eighteen. Similar gender differences appeared in the large, previously mentioned, prevalence study in Oregon (Allgood-Merten, Lewinsohn, & Hops, 1990). The reasons for this gender difference are poorly understood but may involve differences between stressful life events for men and women, styles of coping with stress, negative body image and self-esteem, emphasis on thinness as an ideal for women, and differences in biological vulnerability (Allgood et al., 1990; McCarthy, 1990; NIMH, 1981).

Levels of Depression in Adolescents and their Parents. Kandel and Davies (1982) obtained information from over 5,500 parents about their own depression to understand the relationship between parent and adolescent depression. Self-reported levels of depressive symptoms for adolescent girls older than fourteen were consistently higher than those reported by mothers. Boys older than fifteen consistently reported higher levels of symptoms than did fathers.

Studies of clinical depression in England confirm these American findings (e.g., Rutter, Graham, Chadwick, & Yule, 1976). If depression is indeed higher among teen-agers than their parents, why do such differences exist? Only substantial research can fully answer this question. Developmental changes and unique social stressors associated with adolescence and young adulthood are central to understanding depression and other problems in these populations.

Causes

Cognitive/Developmental Factors in Depression

Object Loss. One of the most widely discussed theories of depression in adolescents and young adults is object or person loss. Derived from psychoanalytic conceptualizations, the notion asserts that adolescence involves a loss of attachment to certain objects, especially parents. As young people pursue independence and autonomy, they may reject parental suggestions and wishes (Berman, 1980). For most teen-agers, becoming independent is natural, and therefore, any depression accompanying this separation from parents exists only transitorily. But, if the adolescent has experienced prior problems with parents and has felt loss of their love or that of another significant person in his or her life, clinical depression will probably develop.

In studies involving historical reports of depressed adults, evidence for the **object loss theory of depression** is scant. Research comparing depressed adolescents with other clinical groups has not discovered any difference between them (Chartier & Ranieri, 1984). Moreover, it is widely agreed upon that not all adolescents become depressed when their parents die or leave them through separation, divorce, or even abandonment. Yet, *longitudinal* studies of adolescents in divorcing families suggest some validity to the object loss theory of depression. In one study, 37 percent of adolescents with divorced parents were moderately to severely depressed five years following the divorce (Wallerstein & Kelly, 1980). Moreover, of sixty middle-class families in California, at eighteen months and then five years after the divorce, depression was the most common pathological finding among the adolescents. Subjects had intense complaints of chronic unhappiness, anger, apathy, restlessness, and emotional deprivation. Almost one quarter of the adolescents were disappointed with the relationship with their noncustodial parent because of their infrequent or emotionally shallow meetings. Surprisingly, at the time of the divorce, the majority of the children and adolescents preferred their parents' unhappy marriage to a divorce.

Although Wallerstein and Kelly's (1980) study did not have a control group of children and adolescents in intact families, depression among adolescents coping with divorce appears more prevalent and severe than in the general adolescent population. (Recall that 8 percent of high school adolescents were clinically depressed in the large prevalence study in Oregon.) The loss of frequent contact with a parent and the associated problems of a family breakup, such as reduction of money to a household, may place adolescents at an elevated risk for depression. In sum, object loss or some loss or frustration associated with family dissolution may contribute to depression in a significant percentage of adolescents coping with divorce.

Learned Helplessness. The **learned helplessness** model (see Chapter 7) has aided researchers and clinicians in understanding childhood and adolescent depression (Petti, 1983). This model suggests that with prolonged exposure to an adverse environment, such as repeated failures or a disadvantaged, abusive, or neglectful home, children and adolescents develop a sense of helplessness. They come to view aversive events as outside of their control and likely to continue, even if they try to change them. Experimental research has shown that adolescents with helpless and nonhelpless beliefs may have equal competence at solving problems, but those with helpless beliefs attribute failure experiences to their lack of competence and are likely to give up in the face of failure. In contrast, adolescents who do not feel helpless believe they can modify failure by increasing their effort (Dweck & Reppucci, 1973). Further, extremely depressed hospitalized adolescents on a hospital ward fail to view positive events as the result of their own effort. They also see such outcomes as unpredictable or unstable (Curry & Craighead, 1990).

Related research indicates that depressed children and adolescents often view their world as determined by external factors outside their control. Tendencies to attribute events in one's life to internal factors such as effort or to external factors such as luck have been measured, using a **locus of control** scale. Depressed adolescents exhibit higher external locus of control scores than nondepressed peers (Moyal, 1977).

Although learned helplessness and external locus of control are not synonymous concepts, they are related to each other and to depression. The significant variable in learned helplessness is that the adolescents perceive aversive events as not under their control. Locus of control refers to people's more general tendency to view events as within or outside their control. Before we can say that cognitive variables will produce depression in adolescents, longitudinal research is necessary. Such research has not yet been conducted. We know, nevertheless, that efforts to change helpless beliefs and attitudes of adolescents can result in behavior change. Dweck (1975) gave adolescents with helpless attitudes daily training, teaching them to take responsibility for failure and to view it as due to lack of effort (as opposed to lack of ability). Following training, these adolescents performed much better on arithmetic problems than a second group of adolescents with helpless attitudes who received training that only provided success experiences. These and related findings indicate that by changing adolescents' helpless attributions about aversive events, they will improve their ability to overcome obstacles and persevere even when faced with some failure experiences.

Relationships with Parents and Peers. Researchers have assessed a number of variables thought to be related to adolescent depression and found the following specific factors closely associated with depression:

1. Lack of closeness to mother.
2. Lack of closeness to father.
3. Almost exclusive intimacy with peers.
4. Minor delinquency (Kandel & Davies, 1982).

When the investigators looked at combinations of variables related to depression, they found that patterns of involvement with peers to the exclusion of parents best predicted depression for both boys and girls. If adolescents get involved with peers to the point that they have little interaction with their parents, their risk of depression increases dramatically. Another team of researchers also observed the family as a more significant source of stress for depressed than nondepressed teen-agers (Larson et al., 1990). Depressed youths preferred to be away from their parents more than non-depressed youths.

The increasing divorce rate and difficulties faced by single parents in the United States are probably related to the rising rate of depression among teens and young adults. Additionally, cross-cultural studies reveal Americans spending less time with their children than parents in any other country in the Western world, except England (Bronfenbrenner, 1970; Nicholi, 1988). With the accelerating divorce rate and increase in out-of-wedlock pregnancies, over half of the children in the United States live in a home with one or both parents missing (U.S. Bureau of the Census, 1988). The divorce rate of approximately 45 percent in the United States and the number of children born to single mothers increase the likelihood of alienation from parents and orientation toward peers. While some adolescents may have very close relationships with their single or divorced parent, the need of a single parent or a parent with custody of his or her adolescents to work and support the family often makes monitoring adolescents' behavior infrequent or difficult. These circumstances may place the adolescents at increased risk for depression and involvement in delinquent activities.

Genetic Factors in Depression. Genetic predisposition for depression was discussed in Chapter 7, and family studies were cited that link biological vulnerabilities to depression. That is, an individual with a relative hospitalized for depression has some elevated risk for depression. Additionally, twin studies have provided the most convincing evidence for a genetic component in depression. Investigators have reported a 40 percent concordance rate for unipolar depression among monozygotic twins (Allen, 1976).

Few studies have specifically examined the role of genetic factors in adolescent depression (Cantwell, 1983). Some evidence does indicate the increased likelihood of depressed adolescents' having a parent with some psychiatric disorder than nondepressed adolescents (Hudgens, 1974). These data suggest a general genetic factor in the etiology of adolescent depression. Since parents of depressed adolescents can have varied histories of psychiatric disorders, not simply histories of depression, the evidence must be considered *supportive* of genetic factors, but not definitive evidence of them.

Instead of examining the family backgrounds of depressed adolescents, some investigators have studied the offspring of parents with known effective disorders. Studies of children of parents suffering from bipolar disorders (manic depressive illness) indicate they are much more likely to be depressed than control children matched on socioeconomic status (Cytryn et al., 1984). On the other hand, a study of children of unipolar and bipolar depressives (Weintraub, Winters, & Neale, 1986) found that children of affectively ill parents (bipolar or unipolar) were not commonly clinically depressed. In fact, less than 21 percent of the offspring of former patients with unipolar or bipolar depression had any diagnostic disorder when they were assessed at age eighteen (Weintraub, 1987). But children of these former patients did have more problems than a control group: They were generally more aggressive, more anxious, and less socially competent. Overall, the findings suggest that children of parents with affective disorders, especially bipolar depression, are at some general risk for social and emotional problems, although they may not show depression.

Treatment of Depression in Young People

Treating depression in adolescents and young adults can differ markedly from the treatment of adults. First, few depressed adolescents are referred for depression and few seek treatment on their own. They generally arrive at clinics or hospitals because of other problems, such as poor school performance, substance abuse, or defiance. Second, because parents usually fail to notice overt behavior problems or the underlying depression of their children, it is often unnoticed in adolescents. Depressed adolescents who display few other problems often do not receive treatment until a crisis occurs, such as running away from home or attempting suicide. Why do parents so often fail to recognize the problem before it gets out of hand? Teen-agers' negativism may simply be puzzling to many parents. After all, aren't these people at the best time of their lives? They have youth, lack of financial responsibility, and few illnesses. When they complain or mope around the house or snarl, parents may conclude they are simply being selfish, lazy, or defiant. Educational efforts to help parents and teachers recognize depression in young people are clearly needed.

When adolescents are brought for treatment, a therapist's first job is often to help the family see their son or daughter is depressed, not defiant. Box 13.1 describes how a therapist met this challenge in treating an adolescent boy.

Dennis Cantwell (1983) has suggested that treatment of children's depression should be multimodal, that is, consist of interventions involving biological, social, familial, and intrapsychic issues. This argument can readily be extended to treatment of adolescents and young adults. While a patient's specific pro-

BOX 13.1 Treatment of Depression

A divorced mother sought treatment for her 12-year-old son, Larry. He was doing poorly in school and had joined in recent neighborhood episodes of truancy, vandalism, and drinking. His mother responded to the unacceptable behaviors with powerful bursts of rage, and prolonged arguments resulted. When she became angry with her son she would think, "He's just like his father," and become even more enraged as she remembered her sociopathic, abusive ex-husband.

Larry meanwhile alternated between angry defiance towards his mother and highly immature, dependent behaviors (such as jumping onto his mother's lap and embracing her during a family session). Both the therapist and the school personnel agreed that the boy concealed his essential fearfulness and inadequacy with a veneer of rebelliousness. He seemed desperate for attention and affection, particularly from adult males.

The therapist worked to sensitize the mother to the numerous manifestations of her son's poor self-image. He emphasized the connection between her son's low self-esteem and his vulnerability to negative peer influences. She began to recognize that the boy's acting out behavior reflected his desire for recognition and peer status, not his inherently antisocial nature. The therapist also encouraged the mother to enumerate the differences between her ex-husband and her son, so that she could begin to resist the tendency to scapegoat the boy. Gradually, she began to react to his provocative behavior in a calmer less hysterical fashion, and thereby avoided a number of destructive confrontations.

From a more detached position, she was able to see more clearly the effects of his strong sense of inadequacy (as opposed to his "bad genes") upon his behavior. As she changed, she was surprised to see his behavior change also. Concurrently, the therapist also worked on an individual basis with the son. For the most part, he ignored the boy's expressions of distrust and hostility early in their relationship. The therapist played games and lifted weights with the boy all the while discussing his relationships with his peers and his parents. For over a year, Larry had nurtured the belief, at times encouraged by remarks from both parents, that he would be able to move in with his father, who lived several states away, if his mother would only allow him to make the transition. He would say, "I'm miserable because my mother won't let me go to live with my father." The therapist enabled the boy to reconsider more carefully who was truly responsible for his living arrangements. He began to acknowledge that the reason he had not moved in with his father was that both parents had agreed it was preferable for him to remain with his mother. Moreover, he recognized that he often raised the issue of custody in order to make his mother angry. As he became more comfortable with the therapist, Larry was able to discuss issues in his life which did not directly involve his mother, such as his poor school performance and his unsatisfying friendships.

Source: Emery, G., Bedrosian, R., & Garber, J. (1983). Cognitive therapy with depressed children and adolescents. In D.P. Cantwell & G.A. Carlson (Eds.) *Affective disorders in childhood and adolescence: An update*, CA: PMA Publishing Corp. Reprinted with permission of publisher.

gram should be tailored to the unique aspects of his or her situation, a clinician using this multimodal intervention might consider medication, individual psychotherapy, family therapy, and often a psychoeducational program. Though antidepressant medication might well be considered in treatment plans for adolescents and young adults, the effectiveness of these medications with adolescents are discouraging while psychological and family therapies show considerable promise (Craighead & Curry, 1990; Lewinsohn, Clarke, Hops, & Andrews, 1990).

SUICIDE AMONG YOUNG PEOPLE

At 6:30 in the evening, Vivienne Loomis, an attractive fourteen-year-old with an unusual talent for writing, hanged herself in her mother's silversmithing studio in the family basement. At the time of Vivienne's death, her parents were a block away attending a farewell party in their honor. The family was moving to the seaport of Gloucester, Massachusetts, where her father was assuming a new position as the minister of a Unitarian church. Vivienne's older sister, Laurel, was playing the piano in the living room filled with boxes in preparation for the move. Their brother was in his apartment in Revere, Massachusetts. Vivienne's best friend, Ann, had gone on a Christmas vacation trip with her parents. John May, a teacher whom Vivienne greatly admired, was 3,000 miles away.

Laurel's comments about her last interactions with Vivienne follow:

> *Vivienne and I had a terrible fight about packing. That week she refused to help. I just wanted to shut everything out. . . . Mummy and Daddy had gone to the party. I was dimly aware of Vivienne. I saw her a couple of times. She walked downstairs, went upstairs, came down again and back up. I just didn't think about it. Finally, she walked to the basement. She must have been down there fifteen minutes when suddenly I thought, "This is strange, something funny is going on here." I had kind of an intuition it had happened. And I walked down and found her.* (Mack & Hickler, 1981)

Following Vivienne's death, her mother understood she had been planning it for at least several days:

> *I had given her the rope on Sunday. . . . She asked me for some rope that day and I didn't even ask why. I thought it had something to do with packing. I remembered that we had some L.L. Bean rope around somewhere and I found it and that is what she used. I think she was down there trying it that Sunday because I was down with a load of wash for the washing machine and she was down there. I said, "Are you getting some clothes or something?" She didn't say much, she just went upstairs. There was only one room that was totally cleaned out in preparation for the move. It was my silversmithing shop. She used a water pipe in my shop and the instrument I had put in her hands.* (Mack & Hickler, 1981)

Why did Vivienne kill herself? She kept a diary called, *My Private Paper Book,* which nobody had read before her death. The diary chronicled Vivienne's inner life as she attempted to cope with the everyday struggles of adolescence, such as getting along with parents, friends, and teachers. It discussed her feelings about sexual morality, drugs, and concerns about her own self-worth.

The diary also revealed that she had told her friend, Ann, of suicide attempts at least five times. Ann was sworn to secrecy, and, moreover, did not believe that Vivienne would really kill herself. Vivienne desperately wanted to escape her depression and sometimes unbearable pain. On December 11, she wrote her former teacher, John May, about her suicide attempts. Because she could not find an airmail stamp for her letter, it was not mailed until two days before her death. John May received the letter one day after she had died.

Besides describing her suicide attempt in detail, Vivienne discussed her failure to connect with the teachers in her new private school to which she had received a scholarship.

In the last paragraph of her letter to John May, she wrote:

> *I hope all is well with you and that the teaching is working out. I know you're over there somewhere giving yourself to so many people like when you were over here. It is hard getting used to teachers whose policies include avoiding getting personally involved with their students. This is more of a dog-eat-dog world every time I turn around again. I know there must be more people like you around here* some-where; *maybe I should put out a "Wanted" ad. Well this whole letter shows you how depressed I really am. But I am not always like that. Write me back a really positive letter and tell me somewhere in it what an ass I am for writing letters like this.*
>
> *Take care, with love,*
> *Vivienne*
>
> (Mack & Hickler, 1981, p. 117)

Vivienne's suicide has several common themes characteristic of other adolescent suicides: She had given warning to at least one person a number of times; she felt hopeless; she was depressed and lonely; she had become isolated.

Prevalence

It has long been assumed that the suicide rate increases with age. This idea can be traced to a well-known French sociologist, Emil Durkheim. In *Le Suicide* (1897), Durkheim presented data suggesting that most suicides occurred late in life, and more than ninety years afterward, many professionals still hold this belief. Durkheim, however, used numbers of people who died from suicide at various ages to arrive at his conclusion. Yet if we look at suicide rates as a percentage of all deaths per age group (rate/100,000 people), they are highest among adolescents and young adults. As Table 13.1 shows, suicide follows accidents as the third leading cause of death among fifteen- to twenty-four-year-olds. While younger children sometimes talk about suicide and school administrators are frequently frightened by youngsters' suicidal threats, each year only two children younger than age ten commit suicide in the United States (Hawton, 1986).

The seriousness of the problem cannot be overestimated. Suicide among American adolescents and young adults has increased over 200 percent since the 1950s, and the rates (proportion of deaths/100,000 people) for males have increased much faster than for females (Peck, 1985). A similar rise in suicide among adolescents and young adults has also occurred in Europe and Australia. Suicide rates among European youths are roughly similar to those in the United States, while that of Japanese adolescents is the highest in the world.

Sex of Victims. Overall, males kill themselves far more frequently than females. Since the 1950s, about 75 percent of all persons committing suicide have been males (Parker, 1974; Hawton & Catalan, 1982). This gender difference also holds for individuals from fifteen to twenty-four years old. Even during early adolescence (ages ten to fourteen), the suicide rate is almost twice as high for males as females. The dramatic difference in suicide rates for males and females is reflected in Figure 13.1 (Hawton, 1986, p. 21). It clearly shows the dramatic increase in suicide in males as largely accounting for the rise in suicide rates among adolescents and young adults.

One reason for males' higher suicide rate may be that they tend to employ more lethal means when attempting to take their own lives. Guns are by far the most common means of suicide for male adolescents and young adults in the United States. Additionally, young females contemplating suicide may be more likely than young males to seek help before the actual attempt.

Race of Victims. White youths commit suicide more often than nonwhites. The suicide rate among white males from fifteen to nineteen years old is, in fact, almost twice that of nonwhite males (National Center for Health Statistics, 1984). Although the differences are not as large among twenty- to twenty-four-year-olds, white males' suicide rate is still higher. Similarly, rates of suicide among white females ages fifteen to twenty-four are higher than those for other females. The reasons for these differences remain unclear, especially as minority groups are generally subject to more stress. Differences in cultural attitudes about suicide may be one factor contributing to this discrepancy. For example, it has been hypothesized that blacks may view suicide much more negatively than whites do. In this context, suicide rates reported for blacks from traditional southern communities have been lower than those reported for blacks in northern states where their attitudes may have become more influenced by the cultural mainstream (Shaffer & Fisher, 1981).

TABLE 13.1 Ten Leading Causes of Death in the United States

Ages Fifteen to Twenty-Four	All Ages
1. Accidents	1. Heart disease
2. Homicide	2. Cancer
3. Suicide	3. Stroke
4. Cancer	4. Accidents
5. Heart disease	5. Chronic pulmonary disease
6. Congenital anomalies	6. Influenza and pneumonia
7. Stroke	7. Diabetes mellitus
8. Influenza and pneumonia	8. Suicide
9. Pulmonary disease	9. Cirrhosis and liver disease
10. Diabetes	10. Atherosclerosis

Source: National Center for Health Statistics: *Monthly Vital Statistics Report* (Vol. 37, No. 13). Hyattesville, MD. U.S. Public Health Service, Washington. U.S. Government Printing Office, 1989, p. 192.

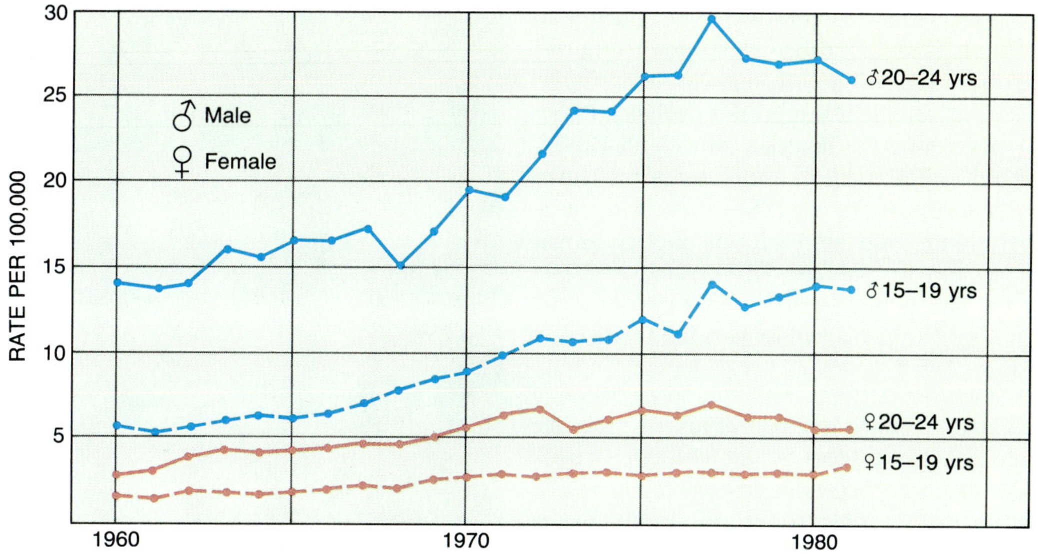

Figure 13.1 Epidemiology of Suicide *As is very evident in this figure, the number of suicides of young males rose steadily from 1960 to 1980. This increase is apparent for both the 15–19 year old group and the 20–24 year old group. Suicides of females, on the other hand, did not change across these two decades.*
Source: National Center for Health Statistics.

Suicide Attempts and Actual Suicides

In many countries data regarding the prevalence of suicide attempts are unavailable. Where records are available, they show the dramatically increased rate of attempted suicide among adolescents and young adults. For example, in the Netherlands, the number of admissions to hospitals following suicide attempts nearly doubled from 1970 to 1980 (Diekstra & Hawton, 1987). In Melbourne, Australia, the rates of suicide attempts among adolescent females doubled from 1963 to 1970 while the rates for adolescent males increased several times (Oliver, Kaminski, Tudor, & Hetzel, 1971).

An astute reader may wonder whether differences exist between teens and young adults who make unsuccessful and successful suicide attempts. Some individuals make nonlethal suicidal gestures, such as superficial wrist slashing and taking quantities of pills insufficient to cause death. Such attempts seem to represent desperate cries for help. Individuals who make them usually suffer from serious immediate stressors but may be less likely to have the intense long-standing problems of suicide attempters employing more lethal means. Overall, however, there are more commonalities than differences between suicide attempters and suicide victims. Attempters and completers share one critical common pattern: Nearly all of them send messages of some kind of their intent to significant people in their lives.

In fact, approximately 80 percent of suicidal people of all ages provide clear clues about their intent to kill themselves. They show their despair and helplessness, ask for help in various ways, and give friends and families opportunities to rescue them. Thus, adolescent suicide does not seem to occur on the spur of the moment very often. Instead, it is usually an outcome of serious emotional problems which typically have gone unrecognized and untreated (Holden, 1986). Further, suicides are not usually acts of hatred or attempts to get even with friends and family. As Schneidman (1985) remarks, "Suicides are individual's attempts to get others to see their pain and stop them from killing themselves." Talk and other hints of suicide should always be taken very seriously.

Causes

Alcohol Use. Alcohol use seems to be a key risk factor associated with suicide. Research on countrywide changes in Western Europe shows a strong correlation between increases in alcohol consumption and rises in suicide rates (Diekstra, 1985). Evidence about individuals who attempt suicide also points to alcohol use as a risk factor. Approximately 15 percent to 30 percent of adolescents and young adults who attempt to kill themselves have a history of alcohol abuse (Hawton, O'Grady, Osborn, & Cole, 1982; Headlam, Goldsmith, Hanenson, & Rauh, 1979).

Separation/Divorce. It has been well documented that young people whose parents divorced attempt suicide more often than those from intact families. In one study, researchers compared family backgrounds of suicidal and nonsuicidal individuals aged six to twenty-one (Garfinkel & Golumbek, 1983; Garfinkel, Froese, & Hood, 1982). Of those who had attempted suicide, less than half lived with both their parents.

Comparison of suicide attempters to other adolescents with psychiatric difficulties shows no difference in the rate of separation and divorce for these two groups (e.g., Spirito et al., 1987). Just as separation and divorce are risk factors for alcohol and drug abuse, so they are for suicide. The critical problem underlying the risk factor for adolescents in divorced and nondivorced families may be overt family discord and fighting.

Death of a Parent. Loss of a parent and an inability to cope with that loss are associated with young people's suicide attempts. We have known for approximately fifty years that a disproportionate number of young people attempting suicide come from homes where a parent has died (Zilboorg, 1936). Further, comparisons of suicides and attempted suicides indicate death of a parent as a more common occurrence in the childhood or adolescence of actual suicides than attempted suicides (Dorpat, Jackson, & Ripley, 1965). Nevertheless, the majority of young people who lose a parent during childhood or adolescence are nonsuicidal. The quality of the parent–child relationship just prior to the parent's death may be a significant predictor of later adjustment, as exemplified in the following clinical account of a young man's trouble coping with his mother's death:

> *He saw his mother as refusing to let him grow up. She would not let him have a door to his room and insisted on her right to open his mail. She seemed to have been particularly fearful of his involvement with girls. He felt his mother tried to live her life through him. As he spoke, it was clear he thought he had performed and lived for his mother at the expense of living his own life. Yet he had felt lost and "out of control" when he went off to college and felt depressed and cut off without his mother. It was in this period, which had preceded her illness, that he first became preoccupied with thoughts of suicide. Nothing outside of his family had much deep, living reality for him. He never dreamt of being in his current apartment; in all his dreams he was in the home where he had grown up with his parents.* (Hendin, 1985, p. 21)

Suicide Attempts by Family Members, Friends, and Celebrities. Adolescents attempting suicide are particularly likely to have relatives or close friends who have made suicide attempts (Jacobs, 1971; Teichner & Jacobs, 1966). One study actually found that suicide attempts by relatives were seven times more common in the backgrounds of adolescents who attempted suicide compared to adolescents in a control group (Garfinkel, Froese, & Golumbeck, 1979). The increased likelihood of suicide attempts following similar behavior by family members suggests the powerful role of modeling. If a close friend or relative has attempted or completed suicide, suicidal behavior may be seen by the adolescent as a viable or even positive option.

Suicide rates rise following the suicide or death of a public or popular personality, such as Marilyn Monroe.

Similarly, data from suicide notes indicates that suicide sometimes occurs after reading of a public figure's suicide (Shaffer, 1974). Suicide rates also rise just after the death of a popular figure, such as the film actress Marilyn Monroe (Shaffer & Fisher, 1981). They also increase following television broadcasts of fictional stories featuring suicidal behavior (Gould, Shaffer, & Kleinman, 1988). In brief, imitation of the suicidal behavior of a family member, friend, or television character is certainly a risk factor for adolescent suicidal behavior.

A related issue receiving recent attention is the role of popular music advocating suicide. In March 1990, Cardinal John O'Connor of New York City denounced Ozzy Osbourne's tune, *Suicide Solution.* The lyrics include:

> Wine is fine but whiskey's quicker
> Suicide is slow with liquor . . .
> Suicide is the only way out.
> Don't you know what it's really about?*

* *SUICIDE SOLUTION:* Words and Music by John Osbourne, Robert Daisley, and Randy Rhoads. TRO—© Copyright 1981 Essex Music International, Inc. and Kord Music Publishers, Venice, CA. Used by permission.

Ozzy Osbourne, famous rock star and heavy metal singer, who sang Suicide Solution.

In 1990, the Pennsylvania state legislature passed a bill requiring printing the lyrics on the packaging of recordings that describe or advocate suicide or morbid violence. Some large chain stores have already announced that they will not sell records that have printed lyrics advocating violence and suicide (*Newsweek*, March 19, 1990).

Psychiatric Disorders and Hopelessness. Relatively few young suicide attempters suffer from clearly defined psychiatric disorders. A study of adolescent suicide attempters in England noted that only 20 percent had psychiatric problems (Hawton, 1986), and these were generally described as mild depression and personality problems. While depression is more common among suicidal adolescents than among nonsuicidal adolescents referred for psychiatric services (Taylor & Stansfield, 1984), it occurs in only about one quarter to one third of adolescents who attempt suicide (Clarkin et al., 1984). Psychiatric problems appear to exist more commonly among suicidal boys than suicidal girls, with character and/or conduct disorders being the most common problems found among suicidal boys.

Depression and suicide are certainly related, but the majority of adolescents who make suicide attempts are not clinically depressed. Nor do the majority of clinically depressed adolescents commit suicide. Hopelessness, or a sense that there are no solutions for one's problems, has been a key predictor of suicide in adults (Beck, Kovacs, & Weissman, 1975). It is also an indicator of adolescent suicidal thinking and suicidal behavior (Kazdin et al., 1983; Spirito, Brown, Overholser & Fritz, 1990). Moreover, while hopelessness is one common symptom of depression, it seems to be a better predictor of suicidal attempts than overall level of depression, probably because a hopeless person sees no way out. No solutions appear viable. In contrast, an individual may be depressed and yet believe that these feelings may diminish or that with effort things will improve. A sense of hopelessness is vividly reflected in the suicide note written by Bill (see Box 13.2).

Academic Pressures. In 1986, three college students attending Massachusetts Institute of Technology (M.I.T.) committed suicide, and in 1987 three more students from that university killed themselves. M.I.T. enjoys the reputation of being one of the best universities in the United States for science and engineering students. Thus, its intensely competitive environment may have contributed to the high number of suicides. The following quotations from an article in *The New York Times* describes some of this pressure (November 26, 1987):

> . . . even the buildings have numbers rather than names. Stephanie Pollack, a Boston lawyer who graduated from M.I.T. five years ago, observed, "I think the problem has gotten worse in recent years because of the widespread use of computers. They're very isolating." "It's the type of people who come here," said Stephen Fillipone, a 25-year-old graduate student in electrical engineering, "very competitive types of students who have been valedictorians, have never gotten a B, and whose whole basis for self-esteem is that they are the best in their subjects. When they get here, they no longer are the best and they lose perspective."

Suicide attempts occur more often among college students than young people not in college. College students who attempt suicide often have relatively high overall grade-point averages, but tend to do poorly in the semester prior to the attempt. Most do not seek psychiatric help, and of those who died, the majority were not recognized as suicidal. Yet, two thirds of students attempting or completing suicide behave differently shortly before the suicidal act or warn friends or teachers of their intentions (Parrish, 1957; Seiden, 1969; Temby, 1961). Pressures to achieve and maintain grades contributes to the higher suicide rate among young adults attending college (Raphael, Power & Berridge, 1937).

Adolescents who attempt suicide also tend to have more school problems than those who do not, and the dangerousness of the suicide attempt seems related

BOX 13.2 A Suicide Note

To my family and friends:

I'm sorry it has to be this way. For some reason, I have set unattainable goals for myself. It hurts to live and life is full of so many disappointments and troubles. What I would really like to say is that I can't face up to problems the way I should. Society is always judging you and telling you what to do. My problem I think is that I have always thought only of Bill [himself]. Everything I have done hasn't satisfied me. Why this is I cannot tell you. It is a very funny feeling that I get inside when I sit down to do something. Maybe like what I write or do won't be accepted by society. Competition is another thing I hate. Maybe I expected too much out of life. Please don't cry or feel badly. I know what I am doing and why I am doing it. I guess I never really found out what love or responsibility was.

Bill

(P.S.) I might also add that I had had in recent years no great desire to continue living. Saying goodbye to all of you who I was close to would only make things harder for me. Believe me I tried to cope with my problems but I couldn't.

Source: Jacobs, J. (1971). *Adolescent suicide.* New York: Wiley-Interscience, p. 88.

to the extent of school difficulties. Adolescents engaging in serious suicide attempts are more likely to be failing in school than those who make less dangerous ones (Garfinkel & Golumbek, 1983). Poor grades, truancy, and disciplinary problems may precede as many as 77 percent of adolescent suicide attempts (Shaffer, 1974). Chronic poor school performance appears to be a larger correlate of suicide attempts in adolescents than in college students, although in the semester before the suicide attempt, declining or failing grades are predictive of suicide attempts in both populations.

Boyfriend/Girlfriend Problems. Rejection by a boyfriend or girlfriend may trigger many adolescent suicide attempts. A study of English adolescents who attempted suicide through self-poisoning revealed approximately half of them were preceded by problems with a boyfriend or girlfriend (see Table 13.2; Hawton et al., 1982). Other findings show that many adolescent suicide attempts occur during the terminal breakup stages of romance (Jacobs, 1971). Girls attempting suicide are more likely to have had problems with a member of the opposite sex than are boys (Otto, 1972), probably because young women place much greater emphasis on relationships than young men do.

Problems with Parents. Indeed, large numbers of adolescent suicide attempters report problems with their parents prior to their attempt (see Table 13.2; Hawton et al., 1982). Psychologists of varied orientations generally agree that disturbed parent–child relationships significantly heighten vulnerability to suicide. According to one psychodynamic view, adolescents in alienated family relationships seek intense teen romances. Such adolescents are searching for the intimacy and openness they always lacked or previously experienced with their parents (Hendin, 1985). Teens without close parental ties may invest most of their energies in a romance while ignoring past friendships. When the romance ends, lacking somebody to turn to, they feel completely isolated and hopeless. Suicide becomes a "solution" to their problems.

Treatment of Suicide Attempters

Because of a suicide attempt's possibly tragic consequences, attempters must be taken seriously. Most professionals recommend the active treatment of ongoing therapy for adolescent suicide attempters. Repeated follow-up visits with a family physician, psychiatrist, psychologist, or social worker are, at the very least, necessary. Parents, friends, and teachers should interpret the suicide attempt as a cry for help. Controlled studies of interventions with young people who have attempted suicide are difficult to conduct because they cannot be compared to nontreated attempters. All suicide attempters should receive professional help if they will accept it, and some may even be forced to enter treatment because professionals feel it is critical for their safety. One study compared the usual hospital emergency-room treatment with a treatment involving a social worker supportively counseling the adolescent and encouraging him or her to make follow-up appointments at the hospital (Deykin, Hsieh, Joshi, & McNamara, 1986). In addition, in the geographic area in which the service was offered, school and police personnel received a special educational curriculum about suicidal issues. Unfortunately, the program did not affect later suicide attempts. A survey of experts on the National Task Force for Youth Suicide revealed great diversity of opinion about the best ways to prevent teen suicide (Eddy, Wolpert, & Rosenberg, 1987). Treatment and prevention programs received the experts' highest endorsement, but the following measures were not far behind: screening youth in schools, hot line and crisis centers, school programs

TABLE 13.2 Current Problems Identified for Fifty Adolescent Self-Poisoners	
Problem Area	**Percentage of Subjects for Whom Each Problem Was Applicable**
Parents	76%
School/work	58
Boy/girlfriend	52
Social isolation	28
Sibling(s)	22
Physical health	22
Psychiatric symptoms	20
Sexual	16
Relationship with peers	14
Alcohol	14
Physical illness of family member	14
Financial	8
Psychiatric disorder of family member	6
Legal	2
Drugs	2

Source: Hawton, K., O'Grady, J., Osborn, M.M., & Cole, D. (1982). Adolescents who take overdoses: Their characteristics, problems and contacts with helping agencies. *British Journal of Psychiatry, 140,* p. 121.

to help teens identify the types of problems that lead to suicide, and restricting access to firearms. Restricting access to medications was not seen as an effective measure by any of the experts. Thus the most economically feasible methods may be the most likely to be developed, but it appears that psychological treatment will almost always be one of those measures if the teen-agers and/or the parents desire such help.

Because family problems are so often at the root of suicide attempts among adolescents living at home, family therapy is frequently the psychological treatment of choice. As described in Chapter 17, Marital, Family, and Medical Therapies, family therapy usually involves individual therapy with the adolescent and sessions with all family members. The therapist attempts to help the family uncover and then overcome the lack of communication and support typifying the families of adolescent suicide attempters. Individual therapy is most often chosen for older adolescents and young adults living away from home. The therapist's first goal is to immediately assure the potential victim of help and hope. A caring, understanding relationship between the patient and the therapist or between the patient, parents, and peers lessens the risk of repeated suicide attempts.

Young people with a combination of depression and conduct problems (defiance of social rules, impulsivity, and aggressive behavior) are also potential suicide attempters. These individuals are at higher risk for suicide than others because their impulsiveness can often have disastrous consequences. Additionally, their frequent drug and alcohol abuse may result in accidental overdose. Barbara exhibits the risk of depression and conduct problems for suicide:

> *By the time she was 16, she was a heavy user of Quaaludes and alcohol. She had started using marijuana at age 12 and had tried PCP, cocaine, and a variety of other drugs. When she first came to therapy at 16, she had already made a suicide attempt and had dropped out of school six months earlier. Her peers were also heavy drug users and tended to be involved in rebellious and acting-out behaviors. Her family history was a chaotic one. Her mother had been twice divorced, the first one occurring when Barbara was seven. Her most recent stepfather drank heavily and physically assaulted various members of the family. (Peck, p. 121)*

Therapy for youngsters like Barbara generally includes a large number of agencies, involvement of the family, and group and individual therapy. Family therapy should be utilized whenever possible since the family members need to take equal responsibility with the patient to prevent further suicidal episodes. Individual therapy with these youngsters must focus on the terrible feelings of pain and boredom they experience when not under the influence of drugs and alcohol (Peck, 1985).

Treating suicidal adolescents who have a combination of depression and conduct problems such as drug abuse, truancy, or defiance of authority tends to be harder than treating adolescents who are able to acknowledge their problems and see their suicide attempt as a call for help. Defiant adolescents are often so deeply troubled that the patient–therapist bond that makes therapy so beneficial is difficult to establish.

Prevention

Suicides account for as many as one third of all deaths of adolescents and young adults (Peck, 1985). Consequently, more than one-on-one psychological and psychiatric services need to be involved. When groups of high school students commit suicide together, as in 1986 in Bergenfield, New Jersey, and when a pair of teen-agers commit suicide together, as in Aslip, Illinois (see Box 13.3), the need for community agencies, high schools, and universities to become actively involved in suicide *prevention* becomes extremely clear. Abnormal psychology books like this text can help, but broad-scale public efforts are also essential to provide information about suicide to as many people as possible. Table 13.3 presents warning signs everyone should be aware of, and Table 13.4 provides guidelines for appropriate action if someone you know appears to be suicidal.

TABLE 13.3 Suicide Warning Signs*

1. Is the person suffering a severe depression that seems to be continuing and that may have been caused by a serious loss of some sort? (Loss of a friend, parent, breakup of a romance, academic or social failure, and so on)
2. Is the person suddenly retreating from people and formerly enjoyable activities – becoming increasingly isolated and unwilling to participate or talk things over?
3. Is the person giving away prized possessions?
4. Is the person suddenly doing poorly in school?
5. Is the person writing or making statements that suggest a wish to die, or to escape, or that hint at a final departure? ("I wish I were dead" . . . "Who needs this world" . . . "soon it'll be all over" . . . "I can't take any more of this" . . . "You won't have to worry about me much longer.")
6. Does the person seem unusually hostile and aggressive, getting into physical fights and uncharacteristically defying those in authority?
7. Has the person threatened to commit suicide?
8. Has the person attempted suicide in the past?
9. Is the person acting in a strange manner, behaving illogically and seemingly out of touch with reality?
10. Is the person suddenly extremely happy after a prolonged episode of depression and despair? (Sometimes the depression has lifted because the person has decided to go ahead with the suicide attempt.)
11. Is there a deterioration in the person's personal appearance and grooming?

* *Note:* If several of these warning signs are evident, the potential victim should be referred for treatment.

Source: Diekstra, R. F. W. & Hawton, K. (1987). *Suicide in Adolescence*. Dordrecht, Netherlands: Martinus Nijhoff Publishers, pp. 177–178.

One early morning in 1906, Reverend Harry W. Warrent received a call from a woman who had urgently requested to see a clergyman the previous evening, while in a hotel. None was available. By the time Reverend Warren, the local Baptist minister, found her the next morning, she was dying from self-inflicted injuries. As he attended to the woman, she told him she would not have tried to kill herself if he had been available to see her the night before. Reverend Warren promised the woman he would establish an organization to prevent such acts by people like herself seeking help. The organization he subsequently founded, the "National Save-a-Life League," became a prototype of the suicide hotlines now operating in most countries.

Since suicide in the United States is the eighth leading cause of death for individuals of all ages and the third leading cause of death for individuals aged fifteen years to thirty-four years, suicide prevention centers have become high priorities in most metropolitan areas. Virtually all these areas in the United States have at least one prevention center, and these centers in turn make referrals to other mental health agencies (Dew, Bromet, Brent, & Greenhouse, 1987).

Suicide prevention centers do attract young people contemplating suicide. People who have killed themselves often have been former suicide center clients (Dew et al., 1987). Therefore, we may con-

TABLE 13.4 What to Do if Friends Seem Suicidal

1. Listen to them and encourage them to talk.
2. See if they have the symptoms of suicide attempters (see Table 13.3).
3. If they have many of the symptoms, especially hopelessness, tell them where they can get help, and, if possible, make certain that they go to a professional or that they make an appointment to see one.
4. If you know family members of the potential suicide attempter, alert them to the risk and enlist their aid in obtaining treatment for the individual. You may be faced with a conflict between keeping your friend's secrets or protecting your friend's life. Saving a life is certainly more important.
5. If you have any doubts about what to do, call a university counseling center, a suicide hotline, or your local mental health clinic and speak to a clinical psychologist or psychiatrist about what you can do.

Source: Diekstra, R. F. W. & Hawton, K. (1987). *Suicide in Adolescence*. Dordrecht, Netherlands: Martinus Nijhoff Publishers, pp. 180–181.

clude suicide prevention centers reach the people they are intended to serve. Yet, the extent of their effectiveness is poorly understood. On the whole, researchers have not found that they affect suicide rate in the general population areas served. Some evidence does suggest that centers focusing exclusively on suicide prevention are more effective in preventing suicide than multipurpose centers that attract suicidal clients. Additionally, certain cohorts or age groups appear to be most helped by suicide prevention centers. Specifically, young women's suicide rates have decreased in areas served by suicide pre-

BOX 13.3 Teen Suicide Pacts

The Bergenfield suicides, which involved two sisters and two male victims, were a deeply troubled group of teen-agers. Three were high school dropouts, and one had been suspended and was considering not returning to school. All of them were alienated from the most accepted groups, associated instead with a highly disgruntled group in school, and had been labeled by peers as burn-outs.

The four victims were close friends of another high school dropout, Joseph Major, who had died some months prior to their suicide by falling off a cliff after a drinking bout. Although his death was ruled an accident, his friends were not convinced he hadn't meant to fall. They had been brooding about his death and frequently visited his gravesite and wept.

The two young men in the group had recently experienced tremendous turmoil. One had watched his father kill himself, and both boys had been treated for drug or alcohol abuse. The two young women were trying to adjust to their mother's new husband and his children. All four of the suicides had been drinking heavily. Nobody was aware of the planned suicide even though the two sisters had contacted about thirty friends on the day of their suicide. The four teen-agers bought three dollars worth of gas and later sat in a car in a closed garage writing their suicide pact on a brown paper bag. A man driving to work heard the car motor running in the apartment complex and called the police, who found the bodies.

A day after the Bergenfield suicides, two young women from Aslip, Illinois, Nancy Gannon and Karen Logan, died in the same fashion. They were found in Nancy's Chevrolet in her family's garage; nearby were eleven suicide notes. The fumes from the garage filled the house, also killing the family dog and cats.

Mourning parents of adolescent who was a member of a group suicide pact. Group suicide pacts recently occurred in Bergenfield, New Jersey, Sheridan, Arkansas, and Aslip, Illinois.

Nancy and Karen may have already decided to kill themselves before they heard of the Bergenfield suicides, but possibly the news of it pushed them over the brink. The following week, another four Ohio youths took their lives in a suicide pact. These teen suicide pacts were not random occurrences across a year; they occurred very close to one another. The "copy cat" teen suicide pacts were likely influenced by the model provided by the Bergenfield suicide victims.

There are some mass suicides of historical note related to religious cults such as the Jonestown mass suicide of over 900 people in 1978. However, with the exception of religious cult suicides followings and group suicides of some prisoners, copy cat suicides appear unique among adolescents and young adults. The causes of these multiple suicides are unknown, but modeling of others seems a plausible precipitant. Nonetheless, other issues like those in the development of individual suicides in this population would likely also be present. Alienation, loneliness, and hopelessness are certainly key features. The unique and as yet unknown aspect is the group dynamic, the role of follower and leader, that operates to implement group suicides among adolescents and young adults.

Source: Adapted from *Newsweek*, March 23, 1987.

vention centers, as compared with control communities (Dew et al., 1987). This result is encouraging since young women are the most frequent users of such centers.

EATING DISORDERS: ANOREXIA NERVOSA AND BULIMIA NERVOSA

> *The child I was baby-sitting lay asleep upstairs. His parents weren't due home for another three hours, ample time for temptation to seize me. The lure of the television, the call of my homework were no competition for the magnet of the kitchen: food. Like a creature obsessed, neither tasting nor thinking, I burrowed through cupboards, refrigerator, cookie jar, and freezer. Grabbing fistfuls of Mallomars and brownies, gulping ice cream, Jello-O, and cheese, I was indiscriminate in my gorging. Frenzied, as though possessed by some malevolent phantom, I raced through the larder and could quit only after collapsing in glutted agony. Then, when the spell finally broke, I loathed myself for such weakness and raged at my failure of willpower.*
>
> *Staggering into the bathroom, I presented myself for penitence. The mirror mercilessly cast its wrath upon me. My reflection resembled that of a bloat-bellied malnutrition victim. I weighed under 90 pounds. My scrawny arms, bony chest, and spindly legs cried out in protest against the distended abdomen of my cruel binge. The sight nauseated me. No doubt about it, eating was evil. My faith in the virtue of abstinence grew the longer I stood examining myself. It sent me into spasms of remorse over my greed and propelled me into a program of redemption.*
>
> *I began by vomiting. Like yoga, my method relied on muscle contraction and concentrated control. But unable to purge myself completely this way, I worked out a backup maneuver. My magic cure was Ex-Lax, taken at three times the recommended dosage. It was like swallowing Drano. The only problem was that the effects were not instantaneous, and I was desperate for immediate relief. I could feel the calories turning to fat as I waited. My last resort was exercise. Like an expectant mother, I bent over my swollen stomach to touch toes, gasped through hundreds of jumping jacks, and struggled through feverish sit-ups. Not even the impending homecoming of my employers could subdue me. Keeping an ear cocked for the sound of the garage door opening, I kept working out for as long as possible. I was haunted by the thought that a single carbohydrate might escape my frenzy and become flesh.*
>
> *My penance lasted days afterward. Rejecting all but the merest taste of food, I raged at my parents as they urged me to eat. My mother worried. My father winced at the sight of my protruding clavicles [collar bones]. But I kept examining the fluctuations of the bathroom scale with the zeal of a religious fanatic. When, at the end of a three- or four-day fast, my pelvis sank to a hollow shell once again. I gloried in this proof of strength and determination. Loss of weight had become my personal path to honor; starvation was the goal of my adolescence.* (Excerpt from SOLITAIRE by Aimee Liu. Copyright © 1979 by Aimee Liu. Reprinted by Permission by HarperCollins Publishers.)

This young adolescent suffered from a combination of **anorexia nervosa** and **bulimia nervosa.** She and other adolescent and young adult females compose the high-risk population for these eating disorders, whose prevalence seems to be increasing rapidly. Both anorexics and bulimics obsessively fear they either are or will become fat. Anorexics shun food to lose weight and thereby fail to maintain sufficient body weight for good health. Bulimics binge-eat, then attempt to purge themselves through vomiting or using laxatives and diuretics. Sometimes, as in the example, anorexia nervosa and bulimia nervosa coexist. Although both disorders can result in severe physical damage, they are unaccounted for by any known physical illness. However, despite the similarities between anorexia nervosa and bulimia nervosa, there are important clinical differences, as discussed later.

The features and prevalence of anorexia nervosa and bulimia nervosa will be discussed below. Following this, factors that may contribute to the development of an eating disorder in general will be reviewed. Finally, we will present the treatments for both anorexia nervosa and bulimia nervosa and some differences between the two problems.

Characteristics of Anorexia Nervosa

Anorexia nervosa is not a new problem. In Medieval times people fasted and starved themselves to attain religious perfection. In the Victorian era, people fasted and curbed their appetite since eating was considered a substitute for sexual desires. Until 1980, anorexia nervosa was generally regarded as an endocrine dysfunction and did not even appear in the *Diagnostic and Statistical Manual* of the American Psychiatric Association. But today it is viewed as a life-threatening eating disorder. The four criteria necessary for a diagnosis of anorexia nervosa in *DSM-III-R* (1987) are:

1. Refusal to maintain body weight over a minimal normal weight for age and height.
2. Intense fear of becoming obese or gaining weight, even when underweight.
3. Disturbance in the way in which one's body weight, size, or shape is experienced.
4. In females, absence of at least three consecutive menstrual cycles when otherwise expected to occur (amenorrhea).

Anorexia nervosa has two peak onset times, ages thirteen to fourteen and seventeen to eighteen. It

Karen Carpenter was one of the most famous anorexia nervosa victims. A well known pop singer in the 1970s and early 1980s, she died from a heart attack at 33 years of age; physicians believed it resulted from her own battle with anorexia nervosa.

typically occurs in teen-agers who perceive themselves as overweight, then begin dieting and become preoccupied with being thin. To keep their weight down, they fast, exercise excessively, and/or take laxatives. Although such adolescents may actually lose weight, they usually feel it occurs too slowly. Other symptoms coexisting with anorexia are depression and a distorted body image; anorexics continue to see themselves as too fat, despite their emaciated appearance. Weight loss in anorexia nervosa is often severe and life threatening. Between 5 percent and 18 percent of victims die as a result of this disorder.

Prevalence of Anorexia Nervosa

The number of people with anorexia nervosa has increased in recent decades. In Switzerland, where anorexia nervosa's incidence among females ages twelve to twenty-five has been recorded since 1956, the percentage of sufferers has quadrupled from the mid-1950s to the mid-1970s (Willi & Grossman, 1983). And in New York State, between the mid-1960s and the 1970s, anorexia rates doubled (Jones, Fox, Babigian, & Hutton, 1980).

Whenever an increase in a psychological problem is reported, we may reasonably ask whether clinicians simply diagnose the problem more frequently. But since those afflicted by anorexia are immediately recognizable by excessive thinness, it is unlikely that we can attribute the dramatic rise in reported cases to greater recognition of the problem. This view is supported by findings that anorexia nervosa's prevalence has increased in private schools for young women, where dangerously low body weight is easily detected during required annual physicals.

Gender Differences. Anorexia nervosa afflicts at least one in every hundred teen-age girls. In female college students, the prevalence may be as high as 10 percent of the population (Herzog, 1988). Yet only 5 percent of individuals with anorexia nervosa are males. Reasons for the gender difference will be discussed later.

Socioeconomic Differences. Anorexia nervosa occurs largely among white adolescent females from middle- and upper-income families. A survey of a psychiatric case register in Monroe County, New York, revealed approximately three quarters of the anorexic population came from the two highest socioeconomic groups (Jones et al., 1980). This register contains nearly all residents of a New York county entering the formal mental health care system (see Table 13.5). This register also includes one of the first reported cases of a black anorexic female. Anorexia nervosa's prevalence in black populations is unknown because there have not been large-scale epidemiological studies of eating disorders in this population. But the New York State case register study and a recent series of case studies of blacks referred for eating disorders indicate the prevalence may be increasing (Hsu, 1987). Other studies suggest, however, that eating disorders are still far less common in

TABLE 13.5 Incidence of Diagnosed Anorexia Nervosa by Socioeconomic Levels, Monroe County, New York: 1970–1976

Social Class	Females Only 15–44 Rate per 100,000
I (Highest)	3.2
II	1.9
III	1.2
IV	0.0
V (Lowest)	0.0

Source: Jones, D. J., Fox, M. M., Babigian, H. M., & Hutton, H. E. (1980). Epidemiology of anorexia nervosa in Monroe County, New York: 1970–1976. *Psychosomatic Medicine, 42,* 551–558. Copyright © by the American Psychosomatic Society.

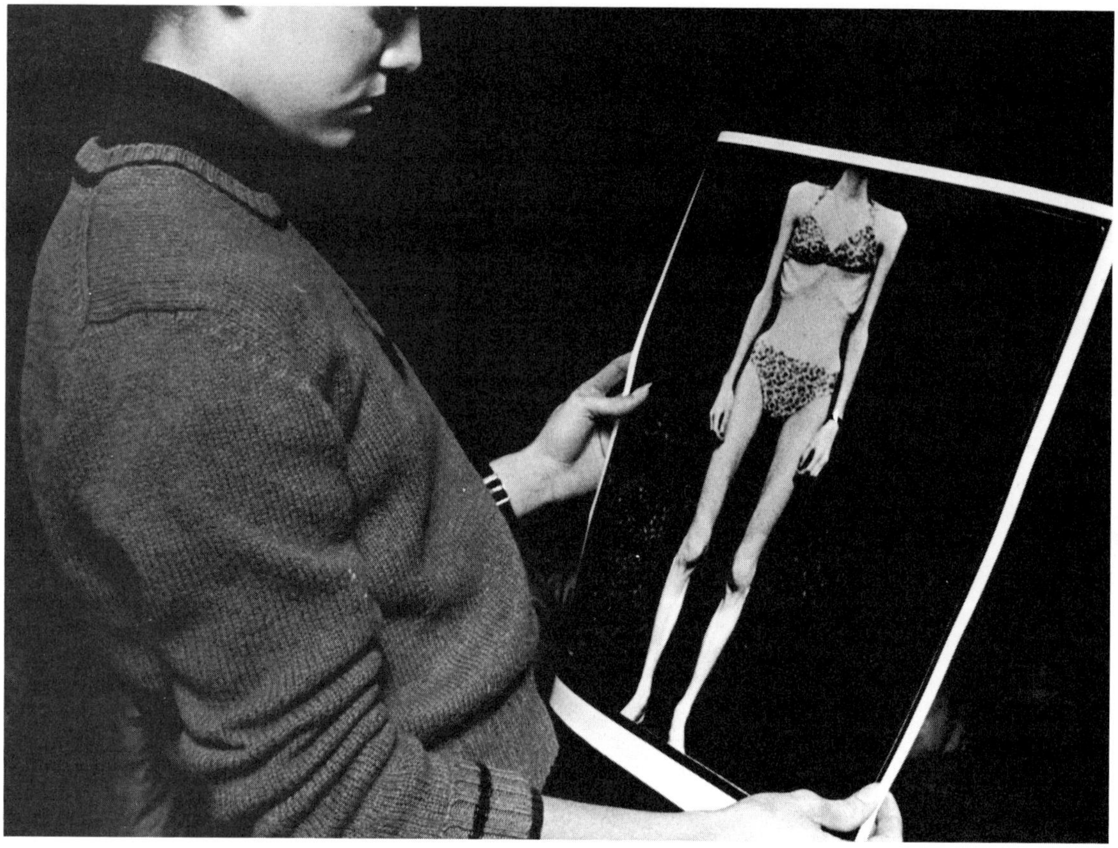

This adolescent ponders over a picture of a female with the disorder, anorexia nervosa. As is evident here, anorexia nervosa can be life threatening. Between 5 and 18 percent of victims die as a result of this disorder.

blacks than in whites. The relatively low prevalence of anorexia nervosa among blacks compared to whites is likely caused by different attitudes toward weight and beauty—not simply a socioeconomic difference (e.g., Gray, Ford, & Kelly, 1987).

As we will see, social emphasis on thinness strongly influences the development of both anorexic and bulimic behavior patterns. If this emphasis on thinness becomes adopted across all socioeconomic and racial groups, both of these disorders will probably become more common. Indeed, some evidence already suggests a rise in anorexia nervosa during the last decade among the lower socioeconomic groups (Garfinkel & Garner, 1982).

Characteristics of Bulimia Nervosa

Like anorexia nervosa, bulimia nervosa primarily afflicts female adolescents and young adults. Additionally, as indicated, anorexics may also be bulimic, and bulimics, anorexic (Andersen, 1985). Despite similarities between the two disorders, there are important clinical differences. Unlike anorexics, bulimics are normal weight individuals, although their weight usually fluctuates because of alternate binge-eating and fasting. Bulimia's mean age of onset is one to two years later than anorexia's (Hsu, 1990), with bulimics using laxatives and diuretics more frequently. While weight loss is not life threatening, bulimics' frequent vomiting results in serious loss of body salts and possible gastrointestinal problems; thus, physical damage can be quite severe. Diagnostic criteria for bulimia nervosa are (*DSM-III-R,* 1987):

1. Recurrent episodes of binge eating (rapidly consuming large amounts of food within discrete periods of time).
2. Repeated attempts to lose weight by severely restricted diets, self-induced vomiting, or the use of cathartics or diuretics.
3. Feeling of lack of control over eating during binges.
4. A minimum of two binge episodes a week for three months.
5. Persistent overconcern with body shape and weight.

Prevalence of Bulimia Nervosa

We do not know how prevalent bulimia nervosa is because no true epidemiological studies of it exist for

Slim models are predominant in popular magazines. Unfortunately, the near exclusive use of such model types present an unrealistic ideal to young women who often try in vain to have the thin appearance of the media models.

the general population. However, a study of women attending a family planning clinic in England indicated approximately 2 percent of that population was bulimic (Cooper & Fairburn, 1983). Since thousands of women from all socioeconomic classes attend such clinics, this prevalence outcome appears to offer a reasonable estimate of the problem in England. As with anorexia nervosa, the prevalence of bulimia may be higher among college students than the general population. Studies of freshman college students in several universities suggest that approximately 3 percent to 4 percent of female college students are bulimic (Drewnowski, Yee, & Krahn, 1988; Stangler & Printz, 1980; Striegel-Moore, Silberstein, Frensch, & Rodin, 1989), with some indications of the problem increasing in this population (Pyle, Halvorson, Neuman, & Mitchell, 1986).

Gender Differences. Like anorexia nervosa, bulimia nervosa is far more common among women than men; at least 90 percent of bulimics are women (Striegel-Moore, Silberstein, & Rodin, 1986). Variables contributing to this gender difference are discussed later.

Causes of Eating Disorders: A Biopsychosocial View

Why certain young people move from normal dieting and exercise regimens to an anorexic or bulimic pattern is unknown. A number of factors appear to be associated with the disorders. At present, no biological, psychological, or social variable by itself seems sufficient to cause either anorexia nervosa or bulimia nervosa. These variables operate together to place individuals at risk for eating disorders, with an intense fear of gaining weight as both eating disorders' primary symptom.

Gender and Differential Risk. Why do far more women have eating disorders than men? Dieting is clearly one culprit. Tremendous social pressures exist for women to be thin in order to be attractive. The greater the pressure to be thin, the more young women and teen-age girls diet, and in turn the more eating disorders exist (Hsu, 1989). The pressure is obviously a cultural phenomenon; anorexia nervosa and bulimia nervosa do not exist to any significant degree outside North America and Europe, except in

Japan, and, as noted, appear relatively uncommon among black women.

From an early age, females learn that their appearance is extremely important. This information comes from diverse sources such as family, friends, and the mass media—all emphasizing physical attractiveness in females much more than in males. Thus, appearance becomes a part of females' self-concept from an early age, and weight seems to be a critical factor in appearance. But with puberty's onset, females gain weight primarily in the form of fat tissue whereas males gain it primarily in muscle and lean tissue. Hence, in the cultural context of the "thin is in" ideal for women, we should not be surprised that adolescent females express greater dissatisfaction with their weight and show lower body esteem than males. For most females reaching physical maturity means being heavier than what is currently considered beautiful (Striegel-Moore et al, 1986).

Besides adolescence's physical changes, it is a time of interpersonal challenges. Females appear to define themselves more in terms of their relations and connections to others than do males. This interpersonal orientation probably causes adolescent females to be more susceptible to others' evaluations and social demands. Popularity is a higher priority for females than males.

If women are at greater risk for eating disorders than men, are certain groups of men more concerned about weight and dieting? Research indicates a higher prevalence of eating disorders, especially bulimia, among jockeys and wrestlers than in athletes involved in sports in which a prescribed body weight does not have to be maintained, such as baseball (Striegel-Moore et al., 1986). Finally, it is interesting to note that this disorder's causative factors generally are different for women and men; for women the issue is appearance whereas for men it is competence mastery.

Biological Factors. Although heredity's role in anorexia nervosa is unclear, increasing evidence indicates that some genetic or biological factor may be important in this disorder's development. A number of studies indicate that when one member of a monozygotic (same egg) twin pair is anorexic, the likelihood of the other twin being affected is approximately 55 percent. In contrast, the concordance rate of dizygotic (different egg) twins is only about 7 percent (Garfinkel & Garner, 1982; Holland et al., 1984; Holland, Sicotte, & Treasure, 1988).

Even less attention has been given to the possibility of a genetic risk factor for bulimia nervosa. Yet two recent studies have reported on the concordance rates of bulimia nervosa in twins, and both strongly suggest genetic factors' importance in bulimia nervosa. The first (actually a series of case studies in which one twin was bulimic) showed bulimia as much more probable in monozygotic than in dizygotic twins (Hsu, Chesler, & Santhouse, 1990). In the second study, 83 percent of female monozygotic twin pairs were concordant for bulimia nervosa, whereas only 27 percent of dizygotic female twin pairs were (Fichter & Noegel, 1990). If these results were replicated with larger numbers of twin pairs, they would indicate that bulimia nervosa, like anorexia nervosa, has some genetic link.

Research is also needed to determine the nature of the genetic risk in both disorders. In a recent study of bulimia nervosa in the first-degree female relatives of anorexic patients, it occurred at a rate almost three times that of first-degree female relatives of affectively disordered patients, and twice the rate of first-degree female relatives of nonaffective, non-anorexic patients. Although these results are preliminary, they suggest that anorexia nervosa and bulimia nervosa may share a genetic link (Strober et al., 1990).

Family Weight History. Family weight history may be a risk factor for developing an eating disorder. This variable may operate through psychological means but biological factors may be alternatively involved. Many bulimics have some history of being overweight before the disorder's onset and have obese parents. The evidence is less clear for anorexics. A number of studies have found the prevalence of parental obesity to be higher in anorexics who are also bulimic, than in anorexics without concurrent bulimic symptoms (e.g., Garner, Garfinkel, & O'Shaughnessy, 1985; Strober, 1981). A family history of obesity could lead adolescents to become highly concerned about their weight and body shape. Yet, the extent to which parental weight may influence bulimia nervosa's onset is not understood. For example, the critical factors moving adolescents from concern about weight to a self-defeating course in regulating it are not known. We may reasonably assume that a young person's family history of weight problems could contribute to his or her fear of becoming fat, an essential characteristic of bulimics. Still, many nonbulimics have overweight parents, and we cannot conclude that being the child of overweight parents per se places someone at heightened risk for bulimia nervosa. Most of the thousands of overweight adolescents also do not become bulimic. In short, a family history of obesity by itself does not cause bulimia nervosa, although it may be a significant risk factor when combined with other variables.

Sociocultural Factors. Societal emphasis on thinness certainly is relevant to the etiology of anorexia

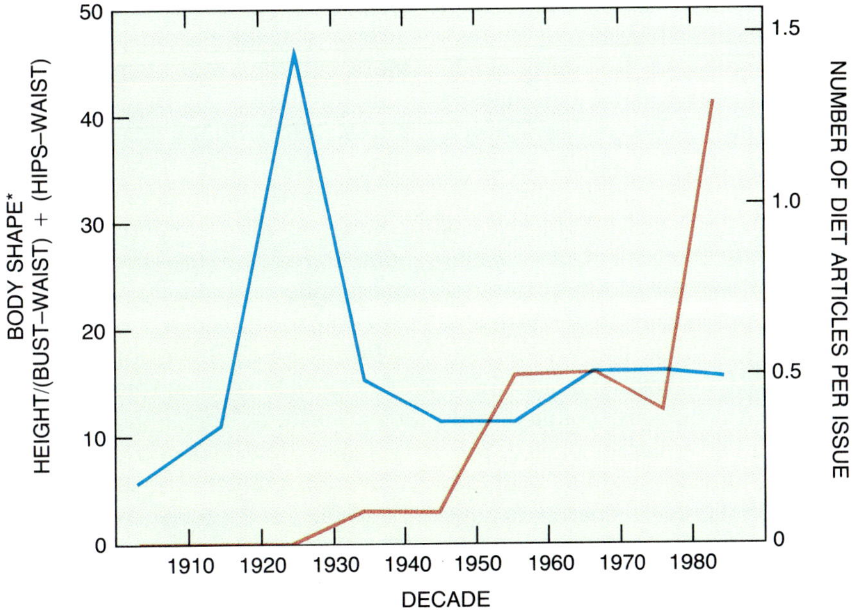

Figure 13.2 Preferred Female Body Shape *The preferred female body shape (blue line) from 1900 to 1983 became straighter or less curvaceous in three women's magazines (*Ladies' Home Journal, Good Housekeeping, *and* Harper's Bazaar*). (*Larger body shape ratios indicate straighter figures.) During the same time, the number of articles (red line) about dieting increased from 1940 to 1980.*

Source: Agras, W.S., & Kirkley, B.G. (1986). Bulimia: Theories of etiology. In K.D. Brownell & J.P. Foreyt (Eds.), *Handbook of eating disorders: Physiology, psychology, and treatment of obesity, anorexia, and bulimia,* p. 370. New York: Basic Books. Reprinted by permission of Basic Books, Inc., a division of Harper Collins Publishers.

nervosa and bulimia nervosa. Their rising prevalence seems to have been paralleled by a shift in societal preferences away from more rounded shapes toward a preference for thinness. This alteration in ideal body images was documented in a recent study showing that the body shapes of women depicted in three popular women's magazines became increasingly thinner from 1910 to 1975, except for a period during the 1940s and 1950s (Agras & Kirkley, 1986). The number of articles about dieting in these magazines also increased markedly from 1950 to 1980 (see Figure 13.2).

Other evidence of the increasing preference for thinness may be observed in the declining average weights of *Playboy* centerfolds (see Figure 13.3) and Miss America contestants from the late 1950s to the late 1970s (Garner, Garfinkel, Schwartz, & Thompson, 1980). Yet despite these trends, the average weight of women in the general population under thirty years old actually *increased* by five pounds over the same twenty-year period.

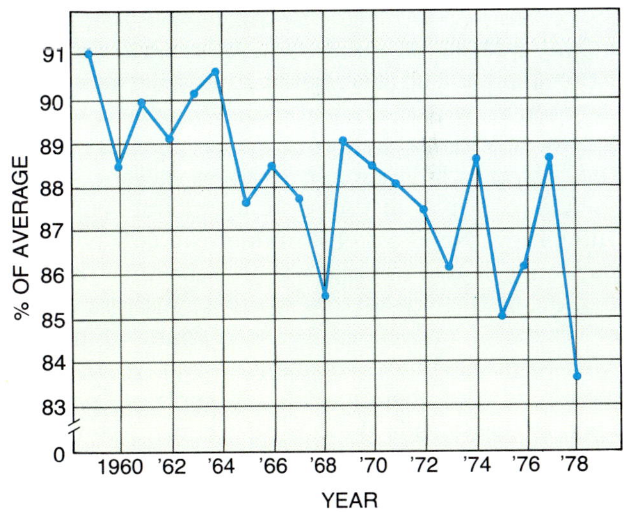

Figure 13.3 Weight Changes of Playboy Centerfolds *The weight of Playboy centerfolds decreased to a point in 1978 when they were only 83 percent of the weight of the average female.*

Source: Reprinted with permission from authors and publisher from: Garner, D.M., Garfinkel, P.E., Schwartz, D., & Thompson, M. "Cultural expectations of thinness in women." *Psychological Reports,* 1980, 47, 483–491.

The extensive use of thin female models in magazines, television, and advertising reflects an ideal emulated by many females. Pressure to be thin is felt especially by young women. It has been repeatedly documented that most of them are generally dissatisfied with their bodies and want to be thinner. One study found that 80 percent of senior high school females desired to lose weight, whereas only 20 percent of male students wanted to. Not surprisingly then, 30 percent of the female students were dieting in comparison to 6 percent of the males (Dwyer, Feldman, Seltzer, & Mayer, 1969). A similar Swedish study found the majority of female adolescents "felt fat," whereas males rarely experienced themselves as overweight (Nylander, 1971). More recent studies indicate that as many as 65 percent of American adolescent females engage in dieting (e.g., Rosen & Gross, 1987).

Vulnerability to anorexia nervosa seems heightened when pressures to be slim are coupled with high achievement standards. By career choice, professional ballet and modeling students must maintain a slim body shape. Not surprisingly, researchers have found that a much higher prevalence of anorexia in such students (approximately 7 percent) than that reported for young women of similar age and socioeconomic status (approximately 1 percent). Moreover, ballet dancers from the most competitive programs, with greater pressure to succeed, weigh less than dancers from other programs (Garner & Garfinkel, 1980). In sum, the data suggest that young women under pressure to be thin are at risk for developing anorexia nervosa, and that both internally and externally imposed high performance demands are causal factors.

Family Interaction Patterns. Although a causal relationship has not been demonstrated between family interaction patterns and eating disorders, laboratory observations of anorexic female teen-agers and their parents indicate it may be associated with a unique pattern of disturbed family interactions (e.g., Humphrey, 1989). Parents of anorexic girls communicated a double message of nuturant affection and neglect of their daughters' needs to express themselves and their feelings. Anorexic young women, in turn, responded more submissively and more ambivalently toward their parents. In contrast, parent–child interactions in the control group showed more helping, trusting, and initiating between the parents and daughters. A related study (Humphrey, 1988) indicated that anorexic young women and their families failed to perceive any excesses and deficits in their parent–child relationships. Instead, they described themselves as loving and happy. This discrepancy is consistent with clinical observations that families of anorexics often present a facade of perfection, thereby failing to acknowledge their problems.

Like anorexia nervosa, bulimia nervosa is associated with family relationship disturbances. The types of interaction problems in families of bulimics may differ markedly from those seen in families of anorexics. During laboratory interactions between teen-age girls and their parents, mothers of bulimics were more belittling and blaming toward their daughters than mothers of anorexics or control subjects (Humphrey, 1989). Bulimic daughters were similarly belittling and blaming toward their mothers. Bulimic fathers were controlling of their daughters while bulimic daughters reacted with sulky resentment. In sum, a greater expression of hostility appears within the families of bulimics than in families of anorexics and control subjects.

Professionals have long speculated family problems' possible causal role in the development of eating disorders. But such disturbed relationships are typically identified *after* an eating disorder has become extremely serious and treatment is sought. Therefore, the precise ways troublesome family interactions may contribute to or result from an eating disorder remain difficult to determine.

Restrained Eating. As noted previously, sociocultural factors contributing to excessive weight concern are relevant to the development of bulimia nervosa and anorexia nervosa. The role of **restrained eating,** or dieting, has recently become a central focus of attempts to uncover bulimia nervosa's causes. Considerable evidence suggests dieting and binge-eating co-occur. Although individuals who binge obviously may diet to compensate for their excessive eating, dieting often precedes binge-eating's onset (Boskind-Lodahl & Sirlin, 1977; Pyle, Mitchell, & Eckert, 1981).

Dieting itself cannot cause an eating disorder but appears to be a substantial risk factor. In a recent study of over 1,000 fifteen-year-old London schoolgirls, 81 percent of these who became either bulimic or anorexic during a twelve-month period had been dieting at the study's outset. Most dieters did not, however, develop an eating disorder. Twenty-one percent of those dieting at the study's outset became eating disordered, 38 percent continued normal dieting, and 41 percent stopped dieting. In this longitudinal study, increased weight, social problems, family history of dieting, family psychiatric history, and obsessiveness also associated strongly with an eating disorder (Patton, 1988).

Negative Emotional States. Several recent studies have characterized bulimics not only by symptoms related to eating and weight but also by depression, anxiety, low self-esteem, social difficulties, and impulse control problems (Katzman & Wolchik, 1984; Williamson, et al., 1985). In comparison to nonbulimic restrained eaters, bulimics demonstrate increased pathology on measures of depression, self-esteem, and interpersonal relationship fears (Laessle, Tuschl,

Waadt, & Pirke, 1989). Higher levels of depression, anxiety, negative feelings about weight, perceived stress, and increasing feelings of ineffectiveness have been found to be risk factors for a worsening of disordered eating symptoms (Patton, 1988; Striegel-Moore et al., 1989).

These negative emotional states may interact with severely rigid dieting practices to transform someone into an eating disordered individual. Studies have indeed indicated negative emotional states' strong effect on eating behavior. A series of observational studies of women who were bulimic, restrained eaters, or actively dieting, demonstrated that episodes of bulimia or overeating were more likely to occur following increases in negative emotional states such as depression, anxiety, loneliness, or boredom (Cooper & Bowskill, 1986).

Treatment of Anorexia Nervosa

Psychological Treatments. Hospitalization is often necessary in anorexia's initial treatment, particularly when the patient's weight has fallen dangerously low. Treatment's first goal is to restore the patient to some near normal body weight to prevent further complications. Forced feeding methods are applied when the anorexic's condition is life threatening, via a nasogastric tube (a tube leading from the nose to the stomach) or an intravenous catheter inserted directly into the large vein near the heart. These methods involve steadily infusing nutrients such as glucose, protein, vitamins, and fat.

Behavioral programs based on operant principles have successfully motivated hospitalized anorexics to gain weight. In a classic study by Bachrach, Erwin, and Mohr (1965), the weight of a severely emaciated woman was influenced when conversation, attention, and praise were made contingent on her eating. Subsequent research has shown that similar reinforcement procedures lead to immediate weight increases (e.g., Agras et al., 1974).

There has been only one large-scale evaluation of inpatient behavioral interventions like those just described as compared to many evaluations of **milieu therapy** (Eckert et al., 1979). The therapeutic milieu program was a hospital-based environment where patients developed group norms, expectations, social support and pressure to motivate each other to reach certain goals regarding weight gain. Eighty-one anorexic patients were randomly assigned to the therapeutic milieu program or to a hospital unit in which behavioral procedures were added to the therapeutic milieu. The treatment lasted thirty-five days. The two therapies did not result in differential weight gain, but both treatments yielded significant improvement, with an average weight gain of about nine or ten pounds.

With some notable exceptions, most anorexic treatment studies have focused on short-term weight gains. Therefore, less is known about the efficacy of various interventions for long-term maintenance of these gains. **Family therapy approaches** seem to help anorexics over the long term. The first illustrations of family therapy's success were provided in 1978 by Minuchin, Rosman, and Baker at the Philadelphia Child Guidance Clinic and by Selvini-Palazzoli in Milan, Italy. Family therapy of anorexics focuses on mealtime activity when parents and family members are instructed to either make the anorexic eat or to decide that the eating is none of their business. Because parents usually fail at getting their adolescent to eat, they realize that changing the anorexic's eating patterns is not their primary responsibility. Family members at this point begin to acknowledge their own contributing problems, such as ambiguous communication patterns.

Family therapy approaches have clearly resulted in weight gain in anorexics, and the gains have been as high as 86 percent (Minuchin, Rosman, & Baker, 1978) at three-month to four-year follow-up. More controlled evaluations suggest that weight gain at the end of treatment is maintained at a one-year follow-up for those anorexics whose illness began at eighteen years or younger, but that the maintenance was not as good when the illness began at nineteen years or older (Russell, Szmukler, Dare, & Eisler, 1987). While family therapy approaches to anorexia nervosa have not yet been thoroughly researched, they probably will be in the next decade. Family therapy is growing rapidly and receiving worldwide attention. Further, it has been very successfully integrated with behavioral systems therapy in treating anorexia nervosa (e.g., Robin & Siegel, 1987).

Pharmacological Treatments. Some controversy exists over using pharmacological interventions with anorexics. Some professionals believe anorexia is a variant of an affective or depressive disorder and thus have viewed antidepressant medication as a potentially useful mode of treatment. Antidepressants result in greater caloric intake and increased appetite in anorexics but have not been shown superior to placebos in promoting weight gain (Lacey & Crisp, 1980). At least one drug with appetite stimulating effects (cyproheptadine) caused significant weight gain in anorexics without bulimia but appears to retard weight gain in anorexics with it. In summary, antidepressant pharmacological interventions with anorexics have proved disappointing because they do not affect a presumed central cause of the disorder—dieting and restrained eating.

Treatment of Bulimia Nervosa

Psychological Treatments. Unlike anorexia nervosa, bulimia nervosa is almost always treated on an outpatient basis. A variety of psychological interventions are successful in treating bulimia nervosa, but cognitive-behavioral therapy has received the most attention (e.g., Fairburn, 1985). This treatment is based on persistent overconcern with body shape and weight as the central feature of this disorder. Most of the other features, such as extreme dieting and vomiting, are seen as secondary to these concerns (Fairburn, 1988; Fairburn, Kirk, O'Conner, & Cooper, 1986). **Cognitive-behavioral interventions** thus focus on changing bulimics' attitudes regarding shape and weight. For example, bulimics examine and try to overcome unrealistic fears and distorted beliefs associated with eating. They also keep records of food intake, binge-eating, and purging. Finally, bulimics and their therapists work together to establish a regular eating pattern, such as eating three meals per day, increasing the amount of food intake during regular meals, and widening the variety of food consumed. Cognitive behavior therapy leads to dramatic reductions in binge-eating and vomiting (e.g., Lacey, 1983; Lee & Rush, 1986; Wolchik, Weiss, & Katzman, 1986). Moreover, these gains are much greater than in nontreated bulimics in a waiting list control condition.

Response prevention is a behavioral treatment for bulimia which reduces binge-eating and vomiting (e.g., Leitenberg, Gross, Peterson, & Rosen, 1964; Rosen & Leitenberg, 1985). It is based on the hypothesis that purging is prompted by the bulimic's fears of gaining weight; purging then apparently diminishes this anxiety. Bulimics become caught in a vicious cycle of purging's anxiety reduction reinforcing binge-eating. Therefore, in response prevention treatments, they can binge-eat during therapy sessions but are prevented from purging afterward. The therapist remains with patients until the urge subsides. Prevention of vomiting helps bulimics learn that their anxiety can dissipate without vomiting.

A number of studies have compared different types of psychological interventions with CBT, the treatment designed to alter bulimic's fear of gaining weight and to normalize eating patterns. CBT has been compared to a form of brief psychotherapy (Fairburn et al., 1986)—**interpersonal psychotherapy (IPT)**—and a form of CBT focusing only on the normalization of eating habits (Fairburn et al., 1989). The brief psychotherapy intervention is patterned after Hilde Bruch's (1973) approach of eating problems as a maladaptive solution for other underlying difficulties. Its major aim is to enable bulimics to identify these difficulties and their relation to eating problems. Originally developed as a treatment for depression, IPT focuses on past and present interpersonal interactions. It is partially rooted in psychodynamic theory but also emphasizes attachment to parental figures and significant others (e.g., boyfriends). On measures of binge-eating, purging, depression, and general psychopathology, cognitive-behavioral therapy and interpersonal therapy are equally effective. However, CBT is superior in modifying bulimics' attitudes about shape and weight.

Though most follow-up periods for the treatment of bulimics have been relatively brief, long-term follow-up evaluations have been very heartening. In two studies, patients were evaluated at least two-and-a-half to three years after treatment (Fairburn, 1988; Mitchell, Pyle, Hatsukami, Goff, Glotter, & Harper, 1988). In both studies, at least 75 percent continued to show improvement. Mitchell et al.'s (1988) follow-up study suggests a number of patients may experience periodic relapses into bulimic behaviors, indicating additional treatment is necessary. However, these and other studies with shorter follow-up intervals (e.g., Wilson, Rossiter, Kleinfield, & Lindholm, 1986) show that the gains evident immediately following treatment are likely to be either maintained or increased.

Pharmacological Treatments. The role of pharmacological treatment for bulimia is unclear. Antidepressants appear to help many bulimics (e.g., Pope & Hudson, 1982). They are more effective than placebos and cause a complete remission of symptoms for some bulimics. In contrast, other bulimics show no improvement with antidepressants, and most of those who do improve later relapse after the medication is withdrawn (Pope, Hudson, Jonas, & Yergelun-Todd, 1985). Results obtained with antidepressants are generally not as good as those obtained with cognitive-behavioral therapy (CBT) (Mitchell, Pyle, Eckert, Hatsukami, Pomeroy, & Zimmerman, 1988). Other studies also indicate that the addition of pharmacological treatment to CBT does not enhance CBT's effectiveness (e.g., Mitchell et al., 1988). Finally, antidepressant medication appears to *increase* dietary restraint and may even be incompatible with the therapeutic goal of having the patient reinstate a normal caloric intake (Craighead & Agras, 1991).

Different Treatments for Different Results? The treatments we have discussed may affect different causes of bulimia nervosa. Behavioral treatments may modify the cognitive and/or behavioral components associated with severely restrained eating, whereas interpersonal therapy may decrease negative emotional states, increase self-esteem, and improve interpersonal relationships. Both results could

BOX 13.4 Problematic Eating

The prevalence of problematic eating appears to be rising. In a survey of Ohio females in the ninth through twelfth grades, 46 percent reported engaging in periods of excessive uncontrolled eating (i.e., binge-eating). Of those reporting binge-eating, 24 percent said that they did so at least once a week. Eleven percent of the sample revealed they vomited and 5 percent used laxatives. While a large percent of these adolescent females engaged in bulimic-like behaviors, only 8 percent of the sample met *DSM-III* criteria for bulimia. Four percent binged frequently enough to meet *DSM-III-R* criteria for bulimia nervosa (Crowther, Post, & Zaynor, 1985).

There have also been several surveys of college students' eating patterns. In one, 43 percent of the women reported a history of binge-eating, and 12 percent purged to control weight. In contrast to these behaviors' frequency, only 4 percent of the women met *DSM-III-R* criteria for bulimia nervosa (Striegel-Moore et al., 1989).

The high frequency of binge-eating among these populations has led several investigators to argue that binge-eating alone is not necessarily abnormal. Nonbulimic binge-eaters reported their eating habits were only moderately disruptive, and only 25 percent of these women expressed a desire for treatment of their eating habits (Katzman, Wolchik, & Braver, 1984). Despite these young women's lack of concern about their eating habits, one survey concluded that 45 percent of nonbulimic women were depressed following an episode of binge-eating (Gray & Ford, 1985). An increased need for social approval also seems to be associated with adolescent females' compulsive eating (Kagan & Squires, 1983). In sum, while binge-eating and purging may be common among adolescent females, these behaviors do not appear to be without negative consequences.

be successful because they provide the bulimic with effective coping strategies and behaviors. Pharmacological interventions, in contrast, have antidepressant and antianxiety effects decreasing negative emotion states and thereby reducing disordered eating. These antidepressant and/or antianxiety effects are only present while the bulimic takes the drug. After medication is withdrawn, negative emotional states, and hence disordered eating, may reemerge because neither the bulimic's coping strategies nor environment (e.g., social pressures) has been modified.

DRUG ABUSE AMONG YOUNG PEOPLE

Alcoholism, drug abuse, and other addictive problems were discussed in some detail in Chapter 11. Yet any discussion of special problems among adolescents and young adults is incomplete without some mention of drug use and abuse. Rising concern about drug use led to "Just Say No" campaigns headed by First Lady Nancy Reagan in the 1980s. Opinion polls like the one shown in Table 13.6 (Barrett, 1989) indicate that drug problems outrank all other issues that the general population is willing to pay money to change, except for providing medical care for young children. Prompted by repeated polls, President George Bush began a "War on Drugs" emphasizing law enforcement and prevention. Public concern about substance abuse has been heightened by the

Some adolescents get hooked on crack, a smokable cocaine derivative, because of its availability in many towns. It is one of the most addictive drugs.

TABLE 13.6 Would You be Willing to Pay Higher Taxes if the Money Were Used for:

	Yes
Feeding and providing medical care for very poor children?	86%
Fighting the war on drugs?	79
Increasing benefits for retired people?	75
Improving public schools in communities like yours?	72
Reducing the federal budget deficit?	57
Ensuring modern weapons and equipment for the armed forces?	50

Source: Time, October 23, 1989, p. 34. "Giving the Public What It Wants" by L.I. Barrett. Taken from a telephone poll of 1,000 adult Americans taken for *Time/CNN* on October 9–10 by Yankelovich Clancy Shulman. Sampling error is plus or minus 3%. *Time* chart by Cynthia Davis. Copyright © 1989 by the Time Inc. Magazine Co. Reprinted by permission.

recent problem of **crack,** a smokable cocaine derivative. Cheap and readily available on many streets, it also has devastating effects: This very potent form of cocaine can reach the brain within seconds after being smoked or injected. A person can experience an intense "high" on crack within fifteen minutes after an injection. It is also believed to be one of the most addictive of all drugs.

Public alarm about drug use stems from more than concerns that America's teens and young adults are destroying their lives. It is also fueled by fear that innocent people may be victimized by robberies and violent acts committed by drug users, either as a result of consuming substances or to obtain money to purchase drugs. These fears are warranted: Forty-eight percent of all persons convicted of a crime in the United States in 1983 had consumed alcohol before committing the crime (see Chapter 11). Further, a twenty-two-city survey indicated illicit drug use by males in approximately two thirds of the cases when crimes were committed (U.S. Department of Justice, 1990).

Prevalence

A national survey of at least 10,000 high school seniors is conducted each year by the National Institute of Drug Abuse. The 1989 survey indicated that marijuana use has *declined* steadily since 1979 (*ADAMHA News*, April 1990). In 1986, 24 percent reported they had used marijuana in the last month; in 1987, 18 percent were users. Cocaine use has declined since 1986: In 1986, 6.2 percent of high school students surveyed indicated they had used cocaine within the past month. In 1989, that figure dropped to 2.8 percent.

Teens' greater concern about marijuana's harmful effects seem to be central to the decline in its use. The change in marijuana's perceived harmfulness is clearly reflected in a markedly increased concern about its damaging effects across the last decade. This concern about harmful effects seems to have also been felt about cocaine, since over half of high school seniors believe cocaine is quite harmful. Moreover, illicit drug use among high school seniors has clearly declined across the last decade (see Figure 13.4).

A major concern of health planners is that alcohol use among adolescents and young adults has *not* declined in several years. Sixty-six percent of high school seniors report being current users, and a striking 5 percent report daily drinking. Moreover, 37 percent report at least one occasion of heavy drinking (five or more drinks in a row) during the past two weeks (ADAMHA Update, March, 1988). Alcohol-related deaths at college fraternity "keg" parties have forced college students and administrators to reconsider the alcohol policies on college campuses (see Box 13.5).

Causes

A combination of biological, psychological, and social factors are risk factors for alcoholism (see Chapter 11). No single biological, psychological, or social explanation can account for alcohol and drug abuse problems among adolescents and young adults. Individuals with a family history of alcoholism themselves are at increased risk for developing problems, although most do *not* become alcoholics. Other key etiological variables include psychological factors

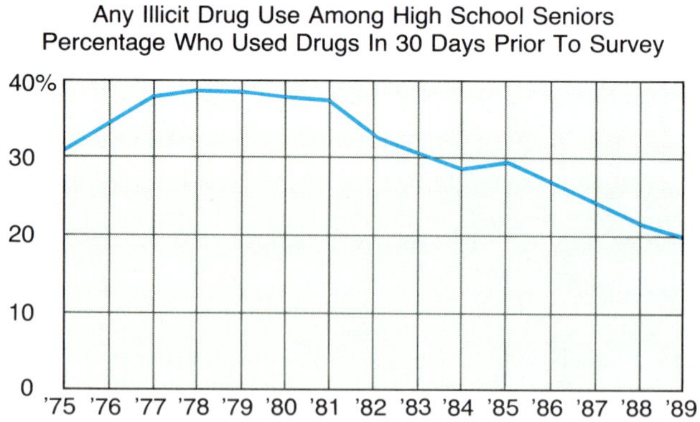

Figure 13.4 Decrease in Use of Illicit Drugs Continues *As can be seen in the figure, illicit drug use declined among high school seniors from 1979 to 1989. "Any illicit drug" includes any use of marijuana, hallucinogens, cocaine, and heroine, or any use of other opiates, stimulants, sedatives, or tranquilizers not under a doctor's orders.*
Source: ADAMHA News, April 1990.

BOX 13.5 Drinking Themselves to Death

Rutgers University has now banned fraternity and sorority parties indefinitely, too late to save James Callahan but maybe soon enough to keep other young people from drinking themselves to death. That's what Mr. Callahan, an 18-year-old freshman, apparently did at an initiation party.

His death followed by less than a week a near-fatality at Princeton, where a student drank himself into a coma during an initiation party at an eating club. Both incidents come at a time of heightened concern among college administrators about alcohol abuse. They point up the difficulty of translating administrative concern on this subject into safe, intelligent student behavior.

Students and alcohol have always been a tricky combination, but as Rutger's late president, Edward Bloustein, observes, there appears now to be "a growing trend of abusive use of alcohol" on campuses. Some experts say that as students turn away from illicit drugs, they see alcohol as a safe, and generally legal, alternative. In Mr. Callahan's case, however, it was neither.

By all accounts, Rutgers has an exemplary program of alcohol abuse education. But Mr. Callahan got none of its benefits because the Lambda Chi Alpha fraternity did not seek a required university permit for its party. At the same time, it was no secret that pledges were being initiated last week.

The same hands-off attitude prevailed at Princeton. For complex legal reasons, the university has distanced itself from the eating clubs. The local police also keep their distance, respecting the constitutional rights of the club members to privacy unless they create a public disturbance.

That is pretty much the case nationwide. Except where they are hosts or landlords, institutions cannot do much except advise and educate their students on the responsible use of alcohol. Whether to follow the advice is for the students to decide. Their lives, as the James Callahan tragedy demonstrates, are in their own hands.

Many adolescents and young adults drink themselves into unconsciousness and death. Because of the alcohol related deaths on college campuses, many universities are changing drinking policies at fraternity parties.

BOX 13.6 Adolescent Runaways and Throwaways

One out of ten American teen-agers runs away from home at least once. Approximately 500,000 leave home annually; these kids are called *runaways*. There are more than one million runaways on U.S. city streets. In order to support themselves, they are often forced to hustle drugs and sex. Many migrate to "hot spots" like Times Square in New York City, the Sunset Strip in Los Angeles, or the beaches of Fort Lauderdale where large enough clienteles enable them to support themselves in this manner. Most, however, run away to places not more than 300 miles from home.

Kids leave home for many reasons, with the most likely being poor relations with their parents, extreme family conflict, little supervision, and lots of parental criticism. Approximately 74 percent of runaways report leaving home because they were not getting along with their parents. Incest and physical abuse are often reasons given by the runaways for their flight. Poor self-esteem, depression, and social isolation commonly characterize these adolescents.

Running away is a special problem of adolescence. Its magnitude is immense, and the problem is very difficult to manage. While depression and poor self-esteem are common problems of runaways, kids who run away do not always have a clearly diagnosable mental or physical illness at the time that they run away. Moreover, many would be more correctly labeled *throwaways*, or kids encouraged or asked to leave home (Adams, Gullotta, & Clancy, 1985). In San Francisco, 68 percent of parents of runaways called by a social worker from the Larkin Youth Center said, "You keep the kid" (*Newsweek*, April 15, 1968).

About 10 percent of adolescents run away from their homes. Most of these adolescents leave because they do not get along with their parents.

such as modeling and expectations of alcohol reducing anxiety. Membership in an ethnic group that traditionally uses alcohol primarily for intoxication purposes (e.g., Irish-Americans, black Americans) also increases risk. Yet, a more complete understanding of alcohol and drug abuse among youths requires consideration of some additional etiological factors.

Peer Pressure. Peer pressure is currently viewed as the primary risk factor for drug use and abuse among teens and young adults. However, several major longitudinal investigations indicate that peer relations and pressure to use drugs and alcohol are necessary but not sufficient to predict drug use. It may be that peer groups are critical at the moment of choice about whether and what type of substance a young person may use.

The inability to resist peer pressure is highly related to substance abuse in white, black, and Hispanic adolescents (Wills, Baker, & Botvin, 1989). Such results are in accord with the prevention programs emphasizing saying "No" to drugs. Moreover, students' lack of skill to say "No" to drugs was associated with drug use as early as seventh grade, and it was hypothesized that this lack of assertiveness may have been rooted in childhood family variables.

Family Background/Personality. Family and personality factors leading teen-agers to identify with particular peer groups are also of special importance in motivating substance abuse. Family and personality variables assessed as early as nursery school and elementary school have been shown to predict later drug use. Drug use in adolescent girls is predicted by unstructured and *laissez-faire* homes where their behavior is poorly monitored (Block, Block, & Keyes, 1988). Lack of emotional control in nursery school and elementary school also predicts adolescent drug use among boys. Longitudinal research from preschool to eighteen years shows important differences between adolescents who experiment with drugs and those who become frequent drug users. Teens abusing drugs had distinct personality styles as early as age seven. As children, they had poor impulse control, were alienated from others, and insecure. They were unable to concentrate and had mood shifts. Their mothers were cold, unresponsive to their needs, and underprotective. These mothers gave their children little encouragement while overtly pressuring them to do well (Shedler & Block, 1990). This research suggests that frequent drug abuse is a *symptom* not a cause of personal problems. The prevention of drug abuse then does not lie in eliminating simple experimentation. The family structure of high-risk populations will have to be addressed before they reach their teen-age years.

Homelessness. Finally, government surveys about drug use and abuse are completed by high school seniors, and, therefore, these figures underrepresent drug use and abuse since many teens have dropped out of school and live on the streets. These runaways and throwaways add significantly to the nation's substance abuse and crime problems (see Box 13.6).

Prevention

School and community-based prevention programs have recently proved effective in reducing experimentation with drugs like crack and cocaine. Since law enforcement efforts have generally failed to re-

Successful programs aimed at preventing drug abuse involve the combined efforts of community members, the media, and the schools. One central message of such programs is that crack is harmful.

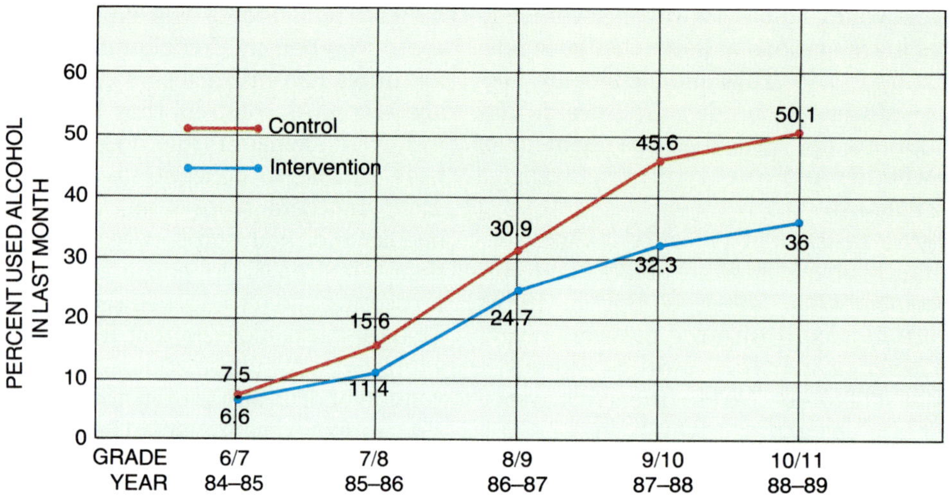

Figure 13.5 Alcohol Use *The Prevention Project was associated with a lesser alcohol use as compared to adolescents who did not receive a prevention program.*
Source: Midwestern Prevention Research Project, National Institute on Drug Abuse, June 1, 1990.

duce cocaine's availability, the recent prevention research is promising. For example, in fifty middle and junior high schools in Kansas City and fifty-seven similar schools in Indianapolis, students randomly picked to participate in the prevention programs used crack half as much as those not in the program. Adolescents in the program also used marijuana, cigarettes, and alcohol less often than those not in the program as shown in Figure 13.5. Unlike most other school prevention programs, this one involved the combined efforts of the media, parents, community, and schools in delivering antidrug messages to the young people. According to Dr. Louis Sullivan, secretary of Health and Human Services, ". . . drug abuse prevention is our first line of defense in reducing this nation's demand for illicit drugs" (Treaster, 1990).

SUMMARY

1. Depression is more common among adolescents and young adults than among any other age group. In the United States and England, it is more common among adolescents than their parents.
2. Depression is more prevalent and more severe among female adolescents and young adults than among male peers.
3. Factors associated with depression in adolescence include lack of closeness with parents, orientation toward peers to the exclusion of parents, and minor delinquent acts. In young adults, depression is often associated with failures in coping with the stresses of becoming independent from parents, relationship problems (boyfriend, girlfriend), and academic and job difficulties.
4. Many symptoms of depression in adolescents and young adults are similar to those in adults. Dejected mood and loss of gratification from pleasurable activities are among the most common symptoms. In adolescents, escape and withdrawal, especially through alcohol and drugs, are quite common. Aggression in varied forms exists simultaneously with many depressed adolescents, especially for males.
5. In accord with a multifactor view of the etiology of depression, a multimodal approach to treatment of depressed adolescents is most desirable, with family involvement as a critical and unique ingredient.
6. Suicide among adolescents and young adults has increased over 200 percent since the 1950s, making it the third leading cause of adolescent death. In Western Europe and the United States, the rates are roughly equivalent, but Japan's suicide rate among fifteen- to twenty-four-year-olds is higher than any other country's.
7. Suicide attempters and completers share one critical commonality: They usually send "messages" about their intent to significant people in their lives.
8. Approximately 75 percent of young people who commit suicide are males, with white males twice as likely as black males to commit suicide. The major risk factors for committing suicide include alcohol use, broken homes, death of a parent, suicide attempts among family members, academic pressure, boyfriend/girlfriend problems, and problems with parents.
9. Suicide attempts must always be taken seriously. One quarter of suicide attempters brought to emergency rooms have made previous attempts. Greater prevention and educational efforts to teach people to recognize suicide's risk factors are urgently required.
10. Anorexia nervosa and bulimia nervosa are eating disorders that develop in adolescence, especially in females. The common problem seen is a fear of being overweight, and the incidence for both problems appear to have increased in the last two decades.
11. Anorexics refuse to maintain adequate body weight. Bulimics binge-eat and use methods such as self-induced vomiting, diuretics, and laxatives to control their weight.

12. Anorexia has predominantly been a problem of upper-class female adolescents, but it will likely become more common among young women of all social classes as pressure to remain slim is adopted by all. The tremendous female–male difference in the prevalence of anorexia and bulimia is due largely to the disproportional pressure on females to remain thin.
13. Twin studies of anorexics and bulimics and family studies of affective disorders implicate biological factors in the etiology of both disorders. Many anorexics and bulimics have histories of being somewhat overweight before they enter a severe course of dietary restriction or binging and purging. Family interaction patterns, restrained eating, negative emotional states, (family psychiatric histories, and personality factors like anxiety and depression) are also associated with the development of eating disorders.
14. Treatment of severe anorexics usually starts with an inpatient intervention. Psychological treatments for anorexics in outpatient clinics involve social reinforcement for eating and changing dysfunctional attitudes toward staying thin. Pharmacological treatments to help stimulate appetite and stabilize weight have proven moderately useful. Family therapy has been effective in aiding some anorexics, especially teenagers.
15. Successful cognitive-behavioral treatment (CBT) for bulimia has involved response prevention, cognitive attitudinal change in eating, self-monitoring of anxiety, and encouragement to consume normal meals. Interpersonal psychotherapy (ITP) has been successful in reducing binging and general psychopathology in the bulimic.
16. Drug and alcohol use among teen-agers and young adults has become a national concern. Crimes against individuals are commonly related to substance abuse.
17. The rising concern of teen-agers and young adults about the dangerous effects of marijuana and cocaine have been associated with decreased use of both in the past few years. Alcohol use, however, has remained steady in teens, with alcohol-related deaths on campuses forcing reconsideration of alcohol policies at colleges and universities.
18. The road to alcohol and drug abuse is complex, and the key etiological variables include peer pressure and immediate situational stressors. Some risk factors for drug use are even evident in nursery and elementary school. Impulse problems of male school children and unstructured early home environments for girls place them at risk for drug use.
19. Prevention programs apparently hold great promise for reducing drug and alcohol abuse.

Pablo Picasso, *Seated Woman (after Cranach)* (1958). Color linoleum cut, composition, 25 11/16 × 21 5/16 inches. Collection of The Museum of Modern Art, New York. Gift of Mr. and Mrs. Daniel Saidenberg.

14 SCHIZOPHRENIA

Schizophrenics think and act in such unusual ways that people often refer to them as "mad," "crazy," or "insane." Schizophrenia is by far the most common of the mental disorders classified as a psychosis. Psychoses are disorders that involve altered perceptions and thoughts. There are many conditions that cause one to lose touch with reality, such as manic-depressive psychoses, organic brain syndrome, and paranoid states. In this chapter we will focus on schizophrenia. Biochemists, geneticists, psychiatrists, psychologists and sociologists have spent billions of research dollars trying to solve the mystery of this disorder. Journals are devoted exclusively to it (e.g., *Schizophrenia Bulletin*), and some federal research hospitals such as St. Elizabeth's Hospital in Washington, D.C. focus almost solely on its causes and treatment. Although considerable progress has been made in unraveling the mysteries of schizophrenia, we have no certain cure for it. We have, nevertheless, many clues about the causes of schizophrenia, and existing treatments enable many schizophrenics to cope with their illness sufficiently well to return to their jobs and families.

Carol North is one of the fortunate who was able to recover from schizophrenia. As a teen-ager, she heard imaginary voices and was diagnosed schizophrenic during college. Yet, having nearly lost her life fighting this disease, she is now a psychiatrist treating other schizophrenics. North's book, *Welcome, Silence: My Triumph Over Schizophrenia* (1987), documents the experiences of her trial with this disorder. Her accounts of coping with voices vividly portray her fear as she revealed them first to her high school counselor and later to her psychiatrist:

> *The voices, reflecting my confusion, kept up running commentaries among themselves. Usually they stayed in the distant background, chattering away nonsensically, like people at a cocktail party in the next room. I generally didn't pay their conversation much attention, but when I heard them talking about me I couldn't help listening in.*
>
> *"She's in here," I heard one of the voices say. "She's on that side," said another voice.*
>
> *What side? I thought. I knew they were talking about me, but I didn't understand what they were saying. I strained to hear every word. I didn't want to be last to know the ultimate truths.*
>
> *"Come to our side," one of the voices enticed me. "You're confused. We know. We have the answers."*
>
> *How did they know all that? If they really did, then they must have cosmic connections. Their words rang of the truth.*
>
> *"What do I have to do?" I asked.*
> *"Dispense with life as you know it."*
> *"Why?"*
> *"You won't need it, there's so much more."*

St. Elizabeth's Hospital in Washington, D.C. is famous for its research and treatment of schizophrenia. John Hinckley, who shot President Reagan, was treated at St. Elizabeth's.

"But how?"

"Pull the plug on the machinery."

"What?"

"Your body. It's a machine . . . lean . . . green . . . obscene . . . ." (pp. 67–68)

I couldn't concentrate on my schoolwork. It was insignificant next to the cosmic matters I was facing. I felt trapped, and there were no solutions. I went to my school counselor.

"I don't like my classes" was the most I could manage to tell her.

"What kind of problems are you having?" she asked.

"Mostly problems with my parents," I told her.

It was true; I thought my mother was reading my thoughts. I often glared at my mother with hostile eyes. She glared back at me. I had been practicing thought-scrambling so much at home that now my thoughts were starting to come out scrambled spontaneously, and I didn't even have to try anymore to produce nonsense. And sometimes when I couldn't produce any thoughts at all, I blamed my mother for stealing them right out of my mind. Yes, I was having problems with my mother.

Just then the voices opened the door to the counselor's office so fast they couldn't be seen, said "Go to hell!" and shut it again. I whipped around to face the door. The counselor looked, too.

"What was that?" she asked.

"People I know," I said.

"But I didn't get to see them."

The counselor referred me to a psychiatrist. (pp. 69–70)

"What kind of problems have you been having?" Dr. Marshall (the psychiatrist) asked me.

"Problems with school and problems with my parents."

Dr. Marshall looked puzzled.

"Can you tell me more?"

This was going to be tough. I didn't even know how to start to explain my real concerns. I didn't know what questions to ask. After a very long pause, I said, "I haven't been able to tell anyone this before." I was trying to buy another moment, hoping I could formulate my questions. . . .

"Well, who do you talk to about what's bothering you?"

I shook my head again. I couldn't seem to start talking. I didn't think I could possibly tell him I talked to voices. Already it seemed that this meeting wasn't going to be too productive. Dr. Marshall asked me several questions about my friends, school, and family. I answered each question briefly, as accurately as I could, trying to avoid exposing any of my scrambled thoughts. No, I didn't socialize with a lot of friends; other people didn't seem to understand me. No, I wasn't in serious academic difficulty at school, I *just couldn't concentrate on the work. Yes, my parents were a problem; my mother was critical of everything. I couldn't seem to find a way to crack the barrier to the important issues. (p. 71)*

During college, Carol North's boyfriend, Steve, became concerned about her hearing voices and her refusal to move from her bed. To him, she seemed almost paralyzed. He carried her to the psychiatric hospital of the university where she was given an intravenous injection to reduce her anxiety and enable her to move.

"What's the matter with my girlfriend?" Steve had asked.

Without looking directly at him, the doctor had said, "She's a catatonic schizophrenic." The doctor felt an obligation to answer Steve honestly, whether or not it meant transgressing my legal right to confidentiality as a mental patient.

"Schizophrenic?" Steve repeated. "You mean, like a split personality? I don't think she's like that." Still looking past Steve toward the far side of the room, the doctor explained, "Schizophrenia isn't a split personality. It's a split from reality, and believe me, buddy, your girlfriend's got it bad." (North, pp. 92–93)

Although schizophrenia is often associated with severely impaired functioning, Carol North's remarkable recovery shows the ability of some people to overcome schizophrenic symptoms and lead productive lives.

The first to describe schizophrenia was Emil Kraepelin, a professor of psychiatry in Munich, Germany. In 1889, he grouped several types of mental abnormalities under one heading, **dementia praecox,** the early term for schizophrenia. The term *dementia praecox* literally meant progressive mental deterioration in early life. All dementia praecox, Kraepelin believed, involved personality deterioration, and he identified three subtypes: catatonia, hebephrenia (later called *disorganized* schizophrenia; *DSM-III-R,* 1987), and paranoia. According to Kraepelin (1971), this disease's causes became evident only during post-mortem brain analyses. He believed that organic changes in the brain were the primary cause of dementia praecox and that psychological factors were of secondary importance in its etiology. Kraepelin suggested the disorder started in early adolescence and was incurable because of the brain's deterioration.

Modern views differ from Kraepelin's about schizophrenia's onset and its prognosis. Most schizophrenics are admitted to hospitals in late adolescence and early adulthood, but the first schizophrenic episode can occur at almost any point in life. Many schizophrenics suffer more than one serious episode although they may also experience long, symptom-free periods. Despite inadequacies, Kraepelin's careful descriptions of symptoms and disorders were very influential, as evidenced by the eight editions of his textbook, *Clinical Psychiatry.* The last edition, published in 1915, included detailed descriptions of thirty-six subcategories of dementia praecox.

Emil Kraepelin, a German psychiatrist, coined the term dementia praecox *and was among the first to classify mental disorders.*

The Swiss psychiatrist Eugene Bleuler, who coined the term **schizophrenia** in 1908, disagreed with Kraepelin about some important features of the disorder. Schizophrenia does not, Bleuler (1951) argued, necessarily have an early onset and does not inevitably lead to mental deterioration. In contrast to Kraepelin's views, Bleuler believed recovery was possible. But, like Kraepelin, Bleuler believed the individual's biological makeup plays an important role in causing schizophrenia, and, consequently, the disorder is likely to recur.

Bleuler placed less emphasis on the prognosis of schizophrenia than Kraepelin did and attempted to identify an underlying psychological feature of the disorder. Bleuler believed that the common denominator in schizophrenia involves a loosening of associations between thoughts and feelings. According to Bleuler, the breaking of these hypothetical associations results in the disrupted and unusual behavior observed in schizophrenic patients.

BOX 14.1 Is Schizophrenia a Split Personality?

The most common misconception about schizophrenia is that it refers to people with "split personalities." The syndrome of split or multiple personalities portrayed in popular movies, such as *The Three Faces of Eve*, is extremely rare and differs from schizophrenia. Multiple personalities is a dissociative disorder in which a person has two or more separate "ego states" which have no contact with each other (see Chapter 6). Each personality exists independently of the other and has a unique set of affective and behavioral styles. Like schizophrenics, people with multiple personalities may complain sometimes of being controlled by voices or other people. However, in contrast to schizophrenia, someone with multiple personality displays two or more highly developed personalities, as if two or more individuals were coexisting in the same body.

Much of the confusion stems from the term *schizophrenia*, which derives from the Greek word *schizein* (split) and *phren* (mind), and literally means splitting of the mind. As originally defined by Bleuler (1950), the split in schizophrenia refers to a separation or loosening of associations. Most critical was a split or separation between thought and feeling, as evidenced when a person laughs and smiles while describing a horrifying event. In sum, the split of associations which Bleuler believed underlies schizophrenics' unusual behavior differs from a split in personality.

PREVALENCE

Approximately 1 percent of the population becomes schizophrenic during their lifetime. Although this figure may seem small in comparison to the prevalence of affective or depressive disorders, schizophrenia has severe effects on behavior. An enormous number of people are incapacitated or maintain a low level of functioning because of schizophrenia. Schizophrenics are the major users of hospital beds in the United States, filling approximately 40 percent of the total number of beds in psychiatric and nonpsychiatric hospitals.

Schizophrenia's onset usually occurs before age forty-five. The median age of first hospital admission for schizophrenia is around thirty years. Its prevalence is approximately equal in developed and underdeveloped countries, appearing in all races, with similar types of symptoms observed across diverse cultures. Still, it is much more common among lower socioeconomic classes, especially among the urban poor (Hollingshead & Redlich, 1958; Kohn, 1968).

Gender Differences

Schizophrenia afflicts approximately equal numbers of males and females. However, the age of first hospital admission in the United States and Europe tends to differ for males and females. Up to age thirty, the rates are much higher for males, whereas after age thirty they are much higher for females (Zigler & Levine, 1981). In adolescence, the male–female ratio of first admissions is about 2:1, whereas at fifty-five to sixty years, the male–female ratio is about 1:2 (see Figure 14.1). We do not know why adolescent males are at higher risk for hospital admission for schizophrenia than adolescent females. Some experts feel boys are more likely to be hospitalized earlier because parents and teachers may react more strongly to disordered behavior in boys than in girls; also, adolescent males with schizophrenia may be more prone to act aggressively than their female counterparts.

DEFINITION AND SYMPTOMS OF SCHIZOPHRENIA

The very definition of schizophrenia has been evolving since the early efforts of Kraepelin and Bleuler. The American Psychiatric Association's *DSM-III-R* (1987) criteria for a diagnosis of schizophrenia include

1. Psychotic symptoms during the active phase of the illness.
2. Duration of problems for at least six months.
3. Deterioration from previous level of functioning.

At some point serious disturbances of thought (delusions), perception (hallucinations), or certain disturbances in affect must be present. Even with these symptoms, the diagnosis is made only when an organic factor, such as a brain tumor, is clearly not the disturbance's cause.

Schizophrenia generally involves impairment in several areas of functioning and multiple symptoms. It is important to note that no single psychotic symptom must be present to make the diagnosis and that a number of schizophrenia's classic symptoms are also seen in other disorders. Impaired functioning at work, home, in social situations, or in caring for oneself distinguishes schizophrenia from disorders involving isolated symptoms, such as a delusional belief

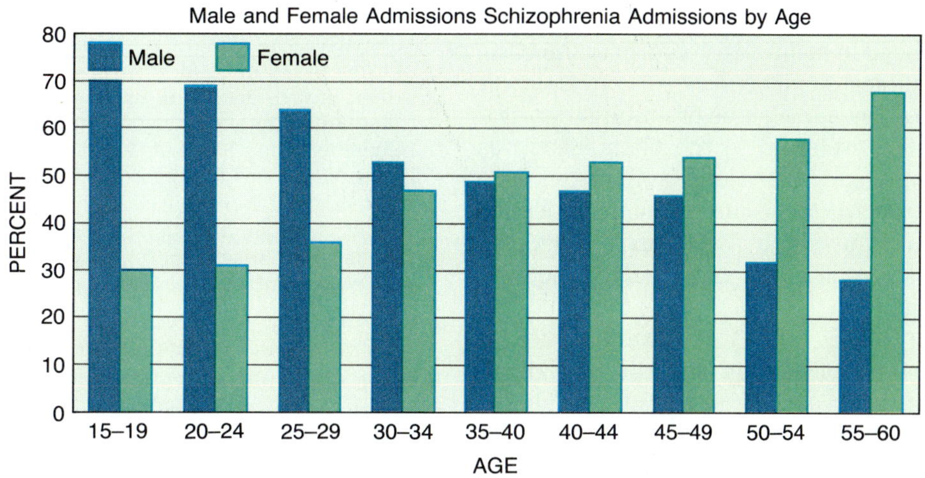

Figure 14.1 **Male and Female Admissions** *Male and female schizophrenia admissions to psychiatric hospitals differ by age groups. At younger ages, males predominate whereas at older ages, females predominate.*

Source: Adapted from Rosenthal, D. (1970). Genetic research in the schizophrenic syndrome. In R. Cancro (Ed.), *The schizophrenic reactions*, pp. 245–258. New York: Brunner/Mazel.

in a person who functions without any impairment at work or in social relations. Interpersonal relations problems are almost always present in schizophrenia, and schizophrenics generally withdraw from others and become emotionally detached. On the other hand, a schizophrenic overwhelmed with fantasies and illogical thoughts may cling to others for validation of these thoughts and, therefore, become excessively dependent on them. Volitional problems—a lack of drive, motivation, and interest—are also characteristic of schizophrenia. In brief, schizophrenics often seem unable to initiate activity, and this inability contributes to their impaired functioning in various areas.

Schizophrenia's classic symptoms include thought disorders, such as illogicality and delusional beliefs; perceptual disturbances, including auditory and visual hallucinations; affect disturbances, including lack of expression and inappropriate emotional expression; and psychomotor disturbances, such as abnormal mannerisms and maintaining uncomfortable poses.

Thought Disorders

Since Bleuler's (1950) original emphasis on loosening of associations, scholars have generally agreed that thought disorder, or disordered thinking, is one of schizophrenia's major features. As previously described, Bleuler viewed thought disorder, or a loosening of associations, as a fundamental psychological dysfunction in schizophrenia. To illustrate this, Bleuler used the example of a schizophrenic's short story "The Blossoming-Time of Horticulture." The unedited story began:

> At the time of the new moon venus stands in the Augutsky of Egypt and lights up with its light rays the merchant-travel-harbours of Suez, Cairo and Alexandria. In this historically famous Caliphcity is the museum of Assyrian statues from Macedonia. Besides pisang, also corn, oats, clover and barley grow there. Bananas, figs, lemons, oranges and olives. Olive oil is an Arabian liqueur sauce which the Afghans, Blackamoors and Moslemites use for ostrich breeding. . . . (Cutting, 1985, p. 309)

Although thought disorder is generally agreed upon as an important feature of schizophrenia, its exact role is still unclear. Harrow and Quinlan (1985) conducted a major research program on thought disorders in schizophrenia for over fifteen years and summed up the state of knowledge:

> Disordered thinking is a prominent and nearly universally agreed upon feature of schizophrenia, and is frequently considered a part of psychosis in general. That illusory agreement breaks down as soon as we ask, "What is the disorder in disordered thinking?" Answers to such a question frequently illuminate more about how or where the responder was trained than about the nature of disordered thinking. (p. 4)

Alternatively stated, no uniform agreement exists about the nature of disordered thought. Yet, clinicians generally agree on two subcategories: (1) disorders of form or process and (2) disorders of content. Disorders of form or process refer to the manner in which ideas are presented, the style and organization of thought, sometimes known as disorders of language and communication. Disorders of content refer to the actual confused ideas often expressed by schizophrenics.

Disorders of Thought Form. Disorders of thought form are evidenced in failures to conform to the basic rules of communication. This lack of conformity is not the effect of low intelligence or cultural deprivation. Meehl (1962) referred to the phenomenon as **cognitive slippage,** or the use of words from ordinary language that, at first hearing, sound as if they were communicating ideas. After quick reflection, however, listeners realize they have understood little of what was said.

Andreasen (1979a; 1979b) reviewed numerous clinical descriptions of thought and language disorders. She combined similar terms and excluded terms clinicians could not agree about. Through this process, she arrived at eighteen mutually exclusive thought, language, and communication disorders. Some of the most common were poverty of speech content, tangentiality and derailment, and illogicality.

Poverty of speech content is speech content that, although adequate in length, conveys little information. This type of speech is characterized by a loss of richness, circumlocution (i.e., going from one topic to another without any logical transition), and general "padding" (i.e., added speech without added meaning). Andreasen (1979a) illustrated poverty of speech content by showing a schizophrenic's answer to the question, "What sort of person are you?"

> Ah one hell of an odd thing to say perhaps in these particular circumstances. I happen to be quite pleased with Who I am or how I am and many of the problems that I have and have been working on are difficult for me to handle or to work on because I am not aware of them as problems which upset me personally. (p. 1318)

Tangentiality and *derailment* are the most typical characteristics of schizophrenic language. Tangentiality refers to oblique or irrelevant responses to questions. Derailment refers to spontaneous speech in which ideas seem to skip to other related ideas. Both processes may be described as loose associations or flight of ideas. Tangentiality and derailment are characterized by abnormal slipping off the initial train of thought. However, tangentiality is seen in the schizophrenic's response to a question whereas derailment is observed in the schizophrenic's spontaneous speech. Cutting (1985) suggests the apt general term of *derailment* describes both processes, for it brings to mind a train gradually slipping off the rails, with the caboose becoming more and more dissociated from the engine on the track. Tangentiality is seen in the response of one of Cutting's schizophrenic patients to the question, "How are things at home for you?"

> What I'm saying is my mother is too ill. No money. It all comes out of her pocket. My flat's leaking. It's ruined my mattress. It's Lambeth Council. I'd like to know what the caption in the motto under their coat of arms is. It's in Latin. It must mean that you've got semen in you, the spunk to do something. The other thing I'm telling you is my birth certificate. Do you remember when I was in that hospital; I was on my knees. Well I was frightened of those nurses. Well they were stealing. Well I burnt all my papers. Look at this now. It is a coin, from Jersey. That's where all the criminals go, Jersey. I'm telling you all this because my wife wants British nationality. (p. 250)

Scores of studies have addressed the specific nature of schizophrenics' thought disorders, and progress has helped refine some of Bleuler's original conceptualizations. For example, we have learned that schizophrenics do poorly on short-term memory tasks. An inability to selectively screen out irrelevant information is thought to contribute to impaired information processing in schizophrenics. Without this ability their train of thought becomes disorganized (Neale & Oltmanns, 1980). However, no single cognitive deficit appears to account for the range of thought disorders observed in schizophrenia.

Illogicality, as the name implies, refers to conclusions that do not follow logically from what has been said. The following example from a chronic schizophrenic illustrates this symptom.

Doctor:	*How long have you been in this hospital?*
Patient:	*29 years.*
Doctor:	*What is the matter with you?*
Patient:	*Pneumonia.*
Doctor:	*That's a long time to have had pneumonia.*
Patient:	*I caught it from a thermometer at Guy's Hospital. The thermometer said that everyone of the age of 20 would get either flu or pneumonia and I got pneumonia. .*
Doctor:	*In my view thermometers only measure temperature. They don't actually specify what illness people have.*
Patient:	*Well you better go back and look up your medical books.* (Cutting, 1985, p. 250)

Disorders of Thought Content. Schizophrenic patients' expressed ideas clearly distinguish them from nonschizophrenic patients. These ideas reflect beliefs not shared by others; as such, they lead the average individual to conclude that the person holding them is crazy. Beliefs seen by most members of society as unusual misrepresentations of reality are called **delusions.** Delusions can take various forms. Their common feature is a firmly held conviction that most people judge to be unusual and false. Delusions are usually idiosyncratic, varying from individual to individual, which distinguishes them from unusual religions or cultural beliefs held in common by a group of people. Delusions are the most colorful and intriguing symptom displayed by schizophrenics. The following are several of the most common.

Delusions of Persecution. The essential theme of delusions of persecution or paranoia is well captured by the statement "people are out to get me." Approximately 65 percent of schizophrenics have such delusions (Sartorius, Shapiro, & Jablensky, 1974). Eileen, a patient described by Andreasen (1984), is one example. A nearly straight A high school student with high SAT scores, Eileen, nevertheless, found her first year of college extremely stressful. She phoned her parents frequently, complaining that the dormitory was "not safe." At home for Christmas vacation, she seemed preoccupied, worried, and aloof. Although she managed to complete her freshman year, Eileen did rather poorly for someone of her ability. Subsequently, she transferred from the large state university to a small college near her family. During weekends at home, she frequently expressed to her parents the fear of people "out to get her." Moreover, Eileen began to overinterpret minor events. When she couldn't find her car keys, Eileen believed her dormitory counselor had hidden them. When an instructor said a midterm exam would be difficult and advised students not to rely solely on lecture notes, Eileen believed he was singling her out and that she would be the only one to flunk the exam. Also, when she walked into a dining hall or a classroom, the young woman felt that people had just been talking about her and laughing at her. Because of her fears of others and their opinions of her, Eileen isolated herself almost totally, studying all the time.

Finally, the paranoid thoughts became focused and so fear-provoking they led to hospitalization. Home from school for the weekend, Eileen became tearful and started to shake and pace on Sunday, the day of her expected return to school. Finally, she confessed that she believed someone was going to take her life if she went back.

> She had been hearing a warning voice, which was an unfamiliar male voice, telling her, "Don't go back, Don't go back." She felt that several of the students were playing "mind games" with her and were controlling her thoughts and actions. For example, even from the distance of fifty miles, she could feel them sending her messages and trying to draw her back like a magnet. She was convinced that when she arrived, she would be physically harmed in some way. Her parents called the dormitory counselor, who indicated that Eileen's fears were obviously unfounded and that Eileen had been behaving in a peculiar and suspicious manner for a number of months, arousing concern in some of the residents that she was having some type of psychiatric problem. Several people, including the counselor, had urged her to see a doctor at Student Health, but she was unwilling to do so. Her parents took her to a local psychiatrist, who recommended hospitalization. **(Andreasen, 1984, p. 55)**

Delusions of Romance (Erotomania). John Hinckley, who was obsessed with actress Jodie Foster, is an interesting example of a schizophrenic displaying **erotomania,** a romantic delusion about someone. He believed he could win Jodie Foster's love by taking extreme measures to impress her (see Box 14.2). Although erotomania is not described in *DSM-III-R* (1987), schizophrenics sometimes display this symptom and it has become a subject of recent interest. The schizophrenic's delusion at times involves believing that a celebrity is romantically interested in him or her, when in fact no such personal relationship exists. The delusion may also involve unrealistic expectations about the likelihood of living with a celebrity; thus John Hinckley wrote on a postcard to Jodie Foster, "One day you and I will occupy the White House and the peasants will drool with envy" (*U.S. News and World Report,* May 17, 1982, p. 15). While not all targets of erotomania are celebrities, the delusion usually is focused on a person respected or highly esteemed because of their looks or power (e.g., a physician, a therapist, a teacher).

Interest in erotomania has been sparked by a marked increase over the last decade in the rate of disturbed individuals who follow and/or menace celebrities, perhaps because of the value our society attaches to celebrities. Psychiatrist Paul Dietz has studied over 5,000 letters to celebrities apparently written by people with delusions (Goleman, 1989). Based on the letters, Dr. Dietz judged that over two thirds of them were written by mentally ill people and approximately 65 percent of them were schizophrenic. The vast majority of letter writers never approach their romantic or otherwise inappropriate target; only one in eight, according to Dr. Dietz, tries to personally approach the celebrity. People with delusions of erotomania are usually withdrawn and lonely, typically have had few sexual encounters, and tend to focus on someone who could give them instant notoriety by virtue of his or her superior status or looks (Segal, 1989).

Delusions of Grandeur. Delusions of grandeur include beliefs that one is an especially important person, such as Jesus Christ, the Queen of England, Elvis Presley, or Michael Jackson. Beliefs that one has special powers, such as the capacity to control the world's destiny, are also considered delusions of grandeur.

Delusions of Control. Delusions of control occur when a person believes his or her thoughts or actions are controlled by external factors, such as forces or people on another planet.

BOX 14.2 John W. Hinckley: A Man Obsessed with Actress Jodie Foster

When most of us imagine a schizophrenic, we think about a person who acts crazy. We may have in mind disheveled people walking the streets, muttering to themselves. We may consider someone we know who was in a mental hospital but is now managing fairly well. Maybe we think also of John Hinckley, who shot President Ronald Reagan. Schizophrenics are all of these people. They are a diverse group of individuals who are victims of a puzzling and crippling disorder. Like John Hinckley, they are suffering from a thinking disorder producing unusual moods and behavior.

Hinckley was raised in a home where he had everything money could buy; yet the material goods provided by his wealthy Evergreen, Colorado, family were not enough to stem the friendless young man's withdrawal into a world of delusional fantasies. Hinckley's withdrawal began as a teen-ager when he spent almost all his free time listening to music in his room. At college, he invented a girlfriend so his parents would send him additional money. As he withdrew further into his own world, Hinckley identified with characters in songs and movies, even modeling himself after the character Travis Brickle, who rescued a twelve-year-old prostitute in the movie *Taxi Driver.* Like Travis, Hinckley began to collect guns. In the process, he became obsessed with actress Jodie Foster, who had played the twelve-year-old prostitute in the film. Following a long period of despair and depression during a summer recess from college, Hinckley hatched a grand scheme to meet his obsession, then a Yale undergraduate. Hinckley told his parents he needed $3,600 to enroll in a writing course. When his parents gave him the money, he headed for Yale to see Jodie Foster, who politely brushed him off. After several rebuffs from Foster, Hinckley withdrew, continued collecting guns, and started target practice. He also began stalking President Jimmy Carter and spent time in New York City looking for prostitutes who needed help.

Hinckley returned to his home in Colorado for sessions with psychiatrist John J. Hopper. Apparently, though, he did not reveal much about his fantasy life, perhaps because the psychiatrist was also treating Hinckley's parents.

On New Year's Eve, 1980, Hinckley recorded a message later made public at his trial:

> It's gonna be insanity if I even make it through the first few days. . . . Anything that I might do in 1981 would be solely for Jodie Foster's sake. And I mean that sincerely. I wanna make some kind of statement or something on her behalf. All I want her to know is that I love her. I don't want to hurt her or anything. I can't hurt anybody, really, I'm a coward, really.

Hinckley identified with another figure, the killer of John Lennon. Following Lennon's murder in 1980, Hinckley wrote, "Inside this mind of mine I commit first-page murder. I think of words that could alter history. . . . This mind of mine doesn't mind much of anything unless it comes to mind that I am out of my mind."

In March 1981, Hinckley's parents, with the consent of Dr. Hopper, told him he should leave their house. Soon after, he boarded a bus for New Haven, with a stopover in Washington, DC. One plan he had was to hijack a plane and demand Jodie Foster as ransom. Another was to commit mass murder at Yale. While in Washington, DC, he found it relatively easy to get close enough to shoot the President. Hinckley then wrote a final love letter to Jodie Foster, saying, "I will admit to you that the reason I'm going ahead with this attempt now is because I just can't wait any longer to impress you. I've got to do something to make you understand."

Shortly afterward, on March 30, 1981, Hinckley shot President Reagan outside the Washington Hilton. Diagnosed as schizophrenic, Hinckley was subsequently found not guilty by reason of insanity and placed in St. Elizabeth's Hospital for the mentally ill in Washington, DC.

Hinckley's delusional beliefs ultimately led to his desperate effort to impress Jodie Foster with his depth of affection for her. Prior to his attempt to assassinate the President, however, Hinckley had no history of aggressive behavior. It is important to note that while some schizophrenics commit violent acts, individuals with the disorder are not on the average more aggressive or dangerous than others. Traditionally, schizophrenics have been called lunatics, maniacs, and madmen, and such terms suggest dangerousness and unpredictability. However, the presumed danger posed by schizophrenics is largely a myth. Most, preoccupied with their own thoughts, withdraw into their own world, and pose little threat to others' safety.

Source: Camper, D., Kasendorf, M., Clausen, P., Monroe, S., Shapiro, D., & Taylor, J. (1982, May 24). The insanity plea on trial. *Newsweek,* pp. 56–61.

Although striking and colorful, delusions have not been extensively investigated. However, we do know that women and married people are the most likely to have delusions with sexual content; foreign-born Americans are the most prone to have paranoid delusions; and people from higher socioeconomic levels are the most likely to have delusions of grandeur. Delusions vary greatly in terms of the strength of belief, the bizarreness of the conviction, and the extent to which they dominate the person's life. Delusions are not unique to schizophrenia; for example, people with affective disorders occasionally have delusions of grandeur. The more bizarre the delusions, though, the more characteristic of schizophrenia.

Some researchers have interviewed recovered schizophrenics in search of the causes of delusions. These people see their delusions as an inability to synthesize perceptions quickly, a failure to be self-critical about the reality of perceptual experiences, a substitute or distraction from fears, and a defense against sin. Yet informative as these self-reports were, they did not explain why some individuals develop delusions whereas others do not.

Perception Disturbances

Hallucinations are abnormal auditory or visual perceptions. Hearing voices which do not really exist is schizophrenics' most common hallucination. Approximately 50 percent of schizophrenics report auditory hallucinations (World Health Organization, 1973). The voices may be single or multiple, male or female. Visual hallucinations are less common than auditory ones, but various types of visual hallucinations occur early in schizophrenia, such as seeing one's hands as larger than usual and one's penis as smaller. Visual hallucinations of a person's image are unusual unless associated with alcohol intoxication. Hallucinations are periodic, rarely have a musical content, and are exacerbated by social isolation (Alpert & Silvers, 1970). In addition, clinical reports of patients during tense or angry periods and continuous monitoring of their autonomic nervous system indicate heightened emotional arousal associated with hallucination (Slade, 1972; Cooklin, Sturgeon, & Leff, 1983).

Research findings indicate that schizophrenics actively engaged in an activity are unlikely to report hallucinations. In one study, Margo, Hemsley, and Slade (1981) restricted schizophrenic patients' visual and auditory input by having them wear goggles and by presenting them with white noise through headphones. As a control condition, patients read passages without goggles and listened to an interesting conversation without headphones. Subjects hallucinated most when their visual and auditory input was restricted. In contrast, they reported few hallucinations while reading prose or listening to an interesting conversation. Self-reports of schizophrenic patients also suggest less of a likelihood of hallucinating when absorbed in an activity, as illustrated in the following remark: "Isn't it funny. When I'm shoveling snow, I don't hear voices" (Strauss & Carpenter, 1981).

Almost everyone has had at least one or two sensory misperceptions during their lifetime. Usually, we quickly recognize these experiences as illusions. For example, we realize that no man was lurking behind the bush; it was just a branch that moved and the silhouette of another bush looked momentarily like a man crouching. These experiences are quite different from hallucinations, which can occur in the absence of any environmental stimulation. Schizophrenics do not recognize their hallucinations as misperceptions but experience them as quite real.

During the 1950s and 1960s, many researchers viewed hallucinations as resulting from faulty or disordered perceptions. Later, researchers saw the perceptual disturbance as a problem secondary to an attention disorder (McGhie & Chapman, 1961). During the last two decades, evidence has supported this view. In brief, schizophrenics appear to concentrate on details at the expense of getting "the broad picture" (Place & Gilmore, 1980). Their ability to screen out irrelevant stimuli seems impaired; as a result, their attention is easily diverted, and thoughts, ideas, and images race through consciousness. Thus, schizophrenics often report, "Everything gets through," or "My mind was filled with thoughts which seemed to dart through my head." Disordered attention may play a critical role in both perceptual disturbances and thought disorders. In fact, some researchers have had difficulty distinguishing hallucinations and delusions (Strauss, 1969; Chapman & Chapman, 1980). In Strauss's view, hallucinations and delusions are on a continuum: At one end are definite abnormal perceptions with clear physical qualities (hallucinations); at the other end are definite abnormal beliefs (delusions). Between them are phenomena reported by schizophrenics which have qualities of each.

Affect Disturbances

Schizophrenics' most typical affective disturbances are blunting or flattening of affect, inappropriate affect, and anhedonia or an inability to feel pleasure. *Blunt affect* is readily apparent in the schizophrenic's lack of emotional expressiveness in gesture, facial expression, and voice tone. Roughly half or more of schizophrenics suffer from flat or blunted affect (Boeringa & Castellani, 1982; Sartorious et al., 1974). Flat affect is also characteristic of patients with mood disturbances, mental retardation, and organic brain disorders; therefore, schizophrenics cannot be distinguished from individuals with other problems solely on the basis of blunted affect.

Inappropriate affect is affect out of context. It is incongruous with a particular situation, such as laughing at the news of a friend's death. This symptom has not been the subject of extensive research, but inappropriate affect distinguishes schizophrenics from other mental patients.

Anhedonia was first described by Rado and his colleagues (1956), who distinguished between physical and social anhedonia. Physical anhedonia is the loss of pleasure in eating, drinking, and sexual activity whereas social anhedonia is the loss of pleasure in

BOX 14.3 Are Schizophrenics Creative Geniuses?

Few, if any, famous politicians, scientists, or performers are known to have been schizophrenic. Artists, such as the painter Vincent Van Gogh, have more often been identified as schizophrenic. Late in his life, Van Gogh spent fifteen months in Arles of southern France, where he had one of the most productive bursts of artistic energy ever recorded. Working feverishly under the bright sun, Van Gogh completed over 200 paintings and scores of drawings between February 1888 and May 1889. Instead of resting at night, he often stuck candles on his hat and painted until dawn. Yet, it was also in Arles that Van Gogh slashed his left ear lobe with a razor and gave the lobe to a girl named Rachael, saying, "Keep this object like a treasure."

The son of a minister, Van Gogh at twenty-five had become an evangelist in Belgium. His attempts to help and serve the common people there were disastrous: The young man was so intense and his interpretations of Christian doctrine so liberal that he could not communicate them to others. He also alienated his superiors and then two years later turned to art. The choice was not entirely surprising; he had sketched since childhood and his brother Theo and several uncles were art dealers. Van Gogh led a relatively isolated life, but he wrote almost one letter a day, mostly to Theo, the only person who may have understood him. Theo was also his lifeline for food, giving him 100 francs per month. The following excerpts taken from Van Gogh's letters and diary reflect the artist's tormented state (Hulsker, 1971):

> July 1882—What am I in most people's eyes A nonentity, or an eccentric and disagreeable man—somebody who has no position in society and never will, in short, the lowest of the low (p. 23).
>
> March 1889—A certain number of people here [Arles] addressed a petition to the Mayor, describing me as a man not fit to be at liberty or something like that. The commissioner of police or the chief commissioner then gave them the order to shut me up again (p. 120).
>
> May 1889—I am again—speaking of my condition—so grateful for another thing. I gather from others that during their attacks they have also heard strange sounds and voices as I did, and that in their eyes too things seemed to be changing. And that lessens the horror that I retained at first of the attack I have had, and, which, when it comes on you unawares, cannot but frighten you beyond measure. . . . If I had not seen other lunatics close up, I should not have been able to free myself from dwelling on it constantly (pp. 126–127).

Vincent van Gogh (1853–1890), *Autoritratto* (1887). Scala/Art Resource.

social contact. Social anhedonia is more characteristic of schizophrenics than the physical type.

Although many schizophrenics display blunted emotions, most also experience intense emotions, particularly at their disorder's outset. These emotions commonly arise from frightening thoughts affecting many schizophrenics. As one schizophrenic explained:

> I think so deep that I am almost out of this world. Then you get frightened that you are going to get in a jam and lose yourself. That's when I get worried and excited. . . . It must look queer to people when I laugh about something that has nothing to do with what I am talking about, but they don't know what is going on inside and how much of it is running round in my head. (Cutting, 1985, p. 236)

Psychomotor Disturbances

Because of their unusual nature, schizophrenics' motor disturbances are obvious, the most common being abnormal mannerisms, grimacing, and posturing (Cutting, 1985; Abrams & Taylor, 1976). Mannerisms may include unusual movements while shaking hands, odd gesticulations, and peculiarities of writing and dress. Some schizophrenics pace like hyperactive adults. Harding, a mental patient in Ken Kesey's novel, *One Flew Over the Cuckoo's Nest* (1962), exemplifies these ritualistic mannerisms and grimaces:

> Harding's face and hands are moving faster than ever now, a speeded film of gestures, grins, grimaces, sneers. The more he tries to stop it, the faster it goes. When he lets his hands and face move like they want to and doesn't try to hold them back, they flow and gesture in a way that's real pretty to watch, but when he worries about them and tries to hold back he becomes a wild, jerky puppet doing a high-strung dance. Everything is moving faster and faster, and his voice is speeding up to match. (p. 58)

In contrast to this speeded up movement, schizophrenics with a symptom called **catalepsy** assume uncomfortable, nearly immobile stances. Catatonics may stand in a stationary position like tin soldiers, or

Van Gogh wanted to marry a pregnant prostitute who was an alcoholic, suffered from gonorrhea, and had a smallpox-pitted face. Theo advised Vincent to become somewhat self-sufficient financially before he married, and Theo was also convinced that Vincent's girlfriend, Sien, was incapable of fidelity. Sien herself also became aware that she and Vincent were probably not meant for each other, and she returned to prostitution.

During his relationship with Sien, Van Gogh was hospitalized for gonorrhea treatment. When he recovered, he attempted to care for himself as well as Sien and her newborn child of another father, but he did not marry her or any other woman. He sought, in vain, for a relationship with a female, but after Sien left him in 1883, he decided to return to his father's protection (Elgar, 1958).

In 1889, Van Gogh was committed to an asylum at Saint-Remy, where he painted prolifically. During the last year and a half of his life (he died in 1890), the artist painted over 300 canvases subsequently proclaimed brilliant. While he was in the asylum, Van Gogh's work was reviewed by the art critic, Aurier:

> What particularizes these works is the excess, excess in strength, excess in nervousness, in violence of expression . . . a kind of drunken giant, better able to move mountains than to handle bibelots (trinkets), an ebullient brain irresistibly pours its lava into all the ravines of art, a terrible and maddened genius . . . almost always on the edge of pathological. (Wallace, 1969, p. 161)

When he ended his life by shooting himself, Van Gogh was only thirty-seven years old. A definitive diagnosis for his illness is still unclear. The term *schizophrenia* had not yet been coined when Van Gogh was hospitalized in 1889. According to official records of Saint-Remy, he was admitted with hallucinations of sight and hearing which had caused him to mutilate himself by cutting off his ear. After he gained posthumous fame, Van Gogh was variously diagnosed as schizophrenic, epileptic, and alcoholic. Perhaps, he had symptoms of all three disorders, and, like many people who suffer from psychological disorders, one diagnosis cannot adequately describe his problems. In any case, it is astonishing that during his illness Van Gogh produced some of the greatest art of all time.

Despite the incredible abilities of individuals like Van Gogh, research attempts to link madness and creativity have generally not been successful. For experimental purposes, creativity is usually defined as the ability to come up with unique or unusual responses to a set of stimuli. For example, unusual responses on word association tests are believed to indicate creative or divergent thoughts, whereas common responses are believed to reflect convergent or impoverished thought patterns. Using varied scoring systems, the responses of schizophrenics and normal control subjects generally do not differ on such tasks (Cutting, 1985; Fuller & Kates, 1969). At least one study indicated that some schizophrenics do score higher than control subjects on tests requiring them to generate unusual uses for objects (Keefe & Magaro, 1980). Overall, however, the notion that schizophrenics are especially creative has not been confirmed by experimenters.

often they assume uncomfortable poses with an arm or leg held outright. It appears they could be pushed over if touched, yet upon approaching someone in such a pose, it becomes apparent that he or she expends a great deal of energy remaining in this motionless stance. In many ways, someone with catalepsy resembles a military guard standing at attention, refusing to speak, look, or even blink if talked to directly.

A few schizophrenics have a symptom called *waxy flexibility,* or a tendency to maintain whatever posture is imposed upon them. Indeed, they resemble a dancer placed in an awkward position by a partner, who then remains in it, to the audience's surprise (Fish, 1967).

Kraepelin accorded movement disorder the highest diagnostic significance of any symptom of dementia praecox. However, the number of schizophrenics presenting the severe movement problems described by Kraepelin is decreasing. In fact, while they comprised 20 percent of Kraepelin's cases, the severe movement disorder, catatonia, now occurs in approximately 5–10 percent of schizophrenics (Cutting, 1985). While the majority of chronic long-term schizophrenics have some movement disorder only a small percentage of acute schizophrenics (those with a sudden episode of psychotic symptoms) have such motor symptoms. For acute schizophrenics not under medication, coordination or tone of movement is generally undisturbed. Impaired fluency of movement and lack of psychomotor coordination, as evidenced in perseverative and involuntary movements, is more common among chronic schizophrenics (Cutting, 1985).

As discussed later, some involuntary movements, particularly lip smacking and tongue protrusion called **tardive dyskinesia,** are known side effects of antipsychotic medication. In general, however, since most schizophrenics receive antipsychotic medication, differentiating the extent movement disorders are related to long-term chronic schizophrenia and the extent they are side effects of long-term medication is very difficult. Although movement disorders can be a side effect of medication, they were observed and documented in patients a century ago, long before the advent of medication. Though the emphasis on severe movement disorders has waned since their original description by Kraepelin, neuropsychologists and neurologists are currently paying special attention to them. As neurological assessment techniques become increasingly sophisticated, research may improve our understanding of these perplexing symptoms.

TYPES AND PHASES OF SCHIZOPHRENIA

Though schizophrenics can present an extensive range of symptoms, any particular patient is likely to exhibit only a subset of the thought, perception, affect, and motor disturbances described. *DSM-III-R* (1987) follows the Kraepelinian tradition of subtyping schizophrenics into groups of patients displaying particular sets of symptoms. After reviewing the types of schizophrenia, we will examine the phases of the disorder.

Catatonic Type

Catatonic schizophrenics have marked psychomotor disturbances. They assume rigid postures and refuse to respond to requests or follow instructions. Often, catatonics seem to be in a stupor or trance-like state; occasionally, they alternate between extreme excitement and stupor. **Mutism,** or refusal to speak, is a common feature. Catatonia's prominent and unusual symptoms make it easy to diagnose. Onset is usually more sudden than other types of schizophrenia. Seen frequently in the 1950s and 1960s, the catatonic subtype of schizophrenia is now rarely diagnosed. The reasons for this decrease are not known; perhaps the widespread use of antipsychotic medications effectively limits the expression of catatonic symptoms.

Disorganized Type

Disorganized schizophrenics are characterized by verbal incoherence, grossly disorganized behavior, marked loosening of associations, and inappropriate affect. Disorganized schizophrenics do not display elaborated sets of delusions, as paranoid schizophrenics do. However, they may exhibit fragmentary delusions or hallucinations, whose content is not organized around a consistent theme. They may also display a variety of motor symptoms, such as unusual mannerisms and grimacing, as well as extreme social withdrawal and social impairment. Onset is early in life, and patients with this subtype seldom experience significant remissions or recoveries.

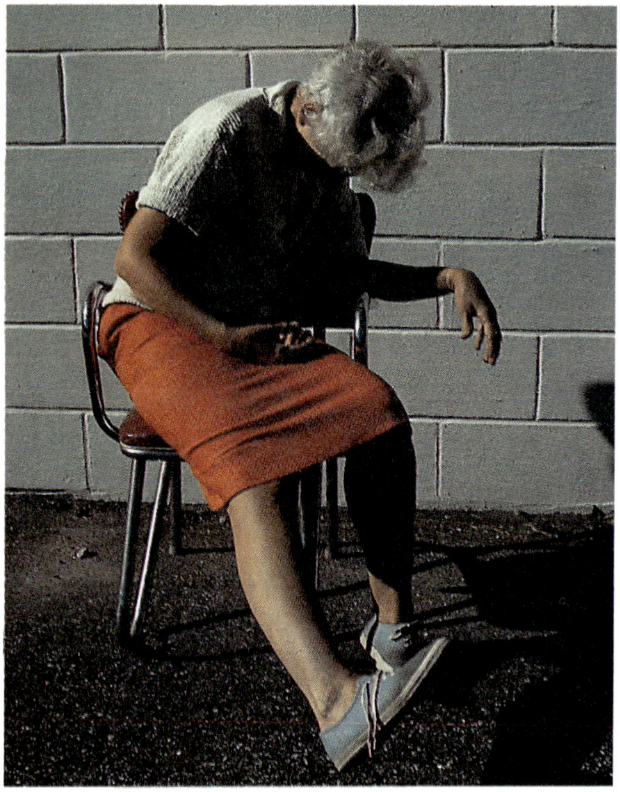

Catatonic patients often assume unusual physical positions and remain stationary in such positions until someone moves them.

Paranoid Type

Paranoid schizophrenics are preoccupied with one or more elaborated sets of delusions. They may also have auditory hallucinations associated with a single theme. Unlike disorganized schizophrenics, paranoid schizophrenics do not have grossly inappropriate affect or disorganized behavior, nor do they display the motor symptoms characteristic of the catatonic subtype. Paranoid schizophrenics sometimes show anger and are occasionally violent, if their delusions are intense and they fear physical harm, they may experience severe anxiety and panic. If they do not act upon their delusions, they continue to function reasonably well. In fact, the prognosis for paranoid schizophrenics may be much better than for the other types of schizophrenia.

Undifferentiated Type

Undifferentiated schizophrenics have psychotic symptoms, such as delusions, hallucinations, and incoherence. They do not, however, meet the specific criteria for the other subtypes.

Phases of Schizophrenia

To make a formal diagnosis of schizophrenia, indications of the disorder must be present for at least six months. Before psychiatric symptoms become clear, the person's level of functioning deteriorates during the *prodromal phase.* The patient often withdraws socially, neglects his or her grooming and dress, has difficulty communicating, shows a lack of initiative, and has some bizarre thoughts. During the prodromal phase, parents and friends are apt to notice a personality change in the individual, that he or she is "no longer the same person." The prodromal phase's exact duration is often difficult to pinpoint, but if the person gradually withdraws and shows increasingly unusual behavior over many years, the prognosis is poor.

During the *active phase,* the patient exhibits psychotic symptoms such as delusions, hallucinations, loose associations, and unusual motor behavior. The active phase's onset may be associated with some life stress such as a move, the birth of a child, the loss of a job, or a promotion. To diagnose schizophrenia, the clinician must observe that active, or psychotic, symptoms have been present for at least one week.

A *residual phase* follows the active phase. Similar to the prodromal phase, it is also characterized by social withdrawal, inactivity, and bizarre thoughts. Psychotic symptoms such as delusions and hallucinations may persist but are generally unaccompanied by strong affect. During the residual phase, flat affect is normally present along with impairment in social and vocational functioning.

POSITIVE AND NEGATIVE SYMPTOMS OF SCHIZOPHRENIA

Many researchers believe an alternative classification scheme may yield more useful information for the understanding and treatment of schizophrenia than the current *DSM-III-R* subtypes. The most popular subtyping scheme among researchers today is the positive and negative symptom division. Positive symptoms are "excess" behaviors such as hallucinations, delusions, and other symptoms of thought disorder. Negative symptoms include "deficits" such as flat affect, lack of drive, and relative absence of speech. Researchers have demonstrated a number of important empirical relationships with this symptom classification. Schizophrenics with negative symptoms, compared to those with positive symptoms, have more cognitive deficits, less education, lower intelligence, and greater problems in social functioning. They are more impaired at hospital admission and at hospital discharge. In addition, negative symptoms seem to be genetically influenced (Crow, 1985).

Positive symptoms appear to respond well to medication, and schizophrenics presenting these symptoms are more likely to function effectively after hospitalization. Biochemical problems involving the neurotransmitter dopamine appear to cause positive symptoms. Since these symptoms may be caused by biochemical imbalances, they may fluctuate with biochemical changes produced naturally or by prescribed medication. In contrast, since structural brain abnormalities are thought to cause negative symptoms, some clinical investigators believe they are irreversible (Crow & Johnstone, 1985).

All classification systems have certain problems, and the positive–negative classification system is no exception. Some researchers believe positive and negative symptoms are negatively correlated; that is, that schizophrenics who have many positive symptoms have few negative symptoms and vice versa. Others see positive and negative symptoms as unrelated; that is, that patients can exhibit several or few or both. More importantly, investigators disagree about the particular symptoms making up the positive and negative symptom clusters (Andreasen, 1985b; Crow, 1985). Such disagreements have led some to believe that researchers would be wise to study specific symptoms, instead of attempting to identify the disorder's subtypes (Smith, 1989). The symptom of affect flattening, for example, discriminates schizophrenic from nonschizophrenic patients and is also a good predictor of post-hospitalization functioning (Endicott et al., 1986).

Even if some researchers choose to study very specific symptoms instead of syndromes, many still will follow the cause of studying syndromes or overall classes of disorders. In any case, the study of positive and negative symptoms has been a fruitful avenue of research.

ETIOLOGY

A variety of biological, psychological, and social factors contribute to the likelihood of becoming schizophrenic. Biological factors contributing to schizophrenia include central nervous system dysfunction and genetic factors. Psychological factors include communication abnormalities and family stressors. Finally, being in a low social class places one at risk for schizophrenia.

Central Nervous System Dysfunction

Brain Imaging. The search for a brain dysfunction in schizophrenics began almost immediately after Kraepelin identified the syndrome. While laboratory tests of brain dysfunction did not exist at the turn of the century, post-mortem brain analyses suggested varied abnormalities in ventricle size and the presence of lesions. In the 1970s, the brain imaging technique called **CAT scanning,** or computerized axial tomographic scanning, allowed researchers to examine the brains of living schizophrenics. The CAT scan sends an X-ray beam through part of the body, such as the brain, to a set of detectors on the other side of the body. The beam is diminished as it passes through body tissue, and its decrease in intensity is measured to develop a picture. The scanner rotates a full 360 degrees around the body, one degree at a time, developing an image of the brain as it rotates.

Brain imaging of schizophrenics has shown atrophy, or deterioration of their frontal lobes, particularly on the left side (Seidman, 1983); the evidence for such brain atrophy is far greater for negative symptom schizophrenics than for positive symptom schizophrenics (Andreasen, 1988). Researchers have hypothesized that factors present at or before birth may be responsible for the observed deterioration (Silverton, Finello, Mednick, & Schulsinger, 1985). Researchers have also found enlarged brain cavities or spaces between brain structures in schizophrenics. These enlarged cavities are believed to result from brain deterioration. Interestingly, however, the presence of enlarged brain cavities does not seem associated with severity of schizophrenic symptoms (Pfefferbaum, 1988). Further, such brain deterioration is not unique to schizophrenics; indeed, abnormalities like enlarged ventricles are evident in various disorders like alcoholism and Parkinson's disease.

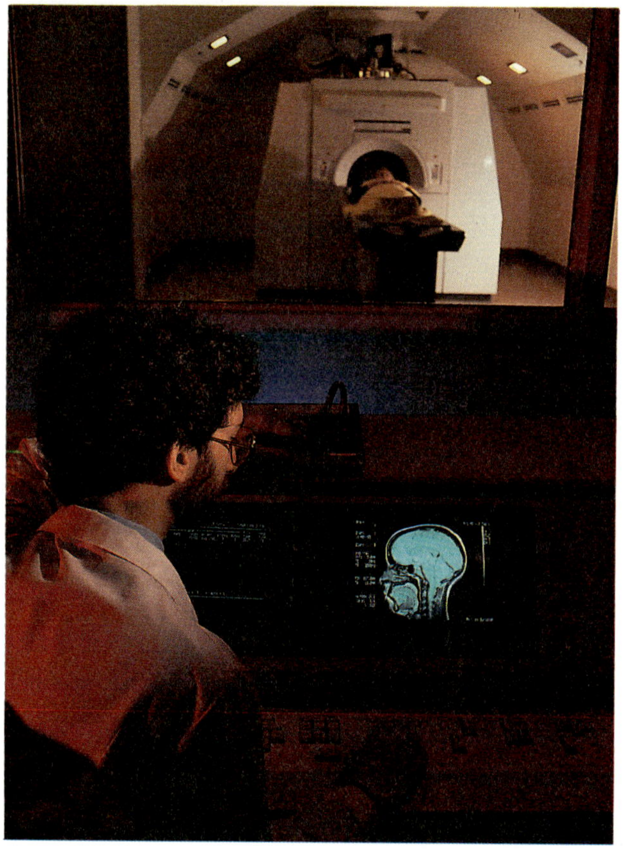

This patient is being moved into the MRI (Magnetic Resonance Imaging) chamber which allows the physician to take pictures of living tissue. A magnetic field encircling the patient's body enables a computer to produce a three-dimensional picture of body tissue.

Magnetic resonance imaging (MRI), first used in the 1980s, has several advantages over the CAT scan. First, it takes a picture of living tissue without risk to the patient's health because it uses no radiation, unlike the CAT scan. Second, MRI produces higher resolution images, enabling small brain structures to be easily seen. MRI works on the principle that our body cells contain hydrogen, phosphorous, and certain elements sensitive to magnetic current. During the procedure, patients are placed inside a huge magnet encircling their body. As a magnetic current passes through the body, a computer creates a three-dimensional picture of body tissue.

Because MRI is a recent development, it has been used in relatively few studies with schizophrenics, but researchers will doubtless employ it widely in the future. Early work with MRI already suggests that schizophrenics have small frontal lobes (Andreasen et al., 1986), a result consistent with CAT scan analyses.

Blood Flow Studies. CAT and MRI scans give images of brain structure, while another procedure, dynamic brain imaging, permits researchers to study cerebral blood flow, oxygen use, and other brain functions. A major method for such analyses is a positron-emission tomographic (PET) scan. In the PET scan, radioactive isotopes are injected into the patient's blood vessels. The radioactive molecules emit particles called positrons, enabling a picture of the isotopes to be projected. The PET technique used most frequently involves the injection of sugar treated with a positron tracer. Since sugar provides energy in the brain, the positron-emitting glucose allows clinicians and researchers to see the most active parts of the brain (using the most energy). The results of PET scan studies generally support the view of schizophrenics having abnormally low activity in the right and left brain hemispheres. Research also suggests that increases in right hemisphere activity are associated with clinical improvement in schizophrenics (Gur et al., 1987; Gur, Resnick, Gur, Alavi, Caroff, Kushner, & Reivich, 1987).

The complex, sophisticated process of PET scanning is prohibitively costly to most patients. At present, it is a research tool, requiring teams of physicists, radiologists, neuropsychologists, and neurochemists. Procedural details of PET scan's use are still being worked out. We still do not know, for example, whether it is more fruitful to study patients at rest or when they are trying to solve problems. Specifics aside, the PET scan is bound to unlock some of the mind's secrets. For example, it will allow scientists a much better idea of the active sites of drug action in the brain. As Andreasen (1985a) remarks,

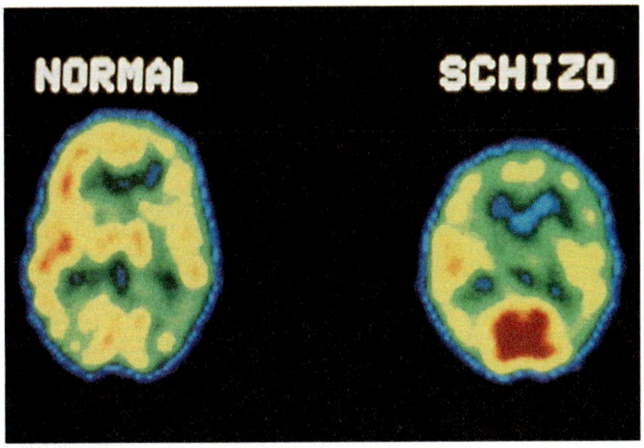

PET (Positron-Emission Tomographic) scans show how radioactive molecules flow through a patient's blood vessels. Often sugar that is treated with a positron tracer is injected in order to assess which parts of the brain are most active and use the most energy. The darker area of the schizophrenic's PET scan reveals an abnormal metabolism of sugar compared to that of the PET scan of a normal control subject.

the PET scan "is a dynamic technique that permits the neuroscientist to watch the brain at work and to observe which parts of it become more active in response to various types of stimuli. Thus, PET scanning is a wonderfully exciting technique that may assist in unlocking many of the secrets of schizophrenia and other major mental illnesses during the next few years." (p. 177)

Genetic Factors

Clear and compelling evidence suggests a genetic influence in schizophrenia. As with other disorders, family and twin studies represent the major methods of assessing genetic predisposition to schizophrenia. We will first review the evidence from these studies and then that from studies of adopted children. Before evaluating the genetic data, we should note that the likelihood of any randomly selected person developing schizophrenia is one in one hundred. This risk for becoming schizophrenic has been known for decades (Book, 1960) and has remained quite constant for the last thirty years in Europe and the United States.

Family Studies. Family studies are the method used the longest to assess genetic predispositions for psychological or psychiatric disorders. It has been noted for centuries that mental illness "runs in families," suggesting it may be inherited genetically. The family study method compares the risk for a disorder in relatives of someone who has the disorder to the risk in a control sample. The risk of developing a disorder is called a *morbidity risk*. The person who has the disorder in question is called the **proband,** or **index case.** If the proband's relatives are still young or are middle-aged adults, they may develop the disorder later in life. The estimate of risk, therefore, has to be corrected on the basis of age. Karlsson (1973) obtained data on diagnosed schizophrenics in Iceland born in the mid- to late 1800s, and only cases with a specific diagnosis of schizophrenia were selected as probands. Data on their relatives were obtained through genealogical records in Reykjavik and mental hospital admission records. This information was then assessed for a diagnosis of schizophrenia or any other psychotic disorder. The data indicated that probands' first- and second-degree relatives were at increased risk for schizophrenia and other psychoses (see Table 14.1), as compared to the general population's 1 percent likelihood of schizophrenia. In brief, using data that spanned over 100 years, Karlsson (1973) concluded that morbidity risk for psychotic diagnoses were elevated for Icelandic people with a relative diagnosed as schizophrenic.

Many family studies of schizophrenia have been conducted in the United States and Europe. Because of variability in diagnostic criteria, statistical procedures used for age corrections, and methods of obtaining data, the specific risk percentage vary from study to study. For example, the estimated risk for becoming schizophrenic if one parent is schizophrenic varies from 7 percent to 17 percent (Rosenthal, 1970). In efforts to provide better risk estimates, researchers have used the data on thousands of schizophrenics, collected across many studies (Slater & Cowie, 1971). Table 14.2 shows these risk values. The astute reader may notice that the risk figures reported in Table 14.1 for siblings, children, and nephews and nieces of schizophrenics are higher than those presented in Table 14.2. Recall that Karlsson considered risk for any psychotic diagnosis (Table 14.1) whereas Table 14.2 shows risk for a specific diagnosis of schizophrenia.

First-degree relatives of schizophrenics (brothers, sisters, children) have approximately a 10 percent chance of becoming schizophrenic. The change is almost 40 percent if both parents are schizophrenic. In contrast, the likelihood of developing schizophrenia if an aunt, an uncle, or a grandparent is schizophrenic

TABLE 14.1 Risk for Psychosis in Relatives of Schizophrenics

Parents	13%
Siblings	14
Children	18
Nephews/nieces	9

Source: Karlsson, J.L. (1973). An Icelandic family study of schizophrenia. *British Journal of Psychiatry, 123,* 549–554.

TABLE 14.2 Risk of Schizophrenia in Relatives of Index Cases	
First-Degree Relatives	**Risk**
Children of two schizophrenic parents	37%
Children of one schizophrenic parent	13
Siblings (brother/sister)	10
Second-Degree Relatives	
Aunts and uncles	5
Nieces and nephews	5
Grandchildren	5

Source: Data adapted from Slater & Cowie, 1971.

is only 5 percent. Each of these percentages is considerably higher than the general population's 1 percent prevalence. Schizophrenia, then, does tend to run in families. As discussed in earlier chapters, however, a shared gene pool is only one common element among family members. They also share experiences, stressors, and behaviors that may be learned from each other and may account for the higher morbidity risks.

Twin Studies. If an identical (monozygotic) twin is schizophrenic, the likelihood that the other twin will also be schizophrenic is roughly 50 percent to 60 percent. If a fraternal (dizygotic) twin is diagnosed as schizophrenic, the likelihood of the other twin developing schizophrenia is only 15 percent to 20 percent. (Kallmann, 1953; Slater, 1953; Rosenthal, 1970; Gottesman & Shields, 1972).

Recall that a twin pair is judged concordant when both meet certain criteria. Estimates of risk are partially determined by how strict or lenient these criteria are. As the criteria for judging concordance become more stringent, concordance rates decrease. Conversely, as the criteria become more inclusive, they increase. Recognizing that varied definitions of concordance will yield different estimates, Gottesman and Shields (1972) devised a three-tier system of concordance criteria. The researchers studied all twin pairs in which at least one twin was hospitalized with a diagnosis of schizophrenia in Maudsley or Betham Hospital in London between 1948 and 1964. The likelihood of twin pairs being judged concordant, they concluded, was 79 percent using the very general criterion that the twin of the index case was also "abnormal, but not necessarily hospitalized." The concordance rate dropped to 54 percent if the criterion was "hospitalized, but not necessarily schizophrenic." And the concordance rate fell to 42 percent if the most stringent criteria, "hospitalized and diagnosed schizophrenic," were used. As Table 14.3 shows, concordance rates for both monozygotic and dizygotic twin pairs decreased as the criteria for judging concordance became more stringent. Regardless of the specific method to judge concordance, however, the rates are much higher for monozygotic than dizygotic twins. Additionally, concordance rates are higher when the index case presents at least one severe schizophrenic symptom than when the index case presents with only mild symptoms (Gottesman & Shields, 1972).

Despite the rather overwhelming evidence suggesting a genetic predisposition for schizophrenia, every twin study poses interpretation problems. Twins are typically reared *together* within a family unit. Thus, exposure to similar familial, dietary, and cultural experiences may partially account for the observed concordance rates for schizophrenia. Some may further argue that identical twins have more similar environments than nonidentical twins, because they look so much alike and are always the same sex, and that this may contribute to the heightened concordance rates among monozygotic twin pairs. To address this issue, researchers have studied identical twins separated at birth and reared *apart* in different homes. However, the number of twin pairs reared apart wherein at least one twin is schizophrenic is extremely small. Of sixteen known cases, ten were judged concordant and six discordant, yielding a concordance rate of 62 percent (Rosenthal, 1970). Because of the unsystematic sampling for these cases and since concordance rates varied according to the years in which the twin pairs were studied (higher before 1960, lower after 1960), these data should be interpreted cautiously. Even so, most experts conclude that studies of twins reared apart provide strong evidence for a genetic component in schizophrenia (Farber, 1981; Vandenberg, Singer, & Pauls, 1986). Yet, these studies also indicate that genetic factors alone cannot fully account for schizophrenia, for if they did, monozygotic concordance rates would be 100 percent.

TABLE 14.3 Concordance Rates of Schizophrenia among Twin Pairs

Definition of Concordance	MZ	DZ
1. Abnormal, but not necessarily hospitalized	79%	45%
2. Hospitalized, but not necessarily schizophrenic	54	18
3. Hospitalized and diagnosed schizophrenic	42	9

Source: Data adapted from Gottesman and Shields (1972).

Adoption Studies. Another way to examine the role of genetic factors in schizophrenia's development is to assess children of schizophrenics who are raised by nonschizophrenic adoptive parents. Such studies eliminate the effects of factors such as modeling the parent's schizophrenic behaviors, stress associated with the parent's hospitalization and treatment, and inadequate parenting during serious episodes. Heston (1966) studied forty-seven children of schizophrenic mothers who were adopted or placed in foster homes less than one month after birth. Of special interest, the Heston study was the first adoption study in the schizophrenia area, and it involved following children of schizophrenics separated from their disordered parent in early infancy. The natural mothers gave birth to their children while hospitalized for schizophrenia at the Oregon State Psychiatric Hospital. No attempt was made to assess the father's psychiatric status, yet none were known to be psychiatric patients. At follow-up, the adopted children were compared to fifty control subjects reared in foster homes. The average age of both groups at follow-up assessment was thirty-six years. Heston interviewed almost all of the index and control cases himself. Two psychiatrists also diagnosed each person and rated him or her on a mental health–sickness scale. Neither psychiatrist knew the nature of the natural mother's illness nor the background of the adult they interviewed. Heston also gave all subjects an IQ test and the MMPI (a personality test). As Table 14.4 shows, the children of schizophrenic mothers were at greater risk than control subjects for developing schizophrenia as well as other mental health problems. None of the control subjects were diagnosed schizophrenic, whereas 11 percent of the children of schizophrenic mothers were.

Another adoption study was conducted by Kety and his colleagues (1968; 1978) in Denmark, where up-to-date records including the addresses and psychiatric hospitalizations of citizens are kept. The researchers attempted to locate all individuals adopted between 1924 and 1927 who were later diagnosed schizophrenic. The psychiatric histories of the biological parents of these schizophrenic probands were then examined and compared to those of the biological parents of the control adopted individuals. A higher rate of schizophrenia and other psychiatric disturbances was found among the parents of the probands than among the parents of the control subjects.

Adoption studies' findings provide evidence of the importance of genetic factors in the etiology of schizophrenia. Nevertheless, only 11 percent of the children born to schizophrenic mothers and then adopted became schizophrenic (Heston, 1966). Like family and twin studies, adoption studies suggest that genetic factors are only one element in schizophrenia's etiology.

Dominant Gene Theory of Schizophrenia. Some researchers believe that eye movement dysfunctions are markers for schizophrenia and that both of these problems may be determined by a single dominant gene. This eye movement dysfunction is a person's inability to track a pendulum or a light with smooth visual movement. While some individuals with other psychiatric disorders also have eye movement dysfunction, it is not as common in other groups as in schizophrenic populations.

Eye movement dysfunction is frequently seen in schizophrenics and their relatives. Even schizophrenics with no eye movement dysfunction themselves often have first-degree relatives with the dysfunction.

TABLE 14.4 Risk of Schizophrenia in Adopted Children

	Adopted Children of Schizophrenic Mothers	Adopted Children Mothers Not Schizophrenic
Number of subjects	47	50
Average age at assessment	36 years	36 years
Number diagnosed schizophrenic	5	0
Number diagnosed sociopathic	9	2
Number diagnosed neurotic	13	7
Number diagnosed mentally defective	4	0
Psychiatric military discharge	8	1

Source: Heston, L.L. (1966). Psychiatric disorders in foster home reared children of schizophrenic mothers. *British Journal of Psychiatry, 112,* 819–825.

Relatives of schizophrenics are thus at increased risk for developing schizophrenia and eye movement dysfunction. Though both problems may be associated with a single gene, twin studies clearly suggest the greater risk of developing eye movement dysfunction than of developing schizophrenia. Thus, eye movement disorders appear to be important indicators of genetic risk for developing schizophrenia.

Using data from offspring of twins who were concordant for schizophrenia and offspring of twins who were discordant for schizophrenia, investigators have concluded that eye movement dysfunction and schizophrenia may be expressions of a single dominant gene (Holtzman et al., 1988). The study of eye movement dysfunction is promising for it may help clinicians identify people at high risk for developing schizophrenia. As important, it may help improve our understanding of schizophrenia's genetic components.

Social and Family Variables

Social Class. For several decades experts have known of schizophrenia's prevalence in the lower socioeconomic groups. In the classic study of social class and mental illness conducted by Hollingshead and Redlich (1958), schizophrenics in New Haven, Connecticut, were three times as likely to be members of the lowest socioeconomic class than of any other class. Schizophrenics were also approximately nine times more likely to be members of the lowest social class than the two highest social classes combined (see Table 14.5). The disproportionate numbers of schizophrenics in lower socioeconomic classes has been similarly observed in New York City (Srole et al., 1962) and in Western European countries such as Denmark, England, and Norway (Kohn, 1968). The highest rates of schizophrenia occur in the centers of large cities, areas generally inhabited by members of the lowest socioeconomic classes, except in cities where large urban renewal projects have attracted the upper and middle classes. In contrast, apparently no relation between schizophrenia and social class exists in small cities (Clausen & Kohn, 1959), probably because small cities generally don't have large impoverished neighborhoods. People from lower socioeconomic classes often migrate to large cities where there are housing projects and free food kitchens. Also, people in small communities may be more apt to pressure citizens to conform to certain standards that inhibit schizophrenic behavior in its early stages.

Despite the discrepancy between small and large cities, schizophrenia is generally much more prevalent in the lower social classes. There are two major hypotheses about this phenomenon. First, factors associated with being a member of a lower class may contribute to developing schizophrenia. Such variables might include poor prenatal care, poor nutrition, unequal access to early treatment, and a relative lack of family, social, and medical support. A second hypothesis is that schizophrenics show downward social mobility; that is, schizophrenics "drift" into poor urban neighborhoods. Schizophrenics withdraw and function less effectively than before the disorder's onset. If schizophrenics become increasingly ineffective at their job, they may earn less than others, may be forced into a lesser paying or lower status job, or may become unemployed. They also may be divorced by their partner or find family pressures very stressful. Any of these factors could cause a transition to poorer housing or homelessness. Evidence of downward social mobility is, however, conflicting: Some studies have found such an association (e.g., Turner & Wagonfeld, 1967) whereas others have not (e.g., Hollingshead & Redlich, 1958).

Examining the occupational status of the parents of schizophrenics is another way to determine the relative merit of the social class and the mobility hypotheses. For example, if fathers of schizophrenics were from the lowest socioeconomic levels, their children would be born into the same level; thus, class would precede schizophrenia. If, however, fathers of schizophrenics were from higher socioeconomic

TABLE 14.5 Incidence and Prevalence of Schizophrenia (rates per 100,000 in New Haven, Connecticut)

		Point Prevalence	Lifetime Prevalence
Social Class:	I/II (High)	6	111
	III	8	168
	IV	10	300
	V (Low)	20	895

Source: Hollingshead, A.B., & Redlich, F.C. *Social Class and Mental Illness.* Copyright © 1958 by John Wiley & Sons, Inc.: New York. Reprinted by permission of John Wiley & Sons, Inc.

classes than their children, schizophrenic offspring could have "drifted" downward. Research has yielded conflicting findings depending upon the city of the subject population. For example, Faris and Dunham (1939) concluded that in Chicago, fathers of schizophrenics were not more likely to come from higher socioeconomic levels than their schizophrenic offspring. Schizophrenics whose fathers are in the lowest socioeconomic groups, moreover, often display upward social mobility, although they typically remain below the general population's average socioeconomic level. Thus poor social conditions appeared to be a causal factor in schizophrenia's development. Yet when Dunham (1965) repeated the same study in Detroit, he came to the opposite conclusion, suggesting that schizophrenics drifted to the slums. Hare (1956), a British psychiatrist, also suggested that living in poor social conditions was a consequence, not a cause, of schizophrenia.

In conclusion, schizophrenia is more prevalent among the lower class than in higher social classes. On the other hand, it is not clear if becoming a schizophrenic is influenced by being a member of a lower social class or if being a schizophrenic pushes the person into the lower social classes. It is possible that this question is not an either/or issue and that both effects operate in certain circumstances.

Stress and Schizophrenia. Possibly, the general stress of society leads some individuals to "break down." The English psychiatrist Roland D. Laing (1967) argues that people who view their social situation as impossible to cope with retreat into the refuge of schizophrenia. Laing asserts, moreover, that the schizophrenic experience is beneficial, and that the majority of the population is simply too close-minded to see it from this perspective. According to Laing:

> If the human race survives, future men will, I suspect, look back on our Enlightened epoch as a veritable Age of Darkness. They will presumably be able to savor the irony of the situation with more amusement than we extract from it. The laugh's on us. They will see that what we call "schizophrenia" was one of the forms in which, often though quite ordinary people, the light began to break through the cracks in our all-too-closed minds. (1967, p. 129)

Elsewhere, Laing writes:

> We do not accept "schizophrenia" as being a biochemical, neuropsychological, psychological fact, and we regard it as a palpable error, in the present state of the evidence, to take it to be a fact. Nor do we assume its existence . . . Our question is: are the experiences and behaviors that psychiatrists take as symptoms and signs of schizophrenia more socially intelligible than has come to be supposed? (Laing & Esterson, 1969, p. viii)

Laing and Esterson (1969) presented eleven cases to illustrate that schizophrenic patients' behavior makes sense within their family context. Conversely, without understanding this context, their behavior appears relatively senseless. Laing's central notion is viewing schizophrenic behavior as a way to cope with confusing and ambiguous communications from family members. These ways of coping, he argues, are understandable reactions and should not be interpreted as signs of illness.

Most British professionals have rejected Laing's position because he and his colleagues did not support it with scientifically convincing evidence. But in America, psychiatrist Thomas Szasz took a similar position in his article, *The Myth of Mental Illness* (1960). Applying the label *schizophrenia* to certain behavior patterns, Szasz argued, implies the presence of a disease or illness. In Szasz's view, this label is simply a linguistic practice allowing medical doctors (rather than priests, witch-hunters, or police officers) to control certain behavior deemed unusual or socially unacceptable. Thus, he sees hospitalization, drugs, brain surgery, and other treatments as methods of control. The odd behavior is not a sign of madness in Szasz's view but reflects a disturbance in communication.

Although Szasz's and Laing's ideas have raised public and professional awareness about methods of hospital commitment and mental patients' rights, they have not significantly influenced the mainstream view of schizophrenia as a mental disorder. (For a discussion of Szasz's ideas about committing individuals to institutionalized care, see Chapter 18.) However, deviant family communication patterns' association with schizophrenia has been a popular focus of research.

Laing died in 1989, but before his death, he rejected his earlier idea that schizophrenics may have a comprehensive or even superior mentality. He also acknowledged that many of his own treatment approaches had failed. To the end, however, he believed that the "snake pit" was still an apt term for many hospital facilities for schizophrenics (*The New York Times,* August 24, 1989).

Communication Abnormalities. In the 1950s, many experts believed that deviant family or parental communication patterns might cause schizophrenia. One influential concept was the **double bind** hypothesis (Bateson, Jackson, Haley, & Weakland, 1956). Schizophrenics, the researchers suggested, have experienced an intense relationship to a mother who sent contradictory messages to them. For example, a mother may complain to her son that he is unaffectionate, and yet she may become tense and anxious when he approaches her. Because of the intensity of their feelings, children find it hard to with-

BOX 14.4 Billy Boggs: Does Society Have a Right to Commit Her?

In the rush to remove the homeless from New York City streets, a street person called Billy Boggs, living in front of a restaurant heating duct to keep warm, was picked up by the police and taken to Bellevue Hospital for psychiatric observation. On arrival, she was disheveled and occasionally incoherent. The forty-year-old black woman had previously been a secretary for the Human Rights Commission in Elizabeth, New Jersey, for ten years. After graduating from high school and business school, she lived with her family for the next five years. According to them, she used cocaine periodically and had been abusive to other family members. Unable to get along with them, she had lived in a New Jersey shelter for several months before being asked to leave because of her abusive behavior (*The New York Times*, November 5, 1987). Next, she lived for several years on the streets of New York, until, under a new city program, the police picked her up. Diagnosed as schizophrenic by Bellevue Hospital's psychiatrists, she was given a trial of antipsychotic medication.

Boggs strongly objected to being hospitalized, and aided by civil liberties attorneys, she sued the city and won her freedom. She has subsequently appeared on numerous national television shows and has lectured about involuntary commitment and the homeless to Harvard Law School students. Consistently coherent on television and in her public appearances, Boggs argued that she was "not harming nobody" and should be free to live where she chooses. News about Billy Boggs appeared frequently as this chapter was being completed. A recent report stated she had been out on the streets panhandling again. Regardless of Boggs's living status, her case clearly illustrates the controversy about an individual's right to roam the streets, beg, act unusual, and even possibly freeze to death if he or she chooses.

draw from such relationships even though they get contradictory messages from their parents. Although subsequent researchers did not find empirical support for the double bind hypothesis, research on communication patterns in schizophrenic families has continued. Investigators such as Wynne (1984) and Rodnick, Goldstein, Lewis, and Doane (1984) developed a **systems approach** to schizophrenia, according deviant communication patterns a central role. A person can be best understood, they argue, within the social systems which they live in, such as marriage, the family, and their broader social network. Systems research has shown that communication deviance, a rejecting or indifferent parental style, and a detached family environment are related to schizophrenic behavior. Yet it remains to be demonstrated if these factors play a causal role in schizophrenia or if they result from living with a child who may be preschizophrenic and grossly deviant at a young age. Communication deviance is probably a partial cause and a partial result of schizophrenia.

Family Stressors: High Expressed Emotion

Doctor: Does he care for himself?
Mother of schizophrenic patient: That's a very sore point with me. . . . He goes beyond being a bit grubby. He doesn't shave, doesn't wash his hair, never changes his underwear—it's quite revolting!

Doctor: How do you get along on a daily basis?
Mother of schizophrenic patient: Music, when he's on the downgrade, would nearly drive you crazy. He'd play the same music over and over again, until you felt if I hear that one more time I'll scream.

Strong negative emotion among family members, like that expressed by these two mothers of schizophrenic patients, is a predictor of relapse in hospitalized patients who have been discharged. In England, Brown and his colleagues (1958; 1959) noticed that how well schizophrenic patients fared after release from a hospital seemed to depend upon the living group to which they went. Discharged patients living with a brother or sister did better than those living with parents or a spouse. Patients who spent a limited amount of time with family members did better than those who had extensive contact with them. In a later study, Brown and his colleagues (1962) interviewed schizophrenic patients' female relatives upon the patients' first admittance to the hospital. The researchers assessed hostility, dominance, and levels of emotion expressed by the patient and his or her family members. After discharge, patients returning to homes with family members who displayed high levels of expressed emotion (EE) were most likely to relapse and return to the hospital.

In dozens of studies during the past two decades, high EE has been reliably associated with relapse. In England, during the nine-month period following hospital discharge, the typical relapse rates have been approximately 55 percent for high EE families and 15 percent for low EE families (Brown, Birley, & Wing, 1972). In the United States, Vaughn and associates (1984) similarly observed that patients discharged to high EE families had a 56 percent relapse rate after a nine-month follow-up, whereas patients discharged to low EE families had a 17 percent relapse rate. We do not know if relatives of schizophrenics have high EE to begin with or whether it develops from their exposure to a schizophrenic individual. High EE ratings of patient's relatives have, nevertheless, been major predictors of relapse (Hooley, 1985). Hooley (1985) noted that relapse rates of patients discharged to high EE families appear to be lessened if they receive antipsychotic medication and if they spend fewer than thirty-five hours per week with family members. The relapse rates of patients spending more or fewer than thirty-five hours per week with family members are portrayed in Figure 14.2.

One possible explanation for the high EE and relapse relationship is that patients returning to low EE families may have been less disturbed than those returning to high EE families. Symptomatology during hospitalization and at discharge, however, do not seem different for schizophrenic patients released to high and low EE families. Thus, it seems that high EE may play a causal role in relapse. Further, as discussed later regarding treatment, at least one intervention study (Leff et al., 1982) has produced convincing evidence of changes in family EE levels affecting relapse rates.

A few recent studies in Australia and Germany have found no association between relapse rates and high or low EE status of discharged schizophrenics' families (Parker, Johnston, & Hayward, 1988). The reasons for these discrepant findings are unclear. Since high EE has been repeatedly associated with relapse in schizophrenics in the United States, further research is warranted to reconcile the differences between the results in the United States and elsewhere.

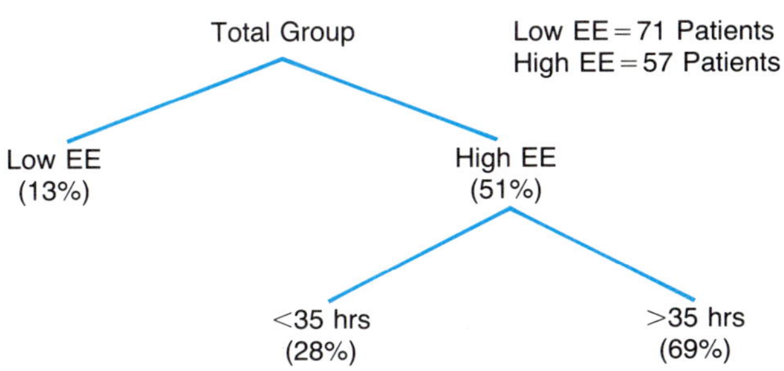

Figure 14.2 Schizophrenic Relapse Rates. *The nine month relapse rates of a total group of 128 schizophrenic patients indicate that those patients who had families with low expressed emotion were much less likely to relapse (13%) than those with high expressed emotion (51%). Further, for those with high expressed emotion, if the patients spent less than 35 hours with family members, they were less likely to relapse (28%) than if they spent more than 35 hours (69%).*

Source: Vaughn, C.E., & Leff, J.P. (1976). The influence of family and social factors on the course of psychiatric illness. *British Journal of Psychiatry, 129,* 132.

High-Risk Studies. Retrospective studies of schizophrenic patients' childhood records has led researchers to hypothesize that children who are more withdrawn, disagreeable, and delinquent than other children are more likely to become schizophrenic (Berry, 1967; Watt, 1974). The records also show lower IQs in preschizophrenic children than in control subjects (Albee, Lane, & Reuter, 1964). These characteristics, however, are found not only in the childhood records of schizophrenics but also in the records of delinquents and criminals. In the search for schizophrenia's risk factors, researchers want to find variables that predict schizophrenia in particular rather than mental disorders in general.

High-risk studies for schizophrenia follow children at risk for developing schizophrenia (usually children with a schizophrenic parent) to determine differences between those who become schizophrenic and those who do not. In many of these studies, children with normal parents form the low-risk control group. Fifteen major research projects have studied large samples of children at risk for schizophrenia. Investigators have tried to identify individual and family variables that make schizophrenics' children more or less vulnerable than children of normal parents for developing the disorder. Pioneering high-risk studies were conducted in the early 1960s by two Danish researchers, Sarnoff Mednick and Fini Schulsinger (1968). They studied 207 high-risk children with adjustment problems whose mothers were chronic schizophrenics. A control group of 104 low-risk subjects whose mothers were not schizophrenic were selected to match the high-risk subjects on variables such as age, sex, race, and socioeconomic status. When the study began, the high-risk subjects averaged fifteen years of age (they ranged from ages nine to twenty). By 1972, seventeen of the now grown-up high-risk subjects were diagnosed schizophrenic, whereas none of the low-risk subjects were. Subjects who later became schizophrenic were distinguished from other high-risk subjects by the following characteristics:

1. Their mothers had a more severe course of illness.
2. They were separated from their parents more often and had been placed in children's homes more often.
3. The perinatal birth difficulties were greater.
4. Their teachers saw them as more aggressive and easily angered.
5. They had higher autonomic nervous system arousal levels, especially those who eventually suffered from hallucinations and delusions.

Since the initial research by Mednick and colleagues, approximately 1,000 children of schizophrenic parents and 500 children at risk for other psychopathologies have been evaluated. Additionally, over 500 matched control children have been studied. As summarized by Watt (1984) in the book, *Children at Risk for Schizophrenia: A Longitudinal Perspective,* children born to schizophrenic mothers have elevated pregnancy complications, show more aggressive and disruptive school behavior, and have lower IQs than control children.

Recall that Danish researchers had reached similar conclusions more than two decades ago by examining adult schizophrenics' school records. The more recent high-risk researchers, however, have now obtained additional information: They have learned that different factors predict behavior problems in children of schizophrenic women as compared to children of depressed women. Marital discord, for example, plays an important role in the development of behavior problems in children with depressed mothers, but not in children of schizophrenic mothers (Emery, Weintraub, & Neale, 1982).

We should not forget that many children of parents with schizophrenia cope extremely effectively. Manfred Bleuler (1984), son of Eugene Bleuler, found that 84 percent of married high-risk subjects in Switzerland had successful marriages and, moreover, that the great majority surpassed their parents' social status. But what crucial types of support, if any, enable them to be so successful? The book, *Children at Risk for Schizophrenia: A Longitudinal Perspective* (Watt, Anthony, & Wynne, 1984), was the result of an international conference of key high-risk researchers, and its dedication may contain an important clue to answer that question.

> Professor Bleuler has published scholarly investigations of the schizophrenic disorder, like most of us. Unlike most of us, he has also treated his schizophrenic subjects clinically, delivered their babies, and cared for their children. This book is dedicated in honor of Manfred Bleuler, for there is nowhere a more faithful champion of schizophrenic people.

Future high-risk research may shed light not only on the precursors of schizophrenic breakdown but also on the adaptive nature of many children of schizophrenics. Researchers have already found that certain factors including peer group acceptance and lack of deviance in family communication seem to buffer, or protect, children from developing schizophrenia.

A DIATHESIS-STRESS MODEL OF SCHIZOPHRENIA

In accord with this book's biopsychosocial framework, a *diathesis,* or predisposition, to develop schizophrenia may interact with ongoing stressors to increase the risk of schizophrenia. Some call this the diathesis-stress model (Zubin & Spring, 1977). The diathesis is a person's genetic, biological, and/or psychological vulnerability whereas the stress is current social or interpersonal stressors, such as poverty or severe criticism from family members.

Using a biopsychosocial model throughout this book, the interaction of these variables in the etiology of many disorders has been discussed (e.g., anxiety, depression, alcoholism, and attention deficit disorders of children). The diathesis-stress model is especially popular in the schizophrenia area, largely resulting from Zubin and Spring's work (1977). They emphasize the interaction of genetic predisposition and social stressors. Basically, Zubin believes any individual can be classified according to his or her vulnerability or predisposition to develop schizophrenia. Some people have almost no likelihood of developing schizophrenia whereas others may be highly likely to develop it. The risk for developing schizophrenia depends in part upon prenatal and postnatal environmental factors as well as one's genetic predisposition. These factors interact with later psychological and social stressors to produce schizophrenia. The diathesis-stress model implies schizophrenia may be preventable or reversible if important stressors are lessened. This contrasts with the view that once schizophrenia develops, it will invariably be a lifetime disorder.

The diathesis-stress model of schizophrenia is supported by information presented earlier in this chapter about schizophrenia's episodic nature for some patients; that is, those who experience symptom-free periods between bouts with the disorder (Bleuler, 1978). Further, as we have seen, schizophrenia is clearly influenced by some social stressors such as high expressed emotion among family members. On the other hand, we have also seen that some schizophrenics' structural brain abnormalities may produce irreversible negative symptoms. Thus, the diathesis-stress model's applicability may vary across individuals with this disorder. Psychological and social stressors may play a bigger role in producing the symptoms of some subgroups of schizophrenia than others.

TREATMENT OF SCHIZOPHRENIA

Like many other serious psychiatric disorders, schizophrenia has been treated historically with many bizarre interventions. In the 1800s, Phillippe Pinel, a French psychiatrist in charge of a mental hospital, concluded that specific moral treatment offered the best course of intervention. For example, if a man believed he had no head, he might be made to wear a heavy helmet laden with lead until he agreed he had a head. If a woman believed she had snakes in her stomach, she might be given an emetic, and a snake might be quickly and secretly placed in the vomit. Early interventions for schizophrenia also included opium in high doses and belladonna (a poisonous herb).

In the earlier decades of this century, especially in the 1930s and 1940s, several somatic therapies were introduced, including injections of insulin or metrazol (a convulsant), **prefrontal leucotomy** (the removal of the frontal portion of the brain), and electroconvulsive therapy (ECT). Also during this period, followers of the famous American psychiatrist Harry Stack Sullivan encouraged the use of psychoanalysis.

The first effective treatment for schizophrenia, a neuroleptic medication called chlorpromazine, was developed in the 1950s. (The general chemical name for this class of medication is phenothiazines). But during the 1960s, at the time of Vietnam War protests and a rising tide of antiestablishment feelings internationally, a number of clinicians and researchers emphasized social causes of schizophrenia and advocated social as opposed to medical treatments. Symptoms such as attentional problems, language disorders, and family issues, rather than schizophrenia per se, became many centers' focus of treatment. In the early 1970s, with the rise of community psychology and psychiatry, increased attempts were made to keep schizophrenics at home with their families or in community group homes, as opposed to hospitalizing them. During the 1980s, this movement, called **deinstitutionalization,** began to be reexamined, as many former mental patients became homeless vagrants in large metropolitan areas (see Box 14.5).

Pharmacological, social, and psychological treatments each have some proven efficacy and have been evaluated in many studies throughout the world. Today, neuroleptic drugs are generally regarded as the most effective treatments for schizophrenic symptoms, and they are now used in combination with psychological and social therapies.

Pharmacological Treatment

Before the 1950s, treatment of schizophrenics basically consisted of confinement to mental institutions. Except in posh private hospitals, "treatment" usually meant custodial care, providing patients with food, shelter, and some exercise and activities. The number of these activities varied according to cost of the hospital stay, but even in mental hospitals for the well-to-do, patients often had little stimulation. Apparently, institutional care had changed little since Van Gogh commented in May 1889 on the food and activities at Saint-Remy in France:

> The food is so-so. Naturally, it tastes rather moldy, like in a cockroach infested restaurant in Paris or in a boarding house. As these poor souls do absolutely nothing (not a book, nothing to distract them but a game of bowls and a game of checkers) they have no other daily distraction than to stuff themselves with chick peas, beans, lentils, and other groceries and merchandise from the colonies in fixed quantities and at regular hours. (Hulsker, 1971, p. 125)

BOX 14.5 Homelessness and Deinstitutionalization

As pressures mounted to release mental patients from hospitals in the 1960s and 1970s, homelessness dramatically increased. Thus, it seemed that one dumping ground, the streets, was substituted for another, psychiatric wards. Rare attempts were made to determine which patients benefitted from hospital care, and unfortunately patients were routinely transferred to local communities without careful planning. Follow-up efforts to assess how patients were faring after their transfer from state hospitals to communities were frequently inadequate. In addition, local residents tended to fear or resent patients coming into their communities and often thwarted state planners' efforts to provide patients with homes and hospital after-care.

Effective community services for outpatient schizophrenics will require public education about the disease. Community members will need to understand that schizophrenics do not generally pose a serious threat to their safety. The community will also need to accept the unusual behavior, dress, and appearance of some schizophrenics who are, nonetheless, able to function outside the hospital. Additionally, successful deinstitutionalization will require staffing of group homes within communities by trained mental health workers able to provide support and skills training to schizophrenics.

The goal of successful community placement of schizophrenics remains far from realized. In large American cities, homelessness is an acute problem. Only 5 percent to 10 percent of the housing placements needed for psychiatric patients are currently available. As a result, the psychiatrically impaired are part of an acute problem of homelessness, representing between 25 percent to 40 percent of the homeless in the United States.

Source: Mechanic, D., & Aiken, L.A. (1987). Improving the care of patients with chronic mental illness. *New England Journal of Medicine*, 317, 1634–1638.

In such institutions, patients were often as afraid of one another as of the hospital itself. They had good reason to be terrified of this environment, for mental hospitals were often filled with frightening sights and sounds: screams and cries, unintelligible speech, hallucinations, mutes and catatonics. Then, as has happened with scientific discoveries, research on a drug for allergies resulted in a remarkable and unexpected finding. Researchers noticed that the drug, an antihistamine, had calming effects on allergic patients. Aware of this, a French surgeon, Laborit, gave his patients an antihistamine compound (antihistamine phenothiazine, or promethazine) in hopes it would prevent a marked drop in blood pressure during surgery, a condition called *surgical shock.* Although promethazine did not produce the desired effect, Laborit noticed that after they were injected with it, patients were able to communicate with markedly less anxiety. Laborit's report triggered chemists to experiment with variations of the drug. They noticed that adding a chlorine atom to the parent compound yielded "chlor-promazine," with a remarkable calming effect on animals. Laborit then tried the new compound chlorpromazine on his patients as a preoperative procedure and found it kept them tranquil about the prospects of surgery. Shortly afterward, two French psychiatrists, Jean Delay and Pierre Deniker (1952), administered chlorpromazine to a variety of psychiatric patients, observing the drug's tranquilizing effect on them. Chlorpromazine not only calmed schizophrenic patients but also markedly diminished their terrifying hallucinations and delusions while allowing them to remain alert. Patients who had been ill for years improved significantly on the drug; as a result, many young hospitalized schizophrenics were able to return to their homes, jobs, and families.

The news of this development in Paris spread like wildfire: A wonder drug of the mental health field had been discovered. Chlorpromazine became the preferred treatment for schizophrenia, and other antipsychotic drugs began to be developed. Because of their use, within twenty years the number of patients in mental hospitals dropped by almost 50 percent, and even those who remained hospitalized led much improved lives.

Beside their immediate positive effects, antipsychotic medications, which Delay called neuroleptics (to distinguish their effects from tranquilizers), have long-term preventative effects, deterring relapse. A review of more than thirty-five published double-blind studies with about 3,500 schizophrenic patients, showed that only 20 percent of those taking neuroleptic drugs relapsed within four to six months and had to be rehospitalized, whereas 50 percent of control patients relapsed within the same period. After a year, 40 percent of schizophrenics taking neuroleptics relapsed, whereas 68 percent of controls receiving placebos did (Hogarty, 1984).

Yet like many medications, neuroleptics have undesirable side effects. After treatment with neuroleptics, many schizophrenic patients develop a largely irreversible and severe side effect called tardive dyskinesia (Kane et al., 1982). Tardive dyskinesia is an extreme neuromuscular disturbance usually characterized by involuntary lip smacking and chin wagging, but it can also affect other areas of the body. In a summary of neuroleptics' side effects, Liberman and Kane (1986) reported that 3 percent to 4 percent of the patients receiving neuroleptics each year develop tardive dyskinesia, and that approximately 20 percent of any psychiatric population surveyed will suffer from it. Fortunately, doctors are learning to prevent or diminish tardive dyskinesia through low or intermittent neurleptic doses (Carpenter et al., 1982; Wegner, Catalano, Gilbralter, & Kane, 1985).

Neuroleptics have clearly and dramatically helped many schizophrenics, yet even with these medications, some relapse and some do not. If we could predict how individual patients might respond to neuroleptics, we would be better able to weigh the costs and benefits of these drugs for particular patients. Without this information, experts generally agree that the possibility of enabling patients to lead productive lives with neuroleptics outweighs their possible negative side effects, especially since the majority of patients respond well to them (Henn & Delisi, 1986).

Psychological Treatment

Psychodynamic Therapy. Like Kraepelin, Freud viewed schizophrenia as an organic problem rather than primarily a psychological one. In 1938, Freud said that "we must renounce the idea of trying our plan of [psychodynamic] cure upon psychotics." In contrast, another influential psychoanalyst, Harry Stack Sullivan, argued in 1924 against the fruitless search for an organic cause of schizophrenia. He felt schizophrenics could respond to a modified version of psychoanalysis. Sullivan worked with schizophrenic patients at a now-famous psychiatric hospital in Maryland called Chestnut Lodge. In his work with young, recent-onset schizophrenics during the 1940s and 1950s, Sullivan concluded their use of language was more a defense than a positive means of communicating. He believed that their speech, or lack of it, served to keep people at a distance, thereby protecting the patients' already low self-esteem. Thus, some patients might maintain their distance by being secretive about their thoughts, some by talking crazily. Sullivan believed that at least some of this avoidance behavior resulted from an unconscious, complicated response to anxiety. In his book, *The Psychiatric Interview* (1954), he commented:

> People who come to be called schizophrenic are remarkably shy, low in their self-esteem, and rather convinced that they are not appreciated by others. They are faced by the possibility of panic related to their feelings of inferiority, loneliness, and failure in living. (p. 206)

The chief impediment to communicating with a schizophrenic, in Sullivan's view, was the patient's anxiety. Therefore, one of the therapist's primary tasks is to avoid provoking unnecessary anxiety in patients during the therapy session. Sullivan believed schizophrenics could benefit from the therapist encouraging them to regress or return to early childhood experiences to gradually yet straightforwardly address the anxieties experienced at critical points in life. Toward the end of his own life, Sullivan began to emphasize the group or social atmosphere of the schizophrenic, especially the tension or anxiety experienced in a group. One of the most influential psychiatrists of his time, Sullivan advocated procedures which constituted the standard psychotherapy for schizophrenia in American until the 1970s.

Few psychotherapy outcome studies were conducted in the 1940s and 1950s, and the effectiveness of Sullivan's approach at Chestnut Lodge was not evaluated with current rigorous treatment standards. Sullivan made one of the first attempts to subject the therapeutic process to close scrutiny. For example, in 1948, he recorded the entire therapy of three patients, each of whom had a different therapist.

Today, few psychodynamic therapists use the specific approaches recommended by Sullivan or his pupil, Freida Fromm-Reichman (1939). Psychodynamic therapies, in general, have become more reality-oriented and increasingly focused on current interpersonal relationship patterns (e.g., Arieti, 1976). Additionally, since the introduction of clearly effective medication for schizophrenics in the 1950s, most individual psychotherapy approaches have become adjuncts to medication. In a psychodynamic treatment study with over 200 schizophrenic patients, however, May, Tuma, and Dixon (1981) showed individual psychotherapy as minimally superior to medication alone in terms of patient adjustment, but that it did not hasten hospital discharge, either as an adjunct to medication or as the sole treatment. In sum, the findings mildly support individual psychotherapy's benefit to schizophrenic patients, though clearly not as a sufficient treatment by itself. However, psychodynamic therapists have always stressed a strong therapeutic relationship or alliance, and it is now clear that a good therapeutic relationship in the first six months of treatment can facilitate compliance with the prescribed medication regimens and better post-hospitalization outcomes for schizophrenics (Frank & Gunderson, 1990).

Milieu Therapy. Before the 1960s, most of the schizophrenics' daily care centered around routine ward management and custodial care. Some experts had intermittently discussed the harmful effects of institutionalization, but in the 1960s a number of writers strongly attacked traditional mental hospitals. Sociologist Irving Goffman published a book, *Asylums* (1961), depicting the similarities between the life of a mental patient and that of a prisoner. Four years later, psychologists Ullmann and Krasner, published *Case Studies in Behavior Modification* (1965), illustrating that schizophrenics' "crazy" behavior was sometimes inadvertently reinforced and thus maintained by simple attention from ward attendants. During sessions too, therapists reinforced "sick talk" by attending to it rather than to "healthy talk." In another influential book, *Institutionalism and Schizophrenia* (1970), British psychiatrists Wing and Brown documented the relationship between a schizophrenic's environment and mental state. Patients were, they observed, more likely to be withdrawn, apathetic, and to speak very little when their living conditions were spartan. The patients' condition was also observed to deteriorate after a superintendent was installed who provided fewer social amenities than they were accustomed to.

In sum, these three books showed the negative effect on patients of traditional care in mental hospitals. Their arguments and findings influenced many professionals to change their attitudes toward the care of schizophrenics. Thus, in the 1960s, clinicians and researchers began to emphasize **milieu treatment** of schizophrenia. Although milieu treatments of schizophrenics vary considerably, they generally emphasize self-care, self-management of ward activities, and group norms for appropriate ward behavior. The new emphasis was on providing as normal a daily routine as possible. Patients were encouraged to care for themselves, seek employment if they did not have a job, and participate in the variety of social activities the hospitals had begun to provide.

Based on the impetus of Ullmann and Krasner's book (1965) and a related book, *The Token Economy: A Motivational System for Therapy and Rehabilitation,* by Ayllon and Azrin (1968), behaviorally oriented psychologists began to use reinforcement principles to promote behavior change in schizophrenics. For example, attention from ward attendants and opportunities to earn privileges such as weekend passes were systematically used to motivate schizophrenics to dress appropriately and to participate in group activities. In fact, in varied forms, such motivational systems or token reinforcement systems are used today not only for schizophrenics but also for motivating developmentally disabled children and adults and in special class settings for children and adolescents.

Paul and Lentz (1977) compared milieu therapy, a social-learning approach, and a standard hospital treatment regime of occupational therapy, group psychotherapy, and medication. The social-learning approach emphasized prompts, instruction, and reinforcement of desirable behavior on the hospital ward for chronic schizophrenics. Twenty-eight chronic schizophrenics were assigned to each of the three treatments, matched for age, sex, symptoms, and length of prior hospitalization. Well-trained observers monitored the extent to which the ward staff followed the various treatment procedures. Patients also were monitored to assess changes in self-care, interpersonal skills, and completion of ward assignments. In contrast to those receiving routine hospital care, subjects in the milieu program and the social-learning program showed significant improvement in interpersonal skills, self-care, and ward activities. Another measure of success was whether patients could be released from the hospital without readmission for ninety days. Subsequently, 96 percent of the social-learning patients, 68 percent of the milieu therapy patients, and 46 percent of the hospital program patients met this criterion of successful treatment.

Milieu and social-learning programs have also been effective in aiding schizophrenics in sheltered or supervised environments such as community group homes (Fairweather, Sanders, Maynard, & Cressler, 1969). Such programs are highly structured, emphasize shared responsibility for the living environment, and stress developing adaptive skills for community living. Their success has led some experts to conclude that *if* community care involves supportive and residential services and is combined with adequate follow-up care from hospitals, then it would be the treatment of choice (Magaro, Talbott, & Glick, 1984). Unfortunately, at present, most communities do not have such support services, and the hospital deinstitutionalization movement of the 1960s has led to accusations of "dumping" patients simply to save money. As we have seen, many former hospital patients have, in fact, swelled the ranks of the urban homeless. Improvement in this regard will undoubtedly require action at the political level to provide the funds necessary for adequate service.

Family Therapy. Family intervention has been one of the most exciting developments of the last two decades in the treatment of schizophrenia. The pioneering work of George Brown and his colleagues (1958; 1972) in England, discussed earlier, led experts to examine the patient's family environment. As previously indicated, patients discharged to families with high expressed emotion (EE) had relapse rates three to four times greater than those discharged to homes with low EE. An intervention study based on these results has shown the beneficial effect of teaching high EE family members to respond less emotionally to family members (Leff et al., 1982). The researchers studied schizophrenic patients from high EE families at four different hospitals in London. All patients received routine hospital drug treatment. The experimental group also participated in a social intervention program consisting of an educational program, a relatives' group, and family sessions, whereas the control group did not. The education program imparted factual knowledge about schizophrenia to the patients. It consisted of four lectures regarding schizophrenia's etiology, course, and treatment. The relatives' group was designed to help high EE relatives cope with family sessions conducted in the home with the entire family, including the schizophrenic. The education program was conducted while the patient was in the hospital. The relatives' groups and the family sessions were conducted after his or her discharge. As predicted, the group receiving the social intervention did better than the control group. The relapse rate for the social intervention group was 8 percent, in contrast to the control group's 50 percent relapse rate. These differences in relapse rates are impressive, and, if replicated, will undoubtedly help to change discharge and after-care procedures for many schizophrenics.

Organized Community Services. The use of neuroleptics to alleviate many psychotic symptoms

Group homes like this one serve as treatment facilities for schizophrenic patients who can return to the community. Patients learn social skills in these homes as they receive instructions and direct feedback from the group home leaders.

and the activism of civil liberties groups reduced the number of involuntary commitments to mental hospitals. Additionally, the community mental health movement led to many mental patients' discharge and community-based treatment. From 1955 to 1987 the number of mental patients in public hospitals fell from 560,000 to approximately 116,000. These people require many services, including some formerly provided by hospitals. An organized system of community services is, therefore, sorely needed. In a review of fourteen studies of patients randomly assigned to community treatment or hospitalization, Kiesler and Sibulkin (1987) concluded the greater effectiveness of community care than hospitalization on a number of dimensions. As already noted, however, the goal of effective, organized community treatment for the majority of schizophrenics is far from realized.

No single intervention or social service can competently address all the needs of schizophrenics. A critical problem for health specialists is how to organize diverse services in the community to benefit schizophrenics (e.g., medication, family intervention, social skills training). To be effective, such services will have to be coordinated with welfare systems, housing authorities, community mental health boards, police departments, and advocacy groups for former mental patients. As Mechanic and Aiken (1987) argue, the "present crisis and future challenge" of caring for mentally ill patients lies in developing a coordinated delivery system for their care.

SUMMARY

1. Only 1 percent of adults become schizophrenic, but 40 percent of all hospital beds in the United States are used by schizophrenics.
2. Equal numbers of women and men are afflicted by this disorder that generally occurs before age forty-five. Males are at much higher risk for hospital admission for schizophrenia before thirty years of age, and females are at greater risk after thirty.
3. Schizophrenia occurs in every race and area of the world, and its symptoms are remarkably consistent across cultures. Kraepelin, who first described schizophrenia (then termed *dementia praecox*), depicted a disease with a deteriorating course, but we now know that many schizophrenics recover, a small percentage without treatment.
4. Schizophrenics think and act unusually. Their odd thoughts and behavior often lead others to call them "mad." The classic symptoms of schizophrenia are thought disorders, perception disturbances, affect disturbances, psychomotor disturbances, sense of self problems, and volitional problems. There are several types of schizophrenia: catatonic, disorganized, paranoid, and undifferentiated, and most schizophrenics progress through phases of the disorder ranging from a prodromal to an active phase and finally to a residual phase.
5. Beliefs seen by most members of society as misrepresentations of reality are delusions. The belief that "everybody is out to get me" is one of the most common delusions. Hallucinations are abnormal perceptions, such as hearing voices and seeing visions.
6. Delusions are called positive, or excess, symptoms, whereas extreme apathy and lack of affect are called negative symptoms. Medication can reduce positive symptoms but does not remedy negative symptoms.
7. There is no single cause of schizophrenia. Most professionals agree that the disorder is produced by a combination of genetic and biochemical factors interacting with the person's environment. Twin studies show a 50 percent to 60 percent concordance rate for schizophrenia in monozygotic twins and a 15 percent to 20 percent concordance rate for dizygotic twins. Other evidence of genetic factors in schizophrenia has been provided by adoption studies showing children of schizophrenics reared in foster homes at higher risk for developing schizophrenia than control children.
8. Schizophrenics are disproportionately represented among the lower socioeconomic classes. Whether schizophrenics drift downward into lower social classes or living in low social classes operates to produce schizophrenia is unclear. Both conclusions are probably accurate to some extent.
9. High-risk studies of children of schizophrenic parents suggest that the majority of their offspring have effective coping and adaptive skills; the likelihood of developing schizophrenia is only 10 percent to 15 percent if a child has one schizophrenic parent. Elevated risk for schizophrenia occurs in children whose mother had a severe schizophrenic disorder, in children separated from their parents when very young, and in children viewed as aggressive and withdrawn at an early age. Children with high autonomic arousal are also at risk for schizophrenia.
10. Treatment for schizophrenia consists of pharmacological, social, and psychological interventions. Neuroleptic medication has become an accepted treatment, calming patients while markedly diminishing hallucinations and delusions. This medication has helped reduce the psychiatric hospital population by almost 50 percent and lessened the likelihood of patient relapse. Milieu and social-learning programs have been successful in allowing schizophrenics to be discharged from hospitals. Psychodynamically oriented psychotherapy has also proven effective in fostering patient adjustment. Finally family therapy is one of the most exciting developments of the last two decades in the treatment of schizophrenia. Schizophrenics in families taught to be less emotional have an 8 percent relapse rate whereas those in families not receiving such training have a 50 percent relapse rate. Regardless of the technological and psychological advances in the treatment of schizophrenia, the development of coordinated health delivery systems with housing authorities, welfare systems, and advocacy groups represent the future challenge in the care of the chronically mentally ill.

Janecek Ota, *The Cell.* Tate Gallery/Art Resource.

15

MENTAL RETARDATION, AGING, AND THE ORGANIC BRAIN DISORDERS

This chapter considers the nature and causes, as well as the treatment and prevention, of the behavioral disorders caused by damage to the normal brain.

A significant number of mentally retarded individuals suffer from demonstrable brain damage. Mental retardation, afflicting about one percent of the U.S. population, is characterized by subaverage intellectual performance and the inability to function in social situations and conform to social norms. A range of factors cause it by permanently disrupting normal brain functioning. Although the brain damage causing mental retardation is irreversible, successful efforts to prevent some brain disorders that lead to mental retardation have been achieved. Advances in institutional and home care for the retarded—enabling them to maximize their independent functioning—have also taken place in recent years.

Because more people throughout the world are living longer, efforts to enable older persons to live happier, healthier, and more productive lives have been given more attention. Research suggests that many "inevitable" features of aging may actually be preventable.

Some organic brain disorders are acute and reversible. Alcohol intoxication most commonly disrupts brain functioning temporarily. Other organic brain disorders, however, are chronic and irreversible. They often involve dementia, characterized by serious memory and learning problems, a marked change in personality and behavior, and deterioration in judgment. The most familiar of these conditions include Alzheimer's disease, a pathological disorder of aging; Korsakoff's syndrome, a consequence of chronic alcohol abuse; the dementias associated with AIDS, Huntington's disease, and Parkinson's disease; and epilepsy. All of these conditions represent major problems for our society. Though we cannot yet cure them, we are making important strides in preventing their occurrence.

MENTAL RETARDATION

Historical Overview

Although ample evidence shows that such psychiatric disorders as schizophrenia, bipolar affective disorder, and alcoholism were recognized, studied, and treated by the ancient Greeks and Romans, neither culture made much mention of mental retardation. About all we know of their views of the condition is that Hippocrates briefly acknowledged the retardation possibly resulting from prenatal and paranatal brain damage and that Spartans and Romans sometimes killed severely mentally retarded infants. And though scientists and society were much concerned with psychosis and demonic possession during and after the Middle Ages, there was still little mention of the mentally retarded. What does seem clear is that they were barely tolerated, often seen as nature's accidents, and sometimes considered in league with the devil. As a result, the mentally retarded were sometimes subjected to the same barbarities as psychotics were during this time, in the name of the Inquisition.

Shortly after Philippe Pinel began to reform hospitals for the insane in France at the end of the 18th century (see Chapter 1), other French physicians (the most famous of whom were Itard and Seguin) and a Swiss (Guggenbuhl) succeeded in bringing the care and study of the severely mentally retarded into the realm of medicine. This resulted in the creation of more humane institutional care for the mentally retarded in both Europe and the United States.

By the mid-1800s, the optimism of the late 1700s about efforts to teach the mentally retarded useful skills had turned into pessimism at the prospects of helping them become more independent and productive. As a result, the institutions for the retarded that had a generation before been reformed, gradually became again more custodial than rehabilitative. At about the same time, efforts to reduce the problem of mental retardation by eugenic (birth) control of various kinds (some of them uncomfortably foreshadowing the Nazi era) began to be considered.

Although continued disinterest in the retarded marked the early part of the twentieth century, discovery of the relationship between inborn errors of metabolism and mental retardation followed shortly thereafter. In the early 1930s, the discovery of phenylketonuria (a metabolically caused form of mental retardation discussed later) raised the possibility of a scientific basis for prevention and treatment efforts. Identification of many other metabolic disorders causing mental retardation has followed these initial discoveries, as has a scientifically based genetics research effort, reflecting the genetic basis of most of the metabolic disorders. Not surprisingly, these advances have been accompanied by a more positive, less judgmental view of retardation. The same change in attitudes toward psychosis followed the recognition, around the time of Kraepelin (1856–1926), that some of these disorders were "real" physical disorders. New laws to ensure proper care for the mentally retarded also followed though, even today, too many institutions for the mentally retarded in the United States reflect legislative neglect and societal indifference.

President John F. Kennedy, whose sister was mentally retarded from birth, sparked a further awakening of America's responsibilities to the mentally retarded and their families in the early 1960s. That interest and concern has continued to the present time.

Problems of Definition and Diagnosis

Definition. Mental retardation can be defined in both biomedical and sociocultural–adaptational terms. The biomedical definition of retardation requires actual changes in the brain's structure and/or function. The sociocultural–adaptational definition sees retardation as an inability to function in social situations and to conform to social norms. This distinction is meaningful: Only 25 percent of the mentally retarded suffer from demonstrable brain damage or dysfunction.

The most widely accepted definition of mental retardation was adopted by the American Association of Mental Deficiency in 1961. It states "Mental retardation refers to sub-average general intellectual functioning which originates in the developmental period and is associated with impairment in adaptive behavior." (p. 14) *DSM-III-R* (1987, pp. 47–48) takes the same position by requiring

1. "Significantly subaverage general intellectual functioning."
2. "Concurrent deficits or impairments in adaptive functioning."
3. "Onset before the age of 18."

Nomenclature. Today we often use the terms *mental retardation* and *mental deficiency* interchangeably. Yet the World Health Organization recommends the term *mental subnormality,* reserving mental retardation for environmentally caused conditions and mental deficiency for biologically determined conditions. The term *feeblemindedness* is still in use in Great Britain though it has generally fallen into disuse in the United States after being the term of choice for many decades. *Oligophrenia* is used frequently in the U.S.S.R., Scandinavia, and other Western European countries.

Diagnosis. *DSM-III-R* distinguishes among four levels of severity of mental retardation:

- Mild mental retardation (IQ 50–55 to approximately 70).
- Moderate mental retardation (IQ 35–40 to 50–55).
- Severe mental retardation (IQ 20–25 to 35–40).
- Profound mental retardation (IQ below 20–25).

Amniocentesis represents a very important recent advance in our ability to diagnose conditions causing mental retardation (Berg, 1986). In amniocentesis, a small amount of amniotic fluid (the protective substance surrounding the fetus in the mother's uterus) is withdrawn toward the end of the fourth month of gestation (see Figure 15.1). The fetal cells floating in

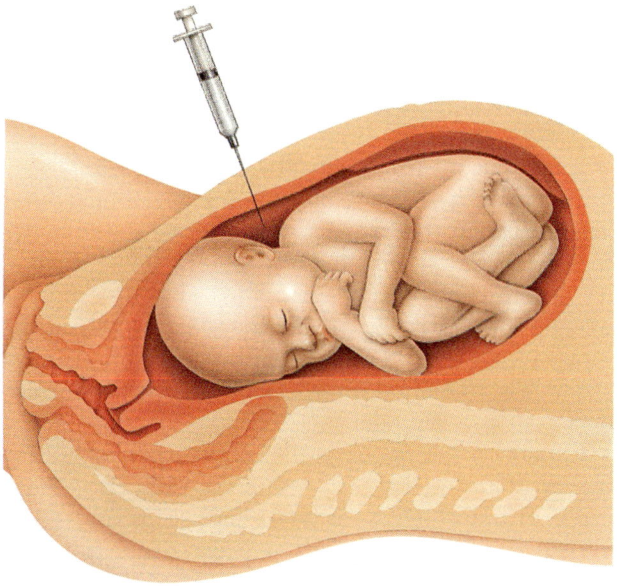

Figure 15.1 *Amniocentesis requires the withdrawal of a small amount of amniotic fluid from the uterus, generally toward the end of the fourth month of gestation.*

the fluid can be carefully analyzed for signs of various fetal abnormalities, including serious hereditary conditions. Parents decide if they should consider a therapeutic abortion if an identified condition would permanently impede the unborn child's quality of life.

As one authority on amniocentesis notes:

> In the absence of universal agreement or even a general consensus on these issues, most professional personnel engaged in the sphere of genetic counseling and prenatal diagnosis are content to accept the choices of termination or continuation of pregnancy from well-informed parents and to be supportive of the decisions they elect to make. Significant deviation from that approach seems uncomfortably akin to donning a "holier than thou" mantle. (Berg, 1986, p. 632)

The Epidemiology of Mental Retardation

In a recent survey of mental retardation's epidemiology, Munro (1986) observed that "mental retardation is the most common lifelong handicap in 'developed' nations and likely consumes more professional and financial resources than any other disabling condition" (p. 593). Although the prevalence of mental retardation in the United States was estimated at 3 percent for many years, more recent epidemiological studies have put the figure at 1 percent. That figure is generally accepted as valid throughout most of the world. With a population of about 250 million, the United States probably has about 2.5 million mentally retarded citizens. Since all of them, to a greater or lesser extent, must receive lifelong special care and attention, it is easy to see the substantial financial and social costs of mental retardation.

Unevenly distributed across age groups, mental retardation represents less than 1 percent of preschool children, as only the more severe forms of retardation are diagnosed then (Shapiro, Palmer, & Capute, 1987). Its greatest prevalence is in school-age children and adolescents between the ages of ten and eighteen, because intellectual and academic performance are most intensively evaluated during those years. Prevalence rates decline steadily through the rest of the lifespan for two principal reasons: Many mildly retarded persons ultimately integrate into society and many of the most severely retarded die before they live out a normal lifespan. Best estimates are that about 75 percent of the retarded are adolescents or younger (Munro, 1986).

Most prevalence studies report higher rates of mental retardation among males than females (Lapousse & Weitzner, 1970). Reasons include males' greater vulnerability to prenatal factors causing retardation, the significant number of hereditary conditions causing mental retardation that are linked to the sex chromosomes, and the social behavior of boys, which is more likely to bring them to the attention of authorities who might then find them to be retarded.

An inverse relationship exists between socioeconomic status and prevalence of mental retardation in the United States (Richardson & Higgins, 1965). This relationship is generally considered a function of the prenatal care the poor receive in this country; their inability to provide their children the same academic milieu, at home and at school, available to middle- and upper-class children; and the greater tendency for school authorities to place poor children in classes for the mentally retarded. Similarly, mental retardation's prevalence in the United States seems higher for nonwhites than for whites (e.g., Jones, 1979).

The overwhelming majority of the mentally retarded, close to 90 percent, are mildly retarded. Almost all can expect to acquire the social and work skills necessary to support themselves. Only 10 percent of the retarded fall into the moderate, severe, and profound categories, which include most of the retarded unable to live independently.

The Nature and Causes of Mental Retardation

The mentally retarded do not suffer from low IQ only—and low IQ alone does not prevent them from effectively functioning in the world (Trites, 1986). Mental retardation caused by prenatal factors, chromosomal abnormalities, and genetic defects, typically involves multiple physical problems that may limit vision, speech, or locomotion (Koranyi, 1986). The retarded may also be burdened by a variety of neuropsychological deficits preventing them from adequately reading, writing, speaking, or perceiving (McCaffrey & Isaac, 1985). Although the retarded experience the full range of psychiatric disorders, they also may be especially prone to depression because of the problems in living their retardation causes them (Pawlarcyzk & Beckwith, 1987; Sovner & Hurley, 1983).

Disorders Caused by Prenatal Factors. The pregnant woman's physical and emotional health, including her nutritional status and use of psychoactive substances, exert marked influences on her unborn child's health and welfare. Some of today's headlines trumpet the indictments of cocaine- and crack-using expectant mothers for threatening their unborn children's welfare. They represent dramatic testimony to our society's sudden recognition of the crucial importance of the unborn child's prenatal environment.

Prenatal factors are important causes of mental retardation. A variety of chronic maternal illnesses, for example, can affect the fetus's developing central nervous system. These conditions include uncontrolled diabetes and high blood pressure. Chronic alcohol or drug abuse during pregnancy can cause the fetal damage and retardation termed *fetal alcohol syndrome* (see Chapter 11). Agents taken during pregnancy to induce immunity to a disease, including antitetanus serum and typhoid vaccine, and incompatibility between the mother's blood and the child's blood also cause retardation. Maternal disorders that lead to premature birth, and birth injuries, including temporary oxygen deprivation, may also cause retardation.

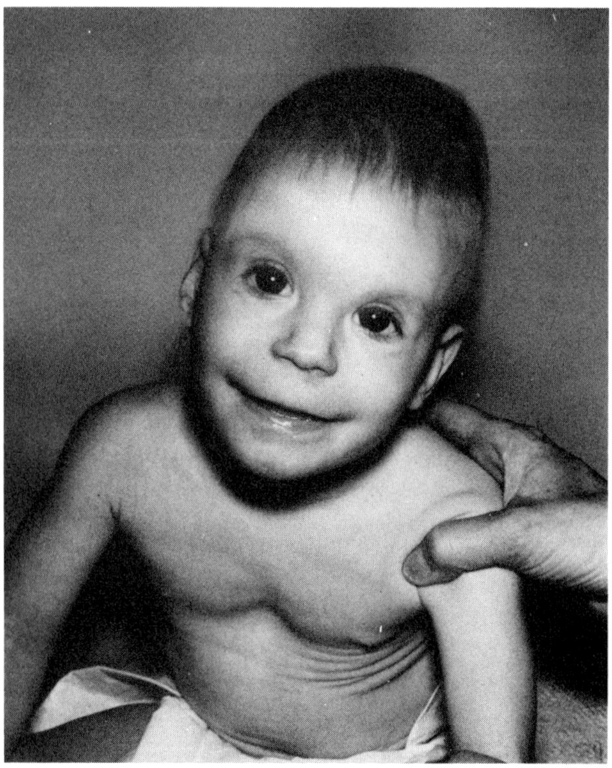

This youngster shows the facial characteristics of fetal alcohol syndrome; mild mental retardation is typically a part of the syndrome.

Infections during pregnancy, especially viral infections, can also seriously damage the developing fetus. The extent of this damage depends on a number of factors, including the kind of viral infection, its severity, and the age of the developing fetus (determining which fetal system is developing most rapidly at the time of infection). The two maternal infections most apt to lead to mental retardation are rubella (German measles) and syphilis.

Rubella is the major prenatal infectious condition responsible for mental retardation. Such serious physical abnormalities as heart disease, deafness, and cranial and visual problems may also result from this maternal infection. Ten to 25 percent of infants born to mothers infected with the rubella virus during the first three months of their pregnancies will develop one or more of these serious problems; when the infection occurs during the pregnancy's first month, the risk of serious damage rises to close to 50 percent.

Syphilis is not a major cause of mental retardation in the United States at this time because it can usually be detected and treated effectively before causing fetal damage. However, the bacterium that causes syphilis (*treponema pallidum*) has become increasingly resistant to antibiotic treatment. As a result, clinicians have become more concerned that the disease will remain untreated in some pregnant women and cause mental retardation.

Disorders Caused by Chromosomal Mutations. Chromosomal mutations in the sperm or ova occur prior to conception. They produce abnormalities in the genes and chromosomes responsible for the body's form and function. Most often induced by X-rays, these chromosomal abnormalities are also significantly more likely to afflict aging mothers and, possibly, fathers. Most chromosomal abnormalities causing mental retardation are located on the autosomal chromosomes though a few are associated with the sex chromosomes.

Down's Syndrome. This common form of retardation was previously termed *Mongolism* because of its victims' Oriental appearance. That term is no longer used due to its negative racial connotations. One of the most studied common forms of mental retardation, the disorder was first described almost 125 years ago by English physician Langdon Down. The child showing Down's syndrome generally has a small, rounded skull with a flattened, moon-shaped face. Openings for the eyes are narrow and have a

This Down's Syndrome teenager takes obvious pride in medals won as a downhill skier.

downward and inward slope. The nose is short. The tongue is often large and may protrude from the mouth. The cheeks are rosy and the hair may be coarse, wiry, and sparse. These children are typically small for their age.

The causes of Down's syndrome include age-related chromosomal abnormalities and radiation-induced chromosomal mutations; there are, probably, other unknown causes as well. Part of the problem of tracing a precise etiology derives from identification of three distinct chromosomal abnormalities responsible for the disorder. The most common is *trisomy 21*. These victims of Down's syndrome have three rather than the usual two chromosome 21's. They have, consequently, 47 rather than the usual 46 chromosomes. A nondisjunction, or separation, during meiosis (the separation of maternal and paternal germ cells prior to fertilization) is thought to account for this form of Down's syndrome.

The incidence of Down's syndrome is estimated at about one in every 700 births. Despite the disorder's severity, only about 10 percent of persons afflicted with it are in institutions for the mentally retarded. Most of the rest, especially children and adolescents, remain at home with their parents. The risk a mother over age thirty-two runs of having a Down's syndrome child is at least seven times greater than that of a younger mother.

Most Down's syndrome sufferers fall into the moderate and severe categories of mental retardation; fewer than half have IQ's over fifty. As children, most of these people are cooperative, friendly, happy, and easy to manage, which explains why most of them are home with their families and greater numbers are being "mainstreamed" in regular public school classrooms. As they grow into adolescence, however, emotional and behavioral disorders are more likely to develop. At that time, the adolescent may perceive more clearly his or her condition's profound impact on prospects for a normal, independent, happy life; depression may be a consequence. The adolescent's increased size and strength, as well as growing sexual feelings, also contribute to the greater likelihood of antisocial behavior, drug abuse, and sexual promiscuity. As a result, institutionalization becomes a prevalent option for some Down's syndrome patients by young adulthood.

Most victims of Down's syndrome die before age 40, often of a presenile dementing condition closely resembling Alzheimer's disease.

Box 15.1 illustrates Down's syndrome's impact on one family. The narrative makes clear how difficult, yet rewarding, parenting a retarded child can be. For some parents, the problems caused by having a mentally retarded child can hasten the end of a troubled marriage. For others, though, like Gary and Mary Wilson, a Down's syndrome child is simply another challenge to be dealt with successfully.

Disorders Caused by Genetic Defects. These genetically transmitted disorders account for between 4 percent and 5 percent of all the mentally retarded. Alkaptonuria, a disorder interfering with the formation of amino acids, was the first of these conditions to be described in 1908. Since then, a significant additional number of disorders have been identified; in many cases, their mechanisms have also been studied. These conditions are caused by genetically transmitted metabolic errors—passed from one generation to the next—which result in the abnormal accumulation of chemical substances preventing the central nervous system's normal functioning.

Phenylketonuria (PKU). The most intensively studied inborn error of metabolism, phenylketonuria or PKU, discovered in 1934, is also a disorder of amino acid metabolism. Because of its thorough study, PKU has become a model for the investigation of other hereditary biochemical disorders.

PKU is transmitted as a simple recessive autosomal trait; it can only appear when both parents carry the recessive gene for the disorder. (This mode of inheritance means that a PKU child's siblings are

BOX 15.1 Why Did It Have to Happen to Us?

Mary and Gary Wilson waited a long time to have their first child. Because both were starting graduate school when they decided to get married, they wanted to wait to have children. Though Gary earned the M.B.A. after two years, Mary still had three more years for her Ph.D. in history. And then, when Mary was awarded the Ph.D., the two made the decision to wait a while longer, so Mary could get a good start up the academic ladder at the prestigious department of history which had offered her an assistant professorship.

Consequently, Mary was almost thirty-four when their first child, David, was born. A smiling, friendly, much-loved newborn, David was the realization of one of Mary and Gary's most precious dreams—until, at the age of four months, he was diagnosed as having Down's syndrome. Gary's reaction included anger, self-pity, and emotional distance from David and Mary. Mary lapsed into unfamiliar depression, blaming herself for having put her own career ahead of the family she had always wanted.

As time went on, though, as David became an affectionate, friendly, easy child, and after his parents had gotten through mourning what might have been, Mary, Gary, and David became a family for the first time. It helped too that David's three living grandparents, all of whom nearby, had understood the couple's decision to postpone parenthood—and had become doting grandparents without much apparent trouble. Mary and Gary's solid, loving marriage helped them get through the postpartum period without destructive mutual recriminations. But it helped most that their son David had become a valued, beloved focus of their lives, despite the burden he—and his family—would have to carry.

also at high risk of developing the disorder.) PKU ranges in prevalence from between one in 10,000 to one in 20,000 persons in the United States. The basic metabolic error involves the body's inability to convert phenylalanine, an essential and plentiful amino acid, into another very common substance, tyrosine, because of the inactivity or absence of the liver enzyme responsible for this conversion. Phenylalanine levels rise, therefore, to between ten and twenty-five times their normal amounts in the blood, resulting in a marked decrease in the essential brain neurotransmitters serotonin, epinephrine, and norepinephrine. Untreated PKU becomes apparent between six and twelve months after birth, when the infant may begin vomiting for unexplained reasons. At about the same time, the urine will begin to have an unusual odor, a skin rash or eczema may appear, and the infant may suffer unexplained seizures.

Most PKU victims are severely or profoundly retarded. Seizures are a particular hazard as well; most sufferers are small in stature, with especially small heads. They tend to be hyperactive and display unusual behavior, including temper tantrums and bizarre movements of the body and upper extremities. Both verbal and nonverbal communication are generally nonexistent.

An effective screening test designed to detect phenylalanine in the blood, now routinely administered to newborn infants in most hospitals, has led to early identification of PKU victims. When placed on a low phenylalanine diet early in life, before blood levels of the substance have risen to and remained at abnormal levels, a PKU victim may avoid most or all of the intellectual deterioration of untreated PKU. However, phenylalanine is also an essential amino acid, and when absent from the diet altogether, proteins necessary for normal muscle growth and development will be lacking. Once brain development has been completed, around age six, a normal diet can be reintroduced.

Disorders Caused by Postnatal Factors. Several serious childhood infections of the brain, such as *meningitis* (which affects the membrane covering the brain) and *encephalitis* (affecting the brain itself), can cause brain damage and mental retardation. Symptoms of these epidemic diseases include a sudden, extreme escalation in temperature, vomiting, disorientation, and complaints of a stiff neck. Without early treatment, delirium may develop and an acute dementia, with permanent effects including mental retardation, may result.

Accidents are the leading cause of death and severe disabling injury—and a prime cause of retardation—in the United States. Head injuries from automobile accidents, falls, and other serious accidents, can cause brain damage severe enough to induce a seizure disorder, which may result in mental retardation. Near drowning, accompanied by a prolonged cutoff of the brain's oxygen supply, can lead to the death of enough brain cells to cause retardation, as can lead poisoning, discussed later.

Disorders Caused by Environmental Factors. Mental retardation caused by biological factors devastates victims, their families, and society. Mental retardation caused by environmental factors may be even worse. First, it seems more easily prevented. Second, it often burdens those least able to bear the hardship—the poor, the vocationally deprived, members of ethnic and racial minorities, and others who have already suffered from society's disdain and neglect. Of course, many people in these groups triumph over the obstacles; others, though, fall prey to their tragic effects.

Although 1 percent of the U.S. population is thought to be mentally retarded, between 10 percent and 30 percent of the poorest members of American society are estimated to meet the criteria for at least mild mental retardation. Whether these people are poor because they are retarded or are retarded because of lifestyle factors associated with their poverty are crucial and still unsolved questions.

A number of factors associated with poverty have been implicated in mental retardation's development. (Obviously, while the poor are not the only ones suffering from the environmental factors associated with mental retardation, they may be at greatest risk because of them.)

A variety of medical problems that rarely burden middle-class Americans often afflict the poor, in large part because they have less access to quality medical care. Poor, pregnant women are more likely to be malnourished and to have little or no prenatal care, thus increasing the likelihood of their unborn children suffering from the consequences of untreated maternal infection, anemia, and birth problems that can produce mental retardation (Koranyi, 1986). Mortality and prematurity are highest among infants born to poor women.

Babies born to lower socioeconomic status (SES) mothers are less likely to have routine checkups or immunizations and are more likely to be treated later rather than earlier for serious illnesses. Again, reasons include inadequate access to competent medical care. A variety of childhood disorders can cause mental retardation if not diagnosed and treated early. The infant's own nutritional status is also more likely to be marginal; severe protein deficiency, caused by dietary deficiencies related to the cost of high-quality food, can cause mental retardation.

As such infants mature into children, the risk of mental retardation from environmental factors continues. One common cause of retardation is lead poisoning, caused by a child's eating paint chips (they taste sweet) from the peeling walls of old tenements covered with lead-based paint.

Beyond the direct effects on the central nervous system of biological and environmental factors, the poor in this country are also subject to a range of emotional and social problems that affect the ability to learn. Being raised in father-absent families by undereducated, underemployed, highly stressed mothers or by a succession of other caretakers is apt to provide a chaotic learning environment (Boodoosingh & Brown, 1986). In such situations,

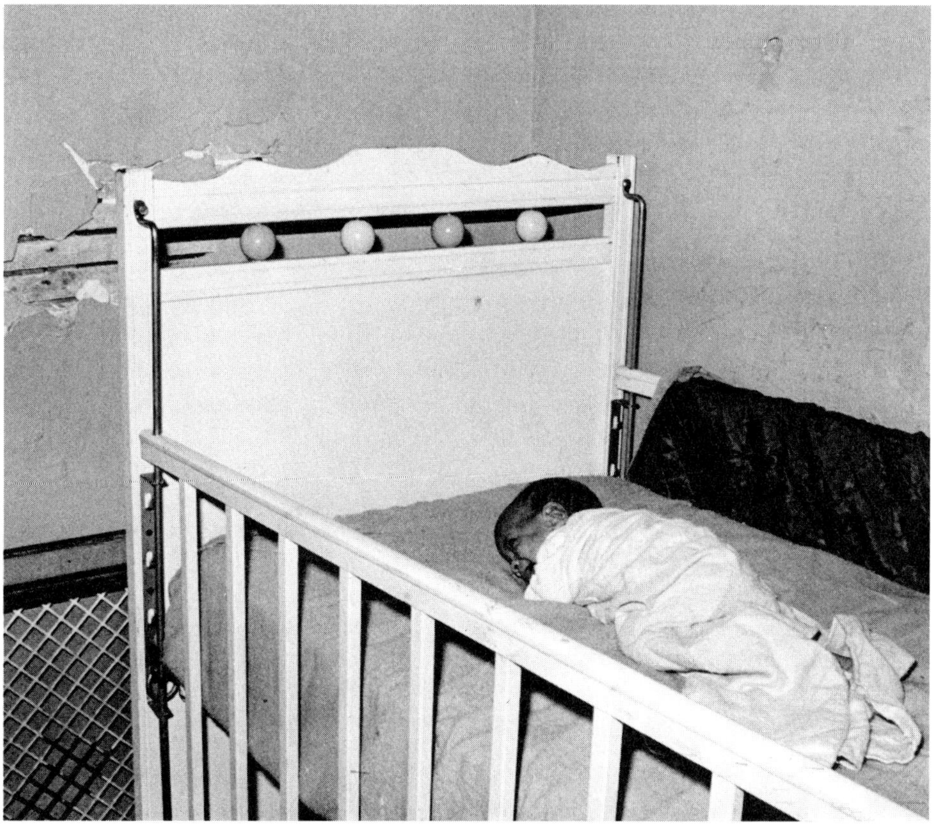

Children born into poverty are at greater risk to develop mental retardation, largely because of the environments in which they are forced to live.

school attendance is likely to be irregular and parental ability to help in the learning process impaired.

Mentally retarded children are also more likely to be born to mentally retarded parents (Feldman, 1986). Familial mental retardation probably accounts for the largest single group of the mentally retarded in this country. Generally mildly retarded, without demonstrable central nervous system damage, these persons are simply less able than the rest of us to acquire new knowledge, remember, reason, and function in school and other learning situations. Although marginally able to function in the world, they pass on their own borderline intellectual capabilities to their children.

Familial mental retardation is also associated with an accumulation of other socially unwanted behaviors, including alcohol and drug abuse and dependence, juvenile and adult crime, promiscuity and teenage pregnancy, and early school dropout. If you are doing badly in school, despair of ever getting a good job, and believe your peers look down on you, you are more likely to express your frustration against society by acting in antisocial ways.

Prevention of Mental Retardation and Care for the Mentally Retarded

At present, no treatment exists enabling a mentally retarded person to achieve a normal intellectual level. For that reason alone, prevention of mental retardation (primary prevention) deserves and receives major emphasis.

Prevention of Mental Retardation. Onc of the most important first steps in preventing mental retardation is education about its nature and causes. In writing this material on mental retardation, for example, the authors of this text hope to alert you to the existence of genetic counseling resources available when you decide to have children. And once a child is on the way, we hope what you read here will help you understand why your physician may, for example, suggest amniocentesis. Perhaps this chapter may have also helped you to appreciate the importance of good nutrition and good health practices during pregnancy. Finally, we hope you will be motivated to do something in your own community about the environmental determinants of mental retardation that put certain societal groups at increased risk.

Efforts to prevent retardation by addressing the factors associated with mental retardation continue. Early intervention—the discovery and modification of biological and environmental factors before they cause a child irreversible brain damage—is particularly valuable. The discovery of the factors associated with phenylketonuria, for example, has led to low phenylalanine diets to prevent the chemical's abnormal levels in the blood associated with retardation. Similarly, the recognition of lead-based paint's toxic effects has led to legislation ordering the removal of lead from paint by manufacturers so that young children no longer will be at risk for lead poisoning should they consume chips of peeling paint.

Care for the Mentally Retarded. Approximately 900,000 retarded children now attend public school in the United States (Schroeder, Schroeder, & Landesman, 1987). That figure contrasts sharply with the 110,000 children and adults residing in institutions for the mentally retarded (Epple, Jacobson, & Janicki, 1985).

Care at Home and in Public Schools. Before reading this section of the text, you may have thought that most of the mentally retarded live in institutions and that few benefit from attending public schools. As we noted previously, however, the vast majority of the retarded suffer from mild retardation. Usually, only the severely and profoundly retarded—and those with marked behavioral problems—cannot be integrated into the public school system.

This does not mean, of course, that every mentally retarded child can simply be placed in a regular classroom and, with a little extra attention, do well. Special education teachers, special classes for the educable mentally retarded, a variety of programs making learning easier for those who find it difficult, associated programs to deal with the emotional problems frequently accompanying retardation, parent-training programs with much the same purpose—all have been developed to keep as many retarded children as possible in society, at home, and in our public schools (Landesman & Butterfield, 1987).

Most experts agree that mentally retarded children's emotional and intellectual development progresses better in a facilitative home environment than in an institution. Of course, if the home environment is not a good one, or if the child is physically assaultive or delinquent, residential care may still be the only alternative. In this instance, it is the child's social misbehavior, though, not deficits in intellectual capacity, that force institutionalization.

Although psychotherapy is still employed with some retarded children to help them deal with the emotional consequences of retardation (Stavrakaki & Klein, 1986), most care and treatment is focused and behavioral. Recently, cognitive-behavioral methods have been used to

1. Identify the retarded person's negative self-statements about his or her intellectual, social, and vocational abilities.

Many mentally-retarded children benefit from special education programs that permit them to attend public schools and live at home.

2. Instill more appropriate positive self-statements.
3. Incorporate more adaptive interpersonal and cognitive behavior into the person's behavioral repertoire.

Promising trials of cognitive methods yielded improved on-the-job problem solving by two severely retarded adults employed by a janitorial supply company (Hughes & Rusch, 1990) and more adequate social and interpersonal behavior in three mentally retarded students working in different nonsheltered work settings (Park & Gaylord-Ross, 1990).

The U.S. Supreme Court, historically the means by which our society's oppressed seek redress, has recently shown interest in expanding the integration of the mentally retarded into society. (Figure 15.2 shows that, in 1979–1980, two-thirds of handicapped, retarded children in the sample studied attended regular classes.) In the 1985 *Cleburne* decision, expanding the rights of the mentally retarded, Justice Thurgood Marshall acknowledged that the mentally retarded had historically been subjected to

> a regime of state-mandated segregation and degradation . . . that in its virulence and bigotry rivaled, and indeed paralleled, the worst excesses of Jim Crow. . . . Prejudice, once let loose, is not easily cabined. As of 1979, most States still categorically disqualified "idiots" from voting, without regard to individual capacity and with discretion to exclude left in the hands of low-level election officials. (*City of Cleburne v. Cleburne Living Center,* 1985, pp. 462, 464)

Shortly before the *Cleburne* decision, the U.S. Congress passed Public Law *94-142,* dealing with the education of handicapped children, including the retarded. Its key provisions ensured all handicapped children between the ages of three and twenty-one the right to

1. Free, appropriate educational opportunity.
2. Individual educational programs reevaluated annually.
3. Education in the least restrictive environment.
4. Due process (if efforts are made to institutionalize them against their wills).

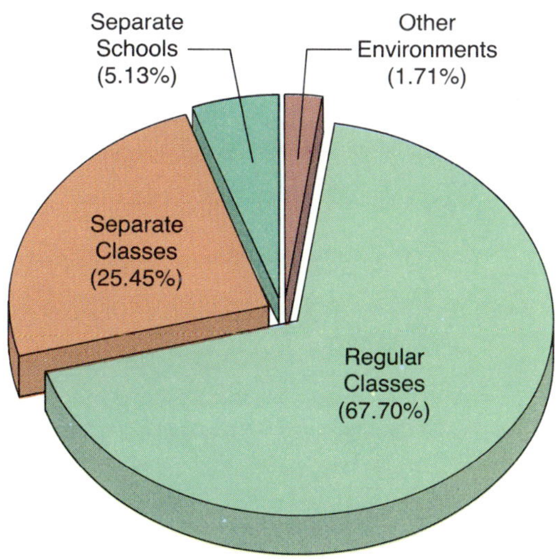

Figure 15.2 *In this 1979–1980 study, two-thirds of the handicapped, retarded children studied attended regular classes, about a quarter were placed in separate special classes, and only about one in twenty had to attend separate special schools.*
Source: Courtesy of U.S. Department of Education.

States that comply with *94-142* receive increased federal assistance for education.

Researchers and clinicians have focused much attention on developing ways to train the mildly and moderately mentally retarded—and their teachers and parents—so they can remain at home and attend public schools. One of the most common challenges is to ease the entry (called *mainstreaming*) of mildly retarded children into regular classrooms. Knapczyk (1989) describes one example, which tested out a program to help three mildly retarded fourth-graders participate in a regular mathematics class. The three were shown videotapes of normal children asking questions in the regular mathematics class. They were also given training in question asking themselves and were provided verbal reinforcement for doing so. As Figure 15.3 shows, the result was a dramatic increase in question-asking behavior (which is essential to a full understanding of the material) during a follow-up posttreatment period.

A wide range of training programs for mentally retarded children's parents have also been proposed (e.g., Dangel & Polster, 1984). Special training programs teach parents to handle the anger and frustration that retarded children often experience, to help them learn self-control and appropriate emotional

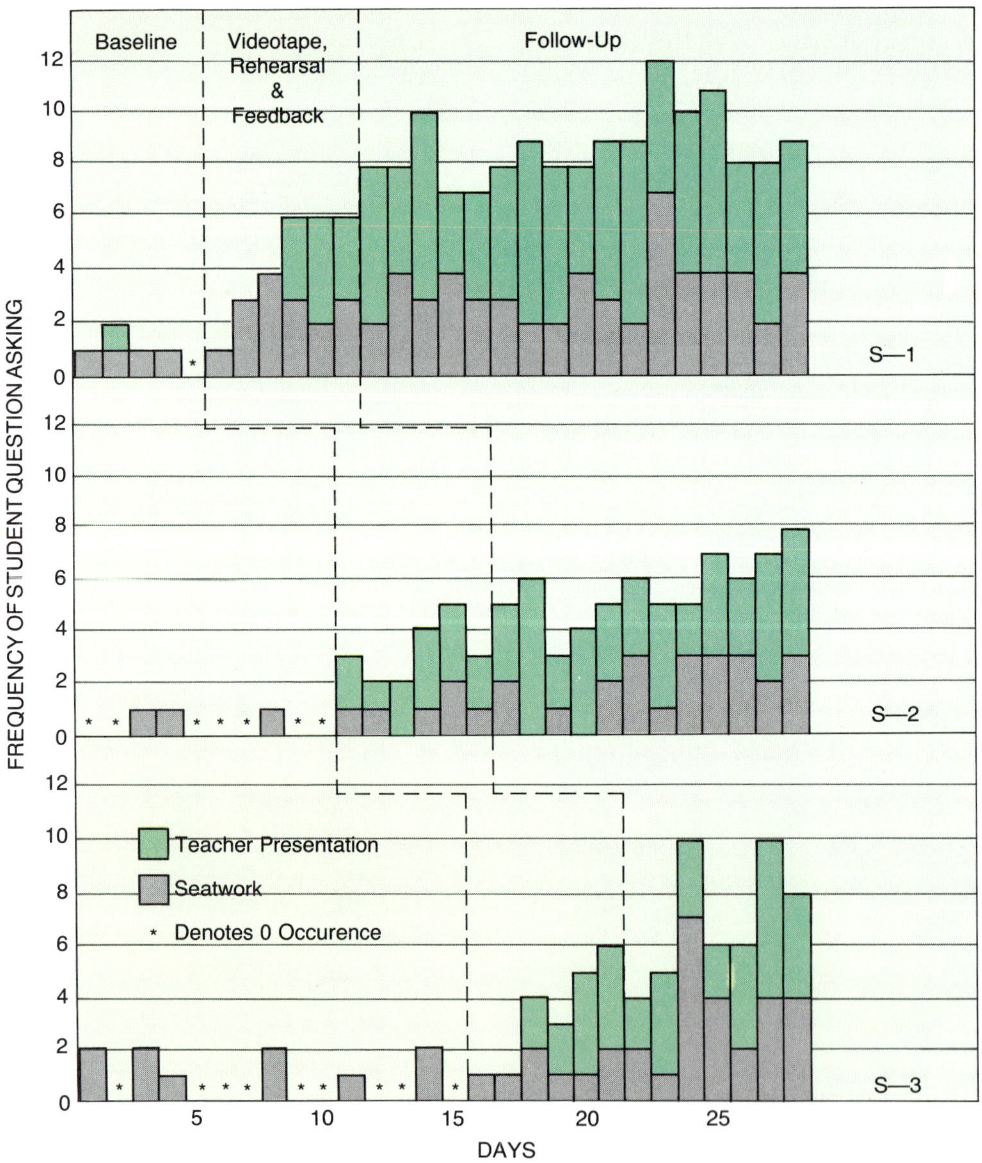

Figure 15.3 *Three mildly retarded children (S-1, S-2, and S-3) markedly increased their question-asking behavior during a lengthy follow-up period after having rehearsed the behavior repeatedly and been reinforced for doing so.*

Source: From Knapczyk, D.R. (1989). Generalization of student question asking from special class to regular class settings. *Journal of Applied Behavior Analysis, 22,* p. 80. By permission of the publisher.

skills, and to aid them in maximizing their learning potential. Most of these programs are behavioral; that is, they emphasize careful assessment of the dimensions of the behaviors to be changed and continuous record-keeping.

Institutional Care. Despite their parents' best intentions, most severely and profoundly retarded persons cannot be cared for at home. Instead, their physical and behavioral disabilities require placement in state institutions for the retarded. (The few private facilities for the retarded are so expensive that—despite their superior care—they serve only a small number of retarded persons.) In recent years, many of these state facilities have made court-ordered improvements in living conditions, staffing, and programs (Hill et al., 1985). As a result, they now represent a more adequate alternative to home and community care than even a decade ago.

Despite these recent changes, though, many state institutions for the retarded remain overcrowded and underfunded. The result, too often, is a custodial institution without the financial or human resources to help make its residents' lives more humane.

One major change for the better in institutional care for the retarded is a marked decrease in the routine use of the major tranquilizers to sedate the severely retarded (McDaniel, 1986) although, in some places, the practice continues:

> A Federal panel of experts on treatment for the retarded . . . said psychiatric medications were used too recklessly with the severely retarded to keep them from injuring themselves. The panel said that all too often the medications were for the convenience of caretakers and did more harm than good for those who took them. (*New York Times*, September 15, 1989, p. B14)

Another recent change involves a marked increase in transitional and community-based programs. These small homelike residences house from three or four to twelve mildly and moderately retarded persons who work in sheltered work settings and do not need constant supervision. Staff in these settings encourage residents to acquire independent living skills to enable them to enjoy as independent a life as possible even though they must live in an institution. Of course, some mildly retarded adults can even live independently, in their own apartments, only occasionally seeing a counselor.

Behavioral Treatment of Self-injury. One of the most serious problems in caring for the severely retarded is self-injury.

> The kinds of self-injury such people engage in include repeatedly banging the head with their hands, slapping the face, poking at the eyes, picking at the skin and pulling at the ears. Some bang the head 100 times a minute or more, and many are in danger of causing permanent damage to themselves. Some have blinded themselves, and others have torn off parts of their ears. (*New York Times*, September 15, 1989, p. B14)

Five behavioral treatment approaches are commonly used to control self-injurious behavior. They include the withholding of social reinforcement, enriched environments (which distract the individual from the temptation to self-injure), sensory extinction (masking the sensory consequences of self-injury to reduce its reinforcement value), punishment, and communication training. (On the assumption that self-injury is communication, this cognitive-behavioral treatment teaches the retarded person more effective means to communicate needs and desires.) Although each method has its supporters and has proven helpful for some individuals, none has been universally successful with the extremely serious problems associated with self-injury by severely retarded persons.

Punishment is particularly controversial. Supporters claim it is sometimes the only way self-injurious behavior can be brought under control while opponents believe it is humiliating, ineffective in the long run, and unnecessary. On weighing the evidence, a federal panel of experts on treatment for the retarded recently recommended that "punishments be used, but only as a temporary measure when there was a need to act quickly, and only in conjunction with more positive approaches" (*New York Times*, September 15, 1989, p. B14).

Behavior Modification in Institutions. Token economies and other behavior modification programs have also been used extensively to manage the behavior of institutionalized retardates, as they have been with institutionalized psychotic patients. These approaches involve the systematic reinforcement of desired behaviors (making one's bed, cleaning one's room, sweeping the hallway, or washing and brushing one's teeth) with staff attention or material reinforcers like candy and food (see Chapter 14). Unwanted behaviors (fighting, poor personal hygiene, or failure to attend to one's assigned chores) are either ignored or punished.

In the twentieth anniversary issue of the journal much of the research on behavior-modification has been published in, one of the developers of this approach to managing severely retarded persons commented on its impact:

> *I visited a well-known program for training social, self-care, and work skills to girls at a state school for the retarded. My request to visit the cottage next door was so pointedly deflected, I sneaked off on my own to see what was going on. That cottage was a snake pit of dirty, unoccupied, and neglected resi-*

dents. Our technology was effective in changing the targeted behaviors of our subjects. Human service administrators were not adopting that technology in general practice at even the most likely settings. (Hopkins, 1987, p. 341)

Despite its successes, then, behavior modification has not been as widely applied to the management problems of the severely retarded as its supporters believe it ought to have been.

NORMAL AGING

This chapter is about the devastating effects to the brain and behavior of pathological changes in central nervous system functioning. Sad outcomes are generally described: The effects of brain disease on behavior are great and treatment efforts overall are not terribly effective.

In contrast, much about the effects of the aging process on the brain (sometimes associated with physical changes in the brain, as discussed later) is not sad at all. It is important that you know about some of these effects.

By now it is a cliché to observe that people are living longer and longer. Yet the facts are impressive. In 1900, there were 3.1 million people in the United States over the age of 65 out of a total population of 76 million, or about 1 person in 25. By the year 2000, less than a decade from now, there will be more than 28 million older people, more than 1 in 10. The population of those 65 and older is, furthermore, growing much faster than the rest of our population—at a rate of 21 percent as against 12.5 percent. For those over age 75, the rate of growth is even more astounding, 37 percent versus 13 percent.

Why is American society aging so rapidly? Part of the reason is demographic: We are having fewer children. Yet advances in medicine are an important element producing this change. So is our society's new and growing concern for better nutrition, more exercise, and healthier lifestyles. New drugs controlling chronic conditions like stomach ulcers, certain forms of cancer, and conditions related to heart disease like hypertension, high cholesterol, and irregular heart rate—all responsible for premature death—have also prolonged life.

Our society then is living longer and living healthier (Woods & Birren, 1984). Persons live active, productive lives at seventy or eighty today that fifty-year-olds did not live two generations ago. We're also learning that older people who have remained healthy and vital are fully as interested in learning, maintaining an active sex life, and remaining involved in society as those much younger. Age truly does seem to be as much a matter of the mind as of the body!

> The old person yearns for, needs, and desires the same satisfactions as the young, differing not in quality though somewhat in degree. Yet the culture has a bias against their expression. What is virility at 25 is lechery at 65. . . . Actually sex in later years correlates strongly with sex in earlier years. It is a timeless drive throughout life even in the 80s and 90s, especially if one's partner is alive. (Braceland, 1972, p. 54)

Aging is truly as much a matter of the mind as of the body!

While we have been able to increase lifespan and extend significantly the productive, healthful years, we have only begun to recognize the need for supportive services to keep pace with the numbers of older people who would like companionship, need specialized housing or transportation, and require comprehensive health-care services. The challenge to American society in the future is to develop cost-effective and humane services for the healthy aged who will increasingly need to call upon them.

The federal government has begun to respond to this challenge (Melcher, 1988). Substantially increased funding for home health-care services through Medicare is now available, permitting aged persons with certain chronic, but not disabling conditions, to remain in their homes whereas they would previously have had to move into institutions. Medicare legislation to increase both acute care and long-term coverage has been passed, helping ease the aged's frequent concern of outliving their health-care resources.

Federal and state governments have also begun confronting *ageism*—prejudicial attitudes, discriminatory practices, and institutional policies directed against certain people only because they are aging (Kimmel, 1988). By legislation, enhanced enforcement of existing statutes, and social pressure, many communities have begun to address systematic discrimination against the aged in health care, housing, and employment.

Aging women are especially susceptible to ageism. They live longer than men and, therefore, are more likely to live alone. Additionally, women of all ages in the United States continue to be discriminated against in obvious and subtle ways (Rodeheaver & Datan, 1988). Women are more likely than men to fall into poverty in their old age, for example, and they are less likely to be aware of available social services and financial aids. Systematic programs to aid aging women, particularly susceptible to old age's problems, have begun.

One of the nation's leading private foundations has recently launched a major research endeavor to explore some of the factors contributing to successful aging. This project reflects leading gerontologists' realization that the nation's focus on aging's adverse consequences has prevented paying enough attention to the millions of individuals over age seventy leading happy, healthy, productive lives. The principal aim of the initiative is to identify the genetic, physiological, psychological, and social factors associated with successful aging.

A recent article by two leaders of the Program on Successful Aging (Rowe & Kahn, 1987), sponsored by the MacArthur Foundation, acknowledges that age does bring limiting changes in physiology and behavior. But the authors point out that certain people age successfully by dealing effectively with these limitations whereas others do not. They ask us to distinguish between usual and successful aging, in the belief that the variability in changes associated with growing older yields a group of people uniquely successful in dealing with these changes. Rowe and Kahn (1987) insist that this understudied group deserves attention.

Thus, they recommend intensive study of transitions in later life as a uniquely valuable way to understand the factors involved in successful aging. Identifying and studying people who deal successfully with the loss of a lifelong partner, a debilitating disease, or a change in economic circumstance may help extend that knowledge to others in similar circumstances.

Finally, recognizing the crucial role of social support in successful aging (people with adequate sup-

This 97-year-old man spent more than 30 years of happy, productive retirement raising prize orchids.

port systems are far more likely to age successfully), Rowe and Kahn (1987) encourage us to study more vigorously extrinsic variables' precise role in determining the degree to which we age successfully.

Of course, we have known for a long time of social support's vital role in the behavior of aging individuals. The disgrace of our nursing homes, for example, stems at least in part from the unwillingness of many of them to recognize the enormous value of maintaining their residents' contacts with family and friends in the community. For cost and convenience reasons, nursing homes have separated their aged residents from the community instead of enabling them to remain interested as long as possible in the world about them.

THE ORGANIC BRAIN DISORDERS

The **organic brain disorders** detailed in this chapter are caused by three different factors: alcohol and drugs, pathological processes associated with the aging process, and physical disease. The signs and symptoms of these disorders involve several of the following organic mental syndromes (a *syndrome* is a distinct group of symptoms; one or more *organic mental syndromes* characterize each organic brain disorder).

Delirium and dementia are the most common and most important organic mental syndromes, resulting in a more or less global deficit in cognitive performance.

Table 15.1 distinguishes between dementia and delirium along several important dimensions.

Delirium is generally the result of brain injury; metabolic or toxic disturbances; including infections causing high fevers, a reduction in oxygen supply to the brain; or alcohol or other drug intoxication. *Dementia* occurs following stroke (which deprives the brain of oxygen for a substantial period of time, thereby destroying part of it), certain serious infections like syphilis and HIV, brain tumors, brain injury, and chronic, progressive brain diseases.

Delirious individuals often don't know what time it is or where they are. They can pay attention for only a few moments and focus on only one thing at a time. They are unable to relate their present circumstance to anything that happened in the past. Their thinking is disconnected and often preoccupied with imaginary experiences. They may experience hallucinations of dreamlike scenes, mainly visual but also involving the other senses. They are typically restless and agitated, constantly moving without purpose.

Demented people suffer a global deterioration in their intellectual, emotional, and cognitive abilities. They almost always experience great difficulty performing tasks requiring remembering, learning, or using facts. Also typical of dementia are changes in personality, emotional balance, and mood. Memory loss is often an initial sign of the syndrome, especially memory for recent events. Attention becomes harder to sustain, fatigue comes more easily, and a general decline in the normal richness of thought becomes

TABLE 15.1 Differential Diagnosis of Delirium and Dementia

Feature	Delirium	Dementia
Onset	Rapid, often at night	Usually insidious
Duration	Hours to weeks	Months to years
Course	Fluctuates over 24 hours; worse at night; lucid intervals	Relatively stable
Awareness	Always impaired	Usually normal
Alertness	Reduced or increased; tends to fluctuate	Usually normal
Orientation	Always impaired, at least for time; tendency to mistake unfamiliar for familiar place or person	May be intact; little tendency to confabulate
Memory	Recent impaired; fund of knowledge intact if dementia is absent	Recent and remote impaired; some loss of common knowledge
Thinking	Slow or accelerated; may be dreamlike	Poor in abstraction; impoverished
Perception	Often misperceptions, especially visual	Misperceptions often absent
Sleep-wake cycle	Always disrupted; often drowsiness during the day; insomnia at night	Fragmented sleep
Physical illness or drug toxicity	Usually present	Often absent, especially in primary degenerative dementia

Source: From Lipowski, Z. J., (1983). Cognitive Disorders (delirium, acute confusional states) in the Elderly, *American Journal of Psychiatry, 140,* p. 1432. Copyright 1983, the American Psychiatric Association. Reprinted by permission.

apparent. Paranoid delusions are common as dementia progresses. Despite them, emotions seem shallow; the death of a loved one may be greeted with apparent indifference during the later stages of a dementing process.

Amnestic syndrome and organic hallucinosis impairment is in two areas of cognitive functioning, remembering and perceiving.

Individuals suffering from *amnestic syndrome*—caused by head trauma, alcohol abuse, malnutrition, brain surgery, oxygen deprivation, stroke, or brain infections—are impaired primarily in short- and long-term memory. Very remote events (those that happened many years ago) are typically remembered better than those that took place a few months ago. Sometimes these persons cannot learn any new information and may be unable to remember something that took place a few minutes before. Recent research by Butters & Stuss (1989) has localized the brain damage responsible for most amnestic syndromes to the medial portions of the diencephalon, specifically, to the dorsomedial nucleus of the thalamus and the mammillary bodies (Figure 15.4).

Persons diagnosed with *organic hallucinosis* have recurrent and prominent hallucinations, generally auditory or visual. Some individuals believe their hallucinations are real while others recognize they are not. Alcohol is a common cause of this organic syndrome, epilepsy another.

The primary disturbance of *organic delusional syndrome, organic mood syndrome,* and *organic anxiety syndrome* resembles, respectively, the schizophrenic, mood, and anxiety disorders.

These disorders are caused by hallucinogens, prolonged alcohol abuse, or toxic or metabolic disturbances. Their victims suffer from prominent and recurrent delusions, mood disorders (either marked depression or mood elevation), or panic or generalized anxiety. These symptoms can be disabling and prolonged, lasting as long as the causal factor is present.

The primary disturbance of *organic personality syndrome* is in personality functioning.

This condition is generally due to structural brain damage caused by a brain tumor, head trauma, stroke, infection, or the effects of drug abuse. Epilepsy is also a cause. Symptoms are a dramatic change in personality functioning or the accentuation of a previous trait (for example, suspiciousness, sexual promiscuity, or moodiness). These persons sometimes seem to have become someone else, so marked is the change in their social behavior and personality.

The disturbance of intoxication and withdrawal is associated either with the ingestion or cessation of ingestion of a psychoactive substance. These organic mental syndromes were discussed in detail in Chapter 11.

Some organic brain disorders last only a few minutes or a few hours. Recovery from them is almost always complete, with generally slight or nonexistent permanent effects. Alcohol intoxication and the de-

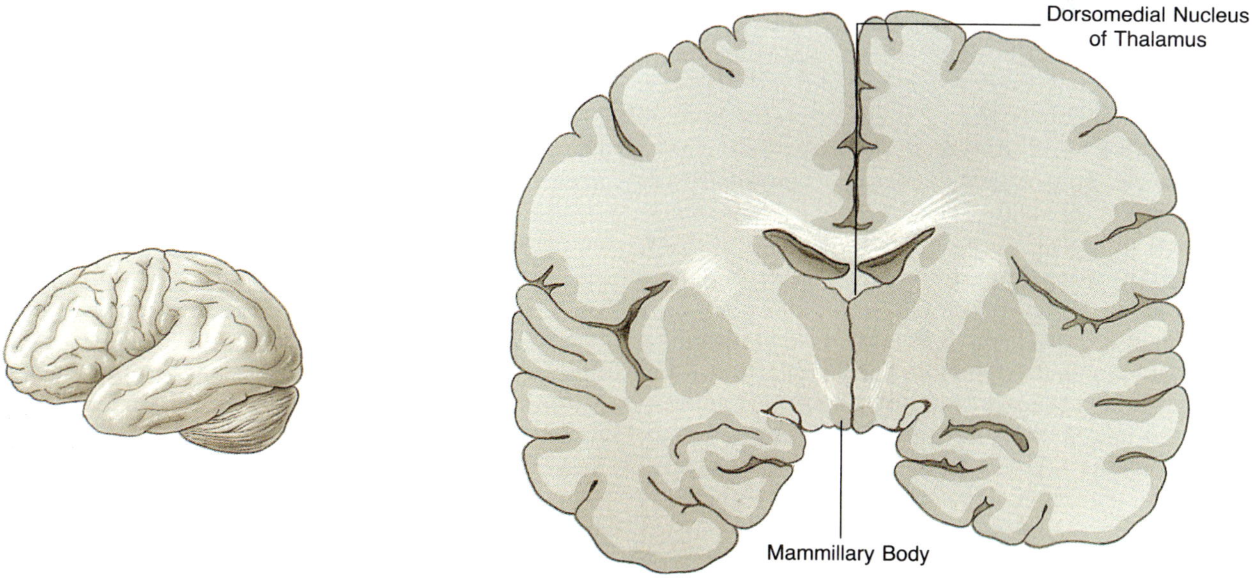

***Figure 15.4** Most amnestic syndromes are caused by damage to the brain in the dorsomedial nucleus of the thalamus and the mammillary bodies.*

Source: From Butters, N. & Stuss, D.T. (1989). Diencephalic amnesia. In F. Boller & J. Grafman (Eds.), *Handbook of Neuropsychology,* Vol. 3, p. 108. Amsterdam: Elsevier Science Publishers B. V. By permission of the publishers.

lirium that young children with high fever from an infection may experience are common examples of these reversible conditions. They are **acute brain disorders.**

Most organic brain disorders, in contrast, last much longer. Typically irreversible, with generally serious behavioral consequences, the **chronic brain disorders** may well endure throughout a lifetime.

Alzheimer's disease is an age-related brain disorder distinguished by profound losses in cognitive ability. Aging is known to affect the functioning of many bodily systems. Changes in muscle tone, in the immune system's ability to defend against infection, and in visual and auditory acuity typically signal aging's pathological effects. The process of aging also causes changes in brain function, usually small and unnoticed. An older man or woman finds it a bit more difficult to remember new names and faces or to solve complex arithmetic tasks without using paper and pencil, and perhaps avoids, rather than as previously confronts and overcomes, novel intellectual challenges. Occasionally, though, more serious changes in memory, cognitive ability, personality, and behavior accompany the aging process. Alzheimer's disease is one of the brain diseases that are a relatively common consequence of aging. The pathological effects of age-related changes to the brain, which include Alzheimer's disease as well as other age-related disorders, are called the **dementias arising in the senium and presenium.** (From fifty to sixty years of age, we are living in the period of the presenium; from sixty years on, we are living in the senium.)

Alcohol and drugs also can cause organic brain disorders (see Chapter 11). Some of these disorders, like alcohol, heroin, cocaine, and amphetamine intoxication, are short-lived, reversible, and of little long-term consequence. Others, the effect on the brain of a lifetime of alcohol or drug abuse, are permanent, irreversible, and serious enough to compromise the person's quality of life. The acute and chronic effects of drugs of abuse on the brain are termed the **psychoactive substance-induced organic mental disorders.**

Problems have been created for society by acquired immune deficiency syndrome, AIDS, caused by a viral infection which neither an effective treatment nor an effective vaccine has been developed for (see Chapter 8). The virus responsible for AIDS (HIV or human immunodeficiency virus) is also capable of inducing changes in brain function with serious behavioral effects. The delirium sometimes a feature of the disease's later stages is one of the **organic mental disorders associated with a physical disorder.** Other important disorders caused by physical disorder include **epilepsy, Huntington's disease,** and **Parkinson's disease.**

Historical Overview

The intoxicating effect of alcohol and most other drugs of abuse has certainly been known for as long as men and women have realized that drinking the fermented liquid of grains and fruits or the exudate of the mature poppy induce tranquil and euphoric feelings.

That some older people may develop problems with remembering and thinking, sometimes of such severity that their personalities may change dramatically, and that a few may even lapse into a total vegetative state from which only death finally spares them have also been known for much of our recorded history.

And that certain physical diseases, whose bacterial or viral causes have only been identified in the last hundred years, affect brain function and cause marked changes in memory, thinking, personality, and consciousness has also been recognized for a long time.

Yet, for all three groups of organic brain disorders, the precise nature of the changes in the structure and function of the brain that are responsible for the changes in behavior remain uncertain. Only recently have we recognized that the brain is centrally implicated in these profound behavioral changes. This belated recognition comes from advancing knowledge of neuroanatomy and investigative techniques, permitting focused study of brain structure and function. Nevertheless, much is still unknown about the precise locus and nature of changes in brain structure and function responsible for the behavioral changes we call the organic brain disorders.

Recently—especially in the last decade—we have rapidly advanced our understanding of the organic brain disorders. More basic knowledge about the brain and its workings relevant to these disorders has been gathered during the past ten years than in all preceding years. Advances in molecular biology, molecular genetics, and the technology of imaging account for much of this knowledge explosion.

The first truly scientific approach to understanding the brain and its role in behavior is generally traced back to the early nineteenth century. Among the earliest researchers were two German phrenologists, Franz-Joseph Gall (1758–1828) and Johann Gaspar Spurzheim (1776–1832), who mapped bumps on the head in the belief that they corresponded to brain centers controlling such specific behaviors as "love of animals," "stubbornness," "patriotism," and "obedience" (see Figure 15.5). Subsequent researchers quickly refuted these claims, making Gall and Spurzheim's status as the first "scientists of the brain" an historical oddity. Yet they did succeed in calling to the attention of our skeptical forebears the brain's central role in behavior. However foolish their

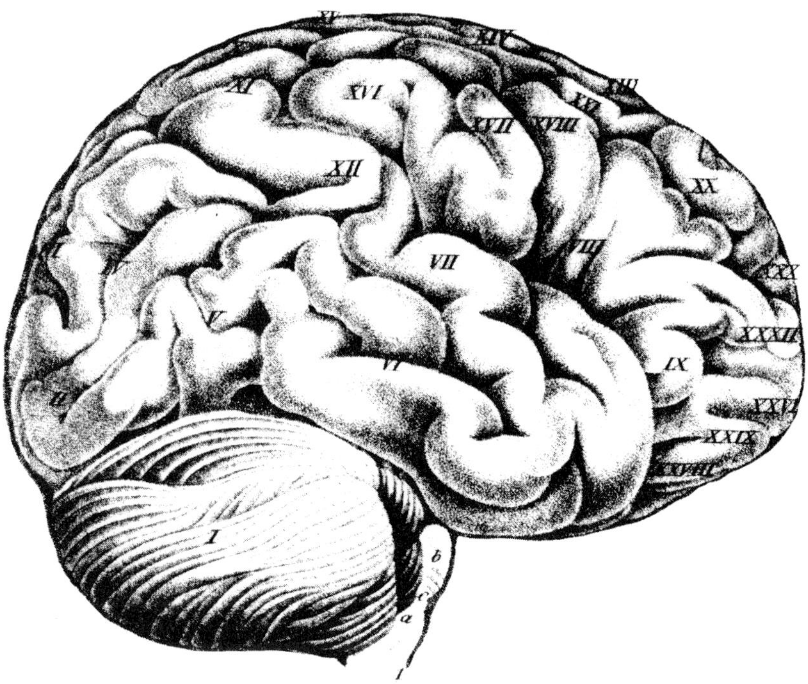

Guide to the Principal Zones

I. Organ of Amativeness
II. Organ of Philoprogenitiveness
III. Organ of Inhabitiveness
IV. Organ of Adhesiveness
V. Organ of Combativeness
VI. Organ of Destructiveness
VII. Organ of Secretiveness
VIII. Organ of Acquisitiveness
IX. Organ of Constructiveness
X. Organ of Self-Esteem
XI. Organ of Love of Approbation
XII. Organ of Cautiousness
XIII. Organ of Benevolence
XIV. Organ of Veneration
XV. Organ of Firmness
XVI. Organ of Conscientiousness
XVII. Organ of Hope
XVIII. Organ of Marvellousness
XIX. Organ of Ideality
XX. Organ of Mirthfulness
XXI. Organ of Imitation
XXII. Organ of Individuality
XXIII. Organ of Configuration
XXIV. Organ of Size
XXV. Organ of Weight and Resistance
XXVI. Organ of Colouring
XXVII. Organ of Locality
XXVIII. Organ of Calculation
XXIX. Organ of Order
XXX. Organ of Eventuality
XXXI. Organ of Time
XXXII. Organ of Melody
XXXIII. Organ of Language
XXXIV. Organ of Comparison
XXXV. Organ of Causality

Figure 15.5 *Spurzheim's 1826 portrayal of the brain's organization and function locates Principal Zones that control 35 specific human behaviors.*

attempts might seem now, they were the first to attempt to localize brain function.

Efforts to localize brain function advanced significantly in the mid-nineteenth century when French surgeon Paul Broca (1824–1880) examined after their deaths the brains of two patients who had suffered strokes affecting their ability to speak. He discovered a damaged area in their brains, specifically in the posterior third of the inferior frontal convolution. Broca concluded that speech is localized in this area of the brain, since called **Broca's area.** Broca's discovery is generally considered the first scientific localization of brain function.

A few years after Broca's groundbreaking discovery, German physiologists Georg Fritsch (1838–1927) and Emil Hitzig (1811–1881) reported that electrical stimulation of specific regions in a dog's cortex resulted in the immediate contraction of specific voluntary muscles. This also demonstrated that specific brain regions control specific bodily movements. Coupled with the development of electrical stimulation, an attractive new method for studying brain localization in experimental animals, it energized clinicians and researchers to widen their study of these relationships in animals and humans.

French neurologist Jean Charcot (1825–1893) is another crucial figure in the history of scientific efforts to understand the brain and its disorders. As a tremendously influential clinician and teacher, he exerted his greatest influence in the late nineteenth century. When he was a professor of neurology in Paris, one of his pupils was Sigmund Freud, who came to work with Charcot at a time in his early career when he was intrigued by neurological disease. Another pupil was George Gilles de la Tourette, who later discovered a rare and striking neurological syndrome in children and named it after himself. Charcot was a keen clinical observer who described

Jean Charcot (1825–1893), demonstrating a neurological patient to students at the Salpetriere Hospital in Paris in the 1880s. Sigmund Freud attended Charcot's demonstrations early in his career.

far more systematically than anyone had before the complex interplay of neurological and psychiatric symptoms characterizing delirium, dementia, and the other syndromes included today among the organic brain disorders. His clinical insights and observations, unparalleled in their day, continue to instruct new generations of neurologists, psychiatrists, and psychologists in training.

The intensive study of relationships between brain and behavior which followed from these early efforts has yielded two principal findings. First, it revealed the degree of control that specific brain regions exert over various bodily functions. Second, it suggested that precise brain localization of many bodily functions is impossible. Two schools of thought on the issue of brain localization developed. Some researchers continued to believe, as did Broca, Fritsch, and Hitzig, that we can localize brain function with great specificity, though not to the degree the phrenologists believed possible. Others were influenced by German neurologist Kurt Goldstein (1878–1965), who studied brain injury's after effects following World War I, and American psychologist Karl Lashley (1890–1958), who examined the ability of rats with experimental brain lesions to solve complex running mazes. These researchers were struck by the brain's ability to compensate for even massive injury. These "holists" rejected the idea of specific localization of brain function. Most researchers today maintain a position somewhere between these two extremes.

Psychologist Howard Gardner, author of *The Shattered Mind* (1974), a graphic description of serious brain injury's effects on behavior, discusses this middle of the road approach:

> . . . neither the extreme claims of the localizers (to every function its own gyrus, or center) nor those of the holists (all areas of the brain implicated equivalently in all activities) are consonant with the facts. Rather, there is a gradient of neural zones, a cluster of functions, each of which is more likely than not to be associated with a certain brain region; at the same time, there exists considerable variability among individuals and across ages, as well as the strong possibility that a specific kind of impairment may result from a rather wide set of lesions. (Gardner, 1974, p. 26)

The Nature and Causes of the Organic Brain Disorders

By definition, every organic brain disorder involves altered brain function and behavior. Yet, as our brief historical overview suggests, the relationship between kind, severity, and locus of disturbed brain function and the behavioral disturbances associated with them is not consistent. For example, severe disruptions in a person's memory and thinking can result from what appear to be minimal changes in his or her brain structure or function. Correspondingly, marked anatomic or physiologic changes in the brain sometimes yield minimal behavioral changes, especially after sufficient time has elapsed to permit nondamaged parts to take over the functions of damaged ones. Clearly, prior learning history, education, chronological and psychological maturity, and the overall psychological and intellectual competence of the brain-damaged person are important determinants of the form a person's brain disorder takes—though this relationship has limits set by the nature and extent of the brain damage.

The extremely varied causes of the organic brain disorders also exert crucial, but not completely fixed, effects on the alterations in behavior accompanying brain damage. Drugs and alcohol, blows to the head, viral and bacterial infections can each cause relatively short-term changes in behavior reflecting acute, reversible, brain damage. Yet precisely the same factors, when sufficiently severe and long-lasting, are capable of inducing irreversible, permanently disabling, life-threatening brain disorders.

Many organic brain disorders are associated with significant mortality. That is, they represent serious, life-threatening diseases. A study of 543 patients with organic mental disorders hospitalized at a large midwestern university hospital over a ten-year period (Black, Warrack, & Winokur, 1985) confirmed this observation: Patients with an organic mental disorder, regardless of age, were at increased risk of early death. (Death generally comes to patients with Alzheimer's disease, for example, within a decade of the initial symptoms' appearance.)

The patients in the 1985 study were especially likely to die from "natural" causes, like cancer and heart disease among women and influenza and pneumonia among men. During the first two years after the diagnosis, men were also at increased risk of death from accidents and suicide. Unfortunately, we do not know, from the design of this study, the direction of causality of these findings (e.g., did cancer and heart disease cause some of the organic brain disorders in these women or did the brain disorders influence the development of the cancer and heart disease?).

Assessment of the Organic Brain Disorders

Psychological Procedures for Assessing Brain Function. Broca's discovery of the brain's speech center in the 1860s inspired his contemporaries to undertake their own efforts to relate localized brain damage to behavioral changes. Shortly after the turn of the century, these efforts began to interrelate with the young science of psychology, especially psychology's brand new subspecialty, clinical psychology, which was devoted at its inception to the definition and measurement of intellectual abilities (see Chapter 3).

In the 1930s and 1940s, growing numbers of clinical psychologists became interested in a related measurement problem, the assessment of the behavioral accompaniments of brain damage. The initial development of this subfield of clinical psychology, now called **clinical neuropsychology,** is generally traced to William Halstead (1848–1931). Working for many years at the University of Chicago, Halstead established the first human neuropsychology laboratory there. He was strongly influenced by the work of neurologist Kurt Goldstein (1878–1965), who had begun to study the inability of World War I brain-injured veterans to think abstractly. With his student Ralph Reitan, Halstead developed a neuropsychological test battery, the *Halstead-Reitan Neuropsychological Battery* (Halstead, 1947; Reitan, 1959; Reitan & Davison, 1974). Despite the development of other neuropsychological test batteries in the decades following this pioneering work, the *Halstead-Reitan Battery* continues as the most widely used measure of the behavioral consequences of brain damage.

The *Halstead-Reitan Neuropsychological Battery* assesses most of the cognitive functions affected by brain damage, including intelligence, attention, concentration, language, problem solving, abstract thinking, basic reading, spelling, calculating, sensation and perception, motor abilities, and vigilance and mental stamina. Because the Halstead-Reitan Battery does not include specific measures of memory, generally affected by brain damage, neuropsychologists often add memory assessment instruments to the battery when they examine patients suspected of brain damage. Table 15.2 describes briefly the specific components of the Halstead-Reitan Battery.

A. R. Luria (1902–1977), another pioneer in brain research, was a world-famous Russian neuropsychologist whose major work was done during the early twentieth century. Luria (1980) developed a detailed theory of cortical functioning that has become widely known in the United States only during the past two decades. Luria's theory of the "functional system" expands on his conviction that although specific areas of the cortex control specific skills, even the simplest human behavior calls on a variety of such skills; accordingly, it is controlled by several cortical centers. To achieve the most accurate picture of disturbances in brain structure and function, then, the neuropsychologist must assess several brain areas and a variety of specific cognitive and behavioral skills.

Luria's theory suggested a more flexible approach to the assessment of brain damage than most American neuropsychologists. He stressed highly qualitative methods, emphasizing clinical description, to evaluate behavior, in contrast to the quantitative, largely statistical and numerical methods developed by Halstead, Reitan, and their coworkers. To Luria, assessment of brain function ought to be ". . . concerned not so much with whether a problem is solved as with the way in which it is solved. In other words, it calls for a careful qualitative analysis of the patient's activity, of the difficulties he experiences, and of the mistakes made" (Luria, 1980, p. 392).

TABLE 15.2 The Halstead-Reitan Neuropsychological Battery

Halstead Category Test

- This nonverbal problem-solving measure requires subjects to use inductive reasoning and form abstract concepts by categorizing a number of objects according to functional class; it also requires immediate and short-term recall and judgment.

Tactual Performance Test

- Blindfolded subjects have to place ten blocks of different shapes in their proper places on a wooden formboard. Motor speed, the ability to use touch cues, learning, and incidental memory (remembering things when not specifically told to do so) are assessed by this measure.

Rhythm Test

- Subjects must compare rhythmic beats in this task, which calls on nonverbal auditory sound pattern recognition, attention, and concentration.

Speech Sounds Perception Test

- Subjects hear sixty nonsense words read to them. They are then asked to describe them, calling on auditory-verbal perception and auditory-visual coordination of language-processing skills, and requiring sustained attention and concentration.

Finger Tapping Test

- This test of motor speed requires subjects to depress a lever connected to a counter repeatedly with the index finger of each hand as rapidly as possible.

Trail Making Test

- Subjects must follow number and number-letter sequences on this paper-and-pencil test, which measures speed, visual scanning, and fine motor coordination.

Strength of Grip Test

- Subjects squeeze a hand dynamometer as hard as they can, using one hand at a time, in order to permit a left-right comparison.

Sensory Perceptual Examination: Tactile, Auditory, and Visual

- The subject must identify a variety of tactile, auditory, and visual stimuli, thus providing both a further measure of perceptual ability and an additional left-right comparison.

Reitan-Indiana Aphasia Screening Test

- This measure, which tests subjects' language ability, is designed specifically to reveal a range of disabilities commonly associated with aphasia.

Wechsler Adult Intelligence Scale (WAIS)

- The WAIS is the most common measure of intelligence (see Chapter 3). It is included in the Halstead-Reitan Neuropsychological Battery because (1) Intelligence influences many of the neuropsychological functions measured by the battery and, therefore, a correct interpretation of strengths and weaknesses in these functions depends on accurate assessment of intellectual capabilities; (2) Some of the subtests of the WAIS, like block design, picture arrangement, digit span, and digit symbol, also reflect neuropsychological performance.

A standardized neuropsychological battery presumably based on concepts and techniques advocated by Luria was developed a decade ago (Golden, Hammeke, & Purisch, 1980). However, the validity of the scales of the *Luria-Nebraska Neuropsychological Battery* and its overall usefulness have been widely questioned (Adams, 1980; Jones & Butters, 1990).

How valid are the neuropsychological measures? Specifically, how accurately do the *Halstead-Reitan Neuropsychological Battery,* the *Wechsler Adult Intelligence Scale* (*WAIS*), and the *Luria-Nebraska Neuropsychological Battery* discriminate between persons who are and are not brain damaged?

Goldstein and Shelly (1984) compared the capacity of the two neuropsychological batteries and the *WAIS* to discriminate presence or absence of brain damage in a group of psychiatric patients. Psychiatric patients were studied because neuropsychologists are most often asked to differentiate behavioral problems associated with psychiatric disorder from problems caused by brain damage.

Table 15.3 summarizes findings from the eighty-four patients given all three measures of cognitive functioning. The Halstead-Reitan and Luria-Nebraska batteries functioned about equally well. Each correctly categorized almost 80 percent of the patients tested. The Halstead-Reitan Battery tended to be more sensitive to the presence of brain damage than to its absence (82.5 percent versus 78.9 percent correct), whereas the reverse was true of the Luria-

TABLE 15.3 Discriminative Validity of Three Measures of Cognitive Functioning

Group	Percent Correct	Number of Cases Classified into Group: Non-brain-damaged	Brain-damaged
	WAIS		
Non-brain-damaged	70.4	19	8
Brain-damaged	63.2	21	36
Total	65.5	40	44
	Halstead-Reitan Battery		
Non-brain-damaged	66.7	18	9
Brain-damaged	82.5	10	47
Total	77.4	28	56
	Luria-Nebraska Battery		
Non-brain-damaged	81.5	22	5
Brain-damaged	78.9	12	45
Total	79.8	34	50

Source: From Goldstein, G. & Shelly, C. (1984). Discriminative validity of various intelligence and neuropsychological tests. *Journal of Consulting and Clinical Psychology, 52,* p. 385. By permission of the publisher.

Nebraska Battery (81.5 percent versus 66.7 percent correct). The WAIS was distinctly inferior to the other two measures; it misidentified patients with normal brain functions as brain damaged and vice versa significantly more often than either of the other two measures did (65.5 percent versus 77.4 percent and 79.8 percent correct).

Imaging Techniques for Assessing Brain Structure and Function. A large part of our information about how brain injury and disease affect behavior has come from neuropsychological studies of brain damage. These provide data, available from no other source, on the pattern of cognitive dysfunction induced by brain damage. We understand much less about how specific changes in brain structure and function cause the behavioral changes that typically accompany them, mainly because of the relative insensitivity of existing techniques, including neuropsychological measures, for studying structure and function.

The past decade, however, has witnessed exciting and productive developments in **imaging procedures** for studying the body's structure and function. These procedures have been especially helpful in brain studies (see Chapter 3). Many of these new imaging techniques are **noninvasive;** that is, they do not, unlike the instruments used by Broca, Fritsch, and Hitzig, have to enter the body physically to study it. These noninvasive procedures permit clinicians and researchers to visualize the structure and, to a limited extent, the function of the brain with impressive sensitivity. Explorations and understandings that were impossible either invasively or noninvasively even five years ago have thus become routine.

The X-ray was the first noninvasive method developed to look inside the body (see Chapter 3). Discovered in the late 1800s by German scientist Wilhelm Roentgen, the X-ray is much better at imaging dense structures like bones and teeth than softer tissues like the brain. The use of contrast materials like air, however, has extended the X-ray's usefulness for brain scientists. By injecting air into the lumbar space in the spinal cord, to produce a pneumoencephalogram, the radiologist positions the patient so that the air rises to his or her cerebrum and provides sufficient contrast on the X-ray to show differences in the brain contours. This procedure, invasive because it introduces a foreign substance into the body, has some risk of brain damage. It also only localizes brain structures with a modest degree of accuracy. Little definition of brain structure and no visualization of brain function, therefore, have been possible from explorations of the brain by means of traditional X-ray technology.

Computerized axial tomography (CAT) has revolutionized the clinical investigation of many brain diseases (see Chapter 3). It was the first procedure to provide detailed images of the living brain's gross cerebral structure. Because this technique sometimes requires the injection of contrast material into the bloodstream, it is invasive. Nonetheless, it is a painless and quick procedure (Jaskiw, Andreasen, & Weinberger, 1987).

One of CAT technology's first achievements was to confirm a long-held suspicion that schizophrenia is associated with enlargement of the lateral and third ventricle spaces and of some cortical surface markings (Shelton & Weinberger, 1986). The net result of these characteristic enlargements of interior spaces in the brain is a reduction in the mass of brain tissue. (To a lesser extent, aged persons—especially victims of Alzheimer's disease—show the same kinds of changes [Brinkman & Largen, 1984]). This reduction in brain volume, called **cortical atrophy,** is presumably associated with the shrinkage in the volume (or, in Alzheimer's disease, the actual loss) of brain neurons. Precisely what mechanisms are responsible for this decrease in the size of neurons in some schizophrenics and some of the aged is unclear, as is how these changes affect behavior.

Magnetic resonance imaging (MRI), an even newer noninvasive technology, may ultimately displace CAT as the imaging technology of choice for the localization of structural brain abnormalities (Jaskiw et al., 1987). MRI provides an extraordinarily clear reconstruction of the brain. Unlike the X-ray and the CAT scan, it does not require the use of ionizing radiation. Repeated scans can be made, consequently, without exposing the body to too much radiation.

MRI studies have extended the CAT data cited previously on the role of brain disorder in schizophrenia (Andreasen, Nasrallah, & Dunn, 1986). Setting out to compare the brains of thirty-eight patients suffering from schizophrenia with those of forty-nine normal control subjects, these investigators ultimately focused their MRI investigations on the frontal lobe because many of the behaviors of schizophrenic patients resemble those of patients with known frontal lobe damage. Among these symptomatic behaviors are decreased spontaneity and fluency of speech, a decrement in voluntary motor behavior, and difficulties with mood and affect, including apathy, indifference, and shallowness.

Comparing the sizes of the two groups' frontal lobes required so much precision that only the MRI could be used. Andreasen and her colleagues (1986) found that schizophrenics had significantly smaller frontal lobes than controls did. Surprising—and unexplained—was finding the especially marked differences between male patients and controls. Andreasen and her coworkers speculate that schizophrenics may have experienced some kind of early developmental abnormality associated with an impaired brain capacity, especially the frontal region, to grow.

Positron emission tomography (PET), one of the newest noninvasive imaging technology, permits direct imaging access to information on brain *function* for the first time (Morihisa, 1987). When used in conjunction with CAT or MRI, PET can help localize a structural abnormality in a region of the brain and then test for possible functional correlates of that regional abnormality, such as reduced blood flow or glucose metabolism.

PET technology brings us closer to realizing the phrenologists' dreams of linking brain regions with behavior, by permitting the study of differences in the activation levels of particular portions of the brain as a function of ongoing behavior. One such recent study (Reiman, Fusselman, Fox, & Raichle, 1989) used PET measurements of regional blood flow, reflecting the activity of brain neurons, to investigate the brain regions responsible for the normal emotion of anticipatory anxiety. Told they would receive a painful electric shock, normal volunteers were studied before, during, and after the shock was delivered. During the time subjects anticipated receiving the shock, PET revealed significant increases in blood flow in the bilateral temporal poles. This is the same region of the cortex where the same investigators had recently reported a significant increase in blood flow following the induction of an anxiety attack by drugs in patients with panic disorder (Reiman et al., 1986).

Organic Mental Disorders

As discussed previously, some organic brain disorders last for only a few minutes or a few hours while others last much longer. The latter conditions, the chronic brain disorders, typically last a lifetime. The chronic brain disorders of known etiology are the organic mental disorders.

Dementias Arising in the Senium and Presenium. For centuries, aging individuals have been recognized to sometimes develop signs and symptoms of brain disorder. *DSM-III-R* (1987) refers to aging's pathological effects on the structure and function of the brain and on behavior, as the dementias arising in the senium and presenium. The *senium,* a Latin word for old age, is generally considered the period in a person's life after the age of sixty. The presenium is the decade directly before that age. Dementias associated with aging occur most frequently well after age sixty-five, especially now that better nutrition and healthier lifestyles are lengthening our lifespans.

Alzheimer's Disease. This disorder is a major and growing health problem in the United States and the other developed countries in the world. It will become an even greater problem in the United States in the future, as more and more Americans live long enough to enter the years of highest risk for its development.

- Alzheimer's disease is the most common cause of organic mental disorder in the elderly (Maletta, Pirozzolo, Thompson, & Mortimer, 1982).
- Of the more than 1 million Americans in nursing homes in 1987, more than half were estimated to suffer from it (Katzman, 1986).
- Older persons living independently also suffer from the disorder. One study found 16 percent of the residents of a southern California retirement community had Alzheimer's disease. Among those over age eighty, 36 percent had the disease (Pfeffer, Afifi & Chance, 1987).
- The incidence of Alzheimer's disease in the U.S. population is about 10 percent over sixty-five years of age and 45 percent over eighty-five years (Davies & Wolozin, 1987).
- In 1983, its estimated cost to American society in health-care costs and lost productivity was between $28 billion and $31 billion (Herrington, 1987).

Table 15.4 lists the array of brain disorders associated with pathological aging that health-care professionals may encounter. It summarizes the diagnoses given to 100 persons consecutively admitted to a geriatric outpatient clinic in Minneapolis following complaints of memory problems, personality changes, confusion, and other symptoms of organic mental disorder (Maletta et al., 1982). Forty-three of these persons—almost half—were diagnosed as suffering from Alzheimer's disease; this finding accords with the disease's national incidence figures. The table also shows that close to one quarter of these outpatients were considered seriously depressed but not suffering from organic brain disease. As discussed later, the symptoms of depression and of organic brain disease closely resemble each other, especially in the elderly.

TABLE 15.4 Diagnoses of 100 Outpatients with Complaints of Organic Mental Disorder in a Geriatric Outpatient Clinic

Diagnosis	Number of Patients
Primary degenerative dementia (Alzheimer's disease)	43
Multi-infarct dementia	10
Dementia associated with alcoholism	7
Dementia associated with specific neurologic disorders	6
Dementia from other causes	3
Delirium	2
Major depressive disorder	24
Schizophrenia	4
Memory problems of unknown etiology	1

Source: From Maletta, G.J., Pirozzo, F.J., Thompson, G., & Mortimer, J.A. (1982). Organic mental disorders in a geriatric outpatient population. *American Journal of Psychiatry, 139,* p. 522. Copyright 1982, the American Psychiatric Association. Reprinted by permission.

The Nature of Alzheimer's Disease. Dementia, an organic mental syndrome, is an important component of a number of organic mental disorders including Alzheimer's disease. Dementia's single essential feature is significantly impaired short- and long-term memory. Frequent accompaniments are disturbances in the ability to exercise sound judgment and to think abstractly, clearly, and effectively. A pronounced change in personality functioning and behavior is also typical of dementia. Although it usually becomes severe enough to interfere markedly with work, family, and interpersonal relationships, dementia generally develops slowly. Its course can be stable or, more often, gradually downward. Dementia is typically lengthy, its duration most often measured in years (Reisberg et al., 1987).

Either subtle or obvious, memory losses are often the first symptoms of Alzheimer's disease (Schneck, Reisberg, Ferris, 1982), as seen in Virginia Armstrong, the seventy-year-old woman whose behavior is described in Box 15.2. Mrs. Armstrong, well known

BOX 15.2 Whatever Happened to Grandmother's Mind?

During the spring of her seventieth year, Virginia Armstrong, a headstrong, efficient, energetic widow who has two grown sons, enough money to last to the end of her life, many friends, and memories of a productive and generally happy life, began to complain to her sons about her failing memory. Previously a person who remembered virtually everything, sometimes to the sorrow of errant friends and family, Mrs. Armstrong now found herself at times forgetting the names of lifelong friends. She also noticed that she could not always remember the day of the week or the number of the bus she took to go downtown shopping. "I guess age is finally beginning to catch up with me," she complained to her sons, when they listened. They began to take her complaints more seriously when she started calling from public phones downtown to ask why she had gone shopping and how she should get home. Once, she forgot which way to walk from the bus stop three blocks from the home she had lived in for forty-five years.

Virginia Armstrong's behavior also began to change in other ways. This efficient, energetic, upbeat person now became lethargic, bad-tempered, suspicious, and sloppy. Her personal hygiene began to deteriorate and, when a friend visited her one day, she noted that Mrs. Armstrong clearly hadn't cleaned the kitchen or the guest bathroom for months. Similarly, her table manners, always impeccable, now had become noticeably bad. And the content of her conversation, which had always been far ranging, informed, and thoughtful, focused almost exclusively on a single topic—her fears of her house being broken into by men intent on raping her.

After finally convincing their mother to see a doctor specializing in geriatrics, Virginia Armstrong's sons took her to Dr. K., who ultimately diagnosed her as suffering from an early stage of Alzheimer's disease. Shortly thereafter, she had to enter a nursing home because she couldn't be trusted to care for herself.

to one of the text's authors, showed a typical array of memory problems early in the history of her organic brain disorder, ultimately diagnosed as Alzheimer's disease. Yet memory problems afflict virtually everyone over the age of fifty or sixty. At this stage of life, people may forget more or less permanently the name of a person met the previous week or the hotel where a vacation was spent the previous summer or even where they live or what their name is. How, then, do we differentiate between normal forgetting and the disorders brought about by Alzheimer's disease?

Memory problems serious enough to cause concern in the aging individual or his or her spouse need to be brought to the attention of someone who can differentiate among changes associated with normal aging, Alzheimer's disease, dementia from other causes, and serious depression (La Rue, 1982). That task is likely to require a mental health professional or doctor who works with the aged.

It is important to recognize that Alzheimer's disease is not simply accelerated aging. This disease's distinct neuropathological picture differs from normal aging. For example, normal forgetfulness and the memory problems associated with Alzheimer's disease are different. Table 15.5 summarizes some of the ways clinicians distinguish between the effects on memory of normal ("benign") and pathological ("malignant") aging.

An Alzheimer's patient checking a memory aid affixed to his door as he prepares to leave his house.

As Virginia Armstrong's case illustrates, changes in other cognitive abilities, judgment, personality, habits, lifelong preferences, and values often accompany the memory loss characteristic of persons with Alzheimer's disease. Because learning and remembering are central to many other cognitive tasks, it is hard to separate them from the other cognitive problems accompanying Alzheimer's disease.

Age-related pathological changes in cognitive functioning run the full gamut: from minimal, barely perceptible changes in reasoning, arithmetic skills, and the ability to bring together diverse kinds of in-

TABLE 15.5 Characteristics of Malignant and Benign Senescent Forgetfulness

Malignant	Benign
Shortened retention time	Recall failures limited to relatively unimportant facts or parts of an experience (such as name, date, or place)
Inability to recall events of the recent past, including not only unimportant facts but the experience itself	Details forgotten on one occasion may be recalled at another time
Distorted recall of some events in the form of confabulations	"Forgotten" data belong to remote as opposed to recent past
Accompanied by disorientation to place and time and, gradually, to person	Subjects are aware of shortcomings and may apologize or compensate

Source: From La Rue, A. (1982). Memory loss and aging: Distinguishing dementia from benign senescent forgetfulness and depressive pseudodementia, *Psychiatric Clinics of North America, 5,* p. 90. By permission of the publisher.

formation to solve a complex problem, with virtually no discernible effect on functioning; to profound deterioration in these processes, resulting in the total inability to function independently (Filley, Kobayashi, & Heaton, 1987). Many people, of course, live their entire lives with no significant cognitive changes of any kind.

Results from the recent intensive neuropsychological examination of three Alzheimer's patients reemphasize the extreme variability in cognitive functioning characterizing the disorder (Martin, 1987). The patients were W, a fifty-eight-year-old male engineer; C, a fifty-four-year-old fireman; and G, a fifty-year-old female music teacher. Although their intellectual levels appeared comparable before the onset of the disease and they had equivalent education, the three differed significantly in their performance on the *Wechsler Adult Intelligence Scale* subtests. W showed a primary deficit in semantic memory (he experienced great difficulty defining words or giving their synonyms). In contrast, his visuospatial and constructional skills were clearly intact (he could readily assemble puzzle pieces to form familiar objects and could identify the missing elements in pictures of familiar scenes). C demonstrated precisely the opposite profile: He was strong in semantic memory and weak in visuospatial and constructional skills. G showed obvious deficits in both semantic memory and visuospatial and constructional skills. Despite these striking differences in cognitive strengths and weaknesses, all three showed equivalent profound deficits in memory when tested with traditional memory tests.

A deterioration in the quality of judgment frequently accompanies the cognitive deficits of Alzheimer's disease. This is not surprising since good judgment requires the ability to choose the best alternative when faced with a range of choices—and making this choice requires the retention of several important cognitive skills. These include being able to remember similar earlier tough decisions and their outcomes as well as to anticipate the consequences of a decision even when a similar decision has never been made before. Alzheimer's patients suffering from impaired judgment may leave their residence inadequately or inappropriately dressed; make absurd accusations or impossible demands in letters to officials, friends, or newspapers; or spend money on expensive, frivolous, and unnecessary purchases.

As Alzheimer's patients become aware of their lessening ability to remember and think clearly and effectively, they commonly respond with depression, anger, and frustration. Remembering and thinking are uniquely human qualities which matter greatly to most of us. People for whom thinking and reasoning are of greatest lifelong importance—teachers, professors, doctors, and lawyers, for example—are likely to react most strongly to a deterioration in these abilities. Box 15.3 describes the catastrophic effects of a loss in thinking ability on a woman, Dorothy Welsh, who throughout her life had valued this ability above all others. Dr. Welsh was a patient of one of the authors of this book.

Depression is a common accompaniment of aging; people react to the losses of friends and loved ones that invariably accompany normal aging and to the

BOX 15.3 A Life without the Mind Is No Life at All

Dorothy Welsh was seventy-two years old and a recently retired university provost when she first noticed her memory beginning to fade. A proud woman with seven honorary degrees, a distinguished record of scholarly achievement, and an administrative style that had consistently created trust, Dr. Welsh had always put the life of the mind at the top of her list of personal and professional values. As she aged, she admitted her greatest fear about getting old was the possibility of her mind failing.

When the family doctor—a former student—told Dr. Welsh and her husband that her memory complaints might represent early signs of Alzheimer's disease, Dr. Welsh's initial response was entirely predictable. She said that she'd work very hard to keep what memory she still had left and watch herself like a hawk to prevent mistakes or misjudgments due to memory loss.

But when Dr. Welsh got home from the doctor's visit, instead of heading to her study to continue working on the scientific paper which had preoccupied her for several weeks, she went immediately to bed, without discussing the visit with her husband. Both the early trip to bed and the failure to talk with her husband about the important doctor's visit were highly unusual for Dr. Welsh.

That evening marked the abrupt beginning of the severe depression accompanying the early stages of her developing organic mental disorder. From a voluble, gregarious, and social woman, she became increasingly isolated, withdrawn, and tactiturn. Previously upbeat and a person of unbounded energy, she adopted a pessimistic outlook unrelieved by effective action. And in another startling change, Dr. Welsh's sole intellectual excitement was generated by television reruns of *Dallas* and the daytime soap, *As the World Turns*.

A few months later, Dr. Welsh's husband found her face down on the floor of their den, a bullet wound in her head. The note by her side said, "A life without the mind is no life at all." Her grieving husband fully understood.

profound problems that characterize age-related organic brain disorders (Lazarus et al., 1987; Reifler, Larson, & Hanley, 1982). The lethargy, psychomotor retardation, disruption in concentration, problem solving, and remembering, and diminished self-esteem of depression may also be early symptoms of Alzheimer's disease. Rovner and his colleagues (1989) reported that 17 percent of a large group of Alzheimer's patients also met diagnostic criteria for major depression. They also found depressed Alzheimer's patients more impaired cognitively and behaviorally than nondepressed Alzheimer's patients.

Because of the relationship among depression, aging, and dementia, differentiating depression from dementia's early stages in the elderly is sometimes difficult. Diagnosis is also difficult because older, severely depressed patients may demonstrate **depressive pseudodementia.** As the following description of Mr. B suggests, their symptoms may mimic the cognitive deficits associated with organic mental disorders (McAllister & Price, 1982). It is important to differentiate between the two conditions because different treatments exist for each.

Mr. B was a 76-year-old man transferred to our mental health center for evaluation of paranoid ideation, social withdrawal, and confusion. His referring physician, an internist, felt that Mr. B had Alzheimer's disease and commented that "very little reasoning is left in this gentleman." The patient had, in fact, been placed in a nursing home because of his symptoms. His past history was notable for four episodes of depressive illness that had responded to ECT (electroconvulsive shock therapy).

On admission Mr. B lay curled up in a fetal position. . . . On mental status testing the patient could recall none of three objects after 3 min., was unable to spell "world," was oriented only to person and place, and would not cooperate with further formal testing.

Mr. B was initially transferred to the medical intensive care unit for treatment of severe dehydration and cardiac arrhythmias. Following resolution of these problems, he showed no improvement in his mental status. B_{12} and folate levels were normal, as was a CT scan of the brain. Because of his previous psychiatric history, the patient was treated with ECT: he received 10 treatments. He demonstrated a dramatic improvement in mood, appetite, and cognitive abilities and was able to resume a normal life at home without medication. (McAllister & Price, 1982, p. 627)

Causes of Alzheimer's Disease. Pathological examination of the brains of Alzheimer's patients reveals two significant findings. First, there is frequently a generalized atrophy of the brain; that is, the brain size of Alzheimer's patients is often diminished (De Leon, Ferris, & George, 1980). Second, the brain of virtually every Alzheimer's patient contains foreign pathological cells, called neurofilbrillary tangles, senile plaques, and granulovacuolar bodies that have taken the place of normal brain cells. Although these nonfunctional brain tissues also appear in other elderly persons, they appear with singular and distinguishing frequency in the brains of Alzheimer's victims (Ball, 1977; Farmer, Peck, & Terry, 1976).

These nonfunctional groups of cells tend to be concentrated at the base of the forebrain, the brain's uppermost and largest region, as well as throughout

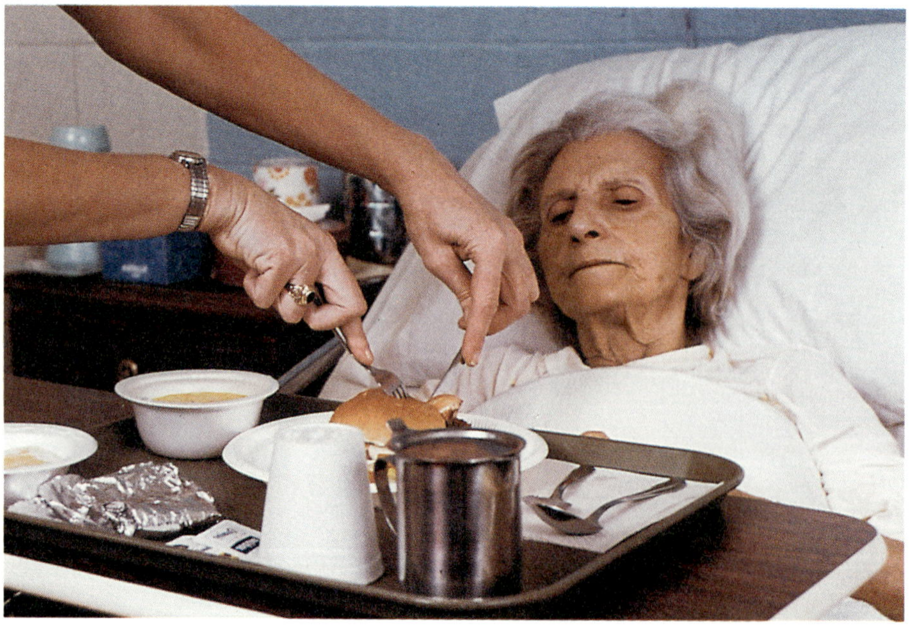

This elderly woman appears to be a victim of both dementia and severe depression.

the cortical association areas. Cells in this area relay nerve impulses to the cerebral cortex, where most of our cognitive activities are localized, and the hippocampus, vital to the formation of memories. The cells affected in the cerebral cortex and the hippocampus areas use the neurotransmitter acetylcholine to communicate; no other brain area relies on this neurotransmitter.

Several hypotheses, none fully supported by existing data, have been put forth to explain Alzheimer's disease. The most widely accepted is that it is caused by viral infection, perhaps by a so-called **slow virus,** taking a very long time to cause symptoms to develop. The hypothesis (Johnson, 1979) is appealing for the following reasons:

1. Viral encephalitis is a relatively common acute disease of the brain.
2. Measles virus infection is thought to cause a delayed progressive neurological disease.
3. Postencephalitic Parkinson's disease is considered a late consequence of influenza.

Most support for this theory, though, comes from the behavioral and pathological resemblance of Alzheimer's disease to two slow virus diseases in humans and one in sheep. Early infection by a slow virus can gradually lead to the development of chronic, dementing disorders akin to Alzheimer's disease (Crapper & De Boni, 1979; Sigurdsson, 1954).

A second etiologic theory of Alzheimer's disease centers on a toxic agent, specifically, aluminum. Researchers have observed markedly elevated brain levels of aluminum in Alzheimer's patients (Crapper, Kirshnan, & Dalton, 1973). They also report that cats injected with aluminum experienced memory loss and abnormal behavior (Crapper & Dalton, 1973). More recent research suggests, however, that brain levels of aluminum are independent of other pathophysiological indices of Alzheimer's disease (Schneck et al., 1982).

An immune system deficiency—essentially, an autoimmune disorder of the body attacking brain cells perceived as "foreign"—has also been hypothesized to account for Alzheimer's disease, though only one group has reported increased brain antibodies in Alzheimer's patients (Tkach & Hokama, 1970). Part of this theory's appeal stems from interest in autoimmune disease, rekindled by the AIDS epidemic.

Finally, it has also been suggested that Alzheimer's disease may be partially a genetic disorder. Supporting evidence of this view includes growing recognition that the disease seems to run in families. All Down's syndrome patients surviving to adulthood also eventually develop the kind of brain lesions characteristic of the disease; Down's syndrome is caused by a genetic abnormality, most often an extra chromosome 21 (Heston, 1979). Perhaps information coded on this extra chromosome is responsible for developing the disorder. Active exploration of the possibility of Alzheimer's disease's having genetic causative factors is currently underway.

Multi-infarct Dementia. Cerebrovascular accidents—strokes, shocks, and CVAs—kill 275,000 Americans a year and disable 300,000 (Yudofsky & Silver, 1985). Affecting six older persons for every one younger one, these catastrophic consequences of high blood pressure, arteriosclerosis, and other cardiovascular diseases are caused by either a leakage of blood into the brain or a blockage of an artery in the brain by a blood clot or arteriosclerotic plaque. In either circumstance, the death of brain tissue results. The most common cerebrovascular accident involves a single episode of rupture or blockage. If the victim survives—about half of those admitted to a hospital with symptoms of stroke die within the first three weeks—he or she is likely to be significantly impaired (Goodstein, 1983), though persons with minor and localized strokes may recover almost completely.

A disruption in blood supply to the brain can also cause **multi-infarct dementia.** Yet, instead of a single rupture or blockage of circulation within the brain, patients with this disorder may suffer literally hundreds of such lesions during the illness. For that matter, many older persons who never receive the diagnosis nonetheless experience one or more interruptions in the brain's blood supply. Howell (1981), for example, found 506 brain lesions—an average of 10.7 per individual—in forty-seven autopsied elderly patients with diagnosed cerebrovascular accidents.

Distinguishing between dementia associated with Alzheimer's disease and multi-infarct dementia may be difficult. While doing so is sometimes possible on the basis of age (Alzheimer's disease typically occurs in older persons), differentiation on the basis of signs, symptoms, and course is more reliable. Alzheimer's disease generally begins very gradually and progressively deteriorates. In contrast, the deterioration in intellectual functioning—as well as movement and sensation—associated with multi-infarct dementia is characteristically "stepwise." Minor symptoms like transient concentration problems and balance difficulties might first appear; later on, gradually but continuously, mental confusion, emotional instability, and more marked personality changes may be noticed. As time goes on, though, cognitive functions (along with psychomotor and sensory ones) become more fully involved until the final stage of severe dementia and total disability.

Patients in the early stages of multi-infarct dementia, like those who have experienced a single, catastrophic stroke, are usually well aware of its impact on their ability to work, relate to others, and remain independent. The stepwise character of multi-infarct dementia is part of the problem; the person has the time to appreciate not only how seriously he or she has been affected but also the disorder's likely future course. Serious depression and suicide are understandable accompaniments of this stage of the disease.

Treatment and Prevention of the Effects of Pathological Aging on the Brain. From the beginning of human history, we have searched for the magical Fountain of Youth, capable of erasing the ravages of time and ensuring eternal vigor. Although there is clearly a limit to what can be done to treat pathological aging's effects, important advances have been made during the past decade. Greater success in preventing and treating the aged's physical diseases, including cancer and heart disease, has helped push the chronological threshhold of old age further into the future. Replacement of worn-out or diseased organs, including the heart and the kidneys, has become almost routine. Mechanical aids to enable people otherwise unable to hear or see continue to be developed. As discussed earlier, as more effective treatments combat age-related diseases and disabilities, more of us live healthier and happier lives long after the biblical "three-score-and-ten."

Despite these advances, age-related brain disorders have remained relatively inaccessible to modification. Once senile or presenile dementia begins, its course cannot be altered, though some of the psychological and psychiatric reactions to it can be treated (Reisberg et al., 1987). Recent reports, however, of drugs which reverse—although for only a few hours—the confusion and dementia associated with these disorders (the drugs replace acetylcholine, a brain neurotransmitter missing in the brain areas most affected by Alzheimer's disease) suggest that chemical agents capable of restoring disordered regions of the brain may ultimately be developed (Jenike, 1986). The search also continues for drugs to enhance both normal memory and memory that has begun to reflect the course of normal aging.

Recent work has also confirmed the importance of aging persons' social support systems—spouse, children, family, and friends. Even the signs and symptoms of Alzheimer's are significantly lessened when patients' needs for care and concern from others are satisfied (Powell & Courtice, 1983). Families, though, must be well informed as early as possible about the disorder and its prognosis so they know what to expect. Families also have to learn how to help their loved ones cope with the resulting gradual loss in function and to help patients limit their activities since they won't always know how to do so themselves. Particularly difficult is the task of convincing caregivers not to exhaust themselves, since the needs of Alzheimer's patients are frequently overwhelming. Finally, family members must learn how to deal with their loved ones' personality and intellectual changes, especially their paranoid delusions and intellectual losses. Both are difficult to handle since they typically contrast so markedly with the patients' earlier behavior.

At present, efforts to prevent age-related organic mental disorders are much more promising than efforts to treat them. Advances in molecular genetics, for example, may permit identification of people with a genetic predisposition to Alzheimer's disease, making it possible to counsel them about this genetic risk. The introduction of increasingly effective treatments for the high cholesterol levels and blood pressure often preceding the disease may also reduce the incidence of multi-infarct dementia. Drugs, diets, and exercise which lower cholesterol levels promise to yield important reductions in the incidence of arteriosclerosis and dementia associated with stroke.

Psychoactive Substance-Induced Organic Mental Disorders. In contrast to the irreversible and disabling senile and presenile dementias, the two most common substance-induced organic mental disorders, **intoxication** and **withdrawal,** represent reversible and generally benign brain conditions. Some of the other effects of alcohol and drugs on the brain, however, are associated with irreversible brain damage as well as with marked and disabling behavior deficits.

Intoxication. Nine of the eleven classes of drugs whose effects on the brain are detailed in *DSM-III-R* (1987) induce intoxication. The two exceptions are the hallucinogens and nicotine. The pleasures of intoxication—the "rush" of amphetamine and cocaine, the euphoria of alcohol and heroin—help explain why people ingest them. In behavioral language, the reinforcing consequences of drug and alcohol ingestion maintain drug-taking behavior in animals and humans.

Why is intoxication a substance-induced organic mental disorder, given its frequency in most societies and its benign outcome for most people most of the time? The reason is because it involves a temporary derangement in brain cell functioning that may in turn cause acute behavioral derangement. Extreme levels of intoxication, resulting from the individual's ingestion of large amounts of a drug, can in fact be life threatening. The drugs most often involved in such situations are the sedatives. Taken in excess, they can cause central nervous system sedation, coma, and even death. Especially dangerous are mixtures of sedatives which reinforce each other's sedative properties, like alcohol and barbiturate or alcohol and Librium or Valium.

Recent studies of the "carry-over" effects of marijuana and alcohol intoxication on aircraft pilot performance suggest that intoxication's behavioral effects can extend long after the substance's disappearance from the brain. Twenty-four hours after ten experienced private pilots smoked a marijuana cigarette, they were still significantly impaired on all measured variables in a flight simulator landing task, which included angle of descent, distance off center on landing, and vertical and lateral deviation on approach to landing. Despite these clear performance deficits, no pilot reported any awareness of them (Yesavage, Leirer, Denari, & Hollister, 1985). A study of ten Navy P3-C Orion pilots who consumed the equivalent of five beers fourteen hours before they were tested in a flight simulator yielded comparable findings: Pilot performance was significantly worse fourteen hours after alcohol consumption than when no alcohol had been consumed for at least forty-eight hours prior to the test (Yesavage & Leirer, 1986).

These studies indicate that intoxication, at least when induced by alcohol or marijuana, can affect central nervous system functioning long after the drug has disappeared from the body.

Withdrawal. Six of the eleven classes of drugs listed in *DSM-III-R* produce withdrawal. These include alcohol, the amphetamines, cocaine, nicotine, the opioids, and the sedative, hypnotic, or anxiolytic drugs. The same drugs also induce **physical dependence** and **tolerance,** when their continued ingestion causes the central nervous system's ongoing metabolic processes to adapt to their presence. Drugs that do not produce physical dependence induce neither tolerance nor withdrawal. Like the six dependency-inducing drugs, however, these drugs—including caffeine, cannabis, the hallucinogens, the inhalants, and phencyclidine (PCP)—do induce **psychological dependence,** most commonly experienced as craving in the drug's absence.

Not everyone agrees on which drugs induce dependency and withdrawal. Though *DSM-III-R* (1987) doesn't regard marijuana (cannabis) as dependency-inducing, the following case report describes a withdrawal syndrome in a woman who had smoked it for twenty-one days during a controlled study of marijuana's effects on hormonal function (Mendelson, Mello, Lex, & Bavli, 1984).

> *Ten hours after cessation of marijuana smoking, Ms. A. developed progressive anxiety, dysphoria (mild depression), insomnia, anorexia (loss of appetite), tremulousness of the extremities, lateral gaze nystagmus (a sign of central nervous system damage), sweating, and exaggerated deep tendon reflexes, which peaked 48 hours after cessation of smoking. The marijuana abstinence syndrome closely resembled mild to moderate alcohol withdrawal.* (Mendelson et al., 1984, p. 1289)

The severity of withdrawal from the drugs which induce physical dependence varies greatly (Hunt, 1985). At one end is nicotine withdrawal, during which new ex-smokers may complain of restlessness, irritability, and difficulty concentrating for a few days; these feelings, though mildly unpleasant, are not dangerous (Hughes, Gust, & Pechacek, 1987; Hughes & Hatsukami, 1986). At the other end, withdrawal from the sedatives can be seriously life threatening and ought to take place in a hospital (Hommer, Matsuo, & Wolkowitz, 1986). Sudden discontinuance of these drugs—including the barbiturates and such popular, widely used tranquilizers as Librium and Valium—once tolerance has developed can precipitate convulsions, coma, and death.

Withdrawal from heroin and the other opioids and alcohol lie somewhere between these two extremes; certainly unpleasant, they are rarely life threatening. Withdrawal from these substances causes nausea and vomiting, muscle aches, tearing, sweating, diarrhea, fever, craving, and insomnia. Hospitalization is indicated for individuals in poor health or with a long history of alcohol or opioid dependence.

Cognitive Functioning after Alcohol Withdrawal. Immediately following withdrawal from alcohol and for weeks or even months afterward, alcoholics' cognitive abilities are disrupted, sometimes seriously (Fabian & Parsons, 1983; Goldman, 1983). Their short- and long-term memories are often impaired, along with coordination and balance. Similarly, their ability to abstract and to learn new information, including information about themselves, is affected, as the central nervous system struggles to adapt to an alcohol-free metabolic environment (Grant, Adams, & Reed, 1984). The impaired ability to take in new information is particularly critical, since treatment for alcoholism typically begins shortly after the abuser has completed withdrawal. It is not surprising, then, that alcohol dependence treatment often appears ineffective, for it starts when abusers seem least likely to be able to call upon either memory or learning to retain what they are taught about their maladaptive way of dealing with abusive substances.

Delirium Tremens. Long-term alcohol abusers also suffer from other serious organic mental disorders, one of the most striking being **alcohol withdrawal delirium.** More familiarly known as **delirium tremens** or **the D.T.'s,** this withdrawal-related phenomenon typically occurs within a week after drinking has stopped.

As discussed earlier, delirium is an organic mental syndrome that can be induced by alcohol or other drugs, fever, or disease. Whatever the cause, its essential features are the same. They include great difficulty in attending to environmental stimuli, as well as in shifting from one stimulus to another. Another key feature is disorganized thinking, signaled by rambling or irrelevant speech or incoherence. Delirium usually develops rapidly, with a highly variable course and brief duration.

Patients experiencing delirium tremens can develop vivid hallucinations, which may be visual ("pink elephants"), auditory (threatening voices of friends or family are common), or tactile (a frequent complaint is of insects crawling over the skin). They may also experience paranoid delusions, becoming convinced that unknown assailants are planning to harm them.

Tom was a forty-seven-year-old truck driver with a fifteen-year history of very heavy alcohol consumption. He had had a number of previous hospitalizations but no known history of delirium tremens. During the first two days of detoxification, he experienced moderate withdrawal symptoms. The symptoms of delirium tremens occurred abruptly on the third day following the cessation of drinking. Tom became extremely agitated, tremulous, disoriented and confused. He could not tell where he was or the date. From time to time, during the period of greatest agitation, Tom started picking at his skin and screaming, "Get them off of me! Get them away! They're all over me! I can't get away from them!" He was experiencing visual and tactile hallucinations, probably of small, crawling insects. Later, Tom's mood became labile — he would be quiet one moment and agitated the next — as he continued to yell at us for plotting against him. He appeared feverish, with an increased respiration rate, a severe tremor, and profuse sweating. (Nathan, in press)

Untreated, delirium tremens can be life threatening, especially for alcoholics in poor health, who are also at greatest risk to develop the condition. Clinicians must thus recognize as early as possible which alcoholics in withdrawal may be at risk of developing delirium tremens. Then they can sedate these patients and thereby prevent further development of the syndrome. Delirium tremens, fortunately, are relatively rare as most alcoholics never experience them.

Alcohol Amnestic Disorder. This condition, usually termed **Korsakoff's syndrome,** is a catastrophic consequence of prolonged, heavy alcohol ingestion and chronic thiamine deficiency. Thiamine is a necessary vitamin in ample supply in many foods. Alcoholics develop a vitamin deficiency when they rely on alcohol rather than food to provide them with all their calories, vitamins, and minerals. Korsakoff's syndrome follows an acute episode of **Wernicke's encephalopathy,** a time-limited brain disorder also caused by thiamine deficiency. Wernicke's encephalopathy is characterized by confusion, balance and coordination problems, eye movement abnormalities, and other signs of neurologic disorder. When these symptoms subside, what may remain is Korsakoff's syndrome, whose main feature is profound and irreversible memory impairment. Butters and Cermak (1980) give excellent descriptions of the clinical features of the Wernicke and Korsakoff stages of this disorder.

Korsakoff's syndrome is marked by four principal cognitive deficits: anterograde amnesia (forgetting of material learned after onset of the syndrome), retrograde amnesia (forgetting of material learned before onset of the syndrome), visuoperceptive deficits (difficulties correctly perceiving aspects of the visual environment), and problem-solving deficits (difficulties figuring out how to solve problems, even simple ones, like putting clothes on in the right order.)

The severe cognitive deficits of Korsakoff's patients prevent them from living independently. In common with patients with moderate to severe Alzheimer's disease, they require lifelong care in a sheltered environment.

Professor Ernest Smith, a colleague of one of the authors of this book, was a distinguished historian, the author of widely recognized volumes of French history, the recipient of several prestigious awards from the American and French governments, and the incumbent of an endowed chair in history at a famous American university. For many years, he had also been alcoholic. While he did no drinking during the day, he would consume most or all of a bottle of bourbon after returning home in the evening. Professor Smith ate very little so most of his daily nourishment came from the alcohol he consumed. (A lifelong bachelor, he lived alone, so no one was home to look after his eating habits.) Despite this regimen, which had lasted for more than a decade, Dr. Smith continued to teach, write, and lecture. Though many colleagues knew he had a "drinking problem," few thought it affected his thinking — that is, until he developed an acute brain inflammation, diagnosed as Wernicke's encephalopathy, which ultimately became Korsakoff's syndrome.

One day Professor Smith was a distinguished historian, with the detailed minutiae of the French Revolution at his fingertips; the next day (actually, a few weeks later, following the resolution of his disorder's acute phase) he could neither learn nor remember anything. He had forgotten how to get from his hospital bed to the bathroom, the name or the face of the doctor he saw every day, as well as which hospital he was in, why he was there, and how long he had been a patient. Friends and colleagues who came to visit were welcomed with Professor Smith's customary courtliness, but he had to be reminded how he knew them and what their names were. Oddly, he was ultimately able to remember more about his childhood — and more about the small events that had taken place in Paris in 1792 — than he could about what he had eaten for breakfast or what day of the week it was.

Delusional Disorders. Notable among the organic mental disorders associated with drugs of abuse other than alcohol are the **delusional disorders.** They occasionally develop following ingestion of the amphetamines, cannabis, cocaine, or phencyclidine (PCP). In such instances delusions—generally persecutory—occur shortly after the person ingests the substance and usually disappear within a day or two, though they have been known to last from a week to more than a year.

When the delusional disorder is caused by a hallucinogen or an amphetamine, the content of the delusions and associated behaviors may be indistinguishable from the behavior of the schizophrenic patient.

Bill W., a seventeen-year-old high school senior and the patient of one of the authors of this book, began using drugs and alcohol when he was thirteen. Initially, his use involved a joint of marijuana after school or some beer with friends over the weekend. As Bill got older, though, he began experimenting with other drugs, trying cocaine, Valium, PCP, and even heroin. But it was amphetamine that worked best for him. At least when he was high, it made him feel that his unhappy home life with a widowed, depressed father might lead to something better.

Bill had been ingesting substantial quantities of amphetamine during the school day as well as on weekends for several months before his friends began to notice worrisome changes in his behavior. The highs he experienced from the drug began to be tinged with a paranoid flavor: A recurrent theme was Bill's concern that his girlfriend was unfaithful to him with his best friend. The crashes that followed the highs also began to last longer, and additional drugs seemed to have lost their capacity to pull him out of the resulting depressions.

Bill began gradually to construct an unbelievable delusion of persecution. He became convinced that his chemistry teacher had slipped dangerous chemicals into the vials Bill worked with in chemistry lab. Bill was also sure these chemicals were causing permanent changes in his thought and the way his body worked. Bill couldn't at first figure out why this teacher, whom he had liked, had done this to him. A week of pondering, much of it when high on his drug of choice, convinced Bill that the teacher was actually an undercover agent for the Drug Enforcement Agency and that he, Bill, was being made an example of for the whole school.

Bill stopped coming to chemistry class. A week later, he dropped out of school. Bill ultimately had to be hospitalized, withdrawn from amphetamine, and given long-term psychotherapy. Only then could he shake the persistent feeling that adults were out to get him.

Other organic mental disorders induced by the hallucinogens and PCP involve serious, time-limited, disturbances of mood, most often, depression. Alcohol and the hallucinogens can also cause changes in perceptual behavior (e.g., alcoholics may experience hallucinations) both during and after these drugs have been ingested heavily for prolonged periods.

Prevention and Treatment of the Effects of Substance Abuse on the Brain. An enormous range of approaches to the prevention and treatment of substance abuse are available (see Chapter 11). Since preventing substance abuse also prevents the consequences of that abuse on brain function, prevention of the former is clearly the most important way to prevent the latter. Next in importance is identification and treatment of an existing abuse problem as early as possible, since the longer it lasts, the more likely it will lead to a substance-induced organic mental disorder.

In this context, two groups of researchers (Leber, Parsons, & Nichols, 1985; Walker, Donovan, Kivlahan, & O'Leary, 1983) have reported a relationship between neuropsychological test performance and outcome of therapy for alcohol abuse. To the extent that outcomes of treatment can be predicted from performance on a neuropsychological measure, assessed before treatment begins, a more efficient allocation of scarce professionals can be made.

A good deal of research has been undertaken on agents to increase the speed at which detoxification—sobering up—occurs in individuals whose level of intoxication is dangerously high. Several substances hastening the removal of ethanol from the blood when infused directly into the blood (the most effective is fructose, a naturally occurring fruit sugar) have been identified. Unfortunately, they cannot be taken by mouth for this purpose because they are then chemically altered before entering the bloodstream because of their passage through the gastrointestinal tract.

Another frequent cause of substance-induced organic mental disorder is withdrawal from dependency-inducing drugs and alcohol after a lengthy period of heavy use. Serious, sometimes life-threatening consequences can ensue. A combination of tranquilizing drugs, to reduce the intensity of the psychological and psychomotor symptoms experienced during withdrawal, and slow and gradual reduction in the abused drug's dosage are usually sufficient to ensure safe withdrawal.

Once a dementia associated with alcohol or other drugs of abuse has begun, no available treatments can alleviate the memory problems and other cognitive dysfunctions associated with irreversible, sometimes progressive, brain damage. The search for drugs capable of reversing dementia's associated cognitive deficits is described in our discussion of treatments for the age-related dementias.

An innovative program designed to teach patients with alcohol-induced organic mental disorder how to compensate for their cognitive deficits has also recently been described (Goldman, 1987). It might well have relevance, as well, to the age-related dementias. When given practice on memory tasks, patients suffering from moderate alcohol-related dementia accompanied by significant memory decrements improve their performance markedly. While the question remains whether practice remembering psychological test items will generalize to improvement in memory in the real world, the possibility is intriguing.

Organic Mental Disorders Associated with Physical Disorders. Many factors other than alcohol, drugs, and pathological aging may disturb the brain's normal functioning. Infections, physical injury to the brain, tumors, and endocrinal, metabolic, and neurological diseases may also affect brain function and behavior. In this section, we will illustrate the organic mental disorders associated with physical disorders by discussing several disorders' effects on the brain and behavior. They include AIDS, a viral infection; Huntington's disease, a genetic disorder affecting neurons in the basal ganglion of the brain; Parkinson's disease, a condition with unknown etiology also affecting the basal ganglion; and epilepsy, an organic brain syndrome which can be caused by a large variety of physical disorders.

Acquired Immunodeficiency Syndrome (AIDS). AIDS is transmitted by a virus (the human immunodeficiency virus, HIV) that is passed from person to person via blood, semen, and other bodily fluids (see Chapter 8). People at greatest risk, then, habitually exchange bodily fluids with persons already infected with the HIV. High-risk individuals include intravenous drug abusers who share needles contaminated with the dried blood of previous users as well as persons who engage in homosexual or heterosexual practices with a high potential for exposing both partners to shared blood or blood and semen.

Neurologic or neuropsychiatric complications occur in most AIDS cases. A generalized brain disorder with dementia as a dominant feature is common (Holland & Tross, 1985). The earliest clinical picture, in such cases, involves depression. Common symptoms at this stage include forgetfulness and poor concentration. Later, psychomotor retardation, decreased alertness, apathy, withdrawal, diminished interest in work, and loss of interest in sex may develop. Over the next several months, in cases where neurologic signs and symptoms are most pronounced, confusion, disorientation, seizures, mutism, profound dementia, coma, and death typically ensue. Neurological complications from other AIDS-related causes, including tumors, circulatory problems, and other infections, have also been observed (Snider et al., 1983). The following excerpt, describing an AIDs-related delirium, is a composite case.

Betty was twenty-seven, the mother of four children, and a "two-time loser" whose decade-long history of intravenous heroin abuse had cost her dearly. As though two prison terms for sale and possession of the drug and the burdens of trying to mother four

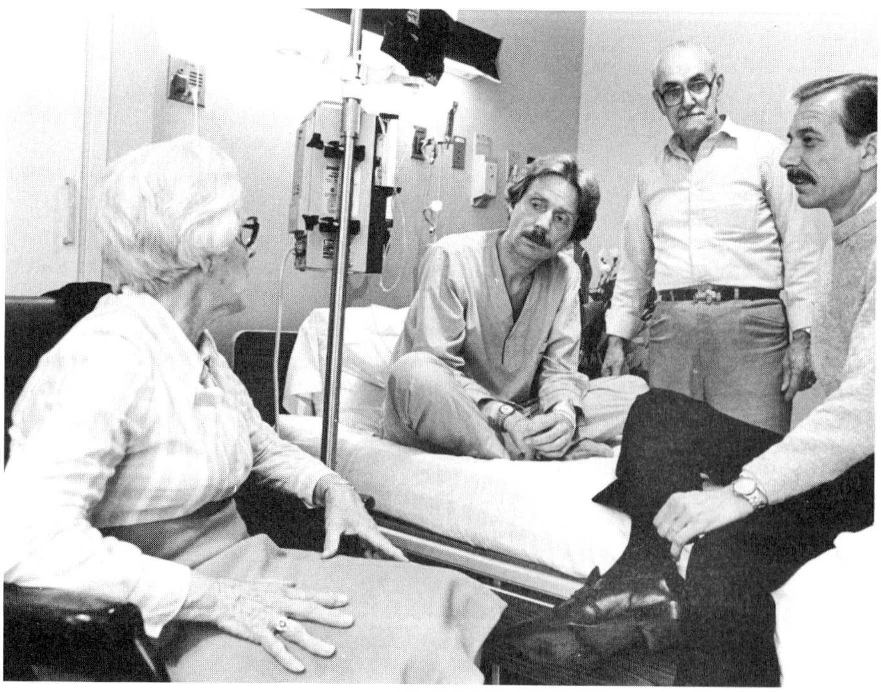

An AIDS patient, surrounded by supportive family and friends.

active children on inadequate state aid were not enough, Betty had learned, a year ago, that she was HIV positive. Now she was in the city hospital because neighbors had begun to observe her acting in very strange ways.

On admission, Betty was quite angry and hostile, refusing to talk to the admitting physician, denying any illness, and demanding to be allowed to go home. She seemed very confused and complained of being unable to remember all her children's names. Before any decision on Betty's request to go home could be made, however, she began complaining that the voices she had begun to hear at home had become more insistent. They were now telling her to go after the heroin addicts with whom she had shared needles and acquired AIDS. Betty also began to pace back and forth in the examining room, telling the emergency room nurse that she was a prominent civic leader and was needed at city hall to attend a meeting on the AIDS crisis. She then picked up a chair and began walking toward a drug cabinet intending, she said, to break in to get the AZT (a drug for AIDS-related symptoms) that she knew was in there (it wasn't).

Not surprisingly, people who test positive for the AIDS virus frequently develop serious psychiatric and psychological complications, such as severe depression and anxiety (Holland & Tross, 1985; Nichols, 1985). That AIDS is often caused by behaviors society strongly disapproves of, specifically homosexual behavior and intravenous drug abuse, increases the AIDS victim's psychological burden. This guilt, which may at times reveal itself in the conviction that the disease is well deserved, adds to the difficulty of preventing or treating the disease's psychiatric and psychological consequences.

The following statement, written by a young man shortly before he died of the disease, is a compelling reminder of the psychological burden AIDS imposes on its victims:

> To those of you not afflicted goes the task of ensuring that our cause is not forgotten by the politicians and civic leaders responsible for allocating funds to carry on the research that feeds our hopes. To you is assigned the work of keeping our plight in the public eye so that those who would ignore the problem in the hope that it will go away, or those who would declare it to be a problem afflicting only a single segment of our society, cannot accomplish what people of good conscience know is patently wrong. It is up to you to correct the public's misperception, fostered by often insensitive media representation, that all AIDS patients are ignoble, drug-abusing people who are undeserving of attention, let alone the benefits of a worldwide quest to save them from a devastating disease. (Ferrara, 1984, p. 1287)

Prevention and Treatment of the Effects of the AIDS Virus on the Brain. At present, an effective treatment for the effects of the AIDS virus on the brain does not exist. As with the other organic brain disorders, however, drugs can ease the agitation, depression, and anxiety associated with a life-threatening disease. Support from family and friends is also of inestimable help to AIDS patients. But support and alleviation of symptoms does not constitute a cure, and a cure for AIDS remains in the future.

AIDS and its consequent brain disorders are, however, preventable. Programs to educate one high risk group, homosexuals, on safe sex practices has led to a marked reduction in their transmission of the HIV (see Chapter 8). We have not been as successful in inducing intravenous drug abusers, another high risk category, to stop sharing needles, though efforts to provide the message to members of this group continue.

Huntington's Disease. This autosomal-dominant disorder invariably afflicts those who inherit the gene if they live long enough. According to Adams and Victor (1981),

> Vessie, in 1932, was able to show that practically all of the patients with this disease in the eastern United States could be traced to about six individuals who had emigrated in 1630 from the tiny East Anglican village in Burres in Suffolk, England. (Adams & Victor, 1981, p. 803)

Woody Guthrie, famed folk singer, a victim of Huntington's Disease.

The defective gene responsible for Huntington's disease ultimately controls the metabolic degeneration of the caudate nuclei of the basal ganglia. The disorder's peak age of onset is forty years. A deteriorating course, which begins with increasingly less subtle changes in personality, intellect, memory, and interpersonal behavior, ultimately leads to chorea (involuntary, jerky movements of the face, arms and legs), depression, dementia, and psychosis. About 90 percent of Huntington's patients ultimately develop dementia during the course of their illness; about 40 percent become clinically depressed. Suicide is common among those doomed to develop the disorder and those who have begun to experience its symptoms (Parsons & Hart, 1984).

At present, Huntington's disease is incurable. Treatment is largely supportive. It mainly consists of drugs to control chorea and combat depression. No treatment for Huntington's-induced dementia exists. For these reasons, prevention of Huntington's disease makes much more sense than trying to treat it. Prevention begins with genetic counseling of persons with a family history of the disorder. Yet counseling for the purposes of prevention is difficult since the disease typically manifests itself after the peak age of childbearing. Education about the disorder is especially helpful for this reason.

Parkinson's Disease. This disorder is caused by the destruction of brain cells producing the neurotransmitter dopamine. The result is a degenerative process that includes tremor (involuntary shaking of the limbs), muscular rigidity, bradykinesis (exaggeratedly slow movement because of muscle rigidity), a stooped posture, and a shuffling gait (Parsons & Hart, 1984).

Age of onset of Parkinson's disease is between forty and sixty years of age. Though etiology is often unknown, the disorder can be caused by encephalitis (a bacterial or viral infection of the brain), carbon monoxide poisoning, or head injury. Parkinson's-like symptoms can also be caused by the long-term use of the major tranquilizing drugs, such as those used most often in treating schizophrenia.

Depression and dementia are quite common in Parkinson's disease. Depression afflicts 50 percent to 90 percent of these patients, while dementia is a complication in 25 percent to 50 percent of them. Some evidence suggests dementia as a more common accompaniment of later-occurring Parkinson's disease (Lavy et al., 1979).

L-dopa, a precursor of dopamine, is given to Parkinson's patients to increase available dopamine. The drug helps alleviate the movement disorders associated with the disease. Yet L-dopa has significant mental side effects including confusion and agitation (Boller, 1980), limiting the drug's usefulness.

Epilepsy. Epilepsy is a chronic condition manifested by repeated and recurrent **seizures.** Seizures are pathophysiological brain disturbances caused by the spontaneous and excessive discharge of neurons in the cortex. The precise nature and frequency of a seizure depend on where and how the responsible cortical neurons are discharged. A seizure may involve abnormal movement or cessation of movement; an unusual smell, taste, or sight; a behavioral disturbance; or a change in the state of consciousness.

Almost any disturbance to the brain can cause epilepsy; as a result, it is considered an organic brain syndrome rather than an organic brain disease. Epileptic seizures may occur at any time, though they appear to be provoked by stress in some individuals. Some people afflicted by seizure disorders experience several seizures a day while others may have one every few months or less (Dodrill, 1981).

One of the most common seizure disorders is **grand mal epilepsy,** involving loss of consciousness and a generalized (tonic-clonic) convulsion of the entire body.

> The individual may or may not have an "aura" (sensory, motor, or psychological changes) preceding the actual convulsion. With the latter, the patient has a sudden loss of consciousness and falls to the floor or ground. The whole musculature is in spasm; the person may emit a piercing cry and bite the tongue. Breathing stops, the bladder may empty, and the pupils are dilated. This is the tonic phase, which lasts for 10–15 seconds. The clonic stage follows, with rhythmic violent muscular contractions; sweating is pronounced; and the pulse is rapid. After one or two minutes, the jerking stops and breathing resumes. The patient is exhausted, confused, disoriented, and amnesic for the episode. (Parsons & Hart, 1984, p. 896)

Petit mal epilepsy involves a brief disruption in consciousness (generally lasting from two to ten seconds) which may be overlooked by observers. The patient may stare vacantly with the mouth open and the eyes blinking or turning up. **Jacksonian seizures** are signaled by a variety of partial motor symptoms involving, initially, the involuntary movement of a finger or a toe, ultimately leading to a period of involuntary jerking of a part of an entire side of the body. Jacksonian seizures typically last from twenty to thirty seconds.

Temporal lobe epilepsy may lead the patient to perform unusual behaviors, sometimes quite complicated and sometimes including episodic violence, during the period of the attack (Westmoreland, 1980). Patients may drive a car long distances, get involved in a complex social interaction, or commit a violent crime in the midst of a temporal lobe seizure; once the seizure ends, they will have no memory of these events. Such patients generally do not remember their behavior after they have recovered from the temporal lobe attack.

Personality disturbances are the most common psychiatric complication of epilepsy (Lishman, 1978); they most often accompany temporal lobe epilepsy. Symptoms include changes in sexual behavior, often involving an increase or decrease in interest in sex; an increased preoccupation with religion; the heightened experience of emotions; and a change in conversation, which becomes ponderous, excessively detailed, and pedantic. Psychosis has also been reported to afflict temporal lobe epileptics between seizures, though much less commonly than the personality disturbance described.

The advent of antiepileptic drugs in recent decades represents a real miracle for older seizure-disorder victims. About 75 percent of epilepsy sufferers experience either complete or substantial remission of their seizures when they begin taking one of the antiepileptic drugs. Although surgical removal of the diseased portion of the brain responsible for the seizure disorder is another treatment option, the antiepileptic drugs are the treatment of choice.

SUMMARY

1. Mental retardation involves subaverage intellectual functioning, deficits or impairment in adaptive functioning, and an onset before the age of eighteen. Only 25 percent of the mentally retarded suffer from brain damage. Mental retardation occurs at four severity levels: mild (IQ 50–55 to approximately 70), moderate (IQ 35–40 to 50–55), severe (IQ 20–25 to 35–40), and profound (IQ below 20–25). The four are associated with differences in social and communication skills, learning ability, and potential for independent living. About 1 percent of the U.S. population is mentally retarded.
2. Mental retardation is caused by prenatal factors (which depend on the pregnant woman's physical and emotional health, including her nutritional status and drug use); rubella and syphilis are maternal infections which cause retardation. Retardation is also caused by chromosomal abnormalities (mutations of the parents' chromosomes, induced by X-rays and aging); the most common such condition is Down's syndrome. Retardation is also caused by genetic defects affecting brain function; phenylketonuria is the most intensively studied of these conditions. Finally, retardation is caused by postnatal factors, including childhood infections and brain injuries, as well as by environmental factors.
3. At present, no treatment has been developed that would enable a mentally retarded person to achieve normal intellectual functioning. By contrast, primary prevention of retardation is possible in many instances. Since most of the retarded suffer from mild retardation, most can be treated at home, especially as children, and integrated into public school systems. Severely and profoundly retarded individuals, however, generally must be cared for in institutions.
4. The United States is rapidly aging. Persons live active, productive lives at seventy or eighty today that fifty-year-olds did not live two generations ago. Many disorders that were thought to be inevitable with aging are now seen as preventable. A variety of supportive services are now available for older people in our society. Federal and state governments, as well, have begun to confront the prejudicial policies of ageism – discrimination based on age alone.
5. Some organic brain disorders last for only a few minutes or hours; they are termed acute brain disorders and recovery from them is almost always complete. Other organic brain disorders last much longer; these chronic brain disorders are often irreversible. Among the latter conditions are Alzheimer's disease, a dementing disease that can afflict older persons; Korsakoff's syndrome, another dementia resulting from chronic alcohol abuse; and the dementias associated with AIDS, Huntington's disease, Parkinson's disease, and epilepsy, all a result of physical disorders.
6. The organic mental syndromes are groups of psychological and behavioral signs and symptoms characterizing a variety of organic brain disorders. They include delirium and dementia, amnestic syndrome, organic hallucinosis, organic delusional syndrome, organic mood syndrome, organic anxiety syndrome, organic personality syndrome, and intoxication and withdrawal.
7. Psychological procedures for assessing brain function include the Halstead-Reitan Neuropsychological Battery, the Luria-Nebraska Neuropsychological Battery, and the Wechsler Adult Intelligence Scale. Imaging techniques for assessing brain structure and function include the pneumoencephalogram, computerized axial tomography (CAT), magnetic resonance imaging (MRI), and positron emission tomography (PET).

PSYCHOANALYSIS AND PSYCHODYNAMIC THERAPIES

Psychoanalytic Concepts and Techniques

Neo-Freudian Therapies

Brief Psychodynamic Therapies

Psychoanalytic Therapies: An Evaluation

HUMANISTIC AND EXISTENTIAL PSYCHOTHERAPIES

Carl Rogers's Person-Centered Therapy

Gestalt Therapy

INTERPERSONAL PSYCHOTHERAPY

The Goals and Strategies of IPT

An Illustrative Case

BEHAVIOR THERAPY

Basic Concepts

Treatment Methods

Clinical and Conceptual Issues

COGNITIVE THERAPY

Rational-Emotive Therapy

Beck's Cognitive Therapy

CURRENT TRENDS IN THE PSYCHOLOGICAL THERAPIES

Theoretical Orientations

Eclecticism

The Effectiveness of Psychological Therapies

SUMMARY

David Hockney, *The Conversation* (1979). Courtesy of Private Collection/Art Resource.

16 INDIVIDUAL PSYCHOLOGICAL THERAPIES

In previous chapters on different clinical disorders we have described some of the methods therapists use to treat individuals with psychological problems. Therapists have a wide range of available treatments: Some involve the use of drugs, but more commonly treatment takes the form of a therapist working with an individual or group. Within these broad categories of individual and group therapy, a variety of approaches can be taken. Some methods are more effective than others with specific disorders. Recall, for example, that exposure treatment seems to be the most helpful therapy for particular anxiety disorders. A psychodynamic approach, together with hypnosis, may be the most useful means of treating dissociative disorders where patients shut off or repress parts of their subjective experience. And specific drug therapies are necessary for treating disorders such as schizophrenia and bipolar depression.

No single type of treatment is appropriate for the widely differing forms of abnormal behavior we have discussed. Just as we need a broad biopsychosocial model to explain the development and maintenance of the various clinical disorders, we also need a range of biological, psychological, and social interventions for preventing or treating them.

Roughly 30 percent of the people in the United States have had some psychological therapy (Meredith, 1986). In the past decade, the number of psychotherapists has jumped from 60,000 to 160,000 (Phillips, 1987). This chapter and Chapter 17 more fully describe the nature of different treatment approaches. The theory behind the different approaches and the specific techniques used in clinical practice are examined. We also take up the questions of the similarities and differences among treatment approaches and discuss how to evaluate their relative effectiveness.

Individuals with psychological problems can be helped in many ways, both formally and informally. Distinguishing between help offered by nonprofessionals on the one hand and mental health professionals on the other, is useful. Nonprofessionals may include friends; a minister, priest, or rabbi; a lawyer or physician; or even a teacher with a personal interest in you. Professionals include clinical psychologists and counselors, psychiatrists, and social workers. Both groups share a deep concern for the well-being of the individual with problems. What separates the professional from the nonprofessional mental health care giver is specific training in, and knowledge of, the biological, psychological, and social foundations of human behavior and its disorders.

Psychological therapy can be defined as a formal interaction between therapist and patient to help the patient with an emotional or behavioral disorder. Box 16.1 summarizes the ethical and professional principles guiding clinicians.

Kanfer and Goldstein (1975) point out that the

Mental health problems are numerous and widespread, and a large number of people in the United States have had some form of psychological treatment.

professional relationship involved in psychological treatment has the following four characteristics: It is unilateral, systematic, formal, and time-limited. The relationship is *unilateral* because the professional exclusively focuses his or her attention on helping the patient, deliberately excluding his or her personal life concerns or problems. The relationship is *systematic* because treatment moves in a purposive manner towards specific objectives. The relationship is *formal* because it takes place at a particular place and time—usually in the therapist's office. Finally, the relationship is *time-limited* because it terminates, by mutual agreement, when treatment goals have been reached.

Informal or nonprofessional helpers benefit most people at one time or another. We feel better and may function more effectively after sharing our problems with someone who cares, listens sympathetically, and offers sound advice. But this level of psychological help is likely to be insufficient in overcoming major clinical disorders of the kind described in previous chapters. These disorders require that the person seek specialized professional treatment by a therapist in private practice, at a university counseling center, in a psychiatric hospital, or at a mental health center.

Who seeks psychological treatment? Until relatively recently psychotherapy tended to be confined to the white upper or middle class with the money to afford it and whose personal values were consistent with the assumptions and goals of traditional psychotherapy. Schofield's (1964) survey of psychologists,

BOX 16.1 Ethical Standards for Mental Health Professionals

1. The goals of treatment should be adequately considered and in the best interests of the client.
2. The choice of treatment procedures should be adequately considered and in the best interests of the client.
3. Whenever possible, the client should be an active and voluntary participant in the therapeutic process.
4. A guardian or an agency responsible for arranging treatment for a client should fully consider whether that treatment is in the best interests of the client.
5. Accurate and complete records are necessary to ensure that a treatment program is achieving its stated objectives.
6. The confidentiality of the treatment relationship between client and therapist should be protected.
7. The professional in charge of the intervention should be qualified in all respects regarding the treatment program.

Source: From L. MacDonald (1987). Ethical standards for therapeutic programs in human services. *The Behavior Therapist,* 9, 213–215. Copyright © 1987, Association for Advancement of Behavior Therapy.

Historically, individual psychotherapy has been limited mainly to middle-class whites. More recently, however, blacks and other minority groups have sought psychological help.

psychiatrists, and social workers revealed that psychodynamic psychotherapy (then the dominant form of treatment) was restricted primarily to patients with the "YAVIS" syndrome, namely those who were young, attractive, verbal, intelligent, and successful.

Times have changed since Schofield's (1964) survey. The development of community mental health centers in the 1960s made psychological treatment more available to society's disadvantaged—the poor and less well educated. A striking change has been psychotherapy's gain in favor among blacks, who once rejected it as a white middle-class solution for emotional problems (*The New York Times,* 1989). Black patients favor goal-oriented treatments with greater interaction between therapist and patient than in the traditional psychodynamic approach.

Numerous systems of psychological therapy or psychotherapy exist. Corsini (1981) identified no fewer than 250 different systems of psychotherapy! Yet the field is not quite as fragmented as this astonishingly high number might suggest. The more developed and influential systems of psychological therapy will be described in this chapter and the next. In this chapter we describe the most influential forms of psychological therapy conducted with individual patients today. In Chapter 17 we describe psychological treatments for more than one individual—marital, family, group, and community-based treatments—as well as the biological treatments of pharmacotherapy, electroshock therapy (ECT), and psychosurgery.

PSYCHOANALYSIS AND PSYCHODYNAMIC THERAPIES

Psychoanalysis originated in Freud's work in Vienna around the turn of the century (see Chapters 1 and 5). Psychoanalysis came to the United States in the 1930s, partly because of the emigration of leading European analysts fleeing Nazi persecution. It came and it conquered. According to Goodwin (1986), "For over 40 years, beginning in the mid-1930s, Freudian psychoanalysis dominated American psychiatry. Almost all the chairmen and professors of psychiatry were psychoanalysts or at least enthusiastic about Freudian theory. Generations of American medical students were taught psychoanalytic theory as received truth" (p. 83). It had a similar impact on clinical psychology.

It is important to distinguish between classical, or pure, psychoanalysis and psychotherapies based on psychoanalytic principles. Classic psychoanalysis is an intensive treatment, usually consisting of four or more sessions a week, for a period of several years. It is conducted by a therapist with formal psychoanalytic training. In today's world pure psychoanalysis is an infrequent choice of treatment; the length and expense of such long-term therapy place it beyond most people's reach.

Psychotherapies based on psychoanalytic principles vary widely in nature, as described later. They differ in structure (e.g., some involve only weekly therapy sessions and may be relatively brief in duration), in content, and in treatment goals. But these treatments have some unifying, core psychoanalytic concepts in common. First, all psychodynamic therapies are concerned with explaining the motives behind why people think, feel, and behave as they do. Second, they all assume that early childhood experiences determine personality development. The bases of subsequent clinical disorders are to be found in problems in these early interactions between the child and his or her parents. Third, they all recognize conflict between opposing psychological forces as an inevitable aspect of human development. Among the sources of conflict are those between a person's identity as a biological/instinctual animal versus as a social being, and those between a person's conscious and unconscious motives. Fourth, they all suggest that the motives behind behavior are mainly unconscious, remaining hidden because our conscious minds find them too threatening or unacceptable. We develop different defense mechanisms to keep these unacceptable motives out of consciousness. And finally, they all suggest that effective psychotherapy's crux is in the development and working through of a special relationship between the patient and the therapist.

Psychoanalytic Concepts and Techniques

Free Association. In the opening phase of treatment the therapist begins to learn about the patient's current life circumstances, family, and past history. Consistent with the principle of providing an open-ended, unstructured situation for the emergence of the patient's underlying motives, the therapist takes a nondirective role. Patients are left to explain their problems. Free association requires patients to talk about whatever feelings and thoughts come to mind—no matter how irrelevant, embarrassing, or personal—without any censoring or editing. **Free association** is an indirect means of exploring the unconscious motives underlying patients' behavior. By remaining passive and letting the patients talk, therapists try to minimize any situational influences so that the patient's associations are determined mainly by internal or intrapsychic processes. The therapists carefully scrutinize what patients say and the manner they express themselves for clues to unconscious conflicts and motives.

Resistance. A basic assumption of all psychoanalytic therapy is patients' unconscious commitment to maintaining the status quo—they resist personal change. **Resistance** is the unwillingness to fulfill the therapeutic contract, which, in this case, involves discussing specific thoughts and feelings. Typical examples of resistance are problems with being able to free associate; refusal to discuss certain topics, silence, disagreement with the therapist's interpretations, missing or arriving late for treatment sessions[1], and failure to pay the therapist's bill.

Resistance occurs despite patients' conscious desire to cooperate with the therapist and overcome their problems. The psychoanalytic explanation is that change is threatening or painful because to change, patients must become aware of previously repressed emotional conflicts. It is easier to repress or avoid these inner conflicts than to confront them. By directly witnessing patients' characteristic defenses in response to threatening topics, the therapist gets clues about unconscious conflicts.

Transference. **Transference** is the developing relationship between patient and therapist where patients respond to the therapist as they did toward significant individuals in childhood, usually parents. Patients, Freud believed, unconsciously reexperience repressed childhood conflicts in the transference relationship, thereby providing the primary means for therapeutic change.

Psychoanalytic therapy's structure promotes the development of transference. Patients are dependent on the therapist who acts in an understanding but strictly neutral, nonjudgmental manner. The therapist tries to provide a "blank screen" on which patients can project ("transfer") their feelings. Patients frequently become frustrated and angry at the therapist's apparent unresponsiveness. Such reactions are seen as a necessary and natural part of therapy. The way patients respond to this frustration helps both patient and therapist understand how childhood patterns of thinking and feeling influence their behavior. The development and subsequent working through of the transference relationship is the most basic and important element of psychoanalytic therapy (Arlow, 1989).

The resolution of the transference relationship is the termination phase of treatment. Here the goal is to wean patients from their unconscious attachment to the therapist so they can function more independently.

Countertransference. Although psychoanalytic therapists remain strictly neutral and do not disclose any information about their own lives, they are not unfeeling. For example, they might find themselves becoming angry or sexually aroused in response to the patient. This emotional response to the patient is known as **countertransference**. The therapist tries to understand the significance of the countertransference, and what his or her feelings might reveal about the patient's motives. For this reason, as part of their training, psychoanalysts undergo a personal analysis to understand their own motives and conflicts.

Interpretation and Denial. Once the transference relationship has been established, and as treatment develops, the therapist shifts from passively observ-

[1] This tendency of psychoanalysts to see unconscious motivation in anything a person says or does has led to the following observation: If patients are late for an appointment, they are hostile; if early, they are defensive; and if on time, they are compulsive. Obviously, not all actions reveal hidden motives. Freud was aware of this problem. "A cigar," he once said, "is sometimes just a cigar" and not a phallic symbol. The problem is how to discriminate this straightforward behavior from telltale signs of unconscious processes. Critics charge that psychoanalysts often fail to make this distinction (Nisbett & Ross, 1980).

ing to interpreting what patients' have said or done. In making an **interpretation,** the therapist confronts patients with information about their behavior which they were previously unaware of. Interpretation produces awareness of unconscious conflicts and thereby induces psychological change.

Analysts usually first interpret the behavior close to the patient's awareness; examples include defense mechanisms and resistance. Only later in treatment will the therapist interpret the content of the unconscious conflicts that give rise to defense mechanisms. These underlying conflicts are less accessible to consciousness and require "deeper" interpretations.

The following example shows how a therapist interpreted a patient's resistance, in this case silence, during the therapy session.

> *Several months of therapy have passed in the case of a hysterical woman suffering from arm and abdominal pains. She begins the hour with a few remarks about her job and then lapses into silence. Her manner and facial expression indicate her feelings of resentment.*
>
> T: *What are you thinking about?*
> C: *[sullenly] Oh, nothing much.*
> T: *You sound angry.*
> C: *I am.*
> T: *What are you mad about?*
> C: *I didn't like your comment last time on my exaggerating things. (In the previous interview she had told of manipulating her boyfriend by threatening to kill herself unless he took her to the beach. One of her typical maneuvers is to heavily dramatize situations in order to get her way. The therapist had pointed out her mechanism of exaggerating the importance of her desires as an interpersonal weapon. At the time she agreed to the truth of the interpretation).*
> T: *But you agreed with me last time.*
> C: *I know it. But thinking about it later I didn't like it.*
> T: *You felt I was reprimanding you?*
> C: *No, not that. You were accusing me of being a phony. That's something I can't stand. Jerry says the same thing. He accuses me of always acting. Once we were at a party and . . .*
>
> *The silence is broken and the patient continues to produce.* (Colby, 1951, cited in Lichtenstein, 1980, p. 112)

Lichtenstein (1980) points out a transference theme in this excerpt: The patient views the therapist as criticizing her the way her boyfriend did. The therapist proceeds to explore the childhood origins of this sensitivity to male criticism. Patients commonly deny the therapist's interpretation. The therapist may see such **denial** as confirmation of the interpretation's accuracy.

Analyzing the transference relationship illustrates the use of a deeper interpretation in showing patients how they misperceive and misinterpret current situations in terms of past conflicts and maladaptive patterns of behavior. By treating patients with respect, yet by refusing to reenact the parental role unconsciously expected of them by the patient, the therapist's detached attitude allows corrective emotional or interpersonal learning to occur. This process is illustrated in the following clinical example:

> *The patient, a young woman suffering from a fairly severe borderline condition who had been seen in long-term therapy, displayed morose affect during the hour, complained of being used, exploited, and criticized by her boss, and eventually communicated in highly indirect ways that she had similar feelings toward me. In a preceding hour she had expressed the wish for my vacation to start soon (I had announced earlier my plan to take a brief vacation). Seeing herself as the victim of an impending separation (= rejection), she experienced herself as dependent and needy but also as wishing to be needed and exploited. While the parallel to a comparable experience with her father was clear, she rejected my attempt at interpreting her current experience in the context of the earlier one. However, she was unable to deny her anger and resentment at me—these were empirical data we could both see. It was also clear to her that I had not been exploiting her and that she had distorted her present experience with me in terms of constructions she had unwittingly placed on it. By pointing out these facts to her, I believe I was able to accomplish a piece of therapeutic work. This was made possible by (a) our basically good relationship, (b) her enactment of a previous experience in the presence of affect, (c) the presence of incontrovertible data we could both see, and (d) her willingness to listen and be confronted, albeit in a painful way, with facts that demanded a reorganization of her cognitions and emotional reactions.* (Strupp, 1980a, p. 298)

Dream interpretation is an important technique in psychoanalytic therapies. Patients are encouraged to report their dreams, which Freud called the "royal road to the unconscious." He assumed that during sleep the person's ego defense mechanisms are lessened, thereby making it more likely that dreams might provide clues about the hidden motives behind clinical disorders and normal behavior. Even then therapists must distinguish between the *manifest content* of dreams, what is consciously remembered, and their *latent content,* the hidden expression of unconscious processes.

Insight. The goal of all psychoanalytic therapies is to help patients gain **insight** into their problems. Insight refers to increased awareness of unconscious conflicts and psychological defenses, resulting in more adaptive behavior.

The couch in Sigmund Freud's office in Vienna.

Insight is not simply an intellectual awareness. It is an emotional process occurring only in the context of a unique, affect-arousing interpersonal interaction. Nor are one or two experiences of insight sufficient to bring about change. Transference's "working through" is continued numerous times in different ways, to increasingly deepen and consolidate the analysis through repetition and elaboration.

Neo-Freudian Therapies

Freud continued to revise his theory until his death in 1939. Psychoanalytic theory and therapy were also modified and amplified by the neo-Freudians, men and women who either had participated in Freud's original Vienna Psychoanalytic Society or had been trained by one of that distinguished group's members. Among the most important Neo-Freudians were Carl Jung, Alfred Adler, Karen Horney, and Harry Stack Sullivan.

Jung (1887–1961) was a psychiatrist who broke ranks with Freud over several basic disagreements and subsequently developed what has been called *analytic psychology.* Most significantly, he rejected Freud's insistence on sexuality as the fundamental source of human motivation. Instead, Jung proposed that sexuality was only one form of a more general psychic energy. In his writings, he focused not only on treating abnormal behavior but also on normal adult development. Consequently, Jung has been regarded as a forerunner of humanistic psychology (discussed later).

Adler (1870–1937), an original member of the Vienna Psychoanalytic Society, also rejected Freud's view of the primacy of biological-instinctive forces and sexuality's overriding importance in personality development. Compared to Freud, he had a more optimistic conception of human development, in which the self most significantly influenced development. Table 16.1 summarizes some of the significant differences between Adler and Freud. Note that Adler anticipated some subsequent developments in psychological therapies, including the emphasis on the concept of self, a subjective sense of personal worth or adequacy (he coined the phrase *inferiority complex*), and the social context of behavior. Adler also discussed the influence of patients' beliefs or personal mythology, which he called basic mistakes. Two examples illustrate the nature of basic mistakes:

1. Overgeneralizations, such as, "People are hostile," or "Life is dangerous".
2. False or impossible goals of "security," such as, "One false step and you're dead," or "I have to please everybody." (Mosak, 1989, p. 87).

Notice the similarity between Adler's basic mistakes and the irrational or dysfunctional cognitions of modern-day cognitive-behavior therapy, described later.

Karen Horney

TABLE 16.1 A Comparison between Freud's and Adler's Psychodynamic Theories

Freud	Adler
1. Individuals can only be understood as intrapersonal, intrapsychic, beings.	1. Individuals can only be understood interpersonally, as social beings moving through and interacting with their environment.
2. The establishment of intrapsychic harmony constitutes the ideal goal of psychotherapy.	2. The expansion of the individual, self-realization, and the enhancement of social interest represent the ideal goals of psychotherapy.
3. People are basically "bad." Civilization attempts to domesticate them for which they pay a heavy price. Through therapy the instinctual demands may be sublimated but not eliminated.	3. People are neither "good" nor "bad," but as creative, choosing human beings, they may choose to be "good" or "bad" or both depending upon their lifestyle and appraisal of the immediate situation and its payoffs. Through the medium of therapy people can thus choose to actualize themselves.
4. People are the victims of their instinctual life and of civilization.	4. People, as choosers, can shape their internal and external environment. Although they are not the complete masters of their fate and cannot always choose what will happen to them, they can always choose the posture they will adopt toward life's stimuli.
5. Women feel inferior because they envy men their penises. Women are inferior. "Anatomy is destiny."	5. Women feel inferior because in our cultural milieu they are undervalued. Men have privileges, rights, preferred status, although in the current cultural ferment, these roles are being reevaluated.
6. Neurosis has a sexual etiology.	6. Neurosis is a failure of learning, a product of distorted perceptions.

Source: Reproduced by permission of the publisher, F.E. Peacock Publishers, Inc., Itasca, Illinois. From Mozak, H.H., Adlerian psychotherapy. In R. Corsini: & D. Wedding (Eds.), *Current psychotherapies,* 1989 copyright, p. 70.

Although Adler seems to have anticipated many later developments in psychological therapy, he is rarely credited as an innovator, and he did not directly influence the major transforming changes in psychological therapies after World War II. Why? We believe it is because Adler remained true to core concepts of psychoanalytic therapy, as outlined earlier, despite going beyond orthodox Freudian theory. Subsequent generations of therapists focused more on Adler's similarity with Freud than on his innovations.

Harry Stack Sullivan (1953) is credited with emphasizing the interpersonal nature of psychological disorders. He used the term **parataxic distortions** to describe the effect of problematic interpersonal relationships in childhood on patients' adult misperceptions of reality. Although Sullivan emphasized the interpersonal nature of early childhood experiences, the concept of parataxic distortions is consistent with basic Freudian principles: Childhood experiences unconsciously affect later adjustment, and therapy's task is to gain insight into these unconscious influences on present behavior.

Sullivan departed more clearly from orthodox Freudian therapy by introducing the concept of the therapist as a "participant-observer." By this, Sullivan meant that patients' behavior during therapy sessions was a product not only of their past experience and personality but also of the therapist's subtle influence. His recognition of the therapist's influence as a "participant" in the treatment process had important therapeutic implications. Whereas Freud insisted the therapist remain nondirective and detached, Sullivan was more directive and focused on events in the here and now.

Ego Analytic Therapies. A major modification of Freudian psychoanalysis was the development of ego psychology and ego analytic therapies (Erikson, 1959; Anna Freud, 1946; Hartmann, 1958; Rapaport, 1960). The neo-Freudians had moved away from Freud's primary emphasis on intrapsychic conflicts within the individual to acknowledge their interaction with the environment. This trend was made even more explicit in the development of ego analytic therapies. In Freud's theory, the ego (conscious part of personality) maintained a balance between the opposing forces of the id (primitive, instinctual impulses) and the superego (conscience). Ego analysts attach greater value than did Freud to current life circumstances and people's ability to adapt to and control their environments. Personal control and adaptive learning are ego functions—hence, the name ego analytic therapies. Erik Erikson became one of the best-known ego analysts. He proposed a series of eight psychosocial stages which people pass through over the total lifespan. At each stage, sociocultural reality confronts the maturing person with new challenges. For example, Erikson saw the adolescent period as when a young person is challenged to develop his or her personal identity or definition of self.

Self Psychology. Another important modification of Freudian psychoanalysis has been Heinz Kohut's development of what is called **self psychology** (Kohut, 1971). According to this approach, problems between mother and child early in life leave the child with low self-esteem. The child grows up trying to compensate for this feeling of vulnerability, resulting in an unrealistic and narcissistic striving for expressions of love and approval from others. Therapy, which is more directive than classical psychoanalysis, is aimed at restoring the patient's sense of self by providing the acceptance the patient never had as a child. The theory and therapy of self psychology was detailed in the description of narcissistic personality disorder in Chapter 10.

Brief Psychodynamic Therapies

One of the major limitations of orthodox, long-term psychodynamic therapy is its length and cost. Only a wealthy few can afford the recommended minimum of four sessions a week for several years. Today, if psychodynamic therapy is to reach a wider population, we need more time-limited and cost-effective treatment methods. In response to these pressures, brief psychodynamic therapies have recently evolved. Different forms of brief therapy have been developed; the best known are associated with the work of Davanloo (1978) in Canada, Malan (1979) in England, and Horowitz (1989) and Sifneos (1979) in the United States. Generally speaking, "brief" therapy in this context means up to forty hours of treatment. (An example of Horowitz's therapy applied to posttraumatic stress disorder was described in Chapter 5.)

Adapting the psychodynamic approach to brief psychotherapy has focused on three parts of the treatment process (Strupp, 1980b):

1. Patient selection.
2. Selection of therapeutic goals.
3. Modification of therapeutic techniques.

Patient Selection. Only carefully selected patients are deemed appropriate for brief psychodynamic psychotherapy. Suitable patients are those with "strong ego resources"; namely, "those in whom the behavioral problem is of acute onset; those whose previous adjustment has been good; those with a good ability to relate; those with high initial motivation" (Strupp, 1980b, p. 221). Unsuitable patients are those who "act out" (i.e., have problems with impulse control), are less mature and responsible, are self-destructive, or are poorly motivated.

Therapeutic Goals. Treatment goals tend to be more modest than in orthodox, long-term psychoanalysis. Instead of fundamental "personality change," the objective of treatment is resolution of the core conflict. As in orthodox psychoanalysis, however, improvement in observable symptoms is viewed not as the primary therapeutic goal, but merely the by-product of the underlying conflict's resolution (Mann, 1980).

Therapeutic Techniques. The therapist is typically more active and directive in this treatment than in orthodox psychoanalysis. In contrast to the more passive and deliberately detached therapist in long-term psychodynamic treatment, in brief treatment the therapist tries to foster the patient's involvement and collaboration in a working "therapeutic alliance." In particular, the therapist frequently interprets what the patient says and does. Different brief therapies favor different types of interpretations, but all focus on actively interpreting the focal conflict or central issue behind the patient's problem. The following is an example of a central or core conflict:

> *A 48-year-old woman was beset with problems with her teen-age daughter. She recognized areas of friction between them and tried desperately but without success to find ways of managing the relationship better. The patient's history revealed an unusual amount of control exercised over her from her earliest years both by her parents and by others. She responded passively, despite intensely frightening fantasies; to the guilt engendered by her anger, she responded with a good deal of reaction formation in the form of being understanding and helpful to others. In her own adolescence she had never rebelled, and now, confronted by an adolescent daughter who had been reared in an atmosphere of understanding and helpfulness and was now typically rebellious, she felt herself to be at her wit's end.*
>
> *The central issue extracted from the patient's history was stated as follows: "You are a person who has been understanding and helpful to your children and to many others. You have always had the inner feeling, however, that you are like a puppet controlled by others, and as a result, you feel and have always felt helpless." How she came to feel this way about herself was the work of 12 treatment sessions* (Mann, 1980, pp. 34–35).

Orthodox psychodynamic therapy moves cautiously from "surface" to "deeper" issues and addresses patients' defenses and resistance in facing their underlying conflicts. Brief therapy goes directly to what the therapist identifies as the focal conflict or central issue behind patients' defenses and resistance.

Psychoanalytic Therapies: An Evaluation

Psychodynamic theory and therapy remain unsurpassed in popularity and influence among mental health professionals in the United States. Its appeal among the broader intellectual community of artists and writers is unrivaled (see Chapter 1). Several reasons help explain psychoanalytic theory's enormous popularity. One is its breadth as it spans normal behavior and the full range of abnormal behavior. Its explanation of the motives behind human behavior is more extensive than any other theory's. It sometimes seems to offer the only comprehensive account of some disorders (see Chapter 6). Also, psychodynamic therapists have reported a wealth of important clinical observations, often the basis for understanding and treating clinical disorders. These observations are significant regardless of the validity of the theories proposed to explain them.

Psychodynamic theory and therapy have, nevertheless, been widely criticized on several counts. First, specific Freudian concepts have been found fault with (Fisher & Greenberg, 1977), and it is easy to be skeptical about some of the more fanciful psychoanalytic notions. Few present-day clinical investigators would agree that agoraphobics become anxious upon leaving their homes because the street represents the place "where it is possible to realize their unconscious wish to be a prostitute" (Arlow, 1989, p. 41), or that bulimia nervosa is really a symbolic form of "oral masturbation" (Schwartz, 1988). It is important to note, however, that many psychodynamic therapists also reject these views and instead point to more enduring contributions, such as the importance of early learning and childhood experience, the indisputable fact that much of our functioning is influenced by unconscious processes, and the way in which personal conflicts can interfere with interpersonal relationships.

Second, Freud rejected evaluating his treatment in controlled empirical research, claiming that individual patients' success sufficiently proved his theory and its therapeutic value. But this reasoning is unacceptable to clinical researchers. There are problems with drawing conclusions from uncontrolled clinical case studies of the sort Freud reported (see Chapter 4). Judgments of treatment effectiveness must depend on independent investigators' experimental evaluations of treatment outcome. Some psychoanalysts claim psychoanalysis is too complex to evaluate by controlled, statistically valid research (Arlow, 1989). But this attitude is not shared by other contemporary psychodynamic therapists who have been actively researching some of psychodynamic treatment's principles and procedures. This research falls into two categories: One is known as process research, the other as outcome research.

Process Research. Deals with interactions between therapist and patient during treatment sessions. It is the dominant type of research on psychoanalytic therapy. For example, Luborsky (1987) hypothesized the existence of a consistent, conflict-producing theme in the relationships patients develop with significant figures in their lives. He called this the Core Conflictual Relationship Theme (CCRT) and has shown its close resemblance to Freud's concept of transference (Luborsky, Crits-Christoph, & Mellon, 1986). To assess the CCRT, Luborsky records therapy sessions and then examines them for consistencies in patients' narratives (descriptions) of different interpersonal relationships.

The numbered circles in Figure 16.1 summarize the relationship patterns from a therapy session of an eighteen-year-old college student suffering from anxiety symptoms. Luborsky had clinicians examine these narratives and infer the underlying CCRT. Their interpretation is summarized in the center circle in Figure 16.1. For this type of analysis to be scientifically useful, the clinical judges' interpretations must be reliable; that is, they must agree with each other about the CCRT's nature.

One of psychoanalytic therapy's basic assumptions is that therapeutic progress depends on therapists accurately interpreting patients' verbal and nonverbal behavior. To study this hypothesis, Luborsky (1987) had one set of clinical judges rate the patient's CCRT, and a second set rate the accuracy of the therapist's in-session interpretations of the patient's CCRT. Luborsky was then able to show that the accuracy of therapists' interpretations correlated significantly with the effects of treatment, thereby providing empirical support for one of the assumptions of psychoanalytic therapy.

Outcome Research. Process research may reveal how treatment works. But this requires evidence of a particular treatment's effectiveness. *Outcome research* evaluates the effectiveness of treatment. To this day there is little controlled research on psychoanalytic treatment's effectiveness. Where it exists it provides relatively little support for psychoanalytic therapies. Two of the best studies in this arena illustrate the nature of the findings.

Can we say that treatment administered by expert psychoanalytic therapists achieves better results than those obtained by kindly nonprofessional helpers? To answer this question, Strupp and Hadley (1979) completed the following study. Patients suffering primarily from anxiety and depression were treated either by highly experienced psychoanalyti-

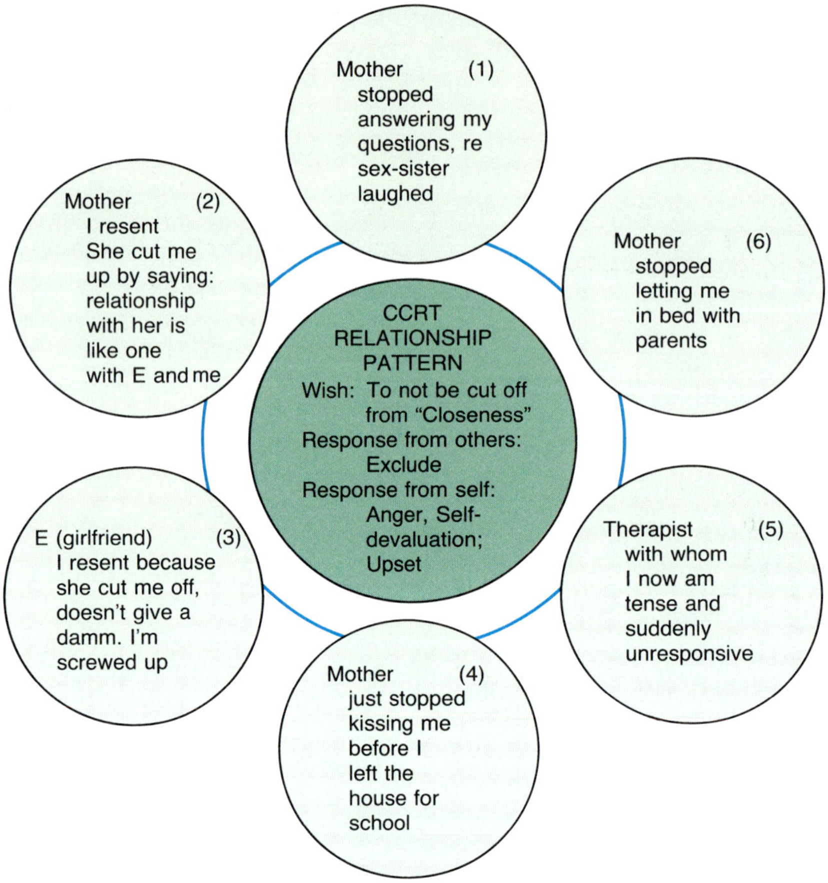

Figure 16.1 Schematic summary of patient's statements about relationships and their Core Conflictual Relationship Theme (CCRT).
Source: From Luborsky L., (1987) Research can now affect clinical practice—a happy turnaround. *The Clinical Psychologist,* 1987, *40,* 56–59. Copyright Division 12, American Psychological Association. Reprinted with permission.

cally oriented psychotherapists or seen for the same period of time by college professors chosen for their ability to form understanding relationships with students. There were no differences between these two groups of subjects across a variety of psychological adjustment measures. The resulting lack of superiority of the expert psychoanalytic therapists damages their claims of specific treatment effectiveness.

In a second study, Sloane and his colleagues (1975) at Temple University Medical School compared psychoanalytically oriented psychotherapy with behavior therapy and a waiting-list control group in treating adults with primarily neurotic (anxiety) disorders. Experts in each approach conducted both treatments. Therapy lasted four months, followed by a posttreatment evaluation and an eight-month follow-up.

This important study's outcome depends on which measure we look at and when. Ratings of each patient's three main symptoms showed that roughly 50 percent of the control group and 80 percent of the behavior therapy and psychotherapy groups improved. Behavior therapy was, however, significantly superior when the overall ratings of improvement were compared. On this global measure of outcome, 93 percent of the behavior therapy group were rated as significantly improved, compared with 77 percent of the psychotherapy and waiting-list patients. On this measure, psychodynamic therapy was no better than the simple passage of time. At follow-up all differences among the three groups had disappeared.

A third, and long-term, concern about psychoanalytic therapy has been its limited applicability to a narrow range of patients—primarily those fitting the "YAVIS" syndrome, as described. The emergence of brief psychodynamic therapies makes the approach more widely available. Yet even the shorter treatment has been criticized as appropriate for only a small percentage of carefully selected patients. Strupp (1980b), one of the leading researchers of these methods, admits that the patients selected for brief psychodynamic therapy are those who tend to improve spontaneously and who might do well with any type of treatment. Until research shows otherwise, all psychodynamic therapies seem restricted to a relatively small range of patients.

HUMANISTIC AND EXISTENTIAL PSYCHOTHERAPIES

Humanistic and existential psychotherapies have in common with psychoanalytic therapies the core assumption that individuals must develop insight into their underlying needs and conflicts. Yet humanistic therapies differ significantly from Freudian theory and therapy. Person-centered therapy and Gestalt therapy are revealing examples.

Carl Rogers's Person-Centered[2] Therapy

The best-known personality theorist and psychotherapist within the humanistic tradition was Carl Rogers (1902–1987). The growth of humanistic psychology and psychotherapy in the 1960s was a reaction against Freudianism and behaviorism. Rogers referred to it as the third force in psychology. Humanistic therapy's essence is the assumption that people are innately good. Rogers believed that behavior is goal-directed and purposive; that is, people are motivated to affect their environment and to achieve personal fulfillment. The tendency toward personal growth is known as **self-actualization.**

Rogers (1961) contrasted this optimistic view of the individual's self-worth and dignity with that of the psychoanalytic model: "I have little sympathy with the rather prevalent concept that man is basically irrational, and that his impulses, if not controlled, will lead to destruction of others and self. Man's behavior is exquisitely rational, moving with subtle and ordered complexity toward the goals his organism is endeavoring to achieve" (p. 194).

Psychoanalytic therapies assume that personality is determined by early childhood experiences. Humanistic therapists believe people are free to shape their own futures. In psychodynamic treatment, the therapist acts as expert, making interpretations designed to give patients insight linking past conflicts to present feelings and actions. Person-centered therapists try to encourage a therapeutic relationship where they listen rather than interpret and they focus on the patient's present experience without attempting to connect it to childhood trauma. Psychoanalysts foster a transference relationship; person-centered therapists do not. Rogers has suggested that "transference relationships develop in an evaluative atmosphere where the patient feels the therapist knows more about him than he knows himself, and therefore the patient becomes dependent. The therapist in person-centered therapy tends to avoid any expression that could have evaluative connotations" (Meador & Rogers, 1984, p. 146). Person-centered therapy rejects techniques placing the therapist in control (e.g., the therapist avoids imposing treatment goals) because they will interfere with patients' experience of self and their developing reliance on their own inner resources. This is why the Rogers's approach was originally known as client-centered therapy.

The essence of humanistic therapy—and the critical mechanism of personality growth and behavior change—is directly experiencing the self in a wide range of ways through an emotionally meaningful relationship with the therapist.

Necessary and Sufficient Conditions of Therapeutic Change. A radical aspect of Rogers's person-centered therapy is the assumption that the techniques of the various psychological therapies (e.g., psychodynamic interpretations, behavioral methods, and cognitive restructuring) are unimportant except to the extent they encourage the expression of three personal qualities of the therapist: empathy, unconditional positive regard, and genuineness.

Empathy. Therapists are empathic when they accurately understand the patient's phenomenological world—the way he or she perceives and emotionally experiences events. Empathy requires more of the therapist than merely understanding the patient's words. The therapist "immerses" him or herself in the patient's world and communicates his or her understanding to the patient at an emotional level.

Unconditional Positive Regard. Therapists show unconditional positive regard when they warmly accept all aspects of the patient's experience in a completely nonjudgmental fashion. They neither probe unnecessarily nor interpret the patient's feelings. They simply communicate a sense of trust in his or her own resources for self-understanding.

Genuineness. This quality is hard to separate from empathy and positive regard. Therapists are genuine, or congruent, when they try to experience what the patient is experiencing. Genuineness goes beyond intellectual understanding; it is a "feel" for what the patient is experiencing emotionally. To be genuine, therapists must first be "real" in trusting their own experience of the relationship. In this way, they allow patients to trust them and to learn from the therapy that they can risk sharing their innermost feelings with another person.

An Evaluation. Rogers's emphasis on personal growth and Skinner's radical behaviorist position that all behavior is a function of external contingencies

[2] Rogers (1951) originally called his treatment client-centered or nondirective therapy. In 1974 he changed it to person-centered therapy, believing that this term most accurately reflected the human values on which treatment is based.

Humanistic approaches to psychological treatment emphasize that people are free to shape their own destiny.

are at opposite ends of the continuum on the issue of whether external forces can or should influence human behavior. Both of these positions are extreme. On the one hand, as indicated in earlier chapters, the majority of contemporary behavior therapists have modified Skinner's extreme position on environmental control and assign fundamental importance to self-control and other cognitive processes in explaining and changing behavior (O'Leary & Wilson, 1987). On the other hand, person-centered therapy was never as free of external (therapist) influence on the patient as Rogers believed. Every form of psychological therapy, irrespective of whether it is described as directive or nondirective, by its very nature involves therapist influence on the patient. Such influence is inevitable and unavoidable.

Truax's (1966) analysis of one of Rogers's clinical cases classically illustrates this aspect of therapeutic interaction. Although Rogers's theory of patient-centered therapy explicitly disavows any directive intervention by the therapist or any contingent use of social influence, Truax showed that this process took place anyway. Without realizing it, Rogers responded to patient talk that he considered "therapeutic" with subtle forms of social reinforcement, such as smiles, nods of the head, or vocal "uh-huhs." Patient material which he viewed as less "therapeutic" was followed by silence and an absence of nonverbal approval cues.

Therapists influence their patients, who, in turn, influence their therapists. Moos and MacIntosh (1970) demonstrated that the therapist–patient relationship should be thought of as an interacting system of mutual social influence. They found that patients exercised significantly greater influence over the behavior of nonbehavioral therapists than vice versa. Therapist behavior was not a function of any behavioral traits or consistently applied technique but was determined by the specific situation. Therapists are confronted with using the naturally occurring social influence process consciously to produce mutually desired change or using it haphazardly in an inefficient or possibly even harmful way (Bandura, 1986).

Critics have also challenged Rogers's fundamental assumptions of the inherent goodness of all people and self-actualization as the major source of human motivation.

Rogers's person-centered therapy's major contribution has been to improve our understanding of how therapists can aid the treatment process. Person-centered therapists have refined specific skills that, ideally, should be important elements of any form of helping relationship. They are an integral part of all humane and effective psychological therapies.

The major limitation of Rogers's approach has been its deemphasis of techniques and the specific nature of the patient's disorder. By themselves, the therapist qualities described by Rogers are simply insufficient to treat the major clinical disorders effectively. The preceding chapters in this book have made it clear that psychological and/or pharmacological techniques are needed to treat specific disorders. For example, cognitive therapy, interpersonal therapy, and certain drugs specifically benefit clinically

BOX 16.2 An Illustration of Person-Centered Therapy

The following example is drawn from a well-known film that Carl Rogers (1965) made, in which he interviews a client for the first time. The analysis of Rogers's comments is adapted from Meador and Rogers's (1984) account of this interview.

The Client

Gloria is a thirty-year-old divorced woman. In her session with Carl Rogers, she says her problem is that she is unable to be open with her nine-year-old daughter (Pam) about her sexual relationships with men since the divorce. She is conflicted about having lied to Pam, and wants to know whether telling her daughter the truth will have a bad effect on her.

The Treatment Session

Several times during the interview, Gloria asks Rogers whether she should say anything to Pam about her sexual relationships. She wants an "authority" to tell her what to do. Each time Rogers communicates to her that he understands her concern. Instead of giving her an answer, he helps her to focus on her own resources. Each request from Gloria and each response by Rogers becomes the occasion for her to explore her own feelings more deeply. The following is an excerpt from the interview:

> In response to Gloria's first request, Rogers replies, "And it's this concern about her (Pam) and the fact that this open relationship that has existed between you, now you feel it's kind of vanished?" and after Gloria's reply he says, "I sure wish I could give you the answer as to what you should tell her." "I was afraid you were going to say that," she says. Rogers replies, "Because what you really want is an answer."
>
> Gloria then explores her feelings about what she calls her "devilish" or "shady" side. She questions whether she accepts this part of her personality. Again she asks Rogers for his advice and says, "You're just going to sit there and let me stew in it and I want more." Rogers replies, "No, I don't want to let you just stew in your feelings, but on the other hand, I also feel this is the kind of very private thing that I couldn't possibly answer for you. But I sure as anything will try to help you work toward your own answer. I don't know whether that makes any sense to you, but I mean it." Gloria says she can tell he really does mean it and again begins to explore her feelings, this time focusing more on the conflict she herself feels between her actions and her inner values.
>
> *[Here Rogers is being real and genuine. He is aware of his own feelings and expresses them in a way that does not impose on Gloria or interfere with her self-exploration. He emphasizes his belief in her ability to find the answer herself and that he cares deeply.]*
>
> Shortly thereafter Gloria again says, "I want you very much to give me a direct answer. . . ." Rogers replies, "I guess, I am sure this will sound evasive to you, but it seems to me that perhaps the person you are not being fully honest with is you, because I was very much struck by the fact that you were saying, 'If I feel all right about what I have done, whether it's going to bed with a man or what, if I really feel all right about it, then I do not have any concern about what I would tell Pam or my relationship with her.'"
>
> *[Here Rogers is communicating empathy and understanding. He is conveying to Gloria that he understands the meaning behind her words, a meaning which is outside of her awareness.]*
>
> In response to Rogers's reflection, Gloria says, "Right. All right. Now I hear what you are saying. Then, all right, then I want to work on accepting me then. I want to work on feeling all right about it. That makes sense. Then that will come natural and then I won't have to worry about Pam. . . ."
>
> *[This last statement by Gloria reveals an important insight into her conflict. "Rogers, in understanding her inner struggle with accepting herself, makes explicit what Gloria has been implying. Her hearing his statement precipitates a real insight for her, as though a light turns on and she understands where she must go for answers, namely, into herself."]*

Source: Reproduced by permission of the publisher, F.E. Peacock Publishers, Inc., Itasca, Illinois. From Meador, B.D., & Rogers, C.R. *Person-oriented therapy*. In R. Corsini (Ed.), *Current psychotherapies*, 1984 copyright, p. 188.

depressed patients beyond the influence of a good therapeutic relationship.

The Effectiveness of Person-Centered Therapy. Another of Rogers's contributions was his role in opening up psychotherapy to empirical research in the 1950s. First, he put forward a clearly stated and testable theory of behavior change that stimulated empirical investigation. Second, Rogers and his colleagues pioneered the tape recording of entire treatment sessions. Investigators could then study the content of sessions and examine systematic interactions between therapist and patient. This methodological breakthrough was the forerunner of today's use of sophisticated videotape recording to train therapists, to assess how well they implement treatment, and even to treat patients.

Rogers's openness to impartial, objective testing of key treatment concepts and therapist behavior contrasts with Freud's unwillingness to submit his theory and therapy to empirical tests. Rogers was a pioneer in the controlled evaluation of psychological therapies' effects. Unfortunately, the collective results of these studies generally failed to support Rogers's predictions. High levels of the three therapist qualities identified by Rogers are insufficient for therapeutic change, as noted previously. Nor are these qualities always necessary to provoke change,

BOX 16.3 Can Psychotherapy Harm as Well as Help You?

Psychological therapy is generally believed to help patients, even though there is disagreement about the extent of its effectiveness. In 1966, Allen Bergin introduced another element into the controversy. He suggested the term **deterioration effect** to describe findings that some patients were worse after treatment. Specifically, he reported that in studies comparing psychological treatment with a control group, the variance in outcome measures was greater for the treatment group than for the control group. He interpreted these data to mean that treated patients both improved and deteriorated. Either treatment techniques or certain therapists, Bergin suggested, caused patients to become worse. Subsequently, Strupp, Hadley, and Gomes-Schwartz (1977) introduced the term *negative effect* to describe therapy-induced worsening of patients' problems.

Certainly, patients' problems have been mismanaged in some cases, and it is tempting to attribute a number of negative effects to incompetent therapists. A small number of patients probably do get exploited. Sexual exploitation of female patients by male therapists is a common example. It is, nonetheless, hard to establish causal link between the worsening of patients and the therapy they received or the therapists who treated them. Establishing this relationship is as difficult as showing that therapy produces improvement. Research incorporating appropriate control procedures is necessary.

One complicating element is the obvious fact that patients get worse spontaneously, that is, without receiving any form of therapy. Consider the following example reported by Rachman and Wilson (1980). In a clinical trial involving the treatment of severe and chronic obsessional patients, two of the patients selected for treatment markedly deteriorated before entering the trial. One patient became severely depressed two weeks before the starting date, and the other had a psychotic episode shortly before she was due to enter the trial. Obviously, if the timing of their entry into the trial had been different, it may have appeared that the intervention of the therapists had provoked their deterioration. Such developments are commonplace in clinical research and treatment. We would need to know the extent and timing of any deterioration in patients before they enter treatment in order to make sense of changes that occur after treatment begins. Because of this and other methodological shortcomings in the literature, some reviewers have concluded that a causal link between therapy or therapist and negative effects in patients has yet to be demonstrated (Mays & Franks, 1985; Rachman & Wilson, 1980).

The opposing view is illustrated by Lambert, Shapiro, and Bergin's (1986) conclusion:

> . . . although there may be many methodological shortcomings and ambiguities in the data . . . , the evidence that does exist suggests that psychotherapy can and does cause harm to a portion of those it is intended to help. (p. 183)

Whatever the evidence, professionals tend to believe in therapy-induced negative effects. A survey of seventy-six expert therapists revealed that virtually all thought it does occur (Strupp et al., 1977). The extent to which subjective bias influenced these reports is unknown.

What types of therapist behavior might cause negative effects? In one of the better studies of this question, Sachs (1983) had trained judges rate therapist–patient interaction in psychodynamic therapy on a scale constructed to assess negative effects. Problems in the therapeutic relationship and therapist skill in using specific verbal techniques significantly predicted treatment outcome. An example of an error in technique was the failure of the therapist to structure or focus the session. Therapists allowed patients to ramble and failed to identify organizing themes in their communication.

even though they are usually desirable and do help the patient to improve (Rachman & Wilson, 1980).

Another prediction that became linked to evaluating person-centered therapy is that the absence of positive therapist qualities or the presence of negative qualities can make the patient worse (Bergin, 1966). This important and controversial hypothesis is discussed in Box 16.3. Strictly speaking, however, the empirical fate of this hypothesis does not necessarily bear on the validity of Rogers's theory, which was formulated well before Bergin advanced his argument.

Gestalt Therapy

Gestalt therapists, like Rogers, believe that human nature is essentially positive, and that people can make meaningful choices about their lives and improve themselves. The two approaches differ, however, in terms of specific therapeutic techniques. Gestalt therapists employ a broader range of treatment techniques than their person-centered counterparts.

The founder of Gestalt therapy was Frederich (Fritz) Perls (1893–1970). Originally trained in medicine and psychoanalysis, Perls fled Nazi Germany for South Africa and later the United States. In these countries he was exposed to Gestalt psychology and a phenomenological-existential perspective from which he developed Gestalt therapy.

Basic Concepts. Gestalt therapists believe that psychological problems develop when, for whatever reason, people's innate positive potential cannot be freely expressed and developed. Gestalt therapy, therefore, like other humanistic therapies, focuses on clients' creative and expressive qualities.

Gestalt is a German term meaning "whole." Perls believed that individuals need to integrate their experience of self (their thoughts and feelings) with their environmental circumstances in a differentiated but harmonious whole. Any dichotomy between different aspects of functioning, such as conflict between conscious and unconscious parts of the personality, interferes with personal growth and happiness and needs to be healed or integrated.

Gestalt therapy, more than any other approach, focuses on *the here and now*. The process of experiencing what is happening at any particular moment is more important than the content of what is being discussed.

The goal of Gestalt therapy is increased *awareness*. This refers to individuals being in touch with, and able to integrate and accept, both their inner feelings and external environment. Awareness involves "not only self-knowledge, but a direct knowing of the current situation and how the self is in that situation. . . . Awareness is cognitive, sensory, and affective. . . . The person who is aware knows what he does, how he does it, that he has alternatives, and that he chooses to be as he is" (Yontef & Simkin, 1989, p. 334).

Personal *responsibility* is emphasized. People must come to own (take responsibility for) their feelings, choices, and behavior. Change is up to each individual. As in person-centered therapy, any attempt by the therapist to impose or direct behavior change will interfere with personal growth. The Gestalt therapist is, however, more active and directive than psychoanalytic or person-centered therapists.

Treatment Techniques. Gestalt therapists may use any technique provided it is aimed at enhancing awareness and is rooted in the immediate interaction between therapist and patient (Yontef & Simkin, 1989).

To keep the patient in the here and now, therapists will often ask basic questions such as "What are you doing now?" or "How are you feeling now?" When patients report a painful or anxiety-provoking thought or feeling they are encouraged to "stay with it" or experience it more fully, thereby overcoming it. Gestalt therapists instruct patients to communicate directly by talking to people rather than about them. To encourage genuineness and personal responsibility for feelings, the therapist uses "I" statements ("I think you are hurting right now") and encourages the patient to do the same.

One of the best-known Gestalt methods is the empty chair technique. For example, a patient might be dealing with unresolved emotional conflict with a dead parent. Instead of simply talking about his or her feelings about the parent, the patient is instructed to imagine the dead parent sitting in the empty chair and to talk directly to the parent. The patient might also switch roles, namely, sit in the empty chair and talk as if she were the parent. This technique's goal is to take care of "unfinished business"—to get in touch with a part of the self not yet fully experienced and accepted.

Dream analysis is another commonly used technique, as the following excerpt from a treatment session illustrates. Lichtenstein (1980) points out that the reader should notice how the therapist, who is Perls himself, uses "what" questions to focus on the here and now, encourages the patient to stay with feelings, and instructs her to communicate directly.

P: *In my dream, I'm sitting on a platform, and there's somebody else with me, a man, and maybe another person, and—ah—a couple of rattlesnakes. And one up on the platform, now, all coiled up, and I'm frightened. And his head's up, but he doesn't seem like he's gonna strike me. He's just sitting there and I'm frightened, and this other person says to me—uh—just, just don't disturb the snake and he won't bother you. And the other snake, the other snake's down below, and there's a dog down there.*

T: *What is there?*

P: *A dog, and the other snake.*

T: *So, up here is one rattlesnake and down below is another rattlesnake and the dog.*

P: *And the dog is sort of sniffing at the rattlesnake. He's—ah—getting very close to the rattlesnake, sort of playing with it, and I wanna stop—stop him from doing that.*

T: *Tell him.*

P: *Dog, stop!*

T: *Louder.*

P: *Stop!*

T: *Louder.*

P: *(shouts) STOP!*

T: *Louder.*

P: *(screams) STOP!*

T: *Does the dog stop?*

P: *He's looking at me. Now he's gone back to the snake. Now—now, the snake's sort of coiling up around the dog, and the dog's lying down, and—and the snake's coiling around the dog, and the dog looks very happy.*

T: *Ah! Now have an encounter between the dog and the rattlesnake.*

P: *You want me to play them?*

T: *Both. Sure. This is your dream. Every part is a part of yourself.*

P: *I'm the dog. (hesitantly) Huh. Hello, rattlesnake. It sort of feels good with you wrapped around me.*

T: *Look at the audience. Say this to somebody in the audience.*

P: *(laughs gently) Hello, snake. It feels good to have you wrapped around me.*

T: *Close your eyes. Enter your body. What do you experience physically?*

P: *I'm trembling. Tensing.*

T: *Let this develop. Allow yourself to tremble and get your feelings . . . (her whole body begins to move a little) Yah. Let it happen. Can you dance it? Get up and dance it. Let your eyes open, just so that you stay in touch with your body, with what you want to express physically . . . Yah . . . (she walks, trembling and jerkily, almost staggering) Now dance rattlesnake (she moves slowly and sinuously graceful) . . . How does it feel to be a rattlesnake now? . . .*

P: *It's—sort of—slowly—quite—quite aware, of anything getting too close.*

T: *Hm?*

P: *Quite aware of not letting anything get too close, ready to strike.*

T: *Say this to us. "If you come too close, I—"*

P: *If you come too close, I'll strike back!*

T: *I don't hear you. I don't believe you, yet.*

P: *If you come too close, I will strike back!*

T: *Say this to each one, here.*

P: *If you come too close, I will strike back!*

T: *Say this with your whole body.*

P: *If you come too close, I will strike back!*

T: *How are your legs? I experience you as being somewhat wobbly.*

P: *Yeah.*

T: *That you don't really take a stand.*

P: *Yes. I feel I'm . . . kind of, in between being very strong and—if I let go, they're going to turn to rubber.*

T: *Okeh, let them turn to rubber. (her knees bend and wobble) Again . . . Now try out how strong they are. Try out—hit the floor. Do anything. (she stamps several times with one foot) Yah, now the other. (stamps her other foot) Now let them turn to rubber again. (she lets knees bend again) More difficult now, isn't it?*

P: *Yeah.*

T: *Now say again the sentence, "If you come too close—" . . . (she makes an effort) . . . (laughter)*

P: *If—if you . . .*

T: *Okeh, change. Say "Come close." (laughter)*

P: *Come close.*

T: *How do you feel now?*

P: *Warm.*

T: *You feel somewhat more real?*

P: *Yeah.*

T: *Okeh . . . So what we did is we took away some of the fear of being in touch. So, from now on, she'll be a bit more in touch. You see how you can use everything in a dream. If you are pursued by an ogre in a dream, and you become the ogre, the nightmare disappears. You re-own the energy that is invested in the demon. Then the power of the ogre is no longer outside, alienated, but inside where you can use it.*

(Perls [1969], cited in Lichtenstein, 1980, pp. 168–169).

An Evaluation. Gestalt therapy only superficially resembles Gestalt psychology, which is primarily concerned with perceptual processes. The theory of personality and psychotherapy behind Gestalt therapy is really a loose amalgam of observations from clinical practice.

Gestalt therapists have traditionally rejected the methodology of quantitative research, claiming that it fails to address change processes within an individual (Yontef & Simkin, 1989). Perls, like Freud before him, argued that the results of therapy need no empirical confirmation—"we present nothing that you cannot verify for yourself in terms of your own behavior" (Perls et al., 1951, p. 347).

What research exists is process research. Greenberg (1986), for example, has studied the processes involved in the empty chair technique. He found that patients rated as achieving greater depth of experiencing during this technique were more successful in resolving conflict during the session. Greenberg (1986) also showed that the empty chair technique was more effective in reducing in-session psychological conflict than empathic reflection, the primary technique of Rogerian, person-centered therapists.

Despite its theoretical and empirical weaknesses, Gestalt therapy has become a leading therapeutic approach, with Perls one of the best-known psychotherapists, as shown later. Much of the interest in Gestalt therapy focuses on its rich range of treatment techniques. Eclectic therapists, and even behavior therapists, frequently use Gestalt methods, such as the empty chair technique, within their own conceptual frameworks (Arnkoff, 1983; Hayes, 1987; Lazarus, 1989). Gestalt methods appeal to these practitioners because of their potential for modifying emotional components of behavior. Gestalt therapists themselves insist that it is the humanistic-existential philosophy of their approach, and not specific techniques, that is important. They are quick to point out that if their techniques are used in an analytic or cognitive style, as they tend to be in behavior therapy, the techniques cease to be Gestalt therapy.

Finally, Gestalt therapy has limited applicability to different patient populations. Lichtenstein (1980) notes that it seems most appropriate for YAVIS patients who are neurotic (anxious), or for inhibited and unassertive individuals who need to express themselves more freely.

INTERPERSONAL PSYCHOTHERAPY

One distinctive trend in psychotherapy after World War II was the shift from virtually an exclusive focus on the Freudian theory of biological-instinctive forces in intrapsychic conflicts to a broader concern with social and cultural influences on personality development and change. As a consequence of this shift, clinicians began to focus on the interpersonal aspects of an individual's functioning. In the early 1900s, Neo-Freudians such as Alfred Adler and Karen Horney recognized the importance of the sociocultural context on human development. But in the postwar period, interpersonal influences began to be accorded primary importance in human functioning.

Several different forms of current psychotherapy, as well as behavior therapy and multimodal therapy (as discussed later), emphasize interpersonal influences. The nature and value of an interpersonal approach is well illustrated by interpersonal therapy (IPT), a form of time-limited psychotherapy developed by Klerman, Weissman, Rounsaville, and Chevron (1984). We focus on IPT here because it provides a "pure" illustration of the interpersonal approach and because controlled empirical research has shown its effectiveness in treating depression (Chapter 7) and bulimia nervosa (Chapter 13).

The Goals and Strategies of IPT

IPT's three distinct phases are the initial, intermediate, and final phases. In the initial phase therapists explore the connection between the patient's problem and interpersonal processes. Current and past relationships are examined, together with the patient's expectations about interpersonal relationships and the changes desired. Therapists identify specific interpersonal problem areas and explain the nature of IPT therapy and the patient's responsibilities in treatment.

In the intermediate phase, therapists focus on different problem areas. The first one is interpersonal disputes. The goals here are to identify conflicts with other people and to resolve them by altering expectations or changing faulty communication patterns. Therapists help patients recognize conflicting feelings, cease avoiding situations that elicit them, and express themselves more directly. Alternative ways of resolving disputes, and their likely consequences, are analyzed.

A second problem area is role transitions. The goals here are to help patients accept the change or the loss of a previous role, and develop self-esteem by acquiring a sense of competence in the new role(s). Patients' feelings about the change in roles are explored, realistic expectations about what has been lost and what novel opportunities now exist are fostered, and efforts to increase social support for coping with the new role are encouraged.

A third problem area concerns interpersonal skills. The goals here are to identify the lack of certain relationship skills and make patients aware of the ways these deficiencies lead to social difficulties. Therapists explore positive and negative aspects of past relationships and analyze their own relationship with the patient as a means of shedding light on other relationships.

In the final phase the therapist discusses termination of therapy and the patient's feelings of loss. The therapist calls attention to evidence of the patient's improvement and to signs of more independent functioning. The goal is to leave patients with an enhanced sense of self-mastery enabling them to cope better with life's problems. Future difficulties are anticipated and ways in which patients might cope are discussed.

An Illustrative Case

The following clinical case summary illustrates how IPT works.

> *Ellen F., a twenty-seven-year-old mother of a six-year-old son, sought treatment after a suicide attempt. She had been in an unhappy relationship with an alcoholic husband who had verbally and physically assaulted her when drunk. The patient's immediate depressive episode was precipitated by an extramarital affair that brought into focus the things missing in her marriage.*
>
> *The patient, although she had long recognized her dissatisfaction with her husband, had been able to ignore it until she experienced what an alternative relationship would be like. She came to treatment wanting to get out of her destructive marriage but not feeling able to make the change on her own. The therapist helped the patient evaluate the new demands, available social supports, and rewards associated with becoming a more independent single parent. The demands of separation from her husband included: (a) tolerating loneliness; (b) maintaining her self-esteem without being identified with a man; (c) managing her child; and (d) making new friends and dating. In each case the therapist helped her examine the fears associated with the demands and determine that she in fact had the resources to meet them. In the situation of disciplining her son, the therapist not only evaluated Mrs. F.'s attitudes about being a single parent but was active in teaching the patient ways to think about and talk with him, information that she had not obtained elsewhere. As to social supports, the therapist helped the patient identify new ones that were less conflicted than her relationships with her mother and in-laws. To help the patient enter the new role the therapist helped her clarify her feelings about the role she wanted to leave—being married to her husband and [being] highly involved with her mother. From this process the patient decided that she lost far more than she gained in these relationships, and this view helped provide incentive for accepting the strain of making the transition she wanted. And in considering the rewards of the new role, the therapist helped the patient recognize the relief and pride she felt in relying on herself.* (Klerman et al., 1984, p. 128)

An Evaluation. Although IPT has much in common with psychodynamic therapy, there are important differences which Table 16.2 summarizes. In IPT the therapist recognizes the intrapsychic conflicts that are the focus of psychodynamic therapy but does not interpret the patient's current problems as expression of them. Instead, the patient's behavior is explored in connection with his or her interpersonal relationships. Unlike psychodynamic therapy's focus on the transference relationship, IPT does not make the therapeutic relationship the primary focus of treatment. The therapist draws parallels between this relationship and others in the patient's life. For example, the relationship between the therapist and patient becomes a focus of attention if the patient's behavior toward the therapist begins to interfere with the treatment's progress.

Psychoanalytically oriented therapists view IPT as a form of supportive therapy—one that fails to address the underlying causes of emotional disorders by focusing primarily on the patient's present problems. Like behavior therapy—and other forms of brief therapy—it is directive (at least in the initial and intermediate stages), focused on well-defined problems, and time-limited. Some of its specific techniques, such as modeling, role-playing, problem solving, and identifying dysfunctional thinking's effects on interpersonal behavior, closely resemble common cognitive-behavioral methods, as discussed later. IPT's procedures are spelled out in a treatment manual, making evaluation of its effectiveness possible (DeRubeis, Hollon, Evans, & Bemis, 1982). The controlled clinical outcome studies that have been completed indicate IPT is an effective form of therapy, particularly in treating unipolar depression (Elkin et al., 1989).

BEHAVIOR THERAPY

Basic Concepts

The history of behavior therapy can be traced to two major developments earlier in this century. The first was the rise of behaviorism in the early 1900s. Preeminent in this regard were the contributions of B. F. Skinner, whose radical behaviorism has had a significant impact not only on parts of behavior therapy but also on psychology in general. Behaviorism is a school of thought emphasizing the objective study of overt behavior and rejecting the use of subjective concepts (see Chapter 2).

The second development was experimental research on the psychology of learning. In Russia around the turn of the century, Ivan Pavlov (1849–1936), a Nobel laureate in physiology, established the foundations of classical conditioning. About the same time in the United States, E. L. Thorndike's (1874–1949) pioneering research on animal learning showed the influence of consequences (rewarding and punishing events) on behavior. Beginning in the late 1930s, instrumental learning was elaborated upon by Skinner in his operant-conditioning research.

Research on conditioning and learning principles, conducted mostly in the animal laboratory, domi-

TABLE 16.2 A Comparison of IPT with Psychodynamic Psychotherapy

IPT	Other Psychotherapies
What has contributed to this patient's depression right now?	Why did the patient become what he/she is and/or where is the patient going?
What are the current stresses?	What was the patient's childhood like?
Who are the key persons involved in the current disputes and disappointments?	What is the patient's character?
Is the patient learning how to cope with the problem?	Is the patient cured?
What are the patient's assets?	What are the patient's defenses?
How can I help the patient ventilate painful emotions—talk about situations that evoke guilt, shame, resentment?	How can I find out why this patient feels guilty, ashamed, or resentful?
How can I help the patient clarify his or her wishes and have more satisfying relationships with others?	How can I understand the patient's fantasy life and help him/her get insight into the origins of present behavior?
How can I correct misinformation and suggest alternatives?	How can I help the patient discover false or incorrect ideas?

Source: Table from *Interpersonal psychotherapy of depression* by G.L. Klerman, M. Weissman, B. Rounsaville, and E. Chevron (1984). Copyright Basic Books, Inc., a division of Harper Collins Publishers. Reprinted with permission.

nated experimental psychology in the United States following World War II. In the tradition of Pavlov and Skinner, workers in this field were committed to scientifically analyzing behavior using the laboratory rat and pigeon as their prototypic subjects.

Isolated and sporadic early applications of conditioning principles to the treatment of clinical problems had scant impact on psychotherapy at the time. Conditioning principles, demonstrated with animals, were rejected as too simplistic and irrelevant to the treatment of complex human problems. There was a gulf between academic-experimental and clinical psychologists. The former were trained in scientific methods, with an emphasis on controlled experimentation and quantitative measurement. The latter concerned themselves with the "soft" side of psychology, including uncontrolled case studies and psychodynamic hypotheses about unconscious motivation. Some efforts were made to integrate conditioning principles with psychodynamic theories of abnormal behavior, but these eclectic formulations had little effect and only obscured the two approaches' crucial differences. The advent of behavior therapy challenged the prevailing status quo and presented a systematic and explicitly formulated clinical alternative that attempted to bridge the gap between the laboratory and the clinic.

Joseph Wolpe, the psychiatrist who has been described as the founding father of behavior therapy.

The formal beginnings of behavior therapy can be traced to separate but related developments in the 1950s in three countries. Joseph Wolpe (1958) in South Africa, developed and tested several treatment methods based on experimental research on the principles of learning theory. Wolpe shocked the world of psychotherapy by claiming that 90 percent of his patients were either "cured" or "markedly improved." This unprecedented success rate was apparently accomplished, not after many years of therapy as deemed necessary by psychoanalysis, but within a few months or even weeks. (Wolpe influenced Arnold Lazarus and Stanley Rachman, both of whom became leading figures in the development of behavior therapy.)

In England, Hans J. Eysenck, at the Institute of Psychiatry of London University, defined behavior therapy as the application of learning principles and procedures to the treatment of emotional disorders (Eysenck, 1959). In Eysenck's formulation, behavior therapy was an applied science, whose defining feature was that it is testable and falsifiable. A testable theory can be specified with sufficient precision for experimental investigation. A falsifiable theory specifies experimental conditions that can result in the theory being disproved or falsified. In 1963 Eysenck and Rachman established the first journal devoted exclusively to behavior therapy, *Behaviour Research and Therapy.* As a result of their continuing research and writings and that of their colleagues, the Institute of Psychiatry of London has remained one of the foremost centers of behavior therapy in the world.

In the United States, operant conditioning and the application of operant-conditioning principles to clinical problems were becoming a third force in behavior therapy. This development was spurred by the publication in 1953 of Skinner's book, *Science and Human Behavior,* in which he criticized psychodynamic concepts and reformulated psychotherapy along behavioral lines.

By the end of the 1960s behavior therapists began to expand their theories and methods. In addition to classical and operant conditioning, they turned to current developments in cognitive, social, and developmental psychology for different ways of conceptualizing their activities and as a source of innovative therapeutic strategies. Particularly noteworthy in this regard was Bandura's (1969) social-learning theory, emphasizing vicarious learning (modeling), symbolic processes, and self-regulatory mechanisms.

Behavior therapy today uses a broad range of heterogeneous methods, often with different theoretical rationales. We have found it useful to distinguish among three approaches within the broad framework of behavior therapy:

1. Applied behavior analysis
2. A stimulus-response model
3. Social-learning theory.

Basically, these three approaches differ in the degree they use cognitive concepts and procedures. At one end of this continuum is applied behavior analysis, exclusively focusing on observable behavior and rejecting all cognitive mediating processes. At the other end is social-learning theory, relying heavily on cognitive theories.

Applied Behavior Analysis. This approach is philosophically consistent with Skinner's (1953) radical behaviorism and relies upon operant-conditioning principles and procedures. Overt behavior is the only acceptable subject of scientific investigation. Skinner (1963) stated that private events such as thoughts should be included in an experimental analysis of behavior. But recognition of private events' role in behavior has always been carefully limited in Skinner's behaviorism. Subjective processes such as thoughts or images can never, according to him, exert a causal effect on behavior. In its strict form, the operant-conditioning viewpoint assumes that apart from genetic influences, human behavior is controlled exclusively by environmental events ultimately beyond personal control.

The operant approach's methodology emphasizes studying the individual organism. Repeated objective measurement of a single subject under highly controlled conditions has been its hallmark. Rejecting statistical comparisons between groups of subjects, Skinner argued that group averages do not adequately reflect actual behavior of individual subjects. His approach became known as the **experimental analysis of behavior,** or **applied behavior analysis,** terms that distinguish it from the traditional scientific strategy of the statistical analysis of group data.

Besides a set of philosophical assumptions about behavior and a methodology for studying it, the operant approach's learning principles have had a decisive impact on the field. Thus it assumes that behavior is a function of its environmental consequences, strengthened by positive and negative reinforcement but weakened by punishment. **Positive reinforcement** refers to the presentation of a stimulus contingent on a response that increases the frequency of that response. If the behavior is emitted, then the reward is given. No behavior, no reward. **Negative reinforcement** refers to an increase in behavior that avoids or reduces an aversive event. **Punishment** is the presentation of an aversive event or the removal of a positive event contingent on a response that results in a decrease in that response's frequency.

Therapists have applied operant-conditioning techniques to a wide range of problems in all age groups in clinical and community psychology, education, rehabilitation, and even medicine (Kazdin, 1984). They have found operant-conditioning procedures most useful in changing the behavior of young children, retarded persons, and institutionalized populations, such as chronic mental patients. Most behavior therapists in clinical practice, particularly with adult patients, would not describe themselves as applied behavior analysts, but see themselves as drawing from much broader theoretical and empirical bases (Barlow, 1985; O'Leary & Wilson, 1987).

The Stimulus-Response Approach. This approach, deriving from the pioneering contributions of Wolpe and Eysenck, attempts to apply the stimulus-response learning theories of Pavlov and other leading learning theorists (such as Clark Hull, Hobart Mowrer, and Neal Miller) to the treatment of clinical problems. Unlike applied behavior analysis or operant conditioning, with the focus exclusively on observable behavior, the stimulus-response approach emphasizes nonobservable or *mediational variables* in explaining and modifying human behavior. A mediational variable intervenes between an observable stimulus and response. The concept of anxiety is a mediational variable; it cannot be measured directly but is inferred to explain an external stimulus' effect on an observable response. For example, an acrophobic who avoids heights does so because the stimulus (high places) elicits anxiety, which, in turn, mediates the response (behavioral avoidance). The treatment technique of systematic desensitization, closely associated with this model, is directed toward the extinction of the underlying anxiety assumed to maintain phobic disorders. The principles and procedures of classical and instrumental conditioning have been this approach's backbone.

Advances in experimental research and psychological theory during the past twenty years have revealed the limitations of conditioning models of complex human behavior (Bandura, 1986). Conditioning principles, while still important, are of more limited usefulness today. Many behavior therapists, especially those who take a social-learning approach as discussed next, have sought broader bases of knowledge (O'Leary & Wilson, 1987).

Another contribution of the conditioning approach has been its commitment to rigorous standards of clinical research and practice. The detailed specification of therapeutic techniques, the use of objective measures of treatment outcome, and the development of innovative single-case experimental designs for studying treatment effects (see Chapter 4) were all directly associated with the methodological behaviorism characterizing the conditioning approach.

Social-Learning Theory. The **social-learning approach** to behavior therapy depends on the theory that behavior is based on three separate but interacting regulatory systems (Bandura, 1977): (1) external stimulus events, (2) external reinforcement, and (3) most important, cognitive mediational processes.

Environmental events' influence on behavior is, according to the social-learning approach, largely determined by cognitive processes, governing which influences people attend to and how they perceive and interpret them. Modeling is one of the best-known and most widely used methods derived from social-learning theory. In this method, behavior is learned or modified by systematically observing the behavior of someone else (the model). We have described how fear is learned by observing the expression of fear in others (see Chapter 5). The important principle in modeling is that learning occurs although the observer does not emit any response nor receives any reinforcement.

Other traditional learning principles are also interpreted within a cognitive framework. For example, reinforcement is seen not as an automatic strengthening of behavior. Rewards work because of the information and incentives they provide (Bandura, 1986). By observing the consequences of behavior, the person learns what action is appropriate in what situation. By rewards, or the symbolic representation of anticipated future behavior outcomes, the person is motivated to initiate and sustain his or her current actions.

Expectations play an important role in social-learning theory. People's expectations and hypotheses about what is happening or will happen to them may often affect their behavior more than the objective reality of the rules and contingencies associated with the behavior. Clinical problems usually arise when a significant discrepancy develops between a person's perception of events and objective reality. Social-learning theory distinguishes between efficacy and outcome expectations. Efficacy expectations are people's confidence that they can cope with a particular situation; outcome expectations are people's belief that their actions will result in a particular outcome. Self-efficacy theory is a critical component of the social-learning approach (see Chapter 5). A social-learning approach to behavior therapy also draws heavily on other cognitive concepts, such as **attribution theory,** which accounts for how we typically explain (attribute causes to) our own attitudes and actions and those of others (Bandura, 1986).

A person's psychological functioning involves an interaction among three interlocking sets of influences: behavior, cognitive processes, and environmental factors. Bandura (1977) summarizes it as follows:

> Personal and environmental factors do not function as independent determinants; rather they determine each other. Nor can "persons" be considered causes independent of their behavior. It is largely through their actions that people produce the environmental conditions that affect their behavior in a reciprocal fashion. The experiences generated by behavior also partly determine what individuals think, expect, and can do, which in turn, affect their subsequent behavior. (p. 345)

In social-learning theory the person is the agent of change: The theory emphasizes the human capacity for self-directed behavior change.

Core Characteristics of Behavior Therapy. Although the three preceding approaches often involve conceptual differences, behavior therapists subscribe to a common core of basic concepts.

Behavior therapy involves a commitment to the scientific approach. This includes the following: an explicit, testable conceptual framework; treatment either derived from or at least consistent with the content and method of experimental-clinical psychology; therapeutic techniques that can be described with sufficient precision to be measured objectively and that can be replicated; experimental evaluation of treatment methods and concepts; and research strategies that rigorously evaluate specific methods applied to particular problems.

Behavior therapy focuses on the current determinants of behavior rather than on the analysis of possible historical antecedents. In other words, understanding the origins of a patient's psychological problem is not essential for producing behavior change.

Treatment Methods

Behavior therapy provides the practitioner with a wide range of treatment techniques. Instead of artificially molding the patient's problems to suit the therapist's preconceived theoretical notions, behavior therapy tailors the principles of social-learning theory to each patient's unique problem. Some techniques are more appropriate with some problems and patients than with others.

In selecting a treatment technique, the behavior therapist relies heavily on empirical evidence about that technique's efficacy applied to the patient's particular problem. Yet this information is frequently insufficient for guiding therapeutic interventions, for in many cases the empirical evidence is unclear or largely nonexistent. The therapist must then rely on the accepted clinical practice—the state of the art—and the basic logic and philosophy of the approach to human behavior and its modification. The therapist also must often use intuitive skill and clinical savvy in deciding not only on the appropriate treatment methods but also when to use a specific technique. Both science and art enter into informed clinical practice, and the most effective therapists are aware of the advantages and limitations of each.

The following are some selective illustrations of the varied methods the typical behavior therapist is likely to employ in clinical practice.

Anxiety Reduction (Exposure) Methods. Exposure treatment can reduce phobic anxiety and eliminate avoidance behavior. Different types of exposure methods are discussed more fully in Chapter 5.

Assertiveness and Social Skills Training. Therapists often see patients who seem unable to express their emotions or stand up for their legitimate rights. They are often taken advantage of by others, feel anxiety in social situations, and suffer from low self-esteem. In behavior rehearsal, the therapist models the appropriate assertive behavior and then asks patients to rehearse, or role-play, the behavior themselves. Attention is focused on developing the patient's nonverbal and verbal expressive behavior (e.g., body posture, voice training, and eye contact). The therapist then encourages the patient to carry out assertive actions in the real world.

Distinguishing among submissive (nonassertive), aggressive, and assertive behavior is important. Submissive people allow others to take advantage of them and then harbor resentment that they do not express openly. Aggressive people take advantage of people; they are often selfish and hurt others. Assertive people express their feelings honestly and directly without exploiting others; they have a positive self-image and feel good about themselves. Assertive behavior is more likely to be effective in interpersonal interactions than nonassertive or aggressive behavior. The differences among these three patterns of interpersonal behavior are illustrated in the following example:

> *Pam is a friendly, outgoing college junior who has been dating an attractive young man for whom she cares a great deal. One evening he invites her to attend a small party with two other couples, both of whom are married. As she becomes acquainted with her date's friends, Pam starts to enjoy herself. After an hour or so, one of the married men brings out several cigarettes which he identifies as marijuana and suggests that they all smoke. Everyone eagerly joins in except Pam, who does not wish to experiment with marijuana. She is in conflict because the young man she admires is smoking marijuana, and as he offers her a cigarette, she decides to be:*
>
> Nonassertive: *She accepts the marijuana and pretends to have smoked it before. She carefully watches the others to see how they smoke. Inside, she dreads the possibility they may ask her to smoke more. The others are speaking of getting "stoned," and Pam is worried about what her friend is thinking about her. She has denied her own feelings, been dishonest with her boyfriend, and feels remorseful for giving in to something she did not wish to do.*
>
> Aggressive: *Pam is visibly upset when offered the marijuana and blasts the young man for bringing her to this "low type" party. She states that she wants to be taken home right away rather than stay with such people. When the others at the party say that she does not have to smoke if she doesn't wish to, she is unappeased and continues to be quite indignant. Her friend is humiliated, embarrassed before his friends, and disappointed in her. Although he remains cordial toward Pam as he takes her home, he does not offer an invitation for a further date.*
>
> Assertive: *Pam does not accept the cigarette, replying simply, "No, thank you. I don't care for one." She goes on to explain that she hasn't smoked pot before and doesn't wish to. She expresses her preference that the others not smoke, but acknowledges their right to make their own choices.* (Alberti & Emmons, 1978).

Besides enhancing assertiveness, the instructional, modeling, and feedback components of behavior rehearsal help the patient develop a broader range of communication competencies, including active listening, giving personal feedback, and building trust through self-disclosure. These communication principles, drawn from nonbehavioral approaches to counseling but integrated within a behavioral framework, are a key ingredient of behavioral marital therapy as described in Chapter 17.

Self-Control Strategies. In behavioral treatment programs, both child and adult patients are taught that they must be active in determining their treatment goals and in implementing the treatment program. Behavior therapists use a number of self-control procedures (Bandura, 1986; Kanfer, 1977). Self-monitoring, a process to make patients more aware of their specific problems and actions, is fundamental to successful self-regulation of behavior. Examples of self-monitoring's use have been discussed in several of the preceding chapters. The therapist helps the patient set goals or standards to guide his or her behavior. For example, in treating obesity, daily caloric goals are mutually worked out, enabling the patient to lose weight safely and effectively. Behavioral research has identified certain properties of goals that increase the probability of successful self-control by patients. For example, goals should be highly specific, unambiguous, and short-term, such as consumption of no more than 1,200 calories each day. Compare this to the vaguer goal of "cutting back" on eating for the "next" week. The value of setting specific short-term goals in order to make difficult behavioral changes is illustrated by the watchword from Alcoholics Anonymous—"one day at a time." Patients' goals also have to be realistic if changes are to be made. Many young women with eating disorders are driven by unrealistic and self-destructive body image ideals (see Chapter 13). We now know that body weight is strongly determined by genetic and biological factors, and attempts to achieve a body weight or shape exceeding biological constraints have adverse physical and psychological effects (Brownell & Foreyt, 1986).

TABLE 16.3 A Monitoring Sheet Illustrating the Eating Habits of a Patient with Bulimia Nervosa in the Early Stages of Treatment*

DAY: Wednesday DATE: 7th November

TIME	FOOD AND LIQUID CONSUMED	PLACE	B	V/L	CIRCUMSTANCES
7:45	1 apple 1 grapefruit 1 black coffee	Kitchen			Depressed. Feel fat.
3:10	1 egg sandwich 1 bread roll 1 doughnut	work " "	* * *		Bought more food from canteen. Shouldn't have eaten the egg sandwich—too much. Bound to be a terrible day now.
3:45	1 doughnut 1 cup tea 1 danish pastry 2 cups of tea	" " " "	* * *	 V	can't stop eating. Help.
8:20	1 slice of toast 1 slice toast	Kitchen "	* *		Weighed myself—130 lbs. Cried. MUST NOT EAT AGAIN TODAY
8:35	1 slice of toast 1 diet coke	" "	*		
8:40	whole packet of shortbread biscuits	"	*		Give up. I can't go on like this. Hate myself.
8:52	1 bowl of cereal 2 glasses of water		*		Feel completely bloated.
9:05	1 bowl of cereal		*	V L	Weighed 131 lbs. Wish I was dead —16 pills

* B = bulimic episodes; V/L = vomiting or laxative use; * = episodes viewed by patient as excessive.

Source: From Fairburn C.G., 1985. Cognitive behavioral treatment for bulimia. In D.M. Garner and P.E. Garfinkel (Eds.), *Handbook of psychotherapy for anorexia nervosa and bulimia.* New York: Guilford Press. Copyright © by Guilford Press. Reprinted with permission.

Once treatment goals have been set, patients self-monitor and evaluate their performance against them. Failure to achieve these goals elicits negative self-evaluation, motivating patients to change their behavior. Successful accomplishment of them produces self-reinforcement, increasing the likelihood that patients will maintain their self-regulatory behavior. The idea of self-regulation explains the observation that human behavior is usually maintained and often altered in the absence of immediate external reinforcement. People generally make self-rewards or self-punishments conditional upon attaining specific standards of performance. The level of self-motivation generated by success or failure in matching self-imposed goals will vary according to the person's specific performance standards, how he or she evaluates performance, and the nature of the incentives to perform. The performance standards are a product of the patient's prior learning history. Dysfunctions in self-regulatory systems seem to play a major role in many of the forms of abnormal behavior discussed in the preceding chapters.

Behavior therapy includes a range of self-control strategies. One we discussed in earlier chapters is progressive relaxation training, widely applied as a self-control method for reducing different forms of stress, including insomnia, tension headaches, and hypertension. Biofeedback methods used to treat a variety of psychophysiological disorders are also self-control procedures.

Reinforcement Procedures. Operant conditioning has demonstrated that behavior is a function of its consequences. By systematically altering the environmental consequences of behavior, we change that behavior. This simple but powerful principle of behavior change has been applied in a variety of ways to help people overcome different forms of abnormal behavior (Kazdin, 1984).

The Token Economy. One of the best illustrations of the value and versatility of reinforcement principles is the use of a **token reinforcement program,** whose main elements can be summarized as follows:

1. Carefully specified and operationally defined target behaviors.
2. Backup reinforcers (the "good things in life," or whatever people are willing to work for).
3. Tokens representing the backup reinforcers.
4. Rules of exchange specifying the number of tokens required to obtain backup reinforcers.

Token economies have been used in a variety of settings, ranging from classrooms with socially disruptive and academically underachieving children (O'Leary & O'Leary, 1977) to psychiatric hospitals with chronic mental patients. In a classic example of the latter, Ayllon and Azrin (1968) at Anna State Hospital in Illinois used a token reinforcement program where patients received special privileges and activities if they engaged in certain behaviors. Desired behaviors, such as, "arriving at work on time, remaining at a job for the entire period, following instructions of supervisors, interacting with fellow employees when necessary" (p. 54), were specified. The researchers observed the patients, and when they engaged in one or more of these behaviors, they were systematically given tokens, plastic chips exchangeable for certain items (e.g., food or cigarettes) or privileges (hospital passes). With the use of the reinforcement program, many of the patients' behaviors changed. For example, their personal hygiene and social behavior improved and their output in various hospital jobs increased.

Subsequent token economy programs used more complex procedures with more ambitious goals, including attempts to ensure the maintenance of behavior change once patients were discharged from the hospital into the community. Paul and Lentz's (1977) study exemplifies the use of a sophisticated and creative token reinforcement program that produced clinically significant and lasting behavior change in schizophrenics (see Chapter 14).

Cognitive Restructuring. These methods are designed to help patients first identify and then modify dysfunctional thinking patterns. We describe them more fully in the following section on cognitive therapy. Because cognitive principles and procedures have been integrated within behavior therapy, the approach is described as cognitive-behavior therapy. Depending on the specific problem in the particular patient being treated, the cognitive-behavior therapist places greater emphasis on the behavioral or the cognitive component (Hawton, Salkovskis, & Clark, 1989).

Clinical and Conceptual Issues

Much of behavior therapy is short-term treatment, but therapy lasting from twenty-five to fifty sessions is common, and still longer treatment is not unusual. Therapy in excess of 100 sessions is relatively rare. There are no established guidelines for deciding on the length of therapy. Most clinicians make a detailed behavioral assessment of the problem(s) and then embark on therapeutic interventions as rapidly as possible. They continually reassess the patient as they evaluate the consequences of initial treatment interventions against the therapeutic goals.

Some behavioral treatment programs have a fixed time course, such as Barlow and Cerny's (1988) program for the treatment of panic and Fairburn's

(1985) program for bulimia nervosa. If treatment is not time-limited from the start, the length of therapy and the scheduling of the treatment sessions are contingent upon the patient's progress. A behavior therapist might typically contract with the patient to pursue a treatment plan for two to three months (approximately eight to twelve sessions) and then evaluate progress. If the patient shows no improvement, the therapist reevaluates whether he or she identified the problem accurately, is using the appropriate techniques or needs to switch tactics, or needs to refer the patient to another behavioral therapist or to some other form of treatment.

In terminating a successful treatment, behavior therapists usually avoid ending it abruptly. Instead, they gradually lengthen the time between sessions, from weekly to biweekly or monthly and so on. These concluding sessions, which progressively phase out the therapist's active involvement, may be shorter than earlier ones, and occasional telephone contact may be interspersed among them.

Behavior therapists attach considerable importance to the therapeutic relationship, but for reasons different from psychodynamic therapists. For psychodynamic therapists, the transference relationship is the crux of treatment. Behavior therapists believe that the interaction between therapist and patient is a part, albeit an often vital part, of total treatment. For therapy to succeed, patients should view therapists as competent and credible. Therapists must be able to convey to patients that they care and understand their problems. Therapists must also inspire trust. If patients do not trust and respect their therapists, they will not open up and disclose highly personal thoughts and feelings. A good therapeutic relationship also makes it more likely that patients will adhere to prescriptions for behavior change. Behavior therapists rely heavily on homework assignments between sessions, and patients' willingness to complete these assignments is directly influenced by the quality of the therapeutic relationship (O'Leary & Wilson, 1987).

A survey of behavior therapists by Swan and MacDonald (1978) reported that the most frequently used clinical methods were those enhancing the relationship between therapist and patient. Patients regard the therapeutic relationship as important in behavior therapy (Mathews et al., 1976; Sloane et al., 1975). Behavior therapists' actions in treatment can be judged by their patients' ratings of their performance or by objective observers' independent ratings of audiotapes or videotapes of sessions. Using ratings by patients, O'Leary, Turkewitz, and Tafel (1973) found that virtually all parents whose children were treated at the Stony Brook Child Guidance Clinic rated the therapists as understanding, warm, sincere, and interested. Several studies have also evaluated therapists' actions by objective ratings of tapes of sessions. For example, Sloane et al. (1975) found that behavior therapists showed higher levels of empathy, warmth, and interpersonal contact than psychoanalytically oriented therapists. The behavior therapists were more directive, more open, more genuine, and more disclosing than their psychoanalytically oriented counterparts. Both sets of therapists used a similar number of interpretations during therapy, but the quality of these interpretations differed predictably, with the psychotherapists focusing on feelings and the behavior therapists on behavior.

An Evaluation. One of behavior therapy's strengths is its foundations in the principles and methods of experimental psychology. As a result, advances in basic and applied psychological research will continue to inform the clinical practice of behavior therapy. Another asset is that treatment methods are carefully specified, and hence can be evaluated in experimental research. Numerous well-controlled studies have shown specific behavioral methods' effectiveness in treating particular clinical disorders, as described throughout this book.

Behavior therapy has been criticized as a superficial form of treatment that treats only the symptoms, not the causes, of the patient's problem. It was alleged, therefore, that behavioral treatment would lead to **symptom substitution**—the replacement of the treated symptom with another because the underlying problem had not been resolved. Yet both behavioral and psychodynamic treatments attempt to deal with the causes of behavior. The difference is in what these respective approaches regard the causes of behavior to be. Psychodynamic theories focus on historical, unconscious determinants of behavior; behavior therapy emphasizes the current causes of behavior—the antecedent, mediational, and consequent variables currently maintaining the patient's problems. Psychodynamic therapists ask about a patient, "Why did he or she become this kind of person?" Behavior therapists ask, "What is causing him or her to function this way now, and what can be done to change that level of functioning?" An adequate behavioral assessment of the problem results in multifaceted treatment that deals with the full range of maintaining determinants' causes.

The charge of symptom substitution has been a confused and confusing notion. For example, even if a new problematic behavior emerged following treatment, it would be difficult to determine if it were a new problem or a substitute symptom. It is more constructive to concentrate instead on objective assessment of therapeutic change, to see if changes in treated problems may be associated with changes in nontreated behavior (Kazdin, 1982). When this is done, we find that the changes are usually positive.

For example, behavioral treatment of phobic disorders usually results not only in the elimination of patients' phobic anxiety and avoidance behavior but also in improvements in nonphobic functioning, such as their interpersonal behavior (see Chapter 5).

Several well-controlled therapy outcome studies have directly examined the nature of correlated changes in nontreated behavior. For example, Sloane and his colleagues (1975) summarized their findings as follows: "Not a single patient whose original problems had substantially improved reported new symptoms cropping up. On the contrary, assessors had the informal impression that when a patient's primary symptoms improved, he often spontaneously reported improvement of other minor difficulties" (p. 100).

Finally, behavior therapy is broadly applicable to a wide range of problems in different patient populations. It is not confined to YAVIS patients. The preceding chapters illustrate how broadly behavior therapy has been applied to the full range of adult and child clinical disorders. The emergence of the field of behavioral medicine was due largely to the extension of the principles and procedures of behavior therapy to medical problems (see Chapter 8).

COGNITIVE THERAPY

The therapies in this category are all based on the assumption that emotional disorders result from maladaptive thought patterns. This can be traced back to the philosopher Epictetus (A.D. 60) who declared that "Men are disturbed not by things, but by the views they take of them." Therapy's task is to restructure these maladaptive cognitions. The two most prominent forms of cognitive treatment are Ellis's rational-emotive therapy (RET) and Beck's (1976) cognitive therapy.

Rational-Emotive Therapy

According to RET, emotional disorders are rooted in people's irrational beliefs, which are distortions of objective reality. Ellis (1970) lists twelve irrational core assumptions at the root of most emotional disturbance. The following are examples of these irrational ideas: "It is a dire necessity for an adult to be loved by everyone for everything he does"; "It is easier to avoid than to face life difficulties and self-responsibilities"; and "One has virtually no control over one's emotions, and one cannot help feeling certain things." According to this approach, then, it is not experience itself, but the patient's perception of that experience that causes neurotic disorders. This process is illustrated by Ellis' A-B-C analysis of depression. "A" refers to a real-life event (e.g., a broken love affair). "B" symbolizes the person's irrational interpretation of that event (e.g., the belief that nothing has meaning anymore; that there will never be anybody else like him or her again). The person catastrophizes, that is, greatly exaggerates the event's negative meaning. "C" is the upset and depression the person then feels not because of the actual breakup but because of his or her extremely negative perception of the broken love affair. Patients do not always consciously or deliberately tell themselves these irrational assumptions in everyday situations. Such assumptions appear to be automatic and pervasive in their influence because people repeat them so often that they become an overlearned response.

In treatment the therapist helps the patient identify irrational ideas and replace them with more constructive, rational thoughts. The therapist directly challenges the patient's irrational ideas and then models rational reinterpretations of disturbing events. The therapist and patient engage in repeated cognitive rehearsals aimed at substituting rational self-statements for previously irrational interpretations. Additionally, the therapist assigns behavioral tasks designed to develop rational reactions to replace the patient's formerly irrational, distress-producing assumptions.

An Evaluation. The theoretical framework for RET is not well developed. In short, RET boils down to the conclusion that thoughts influence behavior. Few doubt that faulty or maladaptive thoughts contribute to emotional disorders, but research does not provide strong support for the loose theoretical assumptions which RET rests on. For example, no convincing evidence exists that Ellis's list of irrational assumptions cause psychological disorders.

The effectiveness of RET remains to be proven. Part of the problem lies in specifying the treatment's precise procedural components. In response to criticism of the conceptual and empirical bases of RET (Meichenbaum, 1977), Ellis (1977) has argued that it has been misinterpreted as a treatment approach restricted to cognitive restructuring using verbal persuasion and logical analysis. He asserts that RET therapists also use behavior therapy techniques and even methods from other approaches, such as Gestalt therapy. But, if RET becomes so all-inclusive, incorporating a wide range of different techniques from other therapies, it also becomes untestable.

Beck's Cognitive Therapy

Beck's cognitive therapy has been used in the treatment of depression (see Chapter 7). Negative or dysfunctional thinking, Beck theorized, causes emotional disorders. It derives from learned, maladaptive assumptions about the self, current experience, and the future. Negative thinking leads to a negative mood, which in turn increases the probability of more negative thinking in what becomes a vicious cycle. The negative assumptions are the target of cognitive therapy.

To help patients challenge their dysfunctional assumptions, therapists raise a number of questions addressing patients' dysfunctional cognitions. Consider, for example, the case of a patient who felt he was a total failure. Beck, Rush, Shaw, and Emery (1979) list the following questions that the therapist would pose:

1. How do you define failure? What are your standards?
2. Have there been degrees of failure: that is, were some failures more total than others?
3. If some experiences were only partial failures, did they also represent partial successes?
4. Were there some areas in your life (friends, family, school work, recreation) in which you did not fail and may, in fact, have reached your goals?
5. Even if you did fail in specific areas, does it follow that you cannot improve and become more successful?
6. Do failures in reaching a goal make you a failure as a person?
7. Should people who have experienced failures be subjected to rejection by other people?
8. Should a person who has suffered defeat subject himself to further pain by rejecting himself (pp. 195–96)

Cognitive therapists require patients to keep and complete written records of homework assignments which are mutually agreed upon with the therapist. For example, they are required to identify and challenge dysfunctional cognitions that are associated with their problems using **Dysfunctional Thought Records** (DTRs). Table 16.4 summarizes dysfunctional cognitions targeted by Beck's therapy. Table 16.5 presents an example of a DTR.

The explicit use of behavioral methods, such as graded task assignments, is a fundamental feature of cognitive therapy. Patients do behavioral tasks to help correct dysfunctional cognitions and disconfirm maladaptive expectations. Instead of arguing with pa-

TABLE 16.4 Dysfunctional Cognitions Targeted by Cognitive Therapy

1. All-or-nothing thinking? You see things in black-and-white categories. If your performance falls short of perfect, you see yourself as a total failure.
2. Overgeneralization: You see a single negative event as a neverending pattern of defeat.
3. Mental filter: You pick out a single negative detail and dwell on it exclusively so that your vision of all reality becomes darkened, like the drop of ink that discolors the entire beaker of water.
4. Disqualifying the positive: You reject positive experiences by insisting they "don't count" for some reason or other. In this way you can maintain a negative belief that is contradicted by your everyday experiences.
5. Jumping to conclusions: You make a negative interpretation even though there are no definite facts that convincingly support your conclusion.
    a. Mind reading. You arbitrarily conclude that someone is reacting negatively to you, and you don't bother to check this out.
    b. Fortune teller error. You anticipate that things will turn out badly, and you feel convinced that your prediction is an already established fact.
6. Magnification (catastrophizing) or minimization: You exaggerate the importance of things (such as your goof-up or someone else's achievement), or you inappropriately shrink things until they appear tiny (your own desirable qualities or the other fellow's imperfections). This is also called the "binocular trick."
7. Emotional reasoning: You assume that your negative emotions necessarily reflect the way things really are: I feel it, therefore it must be true.
8. Should statements: You try to motivate yourself with shoulds and shouldn'ts, as if you had to be whipped and punished before you could be expected to do anything. Musts and oughts are also offenders. The emotional consequence is guilt. When you direct should statements toward others, you feel anger, frustration, and resentment.
9. Labeling and mislabeling: This is an extreme form of overgeneralization. Instead of describing your error, you attach a negative label to yourself: "I'm a loser." When someone else's behavior rubs you the wrong way, you attach a negative label to him: "He's a goddamn louse." Mislabeling involves describing an event with language that is highly colored and emotionally loaded.
10. Personalization: You see yourself as the cause of some negative external event which in fact you were not primarily responsible for.

Source: From David D. Burns, M.D. *Feeling Good.* Copyright 1980. David D. Burns, M.D. New York: Morrow. Reprinted by permission of William Morrow & Company, Inc./Publishers, New York.

TABLE 16.5 An Example of a Dysfunctional Thought Record

Automatic Thought (Self-Criticism)	Cognitive Disortion	Rational Response (Self-Defense)
1. I never do anything right.	1. Overgeneralization	1. Nonsense! I do a lot of things right.
2. I'm always late.	2. Overgeneralization	2. I'm not always late. That's ridiculous. Think of all the times I've been on time. If I'm late more often than I'd like, I'll work on this problem and develop a method for being more punctual.
3. Everyone will look down on me.	3. Mind reading Overgeneralization All-or-nothing thinking Fortune teller error	3. Someone may be disappointed that I'm late but it's not the end of the world. Maybe the meeting won't even start on time.
4. This shows what a jerk I am.	4. Labeling	4. Come on, now, I'm not "a jerk."
5. I'll make a fool of myself.	5. Labeling Fortune teller error	5. Ditto, I'm not "a fool" either. I may appear foolish if I come in late, but this doesn't make a fool. Everyone is late sometimes.

Source: From David D. Burns, M.D. *Feeling Good*. Copyright 1980. David D. Burns, M.D. New York: Morrow. Reprinted by permission of William Morrow & Company, Inc./Publishers, New York.

tients about whether their cognitions are valid or helpful, the therapists collaborate with patients in devising specific behavioral tasks framed as experiments to test the patients' assumptions. The following excerpt from a treatment session (Clark, 1989) illustrates how the cognitive therapist prompts patients to examine their assumptions and how behavioral experiments are a way of challenging dysfunctional assumptions:

Patient: *In the middle of a panic attack, I usually think I am going to faint or collapse.*

Therapist: *How much do you believe that sitting here right now and how much would you believe it if you had the sensations you get in an attack?*

Pt: *50% now and 90% in an attack.*

Th: *OK, let's look at the evidence you have for this thought. Have you ever fainted in an attack?*

Pt: *No.*

Th: *What is it then that makes you think you might faint?*

Pt: *I feel faint and the feeling can be very strong.*

Th: *So, to summarize, your evidence that you are going to faint is the fact that you feel faint?*

Pt: *Yes.*

Th: *How can you then account for the fact that you have felt faint many hundreds of times and have not yet fainted?*

Pt: *So far, the attacks have always stopped just in time or I have managed to hold onto something to stop myself from collapsing.*

Th: *Right so, one explanation of the fact that you have frequently felt faint, had the thought that you will faint, but have not actually fainted, is that you have always done something to save yourself just in time. However, an alternative explanation is that the feeling of faintness that you get in a panic attack will never lead to you collapsing, even if you don't control it.*

Pt: *Yes, I suppose so.*

Th: *In order to decide which of these two possibilities is correct, we need to know what has to happen to your body for you to actually faint. Do you know?*

Pt: *No.*

Th: *Your blood pressure needs to drop. Do you know what happens to your blood pressure during a panic attack?*

Pt: *Well, my pulse is racing. I guess my blood pressure must be up.*

Th: *That's right. In anxiety, heart rate and blood pressure tend to go together. So, you are actually less likely to faint when you are anxious than when you are not.*

Pt: *That's very interesting and helpful to know. However, if it's true, why do I feel so faint?*

Th: *Your feeling of faintness is a sign that your body is reacting in a normal way to the perception of danger. Most of the bodily reactions you are experiencing when anxious were probably designed to deal with the threats experienced by primitive man, such as being approached by a hungry tiger. What would be the best thing to do in that situation?*

Pt: *Run away as fast as you can.*

Th: *That's right. And in order to help you run, you need the maximum amount of energy in your muscles. This is achieved by sending more of your blood to your muscles and relatively less to the brain. This means that there is a small drop in oxygen to the brain and that is why you feel faint. However, this feeling is misleading in the sense that it doesn't mean you will actually faint because your overall blood pressure is up, not down.*

Pt: *That's very clear. So next time I feel faint, I can check out whether I am going to faint by taking my pulse. If it is normal, or quicker than normal, I know I won't faint.*

Th: *That's right. Now, on the basis of what we've discussed so far, how much do you believe you might faint in a panic attack?*

Pt: *Less, say 10%.*

Th: *And if you were experiencing the sensations?*

Pt: *Maybe 25%.* (Clark, 1989)

The use of planned behavioral experiments designed to check out patients' dysfunctional cognitions is central to Beck's therapy. When the therapist points out their dysfunctional thoughts, patients often respond that although they "intellectually" agree with the therapist's analysis, they do not believe it "emotionally." Beck et al. (1979) explain that when patients say they believe or do not believe something emotionally, they are talking about degree of belief. Actually, they are of two minds about some issues. For example, on the one hand, a patient believes that making a mistake is human; on the other hand, he or she believes it's unacceptable. At this point, the therapist can observe,

> What you're really saying is that you don't truly believe my explanation is correct. You don't have a real gut feeling for it, and it is to be expected. These ideas feel foreign to you. What you can do is act upon my suggestions, test them out, see if they're true, discuss them with yourself, look at the other alternatives, consider the evidence. I certainly do not want you to believe it just because I say it or take it on faith; rather, just to try it on for size. Try to have an open mind" (pp. 302–303).

In summary, the therapist helps patients to challenge their dysfunctional thinking, by using both verbal (cognitive) and behavioral strategies.

An Evaluation. A major advantage of Beck's therapy is that it is clearly specified. It has, consequently, lent itself to research on treatment outcome because it is adequately implemented and differs procedurally from alternative methods, a criterion for this kind of research (DeRubeis et al., 1982). This explicit specification of treatment procedure, and the empirical research that this has permitted, can be contrasted with the problems in defining and, hence, testing RET.

Beck's cognitive therapy also differs from Ellis's RET in how therapists attempt to alter dysfunctional cognitions. RET's primary strategy has typically consisted of a verbal attack on the patient's irrational thinking. The therapist actively disputes irrational assumptions and attempts to cajole patients into thinking more logically. In contrast to Ellis's style of direct confrontation, Beck adopts a Socratic approach so that patients discover the inaccuracies and distortions in their thinking for themselves. In Beck's approach, the patient is helped to identify and alter automatic thoughts through a more gentle and strategic progression of therapeutic interventions.

Beck's therapy has been shown to be effective in controlled outcome research. It has been tested extensively in the treatment of depression, and produced consistently positive results. Evidence shows that cognitive treatment for anxiety disorders (e.g., panic disorder) is also effective (see Chapter 5).

Although cognitive therapy has been shown effective, the reasons for its success remain to be established. Beck's (1976) theory of why the therapy works is not well developed. With depression, the treatment is said to modify the dysfunctional cognitive attitudes or schemata which, Beck hypothesizes, cause the disorder. However, it is not clear if the changes in cognitive processes associated with depression are the cause or correlate of successful treatment (see Chapter 7). Moreover, Simons et al. (1984) showed that cognitive therapy and drug pharmacotherapy resulted in the cognitive changes predicted by Beck's theory. Simons and colleagues interpreted these results as indicating such cognitive effects are the consequence rather than the cause of therapeutic change, secondary to the as-yet-undetermined, primary mechanism of change in the treatment of depression.

Beck and Emery (1986) have proposed that cognitive therapy is effective in treating anxiety disorders because it allegedly alters the critical underlying cognitive processes. Experimental analyses of these cognitive mechanisms remain to be carried out. Existing evidence is inconsistent with Beck's position. He has argued that phobic anxiety and avoidance are maintained by negative outcome expectations. In other words, patients are afraid not of a particular object or situation in itself, but of the consequences of their being in the situation or in contact with the object. People with a phobia of heights indicate that they are afraid of falling; people with a phobia of social situations state that they are afraid of being humiliated or rejected. Williams and Watson (1985) have shown the weak relation of these outcome expectations to successful treatment outcome.

CURRENT TRENDS IN THE PSYCHOLOGICAL THERAPIES

Theoretical Orientations

As we have seen, a wide range of psychological therapies exist, often with conflicting concepts and proce-

TABLE 16.6 The Theoretical Orientations of Clinical and Counseling Psychologists

Orientation	%
Psychoanalytic	10.84
Adlerian	2.89
Behavioral	6.75
Cognitive behavioral	10.36
Person-centered	8.67
Gestalt	1.69
Existential	2.17
Rational-emotive	1.69
Family	2.65
Eclectic	41.20
Others	11.12

Source: Adapted from Smith, D. (1982). Trends in counseling and psychotherapy. *American Psychologist*, 37, 802–809. Copyright © 1982 by the American Psychological Association. Reprinted by permission.

dures. But what are the actual practices and attitudes of professionals in the field? In a survey study designed to provide this information and determine current trends in clinical practice (Smith, 1982), a questionnaire was sent to 800 randomly selected members of the Divisions of Clinical and Counseling Psychology in the American Psychological Association. Of the 55 percent of the sample of who responded, 85 percent were male, 65 percent were above the age of forty-five, and 87 percent had earned a Ph.D. The proportion of those in university positions was 41 percent whereas 26 percent were in private practice.

A question in the survey asked respondents to indicate their theoretical orientation. Table 16.6 summarizes the results. The largest percentage described themselves as eclectic in orientation. The trend, then, is away from the exclusiveness and narrowness of particular systems ("schools") of psychological therapy and toward some sort of broader, more flexible approach. Judging from these results, we agree with Smith's (1982) conclusion that the primacy of schools in psychotherapy has passed. Of the particular schools, the two most important today seem to be psychoanalysis and cognitive-behavior therapy.

Related surveys of other professional groups indicate that Smith's was not an isolated finding. Tuma and Pratt's (1982) survey of clinical child psychologists showed that their two major orientations were behavioral and psychodynamic. A similar survey of pediatric psychologists indicated they were more influenced by behavior therapy than by psychodynamic therapy. Fifty-nine percent of respondents chose behavioral psychology as their primary orientation, and 39 percent expressed a preference for psychodynamic psychology (Tuma & Cohen, 1981). In assessing the prevalence of a behavioral or cognitive-behavioral orientation among clinicians, O'Leary (1984) similarly concluded that a behavioral orientation was dominant among clinicians specializing in the treatment of children.

Table 16.7 lists the psychotherapists whom respondents rated as most influential. Note that Carl Rogers heads the list even though his person-centered therapy is not one of the leading schools. Smith (1982) suggests a reason for Rogers's preeminence: All schools endorse his emphasis on the importance of the therapeutic relationship.

Women as Professionals. It will not have escaped our readers' attention that the majority (85 percent) of Smith's (1982) sample were men. This proportion reflects selection and training priorities in previous decades. At present, the majority of graduate students in clinical psychology are women—and were

TABLE 16.7 The Ten Psychotherapists Rated as Most Influential

Rank	Psychotherapist	% of Respondents Assigning a Rank	Cumulative Ranking	Weighted Score
1.	Carl Rogers	37.35	155	363
2.	Albert Ellis	27.23	113	229
3.	Sigmund Freud	10.84	45	117
4.	Joseph Wolpe	11.08	46	87
5.	Arnold Lazarus	9.40	39	84
6.	Fritz Perls	8.19	34	54
7.	Aaron Beck	5.78	24	49
8.	Jay Haley	6.02	25	46
9.	Milton Erickson	4.58	19	40
10.	Donald Meichenbaum	4.34	18	37

Source: Adapted from Smith, D. (1982). Trends in counseling and psychotherapy. *American Psychologist*, 37, 802–809. Copyright © 1982 by the American Psychological Association. Reprinted by permission.

during the 1980s. More women are also becoming psychiatrists. As a result, the number of female practitioners is increasing, and this trend is likely to continue.

Arnold Lazarus, a former student of Wolpe's and one of the founding figures in behavior therapy, who subsequently developed multimodal therapy.

Eclecticism

The trend toward eclecticism revealed by Smith's (1982) survey and others is consistent with the increasing interest of psychotherapists in a rapprochement (a coming together) between the various approaches to psychological treatment. Today's therapists seek to find commonalities among different and often conflicting systems, and, where possible, to integrate divergent methods (Goldfried, 1982).

The extent of the commonalities between psychodynamic therapy and behavior therapy is a major focus of enquiry (Arkowitz & Messer, 1984; Wachtel, 1988). Several reasons exist for the focus on the potential rapprochement between psychodynamic and behavioral therapies: First, they are, as Smith's (1982) survey indicates, probably the two most influential approaches among clinical and counseling psychologists. Second, when self-described eclectic therapists are asked to specify the approaches they most favor, they refer to psychodynamic and behavioral therapies (Garfield & Kurtz, 1976). Third, although eclectic therapists state that they use both approaches, there is a history of conflict and rivalry between psychodynamic and behavioral therapists. For example, psychodynamic therapists have often criticized behavior therapy as superficial, failing to address the real causes of clinical disorders. Similarly, behavior therapists have attacked psychoanalysis as unscientific and lacking any evidence of therapeutic effectiveness. In some ways, these two approaches represent polar opposites in their basic philosophy, theories, and treatment methods. Success in bridging these apparent differences would greatly advance the development of a more integrated approach to psychotherapy. Different solutions have been proposed, and we discuss their advantages and limitations next.

Technical Eclecticism. Lazarus (1989) suggests we are not yet at the stage of development that would permit integrating the different concepts and techniques of varying psychological therapies into a unified, harmonious whole. The preferred alternative, according to Lazarus, is **technical eclecticism.** In this approach, the therapist freely draws upon techniques from any type of psychotherapy without necessarily subscribing to the theoretical tenets that gave rise to them.

The majority of Lazarus's techniques are standard methods within behavior therapy (Wilson, 1982). But, technical eclectism also uses several nonbehavioral methods. An example is the empty chair technique from Gestalt therapy. Lazarus has adapted the technique as a form of role-playing and role reversal, with the goal of modifying current maladaptive behavior patterns.

Despite his openness to techniques from different therapeutic systems, Lazarus (1989) argues that his approach is not atheoretical. The different techniques, he maintains, must be used according to well-conceived guiding principles of behavior change. Technical eclecticism "looks mainly to social and cognitive learning theory for explanatory constructs, since all of its tenets are grounded in research and are open to verification and disproof" (p. 250).

Lazarus (1981) has developed technical eclecticism into what he calls **multimodal therapy.** According to this approach, a patient's problems are assessed across seven different modalities—*B*ehavior, *A*ffect, *S*ensation, *I*magery, *C*ognition, *I*nterpersonal, and *D*rugs (Biology). These modalities are summarized in the acronym of BASIC ID. Comprehensive multimodal therapy requires that interventions be matched to each modality. Table 16.8 is an example of an assessment profile.

TABLE 16.8 Problem Identification in Multimodal Therapy: A Structural Profile

The following is the structural profile of a 40-year-old man who consulted Arnold Lazarus complaining of anxiety and panic attacks:

B. Phobic avoidance
Loss of control
Stays in bed when highly anxious (feigns illness)

A. Anxious
Panicky
Bouts of depression

S. Abdominal cramps
Headaches
Dizziness
Palpitations
Tension
Numbness
Tremors
Dry mouth
Rapid heart beat

I. Images of helplessness
Pictures himself not coping, losing control, failing
Memories surrounding father's death and funeral
Images of himself dying at age 44 like his father

C. Overvalues Protestant work ethic
Preoccupied with thoughts of death and dying
''My life is controlled by outside forces.''
''It is very important to please other people.''

I. Overidentified with father
Wife ''mothers him for somatic complaints and is critical of his ''anxieties''

D. Takes tranquilizers
Spastic colon
Smokes about 20 cigarettes a day
Adverse reaction to Tofranil (Psychiatrist had prescribed it to overcome his panic attacks.) (p. 74)

Source: From A.A. Lazarus, *The practice of multimodal therapy.* (1981). New York: McGraw-Hill. Copyright © 1981, McGraw-Hill. Reprinted by permission.

Respondents in Smith's (1982) survey rated technical eclecticism and multimodalism among the most important trends in the psychotherapy field, and Lazarus among the ten most influential therapists. Nonetheless, multimodal therapy has been criticized. Psychodynamic critics point out its overlap with cognitive-behavior therapy and its theoretical framework, which often fundamentally differs from psychodynamic thinking. Behavior therapists applaud the flexibility of the approach but have questioned the basis for selecting various nonbehavioral treatment techniques in multimodal therapy. They contend that no evidence shows the value of adding these various nonbehavioral methods, such as the empty chair technique, to cognitive-behavioral interventions (Wilson, 1982).

Commonalities and Differences among Psychological Therapies. Goldfried (1980) has proposed a different but related search for rapprochement among the different psychological therapies. He conceptualizes therapy as having different levels of abstraction. The highest level consists of overall theoretical frameworks, a level he rejects as useless for any rapprochement. The lowest level involves specific therapeutic techniques, a level at which

Goldfried feels any commonalities would be "trivial." Instead, Goldfried suggests that the level between theory and practice, which he calls *clinical strategies,* offers the possibility of a consensus among different approaches. As an example of a clinical strategy, Goldfried suggests that providing the patient with new, corrective experiences might be common to all theoretical orientations. Behavior therapy, as has been shown repeatedly in earlier chapters, clearly emphasizes performance-based, corrective learning experiences. The method of exposure, used in treating anxiety disorders and other problems, is a prominent example. Goldfried suggests that other approaches also use corrective learning experiences. In support of this argument, he notes that Freud himself once stated for patients with phobias to improve, they had to engage in new ways of behaving in the real world.

Psychodynamic therapists agree about the significance of new learning experiences but differ from behavior therapists in the experiences they deem therapeutic. The crucial learning experience in psychodynamic therapy occurs within the therapeutic relationship—the development and working through of the transference. Even here, however, commonalities have been suggested between psychodynamic and cognitive-behavioral therapy. Psychodynamic therapists believe that transference allows them to uncover the patient's childhood conflicts, so they can then be resolved. Cognitive therapists, operating from an information processing framework, might describe transference as the use of that relationship experience to access and then alter the cognitive-affective schemata responsible for the patient's problems. Behavior therapists could argue that the relationship elicits anxiety-evoking stimuli associated with interpersonal issues which the patient is then exposed to. Westen (1988) makes this argument using the following clinical example:

> *A borderline patient whom I had been seeing for over a year started to withdraw without clear cause, refusing to talk and sitting glumly in her chair. We had previously discussed a similar pattern in her life of suddenly severing relations with people important to her, but the pattern was now emerging — with corresponding affect — in the transference. She was aware of her actions but angrily told me that she would not and could not explain them. I suggested to her that someone does not pull away from another person like that unless she is afraid of something, at which point she volunteered that she did not know what she feared, but that she was sure something terribly bad would happen if she did not run. The combination of her experiencing this feeling with me and eliciting thoughts and memories congruent with the affect allowed us to explore the fear behind her behavior, and repeated experiences of this sort allowed her both to reanalyze (cognitively) conditions under which fear has been inappropriately evoked, and to see that, in fact, her fears are not confirmed in interaction with me. This latter aspect of use of the transference is similar to* in vivo *exposure techniques in behavioral treatment (p. 175).*

A second commonality identified by Goldfried (1980) is the role of the therapist–patient relationship in effective therapy. All therapies emphasize the therapeutic relationship, but the various psychological therapies differ about which specific elements of the therapeutic relationship are important. For example, in contrast to the neutral and detached role of the psychoanalytically oriented therapist, the behavior therapist is more directive—a problem solver who tries to instigate behavioral change in the patient's natural environment and is a source of personal support. In their comparative study of behavior therapy and psychoanalytically oriented psychotherapy, Sloane et al. (1975) concluded that

> Differences between behavior therapy and analytically-oriented psychotherapy . . . involved the basic patterns of interactions between patient and therapist and the type of relationship formed. Behavior therapy is not psychotherapy with special techniques superimposed on the traditional therapeutic paradigm; rather, the two appear to represent quite different styles of treatment although they share common elements.

Psychoanalytic therapists regard the transference relationship as the primary means of promoting behavior change. Behavior therapists also directly use therapeutic relationship to alter some behavior patterns to a limited degree. We have described Mischel's (1981) criticism of personality trait theory, showing that behavior is situation-specific and not universal across different environmental settings (see Chapter 3). Consistent with these findings, behavior therapists recognize that they must promote corrective emotional experiences within the appropriate situational context. That context, for most patients, is not their relationship with a therapist in an artificial treatment setting; it is more likely the specific interpersonal relationships under particular conditions in their everyday environment. Even if the therapeutic relationship is used to change patients' behavior, behavior therapists do not expect such change to generalize automatically to outside situations. They try to foster generalization by instructing patients to engage in specific interpersonal interactions in the real world.

The issue of commonalities among different psychotherapies can be summarized by stating that there are two distinct views. One is that there are crucial commonalities that are the foundations which we can build a more eclectic and integrated system of psychotherapy upon (Goldfried, 1982; Norcross, 1986). The other is that the consensus on the types of strategies identified by Goldfried and others is limited to only the most superficial aspects of treatment. According to this approach, fundamentally different views on basic issues means that, at least for the present, trying to integrate the diverse forms of psychological therapy is probably futile. An alternative approach would be to devote our energies to developing replicable, testable, and effective methods of therapeutic change within each individual system. Once accomplished, it will be clearer what elements in different approaches would be worthy of integrating into, ideally, an improved and more comprehensive therapy.

The Effectiveness of Psychological Therapies

In a landmark paper, Eysenck (1952) concluded that there was no acceptable evidence that psychotherapy was more effective than no treatment at all. His challenge ignited a controversy that continues today. Some reviewers of the field argue the effectiveness of all forms of psychotherapy (Vanderbos, 1986). Smith, Glass, and Miller (1980), in an influential book, concluded that "Psychotherapy is beneficial, consistently so and in many different ways. Its benefits are on a par with other expensive and ambitious interventions, such as schooling and medicine" (p. 183). Some critics (Prioleau, Murdock, & Brody, 1983), however, conclude that Eysenck's original assertion still cannot be rejected.

Even more controversial is if some therapeutic approaches are more effective than others. The most widely shared view is that, with few exceptions, no one treatment approach is reliably superior to any other (Beitman, Goldfried, & Norcross, 1989; Strupp, 1989).

The alternative view is that some therapies are more effective than others and that specific treatment methods are more effective for particular disorders than others (Lazarus, 1989; Kazdin & Wilson, 1978). In the preceding chapters we have described examples of differences in effectiveness among alternative treatments. For example, exposure therapy has repeatedly been the most effective psychological method for treating phobic disorders. As also shown in preceding chapters, it has become possible to compare the effects of specific psychological methods with those of drug treatments. Depending on the disorder, either psychological or drug treatments may be the preferred method. In some cases a combined biobehavioral treatment approach is called for.

It serves little purpose to inquire whether behavior therapy is more effective than psychotherapy. Many different behavioral and cognitive-behavioral techniques exist, some more effective than others. Similarly, of the many different forms of psychotherapy, each has distinctive qualities. Clinicians and researchers now generally agree that the most useful approach is to ask *what* treatment method, applied by *whom* is most effective for *what* problem in *which* person (Paul, 1967). This formidable question cannot be answered in a single study but provides the framework in which outcome research can be conducted constructively.

Meta-Analysis. An influential but still controversial means of evaluating the effects of psychological therapies is a statistical technique known as **meta-analysis,** a quantitative method for integrating the standardized results of different studies (Smith et al., 1980). The unit of analysis in a meta-analysis is the **effect size** (ES), a statistical index of treatment-produced change. A common way of calculating the ES is by subtracting the mean of the control group from the mean of the treatment group and dividing that difference by the standard deviation of the control group. The larger the ES, the greater the effect of the treatment. ESs from separate studies using different samples and measures can then be combined and analyzed in sophisticated statistical tests of the effects of alternative treatments.

The proponents of meta-analysis argue that it is superior to traditional, "qualitative" reviews of the research literature because it eliminates or at least minimizes the subjectivity which can bias reviews of research evidence (Shapiro & Shapiro, 1983; Smith et al., 1980). Critics charge that this claim of greater objectivity can be illusory (Erwin, 1986; Paul, 1985). For example, Smith et al. (1980) included all studies in their meta-analysis regardless of their individual quality. They then assigned equal weight in their statistical analyses to good and methodologically bad studies. The problem here is that the relatively small number of well-controlled studies in the literature are swamped by the majority of flawed studies (Wilson, 1985). Smith et al. (1980) defend their procedure by claiming that the methodological features of different studies can be systematically related to outcome using statistical techniques. Other experts assert that only studies with adequate controls be included. But *who* decides on the methodological features of specific studies, and *what* criteria are used to judge individual studies? These are human decisions that inevitably involve subjectivity and often create controversy.

In any meta-analysis, a variety of subjective and arbitrary judgments must be made before the data are entered into the computer, such as what studies to include and what methodological features to emphasize. Nevertheless, the process of examining each study in detail to make these judgments makes more public what has usually been a more private process in conventional reviews of the therapy outcome literature (Mintz, 1983). This, and the subsequent ability to carry out sophisticated statistical tests, are the strengths of meta-analysis.

The meta-analysis done to date have not resolved the controversy about the effectiveness of alternative therapies. Different meta-analyses, even of the same set of studies, have yielded inconsistent findings (Searles, 1985). Garfield (1983) has suggested that meta-analyses have simply raised the controversy to a new level. To a large extent, the difficulty has been in how the method has been used, rather than in the method itself. Despite the controversy, it is a widely shared view that meta-analysis will fundamentally change how the medical and behavioral sciences will process large amounts of data from different studies (Mann, 1990).

SUMMARY

1. Psychological therapy is a formal and systematic process of interaction between therapist and patient. The therapist, who may be a clinical psychologist, psychiatrist, or social worker, has specific training in, and knowledge of, the biological, psychological, and social foundations of human behavior and its disorders.
2. Psychoanalytic therapies remain a dominant treatment for abnormal behavior. Traditional Freudian psychoanalysis is relatively rare. The more commonly used methods today are ego analytic and brief psychodynamic offshoots of Freud's approach. Core psychoanalytic concepts emphasize the unconscious motives behind behavior, early childhood experiences, and intrapsychic conflicts. Despite their popularity, psychoanalytic therapies enjoy only limited empirical support.
3. Humanistic and existential therapies assume that people are innately motivated to affect their environment and achieve personal fulfillment. Rogers's person-centered therapy, the most influential humanistic therapy, postulates that if the therapist is empathic, is genuine, and expresses unconditional positive regard for patients, personal growth will occur. Therapists who do not express these relationship qualities may make patients' problems worse.
4. Gestalt therapy is a humanistic-existential approach focusing on the here and now in treatment. The goal of therapy is increased awareness of inner feelings and environmental influences, integrating these opposing forces into a harmonious whole, and taking personal responsibility for one's feelings and actions. Gestalt therapists are more directive than Rogerians and use a range of different techniques to promote awareness.
5. Interpersonal psychotherapies focus primarily on interpersonal relationships. The goals of interpersonal psychotherapy (IPT) are to identify patients' conflicts with others and to help them resolve these conflicts, to help patients move from one role to another, and to remedy interpersonal deficits. IPT has proved effective in treating unipolar depression.
6. Behavior therapy is the application of the principles and procedures of experimental psychology to clinical problems. It focuses primarily on the current determinants of behavior rather than on the analysis of the historical origins of problems. Behavior therapy encompasses a wide range of techniques, variously based on the principles of classical and operant conditioning on the one hand, and cognitive psychology on the other. The increasing emphasis on cognitive principles and procedures has led to the use of the term *cognitive-behavior therapy* to describe the approach. Behavior therapy techniques have been extensively evaluated and are broadly applicable to a wide range of problems in diverse patient populations.
7. Cognitive therapy is based on the assumption that emotional disorders result from dysfunctional thinking. The treatment goal is to identify and then alter the maladaptive thoughts. Both Ellis's rational-emotive therapy (RET) and Beck's (1976) cognitive therapy prompt patients to challenge their dysfunctional thoughts. Beck's approach, however, relies more heavily on behavioral methods to correct dysfunctional thoughts. Instead of debating with them about the validity of their cognitions, therapists collaborate with patients in devising specific behavioral tasks, framed as experiments to test patients' assumptions. Beck's approach has been effective in the treatment of anxiety disorders and depression, whereas RET enjoys little direct empirical support.
8. Clinical psychologists have become increasingly eclectic in their approach to treatment, drawing upon strategies from different approaches rather than relying exclusively on a single system. In multimodal therapy, Lazarus combines techniques from other systems with cognitive-behavior therapy to address each of seven different modalities of functioning—behavior, affect, sensation, imagery, cognition, interpersonal behavior, and drugs.
9. Evaluation of the effectiveness of psychological treatments remains controversial. One group of investigators believes that psychological therapy has been shown to be effective and asserts that no differences exist among different psychotherapeutic approaches. Another group argues that some therapies are more effective than others, and that specific treatment methods are more effective for particular disorders than others.

Mary Joan Waid, *Legacy* (1989). Oil on canvas, 40 × 40 inches. Courtesy of G.W. Einstein Company, Inc.

17

MARITAL, FAMILY, SOCIAL, AND MEDICAL THERAPIES

Why should we devote a chapter to marital, family, social, and medical therapies? First, approximately 40 percent of people seeking help at mental health clinics have serious marital problems—often in conjunction with anxiety, depression, or alcoholism (Gurin, Veroff, & Feld, 1960). Not only do many people ask for help with their marriages, but problems such as depression may be better treated by combining marital therapy with other therapies. Second, many professionals argue that the effects of family and social therapies are more efficient, immediate, and long-term than individual therapies. In fact, individual treatment may be perceived as the therapist's failure to see the patient's problem in a broad perspective. Finally, other clinicians and researchers believe that many psychological disorders have, at least in part, a biological basis; consequently, they argue that medical or biological therapies are indicated. This chapter will first focus on the therapies that move beyond individual treatment, namely marital, family, and social therapies. Then, we will consider medical treatments used to alter some element of an individual's biochemistry to alleviate his or her psychological problems.

MARITAL THERAPIES

Since *DSM-III-R* (1987) does not include marital discord as a separate psychological disorder, we have discussed marital problems only as they may relate secondarily to problems such as sexual disorders and depression. Thus, the prevalence and impact of marital problems will be discussed briefly in order to allow one to appreciate the importance of **marital therapy.**

Prevalence and Impact of Marital Problems

Based on projections from the U.S. Census Bureau, it appears almost half of all recent marriages will end in divorce. Despite these statistics, approximately 90 percent of American adults marry, with approximately three quarters of those divorcing for the first time later remarrying (Spanier & Thompson, 1984). Evidently, divorce in the United States does not constitute a rejection of the institution of marriage or the family but only of a particular marriage. The breakup of that specific marriage, however, often can have serious consequences for the marital partners and/or their children.

Marital problems are among the most common presenting problems of clients at mental health clinics (Gurin, Veroff, & Feld, 1960). As noted earlier, roughly 40 percent of individuals seeking treatment view their problems as marital. Of all the difficulties people face, divorce and marital problems rank second and third, respectively, as the most significant life stressors, exceeded only by the death of a spouse or a close relative (Holmes & Rahe, 1967). At least half the depressed women seeking treatment have clinically significant marital problems (see Chapter 7). Relationship problems are overwhelmingly given as the most common reason for suicide attempts (see Chapter 13). Further, most couples with sexual problems, such as low sexual desire, situational impotency, and orgasmic dysfunction, have marital difficulties. In addition, if one spouse has alcohol or drug dependency problems, significant marital problems are usually present. Marital difficulties are extremely common: In some cases they may result from other problems such as substance abuse or schizophrenia; in others, they may lead to the individual psychological problems discussed earlier. Therefore, during the last two decades, many researchers have concentrated on developing marital therapy either as a primary treatment or as a secondary supplement to other therapies.

Treatment of Marital Problems

Marital therapy is a psychological treatment for couples designed to improve communication, to develop insight into marital problems, and to improve positive feelings between spouses. Marital therapy is conducted by therapists of many different theoretical orientations. Further, marital or relationship therapies are used with unmarried couples, gay or lesbian couples, and sometimes even with couples who wish to separate on amicable terms, keeping their children's best interests in mind. The behavioral, psychodynamic, and cognitive theoretical orientations discussed in the individual therapies are all used to improve marital relationships. Regardless of orientation, marital therapists focus on communication and insight into relationship issues. Behavioral therapists emphasize changing daily behaviors and communication patterns; cognitive therapists focus on changing thoughts and beliefs detrimental to the marriage; and psychodynamic therapists emphasize insight into how each partner's individual problems or styles affect the marriage. (Some psychodynamic therapists emphasize unconscious factors whereas others emphasize the dynamics of current interaction patterns.) The integrated approach we will describe developed from behavioral approaches and now also utilizes therapeutic procedures and ideas taken from psychodynamic and cognitive approaches.

In marital therapy, the therapist usually first meets with each partner separately to understand each spouse's perspective on the relationship. These individual sessions are conducted because the spouses often experience marital problems in different ways. Often, each partner blames the other for the problems. Next, the therapist begins sessions with the couple, called *conjoint sessions*. Although both partners are not always willing to attend marital therapy sessions, treating only one partner is less effective than treating both (Gurman & Kniskern, 1986).

Couples who profit most from marital therapy have some commitment to remain together and some love or caring for each other. Often, the husband or the wife may not have decided whether to remain in the marriage. However, if they share some desire to remain together, marital therapy can help clarify these options. Over 80 percent of couples report their main problem is communication. Decreased interest in sexual interactions and differences over finances, child rearing, and sharing household tasks are also very common. Interestingly, these issues are listed as problems by *both* dissatisfied and satisfied couples. Conflicts are inevitable in marriage; the *manner* of dealing with these conflicts differentiates troubled marriages from happy marriages. Satisfied couples spend more time with each other, respond to both verbal and nonverbal cues for closeness, share the responsibility to resolve problems rather than blaming their partners, and, very importantly, talk more with each other. Distressed couples criticize one another more and display a variety of communication difficulties.

The marital therapies we will describe have been used to treat a wide variety of relationship problems including infrequent sexual interactions, infidelity, and differences over finances, child rearing, and sex roles. Marital therapies have also been used when one partner is an alcoholic, when one partner is depressed, and when one partner is hypochondriacal. In these latter cases, marital therapy is adapted to the particular needs of the partner with the specific disorder. In brief, marital therapy has proven quite useful with diverse groups, either as a treatment itself or in combination with individual therapy for specific disorders (Hahlweg, 1988).

The core of marital therapy is the attempt to change daily interactions of the couple, especially to reduce criticism and increase positive, supportive comments and actions. As progress is made in reducing criticism and anger and in increasing positive comments (e.g., "You really look nice!"), the therapist generally begins to focus on the couple's communication patterns. The individual styles and problematic ways they interact with each other are discussed. The therapist may serve as a model for alternative methods of communicating, and each partner may role-play problem discussions with the therapist acting as the other partner. As the couple gains insight into their problematic ways of interacting, the therapist increasingly focuses on their attitudes and feelings toward each other.

Increasing Positive Behaviors. Increasing positive behaviors in a marriage is often accomplished by having each partner engage in a practice called **caring**

KUDZU by Doug Marlette
Source: By permission of Doug Marlette and Creators Syndicate

days (Stuart, 1980). As each partner shows caring by everyday actions, the husband and wife begin to feel better about each other.

The first step is for each spouse to list things that the other partner could do to demonstrate caring. The caring days list is usually made for a week. Table 17.1 shows a sample of one couple's list.

Once the caring days list is agreed upon, the therapist emphasizes that each partner is responsible for carrying out some of the partner's requests regardless of the partner's behavior. *It is not a tit for tat agreement.* The husband, for example, agrees to do nice things for his wife on particular days even if she did not do the things he requested. An individual may have trouble doing some of the nice things on the caring days list for many reasons, and these are discussed with the therapist at the weekly session. When a husband or wife resists doing things on the list, the therapist uses this to clarify underlying issues, such as jealousy, unresolved anger about past events, or bitterness toward a child or stepchild. These problems are discussed while the couple learns to communicate more effectively.

Caring days prompt positive actions and interactions. In turn, positive interactions often break a cycle where spouses avoid each other. Most importantly, caring days demonstrate that both partners are willing to improve the marriage. Doing things for

TABLE 17.1 Caring Days Lists and a Week of Caring Days*

David's List	Date						
	Mon.	Tues.	Wed.	Thurs.	Fri.	Sat.	Sun.
Give me a backrub	6/13		6/15				6/19
Feed the dog	6/13	6/14			6/17	6/18	
Kiss me	6/13	6/14		6/16		6/18	
Take me out for dinner			6/15				
Call me at work		6/14			6/17		
Play racquetball with me				6/16			
Go to bed when I do	6/13	6/14			6/17	6/18	
Ruth's List	**Date**						
	Mon.	Tues.	Wed.	Thurs.	Fri.	Sat.	Sun.
Tell me that I look nice	6/13		6/15				6/19
Fix lunch for both of us		6/14			6/17		
Put the cap on the toothpaste	6/13	6/14	6/15	6/16	6/17	6/18	6/19
Tell me about your day	6/13	6/14				6/18	
Ask me about my day	6/13	6/14				6/18	
Take me to the movies			6/15				
Look at me when you talk to me	6/13	6/14			6/17		6/19
Sit next to me when we watch TV			6/15	6/16			

* [When a date is noted, David or Ruth agreed to do some specific caring act on that day.]

Source: From Bornstein, P.H., & Bornstein, M.T. (1986). *Marital therapy: A behavioral-communications approach.* New York: Pergamon Press PLC, p. 72. Reprinted with permission.

each other will not solve all marital problems, especially deep hurts resulting from long-standing criticism, mistrust, or psychological and physical abuse. However, caring days is a very important initial step in improving a relationship.

Communication Change. Therapists view poor communication as the most frequent and destructive problem in marriage (Geiss & O'Leary, 1981). Thus, regardless of theoretical orientation, most marital therapies attempt to analyze and change communication patterns. The heart of the communication process is getting each partner to listen to the other with concern and understanding. Generally, such understanding occurs after the husband and wife ask for clarification of certain statements. In the beginning, the therapist often works to clarify meanings, feelings, and messages sent, but as therapy progresses, clarification and restatement of problems come directly from the partners. To develop mutual understanding, the therapist helps each partner express empathy for the other's feelings and needs. Partners learn that agreeing with each other is not always necessary. Once they understand and empathize with each other, the couple can begin to resolve differences and find ways to satisfy each other's needs.

Some couples avoid discussing problems altogether. Others become angry and critical, and although they may get bad feelings "off their chest," they often make no progress toward solving problems. Therapists encourage all couples to communicate their feelings and needs directly. Partners are taught to avoid general, sweeping criticisms (e.g., "You're a lazy bum"), replacing them with specific requests (e.g., "I'd really appreciate some help with the dishes"). They learn to substitute direct expression of their own feelings and desires (e.g., "I would love to go dancing this weekend") for negative or coercive attempts to get their way (e.g., "Are you going to sit in front of that damned TV again this weekend?").

In communication analyses, the therapist asks the couple to describe some of their most characteristic arguments, with *each* partner describing what he or she characteristically does that may lead to avoidance or escalating hostility. If the husband and wife have difficulty understanding what they do that impairs communication, the therapist may ask them to listen to an audiotape or watch a videotape of their interactions. During the communication analyses, the therapist provides his or her understanding of the couple's typical communication styles and of the issues provoking the greatest anger and emotional upset. The therapist will give instructions and feedback, model effective communication styles, and provide support or reinforcement for change. Box 17.1 is an example of how a marital therapist aids a couple's communication efforts.

Once the partners begin communicating feelings and desires more effectively and learn to empathize with each other, therapy often focuses on problem-solving skills. Partners are encouraged to define a problem and then brainstorm possible solutions. Next, they evaluate possible solutions and decide which to implement. Often partners need to negotiate compromises (e.g., "I'll stay home with the kids while you do aerobics on Wednesday if I can go bowling on Thursday"). Sometimes, they have to choose a solution which is only partly satisfactory for each person in order to avoid solutions which are completely satisfactory for one partner and unpleasant for the other.

Attitude Change. Many distressed husbands and wives have irrational attitudes and/or unrealistic expectations of their partners and of marriage. One common unrealistic expectation is "My spouse should always agree with me otherwise he or she does not love me." Another is "A partner should know what I am thinking or feeling without me having to tell him or her" (Eidelson & Epstein, 1982). Some people believe that marriage should satisfy all of a person's needs. They perceive friendships or interests outside the relationship as threatening or upsetting. Distressed husbands and wives also attribute their partner's negative behaviors to stable traits (e.g., He or she is basically a mean person). This attitude can lead spouses to ignore the changes the partner makes in therapy. The therapist prompts each partner to discover unreasonable beliefs or thoughts which produce distressing feelings. According to Epstein, Schlesinger, and Dryden (1988), the therapist tries to get the partners involved in a discovery process by having them adopt certain attitudes for specified time periods in order to see if changing their attitudes affects their feelings and behavior.

Effectiveness of Marital Therapy

If increasing marital satisfaction is the goal, insight-oriented therapies focusing on unconscious factors that influence choice of mate and later marital conflicts are not effective (Beach & O'Leary, 1985). After reviewing all published studies of insight therapies for marital problems, Boelens, Emmelkamp, MacGillavry, and Markvoort (1980) concluded that insight into unconscious issues may be ineffective in increasing marital satisfaction. On the other hand, if the insight concerns the kinds of behaviors that should be changed to make the marriage better, couples improve in their marital satisfaction. Insight alone,

BOX 17.1 Edited Transcript of Communications Skills Training

Therapist: Cal, I can't help but notice that when you talk to Beth in here, you always refer to her in the third person rather than talking directly to her. Because one of the things that we're working on is direct communication, why don't you try speaking to her directly? (Instructions)

Cal: Okay, like I was saying, she never seems able to . . .

Therapist: (interrupts) You mean Beth?

Cal: Right. Beth never seems able . . . (Rehearsal)

Therapist: No, I want you to speak directly to Beth. (Instructions) Here, let me help. Why don't you look directly at Beth and say to her, "You never seem able to. . . ." All right, let's give that a try. (Modeling)

Cal: Yeah, I think I've got it. Beth, what bothers me is that you never seem able to finish things that you start. You always leave things hanging and then expect me to finish them for you.

Therapist: Okay, Beth, I'm sure you want to get in there and respond, but let me say just a couple of quick things. Cal, that was much better! You looked directly at Beth when you spoke, and that was really excellent. In fact, when you talked to her—that was great. (Reinforcement) However, I did notice that even though you spoke to her directly, she was getting pretty uneasy about what you were saying. Isn't that the case, Beth? (Feedback)

Beth: Definitely. (to Cal) I don't like it when you make those sweeping generalizations.

Therapist: (to Beth) What do you mean? Tell Cal.

Beth: (to Cal) When you say I *never* finish things and *always* leave things for you, that's not true. There are some things that I start and don't finish, but not that many things, and I certainly don't leave everything for you.

Therapist: That's a good point. (Reinforcement) Cal, let's try talking directly to Beth again, but this time, rather than saying "always" and "never," maybe you'd be better off giving her a recent example or two of when this kind of thing has happened. (Coaching)

Cal: Okay. (to Beth) Last week, you started stripping the paint on the bathroom cabinets. You worked on it for about 3 hours Saturday afternoon and then you just left it and you haven't been back to it since. It sure doesn't look like it's going to get done soon and that's the kind of thing that's upsetting to me. (Rehearsal)

Therapist: Good.

Beth: I'm not asking you to finish it.

Cal: No, I didn't say you were.

Beth: Well, you said it before.

Therapist: Yes, but he's not saying that now. All he's saying now is that this job was started and it doesn't look like it's getting done. (to Beth) What do you say?

Beth: He's right.

Therapist: No, you're right. (pointing to Cal; Coaching)

Beth: Oh, yeah, You're right. I could definitely finish it. How about if I do 3 hours tonight and 3 hours on Saturday morning?

Cal: Well, you don't need my approval. I'll just be happy if it doesn't get left undone.

Beth: Okay, you've got my word. I'll finish by this weekend for sure.

Therapist: How do you both feel about that?

Cal/Beth: (Describe their pleasure at being able to settle the issue in a reasonable and efficient manner.)

Therapist: I'd like to give you a little homework, not with respect to getting jobs done, but with respect to communicating directly with one another. You got a real good start on it in here today. Now I want you to go home and make sure that you talk *directly* to one another at least 15 minutes per day, every day, until our next meeting. Can you do that? (Homework)

Cal/Beth: Sure, no problem.

Therapist: All right, but remember, you've got to look directly at one another—none of this third person junk. Plus, so that I can get a good idea of how the conversations went, I want you to keep a little notebook and write down when you talked, what you talked about, and how well you did with respect to talking directly to one another. Okay, can you guys do that?

Cal/Beth: Yup!

Therapist: All right, I'll see you next week, and I'll be real interested in looking at the little notebook along with you.

Source: From Bornstein, P.H. & Bornstein, M.T. (1986). *Marital therapy: A behavioral-communications approach.* New York: Pergamon Press PLC, pp. 88–89. Reprinted with permission.

therefore, may be beneficial to couples if it involves current interaction patterns and individual personality styles (Snyder & Wills, 1989; Boelens et al., 1980).

The integrated marital therapy approach we have summarized places emphasis on changing daily behaviors (caring days), communication analysis, and attitude change. In a summary of over a dozen such therapy studies, Hahlweg (1988) reported that the marital therapy consistently increases marital satisfaction. Most couples coming to marital therapy clinics for treatment are extremely dissatisfied with their marriages. Usually, after four to five months of weekly meetings with a therapist, their relationships show significant improvement: Clients are more satisfied with their relationships, and independent judges listening to their interactions as they attempt to solve problems in the therapeutic environment see improvement. Moreover, husbands and wives who receive marital therapy typically feel more love and caring for their partners (O'Leary & Arias, 1983).

In addition to increasing marital satisfaction, marital therapy's effectiveness is evaluated by assessing

Marital therapy is a form of therapy that has become quite popular in the last decade, and there is a great deal of evidence that it is effective in improving marital satisfaction. Moreover, marital therapy appears to be effective in alleviating some individual psychopathology such as depression.

which couples remain married following therapy. In a study of 320 marital therapy couples five years after treatment, 56 percent remained married if the partners had joint therapy. In contrast, if marital therapy services were provided by consulting with either the husband or wife alone, only 29 percent remained married (Cookerly, 1980). Couples who received no treatment did worse than those who received either couple or individual therapy about the relationship. Remaining married, however, is not an end in itself; partners should feel better about themselves and mentally healthy. In some cases, separation or divorce may be a more desirable outcome than remaining together in a stable but highly unsatisfactory marriage. When partners desire to remain together, marital therapy usually helps them feel better about themselves and the relationship. Moreover, strong evidence exists that increased marital satisfaction results in less depression, anxiety, and fewer other psychological problems (Snyder & Wills, 1989).

INTERVENTION WITH FAMILIES

Families certainly play important roles in our lives from birth until death. According to Freud, our personalities are largely formed by the age of five through interactions with family members. The family is the primary influence on development until adolescence when boyfriends, girlfriends, and peer groups become prominent influences. In late adolescence and early adulthood, we may live apart from our families. Their influence, although more subtle, is still powerful. Whether you smoke, drink, or use drugs is likely to be associated with parental behavior and attitudes. Similarly, whether you work hard in college is partially the result of parental expectations and role models. For some college students, use of the family car, spending money, and cosigning student loans may be contingent upon certain grade-point averages. Later, when people marry, they often model their parents' lifestyles, attitudes, and even the way they fight or avoid arguments. For example, many men who are physically aggressive toward their wives or children observed such behavior in their own families as children.

The central unifying theme of all family therapy is treatment of the family as a whole unit. Family therapy, like marital therapy, can be used by therapists of different theoretical orientations, with the general premise that family issues affect us all at points in our lives.

Two prominent approaches to family intervention are family systems therapy and problem-solving therapy. Family systems approaches see each individual family member as part of a dynamic system. Thus, if one family member's behavior changes, the whole system of family relationships can change. The family system as a whole becomes the target of therapy. Problem-solving approaches have somewhat more focused goals than structural (systems) family therapy. While both approaches treat the family as a whole, changes in communication or behavior for a dyad (mother–daughter) or individual (e.g., a child or teen-ager) are acceptable goals for problem-solving therapy. Structural approaches, on the other hand, generally attempt to alter the entire family system and avoid efforts to change only one individual.

FAMILY THERAPY

Family Systems Therapy

In **family systems therapy**—the most common approach to treating families—therapists see the family as a coherent system in which each member has a major role. Therefore, therapists try to see all members of the family for assessment and treatment. The relationships among family members are emphasized more than individual family members' specific difficulties. Rather than viewing an aggressive child as the "problem" and treating him or her alone, every family member is expected to attend treatment sessions because the child may be reflecting pathology within the family unit or system. According to family therapists, the problems do not simply flow from one person to another (e.g., from parent to child), but all family members, even children, influence the other children as well as their parents in complex ways. For example, therapists recognize problem children's impact on individual parents and on the marital relationship.

The particular roles that family members determine for each other influence their mental health. A mother who defines herself and is defined by other family members as the children's caretaker often begins to have certain problems when the children "leave the nest." For example, she might feel unimportant or unwanted. It's likely that she would attempt to find new roles within the family, for example, as a result of entering the work force. Family therapists avoid blaming any particular individual for shaping the mother's role. They emphasize instead that everyone in the family has shaped the mother's role across many years. This is why the therapist may ask all the family members to join the therapy sessions should the mother decide to change her role within the family. Even a mother of college students may need help in changing the expectations for her "adult" children. For example, although she may have taken a job after her children entered college, "Mom" may still be expected to be responsible for all household tasks (cleaning, cooking, laundry, and vacation plans). While she may still enjoy these tasks, she may resent having to bear so many responsibilities unaided by her husband and children.

Structures define boundaries separating parents and children. Such boundaries often become blurred when two family members from different generations form a tight bond and exclude another member. For example, both a mother and a son may harbor resentment against the husband (father) for his temper outbursts and physical abuse of the son. The mother and son then form an alliance excluding the husband

Family counseling is often used to help families cope with parent and adolescent conflicts. It enables a therapist to teach families to use a problem solving approach to address their problems, and it provides a therapist with the opportunity to assess interaction patterns that impede effective communication.

(father) in a coalition against a common "enemy." In turn, the father feels more alienated, defensive, and unsupported, becoming easily angered. The system becomes stable, having a life of its own. Another frequently described structure problem occurs when parents are locked in intense conflict. In an effort to take the heat off themselves, they draw a third member—usually a child—into their system by making him or her a target of criticism; that is, a "scapegoat." Instead of addressing problems between themselves, Mom and Dad yell at their son for minor things (not picking up toys, teasing friends) and provide inconsistent discipline. The parents blame the son for their own frustration and fights, and thus avoid addressing difficult conflicts between themselves.

Regardless of the difficulties, it should now be clear that a family therapist tries to make the family the unit of change even though one family member may have been seen by the others as the problem. Family therapists employ a wide variety of particular strategies. The type of family therapy we will discuss first is called **structural family therapy.** Many people have contributed importantly to this approach's development: Salvadore Minuchin and Virginia Satir are recognized as two important pioneers in this field.

Structural Family Therapy Strategies.

Reframing. Reframing means conceptualizing a problem in a new way. If you sought help from a family therapist, he or she would ask you and each family member to get a new picture, or a new framing, of the problems existing within the family. The therapist would reframe individual problems as family problems, removing blame from the person seen as causing or having the problem. Even though one family member may be hurting the most psychologically, he or she will not be the focus of the family therapy. The general purpose of reframing is to lessen the negative views or attributions that individuals have about the person usually identified as the problem. For example, the therapist may reframe an adolescent's anger and acting out as expressions of insecurity, not hostility. The focus might shift to opening lines of communication and support rather than controlling the teen-ager's behavior through punishment. A wife's refusal to stop looking for a job may be reframed as a need for self-development, not as a desire to become independent or distant from the family.

Validation. Validation refers to the therapist expressing understanding of individual family members' feelings and desires (Satir, 1967). In doing this, the therapist serves as a model—teaching family members to validate each other's feelings. This kind of understanding is necessary before change is prompted or encouraged. Unfortunately, parents often "lower the boom" with rules and restrictions before they even hear or perhaps validate why their children may not have been doing what was expected of them.

Communication. In family therapy, the therapist provides guidelines for communicating with "I feel" statements. Many problems arise when family members assume they know each other's feelings and desires. This is called *mind-reading,* and often results in communicating "You feel" or "You make me . . ." statements blaming others for the way we feel. For example, a college sophomore has been fighting with his parents and makes this statement during a session: "Both of you think I am a lazy bum, sponging off you, drinking and sleeping until noon when my classes start." Instead of expressing his own anger or resentment directly, he blames his parents for his feelings and assumes he knows what they feel. With the therapist's help, he then rephrases his remarks: "I have been angry because I have the feeling that you believe I blow off my studies and stay out drinking. You should know that I work until 3:00 or 4:00 A.M. in the local pizza joint." As you can see, the rephrased statement avoids mind-reading what his parents think and feel. Instead of forcing his parents to respond defensively, the rephrasing makes their response more likely to be empathetic.

A second communication guideline involves "fair fighting" exercises. These specify times when members can vent or release their feelings. During these periods, one person may be a "yeller" while the other family members remain "listeners."

The therapist also teaches each family member to analyze why he or she hears certain messages sent by other members in ways that may have been unintended. The therapist asks them to distinguish between the intent of these messages and the impact of them.

Paradoxical Directives. One of the most complex and unusual strategies of structural family therapy prescribes that clients do *more* of what they describe as the problem. For example, if an adolescent runs away to get away from a stepfather, and if the parents' frequent attempts to get her back have been unsuccessful, the therapist urges that any changes proceed very slowly. Indeed, the therapist may suggest that the parents do more of what they have felt led her to stay away. For example, the therapist may say:

> I suggest that you proceed very cautiously and slowly in attempting to work out this problem with Sue and get her back in the house. Besides being another change to contend with, my biggest concern is that Sue be forced back before she is really ready. This, of course, would result in another blow-up and another runaway, which, as you know would be a difficult situation to deal with. . . . For these reasons, I am

> requesting that you make no attempt with the courts or Sue to get her back. Please hold back and do very little on this issue. (Duncan, 1989, p. 318)

Fortunately, the parents in large part followed this direction to proceed very slowly. They stopped pressuring Sue and the courts. However, they did ask her to attend a family picnic, and to their surprise, she did—and she was quite pleasant. In turn, the therapist expressed concern that they were moving a bit too quickly for his own comfort.

Salvadore Minuchin, a noted family therapist, used this strategy in planning a therapy session with the family of a thirteen-year-old anorexic. The girl and her parents, brothers, and sisters attended the session. Minuchin suggested that the family have lunch so that he could observe their relationships to each other.

> Dr. Minuchin: *I don't think that we have any problem with Laura's eating—she will eat. At the point at which you are 14, Laura, you will eat without any problems. . . . But I think that it is good that you are not eating now, because I think that what is happening is that this is the only area in your family, Laura, in which you have a say-so. And at 14 you'll need to have a say-so in another way. . . . What about—there are some other things, Laura, about which you have a say-so? . . . Around food, at least you can fight. You can say, "That's my body, and that's what I want to eat." Isn't that what you are saying?*
>
> Laura: *Um hmm.* (Aponte & Hoffman, 1973, p. 525)

Instead of forcing the anorexic girl to eat, Minuchin tried to help her feel in control of some part of her life other than eating. The therapist organized the entire family in Laura's presence, giving her permission and even suggesting that she should not eat. In this directive, there is also an implicit directive for Laura's family to "get off her back" for not eating. To many clients' surprise, the intended effect of these **paradoxical directives,** when chosen carefully, is removing the patient's need to have the problem (such as not eating or fighting). The paradoxical directives have been especially effective with resistant teen-agers and young adults, particularly with procrastination, insomnia, and nail biting (Lopez & Wambach, 1982).

As yet, structural family therapy approaches have not been as rigorously evaluated as have other treatments, such as marital and individual therapies. However, they have proven effective when a family member has a drug abuse problem. For example, Stanton & Todd (1982) evaluated family therapy as a supplement to the standard drug treatment program in a Veterans Administration Hospital. The standard drug treatment program consisted of detoxification and methadone maintenance, drug counseling, and occupational therapy. At six months posttreatment, the subjects who received the standard program plus structural family therapy were more likely to be employed and less likely to be using drugs as compared to the standard treatment group.

Initial reviews of family therapy suggested that 65 percent to 76 percent of all clients show improvements (Gurman & Kniskern, 1978; Wells & Dezen, 1978). These reviews, however, often used case studies and the therapies were not compared with control groups. Therefore, the studies provide only suggestive evidence of family therapy's effectiveness (Ganahl, Ferguson, & L'Abate, 1985). On the other hand, a recent study by Markus, Lange, and Pettigrew (1990) provided statistical evidence that family therapy with a diversity of problems was more effective than an alternative treatment (often individual psychotherapy), a minimal treatment, or no treatment. Further, their data suggested that family therapy had better results ten months after treatment than the alternative treatments, though the effects were quite variable across studies. Another review of family therapy with delinquents indicated that it is the treatment of choice with such problems (Todd & Stanton, 1983).

Evaluating the effectiveness of family systems therapy is more difficult than evaluating individual therapy. In addition to assessing improvement in the "patient," the whole family and their complex interactions have to be considered. Compounding this situation, different theoretical ideas within family systems therapy imply different focuses for change in the family system. For these reasons, comprehensive evaluation of this type of therapy awaits the development and widespread acceptance of adequate ways to measure change (Vincent & Carter, 1987).

Problem-Solving Approaches

Another treatment approach directed at changing families is problem solving. Robin and Foster (1988) reviewed problem-solving treatments for families with parent–adolescent conflict and found them useful in changing communication patterns, parental reports of problem behaviors by the adolescent, and adolescent reports of parental hostility and criticism. Problem-solving treatment has somewhat more focused goals than structural family therapy does, though both approaches view the family as the unit to change. Changing communication and reducing problem behavior by either the parent or the adolescent are acceptable goals for problem solving while structural family therapy attempts to alter the entire family system. Problem-solving approaches are built upon the base of structural family therapy but particularly emphasize problem solving and communication. Problem-solving approaches consist of these four basic phases:

1. Defining the problem.
2. Generating alternative solutions to the defined problem before family members criticize solutions (sometimes called **brainstorming**).
3. Evaluating the alternative solutions.
4. Implementing the best available solutions.

The therapist uses his or her clinical skill to help the family reduce intense emotional conflicts through problem solving. For example, a couple may tell the therapist that their problem is their teen-age daughter's being misled by her boyfriend. The father may quickly and hostilely add, "I think the guy is a waste." The daughter may then retort, "He is no more a waste than you when you came home drunk from your pool party and swore at Mom."

At this point, the therapist quickly intervenes to stop the escalating argument and helps the family obtain insight into their dysfunctional communication patterns. In this case, for example, the therapist may point out the father's and daughter's tendency to trade criticisms without defining problems or looking for solutions. Then he or she may help the parents discover what really concerns them about their daughter (her coming home late or failing to do homework; their fear that she is having sex). The therapist also tries to define the problem from the daughter's vantage point (e.g., "Mom and Dad don't treat my boyfriend with respect; they don't even say hello to him when he comes to pick me up; they are critical of his home").

Problem-solving therapies with families have helped to improve the functioning and social skills of depressed and schizophrenic patients (see Chapters 7 and 14). In one family therapy intervention, Falloon and associates (1985) treated the schizophrenic patient as merely one member of a family unit. They emphasized that the schizophrenic patient was not necessarily seen as the most handicapped, and the patient's needs were treated within the context of the whole family system. Families were trained to problem solve in a structured manner of outlining a number of possible solutions, agreeing on a solution, and making detailed plans to implement the solution. When communication problems became apparent during the problem solving, the therapist gave communication skills special attention.

Consider the following discussion of evaluating alternative solutions that a therapist had with Mr. and Mrs. Kasper and their schizophrenic son, Jim (Falloon et al., 1985).

Therapist: *Mrs. Kasper, I would like you to go through the list of alternatives now and to discuss the pros and cons of each possible solution.*

Mrs. Kasper: *Well, the first suggestion was that Jim might go to the church social group Friday evenings.*

Mr. Kasper: *Well, it's free and it's a nice group of Christian, single people.*

Jim: *Yeah, I'd get to meet some people. Probably girls go there.*

Mrs. Kasper: *They plan a lot of different activities that are interesting.*

Therapist: *What do you see as possible drawbacks?*

Jim: *It's a religious group. I'm not into religion myself. But you probably see it differently, Mom.*

Mrs. Kasper: *It might not have a lot of people your age. You know it might be older folks.*

Therapist: *I'd like you to summarize the advantages and drawbacks of that solution, Jim.*

Jim: *The good points in favor are its cheapness and there may be girls there. Against that is the religion, and maybe it's for older people.* (Falloon et al., p. 273)

Family therapy interventions have been used successfully by mental health professionals of varying orientations in aiding schizophrenic patients' families. Because schizophrenic patients usually receive medication as well, the therapist discusses with the family the nature of schizophrenia and the need for antipsychotic medication. Common to many successful programs are the key elements of giving the families information about the nature of the disorder, aiding them in coping with the schizophrenic's problems, and decreasing the intensity of family conflict (Golstein, 1984). In several studies combining family therapy with medication, approximately 10 percent of those treated were readmitted to the hospital within nine months after treatment. In contrast, control groups receiving individual supportive therapy and medication have rehospitalization rates of approximately 50 percent (Golstein, 1984).

Integration of Family Systems and Behavior Therapy Approaches

Sometimes behavior therapy strategies are more effective when combined with family therapies. As early as 1973, Alexander and Parsons developed a "systems-behavioral" approach in dealing with delinquent children and their families. Their model evolved from a behavioral perspective with an emphasis on parental disciplinary strategies, and it has become a dominant force in integrating various therapeutic perspectives (Alexander et al., 1988). The systems perspective added the view that the delinquent and his or her parents were actively trying to change or influence each other. For example, the delinquent attempted to control his or her parents by engaging in delinquent behaviors and, therefore, would resist attempts to change those behaviors. The systems perspective urged the therapist to help families identify the function or value of the problematic and adaptive behaviors within the family context. Family value systems were explored in depth along with ways in which the family might become a more cohesive supportive unit. Finally, special emphasis is placed on bidirectional influences within the family; that is, on the way adults and children influence each other. Patterson (1975), a behavior therapist who has also incorporated family therapy or family systems views into his conceptualizations, argued that children who display deviant behavior are the *victims* as well as the *architects* of their situations. Behaviorally based approaches which incorporate family systems concepts, effectively change aggressive and delinquent children's behavior (Alexander, Mas, & Waldron, 1988; O'Leary & Wilson, 1985).

Interventions combining family systems and behavioral approaches are likely to become increasingly useful. For some problems, each approach appears to change different behavior or attitude domains. Consider a comparison of three different family treatments for child abuse and neglect: (1) behaviorally based parent training programs, (2) family systems approaches, and (3) an integration of the behavioral parent training and family systems approaches. Parent training was more effective in reducing children's specific social problems whereas systems therapy was more effective in restructuring parent–child relations. However, families receiving both therapies showed these benefits as well as reduced overall stress and parental psychiatric problems (Brunk, Henggler, & Whelan, 1987). The integrative approach used by Alexander (1988) combines the cognitive approach, the behavioral approach, and the family systems concepts discussed earlier. This integrative approach makes excellent sense since we know that changing attitudes, specific behaviors, and family interactions are the three factors which appear to most aid families of delinquents (Garrett, 1985).

SOCIAL THERAPIES

Patients suffering from depression, alcoholism, and obesity have traditionally been treated by individual therapy, but they also can be helped by participating in a therapeutic group or community. Group approaches range from small groups for individuals with clinical problems to large-scale community education projects designed to change behavior or to prevent psychological and physical problems. Well-known group approaches now established throughout the world include Alcoholics Anonymous, Weight Watchers, and Gamblers Anonymous. Daytop Village and Phoenix House, residential programs for drug addiction, are also based on the group approach. Although these programs all treat addictive problems, group approaches are employed for almost every psychological problem. For example, groups exist for assertion training, parent training, and couple communication; there are also support groups for coping with diseases such as cancer and kidney failure and self-help groups for former mental patients. Therapeutic communities or communities for people with mental disorders focus on changing attitudes and behavior by group expectation and pressure. Finally, during the 1960s and 1970s, many group approaches like Erhard Seminar Training (EST) developed; these groups encouraged people to get in touch with their inner feelings in beautiful settings like the Big Sur Beach in California. Because of their rapid expansion, EST groups became franchised throughout the United States.

According to one survey, more Americans participate in some form of group therapy, including mutual aid or support groups such as AA, than in any other type of therapy. Approximately 5 percent of Americans have participated in mutual aid groups, 6 percent in group therapy sessions conducted by a mental health professional, and 5 percent in group therapy conducted by a member of the clergy [*Harvard Medical School Mental Health Letter* (1989)].

Why are group therapies so popular? One explanation is that fewer professionals are able to treat more problems at less cost. Also, group approaches have been designed to cope with those problems difficult or almost impossible to treat individually. In general, an individual therapist cannot generate as much pressure to change as the type of mutual support provided by other group members. Moreover, a single therapist can never achieve the type of pressure to change behavior that can be harnessed by working with a whole community. Sometimes merely being with others dealing with the same problems offers comfort an individual therapist cannot provide. Finally, community efforts to change behaviors such as cigarette smoking or dieting habits are much more efficient than attempts to change individuals. The types of social therapies covered in this section include Alcoholics Anonymous, Weight Watchers, therapeutic communities, community psychology and change, and prevention. The chapter progresses from groups to therapeutic communities to the larger community.

Alcoholics Anonymous

Alcoholics Anonymous (AA) has treated alcoholics throughout the world for decades. In the United

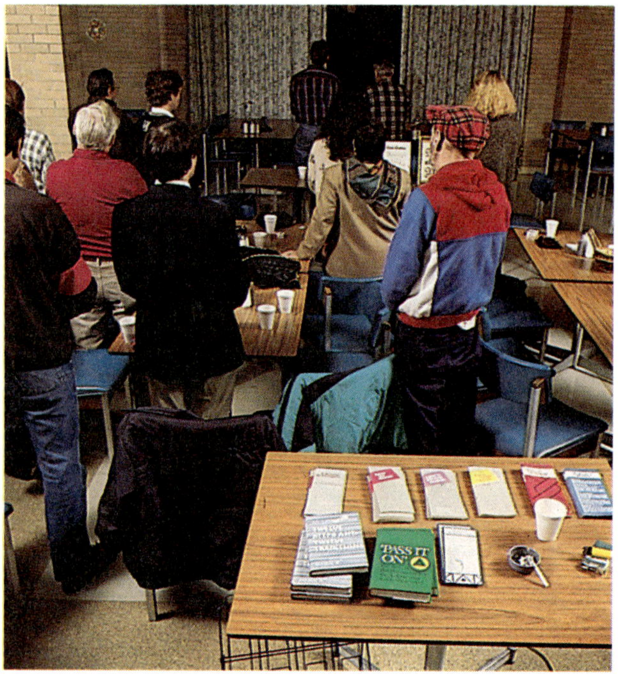

Alcoholics Anonymous is a very effective support group for millions of alcoholics across the world. The group meetings involve self-disclosure (telling one's story) and a focus on accepting the position that there is a higher Power that influences them and can help them remain sober. As seen here, prayer may also be part of the meeting.

States, AA programs are available within thirty miles of almost any citizen. Alcoholics Anonymous (AA) is a social therapy that relies on a group therapy approach and a "buddy system" (see Chapter 11). This involves support and encouragement from a "buddy," a member of AA who has been able to remain sober for some time. Two men from Akron, Ohio, Dr. Bob and Bill W., founded the organization in 1935. A sense of spiritual change had helped Bill recover from alcoholism, and he then helped Dr. Bob to recover. In turn, they both sought to help other alcoholics by starting an organization that has grown to over several million members. AA's basic aim is abstinence, helping to prevent alcoholics from taking a single drink. Meetings involve having members "tell their story," describing how life was while they were dependent on alcohol and how life is without it. First names are used to preserve anonymity, and much of the meetings are spent on problem-focused discussions about how to resist drinking alcohol. AA members are encouraged to accept most, if not all, of the twelve-step program (see Chapter 11). Most importantly, it is essential to admit that alcohol use has become impossible to control and to be able to say: "I am an alcoholic."

AA provides four critical treatment ingredients (Valliant, 1988). First, it offers a substitute for drinking at the barroom because unlike a clinic, AA has hours that compete with barroom hours. Members can usually find an AA meeting every evening near their home and can also attend them on weekends and holidays, the most stressful time for many recovering alcoholics. Second, AA makes it clear that alcoholics delude themselves into thinking they can drink; it serves as a conscience by reminding members they should not drink. Third, by belonging to a group of abstinent individuals, members alleviate loneliness in a setting where they are not made to feel guilty, as often occurs in the presence of family. Many AA groups hold social events such as dances without alcohol. Fourth, sober people who have successfully coped with their desire to have alcohol serve as role models that enhance members' self-worth through identifying with the model.

AA's effects are difficult to ascertain because many members drop out of the program and subsequently may or may not remain sober. For alcoholics who remain in the program for two years, about 50 percent are abstinent, 15 percent drink lightly to moderately, and about 13 percent drink abusively (Alford, 1980). Approximately 20 percent of the groups could not be contacted; thus it is impossible to determine AA's exact success rates. Nonetheless, it clearly helps thousands of people throughout the world daily. It gives members constant social support for resisting that first drink, and for many, it provides an alternative social network to the bar scene formerly used as a base for their social life.

Weight Watchers

Weight Watchers was founded in 1963 to provide support and structure for people wishing to lose weight. Approximately half a million people belong to chapters throughout the world. The program stresses a positive group environment, nutritionally balanced diets, and behaviorally oriented techniques to control eating and the emotions leading to overeating. Participants are also encouraged to exercise more by engaging in natural activities such as climbing stairs and walking.

Studies have attempted to identify the most important elements of Weight Watchers by having participants evaluate difficult parts of the program. Members' responses indicated that the weekly weigh-in with others present combined with a discussion of progress or setbacks was the program's most critical ingredient. Participants felt peer support was next in importance. In fact, they did not want the program to be run by professionals nor did they want their spouses to attend (Stunkard, 1980).

Evaluating Weight Watchers' effectiveness is difficult because it is a commercial operation which does not subject itself to standard experimental testing. Nevertheless, several large-scale surveys of thou-

Weight Watchers is a program involving dietary change, attitude change, behavior modification, group support, and the periodic and public monitoring of weight, as seen here.

sands of participants in the program in Australia (Williams & Duncan, 1976) and the United States (Stuart, 1979) indicate that people who continue with the program and the weekly weigh-in lose, on the average, approximately 10 kilograms, or about twenty-five pounds, across a thirty-week period. Indeed, when compared to psychotherapy groups for weight loss, these findings were so promising that the authors of the surveys questioned if mental health professionals should even be involved routinely in treating obesity. Like most programs for addictive problems, relapse appears high for Weight Watchers participants though formal evaluation of relapse rates is unavailable.

Therapeutic Communities

Historically, **therapeutic communities** arose out of community dissatisfaction with the limitations of traditional hospital treatments for the mentally ill. One of the first therapeutic communities was begun in 1792 by William Tuke, a Quaker tea and coffee merchant, after a patient died mysteriously in an English hospital where patients were often chained or manacled. Tuke's approach called moral treatment emphasized treating an individual in his or her social environment where character qualities were emphasized. He was highly suspicious of treatment offered by "experts." Tuke offered his patients a retreat where they were treated as normally as possible and assigned as many responsibilities as they could handle. Patients lived in a family style environment and were encouraged to develop a routine participating in a variety of chores; they gardened, farmed, and did housework. Restraints and restrictions were used only when patients displayed extremely aggressive or self-destructive behaviors. Taking their minds off their problems was curative. Attendants, instead of physicians, were seen as the primary care givers. In choosing attendants, Tuke emphasized personal qualities such as kindness, caring, and "upright character" (Kennard, 1983).

Records from the late 1800s suggest the moral treatment approach was quite successful. In fact, increasing pressure was placed on the British parliament to build new asylums. The 200-patient limit set by Tuke was gradually increased to 300, 500, then 1,000. The increasing numbers of patients, and a subsequent legal requirement that kept all but the most incurable out of mental hospitals, effectively ended the moral treatment of patients. With only the most severely disturbed individuals in overcrowded hospitals, moral treatment was unable to help them, and this treatment approach waned.

In the 1950s and 1960s, however, a tremendous dissatisfaction arose concerning patients' apathy and listlessness in most hospital wards. Goffman (1961) showed that patients learned to become dependent and docile, taking on what he called "sick roles." Some critics even asserted that hospitals taught patients to become mentally incompetent so they would remain in them. These criticisms became so powerful that a new therapeutic community approach emerged with many similarities to Tuke's moral treatment used in the 1800s.

Residential therapeutic communities generally revolve around regular meetings in a homelike atmosphere. Everyone shares in the work of running the community. Patients, or clients, are on an equal footing with staff members in their ability to influence the behavior of other community members. Part of the therapeutic community's effectiveness lies in its ongoing influence. A great deal of therapy occurs during unofficial meetings and leisure activities. Therapeutic communities differ in their therapeutic emphasis: Some favor active confrontation whereas others simply focus on the patient's responsibility for his or her behavior.

The therapeutic community approach became a model for many halfway houses. A halfway house is a facility for individuals released from a hospital or other treatment program who need more supervision and monitoring than their homes and families can provide. Thus, as the term **halfway house** implies, the individual is halfway between the hospital and home. Halfway houses are usually located in large private residences within a community. Discharged patients sleep and eat in the halfway house and are supervised by one or two people, often a husband and wife, living at the residence. Well-run halfway houses provide skill training in a number of areas. The staff help clients learn to develop and maintain daily routines such as cleaning, meal preparation, and laundry, and they also help them with school and/or job problems. Finally, even after a return to one's family, follow-up from the halfway house staff is often necessary.

If there is adequate community follow-up for individuals placed in halfway houses or group homes, these group approaches are effective in facilitating mental patients' return to the community (Fairweather, Sanders, Maynard, & Cressler, 1969). Compared to standard hospital after-care, halfway houses for mental patients result in less frequent readmittance to mental hospitals and more employment (Fairweather et al., 1969). Whatever effectiveness can be demonstrated, establishing halfway houses is no easy task. Groundwork with local leaders is critical to meet the often intense opposition from neighbors or community members. Remarks like these are common: "The value of my house will drop immediately." "I don't want crazies near my kids." "If they want to house mental patients in communities, let 'em do it somewhere else."

Community Psychology and Change

Therapeutic communities and group approaches such as AA and Weight Watchers focus primarily on changing problematic behavior or conditions. In contrast, community psychology efforts attempt to prevent problems and to teach new skills (Heller & Monahan, 1977). Community psychology developed in the 1960s and 1970s simultaneously with an increased awareness of racial discrimination and poverty's significant contributions to the development of psychological problems. The federal government's "War on Poverty" led by Presidents John Kennedy and Lyndon Johnson was the government's response to this awareness. The ambitious War on Poverty consisted of programs, such as Head Start, which used federal monies to prevent or ameliorate human suffering through broad-scale social interventions to teach academic and social skills to preschool and elementary school children. Private industry was influenced by this atmosphere of social change and programs. For example, *Sesame Street*, an educational television program, was sponsored by many private industries through public television.

More recently, community programs have been offered with television programs and commercials to foster health-promoting behaviors, such as eating properly, exercising, and quitting smoking, in an attempt to reduce the risk of cardiovascular problems. Similarly, police arrests for spouse abuse are a relatively recent strategy designed to prevent and reduce family violence at the community and city level.

TABLE 17.2 Strategies for Change: A Teaching Orientation

Size of Group	Goals of Intervention	
	Maintain "Healthy" Life through Skill Building and Education	Provide Support and Teach Coping Skills for Specific Problems
Individual or small group	1. Well-baby clinics 2. Parent effectiveness training 3. Skill building (athletics, public speaking, etc.)	1. Support groups for physically abused women 2. Assertiveness training groups 3. Support groups for homosexuals
Organizational	1. Sex-education classes in schools 2. Television programs to teach reading and language skills, such as *Sesame Street*	1. Halfway houses for former mental patients 2. Group style living homes for delinquents 3. Shelter services for battered women
Community	1. Community development programs to teach proper eating and dieting habits 2. Fostering support networks 3. Anticipatory guidance through communitywide media	1. Providing legal services for indigent women to obtain divorce 2. Job banks for displaced workers

Source: Adapted from Heller, K., & Monahan, J. (1977). *Psychology and community change.* Homewood, Ill.: The Dorsey Press, p. 18. Reprinted by permission.

These arrest programs serve as a deterrent or warning to men who might physically abuse their spouse that an arrest would occur should they engage in physically violent action (Sherman & Berk, 1984).

Community interventions often were designed to promote competencies rather than to remedy long-standing deficits or problems. As Table 17.2 indicates, community interventions can include various numbers of people extending from small groups, such as parents to organizations like police departments or entire communities.

Another major impetus for community interventions was dissatisfaction with psychotherapy in the 1940s and 1950s. At that time very little evidence existed of psychotherapy's success (Eysenck, 1961). Even if certain types of psychotherapy were found to be helpful, many individuals could not afford the treatment, often lasting a year or more. In the 1960s, many began to feel that effective psychotherapy was limited to clients described as YAVIS: young, attractive, verbal, intelligent, and successful (Schofield, 1964). In addition, traditional therapies treated existing problems rather than preventing problems. In contrast, community efforts can reach people from all economic and racial groups, with the potential to prevent problems before they develop.

Prevention

As reflected in our discussion of community approaches, prevention has been a major focus of community psychologists. It can take various forms. **Primary prevention** is designed to reduce the occurrence of new problems in a population; **secondary prevention** is intended to help detect problems early in their onset and to reduce their intensity; and **tertiary prevention** is designed to reduce a problem's long-term consequences.

Basically, primary prevention focuses on education. One primary prevention program (see Chapter 4) developed by a team of Stanford University researchers consisted of television and radio broadcasts, newspaper announcements and stories—all designed to help people reduce cholesterol intake, exercise more, and stop smoking. Signs and posters placed in major supermarkets reminded shoppers which foods were high in cholesterol and low in calories. Smoking, cholesterol intake, and lack of exercise were chosen because they are known cardiovascular risk factors; that is, they increase the likelihood of an individual developing heart disease. Two California towns, Watsonville and Gilroy, were targeted for the two-year experimental intervention; a third California town, Tracy, was selected as a control because it was separated by a mountain range which blocked radio and television broadcasts from the other towns. At the end of two years, researchers reported that citizens of the two experimental towns showed significantly reduced blood pressure and egg consumption whereas the citizens of the control town did not. Further, on a measure of cardiovascular risk based on exercise, nonsmoking, and cholesterol levels, citizens of the experimental towns significantly improved in contrast to citizens of the control town. The results demonstrate an important reduction in factors contributing to heart disease. The experiment also illustrates the power of harnessing community resources to address a major health problem potentially affecting thousands of residents (Maccoby & Alexander, 1980).

Secondary prevention programs attempt to detect problems early on in order to prevent their further escalation. One example is the diversion program approach for juvenile offenders. Because rehabilitation within the juvenile justice system has not proven successful, this approach attempts to steer adolescents

BOX 17.2 Spouse Abuse: A Call for Primary Prevention

Let us consider the need for community level interventions and primary prevention by looking at another social issue. Spouse abuse can be treated with a combination of individual and marital therapy. However, physical aggression toward a partner occurs in at least 25 percent of all college dating couples and in almost half of engaged couples (O'Leary et al., 1989). Physical aggression, in extreme forms called spouse abuse, occurs in about 10 percent of all couples in the United States (Straus, Gelles, & Steinmetz, 1980). With a problem so pervasive, attitudes of men toward hitting women (and vice versa) need to be changed at an age when dating starts regularly (e.g., high school and college). Men's perceived need for power is of considerable importance. Many men become aggressive when their power or control seems threatened. In addition, it is now well known that a cycle of violence exists across generations; those who observe their parents hit each other or who are themselves abused as children are more likely to engage in physical aggression with their own partners as adults. Unfortunately, by the time spouse abuse issues are addressed by therapists, who are dealing with long histories of physical abuse, therapy often comes too late. Thus, primary prevention efforts directed at teenagers and young adults to help them establish relationships free from violence are greatly needed.

BOX 17.3 Tertiary Prevention for AIDS Victims

The potential for tertiary prevention is seen in the case of a young boy, Ryan White, who contracted AIDS through a blood transfusion. He was subsequently prevented from attending the Western Middle School in Kokomo, Indiana, because of protests by parents, children, and the school board. The school felt they had a responsibility to protect the children against any potential risk presented by Ryan White. Three hundred parents attended a meeting in August 1985, and many signed a petition to be used in a lawsuit against Western Schools should Ryan White be admitted to school in the fall. In turn, the school board president at Western Schools, Mr. Daniel Carter, declared: "We would be negligent [to admit Ryan White]. They [the Health Department] can carry out their tests somewhere else" (Kirp et al., 1989, p. 38).

Despite a prognosis that Ryan would not live, his mother, undaunted, moved to another school district, Hamilton Heights High School in Arcadia, Indiana, where the school and community were willing to accept Ryan. A whole community mobilized to reduce the pain and psychological suffering of this one boy. Under the direction of Mr. Tony Cook, then principal at Hamilton Heights, and with the assistance of Dr. Bob Carnal, superintendent of schools, the community residents developed a program for Ryan that would be used as a model by other communities skeptical of dealing with an AIDS victim in their midst. Their plan was threefold:

Ryan White, and AIDS victim, is here accepted in the school in Arcadia, Indiana, where he studies algebra. Unfortunately, his previous school in Kokomo, Indiana, fought a legal battle to keep him out of school. He became a national hero before he died in the spring of his senior year in high school.

1. Education of School Personnel

They educated the teaching staff and had the State Board of Health assist in addressing questions like: What is AIDS? How is it contracted? Is it communicable? How does one manage an accident if a child with AIDS starts bleeding? A plan was formed to deal with many possible problems that might occur relating to Ryan (Kirp et al., 1989)

2. Inform the School Board and the Public

Anticipating some parental resistance, the school superintendent informed the public about the school's plan to deal with all possible problems that might occur with Ryan attending the Hamilton Heights Schools.

3. Inform the Students

Before school opened in the fall, Ryan's mother was asked to delay Ryan's school entry for three days to allow the school administration time to prepare the students for his arrival. Mr. Cook, the principal, gathered the students into the gym and informed them of the plans to accept Ryan into the school. On the second day, he had representatives of the State Health Department available to instruct and answer students' questions regarding AIDS. Again, they dealt with questions such as, What is AIDS? How is AIDS communicated? How would school personnel handle an accident if Ryan were bleeding? What are the implications of casual contact? To many people's pleasant surprise, the students rallied for parental support and they got it.

Ryan's enrollment was covered by local and national television. The Hamilton Heights Schools had their own cause, and they were determined to show the world that an AIDS victim could live happily with other students. The day of Ryan's enrollment came, and it went extremely well. Moreover, despite the initial dismal medical prognosis, Ryan completed several years at Hamilton Heights High School while in reasonably good health. Unfortunately, he died in the spring of his senior year. (Nov. 1990) away from jail or juvenile detention facilities. **Diversion programs** help adolescents avoid the harmful effect of being labeled a juvenile delinquent. In one study of diversion programs (Davidson et al., 1987), subjects were primarily male teen-age offenders arrested for stealing and breaking and entering. College students worked one-on-one with each juvenile offender for six to eight hours per week over the course of several months, helping him learn communication skills and use community resources such as job placement and recreational services. The results were impressive: The young men diverted from the juvenile court systems were significantly less likely to engage in delinquent acts than those who were part of the normal court processing method. Typically, courts would place these teen-agers in a juvenile detention facility or simply put them on probation for a fixed period, often without any systematic help for the juvenile or his family.

Diversion efforts are a form of social therapy emphasizing early detection and intervention to reduce unlawful behavior. These efforts clearly hold promise for preventing crime in adulthood but early detection and intervention are, nevertheless, very difficult. It is impossible to answer the general question, "Does diversion work?" Some programs do and some don't. However, programs that teach new academic, vocational and social skills seem the most promising for youthful offenders (Davidson, Gensheimer, Gottschalk, & Mayer, 1987).

Tertiary prevention, designed to reduce long-term consequences of a problem, is exemplified by programs helping mental patients get back into the community or helping former mental patients cope with problems. A number of these programs teach social skills both in the hospital and after discharge (Fairweather et al., 1969; Paul & Lentz, 1978). One of these classic studies (Fairweather et al., 1969) showed that chronic schizophrenics can learn living skills enabling them to return to the community. The posthospital care took place in small communal living arrangements with staff supervision called lodges. The staff helped the patients become integrated into the community in many ways, often serving as spokespersons for lodge members with community organizations. For example, the staff members helped the former patients secure jobs in the community by arranging trial job periods in which the patients worked without pay to prove their worth to industry. The lodges can provide excellent service to former mental patients who may otherwise become part of our cities' homeless population. For patients who eventually return home, the lodges function as halfway houses. Moreover, they were developed to deal with discharged patients who had no families to accept them. For them, the lodges became their homes.

Recovery, Inc. is a mutual help group for individuals with mental disorders, many of whom have been in psychiatric hospitals. It is a voluntary self-help nonprofit organization with over 900 chapters in the United States. Members do not discuss medication or psychotherapy even if they are receiving one or both of these treatments from a professional. Instead, they try to identify negative attitudes that cause their problems—the approach suggested by the organization's founder. An evaluation of the program indicated that members generally felt much better since joining the self-help organization. Specifically, over 80 percent said they felt tense and depressed before they participated in the groups sponsored by Recovery, Inc.; after joining, only 10 percent had such feelings. Furthermore, members were much less depressed and anxious than randomly selected nonmembers who had been coping with mental disorders (Galanter, 1988).

Recovery, Inc.'s key ingredient is group cohesion in a context of teaching practical skills for coping with mental problems. Any group which has strong cohesion and sometimes even religious zeal has certain followers who become fanatic about the group. However, if one has a cause which serves a positive function, such as preventing rehospitalization, the fervor or zeal about the group is usually a small price to pay for sanity.

MEDICAL THERAPIES

In the chapters on specific disorders, we briefly discussed various biological means of changing behavior such as the use of antianxiety and antidepressant medication. We will now discuss these attempts to alter behavior by changing the patient's biochemical makeup. Various medications' general effects are discussed because they are effective for a variety of different disorders, not only for a specific problem. For example, antidepressant medication is used to treat depression, anxiety, and obsessive-compulsive disorders. We will also discuss such issues as "Do patients have the right to refuse electroconvulsive treatment?" or "Why is medication prescribed more often for women than for men to alter their feelings and behavior?" Tables are provided of the commonly used **psychotropic medications** used to change feelings, thoughts, and behavior. The general classes of the medications are given along with their generic (general chemical name) and trade (brand) names. This information will help you recognize the medications by one type of name or another so that if you read or hear about one of these commonly used psychotropic medications, you can determine its effects and side effects.

We will cover three major classes of biological treatments: **electroconvulsive therapy (ECT);**

medication (antianxiety medication, antidepressant medication, lithium, antipsychotic medication, and psychostimulants); and **psychosurgery**.

Many biological treatment methods were discovered accidentally. They did not grow out of a gradual development of knowledge about the biochemistry of individuals with specific disorders; they did not develop from biochemical research in which scientists were able to recommend specific medications to alter specific biochemical problems. Thus, although effective biological treatments exist for some disorders, being able to treat a problem does not imply that we understand the problem or its physiology. In fact, just because biological therapies work for a specific problem doesn't necessarily mean the problem is caused by physiological abnormalities. We do not yet know the exact biochemical abnormalities that lead to, or are associated with, various psychological abnormalities.

Electroconvulsive Therapy

In the 1700s, it was observed that body convulsions or spasms "put an end" to some types of madness. For centuries, physicians had known that gross bodily stresses alleviated mental illness, and these observations led to medical interventions such as inducing fever and convulsions for mental patients. Many physicians also began to believe that mental illness was caused by some form of brain illness or pathology. The illness might be cured, or killed, by actually inducing high fevers or other severe stressors.

In the late 1800s, doctors attempted fever cures to treat dementia resulting from syphilis, especially after observing that this disease's symptoms abated in Russian troops after a typhoid fever epidemic. In 1917, nine patients with mental illness from syphilis were injected with active malaria virus in order to induce fevers. With ten to twelve such induced fevers, three patients recovered, three realized temporary relief, and three showed no improvement. The treatment of a disease by this radical method of inducing another disease was widely heralded in the medical community, and its discoverer, Julius Wagner-Jauregg, received the Nobel Prize for medicine in 1927. It became the principal treatment for syphilis until penicillin's discovery in the 1940s.

In 1934, Hungarian psychiatrist Laszlo Von Meduna worked with schizophrenic patients and noted they seldom had epileptic attacks. At that time, it had been reported that in over 6,000 schizophrenic patients, only 20 had a history of epilepsy (Fink, 1979). Meduna also noted a difference in certain cells of schizophrenics and epileptics, from biopsy or tissue research. He reasoned that these were opposite types of biochemical events occurring in the bodies of schizophrenics and epileptics. He felt that this presumed difference in the two patient groups' biological makeup was a key to unraveling schizophrenia's mystery. On reading that two catatonic patients recovered after epileptic attacks, Meduna was convinced that producing epileptic attacks might alleviate schizophrenia's symptoms.

Meduna induced convulsions by injecting patients with camphor, a chemical agent. Then, in 1938, two Italian physicians, Ugo Cerlutti and Lucio Bini, began to induce convulsions electrically, initiating the treatment called electroconvulsive therapy (ECT). From the 1940s through the mid-1960s, ECT became accepted in treating schizophrenia. Then as psychiatrists became optimistic about its use, they started to use it with many disorders, especially severe depression. However, in the 1950s, concern mounted as doctors began to observe bone fractures, panic, memory loss, and heart complications in patients receiving ECT. Anesthesia helped prevent the bone fractures associated with convulsions, but this did not stem criticism when reviews of hospital records revealed that ECT had been used on certain individuals hundreds of times. Critics contended that each ECT treatment killed some brain cells. Others argued that it was used to control violent and aggressive patients on back wards of hospitals (Breggin, 1979).

In some parts of the United States, concern about ECT resulted in hearings and court battles where opponents attempted unsuccessfully to ban it. Nevertheless, public outcry led to federal panels adopting specific guidelines concerning its use. At the same time, the advent of antidepressant medication and the use of lithium in treating manic depression led to decreased interest in ECT. By the mid-1960s, many hospital ECT facilities were closed.

Patients undergoing ECT receive a sedative to make them sleep prior to treatment (see Chapter 7). Patients are also injected with a muscle relaxant to prevent violent muscle contractions. The seizure is then induced by passing 150 volts of electricity through electrodes just above the temple. Unlike the movies, *The Snake Pit* and *One Flew Over the Cuckoo's Nest,* patients show no overt bodily signs of a seizure. After one minute, the seizure is over and within five to ten minutes they awaken. Most patients receive ten to twelve seizure treatments over a three-week period.

Research in the 1960s and 1970s led to insuring safer and more effective ECT treatment. Placing electrodes on only one side of the head resulted in less memory loss than when electrodes were used on both sides, and use of electrical stimulation to one side of the head is as effective as bilateral stimulation. Even with electrical stimulation to only one side of the head, however, there is some memory loss, and some patients report losses for weeks or months. It is unknown whether these reported losses with unilateral placements are due to ECT or other factors (National Institutes of Mental Health Consensus Statement, 1985). Using multiple treatments in one setting with EEG monitoring to record brain waves during the seizures also benefited patients more than numerous treatments across a long period. Monitoring the seizures with the EEG helps psychiatrists know the strength of a patient's seizure. Because the muscle relaxants prevent any overt bodily signs of a seizure, the exact magnitude of the ECT's effect on the brain would be unknown without EEG monitoring. With careful monitoring, however, ECT is generally safe, rapid, and effective in alleviating depression. Even so, 74 percent of patients who are effectively treated would not choose to have the treatment again unless no other alternatives were available (Maletzky, 1981). Despite its effectiveness, people are afraid of ECT (see Chapter 7). As we shall see later, in many instances, their fears appear warranted because professional training in ECT use a decade ago was often minimal and substandard. Many facilities now, however, require specialized knowledge in ECT and agreement between the patient's psychiatrist and the psychiatrist on the ECT team that the patient is a suitable candidate for ECT.

Success rates for ECT vary between 60 percent and 90 percent with psychotic depressives and manic depressive disorders (Fink, 1979). These extremely high success rates are indeed much higher than those of most other treatments. ECT is clearly most effective in treating severe depression characterized by weight loss, difficulty in concentrating, severely depressed mood, and inability to enjoy pleasant events. These types of patients are sometimes referred to as endogenous depressives under the assumption that their depression "arises from within." Within six months after treatment, relapse rates with ECT are judged to be as high as 50 percent, but relapse rates and suicide rates appear to be reduced by use of antidepressant medication following ECT trials (Kiloh, 1982).

Many professionals now feel that ECT should be the treatment of last resort. Some argue that in this case the treatment is worse than the cure. Patients suffering from profound depression or psychotic episodes may still elect to try this radical form of treatment. Death is a possible side effect. It occurs in 1 out of 10,000 patients, but when it happens, it is more commonly a result of the anesthesia than the ECT treatment itself.

ECT treatment may be especially useful for suicidal patients at significant risk for killing themselves. Even in these circumstances, however, ECT should be considered only if the clinician has considerable experience with it. Even in 1981, clinical practice of ECT use was below standard in many facilities. Using guidelines established by the Royal College of Psychiatrists in England, Pippard and Ellam (1981) found that 27 of 100 ECT facilities had serious deficiencies such as poor and indifferent care and obsolete equipment. They rated 31 percent of the psychiatrists as unsatisfactory in their handling of ECT treatments! As the investigators noted:

> ECT is usually left to junior members of the staff . . . with little training and guidance except for nursing staff or anesthetists. . . . Some hospitals regard

BOX 17.4 Electroconvulsive Therapy: Experts' Consensus About a Highly Controversial Treatment

Because of the controversy surrounding ECT, the National Institute of Mental Health assembled a panel of fourteen clinical researchers to arrive at a consensus statement about this treatment. An audience consisting of former patients and health professionals discussed the issues with the mental health experts. The panel's main conclusions about when ECT should be used were as follows:

> . . . ECT is most appropriate in those conditions for which efficacy has been established: Delusional and severe endogenous depressions, acute mania, and certain schizophrenic syndromes. ECT should rarely be considered for other psychiatric conditions. The decision whether to offer ECT to an individual patient should be based on a complex consideration of advantages and disadvantages for ECT and for each treatment alternative. . . . It should be emphasized that for certain patients with very specific and narrow indications, ECT may be the only effective treatment available. In certain circumstances of acute risk to life or of medical status incompatible with the use of other effective treatments, ECT may be the first treatment.
>
> When the physician has determined that clinical indications justify the administration of ECT, the law requires, and medical ethics demand, that the patient's freedom to accept or refuse treatment be fully honored (p. 3).

Source: Electroconvulsive Therapy: Consensus Development Conference Statement, Vol. 5, No. 11, National Institute of Mental Health, Bethesda, MD, 1985.

"supervision" as no more than having the new doctor shown how to press the button. . . . Unilateral ECT is used rarely or never in 80% of clinics (even though unilateral ECT causes less confusion and memory disturbance) (pp. 64–66).

Where the psychiatric staff has special training in ECT methods, ECT must be considered one of the most successful treatments. Some professionals consider it the most effective biological treatment for depression. Risks appear small with well-trained staffs, and the risk in fact is often from the anesthesia, not the ECT itself. Further, the risk is smaller than that of suicide. Finally, since antidepressants often have to be taken for several weeks to be effective, ECT is a very useful treatment for patients under risk of death from dehydration resulting from a refusal to eat.

Theories of ECT Use for Depression. It is believed that ECT alters central brain stem functions by eliciting an increase in hormone levels at the brain sites. Neurotransmitter deficits are believed to be one of the causes of depression (see Chapter 7). Dr. Max Fink, a pioneer and world leader in ECT research, believes that ECT results in release of peptide hormones and that these hormone functions return to normal following ECT treatment (Fink, 1982). In addition, evidence suggests that the hormone cortisol is suppressed in patients receiving ECT treatment (Grunhaus et al., 1987). As you may remember from Chapter 7, failure to suppress cortisol functioning is characteristic of many depressed patients.

Antianxiety Medications

The need for relief from stress is so strong that Americans and Europeans have increasingly sought solace in alcohol, marijuana, and tranquilizers as well as in varied forms of relaxation, biofeedback, and meditation. Audiotapes of babbling brooks and ocean waves pounding the shore can be found in most large bookstores throughout the United States. Flourishing industries produce these somatic and psychological means of anxiety and stress reduction. Minor tranquilizers such as Valium (diazepam) and Xanax (alprozolam) are among the most commonly prescribed drugs. Doctors fill out more than a million prescriptions for antianxiety drugs per year. The cost to the consumer is over $500 million annually (Baldessarini & Cole, 1988). Further, as Figure 17.1 shows, the sale of tranquilizers has been steadily increasing in the United States at what some argue is an alarming rate. Over the past two decades, their use has been so great that the National Academy of Sciences issued a report on the hazards of **antianxiety medication,** especially for inducing sleep.

Figure 17.1 Tranquilizer Sales in the United States. *Sales of tranquilizers in the United States increased between 1979 and 1983.*

1979	428
1980	421
1981	440
1982	482
1983	567

Source: Adapted from Lader, M.H. (1985). Scope of clinical use of benzodiazepines. In M.H. Lader & H.C. Davies (Eds.), *Drug treatment of neurotic disorders: Focus on alprazolam,* pp. 24–35. New York: Churchill Livingstone.

The United States is not the only country where serious concern about unnecessary use of antianxiety medications has been expressed. Approximately 15 percent of the total adult population has used tranquilizers in most Western European countries and in the United States. Often these anxieties are not of major importance. Over 5 percent of the population of France and Belgium have chronically used tranquilizers for over a year or more, as have approximately 2 percent of the U.S. population. (Balter, Manheimer, Mellinger, & Uhlenhuth, 1984). Also, twice as many women as men receive prescriptions for tranquilizers (see Box 17.5).

The search for chemical agents to produce a calming effect without serious side effects continues (see Table 17.3). Barbiturates like phenobarbital, introduced in 1912, were one of the first types of medication used to reduce anxiety, but their serious addictive side effects prevent their common use today. In fact, they are almost never used for anxiety problems because of their severe withdrawal effects. In the 1950s, the propanedoils, or minor tranquilizers, were developed (e.g., Miltown) but were largely replaced in the 1960s by the benzodiazepines (e.g., Valium), another class of minor tranquilizers, primarily because withdrawal from propanedoils after long-term use was associated with grand mal seizures. It was hoped that benzodiazepines would be nonaddictive,

TABLE 17.3 Common Antianxiety Medications

General Class	Generic Name	Trade Name
I. Minor Tranquilizers		
A. Benzodiazepines	Diazepam	Valium
	Chlordiazepoxide	Librium
	Alprazolam	Xanax
B. Propanedoils	Meprobamate	Equanil, Miltown
II. Barbiturates	Phenobarbital	Luminal
	Secobarbital	Seconal

BOX 17.5 Is There Sexual Prejudice in Drug Prescriptions?

Woman far exceed men in their consumption of psychoactive drugs. Almost three fourths of patients prescribed psychoactive drugs in the United States are women (Rossiter, 1983). Moreover, although slightly over half of all visits to a physician's office (58 percent) are made by women, they receive 73 percent of all prescriptions written for psychiatric drugs. Also, male psychiatrists prescribe drugs twice as often as female psychiatrists (Cypress, 1980).

In a study of outpatient services, female patients were 37 percent more likely than males to receive minor tranquilizers, and 62 percent more likely to receive antidepressants. Men and women were equally likely to receive antipsychotic medication (0.08 percent versus 0.10 percent) (Hohmann, Larson, Thompson, & Beardsley, 1988).

To argue that women are prejudicially given more psychoactive medications than men, it is first necessary to compare the likelihood that men and women will receive medication when they present with similar symptoms. In fact, more women receive antidepressant and antianxiety medication than men presumably because significantly more women than men become depressed, and women report more anxiety disorders than men. The differential use of medications by male and female psychiatrists, however, is puzzling and may reflect male psychiatrists' sexual stereotype of helpless women patients.

Instead of suggesting other therapies that may work as well, physicians (especially males), may help female patients with a "quick fix," instead of dealing with the psychosocial issues underlying the depression and anxiety. In that sense, the differential use of psychoactive medications *may be unjustified*. The contemporary psychosocial stressors of differential pay in the work force, spouse abuse, marital discord, and raising children as a single parent can cause some women to become anxious and depressed. These problems, however, require much more than a temporary solution. On the other hand, some psychiatrists argue that some anxiety patients are undertreated and are made to suffer unnecessarily because of fears of dependence on medication for anxiety. At present, there is no simple answer to the question, "Is there a sexual prejudice in the prescription of drugs for men and women?" Nonetheless, the issue will continue to be hotly debated by both patients and professionals.

but as we shall see, no antianxiety medication is risk free. All have some potential for tolerance and addiction.

Minor tranquilizers taken in appropriate doses do have calming effects without sedation. Feelings of reduced anxiety and relaxation are readily apparent; nervousness is lessened. The benzodiazepines are relatively safe, if carefully monitored, unless used with alcohol. Because benzodiazepines and alcohol decrease alertness and central nervous system activity, their combined use is very dangerous and can be fatal. Many medical professionals also continue to be concerned about the risk of dependency, abuse, and addiction with benzodiazepines (Baldessarini & Cole, 1988; Hayward, Wardle & Higgitt, 1989). Tolerance and withdrawal upon abrupt termination of use are problems with these medications (Rickels et al., 1983).

The benzodiazepines (e.g., Valium) generally inhibit the central nervous system. In fact, the benzodiazepines act on specific sites that affect neurotransmitters in the brain and lead to reduced nerve cell firing (Hayward et al., 1989). Relief from anxiety is almost directly proportional to the dosage taken, and the benzodiazepines may activate the behavioral inhibition system. They may also inhibit the reticular activating system, which energizes us (Gray, 1982). As the body develops increasing tolerance, the dosage must be increased to obtain the same level of anxiety reduction. Physiological and psychological dependency on tranquilizers, or addiction, may develop from this increased tolerance. This varies with the type of drug, dosage level, and length of time on the drug. For the barbiturates, physical dependence with severe withdrawal symptoms (similar to withdrawal from alcohol abuse) can occur after about one month of extensive use. For benzodiazepines, physical dependence can occur after several months of such use. In both cases, dosage levels well above the level typically prescribed by doctors are associated with addiction and withdrawal problems (Baldessarini & Cole, 1988). Slow discontinuation is recommended for these individuals.

As noted earlier, the benzodiazepines are less likely to produce dangerous withdrawal effects when given at normally prescribed levels than other sedatives, such as the barbiturates. The most common withdrawal effects from antianxiety medications after having taken them for over a year are anxiety, sleep disturbance, and appetite loss. A small percentage of patients even experience panic, but these feelings generally subside in two to four weeks.

The tranquilizing effects of these drugs have little impact on the hallucinations and mental distortions of schizophrenics and other acutely agitated patients. They do, however, sometimes help acutely agitated psychotic or manic patients cope with their anxiety over new situations and social interactions. Tranquilizers given in combination with antidepressive medication also appear to help seriously depressed, hospitalized patients better than either medication given alone (Cassano & Conti, 1981). The combination of the tranquilizers and antidepressants relieves anxiety, insomnia, and depression.

In 1988, general practitioners and family physicians accounted for 52 percent of the visits for tranquilizer prescriptions in the United States, whereas psychiatrists accounted for only 28 percent (Beardsley et al., 1988). A reason for this difference is that tranquilizers are coprescribed, or prescribed conjointly with other medications, by internists for gastrointestinal and respiratory disorders and for insomnia and stress associated with a variety of illnesses.

Antianxiety agents generally outperform placebos (see Chapter 5). There is, however, little difference in effectiveness among the various antianxiety agents, especially tranquilizers (Cohn, 1981). In addition, Valium can help decrease the depressed mood sometimes associated with anxiety disorders. Some effects of Valium (diazepam) and Xanax (alprazolam) are seen within the first week of use, but they appear to show increasing antianxiety effects until the fourth week of treatment (see Figure 17.2.)

Despite antianxiety agents' effectiveness, when long-term treatment is needed, patients and physicians should consider psychological therapies. Behavioral treatments are particularly effective in treating anxiety (see Chapter 5). Because anxiety agents are potentially addictive, psychological therapies should always be considered as alternatives, or adjuncts, to any long-term tranquilizer use. Also, heated debates continue about whether the symptom relief produced by tranquilizers may actually hamper our understanding of the factors that cause anxiety. Some critics of their usage argue that they are merely a crutch. On the other hand, supporters contend they are useful crutches that help patients regain control over stressful events.

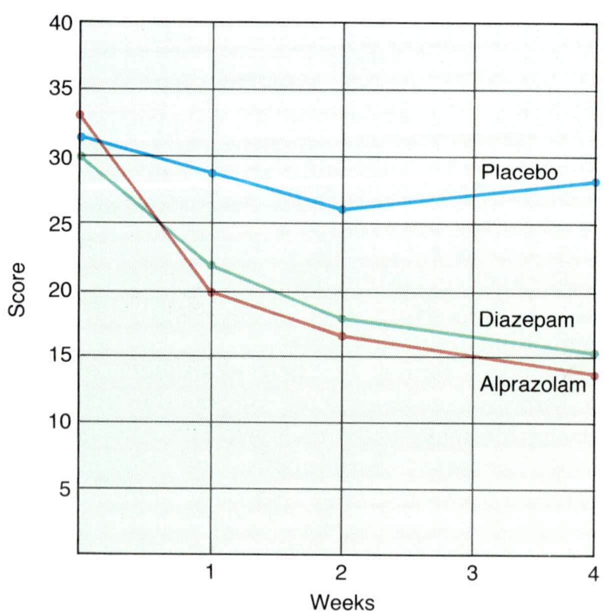

Figure 17.2 Effectiveness of Anti-anxiety Treatments over a Four Week Period. *Two groups of patients receiving anti-anxiety medications, diazepam (Valium) and alprazolam (Xanax), show marked reductions of anxiety scores as compared to patients receiving placebo.*

Source: Fabre, L.F. & McLendon, D.M. (1979). "A double-blind study comparing the efficacy and safety of alprazolam with diazepam and placebo in anxious out-patients." *Current Therapeutic Research, 25(4)*, p. 523.

Antidepressants

According to the ancient Greeks, depression had a biological cause, namely, black bile. Today, many still believe that depression is biological in origin. Recently, there has been an explosion of research into the mechanics of antidepressant medications and the biochemical basis of depression. Increasing evidence suggests that serotonin and norepinephrine deficiencies cause depression (see Chapter 7). You may recall that serotonin and norepinephrine are chemicals called neurotransmitters that transmit messages between nerve cells. Experts believe that some unipolar depressives have a norepinephrine deficiency whereas other depressives have a serotonin deficiency.

There are three types of antidepressant medications: **tricyclic antidepressants, MAO inhibitors,** and a **serotonin uptake inhibitor.** The tricyclics are most commonly used and we will discuss them first.

Tricyclic Antidepressants. The antidepressants' effects were discovered almost accidentally. The major class of antidepressants, called tricyclics, have a three-ring molecular structure similar to that of the phenothiazines used to treat schizophrenics (see Figure 17.3). Because of this chemical similarity, doctors originally tried tricyclics on schizophrenics. Although they did not reduce psychotic thinking, patients taking them showed some mood improvement. Consequently, researchers began to use tricyclic medications to treat depression. Thus, in 1957, the tricyclic medication imipramine was reported to show antidepressant effects in depressed patients (Kuhn, 1958).

Researchers believe that the tricyclics interfere with or block the re-uptake of norepinephrine and serotonin at the nerve cell after it has fired. Figure 17.4 on page 480 shows actions of two antidepressant medications. As you may recall from Chapter 7, deficiencies in norepinephrine and serotonin are believed to be a cause of depression. Norepinephrine is stored in small vesicles inside the messenger neurons, and when the vesicles open, norepinephrine is

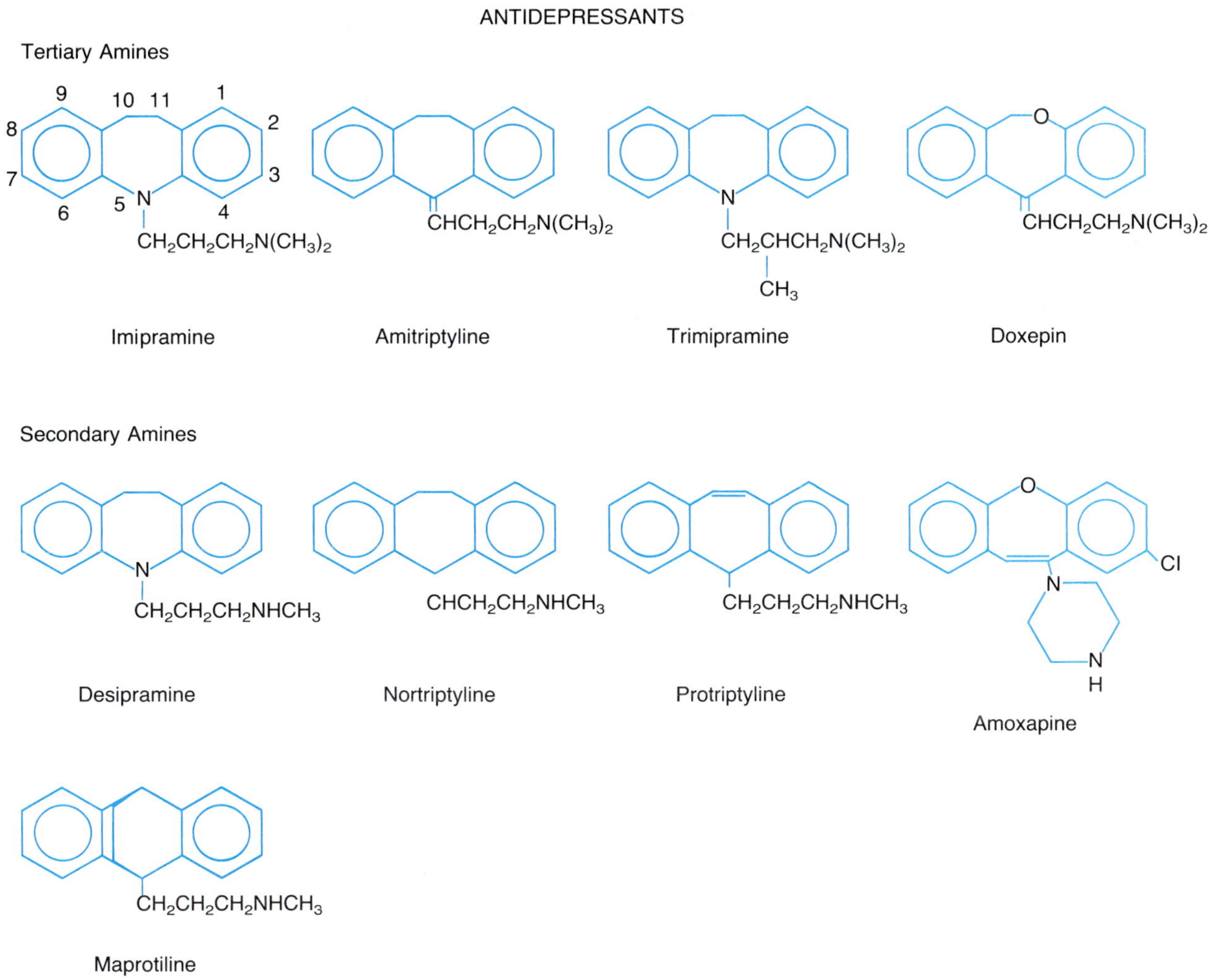

Figure 17.3 Three Ring Structure of Tricyclics. *As seen in this figure, antidepressant medications are called tricyclic compounds because of the two benzene rings (six sided rings) joined by a central compound ring.*

Source: Baldessarini, R.J. & Cole, J.O. (1988). Chemotherapy. In A.M. Nicholi (Ed.) *The New Harvard Guide*, p. 508. London: Harvard University Press. Reprinted with permission.

sent out into the synapse. The transmitter neuron sends messages to the receptor neuron as norepinephrine is released into the synapse, the space between the transmitter and the receptor neuron. First, some norepinephrine travels to the receptor sites on the receptor neuron. Meanwhile, some of the norepinephrine released into the synapse remains in the synaptic area where it gradually reenters the messenger neurons and the vesicles within it. Scientists believe that the reabsorption, or re-uptake, of norepinephrine is one of the body's ways of conserving it. Next, some of the norepinephrine remaining in the synaptic area is broken down or metabolized by the chemical monoamine oxidase (MAO).

The tricyclics operate by making more norepinephrine available within the transmitter system. They prevent it from being returned to the messenger neuron—that is, they deter its re-uptake. One group of depressives fare better when treated with imipramine, which appears to achieve its effect by increasing norepinephrine levels. A second group of depressives fare better when treated with amytriptyline, which acts to increase serotonin.

Tricyclic antidepressants clearly have a positive mood elevating effect on many depressed individuals (Davis, Klerman, & Schildkraut, 1967; Klerman, 1988). Indeed, they are the most widely used medications in treating depression (see Chapter 7). Initial effects on mood usually occur after one or two weeks of treatment. Maximal effects may not be achieved until the third or fourth week. The most common side effects of high doses of tricyclics are dry mouth, fatigue, constipation, difficulty in urination, memory difficulty, dizziness, and weight gain. Optimal duration of treatment is four to six months for an acute episode of depression, with gradual withdrawal of medication advised three months after the depression lifts (Klerman, 1988).

Some depressed individuals respond well to tricyclic medication alone and some respond well to psy-

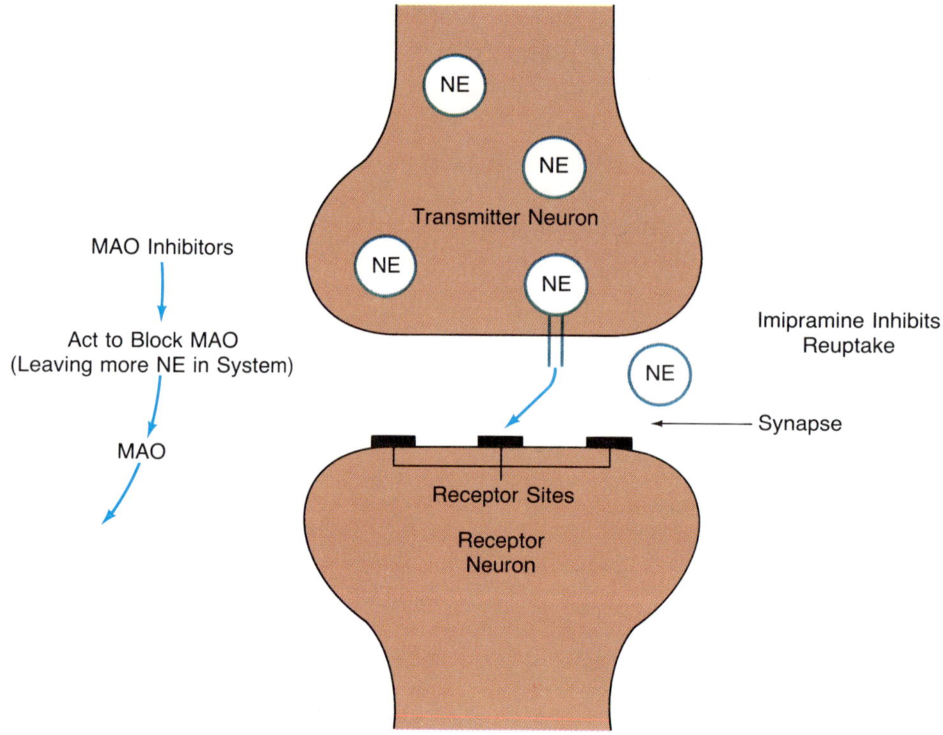

Figure 17.4 Transmission of Message Across Synapse. *Norepinephrine is released into the synapse during the transmission of messages. To increase the amount of norepinephrine available in the system, imipramine is used to prevent its re-uptake and MAO inhibitors are used to block its metabolism.*

chotherapy alone, especially cognitive-behavior therapy. Fortunately, both the pharmacological and psychological treatments of unipolar depression work well (Murphy, Simons, Wetzel, & Lustman, 1984) although severely depressed patients respond best to medication (Elkin et al., 1989). Whether one uses pharmacological or psychological treatments or a combination, it is best to remember that the two types of therapies generally affect different targets. Medication is designed to elevate mood and increase energy directly; psychotherapy is intended to elevate mood through first enhancing interpersonal skills or changing thought patterns.

MAO Inhibitors. The MAO inhibitors are the second major type of medication used to treat depression. True to their name, they block the action of MAO (monoamine oxidase), preventing the breakdown of norepinephrine and serotonin, thereby decreasing depression. Like the tricyclic medications, MAO inhibitors' antidepressant affect were discovered accidentally. They were first used unsuccessfully to elevate the mood of tuberculosis patients.

MAO inhibitors' significant side effect is extreme hypertension (heart pounding, headache, and stiff neck). When taken with certain common foods high in tyramine, such as yeast, chocolate, beer, and various wines, serious physical reactions and even death can result! Such foods cannot be ingested even in small amounts. Because of the toxicity and potential lethal effects of the MAO inhibitors, doctors use them only for individuals who do not respond to other available medications. Even then, however, their use must be carefully monitored and the patient must be totally cognizant of the lethal interaction of the medication with various foods. Because of the hypertensive side effects, and because the MAO inhibitors are often less effective than the tricyclic antidepressants, they are used less often than the tricyclics.

Serotonin Uptake Inhibitor. Prozac is an antidepressant medication that was officially introduced in 1987, and many professionals feel that it is the wonder drug of mental health because it is very effective in treating depression and has few side effects (see Chapter 7). Prozac blocks the uptake or reabsorption of serotonin—making serotonin available for use by the patient. Although Prozac is very effective in treating depressed individuals (Bremner, 1984), a few individuals have intense suicidal thoughts while taking the medication (Teciher et al., 1990). Suicidal thoughts are common in depressed patients, and it is not clear whether the intense suicidal thoughts are caused by the drug use or simply the result of the patient being very depressed. Until this issue is resolved, Prozac will likely be used more cautiously than when it was first introduced as the mental health wonder drug.

Varied Clinical Uses of Antidepressant Medication. Antidepressant medications are also used to treat agoraphobia, obsessive-compulsive disorders, and eating disorders. Antidepressants may do more than treat the symptoms of depression often found to coexist with these anxiety disorders.

MAO inhibitors help some agoraphobics (Sheehan, Ballenger, & Jacobson, 1980). The antidepressant medication clomipramine has reduced the symptoms of obsessive-compulsive children and adults (Leonard et al., 1989; Marks, 1981). The use of antidepressant medication for patients with a primary disorder other than depression can help us learn more about these disorders. For example, clomipramine's use has sparked interest in the idea that obsessive-compulsives have a metabolite serotonin deficiency. Therefore, antidepressant medications and other chemical compounds directly affecting the body's use of serotonin are being evaluated with obsessive-compulsives to try to understand that disorder's mystery (Charney et al., 1988; Zohar et al., 1988).

Antidepressants are also used to treat eating disorders such as bulimia because of the belief that depression plays a major causative role in the development of bulimia. However, professionals now also recognize that anxiety, alcohol abuse, and conduct problems may be quite common in patients with eating disorders (Hsu, 1990; Laessle et al., 1989). Further, while psychotherapy is more effective than pharmacotherapy in the treatment of bulimia (Wilson, 1990), nonetheless, by treating varied disorders with antidepressants some professionals believe that it may be possible to discover some central biochemical and psychological mechanisms that are common to these disorders. More specifically, depression may underlie some eating disorders, compulsions, and even some aggressive disorders. While this position is controversial, if true, some professionals believe that it may be helpful to see these problems as affective spectrum disorders that are at least in part caused by problems of affect or depressed mood (Hudson & Pope, 1990).

Antipsychotic Drugs or Neuroleptics

The antipsychotic effects of chlorpromazine were also accidentally discovered. French surgeon Henri Laborit had used a phenothiazine compound to reduce blood pressure in patients before surgery. Instead of a drop in pressure, he observed that the patients were markedly less anxious. In 1952, after several attempts with variations on the phenothiazine compound, French psychiatrists Jean Delay and Pierre Deniker gave chlorpromazine to a variety of psychiatric patients. As preoperative patients, the psychiatric patients showed reductions in anxiety, with schizophrenics also exhibiting a marked decrease of hallucinations and delusions. A wonder drug of the mental health field, chlorpromazine, had been discovered. After receiving chlorpromazine, many schizophrenic patients who had been hospitalized for years were able to return to their jobs and families (see Chapter 14).

TABLE 17.4 Antipsychotic Medications Used to Treat Schizophrenia

Chemical Name	Generic Name	Trade Name
Phenothiazines	Chlorpromazine	Thorazine
	Trifluoperazine	Stelazine
	Thioridazine	Mellaril
Dibenzodiazepine	Clozapine	Clozaril
Thioaxines	Thiothizene	Navane
Butyrophenone	Haloperidol	Haldol

Source: Adapted from Bernstein, *Handbook of Drug Therapy in Psychiatry,* 1988, pp. 112–114.

Dr. Delay called the **antipsychotic medications (neuroleptics)** (meaning affecting the nervous system) to distinguish their effects from tranquilizers (see Table 17.4). The antipsychotic medications have immediate positive effects and reduce relapse rates (Hogarty, 1984). Between 10 percent and 20 percent of schizophrenics are, however, not helped by neuroleptics. In fact, an estimated 100,000 to 200,000 schizophrenic patients do not respond to standard neuroleptics. Moreover, 20 percent to 30 percent of those who initially respond to the standard neuroleptics relapse during the first year or two of maintenance treatment (Kane et al., 1988).

Neuroleptics like chlorpromazine also produce side effects similar to the symptoms of Parkinson's disease, which include muscle rigidity, stooped posture, unusual shuffling gate, and even occasional drooling. If present, these problems usually emerge in the first few weeks of treatment. Anti-Parkinsonian medications can reduce these side effects, but their use is controversial because of their own side effects. Anti-Parkinsonian medications must be monitored carefully because they can lead to *drug-induced* confusion states difficult to recognize in schizophrenic patients.

A related side effect of neuroleptics is *tardive dyskinesia,* characterized by slowed movements of the face, tongue, and neck muscles. From 15 percent to 20 percent of those who receive neuroleptics for a number of years develop tardive dyskinesia. These symptoms often start as small eye twitches or unusual finger movements. Occasionally, they will be accompanied by strange tongue thrusting movements. These tardive dyskinesia movements not only occur while patients are taking neuroleptics but also are often observed after withdrawal from medication.

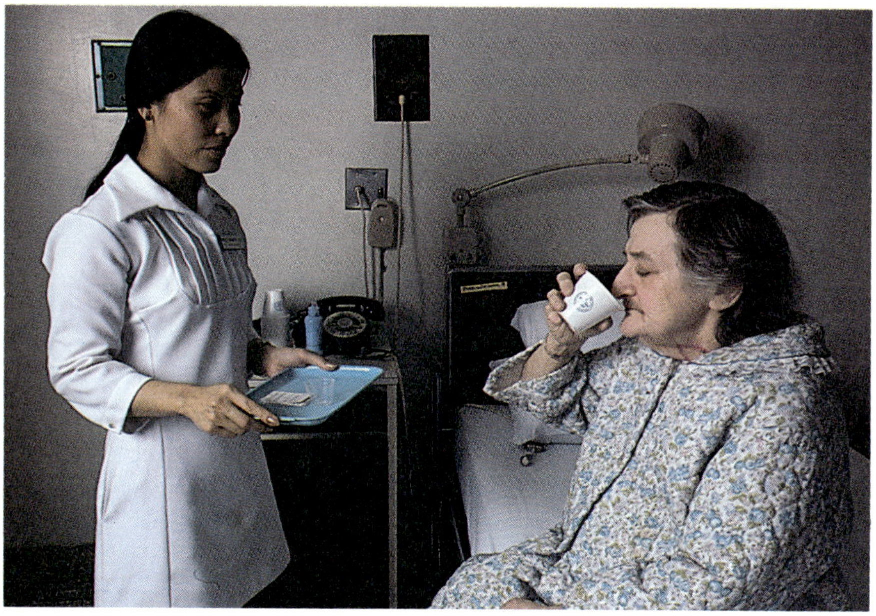

Antipsychotic medications have been very effective in reducing the symptomatology of schizophrenics, and it is necessary to monitor medication use by nurses as seen here.

For many patients, such motor abnormalities are irreversible. As there is no known effective treatment for tardive dyskinesia, careful observation of patients on neuroleptics is necessary to catch the problem when it first begins. The effects can be minimized by finding the lowest efficient neuroleptics dosage to reduce psychotic thoughts. In any case, patients and their relatives should be well educated about these possible side effects.

The serious side effects and the large percentage of nonresponders to neuroleptics led researchers to search for alternatives. Clozapine appears useful for some of the 10 percent to 20 percent of schizophrenics unresponsive to generally available antipsychotic medications. A dibenzodiazepine, clozapine does not generally have significant negative effects on motor functioning. Kane et al. (1988) administered it to over 100 schizophrenic patients who failed to respond to three different neuroleptics. Thirty percent of these patients were classified as "responders" to clozapine: They showed improvements on positive symptoms such as unusual thoughts and conceptual disorganization, and on negative symptoms such as emotional withdrawal and lack of cooperativeness. In another study, the drug caused throat and gastrointestinal tract lesions in about 2 percent of patients (Marder & Van Putten, 1988), but in this study no such lesions developed. Despite this risk of lesions, clozapine is still recommended only for treatment-resistant patients. Further, its use is restricted to certain medical centers, and clozapine is still being monitored by its developer.

Despite the problems associated with neuroleptics, they have led to revolutionary changes in psychiatric hospitals. Most schizophrenic patients can now be treated in open or unlocked wards or in general hospitals with a markedly reduced typical length of hospital stay. With family assistance, many psychiatric or schizophrenic patients do not require hospitalization at all. Although antipsychotic agents have been heralded as the wonder drugs of mental health, the need for concern about the psychological well-being of former schizophrenic patients cannot be overstated. Psychological consultation with families of schizophrenics released from psychiatric hospitals can drastically reduce relapse rates (see Chapter 14). Specifically, when families with high levels of negative emotion decrease the level of criticism and hostility (expressed emotion) toward the former patient, they can greatly reduce the possibility of rehospitalization. Further, a naturally low level of negativity in a family makes the likelihood of relapse within a several-year period quite low also. With such families, maintenance dosages of medication following the patient's release from the hospital may be unnecessary. In sum, although antipsychotic drugs have been a blessing to many schizophrenics and their families, the need to consider the patient's psychological needs became increasingly evident in the 1980s.

Lithium

Lithium carbonate is a naturally occurring salt, similar to sodium carbonate or table salt. Because of its availability in varied natural forms of salts and water, lithium has been used by "medicine men," snake oil peddlers, and modern pharmacologists. In the 1800s, Lithia Water was sold in the United States to treat a variety of nervous and mental problems as well as gout, a disease of the joints (Bernstein, 1988). Lithia Water's popularity declined shortly after the turn of the century when it was observed that preparations of it led to nausea, giddiness, and even poisoning.

In the 1940s Australian psychiatrist John Cade noted lithium salts' calming effect on his experimental guinea pigs. After observing this, Cade tried lithium with agitated psychotic patients and saw the same quieting effect. Today, lithium is used most frequently to treat patients suffering from mania or manic depressive disorder because it normalizes moods and prevents the characteristic swings from extreme highs to extreme lows (Baldessarini & Cole, 1988). Manic episodes can destroy families and personal relationships. During such episodes, people may experience a tremendous high, spend thousands of dollars, have many sexual liaisons, talk incessantly, sleep little, get into fights, or drive recklessly. Episodes are unpredictable and uncontrollable without medical treatment. Lithium is clearly the treatment of choice for manic-depressives, effective in approximately 75 percent of cases. Because lithium is slow acting, doctors often additionally prescribe antidepressant medication to help cope with depressive episodes (Bernstein, 1988). Lithium is not, however, the treatment of choice for major depression, which is better treated with antidepressants.

Most chemical treatments for psychiatric disorders have some side effects. Lithium is no exception, as Table 17.5 shows. It has even led to the death of cardiac patients who used large amounts as a salt substitute. Consequently, it should be prescribed with a careful plan to monitor the lithium ion blood level.

TABLE 17.5 Adverse Effects of Lithium

Therapeutic Dosage	Near Toxicity	Toxic Levels
Nausea	Nausea and vomiting	Heart problems
Dizziness	Hand tremors	Convulsions
Weight gain	Sleepiness	Coma
Mild diarrhea	Vertigo	

In addition to these side effects, manic depressives may not want to take lithium because highs or manias are pleasant and exciting. Some evidence also indicates that artists such as Handel and Schumann were manic. Based on the belief that mania can trigger creativity (see Box 17.6), some patients may simply refuse to take medication that can prevent their manic episodes.

The mechanisms by which lithium works are puzzling partly because of its antimania and antidepressant effects. Depressed people show abnormalities in brain levels of serotonin and norepinephrine (see Chapter 7). Lithium appears to alter serotonin activity in depressed individuals (Baldessarini & Cole, 1988), and this effect underscores the belief that biochemical abnormality produces the disorder.

BOX 17.6 The Value of Mania to a Manic-Depressive Patient

There was an overall sense of motion, a never-being-able to trust that a particular emotional peak once reached would maintain its sharpness—that is with me balancing so precariously in time and space. But there was also the sure sense that I had the wherewithal to conquer every conceivable sort of dilemma—so that insuring my balance wouldn't be difficult, not with me so in charge of myself, in a way, in charge of the whole world. It was only a matter of managing the speed of my ideas, which had somehow managed to change themselves into motion in general—swimming, running, dancing all infusing my body with the proper (or so it seemed) amount of energy. And it was the amount of energy in my body that appeared to increase my level of intelligence. But this is always because I have equated intelligence with mania/speed: a flight towards, a soaring into and above. Nor am I simply speaking of a more mechanical form of intelligence (solving a geometric equation or remembering the dates of the most historical battles of the past five hundred years). No, it is a more exhilarating feeling than that, encompassing the body as well as the mind—more abstract and at the same time more precise. It is as if the eye has been given the facility to see through both a microscope and a telescope at the same time. There is a continual heightened sense of myself as extra competent, in command of more ideas than the average person could ever hope to assimilate. But then the mania, along with linking myself to my intelligence has always been connected in my consciousness with the creative process in general. As a poet I have depended on my mania to keep me functioning at a level high enough to capture not just ideas alone, but the emotions that color and heighten one's sense of reality. The need then is to make the mania last.

Source: S. O'Leary, 1989, patient's file

However glorified the manic phase of a manic-depressive disorder may appear to a patient, these patients are at serious risk for injury to themselves and others because of their hyperactive behaviors and lack of appreciation of the problems associated with their thought processes during the mania.

Psychosurgery

Psychosurgery is probably the most controversial existing treatment for psychiatric disorders. It involves the selective surgical removal of part of the brain or the destruction of nerve pathways to influence behavior. The earliest psychosurgeries removed the frontal lobes from schizophrenic patients. In 1932, American neurosurgeon Walter Dandy removed the frontal lobes of Joe A., a patient who had large growing tumors in both of them. After the operation, many of the patients' intellectual functions slowly returned to normal. At certain times, he was charming and his behavior was impeccable. At other times, however, he acted inappropriately. For example, he often bragged about his sexual prowess although his interest in sex was almost nil (Valenstein, 1986).

About the same time, Carlyle Jacobsen and John Fulton removed the prefrontal areas of the brains of two violent chimpanzees. Following the surgical intervention, the chimps seemed emotionally indifferent to most stimuli. Having heard Jacobsen and Fulton report on their work, Antonio de Egaz Moniz, a professor of neurology in Lisbon, decided that similar psychosurgery techniques might be applicable with schizophrenics, especially to quiet their agitation. Moniz and a colleague, Pedro Almeida Lima, began to remove the frontal lobe tissue from each side of the brain of schizophrenic patients. The two surgeons performed these operations on hundreds of patients for whom other treatments should have been sought. As a result, many patients became apathetic and inactive; over half became mute. It is now estimated that thousands of patients were permanently brain-injured by this procedure. Nonetheless, in 1949, Moniz received the Nobel Prize in medicine for developing the **prefrontal leucotomy,** or **lobotomy.** As a violent ending to this story, one of his patients shot Moniz in 1944, leaving him paralyzed on one side of his body.

In 1936, two physicians in the United States, Walter Freeman and James Watts, began to perform lobotomies. By the late 1950s, Freeman claimed to have performed or supervised over 3,500 of these operations. Freeman and Watts's 1942 book, *Psychosurgery,* helped publicize the operation. Operations by Freeman and Watts usually involved the destruction of significant sections of the frontal lobes. Freeman believed that destroying part of the frontal lobes greatly reduced the emotional responses traveling from the hypothalamus to the cortex. The operation was relatively easy to perform. Some doctors even conducted lobotomies in private offices.

Numerous reasons exist for the growth of psychosurgery, a procedure now considered ineffective for most psychiatric or psychological problems. First, the brain was seen as the cause of abnormal behavior. Second, few effective drug treatments existed for mental disorders at the time. Third, psychotherapy was considered generally ineffective with schizophrenic patients. Recall also that chlorpromazine was not introduced until the 1950s, and psychiatric hospitals were hopelessly overcrowded, especially after the trauma of World War II. Neurosurgery was just being developed, and along with it came the tempting idea to solve difficult problems of mental disorders through surgery. Solving the puzzle of mental disorders meant certain fame and fortune, and Freeman and Watts were determined to find fame through a "great and desperate cure" (Valenstein, 1980).

Early reports by psychosurgeons indicated that most patients improved. A study citing over sixty clinical investigators—recognized experts in the field—found no evidence of an association between the early psychosurgery studied and any permanent memory loss or ability impairment (Freeman & Watts, 1942). This early clinical evaluation had no control group, and the evaluation's emphasis was on the removal of undesirable behavior, not on the lobotomized patient's quality of life. For example, Freeman and Watts's comment on one of their cases, "She is not noisy and is now easy to manage" (Freeman & Watts, 1942, p. 241) illustrates this attitude.

Today doctors perform very limited forms of psychosurgery on patients with specific severe and intractable disorders. Most psychosurgery involves selectively cutting an extremely small area of the brain that provides stimulation to the limbic system. Researchers believe this operation slows the neural firing of the limbic system believed to cause the emotional stimulation resulting in some obsessions (Andreasen, 1984). This type of surgery is largely confined to the treatment of severely obsessive-compulsive individuals or to patients with incapacitating depression associated with severe anxiety. Even this newer operation, however, is controversial in treating obsessive-compulsive behavior (Rachman, 1980). Nonetheless, the treatment holds hope for some patients whose lives have been severely handicapped by obsessions and compulsions. More specifically, it appears to help about 50 percent to 60 percent of obsessive-compulsive patients who did not respond to any other treatment (Andreasen, 1984). Further, a new form of psychosurgery, videolaserscopy, allows surgeons to use a video camera to guide laser surgery to repair vessels in the brain and make cuts smaller than one millimeter. Such surgery may completely replace the scalpel (Cowley, 1990).

Psychostimulants

Military Use and Clinical Discovery. Researchers noted that psychostimulant medications, especially

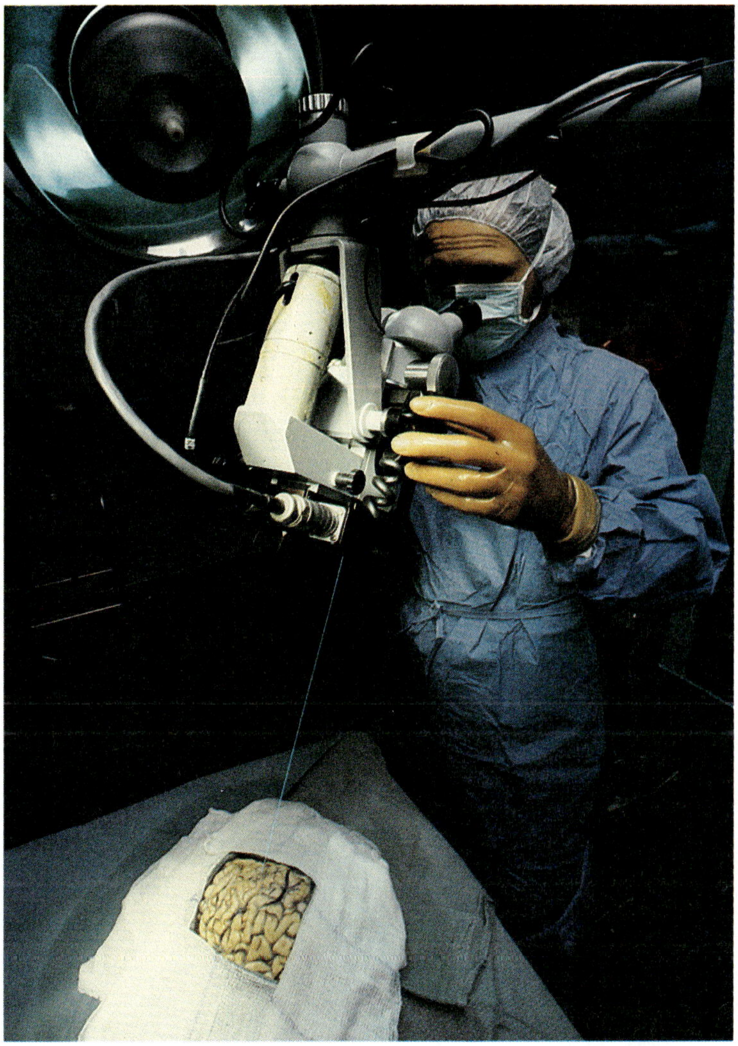

Laser surgery allows physicians to perform brain operations with great precision. Vessels in the brain may be repaired with this procedure with cuts less than one millimeter.

amphetamines, increased alertness, motor skills, and general arousal in laboratory situations. Based on these results, during World War II, pilots, scouts, and foot soldiers were equipped with survival kits containing stimulants. The soldiers took the medication if they were in foxholes and had to remain awake, or if they had to flee from their enemies. Even earlier (1937), Dr. Charles Bradley found that aggressive and hyperactive children responded favorably to the psychostimulant Benzedrine. The children called the medication "arithmetic pills" because they felt they could complete arithmetic assignments more readily when taking their medication. Dr. Bradley reported:

> Possibly the more striking change in behavior during the week of Benzedrine therapy occurred in the school activities of many of these patients. Fourteen (of 30) children responded in a spectacular fashion. Different teachers reporting on these patients, who varied in age and school accomplishment, agreed that a great increase in interest in school material was noted immediately. There appeared a definitive "drive" to accomplish as much as possible during the school period, and often to spend extra time completing additional work. Speed of comprehension and accuracy of performance were increased in most cases. . . . The improvement was noted in all school subjects. It appeared promptly the first day Benzedrine was given and disappeared on the first day it was discontinued (Bradley, 1937).

Thus Bradley joins the long list of clinicians and researchers who made an important medical discovery "accidentally." Bradley had intended to relieve children's headaches by raising their blood pressure with psychostimulants. Although the headaches were unchanged, the children's attentional skills improved. In hyperactive children, **psychostimulants** decrease restlessness and activity level and increase attention span. In the late 1960s and early 1970s, however, a number of studies demonstrated physiological side effects in children and adults of increas-

TABLE 17.6 Common Psychostimulant Medications Used in Treating ADHD Children

Generic Name	Trade Name	Clinical Effects	Side Effects
Methylphenidate	Ritalin	Increase attention	Insomnia
Dextroamphetamine	Dexedrine	Decrease restlessness	Lack of appetite
Magnesiun Pemoline	Cylert	Increase fine motor control	Increase heart rate
			Increase blood pressure

Source: Taken from O'Leary, 1984.

ing heart rate, blood pressure, and central nervous system responsivity. In adults, psychostimulants also produce a marked feeling of euphoria, and increased energy levels and attention span. This increased energy resulted in the nickname "speed" for various psychostimulants. Psychostimulants were misused by many young adults, especially in the 1960s and 1970s. Gradually, it became clear that they were addictive and dangerous. On the other hand, when administered appropriately psychostimulants are not addictive to children.

Clinical Uses. Psychostimulants have been used for decades to treat a sleep disorder called narcolepsy. People with this disorder fall asleep unpredictably. Stimulants have also been used to treat depression in the elderly and as a very controversial treatment for obesity.

We will cover each clinical use of psychostimulants, emphasizing their primary clinical value in treating hyperactive (ADHD) children.

ADHD Children. About 2 percent to 4 percent of elementary school children in the United States receive psychostimulants, primarily Ritalin (Safer & Krager, 1984b). This estimate indicates that almost one child for every primary school classroom in the United States is on psychostimulant medication! In other countries such as Sweden, this medication's use is restricted, and in Italy, Spain and China, its use with children is highly unusual (O'Leary, Vivian, & Nisi, 1985; O'Leary, 1984). Table 17.6 shows the common psychostimulants and their effects.

Problems associated with hyperactive children become most apparent in structured situations like the classroom. Although some mothers complain about their children being wild, frenetic, and always in motion during the toddler stage, the school situation causes hyperactive children the most difficulty (see Chapter 12). Psychostimulants are usually given to such children to focus attention and concentrate on their school work. In over two dozen studies, teachers and classroom observers have consistently noted increased attention in hyperactive children on psychostimulants. The social behavior in a classroom also shows significant improvement. Decreases in fidgeting and walking around the classroom have been repeatedly observed (Conners & Wells, 1986). This medication's effect on motor skills is also often positive. Fifty percent of hyperactive children receiving psychostimulants improved in their handwriting whereas only 5 percent who received a placebo showed handwriting improvement (Lerer, Lerer, & Artner, 1977).

To the surprise of many professionals, increases in academic performance as reflected on standard achievement tests have not been associated with taking psychostimulant medication (Barkley & Cunningham, 1978). Also, hyperactive children who received psychostimulant medication for several years did not fare better than unmedicated hyperactive children (Weiss et al., 1979). These findings have led professionals to believe that hyperactive children's critical problems in learning new academic and social skills cannot be addressed simply with medication. Others have questioned psychostimulant medication's desirability given the positive effects of behavior therapy approaches on social and academic behaviors (e.g., O'Leary, 1980). A combined medication and behavior therapy or family therapy intervention may be the treatment of choice for some. Further, support is increasing for the combination of a low dose of psychostimulant medication and psychological therapies (Satterfield, Satterfield, & Cantwell, 1980; Pelham et al., 1988).

Should We All Get Psychostimulants? We know that various psychostimulants enhance the attention and motor skills of normal adults. As Laties and Weiss stated in 1966, "There is little doubt that amphetamines can improve performance on a wide variety of tasks, especially on those involving an element of fatigue or boredom (p. 806)." These researchers reviewed evidence indicating that swimmers and runners can enhance their speed and endurance by using psychostimulants. They also indicated that performance on simple intellectual tasks such as completing rote arithmetic problems can be improved with psychostimulants. Nevertheless, they concluded that many other ways besides drugs exist to improve performance.

Many experts question the assumption that children who are hyperactive and have attentional problems have a brain dysfunction. In addition, it is now known that children with normal activity level and attention span display the same type of response as hyperactive children to psychostimulants (Rapoport et al., 1978). All children show increased attention spans and somewhat greater fine motor control.

So, if psychostimulants improve adult performance on a variety of tasks, and if hyperactive children have no special brain dysfunction addressed by stimulant medication and no different response to stimulants than other children, should we all be on psychostimulants? One reason against this is that many other ways beside drugs exist to improve performance. We believe that interested consumers with attention and hyperactivity problems should remember that psychostimulants influence all adults. They are not a "magic bullet" for treating a very precisely diagnosed disease. Even as you read this text, you might be able to stay up later, sit stiller, and concentrate longer if you were taking psychostimulants. Such benefits, however, seem misplaced if using a medication with serious psychological and pharmacological addictive qualities is required. If pills for every human problem are theoretically possible, then why aren't pills with no dangers also possible? This issue seems to be more related to the number of human problems than to the nature of pills. Children have long been unnecessarily medicated without proper diagnoses. In some instances, they were so highly medicated that they were called "zombies." If such practices continue, child advocates may have to be assigned by courts to protect children from unnecessary medication. Also, economically disadvantaged children are easily labeled, "medicalizing" a problem, such as hyperkinetic disorder, minimal brain dysfunction, or attention deficit hyperactivity disorder. It is equally easy to treat children with medication when no clear evidence indicates a physical problem. Such medication use may simply delay or prevent necessary attention to social, academic, and family problems.

Kitty Dukakis, wife of Democratic Presidential candidate, Michael Dukakis, unfortunately was a victim of drug abuse. She was addicted to psychostimulants and alcohol.

Appetite Control. Psychostimulants have a strong appetite-suppressing effect on both children and adults. However, research indicates that weight loss associated with psychostimulant use is temporary and weight gain usually occurs once medication is stopped. In the 1970s, there was concern that psychostimulants would retard growth of hyperactive children but with currently prescribed doses, they do not have such an effect (Weiss & Hechtman, 1986; Vincent et al., 1990).

Physicians often prescribed certain psychostimulants as appetite suppressants in the 1970s (Honingfeld & Howard, 1973). In some areas of the United States, it is now unethical (but not illegal) to prescribe them for weight control. We now realize amphetamines' high potential for abuse, and some experts advise their use for weight reduction only when alternative treatments have been unsuccessful (Barnhart, 1988). Even then, such use is advised for only a few weeks, so their limited usefulness must be weighed against the risk of chemical dependency. With very high amphetamine doses, hallucinations, irritability, and aggressiveness occur. Thus other experts argue that psychostimulants, such as dextroamphetamine, should never be used to treat obesity or appetite disorders (Bernstein, 1988).

Narcolepsy. Psychostimulants have been used for decades to treat narcolepsy, a rare disorder occurring in approximately 1 of 1,000 persons. People with this problem fall asleep suddenly at inappropriate times and places. Narcolepsy usually begins between fifteen and twenty-five years of age and lasts for the remainder of the person's life. Because psychostimulants increase the central nervous system's activity, psychostimulants may energize the reticular activating system of the brain and help maintain alertness. A number of psychostimulant drugs decrease the frequency of narcoleptic sleep attacks and drowsiness. Approximately 70 percent to 80 percent of narcoleptics improve with medication and can resume active normal lives (Roth, 1980).

Depression. A common question raised about psychostimulants is whether they help depressed people. Psychostimulants are rarely prescribed for depression because of their psychologically addictive properties and because they often lead to personality changes in adults, such as irritability and aggressiveness. These medications have been used for individuals whose depression appears to be in direct reaction to some major external stressor (Klein & Davis, 1969). Psychostimulant treatment for depression is especially problematic because the physician must find a dosage level to ameliorate depressed mood without producing an emotional high associated with psychological and physical addiction (Greist and Jefferson, 1984).

SUMMARY

1. Marital counseling, family therapy, and social therapies are alternatives to traditional individual psychotherapy. All treat the individual as part of a family or social group.
2. Medical treatments are alternatives or adjuncts to psychological therapies; the medical treatments discussed in this chapter are designed to ameliorate psychological problems through direct changes in the individual's bodily state.
3. Treatments that move beyond the individual are often necessary because an individual's problems are so enmeshed in his or her relationships with others. These therapies are not simply adjuncts to individual therapies. Many professionals see them as the treatment of choice for a variety of problems.
4. Treatments for couples with distressed marriages effectively strengthen the bond between partners and increase marital satisfaction. Marital therapy emphasizes decreasing unrealistic expectations and attitudes, increasing positive daily interactions, and in turn increasing positive feelings toward the partner. These aspects of relationship change not only increase satisfaction with the marriage but also often lead to improvements in other psychological problems, such as anxiety and depression.
5. The very influential types of family therapy are family systems therapy and problem solving. Both therapeutic approaches strongly emphasize changing communication patterns. In family therapy systems the whole family is the unit of change. Central strategies in family systems therapy include reframing, validation, communication, and paradoxical directives. In problem-solving approaches, the unit of change may be a dyad (e.g., mother-son) or a triad (father, mother, son). Moreover, the problem-solving approach limits the focus to changes in problem-solving and communication strategies.
6. Family approaches are one of the most important emerging trends in psychotherapy. While it is the newest on the therapeutic scene, family therapy has become a dominant influence in conceptualizing and treating a variety of psychological problems.
7. The problem-solving approach has had a tremendous impact on treating severely disordered schizophrenic patients and their families, dramatically reducing readmission to psychiatric hospitals. As expected, family approaches have proven very helpful in reducing family conflict, improving communication, and strengthening the supportive bonds between family members.
8. Americans use social therapies more than any other kind of therapy. These therapies include self-help groups for former mental patients, Alcoholics Anonymous (AA) and Weight Watchers. They range from small therapeutic communities and halfway houses for specialized populations, to full-scale community interventions designed to change habits such as smoking or diet. Unlike other therapy approaches covered, social therapists often emphasize prevention. The support, encouragement, and even restraint provided by groups is helpful to millions of people around the world through AA, Weight Watchers, and groups for former mental patients like Recovery, Inc.
9. Many professionals advocate these social therapies as the treatment of choice for certain problems because they have demonstrated effectiveness in helping individuals who remain in these programs. While such groups are difficult to evaluate precisely, AA, Weight Watchers, and Recovery, Inc. exemplify the continuing support that people can receive while participating in these programs. AA has helped approximately two thirds of individuals with alcohol problems to remain abstinent or learn to drink moderately. (While abstinence is their goal, not all accept or achieve this goal.) The average overweight person who remains in Weight Watchers for thirty weeks loses twenty-five pounds.
10. Therapeutic communities had a major influence on treatment in the 1800s, but they faded in importance until the 1960s when it was made clear that many patients played sick roles and were encouraged to do so by the structure of hospitals. With emphasis on taking responsibility, participating in group activities, and changing negative attitudes, the therapeutic community and its by-product, the halfway house, emerged as an important part of the mental health field. Community approaches emphasize prevention. They have had a clear impact on preventing improper dieting habits and delinquent behavior.
11. Medical therapies, especially psychotropic drugs, have dramatically changed the field of mental health. The "wonder drugs," or antipsychotics, have allowed many schizophrenics formerly destined to long-term institutionalization to be released from mental hospitals. Antidepressant medication has clearly proven effective with unipolar depressives and lithium has helped stabilize many bipolar depressives. Antianxiety medication helps many people cope with overwhelming anxiety. The minor tranquilizers can have calming effects with-

out sedation, but they were often misused to help people sleep or avoid normal life troubles. While tranquilizer use continues to rise, growing knowledge about their addictive properties may diminish future use.

12. Electroconvulsive therapy fell from favor in the 1960s and 1970s but became accepted as a treatment for seriously suicidal and depressed individuals in the 1980s. Unlike psychosurgery, ECT has been experimentally evaluated and found to compare favorably to medication for certain seriously troubled patients. Nonetheless, this treatment can easily be misused and prospective patients should be educated about both the clear benefits and risks.
13. Psychosurgery was originally heralded as a medical breakthrough. Today, very limited forms of psychosurgery are used to treat certain extremely disturbed patients, but its effectiveness remains a question except for a few isolated disorders such as extreme obsessive compulsives who are unresponsive to psychological or pharmacological treatment.
14. Psychostimulants aid children with attentional deficit disorders. They decrease restlessness and activity level, and they increase attention span.

LEGAL ISSUES

Mental Health Professionals and the Law

Dangerousness and "the Duty to Warn"

Civil Commitment

Patients' Rights

Competency and Responsibility

ETHICAL ISSUES

Professional Ethics

Ethical Issues in Research

Ethical Standards and the Law

SUMMARY

Jan Sawka, *The Negotiations* (1984). Acrylic on masonite, 75 × 48 inches. Courtesy of the artist.

18 LEGAL AND ETHICAL ISSUES

LEGAL ISSUES

- Your grandfather now forgets more than he remembers. He loses his way home between the grocery store and the house he and your grandmother have lived in for more than forty years. Although he denies he has a problem, your grandmother strongly disagrees. She's not sure she can continue to care for him. Who can help your grandmother? How can she be helped?
- Infuriated by an article in the local paper attacking his best friend, the mayor, your uncle has physically assaulted the paper's editor. An epileptic all his life, your uncle claims that he was in the midst of a psychomotor seizure when he attacked the editor and that his seizure disorder made him act violently. Therefore, he has decided to plead "not guilty by reason of temporary insanity" to the assault charge. Who can help your uncle confront both his seizure disorder and its consequence? How can he be helped?
- After twenty-two years of marriage, your best friend's parents have decided to divorce. Your friend, who is your age, is away at college, but her younger siblings, age fourteen, twelve, and eight, have become the objects of a custody dispute between their mother and father. Each parent claims to be able to provide the best home for them. Who can help the children? How can they be helped?

This chapter is about how these questions and countless others like them are answered every day in courts throughout the United States.

Human beings have always energetically debated the matters we refer to as "legal issues." Not only does every age reach its own conclusions on how to settle such vexing questions, each generation inevitably argues and resolves them anew. Sometimes a new generation answers them the same way the previous generation did; sometimes it does not. Today, we seem to be confronting these problems in far different ways than before.

Essentially, these issues all concern what rights and immunities psychiatrically impaired persons can expect from society—and what society can in return expect from them.

Some of these issues are as old as recorded history. The question of what society ought to do to protect itself from dangerous persons, including people suffering from mental disorders, is one of great antiquity. So is the issue of competency to stand trial: Over 600 years ago, Western societies debated the appropriateness of trying a person for a crime committed during a psychotic episode.

Some of the other issues considered in this chapter, however, are more specific to current concerns. They reflect commitments to civil liberties and civil rights that are rare even among modern Western democracies. For example, many patients' rights issues have only arisen in the past two decades. They ask whether psychiatric patients committed to a hospital against their will have a right to expect treatment, to be treated in the "least restrictive environment," and to be free to refuse possibly harmful treatments. These questions reflect the growing conviction that even seriously disturbed persons have civil rights we cannot ignore.

Our country seems intent on continuing its legal efforts to humanize psychiatric patients' care, at least if that care is protected by constitutional guarantees. One such constitutional guarantee is the right to live under humane conditions. This means that persons committed to a public psychiatric facility have the right to a humane environment—one that is clean, orderly, appropriately furnished, and well staffed.

Some may find these efforts to guarantee the civil rights of mental patients paradoxical. They might seem so in view of America's clear failure to stem the tide of the homeless—many of them mentally ill—in our cities, to provide adequate public hospital facilities in caring for the poor with serious physical and psychiatric disease, and to begin adequately addressing drug addiction in our cities.

Mental Health Professionals and the Law

Most of the issues discussed in this section concern mental health professionals, mental patients, attorneys, judges, and, sometimes, juries. Mental health professionals—psychiatrists and psychologists—are routinely called as expert witnesses during court proceedings. They help determine if a defendant is dangerous and should be involuntarily committed for psychiatric treatment or is competent to stand trial or should have child custody (Curran, McGarry, & Shah, 1986). Although it is the responsibility of a judge and (in cases involving them) jury to finally determine these matters, psychologists and psychiatrists are usually asked their opinions as experts on behavior before a decision is made. In fact, mental health professionals' involvement is legally mandated for certain cases in all states (Bloom & Rogers, 1987).

How useful are mental health professionals in helping courts resolve such complex issues? While nearly everyone agrees they have important roles in resolving them, the quality of their judgments, as Box 18.1 suggests, has sometimes been disappointing (Ennis & Litwack, 1974; Rofman, Askinazi, & Fant, 1980).

Why are these well-trained professionals' efforts sometimes considered inadequate? Partially, this is because of the extremely difficult questions being asked and partially, because of the nature of our adversarial system (Grisso, 1987; Petrella & Poythress, 1983).

Psychologists and psychiatrists serving as expert witnesses are typically asked to answer the hardest human questions imaginable (Perlin & Sadoff, 1982). They include predicting the likelihood that a person will be dangerous to society or himself or herself in the future on the basis of clues from past behavior; deciding which of two loving parents will provide the most competent care for a child during a ten- to fifteen-year period; and judging whether someone's current mental state prevents that individual from understanding the criminal charges against him or her, defending himself or herself against those charges, or both.

Our legal system's adversarial nature requires both sides in a civil or criminal legal matter to try to convince a judge and, often, a jury of the correctness of

Mental health professionals routinely testify as expert witnesses in court cases.

BOX 18.1 How Effectively Do Mental Health Professionals Help Make Mental Health/Legal Decisions?

How effective are mental health professionals in helping judges and juries make predictions of dangerousness or judgments about competence to stand trial? "Not very effective" in the opinion of one prominent psychologist, also trained as an attorney.

- Mental health professionals commit between 100 and 600 false positive errors (by concluding that someone is or will be dangerous who is not or will not be) for every 100 true positives they identify. . . . The art is so inaccurate and the base rate of dangerousness so low that the only known way to improve accuracy would be to categorize each person as nondangerous.
- Of every 1,000 criminal cases prosecuted, the insanity defense is raised in fewer than 10 and succeeds in fewer than 3. A survey showed legislators mistakenly believed that the insanity defense was raised 20 times as often and succeeded 40 times as often as actually occurred.
- Despite the lack of evidence of their reliability or validity, the recommendations of psychiatrists are followed in 98% of cases, but the presence of legal counsel (for the patient) has in some studies been seen to reduce the commitment rate to a fraction of the former rate. Yet only very recently have most states granted involuntary mental patients a right to the assistance of counsel.
- Whatever rights patients may have, one third of mental health professionals believe that patients should be kept ignorant of them.

Source: From Sax, M.J. (1984). Some data to enlighten some doctrines. *Contemporary Psychology, 137,* p. 1061–1064.

their opposing viewpoints. In certain cases—including those involving the prediction of human behavior—where it is not possible to provide answers to difficult questions, each side is usually able to find one or more mental health professionals willing to support it. The apparent ease with which mental health professionals can be found to testify for either side in custody, competency, and dangerousness disputes has convinced some (e.g., Shah & McGarry, 1986) that "expert" testimony is of little use. Others, though, cite data attesting to psychologists' ability to predict suicide attempts, dangerousness, and the likelihood of spouse abuse (e.g., Applebaum & Rosenbaum, 1989).

Dangerousness and "the Duty to Warn"

Predicting Dangerousness. Among the most difficult, common, and important judgments mental health professionals must make concern dangerousness. A patient is dangerous when he or she is likely to commit a violent act against himself or herself or against another person.

For example, confronted with a frantic patient convinced that her psychotic ex-husband will make good on his repeated threat to kill her unless she returns to him, a therapist must decide if the threat poses sufficient danger to justify trying to commit the man. Or, asked by a parole board whether a long-time state prison inmate who has served most of a lengthy sentence for assault with a deadly weapon has been rehabilitated, the prison psychiatrist must determine if the personality traits which led the individual to commit the crime twenty years ago still exist or have disappeared. Requested by colleagues on the adolescent unit of a state hospital to see a young woman, committed to the hospital a month ago after attempting suicide, the ward psychologist must decide whether the patient has gained enough control to ensure she won't try again if released. And, sitting across from a delusional schizophrenic patient who has recently decided that the therapist is conspiring with his family to have him committed, the therapist must decide whether the patient is going to assault her and, if so, what to do about it.

These are some common situations where mental health professionals need to make predictions about future behavior—in this case, behavior potentially dangerous to the patient, to the people around the patient, or both.

Data on mental health professionals' ability to predict long-term dangerousness have tended to be discouraging (Kozol, Boucher, & Garofalo, 1972; Monahan, 1981), largely because the likelihood of violent acts seems to depend more on the immediate circumstances preceding the violence than on the attacker's personality. Recently, however, Applebaum and Rosenbaum (1989) have reported that the more extensive the behavioral data on individuals who might be dangerous, the greater the accuracy of the dangerousness predictions.

It is also very hard to know whether a person with a past history of violence but substantial current treatment will be able to deal with marital discord or stress on the job in five or ten years without resorting to violence. The farther into the future a professional must predict behavior, the less likely it is that he or she will know the factors most likely to influence that behavior. As a result, the prediction of immediate dangerousness is easier. For example, violent behavior by patients committed to an acute inpatient unit because they were considered dangerous to others during the first seventy-two hours of their hospitalization was significantly higher than violence shown by patients in the same hospital for a longer period of time. These findings suggest that the clinicians involved validly predicted the likelihood of violence in their newly committed patients (McNeil & Binder, 1987).

The U.S. Supreme Court has acknowledged the difficulty of predicting dangerousness, estimating, at best, one correct prediction of dangerousness out of three. In *Barefoot v. Estelle,* the Court ruled on a case involving a convicted murderer found to be dangerous by a psychiatrist. That finding had influenced a jury's death penalty deliberations. The Court concluded that "Neither petitioner [Barefoot] nor the [American Psychiatric] Association suggests that psychiatrists are always wrong with respect to future dangerousness, only most of the time."

Tarasoff and the Duty to Warn. Despite the difficulty of predicting long-term dangerousness, psychologists and psychiatrists sometimes must make clinical predictions of behavior they know have only little better odds than chance to happen, even though these judgments are of enormous importance to all concerned (Huber, Roth, Appelbaum, & Ore, 1982). The importance of the judgment of dangerousness to the mental health professional has become far greater since the decision on *Tarasoff v. Regents of the University of California* was handed down by the California Supreme Court in 1976 (Mills, Sullivan, & Eth, 1987).

Prosenjit Poddar, a student at the University of California, Berkeley, became obsessed with Tatiana Tarasoff, another student, after meeting her at a student mixer. He began tape-recording conversations with her, spending many hours listening to the tapes to determine whether she had begun to return his strong feelings of attraction. A friend, worried about the obsession, urged Poddar to seek treatment at the student health service of the university. After an initial evaluation by Dr. Gold, a psychiatrist, he was assigned to Dr. Moore, a psychologist. He received weekly psychotherapy and a tranquilizing medication. Neither Dr. Gold nor Dr. Moore thought Poddar needed hospitalization.

During therapy, Poddar revealed his thoughts of harming, even killing, Tarasoff because she did not return his affections. Dr. Moore also learned from Poddar's friend that he was considering buying a gun. Shortly thereafter, Poddar dropped out of therapy. At this point, Drs. Moore and Gold agreed that hospitalization should be considered and asked the campus police to help bring him to the student health service for evaluation. The campus police went to Poddar's apartment and asked him about his plans; when he denied any intention to hurt Tarasoff, they left.

Two months later, Poddar stabbed Tarasoff to death. He was indicted for first-degree murder and ultimately convicted of second-degree murder. When that conviction was overturned on technical grounds (the judge's improper instructions to the jury), Poddar returned home to India. Subsequently, Tarasoff's family brought suit for negligence against the university, including Drs. Gold and Moore as well as the university police.

The California Supreme Court decided in 1974 that, if the facts in the case were as alleged, Drs. Gold and Moore had had a duty to warn Tarasoff. The court

Tatiana Tarasoff, whose murder by Prosenjit Poddar led to the Tarasoff Decision *and the Duty to Warn.)*

did not find either the doctors or the university policy liable for failing to hospitalize Poddar. This judicial decision thereby established for the first time the legal responsibility of psychotherapists to warn persons threatened during the course of psychotherapy, a responsibility that is now termed the Tarasoff Standard. *(Mills, Sullivan, & Eth, 1987, pp. 69–70)*

The language of Tarasoff *is clear:*

> When a therapist determines, or pursuant to the standards of his profession should determine, that his patient presents a serious danger of violence to another (person), he incurs an obligation to use reasonable care to protect the intended victim against such danger. . . . (This duty) may call for (the therapist) to warn the intended victim or others likely to apprise the victim of the danger, to notify the police, or take whatever other steps are reasonably necessary under the circumstances. (Tarasoff v. Regents of University of California, 551 P.2d 334, 340 [Cal. 1976])

In its decision on *Tarasoff,* the Court specified that only therapists had the clear duty to warn, presumably assuming they know their patients better and can make the difficult judgment of dangerousness more accurately than anyone else.

Fearful of *Tarasoff* liability suits in those states which have adopted the standard, some clinicians have begun hospitalizing patients to prevent violence even though these patients don't otherwise require inpatient treatment. According to Applebaum (1988b), the result is a system of "preventive detention" that uses scarce mental health resources to deal with what may actually be the criminal justice system's responsibility.

Predicting Suicide. Clinicians are more confident they can predict the seriousness of a suicide attempt though, as with dangerousness, data supporting that conviction are not extensive. Psychologists and psychiatrists have, nevertheless, developed criteria for this judgment which many use. Box 18.2 provides one of the most thorough lists of "suicide indicators." It includes most of the factors that are associated with completed, or successful, suicides.

Civil Commitment

What Is Civil Commitment? Despite the turmoil and confusion they may be experiencing, individuals whose behavior represents a danger to themselves or others are often willing to consent to hospitalization. But what if these troubled persons cannot or will not agree to voluntary hospitalization? In such cases, when hospitalization is clearly indicated but the patient refuses it, **civil commitment,** or *involuntary hospitalization,* may be necessary.

Emotionally, legally, and professionally, civil commitment presents dilemmas that most mental health professionals would prefer to avoid. First, the formal process of civil commitment is time consuming and expensive. Second, it may pit patient against family or patient against mental health professional. Third, the legal rules for commitment are sometimes unclear and confusing so professionals might be uncertain about what the circumstances require. At certain times and in certain instances, however, most mental health professionals decide that civil commitment is the only alternative to allowing frightened, psychotic persons to seek their own resolution of a problem, either at their own expense or at the expense of others.

Few legal or ethical issues of concern to mental health professionals have been as hotly debated for as long as those surrounding involuntary hospitaliza-

BOX 18.2 Predictors of Completed Suicides

1. The lack of a therapeutic alliance with the therapist;
2. Severing formerly meaningful relationships and failing to substitute new ones;
3. The presence of severe depression;
4. The presence of psychosis, particularly if auditory hallucinations that command particular actions are present;
5. Prior suicide attempts, particularly a recent attempt;
6. Remission of a psychotic episode but continuance of secondary depression;
7. Advancing age, personal loss, or physical illness, particularly if the latter is chronic;
8. Single or divorced;
9. High lethality potential (dangerousness) of the method used to attempt suicide. (Jumping from a high bridge represents a more dangerous suicide attempt than consuming four aspirin tablets.)
10. Behavior possibly indicative of a finalized decision to die;
11. Presence of a specific plan;
12. Availability of a lethal means;
13. A family history of suicide;
14. Chronic alcoholism;
15. Drug addiction;
16. Age group 15–24;
17. Mental incompetency interfering with the development of a therapeutic alliance.

Source: From Simon, T.R. (1987). *Clinical Psychiatry and the Law.* Washington D.C.: American Psychiatric Press, p. 259. By permission of the publisher.

tion. Few have generated such a volume of rhetoric, some of it reviewed next. And, partly because of this continuing debate, few issues have caused such radical changes in public and professional attitudes during the past two decades (Dix, 1982).

Civil Commitment Criteria. To commit someone to a psychiatric hospital today in most states, he or she must be judged *mentally ill, dangerous to himself or herself or to others, unwilling to enter a hospital voluntarily, capable of benefitting from treatment, or gravely disabled,* and sufficiently troubled that *hospitalization is the least restrictive alternative.* Additionally, some states require that the person *lack the capacity to make a reasoned decision* about the need for treatment. This formidable list of admissions criteria suggests why decreasing numbers of people are being hospitalized against their will nowadays.

Mental Illness. Most states require involuntarily hospitalized persons to be "mentally ill." Some states specifically define mental illness whereas others are more vague. Consequently, it is far easier in some states than in others to satisfy a judge that the mental illness criterion for commitment has been met (e.g., by demonstrating that a competent psychologist or psychiatrist has given the patient a formal *DSM-III-R* diagnosis of schizophrenia or major depressive disorder).

Mental health professionals do partially base commitment decisions on the presence or absence of mental illness. Yet mental illness is generally not as important in that decision as other factors, notably ability to care for self and dangerousness (Appelbaum & Hamm, 1982; Schwartz, Appelbaum, & Kaplan, 1984).

Dangerousness. Before the 1960s, proof of mental illness alone was sufficient to justify most involuntary commitments. Many persons who therefore could have managed on their own or in a sheltered environment outside a hospital were forced to spend some, much, or all their lives in a hospital, simply because someone concluded they were mentally ill and in need of treatment.

Following a California Supreme Court decision in 1969, however, one state court after another considered mental illness alone insufficient to justify involuntary hospitalization. As in California, they required proof that the person was either dangerous to himself or herself or to others, or gravely disabled, and mentally ill.

In our earlier consideration of dangerousness and the legal "duty to warn," we emphasized the difficulties even well-trained psychologists and psychiatrists have in predicting dangerousness, especially if the prediction extends over a lengthy period of time. Box 18.3 compellingly illustrates some of these problems in prediction. As the case example in Box 18.3 suggests, mental health professionals and judges alike must ask themselves a number of questions in evaluating dangerousness.

This is a cell in a hospital for the criminally insane. Most of the patients in the hospital have been judged dangerous to others.

- *How serious is the danger?* Is a person who occasionally exposes his genitals sufficiently dangerous to society to justify his civil commitment? Is a person who steals but has never committed a violent crime against another person dangerous enough to be committed?
- *How imminent is the danger?* If a person threatens to harm someone years after he or she makes the threat, is that threat imminent enough to justify commitment?
- *How real is the threat?* How probable is it that a threat to someone else will be carried out?
- *Can mental health professionals agree on commitment criteria, including dangerousness?*

This important question has begun to be studied. In assessing the reliability of professionals' judgments, recent studies now encourage the belief that mental health professionals working in hospital emergency rooms can be trained to agree on assessments of dangerousness and commitability (Lidz,

BOX 18.3 The Hazards of Predicting Dangerousness

Barker became convinced that the woman he had lived with for ten years (referred to as his "wife") was having an affair with a neighbor. Four events, all occurring within a few months of the hearing, were adduced to show dangerousness. First, Barker tried to punch the neighbor but missed. Second, Barker, who had been drinking, argued with his wife, fired shots from a revolver through an open door, and then feigned an attempt at suicide by firing a blank shell at his head. Third, Barker appeared at his sister's house brandishing a gun, said he was looking for his wife, but then left. Fourth, Barker broke a beer bottle and waved the jagged shards at his wife. The event triggering the commitment was a midnight phone call by Barker in which he charged that the neighbor and his wife were engaged in sodomy. The two examining psychiatrists agreed that Barker suffered from paranoid psychosis characterized by paranoid jealousy delusions, but disagreed about whether he would be dangerous. The court clearly thought that there might be something to Barker's belief that his neighbor was engaged in an affair with his wife. But it concluded that "(e)ven if we assume that the defendant was in fact delusional, we must recognize that the delusion did not produce at the time it happened any violent or dangerous conduct." Even after considering all of Barker's actions together, the court reversed the commitment and ordered his release.

Source: Stromberg, D.C., Haggarty, D.J., Leibenluft, R.F., McMillian, M.H., Mishkin, B., Rubin, B.L., & Trilling, H.R. (1988). *The Psychologist's Legal Handbook*. Washington D.C.: Council for the National Register of Health Service Providers in Psychology, pp. 559–560. By permission of the publisher.

Mulvey, Appelbaum, & Cleveland, 1989; Phillips, Wolf, & Coons, 1988).

Another recent research program has led to an eighty-eight-item questionnaire, *the Index of Dangerousness Indicators* (TRIAD), designed to reliably and validly assess dangerousness to self, others, and grave disability (Segal, Watson, Goldfinger, & Averbuck, 1988a; 1988b). Data from the TRIAD have revealed that clinicians' ratings of dangerousness and of the severity of mental illness are highly correlated (Segal, Watson, Goldfinger, & Averbuck, 1988c). This important latter finding offers empirical data to those who claim that overemphasizing dangerousness in the commitment process neglects persons who are severely mentally ill in favor of those less ill but dangerous.

As unreliable as assessments of dangerousness and diagnoses of mental illness have been until recently, getting clinicians to agree that someone is gravely disabled and cannot provide for his or her own needs has been even tougher. Such a decision turns out to be extremely crucial. As illustrated in Table 18.1, two studies of experienced clinicians' decisions to recommend commitment (Appelbaum & Hamm, 1982; Schwartz, Appelbaum & Kaplan, 1984) indicate that *patients' ability to care for themselves* ("Place to live," "Ability to care for self") had the greatest impact on the clinicians' commitment recommendations. This factor ranked above both *dangerousness to others and to self* and *mental illness* ("Psychotic," "Crazy/sane") in influencing their decision making.

Refusal of Voluntary Treatment. Most states consider patients for civil commitment after they have refused voluntary treatment. This ensures that voluntary efforts to secure needed treatment for seriously disturbed patients are always made first. Most mental health professionals agree that coerced treatment—almost certainly less effective than voluntary treatment—is the second-best choice, to be considered only after noncoercive efforts' failure to arrange needed treatment.

Treatability. Not only must patients considered for civil commitment have refused voluntary treatment—and be both mentally ill and a danger to self or others—they must also suffer from the kinds of

TABLE 18.1 Correlations between Patient Characteristics and the Decision to Seek Commitment

Patient Characteristic	Correlation	Rank
Study 1 (1982)		
Place to live	.55	1
Ability to care for self	.52	2
Danger to self	.52	3
Crazy/sane	.37	6
Danger to others	.36	7
Study 2 (1984)		
Ability to care for self	.58	1
Psychotic	.56	2
Danger to others	.49	3
Place to live	.40	7
Danger to self	.34	11

Source: From Appelbaum, P.S., & Hamm, R.M., 1982, Decision to seek commitment, *Archives of General Psychiatry 39*, p. 449. Copyright 1982, American Medical Association.

psychiatric disorders likely to respond to treatment at the facilities where they would be committed. This civil commitment criterion reflects the importance of "right to treatment," discussed previously. Patients cannot be committed against their wills to hospitals unable to provide them treatment.

What if a person meets all the listed criteria for commitment except for the criterion of treatability? In such cases, the person will typically have to be considered for involuntary referral to a correctional facility (if judged clearly dangerous) or another "supportive environment" (if judged not clearly dangerous).

A study of 102 male inmates of a county jail referred for psychiatric evaluation indicates that correctional facilities may in fact be "dumping places" for the psychiatrically disabled (Lamb & Grant, 1982). Ninety percent of the 102 inmates studied had had at least one psychiatric hospitalization, whereas 92 percent had prior arrest records, 75 percent for felonies. Roughly 80 percent of the 102 showed severe psychopathology; more than 75 percent met the usual criteria for involuntary hospitalization. In other words, the people involuntarily committed to psychiatric hospitals and those sentenced to county and state correctional institutions are unable to function in our complex society in many of the same ways. This fact points up our society's problems in caring for its least competent members.

Gravely Disabled. Mental patients who do not meet the dangerousness criterion but clearly do require and would benefit from treatment can be committed if they cannot exercise the good judgment required to know that they are sick, incapacitated, and in need of treatment.

Least Restrictive Alternative. The courts in most states must consider plans for civil commitment that are least restrictive of patients' freedom and civil rights.

Sometimes, paradoxically, relatively brief periods of hospitalization designed to establish patients on effective antipsychotic drug regimens actually meet least restrictive standards: A period of inpatient treatment might be less restrictive than no hospitalization and no treatment in the long run—if the hospitalization and medication permit the patient to plan for or resume a productive and meaningful place in society.

In the few communities which have them, other less restrictive alternatives include "community residential treatment facilities." These supervised group units generally provide less restrictive and regimented living environments than large, traditional psychiatric hospitals. Although most local political leaders favor such alternatives to hospitalization, many have been unable to mobilize the public support required to produce the necessary public funds and places in the community.

Most states now permit commitment to outpatient treatment. One of outpatient commitment's advantages is the greater choice of least restrictive alternatives it gives judges. Another is its restriction of the flow of patients back to the state hospitals. Why then are commitments to outpatient treatment so rare (Lamb, Weinberger, & Gross, 1988)?

One reason is that many acute psychotic conditions require a hospitalization period so that patients can receive antipsychotic medication and then be monitored and controlled for possibly dangerous side effects. Another reason is that significant concerns over the efficacy of coerced treatment, especially coerced outpatient treatment, have emerged (Geller, 1986; Mulvey, Geller, & Roth, 1987). Antipsychotic medication's effectiveness is likely to be independent of whether patients are in a hospital voluntarily. However, the effectiveness of the psychotherapy often accompanying the medication given to outpatients clearly varies with their motivation for treatment. Moreover, that motivation depends partially on whether they have freely chosen to participate in the treatment.

History of the Concept of Civil Commitment. The laws governing civil commitment have changed dramatically during the past twenty years. Before 1969, involuntary hospitalization of mental patients in most states simply required the patient to be judged "in need of treatment" (Appelbaum, 1985). Assuming that commitment to a hospital for treatment was a benevolent act—in the best interests of all concerned—most courts held legal protections like due process (which includes being able to confront the person responsible for the commitment process, to have a hearing before a judge, to have representation by an attorney) to be unnecessary. Police, families, and society agreed that the best place for some psychotic persons was the state hospital. Even if treatment wasn't provided, at least the person would be taken care of and be out of sight, if not mind (Brakel, 1986).

Beginning in the early 1960s, however, young people began to question many kinds of American social institutions. Old views of mental disorder—of the motivations of the people involved in the care and treatment of mental patients and of civil commitment's standards and purposes—were examined. Inspired by Thomas Szasz's "Myth of Mental Illness," movies like *One Flew Over the Cuckoo's Nest,* and a general dissatisfaction with the status quo brought on by the Vietnam War and the civil rights movement, Americans began to question civil commitment's goals and the relative ease it could be accomplished with (Meisel, 1982).

In 1969, California adopted a radically different commitment standard. To be committed, an individual had to be judged dangerous to self or others or gravely disabled. (Persons clearly suicidal or self-destructive are dangers to themselves. Persons suffering from paranoid delusions that might cause them to assault another person are dangers to others. Persons who are so confused or demented that they cannot provide for their own basic physical needs for food and shelter or who might walk in front of a car or fall into an open construction site are gravely disabled.) Hospitalization simply because treatment seemed indicated was no longer sufficient in California. Since then, virtually every state has adopted the so-called dangerousness criterion (Hoge, Appelbaum, & Greer, 1989).

The authority of psychiatrists, psychologists, the police, and judges to commit has, consequently, been severely narrowed (Hoge et al., 1988). Legal protections for individuals under threat of commitment comparable to those available to persons accused of crimes have also been enacted. A dramatic reduction in the number of persons committed to psychiatric facilities (Figure 18.1) has been one result (Peters, Miller, Schmidt & Meeter, 1987).

Patients' Rights

Patients' Rights through History. Psychiatric patients' living conditions through the ages have often been deplorable. Only after Philippe Pinel mobilized revolutionary France to humanize psychiatric patients' institutional treatment less than 200 years ago did Western society begin to worry seriously about psychiatric patients' living conditions (see Chapter 1). Despite Pinel's efforts, as well as those of reformers in virtually every country in the following 200 years (Dorothea Dix was American society's most energetic psychiatric reformer), psychiatric patients in most countries continue to have poor living conditions by contemporary standards. Why? First, their plight reflects the significant costs of maintaining psychiatric hospitals. Second, it is also the result

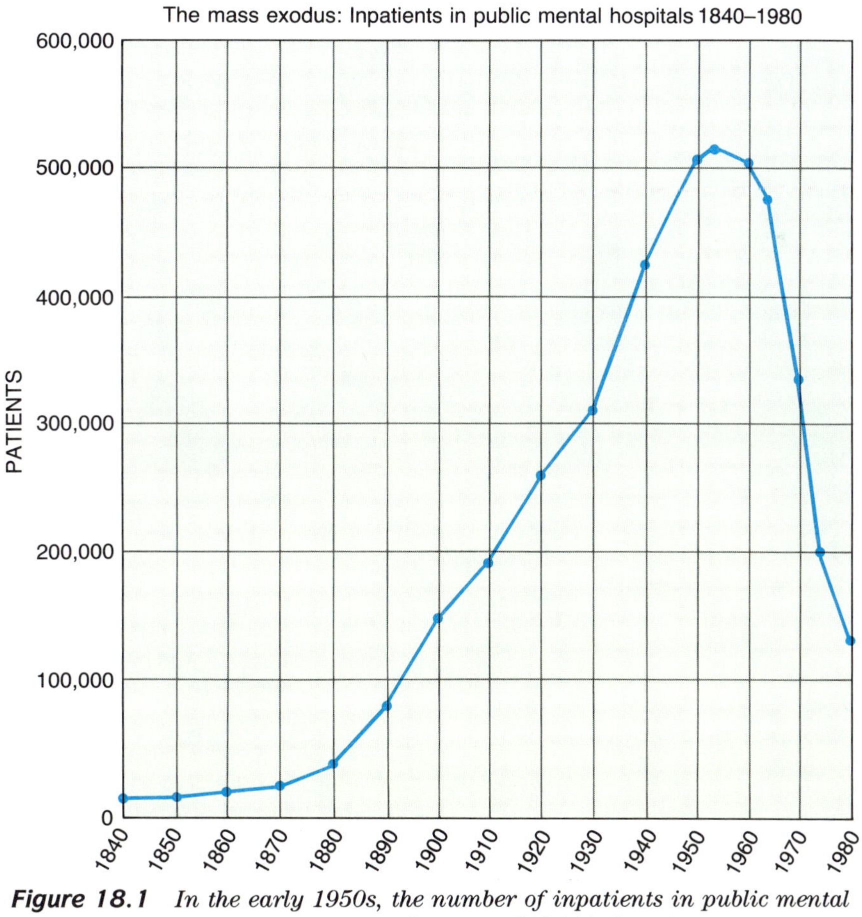

Figure 18.1 *In the early 1950s, the number of inpatients in public mental hospitals in this country peaked at just over 500,000. Shortly thereafter, the number began a precipitous decline.*

Source: Figure from *Nowhere to go* by E. Fuller Torrey. Copyright 1988 by E. Fuller Torrey. Reprinted by permission of Harper-Collins Publishers.

of the stigma most societies have traditionally attached to mental disorder, whereby psychotic patients are seen as less than human—justification of our inhumane treatment of them (Bell, 1980; Goffman, 1961).

Recent Changes in Concern for Patients' Rights. The conditions psychiatric patients have traditionally lived under in many state hospitals in the United States became a major legal battleground in the 1960s, though psychiatric reformers had long been concerned by them.

An important consequence was **deinstitutionalization,** a national movement to empty the state psychiatric hospitals of as many psychiatric patients as possible. Twenty years later, deinstitutionalization had resulted in the release into the community of three quarters of the involuntary (committed) psychiatric patients living in our public psychiatric hospitals at the beginning of the 1960s. Consequently, most public psychiatric hospitals have closed, and the total population of patients still in the remaining facilities represents a small fraction of the number living there twenty years ago. On an average day in 1955, 560,000 people were involuntarily confined in state and county mental hospitals; by 1972, that number had declined to 276,000; and, by 1981, it had dwindled to 138,000 (U.S. Dept. of Health & Human Services, 1981).

One goal of deinstitutionalization is to enable as many patients as possible to live closer to family and friends in apartments and group homes in their home communities, rather than in large, impersonal public hospitals (Shadish, 1984). Idealistically and theoretically a great step forward, deinstitutionalization has been only modestly successful in practice (Bachrach, 1976). One of the most important reasons is the failure of many states to adequately plan and pay for alternative programs for psychiatric patients released from the hospitals to their home communities (Kramer, 1977).

Too few community residences, not enough community mental health centers with staff workers willing and able to care for chronic mental patients, and a shortage of sheltered work environments have led to enormously increased numbers of the homeless, many of them chronically mentally ill. Precise numbers are hard to come by, though. The homeless, by definition, do not have an address at which census takers or community workers can find them.

A recent study of 529 homeless adults in Los Angeles (Gelberg, Linn, & Leake, 1988) reveals some of the consequences of our failure to care for the homeless mentally ill. The 232 persons in that sample (44 percent of the entire sample) with a previous psychiatric hospitalization (1) were least likely to use emergency shelters, (2) had been homeless almost twice as long as subjects without that history, (3) had

One of the unintended consequences of deinstitutionalization was a dramatic increase in the number of the homeless.

The squalor, boredom, and degredation of most public psychiatric hospitals was a prominent cause of the patients' rights movement.

the worst mental health status, (4) abused alcohol and drugs the most, and (5) were most involved in criminal activities.

Another study of the homeless (Bachrach, 1984) focuses on the special problems of mentally ill women, who may suffer even more than men because of our inadequate preparation for the needs of the deinstitutionalized. These women are especially likely to be sexually exploited, targeted as objects of violence, involved in crime, and stigmatized for their mental disorders.

The **patients' rights movement** was another consequence of American society's dissatisfaction with the treatment of the mentally ill. Activists believed it was bad enough for institutionalized patients to live in filth and squalor in the 1960s, as they had for centuries before. But did they also have to be denied most of the civil and legal rights and privileges others in society enjoyed—simply because they were victims of psychiatric disorder? At approximately the same time, research began to suggest that some of the most serious psychiatric disorders had a genetic and biochemical basis. Hence, the essential unfairness of denying basic human rights to patients suffering from disorders with physical causes became even more evident (Suchotliff, Steinfeld, & Tolchin, 1970; Wilson, Beyer, & Yudowitz, 1977).

Thus, when asked to consider the rights of patients committed to public psychiatric hospitals, state courts often concluded that patients had a *right to treatment*—because of the state's obligations owed as part of the hospitalization "contract." The courts also ruled that patients committed to public institutions deserved *humane living conditions* and, when possible, *privacy*. In addition, many judges decided that even committed psychiatric patients deserved a right to many of the same *legal safeguards* as guaranteed in the Constitution to defendants in criminal cases (Meisel, 1982). Among these are the right to be represented by an attorney and the right to confront witnesses whose testimony threatens one's liberty.

During the same period, the 1960s and 1970s, criteria for civil commitment (involuntary commitment to a psychiatric hospital) were made more stringent. Additional legal safeguards and protections were required for individuals threatened with commitment (Dix, 1982).

The General Civil Rights of Mental Patients. Being a voluntary patient in a mental hospital or having been committed to one against your will does not by itself deprive you of your civil rights or prove you incapable of exercising them today. Although these protections have not always been available to patients in mental hospitals, most courts nowadays firmly uphold them (Meisel, 1982). These rights, however, do not guarantee that you may not be judged incapable of doing such things as driving a car, making certain business or legal decisions, or exercising parental rights and responsibilities should a court make such a decision on reasonable grounds.

Specific Rights of Mental Patients. In most states, involuntary mental patients now have legal protection for specific rights.

Right to Treatment. Although common sense may indicate that mental patients have the right to treatment, the law first recognized it in 1971 in the famous *Wyatt v. Stickney* decision handed down by a federal district court in Alabama. Before *Wyatt,* patients involuntarily committed to underfunded public institutions could not and did not receive treatment there. Instead, they languished in the dayrooms of these institutions' closed wards for months or years, receiving no treatment yet remaining there because no one outside would assume responsibility for them.

Living conditions for patients in Alabama state hospitals were particularly deplorable, among the worst in the nation. A history of inadequate state funding for the care of Alabama's state hospital patients had resulted in deteriorating buildings and leaking roofs; poorly paid, poorly trained, poorly motivated hospital workers; few fully trained mental health professionals; frequently inedible food; and filthy bedclothes. Worst of all, state funding inadequacies had condemned most patients to long days with nothing to do—and no treatment for the disorders which had brought them to the hospital. No occupational or recreational therapy, and little or no individual or group therapy, could be provided because persons trained to provide them could not be hired. Instead, patients tended to be heavily dosed with sedating drugs so they could be managed by the few employees staffing each ward.

Wyatt v. Stickney was brought in an effort to force the state of Alabama to meet its responsibilities to these committed patients. The most important was deemed to be treatment, though *Wyatt* also mandated such additional rights as the right of patients to wear clothing of their choice, to interact with the opposite sex (under controlled conditions), and to be free from physical restraints except in psychiatric emergencies.

The reasoning behind *Wyatt v. Stickney* is compelling:

> To deprive any person of his or her liberty upon the altruistic theory that the confinement is for humane therapeutic reasons and then fail to provide adequate treatment violates the very fundamentals of due process.

Besides treatment, state and federal courts have also demanded other improvements in committed patients' care. They have concluded, for example, that patients have the right to prompt and effective medical treatment for illnesses and injuries. Patients also deserve clean, well-heated, and well-lit living units, with as much personal privacy as possible. Finally, courts have found that patients also have the right to protection from physical or verbal threat from disturbed, psychotic patients.

Despite the court decisions requiring these improvements in the quality of life in state mental hospitals, the courts' ability to force improvements in these amenities of life in grossly underfunded public institutions is often limited. In most instances, they cannot force legislatures to provide funds, even for mandated improvements in hospital care. Too often, a standoff has resulted between a federal or state court and overburdened state legislatures unable to bear the additional burden of the funds needed to improve services for state mental patients (O'Reilly & Sales, 1987).

Adequacy of Treatment. Not only did *Wyatt* (and the court decisions on right to treatment that followed it) ensure hospitalized mental patients' right to treatment, it also emphasized their *right to adequate treatment.* This right was originally designed to ensure that the administration of antipsychotic medications to psychotic patients would conform to usual medical practice. Heavy drug dosages given to sedate aggressive, hostile psychotic patients to protect staff from assault are unacceptable when intended only to protect staff and not to benefit patients.

Right to Least Restrictive Alternative. The concerns about humane care for mental patients mobilized by *Wyatt* led a few years afterward to *Donaldson v. O'Connor.* This established that the mentally ill can no longer be confined to a state hospital for an indefinite custodial period simply because no one can or will assume responsibility for them outside the hospital.

At least three quarters of the states have now adopted laws based on a related suit, *Dixon v. Weinberger,* affirming that least restrictive alternative also applies to the locked wards committed patients were previously sent to. Do hostile, threatening patients confined to a locked ward need to be in restraints or in a "quiet room"? How long will they have to remain on the locked ward after medication and a secure environment have helped them calm down? And when can they return to the community, to live in a group home, where they can come and go as they and their caretakers agree is appropriate?

Court decisions on the least restrictive alternative have answered some of these questions. They have addressed the question of behavior within a "specific social context," for example. This phrase refers to the fact that a patient might be considered dangerous if allowed to live alone but not dangerous if he lives in a supervised group home and takes daily antipsychotic medication. Unfortunately, least restrictive alternative also depends on the states' limited capacity to fund housing and other community services for deinstitutionalized patients. If that housing is unavailable, patients either must remain institutionalized or, on being released from the hospital, must join the ranks of the homeless.

Few could object to the humane aims of least restrictive alternative. However, there are times—for example, during an acute psychotic episode's early stages—when people benefit most from a restrictive hospital environment and antipsychotic medication, even though the psychosis may prevent them from acknowledging these needs. Such restrictive, enforced treatment may prove least restrictive in the long run if it prevents a patient from developing a chronic psychotic condition requiring long-term hospitalization.

At present, almost every state permits a new twist on the theme of least restrictive alternative: *involuntary commitment to outpatient treatment* (Bursten, 1986; Mulvey et al., 1987). Despite its appeal from cost-savings and patient rights perspectives, most states employ it relatively rarely, partially because of the difficulty in supervising and guaranteeing it. A recent five-year follow-up of seventy-nine defendants found not guilty by reason of insanity and referred to court-mandated outpatient treatment in Los Angeles (Lamb et al., 1988) eloquently makes this point. During the five-year follow-up, twenty-five of the subjects (32 percent) were rearrested, eighteen of them (72 percent) for violent crimes. In addition, thirty-seven of the seventy-nine had to be rehospitalized and thirty-eight had their conditional release from jail revoked. By any standard, these outcome figures are discouraging.

Nonetheless, as what follows suggests, mandated outpatient treatment of mental patients clearly has a place.

> *Mr. A was a 53-year-old divorced man who had had 29 admissions to his catchment area state hospital and four admissions to (Pennsylvania's) maximum security state hospital. His first admission occurred when he was 26 years old. Mr. A's admissions were generally characterized by grandiose and paranoid delusional ideation, agitation, mania, and threats that sometimes resulted in battery. Mr. A's institutional behavior included innumerable threats against hospital personnel and many episodes of physically attacking staff. . . .*
>
> *Upon his most recent discharge from the state hospital, Mr. A began living in an unsupervised residence and working part-time as a janitor. (He was also given several antipsychotic medications.) In addition to being followed under this protocol, Mr. A was seen by a psychologist in weekly psychotherapy.*
>
> *Mr. A missed neither an appointment with me nor a lithium level determination. He was consistently appropriate . . . and without thought disorder. . . . Despite side effects (from one medication), Mr. A reported that he never wished to consider a change in antipsychotic medication, stating, "I don't want to tamper with success."*
>
> *By the time Mr. A had been out of the hospital 1 year—an event he called a "miracle"—he was motivated to continue his medication regimen. He had come to cherish his nonpathological self—a self not known to him for 26 years. During his tenure in the community, Mr. A has reestablished a relationship with his mother and has developed an intimate relationship with a female peer. As of this writing, Mr. A has been without a psychiatric admission for more than 625 days.* (Geller, 1986, p. 1260)

Right to Refuse Treatment. You may find it strange to learn of the patient's *right to refuse a specific treatment*, just after we have discussed the lengthy history of efforts to ensure their right to it. The theory that committed patients have the right to refuse specific treatments, however, makes as much sense as the theory that they have a right to it.

Indeed, many states recognize the patient's right to refuse treatment. That right arose in recognition of the fact that, for years, some agitated and troublesome psychotic patients were forced to take massive doses of powerful antipsychotic drugs or to submit to psychosurgery or electric shock therapy (and to suffer these treatments' serious side effects) to make them more manageable. Consequently, the courts have now given involuntary patients the right to resist inappropriate or dangerous "treatment" under certain circumstances.

In one of the cases most often linked to the right to refuse treatment, *Rennie v. Klein*, decided in 1978, a depressed schizophrenic patient in New Jersey was given the "qualified right" to refuse antipsychotic medication that he feared would cause him permanent harm. The judge imposed qualifications related to whether, unmedicated, the patient would be more likely to injure himself or others, other treatments were available, and the patient's belief was valid that the medications forced on him were potentially dangerous. The judge in the *Rennie* decision also prescribed a process by which both patient and hospital could appeal a treatment or its refusal if they wished.

A subsequent Supreme Court decision, *Rogers v. Okin*, has questioned the *Rennie* precedent, in view of the proven efficacy of the medications now given to committed psychotic patients. As a consequence, the issue is now back in the state courts, which have taken a number of diverse and, at times, conflicting positions on this right to refuse treatment. Many mental health professionals believe that the right to refuse treatment is of questionable logic under certain circumstances. One such circumstance occurs when seriously disturbed persons with impaired judgment can refuse the treatment that would actually restore them to health and permit their return to freedom (Appelbaum, 1988a; Veliz & James, 1987).

Box 18.4 presents two brief case examples of patients who inappropriately refused treatment and were subsequently found incompetent to make that decision. They illustrate the knotty problems facing mental health professionals and the courts when they are asked to balance patients' rights to refuse treatment with their rights to appropriate treatment.

Privacy, Confidentiality, and Privileged Communication. Privacy, confidentiality, and privileged communication are familiar social and interpersonal concepts that legally define specific relationships between psychiatric patients and mental health professionals, as well as between mental health researchers and their subjects.

Privacy. Privacy, the broadest of the legal concepts discussed here, refers to the right all of us enjoy to the privacy of our own homes and personal lives. Most people value this right for themselves and respect it for others. We do not ask strangers or casual acquaintances intimate details about their lives, nor do we expect them to ask us about ours. Despite the widespread belief that the right to privacy is enshrined in the Constitution, it is not explicitly mentioned. Instead, it has been inferred to be within the scope of certain other explicit constitutional rights.

Psychiatric patients have the right to expect the professionals who care for them to respect their privacy, by only entering into those areas of their lives directly relevant to the clinical situation. Practically, we cannot always distinguish what is relevant in the personal history of a person with a behavior disorder. Patients and psychologists may disagree about where to draw that line.

Certain kinds of privacy-infringing behaviors by professionals are, nevertheless, always out of bounds. These include unnecessarily calling patients at home or inquiring about intimate details of patients' sexual history when they have entered treatment with an entirely different problem.

Research subjects also have the right to privacy (Adair, Dushenko, & Lindsay, 1985; Stanley, Sieber, & Melton, 1987). Primarily, they have the right to expect that their responses to questionnaires, their performance on personality tests, or their answers to interview questions will not be disclosed to others or published in such a way to reveal their identity.

Mental health professionals also have a socially agreed-on and legal right to privacy. Thus, patients are not supposed to interest themselves in their therapists' personal life, even though they are often extremely curious and eager to ask about it.

Social convention usually assures that patients and mental health professionals respect each other's rights to privacy. Sometimes, though, the ordinary, unspoken rules of society are not enough. When that happens, legal sanctions can be invoked to protect whoever is threatened by the invasion of privacy. The ethical standards of the four core mental health professions specifically uphold the right to privacy. The *Ethical Principles of Psychologists* state

> Psychologists who present personal information obtained during the course of professional work in writings, lectures, or other public forums (must) either obtain adequate prior consent to do so or adequately disguise all identifiers (American Psychological Association, 1990, p. 393)

BOX 18.4 Mental Patients' Incompetence to Refuse Treatment

Case 1

A 20-year-old man with paranoid schizophrenia refused his prescribed medications, articulating clearly the side effects and undesirable consequences of these drugs. The court-appointed guardian *ad litem* who had interviewed the patient was convinced that this college-educated, articulate, and well-spoken patient was fully competent. The treating physician, interviewing the patient in front of the guardian *ad litem,* directed her inquiries beyond the simple facts of the medication. The patient in response candidly revealed his elaborate delusions about how the medication was a secret poison administered at the Mafia's orders to get him to betray his country. . . .

Case 2

This 50-year-old man appeared able to grasp cognitively the concept of a 90% success rate for proposed ECT and able to recite back the stated side effects, thereby ostensibly demonstrating his competence to comprehend facts. Due to his depressed state, however, he arrived at illness-distorted conclusions regarding these facts. He assumed that he was doomed to be in the 10% failure group . . . and he expected that the side effects were absolutely certain to occur in him because that was just what he deserved. . . . (T)his patient did not demonstrate competence to weigh risks and benefits. . . .

Source: Gutheil, T.G. & Bursztajn, H. (1986). Clinicians' guidelines for assessing and presenting subtle forms of patient incompetence in legal settings. *American Journal of Psychiatry, 143,* p. 1021. Copyright 1986 by the American Psychiatric Association. Reprinted by permission.

Only under very special circumstances can the confidentiality that protects communication between a patient and a therapist be breached.

Confidentiality. Confidentiality has very specific meaning when applied to relationships between patients and therapists. Only under very special, restricted circumstances can the therapist reveal the content of conversations or other information about the patient gathered during therapy. Without this protection, many patients would be unwilling to reveal the information about themselves necessary for thorough diagnosis and effective treatment.

Confidentiality extends to virtually all information mental health professionals need to perform their jobs. It includes information about a schoolchild gathered by a school psychologist in assessing the child's ability to benefit from a special classroom placement. It includes material about a corporation's employees solicited by an industrial psychologist evaluating management potential. And it includes an evaluation of the fitness of a group of candidates for a city's police force elicited by a consultant psychiatrist. All are protected by confidentiality statutes.

However, *the confidentiality restriction is not absolute.* Mental health professionals may have to breach confidentiality in a number of situations. They include the following:

1. *If the patient agrees that the information can be released, the therapist will do so.* If a prospective employer demands data about a previous hospitalization or the patient's insurance company requires information on the length and focus of treatment, these materials may be released—but only with the patient's permission.
2. *When the law requires disclosure of information acquired by a mental health professional, it must be reported.* Most states now require reporting any suspicion of physical or sexual child abuse within thirty-six hours. Accordingly, if an adult client reports having abused a child or having seen or been aware of it, or a child client reports abuse, this information must immediately be reported to local authorities.
3. *Disclosure of confidential material is also permitted when the clinician is bound by "the duty to warn."* As discussed earlier, in the states which have adopted the *Tarasoff* standard, professionals who learn of a serious threat to another person in a confidential relationship (e.g., during treatment) are legally required to warn the threatened person and, if appropriate, to alert the police (Mills et al., 1987).

Does the duty to warn extend to the spouse or lover of a patient infected with the AIDS virus (Knapp & VandeCreek, 1990)? Does a therapist who learns a patient has AIDS have the duty to inform the patient's lover or spouse that he or she is in clear danger (Totten, Lamb, & Reeder, 1990)? Are research data gathered on AIDS victims protected by confidentiality statutes? Because the AIDS epidemic is so recent, most states have not taken a position on these matters (Gray & Melton, 1985; Melton & Gray, 1988). However, the recent action of a California court in February 1989 may set a new legal precedent. It found the estate of Rock Hudson and his long-time business manager liable for damages totaling more than $24 million for failing to inform Hudson's lover of his disease and the risk it presented him. Only in the future will we know the impact of this enormously difficult legal and ethical problem on confidentiality statutes.

4. *When disclosure of confidential information is required for legal reasons, it will be disclosed.* For example, federal and state laws governing Medicare and Medicaid programs, which pay mental health professionals to provide services to particular groups, require information on the names and addresses of patients, their Medicare or Medicaid numbers, the dates of services, and their nature. Sometimes a diagnosis is also requested.
5. *When the patient brings a lawsuit, confidentiality is not absolute.* The female patient who sues an employer for sexual harassment knows her therapist can be asked to testify about its emotional consequences, just as the passenger who has suffered irreversible brain damage in an automobile accident expects the examining neuropsychologist to report on her findings.
6. *In an emergency, confidential information can also be released.* For example, if a patient receiving drug therapy for a serious psychiatric disorder is injured in an automobile accident, the attending physicians may have to know the drug and its dosage before they can treat her injuries.

Privileged Communication. **Privileged communication** takes place in a confidential relationship, like the relationship between an attorney and a client or a patient and a licensed psychologist or psychiatrist. Communication in these relationships is protected by legal statute: Neither the attorney nor the therapist can be forced to reveal the communication's contents except under very special circumstances (such as a threat against another person or the report of child abuse.)

By ensuring the protection of confidential matters, privilege permits clients to enter into relationships with their attorneys, and patients to enter into relationships with their therapists. In both cases, each party knows that, under all but the most unusual circumstances, what they talk about together cannot be used against them in a court of law.

Competency and Responsibility

Most of our discussion has concerned the rights of mental patients, including what they have a right to expect from those charged with their care. In addition, we have described the responsibilities of mental health professionals.

In discussing competency, however, we must now consider the responsibilities of our criminal and civil justice system and the rights of persons accused of civil or criminal violations. Those rights, enshrined in the Constitution, include the right to understand the charges against oneself, the right to understand and participate in the court proceedings considering those charges, and the right to cooperate with an attorney to defend oneself. Competency for trial, discussed first, speaks to the defendant's mental condition at the time he or she is tried. By contrast, the insanity defense, considered next, concerns the defendant's mental condition when he or she committed the crime.

Competency for Trial. An accused cannot take advantage of his or her constitutional rights unless he or she is *competent to stand trial.* Accused persons must be competent to stand trial because, if they are not, they are unable to assist in their own defense, as the Constitution says they must.

The usual standard employed to assess competency to stand trial in this country was stated back in 1960, in *Dusky v. United States:*

> The test must be whether he (the defendant) has sufficient present ability to consult with his lawyer with a reasonable degree of rational understanding and whether he has a rational as well as factual understanding of the proceedings against him.

Despite the widespread acceptance of this standard, assessment of competency to stand trial is problematic, time consuming, and controversial. Some mental health professionals prefer to leave this determination to the courts because they believe it is a legal not a psychiatric decision. Others refuse to participate in competency assessments because they believe that it is sometimes arbitrary and capricious and, hence, that it goes against their ethical and moral standards (Perlin & Sadoff, 1982). Still others consider competency assessments an unpleasant but legitimate part of their job as mental health professionals and, when asked, will perform them (Homant & Kennedy, 1987).

Despite mental health professionals' reluctance to participate in competency determinations, the process is an important one. More people are probably sent to prison hospitals after being found incompetent than after being found not guilty by reason of insanity. Determination of incompetence is also important because of its long-lasting effects: Incompetent patients are denied many rights that others, including convicted criminals, can claim.

The Insanity Defense. Of the legal issues considered in this chapter, the insanity defense is certainly the most well known and among the most controversial. No reader of this book has not also read about famous insanity defenses in books or newspapers or seen those involved on one side or the other of such cases on television or in the movies. Among the most dramatic events at criminal trials are the jury's deliberations on whether a defendant ought to be judged "not guilty by reason of insanity."

Because of the drama and notoriety of the insanity defense, most of us incorrectly believe it is a common event. On consulting police records, court reports, and clinical files for 2,735 psychiatric referrals from Alaska's criminal justice system from 1977 through 1981, Phillips, Wolf, and Coons (1988) reported a successful insanity defense in 0.1 percent or less of all criminal cases. In Wyoming, "average citizens" thought that 43 percent of all criminal cases involved an insanity defense, students guessed 37 percent, and state legislators—many of them attorneys—said 21 percent. The actual figure was less than one half of one percent of all cases (cited in Stromberg et al., 1988). Also, after an exhaustive survey of all mentally disordered offenders in federal, state, and local correctional facilities, Steadman and his colleagues (1982) found that only 8.1 percent had mounted a successful insanity defense.

Despite its infrequent use, the insanity defense continues to generate heated debate. Contrary to the widespread opinion it is a clever strategy that highly paid lawyers employ to get rich clients off serious charges, the insanity defense is mostly used nowadays on behalf of poor persons defended by public defenders and accused of nonviolent or marginally violent crimes (Lamb, 1982; Phillips et al., 1988). Also, the usual result of a successful insanity defense is commitment to a state hospital's forensic unit for an indeterminate time period, which often turns out to be as long or longer than if the defendant had been sent to jail.

Western society's views on the fairness of trying the insane for actions they had no rational control over has a long history. Insanity as a defense against criminal charges dates back at least to the thirteenth century. During the 700 years following this initial use of the insanity defense, the belief has grown that it is unfair to accuse people of something they cannot comprehend or to convict them of a crime they may not have intended to commit. This notion has evolved into an important humane value despite the relatively small numbers of persons who have been relieved of criminal responsibility through it.

Over the last 150 years, four standards (the M'Naghten, Irresistible Impulse, Durham, and American Law Institute standards) have guided our courts and judges in deciding criminal cases involving the insanity defense.

M'Naghten Standard. In 1843, Daniel M'Naghten mistakenly shot at the secretary to the Prime Minister of England, Robert Peel. (He wanted to shoot the Prime Minister.) When M'Naghten was subsequently found not guilty by reason of insanity, the public was outraged and a great debate ensued. The House of Lords asked a group of distinguished judges to suggest a basis for making such future determinations. Their recommendations included the following:

> Every man is to be presumed sane, and . . . to establish a defense on the ground of insanity, it must be clearly proved that, at the time of committing of the act, the party accused was laboring under such a defect of reason, from disease of the mind, as not to know the nature and quality of the act he was doing; or if he did know it, that he did not know he was doing what was wrong. (8 Eng. Rep. 718, 722–723 [1843])

Soon taken up as the insanity defense's guiding principle by courts throughout the United States, the M'Naghten Standard remains, 150 years later, the exclusive standard for the insanity defense in about a third of the courts.

Irresistible Impulse Standard. The increased understanding of human behavior during the past sev-

Daniel M'Naghten, whose attempt to kill Sir Robert Peel in 1843 led to development of the M'Naghten Standard.

eral decades has caused the M'Naghten Standard's inadequacies—especially its emphasis on cognitive factors ("knowing") to the exclusion of feeling, wanting, or being unable to control impulses—to become more widely recognized. Many states have, therefore, adopted the Irresistible Impulse Standard as an alternative. It asks:

> Did he know right from wrong, as applied to the particular act in question? . . . If he did have such knowledge, he may nevertheless not be legally responsible if the two following conditions concur: (1) If, by reason of the duress of such mental disease, he had so far lost the power to choose between right and wrong, and to avoid doing the act in question, that his free agency was at the time destroyed; (2) and if, at the same time, the alleged crime was so connected with such mental disease, in the relation of cause and effect, as to have been the product of it. (*Parsons v. State,* 2 So. 854, 866–867 [Ala. 1886])

Durham Standard. A 1954 case, *Durham v. United States,* led Presiding Justice David Bazelon of the United States Court of Appeals to propose the following even broader insanity defense standard:

> An accused is not criminally responsible if his unlawful act was the product of mental disease or defect. We use "disease" in the sense of a condition which is not considered capable of either improving or deteriorating. We use "defect" in the sense of a condition which is not considered capable of either improving or deteriorating, and which may be either congenital, or the result of injury, or the residual effect of a physical or mental disease.

The effect of the Durham Standard was to shift the burden of criminal defense from a focus on whether the defendant knew the difference between right from wrong (M'Naghten) or was acting on irresistible impulse. Instead, the Durham Standard required the defense to respond to a clinical judgment: Was the crime a product of mental disorder?

American Law Institute (ALI) Standard. M'Naghten continues to be an influential standard despite its antiquity and the problems associated with it. The American Law Standard (ALI), first proposed in 1962 and an improvement in some ways over its predecessors, became the insanity defense standard of choice in many states. (However, after the ALI Standard's successful use by attorneys for John Hinckley, who attempted to kill President Ronald Reagan in 1981, the standard was replaced in many states by the older M'Naghten Standard.) The ALI Standard provides the following guidelines:

1. A person is not responsible for criminal conduct if at the time of such conduct he lacks substantial capacity as a result of mental disease or defect either to appreciate the criminality of his conduct or to conform his conduct to the requirements of law. (This guideline combines M'Naghten and Irresistible Impulse.)
2. (T)he terms *mental disease* and *defect* do not include an abnormality manifested only by repeated criminal or otherwise antisocial conduct. (This guideline prevents the use of the diagnosis of antisocial personality disorder as a defense.) (American Law Institute Model Penal Code, 1962)

Does the Insanity Defense Have a Future? Politicians and judges have now joined mental health professionals in questioning the insanity defense's legitimacy. Their attacks reflect

1. A rapidly rising, deeply troubling national crime rate.
2. The controversy over John Hinckley's successful insanity defense (the ALI Standard was used) following his attempt on President Ronald Reagan's life in 1981.
3. The continuing difficulty society and the courts have had in deciding what to do with persons whose mental status played a role in their criminal activity.

Competency to Consent to Participate in Research. Though a less controversial matter than competency to stand trial, competency to consent to participate in research also concerns some lawyers and mental health professionals. The necessity of ensuring that subjects of therapeutic and experimental medical procedures are competent to give their consent to be included as research subjects was first recognized in the 1946 Nuremberg Code. The Code, an attempt to set down ethical principles to guide human experimentation, was a reaction to the Nazi atrocities committed in the name of medical science.

Today, the question of competency to consent to participate in psychiatric and psychological research relates most clearly to the inclusion of mental patients and the aged in therapeutic studies. Should such persons be subjects in research on the effectiveness of different kinds of pharmacological or psychotherapeutic treatment of their conditions if they do not clearly understand the purposes of the research or its possible negative effects? While researchers nowadays must solicit fully informed consent from their human subjects, demented or psychotic psychiatric patients cannot fully inform themselves about the possible risks and benefits of participating in the research. Those institutionalized may even feel they are not in a position to refuse to participate in the institution's research program.

A prominent authority on legal and psychiatric issues raised by competency determinations, psychiatrist-attorney Paul Appelbaum (1982) views these questions as legal, not psychiatric. Primarily, he believes that we must choose between conflicting goals before we can agree on how to judge competence to participate in research. Thus, he asks which is more important to us: our respect for the rights of patients or our commitment to the humane goals of research? Appelbaum believes we must decide this question before we can make consistent judgments on competency to consent to participate in research.

ETHICAL ISSUES

Professional Ethics

Most of us feel that we have the right to expect the professionals we consult—for example, our doctor and, if we have one, our therapist—to put our interests and welfare before their own. We believe that professionals give advice and make recommendations on the basis of what is best for us, not for them. Though it would be wonderful to be able to expect consistently ethical behavior from everyone, it is essential to expect it of the professionals with whom we share our most intimate details. As we cannot judge the professional competence of every clinician we consult, we must expect them to do the best for us.

Virtually all professional organizations—such as the American Psychological Association, the American Psychiatric Association, the National Association of Social Workers, and the American Nursing Association—have elaborate sets of ethical standards to guide members. These guidelines detail obvious ethical problems, like the ones arising when a psychotherapy relationship develops into a romantic or business relationship or a mental health professional uses knowledge attained in a confidential relationship for personal gain. The associations' professional standards also consider less clear ethical conflicts like the dilemmas posed by the following situation:

> *A psychologist who specialized in family therapy received a telephone call from an attorney requesting that the psychologist evaluate three children, aged three, five, and seven, while they were on a weekend visit to their father's home, because their father was suing for custody. Rather than schedule a weekend appointment with the children and their father, the psychologist suggested that the mother be requested to bring the children in for an evaluation, or else that the attorney seek a court order for psychological evaluations. The psychologist noted that he would like to evaluate all persons involved in the care of the children, including other adults who might be living in the home and sharing in the care of the children.*
>
> *The mother telephoned the psychologist and agreed to bring the children in for an evaluation and to undergo a psychological evaluation herself as long as her husband was willing to do so.*
>
> *During the psychologist's interview with the father, the father told the psychologist that he suspected his children were being abused sexually and were exposed to illicit drugs by his wife's boyfriend who lived in the home. . . .* (Committee on Professional Standards, 1988, p. 557)

Even such a brief summary of this complicated situation raises several difficult ethical and legal questions. All derive from a single question: Who is the psychologist's client? Is it the attorney who originally contacted the psychologist, the children, their father, or their mother? For that matter, doesn't society have a stake in this assessment as well, especially given the father's accusations?

Also, should the psychologist have accepted the father's request for evaluation, as filtered through his attorney, knowing it would likely be used in the father's effort to gain custody of his children? Should the psychologist have seen the father to evaluate the legitimacy of the father's suspicions before he agreed to meet with the children or have informed the state protective services? How should the psychologist have informed the state of the father's accusations? How should the children's mother have been told? Should the psychologist have agreed to do the evaluation?

You might wonder why intelligent, highly educated professionals need detailed instructions about the right thing to do. Yet knowing what is right and ethical, as the material just reviewed demonstrates, is not always as obvious as it may first appear.

Each professional association's ethical guidelines provide a detailed accounting of the association's expectations of its members, along with extended discussions of solutions to particularly difficult ethical problems. The guidelines also describe the consequences for infraction of the guidelines, typically ranging from admonition for technical violations to expulsion from membership for a serious ethical breach.

To complicate matters, most ethical guidelines contain at least two kinds of standards. Some relate to general behavioral norms intended to set a high standard of conduct for members to aspire to but which, if unattained, do not necessarily justify punishment. For example, the American Psychological Association's *Ethical Principles* state that psychologists are to "act with due regard for the needs, special competencies, and obligations of their colleagues in psychology and other professions." Yet a psychologist doesn't always know a colleague's special competencies, especially if they have never met and do not know each other's work. Hence, failure to recognize a colleague's special competency, for example, by not referring a patient to someone with special expertise in his or her problem, would probably not be viewed as a serious breach of professional ethics.

In general, other standards in most ethical guidelines are more specific and prescriptive. They usually set a minimal or threshold standard of professional behavior which professionals breach only at their own peril. For example, psychologists' ethical standards state that they must not engage in any professional activity their personal problems might interfere with. Thus, an alcoholic psychologist who sees patients in therapy while he or she is intoxicated, would be breaching a specific, precise standard and consequently could reasonably expect sanctions if reported.

Most states have also incorporated ethical guidelines into their licensing laws. Consequently, licensed professionals (psychologists, psychiatrists and nurses are licensed in every state; social workers are licensed in an increasing number of them) can lose their licenses and their means of livelihood should they fail to observe ethical standards. Although it is embarrassing to be dropped from membership in a professional association for unethical behavior, to lose the license to practice and possibly to be also subject to civil or criminal sanctions is disastrous.

Ethical Dilemmas. Ethical issues are much easier to resolve when the difference between ethical and unethical behavior is clear-cut. For example, every association's guidelines conclude that a mental health professional who enters into a sexual relationship with a client is acting unethically. The *Ethical Guidelines* of the American Psychological Association (1990, p. 393) are clear:

> Psychologists do not exploit their professional relationships with clients, supervisees, students, employees, or research participants sexually or otherwise. Psychologists do not condone or engage in sexual harassment. Sexual harassment is defined as deliberate or repeated comments, gestures, or physical contacts of a sexual nature that are unwanted by the recipient.

For a variety of reasons, the ethical problems caused by sexual relationships between therapists and patients are obvious to everyone although, as we note later, they occur with distressing frequency (Gartrell et al., 1988). Some of the reasons include the differences in status and power between therapist and patient, the insoluble conflict of interest such a relationship would pose for the therapist, and the real possibility of seriously harming the patient psychologically.

Other relatively common ethical problems include misrepresentation of professional credentials or training and practicing beyond one's professional competence (e.g., clinicians who agree to provide a particular kind of assessment or therapy even though not fully trained to do so). Another common ethical problem—particularly heart-rending at times—arises when a professional continues to practice even though personal problems (common ones include depression and alcoholism) have begun to interfere with work. Again, the APA *Ethical Guidelines* are quite explicit:

> Psychologists recognize that personal problems and conflicts may interfere with professional effectiveness. Accordingly, they refrain from undertaking any activity in which their personal problems are likely to lead to inadequate performance or harm to a client, colleague, student, or research participant. If engaged in such activity, when they become aware of their personal problems, they seek competent professional assistance to determine whether they should suspend, terminate, or limit the scope of their professional and/or scientific activities. (American Psychological Association, 1990, p. 391)

Unlike these clear ethical violations, many other situations concerning mental health professionals present ethical dilemmas. Such dilemmas demand a choice between two alternatives, neither apparently in the client's best interests. What follows details just such an ethical dilemma, this one relating to marital conflict and intimacy:

> *A counseling psychologist in a university counseling center initiated a therapeutic relationship with a female graduate student. The presenting problems were conflict and general lack of intimacy in the marriage. During the course of therapy, the client began to question her sexual identity and requested a gay or lesbian counselor. The psychologist explained that she was unaware of anyone on the staff who was lesbian or gay, and assured the client that she, the psychologist, was competent to help the client with her issues. Although the psychologist had never sought special training and had not kept current with the literature on gay and lesbian counseling concerns, she felt quite confident with this assertion.*
>
> *The psychologist then listened to the client's concerns in a supportive way and assessed the problem as lack of communication in the marital relationship. Thus, her therapeutic focus was to enhance the emotional and physical intimacy within the marriage. Throughout counseling, the psychologist dismissed the client's sexual identity confusions as unfounded and, therefore, did not explore specific thoughts, feelings, or behaviors related to the client's sexual identity concerns. However, as her focus was to enhance the client's communication with her husband, she did actively encourage her client to talk openly and fully about her sexual identity concerns with her husband, who had previously refused to enter couples' counseling. Six months later, the husband sued for divorce and won custody of their two children on the basis of her "admitted lesbianism."* (Committee on Professional Standards, 1986, p. 689)

By not realizing she needed to consult with someone trained to deal with sexual identity issues, this psychologist may have been practicing outside her competence. By being unaware of the legal or marital problems that might ensue when she suggested the patient discuss her sexual identity feelings with her husband, the therapist didn't adhere to the ethical standard requiring psychologists to know the legal and other consequences of their advice.

The psychologist was firmly convinced she was acting in her patient's best interests. Also, the most appropriate therapeutic approach to the patient's presenting complaints is uncertain, for even more experienced therapists could have anticipated the woman's husband responding much more positively to her disclosing sexual identity feelings than he did.

Figure 18.2 suggests an intriguing visual solution to a different, although equally vexing, ethical/legal dilemma. This novel representation of a familiar problem may also be generally relevant to the task of solving the ethical and legal problems often facing mental health professionals.

The "scale of ethics" shown in this figure (Hundert, 1987, p. 841) schematizes the conflicting values governing the therapist's choice to commit or not to commit. Certain values, shown on the left side of the scale, press for commitment. These values give highest priority to relieving the patient's suffering, assuring the patient's welfare and safety, and assuring the welfare and safety of others in the patient's environment. However, on the other side are such compelling values as respect for the patient's individual liberty and privacy, as well as modesty about the clinician's real ability to predict the patient's future behavior.

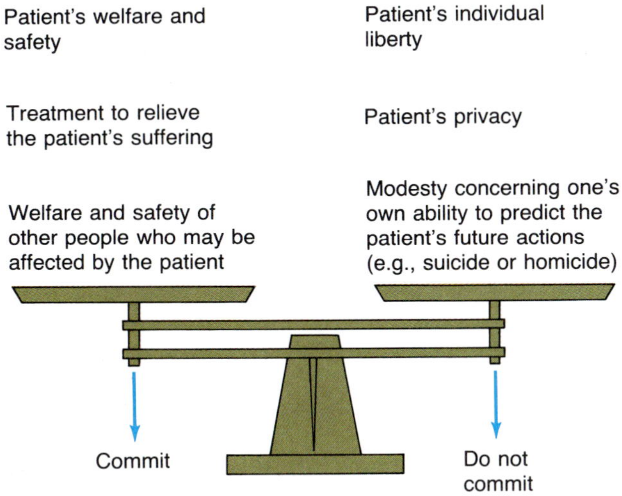

Figure 18.2 *The decisions to commit or not commit a patient involuntarily are equally balanced by compelling arguments.*

Source: From Hundert, E.M. (1987). A model for ethical problem-solving in medicine, with practical applications. *American Journal of Psychiatry, 144*, p. 841. Copyright 1987 by the American Psychiatric Association. Reprinted by permission.

Ethical Issues in Research

AIDS Research. As previously noted, psychological and psychiatric research also raises important ethical and legal issues. Research on AIDS, perhaps our most pressing national health problem, confronts us with particularly troubling ethical problems. For example, we must consider the ethics of requiring research workers to participate in AIDS research, despite the minuscule but real possibility of infection; the ethical problems posed by the researchers' inability to guarantee confidentiality to subjects with AIDS; and the ethical dilemmas created when AIDS is diagnosed but the subject refuses to share this information with his or her past and/or present sexual partners (Melton & Gray, 1988; Melton et al., 1988).

Intentional Deception. AIDS research raises issues specific to it. Many other ethical issues highlighted by psychological and psychiatric investigations into other areas may actually pose greater ethical problems because they involve a greater volume of studies. One such issue is created by research employing intentional deception (Baumrind, 1985). Most researchers ultimately "debrief" subjects who were intentionally deceived during a research project, for example, by informing them they have been given an active drug when, in fact, they have been given an inactive placebo, or telling them they have achieved a high score on a measure of depression when, in fact, they have not. Some observers worry nonetheless that certain deceptions may cause subjects significant problems and believe that deception in research should be permitted only when absolutely necessary or when the issue being studied is extremely critical.

Animals in Research. A public outcry has recently occurred over the ethical issues raised by the use of animals in research, especially if they must be hurt or ultimately killed. Opponents of animal research claim that their use is rarely necessary and that, when animals must be used, far more care can and should be taken to ensure them the least pain possible. Supporters of animal research argue that it has saved millions of human lives, animals can be employed where humans cannot be, and researchers generally care extremely well for their animal subjects. Presently unresolved, this conflict promises to rage on into the distant future.

Psychotherapy Research. The ethical issues raised by controlled clinical trials of psychotherapy and other treatments for psychiatric disorders have also been widely discussed (Imber et al., 1986; Heflinger, 1987). The accepted research method of controlled clinical trials involves giving the active treatment that is being studied—for example, a new form of psychotherapy or a new drug—on a random basis to half the patients with the disorder; the other half of the patients are given either a comparative treatment or a placebo (a substance looking like the active medication but with no clinical effect). The ethical issue arises when the disorder under treatment is devastating—like AIDS or schizophrenia—and a promising treatment must be withheld for comparative purposes.

In other words, this controversy concerns the ethics of giving treatment to some persons, even a treatment with unproven efficacy, and withholding it from others. Although controlled clinical trials are the touchstone of treatment research, the debate on the ethics of their use continues.

Sexism and Ageism in Research. Ethical concerns of ageism and sexism in psychological and psychiatric research have also been raised recently (Denmark, Russo, Frieze, & Sechzer, 1988; Schaie, 1988). Researchers studying older people or women are sometimes unfamiliar with the specialized literature on the elderly and women. As a result, they sometimes conclude that their findings were influenced by subjects' age or gender when an adequate grasp of the research literature would have led them to conclude that age or gender was not responsible for their findings. Responsible instead were variables like socioeconomic status, educational level, the nature of the research instruments, or the experimental setting. Misattributing experimental effects to age or gender reinforces stereotypes about "the elderly" or "most women."

Ethics and Research. Ethical lapses in research present particularly difficult dilemmas because, most of the time, researchers do not intentionally commit ethical violations. Of course, there are always the marginal scientists who "fudge" their data, take credit for the work of someone else, or plagiarize. These serious ethical violations are certainly less common than the lapses we have noted, yet they must also be dealt with. One of the most precious assets scientists have to offer society is their own credibility—the assurance that colleagues reading their papers will believe what is written and, as a result, be willing to incorporate the ideas or results into their own research planning. Without credibility—lost for major or minor deviations from the ethical mainstream—a scientist has nothing to offer.

Ethical Standards and the Law

The relationship between ethical standards and the law, as discussed, is complex.

- There are times when objectionable personal behavior by a psychologist or a psychiatrist is neither illegal nor a violation of ethical guidelines (e.g., when the professional is thoughtless, rude, and ill-tempered to colleagues and staff).
- There are times when the professional runs afoul of the law but is extremely unlikely to be brought up on ethics charges (e.g., if he or she is convicted of a minor traffic violation or a similar misdemeanor not involving other persons or property).
- There are times when an ethics violation does not call for either a civil or criminal complaint (e.g., if a therapist practices a bit beyond his or her competence by employing a psychological technique colleagues believe he or she has not been fully trained to use).
- There are times when a professional violates both ethical standards and the law.

It is to these serious situations that we now turn.

When Ethical Violations Lead to Professional and Legal Sanctions. A recent report of the Ethics Committee of the American Psychological Association (1986) summarized the ethical violations it investigated during the four years preceding the report. The distribution of violations under investigation provides an interesting view of the range and frequency of unethical behaviors of this group of professionals.

- *Inappropriate professional practice:* 35 percent (Includes failure to respect other professionals, practicing outside area of competence, fraudulent insurance claims or exorbitant fees, breach of confidentiality, and testing abuses)
- *Sexual intimacy with client, dual relationship, or exploitation and/or sexual harassment:* 21 percent
- *Inappropriate teaching, research, or administration:* 12 percent (Includes discrimination by age, race, or sex; improper or unsafe use of research techniques; and plagiarism)
- *Cases adjudicated in other jurisdictions:* 10 percent (Includes conviction of a serious crime, loss of license for a serious crime, and expulsion from a state association for an ethical violation)
- *Inappropriate advertising and public statements:* 8 percent (Includes misrepresentation and sensationalism in advertising or public statements and public allegations about colleagues)
- *Other violations:* 14 percent

A review of the Disciplinary Data Reports of the American Association of State Psychology Boards for "adverse licensure actions" against psychologists was reported in 1985, 1986, and 1987 (Stromberg et al., 1988, p. 280). Of the sixty license revocations reported, about one third were for sexual intimacies with a client, 13 percent were for fraudulent billing, and 8 percent each were for a dual relationship (e.g., the patient was also an employee), for unprofessional conduct, and for conviction of a felony.

Therapist–patient sexual intimacy, consistently the most common reason for loss of license to practice and suspension from membership in the American Psychological Association, is a major problem for all the mental health professions (Pope & Bouhoutsos, 1986; Bajt & Pope, 1989). Leaders in all the mental health professions widely agree that sexual intimacy between patient and therapist causes "deep and lasting harm both to the clients and to the integrity of the profession" (Ethics Committee, 1988, p. 564). In view of its frequency and potential to cause serious damage, a variety of efforts have begun to be taken to call the problem to the attention of students in training programs in psychology, psychiatry, and social work (e.g., Gartrell et al., 1988; Glaser & Thorpe, 1986).

A recent analysis of trends in the types of ethics cases brought to the attention of the Ethics Committee of the American Psychological Association (1988) reveals that the number of such ethical complaints has increased over 50 percent during the last few years. About three fourths of complainants are women, many of them alleging inappropriate sexual intimacy. In 1987, 80 percent of the psychologists against whom ethics complaints were filed were male—even though only 64 percent of the association's membership is male.

In about half the ethics cases actually disposed of over the past five years, the Ethics Committee concluded that an ethical principle had been violated. During this period, 23 percent of the violations involved dual relationships with clients (including sexual intimacies), 16 percent involved violation of various APA standards and guidelines concerning practice and research on governmental laws and institutional regulations, 8 percent involved violating or diminishing the legal or civil rights of others, and 4 percent involved a failure to preserve confidentiality. In one third of these cases, the member was dropped from the association; in the rest, lesser membership sanctions were enforced.

SUMMARY

1. In the past two decades in the United States, the conditions psychiatric patients live in have become a legal battleground. Deinstitutionalization, the partial emptying of state hospitals, was one result. Unfortunately, most communities have inadequately provided care for patients from the hospitals, resulting in a marked increase in the homeless chronically ill.
2. When hospitalization is clearly indicated but the patient refuses it, civil commitment – involuntary hospitalization – may be necessary. Most states now impose stringent legal safeguards and protections for persons threatened with commitment. Patients must be judged mentally ill, dangerous to self or others, or gravely disabled, unwilling to enter a hospital voluntarily, capable of benefiting from treatment, and so sick that hospitalization is the least restrictive alternative. The predictions of dangerousness and suicide are among the most difficult judgments mental health professionals must make.
3. The patients' rights movement arose in recognition of their denial of most of the civil and legal rights and privileges enjoyed by others in society. State and federal courts have upheld hospitalized patients' right to the same safeguards the Constitution guarantees to defendants in criminal cases. They also have specific rights to humane living conditions, to treatment (recognized in *Wyatt v. Stickney*), to adequate treatment, to the least restrictive alternative to state hospital confinement if one is available or appropriate, and to refuse treatment (recognized in *Rennie v. Klein*) if it is potentially dangerous.
4. Psychiatric patients also have the right to privacy, confidentiality, and privileged communication. Mental health professionals can only intrude in matters relevant to their clinical responsibilities. They can reveal information acquired in the course of their professional duties only under very special and restricted circumstances. One exception was established by the *Tarasoff* standard: Disclosure of confidential material is permitted when the clinician is bound by "the duty to warn," requiring professionals to warn a person threatened in the course of a confidential relationship and to alert the police. Communication in confidential relationships, such as between a patient and a licensed therapist, is protected against disclosure under most circumstances.
5. Over the past 150 years, four standards have guided courts in deciding criminal cases involving the insanity defense. They include the M'Naghten, Irresistible Impulse, Durham, and American Law Institute (ALI) standards.
6. Most of us expect the professionals we consult to give advice on the basis of what is best for us, not for them. Accompanying these expectations are the ethical standards all organizations of professionals have evolved. The American Psychological Association's standards include prohibitions on inappropriate professional practice; sexual intimacy with clients or dual relationships; inappropriate teaching, research, or administration; and inappropriate advertising and public statements.

Glossary

Abdominal obesity The pattern of obesity, typically shown by men, where there is more body fat above than below the waist.

Acute brain disorders Reversible organic brain disorders lasting only a few minutes or a few hours.

Adherence The extent to which a patient follows professional advice to take certain medication or change behavior patterns.

Agonist A drug or chemical that stimulates activity in particular nerve cells; it facilitates neural transmission between cells.

Agoraphobia A fear and avoidance of being in places or situations in which help might not be available should some incapacitating (e.g., losing control) or embarrassing (e.g., fainting) event occur.

Alcohol withdrawal delirium An acute brain disorder characterized by a pattern of psychological effects, including distorted thinking and even hallucinations, that occurs when someone who is physically dependent on alcohol suddenly stops drinking.

Alpha waves Regular, oscillating waves which represent the EEG pattern of a normal, conscious but relaxed adult.

Alzheimer's disease An age-related chronic brain disorder distinguished by progressive dementia, profound losses in cognitive ability, medical impairment, neurological symptoms, and psychosis.

Anal-erotic personality The Freudian hypothesis that obsessions and compulsions occur in people with a particular personality characterized by orderliness, obstinacy, and stinginess.

Anal stage In Freudian theory, the second stage of psychosexual development, extending from eighteen months to the third year, during which the anus is the main erogenous zone.

Anhedonia Loss of pleasure from previously pleasurable activities; a symptom often exhibited by depressed individuals.

Anorexia nervosa An eating disorder characterized by refusal to maintain adequate body weight, an intense fear of becoming obese, and a body image disturbance.

Antianxiety medications Medications used to treat anxiety. Many types of medication have been used to treat anxiety, including antidepressant drugs (tricyclics), but minor tranquilizers are among the most common.

Anticipatory anxiety The anxiety phobics anticipate they will experience were they to engage in certain activities.

Antipsychotic medications (neuroleptics) Medications used to counter the symptoms of a number of psychotic disorders, especially hallucinations, disordered thought, and agitation. These medications are sometimes called neuroleptics because they affect the nervous system.

Antisocial personality A personality style beginning before the age of fifteen that involves a behavior pattern that seriously violates the rights of others. Individuals with this disorder are extremely irresponsible in their work, school, financial, and personal relationships.

Applied behavior analysis The application of the principles and procedures of operant conditioning to human problems; the analysis of environmental effects on nature.

Arbitrary inference The process of drawing a conclusion from a situation, an event, or an experience when no evidence supports the conclusion or when the conclusion is contrary to the evidence.

Assessment interviews Interviews designed to assess personality, interpersonal behavior, or the functioning of a family unit.

Asylums Institutions first established in the mid-sixteenth century to house the mentally ill.

Attention-Deficit Hyperactivity Disorder (ADHD) A disorder characterized by inattention, impulsiveness, and hyperactivity.

Attribution theory The theory about the cognitive rules people use to infer the causes of behavior they observe in others and in themselves.

Autonomic nervous system (ANS) That part of the peripheral nervous system which regulates the involuntary functions of the glands, heart, blood vessels, and viscera and is responsible for the physiological events associated with the experience of emotion.

Avoidant personality A personality style characterized by an inappropriate fear and avoidance of others, especially in situations where an individual may face failure or rejection. Individuals with this disorder lack self-esteem; they are shy, fearful, and overly self-critical.

Axes The five dimensions on which patients are rated in the DSM-III and DSM-III-R multiaxial diagnostic systems.

Balanced placebo design An experimental design that permits the controlled evaluation of the separate and interactive effects of both a drug and the expectations about having received the drug.

Battered wife syndrome A syndrome experienced by women who are physically abused by their husbands. These women suffer from a fear of unpredictable, violent behavior.

Behavioral medicine The interdisciplinary field concerned with the development and integration of behavioral and biomedical science, and the application of this knowledge to the prevention and treatment of illness and the maintenance of health.

Behavioral model An approach to understanding psychopathology that emphasizes the role of environmental factors and learning in the development of both normal and abnormal behavior.

Bell and pad method A method of treating enuresis in which a bell and pad alarm device awakens the child immediately upon urination. A series of steps are then executed which include visiting the bathroom and cleaning up. Progress is monitored and the child is rewarded for each dry day.

Bilateral stimulation An electroconvulsive therapy technique in which electrodes are attached to both sides of the head to send electrical currents through the brain.

Biofeedback The procedure of using electronic equipment to monitor continuously some feature of physiological response (e.g., heart rate) and convert it into signals that a person can perceive easily.

Biological model An approach to understanding psychopathology that emphasizes the role of physiological and neurochemical processes in the development of both normal and abnormal behavior.

Biopsychosocial perspective The view that both normal and abnormal behavior are products of biological, psychological, and socioenvironmental factors operating interactively.

Bipolar disorder A serious mood disorder which involves extreme mood swings or highs and lows; sometimes termed manic-depressive psychosis.

Body dysmorphic disorder A pathological preoccupation with an imaginary defect in physical appearance.

Borderline personality A highly unstable personality style characterized by lack of a strong sense of identity and by intense personal relationship problems.

Brainstorming A technique often used in the problem-solving approach to marital and family therapy to generate alternative solutions to a defined problem before family members evaluate and criticize solutions.

Broca's area The posterior third of the inferior frontal convolution of the brain where, in the nineteenth century, Paul Broca concluded speech was localized.

Bulimia nervosa An eating disorder characterized by binge eating (uncontrolled consumption of large amounts of food), attempts to compensate for food intake by purging (e.g., self-induced vomiting or laxative abuse) or severe dieting, and persistent overconcern with body weight and shape.

Caring days A practice utilized in marital therapy in which both partners first list various caring behaviors they would like increased by their spouses, and then agree to increase those requested of themselves. These caring behaviors are then charted to monitor the improvement in interaction between spouses.

Case-control study A study in which the person with the clinical disorder is matched with someone without the disorder but who is similar in other respects.

Catalepsy A symptom of schizophrenia in which the individual assumes an uncomfortable, nearly immobile stance for an extended period of time.

Catatonic schizophrenic One of the major types of schizophrenia characterized by marked psychomotor disturbances such as assuming rigid postures and/or being mute.

Categorical approach (to assessment) An approach to assessment that assumes that individuals can be categorized into discrete types of personality styles, problems, or behaviors (contrasts with dimensional approach).

Caudate nucleus A cluster of brain cells in the basal ganglia that is believed to be centrally involved in anxiety disorders such as obsessive-compulsive disorder.

Central nervous system (CNS) The brain and the spinal cord. All sensory impulses are transmitted to the CNS and all motor impulses are sent from the CNS.

Cerebral cortex The thin outer layer of the cerebrum, the brain's gray matter, which is the locus of our ability to think, feel, perceive, and reflect.

Childhood depression. A mood disorder among children that highly resembles unipolar mood disorder of adults; the depressive symptoms are almost identical. The key symptoms include depressed mood, low self-esteem, fatigue, and often suicidal ideation.

Childhood gender nonconformity A sexual disorder in which boys, many of whom seem to become homosexual or bisexual, act in an excessively feminine manner.

Chronic brain disorders Irreversible organic brain disorders which may well endure throughout a lifetime and exert a profound impact on quality of life.

Chronological age The child's age in years, used to determine his or her IQ on the Binet Scale.

Civil commitment Involuntary hospitalization which may be necessary when hospitalization is clearly indicated for a psychiatric patient, but the patient refuses.

Classical conditioning A form of learning, also known as Pavlovian conditioning, in which a neutral stimulus is paired with a second stimulus (the unconditioned stimulus) that naturally elicits a specific response (the unconditioned response). The neutral stimulus becomes a conditioned stimulus (CS), because it signals the occurrence of the unconditioned stimulus, which elicits a conditioned response (CR) that is often similar to the unconditioned response.

Clinical assessment The process clinicians use to gather information to diagnose, plan treatment, and predict the future course of a disorder.

Clinical neuropsychology The subfield of clinical psychology devoted to the diagnosis of brain disorder by means of neuropsychological test batteries and instruments.

Clinical psychologists Core mental health professionals who have earned a doctoral degree in psychology (either a Ph.D or a Psy.D [Doctor of Psychology]) and received extensive clinical training. They are trained in research, assessment, and the application and evaluation of different psychological therapies.

Clitoral orgasm The physiological basis of all orgasms is the stimulation of the clitoris, the female erectile organ which is the main site of female sexual responsiveness.

Cognitive behavior therapy (CBT) A form of psychological therapy that focuses on directly modifying both cognitive processes and behavior. CBT draws heavily on cognitive theory and research, as well as more traditional classical and operant conditioning principles.

Cognitive slippage The use of words from ordinary language that, at first, sound as if they were communicating ideas, but later are recognized to lack conformity to the basic rules of communication.

Collaborative set A term coined by Beck for a relationship between the patient and the therapist characterized by joint exploration of the connection between dysfunctional beliefs and depressed feelings.

Comorbidity The simultaneous manifestation of more than one disorder in the same individual; common comorbid conditions associated with alcoholism include depression and antisocial personality disorder.

Compliance An alternative term for adherence, namely, the extent to which a patient follows professional advice to take certain medication or change behavior patterns.

Compulsions Repetitive, stereotyped acts that a person with the disorder feels compelled to carry out despite some recognition that they are unreasonable.

Compulsive personality Personalities who are unusually tidy and even rigid in their daily behavior. Unlike people with obsessive-compulsive disorder, however, they do not find their behavior distressing.

Computerized axial tomographic (CAT) scanning A brain imaging technique in which an X-ray beam is sent through a part of the body, such as the brain, to provide a picture of the brain. As the beam passes through the body, the different densities of tissue, bone, and water are measured by a scanner that rotates 360 degrees around the body.

Conditioned response In classical conditioning, the response elicited by the conditioned stimulus. Although typically similar to the unconditioned response, it can also be opposite in direction and effect, as in the classically conditioned compensatory responses to alcohol and other drugs.

Conditioned stimulus In classical conditioning, a formerly neutral stimulus which, by being paired with an unconditioned stimulus, comes to elicit a response (the conditioned response) that is often similar to the unconditioned response.

Conduct disorder A persistent pattern of behavior that involves violation of the rights of others; the pattern is seen at home, school, and in the community. Verbal and physical aggression are key features of conduct disorder.

Control group In an experiment, a group of subjects that is functionally the same as the experimental group on all dimensions except the one being manipulated.

Conversion disorder The loss or alteration of physical functioning that suggests a physical disease, but no underlying pathophysiology can be found (e.g., partial or complete blindness).

Core mental health disciplines Members of the mental health team, including clinical psychologists, psychiatrists, psychiatric social workers, and psychiatric nurses.

Coronary angiography A medical procedure in which a fine needle is inserted into the coronary arteries to inject a special dye so that the arteries can then be examined under X-ray.

Correlation coefficient The mathematical expression of the degree of association between two variables. In a positive correlation, a subject who scores high on a measure of one variable will also score high on a measure of the second, correlated variable. In a negative correlation, a high score on one variable is associated with a low score on the other.

Countertransference In Freudian theory, the thoughts and feelings the therapist has for the patient that presumably derive from the therapist's early experiences.

Covert sensitization A behavior therapy technique used to decrease a patient's desire for a particular substance (e.g., alcohol) or activity (e.g., sexual exhibitionism). The patient is instructed to conjure up vivid imagery in which an unpleasant or aversive consequence (e.g., nausea) is systematically associated with the unwanted activity (e.g., consuming alcohol).

Crack A highly addictive smokable cocaine derivative; it is cheap and readily available on the streets and can have devastating effects on the brain and behavior.

Cyclothymia A chronic mood disturbance similar to a bipolar disorder that lasts at least two years; symptoms include expansiveness, irritability, and/or elevation in mood.

Date rape Sexual intercourse is forced on a woman against her will on a date. The male, who is an acquaintance of the woman, overpowers her despite her refusal.

Death instinct In Freudian theory, the id's aggressive and destructive drives, also called thanatos.

Defense mechanisms In Freudian theory, the ego's strategies to defend itself against attack by the id, superego or both.

Deinstitutionalization Beginning in the 1960s, the process by which states markedly reduced the population of their public psychiatric hospitals by returning patients thought to be able to function outside the hospital to their home communities.

Delirium tremens (DTs) An alcohol withdrawal-related delirium typically characterized by difficulty attending to environmental stimuli, disorganized thinking, vivid, often visual, hallucinations, and paranoid delusions.

Delta waves This electroencephalographic pattern of electrical activity in the brain involves a slow brain wave pattern of less than four cycles a second. It is normally recorded when a person is deeply asleep but may also signal the presence of localized brain damage.

Delusional disorders These organic mental disorders, associated with ingestion of the amphetamines, cannabis, cocaine, or phencyclidine, are characterized by persecutory delusions which develop shortly after ingestion of the substance and usually disappear within a day or two.

Delusions Unusual misrepresentations of reality which are a common symptom of schizophrenia and other psychoses. Typical delusions include those of persecution, romance, grandeur, and control.

Demand characteristics Cues in a situation to which people will respond in ways assumed to be socially appropriate to that situation.

Dementia praecox Emil Kraepelin's term, meaning premature dementia, for the psychotic disorder that is now called schizophrenia.

Dementias arising in the senium and presenium Age-related chronic brain disorders that develop during the fifth, sixth, and later decades of life.

Denial A defense mechanism in which a feeling or wish is denied by the person because to consciously admit it would be too painful.

Dependent personality Individuals with this personality style are submissive and dependent; these styles generally begin in adolescence and are evident in diverse settings.

Dependent variable The variable on which experimental effects are measured.

Depressive disorder A mood disorder with depressive feelings that extend into many parts of an individual's life. The disorder is often called unipolar disorder. Symptoms include lack of interest in daily activities, decreased motivation, feelings of worthlessness, and sometimes suicidal thoughts.

Depressive pseudodementia The symptoms of this affective disorder mimic the cognitive and behavioral deficits associated with an organic dementia.

Deterioration effect An outcome of psychotherapy in which patients become worse, presumably because of the therapist's incompetence or insensitivity.

Diagnosis The act of identifying and naming a state or condition according to an agreed-upon system of categorization.

Diagnostic bias Explicit or implicit biases that affect the diagnostic process.

Diagnostic interviews Interviews which produce information on a patient's past and present behavior; useful for diagnostic purposes.

Diagnostic reliability The degree to which a diagnostic system permits clinicians to agree on the diagnoses they confer.

Diagnostic validity The capacity of a diagnostic system to identify and predict disorders accurately.

Dialectical behavior therapy (DBT) A philosophical framework for therapy which assumes that all things are interconnected, and opposing forces within us can be brought together to produce therapeutic change; an approach that has been used with borderline patients.

Diathesis-stress model A model of disorders stating there is an interaction between biological and social events which causes the psychological disorders. The diathesis is the biological or psychological predisposition and the stress is the particular problem the individual encounters.

Dimensional approach (to assessment) This approach to assessment assumes that individuals are best characterized along basic dimensions of personality (contrasts with categorical approach).

Discriminative stimulus In operant conditioning, the information the environment provides on the likelihood a response will be reinforced, ignored, or punished.

Disorganized schizophrenic A type of schizophrenia characterized by verbal incoherence, grossly disorganized behavior, marked loosening of associations, and inappropriate affect.

Diversion programs An approach in which adolescents are sent to therapeutic or community programs in order to keep them from having to go to jail or juvenile detention facilities.

Dizygotic twins Twins almost conceived simultaneously from separate fertilized ova; also termed fraternal twins, they share only a portion of genetic material.

Dominant genes One of a pair of genes (the allele) that dominates the other and determines a particular physical or psychological characteristic in the phenotype.

Double bind A term used to characterize a relationship in which one individual, often the child, receives contradictory messages from another person, often the parent. The parent communicates warmth, but when the child approaches, the parent is cold and withdraws. The child is thus caught in a "double bind."

Dysfunctional thought record A record kept by patients between treatment sessions in which they identify dysfunctional thoughts (cognitions) associated with their emotional problems, and in which they challenge the validity of those thoughts.

Dyslexia A term used to describe Developmental Reading Disorder. The disorder is characterized by impaired word recognition skills and reading comprehension. A common mistake is the reversal of letters (i.e., b for d) or of entire words (i.e., was for saw).

Dyspareunia Burning or itching sensations during vaginal intercourse.

Dysthymia A chronic depressed mood disturbance which includes symptoms such as loss of interest, feelings of hopelessness, poor appetite or overeating, insomnia or hypersomnia, fatigue, low self-esteem, and poor concentration. These symptoms usually last two years or more.

Echolalia The tendency to parrot others' speech, often exhibited by autistic individuals.

Ecological validity The greater the correspondence between an assessment situation and the real world, the greater the ecological validity of the assessment.

Effect size A statistical index of the extent of treatment effects (e.g., subtracting the mean of the control group from the mean of the treatment group and dividing that difference by the standard deviation of the control group).

Ego In Freudian theory, one of three parts of the psychic apparatus and the principal means by which human beings meet societal standards by modifying the id's primitive drives and impulses.

Ego-ideal Ideal image of oneself.

Ego psychologists Psychologists whose theories stressed the importance to personality development and psychology of the ego and its defenses.

Ejaculatory inevitability The point at which a male ejaculates involuntarily.

Electra complex In Freudian theory, a common feature of girls' efforts, during the phallic stage of psychosexual development, to deal with conflicting sexual and aggressive feelings toward their parents.

Electroconvulsive therapy (ECT) A medical procedure for treating depression in which electrical current is sent to the brain; the current produces brief seizures and sleep for five to ten minutes.

Enuresis Bedwetting or an involuntary discharge of urine that occurs at least twice per month and is usually diagnosed between the ages of five and six.

Epidemiologic Catchment Area (ECA) study An epidemiological study of the rates of specific mental disorders of more than 20,000 residents of five American cities and towns, completed in the early 1980s.

Epidemiological surveys Studies of large groups of people typically designed to answer questions about the incidence and prevalence of specific disorders or groups of disorders.

Epidemiology The systematic study of the prevalence, etiology, and consequences of physical disease and mental disorders in a population.

Epilepsy A chronic brain disorder manifested by repeated and recurrent seizures.

Erectile disorder The persistent or recurrent failure to attain or maintain an erection until completion of sexual activity, or the lack of subjective sexual excitement during sexual activity.

Erogenous zone In Freudian theory, the parts of the body which give sexual pleasure during the successive stages of psychosexual development.

Erotomania A romantic delusion in which an individual develops an inappropriate romantic interest in an individual with whom no personal relationship exists.

Etiology The causes of a condition, behavior, or disorder.

Experimental analysis of behavior In operant conditioning, the study of the antecedant and reinforcing environmental events that control the behavior of individual organisms.

Exposure treatment A behavior therapy technique in which patients are guided to gradually confront the situations they avoid to help overcome their phobic anxiety.

Extinction In classical conditioning, a conditioned response extinguishes when the conditioned stimulus is no longer relevant to or paired with the unconditioned stimulus.

Extraversion According to C. G. Jung, the personality type which characterizes persons who are gregarious, social, and emotionally open.

Family therapy A therapeutic method which involves assessment and treatment with all immediate family members. This therapy places emphasis on the family as a system, rather than on one person who might be deemed the identified patient.

Fear of fear hypothesis The hypothesis that patients with panic disorder will panic should they experience anxiety or fear.

Feingold diet A diet free of food additives and preservatives created by Dr. Benjamin Feingold to treat hyperactive children since he believed hyperactive children were physiologically sensitive to these substances.

Femoral obesity The pattern of obesity, typically shown by women, where there is more fat below than above the waist.

Fetal alcohol syndrome A condition affecting the children of mothers who consume large quantities of alcohol during pregnancy; it can involve mental retardation and physical and emotional disability.

Fraternal twins Twins conceived almost simultaneously who develop from separate fertilized ova; also termed dizygotic twins, they share only a portion of genetic material.

Free association A technique in psychoanalysis in which patients are encouraged to talk in therapy about whatever thoughts or feelings they experience without any effort to censor.

Free-floating anxiety An older term used to describe the pervasive anxiety that is characteristic of generalized anxiety disorder.

Frontal lobe One of the four lobes of the cerebral cortex; it is the seat of the capacity to solve problems flexibly and of social cognition.

Gamma waves This electroencephalographic pattern of electrical activity involves an irregular brain wave pattern. It always signals the existence of brain damage.

Generalized anxiety disorder Unrealistic and excessive anxiety about two or more life situations.

Genital stage In Freudian theory, the fifth stage of psychosexual development, It marks the self-identification of a person's gender and the capacity for mature heterosexual relationships.

Genotype The array of genes a person possesses.

Gilles de la Tourette's syndrome A disorder characterized by intermittent bodily tics (e.g., sudden uncontrolled jerks), sounds (e.g., barks), and words (e.g., obscenities).

Global attribution The tendency of depressed individuals to see the causes of negative events as having broad effects in many areas of their lives.

Grand mal epilepsy One of the most common seizure disorders, characterized by loss of consciousness and a generalized tonic-clonic convulsion of the entire body.

Halfway house Facility for individuals released from a hospital or other treatment program who need more supervision and monitoring than their family can provide.

Hallucinations Abnormal auditory, olfactory, visual, gustatory, or kinesthetic perceptions which are a common symptom of schizophrenia; most common are the hallucinations which involve hearing voices or seeing objects that do not actually exist.

Health psychology The application of psychology as a discipline to the promotion of health, and the prevention and treatment of illness.

Hierarchy of needs A concept developed by Abraham Maslow, referring to the hierarchy of physiological, basic social, and complex human needs through which people must progress to achieve self-actualization.

Histrionic personality Individuals with this highly emotional personality style constantly seek attention by exaggerating, overdramatizing, overreacting to situations, and by dressing in unusual attire.

Hormones Chemical messengers secreted by the endocrine glands into the bloodstream; they act on other bodily organs to regulate physiological processes and coordinate internal processes with external events.

Humanistic model An approach to understanding psychotherapy that emphasizes the role of internal psychological processes and our uniquely human strengths and potentialities in the development of both normal and abnormal behavior.

Huntington's disease An autosomal-dominant chronic brain disorder with a deteriorating course, generally beginning in midlife, characterized by changes in personality, intellect, memory, interpersonal behavior, and movement, typically culminating in dementia.

Hyperactivity Behavior marked by high levels of activity and restlessness; such behavior is usually recognized as a problem once the child is expected to sit and attend for a significant period of time, as in a classroom environment.

Hyperkinesis The term used in DSM I and DSM II to diagnose those children now categorized as exhibiting Attention-Deficit Hyperactivity Disorder (ADHD) in the DSM III-R.

Hypochondriasis The belief that one has a serious physical illness despite medical judgments to the contrary.

Hypomania A manic-like episode that is milder than a full manic episode; such an episode does not markedly impair an individual's social and vocational functioning.

Hypothesis An explicitly stated idea or prediction that the experiment is designed to test.

Hypothetico-deductive method The scientific approach of deriving a theory or hypothesis first and then testing it by experiment or observation.

Id In Freudian theory, one of three parts of the psychic apparatus and the source of primitive drives and desires untouched by the real world.

Identical twins Twins who develop from the same fertilized ovum; also termed monozygotic twins, they share all genetic material.

Imaging procedures Procedures by which the structure and function of interior portions of the body and brain can be visualized.

Imipramine An antidepressant medication (a tricyclic) used to treat a number of clinical disorders such as depression, panic disorder, and enuresis.

Immune system The physiological system that protects the body against viral and bacterial disease.

Incidence A public health term that refers to the number of persons within a given population who have acquired a specific disorder within a particular time period, usually one year.

Incomplete penetrance A situation in which a single dominant gene controls the inheritance of a disorder, but not every individual who carries the gene develops the disorder because the gene does not fully "penetrate" the system.

Independent variable The variable which is systematically manipulated or controlled in an experiment.

Index case (proband) In family studies of genetic inheritance of disorders, the individual who has the disorder in question.

Individual therapy interviews Interviews which bring patient and therapist together in an extended relationship based on the patient's willingness to recount and reevaluate past and present behavior, feelings, and attitudes.

Inductive approach The scientific approach of deriving theories to explain a phenomenon only after data have been collected.

Infantile autism A disorder in the subclass of severe developmental disabilities (DSM III-R) which is marked by a lack of social responsiveness and often accompanied by gross speech deficits.

Inhibited female orgasm The persistent or recurrent delay in or absence of orgasm following sexual arousal judged by a clinician to have been adequate in intensity.

Inhibited male orgasm The persistent or recurrent delay in or absence of orgasm following sexual arousal judged by a clinician to have been adequate in intensity.

Insight In psychodynamic therapy, the awareness patients develop, usually in extended psychotherapy, of their unconscious conflicts and psychological defenses.

Instrumental aggression Aggression controlled by positive consequences and rewards. These aggressive behaviors are engaged in to obtain a desired response, which in turn serves to strengthen and maintain the aggressive behavior pattern over time.

Intelligence quotient (IQ) An estimate of intelligence on the Binet Scale produced by dividing the child's mental age by his or her chronological age.

Internal attribution The tendency of a depressed individual to attribute the causes of negative events to his or her own internal failings or incompetency.

Interpersonal psychotherapy (IPT) Therapy which focuses on past and present interpersonal interactions, and emphasizes attachment to parental figures and significant others. IPT has been shown to be effective in treating depression.

Interpretation The technique in which a therapist helps patients address information about their behavior which they were previously unaware of.

Intoxication Behavioral changes associated with acute, reversible changes in brain function brought on by the ingestion of an intoxicating drug.

Intrapsychic conflict In Freudian theory, intrapsychic conflict between the ego and id or the ego and superego.

Introversion According to C. G. Jung, the personality type which characterizes persons who tend to be quiet, shy, and uncomfortable in social settings.

Jacksonian seizures A seizure disorder characterized by a variety of partial motor symptoms initially involving a small part of an extremity, ultimately leading to the involuntary movement of part of an entire side of the body.

Korsakoff's syndrome A consequence of prolonged, heavy alcohol ingestion and chronic thiamine deficiency, characterized by profound memory loss and visuoperceptual and problem-solving deficits.

Latency stage In Freudian theory, the fourth stage of psychosexual development, extending from the sixth year to the onset of puberty, during which Oedipal impulses are repressed.

Law of effect Edward L. Thorndike's demonstration that behaviors associated with satisfying consequences are likely to be repeated, while those linked to unsatisfying consequences are less likely to reoccur.

Learned helplessness The state induced in animals or people as a result of repeated experience that their behavior has no effect on important consequences in their environment.

Libido In Freudian theory, the id's sexual impulses and drives, also called the life instinct.

Life instinct In Freudian theory, the id's sexual impulses and drives, also called libido.

Lithium A naturally occurring salt used as a drug to treat mania and bipolar disorder.

Lobotomy (prefrontal leucotomy) (see prefrontal leucotomy).

Locus of control An individual's assessment of where control for events and circumstances in his/her life lies (i.e., internal vs. external control).

Lovemap A hypothesized pattern of brain functioning that is established early in the psychobiology of sexual development, and which determines sexual imagery and actions later in life.

Low sexual desire The absence of sexual fantasies and the wish for sexual activity.

Magnification A gross error in evaluation involving exaggeration of negative events.

Malingering A pattern of behavior similar to that seen in a genuine clinical disorder, such as conversion disorder, but is deliberately and consciously designed to obtain some reward or avoid some unpleasant situation.

MAO inhibitors Antidepressant medication used to block the action of MAO (monoamine oxidase), preventing the breakdown of norepinephrine and serotonin. This allows for higher levels of these neurotransmitters to remain in the system and thereby decrease depression.

Marital therapy A treatment in which a therapist consults with both the husband and the wife to help them learn to communicate better, to provide more support to each other, and to understand their interactions.

Masked depression A depression not overtly expressed but instead masked or hidden; such depression is thought to be expressed through other behavior and symptoms (e.g., hyperactivity, truancy, or drinking).

Mental age Refers to the number of age-grouped tests and problems the child passes in the Binet Scale; mental age divided by chronological age yields an estimate of IQ.

Mental status examination A semistructured interview designed to evaluate the patient's thinking, feeling, sensing, and perceiving.

Meta-analysis A quantitative method for integrating the standardized results of a large number of separate studies.

Midtown Manhattan study An epidemiological study of the mental health and mental impairment of the 750,000 residents of Midtown Manhattan between 1952 and 1960.

Milieu therapy (see milieu *treatment* definition)

Milieu treatment Treatment for patients within a ward or structured environment that emphasizes self-care, self-management of ward activities, and group norms for appropriate behavior.

Minimal brain dysfunction A term widely used in the 1970s to describe and explain the behavior of hyperactive children with attentional problems; the overactivity and inattentiveness were thought to be due to minimal brain dysfunctions that were not detectable through standard neurological examinations.

Minimization In Beck's cognitive therapy, a dysfunctional form of thinking in which patients minimize the value of their positive characteristics and exaggerate the importance of their negative qualities.

Minnesota Multiphasic Personality Inventory (MMPI) A true-false self-report questionnaire consisting of 567 items in its 1989 revision. It yields useful clinical discriminations and personality formulations for individuals and groups.

Modeling A procedure in which people acquire knowledge and behavior vicariously by observing the actions of other people.

Monozygotic twins Twins developed from the same fertilized ovum; also termed identical twins, they share all genetic material.

Moral anxiety In Freudian theory, anxiety generated by a harsh, punitive superego.

Multiaxial diagnostic system A feature of DSM-III and DSM-III-R by which each patient is rated on five distinct behavioral dimensions or axes.

Multi-infarct dementia This chronic organic brain disorder is caused by repeated disruptions in blood supply to the brain, resulting in the death of more and more brain tissue.

Multimodal therapy An approach to treatment developed by A. A. Lazarus in which each of seven modalities of functioning (behavior, affect, sensation, imagery, cognition, interpersonal relations, and biology) is assessed and then targeted for intervention using an eclectic range of methods.

Multiple baseline across behaviors design Several discrete behaviors are measured over time to provide a baseline to evaluate changes. Each behavior is then successively modified in turn.

Multiple personality The presence of two or more distinct personalities in the same person. The alternative personalities are usually fully integrated with consistent patterns of behavior and attitudes.

Mutism A refusal or inability to speak, often characteristic of catatonic schizophrenia and autism.

Narcissistic personality A grandiose personality style that involves the constant seeking of adulation and exhibition of an exaggerated sense of self-importance, power, brillance, and beauty. It is generally assumed that narcissists have a weak sense of self-esteem and self-worth that is easily threatened.

Needs In Murray's scoring system for the TAT, the respondent's desires and wishes for such things as food, affection, dominance, and sex.

Negative cognitive triad Negative beliefs about the self, the world, and the future maintained by cognitive distortions, as hypothesized in Beck's theory of depression.

Negative correlation The degree to which subjects have different relative standings in the distributions of two variables.

Negative reinforcement An increase in behavior that avoids or reduces an aversive event.

Neuroleptics (antipsychotic medications) Medications used to treat psychotic symptoms.

Neurotic anxiety In Freudian theory, anxiety generated when id impulses threaten to overwhelm the ego.

Neurotransmitters Biochemical substances in the brain which mediate the transmission of electrical impulses across the synapses; excesses and deficits in these substances are believed to be causes of psychopathology.

Noninvasive A characteristic of imaging procedures which do not require that the interior of the body be entered.

Nosologies Schemes for categorizing animals, plants, elements, and other natural phenomena, including diseases.

Obsessions Unwanted, repetitive, and intrusive thoughts, images, or impulses that are distressing to the person.

Objective anxiety In Freudian theory, anxiety generated by the realistic expectation of actual danger.

Object loss theory of depression The psychoanalytic theory that depression is caused when an individual, pursuing independence and autonomy, experiences problems related to a loss of attachment to certain objects, especially parents.

Observational bias An observation of another person's behavior colored by an observer's or a clinician's expectations, attitudes, or convictions.

Observational (vicarious) learning One of three principal modes of learning, closely associated with Albert Bandura, in which learning takes place by watching the behavior of others.

Obsessive-compulsive personality A personality style marked by checking and perfectionistic behaviors that are pervasive and inflexible.

Occipital lobe One of four lobes of the cerebral cortex; it appears to be primarily concerned with visual perception.

Oedipus complex In Freudian theory, the unconscious desire of the four-year-old boy to have sex with his mother and his conflict about eliminating his father, the rival for his mother's affection.

Operant conditioning A form of learning associated with the behavioristic philosophy and research of B.F. Skinner. Behavior is acquired, maintained, and eliminated as a function of its environmental consequences.

Operant response A voluntary response that operates on the environment with an effect that increases the probability of the response being emitted more frequently.

Operational criteria A feature of DSM-III and DSM-III-R in which the distinguishing features of each disorder are clearly listed and carefully described.

Operational definition Definition of a scientific construct in objective, measurable terms.

Oppositional-defiant disorder A disorder of early to middle childhood that may evolve into a conduct disorder, usually diagnosed before the age of twelve; children with oppositional defiant disorder defy adult rules, are angry, and often lose their tempers.

Oral stage In Freudian theory, the first stage of psychosexual development, extending from birth to eighteen months, during which the mouth is the main erogenous zone.

Organic brain disorders Acute or chronic disorders of the brain and behavior caused by one or more factors that interfere temporarily or permanently with brain function.

Organic mental disorders associated with a physical disorder These acute and chronic brain disorders include epilepsy, Huntington's disease, and Parkinson's disease, as well as the delirium and dementia associated with the later stages of HIV infection.

Orgasmic reconditioning A behavior therapy technique used to help paraphiliacs develop sexual arousal to more conventional heterosexual activities. The patient is instructed to imagine engaging in appropriate heterosexual activity just prior to reaching orgasm, so as to classically condition the gratification of orgasm to heterosexual imagery.

Overanxious disorder Children with overanxious disorder have anxieties and fears that are beyond those expected for children of their age; other key symptoms include sleep problems and overreactive autonomic responses.

Overgeneralization An individual's pattern of drawing conclusions about his or her ability, performance, or self-worth based on a single incident.

Overvalued idea An excessive and unrealistic concern.

Panic disorder Unexpected, recurrent attacks of intense anxiety occurring in the apparent absence of situations that would elicit anxiety.

Paradoxical directives A therapeutic procedure often used by family therapists in which a specific suggestion is given by the therapist to do something that seems counterintuitive.

Paranoid personality The personality style of an individual overwrought with the fear that others are against and somehow exploiting or taking advantage of him or her. Paranoids tend to be secretive, jealous, rigid, argumentative, scheming, cold, and frequently sullen.

Paranoid schizophrenic A type of schizophrenia characterized by elaborate delusions.

Paraphilias Sexual disorders in which the individual is sexually aroused by unconventional acts or odd objects.

Parataxic distortion The effect of problematic interpersonal relationships in childhood on the adult's misperceptions of reality.

Parietal lobe One of four lobes of the cerebral cortex; it mediates touch recognition and speech.

Parkinson's disease A chronic brain disorder caused by the destruction of brain cells producing dopamine, resulting in a degenerative process that includes tremor, muscular rigidity, bradykinesis, a stooped posture, a shuffling gait, depression, and dementia.

Passive-aggressive personality A personality style characterized by behavior that expresses hostility in indirect and non-physically aggressive ways.

Patients' rights movement The movement, which began in the 1960s, to restore to hospitalized psychiatric patients most of the rights and privileges others in society enjoy.

Peripheral nervous system The somatic nervous system and the autonomic nervous system.

Personality Although this concept has many definitions, with no one meaning accepted by all psychologists, there is consensus that it refers to the distinctive patterns of thought, emotion, and behavior that characterize each person's adaptation to situations in his or her life.

Personality disorders Maladaptive and inflexible ways of interacting which remain constant despite aging, different environments, and medication; these styles often cause serious difficulties for the disordered individual.

Person-centered theory of personality Carl Rogers' humanistic theory of personality which is based on the proposition that the person is characterized by a fundamental self-actualizing tendency to seek fulfillment in the world as experienced and perceived. The theory holds that the best way to understand behavior is by understanding the inner, perceptual world of the person.

Petit mal epilepsy A seizure disorder involving a brief disruption in consciousness which may be overlooked by observers.

Phallic stage In Freudian theory, the third stage of psychosexual development, extending from the third to the sixth year, during which the primary erogenous zone is the genitals.

Phenotype A person's observable characteristics.

Physical dependence Adaptation of the central nervous system to the continued ingestion of dependency-inducing substances.

Pleasure principle In Freudian theory, the guiding principle of the id, which strives to maximize pleasure and reduce tension.

Positive correlation The degree to which subjects have the same relative standing in the distributions of two variables.

Positive reinforcement The operant conditioning procedure of making an event (the reinforcing stimulus) contingent on behavior so that the probability of that behavior increases.

Post-traumatic stress disorder (PTSD) An anxiety disorder whose symptoms develop following a psychologically distressing event that is outside the normal range of human experiences; the essential features of PTSD include increased arousal, reexperiencing of a traumatic event, and avoidance of stimuli associated with the traumatic event.

Prefrontal leucotomy (lobotomy) Psychosurgery which involves the removal of the frontal portion of the brain.

Premature ejaculation Ejaculation by the male during vaginal intercourse before the female partner is satisfied, and before the man wishes it.

Presses In Murray's scoring system for the TAT, the environmental factors appearing in test responses like poverty, emotional impoverishment and discrimination that prevent a respondent from realizing his or her needs.

Pretreatment assessment The measurement of characteristics of patients and their clinical disorder before they receive treatment for that disorder.

Prevalence A public health term that refers to the total number of persons within a given population who suffer from a particular disorder.

Primary prevention A type of prevention designed to reduce the occurrence of new problems in a population.

Primary process In Freudian theory, irrational and illogical thinking motivated by the pleasure principle, characterized by sexual preoccupations and fantasies, anger, jealousy, selfishness, and envy.

Primitive superego A superego which has not modified parental expectations from childhood; such a superego makes one vulnerable to depression because the expectations of oneself and others are often too high.

Privileged communication Communication between patient and therapist protected by legal statute from being revealed except under very special circumstances.

Proband The individual with a particular problem who is the focus of investigation in a study of familial transmission of a disorder.

Problem solving training A therapeutic method in which the therapist focuses on the patient's cognitive processes, such as expectations, self-statements and problem-solving skills. The core of the method is the problem solving *process,* as opposed to its outcome, or results.

Progressive relaxation A form of relaxation training, involving alternating tensing and relaxing of different muscle groups, now widely used to treat different stress-related disorders.

Projective drawings A projective device which asks respondents to draw pictures without giving them additional explicit instruction.

Psychiatric nurses These core mental health professionals, who have earned a Masters degree in Psychiatric Nursing, typically have extensive training in psychopharmacology and milieu therapy.

Psychiatric social workers These core mental health professionals, who have earned the M.S.W. degree, are trained to appreciate and emphasize the impact of environmental factors on mental disorder.

Psychiatrists These core mental health professionals, who have earned the M.D. degree and received extensive residency training, are trained in psychopharmacology and the other somatic therapies, diagnosis, and, to varying degrees, psychotherapy.

Psychoactive substance-induced organic mental disorders The term used to describe the acute and chronic effects of drugs of abuse on the brain.

Psychoactive substance abuse In DSM-III-R, persons who meet fewer than three of the nine operational criteria for psychoactive substance dependence but have used a substance for a month or more even though it caused them significant problems or who use substances in physically hazardous circumstances.

Psychoactive substance dependence Persons who meet three or more of the nine operational criteria for psychoactive substance dependence in DSM-III-R.

Psychoanalytic theory Sigmund Freud's personality theory, a psychodynamic theory.

Psychobiology Adolf Meyer's theory that organic, psychological, and environmental factors all contribute to psychopathology.

Psychodynamic model An approach to understanding psychopathology that emphasizes the role of internal psychological processes and early childhood experiences in the development of normal and abnormal behavior.

Psychoimmunology The study of the interactions between psychological influences and functioning of the immune system.

Psychological dependence Craving for a substance because of its effects on behavior and the emotions, rather than its physiological effects.

Psychopath An individual who engages in antisocial behavior without anxiety, shame, or remorse.

Psychopathology Mental, psychiatric or emotional disorder.

Psychosis; psychotic disorder A serious mental disorder that involves an actual break with reality; hallucinations and delusions often accompany psychosis.

Psychosomatic medicine The study of the links between psychological processes and physical illness, historically tied to psychodynamic theory.

Psychostimulant medication A medication which increases heart rate, blood pressure, and attention; common side effects are appetite suppression and sleeping problems. This medication is frequently used to treat children with attention deficit disorders and hyperactivity; it also used to treat narcolepsy.

Psychostimulants Medications which increase alertness, motor skills, and general arousal; among some of its various uses are treating hyperactivity and narcolepsy, and controlling appetite.

Psychosurgery The surgical destruction of certain neural pathways in the brain in an effort to control a severe mental disorder.

Psychotropic medications Medications used to alter behavior, thoughts, or feelings.

Punishment In operant conditioning, the presentation of an aversive stimulus or the removal of a reinforcing stimulus contingent on a response, thereby decreasing the probability of that response being emitted in the future.

Quasi-experiment A modified experimental method used to study pre-existing differences in subjects. Possession of specific personal characteristics defines the experimental group.

Reality principle In Freudian theory, the guiding principle of the ego, which recognizes society's realistic demands.

Recessive gene A gene that must be paired with one identical to it in order to determine a trait in the phenotypes.

Recidivism Rate at which relapse occurs.

Reinforcement model Lewinsohn's model of depression which states that depressives experience more aversive events and less reinforcement than nondepressives.

Reinforcing stimulus In operant conditioning, the positive or negative consequences of a response which determine its subsequent frequency.

Relapse A return to alcohol or drug abuse after a period of abstinence or sobriety.

Repetition compulsion The Freudian concept that recurrent, intrusive thoughts or dreams are attempts to overcome psychological fixation on a traumatic event.

Repression A defense mechanism in which the ego excludes threatening impulses from conscious awareness.

Research interviews Interviews which are designed to provide answers to specific research questions.

Resistance The unwillingness on the part of patients to cooperate fully in the process of therapy (e.g., refusal to discuss a certain topic).

Response prevention A behavior therapy technique in which phobic or compulsive behavior (e.g., handwashing) is prevented so that the patient is exposed to the anxiety-eliciting stimuli.

Restrained eating Dieting; a pattern of eating that typically precedes the onset of eating disorders such as bulimia nervosa.

Reversal design An example of a single-case experimental design in which following baseline observation (A), an intervention is made (B), and then withdrawn (A). If the intervention was responsible for change during B, then the effect should disappear during reinstatement of A.

Risk factor A factor that predicts illness, even though the reason for the increased risk is unknown.

Ritalin A psychostimulant medication used to treat hyperactivity.

Rorschach inkblot test A projective test consisting of ten cards, each representing a different ambiguous inkblot design.

Schedules of reinforcement In operant conditioning, the behavioral relationship between a response and its consequences.

Schizoid personality Individuals with this disorder have a restricted range of social and emotional experience; they choose solitary activities, are indifferent to praise and criticism by others, and have few friends.

Schizophrenia A separation or loosening of associations, as between feelings and thoughts, which is believed to underlie the unusual behavior that is exhibited. Serious disturbances of thought and perception, or certain disturbances of affect must be present and cannot be attributed to an organic disorder.

Schizotypal personality A personality disorder with a pervasive pattern of unusual ideation and appearance; individuals with disorders have deficits in interpersonal relationships; they often have paranoid thoughts, suspiciousness, and odd beliefs.

School phobia An inappropriate fear of attending school; this phobic behavior often represents a dependency problem which is reinforced by parental attention.

Scientific theory An explicit and formal statement of a set of propositions designed to explain a particular phenomenon.

Scripted behavior Patterns of behavior following social expectations which often become well-developed and automatic.

Seasonal affective disorder Also called winter depression, this depressive disorder is affected by seasonal changes and/or length of daylight. Its symptoms include weight gain, low energy, and hypersomnia; it is treated by periodic exposure to full spectrum light which simulates the sun's natural spectral qualities.

Secondary prevention Prevention intended to help detect problems early in their onset and reduce their intensity.

Secondary process In Freudian theory, the rational and logical thinking of the ego motivated by the reality principle, characterized by reason and logic.

Seizure Pathophysiological brain disturbance caused by the spontaneous and excessive discharge of neurons in the cortex.

Self-actualization The term used by Abraham Maslow to describe how human beings can achieve their unrealized potential despite the inevitable frustrations of life.

Self-efficacy In social-learning theory, Bandura's term for the beliefs that people hold about their capabilities to exercise control over events affecting their lives.

Self-monitoring In behavioral assessment and behavior therapy, behavioral clinicians typically ask patients to identify and record in writing specific thoughts, feelings, and behaviors.

Self-psychology A modification of psychoanalysis in which the emphasis is on the low self-esteem or vulnerability a child feels because of lack of love. Psychotherapy is directed toward restoring the patient's sense of self by providing the acceptance that was missing in childhood.

Self-report measures These behavioral assessment measures are designed to help clients become aware of self-defeating or self-damaging cognitions.

Self-schemata Beliefs and knowledge about oneself organized into belief systems which function like memory banks to process and organize external information.

Semistructured interviews Interviews which follow an outline but do not prescribe specific questions or require a particular ordering of questions.

Sentence completion measures Projective devices that ask respondents to complete incomplete sentences.

Separation anxiety Intense anxiety experienced by children whenever they are separated from their parents.

Serotonin A neurotransmitter that is thought to be involved in the pathophysiology of different clinical disorders, such as obsessive-compulsive disorder.

Serotonin uptake inhibitor An antidepressant medication used to block the absorption of serotonin in the system; by allowing serotonin to remain in the system, depression is alleviated.

Sexual abuse Sexual contact that is forced or imposed on an individual.

Sexual aversion The avoidance of all or almost all genital sexual contact with a partner.

Sign A characteristic feature of a disease of which a patient may be unaware that is nonetheless noted by a clinician.

Slow virus A viral infection that takes a very long time to produce symptoms; some believe Alzheimer's disease is caused by a slow virus.

Social-consequence model An approach to understanding psychopathology that emphasizes the impact of gender, age, ethnicity, and other sociocultural factors on the development of normal and abnormal behavior.

Social-learning theory Bandura's theory of complex human learning in which behavior is viewed as a product of both internal cognitive mediating processes (e.g., self-efficacy and self-regulation) and external stimulus events (e.g., classical and operant conditioning).

Social support Concern and caring for an individual, including acceptance, offering tangible help, and giving advice about coping with problems.

Sociopathic personality disturbance The catchall diagnostic category that also included antisocial behavior and the sexual deviations under which alcohol and drug addiction were also subsumed in DSM-I.

Somatization disorder Recurrent somatic symptoms causing the person to consult one doctor after another without finding any organic basic.

Somatoform disorders The presence of symptoms typically associated with physical diseases although no known organic basis can be found .

Somatoform pain disorder Extreme pain that cannot be accounted for by any known physiological mechanism.

Specific developmental disorder A disorder diagnosed when children evidence inadequate development of certain academic, language, speech, and motor skills; the child's skills are significantly lower than his/her intellectual capability.

Spectatoring The process whereby a person engaged in sex becomes self-conscious and an observer of his or her sexual response, looking for failure rather than pleasure.

Spontaneous remission Patients experience improvement with a particular problem in the absence of any formal therapy.

Stable attribution The tendency of a depressed individual to believe that the causes of negative events remain consistent across time.

Standardization samples Groups of persons whose responses to new tests are typically analyzed as a function of age, gender, education, socioeconomic status, and other relevant variables; used to test the validity of psychological tests.

Standardized Refers to assessment devices whose validity has been analyzed by means of standardization samples.

Stereotypic movement disorder Habitual, repetitive behaviors that serve no usual social function; the behaviors may include tics, skin picking, teeth grinding, or repetitive vocalizations.

Structural family therapy A form of family therapy made popular by Virginia Satir and Salvadore Minuchin in which family members are asked to reconceptualize problems and to communicate differently.

Structured interview Interviews guided by a detailed set of questions prepared and tested before the interview and always asked in a predetermined order.

Substance dependence syndrome The overarching, empirically-derived concept of dependence that guided the drafting of the psychoactive substance use disorders section of DSM-III-R.

Superego in Freudian theory, one of three parts of the psychic apparatus, the seat of conscience and the ability to distinguish right from wrong.

Surcease The desire to simply give up because living no longer seems tolerable. It is one of the two most common reasons for committing suicide.

Symptom A feature of a disease that a patient recognizes and may complain of.

Symptom substitution The replacement of one symptom with another following a treatment in which the underlying problem is not resolved.

Systematic desensitization A behavior therapy technique for treating phobic disorders. First, the patient is deeply relaxed and then is instructed to conjure-up in imagery a hierarchically-ordered series of events which elicit increasing levels of anxiety.

Systems approach See Family therapy.

Tardive dyskinesia Involuntary movements such as lip-smacking and tongue protrusion which are often side effects of antipsychotic medications.

Technical eclecticism A form of psychological treatment in which the therapist draws on techniques from any system of psychotherapy without necessarily subscribing to the theories behind the techniques.

Temporal lobe One of four lobes of the cerebral cortex; it controls visual information processing, long-term memory, the expression of emotion, and the recognition of sounds.

Temporal lobe epilepsy A seizure disorder that involves unusual behaviors that are sometimes quite complicated and may involve violence.

Tension-reduction hypothesis The learning-based theory that humans consume alcohol to excess primarily to reduce high levels of tension and anxiety.

Tertiary prevention A type of prevention designed to reduce a problem's long-term consequences.

Thanatos In Freudian theory, the id's aggressive and destructive drives, also called the death instinct.

Thematic Apperception Test (TAT) A projective test consisting of thirty-one cards; thirty of the cards portray an ambiguous scene often involving people, while one is blank.

Theory of infantile sexuality Freud's theory that his female patients' accounts of having been sexually abused by family members reflected their unconscious wish to have sex with their father.

Therapeutic communities Social groups designed to treat mental disorders; an approach that was developed in the late 1700s which emphasized personal qualities of staff over medical interventions.

Token reinforcement program An operant conditioning technique in which tokens (conditioned reinforcers) are given to patients contingent on desired behavior. The tokens are later exchanged for the actual rewards the person desires.

Tolerance The phenomenon which requires persons ingesting a drug which has induced dependence to ingest more of the drug to maintain its reinforcing effects; those effects gradually diminish if drug dosage is unchanged.

Transcendental meditation A form of relaxation training in which the person adopts a passive attitude and focuses on a single object.

Transference The special relationship that develops between patient and therapist in which patients respond to the therapist as they did toward significant people (usually parents) in their childhood.

Tricyclic antidepressants A class of medications used to decrease depression; they are called tricyclics because of their three ring molecular structure.

Type A behavior pattern The behavior pattern, marked by aggrressiveness, competitiveness, and impatience, which is hypothesized to be a cause of heart disease.

Unconditioned response (UCR) In classical conditioning, a natural response that is elicited by an unconditioned stimulus (UCS).

Unconditioned stimulus (UCS) In classical conditioning, a stimulus which is naturally capable of eliciting an unconditioned response (UCR).

Unconscious In Freudian theory, psychic material that is out of awareness and cannot be brought into awareness except under special circumstances.

Undifferentiated schizophrenic Individuals with psychotic symptoms such as delusions and hallucinations but who do not meet specific criteria for other types of schizophrenia.

Unstructured interview Interviews which do not follow an outline but occur spontaneously.

Usefulness An assessment method's usefulness is gauged from the assistance in planning or evaluating treatment it provides clinicians.

Vaginal orgasm Freud speculated that orgasm during vaginal intercourse was the mark of psychosexual maturity, whereas clitoral stimulation through masturbation was a sign of psychosexual immaturity. This distinction has been shown to be false.

Vaginismus The involuntary tightening or spasm in the outer third of the vagina that makes it difficult if not impossible for a woman to have intercourse.

Waiting-list control Patients await treatment and undergo repeated assessment for a certain period of time corresponding to the time taken to administer therapy to the treatment group in the study.

Wernicke's encephalopathy An acute brain disorder caused by thiamine deficiency, typically preceding the onset of the symptoms of Korsakoff's syndrome.

Withdrawal The interrelated physical and psychological consequences that accompany the cessation of use of a dependency-inducing drug.

References

Abel, G.G. (1989). Behavioral treatment of child molesters. In A.J. Stunkard & A. Baum (Eds.), *Perspectives in behavioral medicine.* Hillsdale, NJ: Lawrence Erlbaum.

Abel, G.G., Barlow, D.H., Blanchard, E.B., & Guild, D. (1977). The components of rapists' sexual arousal. *Archives of General Psychiatry, 34,* 859–903.

Abel, G.G., Becker, J.V., Cunningham-Rathner, J., Mittelman, J., & Rouleau, J.L. (1988). Multiple paraphilic diagnoses among sex offenders. *Bulletin of the American Academy of Psychiatry and Law, 16,* 153–168.

Abel, G.G., Becker, J.V., Mittelman, M., Cunningham-Rathner, J., Rouleau, J.L., & Murphy, W.D. (1987). Self-reported sex crimes of nonincarcerated paraphiliacs. *Journal of Interpersonal Violence, 2,* 3–25.

Abel, G.G., & Rouleau, J.L. (1990). Male sex offenders. In M.E. Thase, B.A. Edelstein, & M. Hersen (Eds.), *Handbook of outpatient treatment of adults.* New York: Plenum.

Abplanap, J.M., Haskett, R.F., & Rose, R.M. (1979). Psychoendocrinology of the menstrual cycle. I. Enjoyment of daily activities and moods. *Psychological Medicine, 41,* 587–604.

Abramowitz, C.V., & Dokecki, P.R. (1977). The politics of clinical judgment: Early empirical returns. *Psychological Bulletin, 84,* 460–476.

Abramowitz, S.I. (1986). Psychosocial outcomes of sex. *Journal of Consulting and Clinical Psychology, 54,* 183–189.

Abrams, R., & Taylor, M.A. (1976). Catatonia. *Archives of General Psychiatry, 33,* 579–581.

Abramson, L.Y., Metalsky, G.I., & Alloy, L.B. (1989). Hopelessness depression: A theory-based subtype of depression. *Psychological Review, 96*(2), 358–372.

Abramson, L.Y., Seligman, M.E.P., & Teasdale, J. (1978). Learned helplessness in humans: Critique and reformulation. *Journal of Abnormal Psychology, 87,* 32–48.

Adair, J.G., Dushenko, T.W., & Lindsay, R.C.L. (1985). Ethical regulations and their impact on research practice. *American Psychologist, 40,* 59–72.

ADAMHA News. (1990, March-April). "Decrease in use of illicit drugs continues," Volume XVI, no. 2, pp. 1, 14. Rockville, MD: U.S. Department of Health and Human Services.

ADAMHA Update. (1988, March). "Facts from the 1987 National High School Senior Survey." Rockville, MD: U.S. Department of Health and Human Services.

Adams, D. (1989). Treatment models of men who batter: A profeminist analysis. In K. Yllo & M. Bograd (Eds.), *Feminist perspectives on wife abuse.* Newbury Park, CA: Sage.

Adams, G.R., Gullotta, T., & Clancy, M.A. (1985). Homeless adolescents: A descriptive study of similarities and differences between runaways and throwaways. *Adolescence, 79,* 715–724.

Adams, K.M. (1980). In search of Luria's battery: A false start. *Journal of Consulting and Clinical Psychology, 48,* 511–516.

Adams, R.D., & Victor, M. (1981). *Principles of neurology.* New York: McGraw-Hill.

Ader, R. (Ed.). (1981). *Psychoneuroimmunology.* New York: Academic Press.

Ader, R., & Cohen, N. (1985). CNS-immune system interactions: Conditioning phenomena. *The Behavioral and Brain Sciences, 8,* 379–395.

Agras, W.S. (1982). Behavioral medicine in the 1980s: Nonrandom connections. *Journal of Consulting and Clinical Psychology, 50,* 797–803.

Agras, W.S., Barlow, D.H., Chapin, N.H., Abel, G.G., & Leitenberg, H. (1974). Behavior modification of anorexia nervosa. *Archives of General Psychiatry, 30,* 279–286.

Agras, W.S., & Kirkley, B.G. (1986). Bulimia: Theories of etiology. In K.D. Brownell & J.P. Foreyt (Eds.), *Handbook of eating disorders: Physiology, psychology, and treatment of obesity, anorexia, and bulimia.* New York: Basic Books.

Albee, G.W. (1968). Conceptual models and manpower requirements in psychology. *American Psychologist, 23,* 317–324.

Albee, G.W., Lane, E.A., & Reuter, J.M. (1964). Childhood intelligence of future schizophrenics and neighborhood peers. *Journal of Psychology, 58,* 141–144.

Albert, N., & Beck, A. (1975). Incidence of depression in early adolescence: A preliminary study. *Journal of Youth and Adolescence, 4,* 301–307.

Alberti, R.E., & Emmons, M.L. (1978). *Your perfect right.* San Luis Obispo, CA: Impact Books.

Alden, L. (1989). Short-term structured treatment for avoidant personality disorder. *Journal of Consulting and Clinical Psychology, 57,* 756–764.

Alden, L., & Cappe, R. (1988). Characteristics predicting social functioning and treatment response in clients impaired by extreme shyness: Age of onset and the public/private shyness distinction. *Canadian Journal of Behavioral Science, 20,* 40–49.

Alexander, F. (1950). *Psychosomatic medicine.* New York: W.W. Norton.

Alexander, J.F., Mas, C.H., & Waldron, H. (1988). Behavioral and systems family therapies or Auld Lang Syne: Shall old perspectives be forgot? In R. deV. Peters & R.J. McMahon (Eds.), *Social learning and systems approaches to marriage and the family.* New York: Brunner/Mazel.

Alexander, J.F., & Parsons, B.V. (1973). Short term behavioral intervention with delinquent families: Impact on family process and recidivism. *Journal of Abnormal Psychology, 81,* 219–226.

Alford, G.S. (1980). Alcoholics Anonymous: An empirical evaluation study. In W.R. Miller (Ed.), *Addictive behavior* (Vol. 5). Oxford: Pergamon Press.

Allen, M.G. (1976). Twin studies of affective illness. *Archives of General Psychiatry, 33,* 1476–1478.

Allgood-Merten, B., Lewinsohn, P.M., & Hops, H. (1990). Sex differences and adolescent depression. *Journal of Abnormal Psychology, 99,* 55–63.

Alloy, L.B., & Abramson, L.Y. (1979). Judgment of contingency in depressed and nondepressed students: Sadder but wiser? *Journal of Experimental Psychology: General, 108,* 441–485.

Alloy, L.B., Clements, C., & Kolden, G. (1985). The cognitive diathesis—stress theories of depression: Therapeutic implications. In S. Reiss & R.R. Bootzin (Eds.), *Theoretical issues* (pp. 379–410). New York: Academic Press.

Alpert, M., & Silvers, K.N. (1970). Perceptual characteristics distinguishing auditory hallucinations in schizophrenia and acute alcoholic psychoses. *American Journal of Psychiatry, 127,* 298–302.

Althof, S.E., Turner, L.A., Levine, S.B., Risen, C., Kursch, E.D., Bodner, D., & Resnick, M. (1987). Intracavernosal injection in the treatment of impotence: A prospective study of sexual, psychological, and marital functioning. *Journal of Sex and Marital Therapy, 13,* 155–167.

Altura, B.M. (1986). Symposium on cardiovascular effects of ethanol. *Alcoholism: Clinical and Experimental Research, 10,* 557–559.

Ambelas, A. (1979). Psychologically stressful events in their precipitation of manic episodes. *British Journal of Psychiatry, 115,* 883–888.

American Association on Mental Deficiency. (1961). *A manual on terminology and classification.* Willimantic, CT: American Association on Mental Deficiency.

American Psychiatric Association. (1952).

Diagnostic and statistical manual of mental disorders. Washington, DC: American Psychiatric Association.

American Psychiatric Association. (1968). *Diagnostic and statistical manual of mental disorders* (2nd ed.). Washington, DC: American Psychiatric Association.

American Psychiatric Association. (1980). *Diagnostic and statistical manual of mental disorders* (3rd ed.). Washington, DC: American Psychiatric Association.

American Psychiatric Association. (1987). *Diagnostic and statistical manual of mental disorders* (3rd ed., rev.). Washington, DC: American Psychiatric Association.

American Psychiatric Association. (1990). *The practices of electroconvulsive therapy: Recommendations for treatment, training, and privileging*. Washington, DC: Author.

American Psychiatric Association Committee on Drug Abuse. (1987). Position statement on psychoactive substance use and dependence: Update on marijuana and cocaine. *American Journal of Psychiatry, 144*, 698–701.

American Psychological Association. (1986). *Graduate study in psychology and associated fields*. Washington, DC: American Psychological Association.

American Psychological Association. (1990). Ethical principles of psychologists. *American Psychologist, 45*, 390–395.

Andersen, A.E. (1985). *Practical comprehensive treatment of anorexia nervosa and bulimia*. Baltimore, MD: Johns Hopkins University Press.

Anderson, B.J., & Wolf, F.M. (1986). Chronic physical illness and sexual behavior: Psychological issues. *Journal of Consulting and Clinical Psychology, 54*, 168–175.

Anderson, J.C., Williams, S., McGee, R., & Silva, P.A. (1987). DSM-III disorders in preadolescent children: Prevalence in a large sample from the general population. *Archives of General Psychiatry, 44*, 69–76.

Anderson, M. (1984, December 5). Jury clears abused wife of murder. *Fort Lauderdale–Sun-Sentinel*, pp. 1b, 7b.

Anderson, N.B., Lane, J.D., Taguchi, F., Williams, R.B., & Houseworth, S.J. (1989). Race, parental history of hypertension, and patterns of cardiovascular reactivity in women. *The Society for Psychophysiological Research, 26*, 39–47.

Andrasik, F., Holroyd, K.A., & Abell, T. (1979). Prevalence of headache within a college student population: A preliminary analysis. *Headache, 20*, 384–387.

Andreasen, N.C. (1979a). Thought, language, and communication disorders: I. Clinical assessment, definition of terms, and evaluation of their reliability. *Archives of General Psychiatry, 36*, 1315–1321.

Andreasen, N.C. (1979b). Thought, language, and communication disorders: II. Diagnostic significance. *Archives of General Psychiatry, 36*, 1325–1330.

Andreasen, N.C. (1984). *The broken brain: The biological revolution in psychiatry*. New York: Harper & Row.

Andreasen, N.C. (1985). Positive vs. negative schizophrenia: A critical evaluation. *Schizophrenia Bulletin, 11*, 380–389.

Andreasen, N.C. (1988). Brain imaging: Applications in psychiatry. *Science, 239*, 1381–1388.

Andreasen, N.C., & Block, D.W. (1991). *Introductory textbook of psychiatry*. Washington, DC: American Psychiatric Press.

Andreasen, N.C., Hoffman, R.E., & Grove, W.M. (1985). Mapping abnormalities in language and cognition. In M. Alpert (Ed.), *Controversies in schizophrenia: Changes and constancies*. New York: Guilford Press.

Andreasen, N.C., Nasrallah, H.A., & Dunn, V. (1986). Structural abnormalities in the frontal system in schizophrenia. *Archives of General Psychiatry, 43*, 136–144.

Andreasen, N.C., Rice, J., Endicott, J., Coryell, W., Grove, W.M., & Reich, T. (1987). Familial rates of affective disorder. *Archives of General Psychiatry, 44*, 461–469.

Andreasen, N., Nasrallah, H.A., Van Dunn, V., Olson, S.C., Grove, W.M., Ehrhardt, J.C., Coffman, J.A., & Crossett, J.H.W. (1986). Structural abnormalities in the frontal system in schizophrenia. *Archives of General Psychiatry, 43*, 136.

Angell, M. (1985). Disease as a reflection of the psyche. *The New England Journal of Medicine, 312*, 1570–1572.

Annis, H.M. (1986). A relapse prevention model for treatment of alcoholics. In W.R. Miller & N. Heather (Eds.), *Treating addictive behaviors: Processes of change* (pp. 407–433). New York: Plenum Press.

Antoni, M., Levine, J., Tischer, P., Green, C., & Millon, T. (1987). Refining personality assessments by combining MCMI high-point profiles and MMPI codes, Part V: MMPI 78/87. *Journal of Personality Assessment, 51*, 375–387.

Apfelbaum, B. (1988). An ego-analytic perspective on desire disorders. In S.R. Leiblum & R.C. Rosen (Eds.), *Clinical perspectives on desire disorders*. New York: Guilford Press.

Aponte, H., & Hoffman, L. (1973). The open door: A structural approach to a family with an anorexic child. *Family Process, 12*, 1–44.

Appelbaum, P.S. (1982). Competency to consent to research. *Archives of General Psychiatry, 39*, 951–958.

Appelbaum, P.S. (1985). Civil commitment. In J.O. Cavenar, Jr., R. Michels, & H.K.H. Brodie (Eds.), *Psychiatry* (Vol. 3). Philadelphia & New York: J.B. Lippincott & Basic Books.

Appelbaum, P.S. (1988a). The right to refuse treatment with antipsychotic medications: Retrospect and prospect. *American Journal of Psychiatry, 145*, 413–419.

Appelbaum, P.S. (1988b). The new preventive detention: Psychiatry's problematic responsibility for the control of violence. *American Journal of Psychiatry, 145*, 779–785.

Appelbaum, P.S., & Hamm, R.M. (1982). Decision to seek commitment. *Archives of General Psychiatry, 39*, 447–451.

Appelbaum, P.S., & Rosenbaum, A. (1989). *Tarasoff* and the researcher: Does the duty to protect apply in the research setting? *American Psychologist, 44*, 885–894.

Arana, G.W., Baldessarini, R.J., & Ornsteen, M. (1985). The dexamethasone suppression test for diagnosis and prognosis in psychiatry. *Archives of General Psychiatry, 42*, 1193–1204.

Aries, P. (1962). *Centuries of childhood: A social history of family life*. New York: Alfred A. Knopf.

Arieti, S. (1976). The psychotherapeutic approach to schizophrenia. In D. Kemali, G. Bartholini, & D. Richter (Eds.), *Schizophrenia today*. Oxford, England: Pergamon Press.

Arkowitz, H., Holliday, S., & Hutter, M. (1982). Depressed women and their husbands: A study of marital interaction and adjustment. Paper presented at the annual meeting of the Association for Advancement of Behavior Therapy, Los Angeles, CA.

Arkowitz, H., & Messer, S. (Eds.). (1984). *Psychoanalytic therapy and behavior therapy: Is integration possible?* New York: Plenum.

Arlow, J.A. (1989). Psychoanalysis. In R. Corsini & D. Wedding (Eds.), *Current psychotherapies*. Itasca, IL: Peacock Publishers.

Arnkoff, D. (1983). Common and specific factors in cognitive therapy. In M.J. Lambert (Ed.), *Psychotherapy and patient relationships*. Homewood, IL: Dorsey.

Arnow, B., Taylor, C.B., Agras, W.S., & Telch, M. (1985). Enhancing agoraphobia treatment outcome by changing couple communication patterns. *Behavior Therapy, 16*, 452–467.

Arrindell, W.A., & Emmelkamp, P.M.G. (1986). Marital adjustment, intimacy and needs in female agoraphobics and their partners: A controlled study. Unpublished manuscript, State University of Groningen, The Netherlands.

Atkinson, J.W. (1983). *Personality, motivation, and action*. New York: Praeger.

Ayllon, T., & Azrin, N.H. (1965). The measurement and reinforcement of psychotics. *Journal of the Experimental Analysis of Behavior, 8*, 357–383.

Ayllon, T., & Azrin, N.H. (1968). *The token economy: A motivational system for therapy and rehabilitation*. New York: Appleton-Century-Crofts.

Azrin, N.H. (1976). Improvements in the community reinforcement approach to alcoholism. *Behaviour Research and Therapy, 14*, 339–348.

Azrin, N.H., Sneed, T.J., & Foxx, R.M. (1973). Dry-bed: A rapid method of eliminating bedwetting (enuresis) of the retarded. *Behaviour Research and Therapy, 11*, 427–434.

Azrin, N.H., Sneed, T.J., & Foxx, R.M. (1974). Dry-bed training: Rapid elimination of childhood enuresis. *Behav-*

iour Research and Therapy, 12, 147–156.

Babor, T.F., Brown, J., & Del Boca, F.K. (1990). Validity of self-reports in applied research on addictive behaviors: Fact or fiction. *Behavioral Assessment, 12,* 5–32.

Bachrach, A.J., Erwin, W.J., & Mohr, J.P. (1965). The control of eating behavior in an anorexic by operant conditioning techniques. In L.P. Ullman & L. Krasner (Eds.), *Case studies in behavior modification.* New York: Holt, Rinehart & Winston.

Bachrach, L.L. (1976). *Deinstitutionalization: An analytic review and sociological perspective* (DHEW Publication No. ADM 79–351). Washington, DC: U.S. Government Printing Office.

Bachrach, L.L. (1984). Deinstitutionalization and women: Assessing the consequences of public policy. *American Psychologist, 39,* 1171–1177.

Baer, L., Jenike, M., Ricciardi, J., Holland, A., Seymour, R., Minichiello, W., & Buttolph, M. (1990). Standardized assessment of personality disorders in obsessive-compulsive disorder. *Archives of General Psychiatry, 47,* 826–830.

Bajt, T.R., & Pope, K.S. (1989). Therapist-patient sexual intimacy involving children and adolescents. *American Psychologist, 44,* 455.

Baker, C. (1969). *Ernest Hemingway: A life story.* New York: Scribner.

Baker, T.R., Sherman, J.E., & Morse, E. (1987). The motivation to use drugs: A psychobiological analysis of urges. In C. Rivers (Ed.), *The Nebraska symposium on motivation: Alcohol use and abuse.* Lincoln, NE: University of Nebraska Press.

Baldessarini, R.J., & Cole, J.O. (1988). Chemotherapy. In A.M. Nicholi, Jr. (Ed.), *The new Harvard guide to psychiatry.* Cambridge, MA: Harvard University Press.

Bales, R.F. (1946). Cultural differences in rates of alcoholism. *Quarterly Journal of Studies on Alcohol, 6,* 480–499.

Ball, M.J. (1977). Neuronal loss, neurofibrillary tangles and granulovacuolar degeneration in the hippocampus with aging and dementia. *Acta Neuropathologica, 37,* 111–118.

Balter, M.B., Manheimer, D.I., Mellinger, G.D., & Uhlenhuth, E.H. (1984). A cross-national comparison of antianxiety/sedative drug use. *Current Medical Research and Opinion, 8,* 5–20.

Bancroft, J.H. (1974). *Deviant sexual behaviour.* Oxford: Oxford University Press.

Bancroft, J.H. (1983). *Human sexuality and its problems.* New York: Churchill Livingstone.

Bancroft, J., Skrimshire, A., Casson, J., Harvard-Watts, O., & Reynolds, F. (1977). People who deliberately poison or injure themselves: Their problems and contacts with helping agencies. *Psychological Medicine, 7,* 289–303.

Bandura, A. (1969). *Principles of behavior modification.* New York: Holt, Rinehart & Winston.

Bandura, A. (1973). *Aggression: A social-learning analysis.* Englewood Cliffs, NJ: Prentice-Hall.

Bandura, A. (1977a). Self-efficacy: Toward a unifying theory of behavioral change. *Psychological Review, 84,* 191–215.

Bandura, A. (1977b). *Social learning theory.* Englewood Cliffs, NJ: Prentice-Hall.

Bandura, A. (1982a). Self-efficacy mechanisms in human agency. *American Psychologist, 37,* 122–147.

Bandura, A. (1982b). The self and mechanisms of agency. In J. Suls (Ed.), *Psychological perspectives on self* (Vol. 1). Hillsdale, NJ: Lawrence Erlbaum.

Bandura, A. (1986). *Social foundations of thought and action: A social cognitive theory.* Englewood Cliffs, NJ: Prentice Hall.

Bandura, A. (1989). Human agency in social cognitive theory. *American Psychologist, 44,* 1175–1184.

Bandura, A. (1990). Perceived self-efficacy in the exercise of AIDS infection. *Medienpsychologie, 1,* 23–43.

Bandura, A., Adams, N.E., & Beyer, J. (1977). Cognitive processes mediating behavioral change. *Journal of Personality and Social Psychology, 35,* 125–139.

Bandura, A., Grusec, J.E., & Menlove, F.L. (1967). Vicarious extinction of avoidance behavior. *Journal of Personality and Social Psychology, 5,* 16–23.

Bandura, A., & Menlove, F.L. (1968). Factors determining vicarious extinction of avoidance behavior through symbolic modeling. *Journal of Personality and Social Psychology, 8,* 99–108.

Bandura, A., Reese, L., & Adams, N.E. (1982). Microanalysis of action and fear arousal as a function of differential levels of perceived self-efficacy. *Journal of Personality and Social Psychology, 43,* 5–21.

Bandura, A., Ross, D., & Ross, S.A. (1961). Transmission of aggression through imitation of aggressive models. *Journal of Abnormal and Social Psychology, 63,* 575–582.

Bandura, A., Ross, D., & Ross, S.A. (1963). Imitation of film-mediated aggressive models. *Journal of Abnormal and Social Psychology, 66,* 3–11.

Bandura, A., Taylor, C.B., Williams, L., Mefford, I., & Barchas, J. (1985). Catecholamine secretion as a function of perceived coping self-efficacy. *Journal of Consulting and Clinical Psychology, 53,* 406–411.

Bandura, A., & Walters, R.H. (1959). *Adolescent aggression.* New York: Ronald Press.

Bandura, A., & Walters, R.H. (1963). *Social learning and personality development.* New York: Holt, Rinehart & Winston.

Barbach, L.G. (1975). *For yourself: The fulfillment of female sexuality.* Garden City: NY: Doubleday.

Barbanel, J. (1987, November 5). Forcibly hospitalized woman identified. *The New York Times,* pp. B1, B7.

Barber, T.X. (1969). *Hypnosis: A scientific approach.* New York: Van Nostrand Reinhold.

Barefoot, J.C., Dahlstrom, W.G., & Williams, R.G. (1983). Hostility, CHD incidence and total mortality: A 25-year follow-up study of 255 physicians. *Psychosomatic Medicine, 245,* 59–63.

Barkley, R.A. (1981). *Hyperactive children: A handbook for diagnosis and treatment.* New York: Guilford Press.

Barkley, R.A., & Cunningham, C.E. (1978). Do stimulant drugs improve the academic performance of hyperkinetic children. *Clinical Pediatrics, 17,* 85–92.

Barkley, R.A., & Cunningham, C.E. (1979). The effects of methylphenidate on the mother-child interactions of hyperactive children. *Archives of General Psychiatry, 36,* 201–208.

Barling, J. (1990). *Employment, stress and the family functioning.* New York: Wiley.

Barlow, D.H. (1980). Review of Masters and Johnson's "Homosexuality in perspective." *Contemporary Psychology, 25,* 355–357.

Barlow, D.H. (Ed.). (1985). *Clinical handbook of psychological disorders.* New York: Guilford Press.

Barlow, D.H. (1986). Causes of sexual dysfunction: The role of anxiety and cognitive interference. *Journal of Consulting and Clinical Psychology, 54,* 140–148.

Barlow, D.H. (1988). *Anxiety and its disorders.* New York: Guilford Press.

Barlow, D.H., & Cerny, J.A. (1988). *The psychological treatment of panic.* New York: Guilford Press.

Barlow, D.H., Abel, G.G., & Blanchard, E.B. (1979) Gender identity change in transsexuals. *Archives of General Psychiatry, 36,* 1001–1007.

Barlow, D.H., O'Brien, G.T., Last, C.G., & Holden, A.E. (1983). Couples treatment of agoraphobia: Initial outcome. In K.D. Craig & R.J. McMahon (Eds.), *Advances in clinical behavior therapy.* New York: Brunner/Mazel.

Barlow, D.H., Reynolds, E.J., & Agras, W.S. (1973). Gender identity change in a transsexual. *Archives of General Psychiatry, 28,* 569–576.

Barlow, D.H., Sakheim, D.K., & Beck, J.G. (1983). Anxiety increases sexual arousal. *Journal of Abnormal Psychology, 92,* 49–54.

Barnhart, E.R. (1988). *Physician's desk reference.* Oradell, NJ: Medical Economics.

Barrett, L.I. (1989, October 23). Giving the Public What It Wants. *Time,* p. 34.

Barry, J., Mead, K., Nabel, E., Rocco, M., Campbell, S., Fenton, T., Mudge, G., & Selwyn, A. (1989). Effect of smoking on the activity of ischemic heart disease. *Journal of the American Medical Association, 261,* 398–402.

Barsky, A.J., & Klerman, G.L. (1983). Overview: Hypochondriasis, bodily complaints and somatic styles. *American Journal of Psychiatry, 140,* 273–281.

Barsky, A.J., & Wyshak, G. (1989). Hypochondriasis and related health attitudes. *Psychosomatics, 30,* 1–9.

Barsky, A.J., Wyshak, G., & Klerman, G.L. (1986). Hypochondriasis: An evaluation of the *DSM-III* criteria in medical outpatients. *Archives of General Psychiatry, 43*, 493–500.

Barsky, A.J., Wyshak, G., & Klerman, G.L. (1990). Amplification and attribution as mechanisms of hypochondriasis. Unpublished manuscript, Massachusetts General Hospital.

Barthe, D., & Hammen, C. (1981). A naturalistic extension of the attributional model of depression. *Personality and Social Psychology Bulletin, 7*, 53–58.

Bash, K.W. (1986). Psychosomatic diseases and the Rorschach test. *Journal of Personality Assessment, 50*, 350–357.

Bateson, G., Jackson, D.D., Haley, J., & Weakland, J. (1956). Toward a theory of schizophrenia. *Behavior Science, 1*, 251–264.

Baucom, D.H., Sayers, S.L., & Sher, T.G. (1988, November). *Expanding behavioral marital therapy.* Paper presented at the Twenty-second Annual Conference of the Association for the Advancement of Behavior Therapy, New York.

Baumrind, D. (1985). Research using intentional deception. *American Psychologist, 40*, 165–174.

Baxter, L.R., Phelps, M.E., Mazziotta, J.C., Guze, B.H., Schwartz, J.M., & Selin, C.E. (1987). Local cerebral glucose metabolic rates in obsessive-compulsive disorder. *Archives of General Psychiatry, 44*, 211–281.

Beach, S.R.H., Arias, I., & O'Leary, K.D. (1986). The relationship of marital satisfaction and social support to depressive symptomatology. *Journal of Psychopathology and Behavior Assessment, 8*, 305–316.

Beach, S.R.H., Arias, I., & O'Leary, K.D. (1988). *Which comes first? Depression or marital discord?* Unpublished manuscript, University of Georgia, Athens, Georgia.

Beach, S.R.H., Arias, I., & O'Leary, K.D. (1990). Marriage and depression: Longitudinal relationships. Unpublished manuscript. State University of New York, Stony Brook, NY.

Beach, S.R.H., Jouriles, E.N., & O'Leary, K.D. (1985). Extra-marital sex: Impact on depression and commitment in couples seeking marital therapy. *Journal of Sex and Marital Therapy, 11*, 99–108.

Beach, S.R.H., & O'Leary, K.D. (1985). Current status of outcome research in marital therapy. In L. L'Abate (Ed.), *The handbook of family psychology and therapy* (Vol. II). Homewood, IL: Dorsey Press.

Beach, S.R.H., & O'Leary, K.D. (1986). The treatment of depression occurring in the context of marital discord. *Behavior Therapy, 17*, 43–49.

Beach, S.R.H., Sandeen, E., & O'Leary, K.D. (1990). *Marital therapy in the treatment of depression.* New York: Guilford.

Beardsley, R.S., Gardocki, G.J., Larson, D.B., & Hidalgo, J. (1988). Prescribing of psychotropic medication by primary care physicians and psychiatrists. *Archives of General Psychiatry, 45*, 1117–1119.

Beck, A.T. (1963). Thinking and depression: I. Idiosyncratic content and cognitive distortions. *Archives of General Psychiatry, 10*, 561–571.

Beck, A.T. (1967). *Depression: Causes and treatment.* Philadelphia: University of Pennsylvania Press.

Beck, A.T. (1976). *Cognitive therapy and the emotional disorders.* New York: International Universities Press.

Beck, A.T., Brown, G., Steer, R.A., Eidelson, J.I., & Riskind, J.H. (1987). Differentiating anxiety and depression: A test of the cognitive content-specificity hypothesis. *Journal of Abnormal Psychology, 96*, 179–183.

Beck, A.T., & Emery, G. (1985). *Anxiety disorders and phobias.* New York: Basic Books.

Beck, A.T., Kovacs, M.V., & Weissman, A. (1975). Hopelessness and suicidal behavior. *Journal of the American Medical Association, 234*, 1146–1149.

Beck, A.T., Rush, A.J., Shaw, B.F., & Emery, G. (1979). *Cognitive therapy of depression.* New York: Guilford Press.

Beck, A.T., Ward, C.H., Mendelson, M., Mock, J.E., & Erbaugh, J.K. (1962). Reliability of psychiatric diagnoses: 2. A study of consistency of clinical judgments and ratings. *American Journal of Psychiatry, 119*, 351–357.

Beck, J.G., & Barlow, D.H. (1984). Current conceptualizations of sexual dysfunction: A review and an alternative perspective. *Clinical Psychology Review, 4*, 363–378.

Beck, S.J. (1938). Personality structure in schizophrenia: A Rorschach investigation in eighty-one patients and sixty-four controls. *Nervous and Mental Diseases Monographs.* New York: Nervous and Mental Diseases Publishing.

Becker, J.V. (1988). Adolescent sex offenders. *The Behavior Therapist, 11*, 185–188.

Becker, J.V., Skinner, L.J., & Abel, G.G. (1983). Sequellae of sexual assault: The survivors' perspective. In J.G. Greer & I.R. Stuart (Eds.), *The sexual aggressor: Current perspectives on treatment.* New York: Van Nostrand.

Beckett, A., Summergrad, P., Manschreck, T., Vitagliano, H., Henderson, M., Buttolph, M.L., & Jenike, M. (1987). Symptomatic HIV infection of the CNS in a patient without clinical evidence of immune deficiency. *American Journal of Psychiatry, 144*, 1342–1344.

Beers, C.W. (1905). *A mind that found itself.* New York: Longmans, Green.

Begleiter, H., Porjesz, B., Bihari, B., & Kissin, B. (1984). Event-related potentials in boys at risk for alcoholism. *Science, 225*, 1493–1496.

Beitman, B.D., Goldfried, M.R., & Norcross, J.C. (1989). The movement toward integrating the psychotherapies: An overview. *American Journal of Psychiatry, 146*, 138–147.

Bell, A.P., & Weinberg, M.S. (1978). *Homosexualities: A study of diversity among men and women.* New York: Simon & Schuster.

Bell, A.P., Weinberg, M.S., & Hammersmith, S.K. (1981). *Sexual preference: Its development in men and women.* Bloomington, IN: Indiana University Press.

Bell, L.V. (1980). *Treating the mentally ill: From colonial times to the present.* New York: Praeger.

Bemporad, J.R. (1985). Long term psychoanalytic treatment of depression. In E.E. Beckham & W.R. Leber (Eds.), *Handbook of depression* (pp. 82–99). Homewood, IL: Dorsey.

Bennett, W., & Gurin, J. (1982). *The dieter's dilemma.* New York: Basic Books.

Benson, H. (1975). *The relaxation response.* New York: William Morrow.

Berg, F. (1991). Health risks escalate for black Americans. *Obesity and Health, 5*, 1–4.

Berg, J.M. (1986). Prenatal diagnosis of mental retardation and its implications. *Psychiatric Clinics of North America, 9*, 625–634.

Bergeman, C.S., Plomin, R., Pederson, N.L., McClearn, G.E., & Nesselroade, J.R. (1990). Genetic and environmental influences on social support: The Swedish adoption/twin study of aging. *Journal of Gerontology, 45*, 101–106.

Bergin, A.E. (1966). Some implications of psychotherapy research for therapeutic practice. *Journal of Abnormal Psychology, 71*, 235–246.

Berkowitz, A., & Perkins, H.W. (1988). Personality characteristics of children of alcoholics. *Journal of Consulting and Clinical Psychology, 56*, 206–209.

Berman, A.L., & Jobes, D.A. (1990). *Adolescent suicide: Assessment and intervention.* Washington, DC: American Psychological Association.

Berman, S. (1980). The response of parents to adolescent depression. *Adolescent Psychiatry, 8*, 367–378.

Bernard, J. (1972). *The future of marriage.* New York: World.

Bernstein, J.G. (1988). *Handbook of drug therapy in psychiatry.* Littleton, MA: John Wright-PSG.

Berry, J.C. (1967). *Antecedents of schizophrenia, impulsive character, and alcoholism in males.* Paper presented at the 75th Annual Convention of the American Psychological Association, Washington, DC.

Bibb, J.L., & Chambless, D. (1986). Alcohol use and abuse among diagnosed agoraphobics. *Behaviour Research and Therapy, 24*, 49–58.

Bieber, I., Dain, H.J., Dince, P.R., Drellich, M.G., Grand, H.G., Gundlach, R.H., Kremer, M.W., Rifkin, A.H., Wilbur, C.B., & Bieber, T.B. (1962). *Homosexuality: A psychoanalytic study.* New York: Basic Books.

Bigelow, G., Cohen, M., Liebson, I., & Faillace, L. (1972). Abstinence or moderation? Choice by alcoholics. *Behaviour Research and Therapy, 10*, 209–214.

Bigelow, G., Liebson, I., & Griffiths, R.R. (1974). Alcohol drinking: Suppression by a behavioral time-out procedure. *Be-*

haviour Research and Therapy, 12, 107–115.

Biglan, A., Hops, H., Sherman, L., Friedman, L.S., Arthur, J., & Osteen, V. (1985). Problem-solving interactions of depressed women and their husbands. *Behavior Therapy, 16*, 431–451.

Black, C., Bucky, S., & Wilder-Padilla, F. (1986). Interpersonal and emotional consequences of being an adult child of an alcoholic. *International Journal of the Addictions, 21*, 213–231.

Black, D.W., Warrack, G., & Winokur, G. (1985). The Iowa record-linkage study. *Archives of General Psychiatry, 42*, 78–88.

Blackburn, R. (1988). On moral judgments and personality disorders: The myth of psychopathic personality disorder revisited. *British Journal of Psychiatry, 153*, 305–312.

Blake, S.M., Klepp, K.-I., Pechacek, T.F., Folsom, A.R., Luepker, R.V., Jacobs, D.R., & Mittelmark, M.B. (1989). Differences in smoking cessation strategies between men and women. *Addictive Behaviors, 14*, 409–418.

Blanchard, E.B. (1981). Behavioral assessment of psychophysiologic disorders. In D.H. Barlow (Ed.), *Behavioral assessment of adult disorders*. New York: Guilford Press.

Blanchard, E.B. (1982). Behavioral medicine: Past, present, and future. *Journal of Consulting and Clinical Psychology, 50*, 795–796.

Bland, K., & Hallam, R. (1981). Relationship between response to graded exposure and marital satisfaction in agoraphobics. *Behaviour Research and Therapy, 19*, 335–338.

Blashfield, R.K., & Draguns, J.G. (1976). Toward a taxonomy of psychopathology: The purpose of psychiatric classification. *British Journal of Psychiatry, 129*, 574–583.

Blatt, S.J. (1986). Where have we been and where are we going? Reflections on fifty years of personality assessment. *Journal of Personality Assessment, 50*, 343–346.

Blazer, D., George, L.K., Landerman, R., Pennybacker, M., Melville, M.L., Woodbury, M., Manton, K.G., Jordan, K., & Locke, B.Z. (1985). Psychiatric disorders: A rural/urban comparison. *Archives of General Psychiatry, 42*, 651–656.

Blehar, M.C., Weissman, M.M., Gershon, E.S., & Hirschfeld, R.M.A. (1988). Family and genetic studies of affective disorders. *Archives of General Psychiatry, 45*, 289–292.

Bleuler, E. (1950). *Dementia praecox or the group of schizophrenias* (J. Zinkin, Trans.). New York: International University Press. (Original work published 1911)

Bleuler, M. (1978). *The schizophrenic disorders: Long term patient and family studies*. New Haven: Yale University Press.

Bleuler, M. (1984). Different forms of childhood stress and patterns of adult psychiatric outcome. In N.F. Watt, E.J. Anthony, L.C. Wynne, & J.E. Rolf (Eds.), *Children at risk for schizophrenia: A longitudinal perspective*. New York: Cambridge University Press.

Block, J., Block, J.H., & Keyes, S. (1988). Longitudinally foretelling drug usage in adolescence: Early childhood personality and environmental precursors. *Child Development, 59*, 336–355.

Bloom, J.D., & Rogers, J.L. (1987). The legal basis of forensic psychiatry: Statutorily mandated psychiatric diagnoses. *American Journal of Psychiatry, 144*, 847–853.

Blouin, A.G.A., Bornstein, R., & Trites, R. (1978). Teen-age alcohol use among hyperactive children: A 5-year follow-up study. *Journal of Pediatric Psychology, 3*, 188–194.

Blum, J.D. (1978). On changes in psychiatric diagnosis over time. *American Psychologist, 33*, 1017–1031.

Blumenthal, J.A., Williams, R.B., Kong, Y., Schanberg, S.M., & Thompson, L.W. (1978). Type A behavior pattern and coronary arteriosclerosis. *Circulation, 258*, 63–69.

Boelens, W., Emmelkamp, P., MacGillavry, D., & Markvoort, M.A. (1980). A clinical evaluation of marital treatment: Reciprocity counseling versus system-theoretic counseling. *Behavioral Analysis and Modification, 4*, 85–96.

Boeringa, J.A., & Castellani, S. (1982). Reliability and validity of emotional blunting as a criterion for diagnosis of schizophrenia. *American Journal of Psychiatry, 139*, 1131–1135.

Bohman, M., Cloninger, C.R., von Knorring, A.L., & Sigvardsson, S. (1984). An adoption study of somatoform disorders. III. Cross-fostering analysis and genetic relationship to alcoholism and criminality. *Archives of General Psychiatry, 41*, 872–878.

Bohman, M., Sigvardsson, S., & Cloninger, C.R. (1981). Maternal inheritance of alcohol abuse. *Archives of General Psychiatry, 38*, 965–969.

Bollard, R.J., & Nettelbeck, T. (1981). A comparison of dry-bed training and standard urine-alarm conditioning treatment of childhood bedwetting. *Behaviour Research and Therapy, 19*, 215–226.

Bollard, R.J., & Woodroffe, P. (1977). The effect of parent-administered dry-bed training on nocturnal enuresis in children. *Behaviour Research and Therapy, 15*, 159–165.

Boller, F. (1980). Mental status of patients with Parkinson's disease. *Journal of Clinical Neuropsychology, 2*, 157–172.

Boodoosingh, L., & Brown, P. (1986). The culturally deprived child: Social and educational needs. *Psychiatric Clinics of North America, 9*, 767–776.

Book, J.A. (1960). Genetical aspects of schizophrenic psychoses. In D.D. Jackson (Ed.), *The etiology of schizophrenia*. New York: Basic Books.

Borkovec, T.D. (1978). Self-efficacy: Cause or reflection of behavioral change? *Advances in Behaviour Research and Therapy, 1*, 163–170.

Borkovec, T.D., & Mathews, A. (1988). Treatment of nonphobic anxiety disorders: A comparison of nondirective, cognitive and coping desensitization therapy. *Journal of Consulting and Clinical Psychology, 56*, 877–884.

Borkovec, T.D., Mathews, A.M., Chambers, A., Ebrahimi, S., Lytle, R., & Nelson, R. (1987). The effects of relaxation training with cognitive or nondirective therapy and the role of relaxation-induced anxiety in the treatment of generalized anxiety. *Journal of Consulting and Clinical Psychology, 55*, 883–888.

Bornstein, P.H., & Bornstein, M.T. (1986). *Marital therapy: A behavioral-communications approach*. New York: Pergamon Press.

Borysenko, M. (1987). Area review: Psychoneuroimmunology. *Annals of Behavioral Medicine, 9*, 3–10.

Boskind-Lodahl, M., & Sirlin, J. (1977, November). The gorging-purging syndrome. *Psychology Today*, pp. 50–52, 82, 85.

Bovard, E.W. (1985). Neuroendocrine control and behavior. In R.B. Williams (Ed.), *Perspectives on behavioral medicine* (Vol. 2). New York: Academic Press.

Bower, G.H. (1977). *Cognitive psychology and behavior modification*. Paper presented at the Association for Advancement of Behavior Therapy, Atlanta.

Bower, G.H. (1978). Contacts of cognitive psychology with social learning theory. *Cognitive Therapy and Research, 2*, 123–146.

Bower, G.H. (1981). Mood and memory. *American Psychologist, 36*, 129–148.

Bower, G.H. (1986). Prime time in cognitive psychology. In P. Eelen & O. Fontaine (Eds.), *Behavior therapy: Beyond the conditioning framework*. Hillsdale, NJ: Lawrence Erlbaum.

Bower, G.H. (1987). Commenting on mood and memory. *Behaviour Research and Therapy, 25*, 443–456.

Bowlby, J. (1973). *Attachment and loss* (Vols. I & II). New York: Basic Books.

Braceland, F.J. (1972). Senescence—the inside story. *Psychiatric Annals, 2*, 42–56.

Brackett, C.D., & Powell, L.H. (1988). Psychosocial and physiological predictors of sudden cardiac death after healing of acute myocardial infarction. *American Journal of Cardiology, 61*, 797–983.

Bradford, J. (1989). The organic treatment of violent sexual offenders. In A.J. Stunkard & A. Baum (Eds.), *Perspectives in behavioral medicine*. Hillsdale, NJ: Lawrence Erlbaum.

Bradley, C. (1937). The behavior of children receiving benzedrine. *American Journal of Psychiatry, 94*, 577–585.

Brady, J.P. (1976). Behavior therapy and sex therapy. *American Journal of Psychiatry, 133*, 896–899.

Brady, J.P. (1980). Some views on effective principles of psychotherapy. *Cognitive Therapy and Research, 4*, 271–306.

Brady, J.P., & Lind, D.L. (1961). Experimental analysis of hysterical blindness.

Archives of General Psychiatry, 4, 331–339.
Brakel, S.J. (1986). Involuntary institutionalization. In S.J. Brakel, J. Parry, & B.A. Weiner (Eds.), *The mentally disabled and the law*. Chicago: American Bar Foundation.
Branch, C.H.H., & Eurman, L.J. (1980). Social attitudes toward patients with anorexia nervosa. *American Journal of Psychiatry, 137*, 631–632.
Brand, R. (1978). Coronary-prone behavior as an independent risk factor of coronary heart disease. In T.M. Dembroski, S.M. Weiss, J.L. Shields, S.G. Haynes, & M. Feinleib (Eds.), *Coronary-prone behavior*. New York: Springer-Verlag.
Breggin, P.R. (1979). *Electroshock, its brain-disabling effects*. New York: Springer Publications.
Bregman, E. (1934). An attempt to modify the emotional attitudes of infants by the conditioned response technique. *Journal of Genetic Psychology, 45*, 169–198.
Bremner, J.D. (1984). Fluoxetine in depressed patients: A comparison with imipramine. *Clinical Psychiatry, 45*, 414–419.
Breuer, J., & Freud, S. (1895). Studies on hysteria. In J. Strachey (Ed.), *The standard edition of the complete psychological works of Sigmund Freud* (Vol. 2). London: Hogarth Press.
Breuer, J., & Freud, S. (1957). *Studies on hysteria*. New York: Basic Books. (Original work published 1895)
Brickman, P., Rabinowitz, V.C., Karuza, J., Coates, D., Cohen, E., & Kidder, L. (1982). Models of helping and coping. *American Psychologist, 37*, 368–384.
Briddell, D.W., Rimm, D., Caddy, G., Krawitz, G., Sholis, D., & Wunderlin, R. (1978). The effects of alcohol and expectancy set on male sexual arousal. *Journal of Abnormal Psychology, 87*, 418–430.
Brinkman, S.D., & Largen, J.W. (1984). Changes in brain ventricular size with repeated CAT scans in suspected Alzheimer's disease. *American Journal of Psychiatry, 141*, 81–83.
Bronfenbrenner, U. (1970). *Two worlds of childhood*. New York: Simon & Schuster.
Brown, G., & Harris, T. (1978). *Social origins of depression. A study of psychiatric disorder in women*. New York: Free Press.
Brown, G., & Harris, T. (1986). Establishing causal links: The Bedford College studies of depression. In H. Katscnig (Ed.), *Life events and psychiatric disorders:* Controversial issues. (pp. 108–185) Cambridge, U.K.: Cambridge University Press.
Brown, G.W. (1959). Experiences of discharged chronic schizophrenic mental hospital patients in various types of living groups. *Millbank Memorial Fund Quarterly, 37*, 105–131.
Brown, G.W., Birley, J.L.T., & Wing, J.K. (1972). Influence of family life on the course of schizophrenic disorders: A replication. *British Journal of Psychiatry, 121*, 241–258.
Brown, G.W., Carstairs, G.M., & Topping, G.C. (1958). The post hospital adjustment of chronic mental patients. *The Lancet, II*, 685–689.
Brown, G.W., Monck, E.M., Carstairs, G.M., & Wing, J.K. (1962). The influence of family life on the course of schizophrenic illness. *British Journal Of Preventative Social Medicine, 16*, 55–68.
Brown, L.S. (1990). Taking account of gender in the clinical assessment interview. *Journal of Consulting and Clinical Psychology, 21*, 12–17.
Brown, R. (1965). *Social psychology*. New York: Free Press.
Brown, R., & Lewinsohn, P.M. (1984). A psychoeducational approach to the treatment of depression: Comparison of group, individual, and minimal contact procedures. *Journal of Consulting and Clinical Psychology, 52*, 774–783.
Brown, S.A., Creamer, V.A., & Stetson, B.A. (1987). Adolescent alcohol expectancies in relation to personal and parental drinking patterns. *Journal of Abnormal Psychology, 96*, 117–121.
Brownell, K.D. (1988, March). Yo-yo trap. *American Health*, pp. 78–84.
Brownell, K.D., & Foreyt, J. (Eds.). (1986). *Physiology, psychology, and treatment of the eating disorders*. New York: Basic Books.
Brownell, K.D., Hayes, S.C., & Barlow, D.H. (1977). Patterns of appropriate and deviant sexual arousal: The behavioral treatment of multiple sexual deviations. *Journal of Consulting and Clinical Psychology, 45*, 1144–1155.
Brownmiller, S. (1975). *Against our will: Men, women, and rape*. New York: Simon & Schuster.
Bruch, H. (1973). *Eating disorders: Obesity, anorexia nervosa, and the person within*. New York: Basic Books.
Bruch, H. (1978). *The golden cage*. Cambridge, MA: Harvard University Press.
Brunk, M., Henggler, S.W., & Whelan, J.P. (1987). Comparison of multisystemic therapy and parent training in the brief treatment of child abuse and neglect. *Journal of Consulting and Clinical Psychology, 55*, 171–178.
Bryant, R.A., & McConkey, K.M. (1989). Hypnotic blindness: A behavioral and experiential analysis. *Journal of Abnormal Psychology, 98*, 71–77.
Buck, J.N. (1948). The H-T-P test. *Journal of Clinical Psychology, 4*, 151–159.
Buglass, D., Clarke, J., Henderson, A.S., Kreitman, N., & Presley, A.S. (1977). A study of agoraphobic housewives. *Psychological Medicine, 7*, 73–86.
Bulfinch, T. (1979). *Myths of Greece and Rome*. New York: Penguin Books.
Bumberry, W., Oliver, J.M., & McClure, J.N. (1978). Validation of the Beck Depression Inventory in a university population using psychiatric estimate as the criterion. *Journal of Consulting and Clinical Psychology, 46*, 150–155.
Burisch, M. (1984). Approaches to personality inventory construction. *American Psychologist, 39*, 214–227.
Burling, T.A., Lovett, S.B., Frederiksen, L.W., Jerome, A., & Jonske-Gubosh, L.-A. (1989). Can across-treatment changes in cumulative puff duration predict treatment outcome during nicotine fading? *Addictive Behaviors, 14*, 75–82.
Burnam, M.A., Hough, R.L., Escobar, J.I., Karno, M., Timbers, D.M., Telles, C.A., & Locke, B.Z. (1987). Six-month prevalence of specific psychiatric disorders among Mexican Americans and non-Hispanic whites in Los Angeles. *Archives of General Psychiatry, 44*, 687–694.
Burnam, M.A., Stein, J.A., Golding, J.M., Siegel, J.M., Sorenson, S.B., Forsythe, A.B., & Telles, C.A. (1988). Sexual assault and mental disorders in a community population. *Journal of Consulting and Clinical Psychology, 56*, 843–850.
Burns, D.D. (1980). *Feeling good*. New York: William Morris.
Bursten, B. (1986). Posthospital mandatory outpatient treatment. *American Journal of Psychiatry, 143*, 1255–1258.
Burton, R. (1621). *The anatomy of melancholy*. Printed by J. Litchfield & J. Short for Henry Cripps. Oxford.
Buss, A.H., & Finn, S.E. (1987). Classification of personality traits. *Journal of Personality and Social Psychology, 52*, 432–444.
Butcher, J.N., Dahlstrom, W.E., Graham, J.R., Tellegen, A., & Kaemmer, B. (1989). *Manual for the restandardized Minnesota Multiphasic Personality Inventory: MMPI-2*. Minneapolis: University of Minnesota Press.
Butcher, J.N., & Hostettler, K. (1990). Abbreviating MMPI item administration: What can be learned from the MMPI for the MMPI-2? *Psychological Assessment, 2*, 12–21.
Butler, G., Cullington, A., Hibbert, G., Klimes, I., & Gelder, M. (1987). Anxiety management for persistent generalized anxiety. *British Journal of Psychiatry, 151*, 535–542.
Butler, G., Cullington, A., Munby, M., Amies, P., & Gelder, M. (1984). Exposure and anxiety management in the treatment of social phobia. *Journal of Consulting and Clinical Psychology, 52*, 642–669.
Butters, N., & Cermak, L.S. (1980). *Alcoholic Korsakoff's syndrome: An information-processing approach to amnesia*. New York: Academic Press.
Butters, N., & Stuss, D.T. (1989). Diencephalic amnesia. In F. Boller & J. Grafman (Eds.), *Handbook of neuropsychology* (Vol. 3). Amsterdam: Elsevier Science Publishers.
Cadoret, R.J., O'Gorman, T.W., Troughton, E., & Heywood, E. (1985). Alcoholism and antisocial personality. *Archives of General Psychiatry, 42*, 161–167.
Cadoret, R.J., Troughton, E., O'Gorman, T.W., & Heywood, E. (1986). An adoption study of genetic and environmental factors in drug abuse. *Archives of General Psychiatry, 43*, 1131–1136.
Cameron, N. (1963). *Personality development and psychopathology: A dy-*

namic approach. Boston: Houghton Mifflin Company.

Campbell, S.B., Douglas, V.I., & Morgenstern, G. (1971). Cognitive styles in hyperactive children and the effect of methylphenidate. *Journal of Child Psychology and Psychiatry*, *12*, 55–67.

Campbell, S.B., Endman, M.W., & Bernfeld, G. (1977). A three-year follow-up of hyperactive preschoolers into elementary school. *Journal of Child Psychology and Psychiatry*, *18*, 239–249.

Camper, D., Kasendorf, M., Clausen, P., Monroe, S., Shapiro, D., & Taylor, J. (1982, May 24). The insanity plea on trial. *Newsweek*, pp. 56–61.

Canino, G.J., Bird, H.R., Shrout, P.E., Rubio-Stipec, M., Bravo, M., Martinez, R., Sesman, M., & Guevara, L.M. (1987). The prevalence of specific psychiatric disorders in Puerto Rico. *Archives of General Psychiatry*, *44*, 727–735.

Cantwell, D.P. (1972). Psychiatric illness in the families of hyperactive children. *Archives of General Psychiatry*, *27*, 414–417.

Cantwell, D.P. (1983). Depression in childhood: Clinical picture and diagnostic criteria. In D.P. Cantwell & G.A. Carlson (Eds.), *Affective disorders in childhood and adolescence*. New York: Spectrum Publications.

Cantwell, D.P. (1983). Issues in the management of childhood depression. In D.P. Cantwell & G.A. Carlson (Eds.), *Affective disorders in childhood and adolescence: An update*. New York: SP Medical & Scientific Books.

Carlson, G.A., & Cantwell, D.P. (1980). A survey of depressive symptoms, syndrome, and disorder in a child and adolescent psychiatric population. *Journal of Child Psychology and Psychiatry*, *21*, 19–25.

Carpenter, W.T., Stephens, J.H., Rey, A.C., Hanlon, T.E., & Heinrichs, D.W. (1982). Early intervention vs. continuous pharmacotherapy of schizophrenia. *Psychopharmacology Bulletin*, *18*, 21–23.

Carr, M.A., Sweet, J.J., & Rossini, E. (1986). Diagnostic validity of the Luria-Nebraska neuropsychological battery—children's revision. *Journal of Consulting and Clinical Psychology*, *54*, 354–358.

Carroll, B.J. (1979). Neuroendocrine function in mania. In B. Shopsin (Ed.), *Manic illness*. New York: Raven Press.

Carroll, B.J., Feinberg, M., Greden, J.F., Tarika, J., Albala, A.A., Haskett, R.F., James, N.M., Kronfol, Z., Lohr, N., Steiner, M., de Vigne, J.P., & Young, E. (1981). A specific laboratory test for the diagnosis of melancholia. *Archives of General Psychiatry*, *38*, 15–22.

Cassano, G.B., & Conti, L. (1981). Some considerations on the role of benzodiazepines in the treatment of depression. *British Journal of Clinical Pharmacology*, *11*, 23S-29S.

Cassileth, B.R., Lusk, E.J., Miller, D.S., Brown, L.L., & Miller, C. (1985). Psychosocial correlates of survival in advanced malignant disease? *The New England Journal of Medicine*, *312*, 1551–1555.

Cattell, R.B., & Stice, G.F. (1957). *Handbook for the 16 Personality Factor Questionnaire*. Champaign, IL: Institute for Personality and Ability Testing.

Caudill, B., & Lipscomb, T.R. (1980). Modeling influences on social drinking in a laboratory setting. *Journal of Applied Behavior Analysis*, *13*, 355–365.

Centers for Disease Control. (1987). *Morbidity and Mortality Weekly Report, 36.*

Centers for Disease Control. (1989). Prevalence of overweight-behavioral risk factor surveillance system, 1987. *Morbidity and Mortality Weekly Report*, *38*, 421–423.

Centers for Disease Control Vietnam Experience Study. (1987). Postservice mortality among Vietnam veterans. *Journal of the American Medical Association*, *257*, 790–795.

Cermak, T.L. (1988). *A time to heal*. New York: Avon Books.

Cerreto, M.C., & Tuma, J.M. (1977). Distribution of DSM-III diagnoses in a child psychiatric setting. *Journal of Abnormal Child Psychology*, *5*, 147–155.

Chambless, D.L., & Mason, J. (1986). Sex, sex role stereotyping, and agoraphobia. *Behaviour Research and Therapy*, *24*, 231–235.

Chapman, L.J., & Chapman, J.P. (1969). Illusory correlation as an obstacle to the use of valid psychodiagnostic signs. *Journal of Consulting and Clinical Psychology*, *74*, 271–280.

Chapman, L.J., & Chapman, J.P. (1980). Scales for rating psychotic and psychotic-like experiences as continua. *Schizophrenia Bulletin*, *6*, 476–489.

Charney, D.S., Goodman, W.K., Price, L.H., Woods, S.W., Rasmussen, S.A., & Heninger, G.R. (1988). Serotonin function in obsessive-compulsive disorder. *Archives of General Psychiatry*, *45*, 177–185.

Chartier, G.M., & Ranieri, D.J. (1984). Adolescent depression: Concepts, treatments, prevention. In P. Karoly & J.J. Steffen (Eds.), *Adolescent behavior disorders: Foundations and contemporary concerns*. Lexington, MA: Lexington Books.

Chesney-Lind, M. (1987). Girls and violence: An exploration of the gender gap in serious delinquent behavior. In D.H. Crowell, I.M. Evand, & C.R. O'Donnell (Eds.), *Childhood aggression and violence*. New York: Plenum.

Chess, S., & Thomas, A. (1977). Temperament individuality from childhood to adolescence. *Journal of Child Psychiatry*, *16*, 218–226.

Chodoff, P. (1974). The diagnosis of hysteria: An overview. *American Journal of Psychiatry*, *131*, 1073–1078.

Chodoff, P. (1986). *DSM-III* and psychotherapy. *American Journal of Psychiatry*, *143*, 201–203.

Chodoff, P., & Lyons, H. (1958). Hysteria, the hysterical personality and "hysterical" conversion. *American Journal of Psychiatry*, *114*, 734–740.

Christiansen, B.A., Goldman, M.S., & Brown, S.A. (1985). The differential development of adolescent alcohol expectancies may predict adult alcoholism. *Addictive Behaviors*, *10*, 299–306.

City of Cleburne v. *Cleburne Living Center Inc.*, 473 U.S. 432. (1985).

Clark, D.M. (1988). A cognitive model of panic attacks. In S. Rachman & J. Maser (Eds.), *Panic: Cognitive views*. Hillsdale, NJ: Lawrence Erlbaum, 71–90.

Clark, D.M. (1989). Anxiety states. In K. Hawton, P.M. Salkovskis, & D.M. Clark (Eds.), *Cognitive behaviour therapy for psychiatric problems*. Oxford: Oxford University Press.

Clark, D.M., Salkovskis, P.M., & Chalkley, A.J. (1985). Respiratory control as a treatment for panic attacks. *Journal of Behavior Therapy and Experimental Psychiatry*, *16*, 23–30.

Clark, L.P. (1933). *Lincoln: A psychobiography*. New York: Scribner.

Clarkin, J.F., Friedman, R.C., Hurt, S.W., Corn, R., & Aronoff, M. (1984). Affective and character pathology of suicidal adolescents and young adult in-patients. *Journal of Clinical Psychology*, *45*, 19–22.

Clausen, J.A., & Kohn, M.L. (1959). Relation of schizophrenia to the social structure of a small city. In B. Pasamanick (Ed.), *Epidemiology of mental disorder*. Washington, DC: American Association for the Advancement of Science.

Cleaver, E. (1968). *Soul on ice*. New York: McGraw-Hill.

Clements, S.D. (1966). *Minimal brain dysfunction in children—terminology and identification* (USPHS Publication No. 1415). Washington, DC: U.S. Government Printing Office.

Cloninger, C.R. (1986). A unified biosocial theory of personality and its role in the development of anxiety states. *Psychiatric Developments*, *5*, 167–226.

Cloninger, C.R. (1987). A systematic method for clinical description and classification of personality variants: A proposal. *Archives of General Psychiatry*, *44*, 573–587.

Cloninger, C.R. (1987). Neurogenetic adaptive mechanisms in alcoholism. *Science*, *236*, 410–416.

Cloninger, C.R., Bohman, M., & Sigvardsson, S. (1981). Inheritance of alcohol abuse: Cross-fostering analysis of adopted men. *Archives of General Psychiatry*, *38*, 861–868.

Cloninger, C.R., & Gottesman, I.I. (1987). Genetic and environmental factors in antisocial behavior. In S.A. Mednick, T.E. Moffit, & S.A. Stack (Eds.), *The causes of crime: New biological approaches*. New York: Cambridge University Press.

Coates, T.J., McKusick, L., Kuno, R., & Stites, D.P. (1989). Stress reduction training changed number of sexual partners but not immune function in men with HIV. *American Journal of Public Health*, *79*, 885–887.

Cobb, J.P., McDonald, R., Marks, I.M., & Stern, R.S. (1980). Marital versus exposure therapy: Psychological treatments of co-existing marital and phobic-obsessive problems. *European Journal

of Behavioural Analysis and Modification, 4, 3–17.
Coe, C. (1988). Behavioral immunology. In G. Lindzey, R.F. Thompson, & B. Spring (Eds.), *Psychology* (3rd ed.). New York: Worth.
Cohen, A., Rosen, R.C., & Goldstein, L. (1985). EEG hemispheric asymmetry during sexual arousal: Psychophysiological patterns in responsive, unresponsive, and dysfunctional men. *Journal of Abnormal Psychology, 94*, 580–590.
Cohen, F., Horowitz, M., Lazarus, R., Moos, R., Robins, L., Rose, R., & Rutter, M. (1982). Panel report of psychosocial assets and modifiers of stress. In G.R. Elliot & C. Eisdorfer (Eds.), *Stress and human health: Analysis and implications of research*. New York: Springer-Verlag.
Cohen, S., & Syme, S.L. (1985). *Social support and health*. New York: Academic Press.
Cohn, J.B. (1981). Multicenter double-blind efficacy and safety study comparing alprazolam, diazepam and placebo in clinically anxious patients. *Journal of Clinical Psychiatry, 42*, 347–351.
Cohn, P.F. (1989). Another smoking gun linking cigarettes and heart disease. *Journal of the American Medical Association, 261*, 438.
Colby, K.M. (1951). *A primer for psychotherapists*. New York: Ronald Press.
Cole, J.L., & Davis, J.M. (1967). Antidepressant drugs. In A.M. Freedman & H.I. Kaplan (Eds.), *Comprehensive textbook of psychiatry*. Baltimore, MD: Williams & Wilkins.
Coleman, R.W., & Miller, A.G. (1975). The relationship between depression and marital adjustment in clinical population: A multi-trait multimethod study. *Journal of Consulting and Clinical Psychology, 43*, 647–651.
Colliver, J.D., & Malin, H. (1986). State and national trends in alcohol related mortality: 1975–1982. *Alcohol Health and Research World, 10*, 60–64, 75.
Committee on Professional Standards, Board of Professional Affairs, American Psychological Association. (1986). Casebook for providers of psychological services. *American Psychologist, 41*, 688–693.
Committee on Professional Standards, Board of Professional Affairs, American Psychological Association. (1988). Casebook for providers of psychological services. *American Psychologist, 43*, 557–563.
Conger, J.J. (1951). The effects of alcohol on conflict behavior in the albino rat. *Quarterly Journal of Studies on Alcohol, 12*, 1–29.
Conger, J.J. (1956). Alcoholism: Theory, problem, and challenge. II Reinforcement theory and the dynamics of alcoholism. *Quarterly Journal of Studies on Alcohol, 17*, 291–324.
Conners, C.K. (1969). A teacher rating scale for use in drug studies with children. *American Journal of Psychiatry, 6*, 884–888.
Conners, C.K. (1980). *Food additives and hyperactive children*. New York: Plenum.
Conners, C.K., & Wells, K.C. (1986). *Hyperkinetic children: A neuropsychosocial approach*. Beverly Hills, CA: Sage.
Contrada, R., & Krantz, D. (1988). Stress, reactivity, and Type A behavior: Current status and future directions. *Annals of Behavioral Medicine, 10*, 64–70.
Cook, E., Hodes, R., & Lang, P.J. (1986). Preparedness and phobia: Effects of stimulus content on human visceral functioning. *Journal of Abnormal Psychology, 95*, 195–203.
Cook, M.L., & Peterson, C. (1986). Depressive irrationality. *Cognitive Therapy and Research, 10*, 293–298.
Cook, M., Mineka, S., Wolkenstein, B., & Laitsch, K. (1985). Observational conditioning of snake fear in unrelated rhesus monkeys. *Journal of Abnormal Psychology, 94*, 591–610.
Cookerly, J.R. (1980). Does marital therapy do any lasting good? *Journal of Marital and Family Therapy, 6*, 393–397.
Cooklin, R., Sturgeon, D., & Leff, J. (1983). The relationship between auditory hallucinations and spontaneous fluctuations of skin conductance in schizophrenia. *British Journal of Psychiatry, 142*, 47–52.
Coons, P.M. (1986). Treatment progress in 20 patients with multiple personality disorder. *Journal of Nervous and Mental Disease, 174*, 715–721.
Coons, P.M. (1988). Misuse of forensic hypnosis. *The International Journal of Clinical and Experimental Hypnosis, XXXVI*, 1–11.
Coons, P.M., & Milstein, V. (1986). Psychosexual disturbances in multiple personality: Characteristics, etiology and treatment. *Journal of Clinical Psychology, 47*, 106–110.
Cooper, A.J. (1978). Etiology of homosexuality. In J.A. Lorraine (Ed.), *Understanding homosexuality*. New York: Elsevier.
Cooper, G.L. (Ed.). (1989). *Stress and breast cancer*. Chichester, England: John Wiley.
Cooper, P.J., & Bowskill, R. (1986). Dysphoric mood and overeating. *British Journal of Clinical Psychology, 25*, 155–156.
Cooper, P.J., & Fairburn, C.G. (1983). Binge-eating and self-induced vomiting in the community. *British Journal of Psychiatry, 142*, 139–144.
Corsini, R. (1981). *Handbook of innovative psychotherapies*. New York: John Wiley.
Corsini, R. (1989). Introduction. In R. Corsini & D. Wedding (Eds.), *Current psychotherapies*. Itasca, IL: Peacock Publishers.
Coryell, W., & Zimmerman, M. (1988). The heritability of schizophrenia and schizoaffective disorder. *Archives of General Psychiatry, 45*, 323–327.
Costa, P.T., Busch, C.M., Zonderman, A.B., & McCrae, R.R. (1986). Correlations of MMPI factor scales with measures of the five factor model of personality. *Journal of Personality Assessment, 50*, 640–650.
Cowdry, R.W., & Gardner, D.L. (1989). Pharmacotherapy of the borderline personality disorder. *Archives of General Psychiatry, 45*, 111–119.
Cowley, G. (1990, February 12). Hanging up the knife. *Newsweek*, pp. 58–59.
Cox, D.J., Goner-Frederick, L.A., Clarke, W.L., & Carter, W.R. (1988). Effects of acute experimental stressors on insulin-dependent diabetes mellitus. Paper presented at the meetings of the American Diabetes Association, New Orleans.
Coyne, J.C. (1976a). Depression and the response of others. *Journal of Abnormal Psychology, 55*, 186–193.
Coyne, J.C. (1976b). Toward an interactional description of depression. *Psychiatry, 39*, 28–40.
Coyne, J.C. (1986). Strategic marital therapy for depression. In N.S. Jacobson & A.S. Gurman (Eds.), *Clinical handbook of marital therapy*. New York: Guilford Press.
Crahan, M.E. (1969). God's flesh and other pre-Columbian phantastica. *Bulletin of the Los Angeles County Medical Association, 99*, 17.
Craighead, L.W., & Agras, W.S. (1991). Mechanisms of action for cognitive-behavioral and pharmacological interventions for obesity and bulimia nervosa. *Journal of Consulting and Clinical Psychology 59*, 115–125.
Craighead, W.E. (1984). Affective disorders-unipolar. In S.M. Turner & M. Hersen (Eds.), *Adult psychopathology: A behavioral perspective*. New York: John Wiley.
Craighead, W.E., & Curry, J.F. (1990). Depression in children and adolescents. In L.W. Craighead, W.E. Craighead, A.E. Kazdin, & M.J. Mahoney (Eds.), *Cognitive behavioral interventions*. New York: Pergamon Press.
Crapper, D.R., & Dalton, A.J. (1973). Alteration in short term retention, conditioned avoidance, acquisition, and motivation following aluminum induced neurofibrillary degeneration. *Physiological Behavior, 10*, 925–933.
Crapper, D.R., & De Boni, U. (1979). Etiological factors in dementia. In *Abstracts*, Satellite meeting on aging of the brain and dementia, International Society for Neurochemistry. Albano Terme, Italy, FIDIA Research Laboratories.
Crapper, D.R., Kirshnan, S.S., & Dalton, A.J. (1973). Brain aluminum distribution in Alzheimer's disease and experimental neurofibrillary degeneration. *Science, 180*, 511–513.
Crenshaw, T.L., Goldberg, J.P., & Stern, W.C. (1987). Pharmacologic modification of sexual dysfunction. *Journal of Sex and Marital Therapy, 13*, 239–252.
Crewdson, J. (1988). *By silence betrayed*. Boston: Little, Brown.
Crisp, A.H., Hsu, L.K.G., Harding, B., & Hartshorn, J. (1980). Clinical features

of anorexia nervosa: A study of a consecutive series of 102 female patients. *Journal of Psychosomatic Research, 24*, 179–191.

Cronbach, L.J. (1957). The two disciplines of scientific psychology. *American Psychologist, 12*, 671–684.

Cronbach, L.J. (1984). *Essentials of psychological testing* (4th ed.). New York: Harper & Row.

Crow, T.J. (1985). The two-syndrome concept: Origins and current status. *Schizophrenia Bulletin, 11*, 471–485.

Crow, T.J., & Johnstone, E.C. (1985). Schizophrenia: The nature of the disease process and its biological correlates. In V.B. Montcastle & F. Plum (Eds.), *Handbook of Physiology.* American Physiological Society: *The Nervous System, Vol. 5.* American Psychological Society: Bethesda, MD.

Crowell, C.R., Hinson, R.E., & Siegel, S. (1981). The role of conditional drug responses in tolerance to the hypothermic effects of alcohol. *Psychopharmacology, 73*, 51–54.

Crowther, J.H., Post, G., & Zaynor, L. (1985). The prevalence of bulimia and binge-eating in adolescent girls. *International Journal of Eating Disorders, 4*, 29–42.

Curran, J.W. (1985). The epidemiology and prevention of the Acquired Immunodeficiency Syndrome. *Annals of Internal Medicine, 103*, 657–662.

Curran, W., McGarry, A., & Shah, S. (1986). *Forensic psychiatry and psychology.* Philadelphia: Davis.

Curry, J.F., & Craighead, W.E. (1990). Attributional style in clinically depressed and conduct disordered adolescents. *Journal of Abnormal Psychology, 58*, 109–115.

Cutting, J. (1985). *The psychology of schizophrenia.* New York: Churchill Livingstone.

Cypress, B.K. (1980). *Characteristics of visits to female and male physicians: The national ambulatory medical care survey, 1977.* Hyattsville, MD: National Center for Health Statistics.

Cytryn, L., McKnew, D.H., Zahn-Waxler, C., Radke-Yarrow, M., Gaensbauer, T.J., Harmon, R.J., & Lamour, M. (1984). Affective disturbances in the offspring of affectively ill patients—a developmental view. *American Journal of Psychiatry, 140*, 219–222.

Dahlstrom, W.G., Welsh, G.S., & Dahlstrom, L.E. (1972). *An MMPI handbook. Vol. 1, Clinical interpretation* (rev. ed.). Minneapolis: University of Minnesota Press.

Dahlstrom, W.G., Welsh, G.S., & Dahlstrom, L.E. (1975). *An MMPI handbook. Vol. 2, Research applications* (rev. ed.). Minneapolis: University of Minnesota Press.

Dalbo, A., Cedla, A., Brighenti, F., Semenza, C., & Bertolini, C. (1984). Recognition memory in conversion hysteria: Effect of sexual stimuli during learning. *Acta Psychiatrica Scandinavica, 70*, 535–539.

Dangel, R.F., & Polster, R.A. (Eds.). (1984). *Parent training.* New York: Guilford Press.

Darwin, C.A. (1887). A biographical sketch of an infant. *Mind, 2*, 285–294.

Davanloo, H. (Ed.). (1978). *Basic principles and techniques in short-term dynamic psychotherapy.* New York: Spectrum Publications.

Davidson, L.M., & Baum, A. (1986). Chronic stress and posttraumatic stress disorders. *Journal of Consulting and Clinical Psychology, 54*, 303–308.

Davidson, W.S., Gensheimer, L.K., Gottschalk, R., & Mayer, J. (1987). Current status of rehabilitation programs for juvenile offenders. In C. Hampton (Ed.), *Antisocial behavior and substance abuse.* Washington, DC: U.S. Government Printing Office.

Davidson, W.S., II, Gottschalk, R., Gensheimer, L., & Mayer, J. (1987). Interventions with juvenile delinquents: A meta-analysis of treatment efficacy. In C. Hampton (Ed.), *Juvenile offenders.* Washington, DC: U.S. Government Printing Office.

Davidson, W.S., II, Redner, R., Blakely, C.H., Mitchell, C.M., & Emshoff, J.G. (1987). Diversion of juvenile offenders: An experimental comparison. *Journal of Consulting and Clinical Psychology, 55*, 68–75.

Davies, P., & Wolozin, B.L. (1987). Recent advances in the neurochemistry of Alzheimer's disease. *Journal of Clinical Psychiatry, 48*, 23–30.

Davis, B., Krug, D., Dean, R.S., & Hong, B.A. (1990). MMPI differences for renal, psychiatric, and general medical patients. *Journal of Clinical Psychology, 46*, 178–184.

Davis, G.E., & Leitenberg, H. (1987). Adolescent sex offenders. *Psychological Bulletin, 101*, 417–427.

Davis, H. (1975). Crossroads on the pathways to discovery. In F.G. Worden, J.P. Swazey, & G. Adelman (Eds.), *The neurosciences: Paths of discovery.* Cambridge, MA: MIT Press.

Davis, J.M. (1985). Antidepressant drugs. In H.I. Kaplan & B.J. Sadock (Eds.), *Comprehensive textbook of psychiatry* (Vol. 1, pp. 1513–1547, 4th. ed.). Baltimore, MD: Williams & Wilkins.

Davis, J.M., Klerman, G., & Schildkraut, J. (1967). Drugs used in the treatment of depression. In L. Efron, J.O. Cole, D. Levine, & J.R. Wittenborn (Eds.), *Psychopharmacology, A review of progress.* Washington, DC: U.S. Clearinghouse of Mental Health Information.

Davison, G.C. (1976). Homosexuality: The ethical challenge. *Journal of Consulting and Clinical Psychology, 44*, 157–162.

The day of reckoning delayed. (1989, September 11). *Time*, p. 76.

De Leon, M.J., Ferris, S.H., & George, A.E. (1980). Computed tomography evaluation of brain-behavior relationships in senile dementia of the Alzheimer's type. *Neurobiology of Aging, 1*, 69–79.

De Ropp, R.S. (1957). *Drugs and the mind.* New York: Grove Press.

de Silva, P., Rachman, S., & Seligman, M.E.P. (1977). Prepared phobias and obsessions: Therapeutic outcome. *Behaviour Research and Therapy, 15*, 65–77.

deBruijn, G. (1982). From masturbation to orgasm with a partner: How some women bridge the gap—and why others don't. *Journal of Sex and Marital Therapy, 8*, 151–167.

Delay, J., & Deniker, P. (1952). Le traitement des psychoses par une methods neurolytique derivee de l'hibernotherapie. In P.C. Ossa (Ed.), *Congres de medecins alienistes et neurologistes de France.* Paris: Maisson.

Dembroski, T.M., & Costa, P.T. (1987). Coronary prone behavior: components of the Type A pattern and hostility. *Journal of Personality, 55*, 211–235.

DeMonbreun, B.G., & Craighead, W.E. (1977). Distortion of perception and recall of positive and neutral feedback in depression. *Cognitive Therapy and Research, 1*, 311–330.

DeMyer, M.K., Barton, S., DeMyer, W.E., Norton, J.A., Allen, J., & Steele, R. (1973). Prognosis in autism: A follow-up study. *Journal of Autism and Childhood Schizophrenia, 3*, 199–246.

Denmark, F., Russo, N.F., Frieze, I.H., & Sechzer, J.A. (1988). Guidelines for avoiding sexism in psychological research. *American Psychologist, 43*, 582–585.

Depue, R.A. (Ed.). (1979). *The psychology of the depressive disorder: Implications for the effects of stress.* New York: Academic Press.

DeRubeis, R.J., Hollon, S.D., Evans, M.D., & Bemis, K.M. (1982). Can psychotherapies for depression be discriminated? A systematic investigation of cognitive therapy and interpersonal therapy. *Journal of Consulting and Clinical Psychology, 50*, 744–756.

Des Jarlais, D.C. (1988). *Effectiveness of AIDS educational programs for intravenous drug users.* Unpublished manuscript, State of New York Division of Substance Abuse Services, New York.

Dew, M.A., Bromet, E.J., Brent, D., & Greenhouse, J.B. (1987). A quantitative literature review of the effectiveness of suicide prevention centers. *Journal of Consulting and Clinical Psychology, 55*, 239–244.

Deykin, E.Y., Hsieh, C.C., Joshi, N., & McNamara, J.J. (1986). Adolescent suicidal and self-destructive behavior. *American Journal of Psychiatry, 142*, 1299–1303.

Diekstra, R.F.W. (1985). Suicide and suicide attempts in the European Economic Community: An analysis of trends with special emphasis upon trends among the young. *Suicide and Life-threatening Behavior, 15*, 27–42.

Diekstra, R.F.W., & Hawton, K. (1987). *Suicide in adolescence.* Dordrecht, Netherlands: Martinus Nijhoff Publishers.

Digman, J.M., & Inouye, J. (1986). Further specification of the five robust factors of personality. *Journal of Personality and Social Psychology, 50*, 116–123.

Dimsdale, J.E. (1988). A perspective on Type A behavior and coronary disease.

The New England Journal of Medicine, 318, 110–112.

Dimsdale, J.E., & Herd, J.A. (1982). Variability of plasma lipids in response to emotional arousal. *Psychosomatic Medicine, 244*, 413–430.

Dix, G.E. (1982). Major current issues concerning civil commitment criteria. *Law and Contemporary Problems, 45*, 137–159.

Dodrill, C.B. (1981). Neuropsychology of epilepsy. In S.B. Felskov & T.J. Boll (Eds.), *Handbook of clinical neuropsychology*. New York: John Wiley.

Dohrenwend, B.S., & Dohrenwend, B. (1974). *Stressful life events: Their nature and effects*. New York: Wiley.

Doleys, D.M. (1989). Enuresis and encopresis. In T.H. Ollendich & M. Hersen (Eds.), *Handbook of childhood psychopathology* (pp. 291–314, 2nd ed.). New York: Plenum.

Doleys, D.M., Ciminero, A.R., Tollison, C.L., & Wells, K.C. (1977). Dry bed training and retention control training: A comparison. *Behavior Therapy, 8*, 541–548.

Dorpat, T.L., Jackson, J.K., & Ripley, H.S. (1965). Broken homes and attempted suicide. *Archives of General Psychiatry, 12*, 213–216.

Douglas, V.I. (1983). Attentional and cognitive problems. In M. Rutter (Ed.), *Developmental neuropsychiatry*. New York: Guilford Press.

Dressler, W.W. (1985). The social and cultural context of coping: Action, gender and symptoms in a southern black community. *Social Science Medicine, 21*, 499–506.

Drewnowski, A., Yee, D.K., & Krahn, D.D. (1988). Bulimia in college women: Incidence and recovery rates. *American Journal of Psychiatry, 145*, 753–755.

Dubbert, P.M., & Brubaker, R.G. (1987). Assessment of obese patients. In T.D. Nirenberg & S.A. Maisto (Eds.), *Developments in the assessment and treatment of addictive behaviors*. Norwood, NJ: Ablex Publishing.

Dubro, A.F., & Wetzler, S. (1989). An external validity study of the MMPI personality disorder scales. *Journal of Clinical Psychology, 45*, 570–575.

Dumas, J., & Wahler, R.G. (1985). Indiscriminate mothering as a contextual factor in aggressive-oppositional child behavior: "Damned if you do, damned if you don't." *Journal of Abnormal Child Psychology, 13*, 1–17.

Duncan, B.L. (1989). Paradoxical procedures in behavior therapy. In L.M. Ascher (Ed.), *Therapeutic paradox*. New York: Guilford Press.

Dunham, H.W. (1965). *Community and schizophrenia: An epidemiological analysis*. Detroit: Wayne State University Press.

Durkheim, E. (1951). *Suicide*. New York: Free Press. (Original work published 1897)

Duval, S., & Wickland, R. (1972). *A theory of objective self-awareness*. New York: Academic Press.

Dweck, C.S. (1975). The role of expectations and attributions in the alleviation of learned helplessness. *Journal of Personality and Social Psychology, 31*, 674–685.

Dweck, C.S., & Reppucci, N.D. (1973). Learned helplessness and reinforcement responsibility in children. *Journal of Personality and Social Psychology, 25*, 109–116.

Dwyer, J.T., Feldman, J.I., & Mayer, J. (1967). Adolescent dieters: Who are they? *The American Journal of Clinical Nutrition, 20*, 1045–1056.

Dwyer, J.T., Feldman, J.J., Seltzer, C.C., & Mayer, J. (1969). Body image in adolescents: Attitudes towards weight and perception of appearance. *The American Journal of Clinical Nutrition, 20*, 1045–1056.

Eaton, W.W., Holzer, C.E., Von Korff, M., Anthony, J.C., Helzer, J.E., George, L., Burnam, A., Boyd, J.H., Kessler, L.G., & Locke, B.Z. (1984). The design of the epidemiologic catchment area surveys. *Archives of General Psychiatry, 41*, 942–948.

Eckert, E.D., Goldberg, S.C., Casper, R.C., Halmi, K.A., Casper, R.C., & Davis, J.M. (1979). Behavior therapy in anorexia nervosa. *British Journal of Psychiatry, 134*, 55–59.

Eddy, D.M., Wolpert, R.L., & Rosenberg, M.L. (1987). Estimating the effectiveness of interventions to prevent youth suicides. *Medical Care, 25*, 57–65.

Edell, W.S., Joy, S.P., & Yehuda, R. (1990). Discordance between self-report and observer-rated psychopathology in borderlike patients. *Journal of Personality Disorders, 4*, 381–390.

Edleson, J.L., Miller, D.M., Stone, G.W., & Chappan, D.G. (1985). Group treatment for men who batter. *Social Work Research and Abstracts, 21*, 18–21.

Edwards, A.L. (1967). *Edwards Personality Inventory: Manual*. Chicago: Science Research Associates.

Edwards, G., Arif, A., & Hodgson, R. (1981). Nomenclature and classification of the drug- and alcohol-related problems: A WHO memorandum. *Bulletin of the World Health Organization, 59*, 225–242.

Edwards, G., Gross, M.M., Keller, M., & Moser, J. (1976). Alcohol-related problems in the disability perspective. *Journal of Studies on Alcohol, 37*, 1360–1382.

Egeland, J.A., Gerhard, D.S., Pauls, D.L., Susses, J.N., Kidd, K.K., Allen, C.R., Hostetter, A.M., & Housman, D.E. (1987). Bipolar affective disorders linked to DNA markers on chromosome 11. *Nature, 325*, 783–787.

Eich, E. (1984). Memory for unattended events: Remembering with and without awareness. *Memory and Cognition, 12*, 105–111.

Eidelson, R.J., & Epstein, N. (1982). Cognitions and relationship readjustment: Development of a measure of dysfunctional relationship beliefs. *Journal of Consulting and Clinical Psychology, 50*, 715–720.

Elgar, F. (1958). *Van Gogh*. New York: Praeger.

Elkin, I., Parloff, M.B., Hadley, S.W., & Autry, J.H. (1985). NIMH treatment of depression collaborative research program. *Archives of General Psychiatry, 42*, 305–316.

Elkin, I., Shea, M.T., Watkins, J.T., Imber, S.D., Sotsky, S.M., Collins, J.F., Glass, D.R., Pilkonis, P.A., Leber, W.R., Docherty, J.P., Fiester, S.J., & Parloff, M.B. (1989). National Institute of Mental Health Treatment of Depression Collaborative Research Program: General effectiveness of treatments. *Archives of General Psychiatry, 46*, 971–982.

Elkins, R.L. (1980). Covert sensitization treatment of alcoholism: Contributions of successful conditioning to subsequent abstinence maintenance. *Addictive Behaviors, 5*, 67–89.

Elkins, R., & Rapoport, J.L. (1983). Psychopharmacology of adult and childhood depression: An overview. In D.P. Cantwell & G.A. Carlson (Eds.), *Affective disorders in childhood and adolescence*. New York: Spectrum Publications.

Ellenberger, H.F. (1970). *The discovery of the unconscious*. New York: Basic Books.

Ellenberger, H.F. (1972). The story of Anna O: A critical review with new data. *Journal of the History of Behavioral Sciences, 8*, 267–279.

Elliot, G.R., & Eisdorfer, D. (Eds.). (1982). *Stress and human health: Analysis and implications of research*. New York: Springer-Verlag.

Ellis, A. (1970). *The essence of rational psychotherapy: A comprehensive approach to treatment*. New York: Institute for Rational Living.

Ellis, A. (1977). Rational-emotive therapy research data that supports the clinical and personality hypothesis of RET and other modes of cognitive-behavior therapy. *The Counseling Psychologist, 7*, 2–42.

Ellis, E.M. (1983). A review of empirical rape research: Victim reactions and response to treatment. *Clinical Psychology Review, 3*, 473–490.

Ellis, H. (1902). Mescal: A study of a divine plant. *Popular Science Monthly, 61*, 59, 65.

Ellis, L., & Ames, M.A. (1987). Neurohormonal functioning and sexual orientation: A theory of homosexuality-heterosexuality. *Psychological Bulletin, 101*, 233–258.

Emery, G., Bedrosian, R., & Garber, J. (1983). Cognitive therapy with depressed children and adolescents. In D.P. Cantwell & G.A. Carlson (Eds.), *Affective disorders in childhood and adolescence: An update*. New York: SP Medical & Scientific Books.

Emery, R.E. (1982). Interparental conflict and the children of divorce and discord. *Psychological Bulletin, 92*, 310–330.

Emery, R.E., Weintraub, S., & Neale, J.M. (1982). Effects of marital discord on the school behavior of children of schizophrenic, affectively disordered, and normal parents. *Journal of Abnormal Child Psychology, 10*, 215–228.

Emmons, C., Joseph, J.G., Kessler, R.C., Wortman, C.B., Montgomery, S.B., & Ostrow, D.G. (1986). Psychosocial predictors of reported behavior change in homosexual men at risk for AIDS. *Health Education Quarterly, 13*, 331–345.

Endicott, J., Nee, J., Cohen, J., Fleiss, J.L., & Simon, R. (1986). Diagnosis of schizophrenia: Prediction of short-term outcome. *Archives of General Psychiatry, 3*, 13–19.

Engel, G.L. (1977). The need for a new medical model: A challenge for biomedicine. *Science, 196*, 129–136.

English, H.B. (1929). Three cases of the conditioned fear response. *Journal of Abnormal and Social Psychology, 24*, 221–225.

Ennis, B.J., & Litwack, T.R. (1974). Psychiatry and the presumption of expertise: Flipping coins in the courtroom. *California Law Review, 62*, 693–752.

Entwisle, D. (1972). To dispel fantasies about fantasy-based measures of achievement motivation. *Psychological Bulletin, 77*, 377–391.

Epple, W.A., Jacobson, J.W., & Janicki, M.P. (1985). Staffing ratios in public institutions for persons with mental retardation in the United States. *Mental Retardation, 23*, 115–124.

Epstein, N., Schlesinger, S.E., & Dryden, W. (1988). Concepts and methods of cognitive-behavioral family treatment. In N. Epstein, S.E. Schlesinger, & W. Dryden (Eds.), *Cognitive-behavioral therapy with families*. New York: Brunner/Mazel.

Erhardt, C., & Berlin, J. (Eds.). (1974). *Mortality and morbidity in the United States*. Cambridge, MA: Harvard University Press.

Erikson, E.H. (1959). *Identity and the life cycle*. New York: International Universities Press.

Erwin, E. (1986). Establishing causal connections: Meta-analysis and psychotherapy. *Midwest Studies in Philosophy, 9*, 421–436.

Ethics Committee, American Psychological Association. (1986). Report of the Ethics Committee, 1985. *American Psychologist, 41*, 694–697.

Ethics Committee, American Psychological Association. (1988). Trends in ethics cases, common pitfalls, and published resources. *American Psychologist, 43*, 564–572.

Exner, J.E. (1986). *The Rorschach: A comprehensive system* (Vol. 1, 2nd ed.). New York: John Wiley.

Eysenck, H.J. (1952). The effects of psychotherapy: An evaluation. *Journal of Consulting Psychology, 16*, 319–324.

Eysenck, H.J. (1959). Learning theory and behaviour therapy. *British Journal of Mental Science, 105*, 61–75.

Eysenck, H.J. (1961). The effects of psychotherapy. In H.J. Eysenck (Ed.), *Handbook of abnormal psychology*. New York: Basic Books.

Eysenck, H.J. (1976). *Sex and personality*. London: Open Books.

Eysenck, H.J. (1982). The neo-behaviouristic (S-R) theory of behaviour therapy. In G.T. Wilson & C.M. Franks (Eds.), *Contemporary behavior therapy: Theoretical foundations of clinical practice*. New York: Guilford Press.

Eysenck, H.J., & Eysenck, S.B. (1969). *Eysenck Personality Inventory* (rev. manual). San Diego: Educational and Industrial Testing Service.

Fabian, M.S., & Parsons, O.A. (1983). Differential improvement of cognitive functions in recovering alcoholic women. *Journal of Abnormal Psychology, 92*, 87–95.

Fabre, L.F., & McLendon, D.M. (1979). A double-blind study comparing the efficacy and safety of alprazolam with diazepam and placebo in anxious outpatients. *Current Therapeutic Research, 25*, 519–526.

Fabrega, H., Mezzich, J.E., Mezzich, A.C., & Coffman, G.A. (1986). Descriptive validity of *DSM-III* depressions. *The Journal of Nervous and Mental Disease, 174*, 573 584.

Fairburn, C.G. (1985). A cognitive-behavioural treatment for bulimia. In D.M. Garner & P.E. Garfinkel (Eds.), *Handbook of psychotherapy for anorexia nervosa and bulimia*. New York: Guilford Press.

Fairburn, C.G. (1988). The current status of the psychological treatments for bulimia nervosa. *Journal of Psychosomatic Research, 32*, 635–645.

Fairburn, C.G., Jones, R., Peveler, R.C., Carr, S.J., Solomon, R.A., O'Connor, M.E., Burton, J., & Hope, R.A. (1991). Three psychological treatments for bulimia nervosa: A comparative trial. *Archives of General Psychiatry, 48*, 463–469.

Fairburn, C.G., Kirk, J., O'Connor, M., Anastasiades, P., & Cooper, P.J. (1987). Prognostic factors in bulimia nervosa. *British Journal of Clinical Psychology, 26*, 223–224.

Fairburn, C.G., Kirk, J., O'Connor, M., & Cooper, P.J. (1986). A comparison of two psychological treatments for bulimia nervosa. *Behaviour Research and Therapy, 24*, 629–643.

Fairweather, G.S., Sanders, D.H., Maynard, H., & Cressler, D.L. (1969). *Community life for the mentally ill*. Chicago: Aldine.

Falloon, I.R.H., Boyd, J.L., McGill, C.W., Williamson, M., Ranzani, J., Moss, H.B., Gilderman, A.M., & Simpson, G.M. (1985). Family management in the prevention of morbidity of schizophrenia. *Archives of General Psychiatry, 42*, 887–896.

Farber, S.L. (1981). *Identical twins reared apart*. New York: Basic Books.

Faris, R.E.L., & Dunham, H.W. (1939). *Mental disorders in urban areas*. New York: Hafner.

Farmer, A.E., Katz, R., McGuffin, P., & Bebbington, P. (1987). A comparison between the Present State Examination and the Composite International Diagnostic Interview. *Archives of General Psychiatry, 44*, 1064–1068.

Farmer, P.M., Peck, A., & Terry, R.D. (1976). Correlations among neuritic plaques, neurofibrillary tangles and the severity of senile dementia. *Journal of Neuropathology and Experimental Neurology, 36*, 633.

Farone, S.V., Kremen, W.S., & Tsuang, M.T. (1990). Genetic transmission of major affective disorders: Quantitative models and linkage analyses. *Psychological Bulletin, 108*, 109–127.

Farrington, D.P.F., Loeber, R.L., & van Kammen, W.B. (in press). Long-term outcomes of hyperactivity-impulsivity-attention deficit and conduct problems in childhood. In R. Robins, L.N. & M.R. Rutter (Eds.), *Strait and deviant pathways to adulthood*. New York: Cambridge University Press.

Feingold, B. (1975). *Why your child is hyperactive*. New York: Random House.

Feldman, M.A. (1986). Research on parenting by mentally retarded persons. *Psychiatric Clinics of North America, 9*, 777–795.

Feldman, M.P., & MacCulloch, M.J. (1971). *Homosexual behaviour: Therapy and assessment*. New York: Pergamon Press.

Ferrara, A.J. (1984). My personal experience with AIDS. *American Psychologist, 39*, 1285–1287.

Ferster, C.B., & Skinner, B.F. (1957). *Schedules of reinforcement*. New York: Appleton-Century-Crofts.

Fichter, M.M., & Noegel, R. (1990). Concordance for bulimia nervosa in twins. *International Journal of Eating Disorders, 9*, 255–263.

Filley, C.M., Kobayashi, J., & Heaton, R.K. (1987). Wechsler Intelligence Scale Profiles, the cholinergic system, and Alzheimer's disease. *Journal of Clinical and Experimental Neuropsychology, 9*, 180–186.

Fillmore, K.M. (1987). Women's drinking across the adult life course as compared to men's. *British Journal of Addiction, 82*, 801–811.

Fine, R. (1986). *Narcissism, the self, and society*. New York: Columbia University Press.

Fink, M. (1979). *Convulsive therapy: Theory and practice*. New York: Raven Press.

Fink, M. (1982). ECT in anxiety: An appraisal. *American Journal of Psychotherapy, 36*, 371–378.

Finkelhor, D. (1979). *Sexually victimized children*. New York: Free Press.

Finn, S.E. (1986). Stability of personality self-ratings over 30 years: Evidence for an age-cohort interaction. *Journal of Personality and Social Psychology, 50*, 813–818.

Finney, J.C. (1985). Anxiety: Its measurement by objective personality tests and self-report. In A.H. Tuma & J.D. Maser (Eds.), *Anxiety and the anxiety disorders*. Hillsdale, NJ: Lawrence Erlbaum.

Finney, J.W., & Moos, R.H. (1986). Matching patients with treatments: Conceptual and methodological issues. *Journal of Studies on Alcohol, 47*, 122–134.

Fish, F. (1967). *Clinical psychopathology*. Bristol, England: University of Leeds, Wright.

Fisher, E.B., Delamater, A.M., Bertelson, A.D., & Kirkley, B.G. (1982). Psychological factors in diabetes and its treatment. *Journal of Consulting and Clinical Psychology, 50*, 993–1003.

Fisher, L., & Wilson, G.T. (1985). A study of psychology of agoraphobia. *Behaviour Research and Therapy, 23*, 97–108.

Fisher, S., & Greenberg, R.P. (1977). *The scientific credibility of Freud's theories and therapy.* Sussex: Harvester Press.

Flack, J.M., & Sisson, L. (1991). Obesity is a major crisis for African-Americans. *Obesity and Health, 55*, 5–6.

Flynn, N.M., & Rapoport, J.L. (1976). Hyperactivity in open and traditional classroom environments. *Journal of Special Education, 10*, 285–290.

Foa, E.B., Steketee, G., Turner, R.M., & Fischer, S.C. (1980). Effects of imaginal exposure to feared disasters in obsessive-compulsive checkers. *Behaviour Research and Therapy, 19,* 449–458.

Foa, E.B., Steketee, G., & Young, M.C. (1984). Agoraphobia: Phenomenological aspects, associated characteristics, and theoretical considerations. *Clinical Psychology Review, 4*, 431–457.

Fodor, I.S. (1974). The phobic syndrome in women: Implications for treatment. In V. Franks & V. Burtle (Eds.), *Women in therapy: New psychotherapies for a changing society.* New York: Brunner/Mazel.

Folkman, S. (1984). Personal control and stress and coping processes: A theoretical analysis. *Journal of Personality and Social Psychology, 46*, 839–852.

Folkman, S., Bernstein, L., & Lazarus, R.S. (1987). Stress processes and the misuse of drugs in older adults. *Psychology and Aging, 2*, 366–374.

Folstein, S., & Rutter M. (1977). Infantile autism: A genetic study of 21 twin pairs. *Journal of Child Psychology and Psychiatry, 18,* 297–321.

Forehand, R., & McMahon, R. (1981). *Helping the noncompliant child: A clinician's guide to parent training.* New York: Guilford Press.

Foreyt, J., Goodrick, K., & Gotto, A.M. (1981). Limitations of behavioral treatment of obesity: Review and analysis. *Journal of Behavioral Medicine, 13*, 159–174.

Forgac, G.E., & Michaels, E.J. (1982). Personality characteristics of two types of male exhibitionists. *Journal of Abnormal Psychology, 91,* 287–293.

Forsythe, W.I., & Redmond, A. (1974). Enuresis and spontaneous cure rate: Study of 1,129 enuretics. *Archives of Disease in Childhood, 49*, 259–263.

Foster, S.L., Prinz, R.J., & O'Leary, K.D. (1983). Impact of problem-solving communication training and generalization procedures on family conflict. *Child and Family Behavior Therapy, 5*, 1–23.

Foulds, G. (1955). The reliability of psychiatric and the validity of psychological diagnosis. *Journal of Mental Science, 101*, 851–862.

Fowler, R.D. (1969). The current status of computer interpretation of psychological tests. *American Journal of Psychiatry, 125*, 21–27.

Foy, D.W., Cline, K.A., & Laasi, N. (1987). Assessment of alcohol and drug abuse. In T.D. Nirenberg & S.A. Maisto (Eds.), *Developments in the assessment and treatment of addictive behaviors.* Norwood, NJ: Ablex Publishing.

Foy, D.W., Donahoe, C.P., Carroll, E.M., Gallers, J., & Reno, R. (1987). Posttraumatic stress disorder. In L. Michelson & L.M. Ascher (Eds.), *Anxiety and stress disorders.* New York: Guilford Press.

Frances, A., & Widiger, T.A. (1986). Methodological issues in personality disorder diagnosis. In T. Millon & G. Klerman (Eds.), *Contemporary directions in psychopathology.* New York: Guilford Press.

Frank, A.F., & Gunderson, J.G. (1990). The role of the therapeutic alliance in the treatment of schizophrenia: Relation to course and outcome. *Archives of General Psychiatry, 47*, 228–238.

Frank, E., Anderson, B., Stewart, B.D., Dancu, C., Hughes, C., & West, D. (1988). Efficacy of cognitive behavior therapy and systematic desensitization in the treatment of rape trauma. *Behavior Therapy, 19*, 403–420.

Frank, E., Anderson, C., & Rubinstein, D. (1978). Frequency of sexual dysfunction in "normal" couples. *The New England Journal of Medicine, 229*, 111–115.

Frank, E., Kupfer, D.J., Perel, J.M., Cornes, C., Jarret, D.B., Mallinger, A.G., Thase, M.E., McEachran, A.B., & Grochocinski, V.J. (1990). Three year outcomes for maintenance therapies in recurrent depression. *Archives of General Psychiatry, 47*, 1093–1099.

Freeman, R.J., Beach, B., Davis, R., & Solyom, L. (1985). The prediction of relapse in bulimia nervosa. *Journal of Psychosomatic Research, 19*, 349–353.

Freeman, W., & Watts, J.W. (1942). *Psychosurgery: Intelligence, emotional and social behavior following prefrontal lobotomy for mental disorder.* Springfield, IL: Charles Thomas.

Freud, A. (1936). *The ego and the mechanisms of defense.* New York: International Universities Press.

Freud, A. (1946). *The ego and the mechanisms of defense.* New York: International Universities Press.

Freud, S. (1914). On narcissism: An introduction. From *Collected Papers 4,* London: Hogarth Press, 1924–1950.

Freud, S. (1950). Mourning and melancholia. In *Collected Papers,* vol. 4. London, Hogarth Press & the Institute of Psychoanalysis, 152–172. (Original work published 1917)

Freud, S. (1953). Three essays of the theory of sexuality. In J. Strachey (Ed. and Trans.), *The standard edition of the complete psychological works of Sigmund Freud* (Vol. 7, pp. 125–221). London: Hogarth Press. (Original work published 1905)

Freud, S. (1955). Analysis of a phobia in a five-year-old boy. In J. Strachey (Ed. and Trans.), *The standard edition of the complete psychological works of Sigmund Freud* (Vol. 10). London: Hogarth Press. (Original work published 1909)

Freud, S. (1955). Beyond the pleasure principle. In J. Strachey (Ed. and Trans.), *The standard edition of the complete psychological works of Sigmund Freud* (Vol. 18, pp. 7–64). London: Hogarth Press. (Original work published 1920)

Freud, S. (1961). The ego and the id. In J. Strachey (Ed. and Trans.), *The standard edition of the complete psychological works of Sigmund Freud* (Vol. 19, pp. 12–68). London: Hogarth Press. (Original work published 1923)

Freud, S. (1963a). Studies in hysteria. In J. Strachey (Ed. and Trans.), *The standard edition of the complete psychological works of Sigmund Freud* (Vol. 2). London: Hogarth Press. (Original work published 1895)

Freud, S. (1963b). The libido theory and narcissism. Lecture XXVI. In J. Strachey (Ed. and Trans.), *Introductory lectures on psycho-analysis. The standard edition of the complete psychological works of Sigmund Freud* (Vol. 16, pp. 412–430). London: Hogarth Press. (Original work published 1917)

Freud, S. (1963c). The sexual life of human beings. In J. Strachey (Ed. and Trans.), *The standard edition of the complete psychological works of Sigmund Freud* (Vol. 16, pp. 303–319). London: Hogarth Press. (Original work published 1917)

Freud, S. (1964a). An outline of psychoanalysis. In J. Strachey (Ed. and Trans.), *The standard edition of the complete psychological works of Sigmund Freud* (Vol. 23, pp. 141–208). London: Hogarth Press. (Original work published 1940)

Freud, S. (1964b). Femininity. In J. Strachey (Ed. and Trans.), *The standard edition of the complete psychological works of Sigmund Freud* (Vol. 22, pp. 112–135). London: Hogarth Press. (Original work published 1933)

Freud, S. (1964c). The technique of psychoanalysis. In J. Strachey (Ed. and Trans.), *The standard edition of the complete psychological works of Sigmund Freud* (Vol. 23). London: Hogarth Press. (Original work published 1938)

Freud, S. (1970). On the general effect of cocaine. (Lecture before the Psychiatric Union on March 5, 1885). Reprinted in *Drug Dependence, 5*, 17.

Freudenberg, N. (1988). Historical omissions: A critique of "And the band played on." *Health/PAC Bulletin,* Spring, pp. 16–20.

Frezza, M., DiPadova, C., Pozzato, G., Terpin, M., Baraona, E., & Lieber, C.S. (1990). High blood alcohol levels in women: Role of decreased gastric alcohol dehydrogenase activity and first pass metabolism. *New England Journal of Medicine, 322,* 95–99.

Fridhandler, B.M. (1986). Conceptual note on state, trait, and the state-trait distinction. *Journal of Personality and Social Psychology, 50*, 169–174.

Friedman, H.S., & Booth-Kewley, S. (1987). The "disease-prone" personality: A meta-analytic view of the construct. *American Psychologist, 42*, 539–555.

Friedman, J., & Hogan, D. (1985). Sexual dysfunction: Low sexual desire. In D.H. Barlow (Ed.), *Adult clinical disorders*. New York: Guilford Press.

Friedman, M., & Rosenman, R.H. (1974). *Type A behavior and your heart*. Greenwich, CT: Fawcett Publications.

Friedman, M., Thoresen, C.E., Gill, J., Powell, L.H., Ulmer, D., Thompson, L., Price, V.A., Rabin, D.D., Breall, W.J., Dixon, T., Levy, R., & Bourg, E. (1984). Alteration of type A behavior and reduction in cardiac recurrences in postmyocardial infarction patients. *American Heart Journal, 108*, 237–248.

Fromm, E. (1941). *Escape from Freedom*. New York: Farrar & Rinehart.

Fromm-Reichmann, F. (1939). Transference problems in schizophrenics. *Psychoanalytic Quarterly, 8*, 412–426.

Frost, R.O., Sher, K.J., & Geen, T. (1986). Psychotherapy and personality characteristics of non-clinical compulsive checkers. *Behaviour Research and Therapy, 24*, 133–143.

Fuller, G.D., & Kates, S.L. (1969). Word association repertoires of schizophrenics and normals. *Journal of Consulting and Clinical Psychology, 33*, 497–500.

Furman, W., Rahe, D., & Hartup, W. (1979). Rehabilitation of socially withdrawn preschool children through mixed-age socialization. *Child Development, 50*, 915–922.

Gagnon, J. (1977). *Human sexualities*. Chicago: Scott, Foresman.

Galanter, M. (1988, December). Does joining a cult reflect psychopathology in the convert? *The Harvard Medical School Mental Health Letter*. Boston, MA: Harvard Medical School.

Gallant, D.M. (1987). The female alcoholic: Early onset of brain damage. *Alcoholism, 11*, 190–191.

Gallant, S.J., & Hamilton, J.A. (1988). On a premenstrual psychiatric diagnosis: What's in a name? *Professional Psychology: Research and Practice, 19*, 271–278.

Galton, F. (1883). *Inquiries into human faculty and its development*. London: Macmillan.

Ganahl, G.F., Ferguson, L.R., & L'Abate, L. (1985). Training in family therapy. In L. L'Abate (Ed.), *The handbook of family psychology and therapy* (Vol. II). Homewood, IL: Dorsey Press.

Garcia, J., & Koelling, R.A. (1966). Relation of cue to consequence in avoidance learning. *Psychonomic Science, 4*, 123–124.

Gardner, H. (1974). *The shattered mind*. New York: Vintage Books.

Gardner, H. (1983). *Frames of mind: The theory of multiple intelligences*. New York: Basic Books.

Gardner, H. (1986). The waning of intelligence tests. In R.J. Sternberg & D.K. Detterman (Eds.), *What is intelligence?* Norwood, NJ: Ablex Publishing.

Garfield, S.L. (1983). Does psychotherapy work? Yes, no, maybe. *Behavioral and Brain Sciences, 6*, 292–293.

Garfield, S.L., & Kurtz, R. (1976). Clinical psychologists in the 1970s. *American Psychologist, 31*, 1–9.

Garfinkel, B.D., Froese, A., & Golumbek, H. (1979). Suicide behaviour in a pediatric population. *Proceedings of the 10th International Congress for Suicide Prevention and Crisis Intervention*. Ottawa, Canada: M.O.M. Printing, 305–312.

Garfinkel, B.D., Froese, A., & Hood, J. (1982). Suicide attempts in children and adolescents. *American Journal of Psychiatry, 139*, 1257–1261.

Garfinkel, B.D., & Golumbek, H. (1983). Suicidal behavior in adolescence. In H. Golumbek & B.D. Garfinkel (Eds.), *The adolescent and mood disturbance*. New York: International Universities Press.

Garfinkel, P.E., & Garner, D.M. (1982). *Anorexia nervosa: A multidimensional perspective*. New York: Brunner/Mazel.

Garmezy, N. (1978). Never mind the psychologists. Is it good for the children? *The Clinical Psychologist, 31*, 1–6.

Garner, D.M., & Garfinkel, P.E. (1980). Socio-cultural factors in the development of anorexia nervosa. *Psychological Medicine, 10*, 647–656.

Garner, D.M., Garfinkel, P.E., Schwartz, D., & Thompson, M. (1980). Cultural expectation of thinness in women. *Psychological Reports, 47*, 483–491.

Garner, M., Garfinkel, P.E., & O'Shaughnessy, M. (1985). The validity of the distinction between bulimics with and without anorexia nervosa. *American Journal of Psychiatry, 142*, 581–587.

Garrett, C.J. (1985). Effects of residential treatment on adjudicated delinquents: A meta-analysis. *Journal of Crime and Delinquency, 22*, 287–308.

Gartrell, N., Herman, J., Olarte, S., Localio, R., & Feldstein, M. (1988). Psychiatric residents' sexual contact with educators and patients: Results of a national survey. *American Journal of Psychiatry, 145*, 690–694.

Garvey, A.J., Heinold, J.W., & Rosner, B. (1989). Self-help approaches to smoking cessation: A report from the normative aging study. *Addictive Behaviors, 14*, 23–33.

Gauron, E., & Dickinson, J.K. (1966). Diagnostic decision making in psychiatry. *Archives of General Psychiatry, 14*, 233–237.

Gawin, F.H., & Ellinwood, E.H. (1988). Cocaine and other stimulants: Actions, abuse, and treatment. *The New England Journal of Medicine, 318*, 1173–1182.

Geer, J.H., Morokoff, P., & Greenwood, P. (1974). Sexual arousal in women: The development of a measurement device for vaginal blood volume. *Archives of Sexual Behavior, 3*, 559–564.

Geiss, S.K., & O'Leary, K.D. (1981). Therapist ratings of frequency and severity of marital problems; implications for research. *Journal of Marital and Family Therapy, 7*, 515–520.

Gelberg, L., Linn, L.S., & Leake, B.D. (1988). Mental health, alcohol and drug use, and criminal history among homeless adults. *American Journal of Psychiatry, 145*, 191–196.

Geller, J.L. (1986). Rights, wrongs, and the dilemma of coerced community treatment. *American Journal of Psychiatry, 143*, 1259–1264.

Gelman, D. (1987, May 4). Depression. *Newsweek, 44*, 7.

George, W.H., Gournic, S.J., & McAfee, M.P. (1988). Perceptions of postdrinking female sexuality: Effects of gender, beverage choice, and drink payment. *Journal of Applied Social Psychology, 18*, 1295–1317.

Gershon, E.S. (1990). Genetics. In F.K. Goodwin & K.R. Jamison, *Manic depressive illness* (pp. 373–401). New York: Oxford University Press.

Gershon, E.S., & Bunney, W.E. (1976). The question of X-linkage in bipolar manic-depressive illness. *Journal of Psychosomatic Research, 13*, 99–117.

Gershon, E.S., Hamovit, J., Guroff, J.J., Dibble, E., Leckman, J.F., Sceery, W., Targum, S.D., Nurnberger, J.I., Jr., Goldin, L.R., & Bunney, W.E., Jr. (1982). A family study of schizoaffective, bipolar I, bipolar II, unipolar, and normal control probands. *Archives of General Psychiatry, 39*, 1167.

Gerstley, L.J., Alterman, A.I., McLellan, A.T., & Woody, G.E. (1990). Antisocial personality disorder in patients with substance abuse disorders: A problematic diagnosis? *American Journal of Psychiatry, 147*, 173–178.

Gittelman, R. (Ed.). (1986). *Anxiety disorders of childhood*. New York: Guilford Press.

Gittelman, R., & Koplewicz, H.S. (1986). Pharmacotherapy of childhood anxiety disorders. In R. Gittelman (Ed.), *Anxiety disorders of childhood*. New York: Guilford Press.

Gittelman-Klein, R., & Klein, D.F. (1973). School phobia: Diagnostic considerations in light of imipramine effects. *Journal of Nervous and Mental Disease, 156*, 199–210.

Gittelman-Klein, R., & Klein, D.F. (1984). Relationship between separation anxiety and panic and agoraphobic disorders. *Psychopathology, 17*(Suppl.), 56–65.

Gittelman-Klein, R., Klein, D.F., Abikoff, H., Katz, S., Gloisten, A.C., & Kates, W. (1976). Relative efficacy of methylphenidate and behavior modification in hyperactive children: An interim report. *Journal of Abnormal Child Psychology, 4*, 361–379.

Glaser, K. (1981). Psychopathological patterns in depressed adolescents. *American Journal of Psychotherapy, 35*, 368–382.

Glaser, R.D., & Thorpe, J.S. (1986). Unethical intimacy. *American Psychologist, 41*, 43–51.

Glaser, R., Rice, J., Sheridan, J., Fertel, R., Stout, J., Speicher, C., Pinsky, D., Kotur, M., Post, A., Beck, M., & Kiecolt-Glaser,

J.K. (1987). Stress-related immune suppression: Health implications. *Brain, Behavior, and Immunity, 1*, 7–20.

Glueck, S., & Glueck, E. (1968). *Delinquents and nondelinquents in perspective.* Cambridge, MA: Harvard University Press.

Goetsch, V.L. (1989). Stress and blood glucose in diabetes mellitus: A review and methodological commentary. *Annals of Behavioral Medicine, 11*, 102–107.

Goffman, I. (1961). *Asylums: Essays on the social situation of mental patients and other inmates.* Garden City, New York: Doubleday Anchor.

Goffman, I. (1961). *Asylums.* New York: Anchor Books.

Gold, P.W., Goodwin, F.K., & Chrousos, G.P. (1988). Clinical and biochemical manifestations of depression. *New England Journal of Medicine, 319*, 348–353.

Goldblatt, P.B., Moore, M.E., & Stunkard, A.J. (1965). Social factors in obesity. *Journal of the American Medical Association, 192*, 1039–1044.

Golden, C.J., Hammeke, T.A., & Purisch, A.D. (1980). *The Luria-Nebraska Battery manual.* Palo Alto, CA: Western Psychological Services.

Goldfried, M.R. (Ed.). (1980a). Some views on effective principles of psychotherapy. *Cognitive Therapy and Research, 4*, 271–306.

Goldfried, M.R. (1980b). Toward the delineation of therapeutic change principles. *American Psychologist, 35*, 991–999.

Goldfried, M.R. (Ed.). (1982). *Converging themes in psychotherapy.* New York: Springer Publications.

Goldfried, M.R., & Kent, R.N. (1972). Traditional versus behavioral personality assessment: A comparison of methodological and theoretical assumptions. *Psychological Bulletin, 77*, 409–420.

Goldman, M.S. (1983). Cognitive impairment in chronic alcoholics. *American Psychologist, 38*, 1045–1054.

Goldman, M.S. (1987). The role of time and practice in recovery of function of alcoholics. In O.A. Parsons, N. Butters, & P.E. Nathan (Eds.), *Neuropsychology of alcoholism: Implications for diagnosis and treatment.* New York: Guilford Press.

Goldman, M.S., Brown, S.A., & Christiansen, B.A. (1987). Expectancy theory: Thinking about drinking. In H.T. Blane & K.E. Leonard (Eds.), *Psychological theories of drinking and alcoholism* (pp. 181–226). New York: Guilford Press.

Goldman, M.S., Williams, D.L., & Klisz, D.K. (1983). Recoverability of psychological functioning following alcohol abuse: Prolonged visual-spatial dysfunction in older alcoholics. *Journal of Consulting and Clinical Psychology, 51*, 370–378.

Goldstein, G., & Shelly, C. (1984). Discriminative validity of various intelligence and neuropsychological tests. *Journal of Consulting and Clinical Psychology, 52*, 383–389.

Goldstein, I.B., Shapiro, D., Thananopavarn, C., & Sambhi, M.P. (1982). Comparison of drug and behavioral treatments of essential hypertension. *Health Psychology, 1*, 7–26.

Goldstein, M.J. (1984). Family intervention programs. In A.S. Bellack (Ed.), *Schizophrenia: Treatment, management, and rehabilitation.* New York: Grune & Stratton.

Goldstein, P.J. (1985). The drugs/violence nexus: A tripartite conceptual framework. *Journal of Drug Issues, 15*, 493–506.

Goleman, D. (1986, December 2). Major personality study finds that traits are mostly inherited. *The New York Times,* p. C1.

Goleman, D. (1987, March 10). Researcher reports progress against autism. *The New York Times*, Section III, p. 1.

Goleman, D. (1988, November 1). Narcissism looming larger as root of personality woes. *The New York Times*, pp. C1, C16.

Goleman, D. (1989, October 31). Dangerous delusions: When fans are a threat. *The New York Times,* pp. C1, C6.

Goodman, R. (1989). Infantile autism: A syndrome of multiple primary deficits? *Journal of Autism and Developmental Disorders, 19*, 409–424.

Goodman, W., Price, L., Delgado, P., Palumbo, J., Krystal, J., Nagy, L., Rasmussen, S., Heninger, G., & Charney, D. (1990). Specificity of serotonin reuptake inhibitors in the treatment of obsessive-compulsive disorder: Comparison of fluvroxamine and desipramine. *Archives of General Psychiatry, 47*, 577–588.

Goodstein, R.K. (1983). Overview: Cerebrovascular accident and the hospitalized elderly—a multidimensional clinical problem. *American Journal of Psychiatry, 140*, 141–147.

Goodwin, D.W. (1976). *Is alcoholism hereditary?* New York: Oxford University Press.

Goodwin, D.W. (1979). Alcoholism and heredity. *Archives of General Psychiatry, 36*, 57–61.

Goodwin, D.W. (1985). Genetic determinants of alcoholism. In J.H. Mendelson & N.K. Mello (Eds.), *The diagnosis and treatment of alcoholism* (pp. 65–87). New York: McGraw-Hill.

Goodwin, D.W. (1986). *Anxiety.* New York: Ballantine Books.

Goodwin, F.K., & Jamison, K.R. (1990). *Manic-depressive illness.* New York: Oxford University Press.

Gortmaker, S.L., Dietz, W.H., Sobol, A.M., & Wehler, C.A. (1987). Increasing pediatric obesity in the United States. *American Journal of Diseases of Children, 141*, 535–540.

Gotlib, I.H., & Colby, C.A. (1987). *Treatment of depression: An interpersonal systems approach.* New York: Pergamon.

Gotlib, I.H., & Robinson, L.A. (1982). Responses to depressed individuals: Discrepancies between self-report and observer rated behavior. *Journal of Abnormal Psychology, 91*, 231–240.

Gottesman, I.I., & Shields, J. (1972). *Schizophrenia and genetics: A twin study vantage point.* New York: Academic Press.

Gottman, J.M. (1985). Observational measures of behavior therapy outcome: A reply to Jacobson. *Behavioral Assessment, 7*, 317–321.

Gottman, J.M., Gonso, J., & Rasmussen, B. (1975). Social interaction, social competence, and friendship in children. *Child Development, 46*, 709–718.

Gough, H.G. (1969). *California Psychological Inventory* (rev. manual). Palo Alto, CA: Consulting Psychologists Press.

Gould, M.S., Shaffer, D., & Kleinman, M. (1988). The impact of suicide in television movies: Replication and commentary. *Suicide and Life-Threatening Behavior, 18*, 90–99.

Graham, J.R., & Strenger, V.E. (1988). MMPI characteristics of alcoholics: A review. *Journal of Consulting and Clinical Psychology, 56*, 197–205.

Graham, R., & Rutter, M. (1973). Psychiatric disorders in the young adolescent: A follow-up study. *Proceedings of the Royal Society of Medicine, 66*, 1226–1229.

Grandin, T. (1987). Motivating autistic children. *Academic Therapy, 22*, 297–302.

Grant, I., Adams, K.M., & Reed, R. (1984). Aging, abstinence, and medical risk factors in the prediction of neuropsychologic deficit among long-term alcoholics. *Archives of General Psychiatry, 41*, 710–718.

Gray, J.A. (1982). *The neuropsychology of anxiety.* New York: Oxford University Press.

Gray, J.A. (1985). Issues in the neuropsychology of anxiety. In A.H. Tuma & J.D. Maser (Eds.), *Anxiety and the anxiety disorders.* Hillsdale, NJ: Lawrence Erlbaum.

Gray, J.J., & Ford, K. (1985). The incidence of bulimia in a college sample. *International Journal of Eating Disorders, 4*, 201–211.

Gray, J.J., Ford, K., & Kelly, L.M. (1987). The prevalence of bulimia in a black college population. *International Journal of Eating Disorders, 6*, 733–740.

Gray, J.N., & Melton, G.B. (1985). The law and ethics of psychosocial research on AIDS. *Nebraska Law Review, 64*, 637–688.

Graziano, A.M., DeGiovanni, I.S., & Garcia, K.A. (1979). Behavioral treatment of children's fear: A review. *Psychological Bulletin, 86*, 804–830.

Graziano, A.M., & Mooney, K. (1980). Family self-control instruction for children's nighttime fear reduction. *Journal of Consulting and Clinical Psychology, 48*, 206–213.

Green, R. (1978). Sexual identity of 37 children raised by homosexual or transsexual parents. *American Journal of Psychiatry, 135*, 692–697.

Green, R. (1987). *The "sissy boy syndrome" and the development of homosexuality.* New Haven, CT: Yale University Press.

Greenberg, L.S. (1986). Change process research. *Journal of Consulting and Clinical Psychology, 54,* 4–9.

Greenfeld, J. (1972). *A child called Noah.* New York: Holt, Rinehart & Winston.

Greenwood, M.R.C. (1989). Sexual dimorphism and obesity. In A.J. Stunkard & A. Baum (Eds.), *Perspectives in behavioral medicine.* Hillsdale, NJ: Lawrence Erlbaum.

Greist, J.H., & Jefferson, J.W. (1984). *Depression and its treatment: Help for the nation's #1 mental problem.* Washington, DC: American Psychiatric Press.

Grey, S., Sartory, G., & Rachman, S. (1979). Synchronous and desynchronous changes during fear reduction. *Behaviour Research and Therapy, 78,* 137–148.

Grinker, R., Werble, B., & Drye, R. (1968). *The borderline syndrome: A behavioral study of ego functions.* New York: Basic Books.

Grisso, T. (1987). The economic and scientific future of forensic psychological assessment. *American Psychologist, 42,* 831–839.

Gross, A.M. (1988). Oppositional disorder. In M. Hersen & C.G. Last (Eds.), *Child behavior therapy casebook* (pp. 182–183). New York: Plenum Press.

Gross, J., Stitzer, M.L., & Maldonado, J. (1989). Nicotine replacement: Effects on postcessation weight gain. *Journal of Consulting and Clinical Psychology, 57,* 87–92.

Grosz, H.J., & Zimmerman, J. (1965). Experimental analysis of hysterical blindness: A follow-up report and new experimental data. *Archives of General Psychiatry, 13,* 255–260.

Gruen, R.J., Folkman, S., & Lazarus, R.S. (1987). Dyadic response patterns in married couples. *Journal of Family Psychology, 1,* 168–186.

Grunberg, N.E. (1985). Nicotine, cigarette smoking and body weight. *British Journal of Addictions, 80,* 369–377.

Grunhaus, L., Zelnick, T., Albala, A., Rabin, D., Haskett, R.F., Zis, A.P., & Greden, F., Jr. (1987). Serial dexamethasone suppression tests in depressed patients treated only with electroconvulsive therapy. *Journal of Affective Disorders, 13,* 233–240.

Gunderson, J.G. (1984). *Borderline personality disorder.* Washington, DC: American Psychiatric Press.

Gunderson, J.G. (1988). Personality disorders. In A. Nicholi, Jr. (Ed.), *The new Harvard guide to psychiatry* (pp. 337–357). Cambridge: Harvard University Press.

Gunderson, J.G., & Sanarini, M.C. (1987). Current overview of the borderline diagnosis. *Journal of Clinical Psychiatry, 48*(Suppl.), 5–11.

Gur, R.E. (1978). Left hemisphere dysfunction and left hemisphere overactivity in schizophrenia. *Journal of Abnormal Psychology, 87,* 226–238.

Gur, R.E., Resnick, S.M., Alavi, A., Gur, R.C., Caroff, S., Dann, R., Silver, F.L., Saykin, A.J., Chawluk, J.B., Kushner, M., & Reivich, M. (1987). A positron emission tomography study. *Archives of General Psychiatry, 44,* 119–125.

Gur, R.E., Resnick, S.M., Gur, R.C., Alavi, A., Caroff, S., Kushner, M., & Reivich, M. (1987). Repeated evaluation with positron emission tomography. *Archives of General Psychiatry, 44,* 126–129.

Gurin, G., Veroff, J., & Feld, S. (1960). *Americans view their health: A nationwide interview survey.* New York: Basic Books.

Gurman, A.S., & Kniskern, D.P. (1986). Research on marital and family therapy: Progress, perspective and prospect. In S.L. Garfield & A.E. Bergin (Eds.), *Handbook of psychotherapy and behavior change.* New York: John Wiley.

Gurman, A.S., Knudson, R.M., & Kniskern, D.P. (1978). Behavioral marriage therapy: IV. Take two aspirin and call us in the morning. *Family Process, 17,* 165–180.

Gutheil, T.G., & Bursztajn, H. (1986). Clinicians' guidelines for assessing and presenting subtle forms of patient incompetence in legal settings. *American Journal of Psychiatry, 143,* 1020–1023.

Guze, S.B., Cloninger, C.R., Martin, R.L., & Clayton, P.J. (1986). A follow-up and family study of Briques's syndrome. *British Journal of Psychiatry, 149,* 17–23.

Gynther, M.D., & Gynther, R.A. (1983). Personality inventories. In I.B. Weiner (Ed.), *Clinical methods in psychology* (2nd ed.). New York: Wiley-Interscience.

Haas, G.L., & Clarkin, J.F. (1987). Differential therapeutics and treatment format. In R.E. Hales & A.J. Frances (Eds.), *Annual Review of Psychiatry* (Vol. 6). Washington, DC: American Psychiatric Association.

Hafner, R.J. (1986). *Marriage & mental illness: A sex roles perspective.* New York: Guilford Press.

Hagman, C. (1932). A study of fears of children in preschool age. *Journal of Experimental Psychology, 1,* 110–130.

Hahlweg, K. (1988, September). *Behavioural marital therapy: The state of the art.* Paper presented at the Behaviour Therapy World Congress, Edinburgh, Scotland.

Hall, G.C.M. (1989). Sexual arousal and arousability in a sexual offender population. *Journal of Abnormal Psychology, 98,* 145–149.

Halmi, K.A., Eckert, E.D., LaDu, T.J., & Cohen, J. (1986). Anorexia nervosa: Treatment efficacy of cyproheptadine and amitriptyline. *Archives of General Psychiatry, 43,* 177–181.

Halstead, W.C. (1947). *Brain and intelligence: A quantitative study of the frontal lobes.* Chicago: University of Chicago Press.

Hammen, C.L. (1985). Predicting depression: A cognitive-behavioral perspective. In P. Kendall (Ed.), *Advances in cognitive-behavioral research* (pp. 29–71). New York: Academic Press.

Hammen, C.L., Ellicot, A., Gitlin, M., & Jamison, K.R. (1989). Sociotrophy/autonomy and vulnerability to specific life events in patients with unipolar and bipolar disorders. *Journal of Abnormal Psychology, 98,* 154–160.

Haque, M., Ellerstein, N.S., Gundy, J.H., Shelov, S.P., Weiss, J.C., McIntire, M.S., Olness, K.N., Jones, D.J., Heagarty, M.C., & Starfield, B.H. (1981). Parental perceptions of enuresis: A collaborative study. *American Journal of Diseases of Children, 135,* 809–811.

Hare, E.H. (1956). Family setting and the urban distribution of schizophrenia. *Journal of Mental Science, 102,* 753–760.

Hare, R.D. (1970). *Psychopathy: Theory and research.* New York: Wiley.

Hare, R.D. (1983). Diagnosis of antisocial personality disorder in two prison populations. *American Journal of Psychiatry, 140,* 887–890.

Harris, E.L., Noyes, R., Crowe, R.R., & Chaundry, D.R. (1983). Family study of agoraphobia. *Archives of General Psychiatry, 40,* 1061–1064.

Harrow, M., Goldberg, J.F., Grossman, L.S., & Meltzer, H.Y. (1990). Outcome in manic disorders: A naturalistic follow-up study. *Archives of General Psychiatry, 47,* 665–671.

Harrow, M., & Quinlan, D.M. (1985). *Disordered thinking and schizophrenic psychopathology.* New York: Gardner Press.

Harrower-Erikson, M.R., & Steiner, M.E. (1945). *Large scale Rorschach techniques.* Springfield, IL: Charles C. Thomas.

Hartmann, E.L. (1964). *Essays on ego psychology.* New York: International Universities Press.

Hartmann, H. (1958). *Ego psychology and the problem of adaptation.* New York: International Universities Press.

Hartvig, P., & Sterner, G. (1985). Childhood psychologic environmental exposure in women with diagnosed somatoform disorders. *Scandinavian Journal of Social Medicine, 13,* 153–157.

Harvard Medical School Mental Health Letter, 5. (1989, January). Group therapy—Part I. 1–4.

Harwood, H.J. (1984). *Economic cost to society of alcohol and drug abuse and mental illness: 1980.* Washington, DC: ADAMHA.

Hathaway, S.R., & McKinley, J.C. (1943). *Manual for the Minnesota Multiphasic Personality Inventory.* New York: Psychological Corporation.

Hathaway, S.R., & McKinley, J.C. (1951). *Minnesota Multiphasic Personality Inventory: Manual.* New York: Psychological Corporation.

Hathaway, S.R., & McKinley, J.C. (1967). *Minnesota Multiphasic Personality Inventory* (rev. manual). New York: Psychological Corporation.

Hawton, K. (1986). *Suicide and attempted suicide among children and adolescents.* Beverly Hills, CA: Sage.

Hawton, K., & Catalan, J. (1982). *Attempted suicide: A practical guide to its nature and management.* Oxford: Oxford University Press.

Hawton, K., O'Grady, J., Osborn, M., & Cole, D. (1982). Adolescents who take overdoses: Their characteristics, problems, and contacts with helping agencies. *British Journal of Psychiatry, 140*, 118–123.

Hawton, K., Salkovskis, P., & Clark, D. (Eds.). (1989). *Cognitive behaviour therapy.* New York: Oxford University Press.

Hayes, S.C. (1987). A contextual approach to therapeutic change. In N.S. Jacobson (Ed.), *Psychotherapists in clinical practice: Cognitive and behavioral perspectives.* New York: Guilford Press.

Hayes, S.C., Nelson, R.O., & Willis, S.E. (1982). Visual avoidance: The use of slides in a convenient measure of phobic behavior. *Behavioral Assessment, 4*, 211–217.

Haynes, R.B. (1979). Strategies to improve compliance with referrals, appointments, and prescribed medical regiments. In R.G. Haynes, D.W. Taylor, & D.L. Sackett (Eds.), *Compliance in health care.* Baltimore: Johns Hopkins Press.

Hayward, P., Wardle, J., & Higgitt, A. (1989). Benzodiazepine research: Current findings and practical consequences. *British Journal of Psychiatry, 28*, 307–327.

Headlam, H.K., Goldsmith, J., Hanenson, I.B., & Rauh, J.L. (1979). Demographic characteristics of adolescents with self-poisoning: A survey of 235 instances in Cincinnati, Ohio. *Clinical Pediatrics, 18*, 147–154.

Heath, L., Bresolin, L.B., & Rinaldi, R.C. (1989). Effects of media violence on children. *Archives of General Psychiatry, 46*, 376–379.

Hechtman, L., Weiss, G., Perlman, T., & Amsel, R. (1984). Hyperactives as young adults: Initial predictors of adult outcome. *American Academy of Child Psychiatry, 23*, 250–260.

Hedberg, A.G., & Campbell, L. (1974). A comparison of four behavioral treatments of alcoholism. *Journal of Behavior Therapy and Experimental Psychiatry, 5*, 251–256.

Heflinger, C.A. (1987). Psychotherapy research ethics: Continuing the debate on controlled clinical trials. *American Psychologist, 42*, 956–957.

Heiman, J., LoPiccolo, L., & LoPiccolo, J. (1976). *Becoming orgasmic: A sexual growth program for women.* Englewood Cliffs, NJ: Prentice-Hall.

Heiman, J., & Rowland, D. (1983). Affective and physiological sexual response patterns: The effects of instructions on sexually functional and dysfunctional men. *Journal of Psychosomatic Research, 27*, 105–116.

Heimberg, R.G. (1989). Cognitive and behavioral treatments for social phobia: A critical analysis. *Clinical Psychology Review, 9*, 107–128.

Heller, K., & Monahan, J. (1977). *Psychology and community change.* Homewood, IL: Dorsey Press.

Helzer, J.E., Canino, G.J., Yeh, E.-K., Bland, R.C., Lee, C.K., Hwu, H.-G., & Newman, S. (1990). Alcoholism—North America and Asia. *Archives of General Psychiatry, 47*, 313–319.

Helzer, J.E., Robins, L.N., & McEvoy, L. (1987). Post-traumatic stress disorder in the general population. *The New England Journal of Medicine, 317*, 1630–1634.

Helzer, J.E., Spitznagel, E.L., & McEvoy, L. (1987). The predictive validity of lay Diagnostic Interview Schedule diagnoses in the general population. *Archives of General Psychiatry, 44*, 1069–1077.

Henderson, S., Byrne, D.G., & Duncan-Jones, P. (1981). *Neurosis and the social environment.* London: Academic Press.

Hendin, H. (1985). Suicide among the young: Psychodynamics and demography. In M.L. Peck, N.L. Farberow, & R.E. Litman (Eds.), *Youth suicide.* New York: Springer Publications.

Henn, F.A., & DeLisi, L.E. (1987). Conclusions. In F.A. Henn & L.E. DeLisi (Eds.), *Neurochemistry and neuropharmacology of schizophrenia* (Vol. 2). New York: Elsevier.

Herman, C.P., & Polivy, J. (1980). Restrained eating. In A.J. Stunkard (Ed.), *Obesity*, Philadelphia: Saunders.

Herman, C.P., Polivy, J., Lank, C.N., & Heatherton, T.F. (1987). Anxiety, hunger, and eating behavior. *Journal of Abnormal Psychology, 96*, 264–269.

Herman, J., Perry, C., & van der Kolk, B. (1989). Childhood trauma in borderline personality disorder. *American Journal of Psychiatry, 146*, 490–495.

Herrington, B.S. (1987). Alzheimer's costs U.S. billions in care, lost productivity. *Psychiatric News, 22*, 1, 20.

Herzog, D.B. (1988). Eating disorders. In A.M. Nicholi, Jr. (Ed.), *The new Harvard guide to psychiatry.* Cambridge, MA: Harvard University Press.

Heston, L.L. (1966). Psychiatric disorders in foster home reared children of schizophrenic mothers. *British Journal of Psychiatry, 112*, 819–825.

Heston, L.L. (1979). Alzheimer's disease and senile dementia: Genetic relationship to Down's syndrome and hematologic cancer. In R. Katzman (Ed.), *Congenital and acquired cognitive disorders.* New York: Raven Press.

Hetherington, E.M., Cox, M., & Cox, R. (1982). Effects of divorce on parents and children. In M. Lamb (Ed.), *Nontraditional families.* Hillsdale, NJ: Lawrence Erlbaum.

Hilgard, E. (1986). *Divided consciousness.* New York: Wiley.

Hill, B.K., Bruininks, R.H., Lakin, K.C., Hauber, F.A., & McGuire, S.P. (1985). Stability of residential facilities for people who are mentally retarded, 1977–1982. *Mental Retardation, 23*, 108–114.

Hilton, M.E., & Clark, W.B. (1987). Changes in American drinking patterns and problems, 1967–1984. *Journal of Studies on Alcohol, 48*, 515–522.

Hirschfeld, R.M.A. (1990). NIMH collaborative research on the treatment of depression. Comment. *Archives of General Psychiatry, 47*, 685–686.

Hite, S. (1976). *The Hite Report.* New York: Macmillan.

Hjalmarson, A.I.M. (1985). Effect of nicotine chewing gum in smoking cessation. *Journal of the American Medical Association, 252*, 2835–2838.

Hoberman, H.M., Lewinsohn, P.M., & Tilson, M. (1988). Group treatment of depression: Individual predictors of outcome. *Journal of Consulting and Clinical Psychology, 56*, 393–398.

Hofstetter, A.M., Egeland, J.A., & Endicott, J. (1983). Amish study, II: Consensus diagnoses and reliability results. *American Journal of Psychiatry, 140*, 62.

Hofstetter, A., Schutz, Y., Jequier, E., & Warren, J. (1986). Increased 24-hour energy expenditure in cigarette smokers. *The New England Journal of Medicine, 314*, 79–82.

Hogan, R., DeSoto, C.B., & Solano, C. (1977). Traits, tests, and personality research. *American Psychologist, 32*, 255–264.

Hogarty, G.E. (1984). Depot neuroleptics: The relevance of psychosocial factors. A United States perspective. *Journal of Clinical Psychology, 34*, 36–42.

Hoge, S.K., Appelbaum, P.S., & Greer, A. (1989). An empirical comparison of the Stone and dangerousness criteria for civil commitment. *American Journal of Psychiatry, 146*, 170–175.

Hoge, S.K., Sachs, G., Appelbaum, P.S., Greer, A., & Gordon, C. (1988). Limitations on psychiatrists' discretionary civil commitment authority by the Stone and dangerousness criteria. *Archives of General Psychiatry, 45*, 764–769.

Hohmann, A.A., Larson, D.B., Thompson, J.W., & Beardsley, R.S. (1988, November). *Psychotropic medication prescription in U.S. ambulatory medical care.* Paper presented at the American Public Health Association Annual Meeting, Boston, Massachusetts.

Holden, C. (1986). Youth suicide: New research focuses on a growing social problem. *Science, 233*, 839–841.

Holden, C. (1987). Is alcoholism treatment effective? *Science, 236*, 20–22.

Holland, A.J., Hall, A., Murray, R., Russell, G.F.M., & Crisp, A.H. (1984). Anorexia nervosa: A study of 34 pairs of twins and one set of triplets. *British Journal of Psychiatry, 145*, 414–419.

Holland, A.J., Sicotte, N., & Treasure, J. (1988). Anorexia nervosa: Evidence for a genetic basis. *Journal of Psychosomatic Research, 32*, 561–571.

Holland, J.C., & Tross, S. (1985). The psychosocial and neuropsychiatric sequelae of the Acquired Immunodeficiency Syndrome and related disorders. *Annals of Internal Medicine, 103*, 760–764.

Hollingshead, A.B., & Redlich, F.C. (1958). *Social class and mental illness.* New York: John Wiley.

Hollon, S.D., & Beck, A.T. (1979). Cognitive therapy of depression. In P.C. Kendall & S.D. Hollon (Eds.), *Cognitive-behavioral interventions: Theory, research, and procedures*, New York: Academic Press, 153–203.

Hollon, S.D., & Kendall, P.C. (1980). Cognitive self-statements in depression: Development of an Automatic Thoughts Questionnaire. *Cognitive Therapy and Research, 4*, 383–395.

Holmes, T.H., & Rahe, R.H. (1967). The social readjustment rating scale. *Journal of Psychosomatic Research, 11*, 213–218.

Holroyd, K., Penzien, D., Hursey, K., Tobin, D., Rogers, L., Holm, J., Marcille, P., Hall, J., & Chila, A. (1984). Change mechanisms in EMG biofeedback training: Cognitive changes underlying improvements in tension headache. *Journal of Consulting and Clinical Psychology, 52*, 1039–1053.

Holt, P.E., & Andrews, G. (1989). Provocation of panic: Three elements of the panic reaction in four anxiety disorders. *Behaviour Research and Therapy, 27*, 253–262.

Holt, R. (1986). Clinical and statistical prediction: A retrospective and would-be integrative perspective. *Journal of Personality Assessment, 50*, 376–386.

Holzman, P.S., Kringlen, E., Matthysse, S., Flanagan, S.D., Lipton, R.B., Cramer, G., Levin, S., Lange, K., & Lev, D.L. (1988). A single dominant gene can account for eye tracking dysfunctions and schizophrenia in offspring of discordant twins. *Archives of General Psychiatry, 45*, 641–647.

Homant, R.J., & Kennedy, D.B. (1987). Subjective factors in clinicians' judgments of insanity: Comparison of a hypothetical case and an actual case. *Professional Psychology: Research and Practice, 18*, 439–446.

Hommer, D.W., Matsuo, V., & Wolkowitz, O. (1986). Benzodiazepine sensitivity in normal human subjects. *Archives of General Psychiatry, 43*, 542–551.

Honigfeld, G., & Howard, A. (1973). *Psychiatric drugs: A desk reference*. New York: Academy Press.

Hooley, J.M. (1985). Expressed emotion: A review of the critical literature. *Clinical Psychology Review, 5*, 119–139.

Hopkins, B.L. (1987). Comments on the future of applied behavior analysis. *Journal of Applied Behavior, 20*, 339–346.

Hops, S., & Greenwood, C.R. (1981). Social skills deficits. In E.J. Mash & L.G. Terdal (Eds.), *Behavioral assessment of childhood disorders*. New York: Guilford Press.

Horowitz, M.J. (1989). Posttraumatic stress disorders. In *American Psychiatric Association Task Force on Treatments of Psychiatric Disorders* (Vol. 3). Washington, DC: American Psychiatric Association.

Horowitz, M.J. (1988a). *Introduction to psychodynamics: A new synthesis*. New York: Basic Books.

Horowitz, M.J. (Ed.). (1988b). *Psychodynamics and cognition*. Chicago: University of Chicago Press.

Horwitz, R.I., Viscoli, C., Berkman, L., Donaldson, R., Horwitz, S., Murray, C., Ransohoff, D., & Sindelar, J. (1990). Treatment adherence and risk of death after a myocardial infarction. *The Lancet, 336*, 542–545.

House, J.S., Landis, K.R., & Umberson, D. (1988). Social relationships and health. *Science, 241*, 540–544.

House, J.S., Robbins, C., & Metzner, H.M. (1982). The association of social relationships and activities with mortality: Prospective evidence from the Tecumseh community health study. *American Journal of Epidemiology, 116*, 123–140.

Houts, A.C., & Liebert, R.M. (1984). *Bedwetting: A guide for parents and children*. Springfield, IL: Charles C. Thomas.

Houts, A.C., Peterson, J.K., & Liebert, R.M. (1984). The effect of prior imipramine treatment on the results of conditioning therapy in children with enuresis. *Journal of Pediatric Psychology, 9*, 505–509.

Howell, T.H. (1981). Multiple lesions in stroke patients: A study in morbid anatomy. *Journal of the American Geriatric Society, 19*, 246–250.

Hsiao, J.K., Agren, H., Bartko, J.J., Rudorfer, M.V., Linnoila, M., & Potter, W.Z. (1987). Monoamine neurotransmitter interactions and the prediction of antidepressant response. *Archives of General Psychiatry, 44*, 1078–1083.

Hsu, L.K.G. (1987). Are eating disorders becoming more common in blacks? *International Journal of Eating Disorders, 6*, 113–124.

Hsu, L.K.G. (1989). The gender gap in eating disorders: Why are the eating disorders more common among women? *Clinical Psychology Review, 9*, 393–407.

Hsu, L.K.G. (1990). *Eating disorders*. New York: Guilford Press.

Hsu, L.K.G., Chesler, B.E., & Santhouse, R. (1990). Bulimia nervosa in eleven sets of twins: A clinical report. *International Journal of Eating Disorders, 9*, 275–282.

Huber, G.A., Roth, L.H., Appelbaum, P.S., & Ore, T.M. (1982). Hospitalization, arrest, or discharge: Important legal and clinical issues in the emergency evaluation of persons believed dangerous to others. *Law and Contemporary Problems, 45*, 99–123.

Hubert, H.B., Feinleib, M., McNamara, P., & Castelli, W. (1983). Obesity as an independent risk factor for cardiovascular disease: A 26-year follow-up of participants in the Framingham Heart Study. *Circulation, 67*, 968–977.

Hudgens, R.W. (1974). *Psychiatric disorders in adolescents*. Baltimore, MD: Williams & Williams.

Hudson, J.I., & Pope, H.G. (1990). Affective spectrum disorder: Does antidepressant response identify a family of disorders with a common pathophysiology? *American Journal of Psychiatry, 147*, 552–564.

Huesmann, L.R., & Morikawa, S. (1985). Learned helplessness and depression: Cognitive factors in treatment and inoculation. In S. Reiss & R.R. Bootzin (Eds.), *Theoretical issues in behavior therapy* (pp. 361–377). Orlando, FL: Academic Press.

Hugdahl, K. (1978). Electrodermal conditioning to potentially phobic stimuli: Effects of instructed extinction. *Behaviour Research and Therapy, 16*, 315–321.

Hugdahl, K., & Johnsen, B.H. (1989). Preparedness and electrodermal fear-conditioning: Ontogenetic vs. phylogenetic explanations. *Behaviour Research and Therapy, 27*, 269–278.

Hughes, C.C., Tremblay, M., Rapaport, R.N., & Leighton, A.H. (1960). *People of Cove and Woodlot*. New York: Basic Books.

Hughes, C., & Rusch, F.R. (1990). Teaching supported employees with severe mental retardation to solve problems. *Journal of Applied Behavior Analysis, 22*, 365–372.

Hughes, J.O., & Sandler, B.R. (1987). Friends raping friends. *Project on the status and education of women*. Washington, DC: Association of American Colleges.

Hughes, J.R., Gust, S.W., & Pechacek, T.F. (1987). Prevalence of tobacco dependence and withdrawal. *American Journal of Psychiatry, 144*, 205–208.

Hughes, J.R., & Hatsukami, D. (1986). Signs and symptoms of tobacco withdrawal. *Archives of General Psychiatry, 43*, 289–294.

Hulsker, J. (Ed.). (1971). *Van Gogh's "Diary": The artist's life in his own words and art*. New York: William Morrow.

Humphrey, L.L. (1988). Relationships with subtypes of anorexic, bulimic, and normal families. *Journal of the American Academy of Child and Adolescent Psychiatry, 27*, 544–551.

Humphrey, L.L. (1989). Observed family interactions among subtypes of eating disorders using structural analysis of social behavior. *Journal of Consulting and Clinical Psychology, 57*, 206–214.

Hundert, E.M. (1987). A model for ethical problem solving in medicine, with practical applications. *American Journal of Psychiatry, 144*, 839–846.

Hunt, G.M., & Azrin, N.H. (1973). The community-reinforcement approach to alcoholism. *Behaviour Research and Therapy, 11*, 91–104.

Hunt, W.A. (1985). *Alcohol and biological membranes*. New York: Guilford Press.

Hynd, G., & Cohen, M. (1983). *Dyslexia*. New York: Grune & Stratton.

Ignatieff, M. (1988, December). A guide to modern dying. *The New Republic*, pp. 26, 28.

Imber, S.D., Glanz, L.M., Elkin, I., Sotsky, S.M., Boyer, J.L., & Leber, W.R. (1986). Ethical issues in psychotherapy research: Problems in a collaborative clinical trials study. *American Psychologist*, *41*, 137–146.

Ingram, R.E., Lumrey, A.B., Cruet, D., & Seiber, W. (1987). Attentional processes in depressive disorders. *Cognitive Therapy and Research*, *11*, 351–360.

Insel, T.R., Murphy, D.L., Cohen, R.M., Alterman, M., Kilts, G., & Linnoila, M. (1983). Obsessive-compulsive disorder: A double-blind trial of clomipramine and clorgyline. *Archives of General Psychiatry*, *40*, 605–612.

Institute of Medicine/National Academy of Sciences. (1988). *Confronting AIDS*. Washington, DC: National Academy Press.

Irwin, M., Patterson, T., Smith, T.L., Caldwell, Brown, S.A., Gillian, C., & Grant, I. (1990). Reduction of immune function on life stress and depression. *Biological Psychiatry*, *27*, 22–30.

Jacob, R.G., O'Leary, K.D., & Rosenblad, C. (1978). Formal and informal class settings: Effects on hyperactivity. *Journal of Abnormal Child Psychology*, *6*, 47–59.

Jacobs, J. (1971). *Adolescent suicide*. New York: John Wiley-Interscience.

Jacobsen, R. (1986). Female alcoholics: A controlled CT brain scan and clinical study. *British Journal of Addiction*, *81*, 661–669.

Jacobson, E. (1938). *Progressive relaxation*. Chicago: University of Chicago Press.

Jacobson, E. (1971). *Depression*. New York: International Press.

Jacobson, N.S. (1985). The role of observational measures in behavior therapy outcome research. *Behavioral Assessment*, *7*, 297–308.

Jaenicke, C., Hammen, C., Zupan, B., Hiroto, D., Gordon, D., Adrian, C., & Burge, D. (1987). Cognitive vulnerability in children at risk for depression. *Journal of Abnormal Child Psychology*, *15*, 559–572.

Janis, I. (1983). The role of social support in adherence to stressful decisions. *American Psychologist*, *38*, 143–160.

Janowsky, D.S., & Rausch, J. (1985). Biochemical hypotheses of premenstrual tension syndrome. *Psychological Medicine*, *15*, 3–8.

Jaskiw, G.E., Andreasen, N.C., & Weinberger, D.R. (1987). X-ray computed tomography and magnetic resonance imaging in psychiatry. In R.E. Hales & A.J. Frances (Eds.), *Annual review of psychiatry* (Vol. 6). Washington, DC: American Psychiatric Association.

Jeffery, R.W., Folsom, A., Luepker, R., & Jacobs, D. (1984). Prevalence of overweight and weight loss behavior in a metropolitan adult population: The Minnesota heart survey experience. *American Journal of Public Health*, *74*, 349–352.

Jemmott, J.B., III. (1987). Social motives and susceptibility to disease: Stalking individual differences in health risks. *Journal of Personality*, *55*, 267–298.

Jemott, J.B., & Magliore, K. (1988). Academic stress, social support, and secretory immunoglobulin A. *Journal of Personality and Social Psychology*, *55*, 803–810.

Jenike, M.A. (1986). Alzheimer's disease: Clinical care and management. *Psychosomatics*, *27*, 407–416.

Jersild, A.T., & Holmes, F.B. (1935). Children's fears. *Child Development Monographs*, *20*, 1–358.

Johnson, R.T. (1979). Viral etiology in amentias and dementias. In R. Katzman (Ed.), *Congenital and acquired cognitive disorders*. New York: Raven Press.

Johnson, S.B., & Melamed, D.G. (1979). The assessment and treatment of children's fears. In B. Lahey & A.E. Kazdin (Eds.), *Advances in clinical psychology* (Vol. 2). New York: Plenum.

Jones, B.P., & Butters, N. (1990). Neuropsychological assessment. In M. Hersen, A. Kazdin, & A. Bellack (Eds.), *The clinical psychology handbook*. New York: Pergamon Press.

Jones, D.J., Fox, M.M., Babigian, H.M., & Hutton, H.E. (1980). Epidemiology of anorexia nervosa in Monroe County, New York: 1960–1979. *Psychosomatic Medicine*, *42*, 551–558.

Jones, E. (1953). *The life and work of Sigmund Freud. Vol. I: The formative years and the great discoveries*. New York: Basic Books.

Jones, L.A. (1979). Census-based prevalence estimates for mental retardation. *Mental Retardation*, *17*, 199–201.

Jones, M.C. (1924). The elimination of children's fears. *Journal of Experimental Psychology*, *7*, 383–390.

Jung, C.G. (1923). *Psychological types*. New York: Harcourt.

Justice, B., & Justice, R. (1979). *The broken taboo: Sex in the family*. New York: Human Sciences Press.

Kagan, D.M., & Squires, R.L. (1983). Dieting, compulsive eating, and feelings of failure among adolescents. *International Journal of Eating Disorders*, *3*, 15–26.

Kagan, J. (1989). Temperamental contributions to social behavior. *American Psychologist*, *44*, 668–674.

Kaij, J. (1960). *Studies on the etiology and sequels of abuse of alcohol*. Lund, Sweden: University of Lund.

Kallmann, F.J. (1953). *Heredity in health and mental disorder*. New York: W.W. Norton.

Kalucy, R.S., Crisp, A.H., & Harding, B. (1977). A study of 56 families with anorexia nervosa. *British Journal of Medical Psychology*, *50*, 381–395.

Kandel, D.B. (1984). Marijuana users in young adulthood. *Archives of General Psychiatry*, *41*, 200–209.

Kandel, D.B., & Davies, M. (1982). Epidemiology of depressive mood in adolescents: An empirical study. *Archives of General Psychiatry*, *39*, 1205–1212.

Kandel, D.B., Davies, M., Karus, D., & Yamaguchi, K. (1986). The consequences in young adulthood of adolescent drug involvement. *Archives of General Psychiatry*, *43*, 746–754.

Kane, J., Honigfeld, G., Singer, J., Meltzer, H., & and the Clozaril Collaborative Study Group. (1988). Clozapine for the treatment-resistant schizophrenic. *Archives of General Psychiatry*, *45*, 789–796.

Kane, J., Woerner, M., Weinhold, P., Wegner, B., & Kinon, B. (1982). A prospective study of tardive dyskinesia development: Preliminary results. *Journal of Clinical Psychology*, *2*, 345–349.

Kanfer, F.H. (1970). Self-monitoring: Methodological limitations and clinical applications. *Journal of Consulting and Clinical Psychology*, *35*, 148–152.

Kanfer, F.H. (1977). The many faces of self-control, or behavior modification changes its focus. In R.B. Stuart (Ed.), *Behavioral self-management*. New York: Brunner/Mazel.

Kanfer, F.H. (1985). Target selection for clinical change programs. *Behavioral Assessment*, *7*, 7–20.

Kanfer, F.H., & Goldstein, A.P. (Eds.). (1975). *Helping people change*. New York: Pergamon Press.

Kanfer, F.H., & Saslow, G. (1965). Behavioral diagnosis. *Archives of General Psychiatry*, *12*, 529–538.

Kanfer, F.H., & Saslow, G. (1969). Behavioral diagnosis. In C.M. Franks (Ed.), *Behavior therapy: Appraisal and status*. New York: McGraw-Hill.

Kanner, A.D., Coyne, J.C., Schaefer, C., & Lazarus, R.S. (1981). Comparison of two modes of stress measurement: Daily hassles and uplifts versus major life events. *Journal of Behavioral Medicine*, *4*, 1–39.

Kanner, L. (1943). Autistic disturbances of affective contact. *Nervous Child*, *2*, 217–230.

Kanner, L. (1971). Follow-up study of eleven autistic children originally reported in 1943. *Journal of Autism and Childhood Schizophrenia*, *1*, 119–145.

Kaplan, H.I., & Sadock, B.J. (Eds.). (1988). *Synopsis of psychiatry: Behavioral sciences and clinical psychiatry* (5th ed.). Baltimore: Williams & Wilkins.

Kaplan, H.S. (1974). *The new sex therapy*. New York: Brunner/Mazel.

Kaplan, H.S. (1979). *Disorders of sexual desire*. New York: Brunner/Mazel.

Kaplan, M. (1983). A woman's view of *DSM-III*. *American Psychologist*, *38*, 786–792.

Kardish, S., Hillman, E., & Werry, J. (1968). Efficacy of imipramine in childhood enuresis. *Canadian Medical Association Journal*, *99*, 263–266.

Karlsson, J.L. (1973). An Icelandic family study of schizophrenia. *British Journal of Psychiatry*, *123*, 549–554.

Karno, M., Golding, J.M., Sorenson, S.B., & Burnam, M.A. (1988). The epidemiology of obsessive-compulsive disorder in five U.S. communities. *Archives of General Psychiatry*, *45*, 1094–1099.

Karno, M., Hough, R.L., Burnam, M.A., Escobar, J.I., Timbers, D.M., Santana, F., & Boyd, J.H. (1987). Lifetime prevalence of specific psychiatric disorders among Mexican Americans and non-Hispanic whites in Los Angeles. *Archives of General Psychiatry*, *44*, 695–701.

Kasl, S.V., Evans, A.S., & Niederman, J.C. (1979). Psychosocial risk factors in the development of infectious mononucleosis. *Psychosomatic Medicine*, *41*, 445–466.

Kass, F., Skodol, A., Charles, E., Spitzer, R., & Williams, J. (1985). Scaled ratings of *DSM-III* personality disorders. *American Journal of Psychiatry*, *142*, 627–630.

Kaszniak, A.W., Nussbaum, P.D., Berren, M.R., & Santiago, J. (1988). Amnesia as a consequence of male rape: A case report. *Journal of Abnormal Psychology*, *97*, 100–104.

Katon, W., Lin, E., Von Korff, M., Russo, J., Lipscomb, P., & Bush, T. (1991). Somatization: A spectrum of severity. *American Journal of Psychiatry*, *148*, 34–40.

Katzman, M.A., & Wolchik, S.A. (1984). Bulimia and binge eating in college women: A comparison of personality and behavioral characteristics. *Journal of Consulting and Clinical Psychology*, *52*, 423–428.

Katzman, M.A., Wolchik, S.A., & Braver, S.L. (1984). The prevalence of frequent binge eating and bulimia in a nonclinical college sample. *International Journal of Eating Disorders*, *3*, 53–56.

Katzman, R. (1986). Alzheimer's disease. *New England Journal of Medicine*, *314*, 964–973.

Kaufmann, P., & Lilly, M. (1979). A recovering alcoholic speaks and her family therapist introduces her. In E. Kaufmann & P.N. Kaufmann (Eds.), *Family therapy of drug and alcohol abuse* (pp. 243 254). New York: Gardner Press.

Kaye, W.H., Ebert, M.H., Raleigh, M., & Lake, R. (1984). Abnormalities in CNS monoamine metabolism in anorexia nervosa. *Archives of General Psychiatry*, *41*, 350–355.

Kazdin, A.E. (1981). Drawing valid inferences from case studies. *Journal of Consulting and Clinical Psychology*, *49*, 183.

Kazdin, A.E. (1982). Symptom substitution, generalization, and response covariation: Implications for psychotherapy outcome. *Psychological Bulletin*, *91*, 349–365.

Kazdin, A.E. (1984). *Behavior modification in applied settings*. Homewood, IL: Dorsey Press.

Kazdin, A.E. (1985). Selection of target behaviors: The relationship of the treatment focus to clinical dysfunction. *Behavioral Assessment*, *7*, 33–47.

Kazdin, A.E. (1987). *Conduct disorders in childhood and adolescence*. Newbury Park, CA: Sage.

Kazdin, A.E. (1989). *Behavior modification in applied settings*. Pacific Grove, CA: Brooks/Cole.

Kazdin, A.E., Bass, D., Siegel, T., & Thomas, C. (1989). Cognitive-behavioral therapy and relationship therapy in the treatment of children referred for antisocial behavior. *Journal of Consulting and Clinical Psychology*, *57*, 522–535.

Kazdin, A.E., French, N., & Sherick, R. (1981). Acceptability of alternative treatments for children: Evaluations by inpatient children, parents and staff. *Journal of Consulting and Clinical Psychology*, *9*, 900–906.

Kazdin, A.E., French, N.H., Unis, A.S., Esveldt-Dawson, K., & Sherick, R.B. (1983). Hopelessness, depression, and suicidal intent among psychiatrically disturbed in-patient children. *Journal of Consulting and Clinical Psychology*, *51*, 504–510.

Kazdin, A.E., & Wilson, G.T. (1978). *Evaluation of behavior therapy: Issues, evidence, and research strategies*. Cambridge, MA: Ballinger.

Keane, T.M., & Kaloupek, D. (1982). Imaginal flooding in the treatment of a posttraumatic stress disorder. *Journal of Consulting and Clinical Psychology*, *50*, 138–140.

Keefe, J.A., & Magaro, P.A. (1980). Creativity and schizophrenia: An equivalence of cognitive processing. *Journal of Abnormal Psychology*, *89*, 390–398.

Kelly, J.A., St. Lawrence, J.S., & Brasfield, T.L. (1991). Predictors of vulnerability to AIDS risk behavior relapse. *Journal of Consulting and Clinical Psychology*, *59*, 163–166.

Kelso, J.R., Ginns, E.E., Egeland, J.A., Gerhard, D.S., Goldstein, A.M., Bale, S.J., Pauls, D.L., Long, R.T., Kidd, K.K., Conte, G., Houseman, D.E., & Paul, S. (1989). Re-evaluation of the linkage relationship between chromosome 11p loci and the gene for affective disorder in the Old Order Amish. *Journal of Psychosomatic Research*, *21*, 577–580.

Kelso, J.R., Cadet, J.L., Pickar, D., & Weinberger, D.R. (1988). Quantitative neuroanatomy in schizophrenia. *Archives of General Psychiatry*, *45*, 533–541.

Kemeny, M.E., Cohen, F., Zegans, L.S., & Conant, M.A. (1989). Psychological and immunological predictors of genital herpes recurrence. *Psychosomatic Medicine*, *51*, 195–208.

Kendall, P.C., & Braswell, L. (1985). *Cognitive-behavioral therapy for impulsive children*. New York: Guilford Press.

Kendler, K.S. (1986). Genetics of schizophrenia. In A.J. Frances & R.E. Hales (Eds.), *American Psychiatric Association Annual Review* (Vol. 5). Washington, DC: American Psychiatric Press.

Kendler, K.S., Heath, A.C., Martin, N.G., & Eaves, L.J. (1987). Symptoms of anxiety and symptoms of depression. *Archives of General Psychiatry*, *44*, 451–457.

Kennard, D. (1983). *The therapeutic communities*. London: Routledge.

Kennedy, S., Thomson, R., Strancer, H.C., Roy, A., & Persad, E. (1983). Life events precipitating mania. *British Journal of Psychiatry*, *142*, 398–403.

Kennedy, W.A. (1965). School phobia: Rapid treatment of fifty cases. *Journal of Abnormal Psychology*, *70*, 285–289.

Kenny, D.A. (1975). A quasi-experimental approach to assessing treatment effects in the non-equivalent control group design. *Psychological Bulletin*, *82*, 345–362.

Kent, R., & O'Leary, K.D. (1976). A controlled evaluation of behavior modification with conduct problem children. *Journal of Consulting and Clinical Psychology*, *44*, 586–596.

Kern, H.F., & Lewy, A.J. (1990). Corrections and additions to the history of light therapy and seasonal affective disorder. *American Journal of Psychiatry*, *147*, 90–91.

Kernberg, O. (1967). Borderline personality organization. *Journal of American Psychoanalytic Association*, *15*, 641–685.

Kernberg, O. (1970). Factors in the psychoanalytic treatment of narcissistic personalities. *Journal of the American Psychoanalytic Association*, *19*, 451–471.

Kesey, K. (1962). *One flew over the cuckoo's nest*. New York: Viking Press.

Kety, S.S., Rosenthal, D., Wender, P.H., & Schulsinger, F. (1968). The types and prevalence of mental illness in the biological and adoptive families of adopted schizophrenics. In D. Rosenthal & S.S. Kety (Eds.), *The transmission of schizophrenia*. Elmsford, NY: Pergamon Press.

Kety, S.S., Rosenthal, D., Wender, P.H., Schulsinger, F., & Jacobson, B. (1978). The biological and adoptive families of adopted individuals who became schizophrenic: Prevalence of mental illness and other characteristics. In L.C. Wynne, R.L. Cromwell, & S. Matthysse (Eds.), *The nature of schizophrenia: New approaches to research and treatment*. New York: John Wiley.

Keys, A., Brozek, J., Henschel, A., Mickelsen, O., & Taylor, H. (1950). *The biology of human starvation*. Minneapolis: University of Minnesota Press.

Khanna, S., Desai, N.G., & Channabasavanna, S.M. (1987). A treatment package for transsexualism. *Behavior Therapy*, *18*, 193–199.

Khantzian, E.J. (1985). The self-medication hypothesis of addictive disorders: Focus on heroin and cocaine dependence. *American Journal of Psychiatry*, *142*, 1259–1264.

Khantzian, E.J., & Treece, C. (1985). DSM-III psychiatric diagnosis of narcotic addicts. *Archives of General Psychiatry*, *42*, 1067–1071.

Kiecolt-Glaser, J.K., & Glaser, R. (1987). Psychosocial moderators of immune function. *Annals of Behavioral Medicine*, *9*, 16–20.

Kiesler, C.A., & Sibulkin, A.E. (1987). *Mental hospitals: Myths and facts about a national crisis*. Newbury Park, CA: Sage.

Killen, J.D., Fortmann, S.P., & Newman, B. (1990). Weight change among participants in a large sample minimal contact smoking relapse prevention trial. *Addictive Behaviors*, *15*, 323–332.

Kilmann, P.R., Boland, J.P., Norton, S.P., Davidson, E., & Caird, C. (1986). Perspectives on sex therapy outcome: A survey of ASSECT providers. *Journal of Sex and Marital Therapy*, *12*, 116–138.

Kiloh, L.G. (1982). Electroconvulsive

therapy. In E.S. Paykel (Ed.), *Handbook of affective disorders*. New York: Guilford Press.

Kilpatrick, D.G., & Calhoun, K.S. (1988). Early behavior treatment for rape trauma: Efficacy or artifact? *Behavior Therapy, 19*, 421–428.

Kimble, G.A. (1985). Conditioning and learning. In S. Koch & D.E. Leary (Eds.), *A century of psychology as science* (pp. 284–321). New York: McGraw-Hill.

Kimmel, D.C. (1988). Ageism, psychology, and public policy. *American Psychologist, 43*, 175–178.

Kinsey, A.C., Pomeroy, W.B., & Martin, C.E. (1948). *Sexual behavior in the human male*. Philadelphia: Saunders.

Kinsey, A.C., Pomeroy, W.B., Martin, C.E., & Gebhard, P.H. (1953). *Sexual behavior in the human female*. Philadelphia: Saunders.

Kirp, D.L., Epstein, S., Franks, M.S., Simon, J., Conaway, D., & Lewis, J. (1989). *Learning by heart*. New Brunswick, NJ: Rutgers University Press.

Kissin, B. (1982). A historical review of drugs and alcohol use. In J. Solomon & K.A. Keeley (Eds.), *Perspectives in alcohol and drug abuse: Similarities and differences*. Boston: John Wright.

Kivlahan, D.R., Marlatt, G.A., Fromme, K., Coppel, D.B., & Williams, E. (1990). Secondary prevention with college drinkers: Evaluation of an alcohol skills training program. *Journal of Consulting and Clinical Psychology, 58*, 805–810.

Klein, D., & Davis, J.M. (1969). *Diagnosis and drug treatment of psychiatric disorders*. Baltimore, MD: Williams & Wilkins.

Klein, D.F. (1981). Anxiety reconceptualized. In D.F. Klein & J. Rabkin (Eds.), *Anxiety: New research and changing concepts*. New York: Raven Press.

Klein, D.F., Ross, D.C., & Cohen, P. (1987). Panic and avoidance in agoraphobia. *Archives of General Psychiatry, 44*, 377–385.

Klein, D.F., Zitrin, C.M., Woerner, M.G., & Ross, D.C. (1983). Treatment of phobias. *Archives of General Psychiatry, 40*, 139–145.

Klein, M. (1940). Mourning and its relation to manic-depressive states. In *Contributions to Psychoanalysis, 1921–1945* (pp. 311–338). London: Hogarth Press.

Klein, N.C., Alexander, J., & Parsons, B.V. (1977). Impact of family systems intervention on recidivism and sibling delinquency: A model of primary prevention and program evaluation. *Journal of Consulting and Clinical Psychology, 45*, 469–474.

Kleinman, A. (1988). *Rethinking psychiatry: From cultural category to personal experience*. New York: Free Press.

Klerman, G.L. (1982). Practical issues in the treatment of mania and depression. In E.S. Paykel (Ed.), *Handbook of affective disorders* (pp. 438–452). New York: Guilford Press.

Klerman, G.L. (1985). Diagnosis of panic states: A North American view. In M.H. Lader & H.C. Davies (Eds.), *Drug treatment of neurotic disorders: Focus of alprazolam*. New York: Churchill Livingstone.

Klerman, G.L. (1987, May 4). The suicide link. *Newsweek*, p. 52.

Klerman, G.L. (1988). Depression and related disorders of mood (affective disorders). In A.M. Nicholi, Jr. (Ed.), *The Harvard guide to psychiatry*. Cambridge, MA: Harvard University Press.

Klerman, G.L. (1990). NIMH collaborative research on the treatment of depression [Comment]. *Archives of General Psychiatry, 47*, 687–688.

Klerman, G.L. (in press). The psychiatric patient's right to effective treatment: Implications of *Osheroff v. Chestnut Lodge. American Journal of Psychiatry*.

Klerman, G.L., Weissman, M.M., Rounsaville, B.J., & Chevron, E. (1984). *Interpersonal psychotherapy of depression*. New York: Basic Books.

Kluft, R.P. (1986). High-functioning multiple personality patients. *The Journal of Nervous and Mental Disease, 174*, 722–726.

Kluft, R.P. (1987a). An update on multiple personality disorder. *Hospital and Community Psychiatry, 38*, 363–373.

Kluft, R.P. (1987b). First-rank symptoms as a diagnostic clue to multiple personality disorder. *American Journal of Psychiatry, 144*, 293–298.

Klug, W.S., and Cummings, M.R. (1986). *Concepts of genetics*. Glenview, IL.: Scott Foresman & Company.

Knapczyk, D.R. (1989). Generalization of student question asking from special class to regular class settings. *Journal of Applied Behavior Analysis, 22*, 77–84.

Knapp, S., & VandeCreek, L. (1990). Application of the duty to protect to HIV-positive patients. *Professional Psychology: Research and Practice, 21*, 161–166.

Kofoed, L.L. (1987). Chemical monitoring of disulfiram compliance: A study of alcoholic outpatients. *Alcoholism, 11*, 481–485.

Kohlenberg, R.J. (1973). Behavior approach to multiple personality: A case study. *Behavior Therapy, 4*, 137–140.

Kohn, M.L. (1968). Social class and schizophrenia: A critical review. In D. Rosenthal & S.S. Kety (Eds.), *The transmission of schizophrenia*. Elmsford, NY: Pergamon Press.

Kohut, H. (1971). The analysis of the self. *Monograph Series of the Psychoanalytic Study of the Child*. New York: International Universities Press.

Kohut, H. (1972). Thoughts on narcissism and narcissistic rage. *Psychoanalytic Studies of the Child, 27*, 360–400.

Kohut, H. (1977). *The restoration of the self*. New York: International Universities Press.

Kolata, G. (1987). Manic-depression: Is it inherited? *Science, 232*, 575–576.

Kolotkin, R.A., Wielkiewicz, R.M., Judd, B., & Weiser, S. (1983). Behavioral components of assertion: Comparison of univariate and multivariate assessment strategies. *Behavioral Assessment, 6*, 61–78.

Koranyi, E.K. (1986). Mental retardation: Medical aspects. *Psychiatric Clinics of North America, 9*, 635–645.

Kosky, R. (1983). Childhood suicidal behavior. *Journal of Child Psychology and Psychiatry, 24*, 257–468.

Koss, C.A., Gidycz, C.A., & Wisniewski, N. (1987). The scope of rape: Incidence and prevalence of sexual aggression and victimization in a national sample of higher education students. *Journal of Consulting and Clinical Psychology, 55*, 162–170.

Koss, M.P., Dinero, T.E., Seibel, C.A., & Cox, S.L. (1988). Stranger and acquaintance rape: Are there differences in the victim's experience? *Psychology of Women Quarterly, 12*, 1–24.

Kovacs, M., & Beck, A.T. (1977). An empirical clinical approach toward definition of childhood depression. In J.B. Schulterbrandt (Ed.), *Depression in childhood: Diagnosis, treatment, and conceptual models*. New York: Raven Press.

Kovacs, M., & Beck, A.T. (1978). Maladaptive cognitive structures in depression. *American Journal of Psychiatry, 135*, 525–533.

Kovacs, M., Beck, A.T., & Weissman, M.M. (1975). The use of suicidal motives in the psychotherapy of attempted suicides. *American Journal of Psychiatry, 29*, 363–368.

Kozol, B.R., Boucher, R., & Garofalo, R. (1972). The diagnosis and treatment of dangerousness. *Crime and Delinquency, 18*, 371–392.

Kraepelin, E. (1896). *Dementia praecox and paraphrenia*. Edinburgh: Livingston.

Kraepelin, E. (1913). *Psychiatry: A textbook*. Leipzig: Barth.

Kraepelin, E. (1915). *Clinical psychiatry*. New York: Macmillan.

Kraepelin, E. (1971). *Dementia praecox and paraphrenia* (R.M. Barclay, Trans.). New York: Huntington. (Original work published 1896, Edinburgh: Livingstone)

Krafft-Ebing, R. von. (1965). *Psychopathica sexualis*. New York: Putnam. (Original work published 1886)

Krakowski, A.J. (1982). Stress and the practice of medicine: II. Stressors, stresses, and strains. *Psychotherapy and Psychosomatics, 38*, 11–23.

Kramer, J.H. (1990). Guidelines for interpreting WAIS-R subtest scores. *Psychological Assessment, 2*, 202–205.

Kramer, M. (1977). *Psychiatric services and the changing institutional scene, 1950–1985* (DHEW Publication No. ADM 77-433). Washington, DC: U.S. Government Printing Office.

Krane, R.J., Goldstein, I., & DeTejada, I.S. (1989). Impotence. *The New England Journal of Medicine, 321*, 1648–1657.

Krauthammer, C., & Klerman, G.L. (1979). The epidemiology of mania. In B. Shopsin (Ed.), *Manic illness* (pp. 11–18). New York: Raven Press.

Kreiner, S., Simonsen, E., & Mogensen, J.

(1990). Validation of a personality inventory scale: The MCMI P-scale (paranoia). *Journal of Personality Disorders*, *4*, 303–311.

Kroll, J. (1988). *The challenge of the borderline patient: Competence in diagnosis and treatment.* New York: W.W. Norton.

Krull, M. (1986). *Freud and his father.* New York: W.W. Norton.

Kuhn, R. (1958). The treatment of depressive states with G 22355 (imipramine hydrochloride). *American Journal of Psychiatry*, *115*, 459–464.

Kuiper, N.A. (1978). Depression and causal attributions for success and failure. *Journal of Personality and Social Psychology*, *36*, 236–246.

Kumanyika, S. (1987). Obesity in black women. *Epidemiologic Reviews*, *9*, 31–50.

La Rue, A. (1982). Memory loss and aging: Distinguishing dementia from benign senescent forgetfulness and depressive pseudodementia. *Psychiatric Clinics of North America*, *5*, 89–103.

Lacey, J.H. (1983). Bulimia nervosa, binge-eating, and psychogenic vomiting: A controlled treatment study and long-term outcome. *British Journal of Psychiatry*, *286*, 1609–1612.

Lacey, J.H., & Crisp, A.H. (1980). Hunger, food intake, and weight. The impact of clomipramine on a refeeding anorexia nervosa population. *Postgraduate Medical Journal*, *56*, 79–85.

Lader, M.H. (1985). Scope of clinical use of benzodiazepines. In M.H. Lader & H.C. Davies (Eds.), *Drug treatment of neurotic disorders: Focus on alprazolam.* New York: Churchill Livingstone.

Lader, M., & Sartorius, N. (1968). Anxiety in patients with hysterical conversion symptoms. *Journal of Neurology, Neurosurgery and Psychiatry*, *31*, 490–495.

Laessle, R.G., Schweiger, U., Fichter, M., & Pirke, K.M. (1988). Eating disorders and depression: Psychobiological findings. In K.M. Pirke, W. Vandereycken, & D. Ploog (Eds.), *The psychobiology of bulimia nervosa.* New York: Springer-Verlag.

Laessle, R.G., Tuschl, R.J., Waadt, S., & Pirke, K.M. (1989). The specific psychopathology of bulimia nervosa: A comparison with restrained and unrestrained (normal) eaters. *Journal of Consulting and Clinical Psychology*, *57*, 772–775.

Laessle, R.G., Wittchen, H.U., Fichter, M.M., & Pirke, K.M. (1989). The significance of subgroups of bulimia and anorexia nervosa: Lifetime frequency of psychiatric disorders. *International Journal of Eating Disorders*, *8*, 569–574.

LaGreca, A.M., & Santogrossi, D.A. (1981). Social skills training with elementary school students: A behavioral group approach. *Journal of Consulting and Clinical Psychology*, *48*, 220–227.

Lahey, B.B., Hartdagen, S.E., Frick, P.J., McBurnett, K., O'Connor, R., & Hynd, G.W. (1988). Conduct disorder: Parsing the confounded relation to parental divorce and antisocial personality. *Journal of Abnormal Psychology*, *97*, 334–337.

Laing, R.D. (1967). *The politics of experience.* New York: Pantheon Books.

Laing, R.D., & Esterson, A. (1970). *Sanity, madness and the family: Families of schizophrenics.* Baltimore, MD: Pelican.

Lamb, H.R., & Grace, R.W. (1982). The mentally ill in an urban county jail. *Archives of General Psychiatry*, *39*, 17–22.

Lamb, H.R., Weinberger, L.E., & Gross, B.H. (1988). Court-mandated community outpatient treatment for persons found not guilty by reason of insanity: A five-year follow-up. *American Journal of Psychiatry*, *145*, 450–456.

Lambert, M.J., Shapiro, D.A., & Bergin, A.E. (1986). The effectiveness of psychotherapy. In S.L. Garfield & A.E. Bergin (Eds.), *Handbook of psychotherapy and behavior change* (3rd ed.). New York: John Wiley.

Landesman, S., & Butterfield, E.C. (1987). Normalization and deinstitutionalization of mentally retarded individuals. *American Psychologist*, *42*, 809–816.

Lang, P.J. (1969). The mechanics of desensitization and the laboratory study of fear. In C.M. Franks (Ed.), *Behavior therapy: Appraisal and status.* New York: McGraw-Hill.

Lang, P.J. (1985). The cognitive psychophysiology of emotion: Fear and anxiety. In A.H. Tuma & J.D. Maser (Eds.), *Anxiety and the anxiety disorders.* Hillsdale, NJ: Lawrence Erlbaum.

Lang, P.J., Levin, D.N., Miller, G.A., & Kozak, M.J. (1983). Fear, behavior, fear imagery, and the psychophysiology of emotion: The problem of affective response integration. *Journal of Abnormal Psychology*, *92*, 276–306.

Langenbucher, J.W., Nathan, P.E., & Niaura, R.S. (1991). Alcoholic drinking in a normative tavern setting: Tension reduction reconsidered. Unpublished manuscript, Rutgers University.

Lanyon, R.I. (1984). Personality assessment. *Annual Review of Psychology*, *35*, 667–701.

Lanyon, R.I. (1986). Theory and treatment in child molestation. *Journal of Consulting and Clinical Psychology*, *54*, 176–182.

Lanyon, R.I., & Goodstein, L.D. (1982). *Personality assessment* (2nd ed.). New York: Wiley-Interscience.

Lanyon, R.I., & Lanyon, B.P. (1980). Behavioral assessment and decision-making: The design of strategies for therapeutic behavior change. In M.P. Feldman & A. Broadhurst (Eds.), *Theoretical and experimental bases of the behavior therapies.* London and New York: John Wiley.

Lapouse, R., & Monk, M.A. (1959). Fears and worries of a representative sample of children. *American Journal of Orthopsychiatry*, *29*, 803–818.

Lapouse, R., & Weitzner, M. (1970). Epidemiology. In J. Wortis (Ed.), *Mental retardation: An annual review, I.* New York: Grune & Stratton.

Larson, R.W., Rafaelli, M., Richards, M.H., Ham, M., & Jewell, L. (1990). Ecology of depression in late childhood and early adolescence: A profile of daily states and activities. *Journal of Abnormal Psychology*, *99*, 92–102.

Last, C.G., & Blanchard, E.B. (1982). Classification of phobics versus fearful nonphobics: Procedural and theoretical issues. *Behavioral Assessment*, *4*, 195–210.

Laties, V.G., & Weiss, B. (1966, March). Performance enhancement by the amphetamines: A new appraisal. *Proceedings of the 5th International Congress of the Collegium International Neuropsychopharmacologicum.* Washington, DC.

Laudenslager, M.L., Ryan, S.M., Drugan, R.C., Hyson, R.L., & Maier, S.F. (1979). Coping and immunosuppression: Inescapable but not escapable shock suppresses lymphocytes proliferation. *Science*, *221*, 568–570.

Lavy, S., Melamed, E., Cooper, G., Bentin, S., & Rinot, Y. (1979). Regional cerebral blood flow in patients with Parkinson's disease. *Archives of Neurology*, *36*, 344–348.

Laws, D.R. (Ed.). (1989). *Relapse prevention with sex offenders.* New York: Guilford Press.

Lazarus, A.A. (1981). *The practice of multimodal therapy.* New York: McGraw-Hill.

Lazarus, A.A. (1989). Why I am an eclectic (not an integrationist). *British Journal of Guidance and Counseling*, *17*, 248–258.

Lazarus, L.W., Newton, N., Cohler, B., Lesser, J., & Schweon, C. (1987). Frequency and presentation of depressive symptoms in patients with primary degenerative dementia. *American Journal of Psychiatry*, *144*, 41–45.

Lazarus, R.S., & Folkman, S. (1984). *Stress, appraisal, and coping.* New York: Springer-Verlag.

Leber, W.R., Parsons, O.A., & Nichols, N. (1985). Neuropsychological test results are related to ratings of men alcoholics' therapeutic progress: A replicated study. *Journal of Studies on Alcohol*, *46*, 116–121.

Lederer, W.J., & Burdick, E. (1958). *The ugly American.* New York: W.W. Norton.

Lee, N.L., & Rush, A.J. (1986). Cognitive-behavioral group therapy for bulimia. *International Journal of Eating Disorders*, *5*, 599–615.

LeFebvre, R.C., Cobb, G.D., Goreczny, A.J., & Carleton, R.A. (1990). Efficacy of an incentive-based community smoking cessation program. *Addictive Behaviors*, *15*, 403–411.

Leff, J., Kuipers, L., Berkowitz, R., Eberlein-Vreis, R., & Sturgeon, D. (1982). A controlled trial of social intervention in the families of schizophrenic patients. *British Journal of Psychiatry*, *141*, 121–134.

Lefkowitz, M.M., Eron, L.D., Walden, L.O., & Heusmann, L.R. (1977). *Growing up to be violent*. New York: Pergamon Press.

Lehrer, P.M., & Woolfolk, R.L. (1982). Self-report assessment of anxiety: Somatic, cognitive, and behavioral modalities. *Behavioral Assessment, 4*, 167–177.

Lehrer, P.M., & Woolfolk, R.L. (1984). Are stress reduction techniques interchangeable, or do they have specific effects? A review of the comparative empirical literature. In R.L. Woolfolk & P.M. Lehrer (Eds.), *Principles and practices of stress management*. New York: Guilford Press.

Leiblum, S.R., & Rosen, R.C. (Eds.). (1988). *Sexual desire disorders*. New York: Guilford Press.

Leitenberg, H., Gross, J., Peterson, J., & Rosen, J.C. (1964). Analysis of an anxiety model and the process of change during exposure and response prevention treatment of bulimia nervosa. *Behavior Therapy, 15*, 1–20.

Lemere, F., & Voegtlin, W.L. (1950). An evaluation of the aversion treatment of alcoholism. *Quarterly Journal of Studies on Alcohol, 11*, 199–204.

Leohlin, J.C. (1977). An analysis of alcohol-related questionnaire items from the National Merit twin study. In F.A. Seixas, G.S. Omenn, E.D. Burk, & S. Eggleston (Eds.), *Annals of the New York Academy of Sciences, 197*, 117–120.

Leonard, C.V. (1977). The MMPI as a suicide predictor. *Journal of Consulting and Clinical Psychology, 45*, 367–377.

Leonard, H.L., Swedo, S.E., Rapoport, J.L., Koby, E.V., Lenane, M.C., Cheslow, D.L., & Hamburger, S.D. (1989). Treatment of obsessive-compulsive disorder with clomipramine and desipramine in children and adolescents. *Archives of General Psychiatry, 46*, 1088–1092.

Lerer, R.J., Lerer, P.M., & Artner, J. (1977). The effects of methylphenidate on the handwriting of children with minimal brain dysfunction. *Journal of Pediatrics, 91*, 121–132.

Lerner, P.M. (1984). Projective techniques and personality assessment: The current perspective. In N.S. Endler & J.M. Hunt (Eds.), *Personality and the behavior disorders*. New York: John Wiley.

Lesse, S. (1981). Hypochondriacal and psychosomatic disorders masking depression in adolescence. *American Journal of Psychotherapy, 35*, 356–367.

Levenson, D. (1988). Marital violence across cultures. In V.B. Van Hasselt, R.L. Morrison, A.S. Bellack, & M. Herson (Eds.), *Handbook of family violence*. New York: Plenum.

Levenson, R.W., Oyama, O.N., & Meek, P.S. (1987). Greater reinforcement from alcohol for those at risk: Parental risk, personality risk, and sex. *Journal of Abnormal Psychology, 96*, 242–253.

Leventhal, H., Meyer, D., & Nerenz, D. (1980). The common sense representation of illness danger. In S. Rachman (Ed.), *Contributions to medical psychology*. Oxford: Pergamon Press.

Leventhal, H., Zimmerman, R., & Gutmann, M. (1984). Compliance: A self-regulation perspective. In W.D. Gentry (Ed.), *Handbook of behavioral medicine*. New York: Guilford Press.

Levin, A.P., Schneier, F.R., & Liebowitz, M. (1989). Social phobia: Biology and pharmacology. *Clinical Psychology Review, 9*, 129–140.

Levin, S., & Stava, L. (1987). Personality characteristics of sex offenders: A review. *Archives of Sexual Behavior, 16*, 57–79.

Levine, S.B., & Agle, D. (1978). The effectiveness of sex therapy for chronic secondary psychological impotence. *Journal of Sex and Marital Therapy, 4*, 235–258.

Levine, S.B., & Lothstein, L.M. (1981). Transsexualism or the gender dysphoria syndromes. *Journal of Sex and Marital Therapy, 7*, 85–113.

Levy, A.B., Dixon, K.N., & Stern, S.I. (1989). How are depression and bulimia related? *American Journal of Psychiatry, 146*, 162–169.

Levy, D., & Kannel, W.B. (1988). Cardiovascular risk: New insights from Framingham. *American Heart Journal, 116*, 266–272.

Levy, L.H., Knight, B.G., Padgett, V.P., & Wellert, R. (1977, August). *Patterns of help-giving in self-help groups*. Paper presented at the 85th Annual Meeting of the American Psychological Association, San Francisco.

Levy, S.M., Herberman, R.B., Maluish, A.M., Schlien, B., & Lippman, M. (1985). Prognostic risk assessment in primary breast cancer by behavioral and immunological parameters. *Health Psychology, 4*, 99–113.

Lewin, K. (1935). *Principles of topological psychology*. New York: McGraw-Hill.

Lewinsohn, P.M. (1987). The coping-with-depression course. In R.F. Munoz (Ed.), *Depression prevention: Research directions* (pp. 159–170). Washington: Hemisphere.

Lewinsohn, P.M., & Arconad, M. (1981). Behavioral treatment of depression: A social learning approach. In J.F. Clarkin & H.I. Glazer (Eds.), *Depression: Behavioral and directive intervention strategies*. New York: Garland Press.

Lewinsohn, P.M., Clarke, G.N., Hops, H., & Andrews, J. (1990). Cognitive-behavioral treatment for depressed adolescents. *Behavior Therapy, 21*, 385–401.

Lewinsohn, P.M., Hoberman, H.M., Teri, L., & Hautzinger, M. (1985). An integrative theory of depression. In S.R. Reiss & R. Bootzin (Eds.), *Theoretical issues in behavior therapy* (pp. 331–352). New York: Academic Press.

Lewinsohn, P.M., Hops, H., Roberts, R.E., & Seeley, J.R. (1989). *The prevalence of affective and other disorders among older adolescents*. Unpublished manuscript, University of Oregon, Eugene.

Lewinsohn, P.M., & Lee, W.M.L. (1981). Assessment of affective disorders. In D.H. Barlow (Ed.), *Behavioral assessment of adult disorders*. New York: Guilford Press.

Lewinsohn, P.M., Mischel, W., Chaplin, W., & Barton, R. (1980). Social competence and depression: The role of illusory self-perceptions. *Journal of Abnormal Psychology, 89*, 203–212.

Lewinsohn, P.M., Sullivan, J.M., & Grosscup, S.J. (1982). Behavioral therapy: Clinical applications. In A.J. Rush (Ed.), *Short term psychotherapies for the depressed patient*. New York: Guilford Press.

Lewis, B. (1985, August 25). Child sexual abuse. *Los Angeles Times*, p. 1.

Lewis, M., Feiring, C., McGuffog, C., & Jaskir, J. (1983). Predicting psychopathology in six-year-olds from early social relations. *Child Development, 55*, 123–136.

Lewis, O. (1961). *The children of Sanchez*. New York: Random House.

Lewis, O. (1969). A Puerto Rican boy. In J.C. Finney (Ed.), *Culture change, mental health, and poverty*. New York: Simon and Schuster.

Lex, B.W. (1985). Alcohol problems in special populations. In J.H. Mendelson & N.K. Mello (Eds.), *The diagnosis and treatment of alcoholism* (pp. 89–187, 2nd ed.). New York: McGraw-Hill.

Ley, P. (1977). Psychological studies of doctor patient communication. In S. Rachman (Ed.), *Contributions to medical psychology*. London: Pergamon Press.

Lichtenstein, E. (1980). *Psychotherapy*. Monterey, CA: Brooks/Cole.

Lichtenstein, E., & Mermelstein, R.J. (1984). Review of approaches to smoking treatment: Behavior modification strategies. In J.D. Matarazzo, S.M. Weiss, J.A. Herd, N.E. Miller, & S.M. Weiss (Eds.), *Behavioral health* (pp. 695–712). New York: Wiley-Interscience.

Liddle, H.A. (1987). Family psychology: The journal, the field. *Journal of Family Psychology, 1*, 5–22.

Lidz, C.W., Mulvey, E.P., Appelbaum, P.S., & Cleveland, S. (1989). Commitment: The consistency of clinicians and the use of legal standards. *American Journal of Psychiatry, 146*, 176–181.

Liebowitz, M.R., Fyer, A.J., Gorman, J.M., Dillon, D., Appleby, I.L., Levy, G., Anderson, S., Levitt, M., Palij, M., Davies, S.O., & Klein, D.F. (1984). Lactate provocation of panic attacks, I. Clinical and behavioural findings. *Archives of General Psychiatry, 41*, 764–770.

Liebowitz, M.R., Stone, M.H., & Turkat, I.D. (1986). Treatment of personality disorders. In A.J. Frances & R.E. Hales (Eds.), *Annual Review* (Vol. 5). Washington, DC: American Psychiatric Association.

Linehan, M., & Egan, K. (1983). *Asserting yourself*. New York: Facts on File Publications.

Linehan, M.M. (1987). Dialectical behavior therapy for borderline personality disorder. *Bulletin of the Menninger Clinic, 51*, 261–276.

Linehan, M.M., & Wagner, A.W. (1990, January). Dialectical behavior therapy: A feminist-behavioral treatment of borderline personality disorder. *The Behavior Therapist*, pp. 9–14.

Lipid Research Clinics Program. (1989). The Lipid Research Clinics' coronary primary prevention trial results. I. Reduction in incidence of coronary heart disease. *Journal of the American Medical Association, 251*, 351–364.

Lipowski, Z.J. (1983). Transient cognitive disorders (delirium, acute confusional states) in the elderly. *American Journal of Psychiatry, 140*, 1426–1436.

Lipton, D.N., McDonel, E.C., & McFall, R.M. (1987). Heterosexual perception in rapists. *Journal of Consulting and Clinical Psychology, 55*, 17–21.

Lishman, W.A. (1978). *Organic psychiatry*. Boston: Blackwell.

Liu, A. (1979). *Solitaire*. New York: Harper & Row.

Lloyd, C. (1980). Life events and depressive disorder reviewed. *Archives of General Psychiatry, 37*, 521–535.

Loeb, A., Beck, A.T., Diggory, J.C., & Tutill, R. (1967). Expectancy, level of aspiration, performance and self-evaluation in depression. *Proceedings of the 75th Annual Convention of the American Psychological Association, 2*, Washington, D.C., 193–194.

Loney, J. (1987). Hyperactivity and aggression in the diagnosis of attention deficit disorder. In B.B. Lahey & A.E. Kazdin (Eds.), *Advances in clinical psychology*. New York: Plenum.

Loney, J., Whaley-Klahn, M.A., Kosier, T., & Conboy, J. (1981). *Hyperactive boys and their brothers at 21: Predictors of aggressive and antisocial outcomes*. Paper presented at meeting of the Society for Life History Research, Monterey, California.

Lopez, F.G., & Wambach, C.A. (1982). Effects of paradoxical and self-control directives in counseling. *Journal of Counseling Psychology, 29*, 115–124.

LoPiccolo, J., & Stock, W. (1986). Treatment of sexual dysfunction. *Journal of Consulting and Clinical Psychology, 54*, 158–167.

Loranger, A.W., Oldham, J.M., & Tulis, E.H. (1982). Familial transmission of *DSM-III* borderline personality disorder. *Archives of General Psychiatry, 39*, 795–799.

Lothstein, L.M. (1982). Sex reassignment surgery. *American Journal of Psychiatry, 139*, 417–426.

Lou, H.C., Henriksen, L., & Bruhn, P. (1984). Focal cerebral hypoperfusion in children with dysphasia and/or attention deficit disorder. *Archives of Neurology, 41*, 825–829.

Lovaas, O.I. (1987). Behavioral treatment and normal educational and intellectual functioning in young autistic children. *Journal of Consulting and Clinical Psychology, 55*, 3–9.

Lowman, C., Harford, T.C., & Kaelber, C.T. (1983). Alcohol use among black senior high school students. *Alcohol Health and Research World, 7*, 37–46.

Luborsky, L. (1987). Research can now affect clinical practice—a happy turnabout. *The Clinical Psychologist, 40*, 56–60.

Luborsky, L., Crits-Christoph, P., & Mellon, J. (1986). Advent of objective measures of the transference concept. *Journal of Consulting and Clinical Psychology, 54*, 39–47.

Ludwig, A.M., Wikler, A., & Stark, L. (1974). The first drink: Psychobiological aspects of craving. *Archives of General Psychiatry, 30*, 539–547.

Lundy, A. (1985). The reliability of the Thematic Apperception Test. *Journal of Personality Assessment, 49*, 141–145.

Luria, A.R. (1980). *Higher cortical functions in man* (2nd ed.). New York: Basic Books.

Lyles, J.N., Burish, T.G., Krozely, M.G., & Oldham, R.K. (1982). Efficacy of relaxation training and guided imagery in reducing the aversiveness of cancer chemotherapy. *Journal of Consulting and Clinical Psychology, 50*, 509–524.

Lynch, J. (1979). *The broken heart*. New York: Basic Books.

Maccoby, N., & Alexander, J. (1980). Use of media in lifestyle programs. In P.O. Davidson & S.M. Davidson (Eds.), *Behavioral medicine: Changing health lifestyles*. New York: Brunner/Mazel.

MacDonald, L. (1987). Ethical standards for therapeutic programs in human services. *The Behavior Therapist, 9*, 213–215.

Machover, K. (1949). *Personality projection in the drawing of the human figure*. Springfield, IL: Charles C. Thomas.

Mack, J.E.G., & Hickler, H. (1981). *Vivienne: The life and suicide of an adolescent girl*. Boston, MA: Little, Brown.

Madden, J. (1984). *Hey wait a minute: I wrote a book*. New York: Villard Books.

Madsen, C.H., & Madsen, C.K. (1970). *Teaching discipline*. Boston: Allyn & Bacon.

Magaro, P.A., Talbott, T.A., & Glick, I. (1984). The inpatient care of chronic schizophrenia. In A.S. Bellack (Ed.), *Schizophrenia: Treatment management and rehabilitation*. Orlando, FL: Grune & Stratton.

Mahler, M. (1968). *On human symbiosis and the vicissitudes of individuation, Vol. 1: Infantile psychosis*. In collaboration with M. Furer. New York: International Universities Press.

Main, M. (1989). Adult attachment classification system. In M. Main (Ed.), *Behavior and the development of representational models of attachment: Five methods of assessment*. New York: Cambridge University Press.

Main, M., & Goldwyn, R. (1990). Interview Based Adult Attachment Classifications: Related to Infant-Mother and Infant-Father Attachment. *Developmental Psychology*.

Maisto, S.A., Sobell, M.B., & Sobell, L.C. (1982). Reliability of self-reports of low ethanol consumption by problem drinkers over 18 months of follow-up. *Drug and Alcohol Dependence, 9*, 273–278.

Malamuth, N. (1981). Rape fantasies as a function of exposure to violent erotic stimuli. *Archives of Sexual Behavior, 10*, 33–47.

Malamuth, N., & Check, J.V.P. (1983). Sexual arousal to rape depictions: Individual differences. *Journal of Abnormal Psychology, 92*, 55–67.

Malan, D.H. (1979). *Individual psychotherapy and the science of psychodynamics*. Woburn, MA: Butterworths.

Malcolm X (1966). *The autobiography of Malcolm X*. New York: Grove Press.

Maletta, G.J., Pirozzolo, F.J., Thompson, G., & Mortimer, J.A. (1982). Organic mental disorders in a geriatric outpatient population. *American Journal of Psychiatry, 139*, 521–523.

Maletzky, B. (1980). Self-referred versus court-referred sexually deviant patients: Success with assisted covert sensitization. *Behavior Therapy, 11*, 302–314.

Maletzky, B.M. (1981). *Multiple-monitored electroconvulsive therapy*. Boca Raton, FL: CRC Press.

Maltzman, I. (1989). A reply to cook, "craftsman versus professional: Analysis of the controlled drinking controversy." *Journal of Studies on Alcohol, 50*, 466–472.

Mandler, A.V. (1977). Feminism as therapy. In E.I. Rawlings & D.K. Carter (Eds.), *Psychotherapy for women*. Chicago: Charles C. Thomas.

Mann, C. (1990). Meta-analysis in the breech. *Science, 249*, 476–480.

Mann, J. (1980). The core of time-limited psychotherapy: Time and the central issue. In S.H. Budman (Ed.), *Forms of brief therapy*. New York: Guilford Press.

Manson, J.E., Colditz, G., Stampfer, M., Willett, W., Rosner, B., Monson, R., Speizer, F., & Hennekens, C. (1990). A prospective study of obesity and risk of coronary heart disease in women. *The New England Journal of Medicine, 322*, 882–889.

Marcus, M.D., Wing, R.R., Ewing, L., Kern, E., Gooding, W., & McDermott, M. (1990). Psychiatric disorders among obese binge-eaters. *International Journal of Eating Disorders, 9*, 69–77.

Marder, S.R., & Van Putten, T. (1988). Who should receive clozapine? *Archives of General Psychiatry, 45*, 865–867.

Margo, A., Hemsley, D.R., & Slade, P.D. (1981). The effects of varying auditory input on schizophrenic hallucinations. *British Journal of Psychiatry, 139*, 122–127.

Margolin, G. (1983). An interactional model for the behavioral assessment of marital relationships. *Behavioral Assessment, 5*, 103–127.

Margraf, J., Ehlers, A., & Roth, W.T. (1986). Biological models of panic disorder and agoraphobia: A review. *Behaviour Research and Therapy, 24*, 553–567.

Marks, I.M. (1978). Behavioural psychotherapy of adult neurosis. In S.L. Garfield & A.E. Bergin (Eds.), *Handbook of psychotherapy and behavior change* (2nd. ed.). New York: John Wiley & Sons.

Marks, I.M. (1981). Review of behavioral psychotherapy: I. Obsessive-compulsive disorders. *American Journal of Psychiatry, 138*, 584–592.

Marks, I.M. (1985). Behavioral treatment of social phobia. *Psychopharmacology Bulletin, 21*, 615–618.

Marks, I.M. (1987). Comment on S. Lloyd Williams' "On anxiety and phobia." *Journal of Anxiety Disorders, 1*, 181–196.

Marks, M., Gray, S., Cohen, D., Hill, R., Mawson, D., Ramm, E., & Stern, R.S. (1983). Imipramine and brief therapist-aided exposure in agoraphobics having self-exposure homework. *Archives of General Psychiatry, 40*, 153–162.

Markus, E., Lange, A., & Pettigrew, T.F. (1990). Effectiveness of family therapy: A meta-analysis. *Journal of Family Therapy, 12*, 205–211.

Marlatt, G.A. (1985). Relapse prevention: Theoretical rationale and overview of the model. In G.A. Marlatt & J.R. Gordon (Eds.), *Relapse prevention* (pp. 3–70). New York: Guilford Press.

Marlatt, G.A., & Gordon, J.R. (Eds.). (1985). *Relapse prevention*. New York: Guilford Press.

Marlatt, G.A., & Rohsenow, D.J. (1980). Cognitive processes in alcohol use: Expectancy and the balanced placebo design. In N.K. Mello (Ed.), *Advances in substance abuse: Behavioral and biological research* (Vol. 1). Greenwich, CT: JAI Press.

Martin, A. (1987). Representation of semantic and spatial knowledge in Alzheimer's patients: Implications for models of preserved learning in amnesia. *Journal of Clinical and Experimental Neuropsychology, 9*, 191–224.

Martin, B. (1977). *Abnormal psychology: Clinical and scientific perspectives*. New York: Holt.

Martin, J.E., Dubbert, P.M., Katell, A.D., Thompson, J.K., Racqynski, J.R., Lake, M., Smith, P.O., & Webster, J.S. (1984). Behavioral control of exercise in sedentary adults: Studies 1–6. *Journal of Consulting and Clinical Psychology, 52*, 795–811.

Martin, J.L. (1987). The impact of AIDS on gay male sexual behavior patterns in New York City. *American Journal of Public Health, 77*, 578–580.

Martindale, C. (1975). *Romantic progression: The psychology of literary history*. Washington, DC: Hemisphere.

Mash, E.J. (1985). Some comments on target selection in behavior therapy. *Behavioral Assessment, 7*, 63–78.

Mash, E.J. (1987). Behavioral assessment of child and family disorders: Contemporary approaches. *Behavioral Assessment, 9*, 201–205.

Mash, E.J., & Johnston, C. (1983). Sibling interactions of hyperactive children and their relationship to reports of maternal stress and self-esteem. *Journal of Consulting and Clinical Psychology, 12*, 91–99.

Maslow, A.H. (1954). *Motivation and personality*. New York: Harper & Row.

Masson, J.M. (1984). *The assault on truth: Freud's suppression of the seduction theory*. New York: Farrar, Straus & Giroux.

Masters, W.H., & Johnson, V. (1966). *Human sexual response*. Boston: Little, Brown and Company.

Masters, W.H., & Johnson, V. (1970). *Human sexual inadequacy*. Boston: Little, Brown and Company.

Masters, W.H., & Johnson, V. (1979). *Homosexuality in perspective*. Boston: Little, Brown and Company.

Masterson, J.F. (1985). *The real self*. New York: Brunner/Mazel.

Masterson, J.F. (1990). Psychotherapy of borderline and narcissistic disorders: Establishing a therapeutic alliance. (A developmental, self, and object relations approach). *Journal of Personality Disorders, 4*, 182–191.

Matarazzo, J.D. (1990). Psychological assessment versus psychological testing. *American Psychologist, 45*, 999–1017.

Mathew, R.J., Wilson, W.H., Tant, S.R., Robinson, L., & Prakash, R. (1988). Abnormal resting regional cerebral blood flow patterns and their correlates in schizophrenia. *Archives of General Psychiatry, 45*, 542–549.

Mathews, A.M., Gelder, M.G., & Johnston, D.W. (1981). *Agoraphobia: Nature and treatment*. New York: Guilford Press.

Mathews, A.M., Johnston, D.W., Lancashire, M., Munby, M., Shaw, P.M., & Gelder, M.G. (1976). Imaginal flooding and exposure to real phobic situations: Treatment outcome with agoraphobic patients. *British Journal of Psychiatry, 129*, 362–371.

Mathews, A.M., & MacLeod, C. (1986). Discrimination of threat cues without awareness in anxiety states. *Journal of Abnormal Psychology, 95*, 131–138.

Mattes, J.A. (1985). Stimulant therapy of "adult hyperactivity" [Letter]. *Archives of General Psychiatry, 42*, 840.

Matthews, K.A., Glass, D.C., Rosenman, R.H., & Bortner, R.W. (1977). Competitive drive, pattern A, and coronary heart disease: A further analysis of some data from the western collaborative group. *Journal of Chronic Disease, 230*, 489–498.

Matthews, K., & Haynes, S.G. (1986). Type A behavior pattern and coronary risk: Update and critical evaluation. *American Journal of Epidemiology, 123*, 923–960.

Mattick, R.P., & Peters, L. (1988). Treatment of severe social phobia: Effects of guided exposure with and without cognitive restructuring. *Journal of Consulting and Clinical Psychology, 36*, 251–260.

May, P. (1984, December 1). Accused killer says she feared for her life. *Miami Herald*, pp. 1BR, 4BR.

May, P.R.A., Tuma, A.H., & Dixon, W.J. (1981). Schizophrenia: A follow-up study of the results of treatment. *Archives of General Psychiatry, 38*, 776–784.

Mays, D.T., & Franks, C.M. (1985). *Negative outcome in psychotherapy and what to do about it*. New York: Springer.

McAllister, T.W., & Price, T.R.P. (1982). Severe depressive pseudodementia with and without dementia. *American Journal of Psychiatry, 139*, 626–629.

McCaffrey, R.J., & Isaac, W. (1985). Preliminary data on the presence of neuropsychological deficits in adults who are mentally retarded. *Mental Retardation, 23*, 63–66.

McCarley, R.W. (1982). REM sleep and depression: Common neurobiological control mechanisms. *American Journal of Psychiatry, 139*, 565–570.

McCarthy, M. (1990). The thin ideal, depression, and eating disorders in women. *Behaviour Research and Therapy, 28*, 205–215.

McClelland, D.C. (1980). Motive dispositions: The merits of operant and respondent measures. In L. Wheeler (Ed.), *Review of personality and social psychology* (Vol. 1). Beverly Hills, CA: Sage.

McClelland, D.C. (1989). Motivational factors in health and disease. *American Psychologist, 44*, 675–683.

McCord, W., McCord, J., & Howard, A. (1961). Familial correlates of aggression in non-delinquent male children. *Journal of Abnormal and Social Psychology, 62*, 79–93.

McCrady, B.S., Moreau, J., Paolino, T.J., & Longabaugh, R. (1982). Joint hospitalization and couples therapy for alcoholism: A four-year follow-up. *Journal of Studies on Alcohol, 43*, 1244–1250.

McCrady, B.S., Paolino, T.J., Longabaugh, R., & Rossi, J. (1979). Effects of joint hospital admission and couples treatment for hospitalized alcoholics: A pilot study. *Addictive Behaviors, 4*, 155–165.

McDaniel, K.D. (1986). Pharmacologic treatment of psychiatric and neurodevelopmental disorders in children and adolescents, Part 2. *Clinical Pediatrics, 25*, 143–146.

McFall, R.M. (1986). Theory and method in assessment: The vital link. *Behavioral Assessment, 8*, 3–10.

McGhie, A., & Chapman, J. (1961). Disorders of attention and perception in early schizophrenia. *British Journal of Medical Psychology, 34*, 103–115.

McGlashan, T.H. (1986a). Schizophrenia: Psychosocial treatments and the role of psychosocial factors in its etiology and pathogenesis. In A.J. Frances & R.E. Hales (Eds.), *Annual Review* (Vol. 5). Washington, DC: American Psychiatric Association.

McGlashan, T.H. (1986b). Schizotypal personality disorder. *Archives of General Psychiatry, 43*, 329–334.

McGrath, E., Keith, G.P., Strickland, B.R., & Russo, N.F. (1990). *Women and depression*. Washington, DC: American Psychological Association.

McGuire, R.J., Carlisle, J.M., & Young, B.G. (1965). Sexual deviation as conditioned behaviour: A hypothesis. *Behaviour Research and Therapy, 2*, 185–190.

McKeon, J., McGuffin, P., & Robinson, P. (1984). Obsessive-compulsive neurosis following head injury: A report of four cases. *British Journal of Psychiatry, 144*, 190–192.

McKeon, P., & Murray, R. (1987). Familial aspects of obsessive-compulsive neurosis. *British Journal of Psychiatry, 151*, 528–534.

McKusick, L., Horstman, W., & Coates,

T.J. (1986). AIDS and sexual behavior of gay men in San Francisco. In A. Bandura, *Social foundations of thought and action: A social cognitive theory*. Englewood Cliffs, NJ: Prentice Hall.

McMahon, R.J., Forehand, R., & Greist, L. (1981). Effects of knowledge of social learning principles on enhancing treatment outcome and generalization in a parent training program. *Journal of Consulting and Clinical Psychology, 49*, 526–532.

McNally, R.J. (1987). Preparedness and phobias: A review. *Psychological Bulletin, 101*, 283–303.

McNeil, D.E., & Binder, R.L. (1987). Predictive validity of judgments of dangerousness in emergency civil commitment. *American Journal of Psychiatry, 144*, 197–200.

McQuiston, J.T. (1989, August 24). R.D. Laing, rebel and pioneer on schizophrenia, is dead at 61. *The New York Times*, p. D21.

Meador, B.D., & Rogers, C.R. (1984). Person-centered therapy. In R. Corsini (Ed.), *Current psychotherapies*. Itasca, IL: Peacock Publishers.

Mechanic, D., & Aiken, L.A. (1987). Improving the care of patients with chronic mental illness. *The New England Journal of Medicine, 317*, 1634–1638.

Mednick, S.A., Cudeck, R., Griffith, J.J., Talovic, S.A., & Schulsinger, F. (1984). The Danish high-risk project: Recent methods and findings. In N.F. Watt, E.J. Anthony, L.C. Wynne, & J.E. Rolf (Eds.), *Children at risk for schizophrenia: A longitudinal perspective*. New York: Cambridge University Press.

Mednick, S.A., & Moffitt, T.E. (Eds.). (1987). *The new biocriminology*. New York: Cambridge University Press.

Mednick, S.A., & Schulsinger, F. (1968). Some premorbid characteristics related to breakdown in children with schizophrenic mothers. *Journal of Psychosomatic Research, 6*, 354–362.

Meduna, L.J. (1956). The convulsive treatment: A reappraisal. In F. Marti-Ibanez, A.M. Sackler, M.D. Sackler, & R.R. Sackler (Eds.), *The great physiodynamic therapies in psychiatry*. New York: Hoeber-Harper.

Meehl, P.E. (1962). Schizotaxia, schizotypy, schizophrenia. *American Psychologist, 17*, 827–838.

Meichenbaum, D.H. (1966). Sequential strategies in two cases of hysteria. *Behaviour Research and Therapy, 4*, 89–94.

Meichenbaum, D.H. (1977). *Cognitive-behavior modification*. New York: Plenum.

Meichenbaum, D.H., & Turk, D. (1988). *Facilitating treatment adherence*. New York: Plenum.

Meisel, A. (1982). The rights of the mentally ill under state constitutions. *Law and Contemporary Problems, 45*, 7–40.

Melamed, B.G., & Siegel, L.J. (1975). Reduction of anxiety in children facing hospitalization and surgery by use of filmed modeling. *Journal of Consulting and Clinical Psychology, 43*, 511–521.

Melcher, J. (1988). Keeping our elderly out of institutions by putting them back in their homes. *American Psychologist, 43*, 643–647.

Melton, G.B., & Gray, J.N. (1988). Ethical dilemmas in AIDS research: Individual privacy and public health. *American Psychologist, 43*, 60–64.

Melton, G.B., Levine, R.J., Koocher, G.P., Rosenthal, R., & Thompson, W.C. (1988). Community consultation in socially sensitive research. *American Psychologist, 43*, 573–581.

Mendelson, J.H., & Mello, N.K. (1966). Experimental analysis of drinking behavior of chronic alcoholics. *Annals of the New York Academy of Sciences, 133*, 828–845.

Mendelson, J.H., & Mello, N.K. (1985). Diagnostic criteria for alcoholism and alcohol abuse. In J.H. Mendelson & N.K. Mello (Eds.), *The diagnosis and treatment of alcoholism* (pp. 1–20, 2nd ed.), New York: McGraw-Hill.

Mendelson, J.H., Mello, N.K., Lex, B.W., & Bavli, S. (1984). Marijuana withdrawal syndrome in a woman. *American Journal of Psychiatry, 141*, 1289–1290.

Mendelson, M. (1982). Psychodynamics of depression. In E.S. Paykel (Ed.), *Handbook of affective disorders* (pp. 162–174). New York: Guilford Press.

Mendelson, W.B., Johnson, N.E., & Stewart, M.A. (1971). Hyperactive children as teenagers: A follow-up study. *Journal of Nervous and Mental Disease, 153*, 273–279.

Mendlewicz, J., & Rainer, J.D. (1977). Adoption study supporting genetic transmission in manic-depressive illness. *Nature, 268*, 327–329.

Meredith, N. (1986). Testing the talking cure. *Science, 7*, 31–37.

Merikangas, K.R. (1982). Assortative mating for psychiatric disorders and psychological traits. *Archives of General Psychiatry, 39*, 73–180.

Merikangas, K.R. (1987). Genetic epidemiology of psychiatric disorders. In R.E. Hales & A.J. Frances (Eds.), *American Psychiatric Association Annual Review* (Vol. 6). Washington, DC: American Psychiatric Press.

Merikangas, K.R., Spence, M.A., & Kupfer, D.J. (1989). Linkage studies of bipolar disorder: Methodologic and analytic issues: Report of MacArthur workshop on linkage and clinical features in affective disorders. *American Journal of Psychiatry, 46*, 1137–1141.

Meyer, A. (1906). Fundamental conceptions of dementia praecox. *British Medical Journal, 2*, 757.

Meyer, A., Nash, J., McAlister, A., Maccoby, N., & Farquhar, J. (1980). Skills training in a cardiovascular health education campaign. *Journal of Consulting and Clinical Psychology, 48*, 129–142.

Meyer, J.K., & Reter, D.J. (1979). Sex reassignment. *Archives of General Psychiatry, 36*, 1010–1015.

Meyer, R.E., & Hesselbrock, M.N. (1984). Psychopathology and addictive disorders revisited. In S.M. Mirin (Ed.), *Substance abuse and psychopathology* (pp. 1–17). Washington, DC: American Psychiatric Press.

Michaud, S.G., & Aynesworth, H. (1983). *The only living witness*. New York: Linden Press/Simon & Schuster.

Michaud, S.G., & Aynesworth, H. (1989). *Ted Bundy: Conversations with a killer*. New York: Signet Books.

Miklowitz, D.J., Goldstein, M.J., Neuchterlein, K.S., Snyder, K.S., & Mintz, J. (1988). Family factors and bipolar depression. *Archives of General Psychiatry, 45*, 225–231.

Miller, E. (1987). Hysteria: Its nature and explanation. *British Journal of Clinical Psychology, 26*, 163–173.

Miller, N.E. (1969). Learning of visceral and glandular responses. *Science, 163*, 434–445.

Miller, W.R. (1985). Motivation for treatment: A review with special emphasis on alcoholism. *Psychological Bulletin, 98*, 84–107.

Miller, W.R., & Hester, R.K. (1986). The effectiveness of alcoholism treatment: What research reveals. In W.R. Miller & N. Heather (Eds.), *Treating addictive behaviors: Processes of change* (pp. 121–174). New York: Plenum Press.

Millon, T. (1986). A theoretical derivation of pathological personalities. In T. Millon & G. Klerman (Eds.), *Contemporary directions in psychopathology*. New York: Guilford Press.

Millon, T. (1986). The MCMI and DSM-III: Further commentaries. *Journal of Personality Assessment, 50*, 205–207.

Millon, T. (1987). *Millon Clinical Multiaxial Inventory-II: Manual for the MCMI-II* (2nd ed.). Minneapolis, MN: National Computer Systems.

Millon, T. (1987). On the renaissance of personality assessment and personality theory. *Journal of Personality Assessment, 48*, 450–466.

Mills, M.J., Sullivan, G., & Eth, S. (1987). Protecting third parties: A decade after *Tarasoff*. *American Journal of Psychiatry, 144*, 68–74.

Minde, K., Lewin, D., Weiss, G., Lavigueur, H., Douglas, V., & Sykes, E. (1971). The hyperactive child in elementary school: A 5-year controlled follow-up. *Exceptional Children, 38*, 215–221.

Mineka, S., & Cook, M. (1986). Immunization against the observational conditioning of snake fear in rhesus monkeys. *Journal of Abnormal Psychology, 95*, 307–318.

Mineka, S., Davidson, M., Cook, M., & Keir, R. (1984). Observational conditioning of snake fear in rhesus monkeys. *Journal of Abnormal Psychology, 93*, 355–372.

Mineka, S., Gunnar, M., & Champoux, M. (1986). Control and early socio-emotional development: Infant rhesus monkeys reared in controllable versus uncontrollable environments. *Child Development, 57*, 1241–1256.

Mintz, J. (1983). Integrating research evidence. *Journal of Consulting and Clinical Psychology, 51*, 71–75.

Minuchin, S., Rosman, B., & Baker, L. (1978). *Psychosomatic families: Anorexia nervosa in context*. Cambridge, MA: Harvard University Press.

Mischel, W. (1968). *Personality and assessment.* New York: John Wiley.
Mischel, W. (1981). A cognitive social learning approach to assessment. In T.V. Merluzzi, C.R. Glass, & M. Genest (Eds.), *Cognitive assessment.* New York: Guilford Press.
Mischel, W., & Peake, P. (1982). Beyond deja vu in the search for cross situational consistency. *Psychological Review, 89*, 730–755.
Mitchell, J.E., Pyle, R.L., Eckert, E.D., Hatsukami, D., Pomeroy, C., & Zimmerman, R. (1988). Preliminary results of a comparison treatment trial of bulimia nervosa. In K.M. Pirke, W. Vandereycken, & D. Ploog (Eds.), *The psychobiology of bulimia nervosa.* Heidelberg: Springer-Verlag.
Mitchell, J.E., Pyle, R.L., Hatsukami, D., Goff, G., Glotter, D., & Harper, J. (1988). A 2–5 year follow-up study of patients treated for bulimia. *International Journal of Eating Disorders, 8*, 157–165.
Moffitt, T.E., & Silva, P.A. (1988). Neuropsychological deficit and self-reported delinquency in an unselected sample birth cohort. *Journal of the American Academy of Child and Adolescent Psychiatry, 27*, 233–240.
Mogg, K., Mathews, A., & Weinman, J. (1987). Memory bias in clinical anxiety. *Journal of Abnormal Psychology, 96*, 94–98.
Monahan, J. (1981). *The clinical prediction of violent behavior* (DHHS Publication No. ADM 81–92). Rockville, MD: National Institute of Mental Health.
Money, J., & Lamacz, M. (1989). *Vandalized lovemaps.* New York: Prometheus Books.
Moos, R.H., & Finney, J.W. (1983). The expanding scope of alcoholism treatment evaluation. *American Psychologist, 38*, 1036–1044.
Moos, R., & MacIntosh, S. (1970). Multivariate study of the patient-therapist system. *Journal of Consulting and Clinical Psychology, 35*, 298–307.
Moos, R., & Moos, B. (1984). The process of recovery from alcoholism: Comparing functioning in families of alcoholics and matched control families. *Journal of Studies on Alcohol, 45*, 111–118.
Morey, L.C., & Ochoa, E.S. (1989). An investigation of adherence to diagnostic criteria: Clinical diagnosis of the *DSM-III* personality disorders. *Journal of Personality Disorders, 3*, 180–192.
Morey, L.C., & Skinner, H.A. (1986). Empirically derived classifications of alcohol-related problems. In M. Galanter (Ed.), *Recent developments in alcoholism* (Vol. 4, pp. 144–168). New York: Plenum Press.
Morey, L.C., Waugh, M.H., & Blashfield, R.K. (1985). MMPI scales for *DSM-III* personality disorders: Their derivation and correlates. *Journal of Personality Assessment, 49*, 245–251.
Morganthau, T. (1986, March 23). Getting high on crack. Teens fall prey to new cocaine. *Anchorage Daily News*, pp. E1, E4, E5.
Morihisa, J.M. (1987). Functional brain imaging techniques. In R.E. Hales & A.J. Frances (Eds.), *American Psychiatric Association Annual Review* (Vol. 6). Washington, DC: American Psychiatric Association.
Morokoff, P.J., & Heiman, J.R. (1980). Effects of erotic stimuli on sexually functional and dysfunctional women: Multiple measures before and after therapy. *Behaviour Research and Therapy, 18*, 127–137.
Morokoff, P.J., & LoPiccolo, J. (1986). A comparative evaluation of minimal therapist contact and 15-session treatment for female orgasmic dysfunction. *Journal of Consulting and Clinical Psychology, 54*, 294–300.
Morrison, J.R., & Stewart, M.A. (1971). A family study of the hyperactive child syndrome. *Biological Psychiatry, 3*, 189–195.
Morrison, J.R., & Stewart, M.A. (1973). The psychiatric status of legal families of adopted hyperactive children. *Archives of General Psychiatry, 3*, 888–891.
Mosak, H.H. (1989). Adlerian psychotherapy. In R. Corsini & D. Wedding (Eds.), *Current psychotherapies.* Itasca, IL: Peacock Publishers.
Moses, J.A., Cardellino, J.P., & Thompson, L.L. (1983). Discrimination of brain damage from chronic psychosis by the Luria-Nebraska Neuropsychological Battery: A closer look. *Journal of Consulting and Clinical Psychology, 51*, 441–449.
Moskowitz, D.S. (1986). Comparison of self-reports, reports by knowledgeable informants, and behavioral observation data. *Journal of Personality, 54*, 294–317.
Mowrer, O.H. (1947). On the dual nature of learning—a reinterpretation of "conditioning" and "problem-solving." *Harvard Educational Review, 17*, 102–148.
Mowrer, O.H., & Mowrer, W.M. (1938). Enuresis—a method for its study and treatment. *American Journal of Orthopsychiatry, 8*, 436–459.
Moyal, B.R. (1977). Locus of control, self-esteem, stimulus appraisal, and depressive symptoms in children. *Journal of Consulting and Clinical Psychology, 45*, 951–952.
Muehlenhard, C.L. (1989, August). Quoted in *The New York Times*, p. C1.
Muehlenhard, C.L., Julsonnet, S., Carlson, M.I., & Flarity-White, L.A. (1989). A cognitive-behavioral program for preventing sexual coercion. *The Behavior Therapist, 12*, 211–214.
Multiple Risk Factor Intervention Trial Research Group. (1982). Multiple risk factor intervention trial: Risk factor changes and mortality results. *Journal of the American Medical Association, 248*, 1465–1477.
Mulvey, E.P., Geller, J.L., & Roth, L.H. (1987). The promise and peril of involuntary outpatient commitment. *American Psychologist, 42*, 571–584.
Munoz, R.A., & Amado, H. (1986). Anorexia nervosa and affective disorders. *New Directions of Mental Health Services, 31*, 13–19.
Munro, J.D. (1986). Epidemiology and the extent of mental retardation. *Psychiatric Clinics of North America, 9*, 591–624.
Murphy, G.E., Simons, A.D., Wetzel, R.D., & Lustman, P.J. (1984). Cognitive therapy and pharmacotherapy. *Archives of General Psychiatry, 41*, 33–41.
Murray, H.A. (1938). *Explorations in personality.* New York: Oxford Press.
Myers, J.K., Weissman, M.M., Tischler, G.L., Holzer, C.E., III, Leaf, P.J., Orvaschel, H., Anthony, J.C., Boyd, J.H., Burke, J.D., Kramer, M., & Stoltzman, R. (1984). Six-month prevalence of psychiatric disorders in three communities. *Archives of General Psychiatry, 41*, 959–967.
Nasrallah, H.A., Olson, S.C., & McCalley-Whitters, M. (1986). Cerebral ventricular enlargement in schizophrenia: A preliminary follow-up study. *Archives of General Psychiatry, 43*, 157–159.
Nathan, P.E. (1981). Nonproblem drinking outcomes: The data on controlled drinking treatments. *Advances in Alcoholism, 2*, 13.
Nathan, P.E. (1983). Failures in prevention: Why we can't prevent the devastating effect of alcoholism and drug abuse on American productivity. *American Psychologist, 38*, 459–468.
Nathan, P.E. (1988). The addictive personality is the behavior of the addict. *Journal of Consulting and Clinical Psychology, 56*, 183–188.
Nathan, P.E. (1990a). Integration of biological and psychosocial factors in alcohol research. *Alcoholism: Clinical and Experimental Research, 14*, 368–374.
Nathan, P.E. (1990b). Neuropsychological and behavioral consequences of long-term alcohol abuse. In J.J. Boren & J. Spencer (Eds.), *Residual effects of abused drugs on behavior: Clinical-research integration* (pp. 112–123). Washington, DC: National Institute on Drug Abuse.
Nathan, P.E., Andberg, M.M., Behan, P.O., & Patch, V.D. (1969). Thirty-two observers and one patient: A study of diagnostic reliability. *Journal of Clinical Psychology, 25*, 9–15.
Nathan, P.E., & Harris, S.L. (1980). *Psychopathology and society* (2nd ed.). New York: McGraw-Hill.
Nathan, P.E., & McCrady, B.S. (1987). Bases for the use of abstinence as a goal in the behavioral treatment of alcohol abusers. *Drugs and Society, 2*, 109–131.
Nathan, P.E., & O'Brien, J.S. (1971). An experimental analysis of the behavior of alcoholics and nonalcoholics during prolonged experimental drinking. *Behavior Therapy, 2*, 455–476.
Nathan, P.E., & Skinstad, A.-H. (1987). Outcomes of treatment for alcohol problems: Current methods, problems, and results. *Journal of Consulting and Clinical Psychology, 55*, 332–340.
Nathan, P.E., Titler, N.A., Lowenstein, L.M., Solomon, P., & Rossi, A.M. (1970). Behavioral analysis of chronic alcohol-

ism. *Archives of General Psychiatry, 22*, 419–430.

National Highway Traffic Safety Administration, National Center for Statistics and Analysis. (1988). *Drunk driving facts*. Washington, DC: NHTSA.

National Institute of Health Consensus Conference on Obesity. (1985). Consensus conference statement. *Annals of Internal Medicine, 103*, 1073–1077.

National Institute of Mental Health. (1981). *Depressive disorders: Causes and treatment* (DHHS Publication No. ADM 81-1081). Washington, DC: U.S. Government Printing Office.

National Institute of Mental Health. (1990). *Mental health, United States, 1990*. R.W. Manderscheid & M.A. Sonnenschein (Eds.). (DHHS Publication No. ADM 90-1708). Washington, DC: U.S. Government Printing Office.

National Institute of Mental Health Consensus Statement. (1985). *Electro-convulsive therapy* (Vol. 5, No. 11). Bethesda, MD.

Neale, J.M., & Oltmanns, T.F. (1980). *Schizophrenia*. New York: John Wiley.

Needleman, H.L., Gunnoe, C., Leviton, A., Reed, R., Peresie, H., Maher, C., & Barret, B.S. (1979). Deficits in psychological and classroom performance of children with elevated dentine lead levels. *The New England Journal of Medicine, 300*, 689–695.

Needleman, H.L., Schell, A., Bellinger, D., Leviton, A., & Allred, E.N. (1990). The long-term effects of exposure to low dosages of lead in childhood: An 11-year follow-up report. *The New England Journal of Medicine, 322*, 83–88.

Neitzel, M.T., Russel, R.L., Hemmings, K.A., & Gretter, M.L. (1987). Clinical significance of psychotherapy for unipolar depression: A meta-analytic approach to social comparison. *Journal of Consulting and Clinical Psychology, 55*, 156–161.

Nelson, R.E., & Craighead, W.E. (1977). Selective recall of positive and negative feedback, self-control behaviors, and depression. *Journal of Abnormal Psychology, 86*, 379–388.

Nelson, R.O. (1983). Behavioral assessment: Past, present, and future. *Behavioral Assessment, 5*, 195–206.

Nelson, R.O., & Barlow, D.H. (1983). Behavioral assessment: Basic strategies and initial procedures. In D.H. Barlow (Ed.), *Behavioral assessment of adult disorders*. New York: Guilford Press.

NIAAA. (1985). *U.S. alcohol epidemiologic data reference manual, Vol. 2. Liver cirrhosis mortality in the United States*. Rockville, MD: Author.

NIAAA. (1987). *Sixth special report to the U.S. Congress on alcohol and health*. Washington, DC: Author.

Nicholi, A.M., Jr. (1988). The adolescent. In A.M. Nicholi, Jr. (Ed.), *The new Harvard guide to psychiatry*. Cambridge, MA: Harvard University Press.

Nichols, S.E. (1985). Psychosocial reactions of persons with the Acquired Immunodeficiency Syndrome. *Annals of Internal Medicine, 103*, 765–767.

Nichols, W.C., & Everett, C.A. (1986). *Systemic family therapy: An integrative approach*. New York: Guilford Press.

NIDA. (1986). *NIDA Capsules*. Rockville, MD: Author.

Nisbett, R., & Ross, L. (1980). *Human inference: Strategies and shortcomings of social judgment*. Englewood Cliffs, NJ: Prentice-Hall.

Nolen-Hoeksema, S. (1987). Sex differences in unipolar depression: Evidence and theory. *Psychological Bulletin, 101*, 259–282.

Norcross, J.C. (Ed.). (1986). *Handbook of eclectic psychotherapy*. New York: Brunner/Mazel.

Norden, M.J. (1989). Is there an effective drug treatment for borderline personality disorder? *Harvard Medical School Mental Health Letter, 6*, 8.

Nordheimer, J. (1989, January 25). Bundy is put to death in Florida after admitting trail of killings. *The New York Times*, pp. A1, A20.

North, C.N. (1987). *Welcome, silence: My triumph over schizophrenia*. New York: Simon & Schuster.

Noyes, R., Jr., Anderson, D.J., Clancy, J., Crowe, R.R., Slymen, D.J., Ghoneim, M.M., & Hinrichs, J.V. (1984). Diazepam and propranolol in panic disorder and agoraphobia. *Archives of General Psychiatry, 41*, 287–292.

Noyes, R., Clarkson, C., Crowe, R.R., Yates, W.R., & McChesney, C.M. (1987). A family study of generalized anxiety disorder. *American Journal of Psychiatry*, 144, 1019–1024.

Nunnally, J.C. (1984). Self-report measures of personality traits. In N.S. Endler & J.M. Hunt (Eds.), *Personality and the behavior disorders*. New York: John Wiley.

Nurnberger, J., & Gershon, E.S. (1982). In E.S. Paykel (Ed.), *Handbook of affective disorders* (pp. 126–145). Edinburgh: Churchill Livingstone.

Nylander, I. (1971). The feeling of being fat and dieting in a school population: Epidemiologic interview investigation. *Acta Sociomedical Scandinavica, 3*, 17–26.

O'Connor, A.A. (1987). Female sex offenders. *British Journal of Psychiatry, 150*, 615–620.

Oei, T.P.S., & Jackson, P. (1980). Long-term effects of group and individual social skills training with alcoholics. *Addictive Behaviors, 5*, 129–136.

O'Hara, M.W., & Rehm, L.P. (1979). Self-monitoring, activity levels, and mood in the development and maintenance of depression. *Journal of Abnormal Psychology, 88*, 450–453.

Ohman, A. (1986). Face the beast and fear the face: Animal and social fears as prototypes for evolutionary analyses of emotion. *Psychophysiology, 23*, 123–145.

O'Leary, A. (1990). Stress, emotion, and immune function. *Psychological Bulletin, 108*, 363–382.

O'Leary, A., Shoor, S., Lorig, K., & Holman, H.R. (1988). A cognitive-behavioral treatment for rheumatoid arthritis. *Health Psychology, 7*, 527–544.

O'Leary, A., Temoshok, L., Jenkins, S.R., & Sweet, D.M. (1989, October). Autonomic reactivity and immune function in men with AIDS. Paper presented at the annual meeting of the Society for Psychophysiological Research. New Orleans, LA.

O'Leary, K.D. (1980). Pills or skills for hyperactive children. *Journal of Applied Behavior Analysis, 13*, 191–204.

O'Leary, K.D. (1984a). *Mommy, I can't sit still: Coping with hyperactive and aggressive children*. New York: New Horizon Press.

O'Leary, K.D. (1984b). The image of behavior therapy: It is time to take a stand. *Behavior Therapy, 15*, 219–233.

O'Leary, K.D., & Arias, I. (1983). The influence of marital therapy on sexual satisfaction. *Journal of Sex and Marital Therapy, 9*, 171–181.

O'Leary, K.D., Barling, J., Arias, I., Rosenbaum, A., Malone, J., & Tyree, A. (1989). Prevalence and stability of physical aggression between spouses: A longitudinal analysis. *Journal of Consulting and Clinical Psychology, 57*, 263–268.

O'Leary, K.D., & Beach, S.R.H. (1988). *Marital therapy: A viable treatment for depression and marital discord*. Unpublished manuscript, State University of New York at Stony Brook.

O'Leary, K.D., & Beach, S.R.H. (1990). Marital therapy: A viable treatment for depression. *American Journal of Psychiatry, 147*, 183–186.

O'Leary, K.D., & Borkovec, T. (1978). Conceptual, methodological, and ethical problems of placebo groups in psychotherapeutic research. *American Psychologist, 33*, 821–830.

O'Leary, K.D., & Christian, J. (1990). A closer look at the marital discord depression link. Manuscript submitted for publication.

O'Leary, K.D., & Emery, R.E. (1984). Marital discord and childhood behavior problems. In M. Levine & P. Satz (Eds.), *Middle childhood: Development and dysfunction*. Baltimore: University Park Press.

O'Leary, K.D., & O'Leary, S.G. (1977). *Classroom management* (2nd ed.). New York: Pergamon Press.

O'Leary, K.D., Turkewitz, H., & Tafel, S. (1973). Parent and therapist evaluation of behavior therapy in a child psychological clinic. *Journal of Consulting and Clinical Psychology, 41*, 289–293.

O'Leary, K.D., & Vivian, D. (in press). Physical aggression in marriage. In F.D. Fincham & T. Bradbury (Eds.), *The psychology of marriage*. New York: Guilford Press.

O'Leary, K.D., Vivian, D., & Nisi, A. (1985). Assessment and treatment of "hyperactivity" in Italy and the United States. *Journal of Abnormal Child Psychology, 13*, 485–500.

O'Leary, K.D., & Wilson, G.T. (1985). *Behavior therapy: Application and outcome*. Prentice Hall: Englewood Cliffs, NJ.

O'Leary, K.D., & Wilson, G.T. (1987). *Behavior therapy: Application and out-*

come (2nd ed.). Prentice Hall: Englewood Cliffs, NJ.

O'Leary, S.G., & Pelham, W.E. (1978). Behavioral therapy and withdrawal of stimulant medication with hyperactive children. *Pediatrics, 61*, 211–217.

O'Leary, S.G., Pelham, W.E., Rosenbaum, A., & Price, G.H. (1976). Behavioral treatment of hyperkinetic children. *The Clinical Psychologist, 15*, 510–515.

Oliver, R.G., Kaminski, Z., Tudor, K., & Hetzel, B.S. (1971). The epidemiology of attempted suicide as seen in the casualty department, Alfred Hospital, Melbourne. *Medical Journal of Australia, 1*, 833–839.

Olsen, J. (1967). *Black is best: The riddle of Cassius Clay*. New York: Putnam.

Oltmanns, T.F., Broderick, J.E., & O'Leary, K.D. (1977). Marital adjustment and the efficacy of behavior therapy with children. *Journal of Consulting and Clinical Psychology, 45*, 724–729.

Olweus, D. (1979). Stability of aggressive reaction patterns in males: A review. *Psychological Review, 86*, 852–875.

O'Reilly, J., & Sales, B. (1987). Privacy for the institutionalized mentally ill: Are court-ordered standards effective? *Law and Human Behavior, 11*, 41–53.

Orne, M.T. (1962). On the social psychology of the psychological experiment: With particular reference to demand characteristics and their implications. *American Psychologist, 17*, 776–783.

Orne, M.T., Dinges, D.F., & Orne, E.C. (1984). On the differential diagnosis of multiple personality in the forensic context. *The International Journal of Clinical and Experimental Hypnosis, 32*, 118–169.

Ornish, D., Brown, S., Scherwitz, L., Billings, J., Armstrong, W., Ports, T., McLanahan, S., Kirkeeide, R., Brand, R., & Gould, K. (1990). Can lifestyle changes reverse coronary heart disease? *The Lancet, 336*, 129–131.

Orvaschel, H., & Weissman, M.A. (1986). Epidemiology of anxiety disorders in children: A review. In R. Gittelman (Ed.), *Anxiety disorders of childhood*. New York: Guilford Press.

Otto, U. (1972). Suicidal acts by children and adolescents. *Acta Psychiatrica Scandinavica, 48* (Suppl. 233, p. 123).

Overholser, J.C., & Beck, S. (1986). Multimethod assessment of rapists, child molesters, and three control groups on behavioral and psychological measures. *Journal of Consulting and Clinical Psychology, 54*, 682–687.

A panel backs punishment therapy. (1989, September 15). *The New York Times*, p. B14.

Pardes, H. (1979). Future needs for psychiatrists and other mental health personnel. *Archives of General Psychiatry, 36*, 1401–1408.

Park, H., & Gaylord-Ross, R. (1989). A problem-solving approach to social skills training in employment settings with mentally retarded youth. *Journal of Applied Behavior Analysis, 22*, 373–380.

Parker, A.M., Jr. (1974). *Suicide among young adults*. New York: Exposition Press.

Parker, G., Johnston, P., & Hayward, L. (1988). Parental "expressed emotion" as a predictor of schizophrenic relapse. *Archives of General Psychiatry, 45*, 806–813.

Parrish, H.M. (1957). Epidemiology of suicide among college students. *Yale Journal of Biology and Medicine, 29*, 585–595.

Parsons, O.A., & Hart, R.P. (1984). Behavioral disorders associated with central nervous system dysfunction. In H.E. Adams & P.B. Sutker (Eds.), *Comprehensive handbook of psychopathology*. New York: Plenum.

Partanen, J., Bruun, K., & Markkanen, T. (1966). Inheritance of drinking behavior: A study on intelligence, personality, and use of alcohol of adult twins. *Finnish Foundation for Alcohol Studies, 14,* 159.

Pasamanick, B., Toberts, D.W., Lemkau, P.V., & Krueger, D.E. (1962). A survey of mental disease in an urban population. *American Journal of Public Health, 47*, 923–929.

Paternite, C.E., & Loney, J. (1975). *Parenting styles and symptom severity in MBD and hyperactive boys of high and low socioeconomic status.* Paper presented at the annual convention of the Midwestern Psychological Association, Chicago.

Paternite, C.E., & Loney, J. (1980). Childhood hyperkinesis: Relationships between symptomatology and home environment. In C.K. Whalen & B. Henker (Eds.), *Hyperactive children: The social ecology of identification and treatment.* New York: Academic Press.

Paternite, C.E., Loney, J., & Langhorne, J.E. (1976). Relationships between symptomatology and SES-related factors in hyperkinetic/MBD boys. *American Journal of Orthopsychiatry, 46*, 291–301.

Patterson, G.R. (1975). The aggressive child: Victim or architect of a coercive system. In L.A. Hamerlynck, L.C. Handy, & E.J. Mash (Eds.), *Behavior modification and families, I. Theory and research.* New York: Brunner/Mazel.

Patterson, G.R. (1982). *Coercive family process.* Eugene, OR: Castalia Publishing.

Patterson, G.R., & Bank, L. (1986). Bootstrapping your way in the nomological thicket. *Behavioral Assessment, 8*, 49–73.

Patterson, G.R., & Fleischman, M. (1979). Maintenance of treatment effects: Some considerations concerning family systems and follow-up data. *Behavior Therapy, 10*, 168–185.

Patterson, G.R., Littman, R.A., & Bricker, W. (1967). Assertive behavior in children: A step toward a theory of aggression. *Monographs for the Society for Research in Child Development, 32*, 1–43.

Patterson, G.R., Reid, J.B., & Dishion, T.J. (in press). *A social learning approach: 4. Antisocial boys.* Eugene, OR: Castalia Publishing.

Patton, G.C. (1988). The spectrum of eating disorder in adolescence. *Journal of Psychosomatic Research, 32*, 579–584.

Paul, G.L. (1967). Insight vs. desensitization in psychotherapy two years after termination. *Journal of Consulting and Clinical Psychology, 31*, 333–348.

Paul, G.L. (1985). Can pregnancy be a placebo effect? Terminology, designs, and conclusions in the study of psychosocial and pharmacological treatments of behavioral disorders. In L. White, B. Tursky, & G. Schwartz (Eds.), *Placebo: Clinical phenomenon and new insights.* New York: Guilford Press.

Paul, G.L., & Lentz, R.J. (1977). *Psychosocial treatment of chronic mental patients.* Cambridge, MA: Harvard University Press .

Pauls, D.L., Towbin, K.E., Leckman, J.F., Zahner, G.E.P., & Cohen, D.J. (1986). Gilles de la Tourette's syndrome and obsessive-compulsive disorder. *Archives of General Psychiatry, 43*, 1180–1182.

Pavkov, T.W., Lewis, D.A., & Lyons, J.S. (1989). Psychiatric diagnoses and racial bias: An empirical investigation. *Professional Psychology, 20*, 364–368.

Pavlov, I.P. (1928). On conditioned reflexes. In W.H. Gantt (Trans.), *Lectures on conditioned reflexes.* New York: International Publishers. (Original work published 1904)

Pavlov, I.P. (1957). *Experimental psychology and other essays.* New York: Philosophical Library.

Pawlarcyzk, D., & Beckwith, B.E. (1987). Depressive symptoms displayed by persons with mental retardation: A review. *Mental Retardation, 25*, 325–330.

Paykel, E.S. (Ed.). (1982). *Handbook of affective disorders.* New York: Guilford Press.

Paykel, E.S., Myers, J.K., Dienelt, M.N., Klerman, G.L., Lindenthal, J.J., & Pepper, M.P. (1969). Life events and depression: A controlled study. *Archives of General Psychiatry, 21*, 753–760.

Peck, M.L. (1985). Crisis intervention treatment with chronically and acutely suicidal adolescents. In M.L. Peck, N.L. Farberow, & R.E. Litman (Eds.), *Youth suicide.* New York: Springer Verlag.

Pelham, W.E., & Bender, M.E. (1982). Peer interactions of hyperactive children: Assessment and treatment. In K.D. Gadow & I. Gialer (Eds.), *Advances in learning and behavior difficulties.* Greenwich, CT: JAI Press.

Pelham, W.E., & Murphy, H.A. (1986). Behavioral and pharmacological treatment of attention deficit and conduct disorders. In M. Hersen (Ed.), *Pharmacological and behavioral treatment: An integrative approach.* New York: John Wiley.

Pelham, W.E., Schnedler, R.W., Bender, M.E., Miller, J., Nilsson, D., Budrow, M., Ronnei, M., Paluchowski, C., & Marks, D. (1988). A combination of behavioral therapy and methylphenidate in the treatment of hyperactivity: A theory outcome study. In L. Bloomingdale (Ed.), *Attention deficit disorders: III. New research in attention/treatment and psychopharmacology* (pp. 29–48). London: Pergamon Press.

Pelham, W., Schnedler, R., Bologna, N., & Contreras, A. (1980). Behavioral and stimulant treatment of hyperactive children: A therapy study with methylphenidate probes in a within—subject design. *Journal of Applied Behavior Analysis*, *13*, 221–236.

Pendery, M.L., Maltzman, I.M., & West, L.J. (1982). Controlled drinking by alcoholics? New findings and a reevaluation of a major affirmative study. *Science*, *217*, 169–175.

Penk, W., Robinowitz, R., Black, J., Dolan, M., Bell, W., Roberts, W., & Skinner, J. (1989). Co-morbidity: Lessons learned from Post-Traumatic Stress Disorder (PTSD) from developing PTSD scales for the MMPI. *Journal of Clinical Psychology*, *45*, 709–717.

Pennebaker, J.W., Kiecolt-Glaser, J.K., & Glaser, R. (1988). Disclosure of traumas and immune function: Health implications for psychotherapy. *Journal of Consulting and Clinical Psychology*, *56*, 239–245.

Peplau, L.A., Rubin, Z., & Hill, C.T. (1977). Sexual intimacy in dating relationships. *The Journal of Social Issues*, *33*, 86–109.

Perlin, M.L., & Sadoff, R.L. (1982). Ethical issues in the representation of individuals in the commitment process. *Law and Contemporary Problems*, *45*, 161–192.

Perls, F., Hefferline, R., & Goodman, P. (1951). *Gestalt therapy*. New York: Julian Press.

Persky, H., O'Brien, C.P., & Kahn, P.R. (1976). Reproductive hormone levels, sexual activity and moods during the menstrual cycle. *Psychosomatic Medicine*, *38*, 62–63.

Peters, R., Miller, K.S., Schmidt, W., & Meeter, D. (1987). The effects of statutory change on the civil commitment of the mentally ill. *Law and Human Behavior*, *11*, 73–99.

Peterson, C. (1988). Explanatory style as a risk factor for illness. *Cognitive Therapy and Research*, *12*, 117–130.

Peterson, C., Seligman, M.E.P., & Vaillant, G.E. (1988). Pessimistic explanatory style is a risk factor for physical illness: A thirty-five-year longitudinal study. *Journal of Personality and Social Psychology*, *55*, 23–27.

Petit, G.S., McClasky, C.L., Brown, M.M., & Dodge, K.A. (1987). The generalizability of laboratory assessments of children's socially competent behavior in specific situations. *Behavioral Assessment*, *9*, 81–96.

Petrella, R.C., & Poythress, N.G., Jr. (1983). The quality of forensic evaluations: An interdisciplinary study. *Journal of Consulting and Clinical Psychology*, *51*, 76–85.

Petti, T.A. (1983). Behavioral approaches in the treatment of depressed children. In D.P. Cantwell & G.A. Carlson (Eds.), *Affective disorders in childhood and adolescence*. New York: SP Medical & Scientific Books.

Petti, T.T. (1983). Imipramine in the treatment of depressed children. In D.P. Cantwell & G.A. Carlson (Eds.), *Affective disorders in childhood and adolescence*, (pp. 375–415). New York: Spectrum Publications.

Pfeffer, R.I., Afifi, A.A., & Chance, J.M. (1987). Prevalence of Alzheimer's disease in a retirement community. *American Journal of Epidemiology*, *125*, 420–436.

Pfefferbaum, A., Zipursky, R.B., Lim, K.O., Zatz, L.M., Stahl, S.M., & Jernigan, T.L. (1988). Computed tomographic evidence for generalized sulcal and ventricular enlargement in schizophrenia. *Archives of General Psychiatry*, *45*, 633–640.

Phelps, J.R. (1987). Physical activity and health maintenance—exactly what is known? *The Western Journal of Medicine*, *146*, 200–206.

Philips, C., & Hunter, M. (1981). The treatment of tension headache—I. Muscular abnormality in biofeedback. *Behaviour Research and Therapy*, *19*, 485–498.

Phillips, J. (1987). Science in the service of profession. *The Clinical Psychologist*, *40*, 60–62.

Phillips, M.R., Wolf, A.S., & Coons, D.J. (1988). Psychiatry and the criminal justice system: Testing the myths. *American Journal of Psychiatry*, *145*, 605–610.

Pinel, P. (1962). *A treatise on insanity*. New York: Hafner. (Original work published 1801)

Pinsker, H. (1967, May). *The irrelevancy of psychiatric diagnosis, or psychiatric diagnosis in the general hospital*. Paper at the Annual Meeting of the American Psychiatric Association, Detroit, MI.

Piotrowski, C., & Keller, J.W. (1989). Psychological testing in outpatient mental health facilities: A national study. *Professional Psychology: Research and Practice*, *20*, 423–425.

Piotrowski, C., Sherry, D., & Keller, J.W. (1985). Psychodiagnostic test usage: A survey of the Society for Personality Assessment. *Journal of Personality Assessment*, *49*, 115–119.

Piotrowski, Z. (1937). The Rorschach inkblot method in organic disturbances of the central nervous system. *Journal of Nervous and Mental Disease*, *86*, 525–537.

Pippard, J., & Ellam, L. (1981). *Electroconvulsive therapy in Great Britain*. London: Gaskell.

Piran, N., Bigler, E.D., & Cohen, D. (1982). Motoric laterality and eye dominance suggest unique pattern of cerebral organization in schizophrenia. *Archives of General Psychiatry*, *39*, 1006–1010.

Place, E.J.S., & Gilmore, G.C. (1980). Perceptual organization in schizophrenia. *Journal of Abnormal Psychology*, *89*, 409–418.

Plomin, R. (1986). *Development, genetics, and psychology*. Hillsdale, NJ: Lawrence Erlbaum.

Plomin, R. (1989). Environment and genes: Determinants of behavior. *American Psychologist*, *44*, 105–111.

Plomin, R., DeFries, J.C., & Fulker, D.W. (1988). *Nature and nurture during infancy and early childhood*. New York: Cambridge University Press.

Polivy, J. (1976). Perception of calories and regulation of intake in restrained and unrestrained subjects. *Addictive Behaviors*, *1*, 237–243.

Polivy, J., & Herman, C.P. (1985). Dieting and binging: A causal analysis. *American Psychologist*, *40*, 193–201.

Pomerleau, O.F., & Rodin, J. (1986). In S. Garfield & A. Bergin (Eds.), *Handbook of psychotherapy and behavior change*. New York: John Wiley.

Pope, H.G. Jr., & Hudson, J.I. (1982). Treatment of bulimia with antidepressants. *Psychopharmacology*, *78*, 167–179.

Pope, H.G. Jr., Hudson, J.I., Jonas, J.M., & Yurgelun-Todd, D. (1985). Antidepressant treatment of bulimia: A two year follow-up study. *Journal of Clinical Psychology*, *5*, 320–327.

Pope, H.G., & Hudson, J.I. (1988). Is bulimia nervosa a heterogeneous disorder? Lessons from the history of medicine. *International Journal of Eating Disorders*, *7*, 155–166.

Pope, K.S., & Bouhoutsos, J.C. (1986). *Sexual intimacy between therapists and patients*. New York: Praeger.

Popper, K. (1962). *Conjectures and refutations*. New York: Basic Books.

Porjesz, B., & Begleiter, H. (1983). Brain dysfunction and alcohol. In B. Kissin & H. Begleiter (Eds.), *The pathogenesis of alcoholism* (pp. 415–483). New York: Plenum.

Potter, W.Z., Rudorfer, M.V., & Goodwin, F.K. (1987). Biological findings in bipolar disorders. In R.E. Hales & A.J. Frances (Eds.), *American Psychiatric Association Annual Review* (Vol. 6). Washington, DC: American Psychiatric Press.

Powell, L.S., & Courtice, K. (1983). *Alzheimer's disease: A guide for families*. New York: Addison-Wesley.

Preng, K.W., & Clopton, J.R. (1986). Application of the MacAndrew Alcoholism Scale to alcoholics with psychiatric diagnoses. *Journal of Personality Assessment*, *50*, 113–122.

Price, L.H., Charney, D.S., Delgado, P.L., & Heninger, G.R. (1989). Lithium treatment and serotoninergic function. *Archives of General Psychiatry*, *46*, 13–19.

Prinz, R.J. (1985). Diet-behavior research with children: Methodological and substantive issues. *Advances in Learning and Behavioral Disabilities*, *4*, 181–189.

Prioleau, L., Murdock, M., & Brody, N. (1983). An analysis of psychotherapy versus placebo studies. *The Behavioral and Brain Sciences*, *6*, 275–310.

Putnam, F.W. (1984). The psychophysiological investigation of multiple personality: A review. *Psychiatric Clinics of North America*, *7*, 31–39.

Putnam, F.W., Guroff, J.J., Silberman, E.D., Barban, L., & Post, R.M. (1986). The clinical phenomenology of multiple personality disorder: Review of 100 recent cases. *Journal of Clinical Psychology*, *47*, 285–293.

Pyle, R.L., Halvorson, A., Neuman, P.A., & Mitchell, J.E. (1986). The increasing prevalence of bulimia in freshmen college students. *International Journal of Eating Disorders*, *5*, 631–648.

Pyle, R.L., Mitchell, J.E., & Eckert, E.D. (1981). Bulimia: A report of 34 cases. *Journal of Clinical Psychiatry, 42*, 60–64.

Pyszczynski, T., & Greenberg, J. (1987). Self-regulatory perseveration and the depressive self-focusing style: A self-awareness theory of reactive depression. *Psychological Bulletin, 102*, 122–138.

Quay, H.C. (1978). Classification. In H.C. Quay & J.S. Werry (Eds.), *Psychopathological disorders of childhood*. New York: John Wiley.

Rabiner, C.J., & Klein, D.F. (1969). Imipramine treatment of school phobia. *Comprehensive Psychiatry, 10*, 387–390.

Rabkin, J.G., & Struening, E.L. (1976). Life events, stress, and illness. *Science, 194*, 1013–1020.

Rachman, S. (1976). Observational learning and therapeutic modeling. In M.P. Feldman & A. Broadhurst (Eds.), *Theoretical and experimental bases of the behaviour therapies*. New York: John Wiley.

Rachman, S. (1977). The passing of the two-stage theory of fear and avoidance: Fresh possibilities. *Behaviour Research and Therapy, 14*, 125–131.

Rachman, S. (1980). Obsessional-compulsive disorders. In E.S. Valenstein (Ed.), *The psychosurgery debate: Scientific, legal and ethical perspectives*. San Francisco, CA: W.H. Freeman.

Rachman, S., & Hodgson, R.J. (1968). Experimentally induced "sexual fetishism": Replication and development. *Psychological Record, 18*, 25–27.

Rachman, S., & Hodgson, R.J. (1980). *Obsessions and compulsions*. Englewood Cliffs, NJ: Prentice-Hall.

Rachman, S.J., & Wilson, G.T. (1980). *The effects of the psychological therapies*. Oxford: Pergamon Press.

Rachman, S., & Maser, J.D. (Eds.). (1988). *Panic: Psychological perspectives*. Hillsdale, NJ: Lawrence Erlbaum.

Rachman, S., & Wilson, G.T. (1980). *The effects of psychological therapy*. Oxford: Pergamon Press.

Rado, S., Buchenholz, B., Dunton, H., Karlen, S.H., & Senescu, R. (1956). Schizotypal organization. In S. Rado & G.E. Daniels (Eds.), *Changing concepts of psychoanalytical medicine*. New York: Grune & Stratton.

Ragland, D.R., & Brand, R.J. (1988). Type A behavior and mortality from coronary heart disease. *The New England Journal of Medicine, 318*, 65–69.

Ramsey, R.G. (1981). *Neuroradiology*. Philadelphia: Saunders.

Rankin, H. (1986). Dependence and compulsion: Experimental models of change. In W.R. Miller & N. Heather (Eds.), *Treating addictive behaviors: Processes of change* (pp. 361–374). New York: Plenum Press.

Rapaport, D. (1960). *The structure of psychoanalytic theory*. New York: International Universities Press.

Rapee, R., Mattick, R., & Murrell, E. (1986). Cognitive mediation in the affective component of spontaneous panic attacks. *Journal of Behavior Therapy and Experimental Psychiatry, 17*, 245–253.

Raphael, T., Power, S.H., & Berridge, W.L. (1937). The question of suicide as a problem in college mental hygiene. *American Journal of Orthopsychiatry, 7*, 1–14.

Rapoport, J.L., Buchsbaum, M.S., Zahn, T.P., Weingartner, H., Ludow, C., & Mikkelsen, E. (1978). Dextroamphetamine: Cognitive and behavioral effects in normal prepubertal boys. *Science, 199*, 560–563.

Ravussin, E., Lillioja, S., Knowler, W.C., Christin, L., Freymond, D., Abbott, W.G.H., Boyce, U., Howard, B.U., & Bogardus, C. (1988). Reduced rate of energy expenditure as a risk factor for body-weight gain. *The New England Journal of Medicine, 318*, 467–472.

Ray, O. (1990). *Drugs, society, and human behavior.* St. Louis: Times Mirror/Mosby College Publishing.

Redd, W., & Andrykowski, M.A. (1982). Behavioral intervention in cancer treatment: Controlling aversion reactions to chemotherapy. *Journal of Consulting and Clinical Psychology, 50*, 1018–1029.

Regier, D.A., & Burke, J.D. (1987). Psychiatric disorders in the community: The epidemiologic catchment area study. In R.E. Hales & A.J. Frances (Eds.), *American Psychiatric Association Annual Review* (Vol. 6). Washington, DC: American Psychiatric Press.

Regier, D.A., Myers, J.K., Kramer, M., Robins, L.N., Blazer, D.G., Hough, R.L., Eaton, W.W., & Locke, B.Z. (1984). The NIMH epidemiologic catchment area program. *Archives of General Psychiatry, 41*, 934–941.

Rehm, L.P. (1977). A self-control model of depression. *Behavior Therapy, 8*, 787–804.

Rehm, L.P. (1987). Approaches to the prevention of depression with children. In R.F. Munoz (Ed.), *Depression prevention* (pp. 79–91). Washington: Hemisphere.

Rehm, L.P. (1988). Self-management and cognitive processes in depression. In L.B. Alloy (Ed.), *Cognitive processes in depression* (pp. 143–176). New York: Guilford Press.

Rehm, L.P., & Plakosh, P. (1975). Preference for immediate reinforcement in depression. *Journal of Behavior Therapy and Experimental Psychology, 6*, 101–113.

Reich, J., Noyes, R., Jr., Hirshfeld, R., Coryell, W., & O'Gorman, T. (1987). State and personality in depressed and panic patients. *American Journal of Psychiatry, 144*, 181–187.

Reifler, B.V., Larson, E., & Hanley, R. (1982). Coexistence of cognitive impairment and depression in geriatric outpatients. *American Journal of Psychiatry, 139*, 623–626.

Reiman, E.M., Fusselman, M.J., Fox, P.T., & Raichle, M.E. (1989). Neuroanatomical correlates of anticipatory anxiety. *Science, 243*, 1071–1074.

Reiman, E.M., Raichle, M.E., Robins, E., Butler, F.K., Herscovitch, P., Fox, P., & Perlmutter, J. (1986). Application of positron emission tomography to study of panic disorder. *American Journal of Psychiatry, 143*, 469–477.

Reisberg, B., Borenstein, J., Salob, S.P., Ferris, S.H., Franssen, E., & Georgotas, A. (1987). Behavioral symptoms in Alzheimer's disease: Phenomenology and treatment. *Journal of Clinical Psychiatry, 48*, 9–13.

Reitan, R.M. (1959). The comparative effects of brain damage on the Halstead impairment index and the Wechsler-Bellevue scale. *Journal of Clinical Psychology, 25*, 281–285.

Reitan, R.M., & Davison, I.A. (1974). *Clinical neuropsychology: Current status and applications*. Washington, DC: V.H. Winston.

Rekers, G. (1982). *Growing up straight: What every family should know about homosexuality*. Chicago: Moody Press.

Rekers, G.A., & Lovaas, O.I. (1974). Behavioral treatment of deviant sex-role behaviors in a male child. *Journal of Applied Behavior Analysis, 7*, 173–190.

Rescorla, R.A. (1988). Pavlovian conditioning: It's not what you think it is. *American Psychologist, 43*, 151–160.

Resick, P.A., Jordan, C.G., Girelli, S.A., Hutter, C.K., & Marhoefer-Dvorak, S. (1988). A comparative outcome study of behavioral group therapy for sexual assault victims. *Behavior Therapy, 19*, 385–402.

Reynolds, C.F., & Kupfer, D.J. (1987). Sleep research in affective illness: State of the art circa 1987. *Sleep, 10*, 199–215.

Rice, D.G., & Greenfield, N.S. (1969). Psychophysiological correlates of "la belle indifference." *Archives of General Psychiatry, 130*, 102–105.

Rice, J., Reich, T., Andreasen, N.C., Endicott, J., Van Eerdewegh, M., Fishman, R., Hirschfeld, R.M.A., & Klerman, G.L. (1987). The familial transmission of bipolar illness. *Archives of General Psychiatry, 44*, 441–447.

Richardson, W.P., & Higgins, A.C. (1965). *The handicapped children of Alamance County, North Carolina*. Wilmington, DE: Nemours Foundation.

Rickels, K., Case, W.G., Downing, R.W., & Winoker, A. (1983). Long term diazepam therapy and clinical outcome. *Journal of the American Medical Association, 250*, 767–771.

Rincover, A. (1986). Behavioral research in self-injury and self-stimulation. *Psychiatric Clinics of North America, 9*, 755–766.

Rinsley, D.B. (1982). *Borderline and other self disorders*. New York: Jason Aronson.

Robertson, N. (1988). *A.A.: Inside Alcoholics Anonymous*. New York: William Morrow.

Robin, A.L., & Foster, S.L. (1988). *Negotiating adolescence: A behavioral family systems approach to parent/teen conflict*. New York: Guilford Press.

Robin, A.L., & Siegel, P. (1987). *Behavioral family systems therapy for ano-*

rexia nervosa. Unpublished manuscript.

Robins, L.N. (1966). *Deviant children grown up*. Baltimore: Williams and Wilkins.

Robins, L.N. (1978). Sturdy childhood predictors of adult antisocial behavior: Replications from longitudinal studies. *Psychological Medicine*, *8*, 611–622.

Robins, L.N. (1985). Epidemiology: Reflections on testing the validity of psychiatric interviews. *Archives of General Psychiatry*, *42*, 918–924.

Robins, L.N., & Helzer, J.E. (1986). Diagnosis and clinical assessment: The current state of psychiatric diagnosis. *Annual Review of Psychology* (Vol. 37, pp. 409–432).

Robins, L.N., Helzer, J.E., Croughan, H., & Ratcliff, K.S. (1981). National Institute of Mental Health Diagnostic Interview Schedule: Its history, characteristics, and validity. *Archives of General Psychiatry*, *38*, 381–389.

Robins, L.N., Helzer, J.E., Weissman, M.M., Orvaschel, H., Gruenberg, E., Burke, J.D., & Regier, D.A. (1984). Lifetime prevalence of specific psychiatric disorders in three sites. *Archives of General Psychiatry*, *41*, 949–958.

Rodeheaver, D., & Datan, N. (1988). The challenge of double jeopardy: Toward a mental health agenda for aging women. *American Psychologist*, *43*, 648–654.

Rodin, J. (1988, April 29). Control, health, and aging. Invited Address to the Society of Behavioral Medicine, Boston.

Rodin, J. (1989). Personal communication.

Rodin, J., & Salovey, P. (1989). Health psychology. *Annual Review of Psychology*, *40*, 533–579.

Rodnick, E.H., Goldstein, M.J., Lewis, J.M., & Doane, J.A. (1984). Parental communication style, affect, and role as precursors of offspring schizophrenia. In N.F. Watt, E.J. Anthony, L.C. Wynne, & J.E. Rolf (Eds.), *Children at risk for schizophrenia: A longitudinal perspective*. New York: Cambridge University Press.

Rofman, E.S., Askinazi, C., & Fant, E. (1980). The prediction of dangerous behavior in emergency civil commitment. *American Journal of Psychiatry*, *137*, 1061–1064.

Rogers, C.R. (1942). *Counseling and psychotherapy*. Boston: Houghton Mifflin.

Rogers, C.R. (1951). *Client-centered therapy: Its current practice, implications and theory*. Boston: Houghton Mifflin.

Rogers, C.R. (1961). *On becoming a person*. Boston: Houghton Mifflin.

Rorschach, H. (1921). *Psychodiagnostik*. Bern and Leipzig: Ernst Bircher Verlag.

Rose, T.L. (1978). The functional relationship between artificial food colors and hyperactivity. *Journal of Applied Behavior Analysis*, *11*, 439–446.

Rosen, J.C., & Gross, J. (1987). The prevalence of weight reducing and weight gaining in adolescent girls and boys. *Health Psychology*, *6*, 131–147.

Rosen, J.C., & Leitenberg, H. (1985). Exposure and response prevention treatment of bulimia. In D.M. Garner & P.E. Garfinkel (Eds.), *Handbook of psychotherapy for anorexia nervosa and bulimia*. New York: Guilford Press.

Rosen, L.A., O'Leary, S., Joyce, S.A., Conway, G., & Pfiffner, L. (1984). The importance of prudent negative consequences for maintaining the appropriate behavior of hyperactive students. *Journal of Abnormal Child Psychology*, *12*, 581–604.

Rosen, R.C., & Beck, J.G. (1988). *Patterns of sexual arousal*. New York: Guilford Press.

Rosen, R.C., & Hall, E. (1984). *Sexuality*. New York: Random House.

Rosen, R.C., & Hall, K.S. (in press). Behavioral treatment approaches for offenders and victims. In W.O. Donohue & J. Geer (Eds.), *Sexual abuse of children*. Hillsdale, NJ: Lawrence Erlbaum.

Rosen, R.C., & Leiblum, S.R. (1987). Current approaches to the evaluation of sexual desire disorders. *The Journal of Sex Research*, *23*, 141–162.

Rosenbaum, J.F., Biederman, J., Gersten, M., Hirshfeld, D.R., Meminger, S.R., Herman, J.B., Kagan, J., Reznick, J.S., & Snidman, N. (1988). Behavioral inhibition in children of parents with panic disorder and agoraphobia. *Archives of General Psychiatry*, *45*, 463–470.

Rosenberg, S.E. (1985). Brief psychodynamic therapy for depression. In E.E. Beckham & W.R. Leber (Eds.), *Handbook of depression* (pp. 100–123). Homewood, IL: Dorsey.

Rosenbluth, J., Nathan, P.E., & Lawson, D.M. (1978). Environmental influences on drinking by college students in a college pub: Behavioral observation in the natural environment. *Addictive Behaviors*, *3*, 117–121.

Rosenman, R.H., Brand, R.J., Jenkins, C.D., Friedman, M., Straus, R., & Wurm, M. (1975). Coronary heart disease in the Western Collaborative Group Study: Final follow-up experience of 8 1/2 years. *Journal of the American Medical Association*, *233*, 872–877.

Rosenthal, D. (1970). Genetic research in the schizophrenic syndrome. In R. Cancro (Ed.), *The schizophrenic reactions*. New York: Brunner/Mazel.

Rosenthal, T.L. (1976). Modeling therapies. In M. Hersen, P.M. Miller, & R. Eisler (Eds.), *Progress in behavior modification* (Vol. 2). New York: Academic Press.

Rosenzweig, S. (1988). The identity and idiodynamics of the multiple personality "Sally Beauchamp." *American Psychologist*, *43*, 45–48.

Ross, D.M. (1974). *Psychological disorders of children*. New York: McGraw-Hill.

Ross, D.M., & Ross, S.A. (1976). *Hyperactivity: Research-theory-action*. New York: John Wiley.

Rossiter, L.F. (1983). Prescribed medicines: Findings from the National Medical Care Expenditure Survey. *American Journal of Public Health*, *73*, 1312–1315.

Roth, B. (1980). *Narcolepsy & hypersomnia*. New York: Krager.

Rotter, J.B., & Rafferty, J.E. (1950). *Manual: The Rotter Incomplete Sentences Blank*. New York: Psychological Corporation.

Rounsaville, B.J., Kosten, T.R., Williams, J.B.W., & Spitzer, R.L. (1987). A field trial of *DSM-III-R* psychoactive substance dependence disorders. *American Journal of Psychiatry*, *144*, 351–355.

Rovner, B.W., Broadhead, J., Spencer, M., Carson, K., & Folstein, M.F. (1989). Depression and Alzheimer's disease. *American Journal of Psychiatry*, *146*, 350–353.

Rowe, J.W., & Kahn, R.L. (1987). Human aging: Usual and successful. *Science*, *237*, 143–149.

Roy, A., Adinoff, B., Roehrich, L., Lamparski, D., Custer, R., Lorenz, V., Barbaccia, M., Guidotti, A., Costa, E., & Linnoila, M. (1988). Pathological gambling: A psychobiological study. *Archives of General Psychiatry*, *45*, 369–373.

Rush, H.A., Beck, A.T., Kovacs, M., & Hollon, S. (1977). Comparative efficacy of cognitive therapy and pharmacotherapy in treatment of depressed outpatients. *Cognitive Research and Therapy*, *1*, 17–37.

Russell, D.E.H. (1983). The incidence and prevalence of intrafamilial and extrafamilial sexual abuse of female children. *International Journal of Child Abuse and Neglect*, *7*, 133–139.

Russell, G.F.M., Szmukler, G.I., Dare, C., & Eisler, I. (1987). An evaluation of family therapy in anorexia nervosa and bulimia nervosa. *Archives of General Psychiatry*, *44*, 1047–1056.

Rutter, M. (1970). Sex differences in children's response to family stress. In E.J. Anthony & C. Koupernik (Eds.), *The child in his family*. New York: John Wiley.

Rutter, M. (1987). Temperament, personality and personality disorder. *British Journal of Psychiatry*, *150*, 443–458.

Rutter, M., & Garmezy, N. (1983). Developmental psychology. In P. Mussen (Ed.), *Handbook of child psychology* (Vol. 4). New York: John Wiley.

Rutter, M., Graham, P., Chadwick, O., & Yule, W. (1976). Adolescent turmoil: Fact or fiction? *Journal of Child Psychology and Psychiatry*, *17*, 35–56.

Sachs, J.S. (1983). Negative factors in brief psychotherapy. *Journal of Consulting and Clinical Psychology*, *51*, 557–564.

Sack, R.L., Lewy, A.J., White, D.M., Singer, C.M., Fireman, M.J., & Vandiver, R. (1990). Morning vs. evening light treatment for winter depression. *American Journal of Psychiatry*, *47*, 343–351.

Safer, D.J., & Krager, J.M. (1984a). Trends in medication treatment of hyperactive school children. In K.D. Gadow (Ed.), *Advances in learning and behavioral disabilities* (Vol. 3). Greenwich, CT: JAI Press.

Safer, D.J., & Krager, J.M. (1984b). Trends in medication treatment of hyperactive school children: Results of six biannual surveys. *Clinical Pediatrics*, *22*, 500–504.

Salkovskis, P.M. (1989). Somatic problems. In K. Hawton, P.M. Salkovskis, J. Kirk, & D.M. Clark (Eds.), *Cognitive behaviour therapy for psychiatric problems*. New York: Oxford University Press.

Salter, A. (1949). *Conditioned reflex therapy*. New York: Farrar, Straus.

Salzman, C. (1989). Treatment with antianxiety agents. In *American Psychiatric Association Task Force on Treatments of Psychiatric Disorders* (Vol. 3, pp. 2036–2065). Washington, DC: American Psychiatric Association.

Salzman, L. (1985). *Treatment of the obsessive personality*. New York: Jason Aronson.

Sanchez-Craig, M. (1980). Random assignment to abstinence or controlled drinking in a cognitive-behavioral program: Short-term effects on drinking behavior. *Addictive Behaviors*, *5*, 35–39.

Sanchez-Craig, M., Annis, H.M., Bornet, A.R., & MacDonald, K.R. (1984). Random assignment to abstinence and controlled drinking: Evaluation of a cognitive-behavioral program for problem drinkers. *Journal of Consulting and Clinical Psychology*, *52*, 390–403.

Sarrel, P.M., & Masters, W.H. (1982). Sexual molestation of men by women. *Archives of Sexual Behavior*, *11*, 117–131.

Sartorius, N., Shapiro, R., & Jablensky, A. (1974). The international pilot study of schizophrenia. *Schizophrenia Bulletin*, *11*, 21–35.

Satir, V. (1967). *Conjoint family therapy* (rev. ed.). Palo Alto, CA: Science and Behavior Books.

Satterfield, J.H., Cantwell, D.P., & Satterfield, B.T. (1979). Multimodality treatment. *Archives of General Psychiatry*, *36*, 965–974.

Satterfield, J.H., Satterfield, B.T., & Cantwell, D.P. (1980). Multimodality treatment: A two-year evaluation of 61 hyperactive boys. *Archives of General Psychiatry*, *37*, 915–918.

Satterfield, J.H., Satterfield, B.T., & Cantwell, D.P. (1981). Three-year multi-modality treatment study of 100 hyperactive boys. *Journal of Pediatrics*, *98*, 650–655.

Sax, M.J. (1984). Some data to enlighten some doctrines. *Contemporary Psychology*, *29*, 8–9.

Schacht, T.E. (1985). *DSM-III* and the politics of truth. *American Psychologist*, *40*, 513–521.

Schacht, T.E., & Nathan, P.E. (1977). But is it good for the psychologists? Appraisal and the status of DSM-III. *American Psychologist*, *32*, 1017–1025.

Schacter, D.L., Wang, P.L., Tulving, E., & Freedman, M. (1982). Functional retrograde amnesia: A quantitative case study. *Neuropsychologia*, *20*, 523–532.

Schaie, K.W. (1988). Ageism in psychological research. *American Psychologist*, *43*, 179–183.

Schechtman, C., Nahmias, C., Garnett, E.S., Firnau, G., Brown, G.M., Kaplan, R.D., & Cleghorn, J.M. (1988). Effect of neuroleptics on altered cerebral glucose metabolism in schizophrenia. *Archives of General Psychiatry*, *45*, 523–532.

Schildkraut, J.J., Green, A.I., & Mooney, J.J. (1985). Affective disorders: Biochemical aspects. In H.I. Kaplan & B.J. Sadock (Eds.), *Comprehensive textbook of psychiatry* (Vol. 1, pp. 769–778, 4th. ed.) Baltimore MD: Williams & Wilkins.

Schleifer, S.J., & Keller, S.E. (1989). Immunity and major depressive disorder. In A.E. Miller (Ed.), *Depressive disorders and immunity* (pp. 65–84). Washington, DC: American Psychiatric Press.

Schneck, M.K., Reisberg, B., & Ferris, S.H. (1982). An overview of current concepts of Alzheimer's disease. *American Journal of Psychiatry*, *139*, 165–173.

Schneidman, E.S. (1985). *Definition of suicide*. New York: John Wiley.

Schneidman, E.S., & Farberow, N.L. (1957). *Clues to suicide*. New York: McGraw-Hill.

Schofield, W. (1964). *Psychotherapy: The purchase of friendship*. Englewood Cliffs, NJ: Prentice-Hall.

Schopler, E. (1987). Lovaas study questioned. *Autism Research Review*, *1*, 6–7.

Schover, L., & LoPiccolo, J. (1982). Effectiveness of treatment for dysfunctions of sex desire. *Journal of Sex and Marital Therapy*, *8*, 179–197.

Schroeder, S.R., Schroeder, C.S., & Landesman, S. (1987). Psychological services in educational settings to persons with mental retardation. *American Psychologist*, *42*, 805–808.

Schuckit, M.A. (1986). Genetic and clinical implications of alcoholism and affective disorder. *American Journal of Psychiatry*, *143*, 140–146.

Schuckit, M.A. (1989). The relationship between alcohol problems, substance abuse, and psychiatric syndromes: Report for the *DSM-IV* Workgroup on Alcohol and Substance Problems. Unpublished manuscript, University of California, San Diego.

Schumacher, S., & Lloyd, C.W. (1981). Physiological and psychological factors in impotence. *The Journal of Sex Research*, *17*, 40–53.

Schwartz, G.E., & Beatty, J. (1977). *Biofeedback: Theory and research*. New York: Academic Press.

Schwartz, G.E., & Weiss, S.M. (1978). Behavioral medicine revisited: An amended definition. *Journal of Behavioral Medicine*, *1*, 249–252.

Schwartz, H.I., Appelbaum, P.S., & Kaplan, R.D. (1984). Clinical judgments in the decision to commit. *Archives of General Psychiatry*, *41*, 811–815.

Schwartz, H.J. (Ed.). (1988). *Bulimia: Psychoanalytic treatment and theory*. Madison, CT: International Universities Press.

Schwartz, M.S., Blazer, D.G., George, L.K., Winfield, I., Zakris, J., & Dye, E. (1989). Identification of borderline personality disorder with the NIMH diagnostic interview schedule. *American Journal of Psychiatry*, *146*, 200–205.

Searles, J.S. (1985). A methodological and empirical critique of psychotherapy outcome meta-analysis. *Behavior Research and Therapy*, *23*, 453–464.

Sears, R.R., Maccoby, E., & Levin, H. (1957). *Patterns of child rearing*. New York: Harper & Row.

Segal, B. (1988). *Drugs and behavior*. New York: Gardner Press.

Segal, J.H. (1989). Erotomania revisited: From Kraepelin to DSM-III-R. *American Journal of Psychiatry*, *146*, 1261–1266.

Segal, S.P., Watson, M.A., Goldfinger, S.M., & Averbuck, D.S. (1988a). Civil commitment in the psychiatric emergency room. I. The assessment of dangerousness by emergency room clinicians. *Archives of General Psychiatry*, *45*, 748–752.

Segal, S.P., Watson, M.A., Goldfinger, S.M., & Averbuck, D.S. (1988b). Civil commitment in the psychiatric emergency room. II. Mental disorder indicators and three dangerousness criteria. *Archives of General Psychiatry*, *45*, 753–758.

Segal, S.P., Watson, M.A., Goldfinger, S.M., & Averbuck, D.S. (1988c). Civil commitment in the psychiatric emergency room. III. Disposition as a function of mental disorder and dangerousness indicators. *Archives of General Psychiatry*, *45*, 759–763.

Seiden, R.H. (1969). *Suicide among youth: A review of the literature, 1900–1967*. Department of Health, Education and Welfare. Washington, DC: U.S. Government Printing Office.

Seidman, L.J. (1983). Schizophrenia and brain dysfunction: An integration of recent neurodiagnostic findings. *Psychological Bulletin*, *94*, 195–238.

Seligman, M.E.P. (1971). Phobias and preparedness. *Behavior Therapy*, *2*, 307–320.

Seligman, M.E.P. (1975). *Helplessness: On depression, development, and death*. San Francisco: W.H. Freeman.

Seligman, M.E.P., Abramson, L.Y., Semmel, A., & von Baeyer, C. (1979). Depressive attributional style. *Journal of Abnormal Psychology*, *88*, 242–247.

Selvini-Palazzoli, M., Boscolo, L., Cecchin, G., & Prata, G. (1978). *Paradox and Counterparadox*. New York: Jason Aronson.

Selye, H. (1956). *The stress of life*. New York: McGraw-Hill.

Shadish, W.R. (1984). Policy research: Lessons from the implementation of deinstitutionalization. *American Psychologist*, *39*, 725–738.

Shaffer, D. (1974). Suicide in childhood and early adolescence. *Journal of Child Psychology and Psychiatry*, *15*, 275–291.

Shaffer, D. (1986). Learning theories of anxiety. In R. Gittelman (Ed.), *Anxiety disorders of childhood*. New York: Guilford Press.

Shaffer, D., & Fisher, P. (1981). The epidemiology of suicide in children and young adolescents. *Journal of the*

American Academy of Child Psychiatry, 21, 545–565.

Shagass, C., Roemer, R.A., & Straumanis, J.J. (1982). Relationships between psychiatric diagnosis and some quantitative EEG variables. *Archives of General Psychiatry, 39*, 1423–1435.

Shah, S., & McGarry, A. (1986). Legal psychiatry and psychology: Review of programs, training and qualifications. In W. Curran, A. McGarry, & S. Shah (Eds.), *Forensic psychiatry and psychology*. Philadelphia: Davis.

Shamoon, H., Hendler, R., & Sherwin, R.S. (1980). Synergistic interactions among anti-insulin hormones in the pathogenesis of stress hyperglycemia in humans. *Journal of Clinical Endocrinology and Metabolism, 52*, 1235–1241.

Shapiro, B.K., Palmer, F.B., & Capute, A.J. (1987). The early detection of mental retardation. *Clinical Pediatrics, 26*, 215–220.

Shapiro, D., & Goldstein, I.B. (1982). Biobehavioral perspectives on hypertension. *Journal of Consulting and Clinical Psychology, 50*, 841–858.

Shapiro, D.A., & Shapiro, D. (1983). Comparative therapy outcome research: Methodological implications of meta-analysis. *Journal of Consulting and Clinical Psychology, 51*, 42–53.

Shavit, Y., & Martin, F.C. (1987). Opiates, stress, and immunity: Animal studies. *Annals of Behavioral Medicine, 9*, 11–15.

Shedler, J., & Block, J. (1990). Adolescent drug use and psychological health. *American Psychologist, 45*, 612–630.

Sheehan, D.V. (1983). *The anxiety disease*. New York: Charles Scribner.

Sheehan, D.V., Ballenger, J., & Jacobson, G. (1980). Treatment of endogenous anxiety with phobic hysterical and hypochondriacal symptoms. *Archives of General Psychiatry, 37*, 51–59.

Sheehan, D.V., Sheehan, K.E., & Minichiello, W.E. (1981). Age of onset of phobic disorders: A reevaluation. *Comprehensive Psychiatry, 22*, 544–553.

Shelton, R.C., & Weinberger, D.R. (1986). X-ray computerized tomography studies in schizophrenia: A review and synthesis. In H. Nasrallah & D.R. Weinberger (Eds.), *The neurology of schizophrenia*. Amsterdam: Elsevier.

Sher, K.J. (1985). Excluding problem drinkers in high-risk studies of alcoholism: Effect of screening criteria on high-risk versus low-risk comparisons. *Journal of Abnormal Psychology, 94*, 106–109.

Sher, K.J. (1987). Stress response dampening. In H.T. Blane & K.E. Leonard (Eds.), *Psychological theories of drinking and alcoholism* (pp. 227–271). New York: Guilford Press.

Sher, K.J. (in press). *A critical review of the literature on the behavioral effects of parental alcoholism*. Chicago: University of Chicago Press.

Sher, K.J., & Levenson, R.W. (1982). Risk for alcoholism and individual differences in the stress-response dampening effect of alcohol. *Journal of Abnormal Psychology, 91*, 350–368.

Sherman, L.W., & Berk, R.A. (1984). The specific deterrent effects of arrest for domestic violence. *American Sociological Review, 49*, 261–262.

Shiffman, S., Read, L., Maltese, J., Rapkin, D., & Jarvik, M.E. (1985). Preventing relapse in ex-smokers: A self-management approach. In G.A. Marlatt & J.R. Gordon (Eds.), *Relapse prevention* (pp. 472–520). New York: Guilford Press.

Shilts, R. (1988). *And the band played on: Politics, people, and the AIDS epidemic*. New York: Penguin Books.

Siegel, B.S. (1986). *Love, medicine, and miracles: Lessons learned about self-healing from a surgeon's experience with exceptional patients*. New York: Harper & Row.

Siegel, S. (1978). A Pavlovian conditioning analysis of morphine tolerance. In N.A. Krasnegor (Ed.), *Behavioral tolerance*. Washington, DC: NIDA.

Siegel, S. (1983). Classical conditioning, drug tolerance, and drug dependence. In R. Smart, F. Glaser, Y. Israel, H. Kalant, R. Popham, & W. Schmidt (Eds.), *Research advances in alcohol and drug problems* (Vol. 7). New York: Plenum.

Siever, L.J., Haier, R.J., Coursey, R.D., Sostek, A.J., Murphy, D.L., Holzman, P.S., & Buchsbaum, M.S. (1982). Smooth pursuit eye tracking impairment. *Archives of General Psychiatry, 39*, 1001–1005.

Sifneos, P.E. (1979). *Short-term psychotherapy: Evaluation and technique*. New York: Plenum.

Sigurdsson, B. (1954). Rida, a chronic encephalitis of sheep with general remarks on infections which develop slowly and some of their special characteristics. *British Veterinary Journal, 110*, 341–343.

Sigvardsson, S., Von Knorring, A.L., Bohman, M., & Cloninger, C.R. (1984). An adoption study of somatoform disorders. *Archives of General Psychiatry, 41*, 853–859.

Silberman, C.E. (1970). *Crisis in the classroom*. New York: Random House.

Silverton, L., Finello, K.M., Mednick, S.A., & Schulsinger, F. (1985). Low birth weight and ventricular enlargement in high-risk sample. *Journal of Abnormal Psychology, 94*, 410–413.

Simon, R.I. (1987). *Clinical psychiatry and law*. Washington, DC: American Psychiatric Press.

Simons, A.D., Garfield, S.L., & Murphy, G.E. (1984). The process of change in cognitive therapy and pharmacotherapy for depression. *Archives of General Psychiatry, 41*, 45–51.

Sims, E., Goldman, R., Gluck, C., Horton, E., Kelleher, P., & Rowe, D. (1968). Experimental obesity in man. *Transcript of American Physicians, 81*, 153.

Sizemore, C.C. (1986, March). On my life with multiple personalities. *Art Therapy*, pp. 18–21.

Sizemore, C.C. (1989). *A mind of my own*. New York: William Morrow.

Sizemore, C.C., & Pittillo, E.S. (1977). *I'm Eve*. Garden City, NY: Doubleday.

Skinner, B.F. (1938). *The behavior of organisms*. New York: Appleton-Century-Crofts.

Skinner, B.F. (1953). *Science and human behavior*. New York: Macmillan.

Skinner, B.F. (1963). Behaviorism at fifty. *Science, 140*, 951–958.

Skinner, B.F. (1969). *Contingencies of reinforcement*. New York: Appleton-Century-Crofts.

Skinner, H.A., & Jackson, D.N. (1978). A model of psychopathology based on an integration of MMPI actuarial systems. *Journal of Consulting and Clinical Psychology, 46*, 231–238.

Skodol, A.E., & Spitzer, R.L. (1987). *An annotated bibliography of DSM-III*. Washington, DC: American Psychiatric Press.

Slade, P. (1974). Psychometric studies of obsessional illness and obsessional personality. In H.R. Beech (Ed.), *Obsessional states*. London: Methuen.

Slade, P.D. (1972). The effects of systematic desensitization on auditory hallucinations. *Behaviour Research and Therapy, 10*, 85–91.

Slater, E. (1953). *Psychotic and neurotic illness in twins*. London: MRC Special Publication 278, H.M.S.O.

Slater, E., & Cowie, V. (1971). *The genetics of marital disorders*. London: Oxford University Press.

Slater, E.T.O. (1965). Diagnosis of "hysteria." *British Medical Journal, 1*, 1395–1399.

Slater, E.T.O., & Glithero, E. (1965). A follow-up of patients diagnosed as suffering from "hysteria." *Journal of Psychosomatic Research, 9*, 9–13.

Sloane, R.B., Staples, F.R., Cristol, A.H., Yorkston, N.J., & Whipple, K. (1975). *Psychotherapy versus behavior therapy*. Cambridge, MA: Harvard University Press.

Smith, B.K. (1973). *Aging in America*. Boston: Beacon Press.

Smith, D. (1982). Trends in counseling and psychotherapy. *American Psychologist, 37*, 802–809.

Smith, D.A. (1989). *Psychophysiological features of affective flattening among medication-free schizophrenic patients*. Unpublished doctoral dissertation, State University of New York, Stony Brook.

Smith, G.R., Monson, R.A., & Ray, D.B. (1986). Psychiatric consultation in somatization disorder. *The New England Journal of Medicine, 314*, 1407–1413.

Smith, M.L., Glass, G., & Miller, T. (1980). *The benefits of psychotherapy*. Baltimore: Johns Hopkins University Press.

Smith-Rosenberg, C. (1972). The hysterical woman: Sex roles and role conflict in 19th-century America. *Social Research, 39*, 652–678.

Snider, W.D., Simpson, D.M., Nielsen, S., Gold, J.W.M., Metroka, C.E., & Posner, J.B. (1983). Neurological complications of Acquired Immune Deficiency Syndrome: Analysis of 50 patients. *Annals of Neurology, 14*, 403–418.

Snyder, D.K., & Wills, R.M. (1989). Behavioral versus insight-oriented marital therapy: Effects on individual and interspousal functioning. *Journal of Consulting and Clinical Psychology, 57*, 39–46.

Sobell, L.C., Maisto, S.A., Sobell, M.B., & Cooper, A.M. (1979). Reliability of alcoholics' self-reports of drinking and related behaviors one year prior to treatment in an outpatient treatment program. *Behaviour Research and Therapy, 17*, 157–160.

Sobell, L.C., & Sobell, M.B. (1990). Self-reports across addictive behaviors. *Behavioral Assessment, 12*, 1–14.

Sobell, M.B. (1978). Empirically derived components of treatment for alcohol problems: Some issues and extensions. In G.A. Marlatt & P.E. Nathan (Eds.), *Behavioral assessment and treatment of alcoholism*. New Brunswick, NJ: Rutgers Center for Alcohol Studies.

Sobell, M.B., & Sobell, L.C. (1973). Alcoholics treated by individualized behavior therapy: One year treatment outcome. *Behaviour Research and Therapy, 11*, 599–618.

Sobell, M.B., & Sobell, L.C. (1976). Second-year treatment outcome of alcoholics treated by individualized behavior therapy: Results. *Behaviour Research and Therapy, 14*, 195–215.

Socarides, C. (1978). *Homosexuality*. New York: Jason Aronson.

Solomon, G.F. (1989). Psychoneuroimmunology and human immunodeficiency virus infection. *Psychiatric Medicine, 81*, 153.

Solomon, G.F., Temoshok, L., O'Leary, A., & Zich, J. (1987). An intensive psychoimmunologic study of long-surviving persons with AIDS. *Annals of the New York Academy of Sciences, 496*, 647–655.

Sontag, S. (1977). *Illness as metaphor*. New York: Random House.

Sovner, R., & Hurley, A.D. (1983). Do the mentally retarded suffer from affective illness? *Archives of General Psychiatry, 40*, 61–66.

Spanier, G.B., & Thompson, L. (1984). *Parting: The aftermath of separation and divorce*. Beverly Hills, CA: Sage.

Spanos, N.P., Weekes, J.R., & Bertrand, L.D. (1985). Multiple personality: A social psychological perspective. *Journal of Abnormal Psychology, 94*, 362–376.

Spark, R., White, R., & Connolly, P. (1980). Impotence is not always psychogenic: Newer insights in hypothalamic-pituitary gonadal dysfunction. *Journal of the American Medical Association, 243*, 750–755.

Spiegel, D. (1986). Dissociating damage. *American Journal of Clinical Hypnosis, 29*, 123–131.

Spiegel, D., Bloom, J.R., Kramer, H., & Gottheil, E. (1989). Effect of psychosocial treatment on survival of patients with metastatic breast cancer. *Lancet, 14*, 888–891.

Spirito, A., Brown, L., Overholser, J., & Fritz, G. (1990). Attempted suicide in adolescence: A review and critique of the literature. *Clinical Psychology Review, 9*, 335–364.

Spirito, A., Stark, L.J., Fristad, M., Hart, K., & Owens-Stivley, J. (1987). Adolescent suicide attempters on a general pediatrics floor. *Journal of Pediatric Psychology, 12*, 171–189.

Spitzer, L., & Rodin, J. (1981). Human eating behavior. *Appetite, 2*, 293–329.

Spitzer, R.L., & Endicott, J. (1971). An integrated group of forms for automated psychiatric case records. *Archives of General Psychiatry, 24*, 540–547.

Spitzer, R.L., Forman, J.B.W., & Nee, J. (1979). *DSM-III* field trials: I. Initial interrater diagnostic reliability. *American Journal of Psychiatry, 136*, 815–817.

Spitzer, R.L., Skodol, A.E., Gibbon, M., & Williams, J.B.W. (1983). *Psychopathology: A case book*. New York: McGraw-Hill.

Spivak, G., & Shure, M.B. (1982). The cognition of social adjustment: Interpersonal cognitive problem-solving thinking. In B.B. Lahey & A.E. Kazdin (Eds.), *Advances in clinical child psychology* (Vol. 5). New York: Plenum.

Sports Illustrated. (1989, November). 35th anniversary issue, p. cover.

Sprenger, J., & Kraemer, H. (1970). *Malleus maleficarum* (M. Summers, Trans.). New York: Benjamin Bloom.

Srole, L., Langner, T.S., Michael, S.T., Opler, M.K., & Rennie, T.A.C. (1962). *Mental health in the metropolis: The midtown Manhattan study*. New York: McGraw-Hill.

Sroufe, L.A. (1983). Infant-caregiver attachment and patterns of adaptation in preschool: The roots of maladaptation and competence. In M. Perlmutter (Ed.), *Minnesota symposium on child psychology* (Vol. 16). Minneapolis: University of Minnesota Press.

Srull, T.K., & Wyer, R.S., Jr. (1979). The role of category accessibility in the interpretation of information about persons: Some determinants and implications. *Journal of Personality and Social Psychology, 37*, 1660–1672.

Stall, R., McKusick, L., Wiley, J., Coates, T., & Ostrow, D. (1986). Alcohol and drug use during sexual activity and compliance with safe sex guidelines for AIDS. *Health Education Quarterly, 13*, 359–371.

Stamford, B.A., Matter, S., Fell, R.D., & Papanek, P. (1986). Effects of smoking cessation on weight gain, metabolic rate, caloric consumption, and blood lipids. *The American Journal of Clinical Nutrition, 43*, 486–494.

Stangler, R.S., & Printz, A.M. (1980). DSM-III: Psychiatric diagnosis in a university population. *American Journal of Psychiatry, 137*, 937–940.

Stanley, B., Sieber, J.E., & Melton, G.B. (1987). Empirical studies of ethical issues in research. *American Psychologist, 42*, 735–741.

Stanton, M.D., & Todd, T.C. (1982). *The family therapy of drug abuse and addiction*. New York: Guilford Press.

Stavrakaki, C., & Klein, J. (1986). Psychotherapies with the mentally retarded. *Psychiatric Clinics of North America, 9*, 733–743.

Steadman, H.J., Monahan, J., Hartstone, E., Davis, S.K., & Robbins, P.C. (1982). Mentally disordered offenders: A national survey of patients and facilities. *Law and Human Behavior, 6*, 31–38.

Steege, J.F., Stout, A.L., & Carson, C.C. (1986). Patient satisfaction in Scott and Small-Carrion penile implant recipients: A study of 52 patients. *Archives of Sexual Behavior, 15*, 393–399.

Stein, M., Keller, S.E., & Schleifer, S.J. (1985). Stress and immunomodulation: The role of depression and neuroendocrine function. *Journal of Immunology, 135*, 827–833.

Stein, M., Miller, A.H., & Trestman, R.L. (1991). Depression, the immune system, and health and illness: Findings in search of meaning. *Archives of General Psychiatry, 48*, 171–177.

Steketee, G., & Foa, E. (1985). Obsessive-compulsive disorder. In D.H. Barlow (Ed.), *Clinical handbook of psychological disorders: A step-by-step treatment manual*. New York: Guilford Press.

Steketee, G., & Foa, E. (1987). Behavioral treatment of phobics and obsessive-compulsives. In N.S. Jacobson (Ed.), *Psychotherapists in clinical practice*. New York: Guilford Press.

Steketee, G., Foa, E.B., & Grayson, J.B. (1982). Recent advances in the behavioral treatment of obsessive-compulsives. *Archives of General Psychiatry, 39*, 1365–1371.

Sternberg, R.J. (1984a). A contextualist view of the nature of intelligence. *International Journal of Psychology, 19*, 307–334.

Sternberg, R.J. (1984b). Toward a triarchic theory of human intelligence. *The Behavioral and Brain Sciences, 7*, 269–315.

Sternberg, R.J. (1985). *Beyond IQ: A triarchic theory of human intelligence*. New York: Cambridge University Press.

Sternberg, R.J., & Berg, C.A. (1986). Quantitative integration: Definitions of intelligence: A comparison of the 1921 and 1986 symposia. In R.J. Sternberg & D.K. Detterman (Eds.), *What is intelligence? Contemporary viewpoints on its nature and definition*. Norwood, NJ: Ablex Publishing.

Sternberg, R.J., & Soriano, L.J. (1984). Styles of conflict resolution. *Journal of Personality and Social Psychology, 47*, 115–126.

Stevens, V.J., & Hollis, J.F. (1989). Preventing smoking relapse, using an individually tailored skills-training technique. *Journal of Consulting and Clinical Psychology, 57*, 420–424.

Stewart, J., deWit, H., & Eikelboom, R. (1984). The role of unconditioned and conditioned drug effects in the self-administration of opiates and stimulants. *Psychological Review, 91*, 251–268.

Stewart, R.S., Devous, M.D., Rush, A.J., Lane, L., & Bonte, F.J. (1988). Cerebral blood flow changes during sodium-lactate-induced panic attacks. *American Journal of Psychiatry, 145*, 442–449.

Still, G.F. (1902). The Coulstonian lectures on some abnormal physical conditions in children. *Lancet*, *1*, 1008–1012.

Stoller, R.J. (1967). Transvestites' women. *American Journal of Psychiatry*, *124*, 333–339.

Stoller, R.J. (1979). *Sexual excitement.* New York: Pantheon Books.

Stone, M.H. (1983). Psychotherapy with schizotypal borderline patients. *Journal of the American Academy of Psychoanalysis*, *11*, 87–111.

Stone, M.H. (1985). Schizotypal personality: Psychotherapeutic aspects. *Schizophrenia Bulletin*, *11*, 576–589.

Strain, P.S., Young, C.C., & Horowitz, J. (1981). Generalized behavior change during oppositional child training. *Behavior Modification*, *5*, 15–26.

Straus, M., Gelles, R.J., & Steinmetz, S. (1980). *Behind closed doors: Violence in the American family.* New York: Anchor Books.

Strauss, J.S. (1969). Hallucinations and delusions as points on continual function. *Archives of General Psychiatry*, *21*, 581–586.

Strauss, J.S., & Carpenter, W.T., Jr. (1981). *Schizophrenia.* New York: Plenum.

Streater, J.A., Sargent, R.G., & Ward, D.S. (1989). A study of factors associated with weight change in women who attempt smoking cessation. *Addictive Behaviors*, *14*, 523–530.

Stricker, G. (1983). Passive-aggressiveness: A condition especially suited to the psychodynamic approach. In R.D. Parsons & R.J. Wicks (Eds.), *Passive aggressiveness: Theory and practice.* New York: Brunner/Mazel.

Stricker, G., & Healey, B.J. (1990). Projective assessment of object relations. *Psychological Assessment*, *2*, 219–230.

Striegel-Moore, R.H., Silberstein, L.R., Frensch, P., & Rodin, J. (1989). A prospective study of disordered eating among college students. *International Journal of Eating Disorders*, *8*, 499–509.

Striegel-Moore, R.H., Silberstein, L.R., & Rodin, J. (1986). Toward an understanding of risk factors for bulimia. *American Psychologist*, *41*, 246–263.

Strober, M. (1981). A comparative analysis of personality organization in juvenile anorexia nervosa. *Journal of Youth and Adolescence*, *10*, 285–295.

Strober, M., Green, J., & Carlson, G. (1981). Phenomenology and subtypes of major depressive disorder in adolescence. *Journal of Affective Disorders*, *3*, 281–290.

Strober, M., Green, J., & Carlson, G. (1981). Reliability of psychiatric diagnosis in hospitalized adolescents. *Archives of General Psychiatry*, *38*, 141–145.

Strober, M., & Humphrey, L.L. (1987). Familial contributions to the etiology and course of anorexia nervosa and bulimia. *Journal of Consulting and Clinical Psychology*, *55*, 654–659.

Strober, M., Lampert, C., Morrell, W., Burroughs, J., & Jacobs, C. (1990). A controlled family study of anorexia nervosa: Evidence of familial aggregation and lack of shared transmission with affective disorders. *International Journal of Eating Disorders*, *9*, 239–253.

Strober, M., Salkin, B., Burroughs, J., & Morrell, W. (1982). Validity of the bulimia-restrictor distinction in anorexia nervosa: Parental personality characteristics and family psychiatric morbidity. *Journal of Nervous and Mental Disease*, *170*, 345–351.

Stromberg, C.D., Haggarty, D.J., Leibenluft, R.F., McMillian, M.H., Mishkin, B., Rubin, B.L., & Trilling, H.R. (1988). *The psychologist's legal handbook.* Washington, DC: The Council for the National Register of Health Service Providers in Psychology.

Strupp, H.H. (1980a). Some views on effective principles of psychotherapy. *Cognitive Therapy and Research*, *4*, 298.

Strupp, H.H. (1980b). Toward the refinement of time-limited dynamic therapy. In S.H. Budman (Ed.), *Forms of brief therapy.* New York: Guilford Press.

Strupp, H.H. (1989). Psychotherapy: Can the practitioner learn from the researcher? *American Psychologist*, *44*, 717–724.

Strupp, H.H., & Hadley, S.W. (1979). Specific vs. nonspecific factors in psychotherapy. *Archives of General Psychiatry*, *36*, 1125–1136.

Strupp, H.H., Hadley, S.W., & Gomes-Schwartz, B. (1977). *Psychotherapy for better or worse.* New York: Jason Aronson.

Stuart, R.B. (1979). The chances of keeping it off after taking it off: The maintenance of weight loss. In P.O. Davidson (Ed.), *Behavioral strategies for lifestyle change.* New York: Brunner/Mazel.

Stuart, R.B. (1980). *Helping couples change.* New York: Guilford Press.

Stunkard, A.J. (Ed.). (1980). *Obesity.* Philadelphia: W.B. Saunders.

Stunkard, A.J. (1989). Perspectives on human obesity. In A.J. Stunkard & A. Baum (Eds.), *Perspectives in behavioral medicine.* Hillsdale, NJ: Lawrence Erlbaum.

Stunkard, A.J., Foch, T.T., & Hrubec, Z. (1986). A twin study of human obesity. *Journal of the American Medical Association*, *256*, 51–54.

Stunkard, A.J., Sorensen, T., Hanis, C., Teasdale, T.W., Chakraborty, R., Schull, W.J., & Schulsinger, F. (1986). An adoption study of human obesity. *The New England Journal of Medicine*, *314*, 193–198.

Stunkard, A.J., & Stellar, E. (Eds.). (1984). *Eating and its disorders.* New York: Raven Press.

Sturgis, E.T. (1984). Anxiety disorders. In N.S. Endler & J.M. Hunt (Eds.), *Personality and the behavior disorders.* New York: John Wiley.

Styron, W. (1990). *Darkness visible: A memoir of madness.* New York: Random House.

Suchotliff, L., Steinfeld, G., & Tolchin, G. (1970). The struggle for patients' rights in a state hospital. *Mental Hygiene*, *54*, 230–240.

Sullivan, H.S. (1924). Schizophrenia: Its conservative and malignant features. *American Journal of Psychiatry*, *81*, 77–91.

Sullivan, H.S. (1953). *The interpersonal theory of psychiatry.* New York: W.W. Norton.

Sullivan, H.S. (1954). *The psychiatric interview.* New York: W.W. Norton.

Sulloway, F.J. (1979). *Freud: Biologist of the mind.* New York: Basic Books.

Suomi, S.J. (1982). Relevance of animal models for clinical psychology. In P.C. Kendall & J.N. Butcher (Eds.), *Handbook of research methods in clinical psychology.* New York: John Wiley.

Surwit, R.S., & Feinglos, M.N. (1988). Stress and autonomic nervous system in type II diabetes: A hypothesis. *Diabetes Care*, *11*, 83–85.

Sutherland, N.S. (1976). *Breakdown.* New York: Signet Books.

Sutker, P.B., & Allain, A.N., Jr. (1988). Issues in personality conceptualizations of addictive behaviors. *Journal of Consulting and Clinical Psychology*, *56*, 172–182.

Swan, G.E., & MacDonald, M.L. (1978). Behavior therapy in practice: A national survey of behavior therapists. *Behavior Therapy*, *9*, 799–807.

Swanson, T.M., & Kinsbourne, M. (1980). Food dye impairs performance of hyperactive children on a laboratory learning test. *Science*, *207*, 1485–1486.

Sweeney, J.A., Clarkin, J.F., & Fitzgibbon, M.L. (1987). Current practice of psychological assessment. *Professional Psychology: Research and Practice*, *18*, 377–380.

Szasz, T.S. (1960). The myth of mental illness. *American Psychologist*, *15*, 113–118.

Szasz, T.S. (Ed.). (1974). *The age of madness: The history of involuntary hospitalization.* New York: Macmillan.

Tavris, C.A., & Sadd, S. (1977). *The Redbook report on female sexuality.* New York: Delacorte.

Taylor, C.B., & Agras, S. (1981). Assessment of phobia. In D.H. Barlow (Ed.), *Behavioral assessment of adult disorders* (pp. 181–208). New York: Guilford Press.

Taylor, C.B., & Arnow, B. (1988). *The nature and treatment of anxiety disorders.* New York: Free Press.

Taylor, C.B., Sheikh, J., Agras, W.S., Roth, W.T., Margraf, J., Ehlers, A., Maddock, R.J., & Gossard, D. (1986). Self-report of panic attacks: Agreement with heart rate changes. *American Journal of Psychiatry*, *143*, 478–482.

Taylor, E.A., & Stansfield, S.A. (1984). Children who poison themselves: I. Clinical comparison with psychiatric controls, & II. Prediction of attendance for treatment. *British Journal of Psychiatry*, *145*, 127–135.

Taylor, J.R., Helzer, J.E., & Robins, L.N. (1986). Moderate drinking in ex-alcoholics: Recent studies. *Journal of Studies on Alcohol*, *47*, 115–121.

Teasdale, J.D. (1983). Negative thinking in depression: Cause, effect, or reciprocal relationship? *Advances in Behaviour Research and Therapy, 5*, 27–49.

Teicher, M.H., Glod, C., & Cole, J.O. (1990). Emergence of intense suicidal preoccupation during fluoxetine treatment. *American Journal of Psychiatry, 147*, 207–210.

Teichner, J.D., & Jacobs, J. (1966). Adolescents who attempt suicide: Preliminary findings. *American Journal of Psychiatry, 122*, 1248–1257.

Telch, M.J., Agras, W.S., Taylor, C.B., Roth, W.T., & Gallen, C.C. (1985). Combined pharmacological and behavioral treatment for agoraphobia. *Behaviour Research and Therapy, 23*, 325–336.

Telch, M.J., Brouillard, M., Telch, C.F., Agras, W.S., & Taylor, C.B. (1989). Role of cognitive appraisal in panic-related avoidance. *Behaviour Research and Therapy, 27*, 373–383.

Telch, M.J., Lucas, J.A., & Nelson, P. (1989). Nonclinical panic in college students: An investigation of prevalence and symptomatology. *Journal of Abnormal Psychology, 98*, 300–306.

Temby, W.D. (1961). Suicide. In G.B. Blaine, Jr., & C.C. McArthur (Eds.), *Emotional problems of the student*. New York: Appleton-Century-Crofts.

Temoshok, L., Heller, B.W., Sagebiel, R.W., Blois, M.S., Sweet, D.M., DiClemente, R.J., & Gold, M.L. (1985). The relationship of psychosocial factors to prognostic indicators in cutaneous malignant melanoma. *Journal of Psychosomatic Research, 29*, 139–154.

Terman, L.M., & Merrill, M.A. (1960). *Stanford-Binet Intelligence Scale: Manual for the 2nd revision, Form -M*. Boston: Houghton Mifflin.

Terman, L.M., & Merrill, M.A. (1973). *Stanford-Binet Intelligence Scale: 1972 norms edition*. Boston: Houghton Mifflin.

Thase, M.E., Frank, E., & Kupfer, D.J. (1985). Biological processes in depression. In E.E. Beckman & Leber, W.R. (Eds.), *Handbook of depression* (pp. 816–913). Homewood, IL: Dorsey.

Thase, R.G., & Moss, M.K. (1976). The relative efficacy of covert modeling on the reduction of avoidance behavior. *Journal of Behavior Therapy and Experimental Psychiatry, 7*, 7–12.

The New York Times. (1989, November 22). Psychotherapy gaining favor among blacks. Section A, p. 1.

Thigpen, C.H., & Cleckley, H.M. (1954). The three faces of Eve. Kingsport, TN: Kingsport Press.

Thigpen, C.H., & Cleckley, H.M. (1984). On the incidence of multiple personality disorder. *The International Journal of Clinical and Experimental Hypnosis, 32*, 63–66.

Thorndike, E.L. (1911). *Animal intelligence*. New York: Macmillan.

Thyer, B.A., Himle, J., Curtis, G.C., Cameron, O.G., & Nesse, R.M. (1985). A comparison of panic disorder and agoraphobia with panic attacks. *Comprehensive Psychiatry, 26*, 208–214.

Thyer, B.A., Nesse, R.M., Cameron, O.G., & Curtis, G.C. (1985). Agoraphobia: A test of the separation anxiety hypothesis. *Behaviour Research and Therapy, 23*, 75–78.

Tippin, J., & Henn, F.A. (1982). Modified leucotomy in the treatment of intractable obsessional neurosis. *American Journal of Psychiatry, 139*, 1601–1603.

Tkach, J.R., & Hokama, Y. (1970). Autoimmunity in chronic brain syndrome: A preliminary report. *Archives of General Psychiatry, 23*, 61–64.

Todd, T.C., & Stanton, M.D. (1983). Research on marital and family therapy: Answers issues and recommendations for the future. In B.B. Wolman & G. Stricker (Eds.) *Handbook of Marital and Family Therapy,* 91–115. New York: Plenum.

Torgersen, S. (1983). Genetic factors in anxiety disorders. *Archives of General Psychiatry, 40*, 1085–1089.

Torgersen, S. (1986). Genetic factors in moderately severe and mild affective disorders. *Archives of General Psychiatry, 43*, 222–226.

Torrey, E.F. (1988). *Nowhere to go.* New York: Harper-Collins Publishers.

Totten, G., Lamb, D.H., & Reeder, G.D. (1990). *Tarasoff* and confidentiality in AIDS-related psychotherapy. *Professional Psychology: Research and Practice, 21*, 155–160.

Treaster, J.B. (1990, June 2). Programs find adolescents' use of cocaine can be curtailed. *The New York Times: National.*

Trites, R.L. (1986). Neuropsychological variables and mental retardation. *Psychiatric Clinics of North America, 9*, 723–731.

Truax, C.B. (1966). Reinforcement and nonreinforcement in Rogerian psychotherapy. *Journal of Abnormal and Social Psychology, 71*, 1–9.

Trull, T.J., Widiger, T.A., & Guthrie, P. (1990). Categorical versus dimensional status of borderline personality disorder. *Journal of Abnormal Psychology, 99*, 40–48.

Tuma, J., & Cohen, R. (1981). Pediatric psychology. Cited in K.D. O'Leary (1984), The image of behavior therapy: It is time to take a stand. *Behavior Therapy, 15*, 219–233.

Tuma, J., & Pratt, J. (1982). Clinical child psychology practice and training: A survey. *Journal of Clinical Child Psychology, 11*, 27–34.

Turk, D.C., Meichenbaum, D., & Genest, M. (1983). *Pain and behavioral medicine.* New York: Guilford Press.

Turk, D.C., & Salovey, P. (1985). Cognitive structures, cognitive processes, and cognitive-behavior modification: II. Judgments and inferences of the clinician. *Cognitive Therapy and Research, 9*, 19–34.

Turkat, I.D., & Maisto, S.A. (1985). Personality disorders: Application of the experimental method to the formulation and modification of personality disorders. In D. Barlow (Ed.), *Clinical handbook of psychological disorders.* New York: Guilford Press.

Turner, R.J., & Wagonfeld, M.O. (1967). Occupational mobility and schizophrenia. *American Sociological Review, 32*, 104–113.

Turner, R.M. (1989). Case study evaluations of a bio-cognitive-behavioral approach for the treatment of borderline personality disorder. *Behavior Therapy, 20*, 477–489.

Uhlenhuth, E.H., Lipman, R.S., Balter, M.B., & Stern, M. (1974). Symptom intensity and life stress in the city. *Archives of General Psychiatry, 31*, 759–764.

Ullmann, L.P., & Krasner, L. (Eds.). (1965). *Case studies in behavior modification.* New York: Holt, Rinehart & Winston.

Ullmann, L.P., & Krasner, L. (1975). *A psychological approach to abnormal behavior* (2nd ed.). Englewood Cliffs, NJ: Prentice-Hall.

Ullmann, L.P., & Krasner, L. (1969). *A psychological approach to abnormal behavior.* Englewood Cliffs, NJ: Prentice-Hall.

Umberson, D. (1987). Family status and health behaviors: Social control as a dimension of social integration. *Journal of Health and Social Behavior, 28*, 306.

U.S. Bureau of the Census. (1988). Current Population Reports, Series P-20, *Marital Status and Living Arrangements: March 1987.* Washington, DC: U.S. Government Printing Office.

U.S. Department of Education. (1982). *Fourth Annual Report to Congress on the Implementation of P.L. 94-142.* Washington, DC: U.S. Dept. of Education.

U.S. Department of Health and Human Services. (1981). *Toward a national plan for the chronically mentally ill: Report to the Secretary by the Department of Health and Human Services Steering Committee on the Chronically Mentally Ill.* Washington, DC: U.S. Government Printing Office.

U.S. Department of Justice. (1990). *Drug use forecasting.* National Institute of Justice, Research and Action.

Uno, H., Tarara, R., Else, J.G., Suleman, M.A., & Sapolsky, R.M. (1989). Hippocampal damage associated with prolonged and fatal stress in primates. *The Journal of Neuroscience, 9*, 1705–1711.

Vaillant, G.E. (1976). Natural history of male psychological health: V. The relation of choice of ego mechanisms of defense to adult adjustment. *Archives of General Psychiatry, 33*, 535–545.

Vaillant, G.E. (1977). *Adaptation to life.* Boston: Little, Brown.

Vaillant, G.E. (1979). Natural history of male psychological health. *The New England Journal of Medicine, 301*, 1249–1254.

Vaillant, G.E. (1983). *The natural history of alcoholism.* Cambridge, MA: Harvard University Press.

Vaillant, G.E. (1986). *Empirical studies of ego mechanisms of defense.* Washington, DC: American Psychiatric Press.

Vaillant, G.E. (1988). The alcohol-dependent and drug-dependent person. In A.M. Nicholi (Ed.), *The new Harvard guide to psychiatry*. Cambridge, MA: Harvard University Press.

Vaillant, G.E., Bond, M., & Vaillant, C.O. (1986). An empirically validated hierarchy of defense mechanisms. *Archives of General Psychiatry, 43*, 786–794.

Vaillant, G.E., & Schnurr, P. (1988). What is a case? A 45-year study of psychiatric impairment within a college sample selected for mental health. *Archives of General Psychiatry, 45*, 313–319.

Valenstein, E.S. (Ed.). (1980). *The psychosurgery debate: Scientific, legal, and ethical perspectives*. San Francisco, CA: W.H. Freeman.

Valenstein, E.S. (1986). *Great and desperate cures: The rise and decline of psychosurgery and other radical treatments for mental illness*. New York: Basic books.

Valk, J. (Ed.). (1986). *Neuroradiology 1985/1986*. Amsterdam: Excerpta Medica.

Van Arsdalen, K., Malloy, T.R., & Wein, A.J. (1983). Erectile physiology, dysfunction and evaluation—Part II: Etiology and evaluation of erectile dysfunction. *Monographs in Urology, 4*, 165–185.

Van Itallie, T.B. (1979). Obesity: Adverse effects on health and longevity. *American Journal of Clinical Nutrition, 32*, 2723–2733.

Vandenberg, S.G., Singer, S.M., & Pauls, D.L. (1986). *The heredity of behavior disorders in adults and children*. New York: Plenum.

Vandenbos, G.R. (1986). Psychotherapy research: A special issue. *American Psychologist, 41*, 111–112.

Vaughn, C.E., & Leff, J.P. (1976). The influence of family and social factors in the course of psychiatric illness. *British Journal of Psychiatry, 129*, 125–137.

Vaughn, C.E., Snyder, K.S., Jones, S., Freeman, W.B., & Falloon, I.R.H. (1984). Family factors in schizophrenic relapse. *Archives of General Psychiatry, 41*, 1169–1177.

Veliz, J., & James, W.S. (1987). Medicine court: *Rogers* in practice. *American Journal of Psychiatry, 144*, 62–67.

Venn, J.R., & Short, J.G. (1973). Vicarious classical conditioning of emotional responses in nursery school children. *Journal of Personality and Social Psychology, 28*, 249–255.

Verbrugge, L. (1989). The twain meet: Empirical explanations of sex differences in health and mortality. *Journal of Health and Social Behavior, 30*, 282–304.

Vernon, D.J., & Bailey, W.C. (1974). The use of motion pictures in the psychological preparation of children for induction of anesthesia. *Anesthesiology, 40*, 68–72.

Vetter, H., Ramsey, L.E., Luscher, T.F., Schrey, A., & Vetter, W. (1985). Symposium on compliance—improving strategies in hypertension. *Journal of Hypertension Supplement, 3*, 1–99.

Vincent, J.P., & Carter, A.S. (1987). Family assessment: Practical and methodological considerations. In K.D. O'Leary (Ed.), *Assessment of marital discord: An integration for research and clinical practice*. Hillsdale, NJ: Lawrence Erlbaum.

Vincent, J.P., Varley, C.K., & Leger, P. (1990). Effects of methylphenidate on early adolescent growth. *American Journal of Psychiatry, 147*, 501–502.

Vivian, D., Fischel, J.E., & Liebert, R.M. (1987). Effect of "wet nights" on daytime behavior during concurrent treatment of enuresis and conduct problems. *Journal of Behavior Therapy and Experimental Psychiatry, 17*, 301–303.

Vivian, D., & O'Leary, K.D. (1988). *Clients' reasons for seeking marital therapy*. Unpublished manuscript. State University of New York, Stony Brook, New York.

Voegtlin, W.L. (1940). The treatment of alcoholism by establishing a conditional reflex. *American Journal of Medical Science, 199*, 802–809.

Wachtel, P. (1988). *Action and insight*. New York: Guilford Press.

Wadden, T.A., Stunkard, A.J., & Liebschutz, J. (1988). Three-year follow-up of the treatment of obesity by very low calorie diet, behavior therapy, and their combination. *Journal of Consulting and Clinical Psychology, 56*, 925–928.

Wade, T.C., & Baker, T.B. (1977). Questions and use of psychological tests: A survey of clinical psychologists. *American Psychologist, 32*, 874–882.

Walker, L.E. (1977). Battered women and learned helplessness. *Victimology*, Nos. *3–4*, 525–534.

Walker, L.E. (1989). Psychology and violence against women. *American Psychologist, 44*, 695–702.

Walker, L.E.A. (1987). Inadequacies of the masochistic personality disorder diagnosis for women. *Journal of Personality Disorders, 1*, 183–189.

Walker, R.D., Donovan, D.M., Kivlahan, D.R., & O'Leary, M.R. (1983). Length of stay, neuropsychological performance, and aftercare influences on alcohol treatment outcome. *Journal of Consulting and Clinical Psychology, 51*, 900–911.

Wallace, R. (1969). *The world of Van Gogh: 1853–1890*. Alexandria, VA: Time-Life Books.

Waller, N.G., & Waldman, I.D. (1990). A reexamination of the WAIS-R factor structure. *Psychological Assessment, 2*, 139–144.

Wallerstein, J.S., & Kelly, J.B. (1980). *Surviving the breakup: How children and parents cope with divorce*. New York: Basic Books.

Walton, D., & Mather, M.D. (1963). The application of learning principles to the treatment of obsessive-compulsive states in the acute and chronic phases of illness. *Behaviour Research and Therapy, 1*, 163–174.

Warner, R. (1978). The diagnosis of antisocial and hysterical personality disorders: An example of sex bias. *Journal of Nervous and Mental Disease, 166*, 839–845.

Warren, N.T. (1976). Self-esteem and sources of cognitive bias in the evaluation of past performance. *Journal of Consulting and Clinical Psychology, 44*, 966–975.

Wasserman, M.D., Pollack, C.P., Speilman, A.J., & Weitzman, E.D. (1980). Theoretical and technical problems in the measurement of nocturnal penile tumescence for the differential diagnosis of impotence. *Psychosomatic Medicine, 42*, 575–585.

Watkins, J.G. (1984). The Bianchi (L.A. Hillside Strangler) case: Sociopath or multiple personality? *The International Journal of Clinical and Experimental Hypnosis, 32*, 67–101.

Watson, C.G., & Buranen, C. (1979). The frequency and identification of false positive conversion reactions. *Journal of Nervous and Mental Disease, 167*, 243–247.

Watson, J.B. (1913). Psychology as the behaviorist views it. *Psychological Review, 20*, 158–177.

Watson, J.B., & Rayner, R. (1920). Conditioned emotional reactions. *Journal of Experimental Psychology, 3*, 1–14.

Watt, N.F. (1974). Childhood and adolescent roots of schizophrenia. In D. Ricks, A. Thomas, & M. Roff (Eds.), *Life history research in psychopathology* (Vol. 3). Minneapolis, MN: University of Minnesota Press.

Watt, N.F. (1984). In a nutshell: The first two decades of high-risk research in schizophrenia. In N.F. Watt, J. Anthony, L.C. Wynne, & J.E. Rolf (Eds.), *Children at risk for schizophrenia: A longitudinal perspective*. New York: Cambridge University Press.

Watt, N.F., Anthony, J., Wynne, L.C., & Rolf, J.E. (Eds.). (1984). *Children at risk for schizophrenia: A longitudinal perspective*. New York: Cambridge University Press.

Webb, J.T., & McNamara, K.M. (1978). *Configural interpretation of the MMPI*. Columbus, OH: Ohio Psychology Publishing.

Wechsler, D. (1939). *The measurement of adult intelligence*. Baltimore: Williams and Wilkins.

Wechsler, D. (1955). *Manual for the Wechsler Adult Intelligence Scale*. New York: Psychological Corporation.

Wechsler, D. (1958). *The measurement and appraisal of adult intelligence* (4th ed.). Baltimore: Williams and Wilkins.

Wechsler, D. (1967). *Manual: Wechsler Preschool and Primary Scale of Intelligence*. New York: Psychological Corporation.

Wechsler, D. (1974a). *Manual: Wechsler Adult Intelligence Scale—Revised*. New York: Psychological Corporation.

Wechsler, D. (1974b). *Manual: Wechsler Intelligence Scale for Children—Revised*. New York: Psychological Corporation.

Weckowicz, T.E. (1984). Philosophical-moral models. In T.E. Weckowicz (Ed.), *Models of mental illness: Systems and theories of abnormal psychology*. Springfield, IL: Charles C. Thomas.

Wegner, J.T., Catalano, F., Gilbralter, J., & Kane, J.M. (1985). Schizophrenia with tardive dyskinesia. *Archives of General Psychiatry, 42*, 860–865.

Wehr, T.A., & Rosenthal, N.E. (1989). Seasonality and affective illness. *American Journal of Psychiatry, 146*, 829–839.

Weinberger, D.R., & Kleinman, J.E. (1986). Observations on the brain in schizophrenia. In A.J. Frances & R.E. Hales (Eds.), *American Psychiatric Association Annual Review* (Vol. 5). Washington, DC: American Psychiatric Association.

Weiner, A., Reich, T., Robins, I., Fishman, R., & van Doren, T. (1976). Obsessive-compulsive neurosis. *Comprehensive Psychiatry, 17*, 527–539.

Weiner, B., & Litman-Adizes, T. (1980). An attribution expectancy-value analysis of learned helplessness and depression. In J. Garber & M. Seligman (Eds.), *Human helplessness: Theory and applications.* New York: Academic Press.

Weiner, H. (1977). *Psychobiology and human disease.* New York: Elsevier.

Weiner, I.B. (1983). The future of psychodiagnosis revisited. *Journal of Personality Assessment, 47*, 451–459.

Weinstein, E.A. (1981). *Woodrow Wilson: A medical and psychological biography.* Princeton, NJ: Princeton University Press.

Weintraub, S. (1987). Risk factors in schizophrenia: The Stony Brook high-risk project. *Schizophrenia Bulletin, 13*, 439–450.

Weintraub, S., & Neale, J.M. (1984). The Stony Brook high-risk project. In N.F. Watt, J. Anthony, L.C. Wynne, & J.E. Rolf (Eds.), *Children at risk for schizophrenia.* New York: Cambridge University Press.

Weintraub, S., Winters, K.C., & Neale, J.M. (1986). Competence and vulnerability in children with an affective disordered parent. In M. Rutter, C.E. Izard, & P.B. Read (Eds.), *Depression in young people.* New York: Guilford Press.

Weiss, G., Hechtman, L., Perlman, T., Hopkins, J., & Wener, A. (1979). Hyperactives as young adults. *Archives of General Psychiatry, 36*, 675–681.

Weiss, G., & Hechtman, L.T. (1986). *Hyperactive children grown up.* New York: Guilford Press.

Weiss, G., Minde, K., Werry, J.S., Douglas, V.I., & Nemeth, E. (1971). Studies on the hyperactive child, VIII: Five-year follow-up. *Archives of General Psychiatry, 24*, 409–414.

Weiss, R.L., & Aved, B.M. (1978). Marital satisfaction and depression as predictors of physical health status. *Journal of Consulting and Clinical Psychology, 46*, 1379–1384.

Weiss, R.L., & Tolman, A.O. (1990). The Marital Interaction Coding System-Global (MICS-G). *Behavioral Assessment, 12*, 271–294.

Weissman, M.M., Gammon, G.D., John, K., Merikangas, K.R., Warner, V., Prusoff, B.A., & Sholomskas, D. (1987). Children of depressed parents. *Archives of General Psychiatry, 44*, 847–853.

Weissman, M.M., & Klerman, G.L. (1977). Sex differences and the epidemiology of depression. *Archives of General Psychiatry, 34*, 98–111.

Weissman, M.M., Klerman, G.L., Markowitz, J.S., & Pihl, R.O. (1989). Suicidal ideation and suicide attempts in panic disorder and attacks. *The New England Journal of Medicine, 321*, 1209–1214.

Weissman, M.M., Klerman, G.L., Paykel, E.S., Prusoff, B., & Hanson, B. (1974). Treatment effects on the social adjustment of depressed patients. *Archives of General Psychiatry, 30*, 771–778.

Weissman, M.M., Leaf, P.J., Blazer, D.G., Boyd, J.H., & Florio, L. (1986). The relationship between panic disorder and agoraphobia: An epidemiologic perspective. *Psychopharmacology Bulletin, 43*, 787–791.

Weissman, M.M., Merikangas, K., John, K., Wiskramaratne, P., Prusoff, B., & Kidd, K. (1986). Family-genetic studies of psychiatric disorders. *American Journal of Psychiatry, 43*, 1104–1116.

Weissman, M.M., Myers, J.K., & Harding, P.S. (1978). Psychiatric disorders in a U.S. urban community: 1975–1976. *American Journal of Psychiatry, 135*, 459–462.

Weissman, M.M., Leckman, J.F., Merikangas, K.R., Gammon, G.D., & Prusoff, B.A. (1984). Depression and anxiety disorders in parents and children. *Archives of General Psychiatry, 41*, 845–852.

Weller, R.A., & Halikas, J.A. (1985). Marijuana use and psychiatric illness: A follow-up study. *American Journal of Psychiatry, 142*, 848–850.

Wells, R.A., & Dezen, A.G. (1978). The results of family therapy revisited: The non-behavioral methods. *Family Process, 17*, 251–274.

Wender, P.H. (1971). *Minimal brain dysfunction in children.* New York: John Wiley-Interscience.

Wender, P.H., Kety, S.S., Rosenthal, D., Schulsinger, F., Ortmann, J., & Lunde, I. (1986). Psychiatric disorders in the biological and adoptive families of adopted individuals with affective disorders. *Archives of General Psychiatry, 43*, 923–929.

Wender, P.H., Reimherr, F.W., & Wood, D.R. (1980). Attention deficit disorder treatment. *Archives of General Psychiatry, 38*, 449–456.

Wender, P.H., & Wender, E.H. (1978). *The hyperactive child and the learning disabled child.* New York: Crown Publishers.

Werner, E. (1986). Resilient offspring of alcoholics: A longitudinal study from birth to age 18. *Journal of Studies on Alcohol, 47*, 34–40.

Werner, E.E. (1980). Environmental interaction in brain dysfunction. In H.E. Rie & E.D. Rie (Eds.), *Handbook of minimal brain dysfunctions: A critical view.* New York: John Wiley.

Werner, P.D., & Pervin, L.A. (1986). The content of personality inventory items. *Journal of Personality and Social Psychology, 51*, 622–628.

West, D.J. (1982). *Delinquency: Its roots, careers and prospects.* Cambridge, MA: Harvard University Press.

West, M.O., & Prinz, R.J. (1987). Parental alcoholism and childhood psychopathology. *Psychological Bulletin, 102*, 204–218.

West, R.J., Hajek, P., & Belcher, M. (1986). Which smokers report most relief from craving when using nicotine chewing gum? *Psychopharmacology, 89*, 189–191.

Westen, D. (1988). Transference and information processing. *Clinical Psychology Review, 8*, 161–180.

Westen, D., Lohr, N., Silk, K.R., Gold, L., & Kerber, K. (1990). Object relations and social cognition in borderlines, major depressives, and normals: A Thematic Apperception Test Analysis. *Psychological Assessment, 2*, 355–364.

Westmoreland, B.F. (1980). Organic mental disorders associated with epilepsy. In H.I. Kaplan, A.M. Freedman, & B.J. Sadock (Eds.), *Comprehensive textbook of psychiatry* (Vol. 2). Baltimore: Williams & Wilkins.

Whalen, C.K., & Henker, B. (Eds.). (1980). *Hyperactive children: The social ecology of identification and treatment.* New York: Academic Press.

Whipple, S.C., Parker, E.S., & Noble, E.P. (1988). An atypical neurocognitive profile in alcoholic fathers and their sons. *Journal of Studies on Alcohol, 49*, 240–244.

Whisman, M.A., Jacobson, N.S., Fruzzetti, A.E., & Schmaling, K.B. (1988). Treatment for the depressed, maritally discordant clients: A comparison of behavioral marital therapy, individual cognitive therapy, and wait list control. Paper presented at Association for Advancement of Behavior Therapy, New York.

Whitaker, A., Johnson, J., Shaffer, D., Rapoport, J.L., Kalikow, K., Walsh, B.T., Davies, M., Braiman, S., & Dolinsky, A. (1990). Uncommon troubles in young people. *Archives of General Psychiatry, 47*, 487–496.

Whitehall, J.A. (1989). A piece of mind: Wife. *Journal of the American Medical Association, 261*, 3460.

Widiger, T. (Ed.). (1987). Self defeating personality disorders [Special issue]. *Journal of Personality Disorders, 1*(2).

Widiger, T.A., Trull, T.J., Hurt, S.W., Clarkin, J., & Frances, A. (1987). A multidimensional scaling of DSM-III personality disorders. *Archives of General Psychiatry, 44*, 557–563.

Wiedenfeld, S.A., O'Leary, A., Bandura, A., Brown, S., Levine, S., & Raska, K. (1989). Impact of perceived self-efficacy in coping with stressors on components of the immune system. Unpublished manuscript, Stanford University.

Wiens, A.N., & Menustik, C.W. (1983). Treatment outcome and patient characteristics in an aversion therapy program for alcoholism. *American Psychologist, 38*, 1089–1096.

Wikler, A. (1965). Conditioning factors in opiate addiction and relapse. In D.I.

Wilner & G.G. Kassenbaum (Eds.), *Narcotics* (pp. 85–100). New York: McGraw-Hill.

Willerman, L. (1968). Activity level and hyperactivity in twins. *Child Development, 39*, 27–34.

Willerman, L., & Cohen, D.B. (1990). *Psychopathology*. New York: McGraw-Hill.

Willi, J., & Grossman, S. (1983). Epidemiology of anorexia nervosa in a defined region of Switzerland. *American Journal of Psychiatry, 140*, 564–567.

Williams, A.E., & Duncan, B.A. (1976). A commercial weight-reducing organization: A critical analysis. *Medical Journal of Australia, 1*, 781–785.

Williams, J.B.W. (1987). Multiaxial diagnosis. In A.E. Skodol & R.L. Spitzer (Eds.), *An annotated bibliography of DSM-III*. Washington, DC: American Psychiatric Press.

Williams, L. (1989, November 22). Psychotherapy gaining favor among blacks. *The New York Times*, p. 1.

Williams, S.L. (1987). On anxiety and phobia. *Journal of Anxiety Disorders, 1*, 161–180.

Williams, S.L., & Watson, M. (1985). Perceived danger and perceived self-efficacy as cognitive determinants of acrophobic behavior. *Behavior Therapy, 16*, 136–146.

Williamson, D.A., Kelly, M.L., Davis, C.J., Ruggiero, L., & Blouin, D.C. (1985). Psychopathology of eating disorders: A controlled comparison of bulimic, obese, and normal subjects. *Journal of Consulting and Clinical Psychology, 53*, 161–166.

Wills, T.A., Baker, E., & Botvin, G.J. (1989). Dimensions of assertiveness: Differential relationships to substance use in early adolescence. *Journal of Consulting and Clinical Psychology, 57*, 473–478.

Wilson, D.R. (1990). Socioeconomic differentials in health: A review and redirection. *Social Psychology Quarterly, 53*, 81–99.

Wilson, G.T. (1981a). Behavior therapy as a short-term therapeutic approach. In S. Budman (Ed.), *Forms of brief therapy*. New York: Guilford Press.

Wilson, G.T. (1981b). Expectations and substance abuse: Does basic research benefit clinical assessment and therapy? *Addictive Behaviors, 6*, 221–231.

Wilson, G.T. (1981c). The effects of alcohol on human sexual behavior. In N. Mello (Ed.), *Advances in substance abuse: Behavioral and biological research*. Greenwich, CT: JAI Press.

Wilson, G.T. (1982). Adult disorders. In G.T. Wilson & C.M. Franks (Eds.), *Contemporary behavior therapy*. New York: Guilford.

Wilson, G.T. (1984). Clinical issues and strategies in the clinical practice of behavior therapy. In C.M. Franks, G.T. Wilson, K.D. Brownell, & P. Kendall (Eds.), *Annual review of behavior therapy: Theory and practice* (Vol. 8). New York: Guilford Press.

Wilson, G.T. (1985). Limitations of meta-analysis in clinical psychology. *Clinical Psychology Review, 5*, 35–47.

Wilson, G.T. (1986). Social psychological concepts in the theory and practice of behavior therapy. In P. Eelen & O. Fontaine (Eds.), *Behavior therapy: Beyond the conditioning framework*. Hillsdale, NJ: Lawrence Erlbaum.

Wilson, G.T. (1987a). Cognitive processes in addiction. *British Journal of Addiction, 82*, 343–353.

Wilson, G.T. (1987b). Cognitive studies in alcoholism. *Journal of Consulting and Clinical Psychology, 55*, 325–331.

Wilson, G.T. (1988). Alcohol use and abuse: A social learning analysis. In A. Wilkinson & H. Chaudron (Eds.), *Theories of alcoholism*. Toronto: Addiction Research Foundation.

Wilson, G.T. (1990, August). Cognitive-behavioral treatments versus pharmacological treatments of bulimia nervosa. Paper presented at Symposium on Psychological and pharmacological treatments, Bad Pyrmont.

Wilson, G.T., & Davison, G.C. (1971). Processes of fear reduction in systematic desensitization: Animal studies. *Psychological Bulletin, 76*, 1–14.

Wilson, G.T., Leaf, R., & Nathan, P.E. (1975). The aversive control of excessive drinking by chronic alcoholics in the laboratory setting. *Journal of Applied Behavior Analysis, 8*, 13–26.

Wilson, G.T., & O'Leary, K.D. (1980). *Principles of behavior therapy*. Englewood Cliffs, NJ: Prentice-Hall.

Wilson, G.T., Rossiter, E., Kleinfield, E.I., & Lindholm, L. (1986). Cognitive-behavioral treatment of bulimia nervosa: A controlled evaluation. *Behaviour Research and Therapy, 24*, 277–288.

Wilson, H. (1980). Parental supervision: A neglected aspect of delinquency. *British Journal of Criminology, 20*, 203–235.

Wilson, J.P., Beyer, H.A., & Yudowitz, B. (1977). Advocacy for the mentally disabled. In L.E. Kopolow & H. Blood (Eds.), *Mental health advocacy* (DHEW Publication No. 77-455). Washington, DC: U.S. Government Printing Office.

Wilson, J.Q., & Herrnstein, R.J. (1985). *Crime and human nature*. New York: Simon & Schuster.

Wilson-Barnett, J., & Trimble, M.R. (1985). An investigation of hysteria using the Illness Behaviour Questionnaire. *British Journal of Psychiatry, 146*, 601–608.

Wincze, J.P. (1982). Assessment of sexual disorders. *Behavioral Assessment, 4*, 257–571.

Wing, J.K., & Brown, D.W. (1970). *Institutionalism and schizophrenia*. Cambridge, England: Cambridge University Press.

Winn, S., & Merrill, D. (1980). *Ted Bundy: The killer next door*. New York: Bantam Books.

Winokur, G. (1981). *Depression: The facts*. New York: Oxford University Press.

Winters, K.C., & Neale, J.M. (1985). Mania and low self-esteem, *Journal of Abnormal Psychology, 94*, 282–290.

Wirtz, P.W., & Harrell, A.V. (1987). Effects of postassault exposure to attack-similar stimuli on long-term recovery of victims. *Journal of Consulting and Clinical Psychology, 55*, 10–16.

Wolchik, S.A., Weiss, L., & Katzman, M.A. (1986). An empirically validated, short-term psychoeducational group-treatment program for bulimia. *International Journal of Eating Disorders, 5*, 21–34.

Wolf, L., & Goldberg, B. (1986). Autistic children group: An eight to twenty-four year follow-up study. *Canadian Journal of Psychiatry, 31*, 550–556.

Wolfe, D.A. (1987). *Child abuse*. Newbury Park, CA: Sage.

Wolfe, J., Keane, T., Lyons, J., & Gerardi, R. (1987). Current trends and issues in the assessment of combat-related post-traumatic stress disorder. *The Behavior Therapist, 10*, 27–32.

Wolfe, J.L., & Fodor, I.G. (1977). Modifying assertive behavior in women: A comparison of three approaches. *Behavior Therapy, 8*, 567–574.

Wolfe, L. (1981). *The Cosmo Report*. New York: Arbor House.

Wolpe, J. (1958). *Psychotherapy by reciprocal inhibition*. Stanford, CA: Stanford University Press.

Wolpe, J. (1985). *The practice of behavior therapy* (2nd. ed.). New York: Pergamon Press.

Wolpe, J., & Lazarus, A.A. (1966). *Behavior therapy techniques*. New York: Pergamon Press.

Wolpe, J., & Rachman, S. (1960). Psychoanalytic "evidence": A critique based on Freud's case of Little Hans. *Journal of Nervous and Mental Disease, 131*, 135–148.

Wood, D.R., Reimherr, F.W., & Wender, P.H. (1976). Diagnoses and treatment of minimal brain dysfunction in adults. *Archives of General Psychiatry, 33*, 1453–1460.

Wood, J., Saltzberg, J., Neale, J., Stone, A., & Rachmeil, T. (1989). *Self-focused attention, distressed mood, and coping style in everyday life*. Manuscript submitted for publication.

Woods, A.M., & Birren, J.E. (1984). Late adulthood and aging. In J.D. Matarazzo, J.A. Herd, N.E. Miller, & S.M. Weiss (Eds.), *Behavioral health*. New York: John Wiley.

Woods, B.T., Kinney, D.K., & Yurgelun-Todd, D. (1986). Neurologic abnormalities in schizophrenic patients and their families. *Archives of General Psychiatry, 43*, 657–663.

Woody, E.Z., Costanzo, P.R., Leifer, H., & Conger, J. (1981). The effects of taste and caloric perceptions on the eating behavior of restrained and unrestrained subjects. *Cognitive Research and Therapy, 5*, 381–390.

Wooley, S.C., Wooley, O.W., & Dyrenforth, S.R. (1979). Theoretical, practical, and social issues in behavioral treatments of obesity. *Journal of Applied Behavior Analysis, 12*, 3–25.

World Health Organization. (1973). *The international pilot study of schizophrenia* (Vol. 1). Geneva: World Health Organization Press.

Wurtele, S.K., & Martin, J.E. (1987). Assessment of smoking. In T.D. Nirenberg & S.A. Maisto (Eds.), *Developments in the assessment and treatment of addictive behaviors*. Norwood, NJ: Ablex Publishing.

Wynne, L.C. (1984). The University of Rochester child and family study: Overview of research plan. In N.F. Watt, E.J. Anthony, L.C. Wynne, & J.E. Rolf (Eds.), *Children at risk for schizophrenia: A longitudinal perspective*. New York: Cambridge University Press.

Yalom, I.D., Green, R., & Fisk, N. (1973). Prenatal exposure to female hormones: Effect on psychosexual development in boys. *Archives of General Psychiatry*, *28*, 554–561.

Yando, R.M., & Kagan, J. (1968). The effects of teacher tempo on the child. *Child Development*, *39*, 27–34.

Yesavage, J.A., & Leirer, V.O. (1986). Hangover effects on aircraft pilots 14 hours after alcohol ingestion: A preliminary report. *American Journal of Psychiatry*, *143*, 1546–1550.

Yesavage, J.A., Leirer, V.O., Denari, M., & Hollister, L.E. (1985). Carry-over effects of marijuana intoxication on aircraft pilot performance: A preliminary report. *American Journal of Psychiatry*, *142*, 1325–1329.

Yontef, G.M., & Simkin, J.S. (1989). *Gestalt therapy*. In R. Corsini & D. Wedding (Eds.), *Current psychotherapies*. Itasca, IL: Peacock Publishers.

Young, J.E., & Beck, A.T. (1982). Cognitive therapy: Clinical applications. In A.J. Rush (Ed.), *Short term psychotherapies for depression*. New York: Guilford Press.

Young, R.C. (1972). Clinical judgement as a means of improving actuarial prediction from the MMPI. *Journal of Consulting and Clinical Psychology*, *38*, 457–459.

Yudofsky, S.C., & Silver, J.M. (1985). Psychiatric aspects of brain injury: Trauma, stroke, and tumor. In R.E. Hales & A.J. Frances (Eds.), *American Psychiatric Association Annual Review* (Vol. 4). Washington, DC: American Psychiatric Association.

Zarantonello, M.M. (1988). Comparability of the WAIS and the WAIS-R: A consideration of level of neuropsychological impairment. *Journal of Consulting and Clinical Psychology*, *56*, 295–297.

Zigler, E., & Levine, J. (1981). Age of first hospitalization of schizophrenics: A development approach. *Journal of Abnormal Psychology*, *90*, 458–467.

Zilbergeld, B., & Ellison, C.R. (1980). Desire discrepancies and arousal problems in sex therapy. In S. Leiblum & L. Pervin (Eds.), *Principles and practice of sex therapy*. New York: Plenum Press.

Zilbergeld, B., & Evans, M. (1980). The inadequacy of Masters and Johnson. *Psychology Today*, *14*, 28–43.

Zilboorg, G. (1936). Consideration on suicide with particular reference to that of the young. *American Journal of Orthopsychiatry*, *7*, 15–35.

Zilboorg, G., & Henry, G.W. (1941). *A history of medical psychology*. New York: W.W. Norton.

Zimmerman, M., & Coryell, W.H. (1989). DSM III personality disorder dimensions. *Archives of General Psychiatry*. *46*, 682–689.

Zimmerman, M., Coryell, W., & Pfohl, B. (1986). The validity of the dexamethasone suppression test as a marker for endogeneous depression. *Archives of General Psychiatry*, *43*, 347–355.

Zitrin, C.M., Klein, D.F., Woerner, M.G., & Ross, D.C. (1983). Treatment of phobias: I. Comparison of imipramine hydrochloride and placebo. *Archives of General Psychiatry*, *40*, 125–138.

Zohar, J., Foa, E.B., & Insel, T.R. (1989). Behavior therapy and pharmacotherapy. In *American Psychiatric Association Task Force on Treatments of Psychiatric Disorders* (Vol. 3). Washington, DC: American Psychiatric Association.

Zohar, J., & Insel, T.R. (1987). Obsessive-compulsive disorder. *Biological Psychiatry*, *22*, 667–687.

Zohar, J., Insel, T.R., Zohar-Kadouch, R.C., Hill, J.L., & Murphy, D.L. (1988). Serotonin function in obsessive-compulsive disorder. *Archives of General Psychiatry*, *45*, 167–172.

Zohar, J., Mueller, E.A., Insel, T.R., Clarkson, C., Crowe, R., Yates, W.R., & McChesney, C. (1987). A family study of generalized anxiety disorder. *American Journal of Psychiatry*, *144*, 1019–1024.

Zohar-Kadouch, R.C., & Murphy, D. (1987). Serotonergic responsivity in obsessive-compulsive disorder. *Archives of General Psychiatry*, *44*, 946–951.

Zubin, J., & Spring, B. (1977). Vulnerability: A new view of schizophrenia. *Journal of Abnormal Psychology*, *86*, 103–126.

Zucker, K.J., Finegan, J.K., Deering, R.W., & Bradley, S.J. (1984). Two subgroups of gender-problem children. *Archives of Sexual Behavior*, *13*, 27–39.

Acknowledgments

PHOTOGRAPHS

Chapter 1 **2** National Mental Health Association **4** The Vatican Museum (left) **4** Library of Congress (center) **6** Laima Druskis **8** Laima Druskis **9** Will & Deni McIntyre/Photo Researchers **10** Stephen Frisch/Stock, Boston **12** New York Public Library Picture Collection **13** The Bettmann Archive **14** Cornell University Library **15** Boston Atheneum (top) **15** Courtesy of Pennsylvania Hospital (bottom) **17** John Hopkins Medical Institution, Office of Public Affairs **18** Library of Congress

Chapter 2 **31** WHO Photo **32** Topham/The Image Works (top) **32** Karen Thomas/Stock, Boston (bottom) **33** Lew Merrim/Monkmeyer Press **34** The Bettmann Archive **36** © Keystone/The Image Works (left) **36** The Bettmann Archive (center) **36** New York Public Library Picture Collection (right) **36** © Keystone/The Image Works (bottom) **38** Edward L. Miller/Stock, Boston **39** Carl Rogers Memorial Library **40** Courtesy of Marcia Roltner, reprinted by permission of Brooks/Cole Publishing Co. **41** UPI/Bettmann **42** Culver Pictures **44** Courtesy the estate of B.F. Skinner **46** News and Publications Service, Stanford University. Photo by Chuck Painter **48** John Launois/Black Star **49** United Nations photo **51** Courtesy Washington University School of Medicine, St. Louis

Chapter 3 **55** Marc Anderson **57** Susan Rosenberg/Photo Researchers **64** Ken Karp **67** Barbara Rios/Photo Researchers **70** Courtesy Dr. Fred J. Hodges, III, The Edward Mallinckrodt Institute of Radiology, Washington School of Medicine (top left) **70** National Institute of Health (top right) **70** Courtesy Dr. Michael M. Ter-Pogossian (bottom left) **70** Courtesy Dr. Richard J. Feldman, National Institute of Health (bottom right)

Chapter 4 **78** Bob Daemmrich/The Image Works **82** Dan McCoy/Rainbow **83** John Watney/Photo Researchers **89** Harlow Primate Laboratory, University of Wisconsin **90** Courtesy University of Pennsylvania, Department of Psychology

Chapter 5 **98** G. Zimbel/Monkmeyer Press **106** Dan McCoy/Rainbow **114** Catherine Ursillo/Photo Researchers **117** UPI/Bettmann

Chapter 6 **126** Ray Ellis/Science Source/Photo Researchers **131** New York Public Library Picture Collection **134** Ken Robert Buck/Stock, Boston **137** AP/Wide World Photos **140** UPI/Bettmann

Chapter 7 **148** The Bettmann Archive **149** Marc Anderson **163** James R. Holland/Stock, Boston **164** *Newsweek,* illustration by Theo Rudnak **165** James D. Wilson/Woodfin Camp and Associates **166** Courtesy of Aaron Beck **168** Courtesy of Peter Lewinsohn **169** Courtesy of Myrna Weissman **170** Kolvoord/The Image Works

Chapter 8 **175** Courtesy of Judith Rodin **184** Joel Gordon **185** Jeffry Myers/Stock, Boston **188** Hank Morgan/Rainbow **191** Blair Seitz/Photo Researchers **192** Arlene Collins/Monkmeyer Press **193** AP/Wide World Photos (left) **193** AP/Wide World Photos (right) **194** Bob Daemmrich/Stock, Boston **195** Joel Gordon

Chapter 9 **202** UPI/Bettmann Newsphotos **203** UPI/Bettmann Newsphotos **211** W. Hill, Jr./The Image Works **218** Bill Powers/NYT Pictures **219** Laima Druskis **220** AP/Wide World Photos **221** AP/Wide World Photos **224** UPI/Bettmann Newsphotos **227** Laima Druskis

Chapter 10 **234** UPI/Bettmann Newsphotos **235** D.V. Woo/Stock, Boston **237** Menzies/The Image Works **244** UPI/Bettmann Newsphotos **247** Laima Druskis **248** H. Darr Beiser, *USA Today* **251** Ken Karp

Chapter 11 **262** Drug Enforcement Administration **268** Irene Springer **273** Dan McCoy/Rainbow **278** Leif Skodgfors/Woodfin Camp & Associates **279** S. Kerman/Gamma-Liaison **281** Dan McCoy/Rainbow **284** © Gage Taylor **288** Robert Goldstein/Photo Researchers **290** W. Marc Bernsau/The Image Works

Chapter 12 **297** Carl Glassman/The Image Works **300** Michal Heron/Woodfin Camp & Associates **313** Gale Zucker/Stock, Boston **317** Library of Congress

Chapter 13 **326** Stu Rosner/Stock, Boston **334** AP/Wide World Photos **335** Bob Leafe/Star File Photo **339** AP/Wide World Photos **341** Globe Photos **342** Patt Blue **343** Reuters/Bettmann (left) **349** Lawrence Migdale/Stock, Boston **352** Mary Ellen Mark Library **353** David M. Grossman/Photo Researchers

Chapter 14 **358** AP/Wide World Photos **359** New York Public Library Picture Collection **366** Scala/Art Resource **368** Grunnitus/Monkmeyer Press **370** Hank Morgan/Rainbow **371** NIH/Science Source/Photo Researchers **382** Stock, Boston

Chapter 15 **388** From the Journal of the American Medical Association, 1976, Vol. 235, 1458–1460. Courtesy, James W. Hanson, M.D. **389** Linda K. Moore/Rainbow **391** Harry Schlack/Monkmeyer Press **393** Will & Deni McIntyre/Photo Researchers **396** John Isaac/United Nations Photo (left) **396** National Institute of Aging (right) **397** Shirley Zeiberg **402** Culver Pictures, Inc. **408** Mira Wyman/Sygma **416** Alon Reininger/Woodfin Camp & Associates **417** Robin Carson, photographer. Used by permission of Woody Guthrie Publications, Inc.

Chapter 16 **423** Ken Karp **426** Reuters/Bettmann Newsphotos (top) **426** The Bettmann Archive (bottom) **439** Courtesy of Dr. Joseph Wolpe **451** Courtesy of Dr. Arnold A. Lazarus

Chapter 17 **462** Shirley Zeiberg **463** Bob Daemmrich/The Image Works **468** Hank Morgan/Science Source/Photo Researchers **469** Arlene Collins/Monkmeyer Press **473** AP/Wide World Photos **482** Joel Gordon **485** A. Tsiaras/Science Source/Photo Researchers **487** UPI/Bettmann Newsphotos

Chapter 18 **492** Bob Daemmrich/Uniphoto **494** AP/Wide World Photos **496** Peter Southwick/Stock, Boston **500** United Nations photo **501** Marcia Keegan/Woodfin Camp & Associates **505** John Ficara/Woodfin Camp & Associates **507** The Bethlem Royal Hospital

CASES/EXTRACTS/TEXT

Chapter 1: **2** Beers, C.W. *A mind that found itself* (1905). Doubleday & Company. By permission of the publisher. **2** Spitzer, R.L., et al., *Psychopathology: a case book.* By permission of the publisher. McGraw Hill, New York

Chapter 2: **25** Quotation from Willerman, L. & Cohen, D.B., *Psychopathology* (1990) p. 201. New York: McGraw-Hill. By permission of the publisher. **40** Quotation from Watson, J.B. (1913), Psychology as the Behaviorist Views It, *Psychological Review, 20,* p. 158. By permission of the publisher. **48** Quotation from X, Malcolm (1966), *Memoirs,* p. 22. Copyright by Random House, Inc. Reprinted by permission of the publisher.

Chapter 4: **79** Excerpt from Clark (1989), p. 85. Anxiety states. In Hawton et al. (Eds.), *Cognitive behavior therapy for psychiatric problems.*

Chapter 5: **100** *From Hey, wait a minute,* (*I wrote a book!*) by John Madden with Dave Anderson. Copyright © 1984 by John Madden, Inc. Reprinted by permission of Villard Books, a division of Random House, Inc. **106** From Goodwin, D.W. (1986). *Anxiety*, New York: Copyright Ballantine. Reprinted with permission. **104; 112** From Taylor, C.B., & Arnow, B. (1988). *The nature and treatment of anxiety disorders.* New York: Free Press. Reprinted with permission. **113–14** From Foy, D.W., Donahue, C.P., Carroll, E.M., Gallers, J., & Reno, R. (1987). Posttraumatic stress disorder. In L. Michelson & L.M. Ascher (Eds.), *Anxiety and stress disorders.* New York: Guilford Press. Reprinted with permission. **115–16** From Horowitz, M. (1989). Posttraumatic stress disorders. In American Psychiatric Association Task Force on Treatments of Psychiatric Disorders, Vol. 3, 2065–2082. Washington, DC: American Psychiatric Association. Reprinted with permission.

Chapter 6: 127 From P.M. Salkovskis (1989), Somatic problems, p. 254. In K. Hawton, P.M. Salkovskis, J. Kirk, & D.M. Clark (Eds.), *Cognitive behavior therapy for psychiatric problems.* Copyright Oxford University Press, 1989. Reprinted by permission of Oxford University Press. **138–139** From Kluft, R.P. (1986). High-functioning multiple personality patients. *The Journal of Nervous and Mental Disease, 174,* p. 723. Copyright Williams & Wilkins, 1986. Reprinted by permission of Williams & Wilkins.

Chapter 9: 205 From Kaplan, H.S. (1974). *The new sex therapy.* New York: Brunner/Mazel. Copyright Brunner/Mazel, p. 256. Reprinted with permission. **222** From Stoller, R.J. (1967). Transvestites' women. *American Journal of Psychiatry, 124* pp. 333–339. Copyright by the American Psychiatric Association. Reprinted with permission. **224–25** From Green, R. (1987). *The "sissy boy syndrome" and the development of homosexuality.* New Haven, CT: Yale University Press, pp. 124–126. Reprinted with permission.

Chapter 10: 235; 236–37 Masterson, J.F. (1985). *The real self.* New York: Brunner/Mazel, 47, 88. Reprinted by permission. **240** Kroll, J. (1988). *The challenge of the borderline patient: Competency in diagnosis and treatment.* New York: Norton, pp. 197–98. Reprinted by permission. **251–52** Salzman, L. (1985). *Treatment of the obsessive personality.* New York: Jason Aronson. Reprinted by permission. **253** Turkat, I.D., & Maisto, S.A. (1985). Personality disorders: Application or the experimental method to the formulation and modification of personality disorders, pp. 502–570. In D. Barlow (Ed.), *Clinical handbook of psychological disorders.* New York: Guilford. Reprinted by permission. **255** Stone, M.H. (1985). Schizotypal personality: Psychotherapeutic aspects. *Schizophrenia Bulletin, 11,* 576–589.

Chapter 11: 267 Copyright © 1988 by T.L. Cermak. From the book *A time to heal* and reprinted with permission from Jeremy P. Tarcher, Inc., Los Angeles, CA **274** Kaufmann, P. & Lilly M. (1979). A recovering alcoholic speaks and her family therapist introduces her. In E. Kaufmann & P.N. Kaufmann (Eds.), *Family therapy of drug and alcohol abuse,* pp. 243–254. New York: Gardner Press, Inc. By permission of the publisher. **277** From *AA: Inside Alcoholics Anonymous* by N. Robertson. Copyright 1988 by N. Robertson. Reprinted by permission of William Morrow and Co., Inc. **279** From *Getting Clean* by Phoebe Hoban. Copyright © 1991 News America Publishing Incorporated. All rights reserved. Reprinted with the permission of *New York Magazine.* **286** Quotation from Marlatt, G.A. & Gordon, J.R. (Eds.), (1985). *Relapse Prevention.* New York: Guilford Press. By permission of the publisher. **289** Copyright © 1989 by The New York Times Company. Reprinted by permission.

Chapter 12: 299 Gross, A.M. (1988). Oppositional disorder. In M. Hersen and C.G. Last (Eds.), *Child Behavior Therapy Casebook.* New York: Plenum. Reprinted with permission of publisher. **320** From *A Child Called Noah* by Josh Greenfeld. Copyright © 1970, 1972 by Josh Greenfeld. Reprinted by permission of Henry Holt and Company, Inc. **320** Kanner, L. (1971). Follow-up study of eleven autistic children originally reported in 1943. *Journal of Autism and Childhood Schizophrenia, 1,* pp. 119–145.

Chapter 13: 331 Mack, J.E.G. & Hickler, H. (1981). *Vivienne: The life and suicide of adolescent girl.* Boston, MA: Little, Brown & Co.

Chapter 14: 357–59 North, C. (1987). *Welcome, silence: My triumph over schizophrenia.* New York: Simon & Schuster. Copyright 1987 by Carol S. North. Reprinted by permission of Simon & Schuster, Inc. **361, 362, 366** Cutting, J. (1985). *The psychology of schizophrenia.* New York: Churchill Livingstone. Reprinted by permission of the publisher.

Chapter 15: 387 Quotation from Berg, J.M. (1986). Prenatal diagnosis of mental retardation and its Implications. *Psychiatric Clinics of North America, 9* and Table from La Rue. (1982). Memory loss and aging: Distinguishing dementia from benign senescent forgetfulness and depressive pseudodementia. *Psychiatric Clinics of North America, 5.* By permission of the publisher. **395** Quotation from Goleman (1989), p. B14. Copyright © 1989 by The New York Times Company. Reprinted by permission. **395–96** Quotation from Hopkins, B.L. (1987). Comments on the future of applied behavior analysis. *Journal of Applied Behavioral Analysis, 20.* By permission of the publisher. **396** Quotation from Braceland, F.J. (1972). Senescense—The Inside Story, *Psychiatric Annals, 2,* pp. 42–56. By permission of the publisher. **402** Gardner, H. (1974), *The Shattered Mind.* Copyright Alfred A. Knopf, Inc. By permission of the publisher. **410** Quotation from McAllister, T.W. & Price, T.P.R. (1982). Severe depressive pseudodementia with and without dementia, *American Journal of Psychiatry, 139.* By permission of the publisher. Washington D.C.: American Psychiatric Press. **413** Quotation from Mendelson, J.H., Mello, N.K., Lex, B.W. & Bavli, S. (1984). Marijuana withdrawal syndrome in a woman. *American Journal of Psychiatry, 141,* 1289–1290. Washington D.C.: American Psychiatric Press. By permission of the publisher. **417** Quotation from Ferrara, A.J. (1984). My personal experience with AIDS. *American Psychologist, 39,* pp. 1285–1287. By permission of the publisher. **417** Adams, R.D. & Victor, M. (1981). *Principles of Neurology.* New York: McGraw-Hill. By permission of the publisher. **418** Parson, O.A. & Hart, R.P. (1984). *Comprehensive Handbook of Psychopathology.* Behavioral disorders associated with central nervous system dysfunction. In H.E. Adams & P.B. Sutker (Eds.), pp. 841–916. New York: Plenum Press. By permission of the publisher.

Chapter 16: 425; 436 From Lichtenstein, E. (1980, p. 112). *Psychotherapy.* Monterey, CA: Brooks/Cole. Copyright Brooks/Cole. Reprinted with permission. From Lichtenstein, E. (1980, pp. 168–169). *Psychotherapy.* Monterey, CA: Brooks/Cole. **448–49** From Clark, D.M. (1989). Anxiety States. In Hawton, K., P.M. Salkovskis, & D.M. Clark (Eds.), *Cognitive behaviour therapy for psychiatric problems.* Oxford: Oxford University Press. Reprinted by permission.

Chapter 18: 494–95 Mills, M.J., Sullivan, G. & Eth, S. (1987). Protecting third parties: A decade after *Tarasoff. American Journal of Psychiatry, 144,* pp. 68–74. By permission of the publisher. Washington, D.C.: American Psychiatric Press. **503** Geller, J.L. (1986). Rights, wrongs, and the dilemma of coerced community treatment. *American Journal of Psychiatry, 143,* 1259–1264. **509** Committee on Professional Standards, Board of Professional Affairs, American Psychological Association. (1988). Casebook for providers of psychological services. *American Psychologist, 43,* 557–563.

Index

AUTHOR

SUBJECT

ANXIETY DISORDERS (OR ANXIETY AND PHOBIC NEUROSES)

Panic Disorder
  With Agoraphobia
  Without Agoraphobia
Agoraphobia Without History of Panic Disorder
Social Phobia
Simple Phobia
Obsessive Compulsive Disorder (or Obsessive Compulsive Neurosis)
Post-Traumatic Stress Disorder
Generalized Anxiety Disorder
Anxiety Disorder NOS

SOMATOFORM DISORDERS

Body Dysmorphic Disorder
Conversion Disorder (or Hysterical Neurosis, Conversion Type)
Hypochondriasis (or Hypochondriacal Neurosis)
Somatization Disorder
Somatoform Pain Disorder
Undifferentiated Somatoform Disorder
Somatoform Disorder NOS

DISSOCIATIVE DISORDERS (OR HYSTERICAL NEUROSES, DISSOCIATIVE TYPE)

Multiple Personality Disorder
Psychogenic Fugue
Psycogenic Amnesia
Depersonalization Disorder (or Depersonalization Neurosis)
Dissociative Disorder NOS

SEXUAL DISORDERS

Paraphilias

Exhibitionism
Fetishism
Frotteurism
Pedophilia
Sexual Masochism
Sexual Sadism
Transvestic Fetishism
Voyeurism
Paraphilia NOS

Sexual Dysfunctions

Sexual Desire Disorders
  Hypoactive Sexual Desire Disorder
  Sexual Aversion Disorder
Sexual Arousal Disorders
  Female Sexual Arousal Disorder
  Male Erectile Disorder
Orgasm Disorders
  Inhibited Female Orgasm
  Inhibited Male Orgasm
  Premature Ejaculation
Sexual Pain Disorders
  Dyspareunia
  Vaginismus
Sexual Dysfunction NOS

Other Sexual Disorders

Sexual Disorder NOS

SLEEP DISORDERS

Dyssomnias

Insomnia Disorders
Hypersomnia Disorders
Sleep–Wake Schedule Disorder
Dyssomnia NOS

Parasomnias

Dream Anxiety Disorder (Nightmare Disorder)
Sleep Terror Disorder
Sleepwalking Disorder
Parasomnia NOS

FACTITIOUS DISORDERS

Factitious Disorder
  With Physical Symptoms
  With Psychological Symptoms
Factitious Disorder NOS

IMPULSE CONTROL DISORDERS NOT ELSEWHERE CLASSIFIED

Intermittent Explosive Disorder
Kleptomania
Pathological Gambling
Pyromania
Trichotillomania
Impulse Control Disorder NOS

ADJUSTMENT DISORDER

Adjustment Disorder
  With Anxious Mood
  With Depressed Mood
  With Disturbance of Conduct
  With Mixed Disturbance of Emotions and Conduct